MARKETING
Connecting with Customers

MARKETING
Connecting with Customers

Gilbert D. Harrell
Michigan State University

Prentice Hall
Upper Saddle River, NJ 07458

Library of Congress Cataloging-in-Publication Data

Harrell, Gilbert D.
    Marketing: connecting with customers / Gilbert D. Harrell—2nd ed.
        p. cm.
    Includes bibliographical references and index.
    ISBN 0-13-033494-4
    1. Marketing—Management.   2. Consumer satisfaction   I. Title.

HF5415.13 .H356 2001
658.8′12—dc21   2001021309

Acquisitions Editor: Bruce Kaplan
Editor-in-Chief: Jeff Shelstad
Assistant Editor: Anthony Palmiotto
Media Project Manager: Karen Goldsmith
Marketing Manager: Annie Todd
Marketing Assistant: Christine Genneken
Managing Editor (Production): John Roberts
Production Editor: Keri Jean
Permissions Coordinator: Suzanne Grappi
Associate Director, Manufacturing: Vincent Scelta
Production Manager: Arnold Vila
Design Manager: Patricia Smythe
Designer: Kevin Kall
Interior Design: Jill Yutkowitz
Cover Design: Kevin Kall
Manager, Print Production: Christy Mahon
Composition: Progressive Information Technologies
Full-Service Project Management: Progressive Publishing Alternatives
Printer/Binder: Banta

10 9 8 7 6 5 4 3 2 1
ISBN 0-13-033494-4

To my wife, Susanna

contents

about the author

GILBERT D. HARRELL, Ph.D.

Gilbert D. Harrell, Ph.D., is Professor of Marketing, Eli Broad College of Business and Graduate School of Management, Michigan State University. In 2000, Dr. Harrell received a Michigan State University Librarian Computing and Technology Award in recognition of scholarly contributions. He also received the 1997 John D. and Dortha J. Withrow Endowed Teacher/Scholar Award, the 1996 Phi Chi Theta Professor of the Year Award, and the 1995 Gold Key National Honor Society Award for teaching excellence at Michigan State University. His teaching, research, and consulting activities focus on sustainable competitive advantage, building business value, consumer satisfaction, sales management, strategic planning, and relationship marketing. Dr. Harrell's publications have appeared in the *Journal of Marketing, Journal of Long Range Planning, Journal of Marketing Research, Journal of Consumer Research, Journal of Consumer Affairs, Journal of Industrial Marketing Management, Journal of Consumer Satisfaction, Journal of Retailing, Business Topics, Journal of Logistics Information Management, Journal of Health Care Marketing, Journal of International Marketing, Journal of the Academy of Marketing Science,* and others. Dr. Harrell's doctorate degree is from Pennsylvania State University, where he was elected to the Phi Kappa Phi Honorary and the American Marketing Association Consortium. Both his bachelor's and Master's degrees are from Michigan State University.

Dr. Harrell is founder of Harrell & Associates, Inc., a professional consulting group, which specializes in service for strategic marketing management, visioning processes, communication strategies, sales management, and executive strategy development. His firm has helped implement the strategic marketing planning systems for several Fortune 500 companies.

preface

How do you get connected? Compare two shopping experiences. In the first, you visit a large bookstore, look at the books, and choose one or two to purchase. You also look at some music CDs in the store and ask for help from the friendly employees. Then you stop for a cup of coffee at the store's café. In the second shopping experience, you go to a bookstore and are met by a personal shopping assistant, who greets you by name and asks if you would like some help. Based on your previous purchases, she has some suggestions. You listen but decide that none of them are really what you want now. Then the personal shopping assistant tells you that she knows what people in the area have bought. Are you interested? If so, you listen; otherwise, you start moving toward other aisles. As you go along, your personal shopping assistant silently follows. When you stop at a particular subject and pull a book off the shelf, she is ready with recommendations of similar books—no matter how specialized the topic. And she is just as helpful in the CD section. When you go to other stores, another specialized personal assistant will be ready to help.

Which experience do you prefer? By now you have probably guessed that the first visit is to a traditional store—a marketplace. The second is a visit to the Internet—a marketspace. You have a choice about where to shop, and millions of consumers are making that choice daily. Businesses also buy in either the marketplace or the marketspace—everything from computers and paper to steel and jet aircraft. They, too, must decide where to shop. Consider these shopping scenarios from the perspective of a company or nonprofit organization that is developing a strategy to reach purchasers with its goods and services. What is the best way to create a lasting base of loyal customers? You must connect with customers, or your strategy will fail. If you do connect—really connect—your company or organization will thrive. But developing a winning strategy is complex. Both marketplace and marketspace are in constant fluctuation. Everything about your business may change at any time—the products and services offered, the prices charged, distribution, the locations where sales take place, promotions, and information about your customers and competitors. Chances are you will need traditional marketing tools as well as new technologies to get a jump on the competition. That's what *Marketing: Connecting with Customers* is all about.

Everyone knows about the Internet revolution. And every principles of marketing textbook says that the Internet is changing the face of marketing. But our organizing theme is "connecting with customers," and it will give you a better sense of how this change is influencing business actions. You will learn from hundreds of examples how organizations are winning customers around the world—some through innovative applications of traditional marketing tools, some with marketing's newest technology, and some through a unique blend of both.

The connecting with customers theme provides valuable insight into the dynamic world of marketing. Perhaps no other concept better expresses how marketing is changing and will change in the years ahead. The Internet is not the only thing driving change, but it has taken customer relationship management to new heights. Well into the future, customer relationship management will be a major force in marketing. Successful organizations will create the greatest customer satisfaction loyalty possible in creative environments, and they will do this ethically and globally, while recognizing customer diversity. Connecting with customers will be the common thread among the top performers in the coming years. Here is how that theme is featured in the text:

CONNECTING THROUGH TECHNOLOGY

 Technology's effect on marketing is featured seamlessly in every chapter. Chapter 1 introduces the use of the Internet in such areas as scanning, communication, distribution, and research. Internet connections to more than 150 leading-edge companies are provided in opening stories and are highlighted in text examples, boxed examples, and cases.

CONNECTING THROUGH RELATIONSHIPS

 Relationship marketing is a growing trend, and for good reason. By its very nature, a relationship requires a solid, lasting connection. Relationship marketing is introduced early in the book to emphasize the tremendous importance of satisfied, loyal customers. Meaningful relationships with customers happen when all employees within the organization develop the sensitivity, agility, and desire to satisfy customers' needs and wants. The ways to connect through relationships is emphasized throughout the book.

CONNECTING WITH DIVERSITY

 Diversity among organizations and customers is a source of enormous economic strength and opportunity for marketers. Understanding diversity is needed by all marketers, even those who do not specifically target diverse segments. Clearly, progressive companies are moving toward a better understanding of the similarities and differences among various populations. Each chapter has a diversity box, a diversity heading, or both. In addition, diversity is the subject of several chapter-opening vignettes.

CONNECTING GLOBALLY

We live in a world in which the international theme is increasingly recognized as important in all aspects of business. Marketing nearly always takes place in the international arena, so the global connection is woven into numerous principles and examples. You will find headings and references on this subject throughout. Our book is different from others because it covers this material within every chapter, rather than separately.

CONNECTING THROUGH ETHICS

Ethics are critical in all aspects of business, but particularly in marketing, because decisions in this area can affect many groups of people in very different ways. Marketers often face ethical issues. Every chapter of this book identifies ethical dilemmas marketers encounter. In each situation material is provided to help you think about the implications of marketing decisions and resolve inconsistencies. Real-life situations are discussed, and outcomes are identified.

WHAT'S NEW IN THE SECOND EDITION?

The second edition of *Marketing: Connecting with Customers* builds on the foundation of the first edition but extends the customer relationship theme. The third chapter, "The Global Marketing Environment and E-Commerce," provides a framework for talking about e-commerce and the Internet later in the text. For example, we completely revamped chapter 10 to show how the Internet has transformed supply chain management.

We have added a new Bricks or Clicks feature at the end of every chapter to show how companies are embracing—or shunning—the Internet in their efforts to connect with customers. This feature lets us discuss such topics as Web-enabled customer-relationship management at Eastman Chemical Company, Web site visitor analysis through the eLuminate program at Coremetrics, business-to-business marketing at Covisint, and the changing face of intellectual property at Yet2.com.

New vignettes and examples are provided throughout the text to show you how companies—right now—are connecting with customers. These companies range from well-known e-commerce firms, such as eBay, Yahoo!, and Palm Pilot, to lesser-known EnronOnline, an energy company, and Cave, which provides an automatic virtual environment.

A TOTAL TEACHING PACKAGE—IN AND OUT OF THE CLASSROOM

A successful marketing course has many challenges. Students demand a lively presentation with up-to-the-minute examples, technology provides an enormous amount of material that can be integrated into the course, and there is less time to prepare for all of it. Prentice Hall has been conducting research into the most effective ways to deliver ancillary materials and suggestions on the most useful materials to provide to the teaching package for *Marketing: Connecting with Customers*. Your suggestions are most appreciated and will help improve these materials further.

Note: Many of the supplements listed below are available in different formats. Print versions are available through your local PH representative along with 3.5″ diskette versions. You can also download many of these materials from our Web site, www.prenhall.com/harrell. See below for a more detailed description of the Web resources, which have been developed to support the marketing course.

MASTERING MARKETING

It might sound like piano lessons, but it's not. It's more Jimi Hendrix. A complete experience in which students are sucked into a fully interactive movie via a CD-ROM that runs like a TV mini-series. Actors. Lights. Storylines. Student Interaction. Throughout the book, students will follow the exploits of "CANGO," a fictional e-commerce start up. They'll watch (and help) as CANGO launches an IPO, goes global, and handles a myriad of problems. And they'll have fun doing it. The *Mastering Marketing* CD-ROM is available shrink-wrapped with the text at a small additional charge.

INSTRUCTOR'S RESOURCE MANUAL

This helpful teaching resource contains chapter overviews, annotated outlines, class exercises, relevant stories and examples to help in class preparation, discussion notes for in-text company cases, and answers to end-of-chapter questions and exercises. The manual also contains a complete listing of all the ancillary teaching resources available for this course along with an overview of the myPHLIP Web site.

STUDENT LEARNING GUIDE

Prepared by Gil Harrell, this study guide provides students an overview of each chapter, summarizing the major topics and concepts, and strengthens understanding through situational exercises involving cases, chapter highlights, and quizzes. This guide is also available as an online version.

TEST ITEM FILE

The Test Item File, prepared by Gil Harrell, contains more than 1,400 items, including multiple choice, true-false, and essay questions. These questions are graded for difficulty and page references to the text are included. The questions are available in a Test Item File booklet and through the PH Custom Test program (in Windows and Mac versions).

POWERPOINT TRANSPARENCIES

A set of PowerPoint slides is available to adopters. The PowerPoint 4.0 files include over 175 slides and present complete lectures, transitional notes from one slide to the next, and selected key text figures (with accompanying note slides).

ACETATE/OVERHEAD TRANSPARENCIES

The first set of acetates includes hard copy of the PowerPoint slides (for those who prefer to use an overhead projector in class) along with a selection of key graphics from the text.

ADVERTISEMENT TRANSPARENCIES

A complete set of acetates of recent ads, both domestic and international, is available. Over 75 ads have been collected, together with teaching notes for each one.

VIDEOS

A full video library is available to adopters. Over forty segments, focusing on major concepts in marketing, showcase a variety of companies from Nike to Starbucks. These videos are accompanied by written video cases that can be downloaded from the Web site. A custom selection of these print video cases can also be packaged with each student copy of the text at no additional charge (customer value pack). The video segments range in length from 8 to 15 minutes and include up-to-the-minute "inside" stories of companies around the world.

WEB SITE

Both professors and students can visit the Web site for *Marketing: Connecting with Customers!* Go to www.prenhall.com/harrell. The interactive portal contains chapter objectives and faculty resources. Study guide questions for each chapter can be assigned, and students can e-mail results—complete with a grade report—directly to instructors. On the faculty side, the PowerPoint slides, Instructor's Manual, and other resources may be accessed.

ACKNOWLEDGMENTS

I would like to thank many individuals who have made important contributions to this book. Without their help it would not have been produced. Literally every aspect of the project from planning to production has been aided by an exceptional team, which dedicated its time and talent to this project.

Special thanks goes to the following people who contributed in-depth reviews of the first edition. Their reviews made it much easier to write the second edition:

John Durham	*San Francisco State University*
William Flatley	*Principia College*
James S. Gould	*Pace University*
George Kelley	*Erie Community College*
Stephen Koernig	*California State University, Fullerton*
Rex Kovacevich	*University of Southern California*
Felicia G. Lassk	*Western Kentucky University*
Abe Qastin	*Lakeland College*
Deborah Reed Scarfino	*William Jewell College*
A.J. Taylor	*Austin Peay State University*
Mike Welker	*Franciscan University*

I am grateful to these reviewers as I am to the reviewers of the first edition:

David Andrus	*Kansas State University*
Bob Balderstone	*Western Melbourne Institute of TAFE (Australia)*
Richard Brand	*Florida State University*

William Carner	*University of Texas–Austin*
George Chrysschoidis	*University of Wales*
Howard Combs	*San Jose University*
John Cronin	*Western Connecticut State University*
Bernard Delagneau	*University of Wales*
Peter Doukas	*Westchester Community College*
Jim Dupree	*Grove City College*
Joyce Grahn	*University of Minnesota-Duluth*
Robert F. Guinner	*Arizona State*
Pola Gupta	*University of Northern Iowa*
Lynn Harris	*Shippensburg University*
Benoit Heilbrunn	*Le Groupe ESC Lyon/Lyon Graduate School of Business (France)*
Frank Krohn	*Suny, Fredonia*
Ken Lawrence	*New Jersey Institute of Technology*
Chong S. K. Lee	*California State University–Hayward*
Elizabeth Mariotz	*Philadelphia College of Textiles and Science*
Mike Mayo	*Kent State University*
Gary McCain	*Boise State University*
G. Stephen Miller	*St. Louis University*
Herbert Miller	*University of Texas–Austin*
Mark Mitchell	*University of South Carolina*
David Mothersbaugh	*University of Alabama*
Robert O'Keefe	*DePaul University*
Cliff Olson	*Southern State College of SDA*
Stan Paliwoda	*University of Calgary*
Eric Pratt	*New Mexico State University*
Mohammed Rawwas	*University of Northern Iowa*
David Urban	*Virginia Commonwealth University*
Anthony Urbaniak	*Northern State University*
Simon Walls	*Western Washington University*
Ken Williamson	*James Madison University*
Mark Young	*Winona State University*
George Zinkham	*University of Houston*

Elizabeth Johnston skillfully edited the entire manuscript. She made tremendous contributions by making the words come to life, focusing material, and sculpting the sentences to communicate what is intended. I can't thank her enough. Karen Griggs, Amy Kitchen, Amy Kortas, Andrea Moore, Mel Hudson Nowak, Erin O'Conner, Erica Rysberg, Carrie Shimkos, Maureen VanGlabbeek, Jason Vuic, Jane Wichersham, Long Zhang, Michael Yeng, and others tirelessly and enthusiastically did library research, checked sources, found ads, and developed insightful examples. In great spirit, Cindy Seagraves and Sarah Heyer typed the manuscript, which went through many drafts. Somehow they interpreted my scratchings to produce the most professional work. Thank you all so much!

I want to thank my colleagues at Michigan State University for ideas, content, and support including Don Bowersox, Roger Calantone, Tamer Cavusgil, Dave Closs, Bix Cooper, Stan Hollander, and Rich Spreng, to name a few. Thanks to Bob Nason for providing important ideas on positioning content and other support. Additionally, Peter Bennett (The Pennsylvania State University) is a valued mentor. His teaching underpins much that is here.

My gratitude extends to the team at Prentice Hall. Bruce Kaplan, senior editor, launched the second edition with a relevant and innovative positioning strategy. His experience and sensitivity have helped on nearly every front. I especially appreciate his positive demeanor and unhesitating support. Keri Jean, production editor, has done a superb job in producing an attractive text. She has worked long hours to meet almost impossible deadlines and has not compromised a single aspect. I thank her for being so upbeat and professional. Suzanne Grappi, permissions coordinator, did some heroic work obtaining permissions under particularly tight deadlines. The book is "up-to-the-minute" because of her. Donna Mulder, copy editor, did a splendid job on the final editing to make sure the entire manuscript was in alignment. Teri Stratford, photo researcher, coordinated the photo specs, finding photographs that perfectly communicate with the points we made in the text. Anthony Palmiotto, supplements editor, has developed the most comprehensive teaching and learning package in the industry to support this book. Melissa Pellerano, editorial assistant, kept documents flowing smoothly among the numerous parties. Shannon Moore, marketing manager, and Annie Todd, marketing director, have shared their insights and developed marketing and sales plans that connect with our target segments. The marketing and sales team at Prentice Hall has provided important research on the desires of faculty and students, continually emphasizing the critical nature of relationships with those parties. Jerome Grant, president, and Jeff Shelstad, editor-in-chief, have given personal leadership to this venture. Their vision and foresight are truly appreciated.

Due to prior commitments, Gary Frazier was unable to participate in this second edition. I want to thank Gary Frazier for his participation in the first edition. In addition, there has been tremendous support from a broad range of business people, such as Duane Larson and Mike McGorrin at Children's World, Jerry Florence at Nissan, Rich Bell and Bob Gaylord at Cutler-Hammer, Jeanne Cole at Lucasfilms, Kenn Thieff at Flagship Group, and Anita Wiznuik at McDonald's, to name a few. Many of the ideas in the book have been used extensively in classes at Michigan State University and a broad range of executive development programs. Surveys of over 2,000 students indicated that the "connecting with customers" theme does indeed capture their imagination. The feedback from these students and participants has been helpful, and their assistance is appreciated.

Finally, my heartfelt thanks go to my family for their encouragement and loving support; to my wife Susanna and our children Rachael, Nicholas, and Katherine.

Thank you to all!

Gil Harrell
East Lansing, Michigan

chapter 1

MARKETING: CONNECTING WITH CUSTOMERS

1. Understand the concept of marketing, including its definition, purpose, and role in creating exchanges.

2. Learn what is involved in making marketing decisions, including examples of product, price, promotion, and place decisions to create a marketing mix.

3. Contrast the periods of marketing evolution from its early history through the eras of production, sales, and customer marketing, leading up to today.

4. Understand the five key forces that are dramatically influencing how organizations connect with customers.

5. Determine how marketing pertains to you.

◀ *Pop singer Christina Aguilera*

IT'S HARD TO IMAGINE THAT TODAY'S *designer jeans originated as miners' clothes during the California gold rush, but that's exactly what happened. In 1850 Levi Strauss opened a dry goods store on San Francisco's Market Street. Among other items, he stocked blue canvas pants—the original 501 jeans—for hundreds of dusty miners. Soon these jeans were the choice of farmers, mechanics, and cowhands. Levi's now serves diverse segments that span the globe. To date, Levi's has produced more value than all the gold discovered by California prospectors.*

Long before the concept of marketing had evolved, Levi Strauss realized the importance of connecting with customers. He understood that innovation mattered. Therefore, he added patented nonscratch copper rivets on the pocket corners and in the crotch, promising a new pair of jeans if the rivets didn't hold. He also understood how to connect with customers using powerful imagery. In 1886 he added a patch showing two workhorses trying to rip apart a pair of jeans, depicting uncompromising quality.

Today, Levi Strauss & Co. continues to find ways to connect with a new generation of customers. It uses the power of computer technology, telecommunications, global distribution, a vast array of new marketplace options, and flexible manufacturing.

Like most great marketers, Levi's enters a new market looking to satisfy needs and wants. If necessary, it creates a new product to connect with customers. By doing just that, Levi's hopes to establish itself as the maker of the first wearable electronics products. Its European division, along with the Dutch electronics company Philips NV, released IDC+ jackets, which come equipped with a mobile phone and MP3 player. The phone works through a remote control device and ear gear and microphone in the collar. A spokeswoman at the Brussels headquarters says that the jackets are "mostly targeted to people like film directors and television crews—people who like to carry their technology around with them."

*Recently, Levi's has faced a significant loss in sales, forcing the company to rethink some of its marketing techniques. In a somewhat surprising move, Levi's decided in 2000 to stop selling via its own Web site. Rather, Levi's now relies on the Web technology of online retailers. Although this move may seem to be detrimental for any major company in the 21*st *century, Levi's recognizes that Internet customers want an easy shopping experience. The company also realizes that it cannot provide the mechanisms for payment, delivery, and returns so it opted to sell through online retailers. CEO Philip Marineau says of the decision, "We are moving forward aggressively but very strategically, and consistent with what the consumer wants and what our brands are all about."*

In an effort to win back customers who have been buying other brands, Levi's has begun targeting younger markets by portraying itself as a "hip" company. Levi's recently sponsored Lauryn Hill, and in 2000 the company cosponsored Christine Aguilera, affirming its connection to teens' interests. In addition, the company has recently begun a new ad campaign in mainstream lifestyle and fashion magazines to highlight its European-made Engineered Jeans. First sold in specialty stores, this line of jeans is now also sold in department stores. To feature its new line of classic corduroy pants, Levi's began its "Make Them Your Own" campaign with a 52-page supplement in Vogue *magazine.*

The campaign continued with a commercial made by Spike Jonze that ran on MTV and other cable networks popular among youth.

Levi Strauss founded a company that has become one of the world's best-known businesses. From the start, he intuitively adopted concepts that we call marketing. Ideas such as satisfying customers and personalized marketing, which seemed logical to him, have now been proven successful by scores of marketing research studies—and by billions in corporate profits.[1]

career tip Most companies hope to find college graduates with experience directly related to the career they seek. Summer internships are the perfect opportunity to gain such experience. Levi Strauss & Co. offers internships that run from June through August. Most positions are in the home office in San Francisco, but some are available at other locations throughout the country. Contact Levi Strauss & Co. in March to obtain an application for a summer internship.

THE CONCEPT OF MARKETING: CONNECTING WITH CUSTOMERS

Some organizations connect with you. Nike, Coca-Cola, and McDonald's seem to have the uncanny ability to fit into your world. They use the latest technologies to serve you; they are there when you need them—at home or abroad; they understand and accommodate diversity; and they are ethically and socially responsible. They work hard to understand what you want. They take every possible action to relate to you in order to form a lasting connection. In turn, perhaps you will connect with them. That's what they want. These organizations know you have plenty of choices, so they practice marketing at its highest level.

Ideally, organizations are created, grow, and continue to grow. In reality, some decline, and many die. For one reason or another, declining organizations fall out of favor with customers who replace them with more vibrant organizations. The common link: Winning organizations do an exceptional job of connecting with customers. They are extraordinary marketers. They understand the marketing concept and use a full range of marketing tools and techniques. They help customers experience the tremendous satisfaction that occurs when products precisely match their needs and wants. Every time satisfaction occurs, a new connection is made or an existing connection is made stronger.

Today's business environment is global, diverse, and ethically challenging. It is based on technologies that serve customers in ways only imagined a short time ago. Therefore, marketing plays a critical role in determining where, when, and how these technological advances will be applied. Marketing is about much more than just selling a product. It is about connecting with customers in ways that are deeply rewarding for them. Marketing is also about serving the needs of society and accomplishing the goals of the organization. It includes researching potential customers' needs and wants; developing appropriate goods and services; communicating with the market; creating, selecting, and managing channels to reach customers; and pricing to deliver superior customer value. It is about satisfying customers so they will reward the business with the loyalty necessary to reach organizational objectives.

This chapter introduces marketing. As ideas are presented, chapters are referenced to provide a brief overview of the book. We begin by defining marketing and discussing its purpose. Next, we review how marketing creates and facilitates economic exchanges. Then a section on the marketing strategy process introduces the basic elements used to build a marketing plan. This is followed by a short discussion of how marketing has evolved. We then describe how five key factors are shaping the ways in which organizations will connect with customers. Finally, the chapter ends with a note on the personal perspective you bring to marketing.

DEFINITION OF MARKETING

How do you view marketing? Is your impression positive or negative? Because marketing is a broad subject that can be viewed from many perspectives, it can be described in many ways. Most people have been exposed to advertising, point-of-purchase displays, and personal selling, so marketing is often seen strictly as the promotion and sale of existing products. However, marketing is much more extensive. Excellent marketing begins long before a product exists. This allows all marketing decisions—including promotion—to be made with customer needs and wants in mind. Marketing extends far beyond a purchase to ensure customer satisfaction and loyalty. You can gain a good idea about the extent of marketing by understanding each element in its definition.

The American Marketing Association (AMA), an organization of professionals interested in furthering the marketing discipline, developed the following definition. **Marketing** is the process of planning and executing the conception, pricing, promotion, and distribution of ideas, goods, and services to create exchanges that satisfy individual and organizational objectives.[2] Figure 1.1 highlights key elements of the marketing definition.

THE PROCESS OF PLANNING AND EXECUTING

Marketing is an ongoing process. Processes are used to manage complex phenomena that undergo change. New competitors enter the market, customers change, and the economic climate shifts. What works today may be totally wrong tomorrow. Consequently, those who practice marketing must take a long view of events and see the world over time. They must not focus on a single transaction at one moment but on the enduring, systematic management of change. Marketers look for patterns, trends, and surprises that signal what is likely to happen in the future. In fact, later it will be apparent that marketing has its greatest value when it helps guide organizations in highly dynamic environments.

Consider, for example, the computer field in which the marketing plan is crucial. In 1978, the world's fastest computer processed 160 million instructions per second and cost $20 million. Twenty-five years later, most personal computers cost less than $1,000, and many use inexpensive Intel Celeron microchips that process over 600 million instructions per second.[3]

There are literally thousands of similar examples in the computer, telecommunications, and other industries. In the next 20 years, speed compression and cost reduction for computing power will be even more pronounced, and the number of new products and services will be staggering. The computer industry is not alone in rapid change. No company today can enter a major market expecting that a single product and strategy will sustain it for long. Rather, it is the ability to change that separates great marketers from others.

Marketing is concerned with the process of planning, providing the guidance system for companies. Planning sets direction before action takes place. It addresses what is to be accomplished and how to accomplish it. Competition forces marketing plans to be strategic,

ELEMENT	EXPLANATION	THE POINT IS . . .
Process of planning and executing	Is ongoing	→ Marketing is enduring.
	Sets directions before action takes place	→ Marketing is strategic.
	Manages people and events	→ Marketing is action.
Conception (product), pricing, promotion, and distribution (place)	Decisions marketers make	→ Marketing is decisions about products, prices, promotion, and place.
Ideas, goods, and services	What is marketed	→ Marketing is applied to any want—satisfying concept—real or imaginable.
Create exchanges	Focuses on the transfer of value	→ Marketing is relationships among two or more diverse parties.
Satisfy individual and organizational objectives	Helps all parties accomplish objectives	→ Marketing is concerned with the purposeful fulfillment of needs.

FIGURE 1.1 *Key Elements of the Marketing Definition*

to address ways to satisfy customer needs and wants better than competitors. Later we will see that plans are created for a whole organization as well as for select products. No matter what is being planned, marketing involves a broad range of people in order for plans to be relevant. Consequently, marketing usually means working in groups rather than working alone.

Marketing is also responsible for executing or carrying out the plan. Marketing manages people and events in line with the plan, which serves as a guide. To carry out plans, marketing must acquire and develop many of the organization's human resources. Marketers are managers and doers. Marketing is action.

PRODUCT, PRICE, PROMOTION, AND PLACE

Years ago, Professor James Culliton described the business executive as a "decider" and "artist"—a "mixer of ingredients" who sometimes follows a recipe as he or she goes along, sometimes adapts a recipe to the ingredients immediately available, and sometimes experiments with or invents ingredients no one else has tried.[4] This description gave Neil Borden, another noted professor, the idea that there is a list of elements the marketer mixes together. He called these elements the **marketing mix**.[5] Today they are known as the four Ps—product, price, promotion, and place. Several other elements are incorporated within this list. For example, product development, branding, packaging, and service are included in the product area. Leasing, credit terms, and price are all part of pricing. Advertising, personal selling, and sales promotion are included in promotion. Distribution, logistics, retailing, and direct marketing are part of place.

It is through the mixing process that organizations arrive at unique ways of addressing customers. In the process of mixing, marketing creativity and imagination play a key role. For example, Norcom, a school supplies company, found a market among the 40 million Americans who are left-handed. Norcom introduced a notebook with the wire binder and perforation on the right side and three holes punched on the left. Once available only in specialty stores, Norcom's "Left Hander" notebook is now sold in mass-merchandise outlets and over the Internet.[6] A dramatic shift in the mix produces a huge winner and minor shifts create day-to-day competition.

MARKETS FOR IDEAS, GOODS, AND SERVICES

Marketing occurs within markets and is applied to a very broad range of phenomena. A **market** consists of all the organizations and individuals with the potential to have the desire and the ability to acquire a particular idea, good, or service. Generally, we talk about marketing products, which are usually goods that are manufactured or services that are performed. Marketing can also be applied to any idea that can be used in an exchange of value. These include, for example, marketing events, causes, people, and places. Ideas, goods, and services are exchanged in consumer markets, business-to-business markets, nonprofit markets, and internal markets.

Consumer Markets   Literally millions of products are marketed to many diverse consumers. Consumer marketing occurs when organizations sell to individuals or households that buy, consume, and dispose of products. Leading consumer marketers include such companies as Procter & Gamble, Johnson & Johnson, General Mills, Hewlett-Packard, and Nike.

You know the products of these companies very well. You have probably already purchased or used many of them and will continue to do so over the years. Because you buy, consume, and dispose of products such as these daily, you are an important part of consumer marketing. We will learn more about consumer marketing throughout this book.

Business-to-Business Markets   Business-to-business marketing occurs when a business purchases goods or services to produce other goods, to support daily operations, or to resell at a profit. Although there are many more consumers than companies, business-to-business purchases far outweigh the consumer market in dollar amount.

Organizations belong either to the public or private sector. The public sector consists of federal, state, and local government organizations. The private sector includes industrial firms, professionals, retailers, and service organizations. Utility companies, which provide water, electricity, gas, and waste disposal, fall between the public and private sectors because they are regulated by the government but may be privately owned. All these organizations rely on business-to-business marketing to purchase goods and support their operations. For example, Procter & Gamble, a producer of some 400 brands of packaged consumer products,

MARKETING MIX

The four controllable variables—product, price, promotion, and place (distribution)—that are combined to appeal to the company's target markets.

MARKET

All the individuals and organizations with the desire or potential to have the desire and the ability to acquire a particular good or service.

United Technologies participates in business-to-business marketing in the aerospace industry.

spends $26 billion on goods and services purchased from other companies each year. Procter & Gamble recently joined 50 other members of the Grocery Manufacturers of America (GMA) in forming a massive Internet marketplace to streamline their supply chains and do all of their business-to-business purchasing online.[7] George Reilly, a research director at Gartner Group, Inc., predicts that in 2004 business-to-business commerce will be a $7.2 trillion industry.[8] In chapter 8 we will explore many of the topics and issues involved in business-to-business marketing.

Nonprofit Markets   Nonprofit marketing occurs when an organization does not try to make a profit but instead attempts to influence others to support its cause by using its service or by making a contribution. Marketing has many applications in the not-for-profit sector. Churches, museums, hospitals, universities, symphonies, and municipalities regularly create marketing plans in an effort to be more consumer oriented. The National Fish and Wildlife Foundation uses such marketing tools as fund-raisers and conferences to create partnerships with government agencies, universities, individuals, and corporations that will support its cause, which is to solve environmental problems.[9] The U.S. Postal Service competes with private companies, such as Federal Express and United Parcel Service (UPS), to attract consumers, and the U.S. Army, Navy, Air Force, and Marines use their large marketing budgets for recruiting purposes. Sometimes companies work with not-for-profit organizations for mutual benefit. Gatorade Co. partnered with the nonprofit Women's Sport Foundation to promote its line of sports drinks while at the same time encouraging athletic participation in girls under age 18.[10]

Like businesses that seek profit, many of these organizations want to please their constituents, and they have competition. Although they may not be motivated by profit, many are interested in obtaining revenues that equal or exceed expenses. A full range of marketing decisions is often required. We will learn in chapter 11 that, in making these decisions, many not-for-profit groups seek the same quality of marketing talent as for-profit companies do.

Internal Markets   Internal marketing occurs when managers of one functional unit market their capabilities to other units within their own organization. This type of marketing addresses the needs and wants of internal customers, the employees of the firm, so these people can ultimately contribute to the external customers, who are the end users of a company's products or services. For example, Dr. Lew Dotterer, director of learning and organizational development at Sparrow Health System in Lansing, Michigan, is responsible for maintaining the knowledge and skills of employees in all units of the system. Applying marketing techniques, he first identified the key customers—doctors, nurses, administrators, and so forth. Next, he researched each group to determine its learning needs. He then created educational programs to address the learning needs of each group and promoted these programs throughout the organization. Through internal marketing, Dr. Dotterer was able to help employees better serve Sparrow's external customers (patients).

CREATE EXCHANGES THAT SATISFY INDIVIDUAL AND ORGANIZATIONAL OBJECTIVES

How an organization connects with customers has a lot to do with its value. Without customers or the ability to attract them, an organization has absolutely no value. Without customers, an organization's assets are totally wasted. Value occurs for customers and for the organization only when an exchange is created. Thus, marketing creates valuable exchanges. An **exchange** is a process in which two or more parties provide something of value to one another. At the most basic level, an exchange involves a seller who provides a product to a buyer for money or some other item. Most exchanges are much more complex than that. They involve several parties in a social system exchanging all kinds of items.[11] Marketing brings the many parties together and facilitates exchanges. This provides utility. When marketers create utility, value is created. *Utility* is a term economists use to describe the want-satisfying potential of a good or service. There are four fundamental types of utility—form, place, time, and ownership.

Form, Place, Time, and Ownership Utility   **Form utility** occurs when knowledge and materials are converted into finished goods and services. Marketing provides form utility when it guides decisions about what products to create and the attributes those products should possess. When McDonald's created the Grilled Chicken Deluxe for health-conscious consumers, the specific sandwich provided form utility. Quicken.com provides form utility by combining personal finances, including stock tracking, analyst alerts, bank account tracking, financial news, and bill paying into one convenient Web site.[12] Generally, the marketing function is responsible only for specifying what form utility the final product should possess; research and development (R&D), engineering, manufacturing, and other units are responsible for actually building it.

Place utility makes goods and services conveniently available. Fresh bananas on a remote tree are not nearly as want satisfying as those at a local supermarket, convenience store, or restaurant. They are worth many times more at those locations than where they are grown. Marketing brings products to customers for the sake of convenience. When DHL Express, operator of the world's largest international air express network, delivers shipments to 635,000 destinations in 233 countries and territories, it is providing place utility.[13] Place utility can be extremely valuable. Shopping malls provide utility by grouping stores and products together, making it convenient and sometimes fun to shop. For example, Mall.com has brought together over 120 online stores to make shopping by brand or product convenient.[14]

Time utility makes goods and services available when they are wanted. Videotapes can be watched at your convenience, which is one reason for their tremendous popularity. UPS, Federal Express, DHL Express, and other overnight carriers offer outstanding time utility. L. L. Bean now receives an order one day and has the item at your home the next, 15 times faster than the Sears, Roebuck & Co. mail orders that dominated the 1970s and earlier. General Motor's e-commerce site, www.GMBuyPower.com, allows customers to choose a car's make, model, trim, and options and then pinpoints the nearest dealership with that particular model in stock.[15]

Ownership utility makes it possible to transfer the title of goods and services from one party to another. The most obvious way is through cash transactions, but credit card purchases and leasing are other means. Later we will learn about this function internationally. Even airplane travel is a form of ownership utility. By leasing a seat (buying a ticket), you can possess the vast resources of the air transportation system during the time required to reach nearly any destination on the planet. Marketing has progressed by finding better ways to produce increasing amounts of utility.

Organizational Objectives   All organizations have long-term objectives. Many organizations generally focus on financial measures such as profit margins and return on investment to

Experience utilizes a network of companies to provide time utility to their customers.

evaluate performance. Companies must make money when they fulfill consumer needs. Profit provides the financial fuel that allows companies to innovate and grow. Nonprofit organizations, in contrast, use measures such as donation levels, membership, and services provided to evaluate performance. Although nonprofit organizations must be effective and efficient, by definition they do not seek profit as a primary goal. Still, even nonprofit organizations strive to satisfy their constituents in a cost-effective way. For example, the national organizations for Boy Scouts and Girl Scouts have rigorous financial goals. They often strive for growth in sales and in number of members as well as certain levels of customer satisfaction relative to competitors.

THE MARKETING CONCEPT: THE PURPOSE OF MARKETING

Whereas the definition of marketing summarizes what marketers do, the marketing concept provides the underlying purpose. According to the **marketing concept** (philosophy), the purpose of marketing is to understand the needs and wants of customers and to create customer value through satisfaction and quality more effectively and efficiently than competitors in order to increase the value of the organization. Applying the concept helps meet the long-term goals of the organization. The marketing concept provides the guiding reference for appropriate marketing action. In principle, it is simple; in practice, it provides the basis for an awesomely competitive system that dramatically benefits consumers. Because needs and wants are numerous, diverse, and dynamic, the concept points toward unlimited opportunities for marketing. Elements of the marketing concept are summarized in Figure 1.2.

MARKETING CONCEPT
Holds that the purpose of marketing is to identify the needs and wants of customers within markets and satisfy them in ways that ensure the long-run success of the organization.

UNDERSTAND THE NEEDS AND WANTS OF CUSTOMERS AND TARGET MARKETS

Understanding customer needs and wants is central to the marketing concept. It is not possible to implement appropriate marketing without this understanding. Marketers use a **consumer orientation,** an organizational philosophy that focuses on satisfying consumer needs and wants.

CONSUMER ORIENTATION
An organizational philosophy that focuses on satisfying consumer needs and wants.

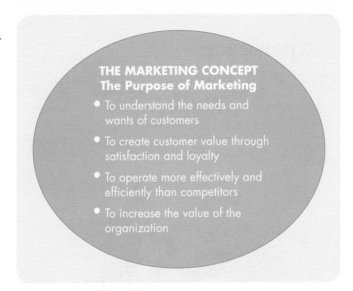

FIGURE 1.2 *The Marketing Concept*

NEEDS

Fundamental requirements the meeting of which is the ultimate goal of behavior.

Needs and wants are not the same. **Needs** are fundamental requirements—meeting them is the ultimate goal of behavior. Of course, there are many needs, ranging from those that allow life to exist to those that produce personal enrichment. A need becomes apparent when there is a gap between a desired state and an actual state. For example, you need proper nutrition on a regular basis to have a healthy and energetic body. When nutrition drops below the desired state, your body signals the deprivation—you feel hungry. When the need is satisfied, the hunger goes away. Needs represent what people and organizations must have to survive and thrive. The degree to which needs are satisfied determines the quality of life for all people and organizations.

WANT

A specific form of consumption desired to satisfy a need.

A **want** is the specific form of consumption desired to satisfy a need. Many different wants can fulfill a need. Each want represents an alternative way to meet goals or requirements. A want is simply one of many desires a person may have to help fulfill a need. For instance, hunger can be satisfied with a candy bar, an orange, or a chicken sandwich. Needs produce many wants. Fulfillment of a huge range of differing wants has the potential to satisfy needs.

Like people, organizations are customers with needs. All organizations have objectives that must be met. They need suppliers and employees. For-profit companies must make a sizable return on the owners' investment or they will go out of business. Nonprofit companies have other needs: The Red Cross, for example, must help increasing numbers of disaster victims if it is to meet its organizational objectives. Every organization needs customers or clients—the people they serve. There are many ways to obtain them, as well as specific types of suppliers, characteristics of employees, and profit objectives. Each way represents a potential want. Boeing addresses the need of United Airlines for aircraft by designing planes the airline will want with attributes that satisfy United's needs. Figure 1.3 shows the relationship between needs and wants.

The marketing concept recognizes the long-run nature of successful marketing. Potential customers continuously search to satisfy wants in such a way as to produce the greatest amount of need satisfaction. Therefore, customers are dynamic. Marketing leaders facilitate and adjust to change rapidly by learning how to serve customers in new and creative ways. Long-term success as a marketer requires change management. The speed and effectiveness with which marketers learn how to serve customers can provide tremendous competitive advantages. Because needs and wants are numerous, diverse, and dynamic, the concept points toward unlimited opportunities for marketing.

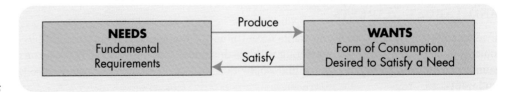

FIGURE 1.3 *Needs and Wants*

CREATE CUSTOMER VALUE THROUGH SATISFACTION AND LOYALTY

The second element of the marketing concept is to create customer value through satisfaction and loyalty. **Satisfaction** refers to the consumer's overall rating of his or her experience with a company and its products. **Loyalty** is a measure of how often, when selecting from a product class, a customer purchases a particular brand. **Customer value** refers to what consumers perceive they gain from owning or using a product over and above the cost of acquiring it—a topic we will consider in more detail in chapter 6. In combination, satisfaction and customer value help create customer loyalty. Loyal customers are a valuable asset. They provide a continuous revenue stream through repeated purchases of a product. They tell others about their satisfaction, which is one of the most effective and inexpensive forms of promotion. To increase customer satisfaction, Amtrak began offering free train rides to passengers who were unhappy with Amtrak's train service.[16] In like manner, Taco Bell placed its 100 percent satisfaction guarantee—"You'll Love It or We'll Eat It!"—on all of its tray liners, whereas Hawaii's Aloha Airlines pledged that if on-time performance, baggage handling, and service weren't up to customers' satisfaction, it would issue a free ticket to anywhere in the Hawaiian Islands.[17]

Southwest Airlines is increasing customer loyalty by simplifying its online ticket ordering process by requiring users to click just 10 times to buy a ticket.[18] Sears now allows customers to request a repair online. These organizations are responding to a request from customers to make their lives easier, thereby adding customer value. Organizations that strive to implement a marketing philosophy that benefits the company develop satisfied, loyal customers. A level of satisfaction strong enough to create product loyalty requires an organizational commitment to customer value in every aspect of the business.

OPERATE MORE EFFECTIVELY AND EFFICIENTLY THAN COMPETITORS

Strong marketers compete, and they measure success by the way their customers judge them, especially relative to competitors. Competition is the key to our economic system. You see aggressive global competition occurring every day: Coke versus Pepsi, McDonald's versus Burger King, and American Airlines versus British Airways. Phil Knight, founder of Nike, has challenged its marketing team to take competition to a new level—replace Coca-Cola as the most recognized brand in the world. Since Coke and Nike don't compete head to head with the same products, this competition is unique. It will be interesting to see whether Nike, Coke, or another company has the number-one position in the next few years.

Don't think that only for-profit companies compete. Even nonprofit groups compete. Mail-order catalogs from the Art Institute of Chicago, the Metropolitan Museum of Art, the Smithsonian Institution, and Boston's Museum of Fine Arts all compete for your purchases. The United Way competes for your discretionary income, and political parties compete for your donations. Marketers outperform competitors by being more effective and efficient. **Effectiveness** means that the organization's activities produce results that matter to consumers. It means doing the right things. **Efficiency** means doing these things with minimal waste of time and money. Baxter International, a hospital products company with over $6 billion in annual sales, is successful on both counts. First, it recognized that customers—hospitals—were spending too much money storing and distributing supplies. Baxter developed an electronic ordering system that indicates what supplies are needed daily and where in the hospital the supplies should go. This system is effective because it meets the needs of Baxter's customers better than the competition. It is efficient because it saves both the hospitals and Baxter substantial amounts of money and time. In many cases hospitals choose Baxter as their only supplier, which leads to higher sales and profits for Baxter.

INCREASE THE VALUE OF THE ORGANIZATION

Both private and public companies strive to increase the value of the organization to its stakeholders. Stakeholders of an organization include customers, suppliers, stockholders, and employees. The single most important role of the marketing effort is to increase the value to the stakeholders by establishing and implementing an effective marketing strategy. Many strategies can be developed. For example, it can involve focusing on a new set of customers or focusing on the types of customers that the company has targeted in the past. Amazon.com targets past customers by e-mailing former customers with book recommendations based on

SATISFACTION
The consumer's overall rating of his or her experience with a company and its products.

LOYALTY
A measure of how often, when selecting from a product class, a customer purchases a particular brand.

CUSTOMER VALUE
What consumers perceive they gain from owning or using a product over and above the cost of acquiring it.

EFFECTIVENESS
The degree to which an organization's activities produce results that matter to consumers.

EFFICIENCY
The degree to which activities are carried out without waste of time or money.

past purchases, e-mailing a best-sellers list to customers, and soliciting book reviews from past customers. All of these activities help Amazon.com secure loyal customers, thereby increasing the value of the organization.

Increasing the value of the organization can also be done by introducing an entirely new product. For example, Smith Klein Beecham recently created a vaccine for Lyme disease in an attempt to limit the 16,000 new cases of the disease that appear each year.[19] The organization was able to increase the value of the organization to all stakeholders: its employees, its customers, its suppliers, and society as a whole. Creating value for the organization and its shareholders is part of the purpose of marketing.

THE MARKETING STRATEGY PROCESS

The marketing concept is implemented through the marketing strategy process, the series of steps the organization takes to interface with the rest of the world. Chapter 4 defines the elements of that process in more depth. Figure 1.4 illustrates the steps of the marketing strategy process.

SITUATION ANALYSIS

Situation analysis includes all the marketing activities required to understand the global marketing environment, the customer's needs and wants, and the competition. It predicts future marketing conditions for the period covered by the strategic marketing plan. Many aspects of the global marketing environment are the same for all organizations, no matter what their line of business. Other aspects are unique to a particular industry. Both types of aspects are addressed in chapter 3.

To enhance their ability to analyze situations, organizations often build elaborate marketing intelligence systems. These capture, distill, and disseminate data to executives on an ongoing basis. Marketers also engage in marketing research, which supplies information about a particular circumstance such as planning for a new product, pricing, or the selling approach.

The situation analysis gives a good idea of the issues an organization must address. It provides the context around which plans are created, altered, and adjusted. This generally requires a thorough knowledge of consumer behavior or, in business-to-business marketing, of organizational buying behavior. Understanding consumer behavior gives marketers insight into why buyers respond to goods and services as they do. As we will see in chapter 7, consumer behavior involves not only their purchase behavior but also the ways in which consumers perceive and use information and how they arrive at feelings of satisfaction and dissatisfaction. Organizational buying behavior is more complex in terms of the functions and personnel involved in the buying decision, and marketer relationships with these buyers are often more direct. Chapter 8 covers organizational buying in the context of business-to-business marketing. An important function of the situation analysis is to provide the information needed to select certain customers for emphasis—targeting—which is covered next.

TARGETING

Markets usually have many types of potential customers with many different needs and wants. It is impractical to attempt to satisfy all customers. Consequently, leading marketers divide customers into groups with similar characteristics. They then select one or several unique groups to address. A **target market** is a group of potential customers with similar characteristics that the company tries to satisfy better than the competition.

The first decision that a customer-driven company makes is to choose its target markets. Fashion designer Ralph Lauren targets upscale consumers with his popular casual line. Lee,

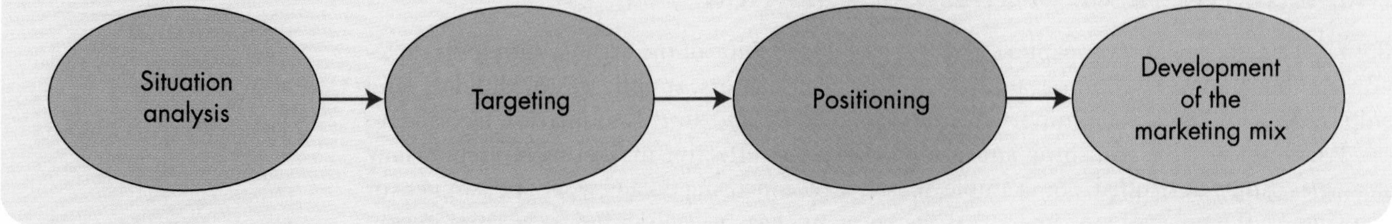

TARGET MARKET

A group of potential customers with similar characteristics that a marketer tries to satisfy better than the competition.

FIGURE **1.4** *Steps in the Marketing Strategy Process*

Goldfish and Sand Dollar
go swimmingly together

Martha's 256 colors offer some inspiring combinations and make decorating a room or an entire house as easy as one-two-three. All you have to do is: 1. Pick a color, Goldfish for example. 2. Flip the paint chip over to find the perfect color to complement it, Sand Dollar for instance. 3. Stand back, and admire.

AVAILABLE AT KMART, SEARS & CANADIAN TIRE

Martha Stewart's line of household products targets customers who are looking for high-quality goods at a low cost.

also with a line of casual clothing, targets a completely different subset of the market. Consider the different target market groups for Rolex and Swatch, Cannondale and Huffy, or Marriott and Motel 6. Many companies are targeting Generation Y by using names and ads with the word "Extreme," or simply "X-." Extreme products include Right Guard's X-treme Sport deodorant, Schick's X-treme III razor, and Burger King's X-treme Double Cheeseburger. As marketers are well aware, Gen Y teens spend an average of $100 billion a year and as a segment are expected to grow to 25 million by 2010.[20]

POSITIONING

One of the most useful concepts to help integrate marketing decisions is positioning. **Positioning** is the process of creating an image, reputation, or perception of the company or its goods and services in the consumer's mind. Although the idea exists in the buyer's mind, it is formed by very specific actions of the marketing organization. First, the company must identify how it wants to be positioned with a target market. Nike says "Just Do It," reinforcing the image of an aggressive, action-oriented company. It's no accident that amateur as well as professional athletes perceive Nike as producing high-quality shoes that help athletes perform to their maximum potential. Everything Nike does is designed to create this impression, including the use of outstanding athletes such as Tiger Woods to spread its promotional message. Positioning is accomplished by creating and adjusting the product, place, promotion, and price variables so that consumers can recognize the distinctiveness of a company or its product. Potential buyers can then better determine the degree to which a product fits their desires. It is this distinctiveness that supports positioning. The next section discusses how companies use the marketing mix to create distinctive positions. Chapter 6 examines positioning strategies in more detail, including the various bases for positioning.

MARKETING MIX DECISIONS

Once the target market is selected, marketing mix decisions have to be made. How do you go about blending the elements into an appealing mix? Clearly, there needs to be a focus and a purpose. That's where the target market enters the picture. Since it is composed of similar

CONNECTED: SURFING THE NET

www.mountaindew.com

"Experience the Dew" on Mountain Dew's "DeWWWeb" site! See how Mountain Dew focuses on Generation Y through its adrenaline-packed ads and "X-treme" Internet activities.

POSITIONING

The process of creating an image, reputation, or perception of the company or its goods and services in the consumer's mind.

FIGURE 1.5 *The Marketing
Mix and Target Marketing*

customers, it is possible to address them with one marketing mix. Adjustments to individual customers then can be made within this framework. Figure 1.5 illustrates elements of the marketing mix and target marketing. Later we'll see that even minor inconsistencies in how marketing mix elements are blended can be disastrous. At the same time, innovation in these areas is what provides opportunities for organizations to excel.

Product Strategy   Product strategy includes decisions about which products to develop, how to manage current products, and which products to phase out. It thereby determines the portfolio of goods and services the organization provides to the market. Because products go through a life cycle, product strategy decisions are ongoing. Most organizations use systematic processes to develop new products and manage products over their life cycles, including decisions regarding product attributes, warranties, package design, and customer service features.

Equally important for many companies is the establishment of brands and the creation of brand equity, the value associated with a brand. Brands send messages to consumers about the unique qualities of products. A great deal of care must be taken to establish brand names and protect their reputation. For example, in the $190 billion beverage industry, brands flourish and die quickly, such as Clearly Canadian flavored water. Coca-Cola has joined with Nestlé to produce a ready-to-drink coffee. National Beverage (with brands Shasta and Faygo) has introduced VooDoo Rain, a line of herbally enhanced, fluorescent-colored beverages. Quaker Oats has purchased both Snapple and Mistic.[21] Techniques for making product decisions will be discussed in both chapter 9, "Product Decisions and Strategies," and chapter 10, "Product Innovation and Management."

Place Strategy   The objective of place strategy is to serve customers by providing products where and when they are needed, in the proper quantities, with the greatest appeal, and at the lowest possible cost. The first task is to determine which distribution channels to use. A distribution channel is a set of independent organizations that make a good or service available for purchase by consumers or businesses. Some companies sell directly, such as your local dry cleaner, whereas others use longer channels with more members. For example, a company may sell to wholesalers, who sell to retailers, who sell to you. Imagine how complicated this becomes in global markets, when numerous channel members are required to move products to customers around the world. In the auto parts business, by the time a single part has reached an installer, been put on a vehicle, and billed to the consumer, more than 50 percent of the price has gone to one or more middlemen! As a result, Internet start-ups such as Carstation.com, MechanicNet.com, and PartsMerchant.com have sought to streamline the auto parts market and sell directly to installers.[22]

Place decisions also involve physical distribution, which is the movement of products through the channels to consumers. To make movement efficient, companies need order entry systems, transportation, and shipping and inventory storage capacity. Sophisticated information systems are creating some extremely innovative ways of serving customers better.

Finally, companies need to manage their interface with customers. Two basic ways are retailing and direct marketing. Retailing involves selling products directly to end users, often in retail outlets such as McDonald's or Kmart. Direct marketing uses an array of nonstore methods of connecting with customers. Marketing via telephone is one of the traditional direct-marketing approaches. However, with the growth and proliferation of the Internet, traditional direct marketers are turning more and more to e-mail marketing, spending almost $300 million on that medium in 2000 alone.[23] Chapter 12, "Marketing Channels, Wholesaling, and Physical Distribution," and chapter 13, "Retailing and Direct Marketing," address the place strategy.

Promotion Strategy   Promotion involves communicating with customers in a variety of ways. Marketers develop integrated marketing communications by coordinating advertising, sales promotion, personal selling, and public relations to get consistent messages to all types of customers. These messages provide information necessary for the choice process. Promotion also increases demand for products, describes unique product characteristics, and helps build customer loyalty by creating expectations and reinforcing buying decisions. For example, Edy's hired race car driver Jeff Gordon to star in a new annual promotion. The first year, Gordon promoted Checked Flag Sundae ice cream. The second year, Edy's ran a promotion entitled "Invent Jeff's Next Flavor," which included asking consumers to invent a new ice cream flavor. Edy's and Gordon chose the best recipe from over 8,000 entrants. For the next year, Gordon promoted the new flavor, Mint Chocolate Sundae, at race car and promotional events throughout the United States.[24]

The promotion strategy includes determining the objectives to be attained, as well as creating messages and the forms they will take. In addition, the communication mechanism or media must be selected. Will two-way communication be used, such as personal selling, the phone, or Internet, or will one-way radio, television, or other media carry the message? Since many messages are carried by numerous media, these decisions can be complex and tremendously interesting. Marketers have a vast number of options when developing promotions, such as training and managing a sales force or creating advertising. Because these mechanisms work together, coordination is vital. The promotion strategy is addressed in chapter 14, "Integrated Marketing Communications"; chapter 15, "Mass Communications: Advertising, Sales Promotions, and Public Relations"; and chapter 16, "Personal Selling and Sales Force Management."

Price Strategy   Price strategy affects nearly every part of a business. The objective is to set prices to reflect the value received by customers and to achieve the volume and profit required by the organization. When prices are too high, customers are dissatisfied and refuse to buy or switch to a competitor. When prices are too low, companies don't have money to cover costs, invest in new development, and provide a fair return to owners. So pricing strategy is extremely important.

Historically, prices were set by adding up costs and tagging on some extra for profit. That approach ignores customers and competitors, two critical elements in determining price. Pricing must focus on determining value, which is based on what customers expect and desire, what competitors charge, and the unique qualities of the products. Marketers must also determine how their prices will influence the volume sold relative to the competition, and what competitors are likely to do with their prices. Consequently, we find many different pricing strategies for new and existing products and for various competitive scenarios.

Prices not only need to be set but also must be communicated and administered. Will warranty charges be extra? What is charged for the base product or add-on? What financing is available? These questions must be answered and factored in. Pricing strategy is covered in chapter 17, "Pricing Approaches," and chapter 18, "Pricing Strategy."

THE EVOLUTION OF MARKETING

When Levi Strauss originally connected with customers, he did it personally—one-to-one. Over time his company moved to mass production and extended its reach to consumers globally. As with most organizations, the connections to customers became more complex and strained as the company expanded. Levi Strauss, much like marketing in general, has come full circle and is again forging connections at a more personal level. Today, companies realize the importance of personal connections and are working to establish and maintain them. In

CONNECTED: SURFING THE NET

www.edys-dreamery.com

Visit the site dedicated to one of Edy's product lines to analyze your dreams, create your dream job, win prizes, learn about the flavors (including Grandma's Cookie Jar and Sticky Bun), or send an electronic postcard.

response to such challenges, marketing has developed a variety of mechanisms over the decades. A brief history will help explain how marketing has evolved in response to changing business conditions and requirements.

Marketing activities, in the broadest sense, can be traced to the trading and barter that occurred thousands of years ago. The ancient Egyptians had vending machines as early as 200 B.C.! But it wasn't until the 1500s in England and the 1600s in Germany and North America that modern marketing began. Most people lived in rural areas and produced all necessary goods themselves. Nevertheless, enterprising businesspeople, who were actually early marketers, discovered they could make money by providing luxury items to the upper class and more practical goods to others in the population.

Although large trading companies had been around for centuries, many merchants and craftsmen built their businesses by satisfying individual customers. You often bought your shoes from a cobbler who knew the exact dimensions of your feet, your preferred shoe style, and your ability to pay. Even if the cobbler had competition, why would you go elsewhere?[25] During the late 1700s and early 1800s, major improvements in production and transportation, along with growing urbanization, fostered the development of mass marketing. **Mass marketing** is the mass production, mass distribution, and mass promotion of a product to all buyers. A free enterprise system based on competition began to develop. Starting in the late 1800s, advertising, marketing research, improved physical distribution methods, and retailing were used to help find and develop markets for mass production. Unlike the days when the consumer came into direct contact with the producer, more goods began to be purchased through an intermediary. The producer had no contact with the end user. During this century, the economy moved through three basic eras in terms of the focus of business: the production era, the sales era, and the customer marketing era as depicted in Figure 1.6.

THE PRODUCTION ERA

During the production era, which lasted until about 1925, companies focused on ways to make products in mass quantities. They achieved production economies that often led to lower prices. This **production orientation** emphasized new products and the efficiency of production. Businesses were primarily concerned with ways to speed physical production. Manufacturers did not address the consumer until after the goods had been made. They assumed a good product would sell itself. Salespeople were more interested in helping the manufacturer take orders than in helping the customer. Demand for these new lower-priced products was often greater than supply, which led to the growth of large manufacturing organizations.

Henry Ford's approach is a prime example of production orientation. Until Ford came along, automobiles were made one at a time in small factories. Often each car was unique; perhaps a few of each type were made. Ford standardized the design of the Model T and mass-produced it on an assembly line. This dramatically reduced costs and made cars affordable to more people. Visualizing a ready demand for this cheap form of transportation, he remarked that people "can have any color they want, as long as it's black."

THE SALES ERA

As production methods improved and more firms entered markets, competition increased. Eventually, the supply of many products outpaced demand. Since businesses had more goods than their regular customers could buy, the need for personal selling and advertising arose. The sales era focused on ways to sell more effectively. This period was marked by the Great Depression of the 1930s when spending power was drastically reduced. Consumers resisted purchasing nonessential goods and services. Sales forces and sales tactics were developed to overcome their resistance.

MASS MARKETING

The mass production, mass distribution, and mass promotion of a product to all buyers.

PRODUCTION ORIENTATION

Historical marketing period that emphasized new products and the efficiency of production.

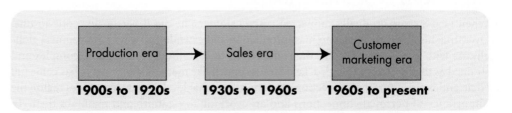

FIGURE 1.6 *Eras of Marketing Since 1900*

The **sales orientation** emphasized that consumers must be convinced to buy. Consumer tastes, preferences, and needs did not receive much consideration. Rather, companies tried to shape consumers' ideals to fit the attributes of the products offered.

After World War II, a vastly different economic environment emerged in the United States. The country was moving from the **seller's market,** in which scarcity of products lets the seller control the market, to a **buyer's market,** in which abundance of products lets the buyer control the market. With the emergence of the buyer's market came rewards to organizations that gave customers a prominent place in their business thinking.

THE CUSTOMER MARKETING ERA

A company with a sales philosophy focuses internally. Emphasis is placed on making the product, then on selling it. The sales force has to push existing products to the consumer through increased promotion and personal selling. In contrast, the customer marketing concept emphasizes customer satisfaction and value. After an organization determines consumer needs, it coordinates its activities so that the product will satisfy customer needs and wants.

During the past 30 years marketing has evolved into a tremendously important business function. Figure 1.7 illustrates this evolution from the viewpoint of top executives. Before the 1960s, the prevailing economic philosophy in the United States was *caveat emptor*—"Let the buyer beware." In other words, consumers had to be cautious when purchasing a product. Once they did, they were stuck with it—and any injuries that might result. It didn't matter if the product was defective.

Led by the efforts of President John F. Kennedy, legislators began to be more responsive to consumer rights. Throughout the 1960s and 1970s, government agencies and private consumer protection groups advanced this cause. Successful companies realized they could gain a competitive edge by treating customers fairly. They also became keenly aware that a loyal repeat buyer is more profitable than a one-time buyer (which you will learn more about in chapter 2). Businesses began to realize that customer satisfaction was paramount.

In the early 1980s, executives turned their attention to competitors. For the first time in U.S. history, foreign rivals seriously threatened the dominance enjoyed for years by U.S.-based global companies. Competition, beyond mere price and promotion, was developed and refined in many ways. During the 1980s, strategic planning became widely accepted. The role of marketing was elevated from understanding consumer behavior to assessing customer expectations, learning about competitors' practices, and determining how to make the organization an industry leader in a continuously changing world.

In the early 1990s, business executives began building teams designed to focus all of the organization's resources on customer satisfaction. Achieving customer satisfaction depends on the entire organization and on how well the various parts work together. A business is like any other team; success is determined not only by individual talents but also by the ability to do

SALES ORIENTATION

Historical marketing period that emphasized that consumers must be convinced to buy.

SELLER'S MARKET

The marketing environment in which scarcity of products lets the seller control the market.

BUYER'S MARKET

The marketing environment in which an abundance of product lets the buyer control the market.

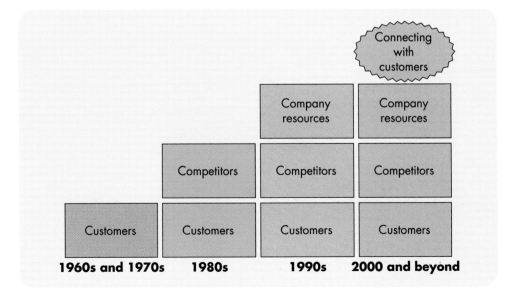

FIGURE 1.7 *Marketing's Recent Past and Immediate Future*

well as a unit. The organization that can form fast, flexible, powerful teams is capable of competing in global markets. It is clear that an organization must be designed to maximize both the speed of its responsiveness to customers and its ability to work as a team.

Customer-driven organizations implement the marketing concept by ensuring that all parts of the organization make the maximum possible contribution toward satisfying customer wants. They make sure that every part of the organization has a clear line of sight to the customer. This often involves using research tools to study customers, their satisfaction, and their loyalty to the company as well as competitors. Customer-driven organizations also make sure that all the costs they incur over the long run provide at least as much value in customer want satisfaction. For example, Microsoft is customer driven. It brings software to market that creates huge amounts of want satisfaction. Its products use the latest technology, such as the latest version of Microsoft Windows Media software. The new Media Player 7 enables customers to copy CDs, listen to Internet radio, and watch videos all with only an integrated player.[26] Microsoft willingly supports millions of users, one at a time, with customer service and 800 numbers to ensure that its products can be used as intended. Customers have rewarded Microsoft with loyalty that yields enormous profits. These, in turn, fuel additional change in Microsoft, making it one of the most competitive companies in the world. Companies such as Microsoft are using their customer-driven approaches to move into the 21st century, which is described in the next section.

In the late 1990s, organizations began to reestablish links with customers on a massive scale. Today they want permanent connections so customers become assets of the organization, not just one-time buyers. How do marketers connect with huge numbers of customers? They certainly can't ask customers what they want one at a time and then provide it—that would be too expensive. So marketers must go through the steps of target marketing, positioning, and development of the marketing mix. Then they can get personal with customers in the target market. Personal attention occurs when organizations are customer driven.

CONNECTING WITH CUSTOMERS IN THE FUTURE

The future will center around better ways of connecting with customers. The single phrase—*connecting with customers*—captures the objective of leading-edge companies. It communicates precisely what outstanding marketers do—they connect. How marketers connect is embodied in the five supporting themes of this book, each of which will shape marketing well into the 21st century. They are:

- Connecting through technology
- Connecting through relationships
- Connecting globally
- Connecting with diversity
- Connecting ethically

These supporting themes were carefully selected to describe how marketers build lasting connections. These five key forces, depicted in Figure 1.8, will reappear throughout the book.

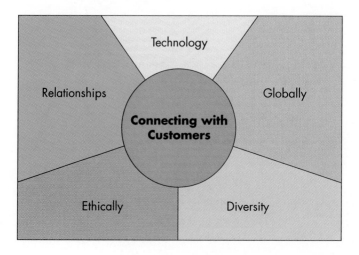

FIGURE 1.8 *Marketing in the 21st Century*

Peter Drucker, renowned educator and author, says that innovation and marketing are the two basic roles of every business, and all other functions (such as accounting, finance, and engineering) support these two business roles. Drucker defines innovation as rearranging the old or creating the new and says that marketing is the process that delivers innovations to society. New technology is all around us, but three types are particularly noteworthy: (1) product technology that spawns new goods and services, (2) process technology that provides flexible manufacturing and distribution to adjust rapidly to customer needs, and (3) the Internet, which facilitates two-way global connectivity with customers. Additionally, we will discuss the concept of a marketspace that is bringing many of these technological forces into a single focus.

Process and Product Technology **Product technology** is technology that spawns the development of new goods and services. Product technology provides the raw material that fuels improvements in our standard of living. Examples of innovative technology that has produced radically new goods and services are everywhere. Olympic swimmers have recently switched to bodysuits such as the Speedo Fastskin because the product's tiny V-shaped ridges allow swimmers to pass more efficiently through the water.[27] Libraries throughout the United States have begun stocking e-books, library books that can be "checked out" over the Internet. [28] Cellular systems support telephone calls, fax, and data transmissions, as well as global positioning from moving vehicles everywhere. Soon digital television and flat-screen technology will support in-home theater systems superior to today's best theaters. We can clone the "best" sheep, tomatoes, and viruses.

Process technology is technology used to make goods and services. Most typically found in manufacturing, it is also used to enter customer orders and make sure that the appropriate products get to the right customer rapidly. Not long ago, the challenge was to forecast the styles and quantity of goods to be produced and have them ready for customers when needed. Today, flexible manufacturing is changing all that. This type of manufacturing is often called *agile production systems*, which describes its versatility. These systems make it possible to respond to customers in a virtual environment—to build a product they request immediately.

Probably the most important marketing development due to process technology is the personalization of products. **Mass customization** occurs when customizing a product for a specific customer is built into a process. Mass customization gives companies the opportunity to produce affordable, high-quality goods and services—but with a shorter cycle time and the lower costs associated with mass production.[29] One form of mass customization occurs at the time of use. When an auto is programmed to recognize one or several drivers and automatically adjust the seat, radio, and ride, customization occurs. Today, mapping systems hooked to satellites provide customized direction finding. Voice-recognition technology will soon make it possible to mass-customize a broad range of items, connecting customers with products that adjust automatically, and with direct verbal links to companies everywhere. [30]

Customization can also occur in conjunction with manufacturing. For example, Reflect.com, a manufacturer of skin and hair care products, allows customers to customize each product they purchase. After taking a short questionnaire, customers receive a tailored product, down to the label and the design. [31] Also impressive is the work done by direct marketer L. L. Bean. By linking a publisher's subscription list with its customer list, L. L. Bean can place ads for customers in certain magazine issues and ads for noncustomers in others. In other words, you may receive the same magazine as your next-door neighbor but with different ads targeting each of you.

The Internet Of the many technological advances that have assisted marketers in their work, perhaps the most significant to date is the Internet. It is a tremendous asset in many ways: Global, interactive, and fully integrated, it creates the opportunity to establish one-to-one relationships with customers. An estimated 360 million people use the Internet worldwide, with 157 million in Canada and the United States alone.[32] By 2003, experts believe that 70 percent of the world population will have access to the Internet. That's up from 28 percent in 1998![33] The Internet is home to content providers, advertisers, and you—the audience.

**CONNECTED:
SURFING THE NET**

www.reflect.com

Find out what products are best for you. Choose your own bottle, label design, and name for your customized product.

One of the many ways in which the Internet serves as a tool for marketers is the use of hand-held computers for marketing surveys.

INTERNET

A global network of computers that enables the transmission of data through the use of a personal computer.

The **Internet** is a global network of computers that has been around since the 1960s, when it was first deployed by the Department of Defense as a means to send messages in case of a nuclear attack. Until the 1990s, the network was accessed primarily by researchers, who shared the capacity of supercomputers as well as electronic mail capabilities. The Web itself, with the use of hypertext, which allowed people to click on text on their screens in order to link to another computer, was introduced in the mid-1990s. The World Wide Web of today—which provides graphics, sound, color, and video—is made possible by graphical browsers, such as the widely popular Netscape Communicator. The structure of the Internet as it pertains to marketing is described in chapter 3.

Throughout this textbook you will learn many ways in which the Internet serves as a tool for marketers—including scanning, research, communication, and distribution. Figure 1.9 highlights a few of the various uses. As a scanning tool, the Internet can be used to evaluate trends, the environment, customers, competitors, and other forces. As a research tool, the Internet can be used to conduct Web surveys, focus groups, observation, and so forth. The Internet is also a fantastic means of distributing products such as magazines, music, and video clips.

Online retailing has become a very popular form of distribution. Marketers communicate with customers through interactive and relationship-building promotions. The Internet is a medium for advertising and public relations, as well.

Marketplace and Marketspace   We tend to think of marketing as activities that occur in a physical marketplace. With the amazing new developments in technology, however, it is possible to market goods and services in **marketspace,** an electronic space where business occurs.

MARKETSPACE

An electronic space where business occurs.

Marketspace transactions take place via the Internet, interactive television or CD-ROMs, ATM machines, online services, shopping channels, 800 numbers, and others. You can travel to Tower Records, Virgin, Strawberries, or any marketplace and buy music on compact discs or tapes. In contrast, you can call a music service in a marketspace—such as Tower On-line—and order the same music. Some marketspaces encourage you to explore new artists and sounds.

Numerous marketspaces available on the Internet are ideal for searching for items such as books and records. Browsing capabilities on Web sites are outstanding. Typing the name of a favorite artist can turn up obscure recordings not easily found in a store. You can even experience music from around the world, including Russian, Pakistani, or Chinese selections. Other Internet marketspaces provide information about nearly every other type of purchase. For instance, while you're browsing the Internet you can listen to your favorite music by artist, by genre, or by radio station. You can also find out what musical events are happening in your area and online listen to interviews, download RealPlayer for free, and buy and review CDs. Broadcast.com offers 30 different categories of radio stations in 138 cities, 24 hours per day, 7 days per week.[34]

Some predict that the growth of marketspace will eventually result in the eradication of marketplaces. Indeed, online retail sales topped $20 billion in 1999 and are expected to grow

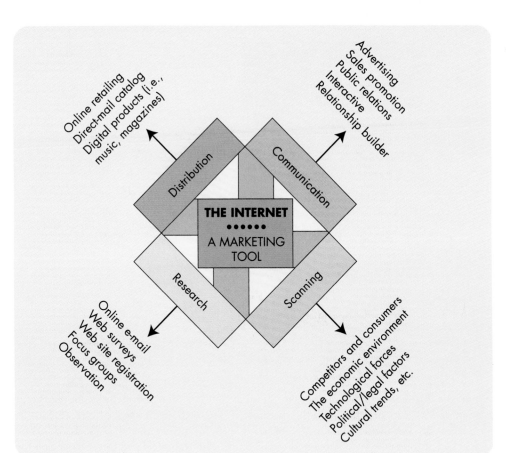

FIGURE 1.9 *The Internet as
a Marketing Tool*

900 percent cumulatively, or 55 percent annually, to $185 billion in 2005.[35] Although this is a significant growth, the eradication of marketplaces altogether is unlikely for several reasons. Technology does not offer the social dimension of shopping in a marketplace where consumers can interact with store personnel and other shoppers. In addition, in a store consumers can physically touch, test, compare, and try on products. Shopping in a marketplace also gives consumers greater reassurance that their credit card transactions will remain confidential.

Connecting through Relationships   Before the production era, marketers embraced the customer orientation. They created products on demand for specific customers. Relationships were built on a personal level. Consumers dealt directly with manufacturers. With mass production began the separation of manufacturers and consumers. As more levels of distribution channels were added—including retailers and wholesalers—the consumer's voice was heard less and less. In an effort to get closer—to become more connected—organizations today are enthusiastically embracing relationship marketing. Figure 1.10 describes a continuum of marketing exchanges from pure transactions to repeated transactions to relationships.[36]

A pure transaction occurs only once. When it is finished, both parties go their separate ways. Repeated transactions occur when customers have strong preferences. Many times they become loyal customers. Relationships create an even stronger connection. **Relationship marketing** is the development and maintenance of successful relational exchanges. It involves interactive, ongoing, two-way connections among customers, organizations, suppliers, and other parties for mutual benefit. Scudder Investment Services, a financial firm, teamed with AARP to create the only investment program geared to the over-50 market. Realizing that aging baby boomers were especially active—and wealthy—Scudder tailored its portfolio programs to meet the particular needs of this segment.[37]

Not all customers are looking for strong relationships in all exchanges. Marketers need to be sensitive to this fact. However, there is a clear trend. In recent years, marketing has evolved from transaction-based exchanges toward relationship-based exchanges. The change goes far

RELATIONSHIP MARKETING
The development and maintenance of successful relational
exchanges through interactive,
ongoing, two-way connections
among customers, organizations,
suppliers, and other parties for
mutual benefit.

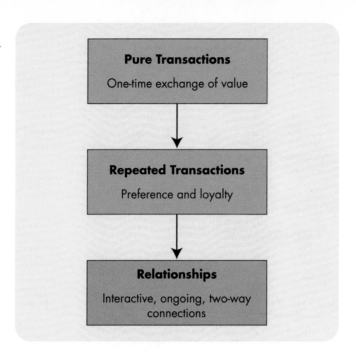

FIGURE 1.10 *Types of
Marketing Exchange*

beyond the interaction between an organization and its customers. It includes suppliers and other parties who are dependent on the customer. These relationships range from informal to contractual or even ownership. On the informal level, incentives make it difficult or inconvenient for customers to switch to a new organization. For example, Land Rover has a club for customers, with a newsletter and invitations to off-road rallies. Service managers call customers to see how their Land Rover Discovery is performing.

*ePresence provides its clients
with the tools to utilize
relationship marketing.*

*Through strategic partner-
ships, Memolink.com attracts
its desired audience.*

*Mr Clean and Econo Lodge
demonstrate a strategic
alliance.*

In business markets, suppliers develop computerized systems that are tied to a customer's manufacturing processes. If the customer selects a new supplier, the computer system will also need alterations. In some cases, these relationships are based on long-term contracts and partnerships. Textron, a manufacturer of auto parts, has multiple-year contracts with Chrysler to supply trim and functional components for the Dodge Viper.[38] This arrangement gives Textron the incentive and security to commit significant investments to technology that will specifically benefit Chrysler.

In some cases, **strategic alliances** occur when a partnership is formed by two or more organizations for a new venture. For example, credit card companies often ally with airlines or automotive companies. American Express has marketed cards in partnership with ITT Sheraton, the New York Knicks basketball team, and the New York Rangers hockey team. The Rangers and Knicks cards offer discounts on games and merchandise, whereas the Sheraton card offers such rewards as free hotel accommodations.[39]

Some alliances may involve actual ownership arrangements. In these cases, several parties form an organization that is owned jointly. For example, America Online, Inktomi Corp., and Adero Inc. formed a global alliance known as "Content Bridge" to compete in the billion-dollar Internet content delivery business. According to their agreement, Inktomi will deliver the content, Adero will update it and oversee transactions, while AOL will provide the network.[40] Since ownership is involved, these relationships strengthen the connections between the parent organizations.

CONNECTING GLOBALLY

Marketers are connecting globally like never before. The global marketplace is tremendously important for U.S. companies, as the United States reigns as the world's leading exporter, shipping $850 billion in goods and services per year.[41] U.S. exports continue to climb dramatically, as demonstarted by $90.6 billion in exports for the month of June 2000 alone.[42] Worldwide marketing opportunities are growing in many areas, including Asia, Latin America, Eastern Europe, the United Kingdom, Germany, Japan, France, Mexico, and Australia. Marketers

STRATEGIC ALLIANCES
A partnership formed by two or more organizations for a new venture.

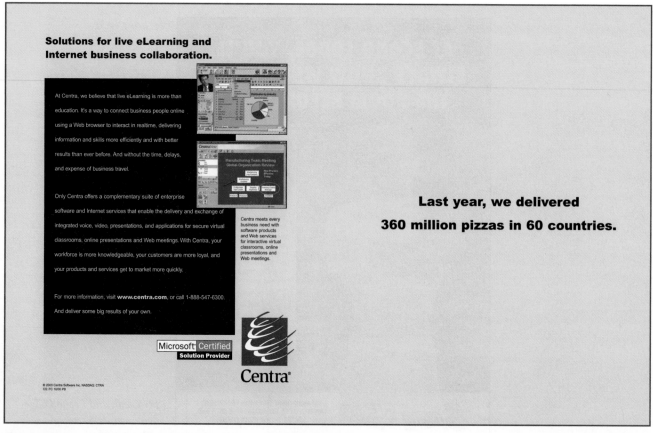

Centra Software aids Domino's Pizza's efforts to market itself worldwide.

should not ignore or lose sight of the importance of a global organization. Compared to domestic firms, global companies have an increased customer reach and a better understanding of diversity and competition. They also offset economic downturns with the implementation of appropriate strategies.

We are surrounded by examples of global marketing. Consider Coca-Cola, which earns more than 80 percent of its profits abroad. Coca-Cola did not achieve such global success without first evaluating numerous global strategies, including the product itself and its packaging, advertising, distribution, and pricing. Coca-Cola's strategy is to customize its product to match local tastes by, for example, varying the degree of sweetness in the formula. Although the signature curved bottle and red packaging are recognized around the world, the scripting is usually changed to reflect the country's language. Ads are also altered or reshot to reflect local standards, people, and customs. Yet the "Always" theme, showing, for example, aspiring chefs, sumo wrestlers, or a supermom, has been prominent everywhere. In contrast, Pepsi has suffered as a result of inconsistent packaging and taste, earning a mere 20 percent of its profits abroad. This led Pepsi to shift its focus to alternative beverages, such as bottled water, orange juice, and tea, and to beef up exports of its Frito-Lay snack chips.[43]

The global marketplace can be very complex. Marketers evaluate many considerations and implement well-planned strategies to ensure their success. The Internet has had a tremendous impact on global marketing. Experts predict that the number of brands around the globe will actually decrease, as companies use the same brand name to market a product regardless of its location. For example, Mars markets 3 Musketeers in the United States, but the same candy bar is called Mars Bar in the United Kingdom. With global marketing emphasized, it is quite likely that Mars will use only one name for the same candy bar. Additionally, Procter & Gamble has decreased the number of its brands from 600 to 400, as it focuses more on global marketing, especially via the Internet.[44] Throughout this book, you will learn that differences need to be researched and accommodated at many levels. These include language, culture, currency, infrastructure, laws and regulations, consumer preferences, and differences in negotiating style. Marketers also need to understand the varying tastes and needs of global customers.

Centra uses its Domino's connection to promote eLearning

*Recognizing the diversity of its
market, Mattel uses ethnic
models to market its Barbie
toy line.*

It can be difficult to gain acceptance in new markets. TheAdStop.com has begun marketing its free-to-use Internet advertising directory to regions of China. To help it gain acceptance, it has hired WebUnion Media Ltd. to develop all Chinese content for its China Web sites, since WebUnion is already a leader in the Asian Internet community. The two companies hope that by working together, they will be able to increase The AdStop.com's market share quickly and more effectively than The AdStop.com could by itself.[45]

CONNECTING WITH DIVERSITY

Professor Warren Plunkett teaches what he calls the "new golden rule." The traditional golden rule states that you should do unto others as you would have them do unto you, but that assumes all people are the same. In an increasingly diverse society, you must be able to see others' point of view. People from different cultures or backgrounds don't necessarily have the same perceptions, needs, and wants. Plunkett's new rule is: Do unto others as they would have you do unto them. In other words, as a marketer you must remember to satisfy your customer on the basis of your customer's desires and social norms—not your own.[46]

As marketers move to a more personalized, one-to-one connection with customers, it is imperative to understand and respect diversity among customers. No two are alike. As you will learn in the consumer behavior chapter, some commonalties exist within the various subcultures and social classes. But marketers today are much more sensitive to the needs of a diverse population. It is important to understand that cultural diversity refers to far more than just ethnic groups. U.S. West Airlines, which recognizes diversity as part of its corporate culture, distinguishes among the following categories: race/color, gender, age, sexual orientation, religion, cultural heritage, veteran status, marital status, liberal/conservative, and national origin. The companies you will work for may have even more distinguishing factors. According to Marsha Farnsworth Riche, director of the U.S. Bureau of the Census, "We're all minorities now. If you count men and women as separate groups, all Americans are now members of at least one minority group."[47]

When marketing to ethnic groups, it is important to distinguish between ethnic background and ethnicity. A person's **ethnic background** is usually determined by birth and

ETHNIC BACKGROUND

Subculture membership usually determined by birth and related to one or more of four elements: country of origin, native language, race, and religion.

related to one or more of four elements: country of origin, native language, race, and religion. Hispanics are an ethnic group, but members have diverse interests and beliefs depending on country of origin, length of time in the United States, geographic placement, and other factors. **Ethnicity** refers to the amount of identification an individual feels with a particular ethnic group. According to Lafayette Jones, president and CEO of Segmented Marketing Services, Inc., marketers should "look at the market not in terms of black and white, but in terms of true ethnicity. We use terms like 'African American' because these terms really describe what we're talking about, without the social and political implications of race. . . . Every culture has its own food, music, and religious practices. They're diverse in competition, flavorings, attitudes, and expressions."[48] In the chapter on consumer behavior, we'll look more specifically at various ethnic markets. Applying what you learn can help you as a marketer cultivate and satisfy customers from varied ethnic backgrounds.

ETHNICITY
The amount of identification an individual feels with a particular ethnic group.

CONNECTING WITH DIVERSITY

BETTY CROCKER: AN AMERICAN MOSAIC

 For 75 years, the most famous face in American grocery stores has been a paragon of white Middle America: a cheery housewife with blue eyes, creamy skin, and June Cleaver features. She has had a makeover every decade or so but has changed little more than the style of her red-and-white wardrobe and her sensible brunette hairdo.

In 1995, Betty Crocker received the wildest face-lift in the history of American marketing. It was immediately clear that when the new Betty emerged, her boss, General Mills, wouldn't be serving up the same old white bread. To mark her 75th anniversary, General Mills selected pictures of 75 real women from across the United States, and digitally "morphed" them into one new super-Betty. Since the contest was open to would-be Bettys of all races and any age from 18 to 118, the hybrid homemaker emerged with more politically correct features. Ethnic diversity, of course, is a holy grail avidly sought by marketers everywhere in the fractious 1990s and the early 21st century. But meshing 75 ethnically diverse women into one face is a new twist.

"We're hoping for ethnic diversity, which is what's happening with homemakers and society as a whole," says General Mills spokesperson Craig Shulstad. Russell Adams, chairperson of African American studies at Howard University in Washington, DC, however, thinks General Mills' high-tech Betty will shrewdly avoid offending anybody. He says the new Betty will look more like the growing market of blacks and Hispanics—"less white bread and more whole wheat," but not be too ethnic, letting General Mills "straddle their conservative core and their emerging market."

The original Betty was born in 1921, when General Mills' precursor, the Washburn Crosby Company, decided it needed to create a spokesperson to respond to its customers' queries about baking. They came up with a fictitious character named after a popular retired director, William Crocker, and held an employee contest to choose a suitable signature for Betty, which the company uses to this day. On Betty's 15th birthday, the company commissioned her first portrait, from prominent New York artist Neysa McMein. She did a bit of 1930s morphing, combining the features of several women in the company's Home Service Department into a "motherly image," according to a General Mills history of Betty.

General Mills continues to develop new ways of marketing the traditionally white Middle American Betty Crocker to ethnic markets. In 1999, the company began an annual "Recipes from the Soul" contest celebrating traditional African American soul food cooking. Likewise, Betty Crocker is reaching out to Hispanic consumers through two traditional Latin-style desserts. These two new dessert mixes, Rice Pudding and Flan, even feature bilingual packaging. Italian foods are also featured in their own *Betty Crocker's Italian Cooking* cookbook. By targeting specific markets such as these, General Mills hopes to affirm its dedication to all of America's kitchens. If Betty Crocker is supposed to be more ethnically diverse, after all, she should be cooking more ethnic meals.

Sources: Reprinted from Rebecca Quick, "Betty Crocker Plans to Mix Ethnic Looks for Her New Face," *Wall Street Journal*, September 11, 1995, pp. A1, A9; "Betty Crocker Announces 2nd Annual Soul Food Cooking Contest," *Business Wire*, January 11, 2000; "Betty Crocker Takes on Italian," *Denver Rocky Mountain News*, August 9, 2000; "Betty Crocker Cooks Up Two New Desserts," *Business Wire*, April 21, 2000; Hector D. Cantu, "Makers of Instant Flan, Spanish Voice-Activated Phones Target Hispanics," *Knight Ridder/Tribune Business News*, April 27, 2000, and www.bettycrocker.com, site visited September 9, 2000.

Marketers recognize that there will be tremendous diversity in marketing in the 21st century. They also recognize the immense spending power of diverse groups. African Americans, Hispanic Americans, and Asian Americans spend in excess of $1 trillion a year—and the amount continues to climb.[49] Mature customers (age 50 and older) control half the U.S. buying power. Young adults spend $150 billion annually, whereas women reportedly buy 80 percent of all consumer goods.[50] These are just a few of the many diverse customers you will be learning about in this book.

It is both profitable and rewarding for marketers to connect and build relationships with every type of customer. By acknowledging, understanding, and accommodating the needs of diverse groups, marketers can create a loyal base of customers for future business. The diversity feature in this chapter, "Betty Crocker: An American Mosaic," highlights the efforts of General Mills to appeal to a broader spectrum of customers.

CONNECTING ETHICALLY

After emerging from the profit-oriented 1980s, marketers began to rediscover the importance of social responsibility and ethical behavior to a company's performance. In fact, ethical initiatives by businesses have more than doubled in the last five years. Responsible marketers make decisions with a clear code of ethics in mind. They must make important decisions about the standards of conduct for an organization. A worldwide poll conducted by Environics International asked 25,000 people in 23 countries to name the factors that most affected their impressions of individual companies. A majority mentioned factors related to social responsibility (i.e., labor practices, business ethics, and the like) and felt that companies should go beyond the traditional goals of "making a profit, paying taxes, and providing employment. . . ."[51] Thus, ethics and social responsibility go hand in hand. We will examine each of these forces more closely in the following sections.

ETHICS

Standards or values that govern professional conduct.

MARKETING ETHICS

The ethics that deal specifically with how moral standards are applied to marketing decisions, behaviors, and institutions.

Ethics   **Ethics** are the values or standards that govern professional conduct. **Marketing ethics** deal specifically with the application of moral standards to marketing decisions, behaviors, and institutions.[52] Nearly every area of marketing has significant ethical dimensions that raise difficult questions.[53] Throughout this book, we will evaluate many different ethical situations, including issues of fairness, equity, conflict of interest, privacy, confidentiality, product safety, and others. You will also find that every area of marketing can present an ethical dilemma, including product development, promotion, distribution, and pricing.

In order to promote ethical behavior in each area of marketing, both large and small businesses implement a code of conduct, sometimes referred to as value statements or management integrity statements. These may provide a wide range of guidelines, depending on the beliefs and values of a particular organization. For example, Johnson & Johnson established one of the first codes in 1947. It embodies a commitment to ethical business practices as well as a responsibility to consumers, employees, the community, and shareholders. You will learn more about Johnson & Johnson in chapter 4.

Aside from implementing a code of ethics, organizations try to build an ethical culture by communicating standards to employees and ensuring that ethics remain a priority. An ethical organization requires the support of top management, and many companies have training programs and seminars on ethics. Columbia/HCA Healthcare Corp., for instance, maintains a senior vice president for ethics, compliance, and corporate responsibility.[54] Boeing incorporates ethical standards into its company objectives through a commitment to integrity:

> Integrity, in the broadest sense, must pervade our actions in all relationships, including those with our customers, suppliers, and each other. This is a commitment to uncompromising values and conduct. It includes compliance with all laws and regulations.[55]

Because the marketing function within an organization relies heavily on interaction with customers, it is often subject to public scrutiny. This emphasizes the power of ethics as a force in making business decisions. Over the long run, it is likely that organizations with a strong ethical culture and code of conduct will be better equipped to handle ethical dilemmas.

SOCIETAL MARKETING CONCEPT

The marketing concept extended to include satisfying the citizen as well as the consumer.

Social Responsibility   Many people believe that a socially responsible business must satisfy the needs of customers in ways that provide profits to the owners or meet other requirements outlined by the owners. Some argue that profits represent the response of consumers to businesses that best serve their needs. As mentioned previously, social responsibility and ethics are closely related. The **societal marketing concept** seeks to balance

**CONNECTED:
SURFING THE NET**

www.benjerry.com

Learn more about Ben & Jerry's efforts to fulfill the societal marketing concept by checking out its Web site. Find out about its most recent social efforts . . . and ice cream flavors!

customer satisfaction against corporate profits and the well-being of the larger society. It extends the marketing concept to include satisfying the citizen as well as the customer. Social responsibility reflects "the consequences of a person or firm's acts as they might affect the interest of others."[56]

Many companies are well known for their commitment to social causes and for acting in the best interest of the citizen as well as the consumer. Consider Ben & Jerry's, which contributes 7.5 percent of its pretax profits to charitable causes.[57] Ben & Jerry's is well known for its environmental initiatives, including innovative recycling, energy saving, and waste reduction. The company incorporated its dedication to societal marketing into this part of its mission statement:

> To operate the company in a way that actively recognizes the central role that business plays in the structure of society by initiating innovative ways to improve the quality of life of a broad community: local, national, and international.

Another example of involvement in social causes is The Body Shop, which is committed to human and civil rights, as well as protection of the environment and animals. It protests animal testing for cosmetics, campaigns for endangered species, and shows support for victims of domestic violence, among others.[58] Numerous companies express their social responsibility through donations. Hewlett-Packard, Intel, and Microsoft donated computers, software, and training to educate more than 400,000 teachers in the area of technology. Intel plans to contribute over $100 million over three years to the program.[59] Even Wall Street investment firms offer socially responsible or "values-based" funds that take ethical stands on everything from tobacco and abortion to sweatshops and whales.[60]

Marketers have many opportunities to correct questionable behavior. Today, television shows often resort to sex, violence, and outrageousness in order to command market share. Procter & Gamble (P&G) and AT&T are taking the lead in cleaning up televised trash, hoping producers will understand that positive topics are more economically viable with advertisers than salacious topics.[61] This chapter's relationships feature describes P&G's initiatives to deal with irresponsible television programming.

MARKETING: YOUR INVOLVEMENT

By now it should be clear that marketing affects you in many ways. Your exploration of marketing begins from many angles—the prospective marketer, member of a target market, customer, and citizen. Each of these roles gives you a slightly different slant, which can lead to the development of valuable marketing skills. Throughout this text we will highlight opportunities in the Career Tip feature. You'll also meet various marketers and learn from their experiences. Some, like Cynthia Palmer, who will be discussed in chapter 13, received a degree

CONNECTING THROUGH RELATIONSHIPS

AVEDA: CONTINUOUS LEARNING TO CREATE SATISFACTION AND LOYALTY

 Founded in 1978 and purchased by Estée Lauder in 1997, Aveda manufactures ecologically correct cosmetics, perfumes, and hair care and skin care products. Additionally, Aveda licenses skin and hair care salons to sell only its products. For these salons, Aveda provides a great deal of education both on general skin and hair care and on its own line of products. Aveda has always been focused on educating customers in order to drive its sales. A great deal of its sales are attributed to customers recommending the products to their friends and families. This free advertising has helped Aveda increase its sales, but Aveda doesn't rely just on customers for referrals. For one hour every Thursday afternoon Aveda employees spend their time trying out all of the latest Aveda products. The goal for CEO Federic Holzberger is to create not only customer loyalty but also employee loyalty to the Aveda products.

To enable the employees to understand the benefits, packaging, features, and part numbers of all of its products, Aveda has established its own salon in the corporate headquarters. Management watches employees use its products in order to determine how customers will use Aveda products. The result is a more effective marketing strategy focused on education, satisfaction, and service. Holzberger believes Aveda's sales are founded in this successful education: "If you're in the business of teaching, then you want to find out how people learn before you try to convey information to them. Both the lifestyle educators and the people we deal with in salons are very creative. So we keep buckets of crayons and markers on tables in our education center. If people have ideas, they can doodle or draw."

Aveda is seeking to satisfy not only its customers' desires for cosmetics but also for inner fulfillment. The "Chakra" line of body cleansers, for example, promises "Fulfillment," "Motivation," "Bliss," or "Attraction," depending on which bottle you select. Aveda even offers "Lifestyle Workshops" specializing in personalized aroma blends, massage, aromatherapy, and self-care for customers who want to make positive lifestyle choices and reduce outer and inner stress in their lives. Combining hair and makeup tips with methods for relieving stress, the company instructs its customers in how to be happy with themselves physically and mentally, all the while using Aveda products. This type of holistic approach to makeup began in the mid-1990s with the explosion of spa culture and aromatherapy, and Aveda is tapping into the growing market of consumers who do not merely want to make themselves look better but also feel and live better. Aveda's sales exceeded $120 million in 1998. Management's goal is to reach $1 billion in the next few years.

Sources: Jill Rosenfeld, "Do Not Disturb . . . Busy Learning," *Fast Company*, June 2000, p. 84; Nina Munk, "Why Women Find Lauder Mesmerizing," *Fortune*, www.fortune.com, May 25, 1998; Tamara Ikenberg, "Good Karma in a Bottle," *Pittsburgh Post-Gazette*, March 26, 2000; and www.aveda.com, site visited September 9, 2000.

in marketing and then applied her knowledge. Others learned through experience to satisfy customers—much like Levi Strauss did 150 years ago.

One in three of you will be in a job that directly involves marketing. Your career may involve strategic marketing planning, personal selling, promotion or advertising, retailing, product development, getting products to market (distribution), or establishing pricing criteria. No matter what career you choose—working for a political campaign, a not-for-profit organization, a religious organization, or a *Fortune* 500 company—your job will require an understanding of marketing. Many of the ideas we will explore in this book can be applied to your personal actions.

In a sense, you are already a marketer through your everyday actions. You market yourself when you apply to schools or pursue a scholarship. You are a marketer when you seek election to an organization or attempt to influence its members. You are a marketer when you interview for an internship or job. In all likelihood, you will be applying marketing in a professional sense in the future. Since marketing is so important, this is true no matter what your college major happens to be.

You also belong to a target market, which makes you tremendously important to other marketers. You are part of a target market when political candidates on MTV ask for your votes, when the Fox network produces a television show designed to appeal to you, and when sports teams, theme parks, and movies compete for your entertainment dollars.

Marketing affects you through your role as a customer. You are a customer every time you purchase. You are a loyal customer when you have a strong preference that results in your repeated purchase of a company's good or service. You are part of a marketing relationship when a company that knows you by name wants to customize its actions to fit your desires precisely.

Finally, marketing pertains to you as a citizen. You are affected by marketing when McDonald's selects paper over styrofoam packaging to reduce pollution. You are affected when Mothers Against Drunk Driving (MADD) reduces your chance of a serious injury from a traffic accident. You are affected when General Motors designs a Cadillac that is completely recyclable.

Marketing is a relevant, fun subject. It is filled with examples that you see every day. It touches your life directly in a million ways. We hope it connects with you—and hopefully you will connect with it.

CHAPTER SUMMARY

OBJECTIVE 1: Understand the concept of marketing, including its definition, purpose, and role in creating exchanges.

Marketing is the process of planning and executing the conception, pricing, promotion, and distribution of ideas, goods, and services to create exchanges that satisfy individual and organizational objectives. The purpose of marketing is to identify the needs and wants of customers within markets and create customer value in ways that will ensure the long-run success of the organization. Many people refer to the purpose as the marketing concept. Marketing works by creating valuable exchanges that provide utility. Utility is produced when products are created or adjusted, when goods and services are placed so consumers can discover and acquire them, when products are delivered at the right time, and when the transfer of ownership is facilitated.

OBJECTIVE 2:   Learn what is involved in making marketing decisions, including examples of product, price, promotion, and place decisions to create a marketing mix.

The marketing strategy process has four steps—situation analysis, targeting, positioning, and marketing mix decisions. Situation analysis provides information about the marketing environment and specific company elements. It is based on insights gained from the use of marketing information systems and marketing research. Targeting occurs when groups of customers with identifiable characteristics are selected for attention. Targeting helps focus resources. The best marketing strategies do an excellent job of addressing the needs and wants of customers within these targets. Positioning is used to determine what image or impression the marketer wants customers within a target segment to possess regarding the organization or its products. By blending the marketing mix—product, price, promotion, and place—marketing decisions are made to support the positioning strategy. These decisions can be blended into a vast array of combinations, each producing different results.

OBJECTIVE 3:   Contrast the periods of marketing evolution from its early history through the eras of production, sales, and customer marketing, leading up to today.

Marketing has progressed through three eras—the production era, the sales era, and the customer marketing era. As the names suggest, the production era focused on ways to efficiently mass-produce new products while the sales era focused on getting people to buy products. The customer marketing era moved management's attention toward satisfying customer needs and wants.

OBJECTIVE 4:   Understand the five key forces that are dramatically influencing how organizations will connect with customers in the future.

Marketing in the 21st century will be influenced by relationships, technology, ethics, diversity, and globalization. Today, more organizations are implementing the marketing concept by forging relationships with valued customers. These are creating loyalty and repeat business that help the organization to achieve its objectives. Product technology develops radically new goods and services, and process technology makes it possible to be more responsive to customers by altering how marketing occurs. The Internet is a particularly noteworthy technological advance because it brings us new distribution, communication, scanning, and research capabilities. The global economy has an impact on all customers and competitors. Consequently, global factors must be considered when making marketing decisions. Ethics and social responsibility are also important forces because they help guide many marketing decisions. Ethics involve making decisions based on what is right and wrong. Social responsibility involves decisions that affect citizens as well as customers.

OBJECTIVE 5:   Determine how marketing pertains to you.

You are intimately involved in marketing—as a marketer, as a member of a target market, as a customer, and as a citizen. Marketing pertains to you personally and you begin your study of the subject having already experienced many of its facets. Professionally, marketing is important no matter what major or career you choose. In a sense, you are often a marketer when you attempt to advance yourself or your views. Along with other people similar to yourself, you are part of a target market toward which certain marketers direct their attention. As a customer, you experience the actions of marketers. As a citizen, you are impacted positively and negatively by organizations whether or not you purchase their products.

REVIEW YOUR UNDERSTANDING

1. What is marketing? What are the key elements in its definition?
2. What are the four basic areas (types of markets) in which marketing is typically applied?
3. What is utility? What are the four types of utility involved in marketing exchanges?
4. What is the difference between a need and a want? Give examples of each.
5. What is the marketing concept? What are its three key aspects?
6. What is a marketing strategy? Describe each of its four steps.
7. How do product, place, promotion, and price decisions form the marketing mix? Give examples of each decision.
8. What are the stages in marketing evolution? Describe each of the three marketing eras.
9. What are the five key forces shaping marketing as we enter the 21st century? Describe each.
10. How does marketing relate to you? List four ways.

DISCUSSION OF CONCEPTS

1. Describe marketing, highlighting examples from your daily life that illustrate each of its four aspects.
2. Identify one company with which you are familiar and describe four ways in which it provides utility.
3. Discuss the activities involved in implementing the marketing concept. How do they pertain to customers, competitors, and the marketing organization?
4. Describe the steps in developing a marketing strategy. Why is it important to target prior to positioning? Why is positioning important prior to marketing mix decisions?
5. Compare and contrast the various eras of marketing, assessing the role each era played in reaching the current relationship era.
6. Discuss the five forces shaping marketing by showing how they help implement the marketing concept.

KEY TERMS AND DEFINITIONS

Buyer's market: The marketing environment that exists when an abundance of product lets the buyer control the market.

Consumer orientation: An organizational philosophy that focuses on satisfying consumer needs and wants.

Customer-driven organization: An organization that implements the marketing concept by creating processes so all parts of the organization can contribute the maximum amount possible toward satisfying customer wants.

Customer value: What consumers perceive they gain from owning or using a product over and above the cost of acquiring it.

Effectiveness: The degree to which an organization's activities produce results that matter to consumers.

Efficiency: The degree to which activities are carried out without waste of time or money.

Ethics: Standards or values that govern professional conduct.

Ethnic background: Subculture membership usually determined by birth and related to one or more of four elements: country of origin, native language, race, and religion.

Ethnicity: The amount of identification an individual feels with a particular ethnic group.

Exchange: A process in which two or more parties provide something of value to one another.

Form utility: A want-satisfying value that is created when knowledge and materials are converted into finished goods and services.

Internet: A global network of computers that enables the transmission of data through the use of a personal computer.

Loyalty: A measure of how often, when selecting from a product class, a customer purchases a particular brand.

Market: All the individuals and organizations with the desire or potential to have the desire and the ability to acquire a particular good or service.

Marketing: The process of planning and executing the conception, pricing, promotion, and distribution of ideas, goods, and services to create exchanges that satisfy individual and organizational objectives.

Marketing concept: Holds that the purpose of marketing is to identify the needs and wants of customers within markets and satisfy them in ways that ensure the long-run success of the organization.

Marketing ethics: The ethics that deal specifically with how moral standards are applied to marketing decisions, behaviors, and institutions.

Marketing mix: The four controllable variables—product, price, promotion, and place (distribution)—that are combined to appeal to the company's target markets.

Marketspace: An electronic space where business occurs.

Mass customization: The customization of a product for a specific customer by means built into a process.

Mass marketing: The mass production, mass distribution, and mass promotion of a product to all buyers.

Needs: Fundamental requirements the meeting of which is the ultimate goal of behavior.

Ownership utility: A want-satisfying value that is created by making it possible to transfer the title of goods and services from one party to another.

Place utility: A want-satisfying value that is created by making goods and services conveniently available.

Positioning: The process of creating an image, reputation, or perception of the company or its goods and services in the consumer's mind.

Process technology: Technology used to make goods and services.

Product technology: Technology that spawns the development of new goods and services.

Production orientation: Historical marketing period that emphasized new products and the efficiency of production.

Relationship marketing: The development and maintenance of successful relational exchanges; it involves interactive, ongoing, two-way connections among customers, organizations, suppliers, and other parties for mutual benefit.

Sales orientation: Historical marketing period that emphasized that consumers must be convinced to buy.

Satisfaction: The customer's overall rating of his or her experience with a company's products.

Seller's market: The marketing environment that exists when scarcity of products lets the seller control the market.

Societal marketing concept: The marketing concept extended to include satisfying the citizen as well as the consumer.

Strategic alliances: A partnership formed by two or more organizations for a new venture.

Target market: A group of potential customers with similar characteristics that a marketer is trying to satisfy better than the competition.

Time utility: A want-satisfying value that is created when goods and services are made available when they are wanted.

Want: A specific form of consumption desired to satisfy need.

REFERENCES

1. "Levi Strauss Has E-Something Up Sleeve of New Jackets," *The Plain Dealer,* August 27, 2000; Michael Liedtke, "That Was Denim, This Is Now: Levi Strauss Aims for Hip Image," *National Post,* July 28, 2000; Naruth Phadungchai, "Levi Strauss Hopes Buttons Will Fly," *Bank Loan Report,* May 22, 2000; and "Marineau's E-Plan: Not a 'Retreat,'" *Women's Wear Daily CEO Summit Supplement,* June 14, 2000.

2. "AMA Board Approves New Marketing Definition," *Marketing News,* March 1, 1985, p. 1.

3. "Faster Chips Unveiled," *Milwaukee Journal Sentinel,* June 26, 2000, p. 15D.

4. James W. Culliton, *The Management of Marketing Costs* (Boston: Division of Research, Graduate School of Business Administration, Harvard University, 1948), cited in Neil H. Borden, "The Concept of the Marketing Mix," *Journal of Advertising Research,* June 1964, pp. 2–7.

5. Ibid.

6. www.norcominc.com/products, Web site visited August 28, 2000.

7. "Moving Procter & Gamble into E-procurement," *Purchasing,* June 15, 2000, p. 5149.

8. Melinda Ligos, "Clicks and Misses," *Sales and Marketing Management,* June 2000, p. 69.

9. www.nfwf.org, Web site visited July 13, 2000.

10. "Gatorade Forgers Alliance to Woo Girl Athletes," *Crain's Chicago Business,* June 12, 2000, crainschicagobusiness.com.

11. Richard P. Bagozzi, "Marketing as Exchange," *Journal of Marketing,* October 1975, pp. 32–39.

12. www.quicken.com, Web site visited June 20, 2000.

13. www.dhl-usa.com/aboutdhl, Web site visited August 28, 2000.

14. www.mall.com, Web site visited June 14, 2000.

15. "General Motors Gears Up for E-customized Sales," *Precision Marketing,* July 3, 2000, www.mad.co.uk/pm/; www.GMBuyPower.com, Web site visited August 30, 2000.

16. "OH& Co Rebrands Railroad Giant," *Design Week,* 14 July 2000.

17. "Well-Placed Messages," *Restaurants and Institutions,* April 1, 2000; www.rimag.com; "Aloha Airlines Launches Oakland-Maui Service," *PR Newswire,* February 28, 2000, www.prnewswire.com.

18. Erick Schonfeld, "Ten Companies That Get It," *Fortune,* November 8, 1999, pp. 115–17.

19. "Shot Can Help Deter Lyme Disease," *USA Today,* August 18, 1999, usatoday.com.

20. "Going to Extremes," *Advertising Age,* July 24, 2000, adage.com.

21. Tara Fatemi, "Beverages Industry," www.hooversonline, Web site visited June 14, 2000.

22. "E-commerce Stalled," *The Asian Wall Street Journal,* July 24, 2000, www.dowjones.com/awsjweekly/.

23. "Can E-mail Turn Internet Users into Shoppers?" *DNR,* May 26, 2000, www.dnrnews.com.

24. "Jeff's Mint Chocolate Sundae Licks the Competition to Become New 'Jeff Gordon' Ice Cream," Edy's Press Release, March 31, 2000.
25. Don Peppers and Martha Rogers, *The One To One Future* (New York: Doubleday, 1993), pp. 21–22.
26. www.microsoft.com/windows/windowsmedia, Web site visited August 28, 2000.
27. "Swimmers Finding Comfort in a Different Kind of Skin," *New York Times,* August 9, 2000, p. 1.
28. "A Public Library in the Palm of Your Hand," *New York Times,* August 28, 2000, p. 1.
29. Christopher Hart, "Mass Customization: Conceptual Underpinnings, Opportunities and Limits," *International Journal of Service Industry Management* 6, no. 2 (1995): 36–45.
30. Peppers and Rogers, *The One to One Future,* p. 2.
31. www.reflect.com, Web site visited August 28, 2000.
32. www.nua.net/surveys, Web site visited August 30, 2000.
33. Justin Fox, "Surprise! Europe Has Web Fever," *Fortune,* June 12, 2000, pp. 219–224.
34. www.broadcast.com, Web site visited June 11, 2000.
35. "Will the Internet Reduce the Demand for Mall Space?" *Real Estate Finance,* Spring 2000, pp. 41–47.
36. See Frederick E. Webster, Jr., "The Changing Role of Marketing in the Corporation," *Journal of Marketing,* October 1992, pp. 1–17.
37. "The Joy of Empty Nesting," *American Demographics,* May 2000, pp. 48–53.
38. www.textron.com/businesses/automotive, Web site visited September 1, 2000.
39. www.americanexpress.com/cards, Web site visited September 1, 2000.
40. "3-Way Web Pact," *Los Angeles Times,* August 24, 2000, p. C-8.
41. "Exporting American Know-How," *World Trade,* April 2000, pp. 42–45.
42. www.census.gov/indicator, Web site visited August 30, 2000.
43. "Returns: Chipping Away," *The Asian Wall Street Journal,* June 16, 2000, www.dowjones.com/awsjweekly/.
44. Kathleen Schmidt, "Outlook 2000: Globalization," *Marketing News,* January 17, 2000, pp. 9–12.
45. "New Web Site Targets China Regions Markets," *Direct Marketing,* May 2000, p. 13.
46. Warren Plunkett, *Instructor's Manual for Supervision,* 7th ed. (Boston: Allyn & Bacon, 1993), pp. 6–7.
47. Marcia Mogelonsky, *Everybody Eats: Supermarket Consumers in the 1990s* (Ithaca, NY: American Demographic Books, 1995), p. 185.
48. Ibid., p. 163.
49. "Putting the World in the Series," *American Demographics,* April 2000, pp. 28–30.
50. "Teens with Money to Burn Are Old Hands at Shopping," *New Orleans Times-Picayune,* July 30, 2000, p. A26; "The Buy Word Is: Women," *New York Post,* August 2, 2000, p. 2.
51. "Great Expectations," *Across the Board,* January 1, 2000.
52. Gene R. Laczniak and Patrick E. Murphy, *Ethical Marketing Decisions: The Higher Road* (Boston: Allyn & Bacon, 1993), p. 3.
53. See John R. Boatright, *Ethics and the Conduct of Business* (Upper Saddle River, NJ: Prentice Hall, 1997), pp. 284–315.
54. "Do the Right Thing," *CIO,* August 1, 2000, www.cio.com.
55. www.boeing.com, Web site visited April 23, 1997.
56. Peter D. Bennett, ed., *Dictionary of Marketing Terms* (Chicago: American Marketing Association, 1995), p. 267.
57. "Ben & Jerry Hope Social Mission Won't Fade; Unilever Sees It as Marketing Tool," *Associated Press Newswire,* May 2, 2000, www.wire.ap.org.
58. www.bodyshop.com, Web site visited June 10, 2000.
59. "Microsoft and Intel Join Forces to Support Training of 400,000 Teachers Worldwide," www.microsoft.com, Web site visited January 10, 2000.
60. "Investing with a Conscience," *Pittsburgh Post-Gazette,* August 28, 2000, p. D-1.
61. Joe Mandese, "Talk Show Stalwart P&G Cans 'Trash,' " *Advertising Age,* November 20, 1995, p. 1.

Bricks or Clicks

ADDING CLICKS TO BUILD RELATIONSHIPS

MANY TRADITIONAL BRICKS-AND-MORTAR companies are taking the Internet plunge. These companies have a big advantage over their Internet start-up rivals—brand identity. Charles Schwab & Company views its Internet site, not as an entirely new business, but as a new way to develop its customer relationships. Internet start-ups tend to focus almost exclusively on name recognition and not on brand building. "These companies spent their go-public money on advertising to get the name recognition instead of putting it into infrastructure and people," says Terry Pearce, co-author of *Clicks and Mortar: Passion Driven Growth in an Internet Driven World.* "The reason Charles Schwab achieved online success is that it's always put the customer first, and it's used technology to effectively strengthen that commitment."

J & R Music World is another bricks-to-clicks success. The e-commerce division, which is run by the founders' son, Jason Friedman, started offering its large assortment of music, electronics, and computers online in 1997. J&R.com can calculate the exact shipping costs for anywhere in the world, which will be useful when the company launches its Web site in South America. The difficulty in determining shipping costs tends to discourage international customers from ordering.

Circuit City has also had success on the Internet. It integrates the traditional retail store into its Web site. The customer gets three shipping choices, one of which is express pickup at the nearest location. This allows consumers to go to the store without having to wait in long lines to pay for their merchandise. They just pay for it online and pick it up at their convenience.

Not all of the bricks-to-clicks stories are happy ones. This combination of Internet and traditional retail can lead to competition within a company for the same customers. Toysrus.com allocated the most popular toys to its distribution channels and undercut the retail stores on price to compete with Amazon.com and eToys.com. These moves led to a lot of resentment in the traditional retail segment.

The Internet provides a powerful tool for traditional retailers to reach out to their customers. Many people prefer shopping online in stores with which they are familiar, and the ability to return items directly to the store is also a plus. In the current Internet climate, with companies exiting as quickly as they entered, the traditional bricks-and-mortar companies have tremendous opportunities available to them.

Sources: Judith N. Mottl, "Schwab Integrates Bricks and Clicks," *Information Week,* June 19, 2000, p. 66; Ellen Messmer, "Family e-ffair," *Network World,* August 14, 2000, p. 20; George Colombo, "Internet-Only Selling Will Fail," *Sales and Marketing Management,* August 2000, p. 29; and Jason Anders, "E-Commerce (A Special Report): The View From Above—Sibling Rivalry: For Traditional Retailers to Succeed on the Web, They Have to Deal with a Big Obstacle—Themselves," *Wall Street Journal,* July 17, 2000, p. R16.

Starbucks

WAKE UP AND SMELL THE coffee! Starbucks is everywhere. According to the company whose largest competitor is less than half its size, coffee is not a trend—it is a lifestyle. Starbucks has been "elevating the coffee experience" since 1971, when three men opened a gourmet coffee shop in Seattle, Washington. Many are unaware that Starbucks has been around for so many years. In fact, it was not long ago that latté, cappuccino, and espresso were not part of America's everyday vocabulary.

Starbucks' success can be attributed greatly to marketing efforts. In 1982, the company hired Howard Schultz as its marketer. After visiting Italy the following year, Schultz was inspired. The relationship he saw between coffee and people in Italy awakened him to the untapped markets in America. In 1987, Schultz added six Starbucks stores and planned to go national with his ideas. The corporation is now the leading retailer and roaster of specialty coffee, with 3,500 Starbucks stores in over 20 markets around the world. Starbucks supplies fine dining, food service, travel, and restaurant accounts with both coffee and equipment. Yet Starbucks remains ambitious: The company plans to reach 10,000 coffeehouses by fiscal year 2005.

Approximately 40,000 employees, known as "partners," undergo multiple sessions of rigorous training. They are taught to educate customers about coffee making, to remind them to purchase new beans weekly, to explain the various blends and beverages, and most importantly to serve only the highest-quality drinks. Employees learn to make drinks in an eight-hour seminar that includes lectures, demonstrations, and hands-on experience. They taste beverages that do not meet quality standards so they can be more sensitive to an unsatisfied customer.

Starbucks has the best success in its top markets—Seattle, Los Angeles, and Chicago—each of which has over 100 stores. Located mostly in urban areas and college towns, Starbucks has also ventured into alliances with other companies. It has recently paired up with Minneapolis-based Target Corp. in a deal that will place Starbucks coffee shops in the new Target supercenters opening across the country. The demographics of a Starbucks and Target customer cross and the companies have both created an upscale image. Its extended line of products includes a coffee-flavored ice cream from Dreyer's Grand, a coffee-flavored beer from Redhook Ale Brewery, and a bottled version of its Frappuccino developed with PepsiCo.

Global expansion has been a large success as well. When Starbucks was introduced in Japan, as many as 200 customers lined up at a time. The company provides informational pamphlets in Japanese and posts menus in both English and Japanese. The world's fourth largest consumer of coffee, Japan is a potential $7 million market for Frappuccino alone.

Despite its rapid growth, Starbucks refuses to compromise quality. The company will not franchise, will not artificially flavor its coffee, and is very selective about business alliances. Schultz intends to maintain the Starbucks upscale image. That is why Starbucks coffee will not be sold in gas stations or convenience stores, among other places.

So how has the name become so renowned? Not only has the company made its logo visible through its products, accounts, and locations, but Starbucks also has received a significant amount of press for community involvement, charity work, and progressive employee policies. Amazingly, traditional advertising has not played a major role in the company's success.

Starbucks seems to have found its way into coffee cups everywhere. Never tried it? There are fewer and fewer people that have not tasted Starbucks coffee. Those who have not yet sampled Starbucks' brew can easily find someone to tell you what you are missing.

1. *The definition of marketing describes four types of decisions made by marketers: product, price, promotion, and place. Identify a place and promotion decision Starbucks has made.*

2. *Based on the types of retail locations selected by Starbucks, what customer characteristics form its target markets?*

3. *The marketing concept holds that the purpose of marketing is to understand the needs and wants of customers and create customer value through satisfaction and quality more effectively and efficiently than competitors. Given the information provided in this case, summarize how Starbucks implements the marketing concept.*

4. *In 1997, Starbucks opened a new store every business day. This includes global expansion into new markets. What factors must Starbucks consider as it continues to pursue global opportunities?*

Sources: www.hoovers.com; Ann Merrill, "Espresso Everywhere: Gourmet Coffee Companies Are Taking Their Product Beyond Coffeehouses to Grocery Shelves, Bookstores and Banks," *Minneapolis Star Tribune*, November 17, 2000; "Starbucks Announces Entry into Continental Europe," *Business Wires*, September 19, 2000.

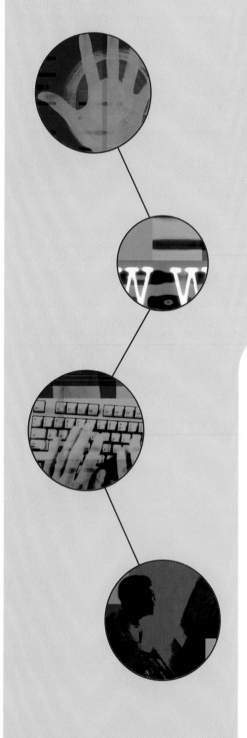

chapter 2

CUSTOMER SATISFACTION AND LOYALTY: BUILDING VALUE WITH QUALITY

1. Understand why customer satisfaction and loyalty are the focus of marketing in winning organizations.

2. Learn how consumer expectations influence satisfaction.

3. See why connecting with customers through relationships achieves outstanding satisfaction and loyalty.

4. Understand the ideas that help organizations market quality goods and services.

5. Define quality and describe how it is obtained.

◀ *Meg Whitman, eBay CEO*

FROM PEZ CANDY DISPENSERS TO POKÉMON cards, from used cars to new homes, eBay (www.ebay.com) auctions offer something for everyone. Pierre Omidyar launched the auction site on Labor Day 1995 to provide a central Internet location where his girlfriend (now his wife) Pam could connect with other collectors of Pez candy dispensers. Now headed by CEO Meg Whitman, eBay has 12 million registered traders and posts an additional 450,000 items in 4,300 product categories every day. The company makes money by charging the seller a small percentage of the price paid by the buyer whose bid wins each auction. Online auctions are so popular that Whitman has set up eBay sites in 53 U.S. cities as well as in Australia, Canada, Germany, Japan, and the United Kingdom.

"We help people trade practically anything on earth" is eBay's mission statement. In line with this mission, the company continually upgrades its Web site and systems to keep auctions running smoothly around the clock. Yet eBay auctions are as much about building relationships as they are about completing transactions, according to Brian Swette, senior vice president for marketing. "From the beginning, community was integrated into our business," he says. "When you make a transaction on eBay, you have to make a ton of personal interactions with other users. It's built into the experience."

From this perspective, every eBay auction becomes an opportunity to strengthen relationships and satisfy both buyers and sellers so they remain loyal. To measure satisfaction, eBay asks users to rate their experience with the site and with customer service representatives. Updated survey results are posted every hour so the CEO, other managers, and the customer service reps can see what customers are saying. eBay's managers pay close attention to these surveys and to other customer feedback so they can spot problems and identify opportunities. Being responsive also shows customers that the company cares. "We learned early on, if you listen to your customers, they will become your greatest evangelists," Swette says. Satisfied eBay customers continue buying and selling—and they encourage friends, family, and colleagues to join in as well.

eBay's ability to build relationships with buyers and sellers depends on safeguarding the integrity of its auctions. This is why eBay uses software to detect outlawed activities such as shill bidding, which occurs when a seller or a seller's agent makes a bid to artificially drive the price up on the seller's item. Shill bidders are suspended from eBay for 30 days for a first offense, and they risk federal prosecution. eBay also offers software to help buyers deal with sniping. A person sniping places a winning bid seconds before an auction closes and thereby does not allow other people the chance to make higher bids. Using eBay's proxy bidding system, a buyer enters the highest price he or she is willing to pay and authorizes the system to bid on his or her behalf. Unless someone tops that price, the buyer can win without having to check the bids every few minutes.

More than ever, eBay needs to reinforce customer loyalty to cope with increased competition. Amazon.com and Yahoo! have entered the online auction business, and specialized sites such as Mobilia.com (which offers automotive collectibles) are also targeting collectors. One way eBay keeps buyers loyal is through its Personal Shopper service, which allows buyers to sign up to receive e-mail notices about upcoming auctions in product categories of their choice.

eBay is also finding new ways to meet customer needs. Consider the acquisition of Butterfield & Butterfield, a traditional auction house known for its expertise in selling antiques and upscale collectibles. Thanks to this acquisition, eBay can now help buyers and sellers authenticate and auction higher-priced items. Car auctions are another growth area for eBay. Knowing that buyers can't easily examine cars auctioned online, the company has formed an alliance with Saturn to offer sellers the option of having cars inspected before auction. Sellers pay less than $100 for an inspection at a local Saturn dealer. Then they post the written report on the eBay site so buyers can get a better sense of each car's condition before they bid.

Sometimes customers prefer to buy at a fixed price or can't wait hours or days to find out whether their bids have been successful. To meet these customers' needs, eBay has acquired Half.com, a Web site where sellers offer books, CDs, and other products at half the regular price. Just as the Internet never stops evolving, eBay is constantly reinventing itself and refining its marketing strategies to satisfy customers and create a virtual community connecting buyers and sellers.[1]

THE CONCEPTS OF CUSTOMER SATISFACTION, LOYALTY, AND QUALITY

If you want to connect with customers, you have to earn their loyalty. That means delivering goods and services worthy of their support. People have millions of choices about where to spend their money. Ultimately, the decision depends on how much value they receive for what they pay. Companies that consistently produce high value are likely to have satisfied customers who reward them with loyalty and repeat purchases.

Winning organizations go to extremes to create customer satisfaction because they know that loyalty is the single most important factor in extraordinary performance. They also know that satisfaction and loyalty are often based on the relationship they have with customers. In this chapter we will learn that satisfaction and loyalty usually go hand in hand, but not always.

We will also learn that leading-edge companies focus a good deal of effort on satisfaction and loyalty. How do they achieve these two goals? There is no question that the ability to produce quality goods and services is required. Without quality, it is almost impossible for goods and services to perform as expected. In order to create superior value, organizations must start with excellent products. That requires the application of total quality management principles to assure that processes throughout the company support the creation and delivery of products that produce satisfaction. Figure 2.1 describes the relationships among all these factors.

What are customer satisfaction and loyalty? What are value and quality? How do relationships and technology play into these factors? As a marketer, you need a strong foundation in these concepts to be able to connect with customers. In this chapter, we'll take a look at each concept in more detail.

CUSTOMER SATISFACTION AND CUSTOMER LOYALTY

Understanding how to achieve customer satisfaction and loyalty is a focal point for scientists who study consumer behavior. A significant amount of marketing research is dedicated to measuring both aspects—but especially customer satisfaction. Satisfaction ratings are a major indicator of an organization's competitiveness. Today every extremely successful company makes a concerted effort to satisfy customers. The race to beat competitors in customer satisfaction is a powerful business objective because satisfaction is an overall indicator of how well customers rate a company's performance. This section begins by exploring why satisfaction and loyalty are important. Next, we look at how customer expectations affect satisfaction. We then tie all of these elements together by describing precisely how connecting through relationships promotes satisfaction and loyalty. We also examine how connecting with diversity and global competition affect efforts to build satisfaction and loyalty.

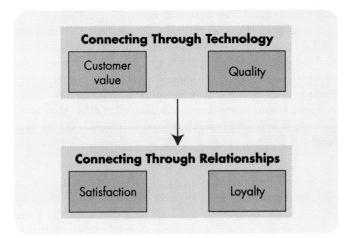

FIGURE 2.1 *Customer Satisfaction, Customer Loyalty, and Quality: Connecting Through Relationships Formed by Organizational Systems and Actions*

WHY SATISFACTION AND LOYALTY ARE IMPORTANT

Customer satisfaction is a customer's positive, neutral, or negative feeling about the value received from an organization's product in specific use situations.[2] In the past, product innovation was the major factor in gaining the competitive edge. That is no longer always true. Now new products are copied by rivals, often within a few weeks or months, and the life span of new products is declining rapidly. Today it is more important for organizations to conduct all aspects of their business to satisfy customers. Favorable satisfaction ratings not only boost sales but can also have a dramatic effect on company performance. For example, Ford estimates that due to a 1 percent increase in customer satisfaction in 1999, it realized a revenue growth of $207 million![3]

Customer loyalty refers to how often, when selecting from a product class, a customer purchases a particular brand. Most business experts believe that customer satisfaction is a critical ingredient in building loyalty. The importance of loyalty cannot be overlooked. It is estimated that U.S. corporations lose 50 percent of their customers in any five-year period.[4] Thus, at this rate, few firms can achieve acceptable volume or profit without a strong base of loyal buyers. On average, 80 percent to 90 percent of a company's profits are generated by 10 percent to 20 percent of its customers.[5] These customers must be retained in the face of ever more challenging competitors. A large number of satisfied, loyal customers results in strong business performance because these customers provide sales to increase revenues, have less concern about price, and help reduce the organization's costs.

Sales to Increase Revenues The revenue stream from one lifetime customer can be tremendous. A loyal Coke drinker can spend as much as $30,000, a buyer of OshKosh B'Gosh baby clothes over $100,000, and a corporate buyer of commercial aircraft equipment literally millions of dollars.[6] When the amount a customer buys is viewed over the lifetime of a relationship, organizations understand why customer retention is so vital. In fact, many organizations develop compensation systems that tie executive and employee pay to measures of customer satisfaction and loyalty.

The importance of satisfied customers for revenue generation is magnified by their influence on other buyers. If a typical customer purchases a new car once every four years and influences one new buyer each year, the loyal, satisfied customer can be worth nearly $1 million in revenues and more than $100,000 in profit. Some companies calculate the **lifetime value of a customer,** which is the amount of profit an organization expects to obtain over the course of a customer relationship. For example, assume you are a marketing manager for a large bicycle equipment manufacturer. One of your customers, Specialized, purchases about $80,000 in equipment each month. If Specialized becomes dissatisfied and selects another supplier, how much will it cost your company? At $80,000 per month for 12 months, Specialized purchases $960,000 annually. Assuming you earn a profit of 15 percent, that equals $144,000 per year. Over two decades, your company would forfeit more than $2.8 million in pure profit and $19.2 million in revenue. If the same problem that dissatisfied Specialized results in the defection of other key customers, you face huge losses!

Less Concern About Price Customer satisfaction has become a key to making sales at appropriate prices. Jeff Bezos, founder of Amazon.com, recently commented on the role of

CUSTOMER SATISFACTION

A customer's positive, neutral, or negative feeling about the value received from an organization's product in specific use situations.

CUSTOMER LOYALTY

A measure of how often, when selecting from a product class, a customer purchases a particular brand.

LIFETIME VALUE OF A CUSTOMER

The amount of profit a company expects to obtain over the course of the relationship.

price: "We're known for competitive prices . . . That's very important online. But we're also known for great customer experience and great customer service. If your brand is based exclusively on price, you're in a fragile position, but if your brand is about great prices and great service and great selection, that is a much better position."[7] Essentially, creating satisfied customers through service and experience is often more important and successful than trying to create satisfied customers through price. In general, customers are willing to pay more because they are certain they will receive valuable benefits. Also, they better tolerate price increases, showing little tendency to shop around. Overall, these factors lead to higher margins and profits.

Reduce the Organization's Costs   The percentage of loyal, satisfied customers is a very important determinant of an organization's costs and revenues. In addition to generating sales, loyal customers affect the **cost structure,** which is the amount of resources required to produce a specific amount of sales. The cost of acquiring a new customer is usually six to ten times more expensive than keeping an existing one.[8] For example, about $3,000 is spent to gain a new auto customer, whereas keeping an existing customer often costs only a few hundred dollars. It's easy to see that you must hold on to a significant number of loyal buyers who make multiple purchases. This is why Ritz-Carlton Hotel Company empowers its employees to spend up to $2,000 to solve problems that may lead to a lost customer.

COST STRUCTURE

The amount of resources required to produce a specific amount of sales.

CUSTOMER EXPECTATIONS

CUSTOMER EXPECTATIONS

Consumers' beliefs about the performance of a product based on prior experience and communications.

Customer expectations play an important role in creating satisfaction. **Customer expectations** are consumers' beliefs about the performance of a product based on prior experience and communications. When companies fall short of those expectations, customers are dissatisfied. When companies exceed them, consumers are delighted. In both cases, customers are emotionally charged by their experience—the delighted are more likely to be loyal, and the dissatisfied are more inclined to switch.

Customer expectations are based on personal experience, observation of others, company actions, advertising, and promotion. Customers also expect companies to offer services to support their purchase decision. For example, because it is difficult for people to assess the quality of products in a catalog, companies such as Williams Sonoma and Crate & Barrel make it easy for people to return products that do not meet their expectations.

Higher and more varied expectations result when competition is intense. When Lexus entered the luxury automobile segment in 1989, expectations were high because Lexus positioned itself against such competitors as Mercedes-Benz, BMW, Cadillac, and Lincoln. Company executives knew the only way to succeed against the competition was to exceed expectations customers had for rival brands. The "Lexus Cares" philosophy treats customers the way they want to be treated.[9] The result has been extremely positive. In 2000, Lexus dealers topped the J.D. Power and Associates Customer Service Index, a position they've held for four straight years.[10]

Each time a company delights a customer, new expectations are created. Similarly, with each change in product, price, promotion, or distribution, expectations can be affected. A major challenge for companies is to create marketing strategies that give buyers high but realistic expectations. Companies must continue to do better in light of competitors' efforts and rising consumer expectations. The technology feature discusses how WebMiles.com is improving customer satisfaction and loyalty by offering frequent flyer rewards.

CUSTOMER DEFECTIONS AND COMPLAINING BEHAVIOR

CUSTOMER DEFECTIONS

The percentage of customers who switch to another brand or supplier.

Organizations look at **customer defections,** the percentage of customers who switch to another brand or supplier. The relationship between customer satisfaction and loyalty is complex. The two often go hand in hand. Yet, loyal customers are not always highly satisfied, and satisfied customers are not always loyal. In some cases customers continue to purchase a brand that doesn't fully meet expectations because defecting would be difficult or an alternative would be no better. In other cases satisfied customers defect because they simply want to try something new. A large number of consumers have many expectations, some of which may be met and others not. Consequently, there are degrees of satisfaction; customers may be highly or only moderately satisfied. One recent study showed that 40 percent of all customers, though satisfied, would be willing to switch to a competitor, whereas highly satisfied customers are

*For five years, J.D. Power and
Associates named Lexus
number one in customer
satisfaction.*

much less willing to do so.[11] The point is that just focusing on satisfaction isn't enough. You must build a bond of loyalty that is based on a relationship.

Figure 2.2 illustrates that, in a study completed in Sweden, 65 percent of customers defect primarily because they are dissatisfied with the way they are treated.[12] Fifteen percent defect because they are dissatisfied with the product. The remaining defect because they prefer a different product or for other reasons unrelated to the product. This is an indicator of how extremely important it is to build relationships.

Companies committed to customer satisfaction will deal with any complaints they receive in a way that still leads to overall satisfaction. On average, nine of every 10 customer problems that are discovered and resolved immediately will result in satisfaction and loyalty. Seven of 10 customers will do repeat business with a company that makes some sort of effort to resolve a problem. In fact, if a problem is handled satisfactorily, the average customer will tell five other

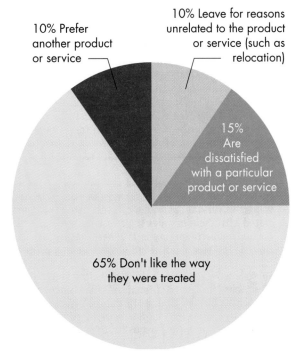

FIGURE 2.2 *Why Customers Leave*

Source: Eugene W. Anderson, Claes Fornell, and Donald R. Lehmann, "Customer Satisfaction, Market Share, and Profitability: Findings from Sweden," *Journal of Marketing* 58 (1994): 53.

people about it. A negative experience will result in nine to 20 people being told about the poor treatment or poor products and services.[13] This suggests that customers who complain and receive satisfactory attention are often more satisfied than those who don't complain at all.

It's not necessarily bad when people complain. Sometimes your most loyal customers are your biggest critics. Toys "R" Us received many complaints from customers after the 1999 Christmas shopping season about the state of disarray and the lack of customer services in its stores. In response, CEO John Eyler developed a plan to make stores more appealing to customers. In the first quarter of 2000, sales at Toys "R" Us retail stores increased 43 percent. Had customers never complained, Eyler would not have known that it was possible to drastically increase sales merely by changing the store layout and environment. Complainers actually increased Toys "R" Us's sales at its stores.[14] Thus, encouraging feedback and responding to complaints are ways to establish a bond of loyalty based on relationships.

SATISFACTION RATINGS AND MEASUREMENT

Because satisfaction contributes so much to the success of an organization, it is no surprise that marketers are very interested in measuring satisfaction. **Satisfaction ratings** provide a way for consumers to compare brands, enable testing agencies to determine how well products

---

CONNECTING THROUGH TECHNOLOGY

WEB MILES: FLYING BY SPENDING

 When David Phillips collected 1.2 million airline miles through a Healthy Choice promotion by peeling the labels off of 12,150 individual servings of pudding, he expected a lifetime of easy flying. However, as he learned when he tried to take his family to Italy for Easter, collecting the miles was easier than using them without problems. Instead of flying directly to Italy, he, his wife, and their children took four separate flights and their luggage was even lost.

WebMiles Corporation is a company seeking to remedy Phillip's problem and the problems of hundreds of traditional airline frequent flyer program members. Customer complaints about these problems include hassles of blackout dates, limited number of allocated seats, required Saturday night stays, expiration of miles, 21-day advance notice, and cost caps. WebMiles rewards, in contrast, are redeemable for unrestricted free travel on any airline.

The WebMiles program began in January 2000 and is based in Salt Lake City, Utah. The program currently helps customers earn free and reduced rate unrestricted travel at more than 60 online companies. Customers at sites such as Dell.com, JCPenny.com, MarthaStewart.com, Nordstroms.com, and ToysRus.com can earn rewards just for shopping. In addition, customers can sign up for the WebMiles MasterCard and earn rewards just for signing up, plus, if they use their card, they earn one reward per dollar spent, allowing them to earn double rewards at participating sites. WebMiles also plans to extend its program to offline companies, further extending its benefits to consumer and company alike.

Consumers aren't the only ones reaping the rewards of the WebMiles program, however; companies like WebMiles because it allows them to distinguish themselves from other companies as ones offering a return for doing business with them. Once customers learn they can earn rewards, they are sure to return to do more business, resulting in valuable customer loyalty. WebMiles sells its rewards to participating merchants, who, in turn, pass them on to their customers.

According to President and CEO Bill Meade, WebMiles succeeds in its mission to please customer and company by taking "the power of airline miles, which are coveted by consumers worldwide, and then enhances them by removing the restrictions commonly associated with them in order to drive long-term customer loyalty and ultimately revenues for businesses participating in the WebMiles network." His plan sure sounds easier than cutting 12,150 labels off of individual pudding containers.

Sources: www.webmiles.com, site visited September 9, 2000; John Flynn, "So . . . Who Wants to Be a Mile-ionaire?" *San Francisco Examiner*, July 23, 2000; "WebMiles Announces 20 New Online Merchants," *PR Newswire*, July 25, 2000; "Loyalty Is No Longer Up in the Air," *PR Newswire*, April 20, 2000; and Don Mogelefsky, "A Rewarding Experience," *Incentive*, August 1, 2000.

perform, and allow companies to monitor how satisfied consumers are with their goods and services.

You may have used a rating system to help choose a stereo component, a car, or even which college to attend. Consumers have been sensitized to the importance of satisfaction by such publications as *Consumer Reports*, which routinely rates many products, and *Motor Trend*, which rates autos. Auto advertisers and others regularly incorporate satisfaction ratings into persuasive messages. The popular press runs major stories on satisfaction ratings. For example, J.D. Power and Associates produces an annual Customer Satisfaction Index for the automotive industry. It is based on evaluations by 52,000 new vehicle owners and is used to determine which vehicles best satisfy customers.[15] The American Consumer Satisfaction Index (ACSI) is a quarterly rating that measures customer satisfaction in seven sectors of the economy broken down into more than 40 industries. Even the U.S. government has entered the scene by sponsoring the Malcolm Baldrige National Quality Award, which is given to outstanding U.S. firms based largely on customer satisfaction.[16] We will discuss this award in more detail later in the chapter.

Competitive advantage comes to companies that can learn and adjust most quickly to market forces. One critical source of information is feedback from customers. It is important to know how they behave and why they feel as they do. A **customer satisfaction measurement program** is an ongoing survey of customers (and competitors' customers) for the purpose of obtaining continuous estimates of satisfaction. Simply looking at sales data can tell us whether more or fewer customers are purchasing, but it does not reveal much about underlying reasons for behavior. Consequently, in addition to sales data, companies measure such items as customer satisfaction and loyalty rates.

Marketers not only should measure their own company's performance but also should monitor that of competitors. What if your company has worked hard to improve product quality, which has been identified as critical to consumer satisfaction, yet the level of satisfaction continues to decline? It is quite possible that competitors have improved their quality much more quickly and that consumers recognize this fact.

The best consumer satisfaction program in the world is worth very little unless it feeds into the strategic and operational planning of the company. This information is then provided to all employees so that adjustments can be made to improve performance in their respective areas. Each functional area at all levels of the organization must be willing to undertake activities that lead to satisfied customers. One of the most important parts of the marketing executive's job is to get the entire organization to focus its decisions on actions that affect how much customers are satisfied. Much of a marketer's time is spent creating strategies that influence satisfaction.

RELATIONSHIPS BUILD SATISFACTION AND LOYALTY

Just a few years ago marketers were content to sell to new customers with the goal of increasing sales faster than competitors. When one company's sales rise faster than all others, that organization's market share increases. Today most companies realize that customer loyalty may be far more important than just market share.

The heart of the marketing concept is to address customer needs and wants. It doesn't stop there. Customer needs and wants should be addressed in a way that produces customer satisfaction and loyalty. Although not every customer seeks a relationship with every purchase, needs and wants more often are best addressed by establishing relationships.

You may try a new item for fun, but if you really like it, you will buy it again or tell others about it. The product becomes a more permanent fixture in your life and has more meaning. Without this loyalty and repeat business from customers, an organization's costs escalate, and in many cases the company fails. Very few organizations can survive on single transactions. Even companies that market products bought once in a lifetime depend on loyalty. The hospital that markets its heart surgery capabilities relies on positive word of mouth from loyal customers. Likewise, a Harley-Davidson dealer who sells a customer that one and only "dream machine" still builds the relationship after the sale. This makes it evident to other potential buyers that the Harley-Davidson organization will continue to connect with its loyal users.

BabyCenter.com, a one-stop shopping and information Web site for expectant and current mothers, established a registry system. This allows the company to track children's ages, birthdays, and favorite products, and to provide relevant information regarding products,

CONNECTED: SURFING THE NET

www.harley-davidson.com

Harley-Davidson even builds relationships with customers on the Web. If you'd like to learn more about Harley-Davidson motorcycles, talk to other Harley owners, or sign up for a tour of its factory—connect to the Harley-Davidson Web site!

child development, and safety to the appropriate parent, based all on the child's birth date. Therefore, immediately before a child's first birthday, BabyCenter.com can automatically e-mail the mother an appropriate and exciting birthday gift, increasing the probability that the mother will remain a customer. Similarly, barnesandnoble.com marketed to member-only associations throughout 2000. It offered discounts for books and music for any of the 85 million consumers that are members of a dues-paying organization. In return, barnesandnoble.com receives information about each customer, including an e-mail address, demographics, and enhanced loyalty.[17]

According to Skip Lefauvre, former CEO of Saturn Corporation, a company "must do things so astonishingly well that customers become not merely loyalists but rather outright apostles."[18] Although Saturn sales have dropped off in recent years, one company in particular has maintained a close relationship with its customers—Harley-Davidson. "It's one thing to have people buy your products," proclaims the Harley-Davidson Web site, "It's another for them to tatoo your name on their bodies."[19] Few companies on Earth have achieved true brand loyalty like Harley-Davidson; however, the point is clear: Connecting through relationships creates a personal bond.

That's what both Harley-Davidson and Saturn want. When you buy a Saturn, your new car is cleaned and polished to perfection and delivered to you in a special location within the dealership showroom. Your salesperson makes sure to take time, without interruptions, to discuss all of the features of your new purchase and answer any questions. And don't be surprised to find cut flowers on the driver's seat. A personal phone call from your salesperson followed by a letter shortly thereafter provides the initial follow-through to begin furthering the relationship.

CREATING A PERSONAL RELATIONSHIP

By its very nature, a relationship is personal. It reflects the connection between two or more parties. Involvement with customers is key in relationship marketing. Chrysler bonded with buyers at its annual "Camp Jeep" weekend in Virginia, where 2,500 Jeep vehicles and 8,500 Jeep owners gathered for three days of family- and Jeep-related activities.[20] Aside from any economic connections, relationships are socially driven as well. Empathy, trust, and commitment are important. This is true whether we are looking at consumer, business-to-business, or other markets.

Empathy   Empathy is the ability to understand the perspective of another person or organization. It means putting yourself in someone else's shoes and seeing the world as that person sees it. Companies that build relationships do this in a number of ways. They use sophisticated marketing research and create a culture within the organization that is sensitive to others. But empathy works best when customers sense and know that they are understood—that the organization has accurate knowledge of their circumstances. Marketers communicate this empathy in nearly everything they do. For example, when you call the telephone company for information and get courteous help, even if you don't spell the name correctly, the company has communicated empathy. When a company goes out of its way to make things work just for you, you experience its empathy.

Trust   Trust is being able to rely on another party to perform as promised and in the way you expect. The communications of marketers are filled with promises. For example: "Levi Strauss & Co. is committed to manufacturing products of the highest quality and ensuring the satisfaction of all our consumers. If any of our products do not meet our stringent quality standards, we want to identify the cause and take whatever corrective action is necessary."[21] Levi's backs up its promises by making it easy for you to return its products for an exchange or replacement. Companies, like people, that keep their promises earn trust. This is a tremendously important element in building lasting connections with customers.

Commitment   Companies that are committed go out of their way to serve customers. They go beyond what is promised to make sure the customer is better off because of the relationship. When things go wrong, they work hard to fix them. This is particularly critical to relationships over time. In the $250 billion telecommunications industry, companies are committed to pleasing customers. By offering new services, Sprint, AT&T, and MCI WorldCom are all attempting to show their commitment to pleasing existing customers. When a recent study indicated that 93 percent of consumers would like bill bundling offered by their telecom company, the three largest telecoms announced plans to bundle bills in the future.[22]

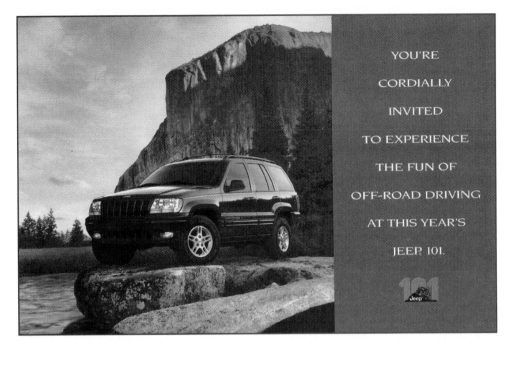

The "Camp Jeep" ads were designed to build a relationship with the end user.

Rewarding Loyal Customers Relationship marketing creates connections that make it unnecessary or difficult for customers to switch to competitors. In order for relationship marketing to work, companies must understand their customers so well that competitors have little chance of offering new or unique items that would entice a trial. This means that companies must be willing to provide superior value for their best customers. Louise O'Brien and Charles Jones, vice presidents with the successful consulting firm of Bain & Company, say that if companies want to realize the benefits of loyalty they must admit that "all customers are not equal . . . a company must give its best value to its best customers. That is, customers who

The Snap-on TRIBUTE CAMPAIGN, which ran for three years, sought to elevate the image and trust level of professional auto technicians.

generate superior profits for a company should enjoy the benefits of that value creation. As a result they will then become even more loyal and profitable."[23] In an effort to reward loyal customers, America Online and American Airlines have developed an alliance called AOL AAdvantage. Members of the program earn miles for every dollar spent shopping on AOL. These miles are later used for travel on American Airlines.[24] By becoming a member of AOL and AAdvantage, customers are rewarded for shopping online and for traveling. Considering that AOL and American Airlines have both had successful reward programs in the past, this program promises to reward customers above and beyond past experiences.

Building relationships may require specific incentives or rewards for loyal customers. In September 2000, Giant Food Inc. launched a frequent shopper "BonusCard" program at all 176 Giant and Super G stores and pharmacies. The BonusCard will allow shoppers to enjoy automatic discounts on store products, make them eligible for random rewards and sweepstakes, and allow them to support local schools without having to save their receipts. "Cards that reward customer loyalty have become very common in retailing," said Giant's CEO. "Through better understanding of our customers, we will be able to improve our services and offer them added value for their grocery dollar. Customers tell us that they appreciate receiving special discounts for products they purchase frequently, and enjoy the advantages they receive for being a loyal customer."[25]

Sometimes competitors attempt to counter loyalty programs of rivals. For example, General Motors gave loyalty coupons worth $500 and $1,000 for repurchase of a GM auto. Chrysler and Ford decided to honor these coupons for price reductions on their vehicles. At the same time, Chrysler and Ford initiated a similar loyalty program for loyal purchasers of their own cars. This neutralized the GM advantage and stimulated many GM customers to shop around.

career tip Employees at Hallmark know firsthand what it means to connect with customers through relationships. Hallmark products directly promote relationships among family and friends. The employee atmosphere within Hallmark reflects this relationship philosophy. Career opportunities at Hallmark are numerous—internships, creative positions, sales, marketing, operations, corporate staff, and others. You can learn more about Hallmark career opportunities by connecting to its online job database at www.hallmark.com. Discover what positions are currently available and obtain application information for your area of interest.

DIVERSITY AND SATISFACTION

The diversity of tastes and preferences presents challenges for customer-centered marketers. Diversity helps explain why companies with the highest overall sales sometimes have lower satisfaction ratings than smaller companies. The latter can design products and services for very narrowly defined segments and can focus all their attention on those customers. These companies may have lower market share but score high satisfaction points with a few customers. As companies gain share by selling to more people, their products and services must appeal to more diversified customers with a broader range of expectations. Large companies must have the flexibility and agility to satisfy many divergent target markets while maintaining or increasing their size. Achieving satisfaction in the face of growth requires using the broadest range of marketing tools and techniques. If an organization expects impressive satisfaction scores, then it must understand all forms of diversity better than even its smallest competitors.

The success of a product or service in one market segment will not automatically transfer to consumers in another segment. The diverse nature of consumers makes universal buying preferences and behaviors very unlikely. Companies such as Coca-Cola, McDonald's, Exxon-Mobil and Levi Strauss address the individual wants and needs of people by acknowledging their unique differences. Attention to the diversity of consumers is often reflected in better market share and product sales.

When McDonald's expanded to the Philippines in 1981, few expected the local, 11-store Jollibee fast-food chain to survive. However, Jollibee reacted by first copying McDonald's business model and then tailoring its menu to better serve the preferences of the local market.

CONNECTING WITH DIVERSITY

TARGETING ASIAN AMERICANS

 The fastest-growing population in the country, Asian and Pacific Islanders (API), is posing new possibilities for companies who recognize the needs and benefits of targeting ethnic groups. Between 1990 and 1999, the API population grew 43 percent to 10.8 million, growing particularly in key areas such as California. This group has traditionally been more educated and wealthier than any other segment of the population, further establishing them as a key market for businesses of all kinds. The Asian American population is by no means homogenous, however, and should not be treated as so. They do not share a common language or culture but speak Chinese, Japanese, Vietnamese, Korean, and other languages, while embracing a variety of cultures as well.

Many companies have recognized the buying power of Asian Americans and have developed promotions catering to their interests. Many of these promotions center around the Lunar New Year, such as Burger King's coupon giveaway, JC Penney's dragon posters, California Bank & Trust and Sears' lunar calendars, and Western Union and State Farm Insurance's red envelopes to use in giving monetary gifts to children. Instead of simply offering promotions, however, many of these companies are paying particular attention to the cultural issues involved. JC Penney, for instance, makes its dragon posters available in the baby apparel departments because many Asian Americans try to plan the birth of their children during the Year of the Golden Dragon. Washington Mutual allows Asian American customers to select their own account numbers so that they can have eights in them, which are considered lucky numbers.

One company in particular has used its ethnic focus on Asian Americans to successfully branch out into mainstream U.S. markets. The East West Bank was founded in 1973 in the Chinatown district of Los Angeles and was the first federal savings and loan specifically chartered to serve the Chinese American community. According to Dominic Ng, East West's current president and CEO, however, the bank has expanded its operations to serve southern California as a whole. "I think of us as the Chinese 'Bank of America' in our community," says Ng. "If you talk to Chinese-Americans and ask 'Do you know of East West Bank?' most of them would say they do. But when you look at our commercial banking business, you'll see that more than half our new business customers are coming from the mainstream population, from outside the Asian-American community." In fact, with $2.3 billion in assets, East West is currently the fourth largest bank headquartered in southern California. As a result, small and medium-sized businesses see East West as an alternative to Wells Fargo or Bank of America, and what's more, East West is locally owned.

The East West Bank has not neglected its Chinese American community, despite its rise to the top. In August 2000, East West Bank took the unprecedented step of offering the nation's first online Internet banking service in Chinese. This service allows customers to open accounts, check balances, transfer money, access transaction history, and pay bills online, all in Chinese. Ng says of the service, "This is a major milestone in the history of East West Bank. With a Chinese Internet-based banking product, our reach to the Chinese community has expanded considerably; not only here in California, but throughout the United States and Asia as well." Even in person, employees continue to reach out to their original audience. Roughly 90 percent of the bank's 100,000 employees, for example, speak Chinese or Cantonese. Presently, East West maintains 23 branch offices in Los Angeles County, 3 in San Francisco, 2 in Silicon Valley, and 1 in Orange County.

East West's methods have produced considerable results for the company. The bank has been profitable for 27 years running, a fact Ng attributes to the bank's close connection with Chinese American customers, as well as its in-depth knowledge of Pacific Rim businesses. With this in mind, East West seems poised to expand beyond California and to serve as an example of successful ethnic marketing to other banks and institutions.

Sources: "Nation's Leading Authority on Marketing to Asian-Americans Comments on Implications of Census Population Estimates Released Yesterday," *Business Wire*, August 31, 2000, Greg Johnson and Edgar Sandoval, "Advertisers Court Growing Asian American Population Marketing," *Los Angeles Times*, February 4, 2000; Pat Maio, "East West Unveils First Chinese-Language Online Bank," *Dow Jones Newswires*, August 31, 2000; "East West Bancorp Introduces Chinese-Language Internet Banking," *Business Wire*, August 31, 2000; and "Dominic Ng—East West Bancorp," *The Wall Street Transcript*, CEO Interview, May 22, 2000.

First, a slightly sweeter hamburger, then a Philippine-style chicken product, and finally a kids-oriented spaghetti plate. Today Jollibee has expanded to 24 overseas stores in 10 countries and, almost unbelievably, has opened up 17 California locations to compete with McDonald's in the United States![26]

Groups based on ethnicity have such tremendous buying power that marketers have begun to recognize the advantages of addressing each group individually. Many have even created marketing positions that focus on this. At Kraft, for example, there is a director of ethnic marketing. According to Steve Bachler, the company's direct-marketing manager: "The closer you can get to the customer, the better—talk their language, represent their lifestyles, make sure the product is relevant to their lives. Targeting makes a lot of sense."[27] Today most of the largest firms in the United States have created diversity management positions in an effort to modify corporate culture to reflect the growth of minority segments. After all, 51 percent of new entrants into the workforce between 1994 and 2005 will be minorities.[28] Targeting Asian-Americans to reach ethnic markets is discussed in the diversity feature.

GLOBAL COMPETITION AND SATISFACTION

The success of global companies is highly dependent on customer satisfaction. Throughout the 1960s and 1970s, domestic firms dominated the U.S. market. By the early 1980s, U.S. businesses were under the false impression that success could be sustained by making only minor adjustments. This resulted in a real lack of focus on customer needs and satisfaction. Foreign companies spotted this weakness and entered U.S. markets quickly, putting customer satisfaction at the heart of everything they did. Some of the strongest U.S. companies saw their market shares plummet because foreign rivals gained strong customer satisfaction ratings. These foreign competitors raised consumer expectations for quality and speed of service to new levels and often at substantially lower overall prices. Essentially, foreign competitors created new levels of customer satisfaction in the U.S. market.

No one knows this better than Xerox. In the early 1960s, Xerox introduced photocopiers to the U.S. business market. It dominated for the next 15 years with high-quality, high-priced copiers that generated satisfaction. With success, however, came a resistance to change, lack of customer focus, fewer product innovations, and unimproved quality standards. Satisfaction with Xerox declined. Japanese competitors entered the U.S. market during the mid-1970s to take advantage of Xerox's lack of customer satisfaction. Although the Japanese first introduced low-end copiers, they slowly increased quality to challenge the high-end copiers marketed by

**CONNECTED:
SURFING THE NET**

www.xerox.com

Discover how Xerox's emphasis on quality has won awards in nearly every major market in which it does business. Learn more about Xerox's newest quality products and business solutions.

Xerox's "Leadership Through Quality" program is designed to focus the entire organization on satisfying customers.

Xerox's "Leadership Through Quality" program is designed to focus the entire organization on satisfying customers.

Xerox. Satisfaction with Japanese copiers was high. By 1981, Xerox had lost 50 percent of its market share, and profits were down by $600 million, or nearly half. To combat these losses, Xerox management implemented the "Leadership Through Quality" program, which was designed to focus the entire organization on satisfying customers. An aggressive goal was set: 100 percent satisfaction across all Xerox business units by 1993. Some units had achieved this goal by 1990, and 10 years later Xerox was the leading digital copier producer in the world. Today many U.S. companies focus on ways to improve customer satisfaction so they can close the gap with and, in many cases, surpass foreign rivals in providing satisfaction.[29]

ORGANIZATIONAL SYSTEMS AND ACTIONS THAT DELIVER QUALITY

As we discussed in chapter 1, the effects of technology are absolutely phenomenal on the creation of customer value. Overall, the functionality of products is increasing while costs are staying the same or decreasing. Today most customer-oriented companies have systems and take actions that deliver quality goods and quality services to customers. And an emphasis on quality—largely made possible through technology and people—brings more satisfaction to customers. Products work as expected, last longer, and are user friendly. This section describes some of the aspects of quality that are used by leading-edge organizations to help accomplish customer satisfaction and loyalty.

QUALITY

In marketing, **quality** describes the degree of excellence of a company's goods and services. It is useful to emphasize both quality in goods as well as the special case of service quality. **Service quality** is the expected and perceived quality of all of the services an organization offers. Quality is necessary for organizations that sell physical products that are manufactured as well as organizations that only sell services. Without quality, it is nearly impossible to achieve customer satisfaction. A quality good or service performs precisely according to specifications that will satisfy customers. Consequently, quality contributes to customer satisfaction. Some companies, such as Packard Electric, believe their product possesses quality to the degree that it meets or exceeds customer expectations. Elmer Reece, a former top executive at the company, introduced the "excellence concept" in a quest to deliver total quality. According to Reece, "being excellent means meeting or exceeding customer expectations in everything." Striving for excellence became a critical part of every employee's job at Packard, and Reece's philosophy turned the company into a real winner. In order to make the concept work, Reece elevated marketing from its traditional sales role to the leading force in every major decision.

<u>QUALITY</u>
The degree of excellence of a company's products or services.

<u>SERVICE QUALITY</u>
The expected and perceived quality of all of the services an organization offers.

A tragic story was used to promote the "unbelievable" quality of the Rubbermaid product line.

SUBJECTIVE ASSESSMENT
OF QUALITY

The degree to which a product does what consumers would like it to do.

Reece often spoke of the problems that occurred when quality was defined from an engineering or manufacturing perspective. He said that the customer, not the company, should be the judge of quality.

No two customers are alike. We all want quality goods and services—but we each may view quality as being slightly different. For example, if you get an urge for a Big Mac® and can even taste its flavor in your mouth, then you might define quality by consistency (which McDonald's has perfected). But if you get an urge for a gourmet meal at a five-star restaurant, you might define quality as uniqueness and variety. Legendary restaurants such as Spago and Lutece take very different actions from McDonald's to accomplish quality.

According to FedEx CEO Frederick W. Smith, "The quality process is the key factor that will allow FedEx to grow because our customers expect 100 percent satisfaction—not 98 or 99 percent satisfaction. And 100 percent customer satisfaction demands 100 percent employee effort to meet that goal." As defined by the customer, 100 percent customer satisfaction means 100 percent on-time delivery and 100 percent accurate information available on every shipment at every location around the world. It also means 100 percent satisfaction every time FedEx comes in contact with its customers, whether helping them locate FedEx in a foreign country or clarifying a billing problem. This is an impressive challenge, considering that FedEx moves approximately 3.3 million packages worldwide—every day![30]

In many markets, a quality product is considered the price of entry. Basically, this means that a company must offer a quality product in order to participate in a market; inferior products or services will not succeed. As more companies build quality into their products as a standard feature, it ceases to provide a differential advantage. This was not always the case, however. In the 1980s, many consumers bought Japanese cars because they were perceived to be of much higher quality than U.S. brands. Today most experts believe that U.S. vehicles are equal in quality to Japanese cars and that U.S. manufacturers are even beginning to take the lead in new areas of quality, such as design and performance. Quality may be evaluated in two ways, subjectively and objectively. Customers are the key to understanding the subjective analysis, whereas technical specifications are the focus of objective assessments.

Assessments of Quality **Subjective assessment of quality** indicates to what degree the product does what consumers want it to do. For example, the hamburger tastes good. In assessing quality, consumers tend to be subjective, whereas companies tend to be objective. After an extensive review of a number of studies, one expert defined quality as "the consumer's judgment about a product's overall excellence or superiority."[31] From this perspective, different groups may evaluate quality altogether differently. When asked, adults may say Wendy's is higher in quality than McDonald's, whereas children may have the opposite response.

Consumers may pay more for brands they perceive have higher value.

Objective assessment of quality indicates to what degree the product does consistently what it's supposed to do. McDonald's and Burger King make what many consider to be high-quality hamburgers because each time one is served it consistently meets company standards. With hamburgers and other physical objects, it's possible to develop objective assessments of quality in the form of standards, such as fat and salt content or nutrition value.

Even objective assessments are open to interpretation. This is particularly true globally. For example, German and Japanese products are manufactured to precise specifications and will not perform in excess of their rating. If a product is rated to lift 1,000 kg, it will do precisely that and no more. In contrast, a similar U.S. product is likely to have a safety factor of 1.5, so the product will lift 1,500 kg. The extra capacity is a sign of quality in the United States but not in many other markets. Consequently, even measures of so-called objective quality are created in response to the subjective desires of various groups.[32]

Static and Dynamic Quality There are at least two types of quality. **Static quality** results when an accepted practice is perfected. **Dynamic quality** results when a major change makes the existing standard obsolete. For example, Smith Corona once dominated the personal typewriter business with an extremely high-quality electric portable. All quality efforts at Smith Corona were directed at improving its typewriters. As consumers shifted to word processors, however, Smith Corona's efforts to achieve static quality became irrelevant. A revolution had taken place as companies in the word-processing business—software and hardware—created value through change, a dynamic quality shift.

Focusing activities on static quality can divert resources from new ventures, and there seems little point in perfecting technology that is about to become outmoded. At the same time, dynamic quality shifts cannot be forced; the technology needs to be perfected and the market prepared. Marketers are a company's advance scouts, signaling what is new and relevant. Marketing is also critical in defining quality from the customer's perspective. Marketers develop estimates of what attributes customers use to define quality, what minimum quality standards must be met, and what various segments are willing to pay for quality.

Total Quality Management **Total quality management (TQM)** is an organizational philosophy that helps companies produce products and services that deliver value to satisfy customers. TQM involves, first, assessing consumer needs and, second, developing products or services that meet those needs. The approach seeks continuous improvement, reduced cycle time, and analysis of process problems. It also includes quality function deployment, which attempts to ensure that customer desires are built into the final product offering.[33] When implemented correctly, TQM involves all company activities that affect customer satisfaction and ends with customer service and feedback. It deals with both deliverables (the goods and services provided) and interactions (how customers experience dealing with the provider).

Continuous Improvement **Continuous improvement** occurs as the organization strives to find better ways of satisfying customers. In discussing the importance of continuous improvement, David Kearns, CEO of Xerox, has described his organization as "being in a race without a finish line."[34] FedEx uses Service Quality Indications (SQI) in its efforts to achieve continuous improvement. The index measures a number of key service factors from the customer's perspective and then weights them as to how seriously the customer will view a failure in any of those areas. Based on SQI, FedEx has set the goal of scoring better year after year. Since 1987, overall customer satisfaction at FedEx has averaged more than 95 percent and is approaching the company's goal of 100 percent.

Milliken & Company, another organization known for superior quality, pays particular attention to constant improvement. It calls its "Pursuit of Excellence" program an evolving process that continuously yields new ideas for enhancing quality, increasing customer satisfaction, and improving business performance. Through Milliken's Policy Committee and Quality Council, management creates the environment and provides the leadership necessary for quality improvement. Relying heavily on employee training and an organizational structure in which employees are called associates, Milliken has instilled in every person a feeling of responsibility to find and implement quality improvement changes. Managers must respond within one day to any suggestion by an associate to enhance customer satisfaction. This form of empowerment gives each associate the opportunity to have a positive influence on quality.

Reduced Cycle Time **Reduced cycle time** is a TQM activity intended to help the company move more quickly from product inception to product delivery in the marketplace.

OBJECTIVE ASSESSMENT OF QUALITY

An evaluation of the degree to which a product does what it is supposed to do.

STATIC QUALITY

Quality that results when individuals or organizations perfect an accepted practice.

DYNAMIC QUALITY

Quality that results from a change that makes an existing standard obsolete.

TOTAL QUALITY MANAGEMENT (TQM)

An organizational philosophy that helps companies produce goods and services that deliver value to satisfy customers.

CONTINUOUS IMPROVEMENT

The enhancement process used by an organization to find the best ways of satisfying its customers.

REDUCED CYCLE TIME

A TQM activity that helps a company move more rapidly from product inception to final delivery of the product to the marketplace.

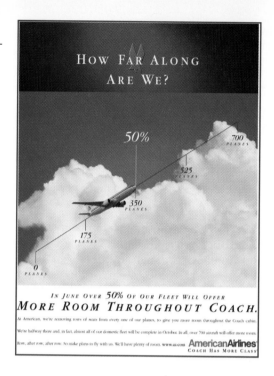

*American Airlines added leg
room—a continuous improvement designed to increase
customer satisfaction.*

The approach pays huge dividends by reducing costs while making possible very quick shipment of products matched specifically to customer requirements. This not only allows customers more flexibility in ordering but also results in lower inventories for business customers
and quicker availability of products for consumers.

Wallace Company, a Houston-based industrial distributor of pipes, valves, and fittings,
has used TQM principles to achieve reduced cycle time and has seen striking results. Wallace
assigns a team of outside salespeople, inside salespeople (customer service and sales representatives in the home office), and accounts receivable personnel to every customer account. This
allows employees and customers to gain a great deal of familiarity with one another. Inventory
turnover improved by 175 percent in five years, sales for newly introduced value-added products increased 75 percent between 1987 and 1990, and profits doubled.

ANALYSIS OF PROCESS PROBLEMS

Methods designed to find and
fix problems that could reduce
quality.

ISO 9000

An inclusive set of standards
established by the International
Standards Organization (ISO) to
ensure that quality requirements
are met.

Analysis of Process Problems   **Analysis of process problems** refers to the activities that
find and fix problems in the production of products and services. For manufactured items this
includes procurement of raw materials and components that go into finished goods, the manufacture of the finished products themselves, and packaging and shipping to ensure that
appropriate products get to their final destination. The International Standards Organization
(ISO) has established an inclusive set of standards, called **ISO 9000,** to determine whether
quality requirements are met. These standards are being introduced into laws in the European
Community to ensure that firms have quality management systems in place that meet specified criteria. Individual products aren't certified. Companies must go through an arduous
process to become ISO 9000 certified. Organizations such as Chrysler and Motorola require
that all their suppliers be ISO 9000 certified.

An important outcome of the analysis is to establish rigid quality control, such as the
Motorola 6 Sigma standard, which sets goals so that virtually all Motorola products perform as
expected. Elaborate efforts are made in product and process design to ensure that the actual
manufacturing activities efficiently produce quality items. In turn, the processes are monitored to make certain that the output is produced according to specifications.

Although quality has been the focus of manufacturing for more than a decade, the same
principles are now being applied to customer service. For example, FedEx handles more than
500,000 calls a day at its state-of-the-art telecommunications center with the sole purpose of
fielding customer service issues. The SQI measures at FedEx approach the mathematical rigor
previously reserved only for manufacturing companies.[35]

**QUALITY FUNCTION DEPLOYMENT
(QFD)**

A process that builds customer
wants and desires into the final
product offering.

Quality Function Deployment   **Quality function deployment (QFD)** is used during the
product or service design process to make sure that features to fulfill customer desires are built
into the final offering. The three most common concerns of QFD are to make the product or

	Faster	Better	Cheaper
COMPANY DELIVERS	Availability Convenience	Performance Features Reliability Conformance Serviceability Aesthetics Perceived Quality	Price
CUSTOMER DESIRES	Responsiveness Access	Reliability Security Competence Credibility Empathy Communications Style	Affordability

FIGURE 2.3 *Faster-Better-Cheaper: What the Company Delivers and What the Customer Desires*

service faster, better, and cheaper. Figure 2.3 shows what consumers desire in their dealings with the company and how those desires are translated into what the company delivers.

It is important to note that not all companies' TQM activities result in performance increases. According to a Bain and Co. research survey, TQM was used in only 41 percent of U.S. companies in 2000, down from 55 percent in 1999. And for the first time TQM is now more widely used in Europe than in the United States.[36] Still, when customer satisfaction is increased (relative to competitors) over time, firms can expect improved profitability.

Benchmarking   **Benchmarking** is the systematic evaluation of the practices of excellent organizations to learn new and better ways of serving customers. Benchmarking of **best practices,** those selected competencies for which leaders are known, has become so important that companies regularly send personnel to study and observe other organizations. Sparrow Health Systems, a leading provider in central Michigan, recently sent executives to Disney World to learn how to improve customer service. They also visited Saturn to obtain ideas for involving employees in the improvement process. Although Disney and Saturn are not in the same business, Sparrow was able to learn several new ways of ultimately improving health care delivery. By comparing its methods with those of known experts in other fields, Sparrow conducted benchmarking.

Quality Awards   To encourage companies to improve their quality and competitiveness, various governments have established awards. These are given to companies that demonstrate the most outstanding quality initiatives. Two very distinguished annual awards are the Deming Prize in Japan and the Malcolm Baldrige National Quality Award in the United States.

The Deming Prize   Everyone has heard of quality inspectors—people who examine finished products as they roll off the assembly line and remove defective goods before they are sold to customers. In the early 1900s, most companies used inspectors as their main source of quality control. Little or no effort was devoted to correcting the manufacturing problems that caused product defects.

In the 1950s, Dr. Edward Deming took a new approach to the issue. He applied the idea of **statistical quality control,** a concept he learned while a statistician at AT&T's Bell Laboratories, to manufacturing. Statistical quality control involves using statistics to isolate and quantify production line problems that may cause defects. The idea was to improve quality in the production process so that faulty goods would not be manufactured. The Japanese openly embraced Deming's philosophy, and this is viewed by many as one of the reasons for Japan's tremendous economic success during the 1970s and 1980s. Deming's work transformed Japan from the maker of inferior products to one of the most powerful economies in the world. To honor Deming's contributions, the Japanese created the Deming Award as their highest recognition of quality.

To help business managers implement quality initiatives within their organization, Deming outlined 14 key issues, listed in Figure 2.4. Deming insisted, moreover, that top

BENCHMARKING
The systematic evaluation of practices of excellent organizations to learn new and better ways to serve customers.

BEST PRACTICES
The competencies of industry leaders that other organizations use as benchmarks.

STATISTICAL QUALITY CONTROL
The use of statistics to isolate and quantify production line problems that may cause product defects.

1. Create constancy of purpose toward improvement of product and service, with the aim to become competitive and stay in business, and to provide jobs.
2. Adopt this philosophy: We are in a new economic age created by Japan. Transformation of Western management style is necessary to halt the continued decline of industry.
3. Cease depending on inspection to achieve quality. Eliminate the need for inspection on a mass basis by building quality into the product in the first place.
4. End the practice of awarding business on the basis of price tag. Purchasing must be combined with design of product, manufacturing, and sales to work with the chosen suppliers; the aim is to minimize total cost, not merely initial cost.
5. Improve constantly and forever every activity in the company in order to improve quality and productivity and thus constantly decrease costs.
6. Institute training and education on the job for everyone, including management.
7. Institute supervision. The aim of supervision should be to help people and machines do a better job.
8. Drive out fear so that everyone may work effectively for the company.
9. Break down barriers between departments. People in Research, Design, Sales, and Production must work as a team to tackle usage and production problems that may be encountered with the product or service.
10. Eliminate slogans, exhortations, and targets for the work force that ask for zero defects and new levels of productivity. Such exhortations only create adversarial relationships; the bulk of the causes of low quality and low productivity belongs to the system and thus lies beyond the power of the work force.
11. Eliminate work standards that prescribe numerical quotas for the day. Substitute aids and helpful supervision.
12a. Remove the barriers that rob hourly workers of the right to pride of workmanship. The responsibility of supervisors must be changed from sheer numbers to quality.
12b. Remove the barriers that rob people in management and in engineering of their right to pride of workmanship. This means, among other things, abolition of the annual or merit rating and of management by objective.
13. Institute a vigorous program of education and retraining. New skills are required for changes in techniques, material, and service.
14. Put everybody in the company to work in teams to accomplish the transformation.

FIGURE 2.4 *Edward Deming's
14 Points of Quality*

Source: Reprinted from *The New
Economics for Industry, Government,
Education* by W. Edward Deming by
permission of MIT and The W.
Edward Deming Institute. Published
by MIT, Center for Advanced
Educational Services, Cambridge,
MA 02139. Copyright 1993 by the
W. Edward Deming Institute.

CONNECTED: SURFING THE NET

www.quality.nist.gov

Discover what it takes to be a winner. Learn more about the Malcolm Baldrige National Quality Award and criteria by connecting to its Web site. Also link to the home pages of several award-winning companies.

MALCOLM BALDRIGE NATIONAL
QUALITY AWARD

A program designed to raise quality awareness and practice among U.S. businesses.

management be involved and supportive. If quality initiatives receive only lip service, without action, they will not be successful.

The Malcolm Baldrige National Quality Award   U.S. businesses have been late to emphasize quality. During the same period that the Japanese excelled in implementing quality initiatives, U.S. firms slipped dramatically in quality. Congress finally moved to establish a quality award for U.S. firms. It was named after the late Malcolm Baldrige, an advocate for quality and a former secretary of commerce. While considering the passage of the Malcolm Baldrige National Quality Improvement Act, the U.S. Senate Committee on Commerce, Science and Technology observed: "Strategic planning for quality improvement programs is becoming more and more essential to the well-being of our nation's companies and our ability to compete effectively in the global marketplace. Such an award would parallel the prize awarded annually in Japan."[37]

The 1987 legislation was enacted by Congress to encourage U.S. businesses and other organizations to practice effective quality control in the production of goods and services. At the time of its passage, the Senate and House produced a declaration reiterating the need for an incentive program for U.S. businesses and affirming that these businesses had been considerably challenged by foreign competitors. Slow growth in productivity and in product and process quality had, in some industries, resulted in annual losses of as much as 20 percent of sales revenues. It was evident that U.S. businesses needed to learn more about the importance of quality.

The **Malcolm Baldrige National Quality Award** is widely acknowledged as having raised quality awareness and practice among U.S. companies. Some consider the Baldrige the most important catalyst for transforming U.S. business because it promotes quality excellence, recognizes

1990 Cadillac Motor Car Company	**1993** Ames Rubber Corporation	**1997** 3M Dental Products Division

1990 Cadillac Motor Car Company
    Federal Express Corporation
    IBM Rochester
    Wallace Co.
1991 Marlow Industries
    Solectron Corporation
    Zytec Corporation
1992 AT&T Network Systems Group
    AT&T Universal Card Services
    Granite Rock Company
    The Ritz-Carlton Hotel
      Company
    Texas Instruments
      Incorporated

1993 Ames Rubber Corporation
    Eastman Chemical Company
1994 AT&T Consumer Communications
      Services
    GTE Directories Corporation
    Wainwright Industries
1995 Armstrong World Industries
      Building Products Operations
    Corning Telecommunications
      Products Division
1996 ADAC Laboratories
    Custom Research, Inc.
    Dana Commercial Credit
      Corporation
    Trident Precision Manufacturing

1997 3M Dental Products Division
    Solectron Corporation
    Merrill Lynch Credit Corporation
    Xerox Business Services
1998 Boeing Airlift and Tanker
      Programs
    Solar Turbines Incorporated
    Texas Nameplate Company, Inc.
1999 STMicroelectronics, Inc.
    BI
    The Ritz-Carlton Hotel Company
    Sunny Fresh Foods
2000 Dana Corporation—Spicer
      Driveshaft Division
    KARLEE Company, Inc.

FIGURE 2.5 *Winners of the Malcolm Baldrige National Quality Award*

achievements by companies that effectively improve quality, and supplies a guideline that business, industry, government, and others can use to evaluate their quality improvement efforts.

Awards are given each year in several categories: manufacturing companies or subsidiaries, service companies or subsidiaries, and small businesses. Figure 2.5 lists companies that have received the Malcolm Baldrige National Quality Award.

In 1999, the Ritz-Carlton Hotel Company was an award winner, making it the only two-time Malcolm Baldrige National Quality Award winner in the service category. The Ritz-Carlton Hotel Company, manages 36 luxury hotels in North America, Europe, Asia, Australia, the Middle East, Africa, and the Caribbean. What makes this company a total quality winner? Among many others, customer focus is a distinguishing achievement. Its outspoken goal is to "Understand Customers in Detail" by relying on extensive data gathering and the dissection of key points where customer satisfaction problems generally occur. The Ritz-Carlton maintains a database of almost a million customer files, which enables hotel staff to anticipate needs of returning guests and to make sure in advance that requests can be honored.[38]

The Malcom Baldrige National Quality Award has raised quality awareness among U.S. companies.

DELIVERING VALUE TO IMPROVE SATISFACTION

Customer-centered marketing requires the development of unique competencies to satisfy customers within selected target market segments and to build their loyalty. Many parties are involved in contributing to the delivery of products that benefit consumers. The value chain is used to describe the chain of activities involved in bringing products to consumers. Additionally, to improve customer satisfaction and loyalty, leading-edge companies operate ethically to fulfill commitments and involve employees and customers in performance improvement efforts.

THE VALUE CHAIN

VALUE CHAIN

All the activities that companies undertake to deliver more value to the ultimate consumer.

Economists use the concept of the value chain, which helps marketers identify ways that the company can do a better job of satisfying the end user. The **value chain** is composed of all the activities that organizations undertake to deliver value to the customer, such as product and service development, and distribution through convenient channels. A simple value chain starts by identifying customer needs. Most people seek products that perform as desired, portray the image they want, are easy to purchase, and are priced fairly. Companies then identify the chain of events that must occur to deliver this value to customers. It is important that quality is built into each link in the chain.

Many activities make a major difference in the amount of customer satisfaction. These include the procurement of raw materials as well as the manufacture and delivery of products to retailers and others in the channel of distribution. Each activity has the potential to deliver added value to the customer. All functional areas—purchasing, operations, manufacturing, marketing, sales, and so on—are involved in delivering customer value. Each area must clearly understand the final consumer. And many separate organizations may be linked in the chain.

Although customers have very little knowledge of these activities, they shape the quality of goods and services as well as the price that will be charged in the marketplace. Think about Nike, whose customers want a good value at a fair price. But Nike knows that manufacturing locations make a big difference in the product cost. In the same manner, the cost of Nike's raw materials, its ability to deliver products efficiently to retail outlets, the effectiveness of its research and development, and many other activities affect the overall quality of the goods and services the company can provide to its customers. Even the quality of the ads for Nike are important, since the image of the product for users is largely shaped by the ads. Nike's competitiveness depends to a great degree on its ability, and the ability of its suppliers and distributors, to perform well on all the factors that influence the amount of value delivered to the marketplace. All organizations in the chain must behave with the intent of creating satisfaction for others in the chain in order that consumers can ultimately benefit to the greatest degree possible.

ETHICAL BEHAVIOR IN FULFILLING COMMITMENTS

Many organizations that promise satisfaction and quality think they should provide a remedy to customers when quality does not meet expectations. Fixing the problem is ethically correct and a good business practice. Although "satisfaction guaranteed or your money back" usually applies to such purchases as clothes or a restaurant pizza, today some colleges believe that a promise of a quality education should be backed by a guarantee as well. They are using statements about quality and satisfaction to attract students from the shrinking pool of high school graduates, which has declined from 3.2 million in 1977 to about 2.8 million today.[39]

In 1986, Henry Ford Community College in Dearborn, Michigan, became the first school to offer a guarantee for its graduates. It provides up to 16 semester hours of further training if an employer feels a graduate lacks the expected job skills. St. John Fischer College, a four-year institution in Rochester, New York, started featuring promotions with "The Fischer Commitment." It gives up to $5,000 in refunds to students who, after a good-faith effort, are unable to find a job within six months of graduation. Of course, many businesses offer satisfaction guarantees. Some pay off with little hassle, like Meijer Thrifty Acres, a regional discount chain with an outstanding reputation for customer service. Others pay lip service to the offer but make it almost impossible for dissatisfied consumers to collect. Despite the satisfaction that results when a customer problem is handled well, a number of companies have tightened their rules and changed generous exchange policies. Best Buy, for example, has quit taking back goods without a sales receipt. Customers who have no receipt must pay a "restocking fee" equal to 15 percent of the purchase price of the item. Wal-Mart has changed its open-ended return policy to one with a 90-day limit.

Customers are partly responsible for these changes. Imagine people returning goods actually purchased at a garage sale or bringing back clothes worn for an entire season. Or what about customers who pull items off store shelves and bring them to the counter for a refund? Nintendo has received returned game boxes containing underwear, soap, and even a lizard. Although these are extreme examples, stores have tightened return policies to help prevent fraud. Since $62 billion in merchandise is returned to retailers annually, the stricter policies may seem reasonable.[40] The important consideration, however, is the consumer response. If the ease of returning a defective or unwanted good is eliminated, then consumers feel negatively about the company or business. Since many aspects of satisfaction are based on how the organization and its products affect customers, it is important to make all employees aware of the importance of the customer to the overall health of the organization. That requires their involvement in knowing why products were returned and nearly every other aspect of customer evaluations.

Employee and Customer Involvement

It's pretty hard to imagine making customers satisfied without having employees who are highly involved in the process. It is also hard to imagine those same employees doing a good job with customers unless they are satisfied with their organization. Satisfied employees are much more likely to produce satisfied customers than are disgruntled employees. Thus, customer satisfaction starts with the company itself. Strong companies involve the entire organization and its customers in efforts to improve performance in ways that will promote customer satisfaction. IBM integrates customers into its improvement planning process by inviting consumers from around the world to give direct input to top-level strategic planners. Executives at Procter & Gamble take time to interview consumers at grocery stores and answer customer service calls. Hewlett-Packard recruits customers to assist in developing products that will replace current offerings. All these companies demonstrate how interaction between consumers and an organization's employees help ensure that the customer is a primary focus.[41]

The job of satisfying consumers cannot be left to the marketing or sales manager alone. According to Robert Schrandt, vice president of customer relations for Toyota Motor Sales, USA, "Achieving customer satisfaction would be impossible without a well-defined process for focusing the entire organization on the customer." As with the most important marketing functions, everyone must participate, from top management to the workers on the factory floor. In fact, most companies that are serious about improving satisfaction consider it critical to involve their top managers. They sit in on meetings about customer satisfaction and demand that everyone "walk the talk"—not just discuss issues but develop plans to address them. Compared to other organizations, managers in these companies spend more time talking with customers, and compensation structures often are based more on satisfying customers than on meeting short-term financial goals. Furthermore, all functional areas are

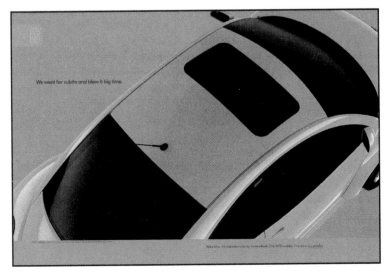

Volkswagen wants consumers to know that its newer Beetle has many new customer pleasing features.

involved, including marketing, sales, engineering, accounting, and purchasing. Other channel members, such as manufacturers' representatives, wholesalers, and distributors, often are made part of the effort. The result is a customer-centered organization working together to create satisfied purchasers.

It isn't enough to involve members of the company and its agents. Customers also must be part of the process. The biggest mistake most companies make is to assume they know what their customers want without asking them. Unfortunately, most companies that guess do so incorrectly. For a true understanding of what consumers want, a company must ask them through some sort of meaningful involvement. It is important to include not only current customers but also potential purchasers and competitors' customers. Each is likely to provide unique and enlightening information. One way to achieve involvement is through formal marketing research, such as interviews or surveys. In addition, many leading companies include customers in their planning teams.

Customer Review, an Internet company that establishes online communities based around sports, electronics, and the home, works to develop relationships with customers of products. An online "facilitator" directs discussion about particular products among the company's 1.2 million Web site visitors. Establishing relationships with its customers is important to the success of Customer Review. However, the quality of these relationships extends to the manufacturers of the products it reviews.[42] The quality of relationships and the accuracy of expectations that manufacturers of products establish with Customer Review's customers are reflected in the product reviews posted on its Web site.

Chapter 4 will focus on how marketing executives and managers develop strategies and plans designed to achieve customer satisfaction more effectively than competitors. Meanwhile, we will take a look at important factors in the global marketing environment that must be accounted for in the strategic planning process.

CONNECTED: SURFING THE NET

WEB MILES
www.webmiles.com

THIS CHAPTER'S TECHNOLOGY BOX DISCUSSED **WebMiles Rewards program. In order to expand your thinking about WebMiles, visit its Web site and answer the following questions.**

1. According to the WebMiles Web site, how does the WebMiles program differ from other frequent flyer programs? How, specifically, does WebMiles provide value for its customers?
2. Decide on a purchase you would make online with your WebMiles MasterCard. How many miles would you earn with your purchase? Could you purchase the same item at a participating site and earn more miles?
3. Visit WebMiles' "Special Member Promotions" section. What additional rewards and bonuses does one attain by being a member?

EAST WEST BANK
www.eastwestbank.com

EAST WEST BANK BUILDS RELATIONSHIPS with customers in many ways, particularly through ethnic marketing, which you learned about in this chapter's diversity box. Here is an opportunity to learn more about East West. Visit its Web site and answer the following questions.

1. Read about East West's personal banking services. What services does it offer?
2. What are East West's import and export services? How would these services target the Asian American community?
3. Look through the news releases on East West's site. Does it seem as though the company is succeeding? Does its success relate to its ethnic focus?

OBJECTIVE 1: **Understand why customer satisfaction and loyalty are the focus of marketing in winning organizations.**

Satisfied, loyal customers generate profits because they are responsible for a large percentage of sales and are less costly to develop than new customers. Loyal, satisfied customers also influence others to buy products. Similar to product innovation, customer satisfaction has become a key to competitive advantage. In addition, satisfaction ratings help consumers compare products. Finally, loyal, satisfied customers will pay more and are less concerned about price and price increases.

OBJECTIVE 2: **Learn how consumer expectations influence satisfaction.**

Customers form impressions about how well companies perform in relation to expectations. If performance falls short, then customers become dissatisfied. Often they defect when they don't like the way they are treated. When customers are delighted, their expectations are likely to increase. Loyal customers are not always satisfied, and they are likely to complain. If their complaint is handled quickly, then their loyalty may be even greater.

OBJECTIVE 3: **See why connecting with customers through relationships achieves outstanding satisfaction and loyalty.**

The personal connection produces loyalty. Relationships are built, first, on empathy—the ability to understand another party and communicate that understanding. Second, trust is important, that is, behaving in line with promises you make and expectations you create. Third, commitment is also important. Commitment means making sure that the customer is better off because of the relationship.

OBJECTIVE 4: **Understand the ideas that help organizations market quality goods and services.**

Diverse customers have different expectations. Creating satisfaction requires paying close attention to various tastes and preferences. Many companies have created units to address specific groups. The variations in customer tastes and preferences are particularly challenging for large companies that want to gain high satisfaction scores. They still need to address each specific segment to achieve high ratings. Satisfaction scores have historically been higher for some foreign companies in this country, reflecting their attention to quality. This has helped them gain a market foothold. Now that U.S. companies also are stressing quality and satisfaction, their scores are improving in marketing to foreign countries.

OBJECTIVE 5: **Define quality and describe how it is obtained.**

Quality can be assessed objectively and subjectively. Objective assessments indicate whether the product performs as designed. Subjective assessments indicate whether the product performs according to what customers want. Businesses must be careful not to focus only on static quality. The quality of change—dynamic quality—is also important. Both build value. Total quality management (TQM) is an organizational philosophy that focuses on quality. It includes several specific actions, such as continuous improvement, reduced cycle time, and analysis of process problems. Benchmarking is also important. It refers to learning from organizations considered to be among the very best and assessing how well you perform relative to them.

1. What is customer satisfaction? What is loyalty? What are four reasons for an organization to stress loyalty and satisfaction? Explain each.
2. How do you calculate the lifetime value of a customer?
3. What are customer expectations? Why do customers defect? Why are complainers often your most loyal customers?
4. What are the three elements that form the personal basis of relationships? Explain each. How do companies reward loyal customers?
5. What are companies doing to address satisfaction with diversified customers?
6. Why is satisfaction important in global marketing?
7. What is customer-delivered value? Explain.
8. What is the value chain? Explain.
9. What are objective and subjective assessments of quality? Static and dynamic quality?
10. What is TQM and what are its four critical components?
11. What is benchmarking?
12. What are the Deming Prize and the Malcolm Baldrige National Quality Award?

1. Why should companies focus on both satisfaction and loyalty? Why is satisfaction alone inadequate?
2. Imagine that you are the marketing director of a local company. How would you use the concept of customer-delivered value to improve the marketing for a product?
3. Discuss how connecting with customers through relationships relates to satisfaction and loyalty.
4. If you observed a large percentage of customer defections from a business, what might the causes be? How would you investigate?

5. Is complaining behavior good or bad? Should you encourage customers to complain?
6. What would you recommend for an organization that wishes to connect with customers through relationships?

7. What is the relationship between quality and customer value? How is quality attained?
8. Do you feel companies should allocate a great deal of effort to apply for the Malcolm Baldrige National Quality Award? Why or why not?

KEY TERMS AND DEFINITIONS

Analysis of process problems: Methods designed to find and fix problems that could reduce quality.

Benchmarking: The systematic evaluation of practices of excellent organizations to learn new and better ways to serve customers.

Best practices: The competencies of industry leaders that other organizations use as benchmarks.

Continuous improvement: The enhancement process used by an organization to find the best ways of satisfying its customers.

Cost structure: The amount of money required to produce a specific amount of sales.

Customer defections: The percentage of customers who switch to another brand or supplier.

Customer-delivered value: The perceived difference between what the customer pays and what the customer gains from a transaction.

Customer expectations: Consumer beliefs about the performance of a product based on prior experience and communications.

Customer loyalty: A measure of how often, when selecting from a product class, a customer purchases a particular brand.

Customer satisfaction: A customer's positive, neutral, or negative feeling about the value received from an organization's product in specific use situations.

Customer satisfaction measurement program: An ongoing survey of customers (and competitors' customers) for the purpose of obtaining continuous estimates of satisfaction.

Customer value: The perception customers have of what they receive from owning and using a product over and above the cost of acquiring it.

Dynamic quality: Quality that results from a change that makes an existing standard obsolete.

ISO 9000: An inclusive set of standards established by the International Standards Organization (ISO) to ensure that quality requirements are met.

Lifetime value of a customer: The amount of profit a company expects to obtain over the course of the relationship.

Malcolm Baldrige National Quality Award: A program designed to raise quality awareness and practice among U.S. businesses.

Objective assessment of quality: An evaluation of the degree to which a product does what it is supposed to do.

Quality: The degree of excellence of a company's products or services.

Quality function deployment (QFD): A process that builds customer wants and desires into the final product offering.

Reduced cycle time: A TQM activity that helps a company move more rapidly from product inception to final delivery of the product to the marketplace.

Satisfaction ratings: Ratings provided by testing agencies that compare purchase satisfaction with specified brands or with how well products perform.

Service quality: The expected and perceived quality of all of the services an organization offers.

Static quality: Quality that results when individuals or organizations perfect an accepted practice.

Statistical quality control: The use of statistics to isolate and quantify production line problems that may cause product defects.

Subjective assessment of quality: The degree to which a product does what consumers would like it to do.

Total quality management (TQM): An organizational philosophy that helps companies produce goods and services that deliver value to satisfy customers.

Value chain: All the activities that companies undertake to deliver more value to the ultimate consumer.

REFERENCES

1. Lee Copeland, "Saturn, eBay Team Up to Boost New, Used Car Sales," *Computerworld*, June 26, 2000, p. 50; "eBay's Bid for Fixed Prices," *Business Week*, June 26, 2000, p. 54; Jim Kerstetter, "Empire Builders: Meg Whitman," *Business Week*, May 15, 2000, p. EB30; Kipp Cheng, "Best Viral Marketing," *Mediaweek*, June 28, 1999, p. IQ/42; Whit Andrews, "eBay Striving to Be More Than a Fad," *Internet World*, May 10, 1999, p. 15; Elizabeth Gardner, "eBay Buys Experience with New Stock Wealth," *Internet World*, May 3, 1999, p. 1; Jason Compton, "Case Study Better Than a Mind Reader," *PC Computing*, December 1999, p. 234; eBay Web site (www.ebay.com).
2. Robert B. Woodruff and Sarah F. Gardial, *Know Your Customer* (Cambridge, MA: Blackwell Publishers, Inc., 1996), p. 20.
3. "Polk Awards: Ford Takes Prize for Fostering Customer Loyalty to Make and Manufacturer," *National Post*, May 19, 2000, p. E-9.
4. "Happy Shopper," *Management Accounting*, July 1, 2000, pp. 28–30.
5. "Customer Care Goes End-to-End," *Information Week*, May 15, 2000, pp. 55–61.
6. "Pay a Little Less Attention to Retention," *Brandweek*, April 10, 2000; p. 34. "Brand Aware," *Children's Business*, June 1, 2000.
7. "We Interrupt This Issue to Remind You That the Internet Is Big," *Wired*, July 2000, pp. 252–57.
8. "Combating Customer Churn," *Telecommunications Americas*, March 2000, pp. 83–85.
9. "Managing Customer Loyalty," *Loyalty-Based Management*, June 1, 1994.
10. "Auto Report: Lexus No. 1 Again for Satisfaction," *Arizona Republic*, July 22, 2000, p. AC1.
11. "Beyond Satisfaction," *CMA Management*, March 2000, pp. 14–15.
12. Clay Carr, *Front Customer Service* (New York: John Wiley and Sons, 1990), p. 31.
13. Ibid., p. 19.
14. "After an Unmerry Christmas, Toys "R" Us Is on the Mend," *Fortune*, July 10, 2000, p. 44.
15. www.jdpowers.com, Web site visited on July 12, 2000.
16. "Judges Panel of the Malcolm Baldrige National Quality Award," *Federal Register*, July 21, 2000.

17. "Barnesandnoble.com to Offer Discounts to More Than 85 Million Customers," *Direct Marketing*, March 2000, p. 14.
18. "It's Party Time for Saturn," *Sales and Marketing Management*, June 1994.
19. www.harley-davidson.com, Web site visited on September 5, 2000.
20. "Nelson Expecting 10,000 for Camp Jeep 2000," *Richmond Times-Dispatch*, August 11, 2000, p. B-2.
21. www.levistrauss.com, site visited on September 2, 2000.
22. "Combo Platter," *Marketing News*, May 22, 2000, p. 15.
23. "Do Rewards Really Create Loyalty?" *Harvard Business Review*, May–June 1995, p. 75.
24. "AOL and American Airlines Create Largest Online Customer Loyalty Program," *Direct Marketing*, May 2000, p. 10.
25. "Giant Introduces Frequent Shopper Program," *PR Newswire*, August 31, 2000, p. 132.
26. "Going Global: Lessons from Late Movers," *Harvard Business Review*, May 1, 2000.
27. "Minority Promotions Pick Up the Pace," *Advertising Age*, February 27, 1995.
28. "HireDiversity.com Joins CareerBuilder Network," *PR Newswire*, August 16, 2000.
29. Excerpted with permission from *The New Economics for Industry, Government, Education*, 2nd edition, copyright © 1994 by the Edward Deming Institute; and from *Out of the Crisis*, copyright © 1986, by the Edward Deming Institute; "Xerox, Once a Symbol of Corporate Success, Struggles to Compete," *Associated Press Newswires*, September 5, 2000.
30. www.fedex.com/us/about/express/facts, site visited on September 5, 2000.
31. "Consumer Perceptions of Price, Quality and Value: A Means-End Model and Synthesis of Evidence," *Journal of Marketing*, July 1988, p. 2; Sandra Vandermerwe, "How Increasing Value to Customers Improves Business Results," *Sloan Management Review*, Fall 2000, pp. 27–37.
32. Michael R. Czinkote, Masaki Kotabe, and David Mercer, *Marketing Management* (Cambridge, MA: Blackwell, 1997), p. 273.
33. Arthur R. Tenner and Irving J. DeToro, *Total Quality Management* (Boston: Addison-Wesley, 1992), p. 733.
34. "Price Achievement," *Nation's Business*, January 1990, p. 29.
35. www.fedex.com, site visited September 5, 2000; Jack Rose, "New Quality Means Service Too," *Fortune*, April 22, 1991, pp. 99–107.
36. "Inside Track: Tools That Do the Business," *Financial Times*, June 15, 2000, p. 16.
37. Malcolm Baldrige National Quality Improvement Act of 1987, report of the Senate Committee on Commerce, Science and Technology on HR 812 (Washington, DC: U.S. Government Printing Office, 1987).
38. www.nist.gov/public_affairs/bald99/ritz.htm, website visited on September 5, 2000.
39. "U.S. Colleges Prepare for Professor Shortage," *Chicago Tribune*, July 16, 2000, p. A-11.
40. "Return to Sender," *Modern Materials Handling*, May 15, 2000, pp. 64–65.
41. Earl Naumann, *Customer Value Toolkit* (Boise, ID: Thomson Executive Press, 1994).
42. "Get Sticky with Your Customer," *Sales and Marketing Management*, May 2000, pp. 26–27.

Bricks or Clicks

WEB-ENABLED CUSTOMER RELATIONSHIP MANAGEMENT

WEB-ENABLED CUSTOMER RELATIONSHIP MANAGEMENT (CRM) initiatives are changing the way that chemical companies serve their customers. Eastman Chemical Company was the first to go online in July 1999 and its Web transactions accounted for up to 20 percent of its business by the end of 2000. One of Eastman's greatest challenges was that many of its customers lacked the necessary modern computer equipment needed to use the new system. In order to correct this, Eastman has partnered with Dell computers to outfit several of its customers with up-to-date computers.

CRM collects data on a company's customers, its customers' customers, and all of the other members of the supply chain. The hope is that CRM will provide the data necessary to anticipate customer needs and thus to meet them in a more timely and efficient manner. Many of the chemical companies are focusing their efforts on an e-supply chain. "The end benefit of developing an e-supply chain is the valuable ability to collect information to improve efficiencies," says Eric Hughey, chief operating officer at e-Chemicals. CRM and e-supply chains will give companies that can manage it properly a sustainable competitive advantage.

The chemical companies are not scrapping their direct sales interactions yet. Many customers are not willing to give up all of the personal interaction with suppliers, so most companies will maintain their direct sales channels for customers with specialized needs. Darryl Plummer, V.P. and group research director at Gartner has said, "People need human contact, they need the reassurance that machines cannot provide. Most of all they need someone to yell at when things go wrong, and successful e-businessess will take this into account." In an industry that sells commodities, customer service is the one true differentiating factor between competitors.

While chemical companies are not trading in all their bricks for clicks, web-enabled CRM is helping the staid industry make strides to improve customer service. These improvements will lead to greater customer loyalty and the ability to create better relationships and generate more wealth at all points along the supply chain.

Sources: Gabrielle Birkner, "Eastman Chemical draws customers online," *Sales and Marketing*, June, 2000, 40–42; "Adding value through web-enabled CRM," *Chemical Week*, July 26, 2000, S22-S23.

The Ritz-Carlton Hotel Company

IMAGINE YOU'RE TRAVELING ON ONE of many overnight business trips. You like your suit pressed by 6 A.M. sharp, and you take your coffee black with one ice cube, among other preferences. How many hotels respond to your needs with consistency and timelines, if at all? The Ritz-Carlton does. The company uses sophisticated information technology to remember your previous requests and provide them for you again and again in any of its hotels where you may be staying. For example, one customer who had regularly stayed in the Ritz-Carlton in Seoul, Korea, checked into a Ritz-Carlton in Palm Beach, Florida, to celebrate his wedding anniversary and had all of his previous requests known and carried out. The Ritz-Carlton prides itself on knowing and respecting your preferences, as well as creating loyalty and satisfaction on a one-to-one basis through its quality services and products.

The Ritz-Carlton Hotel Company manages, develops, and operates luxury hotels. Based in Atlanta, Georgia, it manages 35 hotels on several continents. The Ritz-Carlton primarily targets corporate travelers and affluent vacationers. The Ritz-Carlton is now planning to open 100 additional hotels throughout the Middle East, the United States, Jamaica, Mexico, and the Philippines. Additionally, it is exploring expansion into high-end condominiums, dining clubs, and cruise ships. Ranked in *Forbes* as one of the top 15 U.S. city hotels and in *Fortune* as one of the top six business hotels, the Ritz-Carlton knows about delivering quality. In fact, the company was a winner of the Malcolm Baldrige National Quality Award in 1992 and 1999. Only one other American company has received this award more than once, and the Ritz-Carlton is the only company in the hotel industry to have been recognized. It requires planning, a committed team of employees and management, and implementation of premium service.

How does the Ritz-Carlton Hotel Company accomplish all this? It starts at the top, with a team of senior executives who meet every week to review quality issues. This includes the company's products and services, customer satisfaction and loyalty, growth and profits, and evaluation of the competition. In fact, Ritz executives spend 25 percent of their time working on quality-related issues. Ultimately, however, the responsibility for delivering customer value (and, thereby value to the organization) depends on 14,000 employees. Employees go through a process of orientation, on-the-job training (120 hours per year per employee), and certification. Because employees are extensively trained to observe their guests, the Ritz-Carlton does not have to bother customers with surveys and questionnaires. Instead, each employee is given a "preference pad" that is used to record the personal preferences of each customer. The information is then used to provide more personalized service to the customer in future stays. Employees record the obvious, such as type of room preferred, but they also note the less obvious details, such as a request for extra towels, and note whether the guest took apples or bananas from the fruit basket.

Empowering employees to solve problems is another crucial element in the Ritz-Carlton's quest for quality. They are allowed to do "whatever it takes" to make a customer happy without first seeking management approval. No matter how large or small the problem, all employees, regardless of job description, are expected to resolve potential conflicts and fulfill customer wishes. The Ritz-Carlton believes in rewarding employees and giving recognition for commendable work. The company realizes that their employees come to work with their own personal problems and worries that can prevent the employees from doing their best possible work. To help compensate for this, the Ritz-Carlton has a system of motivation, recognition, praise, and reward.

Teamwork can be found at every level of the company. Each hotel has a "quality leader" who works to design and carry out quality plans. These plans are reviewed with all employees at the start of each shift. This person serves as a resource to coworkers and is an advocate for the company. Each area of the Ritz-Carlton Hotel has threee teams, and these are responsible for both setting and implementing quality standards in their areas. Technology is also integral in achieving objectives. Production reports provide data from 720 different parts of the hotel to indicate progress or potential problems. Automated building, safety, and reservation systems as well as the history profile technology all assist in making customer value a priority.

Although all Ritz-Carlton Hotels work to achieve the same objectives, each can also have a unique identity. For example, the Ritz-Carlton in Kapalua, Hawaii, is considered to be one of the finest hotels in the world. Reflecting the diverse cultural influences of its surroundings, the Kapalua offers native festivals, traditional Hawaiian music and cuisine, and hula dances. In addition, cultural classes are mandatory for all employees.

The Ritz-Carlton Hotel Company is very effective in the implementation of its quality program as a means to achieve customer satisfaction and loyalty. Its 121 quality-related awards in one year alone speak for themselves. With a customer satisfaction rate of up to 97 percent, the high standards are likely to pay off in repeat business.

1. *In this chapter, requirements for creating and delivering customer value were discussed. How does the Ritz-Carlton Hotel Company meet those requirements?*
2. *Relationship marketing creates interactions with customers that make it unnecessary or even difficult for them to switch to a competitor. How has the Ritz-Carlton used this marketing strategy? Invent several ways the company could form one-to-one relationships with customers. How could each of these initiatives influence customer perceptions of quality?*
3. *The diversity of tastes and preferences is a challenge for customer-centered marketers. Identify several different groups (such as those with disabilities or the elderly) and develop initiatives the Ritz-Carlton could use to provide them with superior customer value.*

Sources: The Ritz-Carlton, www.ritzcarlton.com, visited June 19, 2000; Hoover's Online, "The Ritz-Carlton Hotel Company, LLC," www.hooversonline.com, visited June 19, 2000; "Malcolm Baldrige National Quality Award 1992 Winner: The Ritz-Carlton Hotel Company," Winners Showcase, www.quality.nist.gov, as updated May 26, 1998; Gene Sloan, "Hawaii's New Attraction: Her Rich Past," *USA Today,* March 25, 1997, www.usatoday.com; Gene Sloan, "Asia Is Fertile Ground for Resorts," *USA Today,* March 25, 1997, www.usatoday.com; Ed Brown, "The Best Business Hotels," *Fortune,* March 31, 1997, www.fortune.com; Don Peppers and Martha Rogers, "Welcome to the 1:1 Future," *Marketing Tools,* April–May 1994, www.marketingtools.com; Laura Bly, "A Rush to Democratic South Africa," *USA Today,* March 25, 1997, www.usatoday.com; William C. Flannagan, "Where Executives Love to Stay," *Forbes,* September 23, 1996, www.forbes.com; Dave DeWitte, "Ritz-Carlton Hotel Chain Executive Speaks About Customer Service," *The Gazette (Cedar Rapids),* October 18, 2000, and Michael Lohs, "It Pays to Be in the Know," *Business Times (Singapore),* July 4, 2000, p. 32.

chapter 3

THE GLOBAL MARKETING ENVIRONMENT AND E-COMMERCE

1. Describe the marketing environment and the use of environmental scanning.

2. Understand how the roles that stakeholders play influence the accomplishment of marketing objectives. Know why marketing must address stakeholder desires when making decisions.

3. Be able to integrate an understanding of industry competition into environmental analysis.

4. Synthesize aspects of the global macroenvironment, including technological, economic, demographic, cultural, and legal/regulatory elements in order to be in step with long-term trends.

5. Understand the impact that e-commerce is making on the global business environment and understand the structure of Internet marketing.

6. Recognize the importance of ethics and guides to ethical behavior.

◄ Director George Lucas and Actor Jake Lloyd

CHANGE IS CONSTANT. SUCCESSFUL ORGANIZATIONS MUST *keep pace with changes in the environment, and leading-edge organizations often create changes that affect entire industries. Such is the story of George Lucas, who conceptualized and created digital film technology, which revolutionized the film industry and left other film organizations to wonder what he'd come up with next.*

Lucas started building the future back in the 1970s. He wanted to create a truly modern folktale, with appropriate heroes, that would capture the imagination of children at that time. However, the traditional technology prevented George Lucas and his team at Lucasfilm from getting what was in his head onto the screen. To tell his story the way he wanted it told required a new technology. When he began his epic Star Wars *series in 1975, Lucas searched for a company that could create what he envisioned. After scanning the environment and finding a lack of technology to match his creativity, he decided to do it himself. "This was all born out of complete frustration with how the medium worked technically," says Lucas.*

To meet his creative needs, Lucas founded Industrial Light & Magic (ILM), an enterprise that would have profound effects on the entire industry and bring pleasure to millions worldwide. In 1982, ILM created the first computer-generated scene for Star Trek II: The Wrath of Khan. *Three years later came the first digital character, "stained glass man," in* Young Sherlock Holmes. *The first three-dimensional character followed in* The Abyss *(1989), created through the use of Morf, ILM's proprietary technology. Morf techniques were refined in* Terminator 2: Judgment Day *(1991). ILM developed digitally created skin for* Death Becomes Her *(1993) and "real" dinosaurs in* Jurassic Park *(1993).* Forrest Gump *(1995) brought ILM its 14th Academy Award for blending historical footage with modern-day actors.* Casper *introduced the first fully digital character.*

Gordon Radley, president of Lucasfilm, observed that today Lucas is not only the owner of ILM but he is also its most demanding customer. Radley said, "He's a client of his own company. So that when he makes Star Wars, *as he does, he goes to ILM and he negotiates with his own company." This gives Lucas a very unique perspective compared to many other company heads. This orientation toward developing technology to satisfy the creative needs of clients gives ILM the leadership required to continue to be the best and most preeminent company in the business.*

In 1997, Star Wars Trilogy Special Edition, *was released in theaters to celebrate its 20th anniversary, demonstrating how far Lucas and digital effects have come. Lucasfilm restored the original negatives, enhanced the sound and visual, transformed backgrounds, and added a character. Harrison Ford's Hans Solo found himself in a new scene, opposite a digital Jabba the Hut. Digital technology allowed Lucas to produce the movie he had originally imagined.*

Lucas did more than change the way movies are made. With Star Wars, *he created a fantasy world, one with great marketing potential. Like Disney, Lucas told a great story, with great characters, and pushed the technological boundaries. In addition, he provided great value for consumers and a solid business enterprise. When Lucas negotiated with Twentieth Century-Fox in 1975 to make* Star Wars, *he gave up a larger salary in exchange for what the studio then regarded as worthless: ownership of merchandising, music, publishing rights—and all sequels. With that move, Lucas changed the marketing environment for movies with the concept of tie-ins.*

Since 1977, more than $3 billion in licensed Star Wars products have been sold, including toys, books, comics, and even Franklin Mint commemoratives. Bantam Books has shipped more than 15 million copies of novels based on the movie since 1990; 16 of the 19 titles have hit the New York Times best-seller list. "Star Wars is our largest publishing franchise," says Bantam publisher Irwyn Applebaum. Bantam enriched the franchise by publishing series geared toward teens, youth, and children, each with age-appropriate language and content.

Lucas further marketed Star Wars and many other original titles to the computer game industry, creating the LucasArts division. It is one of the largest makers of video games for computers, with about 10 percent of the market share. A key to success has been the application of film techniques (camera angles, lighting, editing, etc.) to make the games look more like a movie. Constant enhancements at LucasArts keep competitors on their toes, further stimulating innovation in the entertainment industry.

Lucas has branched into other digital arenas in movie-making by creating Skywalker Sound, the leader in this area of the industry. Because terrific effects require high-quality sound, Lucas created the THX division. Lucasfilm also released THX Optimode software for DVD, which provides customized audio for individual DVD movies. However, fans won't get the chance to view the latest installment of Lucas's Star Wars series on DVD until the video sales bottom out. Following his pattern of making rather stringent demands on theaters showing The Phantom Menace (released in 1999), Lucas has held off the release of the DVD version of the film until every penny has been squeezed from the more traditional video market.

What's to come? The next step for Lucasfilm is producing the next two Star Wars prequels. With Episode II set for release in 2002 Lucas starts where The Phantom Menace ended by telling the story of how Darth Vader came to be. Lucas is using his old standby films (Episodes IV, V, and VI) to promote the new ones. A 10-minute Episode II preview will be included on a rerelease of the original trilogy while additional marketing will focus on the starwars.com Web site and video/DVD point-of-sale displays.

The marketing environment for the Star Wars films is composed of many forces, technology being one of the most important. It enables organizations to develop a range of products that is often only limited by one's imagination. The success of Lucasfilm shows how one organization is shaping the marketing environment by being there first. In the process Lucas and his organizations have satisfied the needs of fantasy lovers the world over.[1]

CONNECTED: SURFING THE NET

www.lucasarts.com

www.thx.com

Download demos of new games, seek technical support from "Yoda's Help Desk," and learn more about LucasArts.

THE CONCEPT OF THE MARKETING ENVIRONMENT

Change abounds. It can be your friend or enemy depending on how it is handled. Some organizations are reactive—they do not adjust strategies until environmental changes have occurred. That can be dangerous, since it may be too late to construct a successful new strategy. Other organizations are proactive—they anticipate environmental changes and adjust ahead of time. Proactive organizations quickly take advantage of new opportunities and minimize or eliminate damage from negative changes. Connecting with customers is best accomplished with a proactive philosophy because the forces that affect your organization are the same that affect customers. In fact, proactive companies connect best. They are in step with their customers by being in step with the marketing environment. The **marketing environment** is the sum of all factors that affect a business. Figure 3.1 depicts the marketing environment surrounding our theme: connecting with customers. First is the microenvironment, then the all-encompassing global macroenvironment. You will learn about both in the following sections.

An organization does not operate in a vacuum. Many factors can have a dramatic influence. These create opportunities, but they can also prevent the company from pursuing its desired strategy. An organization must be sensitive to its surroundings. **Environmental scanning** collects and analyzes information in order to detect any trends that may affect

MARKETING ENVIRONMENT
The sum of all the factors that affect a business.

ENVIRONMENTAL SCANNING
Collecting and analyzing information about the marketing environment in order to detect important changes or trends that can affect a company's strategy.

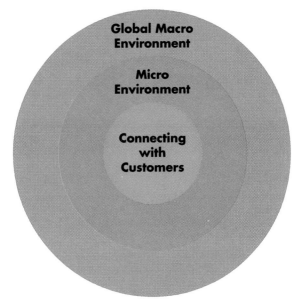

FIGURE 3.1 *The Marketing Environment*

a company's strategy. It can be performed by the company itself, by professional or industry associations, or by one of the numerous consulting organizations that specialize in forecasting.

SBC Communications scans the environment constantly. If not, it might have missed huge opportunities. One key trend is the desire for more visual and voice content in communications. Based on this trend, in an effort to be a leader, SBC Communications will install broadband capabilities in its 36 million business and customer locations. At a cost of $6 billion over the next three years, SBC expects to increase revenues by many billions more. SBC's early monitoring of broadband trends allows SBC to enter the market at precisely the right time.[2]

The Internet is an extraordinary environmental scanning tool. This technology enables marketers to investigate press releases, news stories, online magazines, journals, newspapers, and company Web sites highlighting product offerings, as well as technical and financial data. Even company strategies can be gathered from this public information by a skilled marketing analyst.

Getting information about competitors is much faster and easier on the Internet. The U.S. Bureau of the Census Web site (www.census.gov) provides demographic information, and online magazines such as *American Demographics* (www.marketingtools.com) identify cultural trends. When scanning for legal/regulatory information, marketers can check government sites for relevant material. For example, data on pending designs can be found at the U.S. Patent Office Web site (www.uspto.gov). The most authoritative sources for economic and demographic information about foreign countries are the CIA (www.odci.gov/cia/publications/factbook/index.html) and Economist Intelligence Unit (www.db.eiu.com) Web sites. The Internet also offers research, surveys, and other means for studying Web user behavior and surfing habits. All this is used extensively to collect marketing information, which we will discuss in chapter 5.

If you want help in scanning, there is plenty available. Companies that specialize in competitive intelligence even offer subscriptions to access data they have assembled. Subscribers give a profile of their interests (such as the automotive industry in the Midwest), and the service supplies the latest material. GE Information Services (Global eXchange) and Dow Jones Interactive are two leading providers of these services.[3]

THE MICROENVIRONMENT

The **microenvironment** is made up of the forces close to the company that influence how it connects with customers. As you'll notice in Figure 3.2, stakeholders and industry competition are part of the microenvironment. Stakeholders, as the name suggests, have a stake in an organization. Companies deal with stakeholders daily. Marketers need to understand stakeholders, recognizing that marketing decisions affect them and are affected by their influence. Marketers need to have other parties' needs in mind. Competition is also a daily phenomenon.

MICROENVIRONMENT

The forces close to a company that influence how it connects with customers.

MICROENVIRONMENT

RELATIONSHIPS WITH STAKEHOLDERS
- Owners
- Employees
- Suppliers
- Intermediaries
- Action groups
- Others

COMPETITIVE INDUSTRY
- Competitors
- Competitive groups

FIGURE 3.2 *The Microenvironment*

Competitors challenge your organization—sometimes you win, and sometimes they win. In either case, healthy competition is good because it stimulates change. Competitors, like stakeholders, must be considered in nearly every major marketing decision.

RELATIONSHIPS WITH STAKEHOLDERS

STAKEHOLDER

A group who can influence or be influenced by the firm's actions.

Any group or individual, other than competitors, who can influence or be influenced by an organization's actions is a **stakeholder,** including customers, owners, employees, suppliers, intermediaries, action groups, and many others. In the previous chapter we stressed the importance of building relationships with customers. In this chapter we stress building relationships with other stakeholders. Marketers form interactive, ongoing, two-way connections with stakeholders. They build these lasting relationships so that stakeholders will be a positive influence on the organization. Stakeholders can help serve customer needs and wants as well as help accomplish the objectives of the organization. Consequently, marketers try to act in the best long-term interest of all the firm's stakeholders. But because stakeholders have conflicting objectives, this can be difficult. Let's examine some of these stakeholders.

Owners and Employees Whether public or private, an organization operates for the benefit of its owners, who establish its objectives. For companies, these objectives usually stress increasing the value of the business—making substantial profit. In nonprofit organizations, the objectives usually relate to benefiting constituents. For example, the beneficiaries of Greenpeace are people concerned about the environment. Shareholders have purchased, been given, or inherited a share of the business. Typically, owners either represent themselves or are represented by a board of directors, which is charged with the responsibility to speak for all the owners. Marketers need to understand the goals, risks, and reward levels acceptable to owners, who only invest in a company that continues to reach its objectives.[4] For example, Panera Bread Company had a 100 percent increase in stock price in a single year. It took an aggressive and somewhat risky market approach by introducing several new menu items and announcing plans to open 500 new stores.[5] These actions produced results in line with shareholders' expectations so they were willing to pay more for the stock.

Employees are also key stakeholders. Their livelihood depends on the company. Since every employee helps create and deliver value to the end consumer, each employee has a very important influence on the organization. Companies that connect with their employees to ensure their satisfaction within the organization are often rewarded with satisfied customers. Carlson Hospitality Worldwide, owner of hotels and restaurants such as TGI Friday's and Radisson, treats its employees as a valuable and coveted asset. Besides good pay and advancement opportunities, Carlson offers them a wide range of innovative benefits, including adoption assistance for aspiring parents. "If you have people who want to work for you," says Carlson President Eric Danziger, "keeping them is more important than getting them. Its tough to get the right person. When you get them, you want to keep them." In turn Carlson is able to create marketing strategies that can be implemented with professional, loyal employees.

CONNECTED: SURFING THE NET

www.carlson.com

What other decisions is Carlson making to meet the objectives of its shareholders? Connect to the Carlson Hospitality Worldwide Web site and find out. Visit Carlson's "Consumer Solutions" and plan an extended vacation today!

Management is willing to take care of employees who in turn take care of key aspects of the business.[6]

Contented employees are much more likely to produce contented customers. It is hard to imagine a disgruntled employee being pleasant to customers. Positive connections with customers are a result of positive connections made with employees. Chic-fil-A restaurants reported that during a five-year period, 78 percent of its restaurants with above average employee satisfaction also had above average customer satisfaction.[7]

Suppliers and Intermediaries   **Suppliers** are stakeholders who provide a company with necessary services, raw materials, and components. Very few organizations can exist without suppliers, who also can be a major factor in creating customer satisfaction. Ford has more than 1,700 suppliers in its automotive operations. If you like the dashboard, seats, or electronics on the new Ford Expedition, chances are a supplier worked with Ford to design it. Suppliers manufacture many of the components that go into vehicles—no matter what brand.

Companies rely on suppliers. When they have their own problems, it can mean trouble. Developing and maintaining good working relationships with suppliers can be extremely valuable. After a rash of blowouts in Ford SUVs using Bridgestone/Firestone tires, American automakers began insisting on closer relationships and data sharing with major tire suppliers. The problem was that unlike every other part of the vehicle, automakers traditionally left tire guarantees and maintenance to the tire manufacturers themselves. However, because some 600 people died in wrecks attributed to faulty Bridgestone/Firestone tires, Ford began demanding increased product and complaint information to identify problems earlier.[8]

Since they specialize, suppliers are an excellent source of new technology and are likely to speed the introduction of the latest designs and techniques. They often provide expertise that helps companies compete in ways that would be impossible if they had to rely on their own resources. For example, until 1987, DuPont sold only adhesives to Reebok. Then DuPont technicians suggested that Reebok use a plastic tube technology, originally designed for the automobile industry. The tubes made Reebok shoes "bouncier" and were a hit with consumers.

SUPPLIERS

Organizations that provide a company with necessary services, raw materials, or components.

Suppliers helped Reebok develop a bouncier shoe.

*Ralph Nader, consumer advo-
cate and Green Party presidential candidate in the 2000 U.S.
election, shows off a magazine
cover that supported his platform outside the Franklin
Pierce Law Centre.*

INTERMEDIARIES

Stakeholders who move products
from the manufacturer to the
final user.

ACTION GROUP

A number of people who support
some cause in the interest of
consumers or environmental
safety.

Chances are that Reebok never would have developed this technology on its own at the time. This single idea dramatically influenced the entire industry.

Intermediaries are independently owned organizations that act as links to move products between producers and the end user. They have an important influence on organizations because they dramatically extend the ability of marketers to reach customers at home and abroad. Book wholesalers and campus bookstores help large publishers such as Prentice Hall sell textbooks to students. Beverage manufacturers such as Gatorade, Dole, and Ocean Spray use intermediaries to deliver their goods to outlets that sell them to the final consumer. Chris-Craft, 4Winns, and Sea Ray market their watercraft through dealerships.

Some intermediaries specialize in international markets, using their unique skills and capabilities to give a company global reach. For example, an intermediary with special expertise in an emerging market may provide access to channels necessary to reach select customers. Companies that want to expand into untapped markets find intermediaries invaluable in delivering their product to the consumer. It is very beneficial for companies to establish solid working relationships with their intermediaries.

Action Groups **Action groups** are stakeholders that support some cause in the interest of consumers or environmental safety. They act as "watchdogs," making sure that companies keep the interests of people and the environment in balance with those of profit. There are hundreds of action groups. One of the most vocal and well-known consumer advocates, Ralph Nader, has fought for years to force businesses to produce safer products, and in 2000 he ran for president of the United States campaigning largely for consumer and environmental interests. The late Cesar Chavez challenged large chemical companies to protect the health of migrant workers. Many movie and television personalities lend their names and celebrity to consumer causes.

Marketers are very aware of consumer groups that frequently criticize the pursuits of business. A marketer may have to make difficult decisions when there is a conflict between the desires of action groups and other stakeholders. When Disney extended health benefits to gay couples, the Southern Baptist Convention initiated a boycott, claiming that the policy was counter to family values. The group also condemned Disney's annual "Gay Day" at its park in Orlando, as well as its production of the sitcom *Ellen* with lesbian Ellen Degeneres. Nevertheless, Disney did not give in to protesters, especially over the benefits program, saying that it questioned the integrity of any group wanting to deprive people of health benefits.[9]

Action groups can also help marketers gain positive publicity and may help business make a greater contribution to society. Nike, in response to action groups, founded the Global Alliance for Workers and Communities in 1999. Together with Gap, the World Bank Group, and The Pennsylvania State University, Nike donated $7.7 million to the Global Alliance to deflect criticism that its shoes and other sports products were made in Third World countries under degrading sweatshop conditions.[10] Also, Avon has gained publicity for the 10K walks it sponsors with action groups to fight breast cancer throughout the United States.

INDUSTRY COMPETITION

The word *competition* brings to mind an image of two giant companies vying against each other; however, competition also involves companies of differing types and sizes. These companies, along with potential new companies, suppliers, and customers, form an industry structure that dictates the intensity of competition. Competitors may be individual companies or the industry as a whole.

An analysis of the competitive environment asks several questions. Who are the existing rivals? What new competitors may emerge? What is the relative strength of suppliers and buyers within the industry? Finally, what substitutes are likely to appear? The answers give a complete picture of the overall nature of competition within an industry. Figure 3.3 depicts the forces that shape the competitive environment.

Existing Firms As a marketer, you need a thorough understanding of each major competitor. This includes how each competes against your company and every other in the industry. You should examine each rival's strategy in terms of current and potential products, pricing, promotion, and distribution. You also should identify key customers and suppliers, the types of technologies used, current performance, and strengths and weaknesses. From all this information, the marketing manager attempts to determine the plans of every competitor and how every competitor will react to the marketer's actions. For example, when Air Canada slashed fares on key eastern routes, its competitors AirCan and Royal Airlines immediately did the same.[11]

Potential Competitors At any time a company may enter an industry with similar products. This is nothing new. From the early 1970s to the late 1990s, the number of automobile models grew by 120. The number of over-the-counter pain relievers grew by 124.[12] In 1999, there were 1,983 new products introduced in the candy, gum, and snack foods category, including 83 for beef jerky alone![13] Competitors such as Slim Jim, Red Oak Farms, and Jenny's Jerky were clearly unhappy to see such an increase in competition; however, one advantage is that aggressive marketing by several companies will often draw attention to the product category and cause industrywide sales to increase.

Substitutes A **substitute product** is any good or service that performs the same function or provides the same benefit as an existing one. For example, who competes with Federal Express

CONNECTED: SURFING THE NET

www.slimjim.com

Snap into the Slim Jim Web site and view its latest beef jerky products! Keep up with Slim Jim–sponsored events such as its annual 3-on-3 basketball tournament, indoor snowboard competition, and racing teams. Also watch Slim Jim's latest commercials on the Web-based Slim Jim TV.

<u>SUBSTITUTE PRODUCT</u>

Any good or service that performs the same function or provides the same benefit as an existing one.

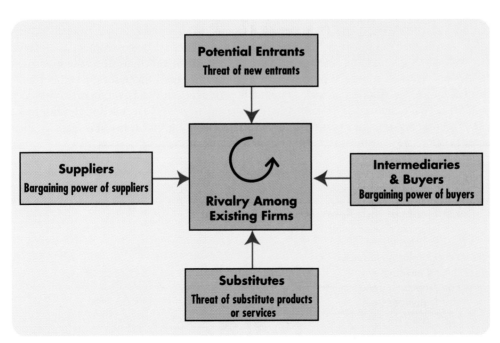

FIGURE 3.3 *Forces Driving Industry Competition*

Source: The Free Press, a division of Simon & Schuster, from *Competitive Strategy: Techniques for Analyzing Industries and Competitors,* by Michael Porter, Copyright 1980.

for overnight delivery of letters? If you said United Parcel Service (UPS), the U.S. Postal Service, Airborne Express, or other overnight delivery companies, then you are correct, but you probably left out two important ones: the fax machine and electronic mail.

Marketers should not limit their analysis to the same industry. Companies in other industries that make or develop substitutes may be an even greater competitive threat. For example, Merrill Lynch, a successful marketer of financial services, faces such industry rivals as Charles Schwab and Paine Webber but also experiences tough competition from insurance companies, banks, brokers, and others. Often information about substitutes can be found on the World Wide Web.

The Bargaining Power of Buyers and Suppliers   Marketers must also ask which group—buyers or suppliers—has the most power in an industry. The answer affects both company strategy and competition. Generally, when there are many suppliers, buyers are the most powerful. Buyers can be more demanding when there are several competing suppliers. For example, Wal-Mart is powerful because there are fewer retailers than in the past and many, many small suppliers. As of 1999, Wal-Mart stores were tied to 96,473 U.S. vendors providing goods for resale. If a vendor does not go along with Wal-Mart's policies, there are many others from which it can select.[14]

When buyers are extremely plentiful, suppliers tend to be more powerful. Since demand is great, suppliers can negotiate contracts on their terms and generally command higher prices. A supplier has the most power when it offers a unique and superior product that buyers are clamoring to purchase.

THE GLOBAL MACROENVIRONMENT

GLOBAL MACROENVIRONMENT
The large external influences considered vital to long-term decisions but not directly affected by the company itself.

Like stakeholders and industry forces in the microenvironment, the global macroenvironment also influences the company but indirectly. The **global macroenvironment** consists of large external influences considered vital to long-term decisions but not directly affected by the company itself. It is critical for marketers to identify, anticipate, and plan for the effect of those factors. These larger forces—each of which constitutes an environment in itself—shift slowly, so they have long-term implications for the organization. Yet, they also affect day-to-day operations. Figure 3.4 lists the most important forces or environments—technological, economic, demographic, cultural, legal/regulatory, and ethical—that make up the global macroenvironment.

TECHNOLOGICAL ENVIRONMENT

TECHNOLOGICAL ENVIRONMENT
The total body of knowledge available for development, manufacturing, and marketing of products and services.

As you know, technology is one of the five key elements in connecting with customers. The **technological environment** is the total body of knowledge available for use in developing, manufacturing, and marketing products. Companies spend huge sums each year to increase this body of knowledge. Merck Pharmaceutical Company, an industry leader, annually invests more than $2.4 billion in research and development activities.[15] The government also plays a role. When President Clinton announced a war against AIDS, it included federally sponsored studies on the disease. Several pharmaceutical companies used this research as the fundamental knowledge required to make patentable products. On their own, many companies would not make the uncertain and risky investment in AIDS research and development (R&D). Basic research is expensive and so time-consuming that it is often years or even decades before any revenue is received from product users.

> **Constituents of the Global Macroenvironment**
> • Technological environment
> • Economic environment
> • Demographic environment
> • Cultural environment
> • Legal/regulatory environment
> • Ethical environment

FIGURE 3.4 *The Global Macroenvironment*

U.S. companies spend nearly $266 billion on R&D annually. This is about 75 percent of the total, and the rest comes from the federal government, academic institutions, and nonprofit organizations.[16] A huge technological effect has resulted from microprocessor R&D. U.S. companies were the first to realize the importance of computers and made large investments in them. Today, leading computer companies spend several billion dollars on research and development annually! For instance, in 2000, Intel Corporation spent $4 billion on R&D alone.[17]

R&D has accelerated the rate of technological change. Products quickly become obsolete. The personal computer (PC) is an example. First introduced on a broad scale by Steve Jobs and Steve Wozniak in 1977, the PC is still evolving rapidly. Many of the first models used the same cassette technology for memory as you might use to record your favorite music. This quickly gave way to floppy disks, then hard drives, then optical disks, and compact disks. Processing capability is also growing phenomenally. At the end of the 1980s, Intel's 20 MHz chip offered state-of-the-art speed. By summer 2000, Intel had introduced three new Celeron processors for PCs costing less than $1,000 of 700, 667, and 633 MHz.[18] Companies are still introducing faster and smaller processors. Recently IBM Corporation unveiled a new microprocessor technology that allows components to be manufactured at the atomic level.[19] The world's first gygabyte disk drive, built in 1980, was the size of a refrigerator and cost $40,000. Today IBM produces a new gygabyte disk drive that is smaller than a matchbox, weighs 28 grams, and costs less than $500.[20] Obviously, changes such as these create great opportunities and challenges for computer companies.

"With new processes and technologies, you want to replace [your own product] instead of letting someone else do it," says Gary Tooker, CEO of Motorola, adding that "success comes from a constant focus on renewal."[21] The rapid rate of change has important implications for businesses today. First, investment in R&D is critical to ensure you're not left behind by the competition. If a computer company cannot build a machine that processes information quickly and accommodates future additions, it will soon be as obsolete as its products. Second, companies must be creative in looking for future technologies. For example, when Microsoft held a conference for 120 delegates from top Asian technology corporations, the gathering provided a unique opportunity for Microsoft to scan the Asian hi-tech environment for new opportunities and ideas.[22]

ECONOMIC ENVIRONMENT

The **economic environment** refers to financial and natural resources that are available to consumers, businesses, and countries. An understanding of consumer economic factors such as income, spending behavior, spending power, and wealth dispersion is essential in assessing opportunities that may emerge. Global marketers must also be familiar with the economic features of the world's major trading blocs.

Income and Spending Behavior   It is said that only two things are certain in life: death and taxes. **Disposable income** is the money consumers have left after paying taxes, and many marketers prefer to use this as the measure of consumer wealth. People spend some of their disposable income on necessities, such as food, clothing, and shelter; anything left over is called **discretionary income.** Consumers may choose to spend all their discretionary income or may choose to save part of it. Marketers of nonessentials, such as vacation packages, jewelry, and stereos, focus on discretionary income, because that is how much consumers have available to purchase nonessential items.

No less important than the amount of income is the willingness, or propensity, to spend. The typical middle-income American family is spending more on luxury goods. According to the U.S. Bureau of the Census, the average income of the top fifth of households rose 38 percent in the last 10 years. The average family income today is almost $52,000, which is significantly higher than in the late 1960s.[23] Marketers have seized this opportunity to promote purchases of nonessential items, especially over the Internet. According to an Ashford.com Luxury Buyer Study, roughly 38 million out of an estimated 75 million Internet users have bought a luxury item online. With more money to spend, consumers use the convenience of the Internet to buy items such as gold, diamonds, leather, and fragrance. Though a new e-accessories start-up, Ashford.com recorded a fourfold increase in luxury sales for 1999.[24]

Spending Power and Wealth Dispersion   Marketers must be careful not to equate a large population with a large marketing opportunity. An important consideration is **spending**

CONNECTED: SURFING THE NET
www.mot.com
Learn more about the company with a "constant focus on renewal." Motorola's Web site provides a chance to go inside the company and learn about its global community, business units, and products.

ECONOMIC ENVIRONMENT
The financial and natural resources available to consumers, businesses, and countries.

DISPOSABLE INCOME
The income consumers have left after paying taxes.

DISCRETIONARY INCOME
The amount of money consumers have left after paying taxes and purchasing necessities.

SPENDING POWER
The ability of the population to purchase goods and services.

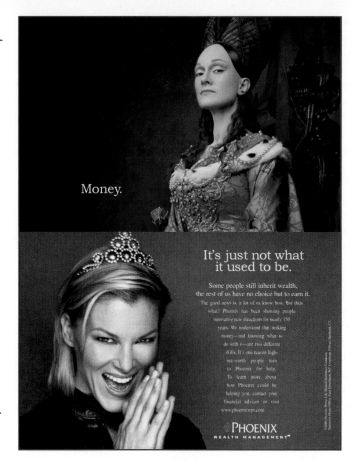

Money.

It's just not what
it used to be.

Some people still inherit wealth,
the rest of us have no choice but to earn it.
The good news is, a lot of us know how. But then
what? Phoenix has been showing people
innovative new directions for nearly 150
years. We understand that making
money—and knowing what to
do with it—are two different
skills. It's one reason high-
net-worth people turn
to Phoenix for help.
To learn more about
how Phoenix could be
helping you, contact your
financial advisor or visit
www.phoenixwm.com.

PHOENIX
WEALTH MANAGEMENT®

*Consumers with high net
worth are the target market for
Phoenix Wealth Management
Company.*

**GROSS DOMESTIC PRODUCT
(GDP)**

The total market value of all
goods and services produced by
a country in a single year.

power, or the ability of people to purchase goods and services. A common measure of spending power is the gross domestic product of a country. **Gross domestic product (GDP)** is the total market value of all final goods and services produced for consumption during a given period by a particular country. The U.S. GDP is approximately $9.7 trillion. The next largest GDP belongs to Japan ($4.9 trillion), followed by Germany ($2.2 trillion), the United Kingdom ($1.6 trillion), and France ($1.5 trillion).[25]

When the GDP of every nation is added together, the gross world product (GWP) today is $39 trillion. That figure is not spread equally among countries, however. Japan accounts for 12 percent of GWP, France and Germany together for about 9 percent, and the United States for around 25 percent. This figure is high, considering that the United States has only about 5 percent of the world's population. China and India, with 38 percent of the world's people, contribute merely 3 percent to GWP.[26]

Many marketers do not look solely at GDP because it does not indicate how much each person in the country has to spend. For example, Mexico and Sweden have approximately the same GDP, but we know that the standard of living is lower in Mexico than in Sweden. Because the population of Mexico is large, a smaller portion of GDP can be allocated to each inhabitant. Consequently, many marketers use GDP per capita (which means "per person") to assess the standard of living. It tells how well off, on average, each citizen of a country is.

Even GDP per capita has limitations because it ignores the dispersion of wealth within a country. Often there are a few rich people and many, many poor ones. In Brazil, for example, 46 percent of the wealth goes to the richest 10 percent of the population, whereas only 14 percent of the wealth goes to the poorest 50 percent.[27] In the United States, approximately 28 percent is owned by the richest 10 percent, whereas 4.2 percent goes to the poorest 20 percent. In Japan and Poland, the dispersion of wealth is much more even.

Trading Blocs   The world's three major trading blocs—Europe, Pacific Rim, and North America—are shown in Figure 3.5. Often called the world's economic superpowers, they will compete for the mastery of international markets well into the 21st century. Combined,

NORTH AMERICA	EUROPE		PACIFIC RIM
Canada	France	Portugal	South Korea
USA	Spain	Greece	Singapore
Mexico	Germany	Ireland	Japan
	Denmark	Luxembourg	China
	Great Britain	Belgium	
	Italy	Netherlands	
	Austria	Finland	
	Sweden		

Combined GDP: $10,803.6 Billion
Combined population: 407,191,000
NAFTA (North American Free Trade Agreement)

Combined GDP: $8,381.5 Billion
Combined population: 377,791,000
EU (European Union)

Combined GDP: $7,999.4 Billion
Combined population: 1,440,005,000

FIGURE 3.5 *The Three Superpower Trading Blocks*

these three regions are responsible for about 80 percent of the world's economic activity. For example, customers in the superpower triad buy a great majority of all computers and consumer electronics. The triad contains over half a billion consumers with converging preferences. Among others, IBM, Motorola, and Gucci are found nearly everywhere in the triad. Today, each of these blocs is basically equal in terms of economic activity, but this will not be true if current trends hold. The Pacific Rim is growing the fastest, Europe next, then North America.

Despite their collective power, the triad's constituent economies are not without difficulties. Many of these countries have a mature economy, rising social welfare costs, an aging population, and escalating research and development costs.[28] Let's look at each of the trading blocs in more detail.

North America In November 1993, when the United States, Canada, and Mexico entered into the North American Free Trade Agreement (NAFTA), they created the largest single market in the world—then 350 million consumers and growing each year.[29] The objective of this economic alliance is to make all three nations more competitive globally by combining their strengths. The United States and Canada have capital, skills, technology, and natural resources; Mexico has low-cost labor. Proponents of NAFTA believe efficient North American companies will be able to offer lower-priced products to consumers. Over all, the open market means removal of tariffs and other trade barriers, increased investment opportunities, stronger protection of intellectual property, and more environmentally sound business practices. Trade among the three NAFTA partners grew from about $300 billion in 1993 to over $500 billion in 1998, an increase of 67 percent.[30] Recently, Central American and Caribbean nations have been pushing to join.

NAFTA is not without critics. Companies will be more mobile, and some will go where labor is cheapest. If U.S. technology does not create enough high-paying jobs at home, U.S. workers will ultimately be fighting for low-paying jobs with fewer benefits.

Pacific Rim The Pacific Rim (PAC Rim), which comprises much of East Asia, is named for the ocean it borders. It is made up of Japan and the four "dragons"—South Korea, Singapore, Taiwan, and Hong Kong, now part of China—known for enormous manufacturing potential. Soon, depending on economic reform, Thailand, Malaysia, and Indonesia could also be included. Economic integration in the PAC Rim is based purely on market forces, not a formal agreement such as NAFTA. Much of the growth in East Asia has been spurred by Japanese investors, such as Matsushita Electric, which has established 10 major operations in Southeast Asia since 1961.

East Asia has undergone explosive economic growth, although it has had a difficult economic period in the recent past. In their classic book, *Megatrends 2000,* authors Naisbitt and Aburdene call it the greatest economic expansion in world history—five times the rate of the Industrial Revolution. These economies, driven by export sales, have been growing three times faster than economies in the rest of the world, although today, with the exception of China, these economies are experiencing slower growth. Yet, China is having growth as its economy benefits from deregulation, the import of new technology, and a shift from farm labor to industrial jobs.[31] China is predicted to experience a 7 to 8 percent annual growth rate to 2010, making it the fastest-growing area in the region. Over all, experts project that the average income of Chinese citizens will double by 2010.[32]

These Asian nations are feeding their home markets with the net gain in money received from other economies, which is possible when a country exports more than it imports. The domestic markets are increasing in size as companies and workers earn more money. With cash reserves of several hundred billion dollars and personal wealth, large amounts of goods can be bought from other countries. In Japan, for instance, annual household savings amount to a hefty $10.3 trillion. As a result, U.S. companies such as Starbucks, Toys "R" Us, and Gap are eager to expand into a Japanese market whose annual contribution to the gross world product outranks that of China and the rest of Asia combined.[33]

Europe The European Union (EU) has occupied much of the news in Europe. Also referred to as the Maastricht Treaty and technically called the Single Market Act, it is of tremendous economic relevance in Europe and around the world. The European Union has the goal of eliminating barriers to the flow of people, goods, services, and money within the union. The objective is to restructure Europe economically so that it can better compete against the United States, Japan, and other developed nations. The EU members are Austria, Belgium, Denmark, Finland, France, Germany, Great Britain, Greece, Italy, Ireland, Luxembourg, the Netherlands, Portugal, Spain, and Sweden. The EU unites 377 million consumers into one market with a GDP of more than $8.3 trillion.

The **Maastricht Treaty** consists of 282 directives that eliminate border controls and customs duties; strengthen external borders; establish a single European currency; coordinate defense and foreign policy; unify product standards and working conditions; protect intellectual property; and deregulate many industries, including telecommunications, airlines, banking, and insurance. This will make it much easier to move products from one region to another. Eventually, a company will be able to create a more unified marketing strategy for all of the EU, whereas today its different market environments still have to be addressed.

General Agreement on Tariffs and Trade and the World Trade Organization In 1947, the General Agreement on Tariffs and Trade (GATT) was founded under the United Nations. GATT is responsible for many of the current trade agreements among its 132 members. This organization has successfully negotiated significant reductions in trade restrictions and import duties that countries would otherwise impose in their own self-interest. GATT has been successful in reducing import duties and tariffs from more than 40 percent in 1947 to less than 5 percent today. Today there are challenges in many areas of foreign trade such as foreign investment and intellectual property rights. In 1995, GATT was absorbed by the World Trade Organization (WTO), which will carry out the traditional role of GATT. The WTO deals with a broad range of issues, including pollution, tariffs, trade agreements, and trade disputes.

Natural Resources The availability of natural sources of wealth (such as timber or oil) within a given region or nation is an important economic factor. For example, the U.S. Pacific Northwest provides a rich source of timber for the paper and construction industries. Similarly, countries in the Middle East control approximately 65 percent of the world's crude oil. In both cases, natural resources provide income to the area's inhabitants. Natural resources also include minerals, plants, wildlife, water, salt, fish, and many others. Resource availability affects a marketer's pricing strategy. If a company operates a large plant in an area where energy or raw materials are expensive, the cost of producing the product will be high, and its price must be set accordingly.

Marketers in quest of natural resources must balance these efforts against preservation of the environment. An example is the spotted owl controversy in the Pacific Northwest. Environmentalists claim that logging is destroying habitat, driving the species toward extinction. The timber industry claims that thousands of jobs and millions of dollars will be lost if its work is discontinued.

Environmental regulations also must be considered by marketers, since these may threaten current business practices or create new opportunities. For example, the Strategic Environment Initiative (SEI) recommends that the government provide tax breaks to companies using environmentally friendly technologies and levy high taxes on those using older,

MAASTRICHT TREATY

Consists of 282 directives that eliminate border controls and customs duties among members of the European Union.

unsafe methods.[34] Product and process innovations often enable companies to comply with environmental regulations. In the product area, for example, companies can retrofit antipollution devices or engineer more environmentally friendly designs. Many marketers are developing strategies with the environment in mind. When it became known that the chlorofluorocarbons (CFCs) released from aerosol cans were thinning the ozone layer, many companies switched to pump spray bottles. Due to environmental concerns, McDonald's discontinued its use of styrofoam sandwich containers.

career tip Need to research a company for an upcoming interview? Check out www.vault.com. Not only does it provide information on sales, number of employees, and market share, but it also contains messages posted by current employees about what it's like to work there. Coupled with all the other research available in placement offices of college campuses, Vault.com can help you develop an idea about the company culture.

DEMOGRAPHIC ENVIRONMENT

The **demographic environment** consists of the data that describe a population in terms of age, education, health, and so forth. Marketers examine such information to gain an understanding of current opportunities and discover trends that may indicate future opportunities. Some frequently studied demographics include population size and density, urbanization, and age structure. Avon Products, Inc. is one company that has adjusted neatly to demographic changes that nearly destroyed the company. The company had to change the way it developed relationships with customers in the United States and had to expand its customer relationships around the world. See the relationships feature entitled "Avon Products, Inc.: Around the World with 2.2 Million Avon Ladies."

DEMOGRAPHIC ENVIRONMENT
The statistical data used to describe a population.

CONNECTING THROUGH RELATIONSHIPS

AVON PRODUCTS, INC.: AROUND THE WORLD WITH 2.2 MILLION AVON LADIES

Do the very words *Avon Lady* make you think of a neatly coifed woman calling on suburban housewives with a suitcase of lipstick samples? Think again. Avon Products, Inc. is in the vanguard when it comes to shifting with the demographic winds and changing the way it reaches and relates to customers.

Until the 1980s, "ding-dong, Avon calling" was the ad line that epitomized the company's strategy for selling cosmetics and other products door-to-door. The only problem was that doorbells began ringing in empty houses. American women had gone to work in droves. Retail chains such as Wal-Mart in the United States and hypermarkets in Europe were also selling similar products at discount prices. With sales plummeting, Avon had to change or die, and change it did. By 2000 the company had healthy earnings and sales, posting increases in sales of 7.4 percent in the third quarter and profit increases of 15 percent. Under the stewardship of James Preston and a raft of top-caliber women executives, Avon accomplished a marketing makeover.

On the home front, Avon instituted the "Four Ways to Be Beautiful" campaign, which gave women more choice in how and when to develop a relationship with an Avon representative. The four ways were by fax, phone, mail, or the trusty Avon Lady. An 800 number also provided a way for working women to contact a representative at a convenient time. Within a month after putting a toll-free number in print ads and catalogs in the early 1990s, consumer inquiries went from 9,000 a month to 90,000. Although many women still want the attention of an Avon representative, now 50 percent of Avon's sales calls are made at the workplace. And Avon is adding a retail presence and Web business.

The environment is changing. Since younger, working women aren't at home to answer when Avon calls, the company, which has built its 115-year-old business on direct sales, is trying to connect to a new customer. It is selling a new line of products, started mid-2001, that is on the shelves at cosmetic counters at JCPenney and Sears, Roebuck and Company. The goal is to attract customers who may not be responding to one of its 3 million independent Avon Ladies calling directly.

Continued

The $5.3 billion company, which announced the venture on September 17, 2000, said it wasn't by any means retiring the Avon Lady, and emphasized that direct sales will continue to represent its core business, accounting for about 95 percent of overall sales.

Previously, direct sales accounted for about 98 percent of overall sales, according to Victor Beaudet, vice president of media relations. Beaudet said that Avon is investing $100 million in Avon's core business, including advertising, revamping its Web site, and developing what it calls its Avon Beauty Advisory Circle, which offers beauty certification to its sales representatives. The separate line of products, tentatively called Avon Gold, will cost 30 to 50 percent more than Avon's traditional lineup.

Yet Avon still confronted a shrinking market. Its smart response has been to train sales reps globally. The majority of Avon's 2.2 million representatives are in developing countries, calling on the growing number of middle-class women who can afford such luxuries as cosmetics. In the 1990s Avon entered 14 new markets, most recently South Africa and India. Combined emerging markets account for 38 percent of company sales and 49 percent of its pretax profit, and the numbers are going up.

In each emerging global market, Avon must adopt new ways for its representatives to contact customers. In countries that lack infrastructure and retail competition, the time-honored door-to-door approach still works wonders. In China, Avon Ladies ride bicycles to key distribution points to pick up products and then pedal off to peddle their wares. In the tiny village of Registro, Brazil, Avon Lady Josina Reis Teixeira visits small wooden shacks outside São Paulo. In Russia, where people are wary of opening the door to strangers, Avon Ladies sell in parks, beauty parlors, and offices. Maria Gerasyova, a former linguist for the Red Army, now commands 15,000 Avon representatives in Moscow, St. Petersburg, and Perm. In India, Avon Ladies will also steer clear of door-to-door selling and market products to their friends, family, and office colleagues.

Avon is proving to women around the world that beauty is more than skin deep. The cosmetics company has invested $500,000 in the cause of breast cancer awareness, and its 2.2 million global reps have helped raise $25 million to combat the disease and promote other women's health issues. About $18 million of that amount came from the sale of pins, key rings, and pens emblazoned with pink ribbons, which have become the symbol for the cause. Avon does no hard-sell for its cosmetics or jewelry at events like its breast cancer summit. Still, such events and grassroots contact give the company yet another way to strengthen ties with customers around the world.

Sources: Cathleen Egan, "Avon Products Beats 3rd Quarter Views by Gains in Most Major Regions," Dow Jones News Service, October 18, 2000. "Avon to sell products in stores; Mall kiosk sales tell company where to expand marketing," *The Detroit News,* September 19, 2000; Dyan Machan, "The Makeover," *Forbes,* December 2, 1996, pp. 135–140; Rasul Bailay, "Avon Tries Twist on Sales Technique for Push into India," *Wall Street Journal,* August 2, 1996, A11; Veronica Byrd, "The Avon Lady of the Amazon," *Business Week,* October 24, 1993, pp. 93–96; Seema Nayyar, "Avon Calling, By Fax, Phone and Infomercial," *Brandweek,* February 22, 1993, pp. 22–23; and Karen Benezra, "Cause and Effects Marketing," *Brandweek,* April 22, 1996, pp. 38–40.

Population   As of September 2000, there were about 6.1 billion people in the world, and there are expected to be over 9 billion by 2050.[35] If marketing opportunities were defined solely by population size, then the prospects would be bright indeed. Other opportunity indicators must be evaluated, however, such as the income available.

Despite such huge cities as Los Angeles, Chicago, New York, and Atlanta, the United States has less than 5 percent of the world's population. China and India account for 38 percent, and they are growing at a higher rate. Population growth depends on the number of live births plus the number of immigrants entering a country. The birthrate, which is measured as the number of live births per 1,000 people, is increasing throughout the world, but the rate of increase has begun to slow. It's estimated that about 80 million people are added to the world population each year. This translates into about 220,000 births a day. In India alone, 1,768 are added to the population every hour.[36] At the same time, advances in medicine and technology mean that people are healthier, and the number of deaths per 1,000 people is decreasing. The longer life spans combined with births result in an even larger world population.

Movement from one country to another redistributes the world's population, and the United States is gaining considerable numbers this way.[37] Although U.S. laws have become more restrictive, immigration is still expected to contribute as much to U.S. population growth as will natural births. This will further diversify the ethnic makeup of the country.

Minority groups accounted for approximately 70 percent of the population growth in the United States in the 1990s.

The U.S. population is expected to grow to 338 million in 2025 and to 404 million in 2050. Nevertheless, the average annual growth rate is expected to decrease by nearly half from 1.1 percent in the 1990s to around .54 percent by 2045. This would be the lowest rate ever. The predicted decline is attributed to numerous factors, including the general aging of the population, increased age at first marriage, delayed childbearing, a growing proportion of childless couples, and the greater participation of women in the labor force.

Density   A country with a large population may seem to offer a large marketing opportunity, but it is important to know where those people live. **Population density** refers to the number of people within a standard measurement unit, such as a square mile. Canada has more than 29 million people but only 3.3 people, on average, per square mile. Yet, because 77 percent of Canadians live in a few large cities, such as Quebec and Toronto, large areas of the country are quite sparsely populated. Singapore's population of 3.5 million is highly concentrated, with an average of almost 6,000 people per square kilometer. Where people are located within a country is also important. When they are concentrated, it's easier and more cost-effective to reach them with advertising campaigns and products. When they are spread out, marketing can be difficult, time-consuming, and expensive. Consider the Pacific Rim countries, where many more people live in the coastal regions than inland. Much the same is true of Australia with its sparsely populated Outback. Imagine the task of delivering products to consumers in these areas. Organizations are likely to focus marketing efforts on densely populated areas.

POPULATION DENSITY
The concentration of people within some unit of measure, such as per square mile or per square kilometer.

Urbanization   **Urbanization** refers to the population shift from rural areas to cities. Many countries have a high proportion of urban population. About half of the world's population lives in an urban area. This is higher in some countries than in others. In Germany, for example, 86 percent of the population lives in urban areas; in Singapore, 100 percent.[38] In the United States, four out of five people live in or near a city. Nearly 40 percent of the U.S. population is concentrated in the 20 largest metropolitan areas. At the top are New York City (20.1 million), Los Angeles (15.7 million), and Chicago (8.8 million). Urbanization is significant to marketers for three important reasons. First, as noted earlier, it is easier to reach a concentrated population. Second, as a group, people in cities tend to have enough income to purchase luxuries and support the arts, such as opera or theater. Third, people in urban areas tend to demand a wider variety of products than do rural inhabitants.

URBANIZATION
The shift of population from rural to urban areas.

When the city population spills into the suburbs, neighboring cities may eventually join together. The U.S. Bureau of the Census has three terms to categorize urban concentrations. A **Metropolitan Statistical Area (MSA)** is a stand-alone population center, not linked to other cities, with more than 50,000 people. Examples are San Antonio, Texas; Montgomery, Alabama; and Spokane, Washington. A **Consolidated Metropolitan Statistical Area (CMSA)** is two or more overlapping urban communities with a combined population of at least 1 million. An example is the area that includes New York City, northern New Jersey, and southwestern Connecticut, with 20.1 million people.

METROPOLITAN STATISTICAL AREA (MSA)
A stand-alone population center, unlinked to other cities, that has more than 50,000 people.

CONSOLIDATED METROPOLITAN STATISTICAL AREA (CMSA)
Two or more overlapping urban communities with a combined population of at least 1 million.

Age Structure   Because generations differ in their tastes, age-related marketing research has become popular. An **age cohort** is a group of people close in age who have been shaped by their generation's experience with the media, peers, events, and the larger society. Often these cohorts are divided into four groups. "Matures" were born between 1909 and 1945, "baby boomers" between 1946 and 1964, "Generation Xers" between 1965 and 1976, and those of "Generation Y" thereafter. Research reveals substantial differences among them in values, tastes, and needs.

AGE COHORT
A group of people close in age who have been shaped by their generation's experience with the media, peers, events, and society at large.

Globally, the average age is less than 25 years and declining. For example, because the Mexican population is growing rapidly, it is getting younger on average. In many industrialized nations, however, the picture is different. Children constitute a declining proportion of the German population, which is aging slowly but is older than the U.S. population. In less than 25 years, over one-fourth of all Japanese will be over age 65. In 2000, the median age in the United States was 35.8 years; by 2030, the average age will be more than 40 years, and about 20 percent of the population will be age 65 or older. This is partly due to the baby boom after World War II, which will affect U.S. demographics for many years. The U.S. age distribution varies according to race. Whereas 82 percent of Americans are Caucasian, fewer than only 76 percent of Americans under age 10 are Caucasian. Among the 12.8 percent of all Americans who are African American, 16 percent are under age 10. Eleven percent of Americans are Hispanic, and 20 percent of them are under age 10.[39]

This ad for Skechers was designed to appeal to the Generation X cohort.

Now that U.S. baby boomers are migrating into midlife, when spending power is substantial, marketers are focusing on older consumers. Thousands of products already are being marketed to help them look and feel their best—such as Oil of Olay moisturizing cream, Just for Men hair coloring, Centrum Silver multivitamins, NordicTrack cardiovascular fitness equipment, and Weight Watcher foods. In fact, Just for Men based an entire promotional campaign on this concept. Targeting men 35 to 54 years old, Just for Men unveiled a new ad campaign with former Washington Redskins quarterback Joe Theismann as its spokesman. Theismann pitched the product in men's lifestyle and sports magazines such as *Men's Health, Sports Illustrated,* and *Playboy.* "We've been marketing to baby boomers for 40 years," says Dominic Demain, a company spokesman. "We recognize this generation of men is different

CONNECTING THROUGH RELATIONSHIPS

McDonald's Is Global

Imagine this scenario. After a long day of work or play, a grumbling in your stomach draws your car into the nearest McDonald's. Relishing the familiar McDonald's atmosphere, you choose a supersized Big Mac value meal or another favorite. The crewmember passes you your food and change, and you find a booth to enjoy your meal. It's a typical scene that we've all been through, but now you can replay it in 109 countries around the world and on every continent but Antarctica. The hamburger is no longer simply an American food.

McDonald's has forged relationships with the world built on the enduring images of Big Macs, Ronald, and the Golden Arches. How do you make a hamburger a global icon?

Continued

McDonald's believes that the customers' experience is critical to business success and growth. In a recent statement to shareholders, Michael R. Quinlan, chairman and chief executive officer of McDonald's, admits that "by focusing on adding restaurants, we took our eye off the basics that made us famous—quality, service, cleanliness, and value." So now McDonald's has three priorities. The first is to improve restaurant operations. The second is to reopen the value gap against competitors by offering the best prices for the total dining experience. The third is to strengthen relationships with franchisees and energize employees. These are all part of a strategy to improve customer satisfaction and enhance loyalty.

McDonald's is a global corporation, and almost half of its 23,000 franchises are located outside the United States. Internationally, service consistency is maintained while modifying products to meet local needs and tastes. In India, the Maharaja Mac replaces the traditional Big Mac's two all-beef patties with mutton, out of respect for the Hindu faith. Also, vegetarian items are offered on a separate menu that is color-coded for simplicity. In Malaysia and many Middle Eastern countries, food is prepared within Muslim guidelines, and in Mexico customers can start their day with a McMuffin à la Mexicana that features an omelet complete with onion, jalapeno, and tomato and topped with refried beans. Many restaurants have decided to follow McDonald's lead into the global eatery environment. Rivals Burger King, Wendy's, and Subway have branched out into foreign countries, and even the "all-American" Applebee's has chosen to alter its menu and strategy to accommodate locations in Kuwait and on the Nile River! "A global strategy is imperative if corporations want to increase revenue bases and defend competitive positions against domestic and foreign-owned [rivals]," says Paul Hazlinger, president of a globally focused Phoenix consulting firm. McDonald's used the global advertising opportunity of a lifetime at the Millennium Olympic Games in Sydney, Australia, to promote its product to customers all over the world.

McDonald's activities, both within its restaurants and in communities around the world, are focused on creating customer satisfaction. This emphasis on customer value and satisfaction has provided McDonald's with a competitive advantage and a way to make a hamburger not just a hamburger, but an institution.

Source: Janice Matsumoto, "Passport to Expansion," *Restaurants and Institutions,* July 15, 2000, pp. 143–144; Mark Kleinman, "Sydney 2000 Hailed as Ad Success," *Marketing,* October 5, 2000, p. 7.

CONNECTED: SURFING THE NET

www.mcdonalds.com

Learn more about its country sites, history, career opportunities and more.

from their fathers."[40] In the years ahead, marketers will face the growing task of serving an aging market and addressing its unique concerns.

CULTURAL ENVIRONMENT

The **cultural environment** consists of the learned values, beliefs, language, symbols, and behaviors shared by people in a society and passed on from one generation to the next. Culture includes morals, values, customs, traditions, folkways, myths, and norms. It also includes religion, laws, economics, history, family structure, knowledge, food customs, art, music, and technology. These and other characteristics distinguish one society from another. They define the way we think about ourselves and the world, what we want, and how we behave. Marketers must be in step with the cultural environment because it helps them to make stronger connections with diverse customers.

Most people are socialized to be part of the culture in which they grow up. The socialization process is so strong that marketers may rely unconsciously on their own values when trying to understand another culture. This is called the **self-reference criterion.** But what we do may not be acceptable elsewhere. For example, most people in the United States would not think twice about eating a candy bar as they walk down the street, but in Japan this is bad manners. In China, when people approach a bus, the first person is expected to buy tickets for the group. It is easy to embarrass yourself and others in a foreign culture unless you take the time to understand it.

Because of people's tendency to use the self-reference criterion, it's often difficult to assess opportunities in other countries—but global success requires precisely that. McDonald's targets the same audience around the world—young families with children—but the basic concept must be "translated" into local conditions. Beer is on the German menu. In India, where cows are considered sacred, McDonald's markets the Maharaja Mac made of two all-mutton patties plus the usual toppings. Understanding different cultures has helped McDonald's establish itself in the new global market.

CULTURAL ENVIRONMENT
The learned values, beliefs, language, symbols, and patterns of behavior shared by people in a society and passed on from generation to generation.

SELF-REFERENCE CRITERION
The unconscious reliance on values gained from one's own socialization when trying to understand another culture.

McDonald's is a global corporation that aims to maintain consistent service while modifying its products to meet local needs and tastes such as in Kuala Lumpur, Malaysia, where food is prepared within Muslim guidelines.

In a classic article, Edward Hall notes that perceptions of time, space, things, friendships, agreements, and negotiations cause the greatest misunderstanding between people of different cultures.[41] If you do not recognize these differences and address them, then you will almost certainly fail to connect in the global marketplace.

Perceptions of Time　　It's extremely important to consider a culture's perception of time, which communicates several subtle points. For example, in some cultures the most significant decisions are given the greatest amount of time. In contrast, Americans tend to operate within deadlines, and time is a scarce resource to be used efficiently. In the United States, if visitors are kept waiting, then they infer that they are unimportant. In a Latin culture, this is not the case; schedules are not rigid, and time is seen as a resource that can be used more flexibly. More recently, many Latin American countries have redefined time for business. In some cultures, a very long time may pass between customer awareness of a product and the actual purchase. Marketers need to plan a longer time frame for recapturing the investment in new-product development. In cultures in which decisions are made quickly, this time frame may be much shorter.

Size and Space　　In the United States, size is equated with importance; the larger and taller a building, the greater the degree of status represented. The dean of a college of business is likely to be located in a spacious office on the top floor; the university president is likely to have a larger office in a taller building. In contrast, the French try to place important executives close to the scene of action, where their influence can be most strongly felt. Thus, a remote office is not equated with high status, but quite the opposite.

The distance between people during conversations also can be culturally related. In many Latin cultures, people stand close and even touch while talking. To communicate friendship, they may come to within two or three inches of one another, whereas an interpersonal space of three to five feet is considered acceptable to most people in the United States. To Latins, that great a distance could be a sign of rejection. Marketers must be sensitive to space. For example, in promotional materials, the wrong interpersonal distance among the actors or models could deliver the wrong message.

Negotiations and Agreements　　Business agreements may have different meanings in various parts of the world. In highly legalistic cultures, they must be written and signed prior to acceptance. In other cultures, legal documents are viewed as inconveniences; more important is a meeting of the minds, sealed with a handshake. When people in the United States consult a lawyer, visit a doctor, or take a taxi, they assume the charge will be at the going rate. This is not the case in many cultures. For example, in the Middle East, it's best to settle the charge in advance or the person providing the service is likely to set an arbitrary price. This can be

Consumer Products Safety Commission (CPSC)
- Enforces regulations to protect consumers from being harmed by products.

Environmental Protection Agency (EPA)
- Regulates business actions to prevent damage to the environment.

Federal Communication Commission (FCC)
- Regulates communications on telephone, radio, television, and other aspects including allocations of frequencies.

Federal Trade Commission (FTC)
- Enforces laws to prevent unfair or deceptive marketing practices.

Food and Drug Administration (FDA)
- Enforces laws to maintain safety in food and drug products.

FIGURE 3.6 *Federal Agencies Regulating Marketing*

important knowledge when developing a pricing strategy for your products. Whereas a predetermined price is expected in the United States, bartering is part of the social process elsewhere, and a preset price upsets or offends consumers.

LEGAL/REGULATORY ENVIRONMENT

The **legal/regulatory environment** is composed of international, federal, state, and local regulations and laws, the agencies that interpret and administer them, and the court system. It also includes the ethical standards and theories that guide marketing decisions. This environment reflects long-standing political and economic philosophies and varies dramatically from one country or region to another. It indicates the general outlook of government toward business practices and ethical issues as well as how cooperative it is likely to be in meeting the requests of business. It also includes the effect that legal/regulatory decisions can have on an organization, individuals, and society as a whole.

In the United States, several agencies are charged with the responsibility of regulating businesses to conform with the intentions of major laws. Among the most important are those listed in Figure 3.6. These agencies must interpret laws and develop policies and procedures to gain compliance. In some cases, the agency gives guidelines so businesses can self-regulate. Those businesses that step out of line may be taken to court by the agency. In other cases, the agency provides approval prior to marketing actions. For example, the Food and Drug Administration (FDA) must approve all drugs prior to their release in the United States.

Although the U.S. legal and regulatory sphere covers hundreds of specific practices, for our purposes these can be divided into four basic types: laws promoting competition, laws restricting big business, laws protecting consumers, and laws protecting the environment.

U.S. Laws Promoting Competition   During the 1800s and early 1900s, a few U.S. enterprises grew to the point of monopoly. Companies such as Standard Oil and Pennsylvania Railroad could exercise economic control over smaller firms, in many cases forcing them into bankruptcy by temporarily lowering prices. In 1890, due to a strong political movement led by midwestern farmers, Congress passed the Sherman Antitrust Act, which prohibits business practices designed to create monopolies or restrict trade across state lines or internationally. The Sherman Antitrust Act is extremely important because it laid the foundation for many laws that followed. The premise behind the legislation is that fair competition allows more companies to serve the market, which in turn keeps prices down and provides a greater number of choices to consumers. As you can see from Figure 3.7, many laws since 1890 are designed to ensure fair competition.

U.S. Laws Affecting Company Size   The U.S. approach to competition has tended to restrict company size and power. The Federal Trade Commission (FTC) has explored numerous accusations of monopolistic control. For example, it recently turned its focus on the pharmaceutical industry, where Mylan Labratories agreed to pay $147 million for conspiring with three other companies to create a monopoly over antianxiety drugs.[42]

In a much publicized case, in July 2000 the U.S. government prevented a $129 billion merger between WorldCom and Sprint. The merger would have created a massive telecommunications and Internet company, one the Department of Justice considered the antithesis

LEGAL/REGULATORY ENVIRONMENT
International, federal, state, and local regulations and laws, the agencies that interpret and administer them, and the court system.

CONNECTED: SURFING THE NET

www.worldcom.com

How does WorldCom remain competitive? At WorldCom's Web site you can explore its extensive services, view its current stock price, and look up such information as international country telephone codes.

Sherman Antitrust Act (1890)
Outlaws monopolies and any business practice that restricts interstate or international commerce.

Federal Trade Commission Act (1914)
Declares as unlawful "unfair methods of competition in or affecting commerce, and unfair or deceptive acts or practices in or affecting commerce."

Clayton Act (1914)
Prohibits mergers and acquisitions that may "substantially lessen competition or tend to create a monopoly"; outlaws tie-in and exclusive dealing arrangements; allows violators to be held criminally liable.

Robinson-Patman Act (1936)
Developed primarily to protect small retailers. Amends the Clayton Act. Makes it illegal to sell "commodities of like grade and quality" to competing buyers at different prices if it will restrict competition. Also makes it illegal knowingly to receive an illegal price break.

Miller-Tydings Act (1937)
Protects interstate fair-trade (price fixing) agreements from antitrust prosecution.

Wheeler-Lea Act (1938)
Outlaws the pursuit of unfair or deceptive practices or actions.

Antimerger Act (1950)
Prevents corporate acquisitions or mergers that may substantially reduce competition.

FIGURE 3.7 *U.S. Laws Promoting Competition*

of fair trade. According to department official Joel Klein, "WorldCom and Sprint used their network power in a number of different fields, the Internet, residential long distance, telecommunications, and data networks of various kinds, separately, and very competitively hard hitting against one another. That loss of competition, I think, would have been very detrimental for the consumer."[43]

Some countries promote monopoly. Many have laws that favor cartels, which are outlawed in the United States. A **cartel** is a group of businesses or nations working together to control the price and output of a particular product. The U.S. government has recognized that laws intended to provide a fair environment for domestic competition may hamper U.S. companies competing globally. Put simply, they may be too small and lack the competitive strength to take on global rivals. In the late 1970s, the Department of Justice began to change its enforcement of traditional antitrust laws. It now permits business cooperation that would have been outlawed in the past.

CARTEL

A group of businesses or nations that work together to control the price and production of a particular product.

U.S. Laws Protecting Consumers   Recall that the early economic philosophy in the United States was typically *caveat emptor*, "Let the buyer beware." Essentially, consumers were responsible for protecting themselves against the unscrupulous acts of sellers. The Pure Food and Drug Act (1906) and the Meat Inspection Act (1906) were the first attempts to protect consumers. For four decades, regulations concentrated on making the food supply safe. Laws then were extended to other products, such as automobiles and toys. Eventually, laws were passed to protect consumers from misleading advertising and deceptive labeling.

By 1960, the consumer movement was so powerful that President Kennedy issued the Consumer Bill of Rights, which guaranteed consumers

1. The right to choose freely from a variety of goods and services.
2. The right to be informed about specific products and services so that responsible purchase decisions can be made.
3. The right to be heard when voicing opinions about products and services offered.
4. The right to be safe from defective or harmful products and services when used properly.

The idea was to impress upon marketers that consumers were not solely responsible for assessing the quality of a product, its safety, and the honesty of the marketer's claim. In 1959, the FTC held a landmark conference at which consumer action groups and businesses discussed harmful practices. This activity led to the FTC assuming responsibility for the enforcement of truth-in-packaging and truth-in-lending laws. The FTC tackled tobacco advertising, forcing manufacturers to include a strong warning about the dangers of cigarette smoking in ads and on packages. Shortly thereafter, the Supreme Court ruled it illegal to create advertising gimmicks that would mislead the public or exaggerate product benefits.

Today the FTC and the FDA aggressively focus on the tobacco industry. In the late 1990s, the FTC investigated the R. J. Reynolds Tobacco Company for unfair advertising with its Joe Camel campaign, allegedly aimed at minors. The campaign was part of the industry's $4.8 billion annual expenditure on ads and promotions.[44] R. J. Reynolds agreed to drop the Joe Camel cartoon figure from such items as hats, lighters, bags, and T-shirts. In addition, R. J. Reynolds will not use Joe Camel in billboard advertising or in the sponsorship of entertainment events. Recently two other tobacco companies, Phillip Morris and Brown & Williamson, agreed to reduce cigarette advertising in magazines read by teens. All told, the companies pulled ads from 42 magazines with more than 2 million readers under 18 years of age.[45] The FTC also examines the Internet for tobacco and alcohol Web sites that may violate advertising guidelines.

There are numerous consumer protection laws, and marketers need to know the ones affecting their company. Consumer safety legislation has a direct effect on important marketing decisions, such as product design, label information and design, and advertising claims. Interest in consumer safety has resulted in the development of seat belts, air bags, shatterproof windshields, antilock brakes, food labels, air quality standards, gasoline restrictions, and others. Consider the effect of air bags on marketing in the auto industry. Although air bags have saved approximately 5,100 lives since 1990, they have caused at least 162 deaths, 96 of whom were children. As a result, Ford Motor Company was the first to introduce less forceful air bags in 1998. Now on-off airbag switches can be found in many vehicles, and automakers have introduced cars with sensors in each seat designed to detect passengers and to measure their size and weight.[46] Figure 3.8 lists several of the most important consumer protection laws.

U.S. Laws Protecting the Environment   By the early 1960s, it was clear that the world's natural resources were being consumed as if the supply were endless. The most basic

Phillips Petroleum Company builds consumer awareness of their environmental protection initiatives.

Pure Food and Drug Act (1906)
Regulates the manufacture and labeling of food and drugs.

Meat Inspection Act (1906)
Permits federal inspection of companies selling meat across state line and allows for enforcement of sanitary standards.

Lanham Trademark Act (1946)
Outlaws misrepresentation of goods and services sold across state lines; forces trademarks to be distinctive.

Automobile Information Disclosure Act (1958)
Forces auto manufacturers to disclose the suggested retail price of their new cars, which keeps car dealers from inflating prices.

National Traffic and Safety Act (1958)
Provides a set of automobile and tire safety standards.

Fair Packaging and Labeling Act (1966)
Permits the FTC and FDA to create standards for packaging and labeling content.

Child Protection Act (1966)
Makes illegal the sale of dangerous toys and children's articles as well as products creating a thermal, mechanical, or electrical danger.

Federal Cigarette Labeling and Advertising Act (1967)
Requires cigarette manufacturers to label cigarettes as dangerous. Outlaws use of television media for cigarette advertisements.

Truth-in-Lending Act (1968)
Also called the Consumer Credit Protection Act. Forces lenders to disclose in writing, before the credit transaction: (1) the actual cash price, (2) the required down payment, (3) how much cash is being financed, (4) how much the loan will actually cost, (5) estimated annual interest rate, and (6) penalty for late payments or loan default.

Fair Credit Reporting Act (1970)
Allows consumers to see free of charge a copy of their credit report. Forces credit reporting agencies to remove any false information. Protects the confidentiality of the consumer.

Consumer Product Safety Act (1972)
Created the Consumer Product Safety Commission. It collects and disperses information on all consumer goods except automobiles, food, and a few others. It also has the authority to develop and enforce product standards, when deemed necessary.

Consumer Goods Pricing Act (1975)
Prevents retailers and manufacturers from entering into certain types of price maintenance agreements.

Magnuson-Moss Warranty/FTC Improvement Act (1975)
Requires the company or individual who offers a warranty to explain fully what the warranty covers and what its limitations are. This information allows consumers to file a lawsuit if the warranty is breached.

Equal Credit Opportunity Act (1975)
Forces creditors to disclose the reason for any credit denial. Credit connot be denied on the basis of sex, marital status, race, national origin, region, age, or receipt of public assistance.

Fair Debt Collection Practice Act (1978)
Prohibits debt collectors from using harassment, abuse, or deceit when collecting a debt.

Toy Safety Act (1984)
Allows the government immediately to remove dangerous toys from the market.

FIGURE 3.8 *Consumer Protection Laws*

resources—air and water—were often so polluted that they were unfit to sustain life. Although little was done internationally, the U.S. Congress enacted the National Environmental Policy Act in 1969 to direct environmental protection activities. The following year, the Environmental Protection Agency (EPA) was formed so that one agency would be responsible for enforcing all federal environmental regulation.

Greenpeace used this message to increase awareness of our need to protect our environment.

U.S. companies are required to make adequate disclosure of potential environmental liabilities. The EPA maintains that those responsible for environmental contamination must pay for the cleanup and subsequently protect citizens' health. The EPA's Water Alliances for Volunteer Efficiency (WAVE) seeks to encourage commercial businesses and institutions to reduce water consumption while simultaneously increasing efficiency, profitability, and competitiveness. WAVE is a part of EPA's long-standing effort to prevent pollution and reduce demand on America's water and energy infrastructure.[47]

Environmental groups such as the Audubon Society, Greenpeace, and the Sierra Club have drawn attention to numerous environmental disasters and are active participants in finding remedies and developing legislation.

ETHICAL ENVIRONMENT

Questions of ethics are not always straightforward. What is acceptable in one part of the world may not be in another. In many countries bribery is regarded as highly unethical, but in others it is considered standard business practice. There is an important difference between what is legal and what is ethical. To determine legality, you must examine the relevant law. If the meaning is unclear, then a court may have to interpret it. Without a precedent, you may have to assess whether the action would be deemed legal or illegal.

Ethical issues are not so easily defined. Is it ethical for a pharmaceutical company to charge a price for a new drug that is much higher than the cost to produce it? After all, the company has poured millions into R&D and is trying to recoup its investment. Yet the high price makes the drug unaffordable to many people who desperately need it. Is the drug company acting unethically?

The matrix in Figure 3.9 shows that marketing decisions may fall into one of four categories: legal and ethical, illegal and ethical, legal and unethical, or illegal and unethical.

	Legal	**Illegal**
Ethical	Market FDA-approved cold medicine	Market a safe AIDS vaccine not yet approved by the FDA
Unethical	Market a harmful drug banned by the FDA in a country with no drug review agencies	Market contraband drugs

FIGURE 3.9 *Ethics Situations*

The appropriate behavior is easy to assess when the proposed action is clearly legal and ethical or clearly illegal and unethical. In the first case you do it, in the second you do not. However, neither legality nor ethics are always clear. What is legal and ethical may also be open to different interpretations. So marketers must be sensitive to both legal and ethical issues.

Perhaps the most difficult circumstances occur when legal and ethical standards conflict. Some people place more weight on the ethical side ("Should we do it?"), while others emphasize the legal ("Can we do it?"). Many people believe it is best to avoid altogether any actions that are either potentially illegal or unethical. Most laws that affect business are interpreted in the courts, which set precedents to be followed. Every legislative session creates new laws that lead to new regulations, which often require new court decisions to set new precedents. So even legal and illegal issues may stretch along a continuum.

Many companies have developed written guidelines for employees. This helps ensure that everyone in the company is following the same set of ethical standards. The American Marketing Association also has a code of ethics, shown in Figure 3.10. Notice that the code goes beyond stating simply "Follow the law." It impresses upon marketers the importance of being honest and acting with integrity. It covers basic responsibilities, including a code of conduct and the importance of fairness. It describes what a customer should be able to expect from an exchange. It also describes ethical dimensions in the areas of product, promotion, place, and price—as well as in marketing research and relationships with others.

Members of the American Marketing Association (AMA) are committed to ethical professional conduct. They have joined together in subscribing to this Code of Ethics embracing the following topics:

Responsibilities of the Marketer
Marketers must accept responsibility for the consequences of their activities and make every effort to ensure that their decisions, recommendations, and actions function to identify, serve, and satisfy all relevant publics: customers, organizations, and society.

Marketers' professional conduct must be guided by:
1. The basic rule of professional ethics: not knowingly to do harm;
2. The adherence to all applicable laws and regulations;
3. The accurate representation of their education, training, and experience; and
4. The active support, practice, and promotion of this Code of Ethics.

Honesty and Fairness
Marketers shall uphold and advance the integrity, honor, and dignity of the marketing profession by:
1. Being honest in serving consumers, clients, employees, suppliers, distributors, and the public;
2. Not knowingly participating in conflict of interest without prior notice to all parties involved; and
3. Establishing equitable fee schedules, including the payment or receipt of usual, customary, and/or legal compensation for marketing exchanges.

Rights and Duties of Parties in the Marketing Exchange Process
Participants in the marketing exchange process should be able to expect that:
1. Products and services offered are safe and fit for their intended uses;
2. Communications about offered products and services are not deceptive;
3. All parties intend to discharge their obligations, financial and otherwise, in good faith; and
4. Appropriate internal methods exist for equitable adjustment and/or redress of grievances concerning purchases.

It is understood that the above would include, but is not limited to, the following responsibilities of the marketer.

Continued

FIGURE 3.10 *American Marketing Association Code of Ethics*

Source: Courtesy of the American Marketing Association.

In the Area of Product Development and Management:
- Disclosure of all substantial risks associated with product or service usage;
- Identification of any product component substitution that might materially change the product or impact on the buyer's purchase decision;
- Identification of extra-cost added features.

In the Area of Promotions:
- Avoidance of false and misleading advertising;
- Rejection of high pressure manipulations, or misleading sales tactics;
- Avoidance of sales promotions that use deception or manipulation.

In the Area of Distribution:
- Not manipulating the availability of a product for purpose of exploitation;
- Not using coercion in the marketing channel;
- Not exerting undue influence over the reseller's choice to handle a product.

In the Area of Pricing:
- Not engaging in price fixing;
- Not practicing predatory pricing;
- Disclosing the full price associated with any purchase.

In the Area of Marketing Research:
- Prohibiting selling or fund raising under the guise of conducting research;
- Maintaining research integrity by avoiding misrepresentation and omission of pertinent research data;
- Treating outside clients and suppliers fairly.

Organizational Relationships
Marketers should be aware of how their behavior may influence or impact on the behavior of others in organizational relationships. They should not demand, encourage, or apply coercion to obtain unethical behavior in their relationships with others, such as employees, suppliers, or customers.

1. Apply confidentiality and anonymity in professional relationships with regard to privileged information;
2. Meet their obligations and responsibilities in contracts and mutual agreements in a timely manner;
3. Avoid taking the work of others, in whole, or in part, and representing this work as their own or directly benefit from it without compensation or consent of originator or owner;
4. Avoid manipulation to take advantage of situations to maximize personal welfare in a way that unfairly deprives or damages the organization of others.

Any AMA members found to be in violation of any provision of this Code of Ethics may have his or her Association membership suspended or revoked.

FIGURE 3.10 *Continued*

MARKETING E-COMMERCE

Internet marketing can be divided into two sectors. **Business-to-consumer (B2C) e-commerce** is trade involving businesses selling to consumers over the Internet. **Business-to-business (B2B) e-commerce** is trade involving Internet sales in which businesses sell to other businesses, including governments and organizations. Marketing is extremely important to both sectors.

Although purchasing on the Web was nonexistent in 1994, sales are estimated to be nearly $8 trillion in 2004. The business-to-business sector will post the largest gains. This kind of e-commerce totaled $336 billion in 2000, which is less than 3 percent of the U.S. business-to-business market, but is expected to grow 20 times that over the next five years, reaching $6 trillion.[48] It will be three times larger than the business-to-consumer sector, which will be about $2 trillion. Before long, a very large percentage of all business-to-business trade in the world will involve e-commerce in some way.

Globally, the United States represents about 41 percent of e-commerce trade. The Asia Pacific area accounts for about 20 percent. Western Europe represents about 19 percent, and

BUSINESS-TO-CONSUMER (B2C) E-COMMERCE
Trade involving businesses selling to consumers over the Internet.

BUSINESS-TO-BUSINESS (B2B) E-COMMERCE
Trade involving Internet sales in which businesses sell to other businesses, including governments and organizations.

the rest of the world makes up about 20 percent.[49] The United States is expected to hold the lead as e-commerce continues to grow, but its percentage of the total will decline slightly.

THE STRUCTURE OF INTERNET MARKETING

Some organizations and individuals benefit from the Internet merely by setting up a Web site. You may have an e-mail address, and nearly every progressive organization can be reached via the Web. Only organizations that are set up to conduct commercial transactions over the Internet are part of e-commerce, which we term the **Internet marketing economy**.[50]

As shown in Figure 3.11, the Internet marketing economy has three components, each with a different role: portals, market makers, and product-service providers.[51] Each contributes to the overall functioning of e-commerce. Together they provide a market space that is globally expansive and personalized.

Web Portals   The purpose of **Web portals** is to direct consumers or businesses to Web sites of product providers or intermediaries. They offer information and Web linkages that enable consumers and businesses to connect with the right commercial sites for their needs. Portals are valuable because they help with this sorting and matching process. Web sites change frequently, and good portals must work constantly to remain current. eTour.com, an Atlanta-based company, spends considerable time looking for addresses that match their members' interests. Because many dot-com companies merge with others or fail, their original Web sites cease to exist.[52] Good portals keep their information timely.

Portals allow users to sort information so that companies, products, and messages can be accessed in useful ways. To help with this process, marketers must classify their Web site with appropriate key words, descriptors, and categories. That begins by selecting a domain name that labels an organization's Internet presence, much like branding is used to identify products. Each domain has a numerical address, and a company may use the same address for several domain names or split them up. For example, Coke can be reached at www.cocacola.com or www.coke.com or by specifying the numerical address (208.134.241.178) directly.

Good portals are powerful search engines that help users reach the sites they want. A search engine like Yahoo! can guide consumers to sites they want to explore in depth. These sites are usually owned by Web market makers or by Web product service providers, both of which are described next.

Web Market Makers   The purpose of **Web market makers** is to help buyers and sellers obtain information about each other and to facilitate secure, low-cost exchanges. Market makers have a great deal of knowledge about domains. In many cases they specialize in certain types of products or exchanges. They also add an element of security and trust to the business transaction. For example, eBay brings consumers together for auctions. It specifies the rules, communicates the auction itself, and provides information about past activities of sellers and buyers, including feedback from each party regarding the other.

Margin definitions

INTERNET MARKETING ECONOMY
All organizations that are set up to conduct commercial transactions with business partners and buyers over the Internet.

WEB PORTALS
Organizations that direct consumers or businesses to the Web sites of product-service providers and intermediaries.

WEB MARKET MAKERS
Organizations that help buyers and sellers by providing information about each party and by facilitating secure, low-cost exchanges.

Type of Player	Role	Business-to-Consumer	Business-to-Business
Web Portals	Bring together information for consumers or businesses and direct them to the Web sites of product-service providers and intermediaries	America Online (AOL) Yahoo! MSN.com	ZDNet Marketsite.net
Web Market Makers	Facilitate transactions between buyers and sellers by providing information about each party and by helping to ensure secure, low-cost exchanges	Ebay.com Priceline.com Travelocity.com	Bloomberg ChemConnect NetBuy.com
Web Product-Service Providers	Deal directly with consumers in an Internet transaction and customize processes to accommodate online customers	Amazon.com Barnes&Noble.com Toys-R-Us.com	Cisco Dell Compaq

FIGURE 3.11   *The Structure of E-Commerce*

Source: Based on *California Management Review,* Vols. 1 & 2, No. 4, Summer 2000.

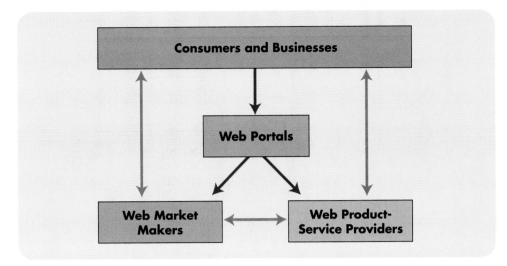

FIGURE 3.12 *Participation in E-Commerce*

In the business-to-business arena, market makers include Chendex (chemicals), HoustonStreet.com (electricity), FastParts (electronic components), and BigBuyer.com (small business products). Experts expect business-to-business market makers to experience tremendous growth. They can organize auctions, set up exchanges, and integrate product and service catalogs from several suppliers.[53] In addition, they can offer **virtual trade shows,** that is, online sites that display new products and technologies from several suppliers to current or potential customers. Industry associations, trade associations, or companies sponsor these trade shows. For example, Plastics Net serves the plastics industry in this capacity.[54]

Web Product-Service Providers   Because they deal directly with customers, **Web product-service providers** customize processes to accommodate online transactions. They go to great lengths to make online buying a major aspect of their business. Minor adjustments to accommodate a small percentage of online orders do not count. Instead, these companies adjust their infrastructure so that Web-based business can become an extensive part of their marketing strategy. These providers connect directly with customers, and the Internet becomes a business channel. Popular organizations in this category are Amazon.com for consumers and Dell for both businesses and consumers.

How the Structure Interacts   Figure 3.12 shows how consumers and businesses interact with the three major parts of the Internet marketing economy. Market makers and product-service providers gain the attention of customers by working with portals as well as through traditional efforts, such as advertising, personal selling, and word of mouth. The revenue stream of a portal depends on how well it supports the Web market makers and product-service providers. At the same time, market makers depend on product-service providers for items to sell, and product-service providers depend on market makers for many of their customers. All parties are roughly interdependent.

New marketing companies have been established just because the benefits of the Internet economy are so great, but the dangers are also high. Some observers believe that 90 percent of the dot-coms developed in the 1990s will be gone by 2001. Some will merge with others, but many will simply fail.[55] Yet, Michael Krauss, a regular columnist for *Marketing News,* notes that traditional bricks-and-mortar firms are increasingly aware of the Internet marketing economy. "The dinosaurs are starting to dance," he says, mentioning such alliances as Wal-Mart Stores and America Online, Kmart and Yahoo!, and Best Buy and Microsoft.[56]

VALUE OF THE INTERNET TO BUYERS AND SELLERS

E-commerce is gaining ground because, as Figure 3.13 indicates, both buyers and sellers receive great value from it. Compared to traditional channels, buyers get better information, greater convenience, wider and customized selection, and better prices. Marketers have access to more customers, reduced supply chain costs, efficient two-way communication with customers, and the ability to personalize messages and products. These advantages are described next.

Value to Buyers   **Better Information** The Internet enables buyers to obtain a great deal of information about products, including availability, costs, attributes, and use instructions, as

VIRTUAL TRADE SHOWS
Online sites that display new products and technologies from several suppliers to current and potential customers.

WEB PRODUCT-SERVICE PROVIDERS
Companies that customize processes to accommodate online customers.

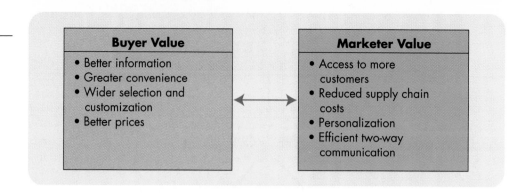

FIGURE 3.13 *Internet Marketing Benefits Buyers and Sellers*

well as information about manufacturers and sellers of particular brands. Some Internet services perform the difficult task of comparison shopping to find the right product configurations at the lowest prices. In many cases, before selecting an item, potential buyers can even obtain other customers' reactions to products: "If you want to hear how other readers evaluate this book, just contact Amazon.com."

Greater Convenience Shopping at home or in the office via computer reduces the amount of travel and time associated with in-store purchases. This is particularly useful for buyers in rural areas or more remote communities around the world. In urban and suburban settings, traffic congestion is high, and consumers may save many hours each week otherwise spent waiting in traffic or on long checkout lines. In addition, savings in gasoline and other vehicle costs can be substantial, not to mention the social benefits of less auto pollution and congestion.

Wider Selection and Customization Online buyers can choose from a wide selection as well as customized products. Retail outlets may carry only certain brands and sizes, but online sources offer all possible configurations. Buyers can compare many more brands and price points. Even unique and scarce products can be sourced quickly. If you need a particular book on some obscure medical topic, contact Amazon.com. Amazon.com will find it if it's in print. At the same time, more customization is possible because buyers can interface with a seller's manufacturing facilities, which in turn are networked with suppliers, so sellers can build or manufacture on demand.

Better Prices Due to the competitive nature of the Internet marketing economy and the efficiency saving, shoppers may benefit from lower prices. One company asks: "Would you like to buy this camera [a popular brand is shown] at $169 or $149 or at $129—Shop at MySimon.com." Internet retailers tend to be driven by price because many buyers go online specifically to obtain price savings. Companies that pioneered in e-commerce used a low-price strategy to attract business and this strategy has continued because online shoppers have become accustomed to the competitive prices.

Values to Marketers **Access to More Customers** On the seller side of the market, Internet businesses have access to a world of customers. A firm in Chicago can communicate with a potential customer in India as easily as with one next door. And communications can be tailored to each party. E-commerce has grown by leaps and bounds, which means that more businesses and customers are being brought together in more uniquely personal ways than could be imagined a decade ago. Internet sellers have access to vastly more customers than their bricks-and-mortar rivals. Even if such marketing forms as retail outlets and catalogs are combined, more potential customers can be reached through the Internet.

According to *Computer Industry Alliance*, by 2002, roughly 490 million people around the world will have Internet access, and by 2005, the figure will be about 750 million. The proportion of users is highest in the United States—estimated at about 40 percent of the population in 2005, compared to 10 percent in other advanced nations. The top 15 economies account for more than 80 percent of worldwide usage.[57] Although in 2002 the United States will have one-third of all Internet users, that means nearly two-thirds will reside elsewhere.

Obviously, not all users make Web purchases. In the United States, 62 percent browse or obtain product information, and 36 percent buy online.[58] These figures are significantly higher than for other parts of the world. A Nielsen survey indicates that in Sweden and Denmark, the next highest Web-using countries, about one-third of users browse for products; 17 percent (Sweden) and 11 percent (Denmark) buy online. The top 17 economies, excluding the United States, have an average product browsing rate of 18 percent and a purchase rate of about 7 percent.[59]

Personalized and Customized Products E-commerce makes it easier for sellers to cater to customer needs. This can be done through product representation and product configuration.[60] Product representation refers to how the product is presented to customers. With the Web it is possible to use the customer's name in a communication or arrange information about the product to reflect more closely the potential buyer's preferences. A more complex customization occurs with product configuration, which promotes selected products or brands directly to a consumer or adjusts attributes to user specifications. In addition, buyers themselves can make adjustments online. For example, computer marketers such as Dell or Compaq allow purchasers to specify precisely what computer configuration they want. Levi-Strauss and other clothing manufacturers can store consumers' personal measurements and manufacture items for each unique body. Broad Vision is a company that helps marketers develop this kind of site.

career tip Andy Jolls, age 34, is an expert in online marketing for Homestore.com. He says experience, not age, is the ticket for success in e-commerce. He believes that "age, meaning total work experience years, is becoming less and less important." Will Frisbie, age 30, account supervisor for the consulting firm Howard Merrell and Partners in Raleigh, North Carolina, says, "Clients increasingly are open to working with young people, and being young, you bring to the table a new enthusiasm and new energy." Advanced beginners (people with an MBA or a couple of years of Internet marketing experience) are being offered $80,000 by prospective employers, plus healthy signing bonuses.[61]

Reduced Supply-Chain Costs E-commerce reduces not only the **supply chain costs** associated with procuring goods and services from suppliers but also the costs of distributing products to consumers. Savings occur throughout the supply chain, including lower inventory costs, due to better demand forecasting, streamlined manufacturing, warehousing, and transportation. Better communication among all members of the value chain reduces errors. Dell has been successful in the computer server market by integrating its supply chain through the Internet. All members of Dell's supply chain are connected online and are given intensive information linked to customer demand. This allows each supplier to operate efficiently while supplying precisely what Dell customers want. Not just part of the supply chain, the Web itself is a marketing channel. What makes this channel unique is that so many customers are within a few keystrokes of a shopping experience. Because many e-commerce companies take advantage of the latest technologies, their supply chains tend to be very efficient.

SUPPLY CHAIN COSTS
Costs associated with procuring goods and services from suppliers and with distributing products from businesses to consumers.

Two-Way Communication A significant benefit of the Internet for marketers is how efficiently it allows two-way communication and customization to take place. It costs less than telephone or mail contact and is significantly less expensive than face-to-face communication. This technology is as revolutionary for communication today as the telephone, radio, and television were when they were introduced. The Web began as a way to present and send information, such as online newspapers or reports. Then it allowed access on demand to all sorts of data, a library function that helped users find information among the most widely ranging sources imaginable. In the most significant communication advance to date, however, the Web can personalize contact. It facilitates dialogue between two parties or among thousands. This two-way, multiple-person communication enables marketers to create dialogues among consumers quickly and inexpensively, so marketers can learn consumers' views on products and issues in real time.

Web communication also facilitates personalization and customization of both products and messages. Marketers can easily collect opinions and test reactions to marketing activities. Also, data on past purchases reveal a lot about what people will buy in the future.

Customers can order and pay for items online. Perhaps even more important, there are opportunities for two-way dialogue about product attributes, ordering, and customer service. The Web even facilitates product customization. The amount and type of communication, including product options and pricing, can be personalized. This kind of contact helps marketers develop and maintain customer loyalty. Connect with Nike (www.nike.com/nike_id/) to build a personal pair of shoes. You can select colors, add a personalized set of initials, and basically design a pair of Nikes just to your taste for approximately an additional $10.

It is important to keep in mind the elements of this chapter when we look at chapter 4, which addresses the strategic marketing planning process. Clearly, leading marketers understand and utilize the global Internet economy.

CHAPTER SUMMARY

OBJECTIVE 1: Describe the marketing environment and the use of environmental scanning.

The marketing environment comprises all factors that affect a business. The factors are divided into two groups—the microenvironment and the global macroenvironment. The microenvironment includes factors that marketers interact with regularly. Consequently, the microenvironment influences and is influenced by marketing. The global macroenvironment includes factors that marketers must take into account when making decisions. However, marketers seldom influence these factors. Together, the environments can facilitate or inhibit organizations from reaching their objectives. Proactive organizations anticipate changes in the marketing environment and plan accordingly. Organizations use environmental scanning in order to keep up with environmental changes. The Web is a great technological tool to help maintain currency in knowledge of the environment.

OBJECTIVE 2: Understand how the roles that stakeholders play influence the accomplishment of marketing objectives. Know why marketing must address stakeholder desires when making decisions.

Stakeholders are important parts of the microenvironment and directly participate in accomplishing the organization's goals. They include owners, employees, suppliers, intermediaries, and action groups. Stakeholders participate with the organization in order to accomplish their own goals; consequently, marketers must take their desires into consideration when making decisions. Because owners are entitled to a fair return on their investment, companies need to make a substantial profit, and nonprofit organizations must accomplish the goals their owners (sponsors) intend. Employees are also important; happy employees produce happy customers. Suppliers provide necessary services, raw materials, and components. They also provide technology in specialized areas. Suppliers have a dramatic influence on your customers. Intermediaries help move products between you and your customers. They often contact customers directly. Since they represent your organization, you must carefully interface with them. Action groups are "watchdogs" that keep the interests of the environment and people in balance with profit seeking. They can help marketers interface better with society. Marketers must address stakeholders' desires because stakeholders support marketers in order to attain their goals. In turn, marketers depend on stakeholders to accomplish their organization's objectives.

OBJECTIVE 3: Be able to integrate an understanding of industry competition into environmental analysis.

An understanding of industry competition provides an integrated picture about the major forces that determine competitive intensity. Competition involves single competitors and groups of company types that compete. We look at the rivalry among existing firms to understand one-on-one competition. Potential competitors are also viewed because firms enter and exit industries. At the same time, substitute products can play a role especially when new technologies bring new ways to perform old functions. The bargaining power of buyers and suppliers determines how a company competes. Suppliers have more power when there are few suppliers and many buyers. All of these aspects of industry competition need to be understood in order to build appropriate marketing strategies.

OBJECTIVE 4: Synthesize aspects of the global macroenvironment, including technological, economic, demographic, cultural, and legal/regulatory elements, in order to be in step with long-term trends.

The global macroenvironment is being influenced by many forces. The technological environment provides knowledge and tools that companies can acquire to produce better products. By phasing in new technology, progressive companies stay abreast of the best ways to create customer value. Economic factors are also important. Changes in income and spending power and other factors help determine which countries have the ability to purchase. The world has three major trading areas. The regions offer large markets, but they also compete

against one another. The natural resources environment also comes into play. It provides raw materials and must be protected. Global demographics are changing. Shifts in population density and dispersion are important, as are age shifts. It is important to grasp the cultural environment and to view things from the other's perspective. The values, beliefs, and behaviors of others may differ from your own. Finally, the legal/regulatory environment is complex. Laws must be interpreted and followed. They help promote competition, influence business size, protect customers, and protect the environment.

OBJECTIVE 5: Understand the impact that e-commerce is making on the global business environment and understand the structure of Internet marketing.

Both business-to-consumer and business-to-business organizations are using the Internet increasingly. However, the business-to-business sector is growing faster. The Internet marketing economy is comprised of three structural elements. Web portals direct consumers or businesses to Web sites of product providers or intermediaries. Web market makers help buyers and sellers enter into transactions on the Web by providing information and making arrangements for selling and buying between parties. Web product-service providers deal directly with customers utilizing special technologies developed to facilitate sales over the Internet. These three entities interact to provide a viable infrastructure to conduct marketing over the Internet in several types of marketspaces, including virtual shopping malls and virtual trade shows. The Internet marketing economy is growing because it offers great value for buyers as well as marketers.

OBJECTIVE 6: Recognize the importance of ethics and guides to ethical behavior.

Marketers often face ethical dilemmas, particularly when legal and ethical standards conflict. Many companies have developed codes of ethics for their employees to help ensure that everyone in the company is following the same standards. The American Marketing Association has a code of ethics that covers the basic responsibilities of marketers in each of the areas in which they are likely to be active. It stresses the importance of fairness and integrity.

REVIEW YOUR UNDERSTANDING

1. What is environmental scanning and what technology is being used for it today?
2. What is the microenvironment and what are its elements?
3. What is the global macroenvironment and what are its elements?
4. Who are stakeholders and why are they important? List five different types of stakeholders.
5. What are the elements of industry competition? Describe each.

6. Why is the technological environment important?
7. What are the elements of the economic environment? List three aspects that are influencing global marketing.
8. What are the three major trading blocs in the world economy?
9. What demographic trends are influencing marketing?
10. What is the self-reference criterion? What are some cultural differences to be aware of?
11. What are the types of laws that affect marketing?
12. What is the difference between unethical and illegal behavior?

DISCUSSION OF CONCEPTS

1. Suppose that IBM and Microsoft announced plans to merge into one company. Would U.S. laws allow this to happen? Do you think that other countries around the world would have the same reaction?

2. What is culture, and how does it affect marketing? Can you think of any products that are successful in the United States but would fail in Japan because of cultural differences?

3. In the 1980s, McDonald's discontinued the use of styrofoam containers for its sandwiches. What other changes have occurred recently in the natural resources environment? What types of legislation do you expect in the future? How would that legislation affect marketing?

4. Do you think that General Motors should invest a significant amount of money in research and development projects? Why or why not?

5. Recently, discount stores such as Wal-Mart and Kmart have become extremely large and powerful. How does this affect industry structure and competitive intensity?

6. As the director of marketing for Dow Chemical Company, you are required to interact regularly with a number of different publics. List these publics, the concerns that each might have, and how you would address each of those concerns.

7. What effect do you expect the new European currency to have on trade among the three superblocs? Which trading relationships will be most affected? In what ways?

8. Which do you feel is more important—ethics or the law? Why?

KEY TERMS AND DEFINITIONS

Action group: A number of people who support some cause in the interest of consumers or environmental safety.

Age cohort: A group of people close in age who have been shaped by their generation's experience with the media, peers, events, and society at large.

Business-to-business (B2B) e-commerce: Trade involving Internet sales in which businesses sell to other businesses, including governments and organizations.

Business-to-consumer (B2C) e-commerce: Trade involving businesses selling to consumers over the Internet.

Cartel: A group of businesses or nations that work together to control the price and production of a particular product.

Consolidated Metropolitan Statistical Area (CMSA): Two or more overlapping urban communities with a combined population of at least 1 million.

Cultural environment: The learned values, beliefs, language, symbols, and patterns of behavior shared by people in a society and passed on from generation to generation.

Demographic environment: The statistical data used to describe a population.

Discretionary income: The amount of money consumers have left after paying taxes and purchasing necessities.

Disposable income: The income consumers have left after paying taxes.

Economic environment: The financial and natural resources available to consumers, businesses, and countries.

Environmental scanning: Collecting and analyzing information about the marketing environment in order to detect important changes or trends that can affect a company's strategy.

Global macroenvironment: The large external influences considered vital to long-term decisions but not directly affected by the company itself.

Gross domestic product (GDP): The total market value of all goods and services produced by a country in a single year.

Intermediaries: Stakeholders who move products from the manufacturer to the final user.

Internet marketing economy: All organizations that are set up to conduct commercial transactions with business partners and buyers over the Internet.

Legal/regulatory environment: International, federal, state, and local regulations and laws, the agencies that interpret and administer them, and the court system.

Maastricht Treaty: Consists of 282 directives that eliminate border controls and custom duties among members of the European Union.

Marketing environment: The sum of all the factors that affect a business.

Metropolitan Statistical Area (MSA): A stand-alone population center, unlinked to other cities, that has more than 50,000 people.

Microenvironment: The forces close to a company that influence how it connects with customers.

Population density: The concentration of people within some unit of measure, such as per square mile or per square kilometer.

Self-reference criterion: The unconscious reliance on values gained from one's own socialization when trying to understand another culture.

Spending power: The ability of the population to purchase goods and services.

Stakeholder: A group who can influence or be influenced by the firm's actions.

Substitute product: Any good or service that performs the same function or provides the same benefit as an existing one.

Suppliers: Organizations that provide a company with necessary services, raw materials, or components.

Supply chain costs: Costs associated with procuring goods and services from suppliers and with distributing products from businesses to consumers.

Technological environment: The total body of knowledge available for development, manufacturing, and marketing of products and services.

Urbanization: The shift of population from rural to urban areas.

Virtual trade shows: Online sites that display new products and technologies from several suppliers to current and potential customers.

Web market makers: Organizations that help buyers and sellers by providing information about each party and by facilitating secure, low-cost exchanges.

Web portals: Organizations that direct consumers or businesses to the Web sites of product-service providers and intermediaries.

Web product-service providers: Companies that customize processes to accommodate online customers.

1. John Lippman, "News Corp.'s Profit Jumped in Period, Aided by Purchase," *Wall Street Journal Interactive Edition*, May 8, 1997; Joshua Levine, "Luke Skywalker Is Back. Let Us Pray," *Forbes*, December 30, 1996, www.forbes.com; Randall Lane, "The Magician," *Forbes*, March 11, 1996, pp. 122–128; "Starman," *Inc. Technology*, 1995, no. 2, p. 44; Joseph Garber, "Virtual Superstar," *Forbes*, March 13, 1995, p. 152; Jeff Jensen, "Star Wars' Empire Shows New Strength," *Advertising Age*, December 5, 1994, p. 33; Thomas Jaffe, ed., "Telephone Assault," *Forbes*, December 5, 1994, p. 20; A.D., "LucasArts Entertainment," *Fortune*, July 11, 1994, pp. 129–130; interview with Jeanne Cole, Lucasfilms, May 1998; Dan Fost, *Marin Independent Journal*, December 29, 1977, p. D5; Philip Van Munching, "The Devil's Adman," *Brandweek*, January 31, 2000, p. 70; "Lucasfilm THX Unveils Now Optimode," *Emedia*, August 2000, p. 22; John Jimenez, "Star Wars Trilogy" to Be Re-Released with Bonus Footage of 'Episode II' Preview," *Video Store*, September 3–September 9, 2000, p. 10; Marco R. della Cava, "Lucas: The Titan of Tech," *USA Today*, February 23, 2001, p. E1, 2.

2. "Why the Biggest Baby Bell Is Wild About Broadband," *Fortune*, June 12, 2000, p. 172.

3. www.gegxs.com and www.nrstg1p.djnr.com, Web sites visited on September 10, 2000.

4. Gene R. Laczniak and Patrick E. Murphy, *Ethical Marketing Decisions: The Higher Road* (Boston: Allyn & Bacon, 1993), pp. 14–15.

5. "Part Fast-Food, Part Casual Dining, Panera Is Thriving," *St. Louis Post-Dispatch*, September 2, 2000, p. 1.

6. Carlo Wolf, "Great Hospitality Is Made, Not Born," *Lodging Hospitality*, March 15, 2000, p. 28.

7. Dana James, "Don't Forget Staff in Marketing Plan," *Marketing News*, March 31, 2000, p. 10–11.

8. "Automakers Mull Closer Relationship with Tire Manufacturers," *Associated Press Newswires*, September 6, 2000.

9. Nicholas Confessore, "Boycotts Will Be Boycotts," *American Prospect*, August 31, 2000, p.10.

10. "Nike-Funded Survey Shows Mostly Favorable Conditions for Overseas Workers," *Associated Press Newswires*, September 5, 2000.

11. "Air Canada Slashes Fares as New Arrivals Take Flight," *National Post*, September 6, 2000.

12. Chad Kaydo, "A Position of Power," *Sales and Marketing Management*, June 2000, p 104–111.

13. Jennifer Timpe, "Sour Power," *Prepared Foods*, April 2000.

14. www.walmartstores.com, Web site visited July 7, 2000.

15. www.merck.com, Web site visited on September 6, 2000.

16. "Resurgence Continues in 2000," *Industry Week*, February 7, 2000.

17. "Intel Post Big Jump in 2nd-Quarter Earnings," *Dow Jones Business News*, August 18, 2000.

18. "Intel Q2 Revenue a Record $8.3 Billion," *Edge: Work Group Computing Report*, July 24, 2000.

19. "IBM, Nikon Shrink Processors with Optics," *PCWeek Australia*, March 20, 2000.

20. "IBM's Big Gig: Fridge to a Matchbox in 20 Years," *Newcastle Herald*, June 26, 2000, p. 44.

21. Terrence E. Deal and Allan A. Kennedy, *Corporate Cultures: The Ethics and Rituals of Corporate Life* (Reading, MA: Addison-Wesley Publishing, 1982), p. 8.

22. "Gates Dismisses Competition During Summit in Seoul," *South China Morning Post*, June 20, 2000, p. 1.

23. "Historical Income Tables, www.census.gov, Web site visited September 12, 2000.

24. "Ashford.com to Take Better Aim at 'Power' Buyers of Luxe Goods," *Women's Wear Daily*, June 12, 2000.

25. Lara L. Sowinski, "30 Top Markets for Trade and Expansion: 2000," *World Trade*, June 2000, p 38–47.

26. "Facts on India," *Asiacom*, January 11, 2000, "China's Long March to Market Economy Continues," *Market Asia Pacific*, April 2000.

27. "Gap Between Rich and Poor as Wide as Ever in Latin America," *Associated Press Newswires*, September 4, 2000.

28. "Becoming a Triad Power: The New Global Corporation," *International Marketing Review*, Autumn 1986.

29. "NAFTA Facts, www.mac.doc.gov/nafta, Web site visited September 12, 2000.

30. David Wernick, "Next Generation NAFTA," *Latin Finance*, July 2000.

31. Andrew Tanzer, "Stepping Stones to a New China?" *Forbes*, January 27, 1997, p. 78–83.

32. "China to Continue with More Reforms to Boost Growth," *Asia Pulse*, January 14, 2000.

33. "Japan Rising," *Adweek*, May 1, 2000, p. 58–64.

34. "How Green Is Al Gore," *The Economist*, April 22, 2000.

35. www.census.gov/ipc/www/img/worldpop.gif, Web site visited on September 12, 2000.

36. "www.censusindia.net," *American Demographics*, May 2000.

37. Claudette Bennett, *Current Population Reports* (Washington, DC: Bureau of the Census, U.S. Department of Commerce, January 1995), p. 2.

38. 2000 World Population Chart www.prb.org, Web site visited July 8, 2000.

39. www.census.gov/population/www/projections/natsum.html, Web site visited September 12, 2000.

40. Mercedes M. Cardona, "Just for Men's New Ad Formula: Take Quarterback, Add Color," *Advertising Age*, July 24, 2000, p 12.

41. Edward T. Hall, "The Silent Language in Overseas Business," *Harvard Business Review*, May–June 1960, p. 87.

42. "Mylan Laboratories Offers to Pay $147 Million to Settle Monopoly Law Lawsuit," *Marketletter*, July 24, 2000.

43. "WorldCom/Sprint Antitrust Issues," CNNfn, August 3, 2000.

44. "FTC and FDA Team Up Against Tobacco," *Wall Street Journal Interactive Edition*, May 1, 1997.

45. Wendy Melillo, "PM Claims Withdrawal of Ads Was Voluntary," *AdWeek East*, June 12, 2000.

46. "Surviving Your Drive," *CNN Newsday*, August 25, 2000.

47. www.epa.gov/owm/faqw.htm, Web site visited on September 13, 2000.

48. Jumper Communications, cyberatlas.internet.com/bigpicture/demographics/article/0,1323,5971402421,00.html October 15, 2000, pp. 1–2.

49. Forester Research, cyberatlas.internet.com/bigpicture/demographics/article/0,1323,5911348161,00.html, January 15, 2000, p. 1.

50. See definitions by B. Mahadevan, "Business Models for Internet-Based E-Commerce," *California Management Review*, 42 Summer 2000, p. 56.

51. Ibid.

52. Julia Angwin, Myline Mangalindan, Nicole Harris, and Sharon Cleary, "Digits," *Wall Street Journal*, November 30, 2000, p. B6.

53. B. Mahadevan, "Business Models," p. 57.

54. Ward Hansen, *Principles of Internet Marketing* (Cincinnati, Ohio: South Western College Publishing, 2000), p. 316.

55. Dana James, "Are You Ready for the Coming Dot-Com Crash," *Marketing News*, January 31, 2000, p. 15.

56. Ibid.

57. "The Market's Guide to Online Facts," Cyberatlas: Internet Statistics and Market Research for Web Marketers, cyberatlas.internet.com/bigpicture/demographics/article/0,1323,591115115,00.html, accessed October 15, 2000.

58. "How the Internet Is Changing Daily Life," *Direct Marketing*, May 2000, p. 51.

59. Cyberatlas, "Guide," p. 3.

60. Hansen, *Principles of Internet Marketing*, p. 197.

61. Laurie Feeman, "Young," *Marketing News*, May 8, 2000, p. 16.

ACQUIRING EXPENSIVE ART ONLINE

Bruce McGaw Graphics (BMG), a world leader in the publishing and distribution of print and poster images, announced today it has signed a letter of intent to acquire Artinside.com, a leading online home art gallery. The acquisition, scheduled to be completed in early 2001, combines the merchandising experience, international fulfillment process, and expanded product offering of a 25-year, profitable, bricks-and-mortar art publisher with the Internet marketing expertise, technological innovation, and engineering talent of a pure art e-tailer. The combined venture creates a robust B2C and B2B entity that will fill the world with art at affordable prices and serve its customers' needs with even greater efficiency.

"Building a robust e-commerce platform to better serve our customers, in addition to offering our wholesale buyers the ability to check the status of an order, payment, and shipping online, has always been a part of our long-term business strategy," stated Bruce McGaw, co-owner and founder of Bruce McGaw Graphics. "When we began looking for an innovative online partner to fulfill our e-commerce strategy, we weren't just looking for technological implementation and presence. We wanted an organization comprised of individuals that shared our passion for art. We're pleased to say that we found those individuals at Artinside.com, complete with superior technology and engineering talent."

Launched earlier this year, Artinside.com delivers an accessible, convenient venue for all consumers to purchase affordable, authentic art. The acquisition by BMG expands the company's product offering to over 5,000 pieces of art. The two companies share a commitment to finding artists whose work they can develop. BMG brings new talent to the Artinside family of artists, including Diane Romanello, Jacques Lamy, and BJ Zhang, as well as the exclusive rights to publish and distribute the collections of many of the world's top museums, including the Museum of Modern Art in New York and the Louvre in Paris.

"There's no doubt that the Internet is the ideal vehicle for helping consumers find the art they love and can afford," said Rengan Rajaratnam, Artinside.com's cofounder and acting CEO. "However, the challenge has always been in recreating an in-person experience so the consumer feels confident that the art that they are selecting will work in their home or office, and will be what they expected when it arrives. BMG has earned worldwide recognition for their customer-focused efforts, established from a true humanity for art and the art community. Together we will revolutionize the art world."

This acquisition is reflective of the trend in the industry of two companies, one a powerful online venture, the other a longtime leader in its sector. Both BMG and Artinside.com uniquely focus on delivering art at affordable prices, efficiently and effectively. This acquisition allows Artinside.com to further strengthen its leadership position and global reach with the addition of 5,000 new pieces of art, while utilizing BMG's extensive international order and fulfillment process, including a sizable in-house framing division. Because BMG manufactures its own quality frames, similar to the ones currently offered by Artinside.com, the merged company will have the ability to quickly turn around orders, while also delivering a broader and more unique product offering to its retail customers and online affiliates.

In addition, BMG immediately gains a solid vehicle through Artinside.com with which to serve wholesale buyers more effectively and efficiently. The anticipated incremental revenue gained by this increased retail activity, coupled with the improved cost efficiencies and reduced operating expenses associated with an e-business, will enable the new entity to foster rapid growth and pursue a public offering in the near future.

Sources: "Bruce McGaw Graphics Signs Letter of Intent to Acquire Artinside.com," *PR Newswire*, October 13, 2000.

CASE 3

The National Basketball Association

Picture an NBA team in 2001, such as the Chicago Bulls, playing for a half-empty arena. Or image the league's premier event—the championship games—being shown on tape delay against *The Tonight Show* due to a lack of interest from fans. Seem impossible? Amazingly, the NBA has not always been the worldwide phenomenon we know today. According to *Sales and Marketing Management*, just 18 years ago the NBA

was "a product about as appealing as a week-old banana." How did it become an international success? Many attribute the transformation to the marketing saucy savy of Commissioner David Stern. He expanded the league from 24 to 29 teams, gross revenues increased from $181.1 million to about $1 billion, and average attendance per game has grown from 11,141 in 1985 to more than 17,000 in 1997. Pat Williams, senior executive vice president of the NBA's Orlando Magic, indicated that "David Stern has a tremendous marketing mind, and he is one of the great sports stories of the twentieth century."

During the 1970s and 1980s, marketing efforts by most NBA teams were minimal. Today, kids are wearing Chicago Bulls T-shirts in Casablanca, Phoenix Suns caps in Punta del Este, and Los Angeles Lakers jackets in London. NBA stars such as Shaquille O'Neal, Steve Smith, and Kobe Bryant are recognized around the globe. And worldwide sales of NBA merchandise amount to more than $1 billion a year.

The NBA has spent more than a decade creating a global brand and has emerged as the first truly global sports league. Commissioner Stern, said, "We're okay in Melbourne, Tokyo, and Hong Kong, but we've got to beef up our operations in Singapore, Jakarta, and Kuala Lumpur." When Stern became commissioner in 1984, he immediately saw the NBA's global potential. In addition to worldwide requests for more games to telecast, Stern noted a number of environmental changes: the collapse of communism and the growth of market economies, the globalization of U.S. consumer products, and a worldwide television revolution that created new cable and satellite channels. A more recent development is the growth of the global Internet, where the NBA has an official Web site. It offers programming in Spanish, French, and Italian and draws 35 percent of its traffic from outside the United States.

How has this vast international opportunity been exploited? Television is the number-one tool. The NBA also sells television rights to local broadcasters, even in countries where it does no other business. In such countries as Spain, France, Mexico, and Japan, the NBA collects more than $1 million in rights fees. Given the intensity of media competition, these numbers are expected to grow. In 1970, the NBA sold cable rights for $400,000. Today, it commands an astounding $660 million just in the United States. Add to that the NBA games that are currently being broadcast to over 200 countries. Each week over 10 hours of NBA games and coverage are broadcast to foreign countries.

A number of factors have facilitated the worldwide growth of the NBA, including electronic media, sports marketing, and foreign-born players. David Stern wants the NBA to be a part of pop culture in "every global medium that matters." He believes "the real-time delivery of data and statistics about the NBA on a global basis via the Web is about as exciting as it gets." Stern himself has participated in online chat sessions. In addition to the popularity of interactive media, sports marketers such as Nike have complemented the NBA's global presence. According to Stern, "they have enormous marketing, distribution and manufacturing capability that we borrow. And to the extent that that's associated with their brand, it makes our brand stronger. We're sort of borrowing each other's equity." Cultural diversity in the league has also facilitated the NBA's global growth. Foreign players intensify the media coverage in their own countries. For example, Arvydas Sabonis brings NBA popularity to Lithuania, Detlef Shrempf to Germany, and Toni Kukoc to Croatia.

Managing the NBA is a dynamic role demanding job. It requires interfacing with apparel companies, licensees, U.S. and global media companies, and corporate giants such as McDonald's, Coca-Cola, Nike, and Disney. The NBA is not just a provider of sports programming; it is also in the sporting goods, sponsorship, consumer products, and trading card businesses, among others. With these relationships comes the need to defend property rights, and the NBA has been the most active league in that regard. This includes even digital rights. Stern says: "I just want to be standing with this big bundle of carefully protected rights . . . I had owners in 1979 that didn't want me to get involved with cable, but if you can be part of the growth pattern, you will always do better."

Growth often brings difficult management decisions. Stern tries to incorporate ethical choices into the league's expansion. "You must be on the ground in every continent exploiting your brand with sensibility towards local issues. But there's nothing easy about that," he says. "We want to play into the existing infrastructure, not supplant it. We do not wish to injure or disrupt the Italian League, Spanish League, or any other league."

The National Basketball Association must confront several obstacles to sustained growth. The players' strike of the late 1990s and the rising player salaries threaten growth for the NBA. One way for the NBA to combat this is to stay abreast of the technological trends to connect with customers. According to Stern, the NBA website (www.nba.com) holds great potential for the organization, both for expanding its market and its sales.

Stern predicts that one-third of the NBA's revenues could come from abroad within the next 10 years. Today's staff of 800 is almost eight times the number that ran the league in the 1980s. The game is played nearly everywhere and is easily understood. The phenomenal popularity and worldwide presence of the NBA are all about marketing. As the league continues to grow, fans will continue to cheer for the *mate* in Latin America, the *trofsla* in Iceland, and the *smash* in France. And the Chinese will continue to root for the Bulls, better known as the "Red Oxen."

1. *The global macroenvironment consists of large external influences vital to long-term decisions but not directly affected by the company itself. Identify these influences and note several ways each has affected or may affect the NBA's global expansions.*

2. *What considerations does the NBA need to address before entering a particular country or region? Suggest several adjustments that may be required to serve customers successfully in those markets.*

3. *Stakeholders include groups such as owners, employees, suppliers, intermediaries, and action groups. Identify the groups with a stake in the NBA, making assumptions as necessary. How may each of these influence marketing decisions?*

Sources: Hoover's Online, "National Basketball Association, www.hooversonline.com, visited June 19, 2000; The National Basketball Association Web site, www.nba.com, visited June 19, 2000; Daniel Roth, "The NBA's Next Shot," *Fortune,* www.fortune.com, February 21, 2000; Marc Gunther, "They All Wanna Be Like Mike," *Fortune,* July 21, 1997 www.fortune.com; Jeff Jensen, "Experiential Branding Makes It to the Big Leagues," *Advertising Age,* April 14, 1997, pp. 20, 24; Terry Lefton, "At Age 50, Stern Looks Ahead," *Brandweek,* October 28, 1996, pp. 34–38; Bob Ryan, "Hoop Dreams," *Sales and Marketing Management,* December 1996, pp. 48–53; and Michael Schrage, "David Stern," *Adweek,* May 26, 1997, pp. 24–26.

THE STRATEGIC MARKETING PLANNING PROCESS: DOMESTIC AND GLOBAL

OVER 65 YEARS AGO, WALT DISNEY founded his company based on three principles: Tell a great story, tell it with great characters, and push the technological boundaries. His characters formed the basis of the movies, cartoons, theme parks, and merchandise that would propel Disney to the forefront of entertainment. His creative vision was easily summed up: Demand the impossible! His marketing vision for the Disneyland theme park, opened in 1955, was far ahead of its time.

On the one hand, Walt's visionary zeal created a number of businesses—movies, cartoons, television shows, theme parks, and merchandise—held together by the Disney brand. On the other hand, the company lacked any real marketing strategy. Walt's autocratic leadership and unchallenged control in every detail of the operation simply did not focus on the long term. When Walt Disney died in 1966, the company floundered. As one senior employee put it, "Everyone looked to the past, asking, 'What would Walt have done?' No one looked to the future and asked the visionary question, 'What if . . . ?' "

It was not until the mid-1980s that a new team of executives, led by CEO Michael Eisner, began strategic and marketing planning for the Walt Disney Company. Eisner separated the organization into strategic business units (theme parks and resorts, filmed entertainment, and consumer products) so that it could focus on what it did best. Instead of short-term planning, long-range plans became the norm. It is not unusual for a Disney division to have 5-, 10-, and 15-year plans to help it stay focused. While the business press was writing off Euro Disney (now called Disney Paris) when it first opened, Disney officials could see that they were actually ahead of their 30-year plan!

One of Disney's strategies is partnering with major marketers. However, in recent years there has been a decline in the worldwide merchandise licensing, which has left Disney with lower revenues. In response to this situation, Disney will be reducing licenses by 50 percent, allowing "a more effective management of key licensee relationships; greater focus on relationships with the most important retailers in the market; and the placing of greater emphasis on consumer research and marketing in order to bring the right product to the right market at the right time." Disney's global strategy continues to expand as well. The Disney Channel is now available in Taiwan, Great Britain, and Germany, among others. The Disney Store has more than 700 retail outlets around the globe. Disney continually searches expansion possibilities. According to plan, the Disney California Adventure, located next to Disneyland in Los Angeles, had its grand opening in 2001. Second parks will soon be open at the Tokyo Disneyland and Disneyland Paris to augment current facilities.

In June 2000, Disney.com premiered "Where the Magic Lives Online." This spectacular Web site provides Disney's home, vacation, shopping, entertainment, and consumer products information. As the top-ranked family entertainment destination on the World Wide Web, the site offers visitors a virtual-theme-park experience complete with "all things Disney." For the Disney California Adventure 2001 introduction, the site features a film with Cindy Crawford.

And Disney continues to recognize diversity. The Disney Store recruiting brochure maintains that it is "committed to supporting cultural diversity in the workplace because . . . 'It's a Small World After All.' " Even the animated films of the 1990s have moved from the exclusively caucasian characters: Aladdin *focuses on Arabs,* Pocahontas *celebrates Native Americans, and* The Lion King *relates to the African experience.*

The "Magic Kingdom" did not become successful through magic. Rather, Disney developed a strategic marketing plan aimed at exceeding customer expectations. Along the way, it also developed short-term tactics to keep the plan in focus.[1]

CONNECTED: SURFING THE NET

www.disney.com

Check out the many features of the Disney Web site. You'll find links to the Disney Store, Walt Disney World, the Disney Channel, Walt Disney Pictures, Disney Publishing, and much more.

S̲T̲R̲A̲T̲E̲G̲I̲C̲ ̲M̲A̲R̲K̲E̲T̲I̲N̲G̲ ̲P̲L̲A̲N̲

The document describing the company's objectives and how to achieve them in light of competitive activities.

THE CONCEPT OF THE STRATEGIC MARKETING PLANNING PROCESS

Connecting with customers requires a sustained, concerted effort by organizations over the long term and the short term. Long-run plans concentrate on developing the resources an organization needs to win. Short-run plans describe how these resources will be deployed. An effective planning system addresses both the development and use of resources. The five forces that determine how well organizations connect with customers can be effective only with careful planning. The strategic marketing plan provides the guidance necessary to build relationships, develop and use technology, court diversity, and ensure ethical behavior in domestic as well as global markets.

Marketing can be described as philosophy, as strategy, and as tactics. Leading-edge businesses such as Children's World, Disney, Eli Lilly, and Johnson & Johnson develop marketing plans that address each of these aspects to help them connect with customers. Figure 4.1 outlines the type of planning that corresponds with each aspect of marketing, including the people who usually implement each.

Marketing as philosophy can be viewed as the organization's marketing concept. It is embodied within the organization's vision statement, which articulates what customer value will be delivered, the codes of conduct guiding organizational behavior, and the resources that will be developed and deployed to build value. The vision describes the fundamental contributions the business intends to make to society, its position relative to competitors, and the attributes that make the organization unique from others. The vision is usually developed by top executives. In many organizations, this often includes the board of directors. Input from all organizational levels may be sought as well.

Marketing as strategy is formalized in the **strategic marketing plan,** a document describing the company's objectives and how to achieve them in light of competitive activities. Essentially, this plan outlines the decisions executives have made about how the vision will be accomplished. The strategic marketing plan generally requires input and guidelines from marketing executives and a planning team of top- and middle-level personnel.

Marketing as tactics refers to precisely how each part of the marketing mix (product, price, promotion, place, and customer service) will be managed to meet requirements of the strategic marketing plan. Marketing mix plans are developed by specialists in each component, such as product managers, advertising executives, and sales personnel.

The owner may perform all these planning roles in a small company whereas several hundred people may be involved in companies such as Johnson & Johnson or General Electric, two global giants known for exceptional marketing planning. You will find that companies

Marketing Aspect	Type of Planning	Responsibility
Marketing as philosophy	Vision	Top executive and top management team
Marketing as strategy	Strategic marketing plan	Marketing executive and other members of the strategic marketing team
Marketing as tactics	Marketing mix plans	Managers responsible for product, price, promotion, and place programs

FIGURE 4.1 *Types of Marketing Planning*

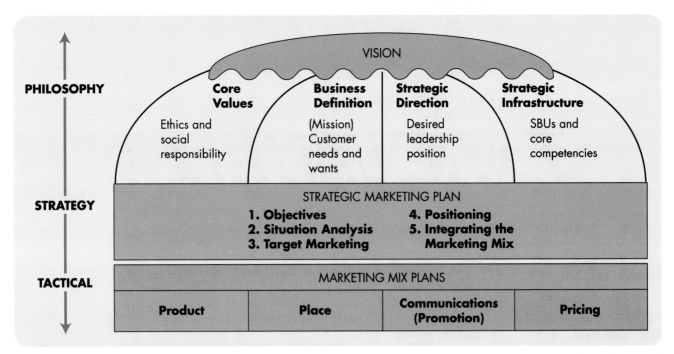

FIGURE 4.2 *Marketing Planning Hierarchy*

tend to blend philosophy, strategy, and tactics into a range of planning appropriate for the organization. Still, all three aspects are found within leading organizations.

The hierarchy shown in Figure 4.2 describes what takes place as companies develop plans to address the three aspects of marketing: philosophy, strategy, and tactics. Each of the major components of the vision, strategic marketing plan, and marketing mix plans depicted here is examined in detail in the following sections. The final section of the chapter focuses on the strategies companies use to enter and build strength in foreign markets.

THE ORGANIZATION VISION

Outstanding performers have a vision that focuses marketing efforts purposefully. The **vision** helps everyone maintain consistent direction despite volatile market environments. When President John F. Kennedy said, "We will put a man on the moon," he created an effective vision. He provided a picture that inspired the U.S. space program, largely because the vision was simple, clear, and easy to remember. If Kennedy had described the enormity of the challenge in detail (how many people were needed, what talents they must possess, what type of equipment would be required), it's doubtful the venture would have succeeded. Instead, Kennedy's vision was fulfilled in 1969, when Neil Armstrong took "one small step for man, one giant leap for mankind," and walked on the moon.

Take a few minutes to visualize your life now and in five years, 15 years, and beyond. You are forming a personal vision. To make that vision a reality, what values will guide your behaviors? What will you contribute to people around you? What is your idea of excellence? What skills and attributes do you possess or will you develop? These same questions must be answered by organizations. This is the visioning process. Discovering the vision is critical for companies (or people) who wish to deliver superior value.

The corporate vision provides a common understanding of what the organization is trying to accomplish in the broadest sense. Duane Larson, president of Children's World Learning Centers, a division of ARAMARK Corporation, says of his company's vision about providing child care:

> Just as the rudder determines the direction a boat will take, our Vision determines what direction our organization will take. Without it there is effort but no progress. At Children's World, it includes our Core Values, which are the things we hold sacred, like our concern for the safety of the children in our care. It also includes our mission, that which we are trying to accomplish. It sounds easy to delineate; it isn't.

VISION

The desired image of the company in the minds of employees.

CORE VALUES

A set of statements describing
the type of behavior expected of
the company and its employees.

**CONNECTED:
SURFING THE NET**

www.lilly.com

**Eli Lilly invites you to learn
more about its global
research-based pharmaceutical corporation. Visit Eli
Lilly's Web site and find out
more about its company philosophy, corporate citizenship, and treatment of
employees.**

Most company visions are composed of four parts: a set of core values, a business definition, the strategic direction of the company, and the strategic infrastructure.

CORE VALUES: THE ETHICAL FOUNDATION

Core values describe the type of behavior expected from a company's employees. Core values are the articulation of ethics and social responsibility, which were discussed in chapter 1. Everyone must live them every day. L. L. Bean's values are to "sell good merchandise at a reasonable price and treat customers like friends." Employees believe that if they do this, business will take care of itself. Core values often express the company's philosophy about societal well-being, good corporate citizenship, and treatment of employees.

"Values are the way a company does things," says Randall Tobias, CEO of Eli Lilly, adding that in order for them to work, "values must be both defined and lived."[2] Eli Lilly executives have clearly articulated the organization's core values.

Eli Lilly Core Values

Long established core values guide us in all that we do as we implement our strategies and pursue our mission

- Respect for the people that includes our concern for the interests of all the people worldwide who touch—or are touched by—our company: customers, employees, shareholders, partners, and communities.
- Integrity that embraces the very highest standards of honesty, ethical behavior, and exemplary moral character.
- Excellence that is reflected in our continuous search for new ways to improve the performance of our business in order to become the best at what we deliver.

Recently, as the first step in their strategic planning process, a team of top executives and managers from Children's World gathered to undertake the difficult task of developing their core values. The result is shown in Figure 4.3. Notice that each of the many stakeholders of the organization is explicitly addressed.

Core values provide an ethical guide that may be particularly useful in a crisis. It is possible Johnson & Johnson would not be around today if it had not adhered to its core values when Tylenol capsules laced with cyanide were linked to several deaths. The company's values are described in a credo, outlined in the early 1940s, which today reads in part: "We believe our first responsibility is to the doctors, nurses, and patients, to mothers and all others who use our products and services. In meeting their needs, everything we do must be of high quality."[3] That credo represents the organization's main purpose: to produce products responsibly with consumer safety in mind.

The tragic Tylenol situation in 1982 is one that few companies could withstand. By following the guidelines set forth in its credo, however, Johnson & Johnson did not just survive, but it emerged stronger. This ethics issue, one of the most heavily covered of this type by the

---

CORE VALUES
We hold sacred...
- Our paramount and uncompromising concern for the safety, health, and emotional and educational well-being of our customers and employees.
- Our dedication to making a positive difference in children's lives.
- Our responsibility to operate with honesty and integrity with all publics:

Parents	Employers
Children	Suppliers
Communities	Management
Employees	Government

- Our respect for the uniqueness of the individual.
- Our commitment to excellence in the delivery of our service to our customers and results to our shareholders.
- The importance of empowering our employees so that they may utilize their creativity and initiative to deliver on the company's commitment to excellence.

FIGURE 4.3 *Children's World
Learning Centers, Inc.
Corporate Vision*

Wall Street Journal, provides a fascinating classic example of core values.[4] Johnson & Johnson owns McNeil Consumer Products Company, the maker of Tylenol, which in 1982 generated $500 million in annual sales and contributed 8 percent of Johnson & Johnson's annual revenues. It was outselling Bayer aspirin, Bufferin, Excedrin, and Anacin combined.

On September 30, 1982, when Extra-Strength Tylenol capsules laced with cyanide were reported as linked with five deaths and one serious illness, McNeil immediately and voluntarily withdrew from the market the lot of 93,000 units from which the two bottles came. That same day, 500 sales agents were sent to remove the product from store shelves. By midafternoon, the company had sent half a million messages to physicians, hospitals, and distributors notifying them of the deaths and indicating the lot number.

Tougher times were ahead. Another death occurred in April that was linked to poisonous Tylenol. The company removed from the market all 22 million bottles of Tylenol capsules, valued at $79 million. To offset the loss in consumer goodwill, the marketing focus shifted to selling Tylenol tablets and voluntarily exchanging these for bottles of capsules. Nevertheless, by October 25, 1982, sales of all Tylenol products had slipped more than 25 percent. A letter was sent to approximately 61,000 doctors nationwide in which McNeil's Dr. Thomas N. Gates outlined the steps taken in response to the product tampering. In addition, 2 million pieces of literature were sent to doctors, dentists, nurses, and pharmacists emphasizing that the company was not the source of the poison. A special promotion offered coupons for Tylenol, and customers who had thrown away their bottles following the scare could have them replaced for free by calling an 800 number. Investor confidence improved and Johnson & Johnson stock, which had fallen 17 percent immediately after the first deaths were reported, bounced back on the New York Stock Exchange. Johnson & Johnson had all stores restocked with tamper-proof capsules by January 1, 1983.

Tylenol's comeback can best be attributed to Johnson & Johnson's early management decision to both stand by its credo and not let the brand die. The credo concludes: "We are responsible to the communities in which we live and work and to the world community as well. . . . We must experiment with new ideas. Research must be carried on, innovative programs developed, and mistakes paid for."

BUSINESS DEFINITION (MISSION)

The **business definition,** also referred to as the company mission, describes the fundamental contributions the organization provides to customers. Merck Pharmaceuticals says: "The mission of Merck is to provide society with superior products and services—innovations and solutions that improve the quality of life and satisfy customer needs."[5] Children's World says: "Our mission is to enrich the quality of family life by providing peace of mind to parents and by enhancing the life experiences of the children in our care."[6]

Noted scholar Ted Levitt has had a tremendous influence on how companies develop their business definition. In a classic *Harvard Business Review* article, "Marketing Myopia," he explains why a customer orientation is absolutely critical to a company's business definition. **Marketing myopia** occurs when executives focus on their company's current products and services rather than on benefits to consumers. Levitt uses U.S. railroads as an example. They didn't stop growing because the need for passenger and freight transportation declined; in fact it grew. They got into trouble because they saw themselves in the railroad business rather than the transportation business. They were product oriented, not customer oriented. Trucking and airline companies took customers away from railroads because they better met their needs. In addition, the railroads' failure to focus on customer needs created a situation whereby they also failed at making railroads themselves as competitive as could be. If the railroads had defined their business as transportation, then maybe Penn Central or some other company would have invented the truck or the airplane or served customers' transportation needs in other innovative ways with the railroads themselves. Levitt adds that "the entire corporation must be viewed as a customer-creating and customer-satisfying organization. Management must think of itself not as producing products but as providing customer-creating value satisfactions."

The organization's business definition should be stated in basic, benefit-rich terms and should focus on consumer benefits, not product features. It should always answer this question: "What business are we really in?" For example, is a cereal company in the "food" business (product focused) or the "nutrition" business (focused on consumer needs)? Benefits

**CONNECTED:
SURFING THE NET**

www.jnj.com

Johnson & Johnson is well known for its adherence to core values set forth by the company. Learn more about Johnson & Johnson and read its credo in its entirety on the company's Web site.

<u>BUSINESS DEFINITION</u>

Describes the contributions the business makes to customers and society; also called the company mission.

<u>MARKETING MYOPIA</u>

A focus on company products rather than on how these products benefit consumers.

THE BUSINESS MISSION
"WHAT IS OUR REAL BUSINESS?"

Myopic Definition	Customer-Centered Definition
Medical Care	Health
Screws	Fasteners
Industrial controls	Productivity
Cars and trucks	Transportation
Computers	Problem solving
Industrial coatings	Protection and aesthetics
Nuclear power	Energy
Cosmetics	Hope
Telephones	Communication

FIGURE 4.4 *The Business Definition*

are based on what customers receive, not on the work companies do. Microsoft has grown dramatically and received substantial profit because of the benefits its software provides. Customers don't care how much raw material Microsoft uses or what it costs to produce the software. Kobe Bryant, Shaquille O'Neal, and Kevin Garnett make hundreds of millions of dollars because of the entertainment they provide, not just the points they score. Figure 4.4 contrasts myopic business definitions with customer-centered business definitions.

> **career tip**   Eli Lilly states that "the company's objective is to attract and retain outstanding people at all levels and in all parts of the organization."[7] As a part of this effort, Eli Lilly offers a summer internship program that has grown and become more diverse each year. Interns are challenged to become actively involved in order to develop individual talents, leadership, and communication skills. Internships are offered in marketing and many other career areas. For further information, you can contact: Summer Intern Coordinator, Eli Lilly & Company, Lilly Corporate Center, Indianapolis, IN 46285.

STRATEGIC DIRECTION (INTENT)

STRATEGIC DIRECTION

The desired leadership position of an organization as well as the measures used to chart progress toward reaching that position.

Strategic direction is the desired leadership position of an organization and the measures used to chart progress toward reaching this position. *Strategic intent* is another term for strategic direction: "Strategic intent captures the essence of winning."[8] Strategic direction addresses the competitiveness of the organization and often sets specific growth, profit, share, or scope goals relative to the competition and market opportunities. Eli Lilly's strategic direction is "to be a leading innovation-driven pharmaceutical corporation." It plans to focus primarily on three strategic dimensions: achieving a global presence, using its critical capabilities, and concentrating its resources on the five disease categories in which the company believes it can have the greatest effect.[9]

Strategic direction may identify competitors by name or by type. Fuji's strategic direction is aimed at overtaking Kodak, and Toyota is intent on surpassing General Motors. Or strategic direction may guide organizations toward becoming one of the largest in an industry. General Electric wants to be either a leader or close follower in each venture it pursues. Netscape and Microsoft's strategic direction involves a battle for dominance of the Web. Both companies have recently introduced new versions of their Internet software, intensifying the competition to be the largest in the industry.[10]

STRATEGIC INFRASTRUCTURE

STRATEGIC INFRASTRUCTURE

The corporate configuration that produces the company's distinctive or core competencies and provides the resources necessary to satisfy customer wants.

Executives must develop and organize the company's **strategic infrastructure,** the corporate configuration that produces the company's distinctive or core competencies and provides the resources necessary to satisfy customer wants. This often means dividing the business into

A cleaner source of energy is coming down the pipe.

It's called the fuel cell. A new, more efficient way to power cars or just about anything else. And so clean that the only thing coming out the tailpipe is pure water. Texaco is helping to make it happen. And the benefits are ... well ... clear.

☆ A WORLD OF ENERGY.

texaco.com

© 2001 Texaco Inc.

Texaco's strategic direction involves a commitment to a cleaner environment.

functional units and determining which core competencies to develop. The idea is to provide the products, services, and talents necessary to satisfy customer needs and create customer value.

Strategic Business Units (SBUs)   Most medium-sized and large companies have several strategic departments or units. A **strategic business unit (SBU)** is a part of the firm that can be managed separately for marketing purposes; it may be a division within the company, a separate product or product line, a distinct group of customers, or a unique technology. Johnson & Johnson has three SBUs: consumer, pharmaceutical, and professional products. The consumer SBU concentrates its efforts on marketing consumer products such as Band-Aids, No More Tears shampoo, and Tylenol. The pharmaceutical SBU mainly markets prescription drugs to the health care industry. The professional SBU produces sutures, surgical equipment, and medical supplies for physicians, dentists, and others. The Walt Disney Company also has three SBUs: theme parks and resorts, filmed entertainment, and consumer products.

Consider the corporation illustrated in Figure 4.5. It has two divisions: ground transportation and air transportation. The ground transportation division can be divided into SBUs according to products (motorcycles, trucks, and cars), types of markets (business, consumer, and military), and technology (electric and gas). The air transportation division can be divided similarly (products are passenger planes, fighter planes, and training planes; markets are military, airlines, and consumers; and technologies are conventional and stealth). The total SBUs possible for this company is 36, but not all combinations would make sense (such as an SBU that produces stealth passenger planes for consumers).

There are several ways to structure the SBUs in this company. Grouped by technology, there would be four (electric, gas, conventional, and stealth); based on products there would be six (motorcycles, trucks, cars, passenger planes, fighter planes, and training planes); according to type of market, there would be four (airlines, other businesses, consumers, and the military). Many companies, lacking a customer focus, form SBUs by product line. In market-oriented companies, SBUs often address specific segments. That's why UPS Logistics Group is organized by the industries it serves: automotive, pharmaceuticals, computer, and so forth.[11]

STRATEGIC BUSINESS UNIT (SBU)

A part of the firm that can be managed separately for marketing purposes; it may be a division, a product or product line, a distinct group of customers, or a unique technology.

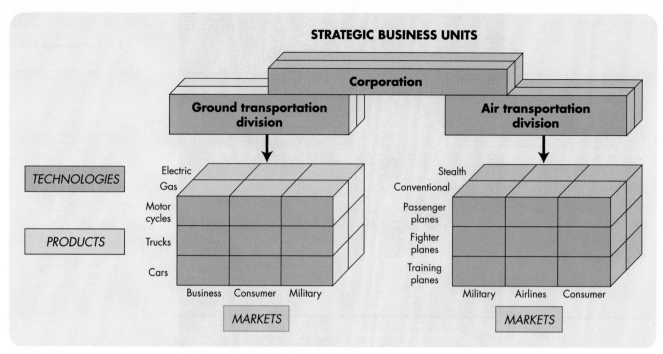

STRATEGIC BUSINESS UNITS

Corporation

Ground transportation division

Air transportation division

TECHNOLOGIES

PRODUCTS

Electric
Gas
Motor cycles
Trucks
Cars

Business Consumer Military

MARKETS

Stealth
Conventional
Passenger planes
Fighter planes
Training planes

Military Airlines Consumer

MARKETS

FIGURE 4.5 *Strategic Business Units*

Typically, an SBU is managed by a team from several different functional areas, such as marketing, accounting, and manufacturing. The corporate executives are responsible for managing the collection of SBUs—often called a portfolio—that makes up the organization. The general health of the company depends on how well the SBU portfolio matches the needs of the market.

Companies such as GE assess its SBUs based on estimates of market share, customer and market knowledge, customer satisfaction, cost efficiency, level of technology, product growth, and financial strength.

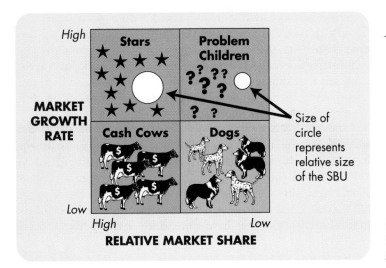

High
Stars **Problem Children**

MARKET GROWTH RATE

Cash Cows **Dogs**

Low

High Low
RELATIVE MARKET SHARE

Size of circle represents relative size of the SBU

FIGURE 4.6 *Boston Consulting Group Growth-Share Matrix*

Portfolio planning tools measure the contribution each SBU makes to the overall performance of the company. We will discuss two that are widely used: the growth-share matrix developed by the Boston Consulting Group (BCG) and the attractiveness-strength matrix developed by General Electric.

Assessing SBUs: The Growth-Share Matrix Marketers need to understand market opportunities and the strength of their organization's resources relative to competitors. The growth-share matrix, shown in Figure 4.6, uses market growth as a measure of opportunity and the company's market share as the measure of resource strength. SBUs are placed in a matrix according to their scores on these two dimensions. Different actions are recommended, depending on the category into which the SBU falls.

In the low-share/high-growth category are SBUs called question marks. Although they are in a market that is growing fast, most have not yet achieved competitive advantage or begun generating substantial revenues. A new airborne transportation vehicle, dubbed "SkyCat," was

PORTFOLIO PLANNING TOOLS
Tools that measure the contribution each SBU makes to the overall performance of the company.

The e-logistics division of UPS is treated as a strategic business unit in this advertisement.

recently introduced by Britain's Advanced Technologies Group. Combining the better qualities of airplanes and hovercraft, the SkyCat could land or fly virtually anywhere. Though experts agree that the SkyCat has "the potential to revolutionize global air transport," a profitable market has yet to be found.[12] Since question marks such as the SkyCat are indeed risky, marketers may choose to (1) invest a little in the SBU and hope for the best; (2) spend time, energy, and patience on developing the SBU; (3) invest everything and keep their fingers crossed; or (4) get more information before doing anything.

Stars (high-share/high-growth SBUs) are a lot like movie personalities—give them lots of attention and expect a lot of success. Because they're growing, stars require a high investment, but it can result in a high return. Products such as Sony PlayStation 2 and Windows 2000 are examples.

Cash cows (high-share/low-growth SBUs) require a relatively small investment but should yield fairly substantial returns. Although the market is growing at a very low rate, the SBU has enough share to generate substantial cash flow. Companies want at least one product in this category and often have more, since revenues from these products can support the development of others. Two huge cash cows are the DOS operating system for Microsoft and Ivory soap for Procter & Gamble.

Dogs (low-share/low-growth SBUs) typically provide less than desirable returns. They're often considered competitively disadvantaged and unlikely to generate profits. They may actually consume resources, becoming cash drains that create negative value for the company. An example is *Playboy* magazine. It loses lots of money, so why keep it? Because it's the cornerstone of the profitable activities of Playboy Enterprises. The astoundingly profitable playmate videos (an SBU star) and other Playboy businesses are possible only because of the magazine.

Assessing SBUs: The Attractiveness-Strength Matrix The growth-share matrix says nothing about competitive behavior or market characteristics, and for this reason most marketing strategists use the attractiveness-strength matrix. As illustrated in Figure 4.7, the marketer first examines such factors as market size, market growth, competitive pressure, price levels, and government regulation to develop a composite industry attractiveness score. Next, the business strengths of each SBU are assessed based on estimates of the company's market share, customer and market knowledge, customer satisfaction with the company, cost efficiency, level of technology, product quality, and financial strength. Each SBU is then graphed in the matrix based on these several measures.

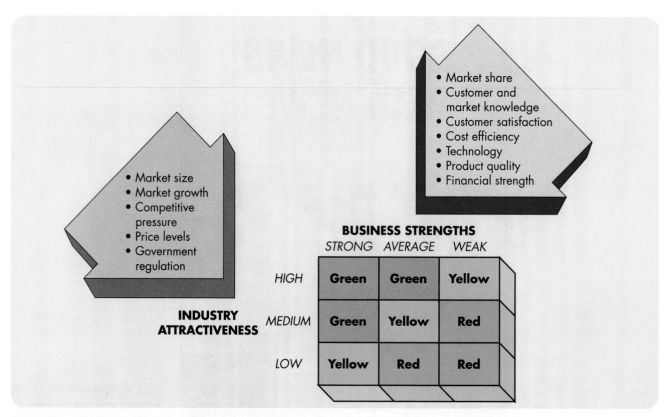

FIGURE 4.7 *The General Electric Attractiveness-Strength Matrix*

The attractiveness-strength matrix uses colors to signal whether executives should stop (red), be cautious (yellow), or go ahead (green) with the SBU. Unfortunately, during the 1960s and 1970s, "red" SBUs were sometimes categorically denied the resources required to compete, dooming them to failure. At the same time, "green" SBUs were allowed to charge ahead, irrespective of the vision of the company. All that was important was the amount of investment required and the SBU's potential return.

Today, portfolio planning tools are considered useful indicators, not predictors. Even SBUs that fall in the same category may need vastly different strategies. Portfolio techniques are helpful in identifying the current business situation, but they are inappropriate for making resource allocations. These, as we shall see later, should be made only after the strategic marketing plan has been developed. Because portfolio techniques say little about strategy, they should be used only as a first step in strategic marketing.

Core Competencies   As shown in Figure 4.2, core competencies are the other important aspect of strategic infrastructures. **Core competencies** are the unique resources a company develops and employs to create superior customer value. They are the fundamental building blocks of competitive advantage. As Duane Larson of Children's World explains:

> In developing a strategic marketing plan for Children's World, it was important that we had a clear idea of what we did well, and how those competencies fit with our overall strategic direction. This process was valuable because more than telling you what we did well, it highlighted the holes we had that needed to be filled in order to deliver on our plan.

Children's World identified several core competencies that are kept confidential as part of their strategy. McDonald's core competencies in food distribution and preparation give it the ability to reproduce precisely the same taste, texture, and service millions of times a day, anywhere in the world. FedEx has developed a core competency in computerized information and tracking system technology so it can determine the location of any package worldwide within seconds.

Core competencies underlie the success of any one SBU and also span several SBUs or corporate divisions. Core competencies allow new products to grow. Marketing's role is to interpret market forces so that the proper core competencies can be developed to provide maximum benefit to consumers in the marketplace. When this role is performed well, companies are rewarded with the profit necessary to support continued improvement and growth. Kodak's ability to thrive through the consolidation of corporatewide technology is discussed in the technology feature.

An understanding of core competencies is necessary to comprehend how technology is shaping marketing practices. Through the rapid growth of technologies, companies build the millions of products and services that produce superior customer value. The many types of core competencies can be grouped into five categories: (1) base technologies, (2) process technologies, (3) product technologies, (4) people systems, and (5) information systems.

Base Technologies The research and development skills of companies can be applied to an endless array of product areas. For example, one of Canon's core competencies, vision optics, can be used to deliver outstanding cameras, copiers, and numerous inventive products. DuPont, known for basic chemistry, has developed multitudes of industrial and consumer products. Raytheon is skilled in the wave technology necessary for radar and other types of vision systems. General Electric has spent billions of dollars developing its extensive knowledge of physics. Base technologies can be applied simultaneously to a number of diverse industries and product areas.

Process Technologies Process technologies allow the firm to produce quality products in the most effective and flexible manner possible. Marketing's job is to make sure that the development of processes is consistent with market trends and is in the customer's best interest. McDonald's has nearly perfected the process of quickly delivering quality food to consumers, but the company does not consider current standards fast enough. Chain executives now boast that they've lowered drive-through times to a mere 90 seconds from the first keystroke of the order until the food is handed to the customer.[13] This improvement requires extensive changes in employee training, as well as the technologies used to process food. ARAMARK set a world record of its own when it used its superior process technologies to serve more than a million meals to athletes, coaches, and officials from 200 countries at the 2000 Olympic Games in Sydney, Australia.[14] WearGuard designs thousands of new products each year for the custom clothing market. An order for a shirt with a company logo or Little League team name can be

CORE COMPETENCIES

The unique resources a company develops and employs to create superior customer value; the fundamental building blocks of competitive advantage.

CONNECTED: SURFING THE NET

www.westinghouse.com

Learn more about base technologies by visiting Westinghouse's Web site. Discover how the company has applied its research and development skills to develop innovative products.

CONNECTING THROUGH TECHNOLOGY

KODAK ADJUSTS ITS FOCUS

 More than a century ago, "You push the button, we do the rest," was the slogan—and vision—that introduced photographic technology to the public and pushed Eastman Kodak to one of the top brands in the United States. By the mid-1990s, however, Kodak had strayed dangerously from its core competency: photo imaging. It had ventured into a host of unrelated businesses, such as household products, clinical diagnostics, and pharmaceuticals, and it posted a $1.5 million loss in 1993. So Kodak made a strategic shift in marketing. In efforts to reinvent the company, top management decided not only to refocus on what made Kodak great in the first place—imaging—but also to push the limits of digital imaging technology to give customers greater value. With respectable earnings of $1.4 billion on $14 billion sales in 1999, it looks like the strategy is paying off.

First, Kodak sold off unrelated businesses. Next, Kodak made leadership in developing digital imaging a priority. Kodak joined forces with competitors Nikon, Minolta, Canon, and Fuji to develop Advanced Photo Systems (APS), hailed as one of the best products of 1996 by *Business Week*. This digital imaging system gives customers easy drop-in film loading, improved print quality, three print formats, and the ability to have certain data recorded digitally on the film. Although the five-company consortium developed APS together, Kodak owns a large percentage of the patents and has contributed the most marketing muscle—a splashy television and print campaign for its own Advantix brand.

Kodak ads now feature the line "Take Pictures Further," and the vision has been as crucial to Kodak's strategic reinvention as was "You push the button" at its founding. The logan expresses Kodak's broader mission to increase the number of photos customers take—whether through digital or traditional technology—and to get customers to use their pictures by enlarging them, putting them on T-shirts, in newsletters, on computer screens—you name it. More than 60 billion pictures are taken each year, but only 2 percent are enlarged, used commercially, or displayed. Part of the APS appeal is the ability to order prints from a contact sheet so that only the pictures customers want get printed.

On June 29, 2000, Kodak launched *Everyday Pictures,* a magazine devoted to picture taking. According to Steve Hallowell, general manager and vice president of cameras and consumer imaging, Kodak hopes to increase the number of pictures people take "by inspiring people to take pictures every day, instead of just on special occasions. We're expanding the role that pictures can play in people's lives and helping them to save even more precious memories." Each issue includes a pull-out section focusing on kids taking pictures.

Kodak's mission, however, is not confined to its digital imaging strategic business unit. Kodak centralized marketing for all nine of the company's SBUs; all report to a chief marketing officer, and each is charged with delivering value to its customers as opposed to delivering technology. "We have a number of technologies, but we have to be technologically transparent," says Bill Gray, manager of corporate branding. "What we deliver is pictures. And how we will get growth and how we will serve people is to explain to them how they can, in our words, 'take pictures further.'" To back up this unified marketing strategy, Kodak is using an ad campaign that spotlights every one of its SBUs—a first for the company.

To prepare for the growth of the digital imaging industry, Kodak has joined forces with several Internet start-ups that focus on digital imaging. For the first time in decades, Kodak will face stiff competition for its core business—photo imaging. The future of Kodak depends on its ability to stay true to its core competency and its ability to again refocus its marketing efforts to meet consumers' demands.

Sources: Linda Grant, "The Bears Back Off Kodak," *Fortune,* June 24, 1996, pp. 24–25; Ginger Conlon, "Getting into Focus," *Sales and Marketing Management,* January 1997, pp. 40–45; Steve Gelsi, "Imaging Is Everything," *Brandweek,* February 26, 1996, pp. 22–23; "New Kodak Everyday Pictures Magazine Provides Inspiration for Picture-Takers," *Business Wire,* June 28, 2000; Dan Goodin, "A New Focus for Kodak," *The Standard,* January 31, 2000.

received over the phone and shipped within 24 hours. In fact, WearGuard maintains a Live Chat service on its Internet site for immediate customer assistance.[15] Its production is tied so closely to the customer order process that no time is spent without contributing value to the customer.

Product Technologies The company's ability to create new goods and services is supported by product technologies. Many organizations have worked hard to develop competency in moving quickly from the idea stage through a series of well-defined steps to commercialization.

DuPont's core competencies in chemistry have enabled it to develop a number of industrial and consumer products.

Others follow the leader, copying competitors' products, possibly improving upon them slightly. Followers benefit from the innovation of leaders without having to invest substantially in developing their own product technology.

The music industry, for instance, has been dramatically affected by recent changes in technology. Thanks to the advent of digital music recording, MP3 players have found a wide and expanding market. MP3 players allow consumers to play and record music in a digital format. Music, therefore, can be downloaded straight from the Internet onto many brands of players, including the Rio from Diamond Multimedia. These players are a result of Diamond Multimedia's desire to expand into a new product line from its formally core group of products that included Internet audio and gaming. Now several entertainment companies, such as Sony, Samsung, and RCA, have all introduced their own MP3 player.[16]

Nokia, second to Motorola in the fierce and fast-growing mobile phone industry, spends less than half the amount of its rivals on research and development. It acquires and copies product technologies developed by others. According to Merrill Lynch analyst Neal Barton, "Motorola and Ericsson are pioneers in technology. Nokia is much closer to customers. It doesn't pioneer technology; it just gives customers what they want." This includes special products, such as phone accessories and unique products for special market segments. Like many companies, Nokia is faced with the challenge of constantly providing better features at increasingly lower prices. It does this by carefully crafting its marketing to meet local tastes and appeal to consumer segments, leaving the responsibility of large-scale innovation to its competitors.[17] Eli Lilly, on the other hand, invests heavily in research and development to retain its status as an innovation-driven company. Currently Lilly produces dozens of "best-in-class" pharmaceutical products, usually for psychotropic or diabetes markets, but it is now expanding agressively into cancer medications.[18]

People Systems The procedures that provide the human connection between companies and consumers are called people systems. Jan Carlzon from Scandinavian Airlines said the "moment of truth" occurs each time an employee has contact with a customer. He meant that the encounter results in either a good or bad impression being formed. Therefore, Carlzon invested in employee training to ensure that the moment of truth resulted in a positive experience for customers. He pulled his company into a leadership position by using people systems that provide outstanding customer service.

The Walt Disney Company has always placed high value on its team of employees. Walt once said: "The whole thing here is the organization. Whatever we accomplish belongs to our entire group, a tribute to our combined effort. I feel that there is no door with which the kind of talent we have cannot be opened." His successor, Michael Eisner, updated those sentiments: "The Disney name—and the image it conveys—is one of our greatest assets, second only to the people who have contributed their talents and dreams toward the achievement of the goals we have set for ourselves."[19]

The importance of Disney's employees is reflected in the organization's retail operation. To foster a spirit of teamwork, employees are called cast members. On the retail floor, they are on stage; in the storeroom they are backstage. Customers are guests. Such role-playing helps employees keep the desired goal in mind: Exceed guests' expectations.[20]

Two companies often cited for excellent people systems are ARAMARK, with over 200,000 employees, and UPS, with nearly 344,000 employees, both of whom have extensive contact with customers and their customers' customers. Scient Corp., an Internet business consulting company with 13 offices worldwide, also has developed a core competency in people systems. Scient Corp. tells new employees, including secretaries, to be bold, up-front, and brassy, demonstrating that in the highly competitive world of e-consulting speed and creativity pay off. In recent years Scient has grown from an Internet start-up to a billion-dollar business, helping such companies as eBay and Chase Manhattan Bank to improve the speed and efficiency of their Internet operations.[21]

Information Systems An exceptional information system can be a core competency. Historically, companies were located close to their customers, so information about them was easy to obtain firsthand. Even executives talked directly with customers. Today, the situation is vastly different because of the increasing diversity of products, customers, and competitors. Especially important in global marketing, information-processing technologies put vast amounts of data at our fingertips rapidly. Companies that don't possess this core competency will be at a dramatic competitive disadvantage.

FedEx has satellite technology that enables it to track packages instantaneously. Route drivers equipped with scanning devices provide information on exactly when a package is picked up or delivered. If you want to know where your package is, simply get on the Web and go to the FedEx home page. This information benefits not only the customer but also FedEx. Management teams determine what types of services are used most often, which destinations are most common, where more drivers may be needed, and so forth.

Basing the marketing strategy on core competency gives companies the longer-term flexibility required for sustained leadership. Technological advances can be shared throughout the company. SBUs should be treated as relatively temporary reservoirs of competencies that may be phased in, phased out, or adjusted radically in accord with strategic marketing conditions. According to Prahalad and Hamel, noted educators, "The real sources of advantage are to be found in management's ability to consolidate corporatewide technologies and production skills into competencies that empower the individual business to adapt quickly to changing opportunities."[22]

THE STRATEGIC MARKETING PLAN

As we have mentioned, implementing the marketing concept is the responsibility of everyone in the organization. Consequently, many people are involved in developing and executing strategic marketing plans. Marketing isn't conducted only within a marketing department. As noted scholar and business consultant Frederick Webster, Jr. says: "Everyone in the firm must be charged with responsibility for understanding customers and contributing to developing and delivering value to them."[23] Marketing is so pervasive in customer-focused, competitively driven companies that it's often carried out in cooperation with marketers by teams from diverse areas of the firm, such as accounting, finance, engineering, and manufacturing.

THE PLANNING TEAM

There cannot be a strategic marketing plan unless someone produces it. In the past, the planning process included only marketing personnel. Today, strong marketers generally assemble a **cross-functional planning team.** This team works together with a total understanding of the

CROSS-FUNCTIONAL PLANNING TEAM
Employees from several areas responsible for developing the company's strategic marketing plan.

TITLE	RESPONSIBILITY
Marketing	Development of strategic plan and team leader
Engineering	Technological product development
Manufacturing	Efficient manufacturing
Finance	Financial modeling of strategies
Marketing Intelligence	Estimate competitor strengths, vulnerabilities
Marketing Research	Customer and consumer requirements
Sales	Potential sales strategies
Promotion and Advertising	Support program development
Procurement	Available supply partners and costs
Human Resources	Union and employee relations
Logistics	Distribution systems approaches
Accounting	Analysis of cost data

FIGURE 4.8 *A Cross-Functional Strategic Planning Team*

market and the organization's capabilities. Just as relationships with stakeholders outside the company are important, so are internal relationships. Since each member of the planning team brings a unique perspective, these people must bring all parts of the picture together. Figure 4.8 gives each person's functional area and a short description of his or her main responsibility.

WHAT IS STRATEGY?

Before we talk about strategic marketing plans, we need to discuss one of the most overused and misused terms in business. The military defines *strategy* as "the art of meeting the enemy in battle under advantageous conditions." Although there are several "correct" definitions of strategy, we will use the following: A **strategy** is the development and/or deployment of resources with the intent of accomplishing goals and objectives in competitive arenas. Because companies have limited resources, executives must determine how best to use them to accomplish organizational goals. Note that "competitive arena" implies the presence of competitors. They are striving to achieve their own goals, perhaps the same ones set by your company. Certainly, their actions affect your ability to achieve your goals. Japanese companies tend to be acutely aware of competitors. Consider Honda's public statement, "Yamaha No Tsubusu" "We will crush, squash, and slaughter Yamaha." But beating competitors with the intent of hurting them is not really what strategy is all about. The idea is to win out by serving customers better—by connecting better—through relationships and technology, with attention to diversity, globally and ethically.

Strategy is not just about meeting competitors fact to face. It's also about seizing the moment to create change in a timely manner. Hang around any group of planners and you're sure to hear someone refer to the **strategic window.** Derek Abell, noted business strategist, coined the term *strategic window* to describe the moment when requirements of the market and competencies of the firm fit together to create a significant opportunity.[24] Now, more than ever, the strategic window is important. Products and technologies are changing so rapidly that organizations late to introduce advances are likely to spend millions in product development only to see it go down the drain. Competitors who get there first will obtain the sales, while the late product sits on the shelf.

For example, in 2000, Lucent Technologies and TeraBeam Networks announced a $450 million joint venture to build communications systems that transmit information directly between city buildings using beams of light, thereby skipping the use of optical fibers altogether. Lucent and TeraBeam realize that light signals have little chance of overtaking fiber-optic cable. However, since less than 5 percent of downtown office buildings are currently "wired" with fiber, there is a strategic window of opportunity. By shooting data-laser beams between medium and large businesses in downtown areas and office parks, Lucent and

STRATEGY
The development and/or deployment of resources with the intent of accomplishing goals and objectives in a competitive arena.

STRATEGIC WINDOW
The time during which market needs and the competencies of the firm fit together to create a significant opportunity.

TeraBeam will provide more data and voice capacity than regular phone lines currently do alone.[25] Savvy marketers such as Lucent and TeraBeam know that the strategic window will be open for a relatively short period as consumers begin to wire their buildings with fiber-optic cables.

Even though strategic windows may open only for a short time, the objective is to create a sustainable strategy. Two generic approaches are a low-cost strategy and a differentiation strategy. **Low-cost strategy** focuses on winning through efficiency. The objective is to be the low-cost leader, which allows the company to have higher margins than competitors and to pass some savings on to customers through lower prices. There are many ways to gain a favorable cost position:

- *Process technology.* Invent a low-cost way to create and deliver a product.
- *Product design.* Create a product that provides the same level of functionality with lower cost, often through new materials or miniaturization.
- *Consolidation of the value chain.* Combine several steps in the value chain into one.
- *Low-cost suppliers.* Lower costs by purchasing materials and other inputs more cheaply.
- *Location.* Put facilities in low-wage areas or nearer markets to lower distribution costs.
- *Economies of scale and scope.* Produce more and market in a larger area so costs are spread over more units and customers.[26]

A **differentiation strategy** involves delivering customer value in a way that clearly distinguishes the product from its competitors. Differentiation works through effectiveness. It is usually achieved by giving superior benefits or reducing customer cost rather than price. There are several ways to achieve differentiation.

- *New functional capabilities.* Create products that do new things.
- *Improved performance.* Make products that work better, have less maintenance, or are cheaper to operate.
- *Product tailoring.* Make products that more closely suit the needs of select groups.
- *Mass customization.* Use a process that creates products precisely to the specifications of individual customers.

LOW-COST STRATEGY
Strategy whose objective is to be the low-cost leader, thereby allowing the company to have higher margins than competitors and pass some savings on to customers through lower prices; works through efficiency.

DIFFERENTIATION STRATEGY
Strategy based on delivering customer value in a way that clearly distinguishes the product from competitors; works through effectiveness.

Wal-Mart is known for their use of low-cost strategy.

These various strategies are meant to create sustainable competitive advantages for the company. **Sustainable competitive advantage** is the cost position or superior value that competitors cannot easily duplicate or surpass. Once it is attained, competitors generally try to copy it or develop their own advantages. Organizations that create sustainable advantages have less volatility and better long-run performance.

COMPONENTS OF THE STRATEGIC MARKETING PLAN

SUSTAINABLE COMPETITIVE
ADVANTAGE
The cost position or superior
value in a product that competitors cannot easily duplicate or
surpass.

Guided by the corporate vision, the strategic marketing plan essentially describes how to accomplish that vision. Keep in mind that many organizations are complex and may have many strategic marketing plans. Similar planning steps are used for the entire company or for an SBU within a company. Delphi, an automotive parts designer, has one strategic marketing plan for the company itself and additional ones for each SBU: engine systems, exteriors, interiors, and chassis. Each plan has a similar structure.

The planning team has to address several areas: objectives, situation analysis, target markets, positioning, and integration of the marketing mix. The first step is to state the objectives the business will pursue and the specific goals it expects to obtain. The second step usually is a situation analysis, which describes the current business environment and how well the company will be able to compete in it. The third step is to determine target markets, or which customers the organization plans to serve. The fourth step is to decide positioning relative to competitors, that is, the image the organization wants customers to have about it and its products. The fifth step is to develop plans for each aspect of the marketing mix and integrate these into the overall strategic plan. We will discuss each step in detail following this logical order, but as actual plans are developed, the various steps usually interact with one another. For example, objectives are stated first but may later be changed to reflect information uncovered during the situation analysis. Finally, like a baseball pitch, a good strategic marketing plan needs follow-through or control measures that provide feedback on how well the plan is working.

Objectives   The strategic marketing plan must support the business definition laid out in the organization's vision. For example, Delphi defines its business as personal transportation. One of its SBUs supplies steering mechanisms for vehicles. Today that SBU manufactures mechanical and hydraulic systems, but because it is moving toward electronic and computerized systems, it is in the business of directional control. Another SBU is in the vision business—headlamps—but is researching other technologies, such as radar, infrared, and satellite positioning. Although each SBU has a separate strategic marketing plan, all contribute to Delphi's business definition of personal transportation.

Since the objectives are an outgrowth of the vision, they tend to be stated up front. But remember, they must take into account all of the remaining parts of the plan as well. Companies usually set objectives in terms of desired profit, market share, or total sales. Profit is the most common choice and may be stated in various ways, such as return on investment, cash flow (amount of cash returned to the business), or profit margins. Market share refers to a proportion relative to competitors that the company captures: the percentage of customers within a given market, the percentage of dollars spent on similar products, or the percentage of all similar product units that are sold (unit sales). Finally, businesses determine a total sales objective, defined as either a dollar amount or a product quantity sold. Most organizations state objectives in one of these ways, but they may add others: number of loyal customers, customer retention rates, and customer satisfaction scores.

A company's market share, profit, and sales objectives are important because managers from various functional areas (such as production and distribution) often base their activities on them. Falling far short of objectives can spell disaster. The objectives stated up front usually are reviewed when the entire plan is completed and adjustments may be made. This makes sense, since implementing a realistic plan is important.

Often, it's appropriate to state very specific objectives such as "44 percent market share by 2008." Ghirardelli Chocolate Company set as its goal for its 150th anniversary in 2002, for example, that it be rated by consumers as the best premium chocolate maker in America. To meet that goal, the company seeks to increase its baking business by 25 percent, to double its squares business throughout all channels, and to grow at least 20 percent a year until 2005.[27]

**CONNECTED:
SURFING THE NET**

www.americaspromise.org

**Learn about Colin Powell's
initiative to help America's
youth and the specific goals
and objectives the organ-
ization has created for its
volunteers.**

Notice that objectives always provide a time frame and must be verifiable. Verifiable means that it will be possible to determine precisely whether the objective has been met or not. You will see why this is important when we talk later about the marketing control process.

Situation Analysis All marketing activities required to understand the marketing environment, customer needs and wants, and the competition are examined in the situation analysis. This analysis predicts market conditions for the period that the strategic marketing plan is in effect. If the plan extends through 2010, for example, then predictions should be made up to that time. Developing possible scenarios generally requires bringing together data and expertise from different parts of the company to provide an accurate picture.

The analysis can be very elaborate or fairly simple, depending on the circumstances. At a minimum, it should give the planning team a general idea about the future, including potential size of the market, types of customers, competitors, technology, channels of distribution, economic conditions, governmental regulations, and the resources the company will have at its disposal, both globally and in individual countries. Mike McGorrin, vice president of marketing at Children's World, describes the major forces that affect his organization.

> Children's World Learning Centers' performance is influenced by demographic trends (e.g., birth rate, number of dual income families, number of single-parent families, delayed childbearing resulting in more disposable income), economic variables (e.g., new job creation and unemployment), parents' expectations/attitudinal factors (e.g., families' preferences for "socialization" and "academic readiness" for their children), competitive activity (e.g., pricing, advertising, promotion and new center development strategies), the public sector (e.g., public elementary school programs, public grants criteria, etc.), the development of new technology (e.g., availability of new computer hardware and software applications which improve our ability to communicate within our organization, etc.).

In order to develop a competitive marketing plan that will succeed, Children's World personnel examine each of these factors and determine their potential influence on the organization. In fact, McGorrin adds, "effective business strategies are rooted in a 'market-driven' mindset. Our new services, pricing, promotions, creative and targeting strategies have all been highly influenced by the marketplace." In other words, Children's World builds effective strategies because it keeps in mind the market forces at work.

As a final step in the situation analysis, the planning team must determine how well the company's skills and resources match the predicted market opportunities. This is typically called a **SWOT analysis,** which is military jargon for strengths, weaknesses, opportunities, and threats. An example is shown in Figure 4.9. Strengths and weaknesses are defined by such measures as market share, number of loyal customers, level of customer satisfaction, and rate of product introduction success. Strengths describe the unique resources or circumstances that can be used to take advantage of opportunities. Weaknesses suggest aspects of the organization or product that need improvement or, if that is not possible, ways to minimize any negative effects. The opportunities portion proposes advances that can be made in new or existing markets and identifies areas in which competitive advantages can be gained. The threats

SWOT ANALYSIS

An analysis of strengths, weaknesses, opportunities, and threats to determine how well the company's skills and resources match the predicted market opportunities.

Children's World
Learning Centers®
Quality Child Care • Preschool School-Age Learning Programs

Children's World Learning Center's vision is "translated" into outstanding learning environments for children.

Strengths	**Opportunities**

Strengths

Assess good use of competencies and results in the market:
- Share increase
- High loyalty and satisfaction ratings
- Excellent sales force
- Unique products, services

Opportunities

Assess areas where advantage may be gained:
- Add a new product
- Promote to new segment
- Sell more to existing customers
- Use a new form of distribution to reach new markets

Weaknesses (Constraints)

Assess poor use of competencies and results in the market:
- Share decrease
- Disloyal customers
- Not enough salespeople
- Product launch delays

Threats (Vulnerability)

Assess external forces that may prevent the company from accomplishing its objectives:
- Competitor with a new technology
- New government regulations
- Changing customer preferences

FIGURE 4.9 *An Example of SWOT Analysis*

section describes how the competition, new technology, the business environment, or government possibly may impede the company's development.

Companies are constrained by their weaknesses. For example, Westinghouse has been hampered in building its defense business because it lacks the capital to fund product development. Companies are also vulnerable to threats. When the government eliminated the use of certain environmentally hazardous resins in the manufacture of recreational boats, irate customers complained that colors faded in the sun. Many stopped purchasing designer-style boats for that reason. White didn't fade, but the lack of color reduced much of the excitement of new models and designs. Today, technological breakthroughs in environmentally friendly but stable colors have eliminated this threat.

Target Marketing   Once the situation analysis is complete, the planning team determines the characteristics of customer groups on whom to focus attention. Businesses cannot be "all things to all people"; given their competencies, they must choose which segments have the greatest potential. **Target marketing** is the process of selecting which market segments the firm will emphasize in attempts to satisfy customers better than its competitors. In late 1999, Ford introduced the new Focus in the United States. Ford specifically aimed at winning Generation Y customers by providing a vehicle with a Sony stereo system, affordable pricing, and fashionable design.[28] The Focus also captured 12.4 percent of all Hispanic car purchases in the second quarter of 2000, up from 11.4 percent. Jan Klug, marketing communications manager at Ford, said the "Focus is a cool car. That's what brings Focus to the party. The car bridges the general market and the Hispanic market. It also gives us a strong entry into the youth market along with the Mustang."[29] Another example is Pontiac, which introduced the Aztec sport recreation vehicle in 2000. Pontiac designed the Aztec so as to combine the image, styling, and utility of the SUV with the ride, performance, and handling of a midsized car. With such an array of options, Pontiac is attempting to satisfy the customer better than its rivals.[30]

Positioning   Planning teams often decide to pursue different positioning strategies with different target market segments. **Positioning,** as you recall, refers to creating a perception in the minds of consumers about the company and/or its products relative to competitors. A common word for positioning is *image,* often evoked by the brand name. For example, the Ralph Lauren Company wants to convey an image of high quality and status. If consumers see the company that way, then the marketing team has been successful in its positioning efforts.

In today's competitive business world, positioning is extremely important. "Everyone is after everyone's business. The mind of your customer or prospect is the battleground and that's where you win or lose," says Jack Trout, author of numerous marketing books and president of Trout & Partners, Ltd. According to him, "just as each product needs to be positioned in the mind [of consumers] against competitors, so does a company need to be positioned. Customers want to know where you're going. So do your employees."

TARGET MARKETING
The process of selecting which market segments the organization will emphasize in attempts to satisfy customers better than its competitors.

POSITIONING
Creating an image or perception in the minds of consumers about the organization or its products relative to the competition.

119

Once the desired positioning is established, the marketing mix—product, place, promotion, and price—must be integrated to make the strategy happen. Taken alone, each mix element does not represent a strategy. A strategy combines all the mix elements to create a unified effect on customers in the market.

There are numerous excellent examples of companies that have integrated all elements of the marketing mix into an effective strategy. Disney offers multiple products—amusement parks, MGM Studios, Epcot Center, Blizzard Beach, Discovery Island, and others. Each

CONNECTING WITH DIVERSITY

KRAFT FOODS: *SU COCINA ES NUESTRA COCINA*

 **Perhaps nothing seems as American as Kraft's Cheez Whiz, yet Kraft Foods USA has been extremely successful in putting its products into the pantries of Hispanic Americans—from Cubans in Miami to Puerto Ricans in New York to Mexicans in Los Angeles. Kraft has long marketed to different ethnic groups, but in 1992 the company realized it couldn't truly focus on the burgeoning Hispanic and African American markets unless it centralized all ethnic marketing activities in one department. Luis Nieto, Jr. headed the team that came up with the idea, and his mission can be summed up in three words: Know your consumer. Kraft uses two strategies to carry out this mission: It looks within the company, tapping its diverse employees for marketing direction, and it looks outside to capture up-to-the-minute data on the buying habits of ethnic consumers.**

"Diverse cultural input is especially important for food companies," says C. L. Reid, director of Kraft's diversity management. "Food is so closely tied to ethnicity and culture . . . Essentially, our Ethnic Marketing people solicit advertising and promotional ideas from blacks and Hispanics inside the company . . . and direct them to the brand groups, who implement them with the sales force, who in turn execute them in specific markets." One example is the company's annual presence at Calle Ocho in Miami's "Little Havana," billed as the biggest block party in the world. With the theme of *Su Cocina es Nuestra Cocina* ("Your Kitchen Is Our Kitchen"), Kraft sponsors on-site food preparation by one of Miami's premier Latino chefs, who cooks up savory items using Kraft ingredients. Kraft also sponsors "Kraft's Hispanic Night" in Chicago where Kraft representatives join members of the National Society for Hispanic MBAs for networking, music, food, and drinks.

Of the $15 million Kraft has invested in targeting over 4 million Hispanic households in the United States, most money goes to ongoing marketing programs. Some capitalize on what the company already knows about the Hispanic consumer. For instance, with data from Strategy Research Corporation, Kraft learned that Hispanics consume twice as many gelatin products as Caucasians and African Americans, so it markets Jell-O aggressively through television ads and samples at events. Other programs seek to introduce Hispanics to Kraft products that are not traditional in their culture, such as macaroni and cheese. Yet others introduce new products developed specifically for Hispanics, such as mango-flavored Tang.

With so much invested in these targeted marketing programs, it's crucial that the company be able to track the results. Until recently, there was a serious lack of data on Hispanic buying habits, but Kraft's Nieto came up with a remedy. The company pioneered with market researcher A. C. Nielsen to create a store scanner system. "What the Nielsen data does," says Nieto, "is give us essentially the same kind of information we have for the general market." For six key Hispanic markets, based on the Nielsen sample, "we're able to read store volume and share results for all our key categories in what we describe as a sample of key stores." The scanner system promises to push Kraft's ethnic marketing into what Nieto calls "the results-driven phase," yet he isn't content to stop there. Kraft is now gathering information on individual Hispanic households to help the company market to this target group more effectively.

Sources: "Opening Doors to Ethnic Category Management," *Progressive Grocer,* May 1996, pp. 124–125; Becky Ebenkamp and Gerry Khermouch, "Why Major Marketers Are Latin Lovers," *Brandweek,* August 5, 1996, pp. 20–24; C. L. Reid, "The Advantages of Taking a Proactive Approach to Diversity," *Executive Speeches,* October–November 1994, pp. 26–28; "Kraft's Hispanic Night," National Society for Hispanic MBAs, www.nshmbachi.org, Web site visited July 3, 2000; "Brand Loyalty," Latin-Pak, www.latinpak.com, Web site visited July 10, 2000.

McDonald's strategy is to provide high-quality, moderately priced food and friendly, fast service to families.

provides a high-quality experience, whether for vacations, weddings, or business meetings. And new products are constantly added, closely related to current consumer lifestyles. Disney carefully chooses theme park locations (place) that are easily accessible to consumers. It also makes information about its products readily available through Web sites and thousands of travel agents around the world. The variety of pricing options—deluxe, moderate, or economy—makes it easy for customers from all walks of life to purchase. And Disney takes care to promote its products to a variety of customers. Some are aimed directly at children, others at young singles, yet others at married couples whose children have left home. This communicates to consumers that Disney parks are for everyone. Clearly, the integrated strategy is paying off: Disney's earnings in 2000 reached $2.8 billion with sales of $25 billion.[31]

A plan is needed for each part of the company's marketing mix: product, place, promotion, and price. The plan for each element often is developed within specific functional areas of marketing, such as the pricing department. In some cases, all these plans are combined into one. Each marketing mix element will be covered in depth in future chapters, but a brief discussion of the issues is provided here. Figure 4.10 illustrates some of the questions marketers face when developing plans for each aspect of the marketing mix. There are many, many more, some of which will be covered in later chapters.

Each plan for an element of the marketing mix deals with both strategies and tactics. For example, the decision to enter a new product area or distribution channel is strategic. Changes to an existing product or the addition of a new retailer in distribution are tactical. Tactics are used to achieve strategies. Strategies are long term and broad in scope; **tactics** are short-term, well-defined actions suited to specific market conditions. Strategies describe how we will compete to serve customers, whereas tactics describe who will do what and when. Duane Larson, president of Children's World Learning Centers, says: "Selling a product or service today is like a war, even in the child care arena. Those armies with the best tactical plan will win more frequently than those without one. Lose enough battles and you won't have to wait for your competitors to put you out of business because the buying public will have already done that."[32]

Companies usually employ several tactics to accomplish a given strategy. McDonald's strategy is to provide high-quality, moderately priced food and friendly, fast service to families. One tactic is to have a miniplayground at some of its restaurants. Another is colorful packaging of children's meals and personal appearances by the popular Ronald McDonald clown. Subway, which targets a more adult audience, pursues a strategy of preparing customized sandwiches quickly. Its assembly-line tactic allows patrons to build their own sandwiches. Subway has also begun focusing on providing healthy alternatives to other fast-food restaurants.[33] Another tactic is to preassemble the meat element of the sandwich, leaving only the toppings to be added, which speeds the process but maintains patron selection. It would be tactically inconsistent for McDonald's to add gourmet items to its menu or for Subway to offer complicated full-course meals.

TACTICS

Short-term actions and reactions to specific market conditions through which companies pursue their strategy.

Marketing Mix Element	Types of Decisions
Product/Service	What new products/services should we introduce? Which ones should we drop? What are our objectives with each product or service? Are any new technologies available to improve our product/service? What type of service do our customers expect or desire? What policies should we implement in terms of product returns, spare parts, or repairs?
Place	Where do our customers shop? Should our product/service be available at all these places or just a few? Should we sell directly to our customers or through middlemen, such as retailers, wholesalers, or dealers? How should we ship the product—by rail, truck, air, ship, or others? How should we handle customer complaints?
Promotion	What are our promotion objectives? Are we trying to create awareness, encourage purchases, or others? What medium should we use: television or radio advertising, coupons, free trials, personal selling, public relations campaign, or a combination of these?
Price	What type of message do we want to send out? What is our overall pricing philosophy? Do we want to exceed, meet, or underprice our competitors? Is our price consistent with the amount of value we deliver to our customers? Should we change our prices? How will this affect demand for our product or service? Do our prices allow the organization to make a profit and invest in improved performance?

FIGURE 4.10 *Examples of Marketing Mix Decisions*

PRODUCT PLANS

A company may sell physical goods (such as automobiles or textbooks) or intangible services (a college education, legal counsel, or health care). Many companies sell both. In the business world, the word *product* has come to mean services as well as physical goods, and when marketers refer to product decisions, they are also referring to services. Unless specified otherwise, we shall use *product* to mean either goods or services. A **product** is any physical object, service, idea, person, event, place, or organization offered to satisfy consumers' needs and wants.

Product decisions are critical for most companies and they are among the most difficult to make. Marketers must help determine which products or product lines to develop and which ones to drop. A **product line** consists of several closely related products marketed by an organization. For example, Nabisco offers many different types of snack foods, including Oreos, Fig Newtons, Chips Ahoy!, and Ritz crackers; each of these is a separate product line. Items are constantly being added, such as Nabisco's Ritz Bitz crackers, a product designed to fulfill customer demand for a smaller snack.

Marketers must take consumers into account when making product decisions. Ford ran into problems when it erroneously claimed that its 2000 SVT Mustang Cobra convertibles and coupes could produce a whopping 320 horsepower. After the company was flooded with customer complaints that in fact the vehicle could not, Ford canceled production of all 2000 SVT Mustang Cobras and implemented plans for a major redesign of all Mustangs for the 2004 model year.[34] Wise Foods, Inc. improved the appeal of its potato chip brands after a thorough review of customer suggestions and complaints. Most centered around poor packaging and

PRODUCT

Any physical object, service, idea, person, event, place, or organization offered to satisfy consumer needs and wants.

PRODUCT LINE

Closely related products marketed by the organization.

*The Rock and Bill Gates are
pictured here at the debut of
the Microsoft Xbox, a console
game player that has its own
individual hard drive.*

bland flavors. Today, Wise has reduced complaints by 32 percent, increasing sales while improving the overall appeal of its products.[35]

Technological product plans challenge marketers to continuously monitor, assess, and make decisions based on the ever-changing technological environment (and other factors). Technological products are developed, introduced, and dropped rapidly. This requires marketers to make frequent and sometimes difficult product decisions. In the $7 billion console game industry, the leading companies have changed often, from Atari and Coleco to Sega and Nintendo. Both Nintendo and Microsoft—a new console game player—announced new game versions to appear in 2001/2002. The Microsoft Xbox will be one of the first to debut with its own individual hard drive. "It is possible to leapfrog the competition in the video game market," said one analyst. "Sony was the last one to do it. But when they came out with the Playstation, they were considered a long-shot. They were coming from the stereo business, but now they are the ones to beat."[36]

PLACE PLANS

Physical distribution is the movement of finished products through channels of distribution to customers. It involves getting the right product, in the right condition, to the right customer, at the right time, for the minimum cost. This is one of the fastest growing and most important areas of marketing. U.S. companies spend more than $800 billion annually on logistics, and that amount is expected to grow.[37]

Physical distribution decisions can greatly affect the profitability of the company. For example, excess inventory in the channel increases storage costs. It is marketing's job to help ensure that an optimal amount of inventory moves through the channel. Of course, some companies are more successful at this than others. Best Buy does an excellent job of inventory control through its "Tailored Logistics Initiative." This program holds products at a distribution center until they are needed at a specific store location, reducing pipeline time and increasing on-time compliance to 60 percent. Best Buy is not satisfied with these improvements, however, and is in the process of selecting a transportation management software system to further improve its supply chain.[38]

Distribution channels are the set of independent organizations involved in making the product available for purchase. A channel describes the route a product follows as it moves from manufacturer to consumers. First, marketers must determine where target customers shop: malls, shopping centers, downtown areas, discount outlets, drive-throughs, or at home via mail or telephone. People also shop in many different types of stores: supermarkets, merchandise marts, hyperstores, specialty shops, and outdoor markets. In each area of the world, consumer shopping patterns are unique. Parisians buy bread baked daily at small shops located throughout the city. The Japanese prefer to purchase fresh fish, caught within hours of eating, from small neighborhood retailers. Suburban Americans usually shop once a week and freeze many items for use days or even weeks later. They like one-stop supermarkets and are

**CONNECTED:
SURFING THE NET**

Xbox
www.msbox.com

**Here's your chance to find
out how Microsoft plans to
leapfrog the competition in
the video game market. Visit
the Microsoft Xbox Web site.**

PHYSICAL DISTRIBUTION
The movement of finished products through channels of distribution to customers.

DISTRIBUTION CHANNEL
A set of independent organizations involved in making the product available for purchase.

willing to drive to them. Obviously, it's important for marketers to know where consumers prefer to shop for the types of products or services that their company makes.

PROMOTION PLANS

The third element of the marketing mix, promotion, provides information about a company's product or service in an effort to encourage purchase. Media advertising, direct mail, coupons and samples, personal selling, or public relations may be used. Many companies employ several forms simultaneously. Broadway shows, once only promoted in theater directories, use several forms of promotion today. Marketing a Broadway show has taken on a new importance. Today ads appear on water towers and subways, while many consumers are reached by direct mail. Jeffrey Seller, a producer of the Broadway show *Rent,* says, "You have to get the word into the consciousness of many different people and that involves many different outlets, like magazines, radio, outdoor, print, publicity." *Rent* used a unique promotional strategy. A major subway advertising campaign was designed to reach teenagers and consumers in their twenties. This market was considered the "non-Broadway-going public." Print ads explained the show's story line and how to purchase tickets. Radio spots were also used on the integrated marketing mix plan to reach consumers.[39] Sometimes other products are marketed in conjunction with Broadway shoes. New World Coffee stores, for instance, introduced a Triple Berry Darkness frozen drink, which is sold as a tie-in to the show *Jekyll and Hyde*.[40]

PRICING PLANS

When Reebok aerobic shoes were first introduced into the women's market segment, demand was disappointing. The product was priced incorrectly, in this case too low. When prices were raised, demand increased. Prices send strong signals to buyers. Consumers equate low price with poor quality, whereas higher prices signal unique and positive characteristics as well as higher quality. Raising price to increase demand is not unusual. Porsche did it in the United States. Ralph Lauren found it worked with men's and women's clothing. The perfume industry has used this technique since its inception.

In other cases, price increases can be devastating to sales volume. Think about the airline industry, with many different providers offering service between the same cities. What do you think would happen to ticket sales at United Airlines if it raised its prices above those of Delta or Northwest? Demand for travel on United Airlines would probably start dropping. That's why a price shift in one airline triggers shifts in most others.

THE MARKETING CONTROL PROCESS

CONTROL PROCESS

Procedures designed to provide feedback on how well the marketing strategy is working.

CONTROL REVIEW MEETING

Meeting of members of the planning team to see whether objectives are being met.

Once a strategic marketing plan is implemented, results seldom occur precisely as expected. The **control process** provides feedback on how well the strategy is working. In a typical **control review meeting,** members of the planning team assemble to see whether objectives are being met. As described in Figure 4.11, the team reviews the original objectives, including sales volume projections, order quantities, customer loyalty rates, customer satisfaction rates, and market share projections. These numbers for each target market segment and in total are compared to actual results. This procedure is often called metrics, which connotes metering what actually happened. This process gives a picture of what has occurred.

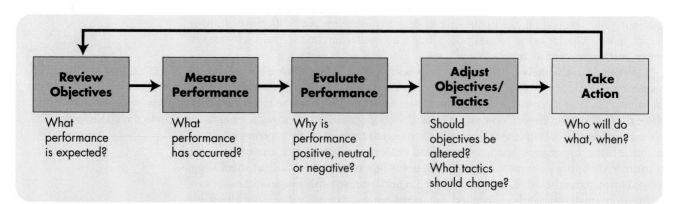

FIGURE 4.11 *The Marketing Control Process: Assessing the Strategic Marketing Plan*

By comparing actual results to the stated objectives, the team can assess the organization's performance. During these reviews, trends can be spotted. For example, sales and market share may be higher than expected because competitors were late in launching a new product, or sales may be low because the company's price was too high in relation to competitors. If it's not apparent what caused the results, additional marketing research may be needed.

Next, the team may decide to adjust objectives or plans. If results are strong, then objectives may be elevated. If not, objectives can be lowered, but the team usually resists this step because it can be viewed as a sign of weakness.[41] Adjustments to the plans usually are tactical rather than strategical, done through changes in the marketing mix elements. If a change in overall strategy is required, then a more involved and lengthy process starts. Sometimes teams go back to ground zero and start fresh. In either case, time is critical. One executive says that adjusting plans and taking action can be "like changing a flat tire on a moving automobile." It happens rapidly in companies that are flexible, efficient, and competitive.

CONNECTING GLOBALLY: ENTERING WORLD MARKETS

Once the domain of a few corporate giants, global marketing is fast becoming a requirement for most companies. Why? First, world markets offer tremendous opportunities. Many foreign market segments are larger and growing more rapidly than segments in the United States. Second, like it or not, U.S. business is no longer safe from global competitors. In comparison with other countries, the United States has few restrictions on foreign entry. Most U.S. companies must deal with some form of global competition, even within local markets. Third, a company intent on becoming an industry leader must operate globally or be placed at a severe competitive disadvantage.

GEOGRAPHIC SCOPE

World trade has skyrocketed in recent years. U.S. exports exceeded $773 billion in 2000. The United States also imports a large amount of foreign goods and services—over $1,222 billion in 1999.[42] From a planning standpoint, marketers must identify the **geographic scope** of the strategy, which is the extent of a company's international activities. Generally, geographic scope is divided into four categories, as outlined in Figure 4.12.

GEOGRAPHIC SCOPE
The extent of a company's international activities.

International Scope When a company conducts business in one or a very few foreign countries, it has an international scope. Generally, international companies treat foreign business as a supplement to their domestic operations rather than as a strategic necessity. Yet expansion in even one country can provide useful experience for further global activity at a later date. For example, Forestry Systems, Inc., of Greensboro, North Carolina, began international operations by selling its handheld computer inventory systems to lumber and logging companies in Canada and Mexico and is now considering additional markets in South America.[43]

Regional Scope Operations in several adjacent countries give a company regional scope. In essence, regional companies are competing within one large market that crosses national borders and generally only in one area of the world. Regional operations tend to be efficient because the markets are close together. The benefits of large market size can be combined with localized production and distribution to provide a viable strategy. This is the approach of Starbucks Corporation, the specialty coffee chain, as it expands outside the United States. The company

International	Operating in one or a few foreign markets
Regional	Operating within countries in close proximity, such as North America, Europe, Scandinavia, or the Pacific Rim
Multinational	Heavy involvement in a few countries located in various regions such as Italy, South Africa, and Japan
Global	Operating in nearly all world markets

FIGURE 4.12 *Geographic Scope*

opened its first Pacific Rim outlet in Tokyo and from there expanded into other regional parts of the Asian-Pacific region, including Singapore, Hong Kong, Taiwan, and Indonesia. According to Kathie Lindemann, director of international operations for Starbucks, "Asia . . . is full of emerging markets; consumers' disposable income is increasing as their countries' economies grow." In 2000, Starbucks opened its largest shop in Seoul, South Korea, with a 200-seat capacity.[44]

Multinational Scope   When companies operate in several countries around the world, their scope is multinational. The markets are not concentrated in one region. For example, Westinghouse sells satellite telephones to Mexico and Australia; nuclear power plants to the Czech Republic, Spain, and Taiwan; and defense-related equipment within North America. It markets many other products to many other countries as well. Multinational companies carefully pick their target areas and choose not to enter many countries. They tend to operate differently within each area of the world. For example, Excite@Home began with operations only in the United States. It slowly began expanding to various countries overseas and plans to receive $80 million in revenues by the end of 2000 from foreign countries. That's a 300 percent increase in only one year![45]

Global Scope   Operations in nearly all countries around the world constitute a global scope. Kenichi Ohmae, global consultant for McKinsey & Company, describes global scope with the mental image of hovering like a satellite over the earth.[46] Global businesses develop totally integrated strategies that maximize competitiveness worldwide over the long term. The Quaker Oats Company has committed to this type of integrated global strategy. Its Quaker International Branding Program is designed to ensure that the Quaker name means "healthy," no matter where you live. The company has a basic advertising, packaging, and promotion plan that is tailored to meet local conditions. This helps keep the Quaker image consistent around the globe. The approach seems to be working, as Quaker's global business outside the United States generated revenues of $4.725 billion in 1999.[47]

A global market reaches nearly all countries. Differences among market areas are recognized, but so are similarities, so that similar segments of buyers within the various regions can be targeted. This helps marketers achieve vast economies of scale, especially in advertising, packaging, and distribution. Consider Gillette, which claims 1 billion people each day use a Gillette product worldwide. The company has always had a worldwide focus. In 1926, King C. Gillette said of the company's safety razor that "There is no other article for individual use so universally known and widely distributed. In my travels, I have found it in the most northern town in Norway and in the heart of the Sahara Desert." However, today, travelers can find Gillette products in far greater places than the founder ever imagined. In 2000, the company led the market in wet shaving tools for men and women, taking approximately 20 percent of the $10 billion global grooming market.[48]

Global marketing is based on the notion that consumers around the world are growing more alike and that modern technology has created a degree of commonality. Travel and communication have exposed more and more people to the same types of goods and services. Global companies appreciate the differences in consumer preferences, shopping behavior, cultural institutions, and promotional media, but they believe that these preferences and practices can and will become more similar.[49]

STRATEGIES FOR FOREIGN MARKET ENTRY

There are several different approaches for entering and developing markets. Small companies may use only one or two methods, whereas larger companies may use several simultaneously. Figure 4.13 outlines the most important approaches.

Exporting and Importing   Exporting and importing are the least risky and most common forms of international marketing. **Exporting** sends domestically manufactured products into foreign countries for resale. **Importing** brings products from foreign countries for resale within the home market, usually as part of another product. Exporting and importing are relatively easy ways to enter foreign trade because the investment is lower than for most other methods. In addition, most governments offer support and expertise to help domestic companies with these activities.

Because foreign trade can involve many complicated details, most firms use **export and import intermediaries,** which are firms with specialized expertise in exporting or importing. There are two types. **Indirect export intermediaries** are located in the domestic market and help send products abroad. They specialize in knowledge about foreign customs, regulations affecting businesses and products, laws, and market conditions. **Direct export intermediaries**

Export—Import	Send products abroad for resale (exporting) or purchase products from foreign companies for resale, usually as part of another product, within the home market (import)
Foreign Licensing and Franchising	Agreements that permit foreign companies to produce and distribute merchandise, often using trademarks and/or selected merchandising and customer delivery approaches
Overseas Marketing and Manufacturing	A marketing infrastructure and/or manufacturing facilities abroad
Joint Ventures and Strategic Alliances	The shared ownership of operations by two or more local and foreign companies (joint venture) or the pooling of resources by two or more companies for the purpose of competing as one entity (strategic alliance)

FIGURE 4.13 *Approaches for Entering and Building Foreign Markets*

are located in the foreign market. Since they are very familiar with the local business environment, they can help clients in special ways, such as offering unique government contacts. Intermediaries can be very beneficial because they assume many of the risks involved with distribution. At the same time, the exporting company must give up a significant amount of control over how its product is distributed.

Trading companies are large intermediaries that facilitate the movement of goods in and out of countries. For example, ESIntertrade is an international trading company that facilitates the sale of goods to and from a variety of regions, such as coffee from Vietnam and tomato paste and tires from other areas.[50]

Foreign Licensing and Franchising   **Foreign licensing** assigns the rights to a patent, trademark, or manufacturing process to a foreign company for a fee, often called a royalty. Licensing allows companies to gain entry into a foreign market at almost no cost or risk, but control of the marketing strategy is turned over to the licensee. **Franchising** is a special type of licensing arrangement whereby the marketer provides not only the product, technology, process, and/or trademark but also most of the marketing program. In nearly any major city around the world, you are likely to find McDonald's, Burger King, and Kentucky Fried Chicken, or Holiday Inn, Hilton, and Marriott. They are there because local entrepreneurs have bought the franchise. Franchising allows companies to maintain marketing control while passing along many of the costs, risks, and responsibilities to the foreign licensees. These often function quite autonomously from the parent company but benefit from being part of a large corporation.

Overseas Marketing and Production   Also called subsidiaries, overseas marketing and production operations are owned by a parent company in foreign countries, whether a small sales office or something more elaborate. A subsidiary operation may simply assemble finished goods or may function as an independent business, responsible for product development, manufacturing, marketing, and so on. For example, General Motors operates assembly plants for automotive components in Mexico, while its German and British subsidiaries produce entire automobiles. Subsidiaries can be very costly to establish and very risky to operate, since the owner is liable for any mishaps. Foreign operations also are subject to a host of circumstances beyond the company's control. For example, several oil companies lost billions of dollars when their Iranian subsidiaries were closed after invasion of Kuwait. The major advantage of a subsidiary is that the parent company retains control and can carry out its own strategy.

Foreign Strategic Alliances   Strategic alliances involve partnering. A **joint venture** occurs when two companies combine resources for a new venture. They are formed to provide products and services more competitively than a single organization could do independently. Typically, a foreign joint venture has one company in each of two countries, but more partners or countries are possible. National laws often require any business to have a certain percentage of domestic ownership. Sony develops many of its innovative computer and communications products through strategic alliances and ventures with companies in the United States.[51] When the Soviet bloc dissolved, joint ventures were formed rapidly as foreign firms attempted to gain

TRADING COMPANIES
Large intermediaries that facilitate the movement of goods in and out of countries.

FOREIGN LICENSING
Assigning the rights to a patent, trademark, or manufacturing process to a foreign company for a fee, often called a royalty.

FRANCHISING
A special type of licensing arrangement whereby the marketer provides not only the product, technology, process, and/or trademark but also the entire marketing program.

JOINT VENTURE
An alliance of two companies that combine resources to provide products and services more competitively than either could do independently.

access to these markets. Often, the first strategy was to buy ownership, which Volkswagen did in the Czech Republic. The Germans beat out other contenders, such as Renault of France, and acquired 31 percent of the Czech auto leader Skoda. Together, Volkswagen and Skoda planned to produce nearly 400,000 autos in 2000, up from 385,330 in 1999.[52]

Global strategic alliances are joint ventures that involve actions taken internationally by two or more companies contributing an agreed amount of resources. The arrangement often resembles a well-funded start-up operation. This approach may be preferred when competition is tough or technology and capital requirements are relatively large for one partner. General Motors has global alliances with Suzuki, Isuzu, and Fiat. Ford has allied with Volkswagon and Nissan, Daimler-Chrysler with Mitsubishi and Honda.[53] General Mills created an alliance with Nestlé in Europe, called Cereal Partners Worldwide (CPW), to compete against Kellogg's growing global share. General Mills and Nestlé agreed to pool part of their product lines and distribution system.

A global strategic alliance may be formed between or among companies that compete in some regions of the world but decide to cooperate in others. Toshiba, for example, has allied with a number of firms in the United States (United Technologies, Apple Computer, Sun Microsystems, Motorola, and National Semiconductor) as well as a number of firms in Europe (Olivetti, Seimens, Rhore-Poulenc Ericcson, and SGS Thomson). Recently, it allied with Integrated Business Solutions, a subsidiary of Lockheed Martin, to provide e-business solutions and data center resources in Japan and the United States.[54] Notice that many of these are rivals in various markets, but each works with Toshiba.

Whether its scope of operations is global or local, the company needs in-depth knowledge of its targeted markets in order to shape the strategic plan and meet its goals. In the next chapter we will look at the important role of marketing research in providing needed information for planning and other marketing decisions.

CONNECTED: SURFING THE NET

Kodak
www.kodak.com

This chapter's technology feature discussed **Kodak's strategic reinvention.** Here is an opportunity for you to learn more about Kodak. Visit its Web site and answer the following questions.

1. In Kodak's annual report you will find the company vision, mission, and values. List them. Discuss several ways Kodak has fulfilled its vision, mission, and values using the Web site as your resource.
2. List Kodak's strategic business units. How are its business units structured? Explain.
3. After exploring Kodak's Web site, products, and services, determine what you think its core competencies are. Explain your choices.
4. Under the "History of Kodak" menu, select and read "Kodak . . . The Company." Which strategy did Kodak use at the firm's beginning, low cost or differentiation? Does it use this same strategy now? Explain.

Kraft Foods
www.kraftfoods.com

Kraft Foods has been very successful at knowing its customers and developing products to meet the needs of various target markets. In order to expand your thinking about Kraft Foods, visit its Web site and answer the following questions.

1. What market does Kraft appear to be targeting with its Web site? What features does the site offer that may be of particular interest to this segment? How might these features help Kraft build relationships with customers?
2. The Kraft strategy is to provide "good food for busy lives." What are some of the tactics Kraft has implemented recently to accomplish this strategy?
3. Peek inside Kraft's virtual refrigerator and pantry, which you'll find loaded with products. Using the Boston Consulting Group growth-share matrix, select a product that is appropriate for each of the four categories—star, question mark, cash cow, and dog.

OBJECTIVE 1: Understand how the strategic marketing planning hierarchy fits together to provide a complete planning system.

Strategic marketing proceeds from a company's vision, to the strategic marketing plan, to the marketing mix plans. The vision describes what the organization is trying to accomplish in the broadest sense. It includes the organization's marketing philosophy. The strategic marketing plan is developed in line with the vision by a cross-functional team representing several business areas, such as manufacturing, accounting, finance, and engineering. The plan describes the company's goals and states how the company will achieve them. Specialists in each component of the marketing mix prepare a plan for that area.

OBJECTIVE 2: Describe the four elements of an organization's vision that provide guidance for all actions.

The vision statement expresses the company's core values, business definition, strategic direction, and strategic infrastructure. Core values reflect the company's beliefs about the types of behavior acceptable from employees and the company as a whole as well as its relationship to employees, customers, and society in general. A business definition describes the contributions a company seeks to make to customers and society. It is important to avoid marketing myopia when developing a mission statement. Marketing myopia occurs when executives focus on the company's goods and services rather than on the benefits these goods and services provide to consumers. Strategic direction is the desired leadership position of an organization as well as the measures used to chart progress toward reaching that goal. It captures the "essence of winning" and addresses the competitiveness of the organization. A company's strategic infrastructure consists of both strategic business units and core competencies. SBUs can be managed using portfolio planning tools, such as the growth-share matrix or the attractiveness-strength matrix. Core competencies are the unique resources a company develops and employs to create superior customer value. They are the fundamental building blocks of competitive advantage and can be developed in one or more of the following areas: base technologies, process technologies, product technologies, people systems, or information systems.

OBJECTIVE 3: Integrate components of the strategic marketing plan with the vision.

The strategic marketing plan describes how to accomplish the vision for a particular part of the business. It has five components: objectives, situation analysis, target marketing, positioning, and integration of the marketing mix. Objectives are developed in line with the vision and the situation analysis. They state aims regarding profit, market share, and total sales as well as customer satisfaction and loyalty. The situation analysis describes the marketing environment for the period that the plan is in effect. It gives all the information required to estimate possible business scenarios, including market size, customer characteristics, competitors, and technology. A key part of the situation analysis is to examine strengths, weaknesses, opportunities, and threats (SWOT). The target marketing phase of strategic marketing planning focuses the organization on select groups of customers. In the positioning phase, the image of the organization relative to the competition is developed. The final step is to integrate the marketing mix plans to accomplish the overall strategy. It is important to look at the total effect of the marketing mix, rather than a single element, on the market.

OBJECTIVE 4: Understand why elements of the marketing mix must be integrated and outline the steps of the marketing control process.

Plans for each part of the marketing mix are usually developed by specialists in the respective areas. Often a separate plan is created for product, place, promotion, and price, but sometimes these plans are combined. Plans for any of these elements are both strategic and tactical. Strategies are long term and broad in scope, whereas tactics are short-term actions suited to specific market conditions. Several tactics may be used to carry out a single strategy.

To determine whether the strategic marketing plan is accomplishing the intended objectives, a marketing control process is needed. It has five steps. First, the original performance objectives are reviewed. Second, measures indicate what performance has occurred. Third, performance is evaluated by interpreting the results obtained and looking for any trends. Fourth, it is decided whether actions or objectives should be altered. Fifth, the strategy proceeds as planned or another course is developed and implemented.

OBJECTIVE 5: Identify the four major ways that organizations enter and cultivate global markets.

Organizations enter and cultivate global markets through exporting and importing, foreign licensing and franchising, overseas marketing and manufacturing, and joint ventures and strategic alliances. Exporting involves sending domestically manufactured products into foreign markets. It is usually the low-risk and low-cost way to enter markets. There are many forms of help for companies just getting started in exporting or importing. Foreign licensing and franchising simply assign the rights to a patent, trademark, or process to a foreign company. Overseas marketing and production involve setting up operations in a foreign country. This requires the commitment of direct investment in a foreign country. Strategic alliances and joint ventures involve sharing resources with a partner to enter markets. Often the partner has strong contacts in the country or region where the venture takes place. Joint ventures can simply involve contracts between companies or shared ownership of new organizations. In some cases these can involve huge investments and substantial risks.

1. What are the elements of the marketing planning hierarchy?
2. What are the components of a vision?
3. What is marketing myopia? How is the company's mission related to myopia?
4. In what ways can strategic business units be structured?
5. What are portfolio planning tools and how are they used?
6. What are core competencies? Give examples of five types.
7. Which people in an organization create the strategic marketing plan?
8. What is the difference between a strategy and a tactic? How do they work together?
9. What are the components of the strategic marketing plan? Describe each.
10. What are the elements of a SWOT analysis?
11. How are marketing mix plans strategic and tactical?
12. What is the marketing control process, and what are its steps?
13. In what four ways can foreign markets be entered? Describe each.

1. Define strategy. Define tactics. How is strategy related to tactics? What strategy do you think Coca-Cola is following? What tactics is it using to support this strategy?
2. How are a company's core values, business definition, strategic infrastructure, and strategic direction interrelated? Do you think it is important for a company to develop an explicit statement about each of these?
3. Imagine that the following companies describe their business as shown: (a) Black & Decker: drills and sanders; (b) Sherwin-Williams: paint; (c) Schwinn: bicycles; (d) U.S. Post Office: mail delivery. Do you think these companies are suffering from marketing myopia? How may they better define their business?
4. Why is it important for a company to have a well-defined strategic direction? In your opinion, what may happen to a company that lacks strategic direction?
5. How would you assess the contribution made by each strategic business unit? Do you think it is important for technology to be shared among SBUs? Why or why not?
6. Who should be involved in the development of a strategic marketing plan? Why?
7. What is the purpose of a situation analysis? What type of information should be included?
8. Why do most companies engage in some type of target marketing? Whom do you think Nintendo is targeting with its Game Boy product line?

Business definition: Describes the contributions the business makes to customers and society; also called the company mission.

Control process: Procedures designed to provide feedback on how well the marketing strategy is working.

Control review meeting: Meeting of members of the planning team to see whether objectives are being met.

Core competencies: The unique resources a company develops and employs to create superior customer value; the fundamental building blocks of competitive advantage.

Core values: A set of statements describing the type of behavior expected of the company and its employees.

Cross-functional planning team: Employees from several areas responsible for developing the company's strategic marketing plan.

Differentiation strategy: Strategy based on delivering customer value in a way that clearly distinguishes the product from competitors; works through effectiveness.

Direct export intermediary: A firm located in a foreign market which specializes in knowledge about foreign customs, regulations affecting businesses and products, laws, and market conditions.

Distribution channel: A set of independent organizations involved in making the product available for purchase.

Exporting: Sending products to a foreign country for sale.

Export intermediary: Domestic or foreign firm that assists with exporting activity.

Foreign licensing: Assigning the rights to a patent, trademark, or manufacturing process to a foreign company for a fee, often called a royalty.

Franchising: A special type of licensing arrangement whereby the marketer provides not only the product, technology, process, and/or trademark but also the entire marketing program.

Geographic scope: The extent of a company's international activities.

Importing: Receiving products from a foreign country.

Import intermediary: Firm set up to help guide importing actions.

Indirect export intermediary: Firm located in a domestic market which specializes in knowledge about foreign customs, regulations affecting businesses and products, laws, and market conditions.

Joint venture: An alliance of two companies that combine resources to provide products and services more competitively than either could do independently.

Low-cost strategy: Strategy whose objective is to be the low-cost leader, thereby allowing the company to have higher margins than competitors and pass some savings on to customers through lower prices; works through efficiency.

Marketing myopia: A focus on company products rather than on how these products benefit consumers.

Physical distribution: The movement of finished products through channels of distribution to customers.

Portfolio planning tools: Tools that measure the contribution each SBU makes to the overall performance of the company.

Positioning: Creating an image or perception in the minds of consumers about the organization or its products relative to the competition.

Product: Any physical object, service, idea, person, event, place, or organization offered to satisfy consumer needs and wants.

Product line: Closely related products marketed by the organization.

Strategic business unit (SBU): A part of the firm that can be managed separately for marketing purposes; it may be a division, a product or product line, a distinct group of customers, or a unique technology.

Strategic direction: The desired leadership position of an organization as well as the measures used to chart progress toward reaching that position.

Strategic infrastructure: The corporate configuration that produces the company's distinctive or core competencies and provides the resources necessary to satisfy customer wants.

Strategic marketing plan: The document describing the company's objectives and how to achieve them in light of competitive activities.

Strategic window: The time during which market needs and the competencies of the firm fit together to create a significant opportunity.

Strategy: The development and/or deployment of resources with the intent of accomplishing goals and objectives in a competitive arena.

Sustainable competitive advantage: The cost position or superior value in a product that competitors cannot easily duplicate or surpass.

SWOT analysis: An analysis of strengths, weaknesses, opportunities, and threats to determine how well the company's skills and resources match the predicted market opportunities.

Tactics: Short-term actions and reactions to specific market conditions through which companies pursue their strategy.

Target marketing: The process of selecting which market segments the organization will emphasize in attempts to satisfy customers better than its competitors.

Trading companies: Large intermediaries that facilitate the movement of goods in and out of countries.

Vision: The desired image of the company in the minds of employees.

REFERENCES

1. "The Walt Disney Company 2000 Annual Report," Disney.com Web site visited on March 1, 2001. The Disney Store recruiting brochure, 1996; Kate Fitzgerald, "License to Sell," *Advertising Age*, February 12, 1996, pp. S1, S40; Matthew S. Scott, "Wonderful World at Disney," *Black Enterprise*, December 1995, pp. 58–64; Rachel Parker, "Disney Finds Upgraded Database System More Agreeable," *Inforworld*, November 13, 1995, p. 94; Patricia A. Scussel, "Disney Tunes Up Catalog Unit," *Catalog Age*, October 1995, p. 6; Wendy Marx, "The Co-Marketing Revolution," *Industry Week*, October 2, 1995, pp. 77–81; George Pitcher, "Disney's Road to Damascus," *Marketing Week*, August 11, 1995, p. 25; Meg Carter, "Disney Shows Its Networking Skills," *Marketing Week*, August 11, 1995, pp. 16–17; and Bill Kelley, "Destination Disney," *Sales and Marketing Management*, July 1995, p. 40.
2. Randall L. Tobias, "Communicating Core Values," *Public Relations Strategist*, Spring 1996, p. 19.
3. www.jnj.com/whoisjnj/crusa.html, Web site visited September 18, 2000.
4. Michael Waldholz and Dennis Kneale, "Tylenol's Maker Tries to Regain Good Image in Wake of Tragedy," *Wall Street Journal*, October 8, 1982; "Johnson & Johnson to Scrap All Capsules in Its Effort to Save the Brand Name," *Wall Street Journal*, October 8, 1982; "It Could Have Been Anyone," *Wall Street Journal*, October 8, 1982; Michael Waldholz, "Johnson & Johnson Officials Take Steps to End More Killings Linked to Tylenol," *Wall Street Journal*, October 4, 1982, p. 16; "Johnson & Johnson Pulls Tylenol Lot from Market in Wake of Five Cyanide Deaths," *Wall Street Journal*, October 1, 1982; "Authorities Say Cyanide-Laced Tylenol Likely Was Planted at Individual Stores," *Wall Street Journal*, October 4, 1982, p. 3; Michael Waldholz, "Johnson & Johnson Can Weather Tylenol Storm—If It Hurries," *Wall Street Journal*, October 5, 1982, p. 22; "Tylenol Containing Strychnine Is Found in California as Consumer Fears Mount," *Wall Street Journal*, October 6, 1982, p. 2; "J&J Tries Ads to Revive Sales of Tylenol," *Wall Street Journal*, October 25, 1982, p. 20; Michael Waldholz, "Drop in Johnson & Johnson Shares Is Linked to Belief That Fears Over Tylenol Will Linger," *Wall Street Journal*, October 29, 1982; Michael Waldholz, "Tylenol Maker Mounting Campaign to Restore Trust of Doctors, Buyers," *Wall Street Journal*, November 12, 1982, p. 33; Michael Waldholz, "Johnson & Johnson Plans to Reintroduce Tylenol Capsules in More Secure Package," *Wall Street Journal*, November 12, 1982, p. 4; and Michael Waldholz, "Tylenol Regains Most of No. 1 Market Share, Amazing Doomsayers," *Wall Street Journal*, December 24, 1982, p. 1.
5. www.merck.com/overview/philosophy.html, Web site visited on September 18, 2000.
6. www.childrensworld.com/about, Web site visited September 18, 2000.
7. www.lilly.com, Web site visited June 6, 2000.
8. "Strategic Intent," *Harvard Business Review*, May–June 1989, p. 64.
9. www.lilly.com visited May 23, 2001.
10. "A Browser Your Mother Could Love," *Boston Globe*, September 14, 2000, p. C-4.
11. www.upslogistics.com, Web site visited September 18, 2000.
12. "SkyCat Transport Carrier to Compete for Airbus Contract," *Financial Times London*, June 30, 2000.
13. "McMakeover," *Advertising Age*, August 17, 2000.
14. www.aramark.com/newsroom/pressreleases/sydney2k.html, Web site visited August 20, 2000.
15. www.wearguard.com, Web site visited September 18, 2000.
16. "In MP3, It's the Rio Thing," *Advertising Age*, November 1, 1999, p. 42.
17. "Nokia Fumbles, But Don't Count It Out," *Fortune*, February 19, 1996, p. 86.
18. "Building Business by Therapeutic Category," *Pharmaceutical Executive*, August 2000.
19. Recruiting brochure for the Disney Store.
20. Ibid.
21. "Clash of the Consultants," *Business Week*, June 18, 2000.
22. "The Core Competence of the Corporation," *Harvard Business Review*, May/June 1990, p. 81.
23. "The Changing Role of Marketing in the Corporation," *Journal of Marketing*, October 1992, p. 14.
24. Derek F. Abell, "Strategic Windows," *Journal of Marketing*, July 1978, p. 21.
25. "Light Signals Direct," *MIT's Technology Review*, August 1, 2000.
26. Based on Michael Porter, *Competitive Advantage: Creating and Sustaining Superior Performance* (New York: The Free Press, 1985).
27. "Ghirardelli Soars Beyond San Francisco," *Candy Industry*, April 2000.
28. "Ford to Make 7,000 'Sony Focus' Cars," *Dow Jones Business News*, January 6, 2000.
29. "Ford Division Leads in Sales to Hispanic Consumers," *PR Newswire*, July 3, 2000.
30. "Industry Nervous About SUV Sales; No Decline Yet," *The Detroit News*, September 13, 2000.
31. CNN the Financial Network, www.cnnfri.cnn.com, "Disney Beats the Street," visited November 9, 2000.
32. Personal interview with Duane Larson, 1995.
33. www.subway.com, Web site visited March 1, 2000.
34. "Ford's Biggest Job: Lift Lincoln," *Automotive News*, July 31, 2000.
35. "Wise Moves," *Snack Food & Wholesale Bakery*, March 2000.
36. "Computing Column," *Houston Chronicle*, August 18, 2000.
37. "What's the Holdup?" *CIO*, January 15, 2000.
38. Mary Aichlmayr and Mike Freeze, "The Quest for Excellence Never Ends," *Transportation and Distribution*, May 2000.
39. Pamela Ellis-Simmons, "Broadway Means Business," Special Advertising Section, *Fortune*, June 9, 1997, pp. 49–56.
40. "New World Coffee Tie-In Has a Split Personality," *Nation's Restaurant News*, July 24, 2000.
41. Jeff Schmidt, Ph.D. dissertation, Michigan State University, 1996.
42. Bureau of Economic Analysis, www.bea.doc.gov, visited May 24, 2001.
43. www.forestrysystems.com, Web site visited September 19, 2000.
44. "Starbucks Considers Expanding Its Chain in Asian-Pacific Area," *Wall Street Journal*, August 29, 1996: "Starbucks CEO Visits Seoul for Opening," *Korea Economic Weekly*, May 8, 2000.
45. Steve Gold, "Excite AtHome Accelerates Global Expansion," *Biz Report*, April 21, 2000.
46. Kinichi Ohmae, *The Borderless World* (New York: Harper Business, 1990), pp. 17–31.
47. "Snacks Made at Columbia, MO, Plant Fueled Quaker Oats Turnaround," *Columbus Daily Tribune*, August 8, 2000.
48. www.gillette.com, Web site visited September 19, 2000.
49. David A. Erickson, "Standardized Approach Works Well in Establishing Global Presence," *Marketing News*, October 7, 1996, p. 9.
50. www.esintertrade.com, Web site visited September 19, 2000.
51. John Blau, "Research Collaborations Drive Global Telecoms Industry," *Research Technology Management*, July/August 1999.
52. "VW-Tochter Skoda Faehrt Gegen Den Trend," *Handelsblatt*, July 19, 2000.
53. "Carmakers Take Two Routes to Global Growth," *Financial Times London*, July 11, 2000.
54. "Lockheed Martin Unit to Form Alliance with Toshiba," *Asia Pulse*, July 18, 2000.

VIRGIN ENTERTAINMENT GROUP

VIRGIN ENTERTAINMENT GROUP IS THE LARGEST multichannel music retailer in the world. It has traditional bricks and mortar stores, such as the megastore in Times Square, an online megastore, and radiofreevirgin.com. The company has an aggressive e-tailing strategy that focuses on customer service and technology rather than on advertising. Virgin recently relaunched a new and improved version of its Virgin Megastore Online, giving a significant boost to their multichannel retail strategy. The Web site, located at www.virginmega.com, was developed to advance the company's ultimate strategy, which is "to provide entertainment customers what they want, how they want it, and when they want it."

The company's strategic direction involves replicating the Virgin Megastore experience in the online environment and does not target any specific consumer segment. A presence on the Internet provides Virgin with the strategic infrastructure necessary to achieve its goals. The Internet site features an impressive, new search engine that is faster and more detailed than search engines for competing retail sites. It also serves as one of the world's largest music reference libraries. The new, easy-to-navigate system gives consumers the ability to track orders, access the catalog, find maps to the nearest store, and enjoy exclusive interviews and reviews.

For the first time, a major retail operation has its "bricks-and-clicks" strategy united under a single CEO and management team, as Virgin recently named its current president of global e-commerce as CEO for the bricks-and-mortar division of North America. Through its strategic business units, Radio Free Virgin, the Virgin Megastores, Virgin Jamcast, and Virgin Megastore Online, Virgin Entertainment Group has incorporated the ways consumers get their music with the ultimate global entertainment service in both the clicks and bricks environments.

Source: "Virgin Entertainment Group Ties MEGA-bricks with MEGA-clicks; Newly Re-launched Virgin Megastore Online Bolsters Company's Multi-channel Retail Strategy," *Business Wire,* July 31, 2000.

CASE 4

Polaroid

REVITALIZING A BUSINESS IS NO small challenge. Polaroid's traditional product line of instant cameras was losing popularity, but the company recently found rejuvenation by focusing more attention on existing and new markets. Often referred to as a tired product, Polaroid's instant camera and film needed to be revived. A four-part strategy was created to restore the company to recognized world leadership in instant imaging.

Historically, Polaroid created innovations with consumer benefits in mind. Founders Edwin Land and George Wheelwright introduced one-step black-and-white photography in 1947. In 1952 they introduced full-color, stereographic movies complete with 3-D glasses. By 1963 the company had the first instant color film, followed by autofocus technology in 1978. Four years later came the first video printer, which could display diagnostic images useful in industrial and medical markets.

Chairman and CEO Gary T. DiCamillo has made a point of listening to Polaroid users, dealers, retailers, employees, investors, suppliers, and even competitors on four continents in order to design the best revitalization strategy. Striving for a competitive plan that would be more responsive, DiCamillo identified opportunities in core consumer markets, selected global commercial markets, developing country markets, and new imaging businesses that required new products. Because all these initiatives were consistent with Polaroid's mission of instant imaging, they worked well together and success in one area helped support strategies in other areas.

Polaroid has come a long way over the past four decades. In May 2000, Polaroid announced that the future of the company will be built "on new products that reinvent traditional instant photography and link this popular technology to advances in digital imaging." Clearly, Polaroid recognizes the role of technology in the success of the organization. It cites the growth of the Internet, broadband technology, and wireless communication advances as key factors that will determine the success of its future products.

Polaroid sees itself as closely tied to digital imaging technology. In reality, it has viewed digital imaging as a competitor to its own innovative images. With the goal of surviving in the digital age, Polaroid seems to be attempting to create brand loyalty among those that will determine its future by supplying fun, innovative products to Gen-Xers and Generation I (Internet generation) before they begin making decisions about digital imaging. Polaroid views instant and digital photography as essentially the same: They both provide immediate and affordable pictures. In 2000, Polaroid announced a business alliance with Picture Works Technology, a software company, to more closely tie Polaroid with the Internet and digital photos. Polaroid also views instant photos as being quite similar to printers. Therefore, Polaroid has launched a wireless printer that receives images transmitted by radio waves from up to 50 feet away.

Polaroid has launched two key new instant cameras in the last two years. The I-Zone product line, which creates thumbnail-size instant photos, was marketed toward Generation I, which consists of teens and young adults who are Internet savvy. Polaroid's goal is to continue launching new products for this target market, focusing on products that can tie into the Internet. Polaroid also created the JoyCam, a camera that creates instant photos as stickers, targeted to Generation X and Generation I. Thanks to these innovations, Polaroid owned the number-one camera brand purchased in 1999 (I-Zone). Additionally, Polaroid has become profitable for the first time since 1994.

Polaroid's goals extend beyond the domestic market. In 1999, approximately 40 percent of Polaroid's sales were outside the United States. Polaroid's goals for the expansion of sales and technology-related products presents quite a challenge. Not only are there many established competitors in the photography industry, the software industry, the printer industry, and the Internet industry, but Polaroid also has to continually update its marketing plan to appeal to its target market. In 1996, Polaroid's average customer was approximately 53 years old and had experience using the product in the past. The new marketing campaign is designed to create awareness among younger consumers as well as a fresh interest in mature markets around the world. For example, Polaroid has hired Britney Spears to help it appeal to Gen-I.

Polaroid has done an excellent job of applying its core competency and is beginning to rejuvenate the organization. DiCamillo is quick to point out the extensive use made of new-product development teams, which bring together key players from marketing, sales, research, engineering, and manufacturing. The teams are required to listen to customers in order to provide them with imaging solutions that meet specific needs. The team approach speeds the product development process, enabling Polaroid to introduce 40 to 50 new products or line extensions annually. These new products are expected to provide up to 25 percent of Polaroid's sales.

Where is Polaroid headed? By focusing on new growing markets and by reinvigorating promotion and product development, Polaroid is trying to stay ahead of competitors, such as Fuji, who have benefited from expirations of Polaroid's patents. The plan is to stick with the company's core competency in instant photography and to maintain about 90 percent of sales and profits in this solid business. Polaroid expects to grow not only in developing markets but also in North America, Western Europe, and Japan. With the introduction of new products and others on the drawing board, Polaroid intends to be a permanent, innovative presence in all the markets.

1. *The corporate vision provides a common understanding of what the organization is trying to accomplish in the broadest sense. Using what you've learned from this case, describe the current vision.*
2. *There are several ways to structure strategic business units. How does Polaroid structure its business units? How could portfolio planning tools be used to assess the effectiveness of the company's business units?*
3. *How can Polaroid ensure that it properly plans its marketing efforts to reach the target markets effectively? How will these plans change as the target markets become older?*
4. *Core competencies are critical aspects of strategic infrastructure. Identify Polaroid's core competencies. Into which categories can they be grouped?*

Sources: Claudia Deutsch, "Polaroid Girds for New Era in Instant Photography," *The New York Times Online,* March 27, 2000, www.nytimes.com; Polaroid Web site, www.polaroid.com, visited June 17, 2000; Shelly Reese, *Marketing Tools,* June 1996 www.marketingtools.com; Mark Maremont, "Polaroid: Ready for a Reshoot," *Business Week,* April 1, 1996, p. 6; Joan Voight, "Polaroid Yuks Up with $40M Push," *Brandweek,* February 26, 1996; Michael Wilke, "Polaroid Pins Its Revival to Brand, Product Lineup," *Advertising Age,* December 2, 1996, p. 20; Otis Port, "Digital Finds Its Photo Op," *Business Week,* April 15, 1996; and Hoover's Online, "Polaroid Corporation," www.hooversonline.com, visited June 16, 2000.

MARKETING INFORMATION AND RESEARCH

◀ *Jeffrey Bezos, Amazon.com CEO*

WHEN YOU ENTER THE BOOKSTORE, YOU'RE met with a familiar greeting: "Welcome back, friend, these are your recommendations." The bookseller suggests several titles that may interest you and points you in the right direction. You quickly find information about the books, author and publisher notes, price information, and even reviews by other customers. You choose two titles, quickly pay with a credit card, and leave the store. The strange thing is you never left home.

Welcome to Amazon.com, one of the hottest online businesses to hit the World Wide Web with 17 million customers in 150 countries. Incorporated in 1995 by Jeffery Bezos, sales have grown dramatically in just six short years. After going public in 1997, sales rose from $147. 8 million (in 1997) to 2.7 billion in 2001. The stock price has increased dramatically, since the initial public offering (IPO) but has since leveled off.

Although a great deal of Amazon.com's success can be attributed to overwhelming growth in the Internet, its use of marketing information systems provides a strong competitive advantage. The ability to record and remember customer preferences allows it to offer specialized services that elude other retailers. Amazon gets to know its customers like few other businesses can.

The Amazon.com marketing information system is a two-way street. While Amazon gathers information about users, users are also given plenty of information about Amazon.com products and even about other customers' tastes and preferences. When customers enter the Web site, they are recognized from their original registration (a simple process that asks for name, e-mail address, and a password), and their buying history is accessed. Next, based on that history and the buying behavior of other Amazon.com customers, a list suggests books and other products that are likely to interest the customer.

For example, users who have never purchased books at Amazon.com are led to six other ways to discover great reads. The most interactive is the BookMatcher system. The simple five-minute process collects information on your reading habits and opinions by asking you to rate genres and specific titles. Once you enter this information, you can rate any book that's recommended or that you find while searching. The data are cross-referenced with the ratings of others to provide an increasingly solid reader profile of you.

Amazon.com delivers information to users even when they are not visiting the site. The service allows readers to choose among more than 40 categories that may interest them. It automatically sends them e-mail with new information about those categories, including recommendations, reviews, author notes, interviews, chapter samples, and best-seller lists.

Another suggestion device is MoodMatcher, which uses an index of themes such as "Fantastic Voyages" and "It Was a Dark and Stormy Night" to guide readers to authors and titles. Customer Buzz lists books by genre that have been heavily reviewed by Web site visitors and separates the list into two categories: "Divided Over" and "Raving About." There also is an option that provides searchers with a way to link well-liked authors to similar writers they may not know about. Yet another section provides title synopses and critical thinking questions that can be used as a framework for group discussion.

The Amazon system also allows users to search for specific titles. The online catalog contains 2.5 million books and is searchable by author, title, subject, publisher, publication date, and ISBN. After you type in the information required, the search engine supplies the three most likely matches, plus any additional items that you may have intended. Each listed title is a link to further information including price and commentary from other reviewers, positive and negative. By posting public reviews, Amazon is able to get feedback on the books it carries, and it makes that information available to customers. Amazon.com now offers more than 18 million products. Besides books and music, the selection of items now includes DVD/video, toys, electronics, software, home improvement products, and video games.[1]

The use of technology to gather information extends beyond the borders of Amazon.com through third-party associates. For example, a Web site specializing in gardening can create a link that takes Amazon.com users directly into a page displaying the latest titles on flowers, lawn care, and botany. The program is growing fast, due in large part to the commissions associates receive for each book purchased in this way. Over 35,000 affiliate sites are earning commissions of up to 15 percent. Jeff Bezos admits, "We're never going to have sofas; we're never going to have latte."[2] Although Amazon.com can't provide the atmosphere of a local bookstore, what it does have can be even more powerful. The information interface allows it to gather customer-specific information and provide users with a more complete service. In a technological age, Amazon.com proves that marketers can understand customers through the Web and perhaps serve them even better than if they were face-to-face.

THE CONCEPT OF MARKETING INFORMATION SYSTEMS AND MARKETING RESEARCH

Connecting with customers requires vast amounts of information. You can't connect if you can't locate, understand, and respond to customers. That's where marketing information systems and marketing research enter the picture. Technology has changed the way the business

This Docent Inc. ad is an example of marketing information.

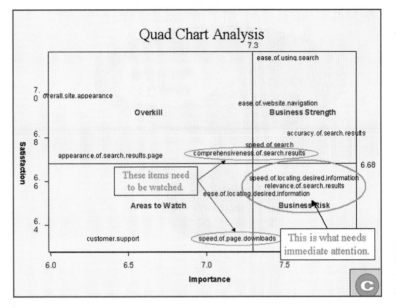

*cPulse software is used to
collect MIS data for large
companies such as Compaq
and AT&T.*

world views marketing information. Data gathering and dissemination occur at the speed of light. Information is at the fingertips of anyone with a personal computer and a modem; access is as easy as dialing the telephone. The director of strategic planning at a large midwestern hospital commented recently: "We have access to more information than we can possibly use. The trick is to determine which information will be useful to us in making decisions that positively affect our future."[3]

In fact, a major problem for executives today is data overload—access to so much that their minds simply can't process all of it. To help decision makers, most companies carefully structure the way data are collected, stored, and made available through marketing information systems and marketing research.

Marketing information systems (MIS) are computerized systems that collect and organize marketing data on a timely basis to provide information for decision making. For example, cPulse provides marketing information services to over 150 clients, such as AT&T and Compaq, focusing on how Web surfers view homepages and how online customer satisfaction can be improved. One research firm predicts that Internet companies will lose $3.2 billion in sales due to poor customer service. cPulse tries to identify these customer service issues by collecting feedback from users of Web sites and assisting companies' marketing departments in making better decisions.[4] The results become part of the MIS so that executives have constant feedback.

Note that the abbreviation *MIS* can be confusing because many organizations have a **management information system,** also called an *MIS.* Many times the marketing information system is considered part of that larger system. Management information systems usually contain additional data, such as employee records and various internal documents.

Marketing research is the formal assembly and analysis of data about specific issues surrounding a marketing strategy. It is called for when managers face a complex marketing situation for which little or no information is available. All the data gathered focus on the problem at hand. For example, Tantau Software Inc., a developer of computer programs for the wireless Internet, recently hired IntelliQuest Research to provide marketing data on the attitudes of current and potential wireless users. After e-mail, IntelliQuest discovered that financial-based transactions showed the most promise of creating a market for the wireless Internet. However, it also found that customers were most concerned with the security of their transactions, and, thus, were hesitant to invest in or use the new medium. As a result, Tantau was able to use IntelliQuest's research to better focus on e-commerce and wireless security software, something that consumers obviously needed.[5]

The type of research just described addresses a specific issue with a clearly identified objective regarding marketing strategy. Once the research is completed, it's typically saved as part of the MIS. Figure 5.1 depicts the relationships of the MIS and marketing research to marketing decision making. This chapter starts with an examination of marketing information systems and their role in marketing decisions. This is followed by a discussion of the

MARKETING INFORMATION SYSTEM (MIS)
A computerized system used to collect and analyze marketing data.

MANAGEMENT INFORMATION SYSTEM (MIS)
A computerized system used to collect and analyze the data needed for management decision making. The marketing information system is often considered a part of this system.

MARKETING RESEARCH
The formal assembly and analysis of information about specific issues surrounding the marketing of goods and services.

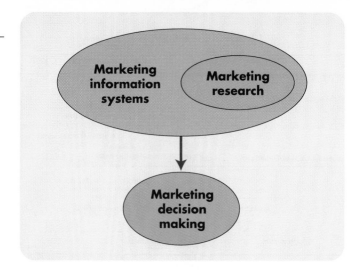

FIGURE 5.1 *Marketing Information and Decision Making*

marketing research process, which is also a key in decision making. The chapter concludes with sections on the all-important technological, global, and ethical dimensions of information generation and usage.

MARKETING INFORMATION SYSTEMS AND DATA

MARKETING DECISION SUPPORT SYSTEM (MDSS)

A two-way communication bridge between the people who collect and analyze information and the executives who use it.

Marketing information systems often include a **marketing decision support system (MDSS),** which allows decision makers to access raw data from the MIS and manipulate it into a useful form. A typical MDSS consists of a computer database, data retrieval and modeling software, and a user-friendly graphical interface. Let's say that a marketing manager wants to know how the price of the company's downhill skis compares to that of a competitor. The information is probably in the MIS on a store-by-store basis. It would be difficult for the manager to wade through all the raw data and draw any conclusions. Instead the manager may sit down at a computer and accesses the company's MDSS. A user-friendly display appears and, through interactive directions, helps the user determine how to manipulate the raw data. The marketing manager may want to compare average prices across the entire country or for one region or state. Once that is decided, the MDSS software retrieves and models the relevant data. Now the manager is able to interpret the data and make an informed decision.

TRANSACTION-BASED INFORMATION SYSTEM (TBIS)

A computerized link between a firm and its customers, distributors, and suppliers.

A specialized type of MIS is a **transaction-based information system (TBIS),** which is a computerized link between a firm and its customers, distributors, and suppliers. Originally designed for ordering, billing, shipping, and inventory control, these systems are now designed to provide data on customer preferences, loyalty, sales trends, and an array of marketing issues.

To develop an excellent MIS and design a useful MDSS, the organization needs to assess its marketing information needs. This assessment begins by identifying the types of executive decisions, what information will help make them, and the best formats and timetables for presenting it. Figure 5.2 describes the types of questions used to assess marketing information needs.

FIGURE 5.2 *How to Determine Marketing Information Needs*

Source: Philip Kotler and Gary Armstrong, *Principles of Marketing,* 9th ed. 2001. Adapted by permission of Prentice Hall, Inc., Upper Saddle River, NJ.

1. What types of decisions do you make regularly?
2. What types of information do you need in order to make those decisions?
3. What types of useful information do you get regularly?
4. What types of information would you like to have that you are not getting now?
5. What types of information do you get now that you don't really need?
6. What information do you want daily? weekly? monthly? yearly?
7. What topics would you like to be kept informed about?
8. What databases would be useful to you?
9. What types of information analysis programs would you like to have?
10. What are the four most helpful improvements that could be made in the present information system?

In order to comprehend marketing information systems and marketing research, you must understand the nature of data and how they become information useful for decision making. Keep in mind that data and information are not the same. Data are simply facts. Information is data that have been analyzed and put in useful form, as depicted in Figure 5.3. "Data served up in tabular form, which is the way business was being done not so many years ago, will no longer suffice," says Gerald Kanovsky, president of Career Consulting Group, Inc. "Today's executives need information they can act on."[6] In other words, market analysts and researchers need to interpret data—turn then into information—to assist upper-level managers and executives in making quick, informed decisions.

Types of Data   Data provide the starting point from which marketing information is derived. **Data** can be any set of facts or statistics obtained from outside (external) or inside (internal) the company. Usually the data are stored in a **database,** which is a collection of material that can be retrieved by a computer.

External data come from outside the company. Popular external databases include LEXIS®-NEXIS®, Dow Jones Interactive, Hoover's Online, and Dialog. They provide raw data as well as articles, newsletters, breaking news stories, financial reports on companies, and nearly any other type of data imaginable. For specific needs, you can use sources such as Forrester Research Group's *Technographic Data,* which provides continuous surveys of 375,000 online households in North America and Europe. *Technographic Data* gives valuable survey information on affluent and young consumers, technology, personal finances, travel, and retail—survey information that many companies need.[7]

To track competitors, one approach is the source in the Nexis® service, which analyzes specific industries and companies. If you're interested in business customers, Dun & Bradstreet can provide information on 58 million businesses in 200 countries.[8] It can give in-depth financial and operational reports on most of the companies. The databases generally have a cost. Companies charge either for time online or for each piece of data, such as a name or news release.

Internal data are found within a company. Sales data, accounting records, and sales force call reports are examples. Internal data are likely to reside in several different departments. For example, the accounting department has detailed records of sales costs and how much cash is generated by each product. In some cases these figures are available for each market segment. The manufacturing and shipping departments track production schedules, amount of capacity utilized, shipping dates, and inventory levels. In many companies the supply chain management department provides detailed records of the flow of goods into the company and out to each customer, including the frequency of orders, stock levels, and purchase rates. The marketing department will usually have such data as type and frequency of sales calls, orders received from each location, and advertising schedules.

Primary data are those gathered for the first time for a particular issue being addressed. As a result, they tend to take longer and be more expensive to collect than other types of data. **Secondary data** are those that already have been collected. Nearly all marketing information falls into this category. For example, the National Trade Data Bank, with data from numerous government agencies, is a wonderful resource for international research.

Data Analysis   Data analysis transforms material into a usable form, so insights can be developed. It usually involves data sorting, statistics, and models. Data sorting uses several tools for grouping data. For example, Burger King may want to know sales by time of day to determine whether certain items are more popular at certain times.

DATA

Facts or statistics obtained from outside or inside the company.

DATABASE

A collection of data that can be retrieved by a computer.

EXTERNAL DATA

Data obtained outside the company.

INTERNAL DATA

Data obtained within the company.

PRIMARY DATA

Information collected for the first time.

SECONDARY DATA

Information that already has been collected.

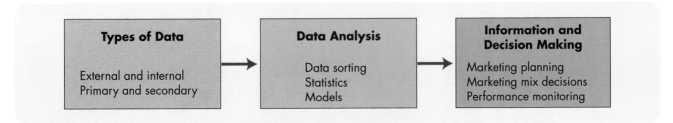

FIGURE 5.3 *How Data Become Information*

Statistics help describe data in more detail or tell us how representative certain occurrences are relative to overall patterns. Most information systems have readily available statistical packages that can easily be applied to the data. In some cases they simply count frequencies of occurrence or describe the averages. For example, 90 percent of J. D. Edwards's revenues comes from installing and configuring software packages. However, 34 percent of that comes from UNIX or Windows software alone.[9] Awareness of such statistical data helps J. D. Edwards to focus its time and resources on that pivotal 34 percent.

Models are miniature representations of marketing phenomena. They simplify complex situations by presenting key facts and ignoring unnecessary details. Marketers need models for the same reasons that architects need blueprints. With a blueprint, the architect can visualize various parts of the building without actually being there. Marketing models describe which variables are important for specific marketing situations. For example, Children's World evaluates consumer satisfaction in order to predict loyalty. Its model indicates that satisfaction leads to customer loyalty. The important thing is that the data analysis should be insightful, so that it will lead to innovative marketing decisions, and easy to use, so executives will be more inclined to incorporate it into their decision making.

INFORMATION AND DECISION MAKING

Using information is not easy; however, it's absolutely critical to have good information if you expect to connect with customers. Marketers have historically relied on their own intuition. Although experience is still important, the world is more complex today. So experience must be supplemented with marketing information. Good information helps executives make key marketing decisions. As was illustrated in Figure 5.3, marketing information is generally used in three key areas: marketing planning, marketing mix decisions, and performance monitoring. Let's take a look at each of these in more detail.

Marketing Planning   Marketing planning requires information at nearly every stage of the process. The situation analysis needs input about customers, competitors, market trends, technology, channels of distribution, and economic conditions. Marketing information also helps marketers make better decisions about which segments to target and how to position the organization. Often, marketing information affects the competitive thrust of the company. For example, research at AT&T indicates that customers want help managing their increasingly busy lives. This includes understanding new technology, convenience in reaching others, and easy access to information and entertainment services. To address these wants, AT&T is working to supply such services as electronic bill payment, bill bundling, automatic redialing on calls that receive a busy signal or no answer, and a message recording system for the home workplace that stores faxes or data on the computer if lines are occupied by personal voice calls.[10] Through marketing information, AT&T is able to better understand consumers in order to build customer relationships and provide consumers with valuable products.

Marketing Mix Decisions   Marketing mix decisions are another area in which marketing information is required. In fact, it is so critical to decisions about product, place, promotion, and price that expertise has evolved in each area. For example, Booz, Allen & Hamilton, a large consulting firm, has a department that focuses primarily on product research. The University of Tennessee funds the Center for Logistics Research, which concentrates on distribution channels. The way marketing information aids each of the marketing mix decisions is discussed next.

Product Decisions Marketing information on new products is essential. Gatorade tests the physiological effects of its popular sports drinks at the Gatorade Sports Science Institute in Barrington, Illinois. There Gatorade researchers examine the physical performance of various athletes who work out and then drink the famed Gatorade blend of water and 6 percent carbohydrates and electrolytes. Such test results help refine the Gatorade formula, expand its flavors and product line, and publicize the benefits of the brand. Presently Gatorade controls 81 percent of the $1.5 billion sports drink market. Gatorade's heavy reliance on scientific testing and product research has allowed it to successfully retain market share despite the introduction of competitors such as PowerAde, AllSport, and 10K.[11]

Marketing information also helps identify opportunities for new products. As a result of product testing, but in particular because of customer research and feedback, Delta Airlines made significant improvements to its meal service. "Our passengers' feedback was key in helping Delta develop this latest round of enhancements in our international meal service," said a company spokesman. "We conducted extensive polling and testing to ensure products were selected that our customers would enjoy the most." Meals now include hot breakfast sandwiches, Quaker Oats cereal bars, Ghirardelli chocolate, bottled water, and Oreo cookies.[12]

In another case, Annette Zientek created Christine Columbus, a mail-order catalog that offers specialty items for women travelers, such as compact curling irons and makeup mirrors. Before leaving on a vacation in Europe, she spent nearly six weeks trying to find the travel accessories she needed. Wondering whether all women had the same difficulty, Zientek set out to collect marketing information. She found that women would soon make up more than half of all travelers. As a result of Zientek's research and marketing decisions, Christine Columbus began.[13] Today the company has nearly $5 million in sales and maintains its product catalog completely online.[14]

Place Decisions Marketing information helps with place decisions such as determining the appropriate distribution channel, either directly to consumers or through intermediaries, such as wholesalers and retailers. It can be used to identify specific distributors or the inventory requirements for selected channels. One form of marketing information tracks every item sold in every store. "It captures the entire retail marketing area," says Donald Stuart, partner at Cannondale Associates. "Manufacturers are able to identify the stores that are most important to their category, least important to their category, or that hold the best opportunities for brand or category development." Marketers can identify similar consumer clusters in individual stores and determine which products do better in particular stores. Information such as this "gives manufacturers a definitive read on their business in any account," says Joe Battoe, president of sales and retail services at IRI Research.[15] Once executives gain a good understanding of market phenomena, they are able to make quality decisions regarding the distribution of their products and services.

Promotion Decisions Vast amounts of information are necessary in the area of promotions. For example, executives must determine the budget required to accomplish desired objectives. They have to decide the proper combination of advertising, personal selling, or other promotion approaches. For advertising, they need to determine the most effective amounts of print, television, and radio ads to reach targeted consumers.

Marketing information also provides valuable feedback. "Without indicators like increased sales or market share gain, we really have no way of knowing how effective our plan for a brand really is," says Dana Anderson, media buyer for United Airlines at Leo Burnett Company, Inc., a major advertising agency. "Marketing information also tells us how well an advertising plan meets specific marketing objectives, like an increase in company or product awareness or an improved image of a brand. . . . We also evaluate the effects of our promotional campaign on competitors."[16]

Pricing Decisions Because prices send strong signals to the market about the value of a product, information on pricing is critical for almost every marketing decision. In many cases, pricing is specific to a region. Wal-Mart and Toys "R" Us advertise that they will meet or beat competitors' prices. They monitor these locally, feeding the information into a centralized MIS. They also collect ads that consumers bring in. Automobile companies look not only at the prices of major competitors but also at finance and leasing terms. Information is collected about the effectiveness of cash discounts and rebates as well as the likelihood of buyers switching from one brand to another at various price points. The airline industry, whose profits are highly sensitive to volume, continually monitors how price affects demand in local, national, and international markets. Internet ticket sellers such as Travelocity.com are especially helpful in this regard, as commercial Web sites are an excellent source of consumer information.

Monitoring Performance The third area supported by marketing information is performance monitoring. This helps managers make sure that plans and programs are moving ahead on target. Information is required to track progress, identify unsuspected obstacles, and make corrections to accomplish objectives. 3M has recently begun examining its ability to build its brand name on the Internet. In order to monitor how well 3M is accomplishing its online goals, short surveys randomly pop up on the screens of 3M Web site visitors. The surveys are focused on 5 to 20 Web site attributes, including the quality of product descriptions, ease of use, and speed of dowloading. 3M is able to receive instant feedback and then immediately make the necessary changes.[17]

Today, nearly every organization monitors customer service levels. Marketing information provides data on customer expectations and how well the company meets them. USAA,

**CONNECTED:
SURFING THE NET**

www.travelocity.com

Need a vacation? See how Travelocity returns search results based on price. Compare this Web site's method of returning available flights to other Web sites, such as those of Northwest Airlines, United Airlines, or American Airlines.

an insurance and financial services organization, places a great deal of emphasis on monitoring the performance of its customer service representatives. After a customer speaks with someone in customer service, he or she can expect to receive a short survey approximately one week later, asking about the quality of information and the helpfulness of the representative. Excellent customer service plays a major role in USAA's marketing plan, so monitoring the quality closely helps management determine whether they are accomplishing specific objectives. Recently USAA began scanning each customer complaint into its company-wide database, making them instantly available to all company reps.[18]

Hyatt Hotels and Resorts monitors its salespeople utilizing five principles of customer service highlighted on a koosh ball. Why a koosh ball? Because it stands for:[19]

- **K**now your customers
- **O**versee your operation
- **O**verachieve your goals
- **S**ell professionally
- **H**ire the best people

Outside rating services can provide unbiased information on how consumers evaluate performance. You're probably familiar with the Nielsen ratings, which usually appear weekly in publications such as *USA Today*. Nielsen Media Research, the leading international television information services company, monitors approximately 5,000 homes. A Nielsen People Meter is installed on each television to record tuning records for every channel: the time of day, duration of tuning, and which household members are watching. The company retrieves the information through the phone lines. The result is television show rankings, weekly ratings, and season to date rankings.[20]

Just think of the usefulness of the Nielsen service to marketers. A company can decide to advertise during programs and time slots when it can be certain targeted consumers are watching. It is important for such services to keep an arm's-length relationship with the companies they rate. To see how J. D. Power & Associates accomplishes this for the automotive industry, check out the relationships feature, "J. D. Power & Associates: A 'Hate-Love' Relationship with Detroit."

THE MARKETING RESEARCH PROCESS

Marketing research is a key aspect of the organization's ability to make good marketing decisions. It starts with a clear understanding of the problem to be addressed and ends with an interpretation of findings that will aid in decision making. Each step is shown in Figure 5.4.

CONNECTED: SURFING THE NET

www.nielsenmedia.com

Explore the Web site of one of the nation's top rating services—Nielsen Media Research. Check out its Web audience measurement presentation, or read the latest company news.

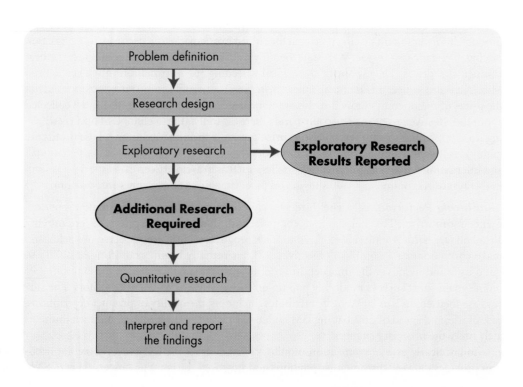

FIGURE 5.4 *The Marketing Research Process*

DEFINING THE PROBLEM

When asked what he recommended for ensuring high-quality marketing research, an experienced executive at Upjohn Corporation answered: "Never begin a research process with a search for market information. Always start by understanding the decisions to be made and the managerial circumstances surrounding those decisions." This isn't as easy as it sounds, but it's a critical step in the research process. As Albert Einstein said, "The formulation of a problem is often more essential than its solution."[21]

The marketing researcher and key decision makers should work together to specify the problem. The researcher usually must ask probing questions to identify objectives. What is the environment of the problem? When must it be solved? What resources will be committed to the final course of action? It does no good to recommend a remedy clearly beyond the capacity of the company.

Care must be taken to isolate the symptoms from the actual problem. Imagine that Pepsi sales decline rapidly. This sounds like a problem, but it's only a symptom. The real problem may be a new promotional campaign by Coca-Cola that Pepsi has failed to address. Or perhaps many Pepsi customers are switching to bottled water. Just as a fever is a sign of the flu, declining sales usually indicate a deeper problem. Once it is isolated, the variables or factors causing it can be identified. This helps define the problem before any marketing research begins.

RESEARCH DESIGN

A **research design** is an outline of what data will be gathered, what sources will be used, and how the data will be collected and analyzed. The research design is, in effect, a master plan for the research project as shown in Figure 5.4.

Most designs call for two types of research: exploratory and quantitative. **Exploratory research** clarifies the problem and searches for ways to address it. **Quantitative research** provides the information needed to select the best course of action and forecast the probable results. Research generally starts with an exploratory study, may include a pilot phase, and ends with quantitative research. A **pilot study** is a small-scale project that allows the researcher to refine and test the approaches that ultimately will be used.

EXPLORATORY RESEARCH

Exploratory research enables investigators to obtain a better understanding of the issues. Specifically, it helps

- determine the exact nature of the problem or opportunity,
- search for causes or explanations for the problem,
- define the magnitude of the problem,
- create hypotheses about underlying causes,
- describe why or how the causes may affect the situation,
- understand competitors' actions and reactions to company strategies, and
- estimate how courses of action may affect the market.

Exploratory research seeks information that will enlighten marketers in the decision-making process. A simple Yahoo! search for sports sites reveals 3,833 homepages for basketball, 3,050 for football, and 4,512 for baseball. By doing this simple bit of exploratory research, companies can learn a lot about sports, such as how fans follow the game, how leagues, teams, and players market themselves, and what products and services sports fans buy.[22]

Exploratory research generally begins by finding and reviewing secondary data. This information already has been collected, so it's usually the quickest and most cost-effective way to get started. Sometimes the entire research question can be answered with secondary data, but the collection of primary data usually is required.

Although exploratory research seldom quantifies the best solution, it clearly defines the problem and suggests options. With that information, the executive may be able to choose a course of action, and many projects end at this stage.

Exploratory research is conducted with focus groups, interviews, projective techniques, observation, and case analysis. Each is discussed next.

Focus Groups   A **focus group** usually involves eight to twelve people whose opinions provide qualitative insights into a problem. This approach is particularly useful in clarifying problems with a company's products, services, advertising, distribution channels, and the like. It's

---

RESEARCH DESIGN

An outline of what data will be gathered, what sources will be used, and how the data will be collected and analyzed.

EXPLORATORY RESEARCH

Research designed to clarify the problem and suggest ways to address it.

QUANTITATIVE RESEARCH

Research designed to provide the information needed to select the best course of action and estimate the probable results.

PILOT STUDY

A small-scale project that allows the researcher to refine and test the approaches that eventually will be used.

FOCUS GROUP

A group, usually composed of eight to twelve people, whose opinions are elicited by an interviewer to provide exploratory insights into a problem.

CONNECTING THROUGH RELATIONSHIPS

J. D. POWER & ASSOCIATES: A "HATE-LOVE" RELATIONSHIP WITH DETROIT

 A common blind spot of marketers is to look for research that confirms what they think, not research that points up what they don't know. This was certainly the case when independent researcher John David Power presented his data to the automotive industry about 30 years ago. Power approached the nation's automakers with extensive independent surveys on customer satisfaction. Instead of embracing Power and his work with open arms, the Big Three gave him the cold shoulder. The surveys highlighted America's dissatisfaction with U.S. made cars, and Detroit didn't want to hear about it. Ironically, it was Power's insistence on maintaining an arm's-length relationship with the auto industry that finally brought Detroit around. Today, the J. D. Power & Associates Customer Satisfaction rating is the most coveted, and credible, seal of approval in the business.

A former financial analyst at Ford Motor Company, Power struck out on his own in 1968. His idea was to pay for his own customer surveys of the automotive industry and later sell the results. Says J. Ferron, a former Power executive and now partner-in-charge of Coopers & Lybrand's auto practice, "Dave's genius was not to depend on companies to finance proprietary studies, but to do independent studies and publish the results." Detroit turned a blind eye, but the Japanese were only too happy to see what the surveys had to say about their competitors. Power's data were a crucial step in their campaign to break into the U.S. auto market, which they did.

By the mid-1980s, Japanese cars were overtaking U.S. models in sales, and the Big Three were forced to listen to Power. "Our goal has always been to improve the quality of cars," says Power. "People like Ralph Nader [the consumer activist] wanted to protect consumers, too, but I always thought he was anti-Detroit. We wanted to work with Detroit." Today, automakers whose cars receive a top rating are happy to fork over the large licensing fee that Power requires when they advertise his results. It's actually a small price to pay, since a J. D. Power & Associates number-one rating has been known to double sales of a particular model.

Drawing on the success of his car ratings, Power is taking his multimillion-dollar company in some exciting new directions. He extended his arm's-length handshake to the nation's 21,000 new car dealerships, giving them the chance to compete for their own J. D. Power awards. The Power Information Network (PIN) is a computerized program that collects details of every transaction made by participating dealers. PIN gives carmakers and dealers an accurate picture of what cars are selling where and at what price. It's a far cry from tabulating survey results at the kitchen table, which is what Power and his wife did when he first started out.

Over the years, J. D. Power has added several other markets for which it conducts market research. Instead of only focusing on the automotive industry, J. D. Power also does work in finance, travel, housing, and telecommunications. In the area of finance, J. D. Power publishes ratings for online broker and credit card ratings. It also publishes ratings for other industries including airlines, home builders, wireless providers, and Internet service providers.

Sources: Larry Armstrong, "Rating J. D. Power's Grand Plan," *Business Week,* September 2, 1996, pp. 75–76; David Carnoy et al., "Know Your Customer," *Success,* February 1997, pp. 36–38; and J. D. Power & Associates, www.jdpower.com, Web site visited July 13, 2000, Winter 2000.

---

possible to gather a wide range of information about customers' feelings on these subjects and discover the reasons for their attitudes or purchase behaviors. Techniques are used that probe into thoughts and feelings. Researchers ask questions and encourage participants to interact with one another to uncover unexpected attitudes, behaviors, and ideas that may suggest innovative marketing strategies. In a sense, the group interviews itself. The social interaction often yields insights that could not be obtained through one-on-one interviews.

Focus groups have been used for a variety of purposes. After the 1992 riots in Los Angeles, the Vons supermarket chain took the lead in opening stores in the central city, an area it traditionally had ignored. Vons conducted extensive focus group research on nearly every aspect of its business—including product mix, security, and hiring policy—in order to develop ideas for matching outlets with the needs of the local community.[23]

Although most focus groups are conducted in person with a facilitator, other formats can be used, such as videoconferencing through television monitors, remote control cameras, and

Focus groups provide qualitative insights.

digital transmission. The Internet has become an excellent—and cost-effective—tool for focus group research. The Atlanta-based ActiveGroup has emerged as one of the leading providers of Internet-based focus group technology. Lately, ActiveGroup has focused on Web site and computer-usability testing by placing a camera above the computer monitor. By doing so, ActiveGroup can record consumer facial expressions of satisfaction, confusion, like, or dislike.[24] You'll learn more about this unique format in the technology section.

When selecting participants for a focus group, it's generally best to choose those with similar demographics, since common experiences provide the basis for more in-depth discussion. Most exploratory research calls for more than one focus group. In fact, a single session is likely to produce erroneous information. The researcher should use several groups to ensure that the findings are somewhat representative. Even though many individuals may be involved, the unit of analysis is the group and not the individual. Six groups with eight people each, in effect, yields six interviews, not 48.

Depth Interviews   **Depth interviews** are relatively unstructured conversations that allow researchers to probe into a consumer's thought processes. Often they are used to investigate the mechanisms of purchase decisions. Although the discussion may appear casual to the participant, the skilled researcher exerts a great deal of control. Often the interview is designed to cover all aspects of the participant's attitudes, opinions, or motivations. The marketer uses these results both as individual case studies and as comparative data to examine commonalities among respondents.

DEPTH INTERVIEW

A relatively unstructured conversation that allows the researcher to probe deeply into a consumer's thoughts.

Projective Techniques   **Projective techniques** enable respondents to project their thoughts onto a third party, or through some type of contrived situation. This is often done using word associations, sentence completion, and role-playing. Because projective approaches do not require respondents to provide answers in a structured format, people are more likely to interpret the situation creatively and in the context of their own experiences and emotions. When asked directly why they purchase a particular item, they may describe a far more rational process than the one that actually occurs. For example, if a recent college graduate is asked why she purchased a Chrysler Sebring convertible, she may cite performance, gas mileage, and overall value of the product. But if asked to project the feelings of a person who purchases this kind of automobile, she may focus on status, self-esteem, and the need to be noticed.

PROJECTIVE TECHNIQUE

A technique that enables respondents to project their thoughts onto a third party or object or through some type of contrived situation.

Observation   **Observation** is a technique whereby the participants are simply watched. In one classic study, researchers stationed themselves in both crowded and uncrowded supermarkets to discover whether buying behavior differed. In uncrowded stores shoppers tended to use the information on labels and shelves, whereas in crowded conditions they tended to make decisions more hastily. This exploratory observation was followed by a more formal survey that enabled conclusions to be drawn about buyer behavior in crowded situations.[25]

Structured observation is made through mechanical means. Galvanometers record electrical resistance in the skin, associated with sweating and other responses. Tachistoscopes measure visual stimuli. Special cameras often are used to study eye movement as a subject reads advertising copy. By observing pupil dilation and blinking responses, it is possible to judge what receives attention in ads or on packaging.[26]

OBSERVATION

A research technique whereby researchers simply watch the participants they are studying.

ELUSIVE YOUTH: RESEARCHERS FIND NEW WAYS TO TRACK THEIR TASTES

 To get a bead on the buying habits of teens and 20-somethings, or to catch the next trend wave before it rolls into the stores, market researchers are now talking to kids in clubs, pizzerias, concert ticket lines, and, of course, the mall.

"We tried focus groups in a traditional conference-room setting," says Mitchell Fox, publisher of the hip New York magazine *Details*. "They understood we were there for something. Teens and youth in their 20s are a tough nut for market researchers to crack. More than previous generations, they are aware of themselves as targets for marketing and advertising. This makes them very knowledgeable and outspoken about what they like and don't like—the perfect focus group subjects—but also very wary of being sold to, conned, or labeled." According to Liz DiPilli, a market researcher who conducts roving focus groups, "Young people want to get their opinions out. They feel that the media perception of them as being these slackers . . . and eating nachos all day is not really them." But who are they, what do they want, and how do you find out without ticking them off?

Companies such as Evian and Comedy Central paid DiPilli a $4,900 fee to take part in "Project X" and get the answers to these questions. In her tour of five U.S. cities, DiPilli ditches the traditional sites and holds partylike gatherings in trendy hotel suites. She also chats up kids on the street, at roller blade rental stands, or at volleyball games. "This way you're dealing with them on their terms," says DiPilli. "There's no client looking at them through a two-way mirror or people taking notes." *Details* publisher Fox holds focus groups in people's living rooms.

Bugle Boy Clothing Company goes a step farther and turns young subjects into researchers of their own life. Working with Chilton Research, Bugle Boy plucked four young men out of obscurity, handed each of them an 8mm video camera, and told them to do a documentary on themselves. The young filmmakers were given only broad categories to work with such as school, home, and shopping. The videos were then used to spur discussions of product and lifestyle issues in free-form focus groups held at unconventional venues, such as restaurants. "I think it really allowed us to get a handle on what these kids do," said Bugle Boy's ad manager, Sue Scheimann. "It lets us see what their lives are all about, their awareness of the Bugle Boy brand, and how they perceive the brand."

Researchers are using unorthodox methods not only to track the tastes of "every kid" but also to spot trends months in advance. Fads and fashions used to be dictated by designers, but now trends are just as likely to pop up from the street, particularly among urban kids. More and more market research firms are getting assignments to seek out today's coolest youngsters. Even MTV has taken note of the importance of getting face-to-face with today's youth. The MTV Campus Invasion is a 20-university music tour that was held in the fall of 1999 and featured sponsors (i.e., Sony Playstation and Neutrogena to name a few), which corresponded to different shows on MTV. For example, MTV airs a show called *House of Style,* and Neutrogena set up a booth, passing out samples of cosmetics and skin care products, in the *House of Style* arena. Sony Playstation was another sponsor that had a booth and allowed students to sample new games at MTV 101. After students viewed the programming themed areas, an MTV concert followed. Although this campus event was not designed specifically as a focus group, it did allow all of these companies to get an inside view of today's youth. At these events, companies can see which products these 20-somethings prefer, what they don't, and can actually speak with them face-to-face about it.

Sources: Cyndee Miller, "Sometimes a Researcher Has No Choice but to Hang Out in a Bar," *Marketing News,* January 3, 1994, pp. 16–17; Roger Ricklefs, "Marketers Seek Out Today's Coolest Kids to Plug into Tomorrow's Mall Trends," *Wall Street Journal,* July 11, 1996, pp. B1–2; Cyndee Miller, "Researcher Reaches Xers with Her Focus Groups on the Road," *Marketing News,* January 2, 1996, p. 10; and T. L. Stanley, "Toyota, PlayStation, Neutrogena backing 20-Campus MTV invasion" *Brandweek,* October 4, 1999, p. 14.

CASE ANALYSIS

The in-depth study of a few examples.

Case Analysis   **Case analysis** is the in-depth study of a few examples. This technique is particularly appropriate for complex buying and competitive situations. For example, how industrial companies make decisions for particular components or capital goods is often studied this way. A single researcher may spend several days interviewing a firm's employees who purchase and use the product in question. In addition, buying policies, documents, and actual purchase history are investigated. When a few (perhaps as many as 10) companies are examined in this way, researchers obtain a more complete understanding of why and how certain

To get a lead on the buying habits of teens and 20-somethings market researchers are now talking to kids and young adults in nontraditional research settings such as the streets.

suppliers are selected. The information can help suppliers determine the appropriateness of various marketing approaches.

Case analysis can also be used to study the competition. Researchers may select two or three activities of key competitors and examine them in depth. By knowing all aspects of the strategies used to introduce a couple of products, researchers can assess competitors' strengths and weaknesses and also predict how they might behave in the future with other products. Benchmarking is also a form of case analysis. Even individual departments can benchmark their expense costs and productivity with those of other companies' departments. For example, the Big Three automakers benchmark such competitors as Nissan, Honda, and Toyota because these companies are substantially more efficient. In fact, one report estimated that if the Big Three could match Nissan's efficiency together, they could save over $8 billion.[27]

QUANTITATIVE RESEARCH

Quantitative research provides information that helps decision makers select the best course of action and estimate the probable results. As the name suggests, numbers are involved. Rigorous statistical procedures allow researchers to estimate how confident they can be about their conclusions. Since quantitative research uses widely accepted methods, duplicating the study should arrive at approximately the same results. Certain techniques also indicate how closely the findings represent the views or attitudes of the whole population at large, not just the sample studied.

Quantitative research played an enormous role in the successful positioning and launch of Kimberly-Clark's Expressions facial tissue line. In the face of increasing competition from products, the company began looking for an innovative way to increase market share for its Kleenex brand. Nearly 37 percent of buyers said they disliked the look of tissue boxes and often hid them in closets or bathrooms, where they wouldn't clash with household decor. The Expressions line introduced packaging with about 18 different motifs that range from Native American animal drawings to Amish quilts to an impressionistic Manhattan skyline. Product testing in eight U.S. cities revealed consumer preferences for six styles: traditional, country, southwestern, contemporary, Asian, and Victorian. Expressions was ultimately a great success, partly because marketers took the time to learn the opinions of consumers.[28]

Quantitative research usually follows the scientific method to ensure that faulty conclusions are not drawn. The **scientific method** is a systematic way to gather, analyze, and interpret data in order to confirm or disconfirm a prior conception. Essentially, it is a two-step procedure. First, researchers develop a hypothesis about an issue based on a limited amount of information. A **hypothesis** is a tentative assumption about a particular event or issue. Second, rigorous tests are conducted to determine whether the hypothesis is supported by the information.

Let us say we have an idea that more men and women shop in malls on the weekend because they're not working, so we hypothesize that greater sales volumes will be obtained on Saturday and Sunday than on weekdays. We then gather information to test the hypothesis.

SCIENTIFIC METHOD

A systematic way to gather, analyze, and interpret data in order to confirm or disconfirm a prior conception.

HYPOTHESIS

A tentative assumption about a particular event or issue.

The key is for researchers to state beforehand what they believe the results may be and why. This enables appropriate data to be gathered and analyzed to assess whether the hypothesis is true.

Data Collection Methods   Two of the most common methods for collecting quantitative data are experiments and surveys. **Experiments** usually take place either where the marketing problem occurs or in a laboratory setting that is contrived to match research needs. To test new packaging for a pain reliever, for example, the manufacturer may invite consumers to "shop" in a simulated supermarket. In that way shopping patterns can be observed to see whether the packaging is eye-catching. Experiments are often used for causal research. **Causal research** attempts to find a cause-and-effect relationship between two events. One of the most important forms of causal research is test marketing. A test market provides a limited trial of a product strategy under realistic conditions.

Surveys are the most popular way to collect data. When researchers want to ensure that each subject is asked for the same information, they prepare a written survey questionnaire. It is a measurement device, much like a thermometer or a ruler. Two common units of measure for questionnaire items are the points along Likert scales and bipolar adjective scales.

Likert scales are simple to develop and easy to interpret. **Likert scales** allow the intensity of feelings to be expressed and tend to provide information about a person's attitude toward something. Subjects are asked to indicate the extent to which they agree or disagree with each statement in the survey. The Likert scale shown in Figure 5.5 has five points (units of measure). A seven-point scale often is used, adding "somewhat disagree" and "somewhat agree" on either side of the middle point.

Bipolar adjective scales allow respondents to choose along a range between two extremes. Figure 5.6 shows a typical bipolar adjective scale. In general, there are three, five, or seven points in the scale. Many dimensions can be measured in a relatively short questionnaire. Perhaps that is why this scale is so frequently used in marketing research.

The wording of an item can make quite a difference. A classic example occurred in the 1980s during the battles between Burger King and McDonald's. Burger King asked respondents: "Do you prefer your hamburgers flame-broiled or fried?" The three-to-one preference for flame-broiled was touted extensively by Burger King in an ad campaign. The results were completely different when McDonald's researchers asked: "Do you prefer a hamburger that is grilled on a hot stainless-steel grill or cooked by passing the warmed meat through an open-gas flame?" McDonald's frying method received a clear majority. When the question was modified to include the fact that the gas-flame burgers were warmed in a microwave oven prior to serving, McDonald's won seven to one.[29]

EXPERIMENT

A test conducted under controlled conditions in order to prove or disprove a marketing hypothesis.

CAUSAL RESEARCH

Research that attempts to prove a cause-and-effect relationship between two phenomena.

LIKERT SCALE

A scale that measures the respondent's intensity of agreement with a particular statement.

INSTRUCTIONS: Please put an X in the space that indicates how strongly you agree or disagree with the following statements about MTV.

	Strongly Disagree	Disagree	Neither Agree Nor Disagree	Agree	Strongly Agree
MTV is fun to watch	___	___	___	___	___
MTV is less educational than most evening programming	___	___	___	___	___
MTV appeals more to those with higher income	___	___	___	___	___
Carson Daly is a real plus for MTV	___	___	___	___	___

FIGURE 5.5 *A Typical Likert Scale*

INSTRUCTIONS: Please put an X in the space that most appropriately indicates your feelings about shopping at Gap.

	Very	Moderately	Slightly	Neither One nor the Other	Slightly	Moderately	Very	
Inexpensive	_____	_____	_____	_____	_____	_____	_____	Expensive
Helpful Salespeople	_____	_____	_____	_____	_____	_____	_____	Unhelpful Salespeople
High-quality Products	_____	_____	_____	_____	_____	_____	_____	Low-quality Products

FIGURE 5.6 *A Typical Bipolar Adjective Scale*

Administering Surveys   A survey can be administered through personal interviews, mall intercepts, telephone, or mail. Each technique has benefits and disadvantages, as shown in Figure 5.7. The researcher needs to select the method most appropriate for the current project.

Personal Interviews Personal interviews require face-to-face, two-way communication between the interviewer and the respondent. This method is particularly useful in probing complex answers or observing the respondent's behavior. The setting usually is comfortable, and the respondent is given undivided attention. Gen-X Press is a leading full-service consulting group that helps companies to better market to Generations X and Y, usually collecting through face-to-face interviews with members of these generations. Questions are asked about motivation, the relationship between pay and happiness, and empowerment in the workplace. Marketers believe that the opinions of individuals can be used to predict future actions among mainstream members of Generations X and Y.[30]

One benefit of personal interviews is the high participation rate. It's unlikely that any questions will go unanswered, and props or visual aids can be used. But there are several disadvantages. Subjects may be influenced by the interviewer, and they give up anonymity when meeting face-to-face, so they may withhold information or answer in unnatural ways. Interviewing is expensive, since professionals must be trained and then sent to the various locations. The cost can range from $25 per average consumer to thousands of dollars per top executive, surgeon, legislator, or others.

Mall Intercepts Mall intercepts, as the name implies, occur at a shopping mall, and the interviewer chooses respondents on some objective basis, such as every fifth person encountered. Mall intercepts are simple to conduct, and data can be collected quickly and cost-effectively. Questions can be asked about actual purchases during some specified period. This helps the researcher determine actual behaviors as well as opinions and attitudes. One variation of this method is a shopping basket study, or simply looking at what a consumer purchases during a particular trip to the store. Grocery stores often want this kind of information in order to

	Personal Interviews	**Mall Intercepts**	**Telephone**	**Mail**
Speed of Completion	Slowest	Fast	Fastest	Moderate
Response Rate	High	Moderate	Moderate	Low
Quality of Response	Excellent	Good	Good	Limited
Interviewer Bias	High	Moderate	Moderate	Low
Geographic Reach	Limited	Limited	Excellent	Excellent
Cost	Very expensive	Moderate	Moderate	Very inexpensive

FIGURE 5.7 *Comparative Advantages of Interviews, Mall Intercepts, Telephone Surveys, and Mail Questionnaires*

identify which products are purchased together, the total amount of spending, and the shopping patterns of individuals while in the store.

Telephone Surveys Telephone surveys offer speed and relatively low cost. Using banks of telephones, marketers can contact a large number of people at approximately the same time. This method is particularly effective with professionals, who tend to be articulate and willing to discuss things over the telephone. By prearranging the call, it's possible to gain considerable cooperation from respondents. Now that fax machines and the Internet are so prevalent, a common procedure is to call ahead, fax the information or ask respondents to get it from a Web site, and obtain reactions over the telephone. This enables interviewers not only to probe for thoughts and ideas but also to elicit responses to printed materials. Another advantage of the telephone is that a second call can be arranged easily if the individual cannot respond at that moment. Today, computer-assisted technology allows respondents to register their answers using the touch-tone pad, which works particularly well with a large panel of subjects. Also, computerized systems that are voice activated save on telephone charges and make online data analysis possible.

The major drawback of telephone interviews is the increase in unlisted numbers, which makes it very difficult to obtain a valid sample. In some cities more than half the population has an unlisted number. One way to overcome this is through random digit dialing by a computer, although many consumers are adding Caller ID service to screen out unwanted surveys. In addition, phone surveys have an obvious limitation if respondents are required to see something, as in evaluating ads or product renderings.

Mail Surveys In mail surveys, a questionnaire is sent directly to the respondent's home or place of business. An advantage is that people can answer at their own pace and at a convenient time. Mailed questionnaires can be extremely useful for surveying professionals, who have a high response rate and tend to give thoughtful answers. Publishers regularly survey professors by mail concerning textbooks they have adopted, teaching methods, and their ideas about innovative materials that can be created. Associations often obtain good response quality and return rates from membership surveys by mail.

Many techniques are used to encourage people to answer mail questionnaires. Often a cover letter explains the purpose of the study and why it will be beneficial to them. A little gift or a small amount of money can improve return rates. Research also reveals that the rate can be boosted considerably by multiple prior notification, while sending only one has no influence. Mailing a second survey has a significant effect on response rates as well. Alloy.com, an online merchant of trendy apparel and accessories, attracts people to its market surveys by offering popular links on its Web site. Alloy "jumps" include celebrity news, MP3 music samples, horoscopes, and trivia.[31]

It helps to have the surveys sponsored by a legitimate organization, such as a professional association. A study reported in *Industrial Marketing Management* examined this effect. The mean response rates for the questionnaires from a university and an honor society sponsor were significantly higher than for those sponsored by a marketing research firm and an unidentified source.[32] Despite every effort to improve the percentage of responses, many people refuse to answer mail questionnaires. This is a serious problem, since those who do respond may differ from the rest of the population. For example, they may be motivated to answer because they intensely like or dislike a product.

Sampling Surveys are conducted to draw insights about the people being studied. The **population (universe)** is comprised of all the individuals or organizations relevant to the marketing research project. For example, if the government wants to know the average number of jobs a U.S. resident holds during the first 10 years out of high school, the relevant population is all U.S. residents age 28 or older. There are millions in this age group. The government could attempt to interview all of them, but that would be impractical, if not impossible, and far too costly. Researchers have developed methods for surveying a subset of people from whom they draw inferences about the larger population.

The first step is to obtain a **sampling frame,** which is a list of people in the universe who potentially could be contacted. From this, researchers select the sample. A **sample** is the group of people who are asked to participate in the research. Since focus groups usually are very small, it is difficult to determine whether the opinions expressed truly represent those of the larger population.

There are two categories of samples: probability and nonprobability. In a **probability sample,** the chance of selecting a given individual can be calculated. One popular method is **simple random sampling,** whereby each individual has an equal chance of being chosen (say,

POPULATION (UNIVERSE)

All the individuals or organizations relevant to the marketing research project.

SAMPLING FRAME

A list of people in the universe who potentially could be contacted.

SAMPLE

The group participating in a research project that represents the entire population of potential respondents.

PROBABILITY SAMPLE

A sample in which the chance of selecting a given individual from the sampling frame or population can be calculated.

SIMPLE RANDOM SAMPLING

A sampling technique in which each member of the study population has an equal and known chance of being chosen.

every third name is selected). Another is **stratified random sampling,** whereby each individual within a selected subgroup of the sample has a known chance of selection (say, every third household with income of $50,000+). This method is often used in marketing since much research focuses on market segments. If some form of random sampling is adopted, then statistics can be used to determine the likelihood that responses from the sample will be similar to the responses of the larger population.

When using **nonprobability samples,** the researcher does not know the likelihood of selecting a particular respondent. The two most common types are judgment and convenience samples. **Judgment samples** are chosen by the researcher based on the belief that these people represent a majority of the study population.

Convenience samples are people who happen to come along, such as shoppers in a given store at a certain time or travelers passing through an airport. Convenience samples are relatively inexpensive, and the selection can be purposely unrepresentative, such as interviewing only females. In general, this method does not provide data reliable enough for quantitative research. Even probability samples can become like convenience samples if care is not taken regarding the smallest details, such as when interviews are conducted. Tom Brokaw remarked during the 1992 elections that polls could not be taken on Friday night. It seems the results would be skewed because so many Republicans go out that evening.

INTERPRETING AND REPORTING SURVEY FINDINGS

Once the research is completed, the results must be reported to the appropriate decision makers. No matter how sophisticated or reliable, marketing research is of little use unless it can be easily understood by the people who act upon it. Most managers and executives have little experience with research techniques and little interest in learning about them. Thus, presentation of understandable research results is an important skill for marketers. Good research moves from data to information to insight. Unfortunately, to demonstrate the hard work that has gone into a project, many researchers give too much extraneous information. A report that describes each table in detail instead of using the information to reach conclusions is not likely to meet the needs of executives.

STRATIFIED RANDOM SAMPLING
A sampling technique in which each member of a selected subgroup of the population has an equal chance of selection.

NONPROBABILITY SAMPLE
A sample in which the likelihood of selecting a particular respondent from the sampling frame cannot be calculated.

JUDGMENT SAMPLE
A sample selected by the researchers or interviewers based on their belief that those chosen represent a majority of the study population.

CONVENIENCE SAMPLE
A sample composed of people who happen to come along, such as shoppers in a store at a given time, whoever answers the doorbell, or travelers passing through an airport.

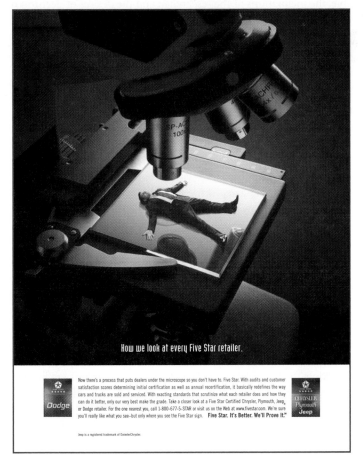

This Dodge advertisement references the results of a customer satisfaction survey.

The Edsel is an example of a marketing mistake.

CONNECTED: SURFING THE NET

www.ford.com

Ford has come a long way since the Edsel. Find out what cars it creates for consumers today by visiting the online "Showroom" at the Ford Web site.

Experience pays off in interpreting research. When the Museum of Fine Arts (MFA) in Boston held focus groups on an upcoming exhibition of Winslow Homer, the researchers found that the public did not know about the artist and would not attend. A museum executive used her experience, including the MFA shop's sales records of items linked to Homer, to demonstrate that the public may not know his name but does know his pictures and would turn out for the show. Because the museum relied on the executive's experience, not the focus groups, it was prepared for the blockbuster. Yet, sometimes research is right when the experts are wrong. Ford didn't listen to marketing research in the mid-1950s. The Edsel was built with features that consumers said they wanted, but the car itself did poorly in several rounds of consumer testing. Ford went ahead anyway, believing it could push the car with a strong sales force. The mistake cost about $350 million (in 1950s dollars)!

There is some debate about whether marketing researchers should recommend action. Whether marketing researchers make recommendations must depend on the total data available, the inclinations of the researcher, and the desires of decision makers. In keeping with the team spirit, most executives would like knowledgeable people to provide as many insights as possible. If recommendations are made, then all the underlying assumptions should be clearly stated.

WHO DOES MARKETING RESEARCH?

The first commercial research department was founded in 1911 at the *Saturday Evening Post,* when Charles C. Parlin completed his now famous study of Campbell's soup users. He undertook the research because Campbell's executives refused to purchase advertising in the *Post,* believing that its working-class readership did not represent a significant market for the company. The soup sold at 10 cents a can, a cost they believed only wealthy consumers could afford. By counting cans in the garbage from different neighborhoods, Parlin proved they were wrong. He showed that canned soup was bought mainly by the time-constrained working class, whereas the wealthy enjoyed homemade soup prepared by servants. Campbell's became a big advertiser in the magazine and one of the top brand names in the United States.

In-Company Research   An American Marketing Association (AMA) survey indicates that three out of four large companies have a formal in-company marketing research department. In fact, nearly all consumer products manufacturers, retailers, wholesalers, advertising agencies, and publishers have such a department. Most were created within the last decade. According to the AMA, the average marketing research budget is about $2 million per firm.[33]

Most in-company marketing research departments are headed by experienced personnel who report to top executives. The research staff usually includes project directors, analysts, and specialists. The project director is responsible for designing projects, which may be conducted within the department or by outside agencies. The position of analyst is an entry-level job with the function of interpreting specific types of data for select decisions. Analysts usually

Rank	Organization	Headquarters	Total Research Revenue (Millions)
1	AC Neilsen Corp.	Stamford, CT	$1,525.4
2	IMS Health Inc.	Westport, CT	$1,275.7
3	Information Resources, Inc.	Chicago, IL	$ 546.3
4	NFO Worldwide, Inc.	Greenwich, CT	$ 457.2
5	Neilsen Media Research, Inc.	New York, NY	$ 453.3
6	The Kantar Group Ltd.	Fairfield, CT	$ 250.2
7	Westat, Inc.	Rockville, MD	$ 242.0
8	The Arbitron Co.	New York, NY	$ 215.4
9	Maritz Marketing Research, Inc.	St. Louis, MO	$ 174.3
10	Marketing Facts, Inc.	Arlington Heights, IL	$ 160.0

FIGURE 5.8 *Top 10 Marketing Research Organizations*

Source: "Top 50 U.S. Research Organizations," *Marketing News*, June 5, 2000, p. 4.

are part of a marketing team from several units or divisions, although they report directly to the head of their department. Marketing research specialists have expertise in one aspect of a project, such as survey design, data collection, statistics, modeling, or marketing science.

Marketing research has become so sophisticated that few organizations are willing to rely entirely on their internal capabilities. Consequently, research is conducted by both in-house personnel and outside agencies, who may or may not work together. Often it's not cost-effective for companies to hire employees with all the different skills required to conduct a broad range of research. This is especially true regarding data collection. Numerous companies offer field services in that area. Even if external agencies are used, however, most companies still need internal staff to help identify the research problem and interface with the outside agency.

External Research Companies often hire out marketing research. As you can see from Figure 5.8, conducting research can be a very lucrative business.

Outside agencies include consulting companies, full-service research firms, specialty research firms, and syndicated data companies. Such consulting companies as Deloitte & Touche and Electronic Data Systems (EDS) often conduct all phases of marketing research but only for clients with whom they have an ongoing relationship. Full-service firms focus on all aspects of data collection and analysis, and their personnel can handle the entire project. Specialty research firms concentrate on certain aspects of a project. There were over 174 research firms in 1999. Companies in the United States spent over $5.2 billion, resulting in a growth rate of 10.1 percent for the research industry.[34]

Some only conduct surveys, relying on others to supply questionnaires and yet others to perform data analysis. Certain specialty research firms help marketers better understand diversity or particular segments. For example, Strategy Research Corporation, a consulting firm based in Miami, studies consumer satisfaction in Spanish-speaking markets in the United States and Latin America. Its monthly telephone research service, Tele-Nacion, interviews consumers in America's 10 largest Hispanic markets: Los Angeles, Miami, New York, Chicago, San Francisco, Houston, San Antonio, McAllen/Brownsville, Dallas/Ft. Worth, and San Diego. SRC's Tele-Nacion interviews 300 Hispanic Americans in each market, usually receiving a fee from companies of $600 per question.[35] Syndicated data companies also research one type of information or a single industry. For example, the Bureau of the Census and the Bureau of Labor Statistics are experts on census data and use the data to model various scenarios for clients. Neurocommunication Research Laboratory specializes in customized information about how broadcast and print advertisements trigger the maximum responses in viewers.

Because marketing research is critical for good decision making but expensive to conduct, most companies build a long-term association with one or more outside sources. This enables the agency to become familiar with the typical problems faced by the organization and to establish a good working relationship with in-company marketing research staff.

career tip   Bob Walker of the market research firm Surveys and Forecasts
says: "Researchers need to be able to synthesize information
from a variety of sources and tell a cohesive story." Marketing research is a challenging and exciting field. Businesses today are not only spending more in this
area but also are adding staff researchers and paying higher salaries.[36] The
increased demand is providing numerous career opportunities. If you think you
might be interested in marketing research, then investigate one of the top 10
organizations listed in Figure 5.8.

TECHNOLOGY'S EFFECT ON MARKETING RESEARCH

Technology has brought many changes to marketing research. Today's marketers can acquire
and analyze more information faster than ever before. Technology also has made it easier for
them to connect with an increasing number of customers and information sources. In the
past, marketing research was a relatively static process in the face of constantly changing markets. Now marketers can know in real time what is happening in the marketplace. Data are
quickly converted to information that can be used in a specific decision.

Technology has not merely speeded up the research process. Advances in computerized
3-D modeling make it easy to simulate retail stores on computer screens. Virtual shopping is
inexpensive to create when compared to the cost of setting up an actual store. Consumers can
make product selections as they scroll through the computer image. You can change brand
assortment or features in minutes. The virtual store gives marketers a no-risk way to exercise
their imagination early in the product development process.[37] Technology helps reduce the
cost as well as the risk of marketing innovations.

INTERNET SEARCHES

The Internet's World Wide Web can be an excellent source of marketing data. In fact, it is
sometimes referred to as the world's largest resource library. It contains information on literally millions of topics and is updated daily. The trick is to sift through all of it to find what you
need. Marketers do this through the use of a search engine such as Yahoo!, America Online,
WebCrawler, or Netscape Navigator Net Search. You type a key word into the search engine,
and it scans all the Web sites to which it's linked, providing you with a list of available information matching the keyword. For example, the keyword *distribution* is likely to produce
thousands of sources ranging from companies that provide distribution services to consultants in the distribution industry. You can scan through the sources and generally find the
information you need. All marketers should learn how to surf using keyword searches. Still,
marketers need to know the limitations of search engines. A single search engine is likely to
find only a third or less of the available information on a topic. Multiengine search devices
such as Metacrawler (www.metacrawler.com) and Google.com give results from several search
engines. The Internet is an amazing research tool. It has two major advantages over traditional
methods—speed and cost-effectiveness. Experts estimate that by the year 2005, over 50 percent of all marketing research revenues will be earned via the Internet, totaling over $3.1 bil-
lion annually.[38] There is information on nearly every industry, from agriculture to zoology. In
addition, quantitative and exploratory research can be conducted through e-mail surveys,
online focus groups, Web site registration, and observation of discussions among Web users.
Marketers often research online to divide Internet users into meaningful segments.

INTERNET SURVEYS AND GROUP RESEARCH

Many researchers are turning to the Internet to gain individuals' participation in surveys.
The main advantage of using the Internet instead of traditional methods is that the information
is available very quickly. Additionally, researchers can survey a greater number of people with less
costs compared to written and mailed surveys, and data can be analyzed as they are collected.

There are four main types of online surveys:

1. *Pop-Up Surveys.* When an Internet surfer leaves a Web site, another window, containing
   a questionnaire, pops up on the screen. Internet users have the option of either completing
   the survey or closing the browser window. The response rate for this type of survey ranges
   from 15 to 45 percent.

Global Crossing's technology affects marketing research.

2. *E-Mail or Web Surveys.* Via e-mail, a company can invite someone for his or her participation in an online questionnaire. The response rates for these surveys range from 25 to 50 percent and are usually completed by the user in two to three days.

3. *Online Groups.* A research company can organize what is essentially a focus group discussion on the Internet. These discussions are held in chat rooms on the Internet.

4. *Moderated E-Mail Groups.* Researchers can carry on long discussions with individuals by communicating through e-mail. Online bulletin boards are an example of this type of research.[39]

Marketers also observe discussions among Web users to gather information about current and prospective customers. Many companies encourage customers to fill out a Web site registration form. The participant is usually asked to volunteer some personal information in exchange for a free gift, coupon, or some other incentive. The information helps the marketer to understand Internet behavior and habits. *The New York Times* Web site, for example, has a Web site registration form that profiles customer interests. Not only can the information be used for research but also relevant e-mail can be automatically forwarded to those who want it.[40]

GLOBAL MARKETING RESEARCH

Global marketing research involves the same process as any other kind—from research design to the interpretation and presentation of results. And usually the same techniques are employed—interviews, focus groups, and surveys. The big difference is that global marketing research is very difficult.

It is not easy to locate secondary data in foreign countries. Sometimes it simply isn't collected in a country. For example, Ethiopia and Chad don't gather population statistics.[41] Many developing countries lack mechanisms for collecting data about retail and wholesale activities. And even if secondary data are available, they may be incomplete or their accuracy questionable. The data may be manipulated by the government for political reasons: In 1994, for instance, Russia reported inflation at two percent when the International Labor

Global Marketing Research uses maps and aerial photos to identify population locations and estimate sizes in countries such as Ethiopia.

Organization found it was actually more than 10 percent.[42] Industrialized nations usually have sophisticated collection procedures, at least for basic statistics on population and economic activity. In developing countries, data are likely to be based on estimates or outdated processes.[43]

Because secondary data are difficult to find, global research most often requires the collection of primary data. This, too, presents many challenges. One of the most obvious is that of language. It's very hard to ensure an exact translation, especially when slang is used. Many researchers use a technique called back translation: The research question is translated into the foreign language by one person, and then it is put back in the original language by a second person. This helps catch any errors. It certainly helped an Australian soft-drink company hoping to market its product in Hong Kong. Its slogan, "Baby, it's cold in here," translated into Chinese as: "Small mosquito, on the inside it is very cold."[44] Needless to say, that would have been an embarrassing marketing blunder!

Once the survey instrument is translated, participants must be found. Again, this isn't easy. In Mexico, there are only eight phones per 100 citizens, compared to 50 phones per 100 people in the United States. And the phone service in Mexico is extremely unreliable. In Brazil, nearly 30 percent of all mail is never delivered. Postal service is equally poor in other developing countries. Even if the mail gets through, literacy can be another barrier. Sometimes even individual interviews present challenges. In many cultures, it's considered embarrassing to discuss personal hygiene, such as which shampoo or soap you use. The Germans tend to avoid conversations about personal finances and the Dutch would rather talk about sex than money.[45]

Nevertheless, companies that avoid global marketing research find themselves in trouble. Consider the U.S. baby care company advertising its bath soap in Hungary. The ad, which showed a mother holding her baby, caused an uproar. Why? Because the mother had a wedding band on her left hand, and Hungarian women wear wedding bands on their right hand. The ad was interpreted as an unwed mother holding her baby, and women refused to buy the product.[46] Marketing research probably would have caught the mistake.

Global marketing research is becoming more and more prevalent as companies expand their scope of operations. The time it takes to conduct worldwide research has been reduced by computer-based interviews via the Internet, the spread of telephones and fax machines, and express delivery services. For example, one software company conducted a worldwide survey of more than 80 clients in only three weeks. This amazing feat involved modeling tasks, computer programming, list development, respondent recruiting, diskette distribution, and data retrieval, analysis, and reporting. As a result of the research, the company was able to improve its pricing strategy.[47]

ETHICS IN MARKETING RESEARCH AND INFORMATION USE

J. D. Power is paid by automakers to provide research on customer satisfaction. This information is then used in publications to promote autos. Some magazine editors receive "consulting fees" from auto companies and write reviews of car performance. These are certainly legal practices, but are they ethical? With the information explosion comes an increasing amount of potentially deceptive research that can be used to alter consumers' opinions. Historically, studies were sponsored by scientists, the federal government, and academic institutions. Today, with government and universities on tight budgets, private companies fill the void with so-called objective research for hire. Corporations, litigants, political candidates, trade associations, lobbyists, and special-interest groups can buy research to use as they like.[48]

A study by the Boston Center for Strategy Research revealed that some marketing managers believe market research is likely to reflect biases rather than present objective information. They also believe much of it is conducted to confirm a preconceived conclusion or validate a client's position. In other words, it arrives at the desired answer, no matter what the facts may indicate. Research of this nature is confirmatory, not exploratory.[49]

The scientific method is supposed to prevent this type of bias because anyone duplicating a study or experiment should come up with the same results. More and more of the information available to consumers is created to sell a product or advance a cause. Buying and selling information to advance a private agenda demonstrates how the modern sense of truth may be warped.[50] Privately sponsored research tends to emphasize positive results and downplay negative ones. Companies obviously want their products to look good.[51] If study results contradict the sponsor's agenda, then they may be suppressed. Yet, if the information indicates potential harm to consumers, then ethical and possibly legal issues arise.

Although consumers are increasingly suspicious about "facts," they often have little basis for questioning them. The average consumer does not have enough personal knowledge to dispute the research that almost daily shapes our beliefs about social, political, economic, and environmental issues. That is why many groups exist to assist and protect consumers. Interested in truth, objectivity, and accuracy, these groups consist of representatives from industry, individual companies, academia, and the government. They have taken action to regulate the content of information and to defend the average consumer from distorted messages. Some industries have collectively formulated policies in order to reduce litigation, prevent mandatory regulation, and increase consumer trust. Still, questionable information finds its way to consumers.

Consider a 1990 study sponsored by Procter & Gamble, the leading maker of disposable diapers. For several years, the company had been fighting a public relations battle against environmentalists and the cloth diaper industry. Between 1988 and 1990, sales of cloth diapers skyrocketed, and more than a dozen state legislatures were considering various regulations for disposable diapers. Under pressure, Procter & Gamble decided to finance a public policy study. The researchers found that disposable and cloth diapers were environmentally equivalent, when factors such as energy and water use were taken into account. The media disseminated the results and the sale of disposables improved. In 1992, Gerber Products, the largest supplier of cloth diapers, closed three plants and laid off 900 workers. Gerber's CEO said: "There was a dramatic change in the cloth diaper market caused by reduced environmental concern about disposable diapers."[52] Procter & Gamble won back lost market share and gained, at least temporarily, acceptance of disposables.

Although a marketer may occasionally benefit from biased information, those who connect ethically are more likely to create a profitable long-term relationship based on trust and loyalty. Often, as companies seek to build such relationships, the first question they must answer is: What customers are we trying to reach and how do we go about it? One concern for parents is the ethical use of information about children under the age of 18. The Children's Online Privacy Act of 1998 covers targeting children. In response, Kibu.com has promised to keep all information regarding its 13- to 18-year-old target market private.[53] In the next chapter we will discover ways in which marketing information supports the selection and targeting of desirable market segments.

Another dimension of the ethical use of marketing research information lies in information obtained about the Internet. Privacy is an important issue for most Internet users. In a recent study by the American Marketing Association, 92.8 percent of Web sites reported that they collect personal information about visitors, while only 65.9 percent post a privacy disclosure on their sites.[54]

J. D. POWER & ASSOCIATES
www.jdpower.com

THIS CHAPTER'S CONNECTING THROUGH RELATIONSHIPS feature discusses J. D. Power & Associates, the international marketing information firm. Learn more about the company by visiting its Web site and answering the following questions.

1. Read "About J. D. Power & Associates." In what two areas has the company been recognized for its marketing information and consulting? What other marketing information services does the company offer? How do these services benefit its customers?
2. Recently, J. D. Power & Associates created "J. D. Clubs." What type of clubs are these? What companies joined with J. D. Power to create them?
3. Since J. D. Power & Associates is an international firm, what difficulties may it encounter when collecting information? In what ways can technology facilitate the company's marketing research efforts?

BUGLE BOY CLOTHING COMPANY
www.bugleboy.com

THE DIVERSITY FEATURE IN THIS chapter discusses the Bugle Boy Clothing Company's unique method of conducting research. To expand your thinking about Bugle Boy, visit its Web site and answer the following questions.

1. Bugle Boy is one of the largest privately held apparel companies in the United States. Read its history. To what does the company attribute its success? What role do you think marketing information and research have played in this success?
2. Read about the evaluation of products at Bugle Boy. How have its products changed through the years? How might exploratory research have contributed to Bugle Boy's product decisions? List ways the company may have collected this research.
3. Read about Bugle Boy's Licensee Program. How will this program help Bugle Boy to grow its business in areas on which it had not previously concentrated?
4. In order to connect with customers, Bugle Boy must understand and accommodate diverse needs. Choose and discuss a press release that shows Bugle Boy connecting with diversity. How does marketing research strengthen this connection?

CHAPTER SUMMARY

OBJECTIVE 1: Understand the roles that marketing information systems (MIS) and research play in marketing decision making.

You can't connect with customers if you can't locate, understand, and respond to them. MIS are critical in making informed decisions about nearly every aspect of marketing. They are used to systematically collect and analyze data to support decision making. An MIS often includes a marketing decision support system (MDSS), which puts information in convenient form for executives to use. MIS are ongoing and encompass all information. Marketing research is conducted to address a particular opportunity, problem, or issue. Marketing information is used in planning, marketing mix decisions, and performance monitoring.

OBJECTIVE 2: Recognize how data are transformed into information to be used in a variety of marketing decisions.

Data and information are not the same. Data must be translated into information before they are useful for decision making. External data come from outside the firm, and internal data originate inside the firm. Both types are stored in databases so they can be retrieved through a computer. Primary data are collected for the first time to address a specific issue. Secondary data already exist and can be accessed immediately by a broad range of users. Once data are assembled, they must be analyzed through data sorting, the use of statistics, and models. All of this is done with particular issues and decision areas in mind.

OBJECTIVE 3: Understand the types of research and the steps of a typical marketing research process.

The marketing research process starts with the problem definition, which focuses on the needs of decision makers to ensure that the research will be useful. The research design is then based on what decisions need what information, what data and data sources will provide that information, and how the data will be collected and analyzed. Next, exploratory research helps investigators better understand issues by defining problems, searching for possible explanations, and creating hypotheses. Quantitative research yields information to help decision makers select the best course of action. Because it is quantitative, estimates usually can be made of the likely results of actions. This requires appropriate measurement and sampling. The last steps are to interpret and report findings. Experience and insight are useful at this stage because the same information can be interpreted in various ways.

OBJECTIVE 4: Describe widely used marketing research techniques.

Exploratory research techniques include focus groups, depth interviews, projective techniques, observation, and case analysis. A focus group usually has eight to twelve people. Several sessions must be used since the group, not individuals, provide the data. Depth interviews are one-on-one conversations. Researchers spend a lot of time probing a few respondents about their opinions and actions. With projective techniques, subjects are asked to analyze contrived situations or to give opinions about how they believe others may respond. Observation provides insights by watching consumers in a range of situations. Finally, case analysis is the study of a few situations in depth. It is particularly useful for benchmarking. Quantitative research often involves using the scientific method. Surveys and test markets are common in this type of research. Survey data are usually collected from a sample of the population. Questionnaire design is important. Likert scales or bipolar adjective scales frequently are used in questionnaires.

OBJECTIVE 5: Explore how marketing information is being influenced by technology and is obtained globally.

Both internal and external marketing research is being dramatically influenced by technology. It facilitates the faster collection and analysis of greater quantities of information than was possible in the past. The Internet is a revolutionary way of interacting with customers. Research in global markets is complicated because secondary data may be scarce. Surveys must be carefully translated, and data collection is often difficult. Still, global research is becoming more and more important.

OBJECTIVE 6: Understand that ethical issues surround the use and dissemination of research.

There are many ethical issues surrounding marketing research. One problem is that it sometimes can reflect the biases of marketers. When research is conducted to confirm a preconceived conclusion or validate a position, the results are not likely to be objective. The scientific method can eliminate this type of bias. A number of groups exist to prevent the manipulation of marketing research. They are interested in accuracy and want to protect consumers.

REVIEW YOUR UNDERSTANDING

1. What is a marketing information system (MIS)? What is a marketing decision support system (MDSS)? What is a transaction-based information system (TBIS)?
2. What is marketing research? How is it different from an MIS?
3. How are data transformed into information? What are the three steps?
4. What are the differences between primary and secondary data? Give examples.
5. What are the three major uses of marketing information? Explain.
6. What are the steps in a typical marketing research project?
7. What is exploratory research? List five exploratory research methods.
8. What is quantitative research? Name two quantitative methods.
9. Give two challenges associated with global marketing research.
10. What are the pros and cons of each type of survey data collection?

DISCUSSION OF CONCEPTS

1. How is an MIS used? What are the two components of a typical MIS? Describe them.
2. What is the difference between data and information? Why is it important for marketers to provide executives with information rather than data?
3. Explain the objective of the marketing decision support system.
4. List and describe the four types of information an MIS provides. What is the importance of each type for decision making?
5. Describe each step of the marketing research process. Why is it so important to lay out each step in detail prior to beginning any research project?
6. Select a marketing problem and design a marketing research approach suitable to address it.
7. After completing an exploratory research study, how would you decide whether quantitative research is in order?
8. What would be the major considerations in developing a marketing research capability for a small company?
9. Under what circumstances would you consider it to be ethical to withhold marketing research from interested consumers? When would it be unethical?

Case analysis: The in-depth study of a few examples.

Causal research: Research that attempts to prove a cause-and-effect relationship between two phenomena.

Convenience sample: A sample composed of people who happen to come along, such as shoppers in a store at a given time, whoever answers the doorbell, or travelers passing through an airport.

Data: Facts or statistics obtained from outside or inside the company.

Database: A collection of data that can be retrieved by a computer.

Depth interview: A relatively unstructured conversation that allows the researcher to probe deeply into a consumer's thoughts.

Experiment: A test conducted under controlled conditions in order to prove or disprove a marketing hypothesis.

Exploratory research: Research designed to clarify the problem and suggest ways to address it.

External data: Data obtained outside the company.

Focus group: A group, usually composed of eight to twelve people, whose opinions are elicited by an interviewer to provide exploratory insights into a problem.

Hypothesis: A tentative assumption about a particular event or issue.

Internal data: Data obtained within the company.

Judgment sample: A sample selected by the researchers or interviewers based on their belief that those chosen represent a majority of the study population.

Likert scale: A scale that measures the respondent's intensity of agreement with a particular statement.

Management information system (MIS): A computerized system used to collect and analyze the data needed for management decision making. The marketing information system is often considered a part of this system.

Marketing decision support system (MDSS): A two-way communication bridge between the people who collect and analyze information and the executives who use it.

Marketing information system (MIS): A computerized system used to collect and analyze marketing data.

Marketing research: The formal assembly and analysis of information about specific issues surrounding the marketing of goods and services.

Nonprobability sample: A sample in which the likelihood of selecting a particular respondent from the sampling frame cannot be calculated.

Observation: A research technique whereby researchers simply watch the participants they are studying.

Pilot study: A small-scale project that allows the researcher to refine and test the approaches that eventually will be used.

Population (universe): All the individuals or organizations relevant to the marketing research project.

Primary data: Information collected for the first time.

Probability sample: A sample in which the chance of selecting a given individual from the sampling frame or population can be calculated.

Projective technique: A technique that enables respondents to project their thoughts onto a third party or object or through some type of contrived situation.

Quantitative research: Research designed to provide the information needed to select the best course of action and estimate the probable results.

Research design: An outline of what data will be gathered, what sources will be used, and how the data will be collected and analyzed.

Sample: The group participating in a research project that represents the entire population of potential respondents.

Sampling frame: A list of people in the universe who potentially could be contacted.

Scientific method: A systematic way to gather, analyze, and interpret data in order to confirm or disconfirm a prior conception.

Secondary data: Information that already has been collected.

Simple random sampling: A sampling technique in which each member of the study population has an equal and known chance of being chosen.

Stratified random sampling: A sampling technique in which each member of a selected subgroup of the population has an equal chance of selection.

Transaction-based information system (TBIS): A computerized link between a firm and its customers, distributors, and suppliers.

REFERENCES

1. Virginia I Postrel, "The Big Uneasy," *Forbes ASAP*, August 26, 1996, p. 32, Kathy Rebello, "A Literary Hangout—Without the Latte," *Business Week*, September 23, 1996, (from online *Business Week*); Michael H. Martin, "The Next Big Thing: A Bookstore?" *Fortune*, December 9, 1996, pp. 168–170; Hoovers Company Profile Database—American Public Companies, Copyright 2001, Hoovers Inc., Austin TX. "Company Research, Key Facts, Amazon.com," *Wall Street Journal*, interactive.wsj.com, Web site visted May 18, 2001.
2. Rebello, "A Literary Hangout."
3. Personal interview with Olga Dazzo, Sparrow Health System, Lansing, MI.
4. Laurie Freeman, "Keeping 'em Happy," *Marketing News*, May 8, 2000, p. 1–2.
5. "IntelliQuest Research Identifies Key Concerns About Mobile eCommerce," *Canadian Corporate Newswire*, August 14, 2000.
6. Cyndee Miller, "Research Spending Up, Staffs Down," *Marketing News*, January 29, 1996, p. 8.
7. www.forester.com, Web site visited on September 23, 2000.
8. www.dnb.com, Web site visited June 28, 2000.
9. Ron Orol, "J. D. Edwards Rethinks Business Strategy," *Forbes*, May 25, 2000.
10. www.att.com, Web site visited on June 28, 2000.
11. Jonathan Eig, "Science and Sweat: Gatorade's Formula for Staying on Top: A Blitz of Research," *Wall Street Journal*, May 5, 2000, p. A1.
12. "Delta Airlines Enhances Meal Service for International Economy Class Passengers," *PR Newswire*, May 1, 2000.
13. Michelle Ortiz, "Catalog Focuses on Women Travelers," *Marketing News*, February 26, 1996, pp. 12–13.
14. Mark Del Franco, "Disappearing Ink," *Catalog Age*, May 1999, p. 1–2.
15. Lean Haran, "Grocery Category Management Made Better by Census Data," *Advertising Age*, May 6, 1996, p. 16.
16. Personal interview with Dana Anderson, Leo Burnett Company, Inc., Chicago, July 3, 1996.
17. Christina Canabon, "Here's Our Site—Are You Satisfied?" *Fast Company*, June 2000, p. 62.
18. Stephen W. Brown, "Practicing Best-in-Class Service Recovery," *Marketing Management*, Summer 2000, pp. 8–9.
19. "Little Things Mean a Lot," *Sales and Marketing Management*, May 2000.
20. www.nielsenmedia.com, Web site visited September 24, 2000.

21. A. Einstein and L. Infeld, *The Evolution of Physics* (New York: Simon & Schuster, 1942), p. 95.
22. Marc Gunther, "You Want a Piece of This?" *Ecompany Now*, October 2000, p. 1.
23. Bradley Johnson, "Supermarkets Move Back to Inner Cities," *Advertising Age*, January 25, 1993, p. 41.
24. "There's No Need to Travel When You Can Watch Your Focus Groups Online," *Wichita Business Journal*, September 8, 2000.
25. Gilbert D. Harrell, Michael D. Hutt, and James C. Anderson, "Path Analysis of Buyer Behavior under Conditions of Crowding," *Journal of Marketing Research*, February 1980, p. 47.
26. For a discussion of human mechanical observation techniques, see Gilbert A. Churchill, Jr., *Marketing Research*, 5th ed. (Chicago: Dryden Press, 1991), p. 349.
27. Valerie Reitman, "Big Three Auto Makers Shrink Productivity, Gap with Rivals," *Wall Street Journal Interactive Edition*, June 12, 1997.
28. Raju Narisetti, "Plotting to Get Tissues into Living Rooms," *Wall Street Journal*, May 3, 1996, p. B1.
29. Christy Marshall, "Have It Your Way with Research," *Advertising Age*, April 4, 1983, p. 18.
30. "Fusing the Generational Gap," *Business Wire*, April 4, 2000.
31. Peter Girard, "Alloy's Online/Offline Dividends," *Catalog Age*, May 2000, p. 12.
32. Sudhir K. Chawla, P.V. (Sundar) Blakrishnan, and Mary F. Smith, "Mail Response Rates from Distributors," *Industrial Marketing Management*, November 1992.
33. Thomas C. Kinnear, ed., *1994 Survey of Marketing Research*, (Chicago: American Marketing Association, 1995) p. 30.
34. Jack Honomichl, "Growth in Research Spending Within the U.S.," *Marketing News*, June 5, 2000, pp. H2–3.
35. www.strategyresearch.com, Web site visited on September 29, 2000.
36. Cyndee Miller, "Study: Firms Adding Researchers but Continue to Outsource," *Marketing News*, June 9, 1997, p. 1–2.
37. "Tru Dynamics Launches E-Commerce Virtual Mall," *Business Wire*, June 20, 2000.
38. Dana James, "The Future of Online Research," *Marketing News*, January 3, 2000, p. 1–2
39. Richard Cross, "Real-Time and Online Research Is Paying Off," *Direct Marketing*, May 2000, p. 61.
40. nytimes.com, Web site visited September 29, 2000.
41. Jeannet Henessey, *Global Marketing Strategies*, 3rd ed. (Boston: Houghton Mifflin, 1995), p. 202.
42. "Politics and Current Affairs," *Economist*, February 5, 1994, p. 32.
43. "The Good Statistics Guide," *Economist*, September 11, 1993, p 34.
44. Sak Onkvisit and John J. Shaw, *International Marketing*, 2nd ed. (Upper Saddle River, NJ: Prentice Hall, 1993), p. 398.
45. "Marketing Shares," *Marketing*, February 22, 1990.
46. Tara Parker Pope, "Ad Agencies Are Stumbling in East Europe," *Wall Street Journal*, May 10, 1996, p. B1.
47. John B. Elner, "Travel the High-Speed Road to Global Market Research," *Marketing News*, June 9, 1997, p. H11.
48. Cynthia Crossens, *Tainted Truth: The Manipulation of Fact in America* (New York: Simon & Schuster, 1994), p 19.
49. "Respondents Assail Quality of Research," *Marketing News*, May 8, 1995, p. 14.
50. Crossens, *Tainted Truth*, p 14.
51. Ibid., p. 19
52. Jeffery Kluger, "Poll Vaulting," *Discover*, May 1995.
53. "They Know What Girls Want," *Marketing News*, March 27, 2000, p. 3.
54. Anthony Miyazaki, "Online Privacy Takes Top Billing in Latest Issue of JPP&M," *Marketing News*, May 22, 2000, p. 22.

Bricks or Clicks

MARKET RESEARCH COMPANIES GO ONLINE

On the consumer side, the internet has undoubtedly changed the way people communicate, shop, and search for information. It has also forced companies to change the way they do business. The industry that links together these two arenas, business and the consumer, has also made strides to understand online consumer behavior. Market research companies are taking their tools online and measuring the effectiveness of online promotion and advertising by tracking Web site usage. Listed below are three examples of how market research companies are using the Internet to communicate and research consumer behavior habits.

One of the major players in the online market information business is a familiar name, Nielsen Media Research. There are now Nielsen families out on the Internet. Nielsen sends software to the families involved in the study. Some companies, such as Relevant Knowledge, have users mail disks to the company on a monthly basis. With Nielsen's system, they plan to send weekly reports on Web usage.

Information Resources, Inc. (IRI) tracks consumer packaged goods by monitoring the UPC labels that get scanned at the grocery store, and also by having a group of people scan everything they buy when they get home. This data allows stores to better understand what is being purchased and who is purchasing it. In the spring of 2000 IRI formed a joint venture with Forrester Research, Netquity, to track online shopping and forecast the impact of online brands. The combination of tracking and forecasting helps companies measure the performance of their bricks and clicks strategies.

The most recent market research technology is from Transactional Data Solutions (TDS). Its technology recognizes the need for bricks and clicks companies to measure their success on both sides of its business simultaneously. The ReTail Ticker can track up to 80 million MasterCard holders and over 4 million transactions in a day. This program will allow companies to see how their different distribution channels are performing in comparison to each other.

Sources: Richard Tedesco, "Net ratings business heats up," *Broadcasting & Cable*, November 2, 1998, 46–47; "Transactional Data Solutions, TDS Launches Free ReTail Ticker Service to Provide Unique Market Intelligence on 'Clicks Versus Bricks' Shopping," *Business Wire*, June 6, 2000, retrieved from the World Wide Web; Jack Neff, "Troubled IRI forms joint venture," *Advertising Age*, May 15, 2000, p. 84.

Reebok

IMAGINE HOW REEBOK MARKETING EXECUTIVES felt when they discovered they had shipped 53,000 pairs of shoes bearing a name that means "an evil spirit that makes sexual advances to women while they are sleeping." The company annually picks about 1,500 new names for products, and "Incubus" was selected after a legal search found that it wasn't trademarked. Unfortunately, no one had taken the obvious first step of looking it up in the dictionary. This is unusual for Reebok, which knows the importance of marketing research and uses it in some very creative ways.

The "Incubus" blooper, however, is minor compared to the many challenges Reebok has faced. In 1995, Paul Fireman, CEO of Reebok International Ltd., told an angry group of shareholders he would resign if he failed to turn the company around within two years. At that time, profits were declining, and sales were relatively flat. In the 1980s Reebok sold about one-third of the sports footwear in the lucrative U.S. market. By the mid-1990s, it commanded a mere 20 percent, while rival Nike had increased by 6 percentage points. Roger Best, senior vice president and general manager of Reebok, says the brand had lost definition. "We've been a little too much like vanilla ice cream, which is a nicer sounding term than mud." This allowed competitors to gain share largely at Reebok's expense.

Part of the company's problems stem from its success in the mid-1980s as a fitness-based brand. By the 1990s, it needed to become a more broadly based sports brand. As a part of this effort, Reebok relied strongly on marketing research and information gathering. Fireman believed that one of the first questions to answer was whether Reebok is a sports/performance brand or a fitness/fashion brand. Based on research, he opted for sports/performance. Reebok needed a leadership product to take on Nike's Air system. The result was the DMX Series 2000, a running shoe that some believe contains breakthrough technology.

How did Reebok use research to design a leadership product? In the 1980s, the company discovered a neglected market niche by studying how women used their leisure time. The results revealed that aerobic exercise was one of the hottest markets for women, so Reebok developed the first women's aerobic shoe. Its success made the company an industry contender and proved the value of understanding time-use methods in identifying needs and creating products. Reebok does a lot of time-use marketing research. Sue Prakken, senior marketing research manager at Reebok, says: "We track what people are doing with their leisure time very carefully, particularly with regard to exercise." Prakken manages an extensive program of telephone interviews, mall intercept surveys, and in-depth interviews at consumers' homes in order to understand precisely how people use their time.

Reebok's time-use research has paid off. In 1991, the company followed the off-season activity of basketball players and found that they played on asphalt rather than indoor hardwood courts. This led to the creation of Reebok's successful blacktop basketball shoes. Research also revealed that adults were spending less time in exercise clubs and more time working out at home. So Reebok marketed a "home step" product and exercise video. When it learned more people were walking for exercise, it responded with a line of walking shoes.

Perhaps Reebok's most interesting research technique today is the Cool Hunt. Who decides what's cool? At Reebok, the answer is certain kids in certain places, and Baysie Wightman, a general merchandise manager, who knows where to find them. Places such as Stratton, Vermont, and California's Summit County are on her list. Cool hunting is not about a clearly defined statement but a collection of observations and predictions. A New Yorker reporter once went on a Cool Hunt with Baysie, who took along a canvas bag with 24 different shoes Reebok planned to bring out. At Dr. J's, the cool place to buy sneakers in the Bronx, Baysie solicited opinions from consumers who gathered around. She asked one question after another as she displayed each pair of shoes. Reebok's new DMX RXT, a low-cut walking and running shoe in white and blue, with mesh and a translucent ice sole, was well received by the men. Interestingly, the DMX RXT was a women's shoe that had not done well, so their interest was particularly useful.

On the surface, it appears that Baysie's research is unscientific. Certainly, it's hard to know whether this method really provides useful marketing data. Is it appropriate for a company that wants to position itself technologically for the serious athlete?

E. Scott Morris, senior designer for Reebok, believes it's important for an organization to stay in touch. "The kid in the store would say, 'I'd like this shoe if your logo wasn't on it.' That's kind of a punch in the mouth. But we have all seen it. You go into a shoe store, the kid picks up the shoe and says, 'Ah, man, this is nice.' Eventually he says, 'Ah, this is Reebok,' and 'I ain't buying this,' puts the shoe down, and walks out." Somewhere along the way, Reebok lost its cool and must rebuild its image.

Reebok's cool hunting takes various forms. For example, a recent Emmett Smith shoe, designed for football players, had a piece of molded rubber on the end of the tongue as a design element. When Reebok gave the shoes to the Boston College football team for wear testing, it got them back with the rubber tongue piece cut out. It wasn't cool, and on the final version of the shoe it was eliminated. The cool hunters at Reebok have a rule of thumb: If kids in Chicago, New York, and Detroit like a shoe, it's a guaranteed hit. When Baysie returns from a Cool Hunt, she sits down with marketing experts, sales people, and designers to reconnect them to the street. She tries to make sure they have the right shoes at the right price. But Baysie isn't alone. Her friend Didi Gordon, who works for Lambiss, an advertising agency in Delmar, California, is also a cool hunter. Didi says to be a good cool hunter you must somehow just know. She said she once tried to hire someone as a cool hunter who was not cool. It was a disaster. He just didn't have the instinct, the sense that told him what was cool.

And finally in 2000, after putting all of this marketing research to use, Reebok seems to be on the right track. It signed on as a sponsor to the very popular Survivor series, which aired in 2000. For 2001, Reebok plans to increase media spending in the United States to $90 million, with a likely Super Bowl launch for one of its brands. You will also see Reebok develop a more unified brand image in its advertising. For instance, ads for Super Bowl 2001 won't be celebrity athlete based. The message will be much simpler and carried out through all of its promotions. It will simply communicate the idea that Reebok has a good design allowing you to look great and have fun.

The stock price has risen 250 percent since the beginning of 2000 and Reebok's 1999 global sales hit about $2.9 billion. "For too many years, we were focused on what the competition was doing instead of just trying to be ourselves," said CMO Angel Martinez.

1. *How do the research approaches and methods described in the case support or not support the positioning being sought by Reebok? Explain.*
2. *Identify the components of a marketing information system you believe are necessary for Reebok to remain competitive.*

3. *What type of research method is a Cool Hunt? What additional steps are required to provide reliable data for making key product development and merchandising decisions within Reebok?*

Sources: www.reebok.com, visited October 30, 1997; Malcolm Gladwell, "The Coolhunt," *New Yorker,* March 17, 1997, pp. 78–88; Joe Schwart, "How Reebok Fits Shoes," *American Demographics,* March 1993; www.marketingtools.com, "What You Didn't Learn in Marketing 101," *Sales and Marketing Management,* April 1997, p. 14; Silvia Sansoni and Lori Bonogiorno, "Reebok Is Tripping Over Its Own Laces," *Business Week,* February 26, 1996, pp. 62–66; Patricia Sellers, "Reebok Gets a Lift," *Fortune,* August 18, 1997, www.fortune.com, Terry Lefton, "Reebok Readies Women's Signature Shoes," *Advertising Age,* April 7, 1997, pp. 3, 53; Randall Laqne, "You Are What You Wear," *Forbes,* October 14, 1996, pp. 42–46; Steve Gelsi, "Everyone's Still Shooting at the Swoosh," *Brandweek,* February 5, 1996, p. 30; Terry Lefton, "Rescuing Reebok," *Brandweek,* September 18, 2000, pp. 1, 61; and Judy Leand, "Reebok Plots Upward Trajectory with New Products, Brand Image," *Sporting Goods Business,* October 11, 2000, p. 21.

chapter 6

MARKET SEGMENTATION, TARGETING, AND POSITIONING

objectives

1. Understand the advantages of target marketing and how it differs from mass marketing and product differentiation.

2. Describe how to do market segmentation and select target markets.

3. Explore three basic target marketing strategies: undifferentiated, differentiated, and concentrated marketing.

4. Know how to do positioning and describe several approaches marketers use to create valuable, lasting images of their products.

◀ *Michael Dell, Dell Computer's CEO*

SMALL BUSINESSES ARE BIG BUSINESS FOR Dell Computer, the leading personal computer company in the United States. Michael Dell was a premed student when he started selling PCs and components from his dorm room. He dropped out of college when monthly sales topped $80,000 and founded Dell Computer to sell PCs and related equipment to consumers and businesses via direct marketing. Now the company, based in Austin, Texas, employs 37,000 worldwide and uses the Internet to ring up half of its $28.5 billion in annual sales. In addition to desktop PCs, Dell sells high-powered workstations, notebook computers, servers for network use, and data storage systems.

Michael Dell and his team understand that different kinds of customers have different computing requirements. For example, families buy lower-priced, basic PCs for daily household needs such as homework and entertainment, whereas corporations need more sophisticated workstations for computer-aided design and other tasks. Similarly, an entrepreneur with a single Web page does not need the high-end server that a large hospital requires to power its sprawling, multiuser Web site. With these differing needs in mind, Dell's marketers use geographic, demographic, and behavioristic variables to segment the consumer and organizational markets for computers and servers. Once they have identified suitable customer segments for targeting, they use differentiated marketing to match the appropriate marketing mix of product, price, place, and promotion to each segment's needs.

Using the geographic variable of national boundaries, Dell has segmented the world market and created product offerings sold through Web sites for dozens of countries. Each country's Web site, presented in the local language, features hardware, software, services, and online content specifically geared to that market's interests and requirements. In addition, Dell divides its overall market into consumer, business, government, and institutional segments. The consumer segment, which Dell calls "home and home office," consists of consumers who buy for personal and home-office use. This is the segment Michael Dell originally targeted during his college days, and it remains both lucrative and highly competitive.

Within the business segment, Dell uses company demographics and product orientation to define specific customer groups. To Dell, a small business is any firm with fewer than 400 employees. Small businesses that buy more than $50,000 worth of Dell goods and services are assigned an account representative, who stays in contact by phone to learn the businesses' needs and suggest solutions to their problems. These customers are also invited to set up Premier Pages, Web pages they can customize for purchasing and tracking orders from Dell.

To stay abreast of this segment's unique needs, Dell periodically brings small business owners to Austin for meetings with top management and factory tours. It also sends the Dell on Wheels mobile showroom to bring the latest technology to small business customers in dozens of cities across the United States. During the day, the Dell salespeople show off their state-of-the-art hardware and software in the showroom, then talk bits and bytes with small business customers over dinner in the evening.

Dell targets the prized big business segment—customers whose annual hardware purchases may total millions of dollars—with a slightly different marketing mix. These customers receive special volume pricing and regular site visits from dedicated account managers; they can also choose from a wide range of purchase and lease options to meet their financing needs. Customized Premier Pages are an even more important part of the marketing mix for this segment. Ford, for example, had Dell set up its Premier Page so employees can place and track online orders for computers, servers, and other Dell equipment built to the automaker's specifications. Its Premier Page also gives Ford employees access to customized technical support services when they need help installing or troubleshooting Dell products.

Other segments targeted by Dell are the health care industry, government agencies, education, and e-commerce. Dell has forged alliances with a number of specialized suppliers to offer a well-rounded menu of goods and services to large hospitals for staff and administrative use. Within the government market, Dell targets federal government agencies (in the United States and other countries) separately from state and local government agencies. Within the education market, Dell targets K-to-12 schools and faculty members separately from administrators, faculty, and students of colleges and universities. Within the world of e-commerce, Dell targets Internet service providers separately from companies that need goods and services for Web-based sales. Through such extensive segmentation and targeting plans, Dell is able to successfully connect with all kinds of computer customers and build mutually satisfying, mutually profitable relationships that last.[1]

THE CONCEPT OF SEGMENTATION, TARGETING, AND POSITIONING

In the early days, the philosophy of General Motors (GM) was "a different auto for every need." At that time, each GM division focused its creative energies and economic might on satisfying loyal customers in separate market segments. They connected with customers by targeting clearly defined groups of buyers. Today, GM's 12 lines of cars and trucks (Chevrolet, Pontiac, Oldsmobile, Buick, Cadillac, GMC, Saturn, Saab, Opel, Holden, Vauxhaul, and EV_1) have several models each. In fact, GM markets over 80 different models of both cars and trucks.[2] When GM was founded, the members of each American social class had a good deal of upward mobility and GM had a brand targeted at each class. Typically, a young family might buy a Chevy, followed by a Pontiac. Years later, a Buick or Oldsmobile would be purchased. Finally, as a mark of economic accomplishment came the ultimate in status and prestige—a Cadillac. America is no longer defined largely by social class, so although the relative costs of GM models still reflect, to some degree, the pricing hierarchy of previous years, their target markets are vastly different.

Among other products, Procter & Gamble (P&G) markets 11 laundry detergents, five body soaps, seven shampoos, five types of dishwashing soaps, and four oral care brands.[3] How many of them can you name? [4]

Why would strong companies such as General Motors and Procter & Gamble develop so many brands? Do these compete with one another or primarily take on rival brands? The answer is that each brand is designed for a different market segment. A **market segment** is a homogeneous group of customers with similar needs, wants, values, and buying behavior. Each segment is an arena for competition. Both GM and P&G have a tradition of building marketing strategies around strong brands that match the uniqueness of diverse segments. And you can bet there's some competition among the organization's own products, but that's minor in comparison to other brands. The approach has worked well—GM is the largest auto company on the planet and P&G dwarfs its competitors.

Through **segmentation,** the market can be divided into several groups of people with similar characteristics. Each segment will vary in size and opportunity. Because it may be difficult to appeal successfully to each segment, companies select certain ones for emphasis and will try to satisfy them more than competitors, which is called **target marketing.** For example, Great Lakes Crossings, an outlet mall with many entertainment destinations was opened in Auburn Hills, Michigan. The mall appeals to the entire family with stores such as Bass Pro Shop's Outdoor World and Neiman Marcus LAST Call. In addition to the shopping, the mall has many family-oriented entertainment options including Game Works, a high-tech indoor playground, Star Theatres, and Jeepers, an indoor amusement park and restaurant. It is targeting value-conscious families who want to make shopping an experience enjoyed by all members.

This ad shows St. Paul's positioning based on "Trust."

Positioning means creating an image, reputation, or perception in the minds of consumers about the organization or its products relative to competition. The company appeals to customers in the target segments by adjusting products, prices, promotional campaigns, service, and distribution channels in a way consistent with its positioning strategy. Great Lakes Crossing has identified a segment of value-conscious families and positioned itself by creating a total entertainment experience for the entire family in its 200 stores and attractions.[5]

Segmentation, targeting, and positioning give organizations the means to connect with customers by identifying and understanding their characteristics, by focusing resources to meet their needs and wants, and by establishing how customers will view the organization. Let us say a company simply compiles data on consumers, averages them, and tries to develop one brand that appeals to the average consumer. In the U.S. marketplace alone, there are approximately 280 million people.[6] You can find the average for certain of their characteristics—age, gender, income, location, and so forth—but what about ethnic origin, home life, and taste in music, clothing, and food? The "average" American represents few, if any, real people. Efforts to connect with this mythical average consumer probably wouldn't have appeal for any customer. Thus, marketers generally cannot use averages. Instead, they use segmentation, targeting, and positioning to define unique consumer groups, select those they wish to serve, and then integrate the marketing mix to establish a unified image of the product relative to the competition.

To be a leader, companies know that they must connect with customers by identifying, selecting, and relating to them in highly innovative ways. That's why segmentation, targeting, and positioning—three sequential stages summarized in Figure 6.1—are critical. You simply can't be a leading-edge marketer without these steps. The activities required to accomplish each stage are described in the sections that follow. Under market segmentation, we include descriptions of mass marketing and product differentiation as general marketing approaches that are contrasted with the more preferred segmentation methods. We also introduce several ways to identify diverse market segments. The section on target marketing describes how to select targets and focus resources where they will accomplish the most. The last section looks at positioning. It also describes how to reposition when things change.

POSITIONING

Creating an image or perception in the minds of consumers about the organization or its products relative to the competition.

167

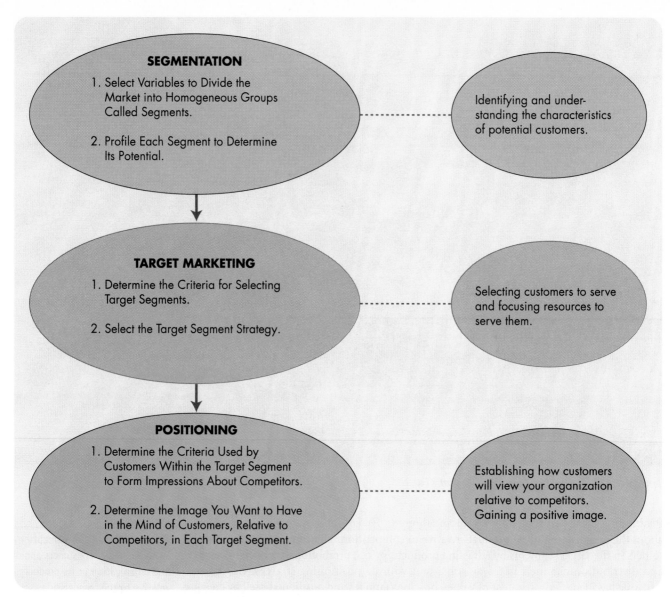

Segmentation

1. Select Variables to Divide the Market into Homogeneous Groups Called Segments.

2. Profile Each Segment to Determine Its Potential.

Identifying and understanding the characteristics of potential customers.

Target Marketing

1. Determine the Criteria for Selecting Target Segments.

2. Select the Target Segment Strategy.

Selecting customers to serve and focusing resources to serve them.

Positioning

1. Determine the Criteria Used by Customers Within the Target Segment to Form Impressions About Competitors.

2. Determine the Image You Want to Have in the Mind of Customers, Relative to Competitors, in Each Target Segment.

Establishing how customers will view your organization relative to competitors. Gaining a positive image.

FIGURE 6.1 *Connecting with Customers by Identifying, Selecting, and Relating to Them*

MARKET SEGMENTATION

Today most leading-edge companies take great care to focus on specific market segments. That hasn't always been the case. Historically, there has been a movement from mass marketing, to product differentiation, to market segmentation, targeting, and positioning. In the following sections you'll explore how these approaches differ.

SEGMENTATION VERSUS MASS MARKETING

We know from chapter 1 that many companies once pursued mass marketing, which is the mass distribution and mass promotion of the mass product to all potential customers. The objective of mass marketing is to reach as many people as possible with the same marketing approach. Coca-Cola, introduced in 1886, pioneered this strategy, and was successful in reaching most consumers with the same product formula, price, promotion, and distribution strategy. Today, however, Coca-Cola's success depends on recognizing the tremendous diversity of the market. During the 2000 Olympic Games, Coca-Cola aired more than 100 different television commercials targeting different market segments.[7]

Although mass marketing was useful decades ago, competition that appeals to consumer diversity prevents this from being a viable strategy for most organizations to use today. While tools are constantly being developed that can reach the mass markets, these tools must be used carefully to get the greatest benefit. For example, GeePS.com, Inc., a New Jersey–based start-up, has developed a means for companies to send marketing materials, such as promotions, coupons, and price comparisons to consumers with wireless handheld devises. CEO Andy Goren says "retailers have the ability to reach their audience anywhere and anytime. It's a great way to achieve customer acquisiton and retention." One research firm indicates that 60.9 million North Americans will have access to wireless devices by 2005.[8] Certainly marketing to this large number of people provides an opportunity for mass marketing as well as the use of segmentation. If marketers simply tried to reach all of these users in the same way, this could be construed as mass marketing. However, what makes it interesting is that this wireless group of consumers may have many unique qualities. These qualities can be organized into specific segments that can be addressed with varying approaches.

Be sure not to confuse mass customization, discussed in chapter 1, with mass marketing. They have nothing in common except the word "mass." Later in this chapter we will see that mass customization is a form of target marketing that takes advantage of many technologies to uniquely serve customers.

SEGMENTATION VERSUS PRODUCT DIFFERENTIATION

Eventually, companies realized that mass marketing didn't provide enough variety and they began to follow a product differentiation strategy. **Product differentiation** makes a product appear unique relative to others, whether produced by the same company or the competition. This uniqueness is then used as a major factor in appealing to customers. The belief is that by offering choices, the company will attract more of the mass market. Notice that product differentiation implies a recognition that consumers may seek variety. But unlike market segmentation, the leading dynamic is a difference in the product, not in buyer characteristics. The pain reliever market is dominated by product differentiation. Aspirin comes in plain formula or with caffeine, buffered or not, with and without sleep aids, with or without a cold remedy, and in standard or extra strength. You can also find it in caplet, liquid, tablet, chewing gum, or capsule form, coated or noncoated, flavored or not. The objective is to offer an aspirin for every preference imaginable. And hundreds of millions of dollars are spent each year by companies such as Bayer to promote its different product configurations.

It is important to keep the distinction between product differences and market segments in mind. Market segments should not be defined by product names or characteristics. Markets are made up of people and organizations. Consequently, market segments are described according to their characteristics, not according to the products they buy. Misunderstanding this distinction is a common and often deadly flaw for the marketing strategist. For example, a marketing consultant once asked the chief engineer of an air-conditioning manufacturer to describe the company's target segments. The engineer responded with product categories: heavy, medium, and light-duty units. When asked questions about the characteristics of current and potential buyers, the engineer had little knowledge. The consultant knew immediately that this client did not fully understand market segmentation, a key reason customers were buying fewer of the engineer's new-product introductions. When executives equate product categories with market segments, they tend to focus attention on what they want to make, which may not meet customer requirements. The result is often products that please the people who make them but disappoint customers.

SEGMENTATION VARIABLES

The total market is **heterogeneous,** meaning it has many types of buyers. Market segmentation divides the total market into **homogeneous** subgroups or clusters with similar characteristics. We then can inspect each subgroup in greater detail. Without a well-focused picture of the market, it's virtually impossible to create a powerful marketing strategy. Essentially, segmentation allows marketers to focus on relevant aspects of potential buyers. It's a critical step in connecting with customers.

How is segmentation done? First, the marketer must select a way to categorize potential customers into subgroups. A **segmentation variable** is any descriptive characteristic that helps separate all potential purchasers into groups. Examples include gender, age, and income. Variables are then subdivided into categories. For example, within the gender variable, the two categories are male and female. Categories may be very broadly or very narrowly defined. Income can be classified generally as low, moderate, and high, or more specifically as, for example, up to $5,000, $5,001 to $20,000, $20,001 to $40,000, $40,001 to $60,000, and above $60,000.

PRODUCT DIFFERENTIATION
A marketing strategy with which companies attempt to make their products appear unique relative to the competition.

HETEROGENEOUS GROUP
Buyers with diverse characteristics.

HOMOGENEOUS GROUP
Buyers with similar characteristics.

SEGMENTATION VARIABLE
Any distinguishing market factor that can vary, such as gender, age, or income.

Tropicana strives to differentiate each of its varieties of juice.

Think about how colleges segment students for recruiting and admissions. Like companies, they do this to gain a better understanding of potential customers. At the most basic level, the segmentation variables are grade point average in high school, SAT or ACT scores, and high school class rank. These variables can be subdivided into categories, as shown in Figure 6.2. The categories then can be grouped together in various ways to form several market segments, which often are named descriptively. For example, the market segment in the third categories column of Figure 6.2 might be called the "cream of the crop." Or students with above average SAT/ACT scores but in the bottom of their class and with a low GPA might be the "underachiever" market segment.

Most colleges add other variables, and these can dramatically change the segmentation structure. For example, what seems to be a fairly uniform market turns out to be a lot of segments. From our example in Figure 6.2, 27 market segments emerge (3 GPA categories ×3 SAT/ACT categories ×3 class rank categories). Adding just two residence categories (in and out of state) would produce 54 segments.

Variables need to be chosen with care because each segment must meet certain criteria in order to be useful to a marketer.

- Members should have similar needs, wants, and preferences, because these are what marketers want to understand and influence.
- Members should have similar information-gathering and media usage patterns, because these allow marketers to communicate with the segment.

Variable	Categories		
High School GPA	Below 2.0	2.0–3.5	3.6–4.0
SAT/ACT Score	Below average	Average	Above average
High School Class Rank	Lowest 25%	Middle 50%	Top 25%

FIGURE 6.2 *Segmenting the College Market*

- Members should have similar shopping and buying patterns, because marketers then can find efficient places to sell and service their products.
- The number of members should be large, because marketers need to generate a profit.
- Data about the segments should be available, because marketers need to know about customers in order to build marketing strategies.

Segmentation typically is based on geographic, demographic, diversity, psychographic, and behavioristic factors and benefits sought. Figure 6.3 lists the variables and categories commonly used to segment. All of these apply to consumer markets. Additional variables and categories that are primarily useful to segment business markets are provided in chapter 8 on business-to-business marketing.

Geographic Segmentation   One of the most common ways to analyze a market is by geography. It can reveal some interesting facts. For example, consider this odd statistic about the difference in the size of men's suits. In New York the most typical size is 42 regular; in Paris, 40 regular; in San Francisco, 38 regular; and in Chicago, a strapping 44 long.[9]

Segmentation by city is often used by global companies. Coke knows that soft-drink consumption relates to population size. With the exception of New York City and Los Angeles, all metropolitan areas of more than 10 million are located outside the United States. So it's no mystery why Coke markets globally. A city's population size alone doesn't always provide enough segmentation information, so marketers think about other factors. Some metropolitan areas are known for their industry expertise: In Hollywood it's movies; in Silicon Valley, computer software; and in Philadelphia, pharmaceuticals. Auto components suppliers, such as Bosch and Eaton Corporation, know that virtually all major buying decisions are made in fewer than 20 cities located in a handful of countries. A presence in Stuttgart, Detroit, Los Angeles, Wiesbaden, Paris, Osaka, and Seoul gives the supplier substantial global coverage.

Geodemography combines geographic information with data on consumer expenditures and demographics to identify segments with common consumption patterns. A geographic information system (GIS) employs computer mapping to identify targets. It uses data from the Bureau of the Census, which provides computerized street maps that contain economic and population data per city block. For a relatively low price you can buy maps and data covering the entire United States. For considerably less, you can buy information for a smaller region of the country. Arby's uses GIS data to select restaurant locations, and the former Chemical Bank used it to target neighborhoods. According to Michael Marvin, an executive at MapInfo Corporation, with this technology, "Quaker Oats found that 80 percent of their ethnic customers lived in 18 of their 55 sales territories."[10] The information allows Quaker to develop highly targeted segment strategies. Many colleges and universities are making use of this type of data to better target prospective students. Information is gathered from questionnaires on the SAT and ACT exams, as well as from former students from the different high schools. Profiles are created and colleges and universities can then target prospective students based on characteristics such as religion, preferred major, and computer savvy.[11]

Zip code segmentation divides the market according to the demographic makeup of the zip code area. One marketing firm grouped all U.S. zip codes into one of 40 clusters based on family size, income, age, age of the home, type of housing, and so forth. Each cluster is described by the typical consumption practices of its residents. For example, in zip code 48236 (Grosse Pointe, Michigan), the cluster type is "Young Influentials":

> Up and coming young professionals living in townhouses and apartments. Residents like to sail, ski, and play tennis, lots of joggers and airline travelers, a good place to sell yogurt and mutual funds but not wall paneling, motorcycles, or guns and ammunition. Residents buy 3.8 times the average number of Rolls-Royces.[12]

Several companies have started to put data on Web sites, where access to information on every zip code in the United States is free.[13] EProject.com uses zip code data to tailor its online radio advertisements to specific groups. For example, an 18-year-old female in Philadelphia might hear an ad for Gap at her local mall while a 25-year-old male in Boston hears a pitch for a J.Crew store down his block. This custom tailoring of advertisements based on zip codes produces a much more effective advertising campaign for eProject.com's clients.[14]

If you need to get even more specific, similar methods can be used to identify customers by city block based on street addresses. The LEXIS®-NEXIS® electronic information database

GEODEMOGRAPHY
Combining geographic information with demographics to identify segments with common consumption patterns.

ZIP CODE SEGMENTATION
Division of a market into specific geographic locations based on the demographic makeup of the zip code area.

	Variable	Examples of Categories
Geographic	World region	Pacific Rim, Europe, North America
	Economic stage	Advanced, developing, subsistence
	Nation	U.S., England, Japan, Mexico
	City	Tokyo, Paris, Mexico City
	City size and density	Large and dense, small and spread out, suburban, rural
	Region	New England, Mid-Atlantic, South Atlantic, East South Central, Midwest, Mountain Pacific
	Climate	Northern Equator, Southern Equator
	Zip Code	10001, 10002, etc.
Demographic	Gender	Female, male
	Age	1–5, 6–11, 12–19, 20–34, 35–49, 50–64, 65–72, 72+
	Income	Poverty, up to $15,000, up to $20,000, up to $30,0000, up to $50,000, up to $100,000, $100,000+
	Family size	1, 2, 3, 4, 5, 6
	Family life cycle	Young single, young married no children, young married with children (under 6), young married with children (over 6), older married full nest, older married empty nest, retired, middle-aged, single, divorced, sole survivor
	Occupation	Unemployed, homemaker, student, retired, clerical, blue collar, white collar, professional, proprietor
	Education	Grade school (or less), some high school, high school graduate, some college, college graduate, postgraduate degree
Diversity	Religion	Protestant, Catholic, Jewish, Muslim
	Race	Anglo, African, Asian, Hispanic, Native American
	Social class	Lower-lower, upper-lower, lower-middle (working class), middle, upper-middle, lower-upper, upper-upper
Psychographic	Lifestyle	Actualizer, Fulfilled, Achiever, Experiencer, Believer, Striver, Maker, Struggler
	Personality	Compliant, aggressive, detached, sensory, intuitive, thinking, feeling
Behavioristic	Readiness	Unaware, aware, interested, knowledgeable, desirous, intend to buy, trial
	Ability and experience	None, novice, expert, professional, nonuser, first-time user, regular user, former user
	Loyalty	Switcher, moderate, high
	Media and shopping habits	Magazine subscriber, cable user, mall, convenience stores
	Usage	Daily, weekly, monthly
	Rates	Heavy, medium, light
Benefit Sought	Delivery	Convenience, speed, flexibility
	Service	No questions asked returns
	Price	Low, medium, high

FIGURE 6.3 *Ways to Segment Consumer Markets*

Source: Philip Kotler, *Marketing Management: Analysis, Planning, Implementation, and Control,* 10th ed. ©2001. Adapted by permission of Prentice Hall, Inc., Upper Saddle River, NJ.

now provides a service called REZIDE, which segments customers by any variable the user requests (zip code, area code, city, and so forth) and supplies the information electronically.

Demographic Segmentation Characteristics such as gender, family life cycle, houshold type, and income are used in **demographic segmentation.** This type of information is readily available. Demographics are very useful in categorizing different tastes and preferences. An added benefit is that it's relatively easy to project the composition and size of demographic segments for the next five, 10, or even 15 years. Consequently, this kind of segmentation is an excellent tool for long-range strategic planning as well as short-term marketing.

Segmentation by Gender The buying behavior of men and women is unique. Some of this uniqueness can be attributed to the roles each performs. Marketers need to be able to adapt their techniques in order to reach one particular gender. For example, LeoShe, an advertising agency, has determined that there are actually four groups of childbearing women that companies can target.[15] By focusing on the specific values and lifestyles that women have, marketers can more effectively reach an entire gender of the population. Women are, in many ways, a prime segment for thousands of products. Judann Pollak has traced the "fitful pursuit of American women" by auto companies.[16] She begins with a 1907 ad for a Franklin showing women in long skirts behind the wheel and the caption "Notice how much room there is to get in or out of the driver's side." In 1930 Chrysler research found women to be a "potent factor" in 75 percent of new car purchases, and themes focusing on them were credited with raising company sales by 33 percent. By 1948, all major automakers were advertising in *Women's Home Companion,* the number-one magazine targeted at women. Robert Austin, director of marketing communications for Volvo Cars of North America, says the industry has come a long way from the "Hi, sweetie, here is a pink car mentality." Today, women are the principal drivers of 26 percent of light trucks, including sport-utility models. According to Sean Fitzpatrick, vice chairman of McCann-Erickson Worldwide advertising agency, the popularity of these vehicles with women is largely due to "straight-shooting" advertising directed at them.[17]

The issue has never been whether to segment by gender—only how to address women. Chrysler formed a Women's Advisory Committee composed of 30 women from disciplines such as finance, manufacturing, and marketing. The company pioneered driver's side sliding doors and integrative child seats on the 1996 minivan. Sometimes women are targeted by accident.

DEMOGRAPHIC SEGMENTATION
Division of the market according to such characteristics as gender, family life cycle, household type, and income.

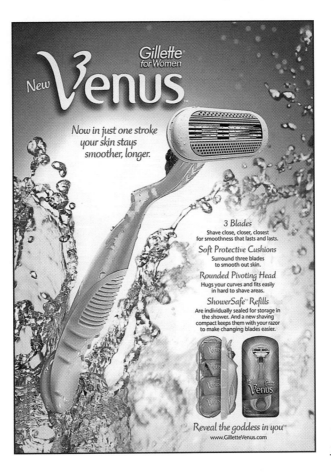

This Gillette product is made for middle-class young woman.

Dianne Romanelli, advertising coordinator at Saturn, says the company didn't start out targeting women: "The strategy was to show people how the Saturn shopping experience is different . . . (i.e., no-hassle, no-haggle policy). It just so happens that women really respond to that."

One key trend in the female demographic segment is the number of women in the workforce. From 1998 to 2008, the number of women working is expected to increase 48 percent. Marketers will have to continue to adjust their techniques in order to reach busy working women in the future.[18]

Men are also a unique segment. Traditional products include sports tickets, hunting and fishing equipment, and auto supplies. Sometimes men buy products traditionally sold to women. Skin care for men is expected to grow 25 percent by 2005. Hair care for men is expected to grow at 5.2 percent annually.[19] In fact, the fastest-growing segment for hair color is men. There are two types of men in this segment, those that dye to cover gray and those that dye their hair because they think it is hip.[20] The growth in these markets is attributed to a redefinition of masculinity and a newfound concern by men for their appearance.[21]

Segmentation by Family Life Cycle Families pass through stages, from young single adults, to marriage, to childbearing, to later life. The next chapter describes the specific categories in depth. For now, it is important to note that these family stages are excellent segmentation categories. Several of the wireless service providers are marketing second and third wireless phones to families. They are targeting parents with teens in particular. Being able to stay in touch with their children and knowing where they are is comforting to parents. In addition, it eliminates the "I couldn't get to a phone excuse" that is frequently used by teenagers.[22] Organic food manufacturers are also seeing the importance of targeting health-conscious parents by offering "fun" healthy convenience meals for children. Many parents that fed their children organic baby food were disappointed in the choices for the children as they got older. Fran's Healthy Helpings' product line includes Wacky Whale Pizza, Dino Chicken Chompers, and Soccer-Oni and Cheese. Parents are willing to pay more for healthier choices.[23] By directing attention specifically to families, these companies have gained leadership in this important segment.

Using the family life cycle as a guide, marketers are beginning to promote adult products to young groups. For example, Mylanta addresses mothers with a children's formula in bubble gum and fruit-flavored chewable and liquid forms.[24] Other adult brands for young people

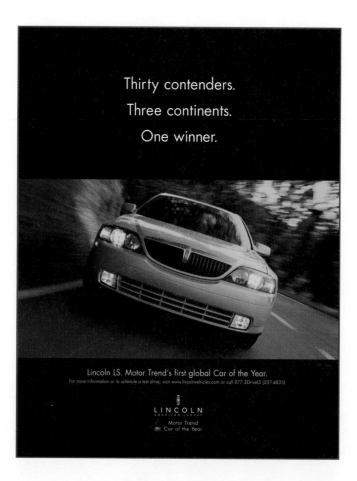

Lincoln targets the baby boomers market segment.

Thirty contenders.

Three continents.

One winner.

Lincoln LS. Motor Trend's first global Car of the Year.
For more information or to schedule a test drive, visit www.lincolnvehicles.com or call 877 2DriveLS (237-4835)

LINCOLN
AMERICAN LUXURY
Motor Trend
Car of the Year

include Benadryl, Sudafed, and Motrin.[25] Kleenex and Dial for Kids are just the tip of the iceberg for children's products.

Segmentation by Age As mentioned in chapter 3, age cohorts are people of similar age and life experience. Heroes, music, and even economic times are somewhat unique for each generation. Tastes, preferences, and product choices reflect those differences. Other generational similarities include physical capacity and earning power. You've probably heard of baby boomers, and baby busters. Figure 6.4 describes various age cohorts frequently discussed today.

The baby boomers are a huge market segment in the United States. By 2010, more than 26.5 percent of the population will be older than 55, an increase of nearly 25 million people in that category compared to today. Several builders in the Chicago area are targeting baby boomers by building age-restricted upscale subdivisions or by including amenities in their subdivisions that appeal specifically to boomers.[26] Travel agents are also targeting the baby boomers. In Pennsylvania, as much as 25 percent of the tourism can be attributed to the senior market. Many companies are offering special senior packages that accommodate the special needs of this rapidly increasing segment.[27]

People with higher spending power, born before World War II, are sometimes called WOOFS (Well-Off Older Folks). This age cohort is often the target of major marketers. JC Penney has a clothing line called Easy Dressing, which uses velcro fasteners instead of buttons and zippers. Barnes & Noble carries large-print paperbacks, and travel agencies market special trips for the elderly. McDonald's introduced the Arch Deluxe to this segment.

As for Gen X, the baby busters, their purchasing power will peak about the time the boomers retire. A survey of 3,000 U.S. citizens has shown that Generation X has done a much better job saving for retirement at a much earlier age. Part of this could be attributed to their lack of confidence in the social security system. Compared to 58 percent of baby boomers, 75 percent of Generation Xers believe that most of their retirement will come from sources other than social security, such as savings and 401(k) plans.[28] Social security payments made over the years by baby boomers were not invested for them. These payments were used to pay benefits to current social security recipients, so little of what they actually paid will remain when they retire. That issue is spurring efforts to change the social security system in the United States. One area that is

Cohort	Born	Comments
GI generation	Before 1930	Came of age during the Depression; many fought in WWII; frugal and patriotic.
Depression generation	1930–1939	Moved from hard economic conditions as children to prosperous postwar years in adulthood.
War babies	1940–1945	The worst-defined generation, it is usually described in terms of those that followed or preceded.
Baby boomers	1946–1964	Largest U.S. generation; also known as the Vietnam, Woodstock, or Sixties generation.
Baby busters	1965–1984	Often described as cynical about their future; also known as Generation X or Gen X.
Millenials	1985–2005	Have also been referred to as generation Y and Generation Next. This generation is predicted to be more than 70 million, dwarfing the 40 million generation X'ers, and possibly surpassing the 76 million post-war baby boomers.

FIGURE 6.4 *Age Cohorts*

Source: Adapted from Diane Crispell, "Where Generations Divide— A Guide," *American Demographics*, May 1993, pp. 9–10. Reprinted with permission. ©1993 American Demographics, Ithaca, NY, and O'Reilly, Brian, "Meet the Future", *Fortune*, July 24, 2000. www.fortune.com

attracting the attention of Gen Xers is the online stock trading industry. Approximately 15 percent of online traders are Gen Xers. Although the average Gen Xer's net worth is only $38, 277, they are trading stocks frequently, even daily, in order to try to get rich quick.[29]

The buying power of the teen segment has increased steadily over the past few years. Teens are expected to spend $155 billion dollars in 2001. Marketers are scrambling to target this young savvy group of consumers, a segment that was largely ignored in the past.[30] Teens receive, on average, about $50 per week from their parents.[31] Approximately two-thirds of this generation have access to the Internet. And they're spending their money online. By 2002, experts predict that the total amount spent online by this group will be $1.2 billion.[32]

Age is a useful segmentation variable for high-technology services. As you would expect, most Internet users have high levels of income and education. Women actually outnumber men online and their habits vary by age. Women ages 24 to 35 spend most of their time on sites that provide information and advice, whereas girls ages 2 to 11 visit television and learning Web sites most often. The growth rate of the female population online has outpaced the overall online growth rate. All categories except females ages 18 to 24 saw a significant increase in their numbers online. Because of this shift in online usage, sites must start to target women, keeping in mind the age-specific differences in their use of the Internet.[33]

Segmentation Based on Diversity   Some people hesitate to segment markets based on ethnic heritage, race, or religious factors. Yet a wonderful fact of life is the world's tremendous diversity. Marketers know that the character of many markets is dramatically influenced by these factors.[34]

It's important to remember that ethnic segments are not homogeneous. There are demographic differences within ethnic groups. For many people of color, race has nothing to do with their buying behavior. Consequently, other forms of segmentation may work much better.

African Americans, Hispanics, and Asian Americans account for much of the current population growth in the United States. Within 25 years, each is estimated to be approximately the same size—about 42 million people. Compared to the general population, African Americans will grow at about twice the overall rate, Hispanics at 4.5 times the rate, and Asians at more than 8 times the rate. Whites will increase at about 60 percent the rate of other groups.[35] Many people will maintain their high ethnicity by living among and associating within these groups. High ethnicity results in attractive market segments.

In 1994, minorities represented nearly 25 percent of the U.S. population, and the Bureau of the Census estimates that figure will rise to nearly 64 percent by 2020.[36] Minorities are now a majority in one of every six U.S. cities. Most immigrants settle in urban areas along with people from their home country. This produces concentrations of new ethnic populations, as the examples in Figure 6.5 show.[37]

Currently, the U.S. Hispanic market consists of 33 million individuals, making up 11 percent of the U.S. population. The total spending power of this group is a whopping $330 billion. So, marketing to this group can be especially profitable for companies. Gateway, Inc. has begun targeting the Hispanic segment since it is expected to make up approximately 25 percent of the U.S. population by 2050. To reach this market, Gateway has begun marketing its products in the Spanish language, including running TV and radio advertisements, and hiring customer service and sales people who are fluent in Spanish.[38]

City	Origin
Atlanta	Vietnam, South Korea
Baltimore	South Korea
Chicago	Mexico, Philippines, South Korea
Denver	Mexico, Vietnam
Dallas	Mexico, Vietnam, India
Jersey City	Cuba
Los Angeles	Mexico
Miami	Cuba
Minneapolis/St. Paul	Laotians
New York City	all immigrants
Seattle	Philippines, Vietnam, South Korea

FIGURE 6.5 *New Ethnic Populations in Selected Cities*

De-ethnicization occurs when a product heavily associated with one ethnic group is targeted at other segments. Products such as bagels, salsa, and egg rolls have become favorites of many people other than Jews, Mexicans, or Chinese. Kikkoman soy sauce was originally marketed to Chinese groceries and restaurants. Now that ethnic foods have become more mainstream, Kikkoman products are sold in grocery chains to consumers from many different backgrounds.

Services also can be de-ethnicized. Many artists, for example, begin by performing for their own ethnic group and then broaden their appeal. Gregory Hines, an African American tap dancer, started out in traditionally black venues and eventually became well known to most of the general public.

Psychographic and Lifestyle Segmentation   Psychographic and lifestyle segmentation links geographic and demographic descriptors with a consumer's behavioral and psychological decisions. Psychographic variables used alone are often not very useful to marketers; however, they can be quite powerful when joined with demographic, geographic, and other data. **Lifestyle** is a person's distinctive mode of living. It describes how time and money are spent and what aspects of life are important. The choice of products, patterns of usage, and the amount of enjoyment a person gains from being a consumer are all part of lifestyle. Consider the difference between people who are physically fit from exercise and proper nutrition and those who are out of shape from high-fat diets, smoking, and sedentary living. Messages such as "Just Do It!" or "No pain, no gain" are received very differently by these two groups. Of course, since there are so many lifestyles, the trick is to identify them in the context of your company's marketing strategy.

Psychographics are marketing approaches and tools used to identify lifestyles based on measures of consumer values, activities, interests, opinions, demographics, and other factors. Figure 6.6 shows one scheme for identifying types of lifestyles, including examples of what people in each category seek, and ways to reach them.

Another way of classifying lifestyles emerged from a Roper/Starch Worldwide survey of about 2,000 Americans for insights into views about money. Seven distinct profiles were discerned: hunter, gatherer, protector, splurger, striver, nester, and idealist. The hunter takes risks to get ahead and equates money with happiness. The gatherer is better safe than sorry, a conservative investor. The protector puts others first and uses money to protect loved ones. The splurger is self-indulgent. The striver believes that money makes the world go around and equates it with power. The nester isn't very interested in money except to take care of immediate need. The idealist believes there is more to life than money; material things aren't all that important.[39]

There are many ways to define lifestyles using psychographics, so marketers must use a combination of research and creativity to develop useful segments.

The best psychographic segmentation approaches are based on accepted consumer psychology and sound research methods. One of the most popular systems is SRI Consulting's VALS™, which stands for *Values And Lifestyles*. This second version of earlier research segments consumers into groups that think and act differently. VALS research found three major

DE-ETHNICIZATION
The result of targeting a product heavily associated with one ethnic group to other segments.

LIFESTYLE
A person's distinctive mode of living.

PSYCHOGRAPHICS
Marketing approaches and tools used to identify lifestyles based on measures of consumers' values, activities, interests, opinions, demographics, and other factors.

Typology	What They Seek	Possible Spokesperson	Source of Advertisement
Intellectual	Superpremium unique products	Luciano Pavarotti	*Wall Street Journal*
Conformist	Products with large market share	Mickey Mouse	*Sports Illustrated*
Popularity Seeker	Trendy products	Bart Simpson	MTV
Active Lifestyle	Good service Healthy body	Barbara Walters	*Travel & Leisure*
Relief Seeker	Fantasy escape	Madonna	HBO
Sentimentalist	Old-fashioned products	Bob Hope	*Family Circle*
Pragmatist	Functional products	Merle Haggard	*Prevention*

FIGURE 6.6 *Psychographic Segmentation*

Source: John Mortan, "Brand Quality Segments: Potent Way to Predict Preference," *Marketing News*, September 14, 1992, IR-8.

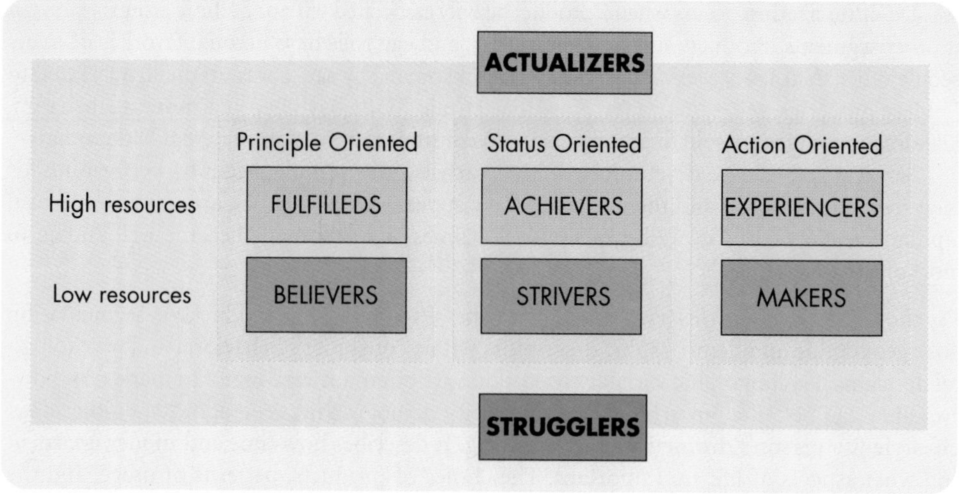

ACTUALIZERS

	Principle Oriented	Status Oriented	Action Oriented
High resources	FULFILLEDS	ACHIEVERS	EXPERIENCERS
Low resources	BELIEVERS	STRIVERS	MAKERS

STRUGGLERS

FIGURE 6.7 *The VALS™ 2 Segmentation System*

Source: Printed with permission from SRI Consulting, Menlo Park, CA.

CONNECTED: SURFING THE NET

www.future.sri.com

Here's a fun way to learn about psychographic segmentation. Learn which VALS™ 2 segment you fit by completing an online questionnaire. You will answer 35 general attitude statements and four demographic questions. In only seconds, you will see a description of your VALS™ type. You'll also be presented with options for exploring the kinds of media, products, and services your segment prefers.

categories of consumers, each with a different self-orientation.[40] Principle-oriented consumers follow their own beliefs; status-oriented consumers are influenced by others, and action-oriented consumers seek variety, action, and risk taking. In addition, VALS considers a consumer's resources, which are education, age, income, energy, self-confidence, eagerness to buy, and health.[41] Figure 6.7 illustrates the VALS™ 2 segmentation system and Figure 6.8 provides summary descriptions of the segments. The VALS battery of attitude items is used in survey research to discover the product choices, media preferences, and leisure activities of each of the VALS consumer groups. Marketers, advertisers, media planners, and new-product designers use VALS to discover who is naturally attracted to their product or service and then to design communication strategies, advertising, and distribution plans that will be attractive to their particular consumer target. VALS refreshes its product media database twice a year.

The Connected: Surfing the Net box describes how you can obtain your profile. If you answer the questions on the VALS™ 2 questionnaire, you can find out whether you are an Actualizer, Fulfilled, Believer, Achiever, Striver, Experiencer, or Struggler. Additionally, you can explore the types of media, products, and services your profile prefers. This is just an example of how psychographic segmentation helps companies connect with customers.

Segment	Orientation	Description	Median Age	Portion of U.S. Population
Actualizer	All	Successful, sophisticated	43	8%
Fulfilled	Principle	Satisfied, comfortable, abundant resources	48	11%
Believer	Principle	Focus on family, religion, and social group	58	16%
Achiever	Status	Committed to jobs, family, in control, abundant resources	26	12%
Striver	Status	Unsure of self, needs approval of others, low resources	26	13%
Experiencer	Action	Fashion-conscious socializers	34	13%
Maker	Action	Practical, traditional, family oriented	30	13%
Struggler	No particular	Older, uneducated, concerned low resources	61	14%

FIGURE 6.8 *The VALS™ 2 Approach to Segmentation*

Source: Printed with permission from SRI Consulting, Menlo Park, CA.

Pontiac utilizes psychographics to reach potential customers.

Using sophisticated computer technology, GeoVALS™ allows marketers to profile a city, metropolitan area, and zip code.[42] It has been adjusted for use in other countries. The Japanese version shows categories of buyers according to product adoption as well as the VALS™ 2 categories.[43]

Behavioristic Segmentation   Behavioristic segmentation categorizes consumers based on people's awareness, product and media uses, and actions. Past behavior is one of the best predictors of future behavior, so these variables require an understanding of what consumers have previously done. The variables include purchase volume, purchase readiness, ability and experience, loyalty, media habits, and shopping behaviors.

Segmentation by Usage Rates You have probably heard about the 80-20 rule: 20 percent of buyers purchase 80 percent of the volume of any product. It is amazing how true this is for many products. Heavy users can be extremely important to companies. Consequently, most marketers divide the market into heavy, moderate, and light users, and then they look for characteristics that may explain why some people consume vastly greater amounts. It usually costs no more to reach heavy users than light users. Therefore, the marketing costs are lower per unit of sales.

Still, marketing strategists need to realize that competition for heavy users can be extreme. If medium or light users are being ignored, they may provide a marketing opportunity. For example, giants such as Coke and Pepsi are always targeting the college crowd. They spend big bucks to be represented on campus in order to capture students. Royal Crown Cola avoids this segment altogether because of the stiff competition. Instead, it concentrates on older adults, who tend to be lighter users of cola.

GM partnered with Bunim/Murray Productions to provide a Yukon with OnStar technology to the cast of *The Real World—New Orleans.* OnStar, which was originally introduced in the Cadillac, provides directions, concierge services, and emergency services. *The Real World*'s audience, 12- to 34-year-olds, is a market that GM wants to tap into. This move will help GM make the transition from providing the service in its luxury vehicles to providing the service in its other models.[44]

Segmentation by Readiness For many products, potential users go through a series of stages that describe their readiness to purchase. These stretch all the way from being unaware of a product, through trial, leading up to loyalty. Readiness is a useful segmentation variable particularly for newer products. This scheme is often used in adjusting the communications mix. Chapter 14 addresses this issue in depth, so it is only mentioned here.

Segmentation by Ability and Experience The performance of products is determined by the ability and experience of its user. Consequently, ability is an excellent segmentation variable for almost any skill-based product. For example, the marketing of skis, tennis racquets, golf clubs, and most other sports equipment is targeted to ability segments. This is due in large part to the performance requirements of these products. As performance requirements increase, new technologies produce products with higher performance capabilities but generally require more skill. A new gadget developed by Inforetech, the Informer 2000, is changing the way golfers play. The device serves two purposes, it displays the entire course on a high-resolution screen providing the golfer with information about the course, and it gives the course managers the ability to monitor the speed of play and course traffic. This will lead to a more efficiently run course, higher revenue, and a more satisfied customer.[45] An accurate rendering of a course is particularly useful for better golfers who want to fine-tune their game.

Segmentation by Loyalty As we have discussed, a key goal of firms is to create brand loyalty. Some consumers are naturally loyal to particular product categories. There are many ways to look at loyalty, but the most popular seems to be the most straightforward. It looks at switchers, moderately loyal, and highly loyal categories. Switchers may select a separate brand with nearly every purchase. They may actually seek variety or they simply don't care which brand they buy. Moderately loyal customers have a preference for a brand but will switch if it is convenient to do so. Loyal buyers have strong preferences. Not all buyers are loyal to a single brand within a product class. Some people have two or three that are equally acceptable. This type of segmentation may include more than the three categories described.

Segmentation by Media and Shopping Habits A broad range of media and shopping habits can be used to categorize shoppers. For example, some people subscribe to cable, others don't; some prefer shopping in malls, others at department stores; and so forth. These variables focus on the accessibility of target customers. Those who shop only in mall settings are accessed differently from those who prefer catalog shopping at home. Shopping habits in the United States changed dramatically from 1996 to 2000. For example, in 1996, 54 percent of all consumers surveyed had visited a supermarket in the past week. In 2000, that number jumped to 80 percent.[46] It would appear that people visiting supermarkets more often are buying less in some trips and are eating prepared meals purchased in supermarkets more.

Segmentation by Benefit   Benefit segmentation divides the market into homogeneous groups based on the attributes consumers seek from a particular product class. Russell Haley popularized this method in the 1960s by dividing the toothpaste market into segments based on whether the consumer wanted flavor, brightness of teeth, dental health, or low price. A benefit segmentation of auto buyers might group them according to the importance they place on economy, performance, styling, or reliability. When a lot is known about the attitudes and perceptions of buyers, it is possible to develop a benefit profile of what product attributes are considered most important. This can be a useful first step in segmentation because customers in a benefit segment are likely to have other identifiable characteristics. For example, people who desire convenience are likely to be members of a dual-career family or single-parent household.

When only benefits are addressed, this technique is not always consistent with good segmentation procedures. Because the benefits are often described according to product characteristics, we learn very little about the buyers themselves. For example, you could say that Apple addressed the user-friendly computer benefit segment. Then again, you could say that Apple products are user friendly. A good rule of thumb is that segments should not be defined solely by product characteristics. In fact, when benefit segmentation is based on product attributes, it may be confused with product positioning, which will be discussed later in this chapter.

Nevertheless, benefit segmentation can be useful when it leads to descriptions of the consumers who prefer each benefit. In order to create these descriptions, researchers generally start with benefit segments and then use the other segmentation schemes to define each group. In this way, the focus is ultimately on buyers, not products.

TWO COMMON SEGMENTING METHODS

Segmentation can be quite complicated because most markets are complex. There are many different types of customers and, as we have seen, literally thousands of variables can be used to segment them. Marketers typically use one of two approaches in selecting variables and grouping customers.

TAKE-DOWN SEGMENTATION METHOD

Method that starts with a set of variables and assigns all consumers to one of them.

The **take-down segmentation method** starts with all consumers and seeks meaningful variables for subdividing the entire market. For example, a cosmetic company may segment by gender. It may choose to target women, believing they have a significantly greater buying potential than men. It then may further segment women by age, type of user, or skin shade. In the early 1990s, cosmetic manufacturer Covergirl recognized the vast potential of marketing to nonwhite women. Until then, it had almost completely ignored the special needs of dark-skinned women. Had it not broken down the market and looked specifically for smaller niches with unmet needs, it might have continued to overlook this huge segment. Today, Covergirl offers more than 72 shades designed specifically for nonwhites, and it leads the ethnic market with over 29 percent of total sales.[47]

The **build-up segmentation method** starts with a single potential customer and adds others with similar characteristics. Anyone without those characteristics is placed in a new segment, and the process continues. In other words, rather than the whole market, the focus is on one segment at a time. For example, Fancl, a Japanese line of natural hair and skin care, is extremely successful with environmentally conscious women in Japan. To expand, it began marketing to Japanese women living in the United States. Now, Fancl is targeting American women by marketing both the idea of using natural products and by proving benefits. Fancl is planning to expand its product line in order to meet the wants and needs of American women.[48] The build-up segmentation method is helping Fancl expand its business.

TARGET MARKETING

While segmentation is an analytical process, target marketing is a decision-making process. The company must choose the segment(s) on which it will focus its energy. At one extreme, all segments may be selected; at the other, only one. Clearly, most companies would like everyone to buy its product. But even giants such as Coca-Cola and Pepsi must battle for customers, and each devotes different effort to specific market segments. Pepsi has a long history of concentrating on youth—"Generation Next." It has spent billions trying to woo the young and nearly young, implying that Coca-Cola is for the older generation. Similarly, The Limited focuses on young, trendy women; Gerber on infants and young toddlers; McDonald's on families; and Lexus on quality-conscious, high-income adults. The relationships feature, "Credit Card Co-Branding: New Shortcut to Hitting the Target Market," discusses a new spin on target marketing.

career tip Interested in a career with PepsiCo? Visit the Pepsi Web site and learn more about the opportunities available in different geographic locations within the Frito-Lay North America, Pepsi Bottling Group, PepsiCo Corporate, Pepsi-Cola North America, or Tropicana North America companies. You can perform a search of the job database and apply online.

SELECTING TARGET SEGMENTS

How do companies decide which market segments to target? Once the segmentation scheme is developed, you need to describe, or profile, each group in more detail. The **market segment profile** compiles information about a market segment and the amount of opportunity it represents. The profile may include (1) the number of current and potential buyers; (2) the potential number of products these buyers may purchase; (3) the amount of revenue the segment may provide; and (4) the expected growth rate. In addition to size and growth, other criteria used to select targets include competitive factors, cost and efficiency factors, the segment's leadership qualities, and the segment's compatibility with the company's vision, objectives, and resources.

Size and Growth   Market segments vary considerably by size and growth rate. Although a segment must be large enough to generate revenues and profits, the biggest is not always the most attractive. Competition may be very tough there. A slightly smaller segment may have enough revenue to ensure a satisfactory profit. In the 1980s, Japanese companies gained strong footholds in many countries (including the United States) by targeting smaller segments that were being ignored. These were large enough to support sustained marketing efforts and included people whose spending power would increase over time.

Competitive Factors   In general, the less competition within a segment, the better. Marketers must be aware not only of who is currently serving the segment but also of who is likely to do so in the future. A company may decide not to serve a particular segment in order to avoid competitors known for their aggressiveness and strength. In other cases, a company may choose to challenge rivals. Church & Dwight decided to take on Procter & Gamble and Colgate-Palmolive by introducing its Arm & Hammer baking soda toothpaste. It felt the product was just different enough to be successful with certain segments.

CONNECTING THROUGH RELATIONSHIPS

CREDIT CARD CO-BRANDING: NEW SHORTCUT TO HITTING THE TARGET MARKET

Credit card issuers are finding it a lot easier to target someone else's loyal customers than to inspire loyalty in their own. After all, with the flood of cut-rate cards filling mailboxes and the ease of transferring balances, consumers have little incentive to stick with a particular one. But what if a card gives something back? That's the principle behind credit card co-branding, a marketing strategy that's taken the business world by storm since it appeared in 1990.

Co-branding works like this: An issuer such as MasterCard or Visa teams up with a partner. It can be a retailer, a mail-order company, an airline, a university, or a nonprofit group. In a typical co-branding program, the issuer develops a marketing campaign that targets the partner's customers. The issuer also contributes about 1 percent of its sales to the partner's reward program, which may be merchandise discounts, cash rebates, gift certificates, or donations to a particular cause. In today's Internet-intensive marketplace, FreeShop.com and NextCard are teaming up with Visa to co-brand a credit card designed to give patrons of Internet commerce perks for utilizing the medium. "Our alliance with NextCard will provide great value to FreeShop.com customers, while creating a significant new revenue opportunity for FreeShop," says Tim Choate, CEO of FreeShop.

Co-branding flourishes because it's a win-win-win situation. The card issuer can easily target and reach a new base of customers and net a steady stream of revenue from transaction fees. The partner gains increased customer loyalty, higher average orders, and more frequent purchases. And the consumer gets free toys, air miles, or a host of other perks for using the co-branded card. During the summer of 2000, MasterCard offered a "win summer vacations for the next 20 years" promotion to go along with its "Priceless" advertising campaign. The program also joined up with ExxonMobil and Alamo Rent-a-Car to offer traveling customers promotional tie-ins.

Of course, perks only draw customers if the brand appeals to them in the first place. The co-branding relationship taps into consumer loyalty or emotional ties to a co-brand sponsor, says Leslie Dukker Dory, senior vice president and director of marketing for Sun Trust BankCard of Orlando, Florida. "A well-established, well-identified, easily reached target, if provided the right perks," says Dory, "will gravitate to a card."

Sun Trust's own specialty is co-branding cards that target leisure-activity niches. Two of the cards it issues are the Cool Country Visa, aimed at fans of 11 major country music artists, and the Daytona USA MasterCard, aimed at motor sports enthusiasts. Sun Trust reaches these people through direct mail as well as promotions, special event tie-ins, album inserts, and take-one dispensers.

Although country music fans and motorcycle mavens represent rather narrow niches, they can be very profitable. Co-branded cards that target populations likely to carry balances can pull in substantial revenues even among a small customer base.

Wal-Mart teamed up with Chase Manhatten Bank to offer a Wal-Mart card, and earlier this year Sears, Roebuck & Co. decided to replace its traditional Sears credit card with a Sears Gold MasterCard. Sears stands to generate large revenues from the changeover, which allows customers to use their Sears cards at any establishment where MasterCard is accepted. The cards can also benefit Sears if it charges fees from the customer as well as the retailers that accept the card.

Sources: Kelly Shermach, "Cobranded Credit Cards Inspire Consumer Loyalty," *Marketing News,* September 9, 1996, p. 12; Kate Fitzgerald and Mark Gleason, "Wal-Mart Leaps into Credit Cards," *Advertising Age,* September 30, 1996, pp. 1, 62; Kathleen Kiley, "Branded!" *Catalog Age,* June 1996, pp. 77–80; Renee Covino Rouland, "Toys 'R' Free," *Discount Merchandiser,* October 1995, p. 70; "Freeshop.com and NextCard Offer Co-branded Credit Card," *Direct Marketing,* July 2000, p. 12; "Mastercard Offers 'Priceless' Summer Vacation," *Bank Advertising News,* June 12, 2000, p. 1; and Mary Vanac, "Sears Switches Credit Card to MasterCard," *The Plain Dealer,* August 15, 2000, p. 6c.

Cost and Efficiency Factors   It is more efficient to target some segments than others. When Citibank set its sights on chief financial officers of several worldwide corporations, costs ran into the millions for research, product development, and personal selling. This sounds expensive, but it was a very efficient use of funds. This extremely compact segment consists of a few known and very influential people, so all the marketing dollars could be aimed directly at the targets. If the message reaches all sorts of consumers, then the result is higher cost and reduced efficiency. For example, alcohol abuse prevention advertisements are seen by responsible drinkers and teetotalers, not just the target audience.

Segment Leadership Qualities   Some segments set the trend for adopting new ideas and products. Professional sports teams influence the dress and equipment of college athletes, who, in turn, influence high school teams. Marketers often choose a target segment with leadership qualities, hoping that other segments will follow suit.

Compatibility Factors   Companies often select segments they believe are particularly compatible with the company's vision, objectives, and resources. Thus, to a significant degree, target segments reflect the qualities and character of the company. In the early 1980s, Honda recognized that Harley-Davidson was attracting customers who didn't appeal to much of the general population. Honda took advantage of this by targeting younger, well-educated buyers with the theme: "You meet the nicest people on a Honda." This segment was consistent with Honda's image. Other Japanese motorcycle companies, such as Yamaha and Kawasaki, did the same and captured a large number of U.S. customers. In the past few years Harley-Davidson has been trying to erase its Hell's Angels image. The old image of tough bikers is definitely a fading emphasis.[49] Today the Harley-Davidson emphasis is on a lifestyle, and buyers include a broad range of responsible individuals. Harley-Davidson executives make the point that "Nobody Needs a Harley" so they attempt to market all of the factors that promote the excitement of a Harley.

FINDING NEW MARKETS TO TARGET

A major innovation occurs when companies discover new market segments. You can probably think of many examples. PocketCard has discovered a novel way to market debit cards. The cards are designed specifically for parents of teenagers. The parents can track all of their teenager's purchases online and revoke privileges at any time. These cards free up parents' time because they aren't constantly running to the ATM to get cash for their children and it gives teenagers a sense of freedom. Several Internet start-ups such as Spendcash.com and Cobalt Card are taking PocketCard's lead and offering credit cards for Internet purchases. These cards are also being targeted to teenagers. It is only a matter of time before big banks start issuing the cards.[50] Thus, a new segment has been discovered.

Hi-Tec is targeted toward young outdoor enthusiasts.

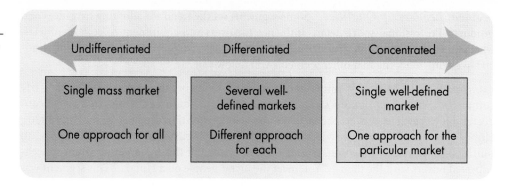

Undifferentiated — Differentiated — Concentrated

| Single mass market | Several well-defined markets | Single well-defined market |
| One approach for all | Different approach for each | One approach for the particular market |

FIGURE 6.9 *Target Market Strategies*

TARGET MARKETING STRATEGIES

TARGETING STRATEGY

The number of market segments and the relative amount of resources targeted to each.

A **targeting strategy** defines the number of target markets and the relative amount of resources allocated to each. Strategies usually fall within one of the three categories shown in Figure 6.9: undifferentiated marketing, differentiated marketing, and concentrated marketing. Two others are used less frequently: niche marketing and micromarketing. Mass customization may be the wave of the future. Figure 6.10 illustrates the way the marketing mix is targeted in each of the three most common strategies.

UNDIFFERENTIATED MARKETING

A strategy that views all potential customers as though they were the same.

Undifferentiated Marketing Similar to mass marketing, **undifferentiated marketing** treats all customers the same. Companies look for desires that are common to most potential customers and then try to design products that appeal to everyone. By focusing internally on a single or a few products, companies can streamline manufacturing, distribution, and even promotion in order to improve quality and gain cost efficiencies. But the standardized product may fail to meet individual customer needs. For years United Parcel Service (UPS) used this strategy. Users benefited from the cost-effective operations but were upset by the company's inability to fulfill unique customer requirements.

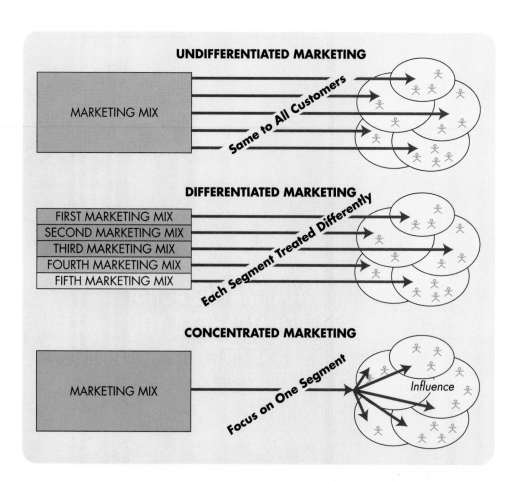

FIGURE 6.10 *How the Marketing Mix Is Used in Common Targeting Strategies*

The Keebler Company utilizes differentiated marketing.

As long as companies keep the price relatively low and competitive alternatives are unavailable, an undifferentiated marketing strategy can be successful. Today, however, competition is tough. Companies that once thrived are being threatened by rivals that use more targeted approaches, such as differentiated or concentrated marketing.

Differentiated Marketing **Differentiated marketing** serves each segment with marketing mix elements matched specifically to its desires and expectations. When Federal Express and others entered the market with differentiated strategies, UPS executives had to make a choice. Should the company settle for slowly eroding sales, or should it choose the risk, hard work, and uncertainty of a new course? UPS decided on a differentiated marketing strategy. It carefully selected targets and designed services to meet their different needs. Some of its operations are applicable to all segments, such as its computerized tracking system and extensive aircraft fleet. Other elements differ, such as product mix, personal selling, and pricing. This approach allows UPS to serve all its customers better.

The advantage of differentiated marketing is that needs and wants are better satisfied for each targeted segment. The disadvantage is that it may also cost more than undifferentiated marketing because several marketing mix strategies are typically required. Differentiated marketing requires decentralized decision making. **Centralized decision making** involves a small group of executives who make all the major decisions for the whole company. **Decentralized decision making** permits numerous groups, each dedicated to a specific segment, to make the decisions for their particular segment. This gives marketers a lead role in the company, as they need to ensure that customers' needs and wants are considered in every decision. When UPS decided to engage in differentiated marketing, the first step was to create a much stronger role for marketing. This meant educating large numbers of executives about the latest marketing techniques.

Concentrated Marketing Focusing the organization's marketing mix on one or two of the many possible segments is called **concentrated marketing.** Companies must make sure they have a great deal of knowledge about their core market segment, as this major target is called. Although most of the marketing is aimed at the core, substantial revenues and profits may be gained from other segments. This is because segments with leadership qualities are often selected for concentrated marketing in the hope that they will influence the behavior of others.

DIFFERENTIATED MARKETING
Marketing to each of several segments with a marketing mix strategy matched specifically to its desires and expectations.

CENTRALIZED DECISION MAKING
Management process in which a small group of executives make all the major decisions for the whole company.

DECENTRALIZED DECISION MAKING
Management process in which numerous groups, each dedicated to a specific segment, make decisions about their segment.

CONCENTRATED MARKETING
Focusing the organization's marketing mix strategy on one or only a few of many possible segments.

Putting them on is easy.
Taking them off is the hard part.

The New Adirondack Boot from UGG Australia. The world's premier brand of authentic sheepskin footwear. 800.847.8447 uggaustralia.com

*This ad by UGG Australia is
an example of concentrated
marketing—it focuses on one
of many possible segments.*

Ralph Lauren has used concentrated marketing successfully to target high-income, well-educated professionals and their families. Wanting to emulate them, consumers in the non-core segment are drawn to Lauren products as well.

Concentrated marketing has worked extremely well for new companies or companies entering new areas of the world. By gaining a foothold in a core market, a company can build the financial strength, experience, and credibility needed for expansion. When Tower Records opened its first music store in Thailand, it concentrated on young people. "They made it a real hip thing to buy a record," says Kamol Su KosolClapp, chief of Bakery Music Company, a popular Thai label.[51] Success in this segment is leading to further expansion in Thailand, including a host of additional outlets catering to listeners of all types.

Niche Marketing and Micromarketing   Niche marketing and micromarketing are two other strategies worth mentioning. A **niche** is a very small market that most companies ignore because they do not perceive adequate opportunity. For example, the advertising firm Johnson & Co. recently designed a campaign for the Information Technology Training Association's Global IT Week conference. Although the audience at the conference was quite small, the company was able to showcase its advertising skills and to have a guaranteed number of individuals in this market.[52]

The smallest possible niche is the individual. Marketing to one customer is called **micromarketing.** Advances in technology have made it possible to adjust marketing strategies to meet individual needs. "Tell me someone's zip code, and I can predict what they eat, drink, drive—even think," claims Jonathon Robbin. He is creator of the PRIZM cluster system, which matches census data and consumer surveys with the 36,000 zip codes in the United States. Consumers are partitioned into 40 lifestyle groups, which in turn are matched with buying behaviors. The information can be used to predict everything from a person's automobile choice to a preference for croissants over Kellogg's Pop-Tarts.[53] Additionally, some retail outlets market directly to niche customers. The Bass Pro Shop in Gurnee, Illinois, allows customers to try out products such as fishing polls in the store's indoor trout stream.[54] Companies are also using computers to sift through billions of bytes and come up with sets of variables and patterns that boggle the mind. See the technology feature, "Mining Data for the Micromarket."

NICHE

A very small market segment
that most companies ignore
because they fail to see any
opportunity.

MICROMARKETING

Marketing to an individual
customer.

Imagine the possibilities of micromarketing. Printing technology is so flexible that neighbors can receive the same magazine with different pages targeted to their own consuming patterns. For example, if the people next door shop at discount stores and you do not, then they may receive a copy with ads featuring price promotions, whereas your copy features upscale items with no mention of price. Even more impressive is the work done to pinpoint loyal

CONNECTING THROUGH TECHNOLOGY

MINING DATA FOR THE MICROMARKET

Data mining and warehousing seems to be a necessity in today's consumer-friendly marketplace. This kind of technology fulfills a dream marketers have had since the 1960s. With these client/server systems, immense volumes of information can be collected in one database. Cross-indexing those data in any combination can be done within minutes—not days or weeks—to get almost any view you can imagine. For instance, Bank of America's data warehouse has 800 billion characters of data, culled by separate computers that handle daily checking, savings, and other transactions. Now, whenever a phone rep fields a customer call—and the company receives about 100,000 calls a day—the rep can reach into the data warehouse and pull up information on that customer's banking patterns. Let's say you call just to check your balance, but the rep notices that you repeatedly bounce checks. You are likely to get a sales pitch on overdraft protection.

The biggest market for these $100,000+ systems (still cheaper than a mainframe, mind you) is retailer powerhouses such as Sears, Wal-Mart, and Burlington Coat Factory. "The retail industry is very competitive," says David Skeels, Computer Science Corporation's retail consultant. "The selling space per person is at an all-time high and consumers are getting smarter—they are highly value driven and not especially loyal."

With its new data-mining capabilities Wal-Mart, the country's largest retailer, is getting smarter, too. The company records every sale for every one of its 2,268 stores in a data warehouse. The corporation uses the data to fashion targeted marketing strategies and to distribute products to the stores where the most people are likely to buy them. It is plausible for the returns on using data-mining software and applications to range anywhere from 10 to 100 percent. Wal-Mart managed to reduce its inventories in 1997 by $1 billion while seeing sales increases of 12 percent. Wal-Mart focuses on an item-per-store basis to determine seasonal data profiles and to predict demand in order to find out what customers will want and when. However, retailers are no longer the only ones using this strategy.

Since the Gramm-Leach-Bliley Financial Services Modernization Act was enacted to allow banking and insurance markets to interact with each other's businesses, the interest in gaining information about customers has become a top priority. A survey done in 1999 found that although average data warehouse users were spending around $6 million per year, insurance companies were close behind at $5.5 million. Insurance companies use this information to gear policies and services toward customers at different stages of their families' lives. As with any company that uses these systems, the ultimate goal is to improve customer service and relations in order to bolster revenue and profits—and it's working.

Every time you make a transaction in a store or over the phone, by snail mail or e-mail, chances are that you're feeding some company's massive data warehouse. In addition, MicroStrategy (a high-profile database service) is poised to begin delivering companies wireless access to their databases through cell phones and other handheld devices. This would mean that sales reps could access any customer information they need on their way to the point of sale and have their customized pitch ready without ever entering the office to do research. These trillion-byte marketing weapons yield so much insight into customer behavior that Bank of America's vice chairman, Luke S. Helms, says, "It's like you're cheating."

Sources: John W. Verity, "A Trillion-Byte Weapon," *Business Week,* July 31, 1995, BW Online; Rosemary Cafasso, "Sears Roebuck and Co.," *Computerworld Client/Server Journal,* special issue, August 1996, pp. 12–13; Laurence Zuckerman, "Do Computers Lift Productivity? It's Unclear, But Business Is Sold," *New York Times,* January 2, 1997, p. C15; John W. Verity, "Coaxing Meaning Out of Raw Data," *Business Week,* February 3, 1997, pp. 134–138; "Discounters Update Data Systems," *Discount Store News,* June 8, 1998, p. 66; Todd R. Weiss, "MicroStrategy, Aether Take Data Mining Wireless," *Computerworld,* November 27, 2000 p. 66; and Mark E. Ruquet, "Data Mining Challenges Cited," *National Underwriter,* December 4, 2000, p. 3.

customers. By linking a publisher's subscription list with a company's customer list, marketers can substitute special ads for loyal customers in place of the general ad being carried in the magazine.

Mass Customization   Probably the most important technological development for marketing is the personalization of mass merchandise. As you learned in chapter 1, mass customization serves one or several markets while efficiently responding to the needs and desires of individual consumers. By creating a process that can respond to uniquely defined needs of targeted consumers, mass customization gives customers tremendous individualized attention. Companies can make affordable, high-quality products tailored to a customer's needs—but with the short cycle time and low costs associated with mass production.[55]

Nike has introduced Nike ID, a custom shoe the consumer creates on its Web site. The consumer starts with a basic shoe and works from there choosing the base and the accent colors. In addition, Nike allows each person to put their own "ID" on the back of the shoe. Customatix.com also creates custom athletic shoes but its Web site affords the consumer many more choices for the colors and the design. Not only do you get to put your name on the shoe, you can pick your own logo. Another small retailer is focusing on the custom market by creating made-to-order clothing, including the hard-to-fit jeans. There are step by step instructions for creating the jeans and for making the measurements to get the perfect fit.[56]

BMW uses mass customization as well. The company believes customer needs are neglected when salespeople are under pressure to sell vehicles off a lot. If you visit BMW's Web site, you can customize your own BMW model, find a dealership, and even process a credit application. The Web site features an easy-to-use interface, immediate updating of manufacturer's suggested retail price, and multiple color views. Choices can also be saved for a return visit. Final transactions will be made with a dealer, but this affords customers the ability to choose exactly what they want in their car.[57]

ETHICAL DIMENSIONS OF TARGETING

It makes sense that manufacturers should want to target ethnic segments, but this creates trouble for some companies. They are coming under fire for campaigns aimed at specific groups. The alcoholic beverage industry frequently is criticized in this regard. For example, in the early 1990s, G. Heileman breweries began distributing a new malt liquor, PowerMaster, in minority neighborhoods.[58] Twenty-one consumer and health groups tried to call a halt. The beer contained 5.9 percent alcohol, compared to no more than 5.4 percent for other malt liquors. Critics denounced the positioning of the beer toward minorities, especially given its alcoholic strength. "The ethics of targeting a single demographic group with a brand is a much stronger issue than even five years ago," says Rob Klugman, vice president of brand marketing at Coors Brewing Company. "The response to PowerMaster should have surprised no one."[59] Shortly thereafter, the product was discontinued.

Similarly, the tobacco industry has come under intense fire due to targeting. With more than 400 cigarette brands and styles available in the United States, many of the products could not survive without appeal to very specific consumer groups. Lorillard, Inc. aims Newport Stripes specifically at women. Cartier Vendome is promoted by Philip Morris as a cigarette for the wealthy or aspiring rich. These brands effectively target subsets of the larger population. When R. J. Reynolds introduced a menthol cigarette for African Americans called Uptown, the result was public scrutiny and condemnation by the U.S. secretary of health and human services and numerous African American and community groups. There were demands that the government bar tobacco companies from designing and promoting cigarettes targeted at this market segment. The fight stopped short of litigation when Reynolds agreed to cancel the brand at an estimated cost of $5 million to $7 million. Not all businesspeople believe this should have happened. Caroline Jones, president of her own advertising agency in New York, a company owned predominantly by blacks, said that it is insulting to ignore the African American community and not target it. "Marketers could and should advertise products to blacks, and that includes cigarettes and alcohol as well as bread and candy."[60]

Are there differences between products such as Uptown cigarettes and Kmart's line of private-label health and beauty care items aimed specifically at African Americans? There are varying opinions among consumer groups and industry manufacturers. One thing is certain. Tobacco and alcohol companies find it increasingly difficult to introduce, position, and market their products to ethnic consumers.

CONNECTED: SURFING THE NET

www.bmwusa.com

Customize a BMW to your specifications on the Internet. You will have an opportunity to select the colors and features you desire in a car. Visit the BMW Web site to check it out.

Major U.S. companies have expanded efforts to reach carefully targeted foreign market segments. Vast amounts are being spent to create a presence in areas where middle-class consumers are growing by leaps and bounds.[61] Frito-Lay is changing the snack food business in Thailand by marketing its traditional potato-based products. It also is changing agriculture. Potatoes weren't traditional food in Thailand, so it is teaching farmers to grow special seeds and educating them on all aspects of potato culture.[62] Anticipating a growth in the Russian middle class, Pepsi is trying to dominate the market for soft drinks. It plans to invest $550 million in building new plants and a new distribution system. There was even a deal in the works to create a "space billboard" on the orbiting Mir before Russia stopped supporting the space station.[63]

Domino's Pizza focuses on various global segments by tailoring its service to different cultural needs. Consider that in Iceland most households are without a telephone, the British consider it rude for a delivery person to knock on the door, and Japanese homes are not numbered sequentially. These cultural differences require Domino's to adjust its strategies. To find addresses in Japan, wall maps up to three times the size of those used in the United States were developed. In Iceland, Domino's paired up with drive-in movie theaters: Employees bring cellular phones to cars with a flashing turn signal, and customers then order pizzas for delivery right to their vehicle.

PepsiCo has been testing the Chinese market, which finds the cheese flavor undesirable, with such Cheeto flavors as Peking duck, fried egg, and dog. Procter & Gamble provides Japanese mothers with thin diapers, since they change their babies twice as often as Americans do. Green Giant advertisements picture corn falling off the cob into salad and pasta in France but being sprinkled over ice cream in Korea.[64]

POSITIONING STRATEGIES

Once the segmentation process gives a clear picture of the market and the target marketing strategy is selected, the positioning approach can be developed. Positioning is the process of creating in the mind of consumers an image, reputation, or perception of the company and its products relative to competitors. Positioning aligns a marketing strategy with the way the marketer wants buyers in a given target market to perceive the value they will receive from the company's products.

Positioning helps potential customers understand what is unique about the company and its products relative to competitors. Most important, it helps buyers connect mentally with the brand by understanding the brand. **Product position** refers to the characteristics that consumers associate with a brand. For example, Snickers is positioned as the snack to give energy, while Three Musketeers can be shared with a friend. BMW is positioned on prestige performance, while Mercedes projects prestige luxury.

THE POSITIONING MAP

A **positioning map** is a diagram of how consumers in a segment perceive specific brand elements they find important. This gives marketers a picture of how their products are viewed. Essentially, the idea is to graph where each brand falls regarding important attributes relative to other brands. To understand this, follow the process used to complete a perceptual map of television talk shows (the product) based on input from executives attending a seminar at Syracuse University.[65] They were asked to give their perceptions of talk shows. The anchors for the graph were social value and intellect. The combined results are shown in Figure 6.11. You can probably think of other talk shows. How do you perceive them relative to the ones listed in the figure?

Once the perceptions are plotted, most marketers want to know the consumer's ideal position. The ideal position is the one most preferred by each consumer. In one example, the star near Larry King marks the positioning many executives preferred. Oprah Winfrey faced a dilemma when she realized that her own show had migrated toward the lower left quadrant, which she felt was out of alignment with her own values. Shows such as Jerry Springer's show have a sensationalism that appeals to many viewers, but many believe their value to society is questionable. Oprah decided to move her show back to its original position in the upper right quadrant. Rosie O'Donnell has been credited with single-handedly saving daytime TV from

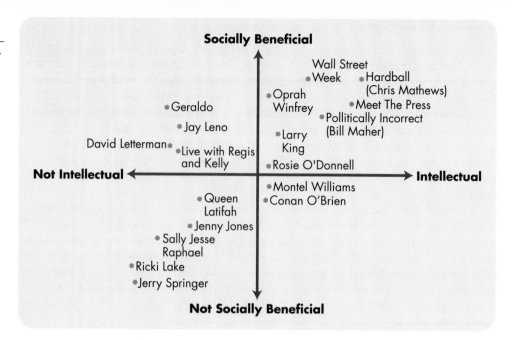

Figure 6.11 *Examples
of a Positioning Map:
TV Talk Shows*

itself by taking the trash out of talk shows. Her program, which is designed to offer intelligence and social value, has won not only great reviews but also huge ratings.[66]

POSITIONING BUSINESS PRODUCTS

In addition to the same positioning methods used by consumer marketers, business marketers look at three other product classifications: commodity, differentiated, and specialty. Commodity products have no uniqueness. These classifications are shown in Figure 6.12. Buyers make selections according to the lowest price and reliable delivery. The differentiated position requires buyers to evaluate, compare, and contrast the products from various suppliers. The specialty position is for a unique product that can be customized to user needs.

Delphi markets auto components to various GM groups such as Oldsmobile, Cadillac, and Opel, as well as to manufacturers around the world. BMW, Renault, and Ford buy components from Delphi. Depending on the product line and target segment, Delphi uses all three positioning strategies. In some cases it positions products as commodities, such as simple wire harnesses that connect parts of the electrical system. For these commodities Delphi tries to keep costs low by using standard technologies. Delphi also markets break systems that are differentiated from those of competitors and require state-of-the-art technology. Delphi's specialty products are unique. By working closely with the designers of drive trains (engines and transmissions) in its customers' companies, Delphi produces engine fuel systems tailored to specifications. These products ensure compliance with EPA standards while producing the performance demanded by consumers.

**CONNECTED:
SURFING THE NET**

www.delphiauto.com

To learn more about new Delphi products and how they are being marketed, visit the Delphi Web site. Click on the "News" button to get the most current information.

Television talk shows, such as Jerry Springer, are positioned by selecting guests and content that appeal to particular target markets.

Category	Commodity	Differentiated	Specialty
Product Characteristics	No hidden qualities, similar to other suppliers	Comparisons with other suppliers show advantages	Unique
Technology	Standard	State-of-the-art	Customized

FIGURE 6.12 *Positioning of Business Products*

STEPS FOR POSITIONING

Consumers' perceptions are influenced by the categories people use to sort through the massive amounts of product information. Music, for example, is categorized as rock, country western, jazz, classical, and so forth, whereas other dimensions help differentiate one artist or group from another. Consumers also evaluate a brand relative to others based on their impression of whether it is more or less similar. Finally, they look at a brand according to their preferences—or how close it comes to their ideal position. The following steps can be used to position a brand.

1. Identify the attributes or characteristics used by buyers in a segment to understand brands.
2. Diagram the most important dimensions on a grid (map).
3. Locate the brand relative to others based on how it is perceived by buyers.
4. Identify the ideal position for buyers in the segment.
5. Determine the fundamental way to position the product.
6. Develop the marketing mix that supports the positioning strategy selected.

BASES FOR POSITIONING

Two noted marketing scholars have identified the following seven fundamental bases that can be used to position products.[67] Each base is described in more detail next.

Positioning by Benefit   Benefits (attributes) can be used to describe the appeal of a product. For example, Procter & Gamble uses medical testimony to position Crest as a cavity-fighting toothpaste. SmithKline Beecham positions Aqua Fresh as a cavity fighter and a breath freshener. Glad trash bags are positioned to be more durable than the competition. Fisher-Price toys are positioned as safe and educational. Energizer batteries are positioned to keep going and going.

You must carefully select the benefits to associate with your product. Describing benefits that satisfy wants tends to work better than merely describing product attributes because consumers can relate the benefits to themselves.

Positioning by Price or Quality   Sam Walton made $25 billion by identifying underserved geographical market segments and then positioning Wal-Mart as being consistently lower priced than competitors. Other retailers, such as Neiman Marcus, position themselves as high priced to signal higher quality. Positioning by price is common in the pharmaceutical industry. Typically, branded drugs (usually marketed by firms that first develop them) are

Positioning Basis	EXAMPLE OF USE	
	Description	Brand/Product
Benefit (Attribute)	Safety	Volvo
Price/Quality	Value	Wal-Mart
Time of Use	After a workout	Gatorade
Product User	Mature	McDonald's Arch Deluxe®
Direct Comparison		MCI vs. AT&T
Product Class	Thirst quencher	Orange juice
Country of Origin	Jamaica	Jamaican rum

FIGURE 6.13 *Examples of Positioning*

priced much higher than generics (usually marketed by companies that copy drugs when the patent expires). The product is basically the same. The generics are positioned on price, whereas the branded products are positioned on quality.

Positioning by Time of Use or Application　Marketers frequently position products on the basis of how they are used or applied. Gatorade, Powerade, and All-Sport are positioned for drinking while exercising. Wrigley's positions its gum for use by smokers when smoking is not permitted—on airplanes, in carpools, or in nonsmoking workplaces.

Often sales can be increased by positioning a product for more than one use or application. For example, McDonald's discovered a huge opportunity when breakfast service was added. Arm & Hammer expanded baking soda sales by positioning the product as an odor fighter in the refrigerator, auto, or cupboard, in addition to its uses in toothpaste, laundry detergent, and baking. V-8 juice, originally consumed at breakfast, is now the "Wow, I could have had a V-8!" anytime beverage.

Positioning by Product User or Spokesperson　In the mind of some people, products take on meanings associated strongly with the spokesperson. For example, Nike used Michael Jordan and Tiger Woods, extraordinary athletes, to position Nike as extraordinary. Andre Agassi and John McEnroe, both considered tennis rebels, were used to help position Nike athletic shoes as an alternative to the conservative models sold by competitors.

Sometimes spokespersons are not even real, such as Betty Crocker and Mr. Goodwrench. At other times, the person's area of expertise may be more significant than the unknown individual. Cat or dog breeders are shown in ads for pet food. The Club, a device to prevent auto theft, was introduced in a national ad campaign by actual police officers.

Positioning by Direct Comparison　Nearly all customers create impressions about a brand by comparing it to another. Marketers need to determine how they want their brand to be evaluated relative to the competition. In a few cases, competitors are named, although many believe they should not be given "free" publicity. More often, the comparison is general—one brand is stronger, brighter, and so forth than "the others." Pontiac brags of "European" performance, inviting comparison with BMW. The "Avis tries harder" positioning strategy moved the company to number two in the car rental industry.

Positioning by Product Class or Category　Cereals can be categorized as natural or sweetened. Consumers are likely to position the natural cereals, such as All-Bran or granola, relative to one another. They tend not to consider sweetened cereals, such as Froot Loops or Frosted Flakes, at the same time. When determining a positioning strategy, it is important to understand how consumers categorize products.

Positioning by Country of Origin　A company's image can be affected by the mental association people make with its country of origin. We think of German precision engineering, Japanese cost and quality, Italian fashion, French taste, and U.S. technology. Certain countries are associated with certain products: the United States with movies, Germany with beer, Japan with electronics, the Netherlands with chocolate, France with wine, and Italy with shoes. Companies may create a subsidiary in a nation associated with a product, or they may use a brand name that sounds like it's from that country. For example, Little Caesar's is a U.S. pizza company with an Italian-sounding name.

REPOSITIONING

For decades, Levi-Strauss & Co. made "the jeans" to wear. However, with many new competitors in the jeans industry, Levi-Strauss has started to suffer. In order to revive its sales of jeans, Levi-Strauss is giving its image a makeover with a campaign entitled "Make them your own." Levi-Strauss hopes the campaign will increase interest in its products, which will include other products, such as corduroys.[68]

Repositioning may become necessary over time as competitive forces, customer tastes and preferences, and the marketing environment change. Repositioning can be difficult and very expensive because it's hard to alter old impressions and create new ones. With a disappointing year in 2000, champagne makers are looking for new strategies to attract more customers to their products. Traditionally, champagne has been the drink for special occasions and this has actually cut into profits in recent years. In addition, the customer base for champagne has steadily gotten older. The companies are trying to reposition their product as the drink for all occasions. They have made smaller, more colorful bottles to attract the younger crowds at clubs to their products. They have also started packaging straws with the champagne to eliminate the formal image and focus on selling individual units of consumption.[69] Whether a company is positioning a new product or repositioning an old one, the ultimate goal of its decision making is to persuade the targeted consumer to make a decision as well—the decision to purchase the product. The complex psychological and social factors that influence consumer decision making and buying behavior will be examined in the next chapter.

CONNECTED: SURFING THE NET

MASTERCARD

www.mastercard.com

THE RELATIONSHIP FEATURE IN THIS chapter discusses credit card cobranding, a popular marketing strategy for developing customer loyalty. One of the many companies teaming up with partners is MasterCard. Visit its Web site and answer the following questions.

1. How many markets does MasterCard target? What specific offerings does the company provide to reach them?
2. In this chapter you learned the variables and categories commonly used to segment consumer markets. Which one(s) does MasterCard use? Select a market the company does not currently target. Does it meet the segmentation criteria listed in the chapter? Do you think this would be a successful market? Explain.
3. MasterCard is accepted in more locations around the world than any other card. List some of its global initiatives. Link to the Web site of MasterCard Australia. How does this site differ in the way it connects with customers?

WAL-MART

www.walmart.com

IN THIS CHAPTER YOU LEARNED about Wal-Mart's use of data mining to identify and target potential customers. Visit the Wal-Mart Web site and answer the following questions.

1. Seven fundamental ways to position products were described in this chapter. Read the overview of Wal-Mart products and services and select three listed. Identify how each is positioned. Explain.
2. Wal-Mart's Web site allows Web users to shop online. What features does Wal-Mart offer to encourage customer involvement with the Web site? How, specifically, do these features help Wal-Mart build relationships with customers?

CHAPTER SUMMARY

OBJECTIVE 1: Understand the advantages of target marketing and how it differs from mass marketing and product differentiation.

Mass marketing treats all customers as though they have the same needs and wants. A single marketing strategy is designed to appeal to all potential customers. This strategy does not generally work well because customers with differing characteristics have different needs and wants. Product differentiation is a strategy that alters products to stress their uniqueness relative to competitors. It recognizes that customers have differing needs and wants, but it doesn't start with an understanding of them. Target marketing focuses on select groups of customers so marketers can more clearly understand their specific needs and wants and adjust accordingly.

OBJECTIVE 2: Describe how to do market segmentation and select target markets.

Market segmentation separates potential customers into several groups or segments with distinctive characteristics. Customers within a segment should have similar needs, wants, and preferences; they should have similar media habits and shopping and buying patterns; the group should be large enough to justify attention; and data about individuals in each segment should be available.

Typical segmentation variables are geographic and demographic factors, ethnic and other diversity-related factors, psychographic and behavioristic factors, and benefits desired. Two common segmenting methods are the take-down method and the build-up method. The take-down method begins by selecting segmentation variables and assigning customers to the category in which they fit. The build-up method starts with the unique characteristics of one potential customer. Each time someone with unique characteristics is discovered, a new segment is added.

Segments are selected as target markets based on such factors as their size and growth potential, competition, cost and efficiency, leadership qualities, and compatibility with the organization.

OBJECTIVE 3: Explore three basic target marketing strategies: undifferentiated, differentiated, and concentrated marketing.

Undifferentiated marketing treats all customers alike and is similar to mass marketing. In order for this strategy to work, companies generally must have significant cost advantages. Differentiated marketing involves serving several segments but adjusting the marketing mix for each. It usually requires decentralized decision making. Concentrated marketing focuses on one segment or only a few. Companies can use all their resources to gain advantage within that group. Because differentiated and concentrated strategies consider customer needs and wants, they are far superior to an undifferentiated strategy.

OBJECTIVE 4: Know how to do positioning and describe several approaches marketers use to create valuable, lasting images of their products.

Positioning creates in the mind of consumers an image, reputation, or perception of the company and its products relative to competitors. It helps customers understand what is unique about a company and its products. Marketers can use a positioning map to depict how customers perceive products according to certain characteristics. For business products, a commodity, differentiated, or specialty positioning strategy can be used. Products are often positioned by benefit, by price and quality, by the time of use or application, by user or spokesperson, by direct comparison with a competitor, by product class, or by country of origin.

REVIEW YOUR UNDERSTANDING

1. Define mass marketing, segmentation, and targeting. How are they different?
2. What are the steps in segmentation, targeting, and positioning?
3. What variables are used to segment markets? Give examples of each.
4. What are the three basic marketing strategies associated with segmentation?
5. What is VALS™ 2? What major categories of consumers does it profile?
6. What is the difference between the take-down and the build-up segmentation methods?
7. What characteristics are used to select target markets?
8. What is micromarketing and how does it differ from mass customization?
9. What are positioning strategies? List three used in business markets.
10. What is a positioning map and how do organizations use it to position products?

DISCUSSION OF CONCEPTS

1. Why do marketers use market segmentation to summarize information about large numbers of consumers? Why not just use averages?
2. Are segmentation techniques used by companies that follow a mass marketing strategy? A product differentiation strategy?
3. Imagine that you are the marketing manager for a company that wants to produce a new line of men's and women's dress shirts. Which segmentation variables would be relevant for this market? What categories would you use? Describe five or six market segments that may emerge.
4. What is a segment profile? Develop one for each market segment you listed in question 3.
5. Which segments in question 3 would you select as target markets?
6. Once target markets are chosen, what different strategies are available? Which would work best for your target markets?
7. Why is positioning important? What are some of the different ways to position dress shirts in your target markets?
8. Positioning is typically done relative to the competition. If you have no important competitors, then how can the concept still be useful?

KEY TERMS AND DEFINITIONS

Build-up segmentation method: Method that starts with a single potential customer's characteristics and adds a segment for each new characteristic found in other customers.

Centralized decision making: Management process in which a small group of executives makes all the major decisions for the whole company.

Concentrated marketing: Focusing the organization's marketing mix strategy on one or only a few of many possible segments.

Decentralized decision making: Management process in which numerous groups, each dedicated to a specific segment, make decisions about their segment.

De-ethnicization: The result of targeting a product heavily associated with one ethnic group to other segments.

Demographic segmentation: Division of the market according to such characteristics as gender, family life cycle, household type, and income.

Differentiated marketing: Marketing to each of several segments with a marketing mix strategy matched specifically to its desires and expectations.

Geodemography: Combining geographic information with demographics to identify segments with common consumption patterns.

Heterogeneous group: Buyers with diverse characteristics.

Homogeneous group: Buyers with similar characteristics.

Lifestyle: A person's distinctive mode of living.

Market segment: A homogeneous group with similar needs, wants, values, and buying behavior.

Market segment profile: Information about a market segment and the amount of opportunity it represents.

Micromarketing: Marketing to an individual customer.

Niche: A very small market segment that most companies ignore because they fail to see any opportunity.

Positioning: Creating an image or perception in the minds of consumers about the organization or its products relative to the competition.

Positioning map: A diagram of how consumers in a segment perceive brands based on specific elements they consider important.

Product differentiation: A marketing strategy with which companies attempt to make their products appear unique relative to the competition.

Product position: The characteristics consumers associate with a brand based on important attributes.

Psychographics: Marketing approaches and tools used to identify lifestyles based on measures of consumers' values, activities, interests, opinions, demographics, and other factors.

Segmentation: Division of a market into homogeneous groups with similar needs, wants, values, and buying behavior.

Segmentation variable: Any distinguishing market factor that can vary, such as gender, age, or income.

Take-down segmentation method: Method that starts with a set of variables and assigns all consumers to one of them.

Target Marketing: The selection of specific homogeneous groups (segment) of potential customers for emphasis.

Targeting strategy: The number of market segments and the relative amount of resources targeted at each.

Undifferentiated marketing: A strategy that views all potential customers as though they were the same.

Zip code segmentation: Division of a market into specific geographic locations based on the demographic makeup of the zip code area.

REFERENCES

1. Chet Dembeck, "Dell Builds a Better Dot-Com Model," *E-Commerce Times,* April 6, 2000, www.ecommercetimes.com/news/viewpoint2000/view-000406-2.shtml; Daniel Lyons, "Make the Little Guys Feel Big," *Forbes,* April 17, 2000, pp. 208+; Michael Dell, "E-Business: Strategies in Net Time," speech at e-business forum at University of Texas, Austin, Texas, April 27, 2000; Dell Computer Web site (www.dell.com), August 22, 2000.
2. General Motors, "The Fleet," www.gm.com, visited July 13, 2000.
3. Procter & Gamble, "P&G Products," www.pg.com, visited July 13, 2000.
4. Bold, Bounce, Cheer, Downy, Dreft, Dryel, Era, Gain, Ivory Snow, Oxydol, and Tide; Camay, Ivory, Coast, Safeguard, and Zest; Head & Shoulders, Mediker, Pantene Pro-V, Physique, Rejoy/Rejoice, Pert Plus, and Vidal Sassoon; Cascade, Cascade Complete, Dawn, Ivory Dish, and Joy; Crest Toothpaste, Fixodent, Gleem, and Scope.
5. "Great Lakes Crossing—Michigan's Ultimate Family Entertainment Destination for Summer Fun," *PR Newswire,* June 1, 2000.
6. Population Reference Bureau, www.prb.org, 2000 World Population Chart, visited July 10, 2000.
7. Dana James, "It'll Be a Wireless, Wireless, Wireless, Wireless World," *Marketing News,* July 17, 2000, pp. 25, 29.
8. Associated Press, "Coke Plans 100 Different Commercials during Olympics Broadcast," retrieved from www.nando.net/newsroom/ap/oth/1996/oth/oly/feat/archive/071596/oly12977, August 29, 1996.
9. *Chicago,* March 1996, p. 22.
10. David Churbuck, "Geographics," *Forbes,* January 6, 1992, pp. 262–266.
11. "Colleges Go All Out in Increasing Effort to Gain Attention," *Omaha World-Herald,* July 30, 2000, p. 9a.
12. Bob Minzesheimer, "You Are What Your Zip Is," *Michigan: The Magazine of the Detroit News,* May 15, 1983, pp. 22–26.
13. Simon Barker-Benfield, "The Florida Times-Union, Jacksonville, Silicon Beach," *KRTBN Knight-Ridder Tribune Business News: The Florida Times Union—Jacksonville,* August 21, 2000.
14. Rebecca Gardyn, "High Frequency," *American Demographics,* July 2000, pp. 32–36.
15. Erin Strout, "Marketing to Mom," *Sales and Marketing Management,* May 2000, p. 11.
16. Judann Pollack, "In Fitful Pursuit of American Women," *Advertising Age,* January 8, 1996, p. 54.
17. Ibid.
18. Andy Cohen, "Does Your Sales Force Need a New Look?" *Sales and Marketing Management,* May 2000, p. 13.
19. Maryellen Lo Bosco, "Cosmetics Makers to Retailers: You've Got Male," *Idea Beat,* www.ideabeat.com, January 31, 2000.
20. Universal Press Syndicate, "Why Men Dye/Guys Increasingly Color Hair to Be Hip or to Hide the Gray," *Houston Chronicle,* July 6, 2000, p. 6.
21. Lo Bosco, "Cosmetics Makers to Retailers: You've Got Male."
22. Steve Alexander, "Families Keeping in Touch with Second Wireless Phone . . . ," *Star-Tribune Newspaper of the Twin Cities,* February 14, 2000, p. 12D.
23. Lisa Sandberg, "Eat Up, Kids. It's Organic: Natural Food Companies Finding New Audience," *National Post,* November 22, 2000, p. B04.
24. Michael Wilke, "Mylanta Targets Children," *Advertising Age,* May 27, 1996, pp. 1–2.
25. Pam Weiss, "Eau de Toilette for the 12-and-Under Set," *Brandweek,* February 13, 1995, p. 30.
26. Mary Umberger, "Chicago Builders See Big Things for Baby Boomers, Suburbanites," *Chicago Tribune,* December 9, 2000.
27. Bill Bergstrom, "Seniors Are Increasingly Valuable Business Market," *Associated Press Newswires,* December 14, 2000.
28. Diane E. Lewis, "Gen X Seen Better at Saving Income," *The Boston Globe,* October 29, 2000, p. J2.
29. Monique Brown, "Fashionable Speaking," *Black Enterprise,* July 2000, p. 75.
30. Frank Green, "Whither the Teen Green?/ Lreport Is Paid to Track Youthful Customers," *The San Diego Union-Tribune,* November 17, 2000, p. C-1.
31. James Heckman, "Random Sampling," *Marketing News,* January 31, 2000, p. 6.
32. Margaret Littman, "How Marketers Track Underage Consumers," *Marketing News,* May 8, 2000, p. 4.
33. "Women Outpace Men Online in Number and Growth Rate According to Media Matrix and Jupiter Communications," *Business Wire,* August 9, 2000.
34. For a review, see Solomon, *Consumer Behavior,* pp. 463–493.
35. Robert Pear, "A New Look at the U.S. in 2050: Bigger, Older, and Less White," *New York Times,* December 4, 1992, p. A1.
36. Leah Rickard and Jeanne Whalen, "Retail Trails Ethnic Changes," *Advertising Age,* May 1, 1995, p. 1.
37. Michael J. McDermott, "Marketers Pay Attention! Ethnics Comprise 25% of the U.S.," *Brandweek,* July 18, 1994, p. 26.
38. Dana James, "Lingua Franca," *Marketing News,* January 3, 2000, p. 17.
39. Robert Sullivan, "Americans and Their Money," *Worth,* June 1994, p. 60.
40. Joel R. Evans and Barry Berman, *Marketing,* 7th ed. (Upper Saddle River, NJ: Prentice Hall, 1997), pp. 270–271.
41. Michael Gates, "VALS Changes with the Times," *Incentive,* June 1989, p. 27.
42. "The Best 100 Sources for Marketing Information," *American Demographics,* January 1995, p. 29.
43. Lewis C. Winters, "International Psychographics," *Marketing Research,* September 1992, pp. 48–49.
44. "General Motors Connects with MTV Generation via OnStar In-Vehicle Technology," *PR Newswire,* June 13, 2000.
45. "Inforetech's Informer 2000 on Par to Change the Way Golfers Navigate on Courses; Inforetech Forges Ahead in Development of New Portable Recreation Device," *Business Wire,* December 14, 2000.
46. "Race You to the Checkout," *American Demographics,* May 2000, p. 9.
47. Leon E. Wynter, "Business and Race," *Wall Street Journal,* July 3, 1996, p. B1.
48. "Reaching American 'Faces,'" *Direct Marketing,* March 2000, pp. 50–52.
49. Associated Press, "Biker Sues Harley-Davidson for Trying to Yank Business," *State News, Michigan State University's Independent Voice,* April 10, 1996, p. 6.
50. Chana Schoenberger, "Big Brother (And Sister): A Debit Card Lets You Spy on Your Kids, in Real Time, as They Spend Money," *Forbes,* January 24, 2000, p. 142.
51. G. Pascal Zachary, "Strategic Shift: Major U.S. Companies Expand Efforts to Sell to Consumers Abroad," *Wall Street Journal,* June 13, 1996, p. A1.
52. Kathleen Schmidt, "Seasoned Agency Exes Recapture Creativity with High-Tech Firms," *Marketing News,* January 3, 2000, p. 8.
53. Michael J. Weiss, *The Clustering of America* (New York: Harper & Row), p. 1.

54. Kathryn Waskom, "Destination Retail Is on Its Way," *Marketing News,* March 13, 2000, p. 3.
55. Christopher Hart, "Mass Customization: Conceptual Underpinnings, Opportunities and Limits," *International Journal of Service Industry Management 6,* no. 2 (1995), pp. 36–45.
56. Carrie Kirby, "Made to Order for Creative Shoppers," *The San Francisco Chronicle,* November 27, 2000, p. F4.
57. Visited BMWUSA.com, December 18, 2000.
58. "Distilling Truth about Alcohol Ads," *Business & Society Review,* Fall 1992, pp. 12–17.
59. Rinler Buck, "PowerMaster Trips ANA's Dewitt Helm," *Adweek's Marketing Week,* July 8, 1991, p. 12.
60. Judann Dagnoli, "RJR's Uptown Targets Blacks," *Advertising Age,* December 18, 1989, p. 4.
61. G. Zachary, "Strategic Shift," *Wall Street Journal,* June 13, 1996, A1.
62. Ibid.
63. "Pepsi Aims for the Stars," *Marketing News,* June 3, 1996, p. 1.
64. Tara Parker-Pope, "Custom Made: The Most Successful Companies Have to Realize a Simple Truth: All Customers Aren't Alike," *Wall Street Journal,* September 26,1996, pp. R22–23.
65. Executive Development Session with Executives sponsored by Syracuse University and Sales and Marketing Executives International, May 4, 2001. The exercise was done for the purpose of creating an example and does not necessarily reflect how executives perceive these shows.
66. Rick Martin, "Coming Up Roses," *Newsweek,* July 15, 1996, pp. 45–48.
67. David A. Aaker and J. Gary Shansby, "Positioning Your Product," *Business Horizons,* May–June 1982, p. 56.
68. "Levi Strauss' New Ads: 'Make Them Your Own'," *Advertising Age,* July 3, 2000, p. 25.
69. Theresa Howard, "Re-Branding Bubbly for the Pepsi Generation: Sales under Pressure," *USA Today,* December 14, 2000, p. C09.

Bricks or Clicks

FAO SCHWARZ IS THE ULTIMATE ONLINE TOY STORE

FAO SCHWARZ IS NOT YOUR garden-variety toy store. Since its founding in 1862, it has specialized in unique, hard-to-find, and exclusive toys and collectibles from around the globe. The company wants to create nothing less than "a magical experience" for its customers. It must be "the ultimate"—the ultimate toys, printed in the "Ultimate Toy Catalogue," from "the world's ultimate toy store."

When FAO Schwarz launched FAO.com in 1995, it faced the challenge of translating this magical, "ultimate" shopping experience into the two-dimensional world of the Internet. It has made great strides toward overcoming this limitation when it relaunched its Web site in August 2000. An interactive "Virtual Playroom" allows customers to "try before they buy." Visitors to the site are able to view and rotate three-dimensional images of selected products 360 degrees. With the aid of a downloadable attachment from FAO.com, "the virtual toy will come to life and perform various actions."

Although electronic bells and whistles are fun and contribute to the desired "magic" of its customers' shopping experience, FAO Schwarz knows that its site would be lacking without a simple and effective means of conducting the sale. Customers visiting FAO.com can check an item's inventory status and leave items in their "shopping bag" for a later time or date. Once the checkout process is complete, customers receive an order number that allows them to track their shipments.

The technical wizardry and the convenience of FAO.com represent the integration of FAO's bricks-and-mortar strategy with the virtual world. The site has become the fastest-growing facet of the company, allowing it to become the "ultimate" online toy retailer.

Sources: "FAO Schwarz Relaunches FAO.com to Bring 'E-Magic' Buying Experience to Online Shopping Community," *Business Wire,* August 21, 2000; see also "FAO Schwarz Leverages Allaire Business Platform to Relaunch FAO.com," *PR Newswire,* August 22, 2000.

CASE 6

Tommy Hilfiger

IN 1984, TOMMY HILFIGER LAUNCHED his line of menswear with an ad campaign that communicated his vision. It proclaimed: "The 4 Great American Designers for Men are: Ralph Lauren, Perry Ellis, Calvin Klein, Tommy Hilfiger." It was a big joke with the New York designer crowd but Hilfiger is now one of fashion's hottest designers. With year 2000 sales of almost $2 billion, he has found tremendous success with his original target— young professional men. Recently, he entered new market segments—hip-hop teens, women, children, and babies.

In the early years, companies such as Calvin Klein, Ralph Lauren, and Bill Blass targeted high-income professionals, so Hilfiger went after younger professionals of more modest means. He positioned his clothing as classic casual wear, with just enough

new style to make it modern, at an affordable price. This meant building in the quality young professionals desired and adding a slight twist to differentiate his product line. The "twist" might be striped fabric lining the inside of polo shirt collars or colored fabric on a traditional oxford shirt. Thanks to the integration of design and manufacturing, Hilfiger could cash in on the Lauren trend with similar quality but for a more price-sensitive market.

The Tommy Hilfiger Corporation was formed in 1989 in partnership with Silas Chou, a member of one of Hong Kong's oldest textile and apparel families. The Chou family had built a fortune on private-label contracting but was beginning to lose business to lower-wage countries such as India, China, and Vietnam. Teaming with former Ralph Lauren executives,

Lawrence Stroll and Joel Horowitz, Chou and Hilfiger integrated design, manufacturing, and marketing. By 1995, the Hilfiger vision was realized; the Council of Fashion Designers of America voted Tommy Hilfiger menswear designer of the year.

In the 1980s, the Hilfiger image was ingeniously associated with such great menswear designers as Ralph Lauren, thereby reaping benefits it had taken those designers years to achieve. Hilfiger has now gained legitimization in his own right, and the Tommy Hilfiger name stands on its own, its positioning based on design themes and association with people who wear the clothes.

Hilfiger often uses a red, white, and blue theme and visualizes his clothes as "celebrating the individuality and creativity that define America." He puts a spin on the classics. Hilfiger positions his designs as an extension of himself. "I want people to feel comfortable yet unique. It's new-age funk combined with traditional style that give my clothing an edge. This enhances people's individuality and enables them to stand out." He notes that "preppy kids started wearing classics in a different way, very oversized. City kids took it another level by going giant sized." So Hilfiger created yet another size category, giant, which is considerably larger than XXL. In keeping with the theme, Hilfiger made his logos bigger and extremely graphic.

Hilfiger is worn by a diverse range of public figures. For example, Bill Clinton, Michael Jackson, Harry Connick Jr., and Mick Jagger all sport his logo. Hilfiger brings together a crossover market of young professionals, preppies, and the urban hip-hop crowd. The prep-urban style runs through many of his lines. Hilfiger says: "I think it's very cool that I can walk down Fifth Avenue and see a messenger wearing my rugby shirt five times too big, and then go to Wall Street and see an investment banker wearing my pinstripes." Hilfiger's street popularity was boosted in March 1994, when Snoop Doggy Dog wore a red, white, and blue rugby shirt on *Saturday Night Live*. Hilfiger has even been labeled "hip-hop's favorite haberdasher."

In advertising, Tommy always wants his models to seem spirited and fun. Referencing to a typical Hilfiger ad, *Adweek* wrote: "Notice the group of wet and wild funsters just up from a dunk in their local quarry, their big ol' WASP prepster style Tommy underwear soaked to the eh—groin. There must be something about the large white teeth gleaming in the mouths of all these nice, clean, young 'ammuricans' that makes the otherwise revealing image seem spirited, as if people pose for their dentist in their underwear."

Sticking to Tradition

RUSSELL SIMMONS, THE FOUNDER OF Def Jam Records, says that "Tommy's clothing represents the American dream to black kids. They're not interested in buying holey jeans; they want high-quality merchandise." Although Hilfiger has been successful in a variety of markets, of particular interest to many is his success among urban youth. Hilfiger focuses on true "hip-hoppers," a group that may seem too small and too poor to target. But millions of suburban kids follow inner-city trends—ranging from music to clothing. Hilfiger has used gangsta' rap to tap into the inner-city market.

Although Tommy has done well in this market, the company is now attempting to move back to its more classical styles. Joel Horowitz, CEO of Tommy Hilfiger, states, "Improvements in our product design and assortments have been at the heart of our repositioning efforts this year, supported by new marketing and advertising programs. We believe that for the Holiday and Spring [2000–2001], consumers will see a strong and more cohesive presentation of traditional Tommy Hilfiger products—'classics with a twist'—as we have refocused our efforts on serving our core customer base."[70]

The company is also using a partnership and new product line to help return to the classic heritage of Tommy. In the fall of 2000, Tommy introduced a line of watches in a licensing deal with Movado. The watch collection includes 230 styles, which range in price from $55 to $175. For the first year of advertising, Movado contributed more than $6 million, which promoted the new line of watches. And Hilfiger's lifestyle campaign featured models Jason Shaw, Tyrone, and Maggie Rizer. "Images are very Kennedy-esque, very nautical, preppie with a twist," Hilfiger said. "It coincides with our return to our classical heritage."[71]

Tommy Targets Women

HILFIGER HAS EXPANDED INTO THE professional women's market with a positioning strategy very similar to that used for men. This could be a very smart move given the strong trend among women toward casual dress. They are also able to target a specific cohort of women, those with very young children and expectant mothers, with a line of Tommy clothes for babies. This line features onesies, bodysuits, overalls, cardigans, pants, and accessories designed like traditional clothing but, of course, with that unexpected twist. Hilfiger gives a face-lift to the very traditional onesie with a large star logo chest motif and contrasting navy and red shoulder, neck, and cuff stitching. He also spruces up the classic bodysuit, adding lap shoulder styles for boys and girls, as well as polo styles for boys and petal-collar styles for girls.

1. *Identify the core target markets of Tommy Hilfiger, historically and today. What subsegments are targeted within each core target?*

2. *Develop an overall segmentation scheme using variables and categories that describe the Tommy Hilfiger market. How do the Hilfiger target market segments differ from those of Calvin Klein?*

3. *Describe the traditional positioning strategy Hilfiger used for the professional men segment. Use a positioning map to represent it. Why did you select each of the axes? How is Tommy Hilfiger differentiated from Calvin Klein and Bill Blass?*

4. *How is Tommy positioned in the women's target market segment? What are the similarities and differences with Tommy Hilfiger's positioning with men?*

Sources: Justin Doebele, "A Brand Is Born," *Forbes,* February 26, 1996, pp. 65–66; Elaine Underwood, "Tommy Hilfiger on Brand Hilfiger," *Brandweek,* February 5, 1996, pp. 23–27; Joshua Levine, "Badass Sells," *Forbes,* April 21, 1997, www.forbes.com; Shelley Reese, "The Quality of Cool," *Marketing Tools,* July 1997, www.marketingtools.com; Marc Speigler, "Marketing Street Culture: Bringing Hip-Hop Style to the Mainstream," *American Demographics,* www.marketingtools.com; Woody Hockswender, "Prep-Urban," *Esquire,* March 1996, pp. 131–132; Martha Duffy, "H Stands for Hilfiger: The Former Menswear Laughing Stock Expands into the Women's Market," *Time,* September 16, 1996, p. 66; and Barbara Lippert, "Beyond Critical," *Adweek,* March 18, 1996; Tommy Hilfiger Corporation Reports Fiscal 2001 Second Quarter Results, PR Newswire Association, Inc., *Financial News,* November 1, 2000; Tommy's Quality Time With Movado, *DNR,* v.30, no. 130, November 6, 2000.

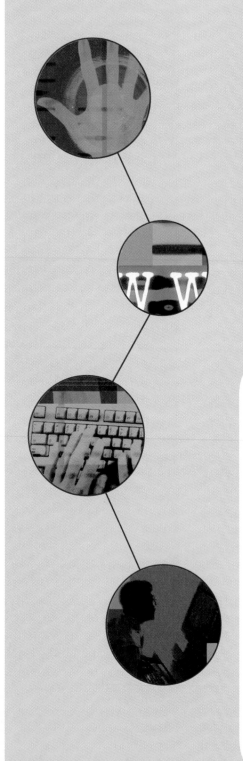

chapter 7

CONNECTING WITH CUSTOMERS: UNDERSTANDING CONSUMER BEHAVIOR

◀ *Richard Braddock, Priceline.com CEO*

CLICK AND SAVE—THE INTERNET IS *transforming the way consumers buy travel-related services. Just a few years ago, vacationers routinely called their local travel agents whenever they wanted to buy airline tickets and reserve hotel rooms. Now a growing number are clicking their way to Travelocity and Expedia, two Web sites that together account for 80 percent of all online travel sales. New travel Web sites are coming online all the time. The five largest U.S. airlines are readying Orbitz, a Web site featuring offerings from 450 airline, car-rental, and hotel partners. Individual airlines are also connecting with customers through their Web sites.*

Despite the popularity of Travelocity and other sites, millions of consumers are listening to those advertisements featuring William Shatner and logging onto Priceline.com (www.priceline.com) to name their own prices for tickets. Priceline.com opened for business on the Internet in 1998 with a simple but compelling premise: Instead of paying the prices established by the airlines, consumers state what they want to pay for tickets. Buying through Priceline.com eliminates the time-consuming hassle of clicking from site to site comparing prices or calling travel agents in search of the best deal.

Here's how the Priceline.com system works. When a customer enters a destination, a date, and a desired fare, Priceline.com's computer switches the inquiry to a special section of the airlines' computerized reservation system, searching for a ticket priced below the customer's figure. If such a ticket is available, Priceline.com buys it, marks it up to the customer's price, and charges the customer's credit card to complete the sale. Under the Priceline.com system, the customer doesn't get to choose the airline or the exact time of departure. In contrast, the customer can select a particular airline or schedule when buying from Travelocity and other Web sites. But the customer expects to get a bargain through Priceline.com, which makes up for the uncertainty. Everybody benefits: Customers get to buy low-priced tickets, Priceline.com earns about 15 percent margins on the tickets it sells, and the airlines fill empty seats on their planes.

Priceline.com's name-your-own-price approach and humorous advertising campaign have brought it considerable publicity and increased consumer awareness of online buying alternatives. The Web site now serves more than 5 million customers, of which more than 800,000 have made two or more purchases. Since the start, travel-related services such as airline tickets, hotel rooms, and rental cars have been Priceline.com's mainstay. But it is also offering new cars, long-distance telephone time, consumer electronics, credit cards, home mortgages, and life and auto insurance, among other goods and services.

Not all of Priceline.com's ventures have been successful. Citing high investment costs, the company shut down its WebHouse Club operation, which had been selling groceries and gasoline online at a discount. In addition, it closed its Perfect Yardsale unit, which had allowed individuals to sell household and personal items online at yard-sale prices because of low volume. Amid slowing sales for its core name-your-price travel unit and problems resolving customer complaints, Priceline.com management has vowed to overhaul its Web site and its customer feedback process.

Consumers are motivated to use the Internet to shop for airline tickets and other products because Priceline.com and other sites offer speed, convenience, and savings. Within a few years, one in five airline tickets will be sold via the Internet, which translates to an estimated $16 billion in yearly consumer purchasing. For their part, the airlines are always looking for ways to fill up to 600,000 empty seats every day. Priceline.com has patented its pricing model, so other sites can't copy it. But can the company successfully extend this type of pricing to dozens of goods and services? The answer depends on whether consumers are willing to put up with some uncertainty in exchange for potential savings. Daniel H. Schulman, Priceline.com's president, believes they are. "When people can save 20 percent to 30 percent on their groceries, don't underestimate how powerful that is," he states.[1]

CONNECTED: SURFING THE NET

www4.nissan.co.jp

Take the Nissan global cyber-cruise. Link to Nissan North America, Asia, Europe, or Japan and then take a plant tour. Read about Nissan milestones, vehicle design, manufacturing, marketing, and much more.

CONSUMER BEHAVIOR

The actions and decision processes of individuals and households in discovering, evaluating, acquiring, consuming, and disposing of products.

THE CONCEPT OF CONSUMER BEHAVIOR

More than ever there is vastly greater diversity among a growing number of consumers in expanding global markets. The challenge leading-edge organizations face is to enhance the life experiences of consumers with products that live up to their expectations. Every action must contribute in some way toward consumer well-being. This doesn't happen with wishful thinking or intuition. It requires a thorough knowledge of consumer decision making and the forces that influence it. To connect with customers, we must understand the societal and psychological factors that determine their decisions. Leading-edge organizations are bundling their knowledge of all these factors into systematic ways of influencing customer satisfaction, loyalty, and relationships.

Connecting with customers requires a thorough understanding of consumer behavior. **Consumer behavior** involves the actions and decision processes of individuals and households in discovering, evaluating, acquiring, consuming, and disposing of products. Consider the key parts of that definition. First, it looks at both actions—what people do—and decision processes—how they think and feel. For example, 52 percent of Gen X women aged 23 to 34 buy hair conditioner regularly, although only 46 percent of baby boomer women aged 35 to 53 do the same.[2] Marketers want to know how often this occurs and for what reasons. Second, the definition refers to individuals and households. Usually an individual makes the purchase, but those decisions are often related to household considerations. When a mother shops, she may buy Pepsi for one person, Coke for another, bottled water for a third, and so forth. Third, evaluating, acquiring, and consuming products are important parts of the process, but we need to remember that consumer behavior starts with discovery and proceeds through disposal.

Figure 7.1 provides an overview of the main topics covered in this chapter. We begin with the relationship between consumer involvement and decision making. Since involvement can be low or high, decision making can be relatively passive or very active. Next we deal with five psychological factors that influence consumer behavior: motivation, perception, learning, attitudes, and information processing. The third major section on social influences describes how culture, subculture, social class, reference groups, and family members affect the decisions of individual consumers. In the last sections, we look at ways in which technology is used to track consumer behavior, as well as ethical issues related to attempts to persuade consumers.

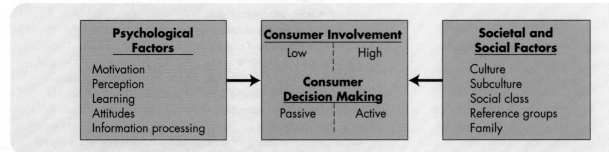

FIGURE 7.1 *Connecting with Customers: Understanding Consumer Behavior*

*The Hummer stretch limo is
an example of a purchase in
The Robb Report magazine,
which specializes in high-
involvement purchases.*

CONSUMER INVOLVEMENT AND DECISION MAKING

Decision making and involvement are closely related processes. Knowledge about them provides insight into how and why consumers behave as they do. Involvement is a function of how important, complex, and/or time-consuming a purchase may be. As we will see, decision making varies with the degree of involvement. For high-involvement purchases, the consumer is likely to devote time and attention to each of five steps in the decision process.

CONSUMER INVOLVEMENT

Think about the difference between buying a box of breakfast cereal and a new home. Which purchase would you spend more time researching and generally care more about? Not all purchases have the same importance; some mean more to us than others. **Low-involvement purchases** require only routine decision making. Cereal, soap, soft drinks, and similar items don't require much thought. Many people purchase the same brand every time they shop, which underscores the importance of brand awareness. **High-involvement purchases** demand more extensive and complex decision making. Buying a car, a computer, or even a television set requires a good deal of thought. The product is expensive, and you probably will have to live with it for a long time. Nontraditional products often fall in this category. An extreme example of high involvement purchases involves Luxury Media Corporation, which publishes magazines, such as *The Robb Report* and *Showcase*. These magazines advertise such nontraditional products as Hummer stretch limousines, an estate in Charleston, South Carolina ($9.5 million), and a 108 foot Mangusta sport cruiser ($10 million). The magazines ask consumers to "experience the other side," while touting themselves as an "Indispensable Luxury Resource."[3]

Figure 7.2 shows how involvement influences decision making. The level of involvement with any product depends on its perceived importance to the consumer's self-image. High-involvement products tend to be tied to self-image, whereas low-involvement products are not. A middle-aged consumer who feels (and wants to look) youthful may invest a great deal of time in her decision to buy a sport-utility vehicle instead of a station wagon. When pur-

LOW-INVOLVEMENT PURCHASE
A routine buying decision.

HIGH-INVOLVEMENT PURCHASE
A complex buying decision made after extensive thought.

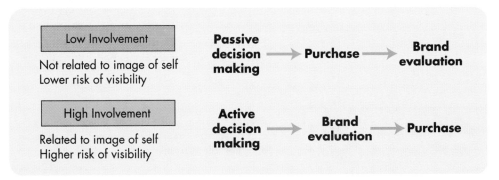

FIGURE 7.2 *Low/High Involvement and Passive/Active Decision Making*

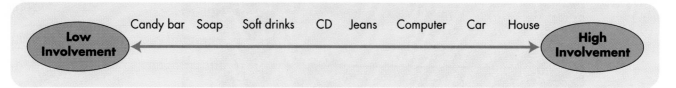

FIGURE 7.3 *Examples of Products on an Involvement Continuum*

chasing an ordinary light bulb, however, she buys almost without thinking because the purchase has nothing to do with self-image. The more visible, risky, or costly the product, the higher the level of involvement.

Involvement also influences the relationship between product evaluation and purchasing behaviors. With low-involvement products, consumers generally will try them first and then form an evaluation. With high-involvement products, they first form an evaluation (expectation), and then purchase. One reason for this behavior is that consumers do not actively search for information about low-involvement products. Instead, they acquire it while engaged in some other activity, such as watching television or chatting with a friend. This is called **passive learning,** which characterizes the passive decision-making process. Only when they try the product do they learn more about it. In contrast, high-involvement products are investigated through **active learning**—part of an active decision-making process—in order to form an opinion about which product to purchase.

Figure 7.3 shows that products fall on a continuum between low and high involvement. Moving toward the high end, decisions are made about more expensive, permanent, and complex products that also are more related to self-concept. Consumers give these purchases more thought.

CONSUMER DECISION MAKING

For a better understanding of consumer buying behavior, marketers have broken the decision process into the five steps described next. These are shown in Figure 7.4, along with a description of how one consumer, Erin, made a high-involvement purchase. For low-involvement

<u>PASSIVE LEARNING</u>

Learning in which little energy is devoted to thinking about or elaborating on information.

<u>ACTIVE LEARNING</u>

Learning in which substantial energy is devoted to thinking about and elaborating on information.

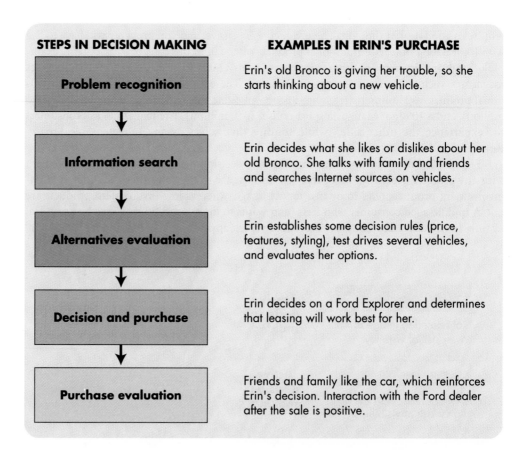

FIGURE 7.4 *The Consumer Decision-Making Process*

purchases, the first three steps may be skipped. As involvement increases, each step takes on greater importance, and more active learning occurs.

Problem recognition occurs when a consumer becomes aware of an unfulfilled desire. In a low-involvement situation, such as the purchase of a compact disc, you might immediately go to a place such as Tower Records and casually select recordings by two or three of your favorite artists. Or, if you're thirsty, you may simply run out and buy a soft drink. In a high-involvement purchase the recognition of a need may arise long before it is acted upon. In the case of a house, the cost may prevent you from acting on your need for several years.

The **information search** consists of thinking through the situation, calling up experiences stored in memory (internal search), and probably seeking information from friends, salespeople, advertisements, online services, and other sources (external search). Each source has its benefits and drawbacks. Experience is a good teacher, but you may not have enough information in memory. External search is beneficial, but friends may have preferences different from yours, salespeople may push the product that earns them the highest commission, and ads are often incomplete.

Alternatives evaluation is based on decision rules about which product or service is most likely to satisfy goals. These rules are personal; that is, they vary according to what the individual consumer considers important. At this point, complex thinking is likely to occur. Using the results of the information search, the consumer weighs the pros and cons of each choice.

The **purchase decision** emerges from the evaluation of alternatives. The consumer may decide not to buy and save the money or spend it on a different item altogether. Or he or she may want to play it safe by deciding to purchase a small amount for trial purposes, or by deciding to lease rather than buy. The decision to buy often occurs some time before the actual purchase. The **purchase** is a financial commitment to make the acquisition. It may take time to secure a mortgage or car loan, or the dealer may be temporarily out of stock.

The **purchase evaluation** stage results in satisfaction or dissatisfaction. Buyers often seek assurance from others that their choice was correct. Positive assurance reinforces the

PROBLEM RECOGNITION

Becoming aware of an unfulfilled need or desire.

INFORMATION SEARCH

Thinking through a situation by recalling information stored in memory or obtaining it from external sources.

ALTERNATIVES EVALUATION

Use of decision rules that attempt to determine which product would be most likely to satisfy goals.

PURCHASE DECISION

The decision of whether or not to buy and which competing product to buy, which is made after carefully weighing the alternatives.

PURCHASE

A financial commitment to acquire a product.

PURCHASE EVALUATION

The process of determining satisfaction or dissatisfaction with a buying choice.

CONNECTING THROUGH RELATIONSHIPS

THE CUSTOMER LOYALTY CARD GAME

More and more people are discovering that there *is* a free lunch—or coffee, haircut, video, or even airline ticket—if you patronize certain shops and get your frequent customer card punched. The average consumer participates in 3.2 loyalty programs and spends as much as 46 percent higher with companies offering loyalty benefits, according to Carlson Marketing Group's study, Loyalty Monitor.

Customer loyalty is in the cards. Retailers realize that building relationships with customers they already have is more profitable than luring first-timers with splashy ad campaigns or costly discounts. Dick Dunn, vice president of business development at Carlson's loyalty operation says, "Organizations that are industry leaders understand their competitive edge lies in their ability to build relations with their best customers and reward them for their loyalty." For their loyalty, customers desire rewards more than anything else—from special rates in telecom and retail to frequent flyer miles in credit card companies. In fact, 42 percent of consumers see discounts as the most important benefit of a loyalty program. Rewards are even connected with the Internet, as in the case of Pittsburgh's Giant Eagle grocery store's Advantage Card Club. Members can find "value and convenience," according to senior vice president Joe Faccenda, through paperless coupons via the Web site. Grocery stores across America realize the benefits of such loyalty programs, with 60 percent of retail grocery stores offering some type of program.

Companies in the customer loyalty business also consider these freebies an investment in an extremely valuable asset—a customer database. Each time someone fills out a card, that person's name, address, and vital stats are punched into a computer. Mailings to advertise specials and new products then go to the people most likely to buy: true-blue customers. However, the government and two-thirds of shoppers with at least one frequent-shopper grocery card are concerned about the use of their personal information. On July 1, 2000, Senate Bill 926, also known as the Supermarket Club Card Disclosure Act, became effective in California, which allows companies to track purchases and analyze

Continued

broad demographic trends but prohibits issuers of the cards from requiring applicants to provide identification such as a driver's license or Social Security card. Even outside the privacy issue, some customers are disgruntled with carrying so many cards in their wallets.

As loyalty programs face some problems, however, companies continue to realize that they benefit the most by providing an immediate reward such as instant promotional discounts or preferential treatment. Standard Register's National Survey found an 8 percent growth in use of loyalty cards from 1999 to 2000 and estimates usage will continue to grow, with 50 percent of customers using loyalty cards within the next five years. These trends seem to indicate, as Nielsen Media Research senior vice president for customer analytics Todd Hale said, "It's no longer enough for the traditional supermarkets just to have the right products consumers want. The most successful chains are those that give their best customers more reasons to shop with them." It seems customers will carry heavy wallets and allow companies to use their personal information to an extent—for a discount.

Sources: "Loyalty Schemes Influence Spending, Says U.S. Report," *Customer Loyalty Today,* July 2, 1999; "Standard Register's National Survey Finds Prepaid and Loyalty Card Use on the Rise," *Business Wire,* April 24, 2000; Barry Janoff, "Private Practice," *Progressive Grocer,* January 2000, pp. 79–83; Robin Clark, "Cards Not Marked for Loyalty Schemes," *Customer Loyalty Today,* June 11, 2000; and "U.S. Consumers Turn Their Backs on Supermarkets," *Customer Loyalty Today,* June 4, 2000.

consumer's decision, making it more likely that such a purchase will be made again. Positive feedback confirms the buyer's expectations.

PSYCHOLOGICAL FACTORS THAT INFLUENCE CONSUMER DECISIONS

Although the decision-making process appears straightforward, it is influenced by many psychological factors. We will look at the most important ones: (1) motivation, (2) perception, (3) learning, (4) attitudes, and (5) information processing.

MOTIVATION

Marketers first conducted "motivation research" during the 1950s and early 1960s in an attempt to identify buyers' subconscious reasons for purchasing various products. This work has since been discredited because it was based on a very limited theory and poor research techniques. Early motivation researchers depended on the ideas of Sigmund Freud. This pioneering psychoanalyst suggested that most human behavior is determined not by conscious thought but by unconscious urges, passions, repressed feelings, and underlying desires. Based on these beliefs, motivation researchers declared that men purchase a convertible as a substitute for a mistress, and women make cakes as a symbol of giving birth. About the best that can be said for this early work is that it inspired marketers to develop new concepts of motivation. Today, motivation theories are much sounder, and they provide several basic insights for marketers.

Motivation is an internal force that directs behavior toward the fulfillment of needs. It involves the needs (or goals) a person has and the energy that is triggered to drive the person to action. The needs that underlie motivation can be classified as either biological or psychological. Biological needs have been called primary or innate needs because they seem to exist in all people, regardless of environment. Needs in this category include food, water, shelter, fresh air, and at least some degree of comfort. Products such as Evian spring water, Kellogg's Special K, and various brands of bedding were developed in direct response to this type of need. **Psychological needs** are often called secondary or learned needs because they result from socialization. Needs in this category include friendship, a sense of self-worth, and achievement or self-fulfillment. The U.S. Army slogan "Be all that you can be" appeals directly to psychological needs.

Maslow's Hierarchy of Needs   Abraham Maslow's famous classification is often used by marketers to help categorize consumer desires. According to Maslow, five basic needs underlie most human goals. He ranked them in a hierarchy to indicate that higher-level needs tend to emerge only after lower-level needs are satisfied. Figure 7.5 illustrates Maslow's hierarchy in the form of a pyramid.

At the base of the pyramid are physiological needs essential to survival such as food, clean air and water, warmth, and sleep. Evian produces bottled spring water to fulfill the need for clean, unadulterated water.

<u>MOTIVATION</u>

An internal force that directs behavior toward the fulfillment of needs.

<u>PSYCHOLOGICAL NEEDS</u>

A need that arises in the socialization process.

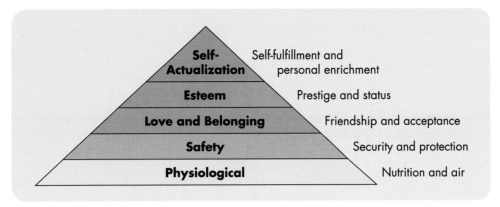

FIGURE 7.5 *Maslow's Hierarchy of Needs*

Source: Adapted from Abraham H. Maslow, *Motivation and Personality,* 2nd ed. Copyright 1970 by Abraham H. Maslow. Reprinted by permission of Harper & Row Publishers, Inc.

On the next level is the need for safety, which includes basic security and freedom from physical abuse. These needs are both biological and psychological. Insurance companies appeal to them with such slogans as "You're in good hands with Allstate" and "Get a piece of the rock" (Prudential).

The third level of the pyramid is the need for love and belonging. Humans seek out companionship to fulfill this psychological need. Family and friends are extremely instrumental in satisfying it. Advertisements for Hallmark cards and FTD florists play on our need for human interaction, love, and belonging.

The fourth level is the need for esteem, which comes from prestige, status, and self-respect. Many consumers maintain and exhibit their social status through high-visibility products. Designer labels or symbols on clothing and recognizable automobile designs are two ways marketers have attempted to fulfill this need.

The final level of Maslow's hierarchy is the need for self-actualization. As people begin to feel physically satisfied, safe and secure, accepted, and esteemed by others, they may need a higher level of personal satisfaction. They are motivated by a desire to develop themselves and

This Timex ad appeals to the need for self-actualization.

use their abilities. Education is directed toward this need by helping people attain knowledge and experiences that improve self-worth, sharpen talents, and promote personal growth. Self-actualization also may come from coaching youth soccer or playing in a basketball league. Backpacking, writing, skiing, painting, and composing are other examples. The Nike ad campaign, "I Can . . . ," is aimed at consumers who are motivated by self-actualization. The Peace Corps offers a challenge as well as a reward: "The toughest job you'll ever love."

Motivational Conflict   People are motivated to attain some ends and avoid others. In marketing terms, consumers approach activities that help them attain desired outcomes but avoid activities that have negative consequences. Yet, because human needs and wants are so varied, consumers may be faced with outcomes that combine both desirable and undesirable features. Three types of such motivational conflict have been identified: approach-approach, avoidance-avoidance, and approach-avoidance. These are summarized in Figure 7.6.

APPROACH–APPROACH CONFLICT
Motivational conflict that occurs when a consumer desires two objectives but cannot have both.

Approach-approach conflict occurs when a consumer desires two objectives but cannot have both. Suppose George wants sports-car styling but family comfort in a new car. Unless he can afford to buy a Viper and a Caravan, he will have to resolve this conflict by choosing one or the other. Nissan Infiniti promotes its QX4 sport-utility vehicle as having "The thrill of a sports sedan. The serenity of a luxury sedan. Capabilities beyond any sedan."[4] This type of promotion is aimed at consumers who want to combine luxury and performance features in one sport-utility vehicle.

AVOIDANCE–AVOIDANCE CONFLICT
Motivational conflict that occurs when consumers must choose between two undesirable alternatives.

Avoidance-avoidance conflict results when a choice must be made between two undesirable alternatives. Elaine's car has a bad muffler. The noise draws disapproving looks from strangers, and her friends are starting to make jokes about it. But the repair will deplete Elaine's savings account. She will have to resolve this conflict by selecting the least adverse choice. Midas muffler says, "America's favorite mufflers are Midas® Mufflers. Period. And quality is one reason." The appeal is to consumers who don't want engine problems yet also don't want to spend extra money on maintenance.

APPROACH–AVOIDANCE CONFLICT
Motivational conflict that occurs when a consumer desires an alternative that has certain negative qualities.

Approach-avoidance conflict occurs when a consumer desires an alternative that has positive and negative qualities. If Jim works out on his NordicTrack, then his body will be stronger but at the cost of time-consuming strenuous exercise. Many types of purchases cause approach-avoidance conflict because they have drawbacks, side effects, or other undesirable features. In a way, all purchases can be considered a mixed blessing, since the buyer must forfeit some money sooner or later. Consider the National Guard, which may offer tuition

Type	Description	Sample Situation	Possible Marketing Response
Approach-Approach	Two objectives are desired, but the consumer cannot have both	Toothpaste ↙ ↘ Health with fluoride Sex appeal with breath freshener	***Provide both benefits:*** Toothpaste with fluoride and a breath freshener.
Avoidance-Avoidance	The consumer must choose between two undesirable alternatives	Muffler repair ↙ ↘ Depleted savings Bothersome exhaust noise	***Stress unpleasantness of one alternative to get desired action:*** Muffler ads that emphasize how embarrassing a defective muffler can be or that offer financing or delayed payments.
Approach-Avoidance	The consumer's goal has both positive and negative aspects	College education ↙ ↘ Hard work and expense Greater earnings opportunities	***Emphasize positive benefits of desired action:*** A college ad campaign that illustrates how long-term earnings compare for a college graduate and a nongraduate.

FIGURE 7.6 *Types of Motivational Conflict*

assistance and enlistment bonuses but requires training obligations and a period of service.[5] The approach-avoidance conflict for people who join up involves positive rewards in exchange for hard work and sacrificed time.

By understanding motivational conflicts, marketers can respond with new products as well as advertising, pricing, and distribution plans that help minimize these buyer conflicts.

PERCEPTION

Human beings use their sensory organs to see, hear, smell, taste, and touch an almost infinite variety of sensations. The sensations are caused by stimuli—the sound of a jackhammer, the fragrance of a flower, the texture of material, and so on. **Perception** is the process of recognizing, selecting, organizing, and interpreting these stimuli in order to make sense of the world around us.

We constantly receive so many stimuli that only a limited number can be processed. Therefore, consumers must select—either consciously or subconsciously—the stimuli on which to focus. Typically, this selection occurs in four stages: selective exposure, selective attention, selective comprehension, and selective retention. At each stage, a product or message may be screened out, disregarded, misinterpreted, or forgotten by the consumer. Figure 7.7 illustrates the perception process.

Selective Exposure   U.S. companies spend more than a billion dollars every day in the hope of communicating messages to consumers. However, a large portion of these messages are screened out in the first stage, when consumers choose whether to ignore or receive the message. How often do you reach for the remote and channel surf whenever an ad appears on television? Marketers call the consumer's ability to seek out or avoid information **selective exposure.** For example, Soloflex advertises extensively on television, but you can choose to watch, tune out mentally, or change the channel. You decide whether to be exposed to Soloflex information. This happens to you hundreds of times a day with other media—billboards, radio, newspapers, and so on.

Selective Attention   Consumers do not pay attention to very many messages. Noticing every one of them would lead to mental exhaustion from information overload. So consumers are extremely skilled at screening out irrelevant messages.

Through **selective attention,** people have a strong tendency to heed information that supports their current views. Democrats listen more often to Democratic than Republican politicians, and vice versa. Similarly, consumers attend to advertising for products they have already purchased or intend to purchase. They screen out much of the information that conflicts with their experience or goals because it is irrelevant and distracting. One of the most important challenges faced by any marketer is gaining the consumer's attention. Without it, no matter how well crafted, the message will have no effect on the intended target.

A good example is the ineffectiveness of smoking prevention campaigns. One million young Americans start smoking each year, despite millions of dollars spent in antismoking campaigns trying to dissuade them, including warnings from the U.S. surgeon general and proof that smoking leads to 400,000 American deaths annually.[6] Smokers may tune into

PERCEPTION
The process of recognizing, selecting, organizing, and interpreting stimuli in order to make sense of the world around us.

SELECTIVE EXPOSURE
The tendency to seek out or avoid information sources.

SELECTIVE ATTENTION
The tendency to heed information that supports current views and behaviors.

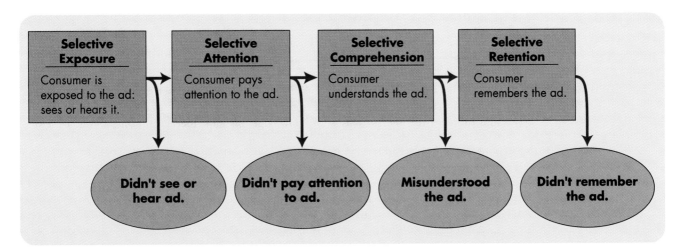

FIGURE 7.7 *Process of Perception*

advertisements about their brand but ignore prevention ads. This selective attention reinforces the likelihood that they will continue to smoke, since the negative messages about health implications do not get through.

To help gain attention, a marketer should initiate the message in a way relevant to the consumer—by using a known sports figure, a common activity, an attractive person, or humor. Then the brand name can be related to that attention-getter. Next, it is important to maintain attention by keeping the ad meaningful or interesting to the consumer. Shimano does an excellent job of attracting attention with its mountain bike ads. The logo is eye-catching and the simple, direct ads have unusual visuals.

Selective Comprehension   Marketers must take care to ensure that their products and messages are understood by consumers in the way intended. **Selective comprehension** refers to consumers' tendency to interpret messages based on their biases. If a message runs counter to a consumer's strong beliefs, then it is perceived as being farther from the buyer's point of view than is really the case. Consumers are likely to reject any information that contradicts their current beliefs or past behaviors. That is why many ads keep it simple and avoid controversial images. A notable exception is political ads, since selective comprehension can work in the marketer's favor.

Selective Retention   **Selective retention** means that consumers remember some messages and forget others. The way information is understood determines how well it is remembered. People tend to recall what agrees with their own beliefs, desires, or behaviors.

Once information is retained, it is held until replaced or altered. Old information may be forgotten when new, conflicting messages are received, or it may be reshaped if the new information is more consistent with the person's beliefs or goals. Joan wants a Macintosh laptop computer but has heard it will be very expensive. She reads an ad comparing the cost of laptops and sees that Macintosh is not the highest. As a result, she discards the idea that Macintosh laptops are expensive and retains the information that other brands cost more. The "Nobody Beats Midas—Nobody" advertisement was designed by the muffler giant to achieve such an effect.

Subliminal Perception   Since our conscious perceptions selectively and routinely filter messages, is it possible to bypass that level and market to the consumer's subconscious? The belief in subliminal persuasion began in 1957 in a New Jersey movie theater. Market researcher Jim Vicary claimed to flash messages such as "Drink Coca-Cola" and "Eat Popcorn" on the screen too fast to be recognized by the naked eye. According to him, the messages still registered in the brain, resulting in sales increases of 18 percent for Coke and almost 60 percent for popcorn. Vicary then coined the term *subliminal advertising*. Researchers were never able to replicate his study, and there is no evidence to support his claim.[7]

We do have evidence that subliminal messages do not work. A 1991 psychology study set out to determine whether self-improvement tapes really help people lose weight, improve memory, raise self-esteem, or quit smoking. Researcher Anthony Greenwald found that roughly half the people who listened to the audio tapes claimed improvement in the area specified on the label. But the labels had been deliberately switched, so any effect has to be attributed to the power of suggestion, not the tapes themselves.[8] It is still debated whether subliminal messages are effective in changing the minds of consumers.

LEARNING

Consumers learn how to acquire and use products. The process starts at an early age and continues throughout life. It is through learning that consumers select the patterns of behavior that determine when, where, and how they purchase, consume, and discard goods. **Learning** is any change in consumers' behavioral tendencies caused by experience. There are two basic types of learning: cognitive and behavioral. Cognitive learning emphasizes perception, reason, and problem solving. It focuses on knowledge, insights, ideas, opinions, and goals. High-involvement and challenging purchases incorporate active learning that focuses attention on problem-solving behavior. The five decision steps outlined in Figure 7.4 dealt with this type of learning. Behavioral learning occurs through either classical or operant (sometimes called instrumental) conditioning when consumers react to external events. Behavioral learning primarily concerns what consumers do, not what they are thinking.

Classical Conditioning   Classical conditioning gets its name from an early (and, therefore, classical) experiment by the Russian physiologist Ivan Pavlov in the 1920s. He presented meat paste to a dog, and the dog salivated. He then presented the paste while ringing a tuning fork.

Again, the dog salivated. Pavlov repeated this several times. Eventually, when the tuning fork was rung without the meat paste, the dog still salivated.[9] The basic idea behind **classical conditioning** is that people can learn to respond to one stimulus in the same way they respond to another if the two stimuli are presented together.

Classical conditioning is used extensively in marketing.[10] Think for a minute about the ad that featured young people on a hot day drinking Mountain Dew and jumping off a steep cliff into a river. Marketers were trying to get consumers to associate the soft drink with excitement and refreshment in summer weather, in much the same way that Pavlov's dogs associated the tuning fork with meat paste. Then, when a hot day comes along (stimulus), you will want to drink Mountain Dew.

Consumer preferences are often influenced by advertising features (stimuli) rather than the product itself. Marketers say that music often helps define the emotional appeal of a certain brand. Classical music is often used to convey comfort, luxury, and distinctive taste.[11] Chevrolet developed an advertising campaign for trucks around Bob Seger's "Like a Rock," which now is identified with the reliability and strength of Chevy trucks.

Marketers need to understand that consumers may generalize stimuli or discriminate among them. **Generalization** occurs when people make the same response to different stimuli. **Discrimination** occurs when consumers make different responses to different stimuli. For instance, when oat bran cereals were first found to reduce cholesterol levels, the oat bran image was generalized to other oat cereals, such as Cheerios, and to other bran cereals, such as Raisin Bran. With experience, however, consumers began to discriminate, aided by advertisers. The Quaker Oats Company says its oat bran cereal is part of a "low saturated fat, low cholesterol diet that may reduce the risk of heart disease."[12]

To take advantage of a strong brand name, marketers establish visual consistency across categories. The various products in ConAgra's Healthy Choice line, including pasta sauces, cereals, breakfast bars, frozen dinners, and ice cream, are branded under the distinctive green Healthy Choice label. Consumers can readily identify the brand and are able to generalize the health benefits of Healthy Choice products even across product categories.

Marketers also try to take advantage of a buyer's ability to discriminate among brands. For example, McDonald's spends over $600 million annually to help consumers distinguish

CLASSICAL CONDITIONING

After two stimuli are presented together repeatedly, people learn to respond to one in the same way as the other.

GENERALIZATION

Making the same response to different stimuli.

DISCRIMINATION

Making different responses to different stimuli.

**CONNECTED:
SURFING THE NET**

www.conagra.com

Visit the Web site of ConAgra, the largest independent food company in the United States. ConAgra produces such brands as Healthy Choice, Hunt's, Van Camp's, Orville Redenbacher's, and many more. Read company information and news or link to the Healthy Choice or Butterball Web sites.

THE BAGEL

NOW HIGHLY EVOLVED

PILLSBURY FILLED BAGELS. They're toaster-shaped. With a tasty bagel crust outside. Delicious cream cheese and jelly inside. And they're *low-fat*. So no cramming bagels into a toaster. No gloppy mess. Next breakfast, it's freezer, toaster, done. **IN YOUR GROCER'S FREEZER.**

*This ad for Pillsbury
toaster filled bagels demonstrates an example of
generalization.*

between its products and those of other restaurants. By naming its products "Mc," as in the case of the new McSalad Shaker and the McFlurry, McDonald's ensures that its food is associated only with McDonald's.[13]

Operant Conditioning Even before Pavlov gained fame, Thorndike, a noted psychologist, published work showing how rewards encourage certain responses and punishment discourages others. Behavior that is intermittently rewarded (positive or negative reinforcement) will be repeated in the expectation of eliciting the reward. Behavior that is punished will be avoided and, thus, will diminish in frequency. Psychologist B. F. Skinner later termed this type of conditioning *operant* because the learning occurs as the subject responds to or "operates on" the environment. Thus, **operant conditioning** is the use of reinforcement or punishment to shape behavior. Today, marketers know that consumers associate positive and/or negative consequences with the items they consume.

There are several ways positive reinforcement can occur. The first is through a product satisfying a need or want. If you drink Lipton's iced tea and your thirst disappears, then that behavior is reinforced. The next time you are thirsty, you are likely to reach for Lipton's. The second reinforcer is information or knowledge. Many organizations publish magazines to support their business: Delta Airlines has *Sky Magazine,* the National Football League issues *NFL Insider,* and AARP publishes *Modern Maturity.*[14] These offer information that will reinforce purchases and stimulate new interests while maintaining brand loyalty. A third way consumer behavior can be reinforced is by seeing results. For example, EAS nutrition products promote "before and after" body-building programs. "It took Michelangelo three years to sculpt a masterpiece" reads one testimonial. "It took me only three months."[15] The 20-minute daily workout required to see results actually becomes a reinforcer because consumers know they are making progress toward getting in shape. Yet another way companies reward purchasers and encourage repeat purchases is the frequent-customer card promotion. This is discussed in the relationships feature, "The Customer Loyalty Card Game."

Punishment may result from such things as a product that fails to perform as advertised; a service agent who acts in a curt, unfriendly manner; or even news stories that cast the corporation in a bad light and undermine the consumer's pride in owning its products.

ATTITUDES

An **attitude** is a state of readiness with cognitive, emotional, and behavioral components, which reflects the beliefs of the consumer with regard to messages, brands, products, product characteristics, or other aspects of life. Attitudes are often described as consumer preferences—a like or dislike for products or their characteristics. Marketers usually think of attitudes as having three dimensions: cognitive, affective, and behavioral. The **cognitive** aspect refers to knowledge about product attributes that is not influenced by emotion. The **affective** component relates to the emotional feelings of like or dislike. The **behavioral** element reflects the tendency to act positively or negatively. In other words, attitudes toward purchasing a product are a composite of what consumers know about its attributes; whether they like or dislike them; and how positively or negatively they feel about the purchase.

Figure 7.8 shows how attitude can affect the purchase of a mountain bike. Attitudes are important because they help us understand why a particular action is taken. And notice that

OPERANT CONDITIONING

The use of reinforcement or punishment to shape behavior.

ATTITUDE

A state of readiness with cognitive, emotional, and behavioral components, which reflects the beliefs of the consumer with regard to messages, brands, products, product characteristics, and so forth.

COGNITIVE (COMPONENT OF ATTITUDE)

Knowledge about a product's attributes not influenced by emotion.

AFFECTIVE (COMPONENT OF ATTITUDE)

Emotional feelings of like or dislike.

BEHAVIORAL (COMPONENT OF ATTITUDE)

Tendency to act positively or negatively.

Product Attribute	ATTITUDE COMPONENT		
	Cognitive (Does the bike have this attribute?)	Affective (Do I like this attribute?)	Behavioral (Am I likely to buy this bike?)
Rapid-fire shifters	Yes	Like very much	Very positive
Light weight	Yes	Like very much	Very positive
Rigid frame	Yes	Neither like nor dislike	Neutral
Durability	No	Like somewhat	Somewhat negative
Vibration absorption	Yes	Like somewhat	Somewhat positive
High cost	Yes	Dislike somewhat	Somewhat negative

FIGURE 7.8 *Attitudes About a Mountain Bike Purchase*

attitudes are not the same as beliefs. A **belief** is a descriptive thought or conviction that expresses an opinion about the characteristics of something. For example, a consumer may believe that rapid-fire shifters are a feature of a Specialized brand bicycle. Beliefs may help shape attitudes but don't necessarily imply like or dislike. Attitudes also influence beliefs: If rapid-fire shifters increase the price, then a consumer who dislikes high cost may believe they are not a very useful feature.

Consumers frequently form attitudes to help evaluate whether products and brands fit into their lifestyle. These attitudes are drawn from a broad range of ideas, not just the characteristics of a product.

Generally, marketers use their knowledge of consumer attitudes to make sure that strategies are consistent with consumer tastes and preferences. From time to time, marketers attempt to change consumer attitudes, usually by influencing one of the three components. A common approach is to use promotion to influence the cognitive component. During the early 1980s, Ford experienced record losses mainly because competitors' products were seen as being of better quality. Consumers thought (cognitive) that if they purchased a Ford, they would not be getting the quality they deserved, which led to negative overall attitudes toward Ford. A companywide strategy was developed to combat the problem. Ford made design and manufacturing changes, enlisted the cooperation of key parts suppliers, and established employee work programs to improve quality. Information about these improvements was communicated to consumers through an advertising theme: "At Ford, Quality Is Job One!" Today, Ford ranks fourth on the *Fortune* 500 list of largest industrial corporations, based on sales, second among motor vehicle producers.[16] These improvements have allowed Ford to jettison its one tagline "quality is job one," and instead spend $1.91 billion in advertising to a variety of buying groups from the young to the old.[17]

Marketers also try to influence the affective component of consumer attitudes. For example, as the health and fitness craze swept the United States, many people developed a dislike for beef, believing it to be high in fat and cholesterol. The industry launched a campaign showing that beef is nutritional and easy to prepare, hoping to make consumers feel good about eating it. "Beef. It's what's for dinner" became a recognizable slogan for millions of Americans and in 1999 Americans spent over $50 billion on an average of 69.2 pounds of beef per person.[18]

To change the behavioral aspect of consumer attitudes, often a coupon or free sample is offered. Research indicates that once a product is purchased or used—even if only a free sample—the likelihood of future purchase is greater. Pepsi's ad campaign "The Pepsi Challenge" takes the product directly to consumers in malls, schools, and athletic events, hoping that once they taste the difference between Pepsi and Coke, they will be more likely to purchase Pepsi.[19]

INFORMATION PROCESSING

Information processing refers to ways in which consumers acquire, store, and evaluate the data they use to make decisions. The human mind has a remarkable ability to process (understand and apply) the information it takes in. Perception, motivation, behavioral learning, and attitudes are integrated into the human thought system, which acquires, stores, and analyzes data to arrive at goal-directed behaviors. Key to information processing is the encoding of information and its use in memory.

Encoding **Encoding** is the process of converting information to knowledge. The brain is sometimes described as having two relatively distinct ways of encoding information.[20] These enable it to handle pictorial, geometric, and nonverbal information as well as verbal, symbolic, and analytical thinking. The mind combines all this information and produces integrated perceptions.

The mental images encoded are thoughts held in "picture" form called episodes. Episodes are not like pictures taken with a camera, and they can be felt and known without words. Aesthetics, tastes, and symbolic meaning are represented this way. Ads and other phenomena are also likely to be retained as episodes.[21] Nike traditionally uses a highly visual format for its advertisements. These images capitalize on consumer emotions and attempt to link personal value to the wide array of Nike products. Advertising is never just about Nike, the brand. It is carefully constructed to draw in consumers. In one recent campaign, famous Nike-sponsored athletes showed their wounds from competition, including scars, missing fingers, and knocked-out teeth. By doing so, Nike connected its own products with the physical and emotional side of athletic competition.[22] The Nike swoosh symbol is a highly recognized trademark that elicits these desired effects because it is an episode encoded in the consumer's brain.

BELIEF

A conviction that something is true or that descriptive statements are factual.

CONNECTED: SURFING THE NET

www.snapple.com

Make the "liquid connection" and visit the Snapple Web site. Create your own Web page, obtain Snapple information, and take an opportunity to play games and win prizes.

INFORMATION PROCESSING

The process whereby consumers acquire, store, and evaluate the data they use in making decisions.

ENCODING

The process of converting information to knowledge.

MERLE NORMAN®
COSMETIC STUDIOS

Pick a shade...free!*

For a limited time, you can receive a FREE, FULL-SIZE LIP COLOR from our inviting array of subtle to stand-out shades in the formula you prefer. Choose from moisturizing LUXIVA® Ultra Lipcolor or LUXIVA® Lasting Lipcolor for a pout with extra staying power. Visit our website at www.merlenorman.com or call (800) 40-MERLE for the location nearest you. Talk about lip service!

FREE LIP COLOR OFFER

To receive a FREE, FULL-SIZE LIP COLOR, fill out the information below and bring this coupon to a participating Merle Norman Cosmetic Studio.

Name _____

Address _____

City _____

State _____ Zip _____

Telephone (____) _____

For Office Use Only

Studio Owner _____

Studio Number _____

*FREE LUXIVA Ultra Lipcolor or LUXIVA Lasting Lipcolor at participating Merle Norman Cosmetic Studios only, while supplies last. Limit one per household. Must be 18 years of age or older to participate. Present original coupon to receive FREE lip color. No photocopies of coupons accepted. Customer must pay sales tax. Redeemable at Studio level only. U.S. residents only. Retailer and Manufacturer coupon. Cash value 1/20 of 1 cent. Void if prohibited, taxed or restricted. Offer expires November 15, 2000.

To overcome the behavioral aspect of consumer attitudes, Merle Norman C.S. offered this promotion.

MEMORY

The brain function that stores and recalls encoded information; includes sensory, short-term, and long-term capacities.

Verbal encoding occurs when words or symbols are stored in semantic memory. General knowledge, facts, and principles gleaned from experience are held there. Many believe that information such as package size, the meaning of brand names, prices, and so forth are stored this way. For example, advertisements for Johnson & Johnson's ultrasensitive products use facts and statistics to appeal to concerned mothers. One ad states that Johnson's baby shampoo is "so gentle that 8 out of 10 pediatricians choose Johnson's for their own babies."[23] Many mothers may form an impression in their semantic memory based on this information and call upon it later to make a purchase decision.

Marketers must remember that consumers encode both verbal and pictorial information about the world.[24] In the early stage of information processing, the pictorial tends to dominate. In later stages, verification and more analytical thoughts dominate. Therefore, visual, musical, creative, and pictorial elements of ads catch the consumer's attention. Then facts, reasoning, and details of product messages are likely to be picked up.

Memory   **Memory** is the brain function that stores and recalls encoded information (knowledge). There are three types of memory: sensory, short term, and long term. Each operates differently and can be considered a separate step in the process of memory formation.

The first and most basic stage is sensory memory, which takes in an almost unlimited amount of encoded information. These sensory impressions decay (are forgotten) within a fraction of a second. But when attention is focused on a few stimuli, sensory information about them is transferred to short-term memory, where it can be coded and interpreted.

Short-term memory interprets what is sent from sensory memory. It usually can hold information for only a short time, and its capacity is much smaller than that of sensory memory—about four to seven chunks of information at once.[25] A chunk is a unit of organized information that can be recalled to solve specific problems of short duration. A chunk may vary greatly among persons focusing on the same object. A first-time buyer of a used car is likely to have a more difficult time than a person who has purchased several. For example, the experienced buyer probably will ask for past service receipts to learn about repair history, whereas the novice may not think of it.

In Derby, Kansas, an exclusive contract with Pepsi will give the school district $1 million over ten years in exchange for exclusive rights to sell its soft drinks in the schools' vending machines.

In long-term memory, a vast amount of information may be held for years or even indefinitely. It remains there until replaced by contradictory information through a process called interference. For example, you go to your favorite restaurant and receive a poor meal or poor service. This interferes with your positive memory of the place, and you then reclassify it to a lower status. Once a brand is stored in long-term memory, consumers can add relevant information to help with future choices. Makers of ChapStick often associate their product with the elements (sun, wind, dryness). That way, when outdoor enthusiasts need lip protection from the elements, they often think of ChapStick.

Consumers are bombarded with promotional messages. Marketers hope that the more often their brand name is seen, the more likely consumers will be to process information about it. In Madison, Wisconsin, school children get unusual exposure to advertising. Coca-Cola was granted exclusive rights to sell its soft drinks in the schools' vending machines, in a "corporate–public school partnership," in exchange for a $100,000 signing bonus and a $515,000 cash advance against three future years' sales. Although some oppose such contracts, arguing against commercialism in classrooms, companies see such contracts as "win-win relationships," hoping that the constant presence of the brand name will reinforce memory and stimulate future purchases.[26]

SOCIAL FACTORS THAT INFLUENCE CONSUMER DECISIONS

Social factors have a great influence on how individual consumers and households behave. Consider something as simple as a pair of earrings. In some societies, children's ears are pierced at birth; other societies frown on ear piercing altogether. Some social groups regard earrings as a symbol of wealth and refinement; others consider them showy and in poor taste. Some people wear them to indicate membership in a group, others to enhance status, yet others to make a fashion statement. Some people have many sets and change earrings almost daily; others wear the same pair forever. Many different social influences affect our purchase decisions, but for marketers the most notable ones are culture, subculture, social class, reference groups, and the family.

CULTURE

Perhaps the most pervasive influence on human beings is culture. **Culture** is the learned values, beliefs, language, symbols, and patterns of behavior shared by people in a society and passed on from generation to generation. It produces manners and actions that are often taken for granted as the "appropriate" way.

Culture changes very slowly unless outside forces intervene. Historically, such forces have included political and religious wars and natural disasters. Today, global economics and technology are having an enormous effect. They have made the world much smaller and culture more uniform. Take television, for instance. The hugely popular CBS programs *Survivor* and *Big Brother* were first major hits in England and Germany, respectively. The show *60 Minutes* is one of the most popular programs in Australia, while U.S. and Latin American soap operas are viewed worldwide.[27] However, globalization extends beyond just entertainment. Global companies such as PepsiCo, Reebok International, CNN, and others pitch products and provide goods and services to consumers throughout the world. Banks, investment firms, and credit

CULTURE
The learned values, beliefs, language, symbols, and patterns of behavior shared by people in a society that are passed on from generation to generation.

VALUES

The shared norms about what is
right to think and do; what culture considers to be worthy and
desirable.

card companies exchange capital and important knowledge-based information 24 hours a day, thus taking advantage of this emergent world culture.[28]

By taking cultural values into account, companies adjust to the particular customs of people in different societies. **Values** are the shared norms about what is right to think and do. They reflect what society considers to be worthy and desirable. Marketers need to understand values so their actions are not counter to what consumers in a given market consider acceptable. Ford must be conscious of the values of Asian consumers in marketing the Taurus. "We know in Singapore that styling is going to be important, and in Hong Kong, it's safety," says John Fitzpatrick, director of sales and marketing for the Pacific Rim. The automaker must make consumers believe that it is sensitive to their values. "The problem with Ford is that it has come to Asia believing that consumers know the brand," says Peter Boardman, a senior industry analyst in Tokyo. "But customers don't know what kind of company it is or what products Ford sells." The plan is to localize in each country, since consumers have different demographic characteristics and buying behaviors. Ford has already started running commercials in South Korea that focus on safety features and environmental policies, two issues important to consumers there.[29]

SUBCULTURE

Understanding a culture provides marketers with an overall picture, but they also need more specific information. A **subculture** is a group of people with shared values within a culture. In the United States, these groups may be defined by ethnicity, age, religion, geographic location, and national origin. In this section we will focus on ethnicity and look at three groups: Hispanic, Asian, and African American consumers.

It should be noted that an ethnic subculture can be a very broad category. For example, the U.S. Hispanic community includes Cubans, Puerto Ricans, Mexican Americans, Tejanos, and Chicanos, among others. Within such groups are further distinctions—low or high ethnicity, length of time in the United States, immigrant or native-born, and place of residence, to name a few. A marketer may want to target Cubans with high ethnicity living in New York City—as Miller beer does.

Marketers know that ethnic subgroups are much more likely to buy branded products and spend more for what they perceive as quality. Immigrants are often perplexed by the wide variety of choices, so they tend to stick with the major brands they knew at home. Gary Berman, president of Miami-based Market Segment Research, says that "these groups define nationally advertised brands as being quality products and are more likely to select quality over price."[30]

Groups with strong ethnicity form some of the most important subcultures. As we learned in chapter 6, marketers are interested in identifying segments of the population with common needs, wants, and buying behaviors. Marketing strategies can then be developed to appeal directly to these segments. Therefore, it's critical for marketers to identify people of high ethnicity—who identify strongly with their ethnic subculture—rather than simply those with a certain skin color or national origin. A thorough understanding of ethnic backgrounds can lead to the formation of homogeneous segments. Figure 7.9 illustrates the spending power, income, and population percentages of several ethnic groups in the United States.

With the increase in ethnic populations, companies that produce, sell, and market ethnic products may see a considerable growth. Use your knowledge of diversity to your advantage in interviews and by writing targeted cover letters. Remember that companies in growth areas may offer you better opportunities for advancement.

Hispanic Consumers   Hispanics are a booming subculture. Their number is growing rapidly due to births and immigration. The U.S. Bureau of the Census predicts the figure of 31 million in 2000 will reach 41 million by 2010—edging out African Americans as the largest U.S. minority group. With an estimated buying power of $383 billion, and 9 percent more likely than Caucasian Americans to be online, Hispanics represent a sizable portion of American consumers, seemingly deserving a sizable portion of marketers' attentions. However, as Christy Haubegger, founding publisher of *Latina* magazine states, Hispanics are "using 16 percent of the lip liner, but there's not a cosmetic company yet that has directed 16 percent of their budget to this audience."[31]

Because Hispanics share Spanish as a common language (except for Brazilians who speak Portuguese), radio or television stations that program in Spanish are obvious media choices for promotional messages. Although many Hispanics are fluent in English, most marketers

	All Groups	White	African American	Hispanic	Asian
Percentage of U.S. Population	100%	72%	12%	12%	4%
Average Household Income	$39,657	$41,591	$26,608	$29,110	$48,614
Annual Spending Power	$3.03 trillion	$2 trillion	$350 billion	$458 billion	$220 billion

FIGURE 7.9 *Subculture Spending Power in the United States*

Source: 2000 Census Race and Hispanic Data, www.census.gov., U.S. Census Bureau; Rachel McLaughlin, "African Americans," Target Marketing, March 1999, pp. 100–101; Nicole St. Pierre, "A Rising Latino Currency in the U.S., "Businessweek Online, March 9, 2001; Alison Wellner and Kimberly Weisul, "Melting Pot of Gold," "Businessweek Online, Nov. 6, 2000; and Bureau of Labor Statistics, www.bls.gov.

believe that it is better to sell in Spanish. According to a pilot study by Skunkworks of New York, advertisers can gain a 20 percent increase in sales among Hispanics simply by advertising on Spanish-language network television. The National Association of Hispanic Publications is even seeking to aid advertisers wishing to reach Hispanics and has begun a "one-stop shopping program" called the Latino Print Network.[32]

Grocery store chains are weighing the benefits of separate labels for Hispanic products besides salsa, such as sardines in tomato sauce and canned spaghetti, with private-label products being offered mainly in areas such as Texas and California where the concentration of Hispanics is high. Difficulties arise, however, because Hispanics are not a homogeneous group. Food preparation as well as vocabulary, for example, vary among Hispanics of different origins.[33]

Companies which are targeting Hispanics should consider the buying power of Hispanic teens. According to Teenage Research Unlimited, America's 4.3 million Hispanic teens spend an average of $375 a month, 7.8 percent more than the average teen. Although these teens could buy the same mainstream products as their friends, some are saying that the mainstream culture does not reflect their physical appearance or lifestyle. Hispanic teenage girls, who are more likely than most teenagers to buy items such as designer jeans, hair spray, and hair gel, are turning to magazines such as *Latingirl,* a bimonthly publication similar to *Seventeen.* The endurance of this magazine, however, will ultimately depend on advertisers' support.[34]

Asian American Consumers Imagine a market segment that's highly educated, affluent, and geographically concentrated. That describes the 11 million Asian Americans, who are the fastest-growing population group, the most affluent, and the best-educated segment of

Although many Hispanics are fluent in English, grocery store chains are weighing the benefits of separate labels for numerous products.

American society. Moreover, they generally spend more than other ethnic groups, particularly in categories such as computers and insurance. Unsurprisingly, advertisement industry executives expect an increased focus on this group.[35]

However, just as with other ethnic groups, marketers must pay careful attention to cultural and language differences. For example, when an airline briefly used the number 1-800-FLY-4444, it failed to recognize that it was offending many in the Asian American community to whom the number 4 implied death. This one instance symbolizes the potential embarrassment and problems that many companies are shying away from as they continue to neglect targeting Asian Americans. Because Asian Americans represent only 4 percent of America's population and are highly diverse as a group, many companies consider the risk not worth the effort.[36]

Cultural differences can pay off when used for profit, however, and some companies are focusing their attention on Asian Americans during important cultural holidays such as the Asian Lunar New Year as a means of recognizing Asian culture and getting paid for it. Hallmark Cards, for example, has developed a line of Lunar New Year products such as greeting cards. According to Kim Newton, marketing manager for Hallmark's Ethnic Business Center, "We wanted to make sure we chose cards that are appropriate for the domestic market but still tie ethnic consumers to who they are. Our goal is to help them keep cultural traditions alive during the holidays that are important to them." Whereas Hallmark's advertising is a large-scale effort, Honest Tea is also realizing the value of the Asian American market and is currently planning to market its products during the Lunar New Year.[37]

Among automobile manufacturers, very little attention is devoted to Asian Americans, whereas other ethnic groups such as Hispanics and African Americans are receiving focus. Even Asian car manufacturers such as Nissan are not devoting specific attention to Asian Americans but rely on name recognition instead.[38]

Through future studies, marketers hope to learn more about the desires of Asian Americans, making advertising to them a more feasible task. The newly founded organization Association of Asian-American Advertising Agencies is seeking to increase the information available to advertisers about this relatively unstudied group.[39]

African American Consumers   African Americans represent about 12 percent of the U.S. population and have an annual buying power of around $400 billion.[40] According to the Buying Power of Black America, a study conducted by Target Market News, African Americans are increasing their expenditures in various areas, from books to automobiles, making them an even more important market.[41] In addition, though they have traditionally been the least active ethnic group in Internet use and buying, they are now the fastest-growing group of Internet users, making their importance to marketers significant in a number of areas.[42]

Demonstrating the power of the Internet in reaching ethnic groups, BET.com has received the highest number of unique visitors among sites designed specifically for African Americans since it began in February 2000. The site even had over 45 percent more visitors than the next two most visited sites, BlackPlanet.com and BlackVoices.com. The site, which provides information for African Americans between the ages of 18 and 44, runs nine content channels, including news, careers, romance, and entertainment. CEO Scott Mills says of the site, "BET.com's leadership position demonstrates the African American online community's affinity for our extensive original content offerings and diverse communities. It's also good news for our partners and advertisers who are investing in BET.com as a primary vehicle to reach African American consumers."[43]

Some companies are seeking to market goods directly to African Americans by focusing on African American culture, much like Hallmark has done through its cards and e-cards celebrating Kwanzaa.[44] However, some consumers are concerned about the lack of major advertising to African Americans outside of January and February, when Martin Luther King, Jr.'s Birthday and Black History Month are celebrated, arguing that advertising only during this time is patronizing. As Clifford Franklin stated in a *St. Louis Post* editorial, "I would hope these companies and their ad agencies realize it will take more than advertising during Black History Month to build a relationship with the African-American community."[45]

Many marketers pay careful attention to cultural issues. JCPenney, for example, targeted African American women through its "white suit" campaign. Designed to tailor to the tradition among African American women of wearing a white suit to church on the fifth Sunday of the month, the company ran ads in black women's magazines and was so successful that urban stores sold out of their white suit inventory.[46] Marketing techniques such as this one, which follow the advice of Suzanne Fuller, president of Pinnacle Associates, support cultural traditions in a sensitive manner. As she says, the African American community is distinct—"marketers should develop advertising and promotions specifically targeted to the African-American community, rather than assuming general-market advertising is enough because this ethnic group speaks English."[47]

SOCIAL CLASS

The third major social influence on consumer behavior is social class. A **social class** is a relatively homogeneous grouping of people based on similarities in income and occupation. Members tend to share values, interests, and behaviors. How would you rank the following occupations by status: salesperson, high school teacher, and accountant? What about a physician, a professor, or a lawyer? Your views agree with research findings if, in both groups, you ranked them from highest to lowest in the order presented. Feelings about the relative prestige of these occupations reflect the tendency in most cultures to make social class distinctions. Figure 7.10 describes various social classes and gives examples of purchases for each.

Global Social Class Dimensions   Marketers increasingly look at social class from a global perspective. In some societies—such as India, South Africa, and Brazil—class distinctions are clear, and status differences are great. In others—such as Australia, Denmark, and Canada—differences are less extreme. In countries with strong class differences, where people live, the cars they drive, the restaurants they frequent, the sports in which they participate, the types of

> **SOCIAL CLASS**
> A relatively stable division of society based on education, income, and occupation.

Social Class	Percentage of U.S. Population	Description	Examples of Purchases
Upper Upper	Less than 1%	Often called the "old rich," upper-upper class families have been wealthy for generations and are born into wealth. People in this group do not have to work for a living.	Jewelry, fine wine, luxury cruises, yachts
Lower Upper	About 2%	Often called the "new rich" because their fortunes are not inherited, these self-made millionaires tend to be executives, athletes, consultants, movie stars, and high-technology entrepreneurs.	Highly visible products such as cars
Upper Middle	12%	Comprised of doctors, professors, lawyers, veterinarians, state politicians, and business executives, this class is upwardly mobile and success oriented.	Condominiums, skiing, travel, home computers, outdoor furniture, camcorders, cellular phones
Middle	32%	In addition to white- and blue-collar workers, the middle class includes such professions as clerk, bank teller, public school teacher, and nearly all nonmanagerial office positions and other such occupations.	Brand-name clothing, family vacations
Working Class	38%	Largely blue collar, the working class has jobs that can be defined as fairly routine and not requiring advanced education. Many in this class are union members.	Used trucks and motorcycles
Upper Lower	9%	Living standards are just above poverty. Work is predominantly unskilled and low wage. The members of this class are often poorly educated.	Fundamental necessities: food, rental housing, medical care
Lower Lower	7%	At the bottom of the social class system are the visibly poor, many of whom are third-generation welfare recipients. Typically underemployed or unemployed, they rely on public aid or charity to survive.	Food, used clothing, minimum necessities

FIGURE 7.10 *A Breakdown of Social Classes*

Source: Based on Richard P. Colenan, "The Continuing Significance of Social Class in Marketing, "Journal of Consumer Research, December 1983, pp. 265–280,© Journal of Consumer Research, Inc. 1983.

clothing they wear, how much they travel, and where (or whether) they go to college are largely determined by social class.

Commercial activity, particularly interpersonal relations, also can be greatly influenced by class associations. For example, the president of a French company expects to deal only with the top executives of another firm. More than once, U.S. companies have failed at marketing in France because they did not know or ignored this. In some cases, the French were offended when the Americans sent lower-level managers to important meetings. In other cases, the Americans lost status when high-ranking executives communicated with middle-level French managers. In a country with a more homogeneous class structure, such as Sweden or Denmark, it is not uncommon for executives from all levels to work as a team, so Americans of various rank are accepted as well.

Marketers study global social class dimensions in order to understand consumer profiles, habits, interests, and purchasing behavior. In 1997–1998, for example, three national surveys costing more than $30 million were mailed to more than 24 million British homes by ICD Marketing Services. The research was designed to give insight into consumer preferences for cars, finance, travel, and other purchases.[48]

REFERENCE GROUPS

Another major influence on consumer behavior is reference groups. We all live with, depend on, and are nurtured by other people. We influence and are influenced by those with whom we have frequent contact—friends, coworkers, and family members. We also are influenced by people we know only indirectly through the mass media. Research shows that groups have an immense effect on the purchasing behavior of their members, including their search for and use of information, their response to advertisements, and their brand choices.[49]

REFERENCE GROUP

A set of people whose norms and values influence a consumer's behavior.

Reference groups are people whose norms and values influence a consumer's behavior. Consumers depend on them for product information, purchase comparisons, and rules about correct or incorrect buying behavior. College fraternities and sororities are examples of reference groups. Although each member is unique, each adheres to certain group norms and standards.

ASSOCIATIVE REFERENCE GROUP

A group with which people want to identify.

Marketers distinguish between two types of reference groups. **Associative reference groups** are those to which people want to belong, although they may be prevented by income, occupation, or education. In contrast, **disassociative reference groups** are those to which people do not want to belong. The same reference group can be associative to some people and disassociative to others. For example, a widely publicized concern about the world of some rock 'n' roll artists is the use of heroin. There is a possibility that teens who are drawn to some rock artists may become more accepting of heroin despite the obvious hazards. Keyboardist Jonathon Melvoin of Smashing Pumpkins died of an overdose, and many other musicians and groups are known to be current or past users, including the Red Hot Chili Peppers, Steven Tyler of Aerosmith, and the late Kurt Cobain.[50] Teens may choose these bands as associative or disassociative reference groups.

DISASSOCIATIVE REFERENCE GROUP

A group with which people do not want to identify.

Advertisers capitalize on the human tendency to rely on groups. In one form or another, groups are a part of almost all mass media advertisements and are used in many personal selling presentations. The "milk mustache" ads by the dairy industry have used a diverse collection of celebrities for a successful campaign. Featuring athletes such as Venus and Serena Williams as well as music celebrities such as Britney Spears and the Dixie Chicks, the campaign targets a number of different reference groups.[51]

Promotions that appeal to associative tendencies command a good deal of attention. Ads in youth-oriented magazines often depict people who belong to admired groups. Because consumers are full of hopes and dreams for the future, the use of associative reference groups is very effective. Consider the number of advertisers that use famous spokespersons to tout their messages about products. Professional athletes are often seen as being members of associative reference groups. A recent survey conducted by Burns Sports Celebrity Service found that Tiger Woods and Michael Jordan were America's top endorsers of products and services, with Woods beating Jordan as the country's top endorser by a three-to-one ratio.[52]

THE FAMILY

How much has your family influenced the way you behave, speak, or dress? Often the family in which you grow up—known as your family of orientation—teaches you certain purchase habits that continue throughout your life. Many consumers buy the same brand of soap, toothpaste, mayonnaise, laundry detergent, or gasoline that their mother or father did. Later people start their own family, called the family of procreation, and it also influences purchase habits.

Model behavior.

Want
strong bones?
Your
bones grow
until
about age
35
and the
calcium
in milk helps.
After that,
it helps
keep them
strong.
Which means
milk is
always in
fashion.

got milk?

*The "milk mustache" ads
use a diverse collection of
celebrities to bring success
to the campaign.*

HOUSEHOLD

Family members (and occasionally others) who share the same
housing unit; for marketers, the
standard purchase and consumption unit.

The family is especially important to marketers because it forms a **household,** which is the standard purchase and consumption unit. If you do not already have a household, chances are great that someday you will purchase or rent a home, buy appliances and durable goods, and require banking and insurance services. In other words, your household will be a consumption unit.

Not all households consist of a mother, a father, and children. Many have only one person, or several nonrelatives, or a single parent with children. This section, however, focuses on the traditional nuclear family. Marketers generally look at three important aspects:

- How do families make decisions as a group?
- What roles can various members play in a purchase decision?
- How does family purchase behavior change over time?

Family Decision Making   Family decision making is "one of the most underresearched and difficult areas to study within all of consumer behavior."[53] How does your family make buying decisions? Most purchases are probably conceived and carried out by one member with little influence from the others. These are called autonomous decisions. In other cases, several family members may be involved. These are called joint decisions.

Marketers must remember that gender roles affect how family decisions are made. Decisions are termed *syncratic* when both spouses are jointly and equally involved; *autonomous* when either one of them makes the decision independently; and *husband- or wife-dominant* depending on which one has the influence. Research has found that gender especially affects financial decisions and that men and women approach finances differently. In general, men perceive themselves as advisors, active in business and in influencing their friends' financial decisions. Men are more likely to take independent financial risks, and they often place value on ego-gratifying opportunities. Women are more likely to discuss finances with friends and others before making a decision. They are less likely to take risks and are more open to advice. Directing marketing activities to the wrong person in the household could be as wasteful as directing them to the wrong market segment.[54] For this reason, it's important for marketers to understand the decision-making roles within a family.

Family Purchasing Roles   When children ask a parent to buy a certain type of cereal, they are influencing the purchase, but the parent still makes the final decision. In contrast, when

**CONNECTED:
SURFING THE NET**

www.whymilk.com

**Want to know how "got milk"
got started? Read the story
behind the award-winning
ads. You also can watch a
30-second ad, courtesy of the
American Dairy Association.**

teenagers go to the mall to buy clothing, while they certainly may be influenced by their parents, they usually make the final decision. Family members play certain roles in certain purchases and play different roles for different products. There are five key roles:

- *Initiator.* First suggests that a particular product be purchased.
- *Influencer.* Provides valuable input to the decision-making process.
- *Decision maker.* Makes the final buying decision.
- *Purchaser.* Physically goes out and makes the purchase.
- *User.* Uses the product.

The role a consumer plays is not always obvious. Although men have been the traditional focus of Black & Decker marketing efforts, research shows that women are a large secondary market. They buy tools not only for gifts but also for their own use.

Children have a significant effect on family decisions. In fact, for certain products, the marketer may decide to focus on them rather than parents. The Coleman Company, maker of outdoor equipment such as tents, sleeping bags, and lanterns, is among the many companies that have formed a club targeting kids. The Coleman Kids' Club offers information on camping and outdoor gear for youths as well as outdoor news, campfire tales, and the like. Kids identify with "their" brand, and the next time a parent purchases camping equipment for them, Coleman can be assured it has developed a young influencer in the purchasing decision.[55] Cereal manufacturers also recognize the important role young children play. Eye-catching boxes and cartoon characters are designed to appeal directly to children. The influence of children continues as they grow but usually for a different set of products—clothes, video or computer games, and such services as family vacations or video rentals.

Family Life Cycle   As families age, they progress through a series of predictable stages, called the family life cycle. At each point, unique problems and life situations must be addressed. An understanding of each stage gives marketers powerful insight into the needs and expectations of families.

Only a few decades ago, everyone was expected to move in orderly progression from youth, to marriage, to childrearing, to retirement. Today, the picture is more complex because of widespread divorce and single parenting, as shown in Figure 7.11. As you can imagine, a family's needs and purchase decisions vary at each stage. Let's look at these in more detail.

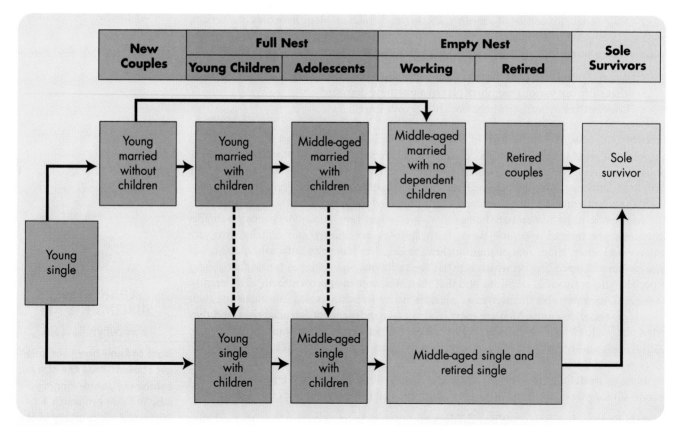

FIGURE 7.11 *The Family Life Cycle*

Young Singles Young singles are in the process of setting up their first household. Items they buy tend to be easily transportable from one location to another as living arrangements change or they find a new job. During this stage, courtship activities make social events, recreation, and entertainment important. Advanced education and training also may be purchased to further a career. This market category, when combined with middle-aged singles and sole survivors, has shown high growth from 18 percent of all households in 1970 to 25 percent in 1990. The U.S. Bureau of the Census predicts the figure will be 27 percent by 2010.

New Couples Young married people without children generally try to build an economic foundation for later responsibilities. By combining resources, a new couple may have enough discretionary income to enjoy recreational activities while still saving for the future. This group spends more than other households on furnishings, new cars and trucks, and alcohol.

Full Nesters Whether you are single, divorced, or married, a great deal changes once children enter the picture. They are expensive and consume great amounts of time. Household budgets for full nesters increase for nearly every category of purchase, and new expenses emerge—diapers, day care, toys, piano lessons, and so forth. As children reach adolescence, their sports activities may cost from several hundred to several thousand dollars per year. Many families prepare for the cost of college, which can consume 30 to 40 percent of annual household income for each child.

Of course, purchase behavior will differ according to family structure—traditional family, divorced or widowed parent, or single parent. The latter group often has very limited spending power. A divorced or widowed parent may have some child support or death benefits to ease the burden a little, but often he or she must work long hours to make ends meet and has very little free time. In traditional families, both parents usually work to provide for their children. Their earnings tend to increase over time as they become well established in a career.

Working Empty Nesters This category consists of three types of consumers: middle-aged singles, married couples with no children, and married couples with grown children who have left home. These households are in their prime wage-earning years. According to the U.S. Census Bureau, the median income of people aged 45 to 54 was $54,148 in 1998, the highest income bracket of any one group. Some 75 percent of Americans in their fifties still

AmericanBaby.com markets to young parents, the young nesters cohort.

work, whereas the baby boomers who were born between 1946 and 1964 are the largest segment of the U.S. population with nearly 80 million people.[56] Without children around, empty nesters are free to travel, pursue hobbies, and explore new lifestyle options. As baby boomers turn 50, this market will grow even more. For details on how to capture it—whether empty or full nesters—see the diversity feature, "How to Satisfy a Senior—Oops—I Mean a Boomer."

Retired Empty Nesters Americans aged 65 and over are worth considerably more than the average American and over the next 20 years, this market is expected to grow by 30 percent. Consumers at this stage in the life cycle have a median net worth of $86,300, compared to the national average of $37,600. Seventeen percent of seniors even have a net worth over

CONNECTING WITH DIVERSITY

HOW TO SATISFY A SENIOR—OOPS—I MEAN A BOOMER

Call them young at heart, in their prime, or maybe even mature. Just don't call them seniors. Marketers who treat the aging baby boomers like previous generations of seniors are in for a shock. Defined as the 80 million people in the United States between 45 and 54, baby boomers are fast approaching traditional retirement age but aren't acting the way retired people traditionally act. With one person turning 50 every 9 seconds, 68.2 million people—one-third of the adult population—are above 50 and this number will jump to 115 million in the next 25 years. These boomers are reinventing senior citizenship in their own young image, and their numbers are too great to be ignored.

The marketing community needs to be reminded that there's gold in those golden years. After all, 50-plus households control 41 percent of all discretionary income and $169 billion is nothing for the business world to ignore. This generation is not buying just hearing aids and prescription medicine, however, but is the leading age group of online purchasers, comprising 48 percent of online shoppers. They also travel more than any other age group, taking approximately 259 million trips annually. It seems as though founder and president of Age Wave Ken Dychtwald is right, "A phenomenal economic opportunity is about to unfold for those that are ready."

Companies that are ready are recognizing the different needs of baby boomers from the needs their parents had. But boomers do seem to have one common denominator: denial of aging. Formerly the American Association of Retired Persons, for example, the organization is now referring to itself simply as AARP to remove the traditional connotations of retirement. Moreover, its monthly publication *Modern Maturity* is now divided into one section for the retired and one for those still working, and covers such diverse topics as grandparenting, dating, midlife career changes, and the 50 greatest adventures in the world. The age group formerly associated with golfing is even becoming interested in sports such as biking, jogging, and in-line skating, and in activities such as yoga and tai chi in its quest for greater health and fitness. Del Webb, a company with 40 years of experience in advertising to adults, recognizes these changes in lifestyles and has altered its advertising campaign to appeal to the subsequent buying habits. Its "Live On" campaign appeals to baby boomers seeking to live as actively as possible. Myprimetime.com, visited by 2.2 million unique visitors monthly, aids baby boomers in making positive changes in their lives through its five content areas—Family, Money, Health, Work, and Play.

But the future for boomers won't be all fun in the sun. According to a Del Webb survey, more than 60 percent of boomers plan to work at least 20 hours per week after they retire. Others plan to volunteer for charities or their communities. Perhaps the most surprising, however, are the 28 percent of boomers who plan to go back to school after they retire. In Sun City, Texas, 350 residents participate in Senior University, learning and discussing topics from foreign policy to French Impressionism. Perhaps companies should also begin rethinking their back-to-school sales.

Sources: Laurie Tarver, "Businesses, Marketers Can Earn from Boomers' Plans," *Memphis Business Journal,* June 16, 2000, p. 33; "Myprimetime.com Surges into Top 300 of All Internet Sites; Dominates Baby Boomer Online Category with More Than 2 Million Unique Monthly Site Visitors," *PR Newswire,* July 24, 2000; Becky Edenkamp and Gina Czark, "Buy Buy Baby Boomer," *Brandweek,* June 26, 2000, p. 18; "TIA 2000 Report: Baby Boomers Prime Movers in Travel Market," *Travel Weekly,* July 20, 2000, p. 10; Marianne Wilson, "Old Money, New Opportunity," *Chain Store Age,* June 2000, p. 136; and Paul Temple, "No Retirement for Boomers," *Workforce,* July 2000, p. 6.

$250,000.[57] This wealthier group has changed the image of the retired couple over the last decade. Retirees are now viewed as financial investors willing to assume some risk, mobile and daring, physically active and health conscious, and willing to pamper themselves. It was once thought that advertising dollars were wasted on this segment but no longer; it's a powerful niche that is targeted in television programming and advertising campaigns. The wealthy elderly are the focus of luxury cruise lines, automobile manufacturers, and land developers.

Sole Survivors Sole survivors are men and women whose spouse has died as well as older single people who never married. Their net worth and buying power have increased over the past two decades due to the stock market boom of the mid-1980s and mid-1990s and the rise in home values. A number of sole survivors are senior citizens, who today are targeted heavily by marketers. The growing number of goods and services designed to appeal to seniors include home health care as well as Internet sites such as CareScout.com, which are devoted to senior needs.[58] Television fitness programs are also targeted to the elderly, as well as a variety of diet supplements.

USING TECHNOLOGY TO TRACK CONSUMER BEHAVIOR

Technology not only helps marketers better understand consumers but also is having a direct influence on how companies build relationships. The number of young people in North America aged 2 to 17 who use the Internet more than tripled from 8 million in 1997 to 25 million in 2000. This "Net Generation" gained more exposure to the Internet as their mothers bought PCs in hopes that their children would derive educational benefits from them and as their schools provided them with increased access to the World Wide Web.[59]

What implications does this have for marketing? Dozens of Internet survey groups such as CyberAtlas, Nua, and Jupiter Communications maintain up-to-date databases and news sites with information on Internet demographics, advertising rates, and industrywide Web spending and usage. These groups allow marketers to effectively track consumer behavior. For instance, Web surfers visited an average of 38 sites in June 2000, typically viewing 36 separate Web pages while spending over 30 minutes per session. Currently the NPD Group maintains an "Online Panel" of consumers, demographically selected, who participate in continuous surveys of the Web. For a fee, companies can access Online Panel reports, including attitude and usage studies, longitudinal tracking, as well as product and concept reviews. Together with names, addresses, and other data requested when a Web site is accessed, such research provides a reservoir of information about consumers.[60]

Marketers also make use of Web-tracking software such as the kind made by Predictive Networks Inc. of Boston, Massachusetts. A new Predictive program released in 2000 allows marketers to track every Web site a surfer visits and to build "a digital silhouette" based on purchases made and sites visited. The resulting silhouette, or profile, provides the kind of precision targeting that marketers so eagerly desire.[61]

Ultimately, the growing use of new technologies will provide marketers with greater insight into consumer behavior. Categorizing user behavior as well as providing consumers with easy Web access enables marketers to reach many of their targeted audiences. This will benefit both consumers seeking information and the companies supplying it.

THE ETHICS OF INFLUENCING CONSUMER BEHAVIOR

For a long time, marketers have used sexual themes to heighten brand awareness and influence consumers. Today, ethical questions are being raised about some of these promotions, which many people find offensive. A notable example was a Calvin Klein campaign using ads with heavy sexual undertones and partial nudity. Despite the bans by television networks, magazines, and retailers, sales of CK products neared $1 billion in the mid-1990s.[62] Recently, Procter & Gamble set up a "sex task force" to examine its policy toward sexually suggestive magazine articles and cover headlines. With nearly $500 million in magazine advertising per year, Procter & Gamble was concerned that it was overly connected with sexually risqué content in magazines such as *Cosmopolitan* and *Glamour*.[63]

Controversial promotion risks losing consumers in the selective comprehension phase of perception. Some people screen out ads altogether that conflict with their values. At the same time, controversy generates free publicity, perhaps worth millions of dollars in the case of

Calvin Klein.[64] Klein was quoted as saying "jeans are about sex," adding that he planned to continue to market his products accordingly.[65]

Although consumers are free to seek out or avoid information, people often feel that children should not be exposed to objectionable images. When these are plastered on billboards or the side of a bus, it is hard to avoid them. Marketers face a challenge when deciding whether to promote a product with a sexual theme or shock tactics. They must weigh the risk of losing customers and crossing ethical boundaries against the advantages of gaining attention and strongly influencing purchase behavior.

Many of the factors that influence consumer decision making also play a role in the buying decisions of businesses because businesspeople are, after all, individuals with psychological motivations, perceptions, and attitudes. Over all, however, the buying behavior of businesses is quite different from consumer buying behavior. As we will see in chapter 8, it often follows formalized procedures, involves many persons and functions, and requires more personalized communication with the selling firm.

CONNECTED: SURFING THE NET

QUARTERMAINE COFFEE ROASTERS
www.quartermaine.com

THIS CHAPTER'S RELATIONSHIPS FEATURE, "THE Customer Loyalty Card Game," discussed how frequent-customer cards help build loyalty. Quartermaine Coffee Roasters is one of many companies that considers freebies a valuable investment. Learn more about the company by visiting its Web site and then answer the following questions.

1. The use of associative reference groups is a very effective way to reach consumers. What groups or spokespersons would be good choices for Quartermaine? Explain.
2. How might global customers differ in their taste and preferences for coffee? How do Quartermaine's coffee varieties accommodate these differences?
3. Marketers develop strategies that form relationships through customer satisfaction. Explain the stages a customer might go through in establishing a relationship with Quartermaine. What actions could the company take to ensure the customer is satisfied?

CLUB MED
www.clubmed.com

THIS CHAPTER'S DIVERSITY FEATURE DISCUSSED baby boomers, a segment marketers are defining by life stage rather than age. Visit the Web site of Club Med, one of the many organizations targeting this group, and answer the following questions.

1. Which three stages of the family life cycle does Club Med present as options for a customized tour of the Web site? How does this feature enable the company to make a stronger connection with customers?
2. Visit the "All You Need to Know" page to learn what Club Med offers. Using Maslow's hierarchy as a guide, explain how the company appeals to each need.
3. What is a Club Med village like? How do these villages differ to meet the diverse needs of customers? How does the Web site help customers select a village that matches their preferences?
4. Imagine you are taking a Club Med vacation. Is this a low- or high-involvement purchase? Explain. Describe the steps you would go through in deciding whether to take the trip. Give examples.

OBJECTIVE 1: Appreciate the importance of involvement in the decisions consumers make.

Marketers know that an understanding of consumer behavior lies at the heart of nearly every successful strategy for connecting with customers. Consumer behavior is the actions and decision processes of individuals and organizations in discovering, evaluating, acquiring, consuming, and disposing of products. Consumers behave differently in low- and high-involvement purchasing situations. When involvement is high, they use an elaborate five-step decision process, and their attitudes are learned actively. When involvement is low, they make choices without much effort, and learning is passive.

OBJECTIVE 2: Evaluate the effect on consumer behavior of such psychological factors as motivation, perception, learning, attitudes, and information processing.

The five important psychological factors influencing consumer behavior are motivation, perception, learning, attitudes, and information processing. Motivation is an internal force that directs behavior toward the fulfillment of needs. Marketers often use Maslow's hierarchy to categorize needs. Consumers may experience one of three forms of motivational conflict: approach-approach, avoidance-avoidance, or approach-avoidance. Perception is the process of recognizing, selecting, organizing, and interpreting stimuli in order to make sense of the world around us. It occurs in four

stages: selective exposure, selective attention, selective comprehension, and selective retention. Learning is any change in behavioral tendencies due to previous experience. The two basic types of learning are cognitive learning and behavioral learning. Behaviors can be learned (conditioned) by classical conditioning and operant conditioning. Attitudes have cognitive, affective, and behavioral components. Information processing involves encoding and memory processes. The human brain encodes information differently depending on the type of data. It processes nonverbal, emotional, and visual concepts in one way, while it handles general knowledge, facts, and justifications in another. Memory consists of sensory, short-term, and long-term memory.

OBJECTIVE 3: Explain how social factors such as culture, subculture, social class, reference groups, and family help explain consumer behavior.

Subcultures are groups that display homogeneous values and behaviors that diverge from the surrounding culture. Social class is a relatively stable division into groups based on such factors as education, income, and occupation. Reference groups provide norms and values that become the perspectives that influence a consumer's behavior. Associative groups are ones with which people want to be associated, whereas disassociative groups are ones with which people do not want to identify. Families have a profound influence on consumer behavior.

1. What is involvement? How does it influence passive and active learning?
2. Describe the five steps in decision making.
3. What is motivation? Describe Maslow's hierarchy of needs.
4. Describe the four elements of the perception process.
5. What is learning? Describe cognitive learning and two types of behavioral learning.
6. What are attitudes? What are their three components? How does knowledge of the components help in creating attitude change strategies?
7. What is information processing and how does it work?
8. What social influences are most important to marketers? List and define each.
9. How is social class measured?

1. Name several subcultures in the United States. Which companies have target-marketed to them?
2. Why must marketers distinguish between a person's ethnic background and ethnicity?
3. How does social class affect consumer behavior? Which social classes exist in the United States?
4. What are the different ways families make purchase decisions? How do these affect marketing?
5. Imagine that you are the marketing manager for the Pontiac Firebird sports car. What product features would you include
to meet each of the five types of needs described by Maslow's hierarchy? (For example, air bags might fulfill the safety need.)
6. What types of motivational conflict might be associated with the purchase of this Pontiac Firebird? How would you try to resolve the conflict?
7. You are in charge of marketing for a major league baseball team. How might you apply the principles of cognitive learning to your job? Could you also apply the principles of classical conditioning or reinforcement learning? How?

Active learning: Learning in which substantial energy is devoted to thinking about and elaborating on information.

Affective (component of attitude): Emotional feeling of like or dislike.

Alternatives evaluation: Use of decision rules that attempt to determine which product would be most likely to satisfy goals.

Approach-approach conflict: Motivational conflict that occurs when a consumer desires two objectives but cannot have both.

Approach-avoidance conflict: Motivational conflict that occurs when a consumer desires an alternative that has certain negative qualities.

Associative reference groups: A group with which people want to identify.

Attitude: A state of readiness with cognitive, emotional, and behavioral components, which reflects the beliefs of the consumer with regard to messages, brands, products, product characteristics, and so forth.

Avoidance-avoidance conflict: Motivational conflict that occurs when consumers must choose between two undesirable alternatives.

Behavioral (component of attitude): Tendency to act positively or negatively.

Belief: A conviction that something is true or that descriptive statements are factual.

Classical conditioning: After two stimuli are presented together repeatedly, people learn to respond to one in the same way as the other.

Cognitive (component of attitude): Knowledge about a product's attributes not influenced by emotion.

Consumer behavior: The actions and decision processes of individuals and households in discovering, evaluating, acquiring, consuming, and disposing of products.

Culture: The learned values, beliefs, language, symbols, and patterns of behavior shared by people in a society that are passed on from generation to generation.

Disassociative reference groups: A group with which people do not want to identify.

Discrimination: Making different responses to different stimuli.

Encoding: The process of converting information to knowledge.

Generalization: Making the same response to different stimuli.

High-involvement purchase: A complex buying decision made after extensive thought.

Household: Family members (and occasionally others) who share the same housing unit; for marketers, the standard purchase and consumption unit.

Information processing: The process whereby consumers acquire, store, and evaluate the data they use in making decisions.

Information search: Thinking through a situation by recalling information from stored memory or obtaining it from external sources.

Learning: Any change in consumer behavior caused by experience.

Low-involvement purchase: A routine buying decision.

Memory: The brain function that stores and recalls encoded information; includes sensory, short-term, and long-term capacities.

Motivation: An internal force that directs behavior toward the fulfillment of needs.

Operant conditioning: The use of reinforcement or punishment to shape behavior.

Passive learning: Learning in which little energy is devoted to thinking about or elaborating on information.

Perception: The process of recognizing, selecting, organizing, and interpreting stimuli in order to make sense of the world.

Problem recognition: Becoming aware of an unfulfilled need or desire.

Psychological needs: A need that arises in the socialization process.

Purchase: A financial commitment to acquire a product.

Purchase decision: The decision of whether or not to buy and which competing product to buy, which is made after carefully weighing the alternatives.

Purchase evaluation: The process of determining satisfaction or dissatisfaction with a buying choice.

Reference groups: A set of people whose norms and values influence a consumer's behavior.

Selective attention: The tendency to heed information that supports current views and behaviors.

Selective comprehension: The tendency to interpret products and messages according to current beliefs.

Selective exposure: The tendency to seek out or avoid information sources.

Selective retention: The tendency to remember some and forget other information.

Social class: A relatively stable division of society based on education, income, and occupation.

Subculture: A subset of people with shared values within a culture.

Values: The shared norms about what is right to think and do; what a culture considers to be worthy and desirable.

REFERENCES

1. Nora Macaluso, "Priceline's WebHouse Club Bows Out," *E-Commerce Times*, October 5, 2000, www.ecommercetimes.com/news/articles2000/001005-6.shtml; Cheryl Rosen, "Transforming Travel," *Information Week*, June 26, 2000, pp. 50+; Wendy Zellner, "Wooing the Newbies," *Business Week*, May 15, 2000, pp. EB116–EB118; Mike Troy, "An On-Line Auction Where the Price Is Always Right," *DSN Retailing Today*, May 8, 2000, pp. 93+; Pamela L. Moore, "Name Your Price—For Everything?" *Business Week*, April 17, 2000, pp. 72–78.

2. "Generation Gaps," *Global Cosmetic Industry*, June 2000, p. 1, www.findarticles.com.

3. *Showcase*, August 2000, p. 108; *The Robb Report*, August 2000, p. 10.

4. Infiniti QX4 advertisement, *Worth*, August 2000, pp. 8–9.

5. The Army National Guard Recruiting Homepage, www.1800gogard.com, Web site visited August 18, 2000., www.cp.org.

6. "U.S. Surgeon General Urges More Money Be Spent on Anti-Smoking Campaigns," *Canadian Press*, August 9, 2000, www.cp.org.

7. John Vivian, *The Media of Mass Communication* (Boston: Allyn & Bacon, 1993), p. 296.

8. A. G. Greenwald et al., "Double-Blind Tests of Subliminal Self-Help Audiotapes," *Psychological Science* 2 (1991): 119.

9. Ivan Pavlov, *Conditioned Reflexes: An Investigation of the Physiological Activity of the Cerebral Cortex*, trans. G. V. Anrep (London: Oxford University Press, 1927).

10. For further discussions, see Walter R. Nord and J. Paul Peter, "A Behavior Modification Perspective on Marketing," *Journal of Marketing* 44 (1980): 36–47; and J. Paul Peter and Walter R. Nord, "A Clarification and Extension of Operant Conditioning Principles in Marketing," *Journal of Marketing* 46 (1982): 102.

11. "Stand by Your Fans," *Advertising Age*, April 29, 1996, p. M1.

12. www.quakeroatmeal.com/products/qobc.shtml, Web site visited August 18, 2000.

13. Greg Johnson, "Did Somebody Say Cheese?" *Los Angeles Times*, June 30, 2000, p. C1.

14. www.delta-sky.com, www.nfl.com/insider, www.aarp.org/mmaturity, Web sites visited August 18, 2000.

15. EAS advertisement, *Muscle Media*, September 2000, pp. 12–13.

16. www.fortune.com/fortune/fortune500, Web site visited August 18, 2000.

17. Karen Lundegaard, "Ford Puts Magazines to Work on Ads for Escape SUV," *Wall Street Journal*, August 14, 2000, p. B2; and Jean Halliday, "Ford's New Ad Gambit: Real People," *Automotive News*, October 25, 1999.

18. John Taylor, "Americans Say It's Beef for Dinner," *Omaha World-Herald*, August 3, 2000.

19. Theresa Howard, "Upfront Markets: Soft Drinks," *AdWeek East*, April 24, 2000, adweek.com; "Pepsi Revives Taste-Test Marketing Campaign," *Daily News*, March 28, 2000; and "Reorganization, Snack Foods Put Pepsi Up to Challenge," *Philadelphia Inquirer*, April 14, 2000, inq.philly.com.

20. Flemming Hansen, "Hemispherical Lateralization: Implications for Understanding Consumer Behavior," *Journal of Consumer Research* 8 (June 1981): 23–36; and Sidney Weinstein, "A Review of Brain Hemisphere Research," *Journal of Advertising Research* 22 (1982): 59.

21. Morris B. Holbrash and William L. Moore, "Feature Interactions in Consumer Judgments of Verbal versus Pictorial Presentations," *Journal of Consumer Research* 8 (1981): 103.

22. Louise Lee, "Take Our Swoosh. Please," *Business Week,* February 21, 2000.

23. Johnson's baby shampoo advertisement, *Parents,* September 2000, p. 79.

24. Allan Piave, "A Dual Coding Approach to Perception and Cognition," in Herbert L. Pich, Jr. and Elliot Saltzma, *Modes of Perceiving and Processing Information* (Hillsdale, NJ: Laurence Erlbaum, 1978), p. 16.

25. Herbert A. Simon, "How Big Is a Chunk?" *Science,* February 8, 1974, p. 183.

26. Peter Maller, "Advertising to Young Minds," *The Milwaukee Journal Sentinel,* August 14, 2000, www.jsonline.com.

27. Richard Pells, "Mass Culture Is Now Exported from All Over to All Over," *International Herald Tribune,* July 12, 2000, www.int.com.

28. "Birth of a Unified Global Culture," *The Korea Herald,* April 26, 2000, www.koreaherald.com.

29. Fera Warner, "Ford Promotes Taurus Model in Asia Markets," *Wall Street Journal,* July 22, 1996, p. A76.

30. Leah Richard, "Minorities Show Brand Loyalty," *Advertising Age,* May 9, 1994, p. 29.

31. Dwight Cunningham, "One Size Does Not Fit All," *Media Week,* November 15, 1999, www.mediaweek.com; and Dick Silverman, "Focus on Ethnic Niches in Internet, Study Urges," *Supermarket News,* May 29, 2000, supermarketnews.com.

32. Dwight Cunningham, "One Size Does Not Fit All."

33. Nancy Brumback, "Salsa Savvy," *Supermarket News,* March 22, 1999, supermarketnews.com.

34. Rachel X. Weissman, "Los Ninos Go Shopping," *American Demographics,* May 1999, www.demographics.com.

35. Stuart Elliot, "Ads Speak to Asian-Americans," *The New York Times,* March 6, 2000, nytimes.com.

36. Ibid.

37. Kelly Gates, "Marketers Tie into Asian Lunar New Year," *Brandmarketing,* May 2000.

38. "Car Makers Rev Up Black and Latino Marketing, But Stall on Asian Effort," *Marketing to the Emerging Majorities,* July 2000.

39. Stuart Elliot, "Ads Speak to Asian-Americans," *The New York Times,* March 6, 2000, nytimes.com.

40. U.S. Census Bureau, Clifford Franklin, "Why Do Companies Only Pay Attention to Black Consumers in January and February?" *St. Louis Post-Dispatch,* February 23, 2000, p. B7, postnet.stlnet.com.

41. Eric L. Smith, "A Time to Buy," *Black Enterprise,* May 2000, blackenterprise.com.

42. Dick Silverman, "Focus on Ethnic Niches in Internet, Study Urges," *Supermarket News,* May 29, 2000, supermarketnews.com.

43. "BET.com Ranked #1 in Unique Visitors Among African American Sites; Leading Web Measurement Firms Release April Figures Citing BET.com as Highest Trafficked," *PR Newswire,* June 6, 2000, prnewswire.com.

44. www.hallmark.com, Web site visited August 20, 2000.

45. Clifford Franklin, "Why Do Companies Only Pay Attention to Black Consumers in January and February?"

46. Dwight Cunningham, "One Size Does Not Fit All." *Brandweek Online,* November 15, 1999.

47. Nancy Brumback, "Ethnic Markets Are Growing Up," *Brandmarketing,* July 2000.

48. "Giant Lifestyle Survey to Hit U.K.," December 4, 1996, www.adage.com.

49. J. Paul Peter and Jerry C. Olson, *Consumer Behavior and Marketing Strategy,* 2nd ed. (Burr Ridge, IL: Richard D. Irwin, 1990), p. 370.

50. Karen Schoemer, "Rockers, Models, and the New Allure of Heroin," *Newsweek,* August 26, 1996, pp. 50–54.

51. www.gotmilk.com, Web site visited August 18, 2000.

52. "Woods Edges Jordan in Pitching Battle," *Chicago Tribune,* December 29, 1999, chicagotribune.com.

53. William L. Wilkie, Elizabeth S. Moore-Shay, and Amardeep Assar, *Family Decision Making for Household Durable Goods* (Cambridge, MA: Marketing Science Institute, 1992), p. 1.

54. Richard E. Plank, Robert C. Greene, Jr., and Joel M. Greene, "Understanding Which Spouse Makes Financial Decisions," *Journal of Retail Banking,* Spring 1994, p. 21.

55. "Coleman Kids' Club," colemanforkids.com/c4k.html, Web site visited August 19, 2000.

56. Daniela Deane, "When the Nest Is Empty. . . ," *The Washington Post,* March 11, 2000, p. G01.

57. Kendra Parker, "Reaping What They've Sown," *American Demographics,* December 1999, demographics.com.

58. www.CareScout.com, Web site visited August 20, 2000; "CareScout.com Launches the Nation's First Ever Unbiased Eldercare Resource on the Internet," *Business Wire,* August 14, 2000, businesswire.com.

59. "Children, Families, and the Internet 2000," www.grunwald.com/survey/index.htm, Web site visited August 20, 2000.

60. "June 2000 Internet Usage Stats," cyberatlas.internet.com, Web site visited August 21, 2000.

61. Julia Angwin, "Web-Tracking Software Raises Issues of Privacy," *The Wall Street Journal Europe,* May 2, 2000.

62. Joshua Levine, "Let Linda Do It," *Forbes,* September 11, 1995, pp. 254–256.

63. Anne Marie Kerwin and Jack Neff, "Too Sexy? P&G 'Task Force' Stirs Magazine Debate," *Advertising Age,* April 10, 2000, adage.com.

64. Robert Gustafson, Johan Yssel, and Lea Witta, "Ad Agency Employees Give Views on Calvin Klein, Benetton Ads," *Marketing News,* September 23, 1996, p. 16.

65. Ibid.

Bricks or Clicks

UNDERSTANDING CONSUMER BEHAVIOR

THE KEY TO DEVELOPING A successful marketing strategy is to understand consumer behavior. This is a challenge for many companies, especially large superstores that have millions of diverse customers nationwide. As the Internet becomes a more significant mode of shopping for many consumers, brick-and-mortar superstores recognize this and have developed online versions of their stores. Now superstores are faced with the even more difficult challenge of understanding online consumer behavior.

The company Coremetrics has developed a Web site visitor analysis service called eLuminate. This service allows online companies to gain a better understanding of their consumers—who they are, what they are buying, and why. The competitive advantage offered by eLuminate is that it is a service. Companies that do their own analyses spend hundreds of thousands of dollars on hardware, software, and the personnel to run them. Many online companies, such as Wal-Mart.com, prefer to analyze Web data using an e-intelligence service such as eLuminate because it requires little up-front investment and can be implemented in days rather than the weeks it can take to install an in-house system.

How exactly is Wal-Mart.com using the technology of eLuminate to track consumer behavior? The service eLuminate provides analyzed information on segmentation and who is entering, buying, and exiting the site. The program sorts through the customers and places them into groups based on their shopping behavior. Wal-Mart.com can identify the value of these visitors by analyzing each

Continued from previous page.

grouping of customers. These data are useful in determining the costs of acquiring new customers and also of retaining previous customers.

However, simply having excellent consumer data is not enough to turn a successful brick-and-mortar superstore into a successful online superstore. "Wal-Mart's future depends on converting the millions who shop at their traditional stores into online customers," says Jim Williamson, an analyst with International Data Corporation in Framingham, Massachusetts. "They also want to take their two most powerful weapons online with them: popular brand names and millions of loyal customers," said Williamson.

Another problem is quantity. Wal-Mart brick-and-mortar stores offer an impressive number of products (approximately 600,000). Yet this quantity online can be cumbersome and has led to some technical issues that have hurt the performance of Wal-Mart.com.

In addition to selecting eLuminate to better understand online consumer behavior, Wal-Mart.com has made many changes in an effort to tackle the many challenges. Improvements in site navigation, new services, and overall customer experience have been made recently, but competition in this arena is still fierce, and sites such as Kmart's Bluelight.com recently reported greater usage than Wal-Mart.com. Yet analysts are not giving up hope for Wal-Mart.com. "Wal-Mart has done a pretty good job of outmaneuvering Kmart on land, and I would imagine over time you would see the same result on-line," said Shari Schwartzman Eberts, a senior research analyst at J. P. Morgan.

Sources: Rick Whiting, "E-Intelligence for Web-Site Analysis," *Informationweek,* March 27, 2000, p. 30; Laura Heller, "Making Walmart.com the Wal-Mart of the Web," *Drug Store News,* June 12, 2000, p. 26; Coremetrics, "Wal-Mart.com Selects Coremetrics™ as eMarketing Intelligence Service Provider of Choice," May 31, 2000; Doug Tsuruoka, "Retailers Look to Lure Customers Online," *Investor's Daily,* June 16, 2000, Section A, p. 12; and Kristen Young, "Wal-Mart Web Site Has Tough Time and Has Already Undergone Several Incarnations," *Los Angeles Times,* August 7, 2000, Vol. 30, No. 92, p. 2.

CASE 7

Viacom—The MTV Networks

THE MTV NETWORKS—MTV, NICKELODEON, and VH1—produce huge profits for Viacom by catering to moody teenagers, fickle kids, and music-loving baby boomers. With nearly $20.04 billion in revenues, $3.54 billion in operating cash flow in 2000, and profit margins that are growing at 25 percent annually, Viacom has become part of the entertainment lifestyles of three consumer generations. How has MTV Networks produced huge profits for Viacom? By constantly keeping a connection with the mindset of each core market segment.

Nearly 342 million households around the world tune into MTV, whose corporate philosophy is "Think Globally but Act Locally." The network stays in tune with a staff of young executives, whose success depends on pleasing young viewers much like themselves. In MTV's free flowing corporate culture, ideas count more than tradition, and even interns get heard. Tom Fredston, CEO of MTV Networks, is confident about the organization's continued growth, as long as it retains the loyalty of kids, teens, and 20-something's—TV's most faddish viewers. This means staying fresh and being open to change. The average employee is age 28, and the corporate climate is more like a college dorm—or romper room, in the case of Nickelodeon. If you walk the halls, you'll see backpacks, not briefcases, and more nose rings than neckties.

To stay current, MTV uses the usual ratings, polls, focus groups, and online chats, but it also sends researchers into the field to dig through dorm rooms, closets, and CD collections of 12- to 34-year-olds. These researchers spotted trouble with fading hits like *Beavis and Butt-head, The Real World,* and *Singled Out.* MTV eliminated several shows and ushered in new ones, such as *Jackass* and *The Andy Dick Show.*

However, the common complaint from viewers is that it is hard to find music on MTV. The problem with music videos is that viewers surf them so rapidly that the ratings don't pick them up, ultimately hurting the network. So even the poorer shows do almost five times better than the video hours because people are least likely to surf during a 30-minute episode. A solution was more live music from studios, instead of videos, on shows such as *Direct Effect (DFX)* and *Total Request Live.* These live shows have music content, but less channel surfing than the video hours.

Despite the lack of music videos, ad rates have grown by 10 percent because sponsors are willing to pay a premium to connect with hard-to-reach consumers age 12–34. Judy McGrath, MTV's president, says that "advertisers want to be on there [MTV] for association, not absolute numbers or eyeballs."

Since 1996, MTV2 has also helped the music loving audience by playing only music videos. MTV2 helps appease some people that are tired of the same videos and looking for the old MTV experience. "It's kind of like the golden days of MTV," says Chris Booker, a VJ for MTV2. "It's a little rough around the edges and that's cool . . ." MTV2 is currently available to selected cable subscribers and carried on 81 college campus cable systems.

Nickelodeon, targeted at 2–11 year olds, is in the enviable position of being able to extend its brand name to everything from kids' toys to macaroni and cheese. Ad spots sell out almost two seasons ahead. Despite a lot of new competition, Nickelodeon has been cable's top-rated network since 1995. Nickelodeon Movies, a partnership with Paramount Pictures, has also been successful. Most recently, *Snow Day,* featuring Chris Elliot and Chevy Chase, was released and grossed almost $60 million in the United States. *The Rugrats Movie,* released in 1998, was "the first non-Disney animated film to gross over $100 million at the domestic box office." Nickelodeon's assets have made it a clear cable star.

VH1 is geared to MTV graduates—the baby boomers and generation Xers who want a channel that plays their music—not just the classic artists, but contemporary artists. VH1 president John Sykes says that "music is in our culture. Music is our social conscience. That's why you see our music selling every product on television today." VH1 tends to have chronically low ratings due to channel surfing, but collects a steady stream of fees from cable operators, who pay up to 10 cents a month for each of the 73 million subscribers.

In developing VH1, Sykes wanted a "focused adult music channel with a singular vision. . . music first. Music drives everything we do. Number one, I saw that the MTV generation had grown up, and had nowhere else to turn for music on cable TV. So I saw a huge opportunity to reach young, active, affluent adults with music." Sykes adds, "We're the generation that grew up with Woodstock, with Vietnam, and with a lot of tension.

The music of those times really stuck to us. It wasn't just pop fodder, it was woven into our culture, and as a result we stay with that music. It's part of our existence." He believes these adults are looking for entertainment with context, such as information about songs. Approximately $50 million was spent on original program production in 1998. Aimed at the inquisitive, sophisticated, adult viewers who watch NBC's *Dateline* or ABC's *20/20,* shows like *Behind The Music, Before They Were Rock Stars, Storytellers,* and *Where Are They Now?* are key elements in the programming.

1. *How are the stages of the family life cycle used by each of the MTV networks in order to reach viewers successfully?*
2. *List three possible viewer reference groups for each MTV network. How do the networks use reference groups to influence consumer behavior?*
3. *Discuss why advertisers would select each of the MTV networks and how attitudes, learning, and perception about the sponsor's brand might be influenced by the network.*

Sources: Marc Gunther, "This Gang Controls Your Kids' Brains," *Fortune,* October 27, 1997, pp. 172–182; Dyan Mcham, "A More Tolerant Generation," *Forbes,* September 8, 1997, pp. 46–47; Donna Petrozello, "VH1: and the Band Plays On; Channel Has Remade Itself to Put Music First for Adults," *Broadcasting and Cable,* September 1, 1997, p. 43; Viacom Networks Web site, www.viacom.com, visited June 18, 2000.

chapter 8

BUSINESS-TO-BUSINESS MARKETING

objectives

1. Describe the types of organizations and products involved in business-to-business marketing and understand the importance of this market.

2. Understand the link between consumer demand and business-to-business marketing.

3. Describe the organizational buying process.

4. Know how buyer–seller relationships work, including informal and contractual partnerships.

5. Learn what functions and roles within organizations influence the purchase of a broad range of products.

Executive Chef Michael Crane of Aramark at the 2000 Summer Olympic Games in Sydney, Australia

WITHOUT EVER KNOWING IT, MOST OF you have been served by ARAMARK. The company sells to thousands of colleges, schools, corporations, convention centers, hospitals, parks, and sports arenas, providing food and support services, uniform apparel, and child care and early education programs. It is principally owned by its employee managers who have worked to produce annual revenues of $7 billion. Every day its 150,000 employees connect with more than 15 million people throughout 15 countries in more than 500,000 worldwide locations.

You may not have heard of the name, however, because ARAMARK partners with businesses to provide expertise on-site. ARAMARK's best-known partnership, for example, is with the Olympic Games. When ARAMARK offered its customized "World Menu from Down Under" at the Sydney Olympic Games in 2000, it marked the twelfth time the company has been selected to serve at the Olympics since 1968.

ARAMARK believes it is qualified to perform a task as lofty as managing the food service of the Olympics. Because of its history with the Olympic Games, almost half of the 2000 team has previously worked at an Olympics. This experience allows ARAMARK employees to successfully prepare and present the more than 600 international recipes offered, all of which represent a wide variety of cultural, religious, and ethnic backgrounds.

Chairman and CEO Joseph Neubauer says, "We take our accountability to the athletes and the countries they represent very seriously. Consider how important the moment is to young athletes who have waited their entire lives for one single event. Their preparation—including how they train and what they eat—in the days leading up to the defining moment of their careers is critical."

Preparing meals for 10,300 athletes, 8,000 coaches and staff, 5,100 officials, and 5,000 media representatives from more than 200 countries involves more than just cooking, however. ARAMARK is responsible for all aspects of the food service at the Olympics, from safety guidelines and office management systems to coordinating suppliers and developing a waste management system.

Experience gained by servicing the Olympics is paying off for ARAMARK in other ventures. For example, the ability to cater to a large international culinary demand prepared the company to service 20,000 employees at two restaurants and a coffee bar at the 2000 World Expo. ARAMARK has also expanded its partnership with the Boeing Company to include food service in addition to outsourcing its uniform services and conference center management.

ARAMARK makes its people responsible to its customers as part of its efforts to ensure customer satisfaction. Each client has an "unlimited partnership" with the company and receives a specially designed program that will work with its own existing infrastructure instead of a prepackaged corporate relationship. The company has even developed "World Class Patient Service," a training program that establishes customer service standards for hourly staff members who have direct contact with the patients of hospital clients.

ARAMARK is an excellent example of an organization dedicated to helping its customers excel in their own businesses.

Although the company seldom sells directly to consumers, its own consumers do. Like many business marketers, the company forms lasting relationships with its clients and plays a major role in how well they compete. This chapter describes the challenges of business-to-business marketing and shows its importance to the world economy.[1]

THE CONCEPT OF BUSINESS-TO-BUSINESS MARKETING

In the 21st century there will be spectacular growth in business-to-business marketing. DuPont, Sun Microsystems, and General Electric, like thousands of other companies, are connecting with customers through selling to other businesses. The marketing of goods and services to other businesses, governments, and institutions is known as **business-to-business marketing.** It includes everything but direct sales to consumers. Globally, it's the largest market by far. Leading research firms predict the business-to-business (B2B) market will reach somewhere between $2.7 trillion and $7.3 trillion by 2004. In comparison, Forester Research predicts business-to-consumer spending will be much less—only $184.5 billion.[2]

Most consumer goods are made from a variety of components and processes. The products are marketed from one organization to another, until the one at the end of the chain sells to the final consumer. Let's follow the production of an automobile. It begins with a steel manufacturer marketing its product to a company that makes rivets and other metal fasteners, which are sold to a company that makes radiators. That business then markets its products to an automobile manufacturer. In the factory, the radiators are combined with other components that have much the same history, and the finished car is shipped to a dealership, where the final customer buys it. At each step, money, time, and effort are spent on marketing, and value is created.

In other cases of business-to-business marketing, a finished product is simply sold and resold down the line until it reaches the end consumer. For example, a deck of playing cards is purchased by a wholesaler, who resells it to a retailer such as Kmart, who then sells it to the final consumer. Again, time, money, and effort are expended at each step. In still other cases, one company sells products directly to another for its own internal use—whether copy machines, laptop computers, or toilet tissue.

Consumers may never take physical ownership of the item at all, but they benefit just the same. A telephone call is one example. Consumers can place a call to and from nearly anywhere in the world, yet they own only their telephone, and sometimes not even that. The switching network, satellite communications equipment, and cable that process the call belong to a company such as AT&T or MCI. With the exception of the consumer's monthly service fee and telephone, the other items are part of business-to-business marketing.

Many types of organizations buy business products. For example, General Motors alone purchases nearly $200 million worth each day from its own divisions and outside companies. Other for-profit and nonprofit organizations—from the *Fortune* 500 to small private firms—do the same and add to this total volume. Finally, the government market makes purchases nearly as large as all private organizations combined, ranging from country road repairs to army boots to toothbrushes. The business market offers tremendous opportunities.

The key elements of the business-to-business market are depicted in Figure 8.1. In the early sections of the chapter we will look at the various industries that comprise the overall market and at possible approaches to segmenting this market. We will see how supply linkages between companies create a supply chain reaching all the way from raw materials extractors to neighborhood retailers, how consumers ultimately determine business market demand, and how the globalization of business markets creates new requirements as well as new opportunities.

We then turn our attention to organizational buying, beginning with an examination of the decisions to be made, and the steps in the buying process. Good buyer–seller relationships are key in business-to-business markets; we will see how these relationships develop in phases and may involve interaction with many functions and personnel in the buying organization. This part concludes with a look at several important factors—including interpersonal conflict—that often influence organizational buying behavior.

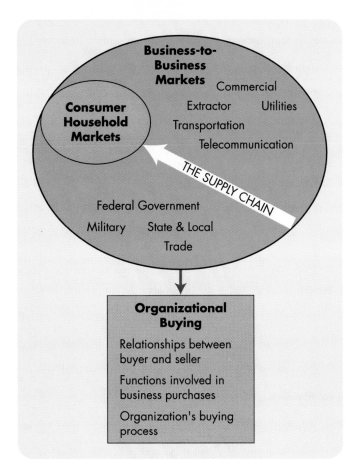

BUSINESS-TO-BUSINESS MARKETS

TYPES OF MARKETS

The business market is divided into the seven categories shown in Figure 8.2: commercial market, extract industries, trade industries, institutions, utilities, transportation and telecommunications, and government. Each category is comprised of organizations with similar business circumstances and general purchasing requirements.

Commercial Market   The **commercial market** category consists of organizations that acquire goods and services that are then used to produce other goods and services. Many of these products are used in finished products purchased by consumers. For example, Ford has more than 3,000 suppliers of products used to build automobiles. These, in turn, have other suppliers. All the marketing activities leading up to and including the sale of goods and services to Ford are part of the commercial market.

Extractor Industries   The **extractor industries** category includes organizations that obtain and process raw materials, as in forestry or mining. Extractor companies are separated from the commercial segment because they acquire much of their supply from the earth. They require expensive equipment such as drilling rigs and instrumentation. These industries are huge consumers of nearly every product imaginable. Many of the companies in this category have global operations, such as Exxon-Mobil.

There are often unique demands on extractor organizations to be environmentally sensitive. An agency of the U.S. Department of the Interior, the Bureau of Land Management, has initiated the Director's Excellence Awards program to recognize environmental sensitivity in the production of fluid materials. Two winners include River Gas Corporation of Utah, which has substantially reduced the impacts of coal bed methane development, and Cross Timbers Operating Company of Wyoming, which has designed facilities that minimize surface disturbance and contamination, preventing the need for surface containment pits.[3] There are numerous opportunities in this category for marketing ecological products. EnviroGroup is a firm that provides both consulting and testing services. Soilsorb, an environmental risk

COMMERCIAL MARKET
Organizations and individuals that acquire goods and services to produce other goods and services sold to an end consumer for profit.

EXTRACTOR INDUSTRIES
Industries that obtain and process raw materials.

CONNECTED: SURFING THE NET

www.envirogroup.com

Learn more about EnviroGroup, the environmental solutions company. Discover how it manages ecological issues for clients worldwide.

Category	Examples of Organizations	Purchase Examples
Commercial	Fabricators Component manufacturers Processors Original equipment manufacturers Designers	Raw materials Component parts Processing equipment Transportation Consulting services
Extractor	Agriculture Forestry Mining Drilling Water	Fertilizer and pesticides, seeds Heavy- and light-duty equipment Pipe Aircraft and transportation Real estate, mining rights Products for resale Loading equipment
Trade	Retailers Wholesalers Dealerships	Computer systems Buildings/real estate Advertising Transportation Warehousing Pharmaceuticals Equipment
Institutions	Hospitals Schools Day care centers Banks and finance organizations Insurance Churches Charities	Food Consulting Health care Suppliers Computer systems
Utilities	Electric utilities Gas utilities Water and waste disposal plants	Nuclear fuel Power generation equipment Electric components Motors Computers Chemicals Testing equipment
Transportation and Telecommunications	Airlines Trucking Rail companies Telephones Cellular	Fuel Equipment Computers Real estate
Government *Federal*	Senate and House Judicial Agencies Military	Consulting Offices Forms Computers Energy Aircraft Radar communications
State and Local	Highway commissions Health and social services Schools and universities Prisons Police Libraries Parks and recreation Museums	Health care items Food Logistics Equipment Energy Books Sports equipment Restoration

FIGURE 8.2 *Types of Business-to-Business Markets*

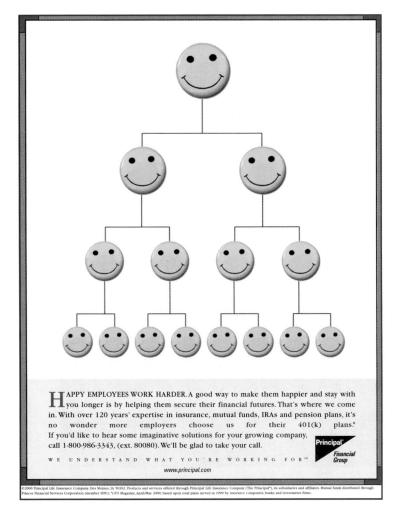

Principal Financial Group targets business-to-business companies.

assessment tool used by EnviroGroup, measures contaminants in soils over time. With its expertise and advanced equipment, EnviroGroup manages environmental issues for clients worldwide.[4]

Trade Industries   The **trade industries** category is made up of organizations that acquire or distribute finished products to businesses or to consumers. It includes retailers, wholesalers, and other intermediaries. These companies play an important role in the "place" component of the marketing mix. The importance of **resellers,** companies that purchase a product and sell it in the same form for profit, has been gaining more and more recognition recently. The computer industry, for example, is now emphasizing the role of resellers in distribution and increasingly relies on them to install and service products. Customers can, for instance, buy Apple computers through any number of resellers. Apple realizes the benefits of reselling, however, and has recently expanded its offerings to resellers by extending its build-to-order (BTO) capabilities to them, now allowing customers to order custom-built computers from their preferred reseller.[5]

In many cases, resellers repackage products to suit the needs of particular market segments. For example, Kroger buys meat in bulk and cuts it into sizes and forms for household use. The Cappuccino Café buys coffee in 100-pound units and sells it by the pound or freshly brewed.

Institutions   The **institutions** category covers public and private organizations that provide health, education, and welfare services to consumers. It includes universities, hospitals, churches, nursing homes, and museums. Institutional buyers purchase a broad range of products with funds of their own or from third parties, such as donors, insurance companies, and government grants.

Because of third-party funding, institutions may have unique purchasing requirements. Consequently, companies often establish very specific strategies for marketing to these organizations. For example, most pharmaceutical firms have separate units that market to hospitals.

TRADE INDUSTRIES

Industries comprised of organizations that acquire finished products and distribute them to others.

RESELLER

A company that purchases a product and sells it in the same form for profit.

INSTITUTIONS

Public and private organizations that provide services to consumers.

Timken, a worldwide leader in bearings and steel, is a part of the commercial market.

ARAMARK has a separate food service division that markets specifically to universities. Its expertise in nutrition, understanding of the college-age population, and knowledge of how universities make decisions combine to create unique, highly targeted marketing programs.

UTILITIES

Companies that distribute gas, electricity, or water.

Utilities   The **utilities** category is comprised of companies that distribute gas, electricity, and water. Once highly regulated by the government, utilities are being given the opportunity to operate more like private organizations. Public service commissions continue to provide oversight, however, because even private utilities are considered to be part of the public sector to some degree. Consolidated Edison and Florida Power & Light are huge buyers of business products. Westinghouse sells billions of dollars in nuclear fuel, power generation equipment, and design services to both public and privately owned utilities.

Transportation and Telecommunications   Transportation and telecommunications make up another business market category. The transportation portion is comprised of companies that provide passenger and freight service such as Union Pacific Railroad and United Airlines. Telecommunications companies supply local and long-distance telephone service as well as cable and broadcasting. CBS, AOL Time Warner, Northwest Airlines, AT&T, and Ameritech are somewhat like utilities. This category was once subject to extensive government regulation that has been relaxed in recent years.

   Although there are relatively few companies in this category, their purchases are huge. In 1998, Boeing alone purchased more than $37 billion worth of parts, components, and systems from more than 30,000 suppliers located in 46 states and 37 countries.[6] The cable and broadcast companies purchase satellite capacity, equipment, and a huge range of services necessary to develop state-of-the-art telecasting.

GOVERNMENT MARKETS

The federal, state, and local governments in their role as purchasers of goods and services.

Government Markets   In the United States, the subdivisions in the **government market** category are (1) the federal government, (2) the 50 state governments, and (3) 8,700 local units. Together, they make more purchases than any other group in the United States. In 2000, the U.S. government spent more than $1.4 trillion. The national military is by far the largest

On the Italian island of Sardinia, protecting all that lives there comes naturally. So when the people challenged us to power their growing economy, they also challenged us to preserve the environment. We combined two technologies, literally taking residue from Italy's largest refinery and returning it as clean energy. What's on your energy wish list? 1-888-55-ENRON, www.enron.com.

Natural gas. Electricity. Endless possibilities: ENRON

Enron sells natural gas and electricity in the utilities category of business-to-business markets.

purchaser of goods and services, accounting for $2.9 billion of U.S. spending.[7] For many corporations, particulary defense companies, the federal government is an essential customer. In December 1999, the U.S. Army awarded a contract for the Wholesale Logistics Modernization Program, worth $681 million over a five-year period, to Computer Sciences Corporation (CSC) of San Diego, California. Under this contract, CSC will develop, implement, and manage a new delivery system to boost efficiency on the battlefield and bases. Other companies, such as General Dynamics Corporation of Falls Church, Virginia, and TRW Inc. of Cleveland, Ohio, have competed for the contract to fix bandwidth problems in the $5 billion Warfighter Information Network-Terrestrial (WIN-T) program, which is part of the army's "battlefield digitization" effort.[8]

BUSINESS MARKET SEGMENTATION

Business markets differ from consumer markets in several important ways: number of buyers, size of purchase, supplier relationships, geographic concentration, purchasing approaches, and buying influences. Figure 8.3 shows the characteristics of each. Although the business market is segmented using procedures much like those used to segment the consumer market (discussed in chapter 6), its distinctive characteristics are used to categorize business consumers along different dimensions—by company demographics, geographic scope, buying approach, and product/technology—as outlined in Figure 8.4.

Segmentation by Company Demographics   In describing a company, we usually think first about its demographics: industry, size, financial stability, place in the distribution channel, and ownership. Industry is defined by the company's products. Ford, GM, and Honda are in the automotive industry, whereas Mack and International are in the heavy truck industry. Large companies may have strategic business units (SBUs) in different industries. Johnson & Johnson, for example, makes consumer health care products as well as medical supplies for professionals. The federal government's Standard Industry Classification (SIC) codes can help identify a company's industrial category. Industry classification reveals a great deal about an organization—the

Characteristic	Business Market	Consumer Market
Number of buyers	Few	Often millions
Supplier relationship	Long-term contracts and supplier involvement	Many single purchases
Size of purchase	Often extremely large	Usually small
Geographic concentration	Usually near population centers	Widely dispersed
Purchasing approach	Technically trained buying agents follow policies and constraints. Tend to buy directly from manufacturer	Nontechnical purchasing to satisfy personal preferences
Buying influences	Committees, technical experts, and management are all involved in decision making	The individual, household members, or friends and relatives

FIGURE 8.3 *How Business and Consumer Markets Differ*

types of problems it is likely to face, the kinds of products it purchases, its economic cycles and regulatory environment, and the types of competitive practices it is likely to encounter.

Company size is based on dollar amount or volume of sales, number of employees, or units produced. Size affects purchase procedures and requirements such as delivery schedules and inventory capacity. Large firms often do much of their own engineering, and their purchasing department uses formal buying arrangements. Medium-sized companies may be interested in value-added services a seller can provide. Small firms often use less formal procedures and may want the seller's help with tracking and restocking inventory.

Another demographic characteristic is financial stability and profitability. Marketing to a company in difficulty may not be worth the effort and risk. If sales volumes are substantial, delays in payments can cause the seller financial hardship. The profitability of a company is often used as an indication of its ability to pay as well as other characteristics.

Channel membership refers to whether the organization is a distributor, original equipment manufacturer (OEM), or one of the tier suppliers. Each type has significantly different needs. Distributors acquire to resell, OEMs want to develop a final product, and tiers typically have unique needs as well.

Basis	Example
Company Demographics	
Industry	food, mining, automotive, computer
Company size	large, medium, small
Financial stability and profitability	strong, medium, weak
Channel	distributor, OEM, first tier, second tier
Ownership	private, public
Industry leadership	leader, close follower, laggard
Geographic Scope	local, regional, national, international, global
Buying Approach	
Centralization	centralized, decentralized
Functional involvement	finance, marketing, manufacturing
Partnering approach	bid, relationship oriented, contracts
Product/Technology	
Level of technology	high, medium, low
Configuration purchased	components, modules, subsystem
Design source	internal, external

FIGURE 8.4 *Segmenting the Business Market*

Ownership influences how organizations buy. Since private companies can set policies as they see fit, we find many purchasing strategies. In the public sector, governmental units and utilities must follow very strict guidelines.

Segmentation by Geographic Scope   When we discussed geographic segmentation in chapter 6, it was in terms of locating clusters of targeted consumers. In the case of businesses, however, we are concerned with the geographic scope of the customer's business, whether local, regional, national, international, or global. The range of operations clearly affects how an organization buys. General Motors has a global scope, so sellers must be able to think in terms of manufacturing plants around the world—and of reaching buyers who may come from various cultures. Saab, which manufactures only in Sweden, has a much more localized set of needs.

Segmentation by Buying Approach   Organizations also can be differentiated according to their buying approach. This takes into account their degree of centralization, what functional areas are involved, and what kind of partnering arrangements they have. A centralized organization generally has one purchasing unit with very set policies, whereas a decentralized organization is likely to allow local buying decisions using various procedures and policies. Functional involvement refers to a company's orientation—manufacturing firms use one set of criteria, whereas a financial institution or a consulting firm may use others. Partnering can range from simple bid purchases to a long- or short-term contract that may or may not contain detailed specifications and other requirements, such as an exclusivity clause.

Segmentation by Product/Technology   Product/technology can affect purchasing in numerous ways, but three of the more important are level of technology, configuration purchased, and design orientation. First, firms vary dramatically in technological capability. This is primarily due to their hiring, training, retention, and technical practices. A high-tech firm has very different expectations from a low-tech firm. Consequently, marketing to each group is different. Second, buying configurations differ. Some companies want to purchase only components and base their decisions on price and delivery specifications. Others buy modules that already combine many components and make it easier to add the supplier's product at the time of manufacturing. Yet others prefer to purchase a system that enhances the functionality of their products, as when Chrysler buys traction-control products from Tevis. This variable is related in some ways to design. Some organizations want to do their own, some want suppliers to do it, and some work closely with suppliers to develop a design. A company such as Delphi Automotive Systems has extensive design capabilities but sometimes relies on suppliers for the design of certain components, modules, and systems.

BUSINESS MARKET LINKAGES: THE SUPPLY CHAIN

The **supply chain** links organizations involved in the creation and delivery of a product. Figure 8.5 is a simplified diagram of the supply chain for automobiles. The original equipment manufacturer, such as GM or Ford, is in the middle of the chain. There are supply activities both upstream and downstream. In business-to-business marketing, the word **tier** refers to the

SUPPLY CHAIN
The linkage of organizations involved in the creation and delivery of a product.

TIER
The degree of contact between the supplier and the OEM.

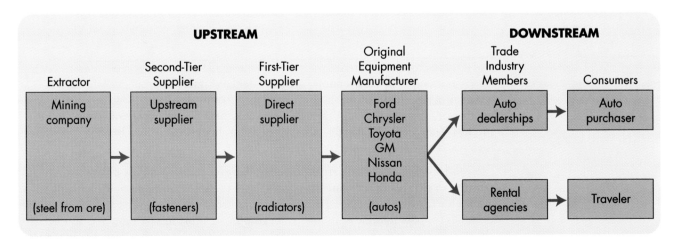

FIGURE 8.5 *An Example of the Supply Chain in Automotives*

*CNF takes a look at the
distribution side of supply
chain management in this
advertisement.*

degree of contact between suppliers and the OEM. In the automotive industry, there are third-tier suppliers (extractors who process steel from ore), second-tier suppliers (manufacturers of components such as fasteners), and first-tier suppliers (makers of radiators). The last is a direct supplier to the OEM. Other examples of direct or first-tier suppliers in this industry are the makers of leather seats, radios, and carpeting, each of whom deals with its own group of suppliers.

Supply chain management involves establishing or improving linkages to maximize efficiency and effectiveness. Marketers view the supply chain in terms of activities that need to be coordinated to provide the greatest value to the consumer, who is at the end of the chain. UPS World Wide Logistics, for example, works with many companies to improve supply chain management. Its experts help clients with systems design, transportation, information systems, and other services.

BUSINESS MARKET DEMAND

The demand for products in the business market is not based solely on what happens in the business sector. As you will see, demand is based largely on what happens to consumers.

DERIVED DEMAND

A demand, such as the demand for business-to-business products, which depends ultimately on the demand of end consumers.

Derived Demand   Business marketers must rely on derived demand to create opportunities for their products. **Derived demand** means that the amount of sales for business-to-business products ultimately depends on (is derived from) the demand for products by consumers. For example, when automobile sales increase, so does the need for materials, components, and subassemblies. The first (original) demand occurs among consumers and is reflected in the business-to-business market. This ripple effect is felt all along the supply chain, and it drives economic growth.

INELASTIC DEMAND

Demand that is influenced little by price changes.

Inelastic Demand   Certain products are so essential that they are less responsive than others to changes in the economy. **Inelastic demand** refers to products so necessary that a change in price has relatively little effect on the quantity demanded. If the price of sugar or another cola ingredient rises, it's doubtful that Coke or Pepsi will use less of it in making their product. The cost has little to do with their decision about what to buy, although it may affect the price charged to consumers.

Fluctuating Demand: The Accelerator Principle   Some business products are highly sensitive to changes in consumer demand. We see the accelerator principle operating when a small fluctuation (increase or decrease) in consumer demand has a larger effect on business demand. Suppose that the economy is sluggish. In an effort to save money, consumers are closely watching their energy consumption—turning off lights when not in use, running the air conditioner as little as possible, and so forth. Obviously, this will affect the revenues of local power plants. A few dollars saved by each customer quickly mount when multiplied by thousands of people in the utility's service area. Even a small drop in consumer demand may be enough to force the plant to postpone the purchase of multimillion-dollar equipment. Of course, if consumer demand exceeds expectations by only a little, the result may be brownouts, power outages, or the need to buy energy from outside the system.

GLOBALIZATION OF BUSINESS MARKETS

The growth of international business has provided companies with a number of business-to-business marketing opportunities overseas. The United Kingdom and the Netherlands, among the first to deregulate their telecommunications industry, are potential markets that AT&T is said to be eyeing. Despite recent economic problems in the Pacific Rim, South Korea is America's seventh largest trading partner, having in 1999 exchanged $54.2 billion in various goods.[9] Indonesia, Malaysia, and Thailand have also provided markets for U.S. goods. Business products being successfully exported from the United States currently include computer hardware and software, aircraft, electronics, medical equipment, oil and gas field machinery and equipment, and analytical instruments.[10]

Strong business marketers must be able to support their customers' business efforts globally. Companies such as International Data Group (IDG), the world's leading publisher of computer magazines and newspapers, are becoming more capable of providing global coverage. IDG currently has 290 publications in 75 countries, which makes it possible for advertisers to connect with more than 90 million customers around the world.[11] IBM, i2 Technologies Inc., and Ariba Inc. have teamed up and launched a $90 million international advertising campaign to promote themselves as the world's leading operator of Internet commerce marketplaces. These three companies are using the slogans "it's b2bx3" and "What a great location for an e-marketplace" as they vie with other similar companies to set up online marketplaces for individual industries throughout the world.[12]

Strong global connections with customers require marketers to establish brand identity. This is just as important in business-to-business markets as in consumer markets. New technologies have created numerous worldwide business opportunities, from supplying satellites to building computer chip factories. Business-to-business marketers must develop and position their brands to differentiate themselves from competitors. In early 2000, JP Morgan, a highly recognized financial services firm in the United States, launched a global branding campaign to expand its customer base to include younger, high-tech, and Web-based firms, which, some fear, may have an outdated sense of the company. Little-known CMGI Inc., owner of a large network of disparate Internet firms, hopes to improve its overall brand recognition through its $76 million purchase of the naming rights for the New England Patriots/CMGI Stadium.[13]

ORGANIZATIONAL BUYING

BUYING DECISIONS

Business-to-business marketing is strongly influenced by two organizational considerations. First, a company must decide whether it is better to seek outside suppliers or to make the product(s) in-house. Second, if suppliers are used, then different types of situations require varying involvement by people within the buying organization. Furthermore, the type of situation also may be a factor in whether competitive bidding is used.

The Make or Buy Decision **Make or buy decisions** occur when companies must decide whether to supply products or services in-house or to buy them from other businesses. **Outsourcing** is the purchase of products from other companies. Many organizations choose this route so they can focus on their core business. A number of factors influence the make or buy decision. A company must evaluate its need for direct control over production or quality, and it must examine the costs associated with supplying internally versus externally. There are also issues of supplier reliability, design secrecy, and workforce stability. Outsourcing could cost thousands of jobs at Delphi. Workforce considerations are very important if a strong union is involved.

Outsourcing has become widely popular—of the 300 largest global companies in 1999, 73 percent had used it in some form, up from 58 percent in 1992. In the year 2000, for instance, IBM Japan was awarded over $3 billion in outsourcing contracts to run the data centers and sales

**CONNECTED:
SURFING THE NET**

www.ibm.com

For more information about IBM's worldwide activities, visit its Web site and select from more than 50 countries. Also discover how IBM is making it safe to shop on the Web.

MAKE OR BUY DECISION
The decision whether to supply products in-house or to purchase them from other businesses.

OUTSOURCING
Purchasing products and services from other companies.

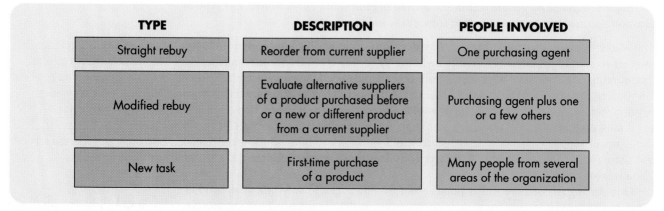

Approximately 86 percent of major corporations use outsourcing so they can focus on their core business.

offices of Mitsubishi Trust, a bank, and Meiji Seika Company, a food and pharmaceuticals firm. Another company, Flextronics, signed a five-year, $30 billion outsourcing agreement with Motorola to manufacture its cellular phones, pagers, and various other communication devices. As for the Internet, Yahoo! recently turned to Google.com to provide a newer and more expanded search engine for Web surfers and consumers.[14] For these companies and hundreds like them, outsourcing can cut costs and allow more attention to be directed toward primary business activities. In order to sustain a competitive advantage, more and more businesses are turning to this option.

The Outsourcing Decision   Outsourcing may involve the purchase of a product on a routine basis, changes in suppliers, or purchase of a product for the first time. This involves the three kinds of situations—straight rebuy, modified rebuy, and new task situations—summarized in Figure 8.6. A **straight rebuy** is a routine purchase with which the organization has had a great deal of experience. For example, an exclusive furniture manufacturer may purchase leather for its sofas from only one supplier, which has a reputation for the highest quality. The two organizations have done business for years, and the manufacturer has made hundreds of purchases. In this case, a buying decision may take less than a week and involve only one or two people from each organization. In fact, it's normal for a purchasing agent to handle the entire transaction.

Suppose that the furniture manufacturer is dissatisfied with the leather supplier or doesn't want to depend on only one. A **modified rebuy** situation involves purchasing a familiar

STRAIGHT REBUY

A routine purchase with which the organization has considerable experience.

MODIFIED REBUY

Purchase of a familiar product from an unfamiliar supplier or a new or different product from a familiar supplier.

TYPE	DESCRIPTION	PEOPLE INVOLVED
Straight rebuy	Reorder from current supplier	One purchasing agent
Modified rebuy	Evaluate alternative suppliers of a product purchased before or a new or different product from a current supplier	Purchasing agent plus one or a few others
New task	First-time purchase of a product	Many people from several areas of the organization

FIGURE 8.6 *Organizational Buying Situations*

product from an unfamiliar supplier or a new or different product from a familiar supplier. Usually more people will be involved in a modified rebuy decision, and more time and energy will be expended.

Finally, let us say the furniture manufacturer decides to add a line of fabric sofas. This **new task situation** involves purchasing an unfamiliar product from an unfamiliar supplier. Because there is a great deal at risk, many people will likely provide input to the decision process, which may take several weeks, months, or even years.

NEW TASK SITUATION

Purchase of an unfamiliar product from an unfamiliar supplier.

Competitive Bidding   Some organizations use competitive bidding, especially for purchases over a certain amount. They want to obtain the lowest price rather than establish long-term relationships with suppliers. Most government purchases must be made this way by law. Many companies, such as General Motors, have purchasing rules that require a minimum number of bids—usually three—for certain types of purchases. Often exceptions can be made so long as the rationale for noncompliance with the bidding policy is documented.

In straight rebuy situations in the private sector, competitive bids are seldom required. They are likely in modified rebuys that involve the evaluation of alternative suppliers and are common in new task situations. In any of these cases, if the amount is very large, then the bidding procedure will probably be used.

Competitive bids may be sealed or negotiated. For the sealed bids, each seller is given a request for quotation (RFQ), which describes all the product and purchase specifications. The responses are due on a given date, when envelopes are opened, and the lowest bidder is awarded the order. Negotiated bids differ in that suppliers may be invited to comment on the specifications, modifications are possible, and the two or three most appropriate bids are then negotiated to determine the best choice—not necessarily the lowest bidder.

STEPS IN THE ORGANIZATIONAL BUYING PROCESS

An organization may go through eight different stages when making a buying decision, but every purchase does not require all of them. New task situations may involve all eight, modified rebuys fewer, and straight rebuys the fewest. The eight possible steps in the organizational buying process are shown in Figure 8.7: problem recognition, general need description, product specifications, supplier search, proposal solicitation, order routine specifications, purchase and use of product, and performance review and feedback.

Problem recognition occurs when the buying organization realizes that a situation can be improved by acquiring a good or service. Potential problems include unsatisfactory materials,

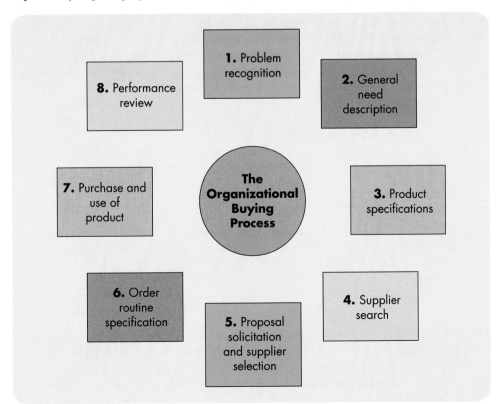

FIGURE 8.7 *Steps in the Buying Process*

machine failure, or development of a new product that requires new equipment. A general need description is developed that identifies the basic characteristics of what is wanted, such as reliability, price, range, and durability. Next, the organization prepares product specifications, which usually are technical and very detailed: Precise dimensions, tolerances, quantity, or the objectives of a consultant's study are examples.

Unless it has been decided to make the product in-house, the search for suppliers now begins. Some may have been involved in the previous stages, but the organization usually looks for more to be certain no options are missed and to encourage price competition. New products may require a lengthy search, and straight rebuys may involve a very limited one. During the proposal solicitation and supplier selection stage, the buying organization invites bids and assesses these according to the criteria set forth in the specifications. The lowest price usually wins, especially in the government sector, but such considerations as a reputation for quality and reliability may enter as well.

When a supplier has been selected, the buying organization negotiates the final terms of the agreement, called order routine specifications. Some fine-tuning may occur, now that a particular supplier has been chosen. During the purchase and use of product stage, the buyer signs the contract, takes the delivery, and begins to evaluate whether the product does the job as anticipated. At this point, follow-through by the seller is critical to resolve any problems that may arise. The final step is performance review and feedback. After making a formal analysis, the buyer lets the supplier know how well the product meets the needs of the organization.

As the buying organization moves through this process repeatedly, creeping commitment may occur. If there is consistent satisfaction with a seller's products, the two parties may begin to build a lasting relationship. In that case, the buying process becomes simpler for both organizations, as modified or straight rebuys are more likely.

RELATIONSHIPS BETWEEN BUYERS AND SELLERS

As in the case of consumers, business marketing relies on connecting through customer relationships. These relationships are built up in phases as the buying and selling organizations learn to work together. A seller that understands the buyer's strategies, problems, and opportunities can help the company be more competitive in its own markets. Authors Don Peppers and Martha Rogers describe a business that treats and interacts with customers individually as a one-to-one enterprise. They say building this type of relationship takes time and effort. Repeated interactions with buyers provide a company with feedback that enables it, over time, to learn how to meet customer preferences even better.[15]

Many business marketers focus on building relationships. Hallmark, known for its excellence in relationship marketing, maintains a Business Solutions program to help companies connect more personally with business customers. Hallmark researchers have worked with clients as large as NASA, the New York Yankees, and State Farm Insurance to identify their marketing goals and then design customized cards with the organization's logo and unique characteristics. These can then be used to mark different events, show appreciation, or simply enhance a growing business relationship.[16]

Relationships in business do not occur overnight. It may take weeks, months, or even years for the companies to understand and trust each other. The typical sequence is the courtship phase, the relationship-building phase, and the partnership phase. Figure 8.8 illustrates these steps. For example, the UPS World Wide Logistics (WWL) group supplies warehousing and shipping services. Usually, a customer begins by purchasing only a few services. As the business comes to realize that WWL services can help satisfy its customers in many ways, more are purchased. Over time it is not unusual for WWL to supply all of a customer's warehousing and transportation needs. WWL's high-technology information systems are not the only reason; WWL works to understand each customer's business thoroughly. This means that strategies and plans must be shared freely, and the client must trust WWL to keep them confidential. In many cases, WWL even helps customers develop the strategies and plans.

The Courtship Phase During courtship, purchasers express their desires to sellers, which develop proposals designed to satisfy the buyers' needs. This phase often begins when a company is placed on the buyer's approved supplier list, which means it meets at least minimum standards. The criteria usually include financial health, size, licensing qualification, and delivery capabilities.

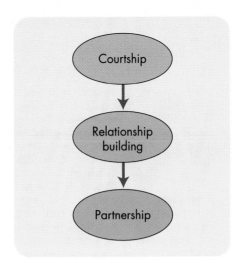

FIGURE 8.8 *Building Business-to-Business Partnerships*

Because quality has become so important, suppliers are often required to demonstrate quality control methods and records as a prerequisite to being approved. Each of the Big Three automakers used to have its own set of standards, but these have been replaced with QS-9000, which specifies requirements to prevent product defects. Uniform criteria for the auto industry simplify compliance for suppliers yet assure quality components.[17]

Unlike many people, businesses tend to look before they leap. Often courtship takes a good deal of time. Each company is trying to understand the other's requirements, so there are many discussions about product specifications, product design, and order routines. Eventually, the social distance begins to narrow. Often the buyer will grant the supplier a small order to test the waters, including the response to any problems that occur.

The Relationship-Building Phase   The buyers and sellers work together for the first time in the relationship-building phase, which strengthens the bond between them. Unlike consumer marketing, business-to-business marketing tends to involve customizing the product, its delivery, and its terms and conditions to each individual buyer. Buyers often grow to rely on suppliers for additional expertise, especially regarding new technologies. That is why trust, loyalty, and compromise become so important in organizational buying activities.

Due to the complexity and technical nature of most organizational purchasing, buyers and sellers must learn to work together. Each party may even adjust its internal practices to better satisfy the other's needs. Understanding the customer—and its customers—is critical. Promotions.com's revenues have been greatly increasing due to its understanding of its customers. The World Wide Wrestling Federation (WWF), for example, outsources its sweepstakes to Promotions.com because the company is successful in increasing traffic to the WWF Web site, facilitating the sign-up process for sweepstakes, and has also increased the site's content.[18]

During the relationship-building phase, the purchasing organization does not always have the upper hand. In fact, the relationship is sometimes said to be symmetrical—that is, the buyer and the seller may have equal power.[19] Both frequently feel a very strong need to interact in order to explore all options before signing a contract. This is particularly the case if a formal partnership is being considered. Sellers generally offer information to help buyers formulate ideas about the purchase decision. Buyers provide information that helps the sellers do a better job of matching products to needs.

Many suppliers expand their business efforts to build stronger relationships. Dell once manufactured only computer hardware but now provides an array of customized Internet products and services to help companies develop a profitable e-business. Its Dell E Works wins customers by asking them what Internet services they need, then customizing entire Internet infrastructures to meet those needs. Because of these strengthened business relationships, Dell's e-business consulting and service revenues approached $1.8 billion in 1999.[20]

In many cases, computerized order entry systems are developed to link the buyer with the seller's manufacturing facilities. Nearly all Kmart suppliers have such a link. Known as the Co-Managed Inventory Program, or CMI, Kmart's order entry system allows its suppliers to monitor its inventory and replenish its stock without prior approval from Kmart. Through this close relationship with its suppliers, Kmart can keep costs down and speed product distribution to avoid lost sales.[21]

CONNECTED: SURFING THE NET

www.kmart.com

Learn more about Kmart's relationships with its suppliers by exploring its Web site. Read the latest headlines, find out more about Kmart celebrities, or window shop in a virtual Kmart.

CONNECTING THROUGH RELATIONSHIPS

CDW PROVES THAT CUSTOMER SATISFACTION EQUALS SUCCESS

Building relationships between buyers and sellers is critical in business-to-business marketing. One savvy company found that customer relationships are profitable to the tune of a whopping 58 percent increase in sales. Perhaps it is this online and catalog company's intimate beginning, however, that has ensured its success.

CDW (Computer Discount Warehouse) began in 1982 when Chairman and CEO Michael P. Krasney put a $3 classified ad in the *Chicago Tribune* to sell his personal computer. When the calls kept coming long after he had sold the machine, he realized the need for a computer business and began selling directly to customers. He soon had so many customers that he began employing technicians. His home-based business has since developed into a billion-dollar company, providing customized computer products, software, accessories, and computing solutions for businesses, the government, and educational institutions throughout the country.

CDW has much to be proud of—its net income, net sales, and Direct Web sales have all greatly increased. It was a finalist for the 2000 Better Business Bureau National Torch Award for Marketplace Ethics, has been named one of the "100 Fastest-Growing Companies in America" by *Fortune* magazine, and in 1999 was ranked 560 on the *Fortune* 1000 list. However, these gains only point in one direction for company leaders, as Krasney states. "The CDW philosophy of creating a coworker-first environment and recognizing the customer as our ultimate employer leads to excellent customer service that creates repeat sales. Our financial success is proof that our commitment to making our customers' day easier continues to make a difference."

CDW calls its focus on customer satisfaction its "clicks and people" strategy and believes that it is the key to its overall mission. Though a leading source of technology products and services for large companies such as Compaq, Hewlett-Packard, IBM, and Microsoft, CDW strives to treat each of its customers in an individual manner. Its CDW@ work Web site program is customized for each customer and is a model for businesses seeking to combine e-business with one-on-one customer relationships.

Recently, CDW offered a seminar focusing on technology innovations for small- and medium-sized businesses. By bringing together experts from Compaq, Microsoft, Cisco, and IDC, the seminar follows the company's mission to make itself a better provider of computer solutions and demonstrates dedication to its customers.

Each company that works with CDW has its own account manager who works with that company and understands its own particular needs. In addition, though much of the company's work is done via the Internet, CDW does not attempt to fully automate the sales process. Believing that customers still want to be satisfied with their service, the company continues to hire sales account managers while Internet sales continue to increase. When phone calls are heavy, it is even common for the CEO to step out of his office and help answer queries. New coworkers at CDW are trained at CDW University, where they learn Krasney's vision of ensuring customer satisfaction. Coworkers are even viewed as part of the satisfaction project because the company believes that happy coworkers lead to happy customers. For example, employees are called coworkers rather than employees. They receive free breakfast on Tuesdays and Thursdays, and have fitness and child care centers at CDW's Vernon Hills, Illinois base.

Of the company's beginnings, Krasney says, "When people would call on the phone, I was excited to talk to them about the machine. I think that's what they enjoyed, and that's what won them over." Apparently, his excitement is still winning them over.

Sources: "CDW in Top Five on Catalog Age 100 List," *PR Newswire,* August 7, 2000; "CDW Computer Centers, Inc. Reports 76 Percent Growth in EPS, 58 Percent Growth in Sales," *PR Newswire,* July 24, 2000; "CDW Named a Finalist for National Better Business Bureau Award for Outstanding Marketplace Ethics," *PR Newswire,* August 8, 2000; "CDW Named to *Fortune* List of 100 Fastest-Growing Companies," *PR Newswire,* August 22, 2000; "CDW Brings Compaq, Microsoft, Cisco and IDC Together to Launch Customer Technology Seminar Series," *PR Newswire,* June 19, 2000; Nick Turner, "Computer Retailer Michael Krasney—He Keeps the Human Touch While Selling High Tech," *Investor's Business Daily,* April 20, 2000; and www.cdw.com, site visited August 27, 2000.

The Partnership Phase   After numerous purchases have been completed satisfactorily and long-term agreements are reached, the partnership phase begins. Because the buyer and seller have extensive experience with each other, they spend less time on the relationship itself and more time on ways to improve the productive aspects of the exchange. The buying process becomes routine. The seller may become an exclusive supplier or blanket orders may guarantee that the buyer will purchase a certain amount within a certain period.

The seller can commit resources to the buyer because the business relationship will continue. Chrysler, for example, gets 70 percent of the value of its vehicles from its regular suppliers. Jeffrey Trimmer, director of operations and strategy, says that the company's challenge is how to continue with its suppliers while using the Internet to facilitate that relationship and to identify and foster technology developments.[22] Another terrific example of connecting with customers can be seen in the relationship feature, "CDW Proves That Customer Satisfaction Equals Success."

career tip   Michael P. Krasney, chairman and CEO of CDW, says the company hires individuals with a zeal for selling computers and satisfying customers. Though the company began with only one person, he attributes its success to the coworkers. Therefore, he looks for people "who have the same goal, the same passion. I need to be able to see that gleam in their eyes." However, according to Krasney, "There's a difference between a gleam in the eye and a hunger in the pocketbook," and so those looking only for employment need not apply. The company's Web site summarizes its qualifications for potential co-workers in the statement: "If you're a high-energy person who's passionate about technology, there's a place for you at CDW."

Partnerships can be informal or contractual. Informally, each party may work without any guarantee of long-term business. Usually, the benefits are such that the relationship is likely to last. A good example is an advertising agency and its client. Both invest a lot of time and energy and share important information, so it's costly for either party to end the relationship.

A contractual partnership is formed when the buyer signs an agreement with a supplier for a specified period, usually three to five years. The trend in purchasing today is toward fewer

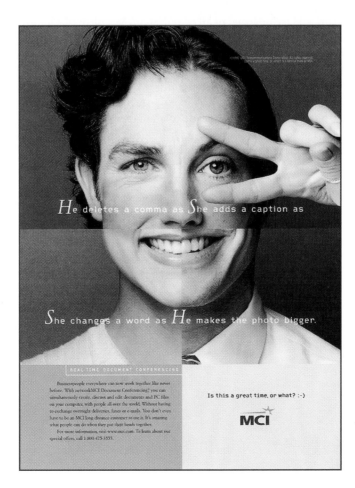

MCI expanded its business efforts to provide a number of additional services, such as real-time document conferencing.

suppliers, the use of programs that certify the qualifications of suppliers, and long-term contracts. Close relationships with suppliers help ensure quality. Many buying organizations find that contractual partnerships have considerable advantages. The long-term relationship with suppliers allows the buying organization to concentrate energy on its customers. The buyer and supplier work as a team, each contributing its own expertise to provide products that better meet consumer needs. The longer the relationship, the better are the results in terms of cooperation, efficiency, quality control, and profits. Contractual partnerships were a major part of Ford's campaign to improve quality and enhance its competitive position in global automobile markets.

Many suppliers also find contractual partnerships advantageous, but there are risks. The organizations often share highly secret market and technological information as well as sensitive strategic marketing plans. Contracts safeguard a supplier against an unethical buyer that might reveal those secrets to the supplier's competitors in an attempt to receive price reductions. When this occurs, most strong suppliers will refuse to market their newest technology to unethical buyers or in some cases refuse to sell to them altogether. Partnerships can have other hazards. Strong relationships mean greater dependence. If one partner experiences downsizing, strikes, or financial failure, then the other party feels the consequences.

Sometimes the partnership phase results in strategic alliances, including joint R&D, licensing agreements, joint ventures, and others. Consider the 10-year deal between Amazon.com and Toys "R" Us, which will open one co-branded toy and video game store and one baby products store. Toys "R" Us will handle inventory while Amazon.com will handle site development, orders, and customer service.[23]

Typically, alliances are formed because each company can offer something of value to the other. Suppose a Frito-Lay supplier has an idea for making chips stay fresh longer but lacks the money to conduct the necessary research. A joint R&D project might benefit both organizations. US West has made a regional agreement with 13 local carriers to share phone lines. In this first multicompany agreement covering an entire region, consumers in 14 states will have access to high-speed Internet and broadband services through shared phone lines for simultaneous transmission of voice and data.[24]

Ethics and Business Relationships   Unethical decisions can have a destructive effect on business relationships. Purchasing agents are often very familiar with the trade secrets, production plans, and technologies of an organization. Misuse of this information has both ethical and legal implications. Consider the legal battle between General Motors and Volkswagen, which began when GM's purchasing chief of North American Operations, José Ignacio López, suddenly moved to Europe's biggest automaker in 1993. López was accused of stealing thousands of pages of documents and computer diskettes from GM. The dispute was resolved when VW agreed to pay GM a $100 million settlement and to purchase $1 billion in parts over seven years.[25]

Turning over trade secrets to a competitor is a serious breech of ethics with numerous repercussions. For example, many industry experts did not expect GM's lawsuit to go to trial because negative publicity was likely to damage the two companies.[26] The image of both the

_Partnerships often result in
strategic alliances such as
the 10-year deal between
Amazon.com and Toys "R" Us._

company and its individual executives may be tarnished. Legal disputes consume large amounts of money as well as management's time and energy. A long-running dispute also can hinder normal business practices and competitive relationships between the companies involved. An individual who steals and betrays company information may face serious criminal charges. Although López was not charged in GM's civil suit, VW agreed not to use his services until 2000, by which time, it was speculated, he would either be exonerated or found guilty.[27]

FUNCTIONS INVOLVED IN BUSINESS PURCHASES

Many employees are important to the purchasing process. Because of their different functions, they do not have the same motives for purchasing and do not use the same criteria. This section highlights those who are most often involved in organizational buying: purchasing agents, functional managers, and the buying center.

Laterally, people at about the same level of management but from different functional areas (such as purchasing, engineering, production, sales, and marketing) may take part in a purchasing decision. Although their status is roughly similar, their influence on a particular purchase can vary considerably. Imagine that several vice presidents meet to select a strategic marketing consultant. Comments by the vice presidents of manufacturing and purchasing are certainly valuable, but the vice president of marketing probably will have the most influence on the final decision.

Vertically, people at different management levels within one functional area may participate in a buying decision. For example, the need for a new piece of equipment may be pointed out by a production floor worker to the foreman, who relays this to the production manager. The production manager seeks approval from the plant manager. If the purchase is costly, then the vice president of manufacturing or even the company president might be involved. If not, then the production engineer may have authority to approve the purchase.

Purchasing Agents   Purchasing agents are hired to help the organization buy a broad range of products most effectively. They establish and enforce policies and procedures that help maintain consistent purchase arrangements with all suppliers. Often they make the initial contact with sellers. They interact with many suppliers and gain a good deal of experience in negotiations. Through training programs, purchasing agents can learn how to obtain the best delivery schedules, prices, and financing, while still meeting product specifications.

Purchasing agents are extremely important executives in some major corporations. In others, they simply process procurement requests. This function has received more attention in recent years, partly because of restricted supply in some industries and a greater general recognition of the cost savings from effective purchasing. College programs emphasizing the buying function have been developed, and graduates with this specialized education are finding increasing opportunities in global purchasing.

Most of us don't think of educational institutions as big spenders, but primary schools, secondary schools, and public universities write an estimated 25 million purchase orders for $115 billion in goods and services annually.[28] In fiscal year 1999–2000, Indiana University processed nearly 29,000 purchase orders and bought $51 million in goods and services.[29] Faculty and staff convey their needs through purchase orders, which are then often processed by purchasing agents.

Functional Managers   Functional managers have a position in a specific operational area of the buying organization. At one time or another in their career, most will be involved in negotiations to buy equipment or supplies. Typically, they come from the following areas:

- *Administration (including accounting and finance).* Help evaluate the cost effectiveness of projects.
- *Design engineering.* Buy equipment and material for products the company is marketing.
- *Research and development.* Look at basic materials and supplies rather than specific applications.
- *Manufacturing.* Often responsible for production equipment and processing approaches.
- *Technical specialists.* Advise others regarding the best brands and suppliers for a particular product type.

The Buying Center   A group of people in the organization who make a purchase decision are said to form the **buying center.** These people may play one of six important roles: gatekeeper, information seeker, advocate, linking pin, decision maker, or user. It's important to note that buying center membership changes, depending on the type of purchase being

BUYING CENTER
The group of people from the buying organization who make a purchase decision.

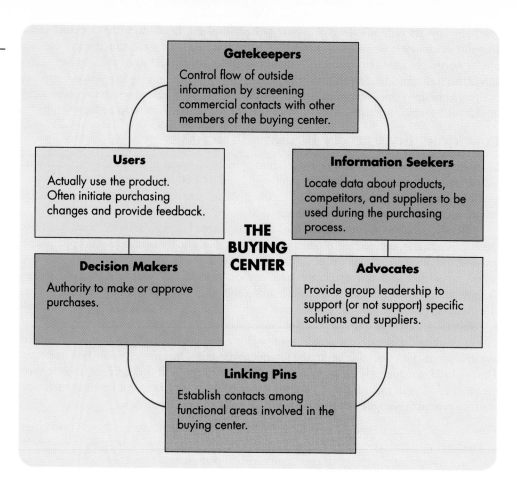

FIGURE 8.9 *The Buying Center Roles*

considered. Often the selling organization that wins the order is the one that has made contact with each of the buying influencers. Figure 8.9 depicts the buying center roles.

Gatekeepers A **gatekeeper** controls the flow of commercial (outside) information into the buying organization. Purchasing agents have been referred to as gatekeepers because they are often the first people that sales representatives contact. They are responsible for screening all potential sellers and allowing only the most qualified to gain access to key decision makers. When the purchasing department is very small and unusual or complicated products are being purchased (such as high-tech parts), the gatekeeper may be a specialist outside the purchasing area. For example, the head of engineering may recommend that only suppliers with which the company has a working relationship should be contacted for engineering consulting services. General Motors uses this approach to control purchases of computer hardware. Because of GM's size, hundreds of selling organizations attempt to market mini- and personal computers to the company. To assure the compatibility of the internal communications system and to obtain the best pricing and delivery terms, GM has its computer experts screen out unwanted vendors. When a department plans to buy computer hardware, it usually calls the gatekeeper to ask which suppliers to contact.

Clearly, a skilled salesperson is one who succeeds in working around and through the gatekeeper. Generally, gatekeepers understand the roles played by various people in the organization. When they are cooperative, they can direct salespeople to the appropriate decision maker.

Information Seekers A great deal of information about products, competitors, and suppliers is required for major purchases. **Information seekers** locate data that they or others can use during the purchasing process. Often the purchasing department is responsible for obtaining lists of firms or alternative types of products, but this task can also be performed by others. Think about the fundamental changes technology has brought to business-to-business marketing. Virtually every company in the world maintains a Web site to provide information about itself. The Web can satisfy some of an information seeker's needs in only seconds.

The role of information seeking differs from that of gatekeeper. The former looks for sources of information, whereas the latter tends to reject sources of information and limits the number of people and companies allowed access to the buying firm. Naturally, marketers can make the job of the information seeker easier by clearly presenting relevant product data in an accessible way.

GATEKEEPER

A person within the buying center who controls the flow of commercial (outside) information into the buying organization by screening all potential sellers and allowing only the most qualified to have access to decision makers.

INFORMATION SEEKER

A person within the buying center who locates data that can be used during the purchasing process.

Advocates The **advocate** exercises a powerful influence over buying center decisions. Advocates participate the most in group discussions, have high status, and play a leadership role. They often obtain their power from the amount of interaction they have with outside organizations and from their expertise on particular topics. Advocates sometimes use their position to inhibit the communications (or recommendations) of less powerful people in the organization. Thus, they may support one seller's offering while restricting the influence of competitors' presentations. Consequently, sellers often seek high-status, knowledgeable, and articulate people within the buying organization to help promote their products. If salespeople are to succeed, then one or more advocates must take their side during purchase deliberations.

Linking Pins Contact among the functional areas involved in a buying center is provided by **linking pins.** They are particularly important to marketers of products that affect several parts of the buying company, such as electronic data-processing and telecommunications equipment. Linking pins communicate with one another both formally and informally. In many cases, information from the seller to one linking pin is then spread throughout the buying organization. A cooperative linking pin makes the seller's job easier.

Users Those within the buying center who actually will use the product being purchased are **users.** In manufacturing firms, for example, they are the employees who operate or service production equipment. When components are purchased, the users assemble the parts. In hospitals and other health care facilities, users may be nurses, physicians, or the technicians who operate medical equipment. In other professional organizations, they may be programmers or technical support staff who interface with computers. There are almost as many types of users as there are job descriptions, and their influence on the purchasing process varies.

Users with a high degree of expertise may help develop product specifications. They are especially important in the last phase of the buying process, follow-through. They can provide valuable feedback to sales representatives about how well the product performs. The sophisticated salesperson seeks out such feedback, in turn providing users with information to make the product function as smoothly as possible.

Decision Makers Sometimes it is difficult for the seller to identify **decision makers,** the persons with authority to make or at least approve the purchase decision. It is also hard to determine when the decision is actually made. Often the selling organization solidifies its relationship with the buying center over time, which is called creeping commitment. The seller gradually wins enough support to obtain the order. In competitive bidding situations, the decision to purchase occurs when the envelopes are opened. In these cases, however, much depends on how the specifications are drawn up in the first place. Some salespeople work closely with the buying organization at that stage to tilt the specs and ultimate decision in their favor. Sellers also spend large amounts of money for promotional items, often unrelated to the product being sold. Companies invest billions in such business-to-business promotional giveaways as hats, key chains, coffee cups, and posters—to keep their name in front of decision makers.

In many cases the salesperson can identify exactly who will make the buying decision. In some organizations the decision maker is the purchasing agent. In most cases, however, the choice is made by a buying center or by someone who has budgetary authority and long-term experience with the product. Retail organizations often use a buying committee. Salespeople are invited to make a presentation or to supply information so that a committee member can decide.

INFLUENCES ON ORGANIZATIONAL BUYING BEHAVIOR

The buying process is seldom the same from one firm to the next, or even from one purchase to the next within a given firm. In each case, the decision-making process of the buying organization is affected by a number of factors.[30]

Background of Buying Center Members   The background of the buying center members affects the buying process. Purchasing agents, engineers, users, and others in the organization have expectations that are formed largely by their experiences. These expectations, in turn, influence the criteria used for decision making. Specialization has a great deal to do with the way people look at problems. Engineers see things differently from financial professionals. Engineers are highly trained in technical areas and are likely to judge a product accordingly. Financial managers are inclined to evaluate products on the basis of profitability.

Role orientation, which refers to the way people see themselves, is also a factor. For example, a member of the buying committee and a minor influencer in the purchase process have a different degree of involvement in the decision. Furthermore, position or rank within the

---

Sidebar:

CONNECTED: SURFING THE NET

www.ups.com

Explore the interactive features of the UPS Web site— from tracking, to quick-cost, to drop-off and pickup. You can also read about UPS services, software, news, and company information. While you're there, take a peek at its global regions.

ADVOCATE

A person within the buying center who exercises a powerful influence over group decisions.

LINKING PIN

A person within the buying center who establishes contact among functional areas formed within the buying organization.

USER

A person within the buying center who actually uses the product.

DECISION MAKER

A person within the buying center who has the authority to make or approve a purchase decision.

organization obviously can have an effect—one vice president among several lower-level managers has a stronger say in buying center decisions.

Finally, personal characteristics play a role. The lifestyles, interests, activities, and general opinions of buying center members affect the buying process.

Information Sources   Organizational buying is influenced by the sources of information—salespeople, exhibitions and trade shows, direct mail, press releases, journal advertising, professional and technical conferences, trade news, word of mouth, and others. Like direct selling, exhibitions provide one-on-one contact with a company's target audience. Although sales calls generally reach only a small number of potential customers per day, exhibitions can

CONNECTING THROUGH TECHNOLOGY

ENRONONLINE—ENERGY AND THE INTERNET'S MARKETPLACE

It's a gold rush on the World Wide Web, and the businesses most likely to get the gold are marketing their wares to other businesses. In fact, business-to-business marketers are leading the way in using new media technologies, particularly Web sites, to promote brand values, reduce paper and printing costs, attract and qualify prospects and leads, and foster customer loyalty. On the purchasing end, Web sites allow corporate buyers to advertise their needs and get the most competitive bids from suppliers. For instance, sites such as Metalsite.com and E-Steel.com allow construction companies around the world to put out their needs to the lowest bidder.

It is expected that these types of global exchangers will soon regulate the rules, standards, and technology of the exchange of many goods and services. Joel Cawley, director of corporate strategy for IBM, says that "Most of this is still happening just below the horizon, and the numbers are still relatively small, so people don't see it yet." However, he predicts that Web marketplaces will quickly assume a position in business, mediating between 30 and 40 percent of industrial e-commerce by 2004.

The most adventurous prospectors in this new terrain are larger cybermarts, such as EnronOnline.com. The world's largest energy trader has become the largest business-to-business Web site, offering a kind of free online marketplace for business buyers and sellers by providing real-time prices of natural gas, electricity, coal, plastics, pulp, paper, and oil. Within the first eight months of its creation, the site handled more than 178,000 transactions worth $84 billion.

Managing Director of EnronOnline Louise Kitchen says of the service, "Buying and selling metals through EnronOnline provides improved pricing, price risk management services and more flexible transactions for our customers. This step is a continuation in the trend of commodity markets to move to web-based trading and a natural extension of our proven business model."

Originally, President and COO Jeffrey K. Skilling said that "This Internet system complements Enron's extensive marketing capabilities and gives our counterparts the choice of transacting over the telephone or instantly through our website." However, this type of online trading has been shown to reduce time that would otherwise be spent in phone conversations. It also reduces transaction costs and provides more detailed and timely market information. Innovations such as these have earned Enron *Fortune's* title of "Most Innovative Company" for five consecutive years.

Moreover, the site has transformed the Enron company. It lost $131 million in 1999 but has earned $338 million in the first quarter of 2000 alone. Enron attributes its success partially to positive customer response to EnronOnline. In July 2000, EnronOnline was averaging $1 billion a day in transactions, frequently even reaching $2 billion a day. Gas trading on the site alone is equivalent to one-third of U.S. consumption.

EnronOnline has also expanded from its original offerings to include bandwidth, used by Internet sites in controlling traffic. CEO Kenneth Lay believes that the bandwidth market will eventually even surpass the other markets for natural gas and electricity. What was a $30 billion market in 2000, he believes, will be $90 or $100 billion by 2003.

Sources: Thomas L. Friedman, "U.S. Grabs the Lead, Global Exchanges Make Up the Rules for Industrial E-Commerce," *The Plain Dealer* (Cleveland, Ohio), January 19, 2000, p. 9B; "Enron Deals in Billions on Web Site," *Houston Chronicle* May 12, 2000; Eric Thode, "Enron Announces First Metals Transaction on EnronOnline," *PR Newswire,* July 6, 2000; "Best of the Web: Energy and Utilities," *Forbes,* July 17, 2000, p. 136; "Enron Posts 34% Jump in 1st-Quarter Profit on Soaring Revenue," *Dow Jones Business News,* April 12, 2000; "Enron Launches Global Web-Based Commodity Trading Site," *PR Newswire,* October 26, 1999; and www.enrononline.com, site visited August 27, 2000.

reach dozens more per hour. Direct marketing is also useful. Of the total spending in this category, 24 percent is used for direct mail, and 38 percent is for telephone marketing.[31]

The Internet is playing an increasing role in business-to-business marketing. Web sites enable organizations to promote brand values, reduce printing costs, attract and qualify prospects and leads, and foster customer loyalty. Sites also can expand the customer database, provide customer service, and showcase and sell products.

The interactive age is providing businesses with the potential to strengthen relationship marketing and generate new customers. The media services available today can be the key to staying ahead and maximizing profits. The reach provided by the Internet is tremendous. Learn more about it in this chapter's technology feature, "EnronOnline—Energy and the Internet's Marketplace."

Product Factors: Time and Risk   Product and company factors tend to influence the organizational buying process. **Product factors** include time pressure and perceived risk. Time pressure relates to the speed with which a purchase must be made. When more members of the buying organization are involved in the decision, more time is required to make it. Perceived risk refers to what can be lost rather than gained when making the purchase. To reduce perceived risk in e-business transactions, PricewaterhouseCoopers' beTRUSTed Internet security program provides cutting-edge security technology to ensure that World Wide Web transactions are secure. beTRUSTed is one of a number of Internet security programs whose overall business will reach an estimated $1.3 billion in 2003.[32]

Five types of uncertainty or risk aversion have been identified among buying organizations:

1. *Acceptance uncertainty*. Buyers are not sure of their need for a product.
2. *Need uncertainty*. The buying organization has not yet established product specifications.
3. *Technical uncertainty*. Buyers are unsure about the performance of a product in their own particular environment.
4. *Market uncertainty*. Buyers are unsure of the possible offerings from which they can select.
5. *Transaction uncertainty*. Buyers are unsure about the terms of the sale and product delivery.

PRODUCT FACTOR

A factor such as time or perceived risk that influences the organizational buying process.

CONNECTED: SURFING THE NET

www.3M.com

Check out 3M's worldwide operations in any industry when you visit the company Web site. Surf its image graphics or obtain information on hundreds of products.

To reduce perceived risk, 3M creates products that meet business needs.

When uncertainty is high, buyers strive to reduce perceived risk by either purchasing less or learning more. Decreasing the amount at stake means smaller orders or a reluctance to pay top prices. When much is at stake, others in the organization may be included in the purchase decision, thus spreading the personal risk.

Company Factors   Three company factors have particular influence on the purchasing process: the organization's orientation, its size, and its degree of centralization. An organization's orientation, or dominating function, is very important. Some companies are production oriented, whereas others are marketing oriented. In still others, finance or accounting controls the decisions. When marketing dominates, sales factors tend to be very important in making purchase decisions. In production-oriented organizations, production factors are most important. In finance-oriented organizations, decisions are likely to be made on the basis of cost and other financial concerns. The seller must understand the organization's orientation in order to determine the basis for purchasing decisions and which members of the buying center are most influential.

The size of the organization is also likely to influence the number of people involved in purchasing. In very small companies, the purchasing process tends to be informal. Decisions are often made by a key executive at the top. Very large organizations use a formal purchasing process, and decisions often are made by members lower in the managerial structure.

Finally, highly decentralized organizations are likely to give various departments or divisions the autonomy to make their own purchases. Nevertheless, owing to the need for accountability, even these companies have formal buying procedures that can involve red tape.

Joint Decisions and Conflict Resolution   Whenever several people are involved in decision making, there is a potential for conflict. Purchase decisions are no exception and can be affected by how conflict is handled. When it occurs, members of the buying organization negotiate with one another to arrive at a solution. These negotiations can be shaped by task or nontask motives. Task motivation refers to solving the organization's problem, whereas nontask motivation refers to the personal needs of the buying group members. Organizations usually attempt to resolve conflicts through problem solving and persuasion. The objective of this task-oriented and constructive approach is to make the best decision for the company. Nontask-oriented approaches to conflict involve bargaining and politicking. Each party is

The American Arbitration Association provides conflict resolution services.

attempting to "get its own way" without considering the organization's goals or engaging in open communication. Sellers who are sensitive to the prevailing negotiating mode can plan their approach accordingly.

Problem solving in the buying context occurs when all decision makers agree on the goals of the particular purchase. Sellers address those goals and show how their product can help meet them. This is very straightforward.

Persuasion occurs when buying center members do not agree on purchase goals, and each tries to convince the others that his or her own goals should take precedence. In the case of buying a computer, for example, the purchasing agent may consider cost most important, whereas a user may put software compatibility first. When the two discuss the merits of the various trade-offs, they are engaging in persuasion. The seller needs to understand both parties and address both sets of goals.

Bargaining occurs when people in the buying center cannot arrive at a solution. Through dialogue, one person may try to obtain his or her preferred product by agreeing that someone else can choose the supplier for a different product. The supplier needs to make sure to address all individuals who might ultimately be in a good bargaining position.

Politicking occurs when buying center members of the organization have strong ego needs. In their search for power or self-esteem, they place their own goals before those of the organization as a whole. Such people are looking for support rather than the most functional purchase choice. What usually results is a "pecking order" within the buying firm, in which an employee's influence on the purchase is proportional to his or her status in the company. The seller's claims about product superiority will go unnoticed because personalities are more important. Sellers must be very sensitive to personalities if they wish to conduct business under this circumstance.

In this chapter we have focused on how buying takes place in business markets. In chapter 9, we will look more closely at what businesses buy in a section devoted to the three categories of business products: capital products, production products, and operations products.

PROBLEM SOLVING
A task-oriented method of conflict resolution whereby all parties agree to put the organization's goals first.

PERSUASION
A task-oriented mode of handling conflicts in which persons with different goals attempt to convince the others that their goals should take precedence.

BARGAINING
A nontask-oriented mode of handling conflict in which one person obtains his or her goal by agreeing to allow the other's goal to prevail at another time.

POLITICKING
A nontask-oriented mode of handling conflict in which personal ego needs take precedence over problem solving.

CONNECTED: SURFING THE NET

CDW
www.cdw.com

THIS CHAPTER'S RELATIONSHIPS FEATURE INTRODUCED you to CDW, a reseller of computer equipment and solutions to businesses, the government, and educational institutions. To expand your understanding, visit its Web site and answer the following questions.

1. What business-to-business markets interest CDW? List the products the company sells. Give examples of likely prospects for CDW.
2. Read "Computing Solutions Built for Government & Education." What personalized services does CDW offer to educational and governmental institutions?
3. Visit "Inside CDW." How does CDW's mission help it build relationships with buyers?

ENRONONLINE
www.enrononline.com

THIS CHAPTER'S TECHNOLOGY FEATURE, "ENRONONLINE.COM—Energy and the Internet's Marketplace," discusses one of the largest online business marts. In order to learn more about it, visit its Web site and answer the following questions.

1. What tools and resources does EnronOnline.com offer? How can these assist a company in the industrial buying process?
2. Recall the five types of purchase uncertainty or risk that buying organizations may experience. How does EnronOnline.com help reduce them?
3. Would EnronOnline.com be most useful in a straight rebuy, modified rebuy, or new task situation? Could it be useful in all three? Explain.
4. After exploring the EnronOnline Web site, do you think businesses can effectively connect with one another in this format? What are the advantages and disadvantages of an online business relationship?

OBJECTIVE 1:   Describe the types of organizations and products involved in business-to-business marketing and understand the importance of this market.

A large number of companies sell most of their products to other companies, which is known as business-to-business marketing. In total volume, business-to-business marketing is much larger than consumer marketing. Types of business markets include the commercial market, extractor industries, trade industries, institutions, utilities, transportation and telecommunications, and government markets. These markets can be segmented according to company demographics, geographic scope, buying approach, and product/technology. Multiple steps bring the final product to consumers as businesses sell materials and processes to each other along the supply chain.

OBJECTIVE 2:   Understand the link between consumer demand and business-to-business marketing.

Business markets rely on derived demand to create opportunities for their products. When consumers purchase more, businesses buy more in order to produce more. The demand for business goods and services tends to be inelastic, which means that a price change does not greatly affect the types of products purchased. The accelerator principle recognizes that some business goods and services are highly sensitive to changes in consumer demand.

OBJECTIVE 3:   Describe the organizational buying process.

Organizations make purchases to support their production requirements and business needs. Buying decisions often start with the make or buy decision. Decisional situations in outsourcing include straight rebuy, modified rebuy, and new task situations. The buying process can involve as many as eight steps: problem recogni-

tion, need description, product specification, supplier search, proposal solicitation and supplier selection, order routine specification, purchase and use, and performance review and feedback. Good buyer–seller relationships are key to facilitating the process.

OBJECTIVE 4:   Know how buyer–seller relationships work, including informal and contractual partnerships.

The buyer–seller relationship between businesses develops over time, usually in three sequential phases: courtship, relationship building, and partnership. During courtship, buyers express their desires to sellers, who propose products to satisfy the purchaser's needs. In relationship building, the two parties work together for the first time, customizing the product, its delivery, and conditions. In the partnership phase, long-term agreements are reached either informally or contractually, and closer cooperation develops lasting relationships.

OBJECTIVE 5:   Learn what functions and roles within organizations influence the purchase of a broad range of products.

Different functional areas may be involved in business purchases, ranging from operational units to a purchasing department. The group of people who make a purchase decision forms the buying center. Having different backgrounds and functions in the company, they have different buying motives and use different criteria in evaluating products. Purchase decisions may be made laterally, through the interaction of people from different functional areas, or vertically, at one or more levels in the corporate hierarchy. Various buying center members play different roles: gatekeeper, information seeker, advocate, linking pin, decision maker, and user. It is important that the salesperson identify exactly who will make the purchase decision, whether the purchasing agent, a buying committee, or someone with budgetary authority.

1. What is business-to-business marketing? How does it differ from consumer marketing?
2. List the types of business-to-business markets.
3. What is the supply chain? Give an example.
4. What is derived demand? Inelastic demand? How do they apply to business markets?
5. What are two ways that globalization affects business marketing?
6. What is a make or buy decision?
7. What are three types of decisional situations in outsourcing?
8. What are the steps in the organizational buying process?
9. List the phases in buyer–seller relationships.
10. List six functions performed in the buying center.
11. What are purchasing agents? Functional managers?
12. List and explain five types of purchase uncertainty.

1. Why is business-to-business marketing larger than consumer marketing? Explain the process of business-to-business marketing.
2. The private sector is composed of several classes of organizations. List examples of these classes, along with companies in each, and explain their importance within business-to-business marketing.
3. Explain the accelerator principle and how it relates to business-to-business marketing. Give an example.
4. When making a purchase, an organization generally goes through a number of steps. Describe these and explain why some purchases require more than others.
5. Describe an informal partnership and a contractual partnership. What are the advantages and disadvantages to both buyer

and seller of each type? How does price-only purchasing come into play?
6. Why are many employees within a buying organization essential to the purchasing process? Explain the different levels of involvement in business purchases. What roles do purchasing agents and functional managers play?
7. Several roles that people play within the buying center are essential to the purchasing process. Define these and explain why they are necessary. Is one more important than the other? Which has the most influence on the purchase decision?
8. Numerous factors influence the buying process. Explain the relevance of each in purchase decisions.

Advocate: A person within the buying center who exercises a powerful influence over group decisions.

Bargaining: A nontask-oriented mode of handling conflict in which one person obtains his or her goal by agreeing to allow the other's goal to prevail at another time.

Business-to-business marketing: Marketing goods and services to other producers of goods and services.

Buying center: The group of people from the buying organization who make a purchase decision.

Commercial market: Organizations and individuals that acquire goods and services to produce other goods and services sold to an end consumer for profit.

Decision maker: A person within the buying center who has the authority to make or approve a purchase decision.

Derived demand: A demand, such as the demand for business-to-business products, which depends ultimately on the demand of end consumers.

Extractor industries: Industries that obtain and process raw materials.

Gatekeeper: A person within the buying center who controls the flow of commercial (outside) information into the buying organization by screening all potential sellers and allowing only the most qualified to have access to decision makers.

Government markets: The federal, state, and local governments in their role as purchasers of goods and services.

Inelastic demand: Demand that is influenced little by price changes.

Information seeker: A person within the buying center who locates data that can be used during the purchasing process.

Institutions: Public and private organizations that provide services to consumers.

Linking pin: A person within the buying center who establishes contact among functional areas formed within the buying organization.

Make or buy decision: The decision whether to supply products in-house or to purchase them from other businesses.

Modified rebuy: Purchase of a familiar product from an unfamiliar supplier or a new or different product from a familiar supplier.

New task situation: Purchase of an unfamiliar product from an unfamiliar supplier.

Outsourcing: Purchasing products and services from other companies.

Persuasion: A task-oriented mode of handling conflicts in which persons with different goals attempt to convince the others that their goals should take precedence.

Politicking: A nontask-oriented mode of handling conflict in which personal ego needs take precedence over problem solving.

Problem solving: A task-oriented method of conflict resolution whereby all parties agree to put the organization's goals first.

Product factor: A factor such as time or perceived risk that influences the organizational buying process.

Reseller: A company that purchases a product and sells it in the same form for profit.

Straight rebuy: A routine purchase with which the organization has considerable experience.

Supply chain: The linkage of organizations involved in the creation and delivery of a product.

Tier: The degree of contact between the supplier and the OEM.

Trade industries: Industries comprised of organizations that acquire finished products and distribute them to others.

User: A person within the buying center who actually uses the product.

Utilities: Companies that distribute gas, electricity, or water.

REFERENCES

1. ARAMARK Web site, www.aramark.com, site visited August 20, 2000.
2. Sandeep Junnarker, "B2B Investing No Certain Road to Riches," *CNET News.com*, March 2, 2000.
3. "Bureau of Land Management Presents Excellence Awards to Industry Leaders in Fluid Minerals Production," *M2 Presswire*, July 25, 2000.
4. www.envirogroup.com, site visited August 22, 2000.
5. www.apple.com, site visited August 22, 2000.
6. "Boeing to Forge 21st Century Partnership with Suppliers," September 22, 1999, www.boeing.com/news/releases/1999/news_release_990922a.html.
7. w3.access.gpo.gov/usbudget/, site visited August 22, 2000.
8. Ed McKenna, "Army Modernizes as It Digitizes," *Washington Technology*, June 19, 2000.
9. www.census.gov/foreign-trade/top/dst/1999/12/balance, site visited August 22, 2000.
10. Sheri R. Lanza, "Around the World in 80 Sites: International Business Research," *Searcher*, February 2000, p. 65.
11. www.idg.com, site visited August 22, 2000.
12. Daniel Golden, "About Advertising: IBM, i2 and Ariba Launch E-Commerce Ad Campaign," *The Wall Street Journal Europe*, August 18, 2000, p. 23.
13. "J.P. Morgan Steps Up Ads in Wake of Online Revolution," *Financial NetNews*, May 15, 2000, p. 3; and Tom Kirchofer, "Company Tries to Stand Out in Its Field," *Boston Herald*, August 24, 2000, p. 35.
14. "In Japan: Outsourcing Without a Capital 'O,'" *New York Times*, July 16, 2000, p. 4; "Flextronics Inks Agreement," *Purchasing*, July 13, 2000, p. 126; "Inside Track: Google Spins Web of Success," *Financial Times London Edition*, July 6, 2000; and John Simke, "Emerging Trends in Outsourcing," *CMA Management*, February 2000, pp. 26–27.
15. Don Peppers and Martha Rogers, "The $15,000 Rug," *Marketing Tools*, May 1997, www.marketingtools.com.
16. Mark Ingebretsen, "Brand Strength Lures Corporations," *Business Marketing*, October 1996, p. 13 and www.hallmark.com, site visited August 27, 2000.
17. "Just Exactly What Is ISO 9000?" *Buffalo News*, August 20, 2000, p. A13.
18. Erika Rasmusson, "Promotional Prowess," *Sales & Marketing Management*, July 1, 2000.
19. Hakan Hakanson and Bjorn Wootz, "A Framework of Industrial Buying and Selling," *International Marketing Management* 8 (1979): 39–49.
20. Paul McDougall, "Dell: Beyond the Box?" *Information Week*, May 22, 2000, p. 49.
21. www.kmartcorp.com/corp/business/vendor/general/cmi.stm, site visited August 23, 2000.
22. Gail Kachadourian, "DCX Relies on Supplier Innovations," *Automotive News*, June 19, 2000, p. 28.
23. "Amazon, Toysrus Team for New Online Stores," *Newsbytes News Network*, August 10, 2000; and Karin Price Mueller, "On the Market: Toys R Us Amazon Play a Good Tack," *Boston Herald*, August 20, 2000, p. 28.
24. "US West, 13 Carriers Reach Line-Sharing Accord," *Newsbytes News Network*, April 25, 2000.
25. Dow Jones News Services, "GM Confirms It Has Settled Dispute with Volkswagen," *Wall Street Journal Interactive Edition*, January 9, 1997; and Gabriella Stern, "Volkswagen to Pay GM $100M in Lopez Settlement," *Wall Street Journal Interactive Edition*, January 9, 1997.
26. Michelle Maynard, "Surprise End to Feud over Trade Secrets," *USA Today*, January 10, 1997, p. B1.

27. Ibid.
28. "Former Education Secretary Lamar Alexander Launches eCommerce Venture to Save Schools Money," *PR Newswire,* January 31, 2000.
29. www.indiana.edu/~purchase/, site visited August 26, 2000.
30. Jagdish N. Sheth, "A Model of Industrial Buyer Behavior," *Journal of Marketing* 37 (October 1973): 50–58.
31. "1999 Direct Marketing Media Spending," *Business Marketing,* January 18, 2000.
32. www.betrusted.com, site visited August 27, 2000 and "Pricewaterhouse Coopers to Go into Online Security," *Newsbytes News Network,* April 20, 2000.

Bricks or Clicks

BUSINESS-TO-BUSINESS MARKETING

THE INTERNET IS HAVING DRAMATIC effects on business-to-business markets, and one industry in particular may see huge changes. Major companies in the automotive industry have partnered to set up Covisint, the world's largest business-to-business online trading site. Originally General Motors and Ford set up their own sites to deal with their suppliers. However, major suppliers found it difficult to work with different sites and threatened to set up their own exchanges. In response, auto manufacturers cooperated to develop Covisint. This site connects the automakers with their suppliers in many unique ways.

Company component buyers can purchase parts online at the site. They can ask for bids from suppliers on various products, use the community catalogs put online by suppliers, or construct their own custom parts and services lists that suppliers can look at. In addition, buyers and sellers can auction off items, such as old equipment.

Additionally, manufacturers can work with their suppliers online, simultaneously viewing the same computer image on Covisint's 3-D imaging program. This service allows the companies to make changes in auto components in a more timely and efficient manner.

These services improve efficiencies in designing and in building vehicles. The savings of time and money will benefit automakers, suppliers, and consumers. This exchange is expected to have about $300 billion in purchasing power, making it by far the largest online exchange site. Covisint itself will be able to generate revenue by charging fees that range from $25 to $100 per sale.

Covisint offers tremendous benefits for all involved parties, but there are challenges. There are concerns about the increased buying power of the automakers, which could cut into the ability of suppliers to make profits. Covisint received close scrutiny from the Federal Trade Commission (FTC) to ensure that the combined purchasing power would not be anticompetitive for suppliers. FTC approval was granted in September 2000, but with a note of caution: Antitrust issues may still be raised, depending on how Covisint conducts business. Covisint has temporary headquarters in Southfield, Michigan, and expects to establish offices in Europe and Asia.

Sources: Associated Press Newswires, "Auto Industry Internet Exchange: Covisint Can Begin Business," *Business News; State and Regional,* September 26, 2000; Ralph Kisiel, "Covisint Dreams Up Tools, Treats for Its Customers," *Crain News Service,* October 9, 2000, p. 11; PR Newswire Association, Inc., "Automotive Trade Exchange to Be Called Covisint," May 16, 2000; Jeffrey McCracken, "Detroit's Proposed Joint Automotive Effort May Alter Carmaking, Commerce," *Detroit Free Press,* May 22, 2000, p. 3; "E-Marketplace: Covisint," *Business Week,* June 5, 2000, p. 6B; and "Covisint Receives Bundeskartellamt Clearance; Automotive Business-to-Business Exchange to Launch Within 30 days" *Business Wire,* September 26, 2000.

CASE 8

Accenture

As of January 1, 2001, Andersen Consulting became known as Accenture. With 1999 revenues of $8.94 billion, Accenture is positioning itself to be the leading organization in the knowledge of intellectual capital, believing this will be the business currency of the 21st century. Accenture differentiates itself from other consulting firms with a service model known as *business integration.* It looks at the client as a total enterprise and attempts to align the client's technology, people, and processes with an overall business strategy.

Management consulting is well over a $20 billion industry that has grown by more than 10 percent annually for almost a decade. To serve this industry, Accenture employs more than 65,000 employees globally. It serves more than 85 of the *Fortune* 100 largest global companies and many of the world's leading governments. That means that Accenture is larger than many of its major clients and one of the largest business-to-business professional organizations in the world.

The "Accenture Way" is to educate and train people to work in teams using very unified approaches. As consultants move from client to client, they execute projects from the same fundamental knowledge platform. This requires spending approximately 6.5 percent of the company's annual revenue on employee education and development. In addition, nearly $50 million a year is spent on R&D to develop knowledge capital.

Knowledge is developed by learning what works in the field and applying it to new challenges. Accenture's information system collects in one centralized location nearly all the project descriptions and reports produced for clients. In this way, teams can tap into what has been done before they work on new projects. Information is applied from client to client, industry to industry, and globally. This is believed to be one of the keys to Accenture's strength.

Consulting can also be specialized, however, so that even a complex organization such as Accenture must form joint ventures with others, in some cases competitors, to satisfy a large client's needs. One alliance was put together by a major customer, J. P. Morgan. Accenture provides applications development, AT&T Solutions does network management, and Bell Atlantic Network Integration is responsible for desktop computing. Called the Pinnacle Alliance, it is an example of a new trend in team outsourcing by many corporations. In another case, DuPont formed an information technology partnership with Accenture and Computer Sciences Corporation. The DuPont contract with Accenture to handle all its data processing is worth $4 billion. Currently, Accenture is working to create a technology services joint venture with Microsoft.

In March 2000, Accenture and Microsoft agreed to a $1 billion alliance. The venture, Avenade, supports Microsoft's desire to establish Windows 2000 as the number-one corporate operating platform. Microsoft will benefit from Accenture's numerous top business contacts and customers.

In April 2000, Accenture and Sun Microsystems announced a joint venture to help companies obtain office supplies, furniture, airline tickets, and computer equipment online. The venture plans to purchase $300 million of hardware from Sun and software from iPlanet E-Commerce Solutions. IPlanet is an alliance between Sun and Netscape Communications, now part of America Online. The venture will be staffed by employees from Accenture, Sun, and iPlanet. The "eProcurement" venture, still unnamed, will help customers cut purchasing costs by as much as 50 percent on certain goods by using the Internet to locate buyers. The venture has garnered $20 billion in letters of intent from 10 U.S. and European companies, which will pay a transaction fee to use the venture's services.

In October 2000, Accenture Ventures, the venture capital unit of Accenture, announced with Softbank Venture Capital that they will invest $50 million each in a network of incubator operations to be known as GameChange. The plan is to open 10 GameChange incubator centers in the United States and Europe during the next two years and create 10 to 20 companies a year at each center. The centers will offer entrepreneurs a place to work as well as advice about recruiting, marketing, public relations, Web design, and accounting. The first was opened on October 4, 2000 at Accenture Ventures' Palo Alto headquarters. GameChange will invest $1 million to $2 million each in individual companies.

To take advantage of the technology trend, Accenture is changing the way it works for and with some clients. Accenture has created a new venture that is focused on expanding the work it does with Internet start-ups and the work it does globally. Within the next three years, Accenture plans to accept stock instead of cash as exchange for consulting services. The organization's hope is that the stock will grow to be worth more than the cash it would receive. Accenture hopes to provide global expansion consulting for Internet companies. To achieve this, Accenture is opening 17 new offices throughout Europe, Asia, the United States, Africa, and South America.

1. *What types of business markets does Accenture serve? How is its business integration approach used to serve these markets?*
2. *Once Accenture has identified a potential client, how do you think the organization goes about developing relationships with key buying influences within the organization?*
3. *What trends are influencing the way Accenture conducts its business? How can Accenture use its knowledge base to predict trends, prepare itself for them, and take advantage of them? What do you think some future trends may be that Accenture needs to watch for?*
4. *What types of issues could be addressed using Accenture's Da Vinci virtual reality simulation?*

Sources: David Whitford, "Arthur, Arthur . . . ," *Fortune,* November 10, 1997, www.fortune.com; Esther Shien, "Outsourcing, Team Style," *PC Week,* November 3, 1997, pp. 84–85; Ann Marsh, "Business Services and Supplies," *Forbes,* January 13, 1997, www.forbes.com; Joanna Glasner, "Andersen Consulting for Stock," *Wired News,* February 9, 2000; Hoover's Online, "Andersen Consulting," www.hooversonline.com, visited June 18, 2000; "Andersen Consulting 1999 Annual Report/Financial Highlights," www.ac.com Web site visited on October 21, 2000; Louise Kehoe, "Microsoft and Andersen Consulting Partner Up in Venture," *Financial Times,* March 13, 2000; "Andersen Consulting, Sun Plan a Venture for Online Supplies," *Wall Street Journal,* April 26, 2000; "Andersen Consulting, Softbank Units to Invest in Incubator Network," *Wall Street Journal,* October 5, 2000; Jon Ashworth, "Andersen Consulting Poised for Split," *The Times of London,* October 14, 2000.

chapter 9

PRODUCT
DECISIONS
AND STRATEGIES

1. Describe the major dimensions used by marketers to differentiate their products from competitors. Understand bundling and unbundling.

2. Understand consumer and business product classifications based on how and why products are purchased and consumed.

3. Know how organizations make product line decisions that determine what will be sold, including the degree of standardization chosen for global markets.

4. Recognize that branding and brand strategies are important aspects of building and maintaining a brand name.

5. Know how to create brand equity — the value associated with a product's name.

6. Discuss the many legal and ethical issues surrounding brand and packaging decisions.

◄ *David Filo and Jerry Young, Yahoo! founders*

FEW INTERNET BRANDS ARE AS RECOGNIZABLE or as lively as Yahoo! Founded by Stanford Ph.D. students David Filo and Jerry Yang, Yahoo! began as a categorized directory of favorite Internet sites. As the directory grew and Web enthusiasts flocked to the site, the two took the next step and formed a corporation they called Yahoo! (the acronym for "yet another hierarchical officious oracle"). Although Filo and Yang wanted to stay active in the technology end, they didn't want to run day-to-day operations, so they tapped the high-tech management expertise of Tim Koogle, who became CEO of Yahoo! in 1995.

Originally, the Yahoo! product line consisted of a categorized directory of Web sites and a search engine for locating sites using specific search terms. The company made money by selling banner and button ads on its pages, so its profitability depended on bringing Web surfers back again and again. While competitors such as Lycos were busy perfecting the next generation of online search technology, Yahoo! followed its mission statement—"to be all things to all people"—and evolved into a one-stop Internet destination with broader product depth and breadth.

Yahoo! arranged to use another firm's search technology—an unusual decision, considering the company's roots—and began adding dozens of useful consumer and business products to its home page. Now users could visit Yahoo! and get one-click access to telephone directories and maps, free Web-page hosting, shopping, auctions, real estate listings, travel services, classified ads, business promotion consulting, group e-mail, and more. The company also began presenting localized content and links through Yahoo! sites for major U.S. cities and country-specific sites for Japan, Sweden, and other nations.

Yahoo!'s extensive customization capabilities have contributed to its ability to attract users and reinforce brand loyalty. With the My Yahoo! option, for example, users can create personalized pages with layout and content tailored to their individual needs and interests. A commuter might set up a My Yahoo! page with traffic reports, news headlines, and weather reports at the top and movie listings and sports scores lower on the page—but no stock quotes or other information that the commuter doesn't need. To make Yahoo! even more valuable and encourage additional visits, users can sign up for a free Yahoo! e-mail address, store their address books and calendars on Yahoo!, send and receive money through Yahoo!, and join online chats with other Yahoo! users—all with a few clicks of the mouse.

By incorporating the Yahoo! family brand into every offering and giving the brand prominent play at every opportunity, the company reinforces brand associations and supports brand equity—a top priority since the early days. "The brand is about being fun, unexpected, and our efforts reinforce that message," comments Luanne Calvert, who holds the official title of buzz marketer at Yahoo! The message starts with the visual look of the brand name: Colorful letters and a bold exclamation point reflect the fun and excitement of the Web world. Yahoo! sends more messages to its target market through irreverent advertising and connections with Ben & Jerry's ice cream, Samuel Adams beer, and other popular consumer brands. "We tried to do as many things as we could to put a human face on this otherwise virtual brand," says Karen Edwards, vice president of brand marketing. "We planted the seeds among people who were curious about the Net

THE CONCEPT OF PRODUCTS

PRODUCT

Any physical object, service, idea, person, event, place, or organization offered to satisfy consumers' needs and wants.

CONNECTED: SURFING THE NET

www.gm.com

At the General Motors' Web site you can select a car, locate a dealer, choose a finance plan, meet the family, discover new terrain, and invest in the company—all in one place! Get connected to learn more.

Product decisions and strategies are challenging and exciting. They affect nearly every aspect of the business and are major factors in connecting with customers. This chapter defines products and how they are managed from a marketer's perspective. The next chapter addresses new-product development, and chapter 11 focuses on services, which are a special case. A **product** is any physical object, service, idea, person, event, place, or organization that can be offered to satisfy consumers' needs and wants. Products can be aggregated into packages that perform important functions for individuals, families, or organizations. In the broadest sense, anything that is purchased or sold can be considered a product. Corn, cornflakes, and Kellogg's Corn Flakes are all products. A silicon chip, a transistor, and a computer are all products. A movie, a baseball game, and airplane travel are also products. For many people, the term *product* refers to a tangible item but may be actually services, a special category of products. Services represent more than 80 percent of U.S. GDP, and nearly 75 percent of the U.S.

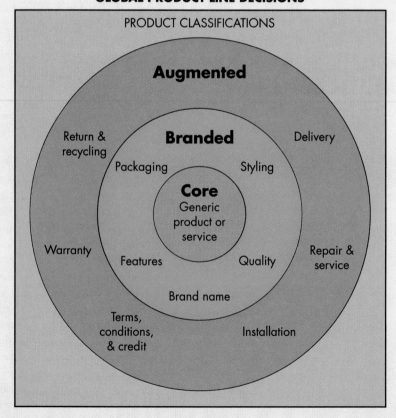

FIGURE 9.1 *Concept of a Product*

workforce is employed in service industries, such as restaurants, lodging, health care, and law. Over 60 percent of the economy of all developed nations is involved in service industries.[2]

Figure 9.1 presents the topics covered in this chapter. First we explore the three dimensions of a product. Then we turn our attention to product classifications and global product line decisions. We will then take a look at branding, packaging, and labeling. The chapter concludes with a discussion of ethical issues surrounding product safety and liability.

PRODUCT DIMENSIONS

Most marketing experts describe products in terms of three dimensions: core, branded, and augmented.

CORE PRODUCTS

A **core product** is the physical item or intangible service that the customer receives. It refers to functions and benefits at the most basic level. A core product can be a tennis racket, a subcompact automobile, a bowling center, a life insurance policy, or a physical examination. The core product is the essential item or service purchased and does not include the brand name, styling features, packaging, or any other descriptive aspects.

A core product is often called the *generic product*, which means it conforms to the basic description that specifies the function it performs. A bicycle has two wheels and can function as a mode of transportation. Although mountain bikes have specifications different from touring bikes and racing bikes, all of them perform the generic function of transportation. One of the most common examples is generic pharmaceuticals, which are drugs sold without reference to a particular manufacturer. Usually the company that discovers or invents a drug will patent and then brand it. Once the patent expires, other companies can simply copy the pharmacological formula and sell it as a generic drug. It usually costs much less than the branded drug since its price doesn't have to reflect the research or marketing costs associated with developing and introducing new drugs.

<u>CORE PRODUCT</u>
The essential physical item or intangible service that the customer receives.

MAKE YOUR MARK

VIRTUALLY ANYWHERE. To produce, your brand needs a whole new approach to custom-branded merchandise. HALO Branded Solutions,™ the world's premier branded merchandise company, combines 28 years of expertise with leading-edge Internet technology and innovation. We provide branded solutions to make your mark on almost anything, in almost no time.

Explore your branding possibilities today. CLICK @ www.halo.com OR CALL @ 888.611.HALO

HALO Industries, Inc. provides solutions for branded products.

BRANDED PRODUCTS

BRANDED PRODUCT

The core product plus the characteristics that allow the consumer to differentiate it from similar products.

A **branded product** is the core product plus the characteristics that allow the consumer to differentiate it from similar products. Most important is the brand name, although styling, quality, features, and packaging are additional ways to distinguish brands. The branded product also can be called the *identified product,* for branding confers an identity on products just as a rancher's brand identifies a herd. Most branded products not only carry the value of the core product but also have a distinctiveness that allows consumers to recognize them and recall their experiences with them. Nearly every teenager recognizes the name Nike. In a 1999 national survey of teenagers, Nike was ranked the "coolest" product brand. Since Teenage Research Unlimited estimates that the teenage market spends around $140 billion a year, marketers seek to establish a "hip" image for their products.[3]

Some branded products are identified purely by the need for the function they perform, such as Morton's salt. Others may be identified through styling. For example, most of us easily recognize the distinctive lines of a Porsche or a Corvette. When Volkswagen dropped the popular Beetle model and used new styling, the result was confusion in the marketplace. Quality and reliability also tend to be associated with brands. For many decades, Maytag has promoted its product reliability by depicting the lonely repairman who never gets to visit a customer. Finally, packaging may differentiate one product from another. We all recognize immediately the distinctive script lettering of Coke.

AUGMENTED PRODUCTS

AUGMENTED PRODUCT

Product with characteristics that enhance its value beyond that of the core and branded products.

An **augmented product** has characteristics that enhance value beyond that of the core and branded products. Delivery methods, warranty terms and conditions, and credit terms are ways to augment a product. A dishwasher from Sears can be delivered, installed, covered by a limited warranty, and paid off on credit. Many products also require extensive installation,

Nicole Miller Eyewear is an example of a branded product.

such as an in-ground swimming pool. Once a product has been purchased, installed, and used, it may require service or repair. That's why warranty conditions and the availability of service are significant in augmenting products. Jackson Hewitt Inc. is offering a Gold Guarantee program that provides tax liability coverage of $5,000 for three years. It is confident that its tax preparation software combined with its skilled tax preparers will eliminate error.[4]

Another aspect of augmentation is product bundling. A **bundling strategy** combines many products into a single offering. Delphi sells engine management systems to automotive manufacturers. Although these systems are made up of several components (products), they are sold as one unit. The functionality of all the products is improved by combining them, and the sale is larger than if they were sold separately. More important, product bundling enables manufacturers to add value.

Consumer marketers also decide whether to bundle. Stereo equipment, for example, can be sold as a system or as individual components. Maybe in the purchasing process you find that Harman/Kardon speakers sound better, but you prefer the Pioneer receiver and a Sony CD player. In this case, you want to buy an unbundled product. Yamaha's strategy is to market a whole stereo system, with components specifically designed to work together for maximum sound quality.

For environmentally conscious consumers, an increasing appeal is augmentation through recycling. Product disposal is becoming a more important issue. Many consumers want a product that can be returned for recycling at the end of its usefulness. A common example of recycling is automobiles that flow to the used car market and eventually into reclamation centers, where usable parts are extracted and such raw materials as metal and rubber are recycled. In response to consumers' environmental concerns, nine European car manufacturers (including BMW, Mercedes, Ford/Jaguar, Rover, and Volvo) cooperate with dismantlers to reduce automotive waste, generate demand for materials currently being sent to landfills, and eliminate pollution risks from the disposal process. Through the program, carmakers and dismantlers are finding new ways to design and recycle vehicles to minimize waste, producing both economic and environmental advantages.[5]

PRODUCT CLASSIFICATIONS

Products are classified according to how they are purchased and used. These classifications usually require a certain type of marketing strategy. We'll start with consumer products and then move on to business products.

CONSUMER PRODUCT CLASSIFICATION

Marketers need to understand the different types of products that consumers buy. One useful scheme divides products into the five categories listed in Figure 9.2.

Unsought Products   **Unsought products** are items not thought about frequently and not perceived as very necessary. The need is usually felt just before purchase and only briefly. These goods may be novelties, such as T-shirts or "over the hill" gag gifts. They also may be things buyers don't like to think about, such as cemetery plots. In any case, consumers don't seek information on their own, so personal selling and prominent promotions are very important. Heavy sales effort may be required to persuade potential buyers to consider the item.

A special category of unsought products is impulse items. As the name suggests, these purchases are made on a whim, with very little thought. In most cases impulse items are relatively inexpensive and have little to do with need fulfillment, other than the buyer's immediate enjoyment at the time of purchase. How many times have you been grocery shopping and tossed into your cart a box of Chips Ahoy! or Twinkies? You're not alone! Many shoppers are now turning to online grocery stores to avoid spending money on impulse purchases they would most likely make if walking the aisles of a supermarket.[6]

Emergency Products   **Emergency products** are purchased when an unexpected event takes place and the consumer has an urgent need for a product. When an ambulance or tow truck is needed, the buyer is unlikely to compare prices and probably has little choice about the supplier. From the marketer's standpoint, it's crucial to have telephone numbers and other means of access available to buyers when an emergency occurs. A good example is the 911 service that local police, fire, and ambulance agencies promote. American Express provides consumers

BUNDLING STRATEGY

A strategy in which several products are combined into a single offering.

CONNECTED: SURFING THE NET

www.yamaha.com

Check out Yamaha's wide variety of products—musical instruments, audio equipment, electronics, computers, and more. You can find out how to write to the company, explore Yamaha worldwide, or inquire about job opportunities.

UNSOUGHT PRODUCT

An item that consumers don't think about frequently and for which they don't perceive much need.

EMERGENCY PRODUCT

A product purchased due to an unexpected event and for which the consumer has an urgent need.

Classification	Repurchase Planning	Number of Comparisons Made	Frequency of Purchase	Location of Purchase	Examples
Unsought	None	Few or none	Seldom	At buyer's home or at store checkout	Cemetery plots Pet rock
Emergency	Unexpected need	None	Very rarely or once	Closest to emergency	Ambulance Towing service
Convenience	Little	Several (but over many purchases)	Often and regularly	Close to home, travel, work	Soft drinks Chewing gum Fast food
Shopping	Moderate	Many	Infrequent	In areas with many similar products	Automobiles Televisions Appliances Furniture Clothing
Specialty	Extensive	Few	Infrequent	Buyer travels to merchant's location	Fine watches Gourmet restaurants

FIGURE 9.2 *A Product Classification Based on Consumer Purchase Behavior*

with phone numbers that allow lost traveler's checks to be replaced immediately. Many automobile companies now provide toll-free numbers for emergency roadside service.

Convenience Products   **Convenience products** are relatively inexpensive items that consumers purchase frequently and with minimum effort. Often they are referred to as staples because people always need them—milk, toilet paper, gum, soft drinks, and so on. Convenience items are usually bought close to home, work, or travel routes. Typically they are purchased only when the consumer's supply is low. For example, when your tube of toothpaste is almost gone, you'll probably buy another. Most of you won't have an inventory of three or four tubes on hand.

Brand name is very important for convenience products because buyers don't spend much time selecting their purchase. They tend to be brand loyal but will choose a substitute if their favorite is unavailable. Consider the national drugstore chain CVS. Since drugstore supplies are items that buyers want to purchase with minimum effort, CVS provides one-stop shopping for a multitude of pharmaceutical and beauty needs. CVS also offers its own brand, which reduces purchase decision time as well as cost. Marketers must ensure that convenience items are widely distributed and prominently displayed so they are noticed and easily purchased. Eye-catching packaging also can be important.

Shopping Products   **Shopping products** are generally purchased only after the consumer has compared several alternatives. Comparisons are made on such elements as style, quality, features, and packaging. Buyers compare prices to select the product providing the best value. Most shopping products are purchased less frequently and cost more than convenience items. Automobiles, televisions, appliances, furniture, and clothing are all considered shopping goods. Although people may do some prepurchase planning at home, they are likely to visit stores to examine shopping goods. That's why stores offering similar types of shopping goods tend to be located near one another. There may be several shoe stores in the same wing of a shopping mall, or several automobile dealerships not far apart on the same street. This makes it easier for consumers to make comparisons and increases the chance that one of the outlets will make the sale.

Because shopping goods tend to be relatively durable, consumers don't want them to clash with what they already own. Selecting just the right piece of furniture to complement a room or finding an item of clothing that coordinates with one's wardrobe can require extensive shopping. Many people take along friends or family to help with the decision, and there

CONVENIENCE PRODUCT

A relatively inexpensive item that consumers purchase frequently and with minimum effort.

SHOPPING PRODUCT

A purchase generally made only after the consumer has compared several alternatives.

Introducing TWIST-n-FILL™. Cherry goo in a watermelon twist.

*Twizzlers is an example of
a convenience product.*

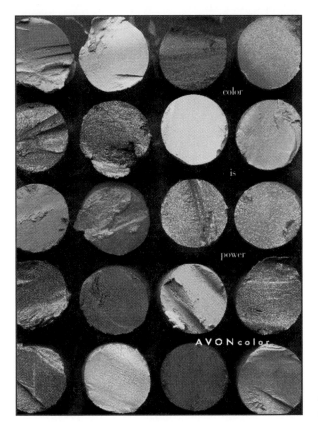

*Avon lipstick is an example of
a "shopping" product.*

tends to be interaction with salespeople. Most of us wouldn't purchase a car or a business suit without first consulting a salesperson. Many retailers and manufacturers recognize this and train their salespeople to identify buyers' needs and help them find exactly the right item.

Because comparisons are made among shopping goods, many manufacturers market several similar products at different price points. Garmin International Inc. has announced the release of three new Global Positioning Satellite units. The units will have different features ranging from city databases to an internal barometric altimeter. The new units give customers more choices at different price points.[7]

Specialty Products   **Specialty items** have unique characteristics that provide unusual value to the purchaser. Most carry meanings that buyers associate with their self-image. Consequently, customers are brand loyal and often refuse to accept substitutes. They are willing to travel long distances and pay high prices to obtain particular products. Some examples are Movado watches, Gucci purses, Godiva chocolates, Louis Vuitton luggage, and Armani suits. A lobster and filet mignon dinner, a dress from Saks Fifth Avenue, a stay at the Plaza Hotel, or a luxury cruise also can be considered specialty items.

Most consumers spend a considerable amount of time on prepurchase planning for specialty items. They must acquire the necessary funds and select a particular style or model of the brand. Marketing a specialty product requires heavy involvement of the retailer to ensure the right fit between the individual model and the customer's needs. To justify the expense of this service, marketers work hard to create customer loyalty. Repeat purchases generate enough profit over time to offset the cost of the first sale.

Service professionals often try to achieve the status of a specialty provider. There are physicians who practice only internal medicine, oncology, or cosmetic surgery. The specialty classification signifies a great deal more value to most customers and in turn commands a much higher price. Certain types of lawyers, architects, consultants, and accountants usually charge more than their nonspecialized counterparts. Buyers often seek these suppliers not only for their status but also because of the unique qualities of the product or service they provide.

A Barbie Collectible doll is an example of a specialty item.

Business products are purchased by an organization for its own use. The seven types listed in Figure 9.3 are grouped into three categories according to function. These are the products needed to start a company and keep it running for a long time.

Capital Products   **Capital products** are costly items that last a long time but are not part of any finished product. They usually are built or used to manufacture, distribute, or support the development of products. For accounting purposes, these items are depreciated over several years. Capital products are subdivided into installations and equipment.

CAPITAL PRODUCT
A costly item that lasts a long time but does not become part of any finished product.

   Installations house operations; examples include office buildings, factories, and distribution centers. Because they cost a lot and are intended to last for a considerable time, they are carefully selected by top management. Salespeople for these products use technical expertise to communicate with buyers. Marketing generally requires a team approach, an understanding of the prospective client's business, and customization of the product to meet the unique requirements of each customer. Providers range from a small construction firm that may put up an office for a local dentist to companies such as Bechtel, a huge multinational. It has offices in most world regions and relies on marketing skills to find opportunities and win business globally.

   Equipment is movable capital goods used to manufacture or maintain other products. Drills, computers, forklifts, and die presses fit this category. ABB and AO Smith sell robotics designed for specific tasks to many types of manufacturers. General Motors (GM), Ford, and Chrysler have purchased thousands of robots for welding alone; other functions include sorting, lifting, and inspecting. Of course, products that bring information to businesses represent a huge equipment marketing opportunity. Companies such as Sun Microsystems sell computerized workstations for professional and clerical workers. These products are connected through elaborate networks that allow personnel around the globe to tie into the company system. Airline reservations in Japan, France, the United States, and the Czech Republic are likely to be made this way. It is not unusual for these equipment systems to cost hundreds of millions of dollars.

Production Products   **Production products**—raw materials, processed materials, component parts, and subassemblies—become part of other goods. Few manufacturers extract the raw materials they need or make all the components for a finished product. Instead, they rely on outside suppliers. Raw materials are basic substances used in the manufacture of products, such as ore or grain to produce steel or flour, or cotton and wool for textiles, or soybeans for

PRODUCTION PRODUCTS
Raw materials, processed materials, component parts, and subassemblies that become part of other goods.

Category and Type	Description	Examples
Capital Products		
Installations	Facilities that contain operations	Office buildings, factories, stores, distribution centers
Equipment	Items used to manufacture products and support the business	Drills, computers, desks, robots, lifts, trucks, airplanes
Production Products		
Raw materials	Substances in natural state	Crude oil, sand, gas, water
Processed materials	Basic substances used to manufacture products	Refined oil, steel, plastic, aluminum
Component Parts and Subassemblies		
Operations products	Products that are elements of other products	Brakes, transmissions, computer chips, switches, lights, cords
Operating services	Activities purchased to help run the business	Consulting, accounting, waste removal, employee food service
Operating supplies	Consumable items used by the business	Paper, pens, file folders, cleaning products

FIGURE 9.3   *A Classification of Business Products*

food products. Companies such as Archer-Daniels-Midland (ADM) claim that they "feed the world" because their agricultural products go into so many food items. Processed materials undergo an intermediate treatment—such as refining, chemical combination, purification, crushing, or milling—before reaching the manufacturer.

Component parts and subassemblies are manufactured goods that are elements of other products. Brake linings are components of antilock brake systems. Since these have several components and are part of still another product—vehicles—they are called subassemblies. Companies such as Eaton and North American Rockwell make components and subassemblies. Although each part is relatively inexpensive, manufacturing companies are likely to purchase large quantities at one time, numbering thousands or even millions of units.

Quality control and delivery of component parts can be very complicated, so successful companies must perform these operations at a high level of precision. Marketers stress this aspect of their product when selling to businesses, which usually is done by highly trained sales representatives. As noted in chapter 8, suppliers frequently form close ties with manufacturers and produce components or subassemblies tailored to their needs.

OPERATIONS PRODUCTS

Products purchased to help run a business and are not included in finished products.

Operations Products **Operations products** are purchased to help run the business and are not included in finished products. These range from very inexpensive items, such as paper clips, to an expensive product like nuclear waste removal from power plants. Operations products are subdivided into supplies and services. **Supplies** are consumable items and may seem relatively unimportant, but in total they can involve large sums. In banks, printed business forms alone often cost several hundred thousand dollars a year. Items such as pens, folders, and cleaning products can contribute significantly to company costs. Even with the increased use of the Internet, the annual market for office paper is estimated to be around $4 billion, and is expected to grow at 6 percent annually.[8]

SUPPLIES

Consumable items used for business operations.

Operations services are activities purchased to help run the business. Examples are legal, accounting, advertising, and billing services. Some companies now outsource their entire logistics operations. Accenture, EDS, and McKinsey & Company all compete for lucrative contracts involving R&D, tactical and strategic plans, and design of information systems. Companies such as ARAMARK and Marriott supply food service and other products. Many companies have outsiders handle customer service; for some of its clients, UPS World Wide Logistics repairs computers returned to the manufacturer. IBM is a world leader in operational services. Its Web site allows companies to view IBM's services according to specific needs, tailoring the services to each company's needs. Companies can choose to have IBM assist them in innovation, integrated technology, and outsourcing, or learn more about e-business.[9]

PRODUCT LINE DECISIONS

Product lines must be configured for domestic and global markets. Decisions about how many lines to carry, how many products in each line, and the degree of standardization across markets shape the overall offering of an organization. A **product line** consists of the closely related products marketed by an organization. A company may have one line or several, but a single line usually focuses on the same type of benefit, such as hair care. An **item** is a specific version of a product within a product line. Each item, in turn, consists of several units. A unit refers to the specific product amount, container size or type, and formula. Retailers call these stock-keeping units (SKUs) to identify the variations they regularly have on the shelves.

PRODUCT LINE

Closely related products marketed by the organization.

ITEM

A specific version of a product within a product line.

Consider a line of products in the hair care category made by Procter & Gamble, Pantene, which includes several items—mousse, styling gel, hair spray, and shampoo. Pantene's 40 SKU shampoo product line consists of five different categories based on the type of look the customer is seeking. The categories are basic, volume, smooth, curl, and color care. Each category has a shampoo, a conditioner, two hairsprays, and various other styling aids. Procter & Gamble carefully manages the entire line and Pantene is the market leader in shampoo and conditioner.[10]

PRODUCT DEPTH AND BREADTH

DEPTH

The number of items in a product line.

Most companies need to consider how broad and deep their product lines should be, as described in Figure 9.4. The **depth** of a product line refers to the number of items. Since the Pantene shampoo product line consists of many items, it is said to be deep. A product line with

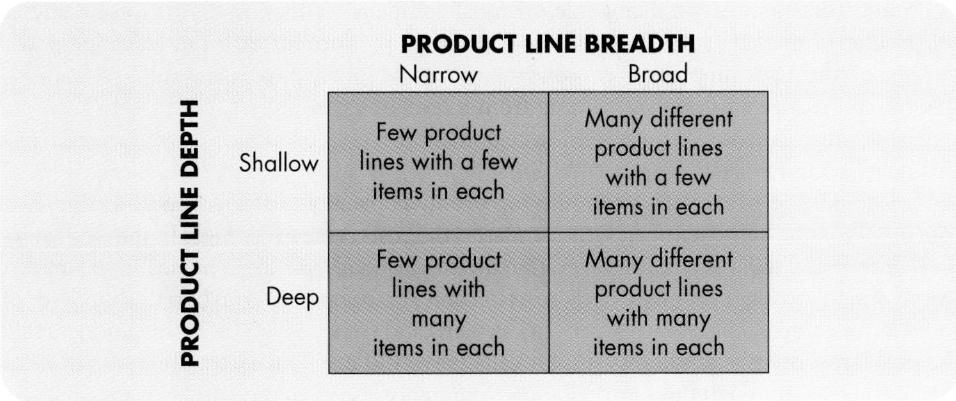

FIGURE 9.4 *Product Line Depth and Breadth*

only a few items is called shallow. **Breadth** of product lines refers to the number of different lines a company markets. Since Procter & Gamble markets many, ranging from laundry detergent to toothpaste to a variety of foods, it is considered to have a broad number of product lines. General Electric has an even broader set of product lines, marketing household products to consumers, nuclear power plants to foreign governments, and hundreds of other product lines as well.

Hershey's candies can be considered a narrow and shallow product line. The products fall in a single product category, candy, and there are a fairly limited number of items—chocolate bars, Kisses, and hard candy, all with a few types each. Organizations such as Kodak compete with narrow but deep product lines. Nearly all of Kodak's products relate to one category: imagery. It manufactures and sells nearly every kind of film imaginable. In addition, Kodak makes products and processing equipment for film development, such as paper and chemicals. Kodak lost money when it attempted to broaden into pharmaceuticals, copiers, and chemicals, lines in which it does not dominate.[11] Additionally, sales fell due to declining use of film by its traditional customer base.[12] Still Kodak is taking its strength in a narrow but deep product line to developing markets. Kodak is planning to sell some products directly via the Internet and is focusing on younger customers as a potentially profitable market. By promoting single-use cameras and digital picture products, Kodak is targeting teenagers who are using lots of pictures to create their own Web sites.[13]

Most companies with a broad product line are large, although there are exceptions. Small organizations usually lack the resources for competing across diverse product categories. Brunswick is a large company that uses a broad and deep product line strategy. One of its lines, recreational boats, is marketed under the brand name Sea Ray. Sea Ray produces several different types of boats, ranging from 12 feet to more than 80 feet. It also owns Brunswick Bowling & Billiards, which markets a line of products ranging from alleys with automatic pinsetters to bowling balls and other equipment. Another Brunswick product line is fishing equipment, marketed under the Zebco brand name, with several types of rods, reels, and related items. Brunswick also markets a number of other product lines with several items each.

Now think about Kmart. It carries a broad product line, but the variety of items within each is limited. In other words, Kmart carries a broad and shallow product line. In some instances, product lines may be too deep or too broad. Procter & Gamble recently sold its profitable Clearasil line of acne products in order to focus on a more specific line of beauty aid products. As part of its Organization 2005 plan, Procter & Gamble has been restructuring its product lines to allow more tailoring to local markets.[14]

GLOBAL PRODUCTS

The globalization of business creates several product-related dilemmas. Among the most critical is determining the optimal amount of standardization for individual products and lines across market regions. Different areas of the world vary greatly in terms of consumer and business purchasing approaches, media exposure, and tastes and preferences. In addition, product standards and regulations, measurements and calibration systems, and economic factors vary immensely. Despite these differences, however, many firms like to standardize products to achieve economics of scale in R&D, production, and marketing.

Standardization plays a major role in global company strategy. In efforts to standardize the products it markets, John Deere, the world's largest producer of agricultural equipment, is also standardizing its suppliers to consolidate worldwide supply purchasing, improve material quality, and reduce costs. By purchasing from a few similar suppliers, John Deere hopes to reduce product variations from region to region and develop relationships with its suppliers that help lead to more customer satisfaction.[15]

Although the advantages of modifying products usually center around meeting customers' needs and conforming to local standards, the costs can be very high. In the electronics area, Europe and the United States are different. Consequently, products made for one market simply will not work in the other. R&D costs to conform to standards run into the hundreds of millions for companies such as Seimens in Germany and General Electric. In an effort to avoid the problem, Ford has developed what it calls the world car, Taurus, which it sells in most major markets. Although there are still minor differences between the European and U.S. versions, Ford believes its costs are reduced enough to pass savings on to consumers, increase market share, and meet profit goals.

The depth and breadth of the product line have a lot to do with successful global competition. Pepsi and Coca-Cola continually compete with each other to expand their product lines. Some believe Coke's global strategy—a narrow line with geographic variations—is one reason for its success. Pepsi, in contrast, has standardized its beverage line globally. Clearly, product line breadth doesn't determine why one company outsells another, but the issue is important in developing global strategy. Although Coca-Cola remains the number-one softdrink company, Pepsi is gaining in popularity through its other product lines. Pepsi recently acquired the South Beach Beverage Company, makers of SoBe, and Quaker Oaks, maker of Gatorade, to broaden its beverage offerings to include fruit blends, teas, and energy drinks, in addition to its already held Aquafina, All Sport, Lipton's Ice Tea, and Frappuchino. Coca-Cola has responded to Pepsi's expansion by purchasing Planet Java coffee, selling its own energy drink KMX, and experimenting with children's milk drinks. Coca-Cola also has its own brands of bottled water, sports drink, and root beer, in addition to other brands sold in various parts of the world. With Pepsi deriving 65 percent of its profits from its snack food line, including products such as Doritos, Cheetos, and Sun Chips, Coca-Cola must continue to promote its products in ways that capture buyers.[16]

IBM also has a global product strategy. It adds products designed to span geographic regions. For the 2001 Australian Open, IBM provided a "virtual seat" to tennis fans around the world by supplying real-time audio and video of the matches and player interviews.[17]

Even some companies with deep domestic product lines find additions are in order when going international. Newell Rubbermaid, known for its large number of products, has expanded its product line to include products marketed globally, which account for more than 20 percent of total revenues. Recently, Newell Rubbermaid implemented a new global group product line strategy with six distinct product lines: storage, organization, and cleaning; home décor; office products; infant/juvenile care and play; food preparation, cooking, and serving; and hardware and tools. The focus is on maximizing operating income, building and enhancing brands, and entering new markets.[18] Experience with a deep and broad product line in the consumer, industrial, and health care fields will be important as companies seek to connect with the needs and tastes of consumers in these diverse regions.

Emerging economies such as China present their own problems from a product standpoint because large and risky investments in design and manufacturing are often necessary. Motorola finished work on a $560 million semiconductor component plant in Tianjin, China, in 1998. Since it is estimated that China will become the world's largest consumer market for new personal computers, television sets, microwaves, and telephones sometime in the 21st century, Motorola believes the plant will position it well to support a broad range of technologically sophisticated products there.[19] In 2000, Motorola obtained official permission from the government to invest $1.9 billion in new and existing telecom facilities. This made Motorola the single largest foreign investor in China.[20]

**CONNECTED:
SURFING THE NET**

www.motorola.com

Learn about "what you never thought possible" by visiting the Motorola Web site. Take a look at the company's product portfolio and business units, or explore its global community.

<u>BRAND</u>

A distinguishing name or symbol to identify and differentiate products from those of competitors.

BRANDS

A **brand** is a distinguishing name or symbol intended to identify and differentiate products from those offered by competitors.[21] Philip Morris purchased Kraft in 1988, the same year Nestlé bought the British company Rowntree. What was unusual about these takeovers was

Sony is a popular brand easily differentiated from competitors.

the tremendous premium paid for the brand name. Philip Morris paid four times more than the tangible assets of Kraft, and Nestlé paid more than five times the assets of Rowntree.[22] Procter & Gamble purchased the Eagle brand name and trademark from Anheuser-Busch for an estimated $10 to $20 million.[23] Why did these companies pay so much? They wanted the long-term cash generation potential of these names. Many brands are now recognized globally, producing dramatic returns around the world.

Can you name the top 10 brands in the world? Does your list match Figure 9.5? No matter what criteria are used in creating such a list, the same brands tend to emerge as leaders.[24]

Brands are very powerful concepts in business. They send strong signals about what the product represents. A brand image can make or break a company's reputation. To a consumer, a trusted brand promises high quality, but a "tainted" reputation means poor quality or bad service. One study by Pricewaterhouse-Coopers found that 80 percent of online shoppers say that their purchasing decisions are strongly influenced by the need to buy brand name products.[25] According to James Lenehan, worldwide chairman of Johnson & Johnson's consumer

Rank	1999	2000
1.	Coca-Cola	Coca-Cola
2.	Microsoft	Microsoft
3.	IBM	IBM
4.	General Electric	Intel
5.	Ford	Nokia
6.	Disney	General Electric
7.	Intel	Ford
8.	McDonald's	Disney
9.	AT&T	McDonald's
10.	Marlboro	AT&T

FIGURE 9.5 *The World's Top 10 Brands*

Source: Interbrand.

pharmaceuticals and professional group: "If you have a brand that you know and trust, it helps you make choices faster, more easily. Can you imagine going shopping without them?"[26]

Historically, brands were used to identify a product's manufacturer. They also protected both the customer and the producer by ensuring that the products met certain quality standards and came from a reputable source. Companies with early success in building brands include Procter & Gamble (P&G), IBM, Anheuser-Busch, Sony, American Express, Volkswagen, American Airlines, Pepsi, and Kodak. Such companies created a brand perceived by consumers as having more intrinsic value.

In the 1960s, the strategy was simple: The greater the perceived value, the greater the sales. This strategy is still used today, but companies must work hard to ensure that the products themselves provide the added value communicated by the name. Brand strategies help businesses such as Coca-Cola, Disney, Gillette, and Hewlett-Packard develop credibility with customers. The role of brands grew in importance in the 1990s. Advertisers spent $331.8 billion in 2000 to promote brands, an increase of 7.9 percent over 1999.[27]

Today, brands do far more than identify the manufacturer. They have become "personalities" with a character much greater than the products they represent. An early example of successful branding is Ivory soap, introduced in 1879 by Harvey Procter. With its claim of "99.44% pure," it has long been the leader. Estimates are that the Ivory brand has brought more than $3 billion in profit to Procter & Gamble over the years. In some cases the brand name becomes the product itself to many people: Xerox, Kleenex, and Rollerblade are synonymous with their functions. And such brands as Nabisco, Kellogg, Kodak, Gillette, Campbell's, and Goodyear have all outlived the specific items they represented when introduced. Although the products themselves may have altered due to changing technology, customer preferences, and modernization, the brand name has stayed the same.

TRADEMARKS

TRADEMARK (BRAND MARK)
A distinctive form or figure that identifies the brand.

People tend to use the words *brand* and *trademark* interchangeably, but there are some notable differences. The brand name is the wording attached to the product. Coke, Pepsi, and Chiquita are brand names. The **trademark** (brand mark) is a distinctive form or figure that identifies

The MGM Grand Lion is a distinctive figure that identifies the hotel.

CONNECTING THROUGH TECHNOLOGY

INTEL BRANDS THE SOUL IN THE MACHINE

 Before 1992—when it wasn't cool to be a cybergeek—not many computer users knew or cared about the microprocessor powering their PC. Then Intel Corporation gave them a reason to care. The company began one of the most revolutionary corporate branding campaigns in history with its "Intel Inside" marketing campaign. Never before had an electrical component company tried to create brand identity with the end user, especially in a commodity market such as computer chips. Through November 1999, Intel had spent a whopping $4 billion on the "Intel Inside" program, and it paid off by raising its market share from 56 percent in 1989 to 82.9 percent in 1999.

The motto of the company owner is "only the paranoid survive," and Intel's success rests on its obsession with making its own products obsolete. The goal is to come out with a new, more powerful microprocessor every 18 months. By 1992, however, Intel needed to convince consumers who had the old 286 chip that a 386 is better—and, looking ahead, that the next generation will be better yet, and the next. So Intel decided to educate buyers with a two-tiered marketing campaign, one aimed at computer manufacturers and the other at end users. For corporate purchasers and PC experts, Intel inserted "technology briefing" pamphlets in PC magazines, featuring a new topic every six to eight weeks. For consumers, Intel television and print ads showed dramatic swooping views of a computer powered by an Intel microprocessor. The goal: Take away the fear and make Intel's technology accessible or, better yet, indispensable.

But the biggest branding brainstorm was Intel's offer of co-op advertising money for every PC maker who put the "Intel Inside" sticker on its products or in its ads. Intel pays up to 5 percent of the ad costs, and now the logos are almost as common as floppies. The move shook up the whole industry. "The microprocessor has become a consumer product," said Intel's hard-driving CEO Andy Grove, adding that "its role in contemporary society is not a passing phenomenon." Said Al Ries, chairman of a consulting firm, "'Intel Inside' will go down in history as one of the more magnificent campaigns of the century. It's brilliant and, in a sense, it pre-empted the branding of personal computers." In 1999, 87 percent of computer print ads displayed the "Intel Inside" logo, which shows the company's success.

There were skeptics when Intel first tried to make consumers care about technology. One analyst asked: "If you buy a BMW, who cares about the spark plugs?" Ironically—and to the distress of PC makers—the consumer now often cares more about the "spark plugs" than the name on the disk drive. Intel has beefed up its brand identity even more by designing and building entire motherboards, the circuitry at the heart of PCs. Dozens of computer companies, including IBM, Digital, Compaq, and Hewlett-Packard, are selling machines with Pentium chips. They were forced to march to Intel's beat since they couldn't produce their own motherboard designs as quickly. And that beat is picking up tempo. According to Gary Stibel, partner of New England Consulting Group, "The marketer has to deliver over and over again over time what a customer expects, which in turn creates a community of passionate consumers about that brand." Intel has managed to do just that.

Sources: **Robert D. Hof, "The Education of Andrew Grove,"** *Business Week Online,* **January 16, 1995; Lawrence M. Fisher, "Intel Doubled Its Earnings in 4th Quarter,"** *New York Times,* **January 15, 1997, p. D1; Tim Clark, "Inside Intel's Marketing Machine,"** *Business Marketing,* **October 1993, pp. 14–19; Robert D. Hof, "Intel Unbound,"** *Business Week Online,* **October 9, 1995; Michael Treacy and Fred Wiersema,** *The Discipline of Market Leaders* **(Reading, MA: Addison-Wesley, 1995), pp. 103–121; Tobi Elkin, "Co-Op Crossroads,"** *Advertising Age,* **November 15, 1999, pp. 1, 24+; and Laurie Freeman, "Who Are You?"** *Marketing News,* **February 14, 2000, pp. 1, 9.**

the brand. A picture is called a trademark symbol; distinctively shaped letters are called a logo: IBM, HBO, GE. Coca-Cola uses white script on a red background. Burger King uses a crown, and McDonald's uses golden arches. Other examples are NBC's peacock, Fila's blue-and-red letter F, Chrysler's five-pointed star, and Nike's swoosh symbol. Intel has found that, in the quickly changing world of technology, the "Intel Inside" symbol has endeared it to customers who have bought many versions of the processor, and are now buying Internet services, audio players, and camera products also. It reassures them about a purchase that is often filled with confusion and anxiety.[28]

The American Cancer Society is selling its red dagger logo for approximately $4 million to endorse NicoDerm antismoking products and Florida Orange Juice. Groups such as the American Dental Association and the American Heart Association have done the same. These endorsements, however, raise an ethical issue. Should nationally respected health groups use their logo to give products instant credibility?[29]

An identifying mark, slogan, or set of words can provide immediate recognition and credibility even when applied to products owned by other companies. FAFSA is commonly known as Free Application for Federal Student Aid, though it is not a trademark. When a company began running a Web site, FAFSA.com, offering financial aid forms online and by phone to students, the Department of Education protested. The Department of Education said that the site deceived customers by associating itself with the government organization and implying that fees were required for financial aid services. The site's operator says that he is not trying to trick students into paying for services, while the Department of Education claims that it should have the rights to the FAFSA.com site by common law. Though not explicitly involving trademarks, this issue demonstrates the effectiveness of name brand association.

TRADEMARK PIRACY

The brand name and the trademark symbol or logo are protected by law if they are registered. That gives the owner sole right to use them any way he or she chooses. Just as most people want to protect their reputation, companies are careful to protect a brand. It is property they own and competitors may not use or imitate it. For example, a federal court in Milwaukee ruled that the Hog Farm, a motorcycle parts and repair shop, had to change its name. It infringed on the rights of Harley-Davidson, whose motorcycles are widely known as "hogs."

Often a company protects materials associated with its brand by copyrighting. Smith + Noble window coverings catalog has had its share of dealings with copyright and brand infringement lawsuits. Most recently, the company has claimed that another window coverings manufacturer, Next Day Blinds, copied the format of its catalog. Bob Perkowitz, founder of Smith + Noble's catalog, says, "You spend years building up a brand with a reputation for quality and service, and you want to protect your brand. And that's all we're concerned about: We don't want our customers to be misled." Though cases such as this one sometimes go to trial, often they are settled out of court.[30]

In the entertainment industry, property rights and reputation are no less important. The wording "Steven Speilberg presents" is used to brand the famous director's cartoon shows, *Tiny Toons* and *Animaniacs.* Networks also brand products. MTV came out with the movies *Joe's Apartment* and *Beavis and Butthead Do America* as well as books, T-shirts, and CDs with the MTV trademark.

Securing trademarks globally can be very tricky. People throughout the world recognize Mickey Mouse and Donald Duck as Disney characters, but a court in Indonesia ruled that the duck's picture could be used by a local company. This situation occurs frequently, particularly in developing countries where more pressing problems command government attention. In advanced economies, trademark protection is considered essential for sound competitive industrial policy. Elsewhere trademarks may be viewed as merely a tool to stimulate commerce. No single world policy has yet been developed that takes into account the perspectives of all nations.

Global losses to brand counterfeiting are thought to be between $200 and $400 billion.[31] Pirated products range from computer software and designer goods to soaps and candies. Packaging closely resembles that of the American-made counterpart, and often logo designs are stolen and used. Individual firms may or may not choose to file an international suit against offenders.

Many problems with brand counterfeiting are occurring in China. Shanghei Volkswagen estimates that two-thirds of the Volkswagen parts market is counterfeit. Henkel, a German food and chemical group, has faced so many problems that it is considering freezing its investment in China if the counterfeiting does not stop. It is estimated that 20 percent of the food and chemical sector is counterfeit, and companies say that cracking down on counterfeiters is harder than it once was. Companies say that counterfeiters are just "too good" to be detected. To protect against such brand counterfeiting and bring the problem to the attention of Chinese officials, 53 companies have joined to form the China Anti-Counterfeiting Coalition.[32]

Counterfeiting has become so widespread that *Fortune* has coined the term *brandnapping* for copying products and affixing illegal labels. An estimated 5 percent of all products sold worldwide fit this category, totaling about $200 billion annually. This represents huge losses to legitimate owners of the brands.

Unfortunately, some fakes can have very serious consequences. For example, the Federal Aviation Administration (FAA) has found quantities of substandard counterfeit airline parts in commercial planes. The FAA estimates that between 1973 and 1993, 166 serious accidents or mishaps were due to counterfeit parts. Though unapproved parts are hard to detect, it is hoped that electronic and bar code tagging will help to slow the sale of bogus parts. The U.S. Congress is taking the problem seriously and is debating legislation that, if approved, would prohibit anyone convicted of counterfeit selling from obtaining future FAA certification or employment in the airline industry.[33] U.S. trade negotiations have lessened the occurrence of infringements, but developing countries have little incentive to enforce laws. Efforts continue through such organizations as GATT and the United Nations to develop international norms.

BRAND STRATEGIES

There are a number of brand strategies, as shown in Figure 9.6. In addition to a generic or nonbranded approach, the most common types are individual, family, manufacturer (national), private, and hybrid.

Generic Strategy   A **generic brand strategy** uses no brand name whatsoever. Firms generally select this approach when they want to gain a low-cost commodity market position. As mentioned before, pharmaceutical companies often adopt this strategy. Some grocery stores devote entire aisles exclusively to generic products, packaged in plain black and white. Many consumers prefer generics because they cost so much less than name brands.

Individual Brand Strategy   An **individual brand strategy** assigns a unique brand name to each major product or product line. There are three situations in which this approach is likely to be used. First, companies may have different product lines that compete against one another. For example, General Motors builds total market share with several individual brands: Chevrolet, Cadillac, Pontiac, Buick, and Oldsmobile. Second, products within one line

GENERIC BRAND STRATEGY
Strategy in which no brand name is used.

INDIVIDUAL BRAND STRATEGY
Strategy in which there is a unique name for each major product or product line.

Type	Description	Reasons for Use	Examples
Generic	No brand name is used.	Lower cost. Commodity position.	Pharmaceuticals Vegetables
Individual	Unique brand name for each major product or line.	Company has dissimilar products. Each product is matched to a segment. Products compete against one another.	Procter & Gamble's Tide, Bold, Cheer, Dreft, Era, Gain, Ivory, Oxydol, and Solo laundry detergents.
Family	Umbrella name covers all products in the line.	Economical way to create one brand identity for all existing and new products. Increase awareness and market presence by using one image for all.	Dole Sony Campbell's Sara Lee Black & Decker
Manufacturer (national)	Brand name synonymous with the owner.	Ties R&D, manufacturing, and company reputation to the product.	McDonald's Kodak Fisher-Price Johnson & Johnson General Motors General Electric
Private (labels)	Brand name applied to supplier's product by wholesaler or retailer.	Lower cost. Builds on and enhances reputation of firm. Enhances firm's buying power.	Meijer A&P: Aunt Jane Wal-Mart: Sam's American Choice ACE Hardware IGA Stores Spartain Stores Sears: Kenmore
Hybrid	Two or more approaches are used.	Merger and acquisition. Gain benefits of all approaches.	Kraft

FIGURE 9.6 *Types of Brand Strategies*

may be matched with unique market segment needs. For example, Procter & Gamble's nine laundry detergents appeal to different segments. Third, a company may make highly dissimilar products. For example, Kellogg markets breakfast cereals under its name, toaster pastries under the Pop-Tarts brand, and pies under the Mrs. Smith's label.

Family Brand Strategy A **family brand strategy** uses a single brand name for the entire group of products in the company's line(s). This can be very cost-effective because advertising, promotion, and distribution resources can be focused to create a single image in the marketplace. The result is increased consumer awareness of the company and its products, such as Black & Decker tools.

The family brand strategy is used when products are similar. Dole markets more than 20 mainstream fruits and vegetables as well as numerous exotic fruits under one name. The Sony name covers hundreds of products, from high-priced stereos to inexpensive alarm-clock radios. The family brand approach has allowed Sony to introduce and eliminate products fairly rapidly while almost guaranteeing that its new products will at least be tried. Both Dole and Sony have sought to make their names synonymous with quality, regardless of the specific product.

Manufacturer's Brand Strategy **Manufacturer's brands,** as the term implies, are named after the maker. Sometimes they are called national brands, since the products often are found throughout the country. We've already mentioned a few in this chapter, such as Kodak and General Electric, but manufacturer's brands also can be local, such as Hanover pretzels. The company's reputation is closely tied to the product. Benetton, McDonald's, and Johnson & Johnson use public relations, advertising, and other means to ensure that the public connects their products with the policies of the firm. Usually this means creating a singular image for the company and the products it makes. Kodak's brand name revolves around imaging; Fisher-Price is known for products that relate to child development and safety; and Gerber is famous for baby food.

Private Brand Strategy When wholesalers or retailers place their own name on a product, it's called a **private brand** (or private label). Since these are promoted locally rather than nationally, they can be sold at a lower price than manufacturer's brands. Private labels allow the reseller to build and enhance its own reputation. By carefully selecting suppliers and developing quality control mechanisms, Wal-Mart can promote Sam's American Choice products as being high quality at a low price. This strategy increases Wal-Mart's buying power, since the company can shop among competing suppliers for the best price and pass on some of the savings to consumers. In addition, private brands enable retailers and wholesalers to differentiate themselves from competitors.

Companies that use private labels believe they understand consumers better than national marketers in several key respects, especially in their knowledge of local or regional consumer needs and shopping habits. Yet they do not have the resources to innovate far beyond current brands.[34] Their goal is to increase in-store brand sales. For their national brand competitors, the challenge is to persuade consumers not to be drawn by the low prices.[35]

The rivalry between in-store and national products has come to be known as the "battle of the brands." The private label market is growing in supermarkets as consumers become more cost-conscious and as private label brands rival the quality of national brands. In 1999, private label food sales in supermarkets accounted for 15.4 percent of total sales and are expected to increase to 18 percent in 2004.[36] The "battle" started when large manufacturers gained power by selling products through a broad range of distribution channels, and their size allowed them to place many demands on retailers. Large retailers retaliated by creating private labels.

Hybrid Brand Strategy Many firms employ a **hybrid brand strategy,** which is a combination of two or more approaches. Often this happens when mergers and acquisitions join organizations using different strategies. In these cases, executives must decide whether to blend the acquired brands into the company's portfolio or let them maintain their identity.

General Motors uses a strategy mix. The individual brand approach generally applies for Chevrolet, Pontiac, Buick, Oldsmobile, and Cadillac, although the Geo individual brand was introduced within the Chevrolet family brand. Saturn cars were introduced as a family brand with loose ties to GM. The company also promotes the manufacturer brand—General Motors automobiles. At the same time, many GM products, such as spark plugs, are sold under the Delco name or to resellers for private branding.

Brand equity refers to the assets linked with the brand name and symbol that add value to the product or service.[37] It indicates how valuable the brand is to the parent company. Be aware that a brand carries denotative and connotative meanings. It denotes (identifies) what the brand is, such as Head & Shoulders or Selsun Blue shampoo. It also connotes (produces an image of) the brand's relationship to the consumer's lifestyle. Connotative meanings grow over time and become tremendously valuable. Ideally, brands will achieve enough connotative meaning to endure forever if they are supported properly. Names such as Gillette, Morton's salt, and Betty Crocker predate your grandparents.

BRAND EQUITY

The assets linked with the brand name and symbol that add value to the product.

DIMENSIONS OF BRAND EQUITY

When people gradually purchase their home from the mortgage company, we say that they are earning or gaining equity. The homeowner is investing in the property. In a similar fashion, companies must invest in developing brands. Through sustained communication of the brand's connotative qualities, value is increased. Brand equity is an intangible asset with five dimensions, as shown in Figure 9.7. Let's look at each dimension in more detail.

Brand Awareness   **Brand awareness** is the extent to which consumers recognize the name and are likely to include it among the set of brands they consider. High awareness means a greater probability of purchase. If consumers are familiar with a brand and like it, they will have positive attitudes about the product(s) with that name. Consider the warmth and no-fail reliability of the Betty Crocker mother figure or Pillsbury's Poppin' Fresh baker. Because strong brands are often global, they may be recognized around the world and provide traveling consumers with ready access to a familiar item. High brand awareness also represents the commitment of the company to maintaining long-term standards of excellence for the consumer.

Even established companies work to sustain brand awareness. Kraft is doing this through its extensive Web site, www.kraft.com, which provides information on nutrition, cooking for specific occasions, mealtime tips, a personal recipe box, and even allows visitors to find recipes based on what main ingredient they wish to use. Online customers who choose to add their

BRAND AWARENESS

The extent to which consumers recognize the brand and are likely to include it among the set of brands they consider.

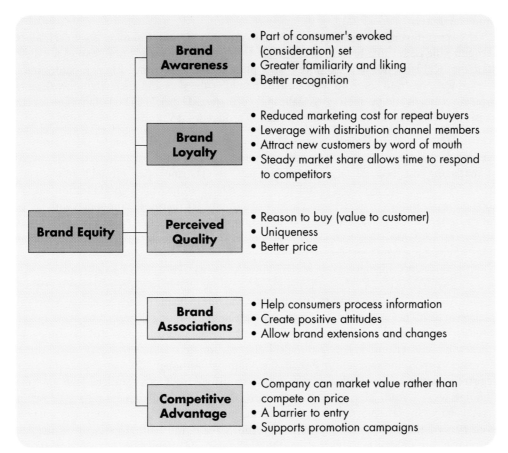

FIGURE 9.7 *The Five Dimensions of Brand Equity*

Source: Adapted from David A. Aaker, *Managing Brand Equity* (New York: The Free Press, 1991), inside cover.

the power to capture spirit

now available in a camera battery

Energizer e^2
lithium technology

take power to the next level™

Energizer is a company that enjoys great brand awareness.

address to a marketing list will receive product information, promotions, and coupons through the mail.[38] This increased accessibility to Kraft's brand name is intended to heighten brand awareness.

Newer companies or brands always have to create awareness. Colorado business leaders recognize the power in a brand name and are trying to decide on a "brand name" for their state that will label the state as more than a place to ski. Two competing companies have worked for months to come up with a catchy name for the state and are trying to work with local government and businesses to establish their preferred label.[39] The relationships feature shows how "Starbucks Extends Its Brand Name Through Joint Ventures."

BRAND LOYALTY

A dimension of brand equity that causes consumers to choose one brand over others available.

Brand Loyalty   **Brand loyalty** occurs when consumers select a particular brand over others on a regular basis. In effect, the firm's customers are an asset. Brand loyalty leads to lower over-all marketing costs because it's much less expensive to persuade repeat buyers than to create new ones. Distribution channel members are more likely to provide a good location within their outlet for the sale of an item with high brand loyalty. Furthermore, companies with faith-ful customers tend to be less susceptible to economic downturns or new competitors. Loyal buyers are not immediately inclined to look at other options, staying with the product even in times of economic hardship.

Brand loyalty is highest among more mature segments who tend to find a brand they like and stick with it, whereas younger generations are more willing to experiment with various brands. Among 20- to 29-year-olds, 59 percent tend to buy the same brands repeatedly, whereas 73 percent of 70- to 79-year-olds stick with the same brands. Among all groups, however, brand loyalty is decreasing.[40] Loyalty produces sales that enhance the earning power of the company. Cheerwine, created in 1917, is a nonalcoholic, carbonated drink produced by Carolina Beverage Corporation and sold mainly in the Southeast. Although Cheerwine does not even register in national market share polls, it has established itself as a southern icon and has found its way of creating loyal customers despite a decline in overall brand loyalty. Cheerwine was taken to Canada as North Carolina hosted the July 4, 2000, celebration in Ottowa and was even part of the 2001 North Carolina governor's inaugural ball. How is this possible? Carolinians are so loyal to the drink that those who relocate often write the company asking

Cheerwine has such a following of loyal customers that 9.4 million gallons have been sold!

where Cheerwine can be bought. Loyalists tell others about their favorite brand, often referred to as the "Nectar of the Tarheels."[41]

Even Mother Nature's own fruits have been branded—bananas by Chiquita and oranges by Sunkist. Why buy these rather than just any banana or orange? Why are names such as Kodak and Coca-Cola so well received in every part of the globe? Customers don't merely know them but prefer them. For a brand to be valuable to a company, a significant number of customers must prefer it over competitive brands.

The best kind of loyalty for a company is when consumers insist on the company's brand. **Brand insistence** means that buyers are not willing to accept substitutes. This degree of loyalty is more likely for specialty items, such as polo shirts or branded pharmaceuticals. Brand insistence is an enviable position and gives the company a valuable asset that will produce significant future cash flows. In recent years, some unlikely products have gained brand insistence status. It used to be that technology products, such as electrical components, did not have much brand awareness to say nothing of brand loyalty. Intel Corporation, the pioneering semiconductor company, gave technology branding a boost. Through an innovative marketing campaign, it has persuaded consumers to insist on Intel microprocessors in their PCs. See the technology feature, "Intel Brands the Soul in the Machine."

Perceived Brand Quality   The third dimension of brand equity is **perceived brand quality,** the degree to which brands consistently produce satisfaction by meeting customer expectations. This is one of the most important reasons consumers buy a product. The high or unique quality of a brand is directly related to what consumers are willing to pay and to whether the firm can charge a premium. A New Zealand study indicates that having and using a major accounting firm is associated with premium audit fees. In effect, names such as Arthur Andersen or Price Waterhouse serve as brand names. Companies are willing to pay higher fees for the perceived higher quality of a Big Eight audit, even when the identical service could be carried out by another firm.[42]

Brand Associations   Brand equity also involves establishing **brand associations** that evoke positive attitudes and feelings in consumers' minds. This enables firms to create messages that gain consumers' attention more easily. It also allows the brand equity to be extended to additional products. Procter & Gamble marketed only 13 advertised brands in 1950. By 1991, there were more than 100, not counting minor variants of major brands, and in 2001, there were more than 300 brands.[43] In a hard-hitting campaign against Yamaha motorcycles, Honda used brand associations with its automobiles. It quickly produced a great number of motorcycles of every type in an effort to crowd Yamaha out of the market. This was a feasible strategy because consumers already had a positive feeling about the Honda brand name.

Brand associations also can facilitate product changes. For example, Tide gradually altered its detergent from a bulky powder to concentrated powder and liquid forms. Positive brand associations help consumers make the transition. Buyers are more willing to try these products and accept them with different features or in new forms.

Competitive Advantage   Finally, brand equity can lead to **competitive advantage,** since a company can sell value rather than compete on the basis of price alone. The firm can charge

BRAND INSISTENCE
A dimension of brand equity that makes consumers unwilling to accept substitutes for the brand.

PERCEIVED BRAND QUALITY
The degree to which a brand consistently produces satisfaction by meeting customer expectations.

BRAND ASSOCIATIONS
The positive attitudes and feelings a brand evokes in consumers' minds.

COMPETITIVE ADVANTAGE
A dimension of brand equity that permits the product to be sold on a value basis rather than a price basis and may serve as a barrier to entrance against competitive products.

The Saab brand commands high perceived quality.

a premium for many of the intangible dimensions associated with the brand. Brand equity also creates competitive advantages by serving as a barrier to entry. In other words, it may be too risky or expensive for another company or brand to compete in the same market. In the 1980s, a battle of the brands among beer companies created an environment in which only the strong survived. Within only 10 years, hundreds of small and local breweries were put out of business by such companies as Anheuser-Busch, Strohs, Miller, and Coors. Nearly every beer company that relied on product processing and procedures rather than building brand equity fell out of contention.

MAINTAINING BRAND VALUE

How many times have you requested a Coke in a restaurant and been asked whether a Pepsi would be okay? Coca-Cola has gone to great lengths to make sure that the Coke brand name does not become a generic name. This is always a danger. Believe it or not, the following used to be brand names: aspirin, escalator, kerosene, nylon, and zipper. To prevent brand names from becoming available for general use, a company must continuously inform the public about its exclusive ownership. Consequently, Coca-Cola waged court battles against retailers who substituted Pepsi when Coke was ordered. Without such efforts, Coke could have lost its trademark exclusivity. Similarly, General Foods, owner of the Jell-O brand, tries to keep the name proprietary.

Often, the first manufacturer of a new technology or product becomes synonymous with the entire product class. How many times has a friend invited you to go Rollerblading, when in fact you would be in-line skating? Did you grow up believing that Kleenex was another name for facial tissue? Do you ask for a Band-Aid when you want an adhesive bandage? Many people say they are going to Xerox something, but they may be using a Canon or some other brand of copier. To avoid the loss of its exclusivity, Xerox runs advertisements explaining that "Xerox" is its registered trademark and should be used only when referring to the company and its products as opposed to a general process.

DEVELOPING A SUCCESSFUL BRAND NAME

Choosing a brand name may not be easy. In 1999, Americans filed over 240,000 trademark applications, 27 percent more than in 1998.[44] This poses a challenge to companies that want a memorable and meaningful brand name.[45] Name Lab, Inc., a specialist in this area, identified Geo as a globally oriented name for GM's Chevrolet Division to use. It also developed Acura for Honda.[46] In both cases the names are easy to remember, distinctive, positive, and can be used around the world. Because every language has a *k, o,* and short *a* sound, names such as Acura, Geo, Coca-Cola, Compaq, and Kodak fit well on the international scene.

Some firms have chosen brand names that communicate product attributes or benefits. For example, Wheaties describes the ingredients of the cereal. When "Breakfast of Champions" is added, we get an image of wholesomeness or goodness. The name Weight Watchers communicates a direct consumer behavior, and it carries strong associations with weight control and health. Recognizing the company's value, Heinz purchased it in 1978 and built it into a major product line by the 1990s.[47] Figure 9.8 identifies several products whose brand names are related to particular benefits.

Brand names must represent quality and commitment. That's why extensive research is usually conducted to identify whether the name is appropriate and can be used internationally. Standard Oil tested Exxon in 54 languages and more than 150 foreign markets before making a final decision. Marketers must be acutely aware that not all brand names carry the same meaning when translated. For example, the new General Mills cereal, Fringos, designed to be eaten with your fingers, translates into a less than appetizing word for Hungarians. Also consider Chevy Nova, which in Spanish-speaking countries meant "no va" or "no go."

Some brand names are successful because of what they say about the user. Many convey a personality trait that makes the connection directly. Magazines such as *Playboy, Cosmopolitan,* and *Glamour* represent attributes readers consider desirable.

JOINT MARKETING OF BRANDS

Joint marketing is cooperation between two companies to sell their brands. A common form of partnership occurs between two goods manufacturers. Since coupons and short-term promotions (such as refund certificates) often cause disloyalty and confusion among customers, replacing those tactics with joint marketing can build business for the cooperating companies. Kraft and Kodak, for example, teamed up in a "Holiday Homecoming" promotion. The partnership hoped to accomplish increased supermarket sales for Kodak products as well as 25 Kraft food items. This type of cooperation is expected to become more frequent.

Some partnerships are established between manufacturers and retailers, such as the team promotion of Tide laundry detergent and the Target brand name. Rubbermaid is another

JOINT MARKETING
Cooperation between two companies to sell their products, which tend to be complementary.

Product/Service	Brand Name
Exercise equipment	Soloflex
Vegetables	Green Giant
Batteries	Eveready
Fabric softener	Stay Fresh
Refrigeration trucks	Thermo King
Sweetener	NutraSweet
Oil change service	Jiffy Lube
Reclining chair	La-Z-Boy
Mufflers	Midas
Internet stock trades	eTrade
Internet travel	Travelocity.com

FIGURE 9.8 *Brand Names That Communicate Benefits*

CONNECTING THROUGH RELATIONSHIPS

STARBUCKS EXTENDS ITS BRAND NAME THROUGH JOINT VENTURES

With over 2,800 stores around the world and its beans sold in hotels, restaurants, and on airlines, Starbucks coffee seems to be everywhere. The Starbucks brand was recently designated as one of the 25 great brands in the next 25 years and one of the top 75 global brands by Interbrand, the world's leading brand consultancy. Brand extension products have been a key force in the process of expanding coffee giant Starbucks' global presence.

Rather than spending money and energy developing new products, Starbucks has formed relationships with key organizations in the product categories or venues it chooses to enter. One of the company's most ambitious joint ventures is its partnership with PepsiCo. Beginning in 1994, the program illustrated both companies' desire to benefit from the other's strength: PepsiCo has benefited from Starbucks' reputation for specialty coffee and Starbucks has profited from Pepsi's bottling and distribution muscle. Their first product, a carbonated coffee drink called Mazagran, was a flop. "Weird," "nasty," and "strange" were some of the unpromising comments when it was test-marketed. But the companies have cashed in on their newest ready-to-drink coffee, a bottled version of Frappucino. This frothy blend of ice, milk, and coffee sent summer sales through the roof at Starbucks stores when it was introduced in 1996. Four years later, the drink is still winning awards. Most recently in Japan, the drink received the Super Goods of the Year 2000 award for the food category by *Mono Magazine.*

After making the leap from hot coffee to cold bottled drink, Starbucks figured a cold coffee dessert was a natural next step. It teamed up with Breyer's Grand Ice Cream, Inc., in another partnership. Espresso Swirl, Javachip, and three others flavored with Starbucks coffee hit grocery store freezers in the summer of 1996. Within eight months, the brand became the nation's top-selling coffee ice cream.

Starbucks also followed through with plans to package the atmosphere of its coffee bars. The company collaborated with Capitol Records, Inc., on two jazz CDs played and sold in Starbucks stores. Most recently, Starbucks and Microsoft have formed a partnership, giving customers the famous Starbucks coffee experience with state-of-the-art technology. Customers will be able to download information and shop online as they relax in the coffeehouse.

There is a risk that Starbucks may extend its name too far and dilute its brand identity, but as time goes on that risk diminishes. Allan Hickock, managing director of Piper Jaffrey in Minneapolis, cautions: "Leaving your concept in the hands of people who don't share your culture is a big risk." Some Starbucks-struck stock analysts were a tad nervous about a deal with United Airlines' food service. The company that made its name marketing, preparing, and serving coffee handed the job over to United flight attendants. Starbucks viewed the deal differently, seeing the chance to reach about 80 million travelers a year in an environment in which coffee traditionally has been crummy. Even Hickock thinks that if any company can pull it off, Starbucks can. "They pay a lot of attention to detail," he says, "and everything the consumer touches drips with quality."

Sources: Kelly Shermach, "Coffee Drinking Rebounds; Specialty Blends Lead Way," *Marketing News,* September 12, 1994, p. 2; "Starbucks Has Breyer's Over for Dessert," *Los Angeles Times,* November 1, 1995, p. D2; Ian James, "One Part Coffee, One Part Soda, Mix in Some Marketing Muscle," *Los Angeles Times,* September 20, 1995, p. D4; Seanna Browder, "Starbucks Does Not Live by Coffee Alone," *Business Week Online,* August 5, 1996; Jennifer Reese, "Starbucks: Inside the Coffee Cult," *Fortune,* December 9, 1996, pp. 190–200; Edward Alden, "US Offered Coffee with a Conscience," *Financial Times,* October 4, 2000, www.hoovers.com visited January 8, 2001; and www.starbucks.com/aboutus/ visited January 8, 2001.

company that has collaborated with large retailers, such as Wal-Mart, Home Depot, and Venture Stores. Kraft Foods, among others, intends to follow suit.[48]

DIVERSITY IN BRAND MARKETING

As U.S. society becomes more diverse, companies are turning their attention to increasing brand equity by meeting the needs of various cultures, nationalities, and age groups. Since minority groups represent about 20 percent of the buying power of Americans, they are a target of many companies.[49]

Marketers are spending increasing amounts of money to promote their brands to ethnic markets. American Greetings Corp. expanded its product line to target Chinese Americans who celebrated the arrival of the Year of the Dragon in 2000. By selling greeting cards to celebrate the holiday, the card company hoped to establish itself as culturally conscious. Hallmark similarly expanded its product line in hopes of promoting its brand of greeting cards to the Hispanic population. Hallmark en Espanol features cards for Quinceanera and Dia de los Santos Reyes.[50]

The younger generations are also being targeted to increase brand equity. Clothing companies are familiar with marketing to younger generations. Tommy Hilfiger Corp. experienced rapid growth in the 1990s by aligning itself with famous rappers and as accessible by all races and economic groups. American Eagle similarly established itself as the store for a rugged, adventure look but revamped its image into a more collegiate, preppy look. By establishing themselves as different from their competitors, clothing companies capture specific components of the teenage population. The plan is to lure younger buyers, who often have mixed brand loyalties.[51]

PACKAGING AND LABELING

"People don't buy spray paint, they buy spray paint cans." That statement was made in a marketing research report for a major manufacturer in the industry to dramatize the importance of packaging. The research found that most buying decisions were made at the point of purchase. By looking at the color and design of the cans and by reading labels, consumers quickly determined which spray paint would best suit their needs.

Packaging and labeling once served simply to protect and identify the product inside. Now their role has been expanded to seven functions:

- Contain and protect items
- Communicate messages to customers
- Make the product more convenient to use
- Facilitate product storage
- Be environmentally friendly
- Contain product codes
- Protect against misuse

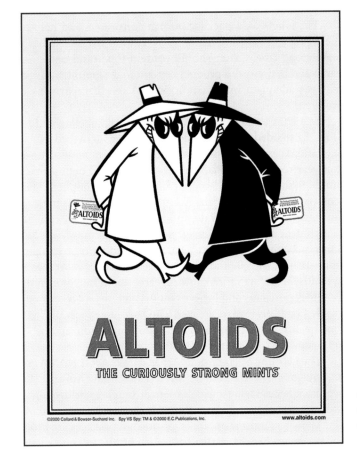

©2000 Callard & Bowser-Suchard Inc.   Spy VS Spy: TM & ©2000 E.C.Publications, Inc.   www.altoids.com

Altoids packaging prominently displays/information to inform consumers and help promote the product.

*Procter & Gamble's Oil of Olay
skin care products display
labels/information to inform
consumers and help promote
the product.*

<u>L</u>ABELS

Information printed on a product's package to inform consumers and help promote the product.

The **labels** on a package inform consumers and help promote the product. The Fair Packaging and Labeling Act of 1966 requires that consumer products carry clear and easily understood labels. They should contain the brand name and symbol, the manufacturer's name and address, the product content and amount, and recommended uses. The law also requires adequate information when value comparisons are made among competitive products.

In 1990 Congress passed the Nutritional Labeling and Education Act, which applies to food.[52] Excluded are meat, poultry, and eggs (covered by U.S. Department of Agriculture regulations) as well as restaurants, delicatessens, and infant formulas. Additional legislation that year required the FDA to develop standard definitions of terms commonly found on products, such as *reduced calories, high fiber,* and *low fat.*[53] These laws affect about 15,000 U.S. food packagers as well as many importers. Food labels must say how much fat and saturated fat, cholesterol, carbohydrate, and protein the product contains. They also must specify vitamin content and the percentage of the daily recommended allowances a serving represents. European standards on "diet" claims are even more strict than in the United States. Research shows that the people most likely to read food labels are women who have more education, live with others, are more knowledgeable about nutrition, are concerned about the quality of food they purchase, and believe that current dietary recommendations are important to their health. Less likely readers are men who have less education, live alone, are less concerned about food quality, are less knowledgeable about nutrition, and believe that the current dietary recommendations are unimportant.[54]

The Labeling of Hazardous Art Materials Act (LHAMA) of 1990 addresses another product category. The U.S. Public Interest Research Group (PIRG) lobbied for this legislation because it believed that a wide variety of suppliers inadequately warned consumers of chronic and long-term health risks related to certain chemicals used in their products.[55]

Marketers must take care to ensure that packages are properly labeled.[56] Both consumers and marketers benefit, particularly when health and safety issues are involved.

ETHICAL ISSUES SURROUNDING PRODUCT SAFETY AND LIABILITY

The Consumer Product Safety Act of 1972 created the Consumer Product Safety Commission (CPSC) to police consumer goods. It has broad authority over the end product, can require recalls and redesigns, and even inspects production facilities. For example, Dell Computer Corporation recalled 27,000 batteries for its notebook computers in 2000 after one notebook computer overheated and caught fire.[57] Of significance is its ability to bring criminal charges against companies and individuals who develop unsafe products.

Product liability refers to the fact that marketers and manufacturers are held responsible for injuries and damages caused by a faulty product. In one case the CPSC found that more than 7,000 people were being injured monthly on three-wheel all-terrain vehicles (ATVs), most of them made by Honda and Kawasaki. Although the number of accidents was well known to dealers and distributors, only when the CPSC applied pressure did the makers agree to stop marketing the product in the United States. Many people believe consumers had the right to know about the ATV injuries. Clearly, wider publicity about the hazards would have meant lost sales.

The liability issue involves the right to safety and the manufacturer's responsibility for designing safe products and for informing the public about any dangers. Most companies fulfill this obligation through the product warranty and, in extreme cases, product recalls.

PRODUCT LIABILITY
The responsibility of marketers and manufacturers for injuries and damages caused by a faulty product.

PRODUCT WARRANTIES

Warranties are written or implied expectations about product performance under use conditions. An express warranty is a written statement about the content or quality of a product and the manufacturer's responsibility to repair or replace it if it fails to perform. For example, an express warranty may indicate that an item is handcrafted in the United States, or may use such general terms as "unconditionally guaranteed" or "fully guaranteed," or may be a technical description of the goods. In the past, when consumers made claims under a warranty, some unethical manufacturers made it very difficult for them to receive satisfaction. General warranty statements came to lack meaning in many cases.

To combat this problem, Congress passed the Magnuson-Moss Warranty–Federal Trade Commission Improvement Act in 1975. Essentially, the law requires that express warranties be written in clear language and indicate which parts or components are covered and which are not. If repair is included in the express warranty, it must occur within a reasonable time, free of charge. A full warranty states that either the merchandise will be repaired or the purchase price refunded if the product does not work after repair.

Many retailers pressure their suppliers to take back any product a customer returns for any reason. Companies such as Wal-Mart have a very liberal return policy. This provides feedback on product performance and builds good customer relations, which in turn helps gain market share.

An implied warranty is an unwritten guarantee that the product or service will do the job it is intended to do. All products, even if not accompanied by a written statement, have an implied warranty based on the Uniform Commercial Code (UCC). Adopted in 1952, the UCC is a federal statute affecting the sale of goods and giving consumers the right to reject a product if it does not meet their needs. Many states also have laws protecting consumers.

WARRANTIES
Implied or written expectations about product performance under use conditions.

PRODUCT RECALLS

A **product recall** is the withdrawal of a potentially harmful product from the market, by either a manufacturer or the federal government, for its repair, replacement, or discontinuation. The Consumer Product Safety Commission (CPSC) is the federal agency responsible for protecting consumers from product-related injuries. It establishes standards for product design and instructions. It also requires manufacturers to meet safety standards through product testing. Manufacturers and retailers are required by law to notify the CPSC if they find a defective product that may result in injury.

When a manufacturer realizes a product is defective, its response can inspire consumer confidence and actually promote sales. In chapter 4 we described the actions of Johnson & Johnson during the Tylenol scare in 1982.[58] The unprecedented recall brought tremendous positive publicity to the company. When Tylenol went back on the shelves, consumers made it the top-selling pain reliever.

Just because a recall is made does not guarantee that consumers do not remain at risk. Consumers do not always respond to product recalls. For instance, Chrysler recalled

PRODUCT RECALL
The withdrawal from the market, by either a manufacturer or the federal government, and repair, replacement, or discontinuation of a potentially harmful product.

4.5 million minivans with defective tailgate latches. After 12 months, only 28 percent of affected customers had responded. A recall of defective seat belts by 11 automakers, which involved 8.8 million vehicles, received an even weaker response—only 5.7 percent among Nissan owners.[59] Much disinterest may be due to a notice that doesn't convey a sense of urgency. In its recall letter, Chrysler did not mention a "defective" part or that passengers had fallen out the back of the vans in accidents, as was shown on news broadcasts.[60] In contrast, Sears realized that dishwashers manufactured for it by Whirlpool had a defective wiring harness that could cause a fire. The Sears recall proclaimed in large red letters: "Important Safety Notice. Dishwasher Rework—Potential Fire Hazard. Please Give This Your Immediate Attention." Within three days the response rate was 20 percent.[61] In other cases, product recalls claim national attention, as did the Bridgestone tire recall in the fall of 2000. When the tires were linked to over 100 automobile deaths, mostly in Ford sport-utility vehicles, Bridgestone recalled over 6.5 million of its Firestone tires and became the center of a debate about responsibility for the accidents.[62] Even when a company meets its legal obligations, consumer awareness and other factors may have a lot to do with ethical considerations that must be addressed.

In some cases product recalls cannot be made. The Consumer Product Safety Commission sometimes faces problems in issuing product recalls, as it did with various brands of defective attic furnaces made by Consolidated Industries from 1984 to 1992. Because the company went bankrupt, it could not finance the product recall actions as required, and a recall was prohibited.[63]

Throughout this chapter we have explored a wide range of strategies—from bundling products into special value units to assuring product safety—that marketers employ to build strong brand equity and give appeal to existing products. In chapter 10 we will look at the special challenges involved in introducing new products and managing products appropriately throughout their life cycle.

CONNECTED: SURFING THE NET

INTEL
www.intel.com

INTEL, THE TOPIC OF THIS chapter's technology feature, was the first electronic component company to create a brand identity with end users. To learn more about Intel, visit its Web site and answer the following questions.

1. Examine Intel's home page. Without exploring the site farther, what features can you identify that may help the company connect with diversity? Now try the features. How do they appeal to diverse consumers? Explain.
2. How does the PC Buyer's Guide help the company build customer relationships? Are there any other features on the site that facilitate this connection?
3. Check out the products and services link. Use a product line depth and breadth matrix (introduced in Figure 9.4) and position Intel in the appropriate box. Explain your choice.
4. Which type of brand strategy does Intel use? Also note its branding approach and the possible reasons for this particular choice.

STARBUCKS
www.starbucks.com

THIS CHAPTER'S RELATIONSHIPS FEATURE IS "Starbucks Extends Its Brand Name Through Joint Ventures." Learn more about Starbucks at its jobline site and answer the following questions.

1. The company's objective is to establish Starbucks as the most recognized and respected brand in the world. Relate its current strategy to what you have learned about branding in this chapter.
2. Read about the history of Starbucks, in which you will also learn about locations, accounts, business ventures, product line, and so forth. One useful marketing scheme to help develop effective strategies is consumer product classifications. How can Starbucks' products be classified? Explain.
3. How do you think the company's community involvement supports connections with customers?
4. What other Starbucks business ventures are not mentioned in this chapter's relationships feature? How can they help build business for the company?

OBJECTIVE 1: Describe the major dimensions used by marketers to differentiate their products from competitors. Understand bundling and unbundling.

Products can be core, branded, and augmented. The core product represents the most basic functions and benefits. Some call this the generic product. The branded product adds characteristics that help consumers differentiate it from others. The augmented product includes such features as delivery, warranty, and customer service. A bundling strategy combines several products into one offering sold together. When products are bundled, they provide more value to the buyer than if each were sold separately.

OBJECTIVE 2: Understand consumer and business product classifications based on how and why products are purchased and consumed.

Five categories are used to classify consumer products. Unsought products are bought on the spur of the moment. They include novelty, impulse, and low-involvement items. Emergency products are bought because of unexpected events, such as an accident or theft. Convenience products are inexpensive and are usually purchased near home. Brand name and wide distribution are very important for these items. Shopping items are selected after comparisons are made. They tend to be carefully chosen and are kept for a long time. Specialty products have unique characteristics and value. They are often high-involvement purchases.

Business products are divided into capital, production, and operations products, depending on their primary use. Capital products include installations, such as offices and factories, and equipment, such as delivery vans and computers. These products last for a long time. Production products become part of other products. This category includes raw and processed materials, components, and subassemblies. Operations products help run the business. These include services such as accounting and waste removal, and office supplies such as business forms and cleaning products.

OBJECTIVE 3: Know how organizations make product line decisions that determine what will be sold, including the degree of standardization chosen for global markets.

A product line may comprise one item or a number of related products. Companies may have one or more product lines, each with many or few items. The term *depth* refers to the number of items in a product line; the term *breadth* refers to the number of lines the company offers. Most companies with broad lines are relatively large; those with narrow lines may be large or small. The degree to which products should be standardized is a major consideration for global firms. Some organizations pursue standardization to benefit from the resulting scale economies whereas others use a local strategy to respond to local needs.

OBJECTIVE 4: Recognize that branding and brand strategies are important aspects of building and maintaining a brand name.

A brand is distinguished from the product in general or other brands. Brands signify the "personality" of a product. The brand name and trademark can provide immediate recognition and credibility. Consequently, companies must register and protect trademarks. This is particularly challenging in global markets because stolen brand names and counterfeit products are so prevalent. There are several brand strategies. The generic approach involves no brand name. The individual strategy uses a unique name for each product line. The family brand is one name that covers all products in the line. Manufacturer brands are synonymous with the company that owns them. Private label brands are names used by wholesalers or retailers for products supplied to them. Combining two or more of these strategies is called a hybrid approach.

OBJECTIVE 5: Know how to create brand equity—the value associated with a product's name.

A strong brand name is extremely valuable, but developing that name is not simple. First, the name must be selected with care. It should be acceptable globally, represent quality and commitment, and be protected legally. A good brand can easily be extended to additional products as they are developed. Second, brand equity must be created by devoting company resources to each of its five dimensions: brand awareness, brand loyalty, perceived quality, brand associations, and competitive advantage. Third, care must be taken to protect the brand so it does not become a generic name for the product.

OBJECTIVE 6: Discuss the many legal and ethical issues surrounding brand and packaging decisions.

Federal laws and codes require that labels clearly identify the brand and manufacturer and warn consumers of safety hazards associated with use. Product liability holds marketers responsible for injuries and damages caused by a faulty product. Warranties refer to how products perform when used. In many cases, manufacturers are legally obligated to replace or repair faulty products. Express warranties are in writing. An implied warranty is unwritten. Essentially, a product should perform as it was designed. A product recall is instituted by the government or manufacturer to withdraw or modify a product. This occurs when a product is defective, especially if the potential for injury exists.

1. What is a product? Give several examples.
2. What are core, branded, and augmented products?
3. What are bundling and unbundling?
4. What are five categories of consumer products? What are three categories of business products? Give examples.
5. What is a product line? Unit? SKU?
6. What is a broad and deep product line? What is a narrow and shallow product line? Give examples.
7. What are global products and brands?
8. What is joint marketing of products? Give an example.
9. What is brand equity? How is it developed?
10. Why is it important to secure trademarks?
11. Name and describe five brand categories.
12. What are the functions of packaging?
13. What is product liability?

1. Imagine that you are a marketing manager at IBM responsible for the sale of personal computers to individual consumers. How would you describe your product in terms of core, branded, and augmented characteristics? Which of these do you feel is most important?
2. What are some advantages of a bundling strategy over an unbundling strategy? Disadvantages?
3. Name the five categories of products based on consumer buying behavior. Why is it so important for marketers to understand the category of their product?
4. Discuss the differences between product line breadth and depth. What are some advantages and disadvantages of each combination of breadth and depth?
5. Classify each of the following companies in terms of product line breadth and depth and explain your reasoning: Sears, 7-Eleven, Hallmark Cards, Wal-Mart, Kmart, Victoria's Secret.
6. If you were the marketing manager at a company with a broad product line, which of the six brand strategies would you likely select? What factors would affect your decision? What if the product line were narrow?
7. What are the most important activities involved in developing a successful brand name? Once the name is developed, how is brand equity formed?
8. Name the key functions of packaging. Which do you feel is most important? Does this vary by product?
9. The Consumer Product Safety Commission is a government entity with the power to bring criminal charges against companies and individuals who develop and market unsafe products. Is it fair to consider marketers criminals if consumers are injured by their company's products? Why or why not?

Augmented product: Product with characteristics that enhance its value beyond that of the core and branded product.

Brand: A distinguishing name or symbol to identify and differentiate products from those of competitors.

Brand associations: The positive attitudes and feelings a brand evokes in consumers' minds.

Brand awareness: The extent to which consumers recognize the brand and are likely to include it among the set of brands they consider.

Branded product: The core product plus the characteristics that allow the consumer to differentiate it from similar products.

Brand equity: The assets linked with the brand name and symbol that add value to the product.

Brand insistence: A dimension of brand equity that makes consumers unwilling to accept substitutes for the brand.

Brand loyalty: A dimension of brand equity that causes consumers to choose one brand over others available.

Breadth: The number of different lines a company markets.

Bundling strategy: A strategy in which several products are combined into a single offering.

Capital product: A costly item that lasts a long time but does not become part of any finished product.

Competitive advantage: A dimension of brand equity that permits the product to be sold on a value basis rather than a price basis and may serve as an entry barrier to competitive products.

Convenience product: A relatively inexpensive item that consumers purchase frequently and with minimum effort.

Core product: The essential physical item or intangible service that the customer receives.

Depth: The number of items in a product line.

Emergency product: A product purchased due to an unexpected event and for which the consumer has an urgent need.

Family brand strategy: Strategy in which a single brand name covers the entire group of products in the company's line(s).

Generic brand strategy: Strategy in which no brand name is used.

Hybrid brand strategy: A combination of two or more brand strategies.

Individual brand strategy: Strategy in which there is a unique name for each major product or product line.

Item: A specific version of a product within a product line.

Joint marketing: Cooperation between two companies to sell their products, which tend to be complementary.

Labels: Information printed on a product's package to inform consumers and help promote the product.

Manufacturer's brand (national brand): Brand named after the manufacturer.

Operations products: Products purchased to help run a business that are not included in the finished products.

Perceived brand quality: The degree to which a brand consistently produces satisfaction by meeting customer expectations.

Private brand (private label): The name wholesalers or retailers attach to products they resell for numerous suppliers.

Product: Any physical object, service, idea, person, event, place, or organization offered to satisfy consumers' needs and wants.

Product liability: The responsibility of marketers and manufacturers for injuries and damages caused by a faulty product.

Product line: Closely related products marketed by the organization.

Product recall: The withdrawal from the market, by either a manufacturer or the federal government, and the repair, replacement, or discontinuation of a potentially harmful product.

Production product: Raw materials, processed materials, component parts, and subassemblies that become parts of other goods.

Shopping product: A purchase generally made only after the consumer has compared several alternatives.

Specialty item: A product with unique characteristics that provides unusual value to the purchaser.

Supplies: Consumable items used for business operations.

Trademark (brand mark): A distinctive form or figure that identifies the brand.

Unsought product: An item that consumers don't think about frequently and for which they don't perceive much need.

Warranties: Implied or written expectations about product performance under use conditions.

1. Valerie Seckler, "Yahoo Mounts Custom Shopping Feature," *WWD,* July 11, 2000, p. 13; "Yahoo's Got Mail," *Computer Reseller News,* July 10, 2000, p. 8; Brent Schlender, "How a Virtuoso Plays the Web," *Fortune,* March 6, 2000, pp. F-79–F-83; Jeffrey M. O'Brien, "Behind the Yahoo!" *Brandweek,* June 28, 1999, pp. IQ17+; Becky Ebenkamp, "Not Waiting for Anybody," *Brandweek,* September 27, 1999, p. 48.

2. Faglan Du, Paula Merganhagen, and Marlene Lee, "The Future of Services," *American Demographics,* November 1995, pp. 30–47; Ronald Henkoff, "Service is Everybody's Business," *Fortune,* June 27, 1994, pp. 48–60; Thomas G. Scott, "Service Sector Drives Job Gowth," *Business First,* July 7, 2000, p. 63.

3. Bill Briggs, "Teen Money Machine Retailing Gurus Track Youth Trends If They Hope to Survive," *Denver Post,* April 26, 1999, p. F-01; "Targeting Teens Using Custom Publishing," *Drug Store News,* November 27, 2000.

4. "Jackson Hewitt Inc. Releases Its Gold Guarantee Program," *PR Newswire,* January 9, 2001, as retrieved from the World Wide Web, ptg.djnr.com.

5. www.tecWeb.com/wlibrary/dismant00.htm, site visited January 9, 2001.

6. Jody Schwartz, "Packaged Goods," *Adhesives Age,* August 2000.

7. "Garmin® Debuts the eTrex Venture, eTrex Legend and eTrex Vista," *PR Newswire,* January 9, 2001, as retrieved from the World Wide Web, ptg.djnr.com.

8. "High Demand for Office Paper Prompts Unique New Business Venture," *Business Wire,* April 25, 2000.

9. www.ibm.com, site visited January 17, 2001.

10. Veronica MacDonald, "The Hair Care Market (1)," *Household & Personal Products Industry,* December 1, 2000, p. 108.

11. Riccardo A. Davis, "Kodak Rethinks Strategy: Marketer Will Focus on Core Photo Brands, New Products," *Advertising Age,* May 10, 1993, p. 48.

12. "Kodak Zooms in on Younger Customers," *Wall Street Journal,* April 12, 1996, p. B5.

13. "Kodak Explains Retail Strategy," *Photo Marketing,* January 2001.

14. Liz Jones, "Procter & Gamble: Big Brands, Big Markets," *European Cosmetic Markets,* December 2000.

15. Tom Stundza, "Buy Steel Better," *Purchasing,* December 8, 2000, pp. 42–46.

16. Jessica Wohl, "USA: Yearahead—U.S. Consumers Thirst for Soft Drink Variety," Reuters English News Service, December 28, 2000, as retrieved from the World Wide Web: ptg.djnr.com; www.pepsi.com, site visited January 17, 2001; Betsy McKay, "Coca-Cola Acquires Maker of Coffee, Bottled Drinks," *The Asian Wall Street Journal,* January 15, 2001, p. N4; www.cocacola.com, site visited January 17, 2001; Hillary Chaura, "Pepsi, Coke Still at War, but on Different Fronts," *Advertising Age,* December 11, 2000.

17. "IBM Serves up E-Business Hosting Solutions for Australian Open," www.ibm.com, site visited January 17, 2001.

18. "Newell Revamps Staff of Plastic Storage Unit," *The Weekly Newspaper for the Home Furnishing Network,* December 18, 2000, p. 4; www.newell-rubbermaid.com, site visited January 17, 2001.

19. Karl Schoenberger, "Motorola Bets Big on China," *Fortune,* May 27, 1996, pp. 116–124.

20. "City:Motorola Coup," *The Daily Telegraph,* August 22, 2000, as retrieved from the World Wide Web: ptg.djnr.com.

21. David A. Aaker, *Managing Brand Equity* (New York: The Free Press, 1991), p. 7.

22. David Arnold, *The Handbook of Brand Management* (Reading, MA: Addison-Wesley, 1992), p. xvii.

23. "Can P&G Make Eagle Fly in Snack Market?" *Chicago Tribune* (National Edition), May 8, 1996, p. B3.

24. "Broad, Deep, Long, and Heavy," *Economist,* November 16, 1996, p. 72.

25. Diane Crispell and Kathleen Brandenburg, "What's in a Brand?" *American Demographics,* 1993, pp. 26–29, 31–32; Glenda Shahso Jones, "Your New Brand Image," *Catalog Age,* July 2000, pp. 175–178.

26. Betsy Morris, "The Brand's the Thing," *Fortune,* March 4, 1996, p. 72.

27. "Forecasters See Less Ad Growth in Coming Year," *The Plain Dealer,* December 5, 2000, p. 2C.

28. Betsy Morris, "The Brand's the Thing," *Fortune,* March 4, 1996, p. 72; www.intel.com, site visited January 17, 2001.

29. "Cancer Society's Deal to Sell Its Name Sparks Protests," *Marketing News,* September 23, 1996, p. 5; and Ron Harris, "Education Dept. Upset About Web Service on Financial Aid," *Associated Press Newswires,* January 17, 2001.

30. "Smith + Noble's New Creative Battle," *Catalog Age,* January 2001, p. 6.

31. "Around Rip-Off Britain," *Financial Times Surveys Edition,* November 7, 2000.

32. "Why China Is a Copybook Case," *Financial Times London Edition,* December 2, 2000.

33. "Junk Parts Behind Many Air Mishaps," *Irish Times,* October 7, 2000, p. 11.

34. Gerry Meyers, "Another View on Private Labels: They're Not Going to Fade Away," *Advertising Age,* April 25, 1994, p. 26.

35. Jonathon Berry, "Attack of the Fighting Brands," *Business Week,* May 2, 1995, p. 125.

36. William A. Roberts, Jr., "More Than a Name," *Prepared Foods,* September 2000.

37. Adapted from Aacker, *Managing Brand Equity,* p. 4.

38. www.kraft.com, site visited January 17, 2001.

39. Jennifer Beauprez, "Shopping for a New Brand," *Denver Post,* June 20, 2000, p. C-01.

40. David J. Lipke, "Pledge of Allegience," *American Demographics,* November 2000, pp. 40–42.

41. Hannah Miller, "Soft Drink Has No Wine, but Plenty of Cheer," *Advertising Age,* June 1, 1992, pp. 3, 4. www.cheerwine.com, site visited January 17, 2001; "Easley Plans Family-Themed Inauguration," *The Associated Press Newswires,* December 15, 2000; "N.C. hosts July 4 celebration in Ottowa," *Associated Press Newswires,* July 12, 2000; Mike Foley, "A Little (Soda) Pop Culture from the Bubbling South Cola Country," *The Greenville (S.C.) News,* August 11, 1999.

42. Michael Firth, "Price Setting and the Value of a Strong Brand Name," *International Journal of Research in Marketing,* December 1993, pp. 381–386.

43. William M. Weilbacher, *Brand Marketing* (Lincolnwood, IL: NTC Business Books, 1993), p. 51; www.pg.com, site visited January 17, 2001.

44. 1999 Annual Report, located at www.uspto.gov, site visited January 17, 2001.

45. Gene Koprowski, "The Name Game," *Marketing Tools,* September 1996, www.marketingtools.com.

46. Susan Moffat, "Foreign Car Sales Go Vroom in Japan," *Fortune,* April 9, 1990, p. 10.

47. Warren Burger, "The Big Freeze at Heinz," *Ad Week's Marketing Week,* August 21, 1989, pp. 20–25.

48. Raju Narisetti, "Joint Marketing with Retailers Spreads," *Wall Street Journal Interactive Edition,* October 24, 1996.

49. "Melting Pot of Gold," *Business Week,* November 6, 2000.

50. "Category Mirrors Diversity of US," *MMR,* February 21, 2000.

51. Leslie Kaufman, "Is Hilfiger Losing the Beat?" *The Arizona Republic,* January 31, 2001, p. D1; "American Eagle's New Teen Focus Has Styles Selling, Stock Soaring," *Chicago Tribune,* December 24, 2000.

52. Chris Baum, "NLEA Compels Food Packagers to Redesign," *Packaging,* May 1994, p. 21.

53. Andrea Dorfman, "Less Bologna on the Shelves," *Time,* November 5, 1990, p. 79.

54. Pam Demetrakakes, "Packaging Field Gears up for New Labeling Rules," *Packaging,* January 1993, p. 3.

55. Mark Hartley, "For the Sake of Invisible Ink," *Occupational Health & Safety,* December 1993, p. 4.

56. Frances J. Cronin, Cheryl Achterberg, and Laura S. Sims, "Translating Nutrition Facts into Action: Helping Consumers Use the New Food Label," *Nutrition Today,* September–October 1993, p. 30.

57. "Dell Computer Is Set to Recall Laptops' Batteries," *Austin American-Statesman,* October 13, 2000.

58. "Tylenol Containing Strychnine Is Found in California as Consumer Fears Mount," *Wall Street Journal,* October 6, 1982, p. 2.

59. Oscar Suris and Nichole M. Christian, "Will Consumers Respond to Ford's Recall Notice?" *Wall Street Journal,* May 8, 1996, p. B1.

60. Ibid.

61. Recall letter from Sears, on file with authors.

62. www.bridgestone-firestone.com, site visited January 17, 2001.

63. Jennifer Oldham, "Faulty Furnaces Set Scores of Fires," *Times Staff Writer,* September 27, 2000.

BRICKS-AND-MORTAR COMPANY BRAND RECOGNITION ON THE INTERNET

INTERNET-ONLY COMPANIES HAVE BEEN SUCCESSFUL in marketing products by focusing solely on a low-cost strategy. These products are generally not associated with high brand recognition or brand equity. However, bricks-and-mortar retailers often rely on a brand name developed over many years. When these companies decide to develop an Internet presence, they risk losing some of this established brand equity. If a well-established bricks-and-mortar company traditionally offers a quality product at a good value, customers' perceptions of brand equity will decline if that same company were to offer its products on the Internet at rock-bottom prices. Brand equity is further lost if product breadth and depth are much greater in the store than on the Internet. In addition, loss of brand recognition can also occur if the Web site portrays a vastly different image of the company than what is perceived in the bricks-and-mortar store. The issue of maintaining brand equity on a Web site has been a major challenge for bricks-and-mortar stores attempting to create an Internet site. Some companies, such as JCPenney, have been more successful with this challenge than others.

JCPenney was one of the first midtier retail chains to launch an Internet site. Its Internet strategy is designed to combat the risk of losing brand equity in three ways: through a special pricing strategy that does not focus solely on low cost; by having a large number of products available on the site; and by maintaining a consistent brand image across all channels.

The first of these brand equity protection measures has been its unique pricing strategy. ". . . JCPenney launched Red Alert, a site that offers any of three pricing models for surplus goods. It can mark products at clearance prices, operate conventional English auctions similar to eBay, or price items using 'auto-markdown' technology that tracks inventory at timed intervals and sets prices accordingly." With this strategy customers receive rock-bottom prices without losing brand equity that has been established in the product. These items are discounted due to surplus, not because the product is cheaply made.

The second measure to maintain brand equity has been to offer a great breadth and depth of product line on the Internet. JCPenney knew that if its site did not offer enough products, customers would be dissatisfied and choose to go to the store for better selection. This is why it offers 200,000 SKUs and plans to increase its selection in the near future.

The third measure for success has been to create a uniform image throughout its many sales channels, storefront, Internet, and catalog. This is the most significant measure to maintain brand equity and JCPenney tackles it from three avenues. First is its slogan, 'Come in, Call in, Log on,' "leverages its [JCPenney] high-profile, store-as-a-brand presence . . . transforming itself into an omnipresent retailer that serves its consumers wherever, whenever, and however they choose." In the infancy of site development, the core team found it especially challenging to translate its well-established catalog, containing hundreds of thousands of SKUs, onto the Web. "They struggled to repurpose two-page paper spreads with shared headlines and a common feel to electronic pages that might only highlight a single or handful of items simultaneously."

JCPenney advertises the Web site on everything from national ads to in-store shopping bags. Every other page of the catalog contains a URL, and post cards are placed in the catalog to advertise particular products on the Internet site at half the cost of stand-alone mailings. While other Internet companies are required to run costly ad campaigns, JCPenney saves billions in "free tag-on exposure." By combining these advertising strategies, the consumer views the store, the Web site, and the catalog as *one* JCPenney.

It also creates a uniform brand name through something called a "sweet spot." Bricks-and-mortar retailers have long known the importance of product placement to sales. Every store has a "sweet spot" and a product is more likely to sell if it is placed there. What Internet retail experts, such as Mark Doss, national director of e-tailing for Ernst & Young, have realized is that the effectiveness of product placement holds true for Web pages as well. The home page is the "sweet spot" because most customers do not buy products placed three clicks away. JCPenney offers most of its products no more than two or three clicks off the home page and is working on designing home pages that are specifically tailored to a customer when he or she logs in. This allows the company to create the same "feel" on the site that customers experience when they walk in the door. When shopping at a store, most customers walk directly to the department that interests them most or even park their cars near the entrance closest to it. The "sweet spots" are generally noticed first and products are more likely to sell. This is also what is done to the Web pages. Products that need to be sold are placed on the home page, or just a few clicks away.

Sources: Corinth Estienny, "Online with the Frontline," *Discount Merchandiser,* January 2000, pp. 37–40; and Ted Kemp, "Wal-Mart No Web Mart—Sudden Site Closure Magnifies Online Superiority of Retail Rivals," *Internetweek,* October 9, 2000, p. 1.

Gap

GAP (AS IN "GENERATION GAP") WAS founded in 1969 in San Francisco with only one store. Today, there are over 3,300 stores throughout the United States and internationally in locations such as Canada, France, Germany, Japan, and the United Kingdom. Gap employs over 140,000 employees within its online, in-store, and corporate operations and had revenues of over $11.6 billion in 1999.

Composed of three different brands—Banana Republic, Old Navy, and Gap, which includes GapKids and BabyGap—Gap strives to "deliver style, service, and value to everyone." That goal extends throughout all of Gap's enterprises; however, specific goals and branding techniques differ for each of the three brands. The three brands are separately housed in different locations in San Francisco to more easily keep the focus and goals of each entity distinct.

Gap purchased Banana Republic in 1983, when it consisted of only two stores that specialized in safari-inspired clothing. Since then, Banana Republic has become the brand for "the modern, versatile wardrobe." Banana Republic boasts the most expensive product line of the three brands, with clothing made from superior fabrics. The product line includes women's and men's clothing, shoes, accessories, personal care products, intimate apparel, jewelry, and home accessories.

Old Navy was created by Gap in 1994. Old Navy has become the brand for "fun, fashion, family, and value." The goal is for Old Navy to be the shopping destination for value for the entire family. This division offers clothing at a lower price point than Gap and Banana Republic for men, women, children, and babies. Old Navy stores have been using what has recently been termed *enter-tailing,* the combination of entertainment and retailing. By playing loud, energetic music, Old Navy hopes to bring younger generations into the stores—and maybe have them bring their parents along.

The Gap brand sits somewhere in between Banana Republic and Old Navy with pricing and quality. Its goal is to "offer a balance of modern and seasonal styles" to men, women, children, and babies in a pleasant and calm shopping environment. Gap specializes in basics such as T-shirts, jeans, and khakis, but it attracts customers by showcasing the latest trends. Many companies would be nervous about having three brands that have similar products. After all, it is possible that Gap customers would decide to purchase lower-priced clothing at Old Navy. That means a decrease in revenues for Gap. But CEO Mickey Drexler is not concerned. According to Chief Operating Officer John Wilson, "We'd rather cannibalize our own business than have the competition do it." Drexler's main goal is to make buying a Gap product just like buying a carton of milk—automatic. He has tried to simplify clothes shopping by always including clothing staples in the product assortments. While some clothing companies actually market an image (youth, sex, money, power, etc.), Gap brands actually market the products they sell: T-shirts, khakis, and sweaters. Drexler also wants to make Gap a global brand, which is as easily recognized in Germany as it is in Japan, San Francisco, and New York City.

Recently, Gap has focused on bringing the brands to the consumer via Internet sites. Banana Republic's and Old Navy's Web sites opened in 1999, and Gap's opened in 1997. The results have been good with total sales from Gap's Web site (www.gap.com) almost tripling in three years to approximately $90 million in 1999!

The future of Gap's products will depend on it providing a product assortment that meets customers' needs with an effective marketing plan. Additionally, Gap will need to continue its focus on creating customer satisfaction and loyalty through its marketing campaigns. With brands that cover many price points and meet the differences in customer needs, Gap should be able to continue its success well into the future.

1. *How has Gap achieved global status and brand equity, especially in an industry that relies so heavily on trends? Do you think that one brand will be more successful globally than the others? Why?*

2. *How can Gap maintain equity in its brands in the future? What are some of the obstacles it will face? Are the obstacles the same for each brand?*

3. *What do you think would happen if the three brands were marketed together? What are some ways that Gap could market them together successfully?*

4. *Which brand do you think is the easiest to market? Why?*

5. *Gap also has discount outlet stores across the United States. Where do those stores fit in with the others?*

Sources: Nina Munk, "Gap Gets It," *Fortune,* www.fortune.com, August 3, 1998; Gap Web site, www.gap.com, visited June 18, 2000; Hoover's Online, "The Gap, Inc.," www.hooversonline.com, visited June 18, 2000; Stacy Permna, "Mend That GAP," *Time,* www.time.com, February 14, 2000; and Julie Creswell, "The Next Big Things," *Fortune,* www.fortune.com, December 20, 1999.

PRODUCT PLANNING, DEVELOPMENT, AND MANAGEMENT

◀ *Model Claudia Schiffer and her own edition of the Palm Vx*

THE PALMPILOT HANDHELD COMPUTER, A FAVORITE *of many business-people and entrepreneurs, began life as a block of wood. When Jeff Hawkins and Donna Dubinsky formed Palm Computing to develop a palm-sized device for mobile computing, they were aiming to provide two major benefits for business users. First, the new device had to be truly portable, easily slipped into a pocket or purse for access at any time. Second, it had to be simple to use—no bulky keyboard, no confusing commands. These two benefits drove the development of the first PalmPilot and have guided product enhancements throughout the product's life.*

To keep the new product compact yet functional, Hawkins and Dubinsky resisted the temptation to add fancy extras. Instead, they focused on a limited number of features they believed business users would most value. One was the ability to jot memos directly on the touch-sensitive screen, using a penlike stylus and a shorthand system developed especially for the PalmPilot. Another was the ability to instantly store and retrieve names, addresses, and detailed contact information. As the PalmPilot took shape, Hawkins began carrying a wooden model of the product wherever he went. Although he felt odd walking around with a chunk of wood in his shirt pocket, the experience helped him better gauge the right size, shape, and weight for the new product.

At the product launch, Palm introduced both a basic and a more powerful version of its palm-sized computer. The PalmPilot became an instant success, popping up in the pockets and briefcases of salespeople, top executives, and other busy professionals. In response to the strong demand, Palm continued to introduce advanced models with improvements such as larger storage capability, brighter display screens, rechargeable power supplies, and wireless Internet access. Within four years, Palm had sold about 7 million PalmPilots and captured most of the U.S. market for handheld computers. According to the company's research, more than 60 percent of its buyers are high-income men living in big cities who use their PalmPilots to check e-mail every hour or two.

The PalmPilot's wild success attracted a number of competitors—including Hawkins and Dubinsky, who sold Palm to U.S. Robotics and left not long after that company was acquired, in turn, by 3Com. Their new company, Handspring, focused on developing a lower-priced handheld device for the consumer market. Meanwhile, Palm was seeing slower sales growth as the market matured. So Palm decided to move beyond business users and broaden its target market to include consumers as well. On the high end, Palm introduced a more stylish version of its most powerful PalmPilot—available only on supermodel Claudia Schiffer's Web site. On the low end, Palm launched a more colorful, limited-function model for consumers, priced in direct competition with Handspring's low-priced Visor model.

Even if Handspring winds up taking significant market share away from the PalmPilot, Palm stands to make money because it licenses its technology to Handspring. It also licenses its technology to IBM, Sony, Nokia, and other manufacturers of handheld computers and electronic devices such as digital cameras and mobile phones. Still, Palm makes a higher profit by selling its own Palm Pilots, so the company may decide to change its licensing strategy once the agreement with Handspring expires in 2005.

Although Palm intentionally limited the number of features on the PalmPilot, it realizes that a multifunction product is more valuable to users. Therefore, Palm is battling to maintain market share and extend product life by encouraging outside developers to create all kinds of new software for the PalmPilot. Already PalmPilot users can choose among 5,000 software add-ons for schedule management, sales force automation, team communications, financial management, and many other functions. The PalmPilot has come a long way from its beginnings as a plain block of wood. Now Palm's challenge is to build on the strength of the PalmPilot brand by continuing to develop innovative new products that meet the mobile computing needs of the target market.[1]

CONNECTED: SURFING THE NET

www.palm.com

Visit the Palm, Inc. Web site to see the large variety of features, products, and applications that are available. You can even customize and purchase your own Palm handheld online.

THE CONCEPTS OF PRODUCT DEVELOPMENT AND PRODUCT MANAGEMENT

A winning company doesn't rest—it innovates. New products invigorate organizations. They create enthusiasm among employees even before they excite the market. They are absolutely essential to competitive advantage. Companies that fail to innovate usually fail, period. Even those that are slower than competitors will find their customer connections strained or broken as leading-edge organizations step in and step ahead. At the same time, winning companies don't prematurely abandon their existing products. They nurture and support them like old friends. Organizations make direct connections with customers through products. Without these, no relationship can exist. Products form the fundamental substance of all business exchanges. Whether these connections remain solid depends largely on the ability of

This FedEx ad displays a few of the company's shipping services.

marketers to introduce and manage products. For example, to be more competitive, Shiseido Cosmetic Co., Japan's largest cosmetic company, recently opened its largest research and development center, a $108 million lab devoted to testing and developing state-of-the-art, environmentally friendly cosmetics for its domestic and global markets.[2] This chapter explores how long-term, tight connections are made through technological innovations and product management that fulfill market potential.

Speed and responsiveness make sheer company size a major force shaping the marketplace today. The ability to develop products quickly is extremely important in gaining a competitive advantage.[3] Companies are compressing the amount of time required to turn an idea into a marketable product. This is multiplying the number of products offered as well as shortening the life of products in the market. Because of these trends, executives are emphasizing the firm's **product mix**—all the product lines and products a company offers. They also are adjusting the depth and breadth of product lines in response to rapidly changing market forces. Excellent product management is considered essential for creating superior customer value.

PRODUCT MIX

All the product lines and products a company offers.

Organizations must continue to manage existing products, and they must have the ability to identify, find, or create new ones. In a classic study, the consulting firm of Booz, Allen & Hamilton found that 28 percent of company growth comes from products introduced in the past five years.[4] Yet, new-product development is risky and expensive. About 56 percent of introductions fail within five years, and about 45 percent of new-product development resources are spent on failures. In fact, companies usually have to come up with 13 new-product ideas before they hit on one that works.[5] Research shows that a common reason innovations fail is the lack of strategic direction.[6] With the right strategy products can provide sufficient profits necessary to reach the organization's objectives and cover the costs of developing and growing new products.

The main objective of product management is to ensure a steady flow of products that supports the company's mission. New technologies that were once restricted to a few giant corporations are now accessible to numerous small and midsized firms. In addition, markets are expanding both domestically and internationally through global networks of communication, distribution, and business relationships. All these factors allow both large and small organizations to introduce products very rapidly. Companies in the 21st century are making even more new and innovative product introductions.

There are many important elements to consider in product development and management as shown in Figure 10.1. This chapter begins with a look at how the product mix affects growth. Organizations sometimes grow by focusing on existing products and segments, but much more growth comes from innovation in products and markets. Next we explore types of innovations and factors that affect how rapidly they are accepted by potential customers. Once a company decides the role of new products for accomplishing objectives, it employs a new-product development process. We explore a successful process—from formulation of new-product strategy to product launch. This is followed by a section on product management approaches, particularly the policies and organizational structures that foster innovation. Finally, we examine how the product life cycle and the diffusion process relate to decisions ranging from introduction to discontinuation.

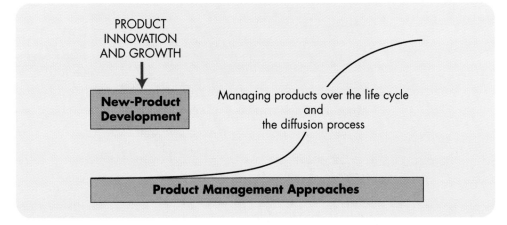

FIGURE 10.1 *The Concepts of Product Planning, Development, and Management*

PRODUCT PLANNING

The focus given to core businesses, market development, product development, and diversification.

PRODUCT PLANNING

Every business needs to develop a product plan consistent with its overall marketing strategy. **Product planning** outlines the focus given to core businesses (current products in current segments), market development (new segments for current products), product development (new products for current segments), or diversification (products totally new to the company for new segments).

Product planning decisions are influenced by market segment strategies. Marketers must decide how much emphasis to place on the existing product lines and segments and how much on developing new products and markets. Figure 10.2 depicts these fundamental choices.

Core Business Focus   A core business focus emphasizes the marketing of existing products to existing market segments. Even this requires careful decisions about whether to maintain, expand, or eliminate current products, depending on market conditions, the age of the product, and competitive factors. Firms that do not make these adjustments usually must retreat.[7] This may become evident in plant consolidations, fewer and fewer products, divestment of lines of business, and withdrawal from certain markets.

Many strong companies achieve success by focusing on their core products and market segments. This doesn't mean that all avenues for expansion are closed off. The core business can provide earnings to support other options, such as Coke's aggressive global strategy. Rather than rely on its U.S. operations, Coca-Cola moved into new markets to become one of the best-known companies in the world. Sometimes companies move away from their core business and then return to their traditional focus. Amazon.com, an Internet company originally based on book and music sales, has branched out to sell everything from stereos, lawn and patio equipment, and cellular phones to cars. However, these new products have not yet produced the results that CEO Jeff Bezos hoped they would. In fact, Amazon's stock has dropped from a high in December 1999 of $113 to a low of about $16 in June, 2001. Though Bezos is confident in the company's ability to make more than its book sales profitable, time will tell if Amazon will be forced to return to its core business.[8]

MARKET DEVELOPMENT

Offering existing products to new market segments.

Market Development   **Market development** occurs when existing products are offered to new segments. Firms may sell directly to these or use new channels of distribution. They also may expand from local markets to regional, national, international, or global markets. Nike has recently expanded its markets by specializing on a new segment of the population. The well-known athletic equipment company has teamed up with Dynastream Innovations of Canada to focus on new products for what they call "digital athletes." Its new division, niketechlab, is devoted to developing new high-tech products for the athlete wanting to combine sports and technology. It has, for example, recently developed a foot-mounted speed and distance gauge called SDM Triax 100. Other products Nike has produced for this market include a heart rate monitor, digital compass, and a handheld sports communication device that works like a two-way radio.[9] Studies have shown that successful market development

	Existing Products	New Products
Existing Market Segments	**Core Product Focus** Maintain, expand, or harvest current products	**Product Development** Improve products Add to product line
New Market Segments	**Market Development** Add new market segment(s)	**Diversification** Add new-product lines Expand into unrelated businesses

FIGURE 10.2 *Product Planning Options*

need not involve the same products as long as there is a fit between brand concept and the extension products.[10] For example, Nike could decide to produce virtual sports games and easily connect its reputation for "real" sports equipment with "virtual" sports equipment.

Product Development **Product development** occurs when companies make new products for existing market segments. This may take the form of simple improvements to older products or extensions of the product line. A **line extension** is an innovation closely related to other products in the line. Most software companies are continuously introducing improved versions. For example, Microsoft has upgraded its popular Word software several times. Examples of extensions are also numerous. Autodesk has recently developed an innovation that will complement its existing AutoCAD 2000i programs. The XML/Data Extension will facilitate the delivery of design materials to the Web by ensuring compatibility between different segments of the design industry. The XML/Data Extension was created to enhance the AutoCAD 2000i platform making it more than an improved version of the platform.[11]

Whether in the consumer or business market, product lines are continuously expanding. Faber SpA established its presence as a premium Italian manufacturer of kitchen chimneys, cooking ranges, and glass hobs and ovens, and has now extended its product line downward. Faber SpA is launching an affordable line targeted for lower income consumers with a new range of kitchen gas stoves.[12] Pizza Hut is always developing new products and recently added yet another type of crust to its standard line—the "Insider" that features six types of cheeses stuffed between two layers of crust.[13] Internet companies also expand their product lines to keep with a demanding market. The Internet's leading provider of discounted hotel accommodations, Hotel Reservations Networks (www.hoteldiscount.com), expanded its product line by offering vacation rentals through a new Web site (www.condosavers.com). This new product will provide customers with ready access to discount vacation rental inventory even during sold-out periods, with a low-price guarantee and an objective rating system, floor plan, description, and photo for each property.[14]

Diversification Diversification occurs when new products are introduced into new market segments. Sometimes this is done with extensions of the current business, and sometimes it occurs with totally new ventures. Many clothing companies and department stores are diversifying their product lines with plus-size clothing for women. I.N.C. label clothing, sold in Macy's and Bloomingdale's, is offering plus-size clothing that is designed exactly like regular-sized clothing, and also styles designed to provide more coverage. Liz Claiborne's Elisabeth line follows mainstream fashion trends by offering styles in leather, suede, and faux suede, while The Casual Corner offers the same prints in heavier fabrics that are softer and more flowing than the fabrics used for regular-sized clothing. Each of these lines responds to a recent survey that shows women's plus-size clothing as the fastest-growing category of women's clothing.[15]

Often companies diversify by expanding into totally new business product areas. The multibillion-dollar conglomerate Philip Morris has acquired several food companies in order to diversify from its leading brand, Marlboro cigarettes. Given the potential legal liability and poor reputation faced by the tobacco industry, the company may be making wise investments in Miller beer, Kraft Foods, and Nabisco.[16] Consistent with the old adage about not putting all of the eggs in one basket, diversification spreads the risk associated with one industry. One Japanese beer company is even seeking to diversify itself to gain profits by expanding into additional beverage products. Moody's Investors Service says of the company's diversification, "We believe that the shift to becoming comprehensive drink providers will give the beer companies business opportunities in the broader categories and therefore increase sales." To maintain profits during the initial buildup period and reduce the risk involved in such diversification, however, brewers must reduce the base cost of their core beer operations.[17]

TYPES OF PRODUCT INNOVATION

Marketers classify innovations according to the effect they are likely to have on consumers. **Continuous innovation** is a minor change in an existing product, such as a new style or model, that can be easily adopted without significant alterations in consumer behavior. The product usually is familiar. Campbell's Soup improved on its already easy-to-make canned soup by removing the one step involved—adding water. The new line of soups, Simply Home Soups, come in a glass jar, ready to heat and eat, and are available in six different varieties, including chicken vegetable pasta, hearty minestrone, and chicken noodle.[18] The product is new, but it requires little or no consumer behavior change.

PRODUCT DEVELOPMENT
Offering new products to existing market segments.

LINE EXTENSION
A new product closely related to others in the line.

CONNECTED: SURFING THE NET
www.condosavers.com

Visit this convenient Web site that will walk you through the process of finding a vacation rental place, at a good price, for even the busiest seasons.

CONTINUOUS INNOVATION
A minor alteration in an existing product, such as a new style or model, that can be easily adopted without significant changes in consumer behavior.

DYNAMICALLY CONTINUOUS INNOVATION

A familiar product with additional features and benefits that require or permit consumers to alter some aspect of their behavior.

DISCONTINUOUS INNOVATION

An entirely new product with new functions.

Digital securities services firm Guardent, Inc. is also using continuous innovation simply by applying its knowledge and assistance to the Internet world. When Microsoft became the victim of a cyberattack and lost the source code for an application still in development, Guardent stepped in to provide its expertise on the event. By offering its assistance in such areas as identity theft, Web defacements, and virus threats, Guardent assists in the continuous innovation of an IT security infrastructure.[19]

A **dynamically continuous innovation** endows a familiar product with additional features and benefits that require or permit consumers to alter some aspect of their behavior. When auto companies introduced the antilock braking system (ABS), consumers needed to adjust driving habits. Rather than pump the brakes in an emergency, they had to learn that ABS works best when the brakes are totally compressed. Manufacturers were careful to educate drivers about the benefits and requirements of ABS so that reaction to the new system would be positive. Another example is plain paper fax machines. Users no longer had to stock special heat-sensitive paper. Regular paper would do, which made it easier to write on and photocopy a fax.

A **discontinuous innovation** is an entirely new product with new functions. Sometimes called "new to the world," these products require behavioral changes by users. The high degree of novelty makes consumers think about the product's benefits and costs prior to adoption. Examples include cellular telephones, satellite-transmitted maps for autos, and heart pumps. When automobile airbags were introduced, buyers had to evaluate the benefits carefully before committing the additional funds for the optional purchase. Eventually airbags became standard equipment and were included in the vehicle price.

The Internet is a discontinuous innovation that has affected nearly every aspect of life, including entertainment, education, and business. It has led to the development of other entirely new products, such as Internet kiosks, sometimes called Internet cyberbooths. Todito.com, a leading Internet portal for North American Spanish speakers, has expanded its Internet kiosks to 150 Elektra stores in Mexico. The Todito kiosks sell low-cost computers with Todito Internet connections, with the hope that it will increase Internet useage and familiarity through its stores.[20]

Lucent offers dynamically continuous innovation with their work on creating a Mobile Internet.

The speech technologies industry is another example. Though speech recognition programs have promised beneficial results, most customers have not yet been completely satisfied. However, new innovations are still being made and could prove to be very popular. SpeechMail, for instance, would allow individuals to receive their e-mail by telephone, and SpeecHTML would allow people to receive information from a Web site by telephone.[21] These revolutionary programs are not widely available yet, but once their benefits become apparent to consumers, they may be as commonplace as the Internet.

WHY INNOVATIONS SUCCEED

Research reveals novelty alone does not ensure new-product success. What matters most is how well innovation meets customer needs.[22] Several specific factors influence consumer acceptance of new products: relative advantage, compatibility, complexity, trialability, and observability.

Relative Advantage   Relative advantage is the amount of perceived superiority of the new product in comparison to existing ones. Marketers must make it easy for consumers to recognize the benefits of switching from the old product. Often this entails a trade-off. A new word-processing program may be easier to use but requires additional training. Consumers need to be persuaded that the training investment will yield benefits, such as time savings and ease of use. Otherwise, they probably won't purchase the new program.

To increase the perceived superiority of its upgraded software versions, Microsoft offers online support that explains product updates[23] and how the upgrade will meet user needs. It's especially important for computer software to have a relative advantage, considering the overwhelming number of offerings. Microsoft's Office 97 was designed to be more "Web savvy" and includes tools to import Web site graphics. Considering the Web's popularity and usefulness, consumers easily saw the advantages of this updated version.[24] In 1998, the U.S. Department of Justice filed suit against Microsoft, claiming essentially that it uses Windows to dominate other markets—for example, to gain a choke hold on the Internet. According to the Department of Justice, by combining a Web browser with the Windows operating system, Windows 98 would have an unfair advantage over companies such as Netscape that only has a browser. According to this claim, ultimately the consumer suffered because of less competition in the market. Microsoft countered that it was doing what the consumer wants, which will help increase its market share. The Justice Department prevailed and in June 2000 a U.S. District Judge ordered a breakup of Microsoft into two separate companies. A case appeal by Microsoft was started in a U.S. Court of Appeals in February, 2001.[25]

Compatibility   Compatible products fit easily into the consumer's current thinking or system. To succeed, a new product should be consistent with the values and beliefs of target consumers. Furthermore, if additional products are required to make a product usable, they

In June 2000, U.S. District Judge Thomas Penfield Jackson ordered Microsoft to split into two separate companies, declaring that the software giant had violated U.S. antitrust laws and that it had "proved untrustworthy in the past."

should be included in the package. Consumers who have to seek out these additions or who find installation difficult are likely to reject the product. This is one reason many organizations now have 800 numbers to answer questions.

Most people consider safety important when deciding to purchase an automobile. Understanding that this is of value, companies are working on high-tech ways to make driving safer. For example, GM's Delco division has created a blind-spot radar to warn drivers when it's unsafe to change lanes. Texas Instruments has developed a thermal-image camera that eliminates glare from oncoming headlights. These innovations provide consumer value. Since the products are included in the vehicle purchase, the issues of installation and additional purchase are avoided.

Product Complexity   Complexity is the degree to which a new product is easy to understand and use. User-friendly items have a great advantage over products with many parts and difficult instructions. It's important for designers to keep the user in mind, a major factor in the success of Macintosh computers. Many people have sat down at a Macintosh, followed the simple instructions, and quickly learned to use elaborate programs. It wasn't until Microsoft developed its Windows interface that the DOS platform provided similar ease of use.

For complex products, understandable owner's manuals and directions are essential. The streamlined layout of switches, buttons, and knobs is also important. A major innovation in cameras was the automation of complicated focusing and lighting mechanisms. By designing a product that matches the photographic needs of most people, companies substantially reduced the complexity and promoted huge growth in 35 mm equipment and films.

IDT Corporation has recently launched what it hopes will be the newest entrant in entertainment. TV.TV will pipe television over the Internet to those with high-speed Internet connections. This system of entertainment will bring many benefits to viewers and producers alike, ensuring audiences for even obscure shows and costing less in production than shows captured on film. Many potential problems still exist, but President James Courter is hopeful that he will be able to transform the motion picture industry.[26]

Trialability   Trialability refers to the ease with which potential users can test a new product at little or no expense. New-product acceptance can be speeded up through free samples,

This Ferrero Rocher ad includes a coupon that increases the trialability factor of their product.

low-cost trials, interactive showroom techniques, or loaners. Computer retailers usually place equipment on display so consumers can interact with it. Nearly every car buyer test drives an automobile before purchasing it.

Trialability is critical for software vendors, because only through use can potential buyers understand the features they would gain. Several software programs can be downloaded for free from the Web, used a few times or in a limited way, and then purchased. In the magazine world, free trial issues are common. Food companies often provide free samples in supermarkets. A Singapore-based IT management consultant advises banks to offer some services on a trial basis to customers in order to allow them to adapt to Internet banking as another banking option. Services such as online balance inquiries and fund transfers are designed to do just this.[27]

Observability   Observability means that the product's benefits can be easily seen by potential buyers. It is particularly useful to be able to see others using the product. New products with obvious advantages are adopted rapidly. When benefits are more subtle, it's more difficult to gain acceptance. Weight-loss plans that show quick results are popular because users can see the results and acquaintances are likely to make positive comments. In comparison, the effects of fitness training may not become apparent for some time, so it's more difficult to gain consumer acceptance.

When Qualcomm released an early version of pdq, a combination cell phone and palm organizer, it did not meet with much success because of its price and bulky size. Since Kyocera Wireless Corp. bought Qualcomm, however, they are trying again, only this time, they have made the new QCP 6035 Smartphone smaller, lighter, and with more features. The benefits of the new model are obvious both to the eye and to the user.[28]

THE NEW-PRODUCT DEVELOPMENT PROCESS

Success with new products depends on translating the organization's core competencies into goods or services that provide superior value to the customer.[29] The competitiveness of most markets requires a stream of new products, processes, and ventures. It's difficult to pinpoint exactly why some organizations are more innovative than others. Nevertheless, researchers have suggested the following will improve the chances of bringing innovations to market successfully:[30]

- A champion who believes in the new idea and will keep pushing no matter what the roadblocks
- A sponsor high enough in the organization to provide access to major resources: people, money, and time
- A mix of bright, creative minds (to generate ideas) and experienced operators (to keep things practical)
- A process that moves ideas through the system quickly so that they get top-level endorsement, resources, and attention early in the game
- A focus on customers at every step
- A team orientation

Figure 10.3 describes the elements in the new-product development process beginning with the new-product strategy and going through commercialization.

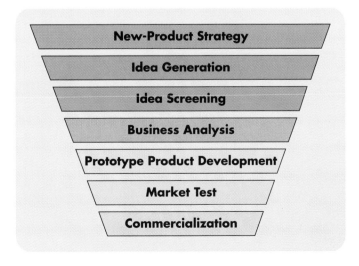

FIGURE 10.3 *The New-
Product Development Process*

NEW-PRODUCT STRATEGY

Leading-edge companies have a strategy for new-product development. In forming that strategy, top executives must answer a number of questions: Will the organization be a market leader, close follower, or also-ran? Will it have broad or deep product lines? How rapidly must the product stream flow, given competitive conditions and market expectations? How much will be invested in R&D over time? The business vision discussed in chapter 4 is the beginning point, since most company missions require that new technologies and innovative processes be used to create superior customer value.

AT&T's business vision of "anywhere, anytime communications" clearly implies that new products must be developed. Fulfilling that vision requires increasingly smaller, more powerful devices for access to data, audio, and visual communications globally. Telephone wire lines are being replaced with fiber-optic cable, which is being replaced by wireless radio frequencies, which are being replaced by satellite beams.

Fulfilling the company mission requires that marketers have the courage to bring out newer and more advanced technologies. The value statements of many corporations recognize the social responsibility of providing more functional, cost-effective, environmentally sound, and safe products. How do those goals become a reality?

IDEA GENERATION

Organizations will not find an adequate number of significant new-product ideas without an appropriate system. **Idea generation** is the use of a range of formal and informal methods to stimulate new product concepts from a number of sources. Among the many possible sources are employees, customers, technology analysis, distributors and suppliers, competitors, R&D, environmental trend analysis, and outside consultants. Marketers must ensure that ideas flow continuously from these groups. Often a reward is provided to individuals who make significant contributions.

A system based on four general principles seems to work quite well.[31]

Scotchgard is an example of a 3M innovation.

- Systematically seek and ask for new-product ideas.
- Make sure that all ideas, no matter how trivial or elaborate, reach the individual or group responsible for collecting them.
- Provide timely feedback to all people contributing ideas.
- Build rewards and recognition into the organization scaled according to the number and quality of ideas.

Employees, who work with products every day, are likely to identify many minor improvements that can result in cost savings, better quality, and higher sales. They should constantly be encouraged to submit ideas. The 3M company breeds a culture of creativity among its employees in many ways. First is a requirement in the company that 40 percent of its sales come from products developed within the last four years. Beyond this, the company ensures that its employees do not become static by allowing them to change jobs and move into areas that they find more interesting. Moreover, each employee is encouraged to devote 15 percent of his or her time to any product idea that could benefit the company.[32] Company salespeople are in the field where they can learn about new trends or ideas that may lead to the development of a new product.

Customers are a logical source of new-product ideas. This is particularly true in business-to-business marketing, since customers rely on suppliers to improve their own products and processes. By training salespeople to explore customer problems, and creating a system for feedback, companies are likely to discover numerous new concepts. Surveys, focus groups, and other marketing research techniques can be used. Technology company Tradient and 10 major oceancarrier companies are joining forces to improve their e-commerce platform in response to customer needs. The carriers are responding directly to customer requests and developing products to provide a better system for managing shipping transactions and tracking cargo.[33]

A technology analysis forecasts the speed of advances as well as possible areas of application. The result can be novel products to improve the standard of living. Any number of products have changed the way people live, from indoor plumbing and telephones to four-wheel-drive automobiles and personal CD players. True innovations such as the Internet are rare, but in the consumer and services sector they tend to be in areas where the bulk of exploration is focused, such as electronics or pharmaceuticals.[34]

**CONNECTED:
SURFING THE NET**

www.3m.com

Visit the 3M Web site and read about many of the company's pioneers in products and technology. You can also find out about the latest 3M innovations that are helping people and businesses around the world.

Dryel is an example of a Procter & Gamble innovation.

Distributors and suppliers have a personal interest in the number of products a company makes. They often are asked to serve on the council that many organizations establish to generate new-product concepts. At semiannual meetings, ideas are exchanged, and concrete lists of innovations and new approaches are developed. Sun Microsystems involves suppliers at the idea stage and allows them to qualify as providers of the new product. These suppliers help Sun introduce new technology into its own workstations.[35]

Competitors can be a major source of ideas. It's not enough for marketers simply to compare products and prices. They need to anticipate rivals' innovations by systematically monitoring and projecting the approach the competition is likely to take. For example, by recognizing progressive changes in miniaturization, Allen-Bradley Corporation has been able to surpass competitors and develop new robotics that leapfrog entire generations. Japanese firms often imitate and improve on the products of U.S. companies rather than develop their own.

R&D personnel—scientists, engineers, designers, and others—have a clear interest in new-product development, since that's a large part of their job. Companies that encourage innovation make sure they provide ample opportunity for scientists to explore on their own. When a percentage of their time is free from routine tasks, R&D staff often identify major breakthroughs. As mentioned previously, one company famous for this is 3M. In addition to allowing employees to work on projects they choose, management urges them to seek new-product ideas from everywhere, even failed experiments. The very successful Post-it notes were invented this way. Scientists were trying to invent a strong adhesive but kept failing. Rather than scrap the research, a way was found to use the less sticky glue.[36]

career tip 3M says: "We foster an individual, entrepreneurial spirit that leads to the development of innovative processes and products. We encourage the exchange of ideas, teamwork across different functions, and empowerment of our employees with the freedom to take risks." 3M is famous for its product development and innovations. You can get a detailed look at the company's employment opportunities online. The company's Web site will fill you in on the varied career opportunities and corresponding job requirements. You can also obtain an application online, or send an e-mail directly from the site for further inquiries. Check it out at www.3m.com.

An environmental trend analysis estimates how major social forces may affect an industry. The organization then can project ways in which it can provide timely products. One example is to identify pollutants in a current product, find substitute ingredients and components, and develop a new version that will appeal to "green" consumers. Seventh Generation is a company that sells bathroom tissue made from 100 percent recycled paper rather than trees.[37] Internet shopping site Respond.com has an "Eco" category for environmentally conscious customers featuring environmentally friendly baby care products, recycling products, and organic clothing.[38]

Outside consultants specializing in new-product development obviously focus much of their work on idea generation. They use a broad range of techniques to help companies develop concepts: surveys, brainstorming, focus groups, and others. Each method provides a structured way of discovering innovative products. The consulting firm Booz, Allen & Hamilton has gained a global reputation for its ability to identify commercially viable solutions to customer problems.

IDEA SCREENING

IDEA SCREENING

Identifying the new-product
ideas that have the most
potential to succeed.

A good system will provide hundreds of new-product ideas each year. The **idea screening** process identifies those with the strongest potential for success. Companies usually apply certain criteria to judge each concept. The criteria generally fall into several categories: the market, competition, required resources, technology, the environment, legal and liability issues, and financial factors. Multiple scales measure how well a product performs on each dimension.

Usually, a cross-functional team examines the limited information about the idea, using both experience and subjective judgment. The team may weight certain factors more than others, and a summary total is provided with qualitative comments to support the evaluation. Once this is completed, the team looks at the scores for all new products under consideration. As a rule, those with higher scores are chosen for further development. The team then provides feedback to everyone who contributed an idea, including an explanation of why it was accepted or rejected. The various team members take different responsibilities over the course of a new-product project. Involving several functions at the idea stage greatly increases the likelihood of picking the best ideas and developing a great product. Each member of the team has specific skills (engineering, marketing, manufacturing) that contribute to product success.[39]

BUSINESS ANALYSIS

A **business analysis** assesses the attractiveness of a product from a sales, cost, profit, and cash flow standpoint. Business analysis starts with the **product concept,** which refines the idea into written descriptions, pictures, and specifications. Marketing and R&D work diligently to define the benefits, form, features, and functions the product will have. The product concept is then presented to consumers, distributors, and retailers, who provide input regarding the product's potential as well as its description and visual representations. In the process, the description is likely to undergo changes. **Concept testing** helps identify the facilitators and inhibitors to a product's success. While testing concepts to sell its new cake batters, Duncan Hines stumbled on the theme of moistness. After hundreds of hours of concept testing, one homemaker said the cake was so moist, it stuck to the fork. From this, a successful campaign emerged.

Once the concept has been fully defined, an initial marketing strategy is developed. Success depends not only on the product but also on the strategy for marketing it. This includes examining the opportunities for segmentation, product positioning, and other aspects of the marketing mix. It's also important to look at production and materials acquisition needs as well as the time required before launch. A key feature of strategy development is to project long-term profitability under different scenarios. At this point, the likelihood of success or failure becomes more apparent. Doubtful products must be weeded out because the next stages can be very expensive.

PROTOTYPE PRODUCT DEVELOPMENT

A prototype is a working model of the product, usually created by a team of marketing, manufacturing, engineering, and R&D personnel. Prototypes can be extremely expensive because handwork rather than automation is used. They may cost 10 or even 100 times more than a product made on the production line. Although costly, these models are necessary for the all-important next step, market testing. Openness among team members and a clear sense of direction, led by a product champion, greatly increase the chances for prototype success regardless of the competitive situation.[40]

Prototype development has been influenced greatly by technology, which has made the design and building process faster and less expensive. Three-dimensional (3-D) digitizers that translate physical models into a computer model enable cross-functional teams to thoroughly understand and adjust the design. Augmented reality systems are emerging that will allow diagrams or textual information to be superimposed on a prototype as if it were painted there. These systems are the joint project of Boeing Computer Services, Honeywell, Virtual Vision, and Carnegie-Mellon University.[41] The technology feature, "Don't Just Look, Step Inside: Virtual Reality in Product Design," discusses this fascinating area.

MARKET TESTING

Test marketing is a limited trial of the strategy for the product under real or simulated conditions. Up to this point, champions may be able to push a weak product through the system. Now reality sets in. A **test market** is a small geographical area, with characteristics similar to the total market, where the product is introduced with a complete marketing program. Test marketing allows companies to implement the product strategy on a limited basis under real conditions. In fact, a test may involve trying two or more marketing strategies in separate areas to identify which works better.

In carefully designed test marketing, consumers are unaware that they are part of an experiment. Retailing, distribution, and promotion activities are similar to what would occur at the national or international level. When the results are in, marketers can forecast how long it will take for the product to be adopted in the general market. That kind of feedback was

BUSINESS ANALYSIS

Assessment of the attractiveness of the product from a sales, cost, profit, and cash flow standpoint.

PRODUCT CONCEPT

A product idea that has been refined into written descriptions, pictures, and specifications.

CONCEPT TESTING

Testing the new-product concept to evaluate the likelihood of its success.

TEST MARKET

A small geographic area, with characteristics similar to the total market, in which a product is introduced with a complete marketing program.

Rank	Place	1990 Population
1.	Tulsa, OK	367,000
2.	Charleston, WV	57,000
3.	Midland, TX	89,000
4.	Springfield, IL	105,000
5.	Lexington-Fayette, KY	225,000
6.	Wichita, KS	304,000
7.	Bloomington, IL	52,000
8.	Oklahoma City, OK	445,000
9.	Indianapolis, IN	731,000
10.	Rockford, IL	139,000
11.	Longview, TX	70,000
12.	Lafayette, LA	94,000
13.	Omaha, NE	336,000
14.	Phoenix, AZ	983,000
15.	Gastonia, NC	55,000
16.	Dallas, TX	1,007,000
17.	Jacksonville, FL	635,000
18.	Edmond, OK	52,000
19.	High Point, NC	69,000
20.	Salt Lake City, UT	160,000

FIGURE 10.4 *Top 20 Test Markets with at Least 50,000 Residents*

obtained when Orbit Canada tested its new Canadian Internet Telephony Service that provides Internet access and unlimited long-distance calling within Canada and the United States for a flat monthly fee.[42]

Test market sites are selected very carefully to represent the segments that eventually will be targeted. For example, manufacturers testing toys would avoid Sarasota, Florida, which has a large elderly population. Snowshoes are more likely to be tested in Wyoming than in Georgia. A popular site is Boise, Idaho, where there may be up to 15 test products on the shelves at once. Pillsbury tried its All Ready pie crust there. The idea of selling kitchen towels and oven mitts in supermarkets was tested in Boise. Audit services in more than 125 cities throughout the United States monitor test market results. Figure 10.4 lists the top 20 test markets with a population of 50,000 or more.

By the time an organization enters a test market, substantial funds have been spent on the new venture. There is a very strong probability of committing to a full-scale product launch—unless the test is a total failure. The results mainly help predict adoption rates among consumers and channel members. Testing products can also be very beneficial to companies that do not have large amounts of money to spend on research, however. Alfonso Porras began his candy store Sir Walter located in Monrovia by testing different batches of candies on people at street fairs. He and his wife then began selling their candies from their own booth and continued to perfect their recipes based on customer comments and suggestions. Eventually, they started selling their candies to retailers and opened their own shop on the same street where they started their testing.[43] Such experiments also help identify factors that facilitate or hinder product adoption and may yield surprises about who the users will be.

There are several drawbacks to using test markets. First, it takes time, and product development costs rise with every delay in full-scale launch. Second, competitors become aware of the new product, and the element of surprise is lost. Sometimes a rival will jump in with a similar product or use tactics that spoil the results. For example, when a competitor test-marketed a new item, Vicks pulled all its similar products off the shelves, leaving no basis for judging whether the test was successful. Other tactics are flooding the market with unusual promotions, point-of-purchase displays, and price cuts. Third, it's impractical to use test marketing for many products because prototypes are too costly. Automobiles are an example. Fourth, it is extremely expensive to make the trial products, stock stores, train salespeople, run ads, and so forth.

CONNECTING THROUGH TECHNOLOGY

DON'T JUST LOOK, STEP INSIDE: VIRTUAL REALITY IN PRODUCT DESIGN

 Sometimes a product designer has to go into a cave before the "Eureka!" light goes on. We're not talking about homes for bats, but a Cave Automatic Virtual Environment (CAVE). CAVE is a projection-based virtual reality (VR) system that surrounds the viewer with screens arranged in a cube. Images, with correct perspective and stereo projections, are displayed on the front and side screens and on the floor. The images change in response to the operator's head motion and use of controls, creating a truly interactive environment. As would be expected, academic institutions taking CAVE to the next level receive funding from engineering companies and manufacturers that will benefit from the technology. Some of the big names with interests are John Deere, Ford, and the United States military.

In the old days car companies had to build physical prototypes. With the VR system, it not only saves time and money but also frees up designers to try more innovative ideas. Auto supply company, Carcerano, uses a form of virtual reality with 3-D simulations to develop ideas on structural strength, visibility, and other important factors of automobile design. Clients of Carcerano buying into these ideas are well-noted carmakers such as BMW, Mercedes-Benz, and Mitsubishi. While only a few pioneering and capital-rich companies can afford to use VR technology, it is generally considered the wave of the product development future. Other organizations forging ahead with the technology range from Boeing and McDonnell Douglas to Honeywell and NASA.

Virtual reality not only spurs innovation but also complements the trend toward concurrent engineering: using multidisciplinary teams to design products. For many team members, especially those without an engineering background, visualizing designs in 3-D can be difficult. Helping them "see" the product early in the development cycle means that changes can be made faster and at less cost. When a marketer looks at the chassis of a virtual car and asks how it would look if the hood were sleeker, the designers don't stomp back to the drawing board to prepare a sketch by next week. According to Joshua Larson-Mogal, manager of the Enabling Technology Group of Silicon Graphic's Advanced Systems division: "Before, to design the interior of a car, you had maybe three or four revisions you could do with the mock-ups before you had to commit to something. With VR you could do 20, maybe 30 or more." It also is easy to incorporate feedback from potential customers about product design long before anything is built. After customers "try out" a VR prototype, designers can make revisions and ask those same customers to reevaluate the update within a matter of hours. The certain result, says Larson-Mogal, will be "products that are better accepted by the market."

Sources: Barbara M. Schmitz, "Great Expectations: The Future of Virtual Design," *Computer-Aided Engineering,* October 1995, pp. 68–74; Joshua Larson-Mogal, "VR at Work Today," *Computer-Aided Engineering,* October 1994, pp. 64–68, 70; Jean Thilmany, "Walkabout in Another World," *Mechanical Engineering,* November 2000, pp. 98–101; and Luca Ciferri, "Carcerano Uses Virtual Reality to Design Cars," *Automotive News,* November 20, 2000, p. 22H.

A **simulated product test** is an experiment in artificial conditions. This may be done before or instead of a full test. GHI, the most authoritative product testing center in Great Britain, performed tests on vacuum cleaners by comparing consumer use performance by cleaning carpets and hard flooring covered with measured amounts of a sand and flour mixture that simulated actual conditions.[44] This simulated product testing helps identify flaws and provides feedback. It can also be used to make evaluations against competitors. The food industry often sets up a replica of a supermarket, asks consumers to shop as if they were in a natural environment, and interviews them afterward. Although simulations are not as effective as a test market, they do provide useful information at dramatically reduced costs. Furthermore, competitors are less likely to find out about a company's plans prior to product launch.

COMMERCIALIZATION

During the final stage of the process, **commercialization** introduces the product to the market. Launching consumer products requires heavy company support, such as advertising, sales promotions, and often free samples and price promotions. Consider the $30 million commercialization of Frito-Lay's Sunchips brand, which included television spots and the company's largest ever direct-mail sampling program to more than 6 million households. After a decade of development, Sunchips breezed through test marketing in six months, indicating to Frito-Lay executives that this multigrain snack had the potential for overnight success. In this industry new products rarely achieve even $40 million in sales, but Sunchips topped $100 million in the first year and continues to bring in huge profits.[45]

THE ETHICS OF PRODUCT IMITATION

Some argue that since companies make substantial investments in new products, they should be the only ones allowed to market them. Recognizing this, intellectual property laws and patent laws afford some protection. Others argue that imitation results in healthy competition. It forces market leaders to keep up with technology, contend with lower-priced substitutes, and respond to smaller and faster challengers. Organizations that want to remain competitive need to keep a keen eye on competitors' new products. Many times it helps to emulate their products, a totally ethical approach under many circumstances.

Protecting a firm's products from imitation is increasingly difficult. This tactic has become a recognized part of business strategy across the globe. Software development giant and market leader Microsoft is said to have greatly benefited from the inventions of others.[46] Its Windows operating system, which has become the standard program that runs nearly all personal computer operations, is considered very similar in user friendliness and visual format to Apple's Macintosh system.

Not all imitations are created equal. Some are illegal duplicates of popular products, and some are truly innovative products merely inspired by a pioneering brand.[47] The makers of knockoffs or clones often copy original designs but may leave off important attributes. In the computer industry, reproductions of IBM PCs carry their own brand names. The clones are often the same basic product, but they retail at lower price and without the prestigious IBM label. Clones are legal because protective patents, copyrights, and trademarks are absent or have expired.

Some copies play on the style, design, or fashion of a popular product. This type of imitation is common in the automobile industry. In the 1980s several Japanese automakers introduced lines to challenge Mercedes-Benz and BMW. Toyota's Lexus, Nissan's Infiniti, and Honda's Acura closely mirror the design and features of the German luxury cars. When technical products are copied, reverse engineering is often used to learn how the original was designed or made.

In the 1980s Toyota introduced their Lexus line which mirrors the design and features of the German luxury cars.

Creative adoptions innovate beyond an existing product. These may occur as a technological development or as an adaptation to another industry. Initially, DuPont developed Teflon for the nose-cones of spacecraft but soon extended its uses to coatings for consumer products. W. L. Gore, who was researching Teflon uses, left DuPont in 1958 and eventually developed Gore-Tex fabric. It is used in clothing that keeps rain out but "breathes" to let body moisture escape.[48] Gore-Tex fabric is frequently used in sports clothing and can be bought at such stores as Eddie Bauer, Bass ProShops, and L.L. Bean.[49]

ORGANIZATIONAL STRUCTURES AND PRODUCT MANAGEMENT

Simultaneous new-product development occurs when people from a number of functional areas work together. Marketing coordinates the team, which usually represents R&D, engineering, production, procurement, legal and human resources, financing, and so on. This approach has many advantages over the old technique of **sequential new-product development,** which passes responsibility from one functional area to the next. Companies can produce better products at lower cost and gain returns more quickly. Consequently, the marketing function should attempt to ensure teamwork across all major departments of the business.

Recent Organizational Trends   There are many ways to manage existing and new products. Today, companies make creative use of computer and communications technologies to support a flexible organizational structure. This enables them to respond quickly to buyer demands. It also provides access to global technologies and the ability to adapt to competitive forces. There are three notable organizational trends.

1. *Downsizing.* Several product lines are brought under a single management team, or product offerings are reduced to those that generate strong and increasing revenues.
2. *Delayering.* The number of personnel and positions between top executives and those who manage market activities is reduced.
3. *Fewer functional silos.* When one function works in isolation from others, it is called a functional silo. Organizations are stressing cross-functional synergy and personnel with experience in multiple areas. Marketers no longer work only with other marketers or accountants only with other accountants.

Fundamental Structures   There are many acceptable organizational structures. Today, most companies prefer a structure that supports strategy changes. As strategies alter to meet new challenges, organizational structures need to change with them. The most fundamental structures for new-product development are the product or market manager, the new-product department, the new-product committee, and the venture team. Companies may combine elements of several of these and may use consulting organizations as well.

Product or Market Managers Some of the most successful organizations have used the product manager or market manager structure. **Market managers** are responsible for one or several similar product lines targeted at defined market areas. **Product managers** oversee one or several products targeted at all market segments. In either case the structure is similar. The manager works closely with individuals from a range of functions to build integrated strategies. The system was pioneered by Procter & Gamble, which developed teams of experts loosely tied but headed by a very strong manager. Each team was responsible for building the equity of a given brand. Product managers compete almost as strongly with other teams in the organization as they do with competitors on the outside. For example, the Crest product manager is in competition with the Gleem product manager, and the Tide product manager is in competition with all product managers for the other detergents made by Procter & Gamble. However, since each product is positioned to address a particular benefit—Crest for tooth decay prevention and Gleem for brightness—competition may not be direct.

Product managers or market managers have the following specific responsibilities:

- Achieve the sales, profit, market share, and cash flow objectives for the product line.
- Develop the market strategy for the product.
- Prepare a written marketing plan, develop forecasts, and maintain timely updates of progress.
- Integrate all functions necessary to implement a synergistic marketing strategy.

One difficulty with this system is that the manager has responsibilities beyond the traditional lines of authority. The product manager can be described as the hub of a wheel. Notice that the spokes are all the functional areas that help make a good marketing strategy work. Product managers have no formal authority over these people, who report directly to managers in their own functional area.

What makes the system work? First, the product or market manager must have the necessary interpersonal and business skills to gain the team's respect. In fact, the lack of direct authority is what makes this system effective. Through team play and networking, strong product or market managers can tap into very specialized talents from a range of people. Second, the manager must report to someone high enough in the organization to obtain the status required. Although unable to govern the activities of team members, product and marketing managers can make their presence felt through communication with top executives and across functional areas of the company.

The system's strength is also its weakness. Product managers must rely on functional managers from various areas of the organization to help them build a strong team. New-product prospects may receive low priority from managers in the spokes. Their reward structures may inhibit working on innovations. Experience has shown that without proper attention by top management, the product or marketing manager may be relegated to relatively mundane tasks. When there is appropriate executive leadership, the system can be a flexible way to address numerous market situations.

NEW-PRODUCT DEPARTMENT

The organizational unit responsible for identifying product ideas and preparing them for commercialization.

New-Product Department The **new-product department** is responsible for identifying ideas, developing products, and preparing them for commercialization. The members generally report directly to top executives and include individuals with experience in many aspects of the business. This structure separates the responsibility of new-product development from the rest of the organization. It helps eliminate redundancies that occur when the same ideas are developed in different product areas. These personnel have a firm grasp of the methods and risks involved in developing new products. In reality, these departments are often formed with great expectations but some quickly become a functional silo neglected by top management. This is particularly the case when top management is preoccupied with current products or when the new-product department does not set aggressive goals regarding commercializable products. Such a department usually operates best when it has strong executive involvement and concentrates its efforts on finding strategies to make product ideas commercial successes.

NEW-PRODUCT COMMITTEE

A group of key functional personnel who are brought together periodically to develop new products.

New-Product Committee The **new-product committee** consists of key functional personnel who are brought together from time to time to develop new products. Because this activity is often not considered a strong factor in building a career, participants may give it less attention than required. Furthermore, the committee often lacks the authority to make things happen. However, ideas and expertise can be contributed by many different key people, and committee members can be brought into a project as needed.

VENTURE TEAM

Personnel from various areas of the company who are given release time to work on a specific assignment.

Venture Team A **venture team** is a group formed for a set period to accomplish a set objective. A venture team is headed by a manager who reports very high in the organization. The manager selects team members from various areas of the company, and each is given release time for the assignment. Because the venture team has very specific objectives and a limited time frame, it tends to focus on getting the job done. Strong leadership and decision-making power allow the team to commit resources in a timely fashion. And the release time enables members to devote attention to the project. Unfortunately, in many organizations managers are unwilling to permit their best people to participate. In addition, the team is dissolved once a given task is completed. The new venture team must start over without the benefit of experience. Hewlett-Packard used this approach to develop the first low-cost laser printer.

Consulting Organizations Full service or specialty consulting firms can be hired to set up new-product development systems, facilitate the process, or conduct all or part of the development task. In many cases, consulting groups have outstanding talent with experience in the area of new products. Because of that experience, companies can save vast amounts of time and money in the innovation process. Unfortunately, employees sometimes resist implementing consulting firm recommendations because they were not involved in the decision-making process. Consulting organizations such as Booze, Allen & Hamilton, and McKinsey and Company often make strong efforts to involve their clients in all phases of their new-product consulting.

MANAGING PRODUCTS OVER THE LIFE CYCLE

One of the oldest and most useful concepts for marketers is the product life cycle, depicted in Figure 10.5. Like living organisms, products move from birth to infancy, adolescence, maturity, old age, and death. The **product life cycle** consists of four stages: introduction, growth, maturity, and decline. It's important to recognize that this is only a conceptual tool, and not all products move through a complete life cycle. Some marketers question the usefulness of the idea, but it remains one of the most common notions in marketing strategy. It has been applied to generic products, suppliers, industries, and individual brands.

Recall from our definition of marketing that firms seek to satisfy customers more profitably than competitors in order to increase the value of the business. Figure 10.5 illustrates the sales and profits for a typical product as it moves through its life cycle. Before introduction, large sums are likely to be expended on development. In the pharmaceutical industry, it may take 15 years or more for R&D, testing, and FDA approval. Eli Lilly, a leading pharmaceutical company, says that it spends $2 billion annually in the research and development of new drugs.[50]

Motorola will devote $55.4 million over the next five years to a software development center in Perth, Australia. The twentieth of its research facilities, Motorola says this facility will work on the research and development of software for cellular phones, silicon chips, and in-vehicle navigation systems.[51] In other industries the development process may be less costly, but every product begins its life by taking cash from some other part of the business.

STAGES IN THE PRODUCT LIFE CYCLE

Each of the four stages in the product life cycle is associated with its own opportunities, costs, and marketing strategies. In this section we examine each stage in more detail.

Stage 1: Introduction   During the introductory phase of the product life cycle, sales slowly take off and grow. Shipments from the factory may be high, and channels of distribution are filled as wholesalers and retailers stock the item. Since the product is new, marketers scramble to create consumer awareness and encourage trial. This often involves heavy advertising campaigns, samples, and educational sales techniques. During this critical period, marketers attempt to build share quickly to gain first-mover advantages. As numerous studies have shown, whoever introduces a product is likely to become the future industry leader in that area. Chrysler introduced minivans and now controls more than half the market. Yet, Chrysler as a whole accounts for only 10 percent of the car market. The first products on the market often are so dominant that they become generic names: Kleenex, Jell-O, Xerox, Formica, and Gore-Tex.[52]

Typically, there are few competitors during introduction, so marketers concentrate on achieving customer acceptance of the entire product class. Less emphasis is placed on gaining competitive advantage through differentiation. When car phones were introduced, most

Managing Products Over the Life Cycle

PRODUCT LIFE CYCLE

The four stages a product goes through: introduction, growth, maturity, and decline.

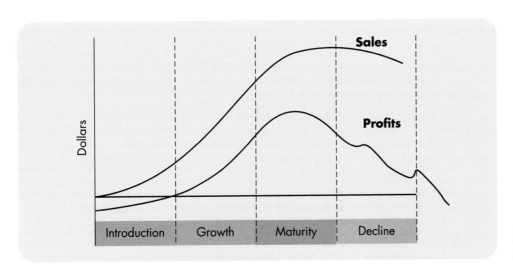

FIGURE 10.5 *Traditional Life Cycle Curves*

advertising focused on selling the idea. Later advertising attempted to distinguish the various products from one another. Most organizations introduce only one or two items in a new-product line so they can gain experience and monitor progress. Furthermore, global markets offer such vast opportunities for new products that some rivals may elect to avoid confrontations by selecting an untapped area.

As a rule, introductions represent advances in technology, manufacturing, and service. Product design also tends to be very innovative. Firms should make sure, however, that the design is easy to try and to use. It's also important to have flexible manufacturing that can match production to highly uncertain demand. Distributors don't want to be left with unsold units. But if demand is not met, buyers may lose interest, or competitors may enter the market. Finally, customer service efforts must seek out and correct problems.

Profits may be negative during all or most of the introductory phase. Sales usually grow slowly, and consumers need to be made aware of the product's existence, which requires relatively costly promotion. It can also be very expensive to develop distribution channels and to educate people about the product's use.

Stage 2: Growth During the growth stage, the pace of consumer acceptance and sales quickens. This is an especially critical time because rivals, noticing the increase in sales, will develop competitive products and aggressively pursue distribution channels. Consumers begin to make comparisons among the various products, so companies attempt to gain preferred status and brand loyalty. Strong companies such as Microsoft and Dell Computers seek dominance during this period. Many organizations believe that if they don't emerge from the growth stage as number one or two, then they should abandon that line of business. Competition is extremely aggressive. Honda, an automobile company which began in 1959 as a motorcycle company, has continued to grow beyond its original product line. Honda is now famous for its automobiles, motorcycles, and power equipment and has even expanded its market to include Internet shoppers through its site at www.ehonda.com.[53] The company has gained preferred status and brand loyalty among consumers and continues to seek dominance among new users and market areas.[54]

Product technology often enters its second generation during the growth stage. The first-generation technology applied to the original products is improved as companies gain experience. Usually, second-generation technology produces greater customer satisfaction through both cost savings and enhanced functionality. The first car phones had to be mounted permanently, and an antenna was attached to the outside. The next generation included bag phones that could be transferred from vehicle to vehicle. Now, handheld phones fit in your pocket.

With growth comes product designs that differ substantially from one manufacturer to the next. Building on the technology of short-range wireless connections and electronics, Hewlett-Packard has developed a second-generation technology it calls Bluetooth Strategy. This strategy allows data to be transferred from mobile phones, computers, personal digital assistants, and networked peripheral devices such as printers and scanners by short-range wireless connections.[55]

Manufacturing processes undergo change during the growth phase. The flexibility of the previous stage gives way to assembly lines and more automation. Higher sales volumes mean that standardized production can be used to achieve economies of scale and cost savings. Since forecasting is more accurate, just-in-time delivery and advanced quality control systems are possible. Motorola strives for six sigma quality rates, which equates to 3.4 defects per 1 million products. Of course, it's important that firms have the manufacturing capacity to meet increasing demand. Otherwise, competitors may step in.

Promotion and sales take on a whole new dimension during growth. Aggressive, head-to-head competition forces organizations to show their uniqueness, and the augmented product becomes extremely important. Financing, installation, and training in product use are critical promotion activities. Advertising shifts to substantive messages that describe the benefits, functions, and features of the product relative to competitors' offerings.

The companies that emerge as leaders tend to provide uncompromising customer service. They build trust in the distribution channel and with end users. Sometimes repeat purchases are based more on service satisfaction than on product performance and styling. Most consumers expect problems with any product. How they are handled makes the difference. If service is performed correctly the first time, then consumers are likely to feel an affinity toward the supplier. In fact, as discussed in chapter 2, loyalty may be strengthened when problems occur and are handled well.

Stage 3: Maturity   As products mature, sales level off and may remain flat for long periods. Overall market growth is relatively small, so a sales increase for one company usually comes at the expense of another. That's why firms with loyal buyers tend to have the greatest longevity. Yet, loyalty also indicates that consumer interest in the product is subsiding, which makes it very difficult and costly to build market share. Most firms are happy if they simply hold their own in this phase. Weaker competitors are likely to lower prices, while stronger rivals may sacrifice market share to maintain a satisfactory profit level. Strong rivals also engage in dramatic cost containment to preserve profits. Often this results in a standardized product design with less costly components and more efficient manufacturing.

At maturity, weaker rivals may drop out and use resources on more promising products. Even strong companies may exit if profit margins suffer too much, as GE did with its consumer line of light bulbs. The maturity phase may last several months, years, or even decades, and a low-cost position is critical for long-term success. This is particularly true if low-cost foreign competitors enter the business.

Product line size becomes especially important during the mature phase. Companies need to drop products with low-volume sales, high production costs, or little competitive viability. But many buyers want to deal with a supplier who offers a full product line. This leads many organizations to employ outsourcing; that is, they purchase certain items from other companies and affix their own label. In this way they continue to mass-produce the lower-cost standardized items while depending on smaller firms to make the rest. Competitors may even buy from one another during the mature stage in order to gain an overall cost advantage, sometimes called co-opetition. For example, Japanese semiconductor makers are outsourcing to reduce spending on production facilities. Hitatchi outsources its semiconductor production to Taiwanese company United Microelectronics Corp. and Episil Semiconductors, Inc.[56] Two Canadian entrepreneurs combined their talents beginning in 1993 to begin a different kind of outsourcing business, one that meets the personnel needs of various companies. Consumer Impact Marketing (CIM) has a continuous training program that trains its personnel to meet the outsourcing needs of its clients—from Legos Canada to Quaker Oats and Imperial Oil.[57]

The technology used for mature products tends to be older. Many firms have invested so heavily in the past technology that they resist committing more resources to an aging product. The primary focus is on improving the manufacturing process. For example, some organizations move from assembly-line and batch-oriented production to a continuous-flow system. This integrates people, paperwork, computerization, and manufacturing into a seamless operation that maintains production at the greatest level of efficiency.

Promotional campaigns focus more on reminder advertising than on new themes, since most buyers are now loyal to a particular brand or company. Sometimes companies resurrect messages that were used to build the brand's name. By adding a novel twist, the firm can keep its product in the forefront. For example, Wheaties, the traditional "Breakfast of Champions," regularly updates its package to show the latest sports superstars. The objective is to create a link to younger consumers while maintaining its strong brand identity.

Service usually is standardized for mature products. In many cases, new service firms are formed to specialize in a particular product area. Even though Otis or Westinghouse installs most of the elevators we use, it is private service companies that keep them in tip-top condition. Many organizations elect to hire local service firms to perform repairs. The marketing of replacement parts may become extremely profitable at this stage. During economic recessions, customers often prefer to fix an existing product rather than buy a new one. In the United States, movable furniture systems from such companies as Steelcase, Herman Miller, and Hayworth have entered the maturity phase. Local firms are now purchasing and refurbishing the units for resale.

The rapid sales increase in the growth stage peaks during early maturity. Profits are likely to decline because of price competition, both domestically and internationally. This is particularly true in industries with high exit barriers. That means it costs companies a lot of money to leave the line of business because of their high fixed investment. Since it is costly to stop making the product, prices often are lowered to maintain demand. Furthermore, such trade promotions as point-of-purchase sales and discounting may be used. By the end of the maturity phase, a product may be losing money or have a very thin profit margin because of low demand.

Stage 4: Decline   In the decline stage of the product life cycle, sales of new units diminish. For some products, such as earlier models of computers, the decrease may be very rapid. For others, it may be slow and steady, as with black-and-white television sets. Or it may be slow and then rapid, which was the case with vinyl records. Their sales dropped gradually and then plummeted as more and more titles became available on CDs. The speed of decline is related to the types and value of substitute products.

Most companies with a declining product want to maintain the lucrative replacement market but are willing to give up market share in exchange for earnings. Fierce price wars are likely to result in losses for all competitors. Low-cost producers that minimize new activities are in a much better position than high-cost competitors. Product design is nearly always standardized. Changes are intended to reduce the cost of components, which helps the company maintain earnings.

Companies are likely to return to a much shallower product line at this stage, focusing on the products that generate adequate cash flow. Old technology is kept in place, and manufacturing runs are limited, which frees up production capacity for more profitable items. To keep costs down, very little promotional activity occurs, so buyers may have to seek out the product themselves. Service is likely to be handled by independent companies. Because replacement parts still generate a profit, the firm is likely to maintain a supply that affords some level of earnings.

The profit life cycle implies that companies should have products in all stages at all times. Firms with only mature and declining products can expect dwindling profitability. Yet product development and the introductory stage are likely to absorb much of the profit generated from growing and mature products. Strong companies plan ahead and add products at various stages in the life cycle to ensure a viable business. This is particularly important for companies whose products are patented. In 1993, Pharmacia faced such a challenge. The patents on four drugs that made up 32 percent of its 1992 sales were due to expire in mid-1994, opening the door for generics. Analysts speculated that the company didn't have any new drugs in the works to offset the sales decline that was sure to occur. Pharmacia then purchased the rights to market several new ibuprofen products that had been developed but never sold. The market for these general pain relievers was growing, and this move gave Pharmacia products in the introductory and growth stages.[58]

VARIATIONS IN PRODUCT LIFE CYCLES

By looking at extinct products, we know that several kinds of life cycles are possible as depicted in Figure 10.6. By understanding the different types, marketers can make general predictions about the challenges they face. The first curve is typical of high-tech products, such as computer software. Just when sales achieve a healthy pace, another generation hits the market. General acceptance of the product grows with each wave, however, which explains the successively higher peaks. Each generation usually lowers the cost to consumers.

The second curve illustrates the life cycle of a fad. Sales rise sharply in the introductory and growth phases and then quickly fall. Marketers of such products are careful not to base the longevity of their company on one or two items. They realize the fad is likely to be a passing windfall. When scooters appeared to be the latest fad for the holiday season in 2000, even Krogers grocery stores in Texas wanted to cash in on the fad. However, Jerry Kaiser ordered only 5,000 for the state of Texas, averaging out to 20 per store, and 50 for the larger stores, making sure to not order too many or too few.[59]

Clothing fashions follow yet another kind of curve. When a style is first introduced, it is likely to experience relatively fast growth and then trail off, only to be resurrected a few years later. The width of neckties has gone from narrow, to medium, to wide, and back to narrow. Skirt lengths rise and fall. Marketers of these products must be aware of constantly changing consumer preferences and build strategies accordingly.

Although the product life cycle gives marketers a rule of thumb, it is not an exact science. To obtain more precise forecasts, researchers have developed mathematical and statistical models that examine market size, the number of initial buyers, and the time between first and

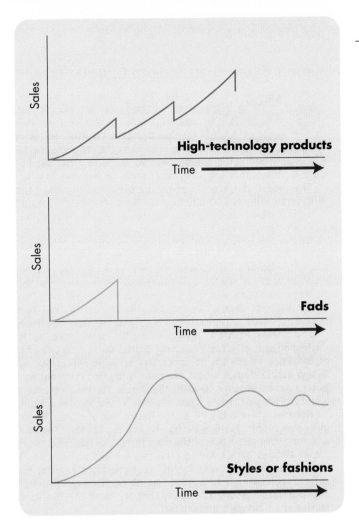

FIGURE 10.6 *Life Cycles for Various Types of Products*

repeat purchase. These can be very useful, particularly for products that behave similarly to those modeled.

EXTENDING THE PRODUCT LIFE CYCLE

Firms that resist change sometimes keep products going far beyond their usefulness. But there are times when it's good business to extend the product life cycle. The four most common ways to do this are to sell to new market segments, to stimulate more frequent use, to encourage more use per occasion, and to promote more varied use.

Selling to New Segments   One way to give a product a new lease on life is to find new buyers. For example, in-line skates were originally used primarily by males to simulate ice hockey, but now they have been adopted widely by females. The automobile industry is no longer geared toward only men but now must direct itself also to women. One Internet site, www.womanmotorist.com, is a site devoted entirely to issues facing women drivers and features such things as buying automobiles, maintenance, and a glossary of related terms.[60] The diversity feature centers on how Mattel entered the market segment of CD-ROM games for girls.

Stimulating More Frequent Use   After a decade of declining sales nationwide, the milk industry needed a marketing campaign to stimulate use. From this the well-known "Got Milk?" campaign was born. Research indicated that the product played only a peripheral role in people's lives. The only time they gave it a second thought was when they didn't have any. The campaign theme chosen was "milk deprivation"—a man agonizing over a milkless bowl of cereal, deciding whether to rob his baby's bottle or his cat's dish. Or Santa entering a home, eating a brownie, finding no milk, and taking the Christmas presents away. Recently, the ads

MATTEL'S BARBIE LURES GIRLS TO COMPUTER GAMES

 Developing a successful new product is hard enough, but what about creating one for a market that doesn't exist? This was the challenge faced by Mattel, Inc., when it came up with its Barbie Fashion Designer CD-ROM. Males accounted for more than 80 percent of the CD-ROM game market, and no company had yet successfully marketed one of these products to girls. But had they stayed away because there were no appealing products or because they simply weren't interested in computers?

The spectacular success of the Barbie CD-ROM proved that appeal was the problem. With retail sales of 200,000 units in November 1996, Barbie Fashion Designer sold more in its first month than any other educational CD-ROM and shook up an industry dominated by products for boys.

One of the keys to Mattel's success was paying attention to girls' computer use and play patterns. Until age 6, they use computers as much as boys and even develop superior concentration and skills. Around age 7, when gender differences begin to emerge, girls drop out of the market. They become more interested in socializing, storytelling, and particularly emulating heroines they read about and see on screen. In sharp contrast, games on the market—such as Doom, Duke Nukem, or Quake—feature kick-boxers, guns, and buckets of blood to capitalize on boys' interest in competitive, spatial games.

The Barbie Fashion Designer CD-ROM, developed by Mattel in conjunction with Hollywood special-effects company Digital Domain, is one of the few titles that addressed girls' desire to use the computer for creative expression. Girls age 5 and older could design Barbie clothes on the computer and print them out on a light fabric with any computer printer. Another CD-ROM, the Barbie Storymaker, uses a number of favorite Barbie haunts to let girls create hundreds of different stories around Barbie and her friends.

However, there was still a significant lack of games targeting the 10- to 15-year-old girl demographic. Fashion Designer was a first in the CD-ROM for the preteen girl industry and continues to be one of the only to have major success with this market. Even recent games such as Barbie Riding Club (ages 5 and up) and the European CD-ROM featuring a character called "Reader Rabbit" that promotes physical education still have their aim set on younger girls or boys. In an attempt to recapture the market, Mattel recently acquired Purple Moon, a company that produced the "Rockett's World" CD-ROM featuring stories of an awkward preteen girl.

Developing a unique product is only half the battle. Mattel and other makers of new CD-ROMs for girls have had an added challenge of reaching this huge untapped market. Girls don't hang out at CompUSA. They don't cruise the CD-ROM aisle of Toys "R" Us or read techie magazines. One tactic is to leverage the power of an established brand, as Mattel has done by basing its product on the popular fashion doll. Using its considerable clout, Mattel persuaded retailers to place the product in both the toy and computer departments.

Her Interactive was not so fortunate when it launched its McKenzie & Co. CD-ROM a full year before Barbie's debut. Designed for the 10–15 age group, it features a group of girls dating, shopping, and applying makeup. McKenzie & Co. couldn't find shelf space. Retailers didn't know where to place it. When the Barbie Fashion Designer was launched, Her Interactive rode happily on Barbie's coattails. Marketers at Simon & Schuster Interactive adopted a grassroots approach, using nontraditional sites to attract preteens and teenagers. Their interactive girls' handbook *Let's Talk About Me* is available in Contempo Casual and Wet Seal clothing stores and is sold right next to clothes and makeup.

It's clear that Barbie's success will spark a host of other companies to develop CD-ROMs for girls, a market with $42 million in disposable income. And girls who want to have fun on the computer couldn't be happier. "The great thing about these products is they put the girl in control," said Barbie media marketing vice president Pam Kelly. "She's making the decisions, and she can use the products to interact with friends, which is how girls like to play."

Sources: Lisa Bannon, "Barbie, Dressed to Kill, Beats CD-ROM Rivals," *Wall Street Journal,* December 18, 1996, p. B1:3; Lisa Bannon, "Mattel Bets Barbie Can Sell Girls on Computer Games," *Wall Street Journal,* February 9, 1996, p. B1:3; Maria Matzer and Bernhard Warner, "Newmedia: Where the Girls Are," *Brandweek,* October 14, 1996, pp. 18–24; Cyndee Miller, "Guys on Games for Girls Don't Do Karate Kicks," *Marketing News,* December 4, 1995, p. 2; "Girls Just Want to Have Fun—New Software Gives It to Them," *Discount Store News,* January 1, 1996, p. 43; John R. Quain, "Where the Girls Are," *Entertainment Weekly,* December 18, 1998, pp. 95–96; Anne Reeks, "Barbie Riding Club CD-ROM," *Parenting,* March 1999, p. 75; Noah Robischon, "Rockett Attack," *Entertainment Weekly,* April 16, 1999, p. 66; and Ian Darby, "Mattel in $6.5 Million 'Fitness for Kids' Project," *Marketing,* February 17, 2000, p. 12.

have appealed to potential milk drinkers by showing celebrities such as Britney Spears, the Dixie Chicks, and Serena and Venus Williams, and even have a Web site selling "Got Milk?" paraphernalia.[61] These award winners not only heightened awareness by 91 percent but also increased the frequency of use.[62]

The makers of cellular phones encourage more frequent use by marketing the importance of owning several instruments. Telephone communication once was limited to the home, office, or a pay phone. Now people can have constant access. Motorola has now taken its communication to another level and offers gadgets that allow one to send and receive e-mail through the Timeport Personal Interactive Communicator. Advertising the device, Motorola says that it is "For the Career Minded," suggesting to serious employees that if they are indeed serious, they need to purchase the Personal Interactive Communicator.[63] Marketers want to convince consumers to purchase several types of communication devices for the sake of both convenience and work.

Encouraging More Use per Occasion   Have you ever purchased a Snickers bar offering 20 percent more candy for free? That is one way to encourage more use per occasion. Many companies promote on this basis. McDonald's offers a "Super Sized®" meal, with a larger order of french fries and a larger beverage. Coca-Cola encourages greater consumption with 20-ounce sizes in vending machines. Claussen, a division of Campbell's, sells a giant crinkle-cut pickle slice to "blanket" hamburgers. The 69 percent of Americans who enjoy pickles on their burgers have a bigger option.[64]

Promoting More Varied Use   Arm & Hammer dramatically extended the life cycle of baking soda by using it as an ingredient in toothpaste, laundry products, room fresheners, and deodorant. Furthermore, ads recommend it for absorbing odors in refrigerators and closets. Once used only for cooking, today baking soda has far more applications. Even when it is being disposed, it helps sanitize the drain. Another example is the "I could have had a V-8" campaign, which popularized the traditional breakfast drink as a refreshment for any time of day. And Yellowstone Park, traditionally viewed as a summer attraction, now advertises snowmobile trips in the winter.

THE PRODUCT LIFE CYCLE IN INTERNATIONAL MARKETS

A product's stage in the life cycle has important implications for international trade, not only in terms of marketing but also in terms of design and manufacture.

New products tend to be designed, manufactured, and sold first in advanced economies, where there is sufficient wealth to underwrite development costs, and where markets accept innovation more readily. For example, personal computers were developed largely in the United States and sold primarily in the more upscale U.S. and Western European markets. As sales grew, however, Pacific Rim manufacturers developed clones, produced them with lower-cost labor, and became important competitors in Western markets. The lower prices that resulted in turn opened up new international markets in less advanced economies such as Russia and Eastern Europe.

A product at the peak of its popularity, with many brands competing for market share, may be manufactured far from its primary market if it can gain a competitive advantage through lower manufacturing costs. Athletic shoes, for example, were pioneered in the United States—which remains their largest single market. But as product sales burgeoned and new competitors entered the market, both Nike and Reebok moved their production to low-wage countries to reduce costs.

Maturing products tend to be exported to less advanced economies looking for lower-priced goods. As these markets grow, companies are likely to establish production facilities there, using their already standardized processes. We see this in Mexico, where both Nissan and Volkswagen have assembly plants that produce for the local market—and export to the United States as well. As manufacturing skills and processes are absorbed locally, local companies may set up their own plants and begin producing for the home market, thereby increasing competition.

Products that have reached the end of their life cycle in one economy may still be needed in another. Few U.S. households still do their laundry with washboards and tubs, but in poorer parts of the world, particularly in rural areas that have no access to electricity, such products remain useful and desirable.

Some countries are more suitable markets early in a product's life and others are more suitable later. Where products are made and marketed depends on their stage in the life cycle and on the economic characteristics of the location.[65]

CONSUMER ACCEPTANCE OF INNOVATION

ADOPTION

The **adoption process** comprises the five steps that consumers go through in making a product choice: knowledge, persuasion, decision, implementation, and confirmation. First, the consumer becomes aware of the product and learns about it. Second, the person forms a favorable or unfavorable attitude toward the product. Third, the product is chosen or rejected. Fourth, the consumer tries the product. Fifth, experience confirms or disconfirms the wisdom of the choice and whether the item will be purchased again.[66]

The major point is that product adoption takes time. The speed of adoption depends on buyer characteristics and other factors. Because people are different, it is possible to categorize them according to how long it will take them to adopt an idea. We know, moreover, that product acceptance is passed from one group of consumers to the next. To explain this process, marketers have developed a concept similar to the product life cycle except that it focuses on consumers: the diffusion process.

DIFFUSION

The **diffusion process** describes the spread of innovations from one individual or group to another over time. Marketers are keenly aware of how diffusion affects the introduction and long-term adoption of products. We know that sales are influenced dramatically by the interaction of buyers, through word of mouth, as well as by promotions and messages from marketers. Often managers focus only on organizing the firm to develop new or improved products. Yet they must also pay attention to understanding how consumers evaluate innovations. Otherwise even very beneficial products may not be diffused throughout the market.[67]

Figure 10.7 illustrates the five groups of consumers who can be expected to purchase a product over time. The approximate distribution is 2.5 percent innovators, 13 percent early adopters, 34 percent early majority buyers, 34 percent late majority buyers, and 16 percent laggards. The illustration is based on standard deviations, but the proportions may differ with various products.

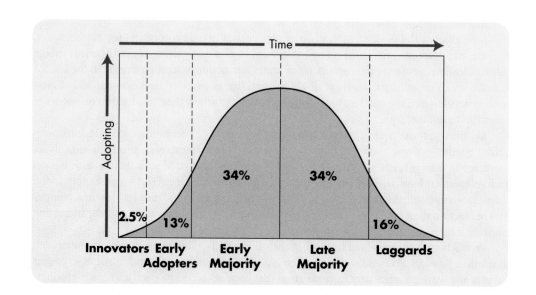

FIGURE 10.7 *The Product Diffusion Cycle*

Innovators   The first consumers to purchase a new product are **innovators.** As you can guess, they are more adventurous than most of the population. They have higher incomes and, thus, can afford to try relatively expensive introductions. They are technically competent and in some cases are almost obsessed with the details of new products. At the same time, many innovators are rather eccentric. This small group has only minor influence over others, but it provides proof that the product functions properly. Marketers can point to that experience in attempting to educate other buyers. The marketer of a new computerized vision system for detecting manufacturing flaws first installed the system at a small innovative firm that makes electronic parts. The company later cited successful use there in selling the product to a leader in the industry.

Early Adopters   **Early adopters** are the second group to purchase new products and are critical to marketers. They are the key to good word-of-mouth publicity and wider acceptance. They are well respected in their community, so other categories of buyers are likely to emulate them. Digital cameras, for example, are quickly increasing in sales and are expected to outsell conventional cameras in four to five years. Much of the success of these cameras lies in the early adopters who rushed to buy them and continue to upgrade their equipment every year.[68] Early adopters help determine the success and adoption rate of such offerings.

Early Majority Buyers   **Early majority** consumers tend to be more risk averse than innovators and early adopters. They wait to see how something new works for others before purchasing it themselves. They also tend to read extensively about various products and compare different brands before reaching a decision. For the most part, these consumers are followers rather than leaders. Casio's MP3 watch, which plays up to four hours of music and costs around $250, is a digital music device that transcends the days of the Walkman.[69] Early majority consumers are likely to wait until a technology such as the MP3 watch is in widespread use before making the purchase, despite the extensive benefits it offers.

Late Majority and Laggards   The more skeptical consumers tend to fall into the **late majority** group. They have little faith in new products, so they wait until half the population has purchased it before they do. However, even more resistant to new products is the last group of consumers to purchase, the **laggards:** little, if anything, can be done to convince laggards to purchase a new product.

U.S. farmers can be viewed using the diffusion cycle. Innovators and early adopters stay current on all developments in agriculture. They go to trade shows and read everything they can get their hands on. These consumers are the first to buy a new piece of equipment or pesticide. At the other extreme lie the laggards. They feel "if it ain't broke, don't fix it" and tend to stay brand oriented. They influence little or none of the market. Marketers have used different strategies to reach each group. The innovators and early adopters prefer advertising with a lot of good information or copy. Laggards, on the other hand, need attention-grabbing ads and coupons as an incentive to purchase new products.[70] Since laggards often have low incomes and are a relatively small group, many marketers simply avoid marketing to this group completely. The fact that they have low education and low income often makes them bad credit risks as well.

The diffusion cycle can also be applied to the pharmaceutical industry. When a pharmaceutical firm introduced a new pain reliever, salespeople were asked to identify physicians who fit the early adopter profile: younger, heavy prescribers, on hospital boards, with modern offices and equipment. Special attention was given to these physicians through direct mail, sampling, and sales calls. Because early adopters are more cosmopolitan than average, they are more inclined to accept information and interact with innovative firms. They agreed to test and evaluate the new product, quickly gave it their support, and set in motion rapid diffusion throughout the medical community.

When we think of product innovation and new-product introductions, our tendency is to think in terms of manufactured goods. But services, too, are products—as you are aware from the marketing definition in chapter 1 and the many examples of services encountered thus far. The next chapter is devoted to exploring the distinctive features of service products, including the functional and interactive features that marketers need to consider when developing new services.

INNOVATORS
The first group of consumers to purchase a new product.

EARLY ADOPTERS
The second group of consumers to purchase new products.

EARLY MAJORITY
The third group of adopters, who are more risk averse in purchase decisions than innovators and early adopters.

LATE MAJORITY
The more skeptical consumers who purchase products after the early majority.

LAGGARDS
Consumers who resist new products the longest.

CHAPTER SUMMARY

OBJECTIVE 1: **Provide a framework to evaluate the extent to which existing or new products are marketed to existing or new market segments.**

Every organization needs to develop a product mix consistent with its overall strategy. It must match current and new products with current and new segments. This produces four basic options for marketing mix management. A core business focus maintains, expands, or harvests current products in current markets. Market development seeks new market segments for existing products. Product development improves or adds new products for sale to current segments. Diversification introduces new products into new market segments. Organizations can use this framework to help allocate resources to obtain the best overall performance.

OBJECTIVE 2: **Understand how the characteristics of innovation influence the speed with which product innovations are accepted.**

Product innovations are of three types. Continuous innovations are minor changes in existing products that require no alterations in how consumers use them. Dynamically continuous innovations have added features and benefits that require minor changes in

behavior. Discontinuous innovations are new to the world and may require major changes.

How rapidly a product is accepted depends on several factors. If its relative advantage over other products is high, then faster acceptance can be expected. If the product is compatible with current thinking, then quick adoption is likely. Also, less complex products and those that can be easily tried are more readily accepted. Finally, if the product can be observed in use by others, then it is more likely to be adopted rapidly.

OBJECTIVE 3: **Know the steps used to develop new products from the initial idea through commercialization.**

The new-product development process has seven steps. First, a strategy is outlined by top management. This indicates the importance of new products to the organization. Second, idea generation provides a list of possibilities. These can come from numerous sources, especially if they are actively sought. Third, idea screening narrows the list to those most compatible with the organization's need. Several criteria are used in screening. Fourth, business analysis develops a product concept and performs a financial analysis to assess feasibility and estimate profitability under numerous assumptions. Fifth, prototype product development involves all the steps leading up to and including the creation of a working model. Sixth, test marketing provides a limited trial of the marketing strategy under real or simulated conditions. The objective is to see whether the strategy will work or needs to be refined before full-scale launch. Seventh, commercialization occurs when the product is formally introduced into the market.

OBJECTIVE 4: Show how the product life cycle concept can be used to build and adjust marketing strategies over time.

Products can be viewed as moving over a life cycle with several stages. In the introduction phase, sales usually take off slowly despite heavy promotion. Marketers concentrate on getting consumers to be aware of and accept the product class. During the growth stage sales increase, and product technology often enters its second generation. Manufacturing and promotion are adjusted. Leading producers focus on customer service. At maturity, sales begin to slow and level off. Gains in market share for one company come at the expense of another. A few companies exit at this point.

Low cost really counts now in manufacturing and marketing. The decline stage is marked by a downward sales trend. Although a good replacement parts market may exist for some products, many companies choose to exit or harvest.

OBJECTIVE 5: Recognize how innovations are adopted by consumers by being spread from group to group.

People go through a series of steps in adopting a new product. The speed depends on personal characteristics. Individuals can be grouped into five categories that comprise the diffusion process. Innovators are the first to adopt. They are usually a small group and tend to be eccentric. Early adopters, a larger group, are next. They have high income and education levels, and others respect them. This group is key to the success of new products. The third category is early majority buyers, a larger segment that generally follows the leadership of the early adopters. The last two categories, late majority buyers and laggards, are the last to adopt. The late majority group is numerous, so it is important.

REVIEW YOUR UNDERSTANDING

1. What are the four product mix options? Describe each.
2. What are the three product innovation categories? What are the characteristics of each?
3. What product characteristics speed the adoption of an innovation?
4. What are the steps in new-product development? Describe each.
5. What are test markets?
6. List five organizational structures for new-product development.
7. What are the differences between simultaneous and sequential methods of new-product development?
8. What is the difference between a product manager and a market manager?
9. What are the stages in the product life cycle? Describe them.

DISCUSSION OF CONCEPTS

1. Explain the differences among continuous innovation, dynamically continuous innovation, and discontinuous innovation. What are the main activities for marketers when introducing each type?
2. Assume you are senior vice president of marketing for General Electric. What four product mix management options might you consider? Give specific examples of each.
3. Describe the typical profit scenario as a product moves through its life cycle. Do you think it's important for companies to have products in all stages? Why or why not?
4. What are some problems with using the product life cycle concept to make marketing decisions? Why do you think so many companies use the concept?
5. What are some ways to extend the product life cycle? Can you think of any companies that have used these techniques?
6. Many marketers use the diffusion cycle concept and the product life cycle concept. How are they different?
7. When introducing a new product, how may a marketer facilitate consumer acceptance?
8. Describe each organizational structure for new-product development. What factors would influence your decision to select one structure over another?

KEY TERMS AND DEFINITIONS

Adoption process: The steps an individual consumer goes through in making a product choice.

Business analysis: Assessment of the attractiveness of the product from a sales, cost, profit, and cash flow standpoint.

Commercialization: Final stage in the new-product development process, when the product is introduced into the market.

Concept testing: Testing the new-product concept to evaluate the likelihood of its success.

Continuous innovation: A minor alteration in an existing product, such as a new style or model, that can be easily adopted without significant changes in consumer behavior.

Diffusion process: The spread of innovations from one group of consumers to another over time.

Discontinuous innovation: An entirely new product with new functions.

Dynamically continuous innovation: A familiar product with additional features and benefits that require or permit consumers to alter some aspect of their behavior.

Early adopters: The second group of consumers to purchase new products.

Early majority: The third group of adopters, who are more risk averse in purchase decisions than innovators and early adopters.

Idea generation: The gathering of suggestions for new products from a number of sources using a range of formal and informal methods.

Idea screening: Identifying the new-product ideas that have the most potential to succeed.

Innovators: The first group of consumers to purchase a new product.

Laggards: Consumers who resist new products the longest.

Late majority: The more skeptical consumers who purchase products after the early majority.

Line extension: A new product closely related to others in the line.

Market development: Offering existing products to new market segments.

Market manager: A manager responsible for one or several similar product lines targeted at specific market segments.

New-product committee: A group of key functional personnel who are brought together periodically to develop new products.

New-product department: The organizational unit responsible for identifying product ideas and preparing them for commercialization.

Product concept: A product idea that has been refined into written descriptions, pictures, and specifications.

Product development: Offering new products to existing market segments.

Product life cycle: The four stages a product goes through: introduction, growth, maturity, and decline.

Product manager: A manager who oversees one or several products targeted at all market segments.

Product mix: All the product lines and products a company offers.

Product planning: The focus given to core businesses, market development, product development, and diversification.

Sequential new-product development: People from various functional areas work on different stages of product development.

Simulated product test: Experimentation with the marketing strategy in artificial conditions.

Simultaneous new-product development: People from all functional areas work together to develop products.

Test market: A small geographic area, with characteristics similar to the total market, in which a product is introduced with a complete marketing program.

Venture team: Personnel from various areas of the company who are given release time to work on a specific assignment.

REFERENCES

1. Mark Gimein, "Palm and Handspring Go Hand to Hand," *Fortune,* September 18, 2000, pp. 319–320; Jon Fortt, "Palm Redesigning Handhelds for Broader Appeal," *San Jose Mercury News,* August 6, 2000, www.mercurycenter.com; Rex Crum, "Palm and Handspring: The Whole World in Their Hands?" *Upside Today,* August 17, 2000, www.upside.com; "Media Backgrounder," Palm Web site, www.palm.com; "Big Fish: Jeff Hawkins Fights Off Feature Creep," *Red Herring,* October 28, 1999, www.redherring.com/companies/1999/1028/cip-bigfish.html.

2. Ichiko Fuyuno and Merle Linda Wolin, "Young Inventors Awards—Research: Products With Polish—A Japanese Make-up Manufacturer Runs a Think-Tank for Ideas That Aren't Merely Cosmetic," *Far Eastern Economic Review,* December 14, 2000, p. 68.

3. George Stalk, Jr. and Thomas N. Hout, *Competing Against Time* (New York: The Free Press, 1990), p. 253.

4. Booz, Allen & Hamilton, *New Product Management for the Eighties* (New York: Booz, Allen & Hamilton, 1982).

5. Christopher Power, "Flops—Too Many New Products Fail. Here Is Why—And How to Do Better," *Business Week,* August 16, 1993, pp. 76–82.

6. Edwin E. Bobrow, "Innovation Is a Strategic Move," *Marketing News,* March 17, 1997, p. 13.

7. Stalk and Hout, *Competing Against Time,* p. 253.

8. Lynn Marshall, "The Cutting Edge: Focus on Technology, Amazon.com Chief Plunges Ahead Despite Turbulent Waters," *Los Angeles Times,* December 4, 2000, p. C-5.

9. Ian McKinnon, "Alberta's Dynastream Hopes to Profit as Nike Takes High-Tech Direction," *National Post,* May 11, 2000, p. C03.

10. N. Dawar and P. Anderson, "Order and Direction of Brand Extension," *Journal of Business Research* 30 (1994): pp. 119–129.

11. "Autodesk Delivers XML Tool for AutoCAD 2000i Products with New Product Extension," *PR Newswire,* December 5, 2000.

12. Gouri Agtey Athale, "The Heat Is On," *Economic Times,* November 22, 2000.

13. www.pizzahut.com, site visited December 13, 2000.

14. "Vacation Rentals Come to the Internet Via Hotel Reservations Network's Condosaver.com," *PR Newswire,* December 5, 2000.

15. "Gearing up for Larger Women," *The Star-Ledger Newark,* August 27, 2000, p. 17.

16. www.PhilipMorris.com, site visited December 13, 2000.

17. "Japan Beer Cos Diversified Strategies Hazardous: Moody's," *Capital Markets Report,* December 12, 2000.

18. www.simplyhomesoups.com, site visited January 13, 2001.

19. "Guardent's World-Class Security Experts Available for Comment on Microsoft Hack and QAZ Trojan Horse," *PR Newswire,* October 27, 2000.

20. "Todito-Branded Internet Kiosks Expand to 150 Elektra Stores; Kiosks Offer Low-Cost Computers Packaged With Internet Connection Service," *PR Newswire,* December 13, 2000.

21. Tony Dawe, "Hello, Is Anybody There," *The Times of London,* October 27, 2000, p. 1DD.

22. R. J. Calantone, C. A. DiBenedetto, and S. Bhoovaroghaven, "Examining the Relationship between Degree of Innovation and New Product Success," *Journal of Business Research* 30 (1994): pp. 143–148.

23. windowsupdate.microsoft.com, site visited December 13, 2000.

24. Chris Jones, "Excel, Power Point to Pack Interactive Tools," *Infoworld,* September 23, 1996, p. 29.

25. Michael Krantz, "The Main Event," *Time,* June 1, 1998, pp. 32–37; "A Decade of Microsoft's Antitrust Battles," *The Seattle Times Company,* seattletimes.com, February 25, 2001.

26. Jeff May, "Newark, N.J.-Based Internet Access Services Firm to Launch Web TV Service," *Knight-Ridder Tribune Business News: The Star Ledger—Newark,* December 12, 2000.

27. Wendy Lim, "Offer Internet Banking Trial Products' Advice," *Business Times (Malaysia),* February 27, 1999, p. 5.

28. "Organized Cell Phones," *Star-Tribune Newspaper of the Twin Cities Minneapolis-St. Paul,* December 8, 2000, p. 17E.

29. George Stalk, Philip Evans, and Lawrence E. Shulman, "Competing on Capabilities: The New Rules of Corporate Strategy," *Harvard Business Review,* March–April 1992, pp. 57–69.

30. Power, "Flops"; and Howard Schlossberg, "Fear of Failure Stifles Product Development," *Marketing News,* May 14, 1990, pp. 1, 16.

31. Michael J. McCarthy, "U.S. Companies Shop Abroad for Product Ideas," *Wall Street Journal,* March 14, 1990, pp. B1, B4; Jack Wagner, "New Products Are Not the Only Way to Grow," *Marketing News,* May 14, 1990, p. 17; and Power, "Flops."

32. Prasanna Raman, "Culture Promotes Innovation," *The New Straits Times,* October 17, 2000, p. 38.

33. "Carriers Forming E-Group" *South China Morning Post,* December 6, 2000, p. 1.

34. William M. Weilbacher, *Brand Marketing* (Lincolnwood, IL: NTC Business Books), p. 22.

35. James Carbone, "Sun Shines By Taking Time Out," *Purchasing,* September 19, 1996, pp. 34–35.

36. Power, "Flops."

37. "Seventh Generation, Inc.," *Marketing News,* April 25, 1994, p. E8.

38. "In Celebration of Earth Day, Respond.com Announces New Categories for Environmentally Friendly Products and Services," *Business Wire,* April 19, 2000.

39. R. Calantone, S. Vikery, and C. Droge, "Business Performance and New Product Development Activities: An Empirical Investigation," *Journal of Product Innovation Management* 12 (June 1995): pp. 214–223.

40. T. Haggblom, R. Calantone, and C. A. DiBenedetto, "Do New Product Managers in Large or Hi-Market Share Firms Perceive Marketing R&D Interface Principles Differently?" *Journal of Product Innovation Management* 12 (September 1995): pp. 323–333.

41. "Wearable Computer Systems with Head-Mounted Displays for Manufacturing, Maintenance, and Training Applications," eto.sysplan.com/ETO/TIA/Factsheets/BoeingTRP.html, November 1996.

42. "Orbit Canada Announces Success of Marketing Program for Canada's First Phone-to-Phone Internet-Based Telephony Network," *Canada Newswire,* December 13, 2000.

43. Karen E. Kline, "Your Company Learning Curve," *Los Angeles Times, Home Edition,* December 13, 2000, p. C-5.

44. "Consumer: Suck It and See: Dyson Has Triumphed over Hoover in the Great Vacuum Cleaner Legal War, but Which Are the Best Dust-Busters?" *The Guardian,* October 5, 2000.

45. Jennifer Lawrence, "The Sunchip Also Rises," *Advertising Age,* April 27, 1992, p. S2; and Jennifer Lawrence, "Big Push for Sunchips," *Advertising Age,* February 24, 1992, p. 2.

46. Bob Trott and Ed Scannell, "Courtroom Showdown: Antitrust Action Already Affecting Microsoft Rivals," *InfoWorld,* May 25, 1998, pp. 1–7.

47. Steven P. Schnaars, *Managing Imitation Strategies* (New York: The Free Press, 1994), p. 5.

48. Frank Shipper and Charles C. Manz, "WL Gore and Associates, Inc.," in Henry Mintzberg, James Brian Quinn, and John Voyer, *The Strategy Process* (Upper Saddle River, NJ: Prentice Hall, 1995), pp. 488–498.

49. www.gorefabrics.com/shop-online/usa_shops.html, site visited December 20, 2000.

50. www.lilly.com/health/innovation/index.html, site visited December 13, 2000.

51. Cathy Bolt, "Perth Wins Battle for $55m Motorola Centre," *Australian Financial News,* December 13, 2000, p. 17.

52. Al Ries and Jack Trout, *The 22 Immutable Laws of Marketing* (New York: Harper Collins, 1993), pp. 6–7.

53. www.honda.com, site visited December 13, 2000, "Honda Launches Streamlined e-Commerce Web Site," *PRNewswire,* December 13, 2000.

54. Valerie Reitman and Reginald Chua, "Honda's Cub Reigns as King of the Road," *Wall Street Journal,* July 26, 1996, pp. B1, B13.

55. Bien Perez, "HP Bluetooth Strategy to Widen Links for Its Hardware Products," *South China Morning Post,* November 21, 2000, p. 8.

56. Masayoshi Kanabayashi, "Taiwan Becomes Asia's Main Supplier of Chips to Japan," *The Asian Wall Street Journal,* December 14, 2000, p. 6.

57. Lesley Young, "A Phone, a 386, a Table and a Vision: Outsourcing Success Story," *National Post,* December 13, 2000, p. E14.

58. Ron Stodghill II, "At Upjohn, a Grim Changing of the Guard," *Business Week,* May 3, 1993, p. 36; and Patricia Winters, "Upjohn Buys McNeil's R&D and Runs," *Advertising Age,* January 25, 1993, p. 4.

59. Greg Hassell, "Gaggle of Grocers Scoot on New Craze," *Houston Chronicle,* November 29, 2000, p. 1.

60. www.womanmotorist.com, site visited December 14, 2000.

61. www.gotmilk.com, www.whymilk.com, sites visited December 14, 2000.

62. Paula Mergenhagen, "How 'Got Milk' Got Sales," *American Demographics,* September 1996, www.marketingpower.com/publications/MT/96 MT/9609_MT/9609MD02.HTM.

63. www.commerce.motorola.com/consumerQWhtml/home.html, site visited December 14, 2000.

64. Ian P. Murphy, "Super-size It Was the Answer," *Marketing News,* June 9, 1997, p. 2.

65. Raymond Vernon, "International Investment and International Trade in the Product Life Cycle," *Quarterly Journal of Economics* (May 1986), p. 199.

66. Evertt M. Rogers, *Diffusion of Innovations,* 3rd ed. (New York: The Free Press, 1982), pp. 164–175.

67. R. Olshavsky and R. Spreng, "An Exploratory Study of the Innovation Evaluation Process," *Journal of Product Innovation Management* 13 (November 1996): pp. 512–529.

68. Kevin Marron, "Digital Cameras Move On Up Consumer Wish Lists," *The Globe and Mail,* December 1, 2000, p. T5.

69. Andy Goldberg, "Sales Record for Chips with Everything," *The Daily Telegraph,* December 7, 2000.

70. Brian F. Blake, "They May Be Innovative, But They're Not the Same," *Marketing News,* April 15, 1991, p. 12.

Bricks or Clicks

YET2.COM IS THE NEW WAY TO CAPITALIZE ON INTELLECTUAL PROPERTY

Yᴇᴛ2.ᴄᴏᴍ ɪs ʀᴇᴠᴏʟᴜᴛɪᴏɴɪᴢɪɴɢ ᴛʜᴇ ᴇxᴄʜᴀɴɢᴇ of intellectual property. The companies involved, which make up 15 percent of the total worldwide research and development expenditures, range from university professors with a single technology to large corporations with thousands of technologies. The premise behind the site is that these companies have technologies that are being underutilized. The site allows companies from very different industries to exchange information in the form of licensing the technologies. For example, Boeing licensed an optical coating to Touchbridge, a touch screen manufacturer. Boeing used the coating to reduce the dirt and fingerprints on its cockpit instruments. The two companies would not have connected without yet2.com.

This example illustrates the untapped assets many companies have sitting in drawers. Many inventions or new technologies are not useful for the company, but that knowledge may be extremely profitable in another industry. Intellectual property and how to manage it is a difficult issue facing many companies. The push to maximize shareholder value and, thus, make a return on the money invested in research makes this exchange system an important tool.

Yet2.com has made another smart move by partnering with Deloitte & Touche to offer intellectual asset management (IAM) to its companies. Deloitte & Touche has the IAM capabilities to determine the market value of different technologies, facilitate the licensing process, and most importantly, it has a portfolio mining group that assists in determining the technologies with the most potential.

Confidentiality is a major concern for the companies involved with yet2.com. At a recent conference, the participants barred the media until the concluding session. All of the technologies offered on the site are described without giving away the details on how they work. Those details are not revealed until the deal is nearly complete.

Yet2.com is revolutionizing the way companies view their intellectual property and facilitating the exchange of information that ultimately leads to better products.

Sources: "Four Korean Companies Join the World's Premier Technology Exchange," *Business Wire,* October 19, 2000, retrieved from the World Wide Web, www.lexis-nexis.com; "E-Biz: IP: Bringing the Old and New Economies Together: Yet2.com

Finds Common Ground Between Giants of Industry and Internet Specialist Companies," *Sunday Business Group,* October 1, 2000, retrieved from the World Wide Web, www.lexis-nexis.com; and "Deloitte & Touche Brings Intellectual Asset Management to the Web via Partnership with Yet2.com, Internet Showcase and Global Sales Exchange for Patented Technologies, Processes," *Business Wire,* October 10, 2000, the World Wide Web, www.lexis-nexis.com.

CASE 10

Innovation at Minnesota Mining and Manufacturing

INNOVATION IS REQUIRED AT 3M, where 30 percent of annual sales must come from products less than four years old. New products are a critical part of 3M, but the company also believes in forming innovative relationships with suppliers and customers. 3M made the top 10 list in *Fortune*'s "Most Admired Corporations" many times during the 1990s. Much of its success can be attributed to aggressive new-product development. 3M is frequently ranked among the top 10 U.S. corporations for number of patents received annually.

According to Dave Beal, a business reporter in Minneapolis-St. Paul, where 3M is headquartered, the company is "stepping up its effort to leverage its technology, in a sweeping drive to boost its sales." Essentially, the strategy is to get to market first with one-of-a-kind products that can be premium-priced to increase the company's profit margins. To help accomplish this, 3M restructured the organization in the late 1990s. Many traditional products that faced price competition were put into a separate company, Emation, whereas less price-sensitive products remained with the parent. In this way, 3M executives can focus attention on higher value-added, unique products.

With a new worldwide technology and product development process, "Pacing Plus," 3M is enhancing its competitiveness by bringing successful products to market more rapidly. The program is designed to bring ideas to successful commercialization in half the amount of time that used to be necessary. This means products with significant functionality for customers and value that can generate high profits for the corporation. Pacing Plus cuts through the red tape and focuses on products with a high probability of success. Successful Pacing Plus products have included Microflex Circuits, paper-thin circuits used in disk drives and ink-jet printer heads, and Brightness Enhancement films that are used in laptop computer screens. With at least $1 billion a year invested in R&D, these new products continue to be successful in the global marketplace. By 2004, the company

expects sales from Pacing Plus products to account for $1 billion in annual sales.

3M certainly has the talent to make things happen. Its 6,500 R&D personnel have backgrounds in chemistry, electronics, biochemistry, microbiology, genetics, pharmacology, and material sciences. They are scattered among 71 R&D laboratories around the world, the largest of which houses approximately 4,000 at 3M's Maple Wood campus in Austin, Texas. Many new-product ideas emerge from scientists working closely with customers who have specific needs. 3M also gives scientists the freedom to pursue their own projects with the corporate "15 percent rule." This rule says that scientists can spend up to 15 percent of their time working on individual initiatives, which has resulted in many new products for the company.

3M R&D chief, William Coil, says that "one of our goals is to increase our speed to market. But we're not trying to increase our speed before we decide to take something to market, because that could have a real negative implication for innovation." 3M spends a good deal of time making sure that market conditions can support a new product. The risks are gigantic, given the large number of people and huge budgets involved, but 3M personnel are taught to understand and assume risk. In one training session, students are given real money and asked to wager it. In one scenario, a small amount of cash is placed at the end of a long plank laid on the floor, and an employee is given the opportunity to walk along the plank to get the loot. Then the students are asked that if a huge amount of money were at stake, would they walk the same plank if it were stretched between two seven-story buildings. "The downside risk . . ." someone might begin; but the leader responds, "What risk? You've already proven it's very easy to do it."

By creating a safe environment for risk-taking entrepreneurship, 3M has been able to accomplish 30 percent of sales from very young products. Still, it is interested in raising the bar, and Pacing Plus has begun to do this. It requires coordination throughout the organization. According to Marc Adam, head of marketing, "there's progressively more in common between R&D and marketing." 3M's major customer teams include representatives from R&D all the way through sales. This helps the company understand even unarticulated customer needs, so it can create products to meet them.

1. *Imagine you are in charge of product development at 3M. Explain why innovation is a critical part of your company's strategy.*
2. *How is Pacing Plus expected to improve 3M's product development process?*
3. *How does 3M manage risk? Suggest additional ways the company can promote risk-taking entrepreneurship.*
4. *How might 3M use the product life cycle concept to build and adjust its marketing strategies over time?*

Sources: Dave Beal, "Dave Beal Column," *Saint Paul Pioneer Press, Minnesota,* December 6, 2000, retrieved December 21, 2000 from the World Wide Web, ptg.djnr.com; Terry Fiedler, "3M Innovation to Be Tested," *Star-Tribune Newspaper of the Twin Cities Minneapolis,* December 10, 2000, p. 1D; Scott Scholten, "3M Sees Sales Increasing by 6% to 7% in 2000," *Dow Jones News Service,* January 26, 2000, retrieved December 21, 2000 from the World Wide Web, ptg.djnr.com; Dave Beal, "To Boost Sales, 3M Steps Up Effort to Capitalize on Its Technology Edge," *St. Paul Pioneer Press-KnightRidder/Tribune Business News,* March 31, 1997, p. 331; Thomas A. Stewart, "3M Fights Back," *Fortune,* February 5, 1996, www.fortune.com; and 3M Web site, www.3m.com, visited on December 22, 2000.

chapter 11

SERVICES AND NONPROFIT MARKETING

1. Identify the forces that have produced and will continue to create tremendous growth in the service economy.

2. Understand which characteristics of services must be adjusted for successful marketing.

3. Know how to develop the service mix.

4. Explore the expanded concept of services.

5. Appreciate the importance of nonprofit marketing and the uniqueness of this important marketing arena.

◀ *The original IBM (International Business Machines) world headquarters*

IBM WAS A PIONEER OF THE *digital age, when computers were room-sized and powered by vacuum tubes. It was also in the forefront of the personal computer revolution, bringing computing power to the desktop with the 1981 introduction of its PC. Now the company is moving beyond hardware and software toward another transformation, harnessing the specialized technology expertise of its employees to become a worldwide provider of technology services. IBM still sells more than $30 billion worth of computer equipment every year, but these days, its fastest-growing division is focused on delivering services. Multinational corporations, giant Web retailers, government agencies, and e-business start-ups are just some of the organizations that have hired IBM Global Services to work on a variety of technology projects.*

Within the Global Services division, the Business Innovation Services group specializes in Internet-related services; the Integrated Technology Services group puts together sophisticated hardware and software systems; and the Strategic Outsourcing Services group operates computer installations on behalf of corporate customers. In all, the 140,000 employees of IBM Global Services have the training and skill to configure a communication network for the international space station, create a Web site for an earth-based e-tailer, and provide complete computer support as an outsourcing supplier to numerous companies. This IBM division holds nearly 10 percent of the rapidly expanding $450 billion worldwide market for information technology services. If it were a stand-alone business, the division would be the world's largest high-tech service firm.

IBM's long-standing relationship with many corporate customers and its reputation for reliability and responsiveness are definite pluses when the Global Services division competes for service contracts. Yet as a service provider, the division is only as good as the personnel who actually deliver its services to customers. To keep up with the burgeoning demand and compete against eager rivals such as Electronic Data Systems and Computer Sciences, IBM must continue to hire, train, and retain at least 20,000 additional technology specialists every year—a difficult challenge when so many other businesses are actively recruiting the same kind of specialists.

IBM Global Services is often perceived as a service provider for larger organizations, but it is also eager to cash in on opportunities in the small and midsized business segments. To help service this segment, IBM is partnering with 45,000 distributors, developers, Internet experts, and other specialists who will provide systems design and support, education and training, e-commerce connections, and technology operations. IBM earns 20 percent of the revenue from any services performed by its partners, and it can try to sell its own services to the same business customers. With sales of services to the small and midsized business segments growing by 20 percent per year, this is a good way for the Global Services division to supplement its own efforts in following up sales leads, providing technical support, customizing systems, and taking over outsourced operations as needed.

As evidence of its reliability and responsiveness—two highly prized dimensions of service quality—IBM Global Services stands ready to provide 24-hour, seven-day service. Customers with business offices on every continent, such as Lucent Technologies, expect to be able to access their outsourced computer systems at any hour of the day or night. Similarly, Web retailers are always open for business, so they need to be able to contact IBM service personnel around the clock. Regardless of the size of the customer or the complexity of the problem, IBM is able to offer service support through its Web site, through technical hot-line operations, or through another approach to each customer's individual needs.

Knowing that tangible elements contribute to perceptions of service quality, IBM Global Services is establishing a series of cutting-edge design and consulting centers where businesses can sit down with IBM tech specialists to discuss their Internet-related service requirements. In addition, the division is building credibility by promoting its ability to help customers with critical issues such as Internet security and wireless communication. As one example, Global Services created a new system that allows travelers holding tickets on Swissair flights to avoid long lines at the airport by completing the check-in process using their mobile phones. This is the kind of innovation that keeps IBM Global Services in such demand as a provider of technology services.[1]

THE CONCEPT OF SERVICES

SERVICE

An idea, task, experience, or activity that can be exchanged for value to satisfy the needs and wants of consumers and businesses.

Products can be either goods or services. Goods are physical objects. **Services** are intangible ideas, tasks, experiences, performances, or activities that one party can offer another. A major difference between a service and a good is that services generally involve suppliers connecting directly with consumers for performance of the service. Your barber, your doctor, and your professor all require your involvement in order to perform their service. They connect with you personally. When you think about it, even goods are more valuable when accompanied by excellent service. Consequently, goods and services often go hand in hand.

To serve means to benefit a receiving party through personal acts. The marketing of services, by its very nature, concerns the development of beneficial relationships. Interpersonal skills are critical, because for a service to be performed well, these skills must help support the customer relationship. And the marketers of services are likely to fail if they do not embody all the principles of good marketing in their activities.

For more than a quarter century, the dollar volume of services in the U.S. economy has grown at nearly 4 percent annually, approximately double the growth rate for products. This torrid pace is expected to continue well into the 21st century. Services were responsible for 80 percent of the GDP and for more than 73 percent of all jobs in the United States at the end of 1999.[2] More than 33.8 million people have been employed in the service sector in the United States since 1997.[3]

Countries such as the United States and Great Britain rely on the production, sale, and consumption of services for domestic growth; Great Britain, the United States' nearest

TGI Friday's is an international service provider that has done especially well in the Far East.

competitor in service sales, generates about $100 billion a year. The United States, in comparison, sold $250 billion last year in services. Since services account for $1.3 trillion, the global market is also very important. The United States has emerged as a world leader in services. Foreign countries pay approximately $80 billion more for U.S. services than Americans pay them for theirs. That trade surplus is five times greater than it was in 1986, and some analysts expect it to be even greater by 2010, when the sale of services by U.S. companies is expected to reach $650 billion.[4] Global marketing, therefore, is particularly important for many U.S. service providers. The Carlson Company is a good example of how U.S. service companies have gone international. Carlson owns T.G.I. Friday's, a popular "all-American" restaurant chain with a casual format that has done well at home and abroad, including the Far East. Sales volume in Seoul, Korea, for example, is double that of the chain's average U.S. restaurant. The atmosphere is the same, the walls are decorated with remnants of American culture, and the staff is just as lively as in the States.[5]

Figure 11.1 provides an overview of this chapter. We begin by looking at forces that have created and will continue to produce explosive growth for services. This is followed by a section that explores service characteristics in depth. It will show how services are differentiated, their relationships to goods, the attributes consumers use to judge them, and what quality service is. Next, we will describe the aspects marketers consider when developing the service mix. You will extend what you learned in chapters 9 and 10 to services by looking at core, augmented, and branded services and the development of new offerings. Keep in mind that services are as important in business-to-business marketing as they are in consumer marketing. Such traditional services as health care, insurance, energy, telecommunications, garbage and snow removal, accounting and tax preparation, auto service, and restaurants have been the backbone of the service economy for a long time. The first part of the chapter provides an understanding of how these kinds of services are marketed. The next sections discuss the expanded concept of services, which includes person, entertainment, event, place, political, cause, and internal marketing. We conclude by looking at the important area of nonprofit marketing.

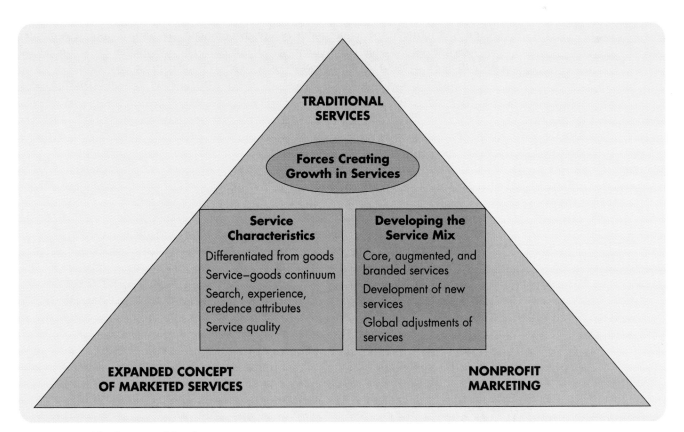

FIGURE 11.1 *The Concept of Services*

GLOBAL FORCES CREATING GROWTH IN SERVICES

The service economy is not unique to the United States. In developed countries around the globe, more and more of total economic well-being is based on services. As nations become more sophisticated, the demand for services grows. The Industrial Revolution brought about productivity gains through the substitution of machines for human and animal labor. The technology revolution that followed went far beyond the mere substitution of labor. It resulted in the creation of products that exceeded human and animal capabilities. A century ago, who would have imagined that millions of business travelers would routinely fly six miles above the earth and use plastic cards to charge phone calls while in flight? Air transportation and telecommunications, including the recent explosion of the Internet as a means of global communication, are examples of services that have brought us closer to the reality of a global community. Figure 11.2 depicts the global forces that are influencing growth in services.

TECHNOLOGY

Technology is producing more sophisticated services more rapidly. Until recently, more advanced nations were still dedicated to the production of goods. Today, many of the goods that are produced support services for thousands and even millions of consumers. The technologies of today can't be used by consumers without the services of highly trained professionals. For example, jet aircraft produced in the 1960s still carry millions of passengers annually, and planes being produced today are likely to still be flying halfway through the 21st century. Smaller percentages of the population are now able to produce greater quantities of more valuable goods, thereby shifting the emphasis to value-added services. Some of these services in the consumer sector include entertainment, travel, health, and education and consulting and environmental controls in the business-to-business sector.

The technological revolution is making an information revolution possible, which now facilitates nearly every human endeavor. Soon transmitters in today's microprocessors will be replaced by transmitters that operate 10 million times faster. This could alter the commercial landscape to a point nearly unrecognizable by many of us.[6] Today one of the largest service industries is computer software, and this sector will almost certainly expand exponentially in future decades. Consider the impact of MP3 technologies such as Napster and peer-to-peer networking. Not only is this having a huge impact on the way information is distributed, but it is also forcing the recording and publishing industries to completely rethink their distribution channels. Amazingly, the service industry already dominates spending for online computer services, totaling $520 million and topping 25 industries.[7] The information and technological revolution will assist in the creation of services presently unimaginable.

In many cases, technology eliminates the need for personal interaction between a buyer and seller. For example, according to the Federal Deposit Insurance Corporation, the number of commercial banks has declined from 14,200 in 1986 to 8,581 in 1999 (www.fdic.gov). This can be attributed in part to automated teller machines, online banking, and other services.

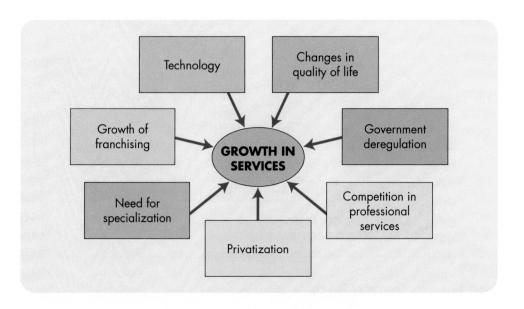

FIGURE 11.2 *Global Forces Creating Growth in Services*

With the increase in technology, there is less need for customer contact. As shown with Autotrader.com, customers don't need to go to the dealership to look for a car.

Despite the decline, consumers still prefer to do business face-to-face. A study by KPMG Peat Marwick indicated that 73 percent of consumers prefer to bank in a staffed branch. Another 64 percent said they would rather not use technology for certain transactions.[8]

QUALITY OF LIFE

Quality of life is not defined by how much is consumed but by how people feel and experience life. For example, our thinking about basic services such as health, education, and mobility has expanded dramatically. Health once meant the absence of sickness but today's perception of health has expanded to include fitness, increased physical performance, and enhanced mental well-being. Education, once the domain of the elite few, has become accessible to a significant percentage of the population. Many people find expenditures at bookstores as valuable as the purchase of a microwave oven was in the 1970s. Mobility, expressed in the 1950s by a high-performance car, now includes psychological mobility provided by movies, cellular phones, and the Internet. Internet cafes illustrate yet another change in the quality of life, providing customers with two popular services in one—specialty coffees and the worldwide computer network.

The fast pace of family life has placed a tremendous premium on services of all types. As more women move into the workforce, there is less time available for traditional responsibilities such as child care and cooking. Nearly all the women who entered the workplace in the last two decades have joined the service sector, which has increased the demand for services. Most people would prefer to use their leisure time for activities other than shopping and cooking. Today, Americans' eating patterns are changing from three square meals a day to five smaller meals. An increasing percentage of these meals are consumed in the car. This has resulted in an increase in the availability of convenient food options for on-the-go consumers; most Americans spend 7 percent of their total income on food not cooked in the home.[9] Because of time constraints, sales in traditional supermarkets are declining dramatically, while companies such as Peapod Delivery Systems, which delivers full grocery baskets to people's homes, are surviving despite some growing pains. Others, such as Waiter on Wheels, Room Service Deliveries, Takeout Taxi, and Door 2 Door, work with restaurants to deliver meals. Even services such as Kozmo.com and Urbanfetch are tapping into the increased need for convenience. Many travelers in the future may not have to wait at baggage claim. Baggage Direct, a company operating out of Heathrow Airport in London, delivers baggage to any location in London in about three hours for a $40 fee, using an RFID label to scan and identify baggage, thereby saving time for the traveler anxious to get to work or home to the family.[10] Today, 42 percent of preschool-age children are in day care facilities, allowing both parents to work. As a result of the increase in dual-career families, the need for quality day care services has grown dramatically and services to support the family in leisure time have also become more valuable.

GOVERNMENT DEREGULATION OF SERVICES

Another factor profoundly influencing growth in services is industry deregulation that has occurred over the past 20 years. This trend, started in the United States, has now spread throughout Europe. Understanding that competition provides vast opportunities for economic growth, legislators have deregulated many services that were traditionally controlled by government agencies. As expected, numerous private companies have stepped in to seize and create opportunities. For example, the spectacular growth in cellular phones was stimulated by deregulation of the telephone industry. In fact, the deregulation of the telephone industry led to competitive phone wars. Some of the smaller companies, however, bought each other out to emerge as larger, more consolidated telecommunications companies. With more resources at their disposal, they were able to compete with older companies for customers. For example, AT&T's wireless phone sales rank only third in the country behind Verizon, who bought Vodafone to expand services, and Cingular, an alliance of SBC and BellSouth. Most of these companies sell services as a part of a total package, a "bundle" that offers several services that appeal to a particular group, such as business customers, at a special price, in order to attract customers. The realignment of companies and services can sometimes be difficult for consumers, as companies stretch resources to attract more customers.[11] But consumers should eventually emerge as winners in the midst of increasing competition due to improved services and lower prices. Major deregulation also has occurred in:

- Transportation—air freight, airlines, trucking, and shipping
- Finance—banking, securities, and insurance
- Telecommunications—radio, television, and telephones
- Energy—electricity and gas

Competition stimulated by deregulation results in a better selection at a better price, which improves demand and creates jobs. For example, when the government deregulated the airline industry, companies expanded the number, location, and pricing approaches of flights, among other changes. The result has been better prices, better schedules, and overall improved service levels for consumers. Increased competition has made it necessary for companies to deliver greater value to consumers, which in turn has stimulated demand for these services. For example, the telecommunications industry has become one of the three fastest-growing industries in the United States. Spending on communications alone was expected to reach $400 billion by the year 2000.[12] Over all, consumers and businesses both win.

COMPETITION IN PROFESSIONAL SERVICES

Not long ago, doctors, lawyers, and other professionals were prohibited from marketing their services in the media. Only subtle means were allowed, such as sports team sponsorships or word of mouth. All of this changed in 1974, when the Supreme Court ruled that a ban on lawyer marketing was unconstitutional.[13] Today, nearly every profession engages in some form of marketing. Health care is a good case in point.

Hospitals, preferred provider organizations, and health maintenance organizations compete vigorously for patients, and there are elaborate educational campaigns designed to teach doctors how to market services. The availability of information via technology has enhanced marketers' opportunities to promote health care services. Users will be able to access medical specialists and information as well as interact with visuals and audio. Marketers must exercise care in the promotion of health goods and services. Since the health care industry is complex and often confusing, consumers usually know very little about products and services offered. Without this knowledge and expertise about the industry, consumers must rely, to some degree, on marketers to inform them. This places great emphasis on the importance of truthful and reliable information, even with well-known and trusted Web sites such as WebMD. The recent explosion of drug companies advertising on television has caused some problems. For example, Pfizer and Pharmacia corporations, the makers of Celebrex, an arthritis drug, were ordered to pull an advertisement from television by the FDA. The ad showed "Bill," a person with "arthritic knees," zipping around a park on a scooter. The FDA claimed that this ad overstated to consumers the actual efficacy of the drug.[14]

The legal profession also promotes itself. The largest section in most urban Yellow Pages is Attorneys. Although prestigious law firms still tend to use community activities as their main source of promotion, many attorneys use all forms of promotion, pricing, and distribution approaches. In some areas, lawyers distribute their services through 900-number phone lines, which consumers call for advice at $3.00 per minute or more. However, some states want to restrict legal advertising by prohibiting jingles, reenactments, and other devices deemed inappropriate or misleading.[15]

PRIVATIZATION

Privatization occurs when government services are contracted to private organizations for them to manage. The concept originated in the United Kingdom as an effort to revitalize the economy by shifting many bureaucratic services to aggressive private firms. The British railroad, telecommunications, and transportation industries were privatized, among others. Privatization also occurred in East Germany when the Berlin Wall came down and in Russia when the Soviet Union was dissolved. Both countries immediately began to transfer ownership of huge, government-controlled service institutions to private companies. Consulting organizations from the United States, Europe, and Japan have been working diligently to help these private companies succeed. The Italian government, for example, has recently begun privatizing many state companies by selling stock shares in Alitalia, the state airline, and in Eni, the state-owned oil and gas group. Recent Italian governments, finding the entirely state-owned companies inefficient and, therefore, more expensive, decided that privatization and allowing competition between companies would increase efficiency and lower prices for the Italian consumer.[16]

In the United States there is a definite trend toward privatization of local, state, and federal government services. Many hospitals and jails, once owned and maintained by cities and counties, are now operated by private companies. Likewise, prisons are often run more economically by private firms than by the government, although there are some doubts as to their efficacy at rehabilitating prisoners. The Edison Project is a company that runs public schools on a management contract basis. It operated 77 schools with 37,000 students in 1999. Edison schools receive the same funding as public schools, but operate 90 more minutes a day and 25 days longer a year by lowering administration costs. One study has shown that 10 percent of all schools will be operated by management companies in 10 years' time, accounting for $36 billion a year.[17]

THE NEED FOR SPECIALIZATION

Specialization occurs when an organization chooses to focus its resources on core business activities. In order to utilize resources and build strength in their core business, many organizations rely on service providers for basic support of their business. Personnel agencies hire and assess employees, accounting firms do the books, systems consultants set up the computers, and so forth. Most companies find it economical to farm out some of the services they previously performed themselves. ARAMARK, featured in chapter 8, is one of the world's largest service companies. It has chosen the strategy of marketing services that are not core to their clients' business. For example, ARAMARK offers security, cleaning, grounds maintenance, catering, and snow removal services. For large stadiums and amusement parks, it handles everything from parking lots to food, maintenance, and cleaning. The firm even supplies hospitals with physicians for emergency rooms, a particularly difficult area of hiring and management for hospitals. Companies realize that just as they specialize in a certain aspect of business, there are service providers who do the same.

*ServerVault provides companies
with "secure, reliable and
wicked fast" Web hosting.*

career tip ARAMARK is the world's leading managed services provider with
a portfolio of career opportunities in nearly every service area.
Since ARAMARK has units in thousands of locations, it can offer companywide,
nationwide, and worldwide opportunities. Check out current employment listings
and submit your qualifications online at www.aramark.com/careers/submit.htm.

ACCESS TO KNOWLEDGE

Today, fundamental competencies required to run many service businesses are accessible to
individuals or small groups of experts. At one time, these competencies were only available to
large corporations. Through computerized subscription services on the Internet, experts
everywhere have access to vast quantities of information. At one time, General Motors (GM)
provided its own internal information service, but as it grew more complex, GM acquired
EDS, a service group, to help develop and maintain its information system. By providing
expertise in mainframe computers and centralized control, EDS brought many unique skills
that GM required to manage its vast information needs. Today, much of that same type of
information is available to anyone with a good PC. Although GM recently sold EDS, it now
helps GM connect a vast array of PCs in a distributed information system. The system allows
thousands of GM employees access to company information. This increased accessibility to
the system gives employees all the information that is needed to do their jobs right at their
fingertips. The advent of the Internet has caused even more outsourcing in information
technologies; one study found that in 2001, 45 percent of all customer service needs would be
met online. Therefore, many companies need Internet experts to develop programming and
run services to meet consumer needs.[18]

GROWTH OF FRANCHISING

A **franchise** is a contractual agreement in which an entrepreneur pays a fee and agrees to meet
operating requirements in exchange for the franchise name and marketing plan. Franchising is
another major trend influencing the service industry. National and international franchisers

FRANCHISE

A contractual agreement
whereby an entrepreneur pays
a fee for the franchise name
and agrees to meet operating
requirements and use the
organization's marketing plan.

have developed aggressive growth strategies, particularly in the sectors of fast food and cleaning. Franchising allows companies such as McDonald's, Subway, Service Master, and Jiffy Lube to increase quickly the number of locations where customers can purchase their services. Food service chains were expected to see a growth of about 5 percent in 2000, which would contribute to the $350 billion restaurant industry.[19] Of course, this also means that more and more employees are required to deliver the service.

Another area of franchise growth will be seen in the distribution channels for car sales. Since customers value pressure-free shopping when purchasing an automobile, online car sales have become increasingly popular. These alternatives have taken a fixed-price approach without aggressive sales tactics. Traditional dealerships have responded by starting their own Web sites. Most consumers use the Web sites devoted to cars to decide what models they are interested in buying but still visit showrooms to buy a car. As one salesperson said, "[Cars and trucks] are still a commodity that people like to touch and drive and feel."[20]

SERVICE CHARACTERISTICS THAT AFFECT MARKETING STRATEGY

Several aspects of services should be considered when marketing strategies are developed. First, services can be clearly contrasted from goods in several ways. Second, services should be looked at from the perspective of a service–goods continuum, not simply as services. Some products are all service, others are a combination of each, and still others are pure goods. Third, consumers use several strategies to evaluate a service. They look at its attributes to find clues about its expected performance. Fourth, service quality plays a key role in success.

THE CONTRASTS BETWEEN GOODS AND SERVICES

Most of our discussion in this book has referred to products, meaning both goods and services. This is because the marketing of both is very similar. What works for one generally works for the other. In addition, as we will see later, an organization's product mix usually has products with characteristics of both goods and services. Even so, there are six sharp distinctions between the two. The uniqueness of services lies in their intangibility, the relationship with the consumer, the importance of the service encounter, their aspect of simultaneous production and consumption, their perishability, and the type of quality controls they entail.

Marketing Intangibles   Physical goods have form and mass; they can be seen and touched. Prior to sale, services exist primarily as an offer or promise of some experience that will occur in the future. They only become "real" when performed. Insurance is a good example of an intangible product. The paper on which the policy is printed describes the promise the company makes to the person paying the premiums. Only when the consumer suffers a loss is the product delivered—in the form of money or a replacement for an insured item.

Many services take shape in unexpected ways over time. Think about a computerized dating service. The purchaser may have high expectations, but it may be weeks, months, or even years before the potential benefit is realized. This intangibility makes it difficult to assess the value of services or compare alternatives prior to purchase. After the service is performed, it is too late to change the decision. Consider bungee cord jumping. Until you step onto the platform, have the cord attached, and jump, you cannot experience the sensation. Once you leave the platform, it is too late to reject the service.

Relationship of Provider to Customer   Services are performed on or with customers personally or on what is theirs—children (day care, youth sports camps), animals (vets, stables, feedlots), things (lawn care, car wash, auto repair), and so forth. Whereas most goods are manufactured at a plant far from customers, most services are created in their presence or with their personal knowledge of how they were performed. Consequently, there is an inseparable relationship between the provider and the user. In some cases this interaction may be very personal, such as the relationship between parents and the provider of their child's care. Consumers may develop a strong preference about who performs the service. Most of us have a favorite barber or hair stylist and dread trying someone new. In fact, we may be willing to pay extra to have our usual stylist cut our hair. Much the same holds true for the family dentist, lawyer, and doctor.

The Service Encounter Connection   One of the most important aspects of service marketing is the **service encounter,** the contact between the consumer and the seller. Jan Carlzon,

CONNECTED: SURFING THE NET

www.subway.com

Learn about Subway franchise opportunities by visiting its Web site. Browse the electronic library, read about international Subway franchises, or request a brochure. And, for fun, play the amazing virtual Subway game.

SERVICE ENCOUNTER

The interaction between the consumer and the seller.

*Liberty Mutual markets an
intangible item—insurance
coverage.*

former president of Scandinavian Airline Systems (SAS), speaks of service encounters as "moments of truth." Carlzon led SAS toward a strong customer focus, pointing out that the airline came face-to-face with consumers 65,000 times each day. He estimated that each passenger had contact with five SAS employees over the course of a year. Although the typical service encounter lasted only about 15 seconds, the outcome of each one ultimately translated into success or failure for the company. His fervent conviction has made SAS one of the most customer-oriented carriers in the industry.

The service encounter concept reinforces the importance of customer relationships in marketing a service. Employees not only must have the interpersonal skills to treat consumers well but also must be oriented toward solving the customer's problem. At the most elementary level, salespeople need to be cordial and gracious. At a more fundamental level, they have to be helpful in discovering and meeting service needs during the encounter. Each moment contributes to the customer's experience with the service. If these moments are positive, then satisfaction with purchase and service delivery is likely to be positive as well.

At SAS, Carlzon realized that in order to satisfy a customer in 15 seconds, employees had to have the tools and the authority necessary to make certain decisions. He rearranged the organization so that frontline personnel could quickly serve any customer. Managers, who typically hold power and responsibility, became supporters for those employees. Similarly, Wal-Mart managers support employees in efforts to maintain exceptional service encounters. At Wal-Mart, the company receives letters daily from customers pleased with their service encounter, which may include an associate who remembers their name or carries out a purchase for them. Some customers write letters in appreciation of a simple smile. Sam Walton, the company founder, insisted that associates practice "aggressive hospitality" in order to offer better service. Wal-Mart believes even brief service encounters can make enough difference to keep the customer coming back.[21] The diversity feature, "Beyond Accessibility: How Hotels Win Over the Disabled Traveler," shows how crucial the service encounter can be.

Simultaneous Production and Consumption   The fact that many services are made and used at the same moment creates interesting situations. First, the buyer and seller have to cooperate. In some cases this involves power dynamics. When you tell your stylist how you want your hair cut, you accomplish a managerial act. Second, since buyers vary and services depend on the recipient, the same service may be dramatically different from one situation to the next. A provider may operate one way with one consumer and then adjust the service considerably to meet the needs of another. Consider the role of a personal fitness trainer. Since people have different goals and varying personal needs, a trainer must adjust a fitness program to suit each individual. Finally, since the buyer must be present in order for at least part of the service to be performed, consumers invest time. This places a premium on the speed of delivery and the importance of correct performance the first time. For example, satisfaction with automobile repair services depends largely on whether the car is ready when promised, or think about how annoying it is to wait in a physician's crowded office when you have other things to do.

No Storage and Inventory   Although goods can be stored until needed, services cannot. Services are extremely **perishable**—their value exists for a short time. When an airplane takes off with several empty seats, those fares can never be recovered. Therefore, accurate forecasting and the need to match supply with demand are important. When the demand for a service is stable, there is little difficulty in meeting supply requirements, but most services have erratic demand. For example, on very hot days almost all consumers turn on their air conditioners, creating a surge in energy demand. Should the utility company build enough capacity to supply its peak load or its average load? In the first case, there will be many periods when resources are unused; in the latter case, blackouts can result. When you telephone on Mother's Day or Thanksgiving, it may be difficult to get through right away because of an unusually high demand for connections. At peak hours of Internet demand, the speed at which you can access information decreases significantly. Similarly, cellular phone users often have problems during rush hour, when everyone tied up in traffic decides to make calls. If the service provider cannot meet the peak load, then customers are likely to go elsewhere.

PERISHABLE
The temporal nature of services, whose value exists for only a short time.

CONNECTING WITH DIVERSITY

BEYOND ACCESSIBILITY: HOW HOTELS WIN OVER THE DISABLED TRAVELER

 To prepare for the 1996 Little People of America Conference, the Adams Mark Hotel in Indianapolis spent thousands of dollars to make check-in desks, elevator buttons, urinals, and other fixtures accessible to people as short as three feet. It also coached employees in being sensitive to dwarves, who often face rejection and ridicule. The Adams Mark is one of a number of hotels taking a proactive approach to the Americans with Disabilities Act (ADA) passed in 1990. With no federal enforcement—but the threat of a lawsuit if a hotel is found not to be accessible—some facilities have only grudgingly complied. Others, such as the Adams Mark, are finding there is good reason not just to meet but to exceed the expectations of disabled customers.

The almost 50 million Americans with disabilities comprise a virtually untapped and ignored market. Furthermore, about 77 million baby boomers are approaching the age at which chronic illness sets in. As the disabled organize for social, legal, and educational purposes, they are holding more and larger conventions, and these tend to last longer than a week. While staying at a hotel, the disabled make more use of dining and bar facilities than other guests do. As Oral Miller, executive director of the American Council of the Blind, points out: "Because 98 percent of our members are blind or visually impaired, we're not as likely to go out and hit the town." After hosting the sixth annual meeting of the Society for Disability Studies, the Embassy Suites hotel near Seattle had the most profitable week of the year in its restaurants.

This doesn't mean that hotels can treat the disabled as a captive market. Like any guests, the disabled complain if they're unhappy, but their complaints can escalate into ADA-related lawsuits. Hotels that court these travelers consult with several disabled groups before they make structural changes, train employees, or host conventions. The Chicago Hilton & Towers talked with several before it undertook a $1.5 million full-scale ADA renovation. Lighthouse, an organization that works with the visually impaired, had very practical suggestions, such as Braille and enlarged-letter information sheets at the front desk. The hotel has since won kudos from *Access to Travel* magazine for successfully hosting a convention of more than 3,000 blind people.

Carol Duke, creator of Opening Doors, a training program for hotel employees, emphasizes that the hospitality industry must go beyond structural issues, such as making a toilet

Continued

seat low enough or doors wider. "You can have the Taj Mahal of accessibility and a manager who can recite every nuance of the law," she says, "but if your employees are uncomfortable around persons with disabilities, it doesn't matter." Duke's program is based on what she calls the "forgotten section" of the ADA, requiring businesses to modify behavior, practices, and policies to overcome fear and ignorance of the disabled.

Accessible and sensitive, hotels are rewarded with a loyalty surpassing that of most guests. Disabled people tend both to return to trusted hotels and to spread the word fast among other groups. The Little People's convention at the Adams Mark ended with hugs between happy attendees and staff and an assurance that the 900-plus group would return and recommend the hotel to others. Beyond these tangible rewards, however, is the simple pleasure service employees feel when they give someone a week of feeling "normal," surrounded by their peers in an hospitable atmosphere.

Sources: Grace Wagner, "Taking a Lead on ADA," *Lodging Hospitality,* October 1993, pp. 47–48; Kevin Helliker, "Catering to the Disabled at Convention Time Is a Lucrative Niche," *Wall Street Journal,* September 19, 1996, p. A1; and Grace Wagner, "Hilton's Leading Role," *Lodging Hospitality,* April 1994, pp. 55–56.

Service Quality Control   The quality of goods is usually monitored by human inspectors or the electronic eye of machinery. That close monitoring is virtually impossible in the case of services. Unique quality control techniques, which are discussed in detail later in the chapter, are necessary for services. For now, it is important to remember that many services cannot be performed again if a mistake is made. An 18-year-old who emerges from high school poorly educated is unlikely to start all over again. In addition, because services are so people intensive, quality can depend directly on service suppliers. For example, companies such as National Seminar Group, Skill Path, Inc., and Career Trak provide educational services nationally, and much of the quality relies on the competence of individual instructors. In some service companies, people at one level of the organization train others, who train others, and so on. But despite all efforts to ensure good training, it may not be possible to standardize a service and ensure quality every time. If one employee at a dry cleaning shop ruins your suit or dress, then you probably will go elsewhere the next time.

Globally, training methods often need to be adjusted to ensure quality service. For example, sales reps in China often sell products solely on price, fail to ask consumers business-related questions, and demonstrate little product knowledge. They also have little training or marketing support. In the United States, sales reps are trained to understand customer's needs and emphasize product benefits, have extensive product knowledge, and help the customer understand the value of the potential purchase. The Chinese and American training methods produce two distinct types of service. Differences in culture also play an important role in consumer perceptions of quality service.[22] French salespeople, for example, are traditionally rude, show little knowledge of the product, and are generally unhelpful to the customer. Recently, however, some French companies have begun to import American consultants to retrain sales staff in the American style.[23]

Service quality control is monitored by trained observers during and after service delivery. Chances are that you have phoned a company and heard a recording saying the call may be monitored to be sure you receive appropriate service. This type of feedback lets the organization know whether service is being performed consistently and as it was intended. When there are difficulties, most customer-oriented service providers give employees additional training, supervision, and help.

THE SERVICE–GOODS CONTINUUM

Although there are differences in marketing goods and services, there are also many similarities. In fact, few organizations market only one or the other. Most purchases fall somewhere along the continuum between almost pure goods and almost pure services, as illustrated in Figure 11.3.

Notice the word *almost* at each end of the continuum. Even in their purest form, goods and services still contain some aspect of the other. Almost pure goods are physical products that can be described by their form, mass, and function. There are thousands of types, ranging

ALMOST PURE GOODS	GOODS WITH SERVICES	HALF GOODS, HALF SERVICES	SERVICES WITH GOODS	ALMOST PURE SERVICES
Physical products that are purchased and consumed with little or no service	Products supported with repair, mainten-ance, add-ons, and advice	Products that consist of both goods and services	Intellectual property or equipment to make goods work	Experiences that are consumed during delivery
Groceries Gasoline (self-serve) Steel	Autos Auto repair Video games	Restaurants Bookstores Movie theaters Prepared food delivery	Rental movies Training books Software Electronic mail Fax service	Health clubs Medical care Consulting Legal services Day care

FIGURE 11.3 *Continuum of Goods and Services*

Source: Valarie A. Zeithaml, "How Consumer Evaluation Processes Differ between Goods and Services," in *Marketing of Services,* eds. James H. Donnelly and William R. George. Reprinted with permission of the American Marketing Association.

from computer chips to ocean liners. A gym supplies several different products that can be considered almost pure goods, such as clothes, equipment, and health food.

Next along the continuum are goods with services. These are physical products accompanied by the supportive services required to make them work. For example, automobiles play a major role in our economy not only because of their sales revenues but also because of the services they require. Saturn's success has been due in part to its policy of involving the customer in many steps of the production process. Gateway Inc. remains a very profitable computer company, when other manufacturers are experiencing a business downturn, because of the extensive customer service support it offers to consumers.[24]

Half goods and half services are products that require both elements equally to succeed. Restaurants provide a certain level of service, which includes the atmosphere, and goods such as food and beverages. Key topics at a National Restaurant show emphasized just that. Customers want to anticipate as well as enjoy their dining experiences, which means it is important for marketers to appeal to customer expectations about entertainment, a unique atmosphere, or interactive opportunities. Since people "want to be in a warm, human environment" as well as eat good food, ambience is just as important a factor as the quality of the food itself.[25] Bookstores provide not only products (books) but also guidance in searching out unique topics. In addition, their spatial arrangement, background music, and atmosphere all contribute to the "feelings" that sell. Coffee and beverage shops have been added to many bookstores to encourage customers to spend hours on a self-actualizing experience.

Services with goods are usually intellectual properties or equipment required to make goods work. Examples include rental movies, training books, and software. They are significant not so much because of their physical aspects but because of the messages they contain. Electronic mail or Internet services such as Netscape can be included in this category. In 1995 the consumer market for online services was very attractive, but the original Microsoft Network failed due to a lack of Web content. Microsoft has since reintroduced its network to include communications, technical information, references, and other services lacking in the previous version.[26] Another example of services with goods is importing and exporting companies. Export services are the fastest-growing sector of global businesses for both industrialized and less advanced economies. Countries such as the United States, Great Britain, and Ireland rely on service industries for economic growth.[27]

Almost pure services provide consumers with experiences that are consumed during the delivery process. Among the many items in this category are health clubs, legal services, and

CONNECTED: SURFING THE NET

www.BarnesandNoble.com or bn.com

Browse for your favorite books in a virtual shopping atmosphere by visiting Barnes and Noble online. You can receive personalized book recommendations and fast delivery of more than 400,000 in-stock titles.

education. Although a haircut is considered the classic example of a pure service, even that ordinarily takes place in an establishment selling styling and beautification products. Services such as air and train travel involve such goods as meals and soft drinks as well as tickets that can be exchanged. Even though Southwest Airlines does not offer meals or assigned seats, consumers still have a very high perception of quality and service value. How can this be? When asked, customers usually cite the great service, such as frequent departures, on-time arrival, friendly employees, and low fares. Southwest has achieved the highest level of on-time arrivals and the fewest complaints of any airline.[28] This is an almost pure service that passengers value highly, which contributes to customer loyalty at Southwest.

CONSUMER EVALUATION OF SERVICES

Product Qualities Affecting Consumer Evaluation   Products can be viewed as having three types of qualities—search, experience, and credence—that affect consumer evaluation. Search attributes can be evaluated prior to purchase. Experience qualities can be assessed only during or after consumption. Credence qualities are almost impossible to evaluate even after purchase and consumption. As Figure 11.4 illustrates, most goods are high in search and experience qualities, whereas most services are high in experience and credence qualities.[29]

Search Qualities Search qualities are found mostly in goods. They make it easy for consumers to judge one product relative to another. People can use their senses of smell, hearing, sight, touch, and taste to note differences in attribute quality. Many products are compared and studied in detail before a selection is made. For example, if you are shopping for new stereo speakers, you can listen to different models at the retail store to decide which pair sounds best. Similarly, you can test-drive different cars or try out a pair of in-line skates in the store parking lot. Even after purchase, items high in search qualities allow the consumer to assess their value. Best Buy, the nation's leading volume specialty retailer, offers demonstrations of video games and other products in their stores.[30] These are meant to increase the customer's knowledge of product features. Since Best Buy offers a number of items high in search qualities, its format enables consumers to compare and contrast products easily.

Experience Qualities In the combined categories (goods with services, half goods and half services, and services with goods), products are high in experience qualities. Consumers cannot assess the amount of pleasure or satisfaction derived from them until they have used them. Then they can decide whether the product met or exceeded their expectations and can

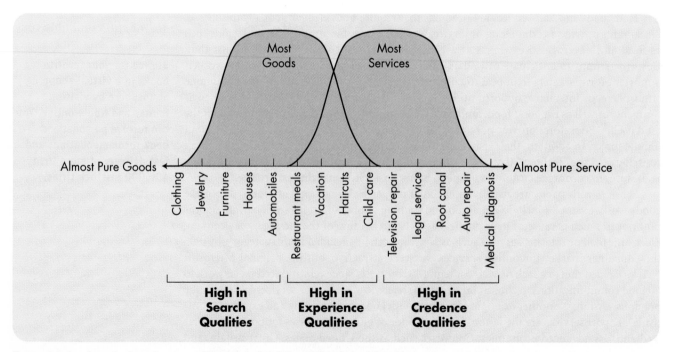

FIGURE 11.4 *Search, Experience, and Credence Qualities of Goods and Services*

Source: Valarie A. Zeithaml, "How Consumer Evaluation Processes Differ between Goods and Services," in *Marketing of Services,* eds. James H. Donnelly and William R. George. Reprinted with permission of the American Marketing Association.

*Carnival possesses experience
qualities that cannot be
assessed until consumers have
used the service.*

**CONNECTED:
SURFING THE NET**

www.carnival.com

**Check out the Carnival
Corporation's new and exciting
cruises, ships, fun, and
news—all on its Web site.
Also read about the company's
vacation guarantee—
"the best guarantee you'll
never use."**

describe desired improvements or changes. As the name suggests, products high in experience qualities involve the customer, and promotional efforts usually create an image of people taking part in the experience. Cruises are a good example. Advertising campaigns for Carnival Cruise Lines often display consumers participating in a wide variety of activities. Carnival attracts more clients than any other line—more than a million per year from all over the world. These consumers can assess their experience only after the cruise has ended, but more than 98 percent of Carnival customers say they were well satisfied.[31] Disney recently created its own cruise line, designing the ships to transport customers not only to new ports but also back in time to the era of glamour. The cruise offers not only amenities, but style, and has been quite successful.[32]

Credence Qualities The credence qualities are found only in services and cannot be evaluated before, during, or after consumption. A medical diagnosis, for example, is almost impossible for consumers to assess, since most people have little or no knowledge of pathology and must trust in the ability of others. The outcomes of credence qualities are largely unobservable to the customer until indirect benefits emerge, such as higher sales as the consequence of hiring a consultant. Of course, there can be negative effects from the service, such as an IRS audit because of an accountant's error. The more intangible the result, the higher the credence qualities involved. In other words, customers must have a high degree of faith that the exchange has been worthwhile.

Consumer Evaluation and Buying Behavior Because services are high in credence qualities, consumer buying behavior tends to be different for services than for goods. Specific differences, described next, range from the more personal nature of the information sources relied upon to the fact that the customer is often a competitor of the service provider.

The Personal Factor In selecting services, buyers rely more on information from personal sources. Because services tend to be personal, this is not surprising. Suppose you are going to court in an important lawsuit. Would you select your lawyer from an ad on television or a recommendation from your best friend? Consumers not only relate better to personal information sources but also give them more credence.

Postpurchase Evaluation Because services are not easily evaluated before purchase, most assessments are made during or after the fact. Lawn care companies are careful not only to do a good job of mowing and trimming but also to clean away the clippings, leaving a well-manicured look with very little the consumer can criticize.

Surrogates for Judgment When a product is high in credence quality, consumers use surrogate cues to make judgments. One such cue is price. Many people equate high-priced services with greater value and low-priced services with less value. Another cue is physical features, such as how the service provider dresses or the appearance or location of offices. The quality of car service may be judged by such a small thing as the cleanliness of the shop's restroom. An inefficiently run physician's office with new furniture may send off more positive cues than one that is better run but has poor lighting, outdated furniture, and clutter. In this case, the cues are used to make judgments about the quality of medical treatment the consumer will receive, and the office decor is a surrogate for measuring the skill and success of the physician.

Small Sets of Acceptable Brands or Suppliers Because services are personal and difficult to judge, consumers are likely to consider a small set of providers when seeking a service. Since services have no search qualities, consumers will not benefit from elaborate comparisons. Furthermore, their personal sources of information are likely to yield relatively few options. And once a reliable provider is found, customers tend to be loyal. For example, most of us use only one or perhaps two dry cleaners all the time. The same is probably true for hair stylists, tailors, party planners, and other types of providers. Some business travelers limit their choice when selecting a hotel, booking only Marriott or Sheraton because they are confident they will receive acceptable service.

Slow Adoption Because prepurchase evaluation is almost impossible, the risk of buying a service is greater than for goods. Therefore, many new services are adopted very slowly by consumers. People want to wait and see how the new service performs. Many consumers were initially reluctant to use the automatic teller machines (ATMs). They anticipated problems such as lost deposits or theft and preferred contact with a human being. Over time these fears diminished, and many consumers now do all their banking through ATMs. Shopping on the Internet caused similar security concerns among consumers, but several Web sites and credit card companies developed new security devices to ensure consumer safety while shopping on the Web.[33]

The situation is the same when the service is not an innovation but simply new to the consumer. Someone who has never had a facial or a body massage may be reluctant to try it. To overcome this reluctance, gyms may offer a free month of membership to encourage customers to join. Hair stylists often give discounts to first-time clients, and financial planners frequently offer free consultations before charging for their services.

Strong Brand Loyalty As noted previously, the personal nature of services includes a built-in loyalty factor. People are more loyal to other people than to things. They also tend to stick with what they know. In addition, because consumers participate in the service, they may attribute any problems that occur to their own behavior, relieving the provider of some responsibility. For example, if your hairdresser cuts your bangs too short, you may partially blame yourself for not being explicit about what you wanted. Furthermore, the high degree of credence qualities in services makes it difficult to know whether the provider has done a poor job unless something goes wrong, such as your car failing to start the day after it was fixed. Without a negative signal, consumers are likely to assume that the provider did at least a good job. In general, there is less complaining behavior from consumers about services as opposed to goods. We know from earlier chapters, however, that it is very important to seek out and respond to consumer complaints about any type of product.[34]

The Customer as Competitor Services usually involve activities that consumers can do for themselves. Parents may elect to stay home with their young children or have relatives take care of them, in which case, they are "competing" with day care centers. People can mow their own lawns, clean their own cars or homes, prepare their own tax returns, or prepare food for their own parties. Or they may select a service provider to do it for them. In many instances the trade-off is between time and money. This is why so many providers stress the amount of time their services will save consumers. For example, online grocery shops hoped that offering products, bought on the Internet and delivered to the consumers' homes, would appeal to the average American's desire to save time. Although distribution and delivery problems have limited the idea's appeal, many still believe that online grocery shopping will grow into a profitable service industry.[35]

Providers also may emphasize the improvements possible through an outside service compared to what consumers can do for themselves. Such claims may be based on larger and more sophisticated equipment or safety, as in tree removal. Especially in business-to-business marketing of services, cost savings may be cited. For example, companies too small to have a personnel department may hire a résumé bank, such as 104 Job Bank, an online résumé bank based in Taiwan. Potential employers pay a fee to 104 Job Bank in order to access the company's online databank of résumés.[36]

SERVICE QUALITY

Since service quality plays a significant part in the purchase decision for most consumers, it is crucial for marketing success. One study shows that service is "irrelevant" to customer perception of quality in only 15 percent of markets.[37] The Marketing Science Institute, through

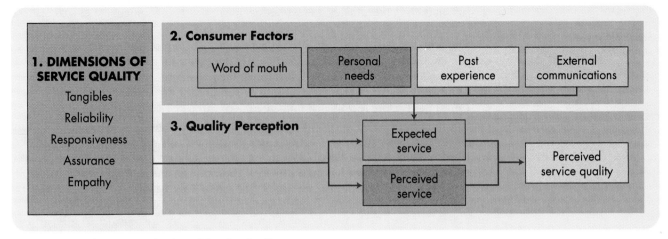

Figure 11.5 *The Customer's View of Service Quality*

Source: Adapted from Valarie A. Zeithaml, A. Parasuraman, and Leonard L. Berry, *Delivering Quality Service, Balancing Customer Perceptions and Expectations* (New York: The Free Press, 1990), p. 26.

international conferences and research with major corporations, has identified how consumers assess overall service quality. The results, outlined in Figure 11.5, indicate that assessments have three aspects: dimensions of service quality, consumer factors, and quality perception. Dimensions of service quality are elements that consumers are most likely to perceive when making judgments, such as reliability and responsiveness. Consumer factors refer to customer needs and information acquisition. Quality perception depends on how closely the buyer's expectations are matched (or exceeded) by the service actually delivered, a concept very similar to customer satisfaction. Each of these is discussed next.

Dimensions of Service Quality   The dimensions of service quality fall into five categories: tangibles, reliability, responsiveness, assurance, and empathy. It's important for marketers to consider each of these as they evaluate the quality of the services they provide to consumers.

Tangibles It has been noted already that services are intangible but often are associated with physical facilities, equipment, personnel, and promotional materials. These tangibles have a very significant effect on customers. Organizations that provide tangibles of high quality communicate an impression of their nontangible offerings as well. For example, the way an office is designed and equipped, its cleanliness, and the personal appearance of employees all play a major role in conveying quality.

Reliability The ability to perform the promised service dependably and accurately is critical to service quality. Reliability involves, for example, returning calls and meeting deadlines. It also means performing activities precisely as outlined, such as sticking to the script in training programs, producing credit card statements free of errors, and doing a task correctly the first time. Research has shown that completing all car repairs when promised is more important than the quality of the work itself.

Responsiveness The willingness of providers to be helpful and give prompt service is very important to buyers. Waiting time is critical to buyer satisfaction and evaluation of service quality. What managers view as a short wait may seem long to customers.[38] It is important to respond in a timely manner to customer requests and needs. If the customer finds an error on a financial statement, is it resolved quickly and with an adequate explanation? Are salespeople willing to answer questions about what to expect from a service? Do they help resolve difficulties if they arise?

Assurance The knowledge and courtesy of employees and their ability to convey trust and competence are essential for services which have high credence qualities. A very important factor is whether customers are treated with dignity and respect. Another is credibility—whether the provider conveys sufficient knowledge, experience, and trustworthiness to perform the service. Finally, assurance is related to security, the belief that the services will be performed safely and confidentially and that a free exchange of ideas between the provider and the consumer is possible. Relationship marketing has become an integral part of services during the last several years. The effort to cut costs, however, threatens these relationships. A recent study showed that declining numbers of customer service staff have led to a lower average of consumer satisfaction in the United States.[39] Providing assurance is a major component in a company's ability to build and maintain these relationships.

Empathy The caring, individualized attention that a firm provides its customers encompasses a number of dimensions. It is particularly important for service providers to convey that they understand the customer. It is through their ability to listen, communicate clearly, and relate well to the client that they transmit empathy.

Consumer Factors Factors that influence the consumer's view of service quality include word of mouth, personal needs, past experience, and external communication. Word of mouth is particularly important because services are not readily observable and must be described verbally. Because they lack search qualities, they are likely to be discussed with friends when consumers are seeking a provider. These discussions tend to carry considerable credibility. Personal needs are also important. These deal with the motives that determine the nature and strength of what a consumer wants from a service. Past experience refers to what consumers have learned through personal interaction with a service provider. This is particularly important in shaping expectations, a topic covered next. The final element is external communication, that is, such marketer-dominated sources as personal selling and advertising. How a service is positioned and what is communicated through paid messages can influence consumer perceptions.

Quality Perception Because perceptions of service quality depend on the service meeting or exceeding customer expectations, service providers must take care in shaping those expectations. Because the product is intangible and people cannot readily observe for themselves what to expect, the messages and examples from service providers contribute much to developing expectations. It is critical that the provider describe outcomes as clearly and accurately as possible before purchase. Organizations that create unrealistic expectations in an effort to sell a service are likely to find that customer satisfaction is low. Those unhappy consumers will tell others, and the credibility of the business will be hurt.

To ensure high perceived quality and a loyal customer base, providers need to be accurate and reasonable about what they lead customers to expect. They also need to do a good job in the areas of tangibles, reliability, responsiveness, assurance, and empathy. Because the personal nature of services makes them very difficult for competitors to emulate, those companies that invest resources and energy in building strong service quality are most likely to be winners. Steak 'N' Shake, recognizing consumer interest in quality service, promotes the atmosphere of its restaurants as a higher-quality, more personal alternative to "fast-food" establishments. The friendly, prompt service encourages revisits.

DEVELOPING THE SERVICE MIX

Services, like goods, usually occur as a mix. They often rely on branding to communicate uniqueness. At the same time, several qualities must be considered when developing a new service. These include the service itself, the brand, and factors that enhance the fundamental service. This section explores these dimensions more extensively.

CORE, AUGMENTED, AND BRANDED SERVICES

Recall from chapter 9 that products have core, augmented, and branded dimensions. Let's relate these concepts to services. We can use the example of birthing in a hospital, as depicted in Figure 11.6. The **core service** is the basic benefit, in this case delivery of a healthy baby and safety for the mother. That is the main objective of the service. But, in today's competitive health care arena, the augmented and branded product also plays a key role. The augmented service is the package of bundled goods and services that differentiates one provider from another. It has a great deal to do with how well service providers connect with customers. Since the core service is the same for all providers, the augmented features are critical.

In chapter 9 we discussed the importance of brand equity for goods. It is equally if not more important to build brand equity for a service. Because a service is intangible, a customer comes to know its value through the symbols and cues around it. McDonald's has achieved name recognition not only because of the reliability of its products but also because of its customer service, personnel management, cleanliness, child-oriented image, and so forth. Its brand equity reflects the interactive service element as well as the functional dimensions of the physical goods sold. Consider the growing brand equity of Kinko's, which now has more than 900 locations in the United States, Canada, Netherlands, Japan, South Korea, Australia, United

**CONNECTED:
SURFING THE NET**

www.steaknshake.com

Find out why "in sight, it must be right" is the foundation of Steak 'N' Shake's customer service philosophy.

CORE SERVICE

The basic benefit delivered.

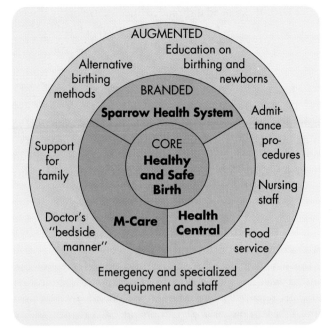

FIGURE 11.6 *Example of a Core, Augmented, and Branded Service*

CONNECTED: SURFING THE NET

www.kinkos.com

Visit www.kinkos.com and learn how to publish and send documents online. You can also download software to make any document print-ready.

Arab Emirates, China, Ukraine, and Great Britain (www.kinkos.com). Others provide copy services, but Kinko's has become synonymous with a customer-oriented philosophy. It has expanded services to include desktop publishing, computer rental with high-speed ISDN Internet access, and worldwide network videoconferencing, among others. Customers rely on the Kinko's name for value and service.[40]

Kinko's provides a range of services to more than 700 copy centers in the United States, Canada, Japan, and the Netherlands.

Marriott extended its branded line by developing three chains with lower complexity than the original service. Courtyard has become an identifiable service mark associated with high-quality motel accommodations and limited services. Fairfield Inns are positioned as the least complex, no-frills part of the chain. Residence Inns cater to an extended stay of five days or more; 80 percent of their guests are business travelers. With these three brand names, the company has developed services consistent with the target markets for which each is intended.[41]

The U.S. Postal Service provides a core service of mail delivery. It leverages a certain amount of brand equity (for example, by sponsoring the cyclist Lance Armstrong) and maintains high quality by being dependable. It augments its services through 50 nationwide business centers. These are designed to help small and medium-sized companies improve the efficiency of their mailings as well as learn new techniques, such as how direct mail can benefit them.

DEVELOPING NEW SERVICES

Just as with goods, new services need to be developed. Certain functional and interactive elements have to be considered. The **functional element** of a service relates to whether it accomplishes what it is intended to do. (Does the orthodontist straighten a patient's teeth? Does a shoe get repaired?) The **interactive element** involves the personal behaviors and physical atmosphere of the service environment. Each element is discussed next.

Functional Elements in Service Development   The functional element in service product development is influenced by the complexity and divergence of the service. **Service complexity** refers to the number and intricacy of steps involved in producing a service. For example, a muffler shop that adds brake lining and transmission repair to its services is increasing complexity. The service a defense lawyer provides a murder suspect is much more complex than a house cleaner's activities. **Divergence** relates to the amount of routine procedure involved in providing a service. A very customized service has high divergence, such as a consultant who tailors staff development advice to each person in a company. A standardized service has low divergence. For example, Fred Pryor Seminars, Inc. (www.pryor.com) gives a set presentation on various topics to groups representing many organizations.[42]

Figure 11.7 illustrates complexity and divergence for four services. Since most local barbershops do approximately the same thing, and cutting hair is not highly complicated, divergence and complexity are very low. Dentistry has low divergence due to standardized procedures, but it tends to be high in complexity. House cleaning is highly customized (divergent) but low in complexity, whereas litigation tends to be high in both divergence and complexity.

Interactive Elements in Service Development   The interactive element is often more important than the functional aspect in creating service excellence. Walt Disney Enterprises has attempted to produce a strong interactive service by using a stage (the environment) with actors (Disney employees) to involve the audience (consumers). Through extensive role-playing, the Disney people have learned to connect in a way that produces strong customer satisfaction. One part of this interaction is simply the desire to help customers have fun.

Many companies use atmospherics, the environment in which the service is performed, to enhance the interactive element.[43] Originally applied to retail stores, atmospherics has important implications for all types of services outside the consumer's home. Such features as color, music, and layout are all part of the atmosphere. It not only influences the selection of a service provider but also, and more important, determines whether service outcomes are satisfying.

FUNCTIONAL ELEMENT

What a service is supposed to accomplish.

INTERACTIVE ELEMENT

The personal behaviors and atmosphere of the service environment.

SERVICE COMPLEXITY

The number and intricacy of steps involved in producing a service.

DIVERGENCE

The degree to which a service involves customization beyond routine or standardized procedures.

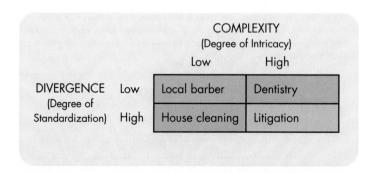

FIGURE 11.7 *Complexity and Divergence in Services*

Lower Complexity/Divergence	Current Process	Higher Complexity/Divergence
No reservation	← Take reservation →	Specific table selection
Self-seating; menu on blackboard	← Seat guest, give menu →	Recite menu; describe entrees and specials
Eliminate	← Serve water and bread →	Assortment of hot breads and hors d'oeuvres
Customer fills out form	← Take orders; prepare orders →	Taken personally by maitre d' at table
Prepared; no choice	← Salad (4 choices) →	Individually prepared at table
Limited to 4 choices	← Entree (15 choices) →	Expand to 20 choices; add flaming dishes; bone fish at table; prepare sauces at table
Sundae bar; self-service	← Dessert (6 choices) →	Expand to 12 choices
Coffee, tea, milk, and sodas	← Beverage served (6 choices) →	Add exotic coffees; wine list; liqueurs
Serve salad and entree together; bill and beverage together	← Serve orders →	Separate course service; sherbet between courses; hand-grind pepper
Cash only; pay when leaving	← Collect payment at table →	Choice of payment, including house accounts; serve mints

FIGURE 11.8 *Structural Alternatives in the Restaurant Business*

Source: Adapted with permission from G. Lynn Shostack, "Service Positioning through Structural Change," *Journal of Marketing* 51 (January 1987): 34–43.

The physical components of atmosphere have an emotional dimension. The mood created greatly influences whether consumers want to enter and explore the environment, communicate with personnel, and gain satisfaction from the service encounter.[44] Retail stores such as Banana Republic, Victoria's Secret, and Eddie Bauer emphasize music as a way to increase sales. AEI Music Network, Inc., a service provider to many retailers, researches the demographics and psychographics of a store's customers and then creates suitable sound. The music is designed to encourage customers to shop longer and also creates an atmosphere for each retailer.[45] The next time you visit a Nine West, Coach, or Victoria's Secret outlet, note the music program created especially to appeal to you.

Structuring New Services   The functional and interactive aspects of services affect how organizations structure new offerings. Marketers determine where each new service attribute fits on the continuum from low complexity/divergence to high complexity/divergence. Figure 11.8 shows an example of structural alternatives in the restaurant business. The standard restaurant can be viewed as falling in the middle. The restaurant's marketing manager can choose to move in one of two directions for each area shown: more upscale (higher complexity/divergence) or more downscale (lower complexity/divergence). By conducting this type of analysis, the organization can make clear choices in developing new services.

AN EXPANDED CONCEPT OF SERVICES

Services of all types are marketed to you daily. In addition to the traditional offerings, service marketing is used to promote people, entertainment and events, places, political candidates and ideas, and different causes. It can even be used within an organization, through internal marketing, to promote one group's capabilities to another. The following sections describe these additional types of service in more detail.

PERSON MARKETING

Person marketing involves promoting an individual's character, personality, and appeal, which in turn may be used to promote a service or product. Michael Jordan, whose endorsements may have a lifetime value of more than a billion dollars, is one of the most notable sports figures to date. Even the Internet makes use of his appeal. Jordan has a 10-year contract to create and manage his own official Web site for SportsLine USA (jordan.sportsline.com), a news and information service. SportsLine believes that Jordan, among other big-name athletes, attracts advertisers and boosts the number of paying subscribers.[46]

The multiethnic appeal and charisma of Tiger Woods have struck a chord with diverse customers across the globe, creating opportunities for companies to market Tiger's image to promote golf-related products. This includes Nike, which will pay him $100 million over five years.[47] According to Phil Knight, Nike CEO: "Today's world is a lot more wired. There are so many ways for [Tiger] to touch people . . . that he could easily be as widely known around the world as any athlete today—and in a fraction of the time."[48] The entire golf industry is making connections with customers, hoping to sell more rounds of golf, apparel, and equipment than ever before; golf equipment sales, however, haven't exploded as expected, and as a result golfers less famous than Woods are having trouble finding endorsement deals.[49]

Michael Jordan and Tiger Woods both have agents who help market their exceptional appeal to various companies and to consumers. For them and other Olympic or professional athletes, much of their attraction is due to their skills and character. In addition, however, service providers who market sports personalities contribute a great deal. Person marketing is often a two-way process in which promotion of the individual increases his or her value as a product endorser. Public exposure that enhances reputation leads to more lucrative endorsements, contracts, and vice versa.

ENTERTAINMENT AND EVENT MARKETING

During the 1999 Thanksgiving weekend, Disney's sequel *Toy Story 2* opened at theaters. It immediately brought in $57 million dollars at the box office, or more than $17,000 per theater. Nothing was left to chance. Nearly every aspect of the movie was the result of careful planning, from promotion to the precise timing of its introduction. Tim Allen and Tom Hanks, huge draws in their own right, were selected for the leads and were featured prominently in every advertisement. The two target audiences, young children and their parents, were both drawn in by the star power of the movie.[50]

Television and radio also thrive on sophisticated marketing. The popular television show *Seinfeld* was successful because it provided comic relief. Jerry Seinfeld wrote much of the show, being careful not to let intellectual material interfere with the light humor enjoyed by so many loyal viewers. At the other end of the spectrum is *ER,* whose appeal is serious drama, but both shows are designed with target audiences in mind. Careful monitoring makes sure that from week to week a show reaches the audiences advertisers desire.

Event marketing is the promotion of an event in order to generate revenues and enhance the reputation of an organization. It has become a huge factor in the entertainment world, with sporting events at the forefront. Ohio State University characterizes its athletic department as being in the entertainment business; the university has an annual athletics budget of $64.9 million.[51] As at many universities, sports at Ohio State are big business. They generate the revenues that support student athletes and contribute positively or negatively to the university's reputation. College athletics are a multibillion-dollar industry, with revenues from stadium attendance, television and radio, concessions, apparel, and signage at stadiums. Michigan State University earns several million in royalties.

One of the most successful event marketers is the National Basketball Association, which in 1985 had earnings of $181 million from tickets, television contracts, and sponsors. By 1995 that figure was $1.1 billion and was expected to be $2.85 billion for the 2000 season. NBA-licensed products (mostly apparel) went from $200 million to more than $3 billion.[52] Although most NBA games are played in the United States, the 2000 NBA All-Star game was televised in 205 countries in 42 languages.[53] With an average attendance of 17,000, arenas are filled at 90 percent capacity, and more than half a billion households in 180 countries watched the games on television during the 1996–1997 season. Given these numbers, Shaquille O'Neal gets the equivalent of about 20 cents per household with his $100+ million salary from the Los Angeles Lakers. The NBA has assisted in basketball theme movies as well: *Forget Paris* starring Billy Crystal, *Celtic Pride* starring Whoopi Goldberg, *Space Jam* starring Michael Jordan, and *Kazzam* starring Shaquille O'Neal.

Sponsorships allow companies to link their names with the outstanding experience people associate with the event. Coke, Pepsi, and General Motors are likely to be seen supporting college athletics. A great example is Coca-Cola's sponsorship of the 2000 Summer Olympics torch relay. Aside from seeing the torch, few spectators could forget the sponsor. Coca-Cola lined the streets with posters announcing when the relay would arrive, while advance trucks sold bottles of Coke. The company also gave out posters and stickers to kids and handled press coverage.

PLACE MARKETING

Place marketing enhances a location in order to appeal to businesses, investors, and tourists. Check out "The Smart State For Business" at www.smart.state.ia.us and you'll learn about Iowa's cutting-edge business environment, such as technology centers at the University of Iowa, Iowa State University, and the University of Northern Iowa. With the theme "Pride and Prosperity," Iowa is marketed as "the smart state for business." Partners in the endeavor are Pella Windows and Doors, Maytag, the Principal Financial Group, MidAmerican Energy, Monsanto, John Deere, Rockwell, and Amana. Other possibilities include Alliant Energy, CertainTeed, EAI, Fisher Controls, Lennox, Pioneer, Quaker Oats, and Wells Fargo Mortgage (www.smart.state.ia.us/industry). Iowa is also trying to persuade other businesses, cities, and counties to join in.[54]

Maybe you want to find an area for financial investment, locate a company, or explore tourism. Brazil, like many countries, is marketing itself to appeal to all those interested.

PLACE MARKETING
Promoting a geographical location in order to appeal to businesses, investors, and tourists.

Hawaii uses place marketing to draw people to their island, Maui.

It points to its location as a global hub for international shipping, and to its valuable real estate and government privatization policies. It also targets consumers and travel agencies by catering to people who want cruises and ecotourism destinations of natural landscapes, rain forests, and undeveloped beauty. Brazil's dismal economic performance in the last 10 years and lack of infrastructure to serve businesses or tourists make the country's marketing strategy, designed to attract investments as well as people, very important to the nation's overall development.[55]

Vacation places receive tremendous marketing attention. Countries, states, cities, and resorts all participate. Few put it all together as well as Disney does. "It's a small world after all" in any one of several unique resort hotels at Walt Disney World near Orlando, Florida. You can walk from country to country experiencing, for example, a British pub or German restaurant. The Theme Parks and Resorts division of Disney had revenues of nearly $4 billion in recent years. This includes Disneyland near Paris and Tokyo, two newer developments.

POLITICAL MARKETING

POLITICAL MARKETING

Promoting an individual or idea
motivated by the desire to influence public policy and voters.

Political marketing involves the promotion of an individual or idea with the aim of influencing public policy and voters. Politicians use political marketing in order to present themselves and their ideas in the best possible way. The 1996 presidential campaign brought two political unknowns into the race for the nation's highest office. Following the same approach of Ross Perot in 1992, Steve Forbes and Morry Taylor used their personal fortunes to fund their quest. And they did what most businesses do for products—they developed carefully planned marketing strategies. Both candidates used a full array of marketing tools to communicate their ideas.[56] Many political analysts feel that Al Gore eventually lost the 2000 presidential campaign because Green Party candidate Ralph Nader appealed to the younger Democrat constituents with his platform. Nader marketed his political message without the benefit of personal fortune or large donations.[57]

Of course, elections are not always won or lost based on the character of candidates or their ideas. In 2000, the advertising spent on the presidential campaign reached over $300 million. The political arena is a highly competitive environment, and both positive and negative advertising is accepted. Few companies would ever bad-mouth competitors' products so aggressively. At least one political commentary indicated that Steve Forbes forgot a basic lesson: Consumers are unlikely to support marketers "whose sales pitch relies on trashing the competition."[58] In the 2000 elections, the American public began to complain about the overwhelming negativity of political advertising; some candidates even accused their opponents of engaging in "bashing" as a new campaign tactic.[59]

The marketing talent a candidate can attract may have a lot to do with the number of votes he or she is likely to receive. For example, less than a month before the election, trailing in the polls, Bob Dole found it difficult to hire a top-quality marketing firm. Phil Dusenberry, who headed Ronald Reagan's team, and Tom Messener, who worked with George Bush, rejected Dole because they said they were busy with consumer products campaigns.[60]

*Nader marketed his political
message without the benefit
of personal fortune or large
donations.*

Just how commercial is the political process? Political marketing involves the same steps we find in other areas. The objectives should be clearly stated in terms of influencing issues and getting elected. Just as mass marketing of products seldom works, mass marketing of issues or candidates will likely fail. The first step is to identify the various target segments, called *constituencies* in political terms. Then it is important to pinpoint the salient issues for each constituency and understand their thoughts and feelings. This usually involves considerable marketing research, including surveys (political polls) and focus groups. Of course, the campaign itself usually requires advertising and direct marketing, with an army of volunteers making calls in person or by telephone to targeted voters.

CAUSE MARKETING

Cause marketing involves gaining public support and financing for a cause in order to bring about a change or a remedy. You are familiar with many of the marketing campaigns to combat AIDS, drunk driving, drugs, domestic violence, and smoking among teens; to promote the use of seat belts; and to prevent cruelty to animals, to name a few. Cause marketing is used for blood drives, Community Chest drives, and charities that feed and clothe the homeless or combat various diseases. The overall objective is to remedy a situation by gaining public support for change.

CAUSE MARKETING
Gaining public support and financing in order to change or remedy a situation.

Cause marketing is challenging because it usually confronts two very difficult tasks: raising money and changing harmful behavior. For example, AIDS activists have been somewhat successful in educating people about the disease to help reduce its spread. Personalities such as Earvin "Magic" Johnson have heightened awareness. Efforts by the gay, lesbian, and heterosexual community have pressured the government into allocating more money to HIV and AIDS research.

INTERNAL MARKETING

Internal marketing occurs when one part of an organization markets its capabilities to others within the same firm. For example, imagine that you are a human resources manager. Your job, among other responsibilities, is to provide training and career development for employees in all the company's different divisions and departments. An effective approach is to use marketing concepts. The only difference is that you are aiming your efforts at internal customers—the employees of the firm—rather than end users of the company's products. This is not the same as internal communications, which are also important; all the marketing tools and techniques tend to be used, even marketing plans.

INTERNAL MARKETING
The marketing of a business unit's capabilities to others within the same firm.

For example, Dr. Lew Dotterer at Sparrow Health System in Lansing, Michigan, was responsible for developing learning programs for the organization. He employed marketing concepts to make this happen. First, he identified the key customers—doctors, nurses, administrators, and so forth. Next, he spoke with each group to determine its learning needs. He then created training programs that addressed those needs and promoted them throughout the system. Through internal marketing, Dr. Dotterer helped his internal customers better serve their external customers.

CONNECTING THROUGH RELATIONSHIPS

THE POINT: CELEBRATING THE LIFE AND CULTURE OF THE SOUTH BRONX

"We're the hottest, most interesting nonprofit in the country," says Paul Lipson. That's how the Point's cofounder likes to describe this emergent community development corporation in the Hunt's Point section of New York's South Bronx. And his description is not just the boasting of a proud father. In the three years since its inception, the Point has garnered almost $400,000 from a wide array of donors and captured the attention of ABC's *Nightline*. More important, it has harnessed the talents of the community it serves—from the young people who participate in and stage its hugely popular hip-hop performances to the budding entrepreneurs who use street-corner smarts to sell their wares in the Point's Marketplace.

Continued

According to Paul Quintero, chairman of the board, the Point has succeeded by turning the standard nonprofit model on its head. In the past, most social agencies used a "What's wrong with this picture?" approach to the South Bronx. They saw the neighborhood only in terms of its crime, poverty, poor schools, and substandard housing. They tried to put a Band-Aid on problems or fill in gaps. In contrast, the Point's four cofounders asked: "What are the assets—the raw assets of the community?" The answer was simple: a wealth of abandoned buildings and the passion and talents of at-risk youth.

With seed money from the Kaplan Foundation, the Point's first project was to turn an abandoned old mint, the former American Banknote Company, into its headquarters. Now a stylishly renovated building, it has a 220-seat theater for its "Live from the Edge" performance series and a 4,000-square-foot arts and business incubator. For the renovation and for every program housed within it, the Point has drawn on the assets of the neighborhood and its residents. Where someone else might see a boiler room, the Point's young aspiring hip-hop and rap artists see a future recording studio. Where someone else might see an abandoned lot full of wood and debris, the Point sees a business enterprise. At the Hunt's Point Farm, local youths use a machine to chop up wood, which they sell for use in fireplaces at restaurants in the metropolitan area.

Developing proposals for concrete projects such as these is a big factor in the Point's success in obtaining funds. "We're building incrementally, project by project, in a very tangible way," says Quintero. "People can relate to that, and that has been a very key piece of our marketing approach. We're not saying 'buy our vision.' The vision is nice, but people can't relate to it." For instance, rather than say "We want to develop arts and enterprise in the community," they go to a donor with a specific proposal and say, "We want to have a cross-cultural theater exchange with a group in Poland" (now a reality), or "We want to start an Internet center."

The Point is also able to attract donors because of its joint ventures with more established nonprofit partners. Working with the renowned International Center for Photography, the Point will soon have a darkroom, photo studio, monthly exhibitions in the atrium, and a budding photography business. Kids who never held a camera will be selling their photos in calendars, date books, and postcards. This ability to help turn interest into skills and then into enterprise is what is most exciting to Quintero. "There's new life, new activity, and new hope. That's the bottom line. For so many people, there is hope now where there wasn't any before."

Sources: Patrick Queen, "Paul Quintero: Making a Difference at the Point," *Columbia,* Winter 1997, pp. 38–39; and interview with Paul Quintero, the Point's chairman of the board.

THE MARKETING OF NONPROFIT SERVICES

Marketing of nonprofit services is a huge area. Today, the more than 1 million nonprofit organizations in the United States generate $621.4 billion. About $130 billion is contributed by private donors. Americans allocate almost 3 percent of their income to charitable giving, and nearly everyone gives something. About 70 percent of all households give an average of $754 dollars per year.[61] Nonprofit services account for more than 6 percent of all economic activity in the United States. As you can see from Figure 11.9, the United States has the highest

FIGURE 11.9 *Nonprofit Jobs as a Percentage of Total and Service Employment*

Source: Stephen Greene, "Nonprofits Group Expanding World," *Chronicle of Philanthropy,* June 28, 1994, pp. 1, 28–29. Reprinted with permission of *Chronicle of Philanthropy.*

	Percentage of Total Employment	Percentage of Nonprofit Service Employment
United States	6.8	15.4
France	4.2	10.0
United Kingdom	4.0	9.4
Germany	3.7	10.4
Average	3.4	8.9
Japan	2.5	8.6
Italy	1.8	5.5
Hungary	0.8	3.0

percentage of nonprofit workers to total employment and to total service employment in the world. The U.S. nonprofit sector employs 10.2 million people, compared to 1.4 million in Japan and about 1 million in France.

Nonprofit marketing is performed by an organization that is not motivated by profit and is exempt from paying taxes on any excess revenues over costs. Marketing has many applications in the nonprofit sector. Churches, museums, foundations, hospitals, universities, symphonies, and municipalities regularly create marketing plans in an effort to gain funds and public support. Nonprofit organizations often use person marketing, entertainment and event marketing, and place marketing. Nearly all political and cause marketing, as well as marketing of the arts, fits the nonprofit description. Most nonprofit organizations have begun advertising and soliciting donations and volunteers on the Internet, in an effort to maximize fundraising at little cost.[62]

NONPROFIT MARKETING
The activities performed by an organization not motivated by profit in order to influence consumers to support it with a contribution.

TYPES OF NONPROFIT SERVICE PROVIDERS

Figure 11.10 shows several categories of nonprofit service providers and gives examples of each. As you can see, marketing skills are required by a very broad range of nonprofit organizations. For example, your university probably has a fairly elaborate marketing plan, and chances are that many of the administrators have attended American Marketing Association seminars on how to promote higher education. Many athletic directors and university presidents are currently being advised to view their positions as similar to that of a CEO of a major corporation.[63]

Category	Example	Product
Arts/Culture/Humanities	Metropolitan Museum of Art, New York	Exhibits
	Chicago Symphony	Musical programs
Education/Instruction	Michigan State University Executive Education	Executive programs
	University of Southern California Undergraduate Program	Classes, degrees
Environmental Quality/ Protection/Beautification	Smokey the Bear (U.S. Forest Service)	Fire safety
	Greenpeace	Saving the environment
Animal Related	San Diego Zoo	Species preservation
	People for the Ethical Treatment of Animals (PETA)	Animal rights
Health	Listening Ear	Cure for AIDS
	Alcoholics Anonymous (AA)	Stop alcoholism
Consumer Protection	Consumer Hotline	Legal aid
Crime Prevention	Neighborhood Watch	Discourage criminals
	Crime Tip Hotline	Catch criminals
Employment/Jobs	U.S. Army	Volunteer recruitment
Public Safety	State of Michigan	Drive safely
	State of Florida	Wear seat belts
Recreation/Sports	Silverdome	Football
	American Youth Soccer Organization	Youth sports programs
Youth Development	Boy Scouts of America	Scouting jamborees
	Big Sister/Big Brother programs	Companionship and role models
Community/Civic	Bring Your Company to . . .	Community enhancement
	Kiwanis Club	Economic development
Grant Agencies	Rockefeller Foundation	Arts development
	Robert Wood Johnson Foundation	Medical research
Religious Organizations	Catholic Church	Membership
	Evangelists	Spirituality
Other Cause-Based Groups	National Organization of Women (NOW)	Women's rights
	American Civil Liberties Union (ACLU)	Individual rights

FIGURE 11.10 *Types of Nonprofit Service Providers*

THE NEED FOR EXCESS REVENUES

Nonprofit service organizations are usually tax exempt and may appear to be less concerned about pricing and cost structures. Yet they need to generate revenues in excess of costs for several reasons. First, their revenues (money for services and from contributions) tend to fluctuate from year to year. For example, the Museum of Fine Arts in Boston, discussed in more detail in chapter 14, relies on blockbuster shows every few years to boost revenues. Every year, the U.S. Open for tennis holds a children's day before the start of the tournament; celebrities perform or play tennis professionals in charity matches, and the event raises $1.5 million for nonprofit organizations. Thus, tying a nonprofit event to a profit-making organization, especially a well-known one, can provide fund-raising opportunities.[64]

Second, you can't raise money if you aren't solvent. The United Way wants the organizations it supports to have at least a three-month safety net. That means a full quarter's expenses have to be earned and set aside—no small task for most organizations! Fund-raising operations must be run in a financially sound manner in order to gain support from large donors. That requires efficiency and documentation identifying the costs of items as well as the revenues received.

Third, nonprofits hire professionals to help the organization grow. Similar to any business, growth generally requires capital and the ability to access funds from financial institutions. Lenders look at nonprofits much the same way they look at any other organization. The Red Cross makes significant positive cash flows.[65] This type of financial performance not only attracts managerial talent but also affords the company access to all the services required by a for-profit company.

FUND-RAISING AND REVENUE GENERATION

Nonprofit organizations may raise revenues in two ways. First, they acquire funding from third parties, such as governments, private and public agencies, and individual contributors. Second, they may expand into a number of business operations.

A considerable amount of funding comes from donations by individuals, families, or businesses. Microsoft CEO Bill Gates is recognized for making contributions to nonprofits. He recently formed his own nonprofit, the Gates Library Foundation, which has contributed $33 million to public libraries in low-income communities for computer hardware and software to access the Internet.[66] Microsoft Corporation pledged to match the donation.[67]

Understanding donor profiles helps nonprofit groups target fund-raising efforts. Figure 11.11 lists six categories of donors, the types of charities they most often support, and why they give. The largest group, communitarians, believe in supporting their community. As government has decreased its support of social services and the arts, nonprofits in these areas must compete against one another for private dollars. Just as new ventures need a well-honed marketing strategy and innovative approach to entice venture capitalists, new nonprofits need to do the same to capture the attention of donors besieged by requests. The Point Community Development Corporation in the Hunt's Point section of New York's South Bronx has rustled up a significant amount of funding. It uses "out of the box" thinking and cultivates relationships within both the neighborhood and the nonprofit community. See the relationships feature, "The Point: Celebrating the Life and Culture of the South Bronx."

In addition to fund-raising, many organizations develop business ventures that provide substantial revenues. These are often unrelated to the basic nature of the core activity. Your high school band, drama club, or sports team probably has used some type of retail operation at one time or another—a car wash, a food stand at the local fair, or a candy sale—to raise money for uniforms or a special trip. We all are familiar with Girl Scout cookie sales. In fact, these activities often compete with the for-profit sector. Because the service labor is donated, the price charged by the nonprofit group can be substantially lower than the normal retail price. In some cases, for-profit businesses simply cannot compete while the fund-raiser is going on. At the same time, nonprofits are good customers for many for-profit businesses.

Sometimes the revenue-generating venture fits nicely with the core activity of the nonprofit. For example, private schools and universities have bookstores and other merchandising operations. Museums and musical organizations (symphonies, opera companies) may have

Category	Percentage of All Major Donors	Who They Are and What They Support	Why They Give
Communitarians	26%	*91% male* Local charities, cultural, religious, and educational concerns	To improve the community Good for business relationships
Devout	21%	*80% male and business owners* Religious organizations	Moral obligation
Investors	15%	*87% male, 75% business owners* Wide variety	Rather support them than the government No moral obligation
Socialites	11%	*62% female* Arts, education, and religious projects	Believe that giving is part of personality and provides entry into a desirable social circle
Repayers	10%	*65% male* Educational institutions and medical facilities	Loyalty or obligation due to an event that happened later in life
Dynasts	8%	*50% male, 50% female* Many have inherited wealth and give to wide range of groups	Believe everyone should support nonprofits Family traditionally supports nonprofits

FIGURE 11.11 *Categories of Donors to Nonprofit Groups*

Source: Adapted from "One Study's Analysis of 7 Types of Wealthy Donors," *Chronicle of Philanthropy,* March 8, 1994, p. 14. Reprinted with permission of *Chronicle of Philanthropy.*

shops and mail-order catalogs. Some groups license their name or logo for a fee. Zoos, museums, sports teams, and others often charge admission.

Finally, membership fees represent a large source of revenue. Most associations are formed for the benefit of members, whether individuals or organizations. For example, a member of the American Marketing Association pays $155 annually to the AMA in addition to chapter dues. Students are given a special rate. This entitles the member to obtain AMA publications and attend conferences at substantially reduced rates. The AMA is the world's largest professional society of marketers, with more than 45,000 members in 92 countries; there are 500 chapters in North America. The association works to promote education and assist in career development among marketing professionals.[68]

Most professions have a similar organization, and in many cases companies can be members. For example, firms interested in service quality are likely to join the Center for Services Marketing and Management at Arizona State University. It is North America's leading university-based program for the study of services marketing and management. The center conducts research, offers specialized education and training, and works to provide firms with applicable principles, concepts, and tools.[69]

PROVIDING POSITIVE SOCIAL BENEFITS

Another challenge for nonprofits is to provide maximum positive social benefits to their constituency. This can be difficult because constituents may have differing objectives and needs. For example, the San Diego Zoo must balance the public's desire to see certain animals with the interests of environmentalists in species preservation. Expenses to house, care for, and in some cases help rare animals reproduce can be very high. Recently, zoos in South Africa and Australia completed an exchange of animals; the South African zoo sent a pair of rare red pandas, who will hopefully breed and leave the Australian zoo with red pandas of their own.[70] Likewise, groups concerned with spouse or child abuse must allocate funds to serving families as well as to promoting their cause.

Having a good understanding of constituent needs is not always easy. The Internet is a particularly useful marketing tool for nonprofit groups. Many use it as a virtual community to communicate, share information, educate, collaborate, and interact. It is an excellent format for publishing, sharing perspectives on issues, assisting in community development, and increasing participation.[71]

A good example of the importance of serving constituency needs can be found in the arts. These include a long list of services—museums, theaters, opera, symphonies, dance companies, exhibitions, public radio and television, and others. A major indicator of the quality of life in many communities is the availability of the arts. Numerous cities have a symphony orchestra, which can be an important factor in attracting businesses and people to the area.

Customers for the arts are called patrons. Attracting them is a critical aspect of marketing the arts, but that is only part of the challenge. Equally important is finding sponsors of all types, since revenues from ticket sales seldom generate enough money. Yet patrons may have many choices about which arts events to attend, and sponsors may have a broad range of requests for donations. Ultimately, successful organizations are those that can show the benefits they bring to their constituents.

ETHICAL ISSUES SURROUNDING NONPROFIT ORGANIZATIONS

Today, many types of organizations claim nonprofit status, which entitles them to tax exemption. While a majority of these benefit society, a growing number have little or no resemblance to traditional charities. In fact, of the 45,000 new organizations that apply for tax-exempt status each year, many make a considerable profit. This raises the question of whether it is ethical for money-making nonprofits to pay no taxes. Consider professional golfing's PGA Tour, which grosses $180 million a year. It could afford to pay its commissioner $4.2 million over the last year, partly at the expense of the American taxpayer. The PGA Tour, Inc., is a nonprofit organization and is not required to pay federal tax on tour operations. Some nonprofits are very rich, indeed. The J. Paul Getty Trust in Los Angeles has $8 billion in assets.

Although nonprofits are taxed on income from businesses unrelated to their function, fewer than 5 percent report such income. The revenue for most nonprofits comes from investments and business operations. Nonprofit executives say they have shifted toward profit-making schemes in order to survive. Many others feel that there are too many nonprofits taking advantage of tax-exempt status, but efforts to change the law have failed repeatedly in Congress.

You may be familiar with many nonprofit organizations, such as National Geographic, the Academy of Motion Picture Arts and Sciences (which presents the Oscars), and the Humane Society. Nonprofits are not limited to charity, however. Many are found in retail, restaurant, hotel, insurance, and even laundry services. Most nonprofits do not pay taxes on investment income as well. Competitors of these organizations find the tax exemptions unfair and unethical. Nonprofits in competition with for-profit companies have a clear financial advantage. Consider the difference between a nonprofit hotel operated by George Washington University and other tax-paying hotels in the area. In fact, Washington, DC, houses 1,800 nonprofits. If they were to pay taxes on the land and buildings they use for operations, then approximately $94 million a year would flow to the city. Critics point out that they use city services just as other organizations do.

The nation's nonprofit sector generates an amazing $190 billion every year and controls $1.475 trillion in assets. While many of these organizations directly benefit Americans, for others the tax-free status remains an ethical issue.[72]

This chapter dealt with services and nonprofit organizations. The next chapter explores how products and services are made available to customers by looking at marketing channels, wholesaling, and physical distribution.

CHAPTER SUMMARY

OBJECTIVE 1: Identify the forces that have produced and will continue to create tremendous growth in the service economy.

The service economy is growing at about twice the rate of the sale of goods. First, technological advances and the accompanying information revolution are creating vast opportunities in the service sector. Technology often can only be used with the help of service specialists who have the necessary knowledge and skills. Second, the quality of life is being measured by how people feel and experience life. Third, governments around the world have deregulated services. Fourth, professional service providers such as lawyers are turning to marketing as a way to conduct their business operations. Fifth, privatization of government functions is opening up service opportunities. Sixth, there is a need for outside specialists by companies that want to concentrate resources on their core business. Finally, there is a strong growth in franchising, which tends to focus on service-based products.

OBJECTIVE 2: Understand which characteristics of services must be adjusted for successful marketing.

Services are differentiated from goods on five key dimensions that must be considered in successful marketing. First, services are intangible, so evidence of benefits may occur long after purchase and may be difficult to assess. Second, there is a unique relationship between the service provider and customers, who are either present when the service is performed or have knowledge of how it was performed. Third, the service encounter is a crucial point of connection between provider and consumer, in which each moment must contribute to meeting customer needs. Fourth, since production and consumption often occur simultaneously, the same service may be different each time it is performed and may be adjusted to the unique circumstances of each consumer. Fifth, because there is no storage or inventory with a service, demand forecasting is important so that service providers are ready when needed. Finally, service quality control is extremely important but it is complicated. It requires thorough training of personnel and careful monitoring.

Most products contain elements of both goods and services and can be placed on a service–goods continuum. Consumers tend to evaluate services differently from goods. Generally, services are high in credence qualities, which means it is difficult to evaluate them even after they have been consumed. Therefore, consumers tend to rely on personal references for information, engage in post-purchase evaluation, develop surrogates for judging quality, select providers from a small set of choices, and actually serve as a competitor to the service provider. They are slow to adopt new services but eventually develop strong brand loyalty.

Judgments of service quality usually have three aspects: the dimensions of service quality, consumer factors, and quality perceptions. The dimensions of service quality include tangibles, reliability, responsiveness, assurance, and empathy. Customer factors—word of mouth, personal needs, past experience, and external communication—help form customer expectations. Quality perception is based on the difference between what is expected and what is received.

OBJECTIVE 3: Know how to develop the service mix.

Service mix development requires understanding in two areas. First, services have core, augmented, and branded dimensions similar to goods. Brand equity is equally if not more important for services than for goods. Second, when developing new services, marketers must give careful consideration to both functional and interactive elements. The functional element is influenced by the complexity and divergence of a service, which must provide benefits that match customer needs and wants. The interactive element involves such concerns as the consumer's personal behaviors and the atmosphere in which the service will be performed.

OBJECTIVE 4: Explore the expanded concept of services.

There are many types of service marketing including person marketing, entertainment and event marketing, place marketing, political marketing, cause marketing, and internal marketing. Person marketing promotes an individual, often a sports figure or movie personality, who in turn generally helps market another product. Entertainment marketing promotes movies, television programming, and the like. Event marketing, like that for sporting events and concerts, is a major category. Through sponsorships of events, companies also market other products. Place marketing promotes a geographic location, such as a city, state, or country. It is often connected to investment or travel products. Political marketing promotes politicians or political ideas and policy issues. Cause marketing attempts to gain support for a cause, such as research on HIV and AIDS. Internal marketing occurs when one business unit markets its capabilities to others within the same firm.

OBJECTIVE 5: Appreciate the importance of nonprofit marketing and the uniqueness of this important marketing arena.

Nonprofit marketing accounts for more than 7 percent of economic activity in the United States and is growing. It is performed by organizations that are tax exempt, such as churches, museums, foundations, hospitals, universities, and orchestras. Even nonprofits need revenues in excess of their costs. These revenues provide service continuity from year to year and allow nonprofits to access the talent and funding required to serve their constituents. Consequently, fundraising and revenue generation from donors, patrons, and members are often a focal point. At the same time, nonprofits must provide benefits to all constituents, which can be difficult because different parties have varying expectations and needs. Ethically, there is a question about tax-exempt status for at least some nonprofits, especially when they compete with for-profit organizations.

REVIEW YOUR UNDERSTANDING

1. List the seven forces that are producing explosive growth in services. Very briefly describe each.
2. What are the differences between goods and services?
3. What is the service–goods continuum? What are the categories of the continuum?
4. What are search, experience, and credence attributes of services? List a product example in each attribute category.
5. What are the five dimensions of service quality, the four consumer factors, and the three elements of quality perception that shape the customer's view of service quality?
6. What are the functional and interactive elements of services?
7. List three examples of person marketing.
8. What is entertainment and event marketing?
9. Give an example of cause marketing.
10. What is internal marketing?
11. What differentiates nonprofit services?
12. Why do nonprofit organizations need excess revenues over costs?

DISCUSSION OF CONCEPTS

1. List three of the seven forces driving the explosive growth of the service economy. How will each force influence the nature of college education?
2. Select two differences between services and goods and detail how each affects marketing strategy development.
3. Do you think it is possible for a product to be either a pure good or a pure service? Why or why not?
4. What are the differences between search, experience, and credence qualities of products? How does each affect marketing strategy development?
5. Name a service high in credence quality. What type of buyer behavior would you expect to encounter?
6. Imagine that you are the marketing manager for a major hotel chain. What steps would you recommend to help ensure success in each of the five dimensions of service quality?
7. Select a target market and design the core, augmented, and branded aspects of a restaurant.
8. Do you consider it appropriate for politicians to develop sophisticated marketing campaigns in order to be elected to office?

Cause marketing: Gaining public support and financing in order to change or remedy a situation.

Core service: The basic benefit delivered.

Divergence: The degree to which a service involves customization beyond routine or standardized procedures.

Event marketing: Promoting an event in order to generate revenues and enhance the reputation of an organization.

Franchise: A contractual agreement whereby an entrepreneur pays a fee for the franchise name and agrees to meet operating requirements and use the organization's marketing plan.

Functional element: What a service is supposed to accomplish.

Interactive element: The personal behaviors and atmosphere of the service environment.

Internal marketing: The marketing of a business unit's capabilities to others within the same firm.

Nonprofit marketing: The activities performed by an organization not motivated by profit to influence consumers to support it with a contribution.

Perishable: The temporal nature of services, whose value exists for only a short time.

Person marketing: Promoting an individual's personality, character, and appeal, which in turn may assist in the promotion of a product.

Place marketing: Promoting a geographical location in order to appeal to businesses, investors, and tourists.

Political marketing: Promoting an individual or idea motivated by the desire to influence public policy and voters.

Service: An idea, task, experience, or activity that can be exchanged for value to satisfy the needs and wants of consumers and businesses.

Service complexity: The number and intricacy of steps involved in producing a service.

Service encounter: The interaction between the consumer and the seller.

REFERENCES

1. David Rocks, "IBM's Hottest Product Isn't a Product," *Business Week,* October 2, 2000, pp. 118, 120; Terry Schwadron, "They Stay Up Late So Your Site Does, Too," *New York Times,* September 20, 2000, p. 16; "Big Blue Partners Win Slice of Services," *CNet News.com,* February 23, 1999, www.cnet.com/news.
2. CIA, *The World Factbook 2000—United States,* www.odci.gov/cia/publications/factbook/geos.us.html.
3. Thomas G. Scott, "Service Sector Drives Job Growth," *Business First,* July 7, 2000, p. 63.
4. Joel Millman, "Services May Lead U.S. to Trade Surplus," *Wall Street Journal,* December 4, 2000, p. A1.
5. Howard Banks, "Surprises in Foreign Sales of U.S. Services," *Forbes,* March 28, 1994, p. 41; Ralph T. King Jr., "U.S. Exports Are Growing Rapidly but Almost Unnoticed," *Wall Street Journal,* April 21, 1993, pp. A1, A6; and James E. Ellis, "Why Overseas? 'Cause That's Where Sales Are," *Business Week,* January 10, 1994, p. 62.
6. Bill Gates, *The Road Ahead* (New York: Viking, 1995), p. 33.
7. Char Kosek, "On-line Spending in Expansion Mode," *Business Marketing,* June 1996, p. S5.
8. Eleena De Lisser, "Tellers vs. ATMs: People Prefer Doing Business Face to Face," *Wall Street Journal Interactive Edition,* May 16, 1997.
9. Ann Therese Palmer, "Food," *Business Week,* January 10, 2000, p. 132.
10. "RFID Delivers for Baggage Service Start-Up," *Frontline Solutions,* November 2000, p. 8.
11. Tim Greene, "Those Baby Bells Are Growing Up Fast," *Network World,* November 20, 2000, p. 36.
12. Ian Murphy, "Yearly 7% Growth Seen for Communications Spending," *Marketing News,* October 7, 1996, pp. 8, 11.
13. Adam Shell, "7 Years after Landmark Ruling, Professional Firms Look to Marketing," *Public Relations Journal,* February 1992, p. 10.
14. Kirk Davidson, "Health Care Industries Pose Ethical Problems," *Marketing News,* December 2, 1996; Chris Adams, "Pharmacia Corp. Pfizer Are Warned on Celebrex Ads," *Wall Street Journal,* December 12, 2000, p. A4.
15. John D. McKinnon, "Ads Are Under New Scrutiny," *Wall Street Journal,* January 28, 1998, p. F1.
16. "Italy to Sell Stakes in Eni, BNL, and Alitalia as State Sales Pick Up Speed," *Euroweek,* May 8, 1998, p. 9.
17. June Kronholz, "Desk Sergants: Tesseract and Others March Briskly Ahead in School Privatization," *Wall Street Journal,* August 13, 1999, p. A1.
18. Randy Mysliviec, "Can Your Business Afford Not to Outsource," *America's Network,* November 2000, p. 18.
19. Palmer, "Food."
20. "Online Auto Sales Altering the Future of the Car Salesman," *Birmingham Business Journal,* September 9, 2000, p. 4.
21. www.wal-mart.com, site visited on December 17, 2000.
22. Chip E. Miller, "U.S. Techniques Not Best for Chinese Sales Reps," *Marketing News,* November 4, 1996, p. 5.
23. "French Salespeople Get a Rude Awakening," *The New York Times,* December 24, 2000.
24. Steven V. Brull, "Gateway's Big Gamble," *Business Week,* June 5, 2000, p. EB27.
25. Amy Spector, "Customer Satisfaction: Ambience," *Nation's Restaurant News,* September 13, 1999, p. 118.
26. Peter Burrows, "David vs. Goliath on the Infobahn," *Business Week,* December 5, 1994, p. 94E.
27. Rhonda Cornell, "Emerald Isle Has Become U.S. Gateway to Europe," *Electronic Buyers' News,* October 23, 2000, p. 52.
28. Scott McCartney, "Airlines' Reputations Hinge on the Basics, Study Shows," *Wall Street Journal,* April 27, 2000, p. B4.
29. Valarie A. Zeithaml, "How Consumer Evaluation Processes Differ between Goods and Services," in *Marketing of Services,* eds. James H. Donnelly and William R. George (Chicago, IL: American Marketing Association, 1981).
30. www.bestbuy.com, site visited on December 18, 2000; and Katie Haegele, "Hitting the Bullseye: DM at the Point of Purchase," *Target Marketing,* May 2000, p. 17.
31. "What to Expect on Carnival Cruises," www.bvt-usa.com/cruises/c-expect.html, site visited on January 13, 1997.
32. Joy Anderson, "Discover Uncharted Magic with Disney Cruise Line," *Incentive,* October 2000, p. D14.
33. Rutrell Yasin, "Security First for Visa," *Internetweek,* November 13, 2000, p. 35.
34. Zeithaml, "How Consumers Evaluation Processes Differ."
35. Sharon Cleary, "E-Commerce (A Special Report)," *Wall Street Journal,* October 23, 2000, p. R54.
36. Julian Baum and Steve Chen, "Jobs and More," *Far Eastern Economic Review,* September 21, 2000, p. 50.
37. Sundar G. Bharadwaj and Anil Menon, "Determining Success in Service Industries," *Journal of Services Marketing,* 7, no. 4 (1993): pp. 19–40.
38. Kelly Baron, "Hurry Up and Wait," *Forbes,* October 16, 2000, p. 158.
39. Darren McDermott, "Customer Satisfaction: Quality, Service Barely Pass Muster with Consumer," *Wall Street Journal,* August 16, 1999, p. A2.
40. www.halcyon.com/dbonner/kinkos/welcome.html, site visited on December 2000.
41. Mike Beirne, "Breaking out of the Hotel Rut," *Brandweek,* June 5, 2000, pp. 36–38.
42. G. Lynn Shostack, "Service Positioning through Structural Change," *Journal of Marketing* 51 (January 1987): 34–43.
43. Philip Kotler, "Atmospherics as a Marketing Tool," *Journal of Marketing* 40 (Winter 1973–1974): 50.
44. M. Mehrabian and J. A. Russel, *An Approach to Environmental Psychology* (Cambridge, MA: MIT Press, 1974).

45. Chad Rubel, "Marketing with Music," *Marketing News,* August 12, 1996, pp. 1, 21.
46. Stefan Fatsis, "Can NBA Star Michael Jordan Score on the World Wide Web?" *Wall Street Journal Interactive Edition,* June 24, 1997.
47. Mark Hyman, "The Yin and the Yang of the Tiger Effect," *Business Week,* October 16, 2000, p. 110.
48. Roy S. Johnson, "Tiger!" *Fortune (Interactive Edition),* May 12, 1997.
49. Hyman, "The Yin and the Yang of the Tiger Effect."
50. www.boxofficemojo.com/toystory2.html, Web site visited December 2000.
51. Mission statement of Ohio State University Athletic Department; and Roy S. Johnson, "How One College Program Runs the Business," *Fortune,* December 20, 1999, p. 163.
52. Bob Ryan, "Hoop Dreams," *Sales and Marketing Management* (December 1996), pp. 48–51; and Craig Copetas, *Wall Street Journal,* November 29, 1996, p. B5; and www.nba.com, Web site visited December, 2000.
53. www.nba.com/allstar2000/asgame/global_broadcast_000203.html, Web site visited December, 2000.
54. "Iowa," *Fortune,* March 4, 1996, special edition section.
55. Thomas Hayden, "Safaris and Sensitivity," *Newsweek,* June 5, 2000, p. 56; Craig Karmin, "Brazil Prepares Launch of Market to Encourage Foreign Investment Through Good Governance," *Wall Street Journal,* December 14, 2000, p. C16.
56. Judy Keen, "Two Unknowns Sink a Fortune into Recognition," *USA Today,* October 15, 1996, p. A2.

57. Paul Magnusson, "The Punishing Price of Passion," *Business Week,* November 20, 2000, p. 44.
58. Steven W. Colford, "Forbes' Faux-pas," *American Advertising,* Spring 1996, pp. A2, 23.
59. James Poniewozik, "Campaign ad Nauseam," *Time,* November 13, 2000, p. 40.
60. Martha T. Moore, "Dole Campaign Looking for Messenger for Its Message," *USA Today,* October 15, 1996.
61. *The Independent Sector,* www.independentsector.org, December 28, 2000; figures the latest from 1998.
62. Alessandra Bianchi, "The New Philanthropy," *Inc.,* October 2000, pp. 23–25.
63. Magnusson, "The Punishing Price of Passion."
64. "US Open Kicks Off," *Wall Street Journal,* June 26, 2000.
65. www.redcross.org, site visited December 20, 2000.
66. gatesfoundation.org, site visited December 20, 2000.
67. "Gates to Give $200 Million for Library Computers," *Wall Street Journal Interactive Edition,* June 24, 1997.
68. www.ama.org, site visited on December 18, 2000.
69. www.cob.asu.edu/smmcenter visited December 18, 2000.
70. www.sandiegozoo.org/special/pandas/pandacam/index.html, visited December 18, 2000; africacentury.com/bushcraft/dailynews/i.../archive_19990708_redpandasemigrate.htm.
71. "Establishing a Presence: Local Nonprofits Online," www.uwm.edu/People/mbarndt/npdev.htm, site visited on December 18, 2000.
72. Bianchi, "The New Philanthropy."

Bricks or Clicks

PBS GOES ONLINE

SINCE ITS FOUNDING AS A nonprofit corporation in 1969, the Public Broadcasting Service (PBS) has become a welcome guest in many homes. The network reaches over 99 percent of television-owning homes in the United States and provides quality educational and community service programming such as *Nova, Masterpiece Theatre,* and *Sesame Street.* With such recognizable titles to its credit, why would PBS need to turn to the Internet and e-commerce?

The answer lies in the changing political and market environment of the mid-1990s. PBS faced increasing competition from for-profit cable networks specializing in educational programming such as the Discovery Channel, the Learning Channel, and the Arts & Entertainment Network (A&E). A more immediate concern came from Congress, which was then considering the removal of PBS's federal subsidies. PBS created PBS.org to provide additional resources for its viewers (e.g., broadcast schedules and educational material) in an effort to maintain its relevance to its audience and, in 1997, to supplement its income through an online store. PBS executives hoped that the online store would provide a more efficient way of taking orders for PBS merchandise and videos than the network's 800-number operation.

The online store at PBS.org exceeded all expectations. The Web site updated in June 2000 to accommo-

date increased programming- and affiliate-related content and the expanding store, selling over 1,500 CDs, books, and videos related to its programming. Don Jalbert, vice president of PBS Learning Media, notes "We're already profitable. It's tight, but it's profitable." The future looks bright. Revenues are increasing "significantly" and Jalbert predicts continued growth as PBS promotes the site.

It looks as if this growth in sales will soon produce dividends. Earnings from the site will go to reducing the membership fees charged to PBS's 348 member stations. Even so, the affiliates have expressed some concern about the advent of the PBS.com e-shop. Many of them have their own sites and shops and are worried about a loss of visitors and sales. Items sold on the affiliates' Web sites provide "a more immediate tonic for member stations' ledgers." Although the details of the relationship between PBS and its affiliates have yet to be worked out, it is clear that growth of revenue from PBS.com is helping ameliorate some of the network's financial woes.

Sources: www.pbs.org; and Bob Tedeschi, "PBS and NPR Find Unexpected Success Selling on the Web," *The New York Times— E-Commerce Report,* October 23, 2000, p. C12.

Ticketmaster

TICKETMASTER KNOWS WHAT IT MEANS to serve customers through the development of beneficial relationships. It is the world's leading computerized ticketing service, with more than 3,750 clients—including 3,400 outlets in nine countries. The company generates revenues by adding $1.50 to $7.00 to the more than 75 million tickets it sells each year. That added up to $341 million in sales in 1998. Ticketmaster experienced a 47 percent growth rate in 1998 alone. It employs over 6,400 employees worldwide. Its customers fill hundreds of leading arenas, stadiums, performing arts venues, and theaters.

Not long ago, buying tickets for a major event was often associated with a long drive, standing in an endless line, and sometimes even camping out overnight. In 1985, *Time* magazine wrote a story about computerized ticketing, which was quickly becoming the industry standard: "Queuing for hours in the subfreezing cold to buy a pair of hard-to-get tickets may have once been a mark of theater-going dedication, but increasingly, it is a mere sign that you are behind the times." Ticketmaster, formed in 1978 by two Arizona State University students, had a competitive drive to be at the forefront of improvements in its industry. Arenas often had poor inventory control, and concert organizers could not accurately predict demand for shows. Ticketmaster helped change all this and became the industry benchmark.

Ticketmaster's computerized operating system is upgraded approximately five times a year. Buyers can order by phone, through ticket centers, from box offices, or via the Internet. Ticketmaster Online enables customers to check event schedules and seating charts, chat with celebrities, shop for tour merchandise, or check on breaking tour information. Through the Ticketmaster system, customers can obtain the best available tickets, no matter where they live.

Ticketmaster has expanded from its core ticketing business into related entertainment and marketing opportunities through the creation of sponsorship and promotional programs. The company publishes *Live!*, a monthly event guide, and sells merchandise through Entertainment to Go. It continually looks for new markets and new ways to serve customers with a wider variety of events.

Ticketmaster introduced its Mobile Ticket Van, donated by General Motors, at Lollapalooza in August 1997. This specially equipped vehicle gives the company yet another way to reach consumers who may not live near a Ticketmaster outlet. Ticketmaster believes "there is an unlimited number of promotional tie-ins we could initiate. [We think we will] find so many uses for this that one won't be nearly enough to cover L.A., and wouldn't be surprised if we roll them out in major cities throughout the country."

Ticketmaster's alliances and ventures are numerous. In addition to ventures with Intel and MasterCard, the company has paired up with Samsung Electronics, Calvin Klein, R. J. Reynolds, Microsoft, Pepsi, Ford, Apple Computer, and others. The aggressive pursuit of marketing opportunities has sometimes been perceived as monopolistic, especially since Ticketmaster has acquired at least 12 of its closest competitors in the past decade and controls approximately two-thirds of major stadiums, arenas, and amphitheaters in urban centers.

In May 2000, Ticketmaster Online-CitySearch, Inc., purchased a competitor, Ticket Web, Inc., in a stock deal valued at $35.2 million. Ticket Web, which has about 700 of its own customers, including New York's Bowery Ballroom and the San Diego Zoo, will be maintained as a separate entity from Ticketmaster. Ticketmaster itself is owned by USA Networks. Other subsidiaries include CitySearch, the Home Shopping Network, and the Hotel Reservations Network. This group of entertainment companies is now being bought by Seagram, a family-owned liquor business. It is through such purchases that the parent company hopes to develop an entire entertainment network.

1. *Discuss how the forces creating growth in services may have affected Ticketmaster's business over time. Which has probably been the most significant influence?*

2. *How does Ticketmaster address each of the five dimensions of service quality? Make assumptions when necessary.*

3. *What are some other ways that Ticketmaster can reach more customers? What will be some potential obstacles for Ticketmaster to overcome to reach these additional customers?*

Sources: Steve James, "Vivendi-Seagram Merger Looks a Good Deal for Diller," *Yahoo! Finance*, biz.yahoo.com, June 15, 2000; Reuters, "Ticketmaster Online Buys Ticket Web in $35Mln Deal," www.reuters.com, May 30, 2000; Hoover's Online, "Ticketmaster Group, Inc.," www.hooversonline.com, visited June 18, 2000; Doug Reece, "Ticketmaster Offers Sales on Wheels," *Billboard*, August 30, 1997, p. 74; "Ticketmaster and Intel Jointly Developing Advanced Online Ticketing Service," September 30, 1997, mktnews.nasdaq.com; United Press International, "Ticketmaster to Issue Credit Card," *USA Today*, November 3, 1997, www.usatoday.com; Ticketmaster Web site, www.ticketmaster.com; and Linda Himelstein and Ronald Grover, "Will Ticketmaster Get Scalped?" *Business Week*, June 26, 1995, pp. 64–68.

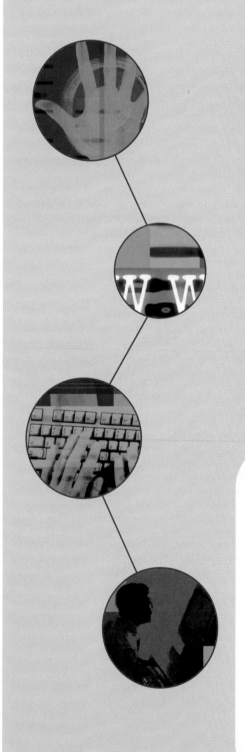

MARKETING CHANNELS, WHOLESALING, SUPPLY CHAIN MANAGEMENT, AND PHYSICAL DISTRIBUTION

objectives

1. Learn why companies frequently use intermediaries to reach targeted customers.

2. Attain insight into how channel relationships should be managed over time.

3. Appreciate the economic importance of wholesalers.

4. Know the different types of wholesalers and the distinct roles they play.

5. Understand supply chain management activities and objectives and how they improve business performance.

6. Identify what physical distribution entails and why it is critical for any business organization.

7. Learn the steps in the order management process.

◀ *Exterior of a Coach store*

WHEN MILES CHAN FOUNDED COACH IN 1962, he needed a way to get his leather goods to consumers. He knew his choice of distribution channel would influence where and when the new products were sold. His line of designer handbags was unique, and he believed the best outlet would be department stores. Because his company was new, Chan decided on personal selling as the best way to persuade buyers for the stores to give his products a chance. So he hired Dick Rose as his lone salesperson, and they put together what was probably the first "designer" collection of handbags under the Bonnie Cashin label. She was a top sportswear designer of that era, and she created for Chan a highly innovative line of soft, squishy leathers.

Rose fondly recalls his start. "I had been selling encyclopedias door-to-door and didn't know a thing about merchandising or retailing. But I was young and brash and bold and newly married—so very desperate for a real job. So I sold myself. I think Miles saw a freshness in me." Rose quickly confronted his first major obstacle: Handbag buyers had no interest because they were unfamiliar with a designer from the sportswear area. He then changed his strategy.

Rose recalled, "My first call was to Norman Wexler at Saks Fifth Avenue because I knew Bonnie [Cashin] had a shop there on the third floor." Wexler returned the phone call with the comment, "I didn't know Bonnie Cashin was making handbags," to which Rose responded, "Yes sir, she is, and I'm just trying to figure out whether you'd prefer to house them on the third floor with the sportswear or in the main floor handbag department." Rose's first order from Saks was for $900 and with that ammunition he called on the handbag buyer at Neiman Marcus and told her that Saks was featuring the bags in both the sportswear and handbag departments. Before he knew it, Rose was up in Stanley Marcus's office. He laid the bags down, and Marcus sat there studying them. Finally he said, "You know, this is something very different: I want to feature it in the windows on Main Street; can I get an exclusive in Dallas and Houston?" Could he get an exclusive? Coach had no other customers! So that was the beginning. From there, Rose got on planes to every department store in the country. Although the collection was offered in a couple of dozen department stores, it died in all of them. The country wasn't ready for it yet.

Times changed, and so did the Coach strategy. Rose did all he could to see that the stores stayed with it, and eventually the products began selling. The leather bags were repositioned as "not for every woman but only for those who truly love the smell and feel of genuine leather. It was a whole new concept." And it worked. But with continued growth, Coach needed more than one salesperson to get its product out. Then it added its own chain of outlets across the country. After its acquisition by Sara Lee in 1984, Coach began to reach customers through a mail-order catalog. Ads featuring the bags and an 800 number underscored the direct-marketing approach. Eventually, Coach factory outlet stores were created to handle the product returns from department stores. As the need arose, Coach altered its distribution channel strategy, always in the interest of finding the best way to reach the customer. The multiple or "hybrid" channel approach has proven successful for Coach. By 1995, sales reached $500 million and remained slightly above that through 2000. Sara Lee has started spinning off Coach

This example illustrates the importance of distribution channels to all manufacturers and service providers. Most customers must have access to goods before they can be observed, evaluated, and purchased. New companies face a major challenge in getting their goods distributed. Once established, distribution channels must be adapted over time to parallel changes in customer needs and competition. Frequently, more than one channel is needed to make a product available to targeted customers.

THE CONCEPT OF DISTRIBUTION CHANNELS

DISTRIBUTION CHANNEL

A set of interdependent organizations involved in making a product available for purchase.

INTERMEDIARY

Independently owned organization that acts as a link to move products between the producer and the end user.

BROKERS

A firm that does not take title to the goods it handles but actively negotiates the sale of goods for its clients.

WHOLESALER

A firm that takes title to products for resale to businesses, consumers, or other wholesalers or distributors.

RETAILER

A firm that takes title to products for resale to ultimate consumers.

DIRECT CHANNEL

A distribution channel in which the producer uses its own employees and physical assets to distribute the product directly to the end user.

INDIRECT CHANNEL

A distribution channel in which the producer makes use of independent organizations to distribute the product to end users.

CHANNEL LEVELS

The number of distinct units (producers, intermediaries, and customers) in a distribution channel.

A **distribution channel** is a set of interdependent organizations that make a product or service available for purchase by consumers or businesses. The distribution channel serves to connect a manufacturer, such as Coach, or a service provider, such as AT&T, with consumers or users. In simple terms, a distribution channel is a pipeline or pathway to the market.

Distribution channels are needed because producers are separated from prospective customers. An example is Mattel's star product, Barbie, which is targeted to girls age 4 through 10 and, of course, their parents. Barbie is made available to consumers in 140 countries through a host of different retail establishments, such as Wal-Mart, Toys "R" Us, Kay-Bees, and neighborhood toy stores. These retailers are both members of the distribution channel and customers of Mattel.

A distribution channel that enables a company to deal efficiently and effectively with separations in time, place, form, and possession will be successful. To accomplish that end, the channel must be organized and managed properly. Physical distribution activities, such as inventory management and product delivery, are essential for connecting with customers.

A distribution channel consists of at least a producer and a customer. Most channels, however, use one or more intermediaries to help move products to the customer. **Intermediaries** are independently owned organizations that act as links to move products between producers and the end user. The primary categories are brokers, wholesalers-distributors, and retailers. **Brokers** do not purchase the goods they handle but instead actively negotiate their sale for the client. A familiar example is real estate brokers, who negotiate the sale of property for their customers. Companies have more control over the activities of brokers, including the final price to the customer, because brokers do not own the goods they sell. **Wholesalers** (also referred to as distributors) take title to products and resell them to retail, industrial, commercial, institutional, professional, or agricultural firms, as well as to other wholesalers. A good example is Ingram Micro, Inc., a large wholesaler of computer hardware and software based in Santa Anna, California. Its salespeople contact a variety of companies to sell and distribute such products as IBM personal computers, Hayes modems, and Microsoft Windows 2000.[2] **Retailers** take title to products for resale to the ultimate consumer. These range from discounters such as Wal-Mart and large department stores to specialty chains such as The Limited and local boutiques.

CHANNEL STRUCTURE

Direct and Indirect Channels   Distribution channels are of two fundamental types. In **direct channels** (also called integrated channels) companies use their own employees (e.g., salespeople) and physical assets (e.g., warehouses, delivery vehicles) to serve the market. For example, IBM's sales force sells computer systems and software directly to large companies such as Bank of America. Sherwin-Williams owns and operates a majority of the outlets where its paint is sold. In **indirect channels** (also called nonintegrated channels) companies make use of independent agents to serve markets. General Motors sells aftermarket components through a variety of channels such as independent parts distributors, auto body repair shops, and independently owned dealerships.

Distribution channels can be described by the number of **channel levels** or the number of distinct units (producers, intermediaries, and customers) in a distribution channel. By definition, a direct channel has two levels: the producer and its targeted customers. Indirect

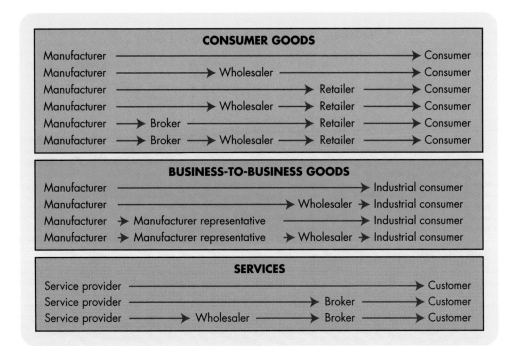

FIGURE **12.1** *Common
Channel Configurations*

channels are longer with at least three levels. Figure 12.1 illustrates common channel arrangements for consumer goods, business-to-business goods, and services.

Companies must decide whether to use direct channels or intermediaries. Direct channels are more attractive when the following conditions obtain:

- Customers and orders are large, especially if concentrated in a few geographical areas.
- Resource constraints are not severe.
- Environmental uncertainty is low to moderate.
- Investments in direct distribution will produce a high return.
- Significant value-added activity is required in the channel, including specialized investments.
- Customers prefer or demand to deal directly with manufacturers, Wal-Mart being a prime example.

Many markets are simply too small to make it economically feasible for companies to establish a direct channel. Consider independently owned convenience stores, whose average order from a company such as Procter & Gamble or Gillette would be tiny relative to supermarket or discount chains. The manufacturer's costs of selling, processing orders, and delivering products to mom-and-pop stores would be larger than the revenues generated. The problem is intensified because convenience stores are so geographically dispersed.

Intermediaries assemble merchandise from a variety of manufacturers and sell in smaller lots at a regional or local level. Therefore, an order from a small convenience store represents a relatively larger sale to a wholesaler than to an individual manufacturer. Moreover, wholesalers often have greater cost efficiencies than manufacturers due to their smaller size (lower overhead) or proximity to customers (lower selling and logistics costs). The result is that wholesalers can make money serving smaller customers whereas manufacturers cannot. The same rationale applies to retailers. Figure 12.2 shows that four manufacturers selling directly to 10 retailers would need to make 40 contacts to conduct business. Each one consumes resources. That compares to four contacts if they do business with one wholesaler, who in turn makes 10 contacts with the retailers for a total of 14.

Intermediaries tend to require less of the company's resources. Intermediaries make investments in inventory, offer credit to customers, and manage accounts receivable. They also pay for sales personnel and other employees, allowing the producer to avoid these costs. More and more companies are relying on the use of intermediaries. Honeywell, recently bought by General Electric, Intel, and Texas Instruments are among those who have increased the use of intermediaries as opposed to using company-owned or direct channels.[3]

**CONNECTED:
SURFING THE NET**

www.coach.com

Learn more about Coach's history, craftsmanship, and distribution by connecting to its Web site. Locate a Coach store near you, request a catalog, or visit the questions and comments page.

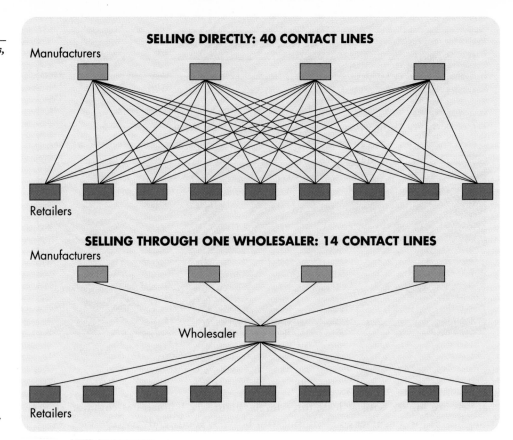

FIGURE 12.2 *Contractual Efficiency*

Source: Louis Stern, Adel El-Ansary, and Anne Coughlan, *Marketing Channels,* 6th ed. © 2001. Adapted by permission of Prentice Hall, Inc., Upper Saddle River, NJ.

The use of intermediaries is attractive to companies when it is difficult to make accurate predictions about the future. This lowers the risk level for the company because the intermediary is sharing the investment burden. Adapting to change is also easier, since companies have less fixed investment and, therefore, more financial flexibility. Warehouse facilities are an obvious example. If owned by the company, then the building, equipment, and personnel are a significant drain on resources when the economy takes a downturn.

Many customers prefer to deal with intermediaries to save money and time. For example, Price Club–Costco prefers to buy computer products and software from wholesalers such as Ingram-Micro, Tech Data, and Merisel rather than deal directly with manufacturers. This avoids the expense of hiring professional buyers who are knowledgeable about features and comparative value. Price Club–Costco notifies wholesalers about the quality, quantity, and price it needs, and the intermediaries locate the best deal. Manufacturers such as IBM, Compaq, and Hayes have little choice but to use these wholesalers if they want to do business with Price Club–Costco.[4]

Multiple Channel Systems   Many manufacturers want to connect with customers in as many ways as possible. **Multiple channel systems** make use of more than one channel to access markets for the same product. For example, Ben & Jerry's distributes its premium ice cream through company-owned stores, wholesalers that resell to supermarkets and convenience stores, and franchised outlets. It even sells by mail, packing the order in dry ice. Ben & Jerry's was recently bought by Unilever PLC, however, due in part to distribution problems. Perhaps too may channels of distribution create as many problems as too few channels of distribution.[5]

A leading manufacturer of personal computers, Compaq uses direct channels to reach large companies such as Goodyear or large government agencies that want to deal directly with producers. It also uses wholesalers such as Ingram-Micro and Intelligent Electronics to reach companies that prefer one-stop shopping for all their computer and software needs. Compaq deals with value-added distributors that assemble customized hardware and software packages to reach specialized markets (such as dentists). Through retailers such as Best Buy, CompUSA, and Computer City, it reaches small to medium-sized businesses as well as consumers. In addition, Compaq sends mail-order catalogs out to certain customer groups.[6]

MULTIPLE CHANNEL SYSTEMS

The use of more than one channel to access markets for the same product.

Reverse Channels   Most distribution channels flow from the manufacturer to the end user, but goods sometimes move in the opposite direction. A **reverse channel** flows from the end user to the wholesaler or the manufacturer. An example is the recycling of bottles and cans. A company called Advanced Recovery takes computers apart and sells the semiconductor chips to parts wholesalers and maintenance shops.[7]

Channel Dynamics and Technology   Companies must continually evaluate whether their channels need adjustment to deal with changing conditions. If this is ignored, then the whole foundation of the company can be weakened. Alterations are required as products progress through the life cycle. For example, Intel introduces new microprocessors about every two years. In the introductory phase, only a direct channel is used. The supply of new chips is limited until production is slowly scaled up. Large computer manufacturers get them first, as a reward for being very important customers. In the growth and maturity phases, both direct and indirect channels are used; wholesalers sell to smaller manufacturers and the replacement market. Finally, Intel relies primarily on indirect channels in the decline stage. Then the next generation of microprocessors is launched and the cycle repeats. The recent downturn in profits may be causing makers of technological products to speed up the cycle of introducing new products, but important customers still get the products first.[8]

Companies also need to alter their channels as the industry evolves. AirTouch Communications began offering cellular service in the Los Angeles market in 1984. Its channel mix at the time consisted of four salespeople who focused on *Fortune* 100 accounts, wholesalers who bought airtime and resold it under their own names, and a group of independent agents. Since the small to medium-sized business segment was not being covered very well by existing channels, AirTouch also established direct sales offices in several communities in the late 1980s.

Technology is also having a tremendous influence on channel operations. Many companies now send orders electronically rather than have salespeople submit handwritten sheets. Caller-identification systems give inside salespeople updated information on customers when they phone in orders. Handheld computers let sales reps take inventory on retail shelves and submit orders to manufacturers via satellite. For about $3,000 to $5,000, a company can print

REVERSE CHANNEL

A distribution channel that flows from the end user to the wholesaler or producer.

CONNECTED: SURFING THE NET

www.airtouch.com

Around the world, demand for wireless communications is on the rise as more people everywhere discover the benefits of wireless services for business and personal uses. AirTouch Communications has emerged as a global leader in this dynamic, fast-growing industry, and at the end of the second quarter of 1997 it reached over a million customers worldwide. Visit the company's Web site and learn more about how it manages its diverse mix of channels.

eSupportNow uses technology to offer supply chain solutions to companies in order to increase their profitability.

its own bar code labels for incoming goods and use scanners to find and retrieve them.[9] Automated conveyor systems and robots have brought enormous efficiencies to many companies. Fax machines, toll-free numbers, e-mail, and the Internet have made it much easier and more efficient for all companies to reach customers all over the world. For example, Ingram-Micro holds a global distribution network of about 140,000 providers in over 130 countries.[10] Technology that improves sales and distribution capability is helping to level the playing field for smaller competitors.

CHANNEL ORGANIZATION AND FUNCTIONS

CONVENTIONAL CHANNEL SYSTEM

A channel system in which efforts to coordinate the actions of channel members are seen as unimportant.

In a **conventional channel system,** efforts to coordinate actions are seen as unimportant by channel members. Loosely aligned and relatively autonomous manufacturers, wholesalers, and retailers bargain aggressively with one another over each transaction.[11] Once a deal is reached, there is not much concern about what others in the channel are doing. Most giftware, furniture, and motion pictures move through conventional channels, where channel members tend to follow traditions.

VERTICAL MARKETING SYSTEM (VMS)

A system in which channel members emphasize coordination of behaviors and programs.

In contrast, **vertical marketing systems (VMS)** are networks that emphasize channel coordination. VMS have grown in importance over the past two decades. More and more companies realize that customer satisfaction is impossible without efficient and effective distribution. There are three types of VMS: administered, contractual, and corporate.

ADMINISTERED CHANNEL SYSTEM

A vertical marketing system in which channel members devote effort to coordinating their relationships.

Administered Channel Systems   Members of an **administered channel system** coordinate with others in the channel and facilitate activities. Marketing programs, such as cooperative advertising and sales training, are developed and offered to channel members.[12] Black & Decker, General Electric, and Sealy (the mattress company) are among the manufacturers known for their administered channel systems. Wal-Mart has invested heavily in coordinating relationships with its suppliers. The Internet has opened new selling spaces in which companies and wholesalers can develop strong relationships, such as the shopping sites in Yahoo! or America Online. When channel members have roles that are rather complex and challenging, greater coordination is needed.

CONTRACTUAL CHANNEL SYSTEM

A vertical marketing system in which relationships among channel members are formalized in some fashion, often with a written contract.

Contractual Channel Systems   In a **contractual channel system,** relationships are formalized, often with a written contract. Retail cooperatives, wholesaler-sponsored voluntary chains, and franchises are three common forms.

RETAIL COOPERATIVE

An alliance of small retailers for wholesaling purposes.

Retail Cooperatives A **retail cooperative** unites a group of small retailers into a wholesaling operation to increase buying power. Compare a hardware retailer who buys 20 Black & Decker power drills a year to 100 stores that buy 2,000. Obviously, the group will have more clout in bargaining on price. Ace Hardware and SERVISTAR are examples. Retail cooperatives also are common in the grocery industry, such as Associated Grocers and Topco Associates.

WHOLESALER-SPONSORED VOLUNTARY CHAIN

A group of retailers that have been united by a wholesaler.

Wholesaler-Sponsored Voluntary Chains In a **wholesaler-sponsored voluntary chain,** a wholesaler takes the initiative to unite a group of retailers. Typically, the wholesaler remains under private rather than cooperative ownership.[13] Again, enhanced buying power is the main objective. Such channels are prominent in the automotive accessory market (Western Auto), the grocery trade (Independent Grocers Alliance, Red and White, and Super Value), and the hardware arena (Pro, Sentry). More than 3,000 independent drugstores are aligned with McKesson Drug Co., a wholesaler of pharmaceuticals and health care products, under the Valu-Rite name. McKesson Drug Co. is the largest in the United States; it captured 17 percent of the market in 1999, which was more than any other company.[14]

FRANCHISE SYSTEM

A type of distribution channel in which the franchiser holds the product trademark and licenses it to franchisees who contract to meet certain obligations.

Franchise Systems In a **franchise system,** a formal contract ties the franchiser to franchisees. The franchiser holds the product trademark and licenses it to franchisees. They pay royalty fees and promise to conform to standards and guidelines laid out in the contractual agreement. This usually covers such issues as the fees required, rights and responsibilities of both parties, transfer of the franchise, and grounds for termination.

There are two types of franchise systems. In product and trade-name franchising, the franchisee acquires some of the identity of the franchiser. Automobile dealerships, gasoline stations, motorcycle dealerships, and soft-drink bottlers are a few examples. Business format franchising involves not only the product and trademark but also the entire business concept—marketing, strategy, training, merchandising, and operating procedures.[15] This is especially prevalent in the service arena: fast-food restaurants (McDonald's and Burger King), hotels and motels (Holiday Inn), diet programs (Nutri-Systems), real estate (Century 21), travel services (Uniglobe), and vehicle rental (Hertz).

About 600,000 franchise outlets in the United States account for more than $800 billion in annual sales.[16] About 50 percent of all U.S. retail sales flow through a franchise system. Business format franchising is growing at a phenomenal rate. U.S. franchisers have been particularly successful in establishing indirect channels in global markets. For example, Coca-Cola gets 64 percent of its beverage profits from overseas, where it commands a three-to-one market share lead over Pepsi. The main reason is its long relationships with independent franchised bottlers in each market, who buy the syrup concentrate and then carbonate, package, and sell the product to retailers. Coke's new breed of regional intermediaries, called anchor bottlers, have deep local ties, huge capital budgets, and finely tuned distribution systems.[17] On a broader scale, McDonald's has developed an excellent program for recruiting and developing a diverse mix of franchisees. See the diversity feature, "McDonald's: Serving Diverse Communities in More Ways Than One."

Corporate Channel System   In a **corporate channel system,** the corporation runs and operates organizations at other levels in the channel. It is very similar to a direct channel, and great emphasis is placed on coordinating activities. Examples are Goodyear, Hart, Shaffner & Marx, Sherwin-Williams, and Tandy, which operate such systems in whole or in part.[18]

Channel Functions   Channel functions are the tasks that must be performed within a distribution system to facilitate sales with ultimate customers. Common channel functions are illustrated in Figure 12.3, broken down into four categories: selling, financing, order management, and postsales service.

Based on the nature of the target market and products, the company must determine the functions to be performed in the channel. For example, Timex does not have to worry much about the product repair function, since its watches are priced so low that customers merely discard them once they stop working. Rolex, in contrast, must ensure that customers have access to reliable repair services.

Distribution Intensity   **Distribution intensity** refers to the number of locations through which a company sells its products in a given market area.[19] There are three strategic options.

CONNECTED: SURFING THE NET

www.wal-mart.com

Learn more about Wal-Mart's relationships with suppliers by visiting the company's Web site. And stop by its virtual store, where you'll find everything from music to automotive, lawn and garden, jewelry, and pet products.

CORPORATE CHANNEL SYSTEM
A vertical marketing system in which a company owns and operates organizations at other levels in the channel.

DISTRIBUTION INTENSITY
The number of locations through which a company sells its product in a given market area.

Selling
- Advertising
- Generating leads
- Qualifying leads
- Personal selling (face-to-face)
- Personal selling (over the phone)
- Customer education

Financing
- Offering credit
- Collecting accounts receivable

Order Management
- Holding inventory
- Transmitting and entering orders
- Screening and prioritizing orders
- Filling orders
- Invoicing
- Loading
- Delivering

Postsales Service
- Training in product use
- Installing
- Assisting with applications
- Handling product returns
- Repairing product

FIGURE 12.3 *Common Channel Functions*

Maybelline utilizes an intensive distribution system.

Intensive distribution uses many outlets in each geographical area. **Selective distribution** uses several outlets per area. **Exclusive distribution** uses only one outlet in each trading area.

The choice is driven to some extent by the nature of the product. Many consumer and business-to-business products are relatively low price and are purchased frequently, requiring little value-added activity in the channel. Commonly referred to as convenience goods, they require intensive distribution.[20] Numerous sales outlets per trade area will minimize travel time and acquisition costs for customers. Examples are most brands of coffee, detergent, chewing gum, motor oil, soft drinks, and toilet tissue. Other products, referred to as shopping goods, require some search on the part of the customer. Different brands are compared on price, quality, and other features at the time of purchase. Selective distribution is appropriate for these goods, which include bicycles, cameras, and motorcycles. Finally, specialty goods have unique qualities that induce high customer loyalty. Since people are willing to exert considerable effort to seek out and purchase them, exclusive distribution can be used. Luxury items and top-of-the-line cosmetics are examples.

The brand strategy of the company also will influence the decision. As Figure 12.4 indicates, different brands of the same product can have widely differing distribution patterns. Brands positioned for high quality and price, and requiring significant value-added activity in the channel, require more selective distribution to protect them against rampant price competition.[21] Generally, the more prestigious the brand, the fewer the number of outlets used by the manufacturer.

When a company uses independent wholesalers and retailers in its channel system, selective and especially exclusive distribution breeds considerable loyalty. For example, Caterpillar uses only 80 dealers in North America and about 200 worldwide. Some dealers have two or three entire states as their exclusive domain. They are like extensions of Caterpillar, willing to support the company in any way they can.

Companies that use independent intermediaries must be careful in moving from a selective to a more intensive strategy. The loyalty of traditional channel members can quickly vanish. For example, Vidal Sassoon hair care products used to be distributed only in beauty salons. When the company decided to distribute through major supermarket and drugstores,

Product Category	Exclusive-Selective Distribution	Intensive Distribution
Bicycles	Cannondale Kestral Klein	Huffy Murray Ross
Cameras	Hasselblad Leica Rolleiflex	Minolta Pentax Polaroid
Golf equipment	Callaway Power Bilt Taylor Made	Dunlop Spalding Wilson
Hair care products	Joico Matrix Paul Mitchell	Clairol Helene Curtis Vidal Sassoon
Stereo speakers	Audiophile N.E.A.R Theil	Advent Bose KLH
Pet food	IAMS Nutro Science Diet	Alpo Friskies Purina
Ski equipment	Lacroix OTA Wolf	K2 Rossignol Solomon
Watches	Ebel Rolex Toumeau	Bulova Citizen Timex

FIGURE 12.4 *Variation in Distribution Intensity Across Brands*

Source: Gary Frazier, consulting project in conjunction with Economic Analysis Corporation, Century City, California, conducted in 1995.

the salons dropped the line in a flash.[22] Similarly, when Gitano Group made its jeans and sportswear available to discount stores such as Wal-Mart and Kmart, full-priced retailers no longer wanted to carry the line for fear of hurting their store image.[23] Recently, Calvin Klein sued licensee Warnaco for selling goods bearing his name to discount outlets such as Costco; he was trying to prevent his own brand from being devalued in a similar fashion.[24] Also, wider distribution is likely to increase price competition and, thus, reduce profit margins of current channel members.

CONNECTING WITH DIVERSITY

McDonald's: Serving Diverse Communities in More Ways Than One

 During the Los Angeles riots in spring 1992, one company remained untouched. Of the 30 McDonald's restaurants located in the inner city, not one was torched. "We were spared—if we can use that term—because of our involvement in the community," said Leighton Hull, owner-operator of two McDonald's in the Lynwood section of Los Angeles. "The folks know we're involved in the community. To them, we aren't the guys who just take the money and leave."

Founder Ray Kroc said that owner-operators should reflect the diversity of the communities in which they do business; he even insisted that all restaurants and company officials participate in community affairs. Since that time, McDonald's has gained kudos for effectively bringing in minorities and women at all levels. Those two groups account for 25 percent of franchisees. McDonald's also has a program that encourages select managers to buy franchises for less than one-third of the usual start-up cost of around $610,000. Many in the program are minorities. In fact, McDonald's has the best record in the fast-food industry for helping African Americans advance. In many black neighborhoods, overwhelmed by crime and poverty, fast-food restaurants have emerged as one of the more stable institutions, offering jobs and role models.

Continued

A case in point is Phil Hagans, who started by flipping burgers at a Houston McDonald's and eventually realized his goal of owning a franchise—now two—in his old neighborhood. When he was promoted to manager, Hagans spurred sales in ways a white manager in the same neighborhood might never have done. He doubled sales by hiring a gospel group to serenade black churchgoers while eating Egg McMuffins® on Sunday morning. The gospel breakfast became so popular that local ministers complained their parishioners were showing up late for church. To avoid upsetting these powerful community leaders, Hagans moved the gospel sessions to Sunday afternoon. In 1992 he bought his first franchise, and he's planning a third. The days of buying furniture one piece at a time are over—Hagans now pulls in six figures.

In 2000, Livia Combs became the first Hispanic woman in the nation to reach the position of regional manager. Combs oversees restaurants with sales that total almost $400 million. Her focus is on career planning and advancement of her employees. She wants to eliminate the perception that there are no opportunities for advancement at McDonald's. Combs says, "I tell them to get a development plan, that they need to grow their skills and competencies. Then they take ownership and responsibility for their careers."

Clearly, businesses can thrive in the inner city when they capitalize on the strengths of community members and give neighborhood youth role models with whom they can identify.

Sources: Charlene Marmer Solomon, "McDonald's Links Franchisees to the Community," *Personnel Journal,* March 1993, pp. 61–64; Jonathan Kaufman, "A McDonald's Owner Becomes a Role Model for Black Teenagers," *Wall Street Journal,* August 23, 1995, pp. A1, A6; Barbara Robie, "The Women Behind McDonald's," *New York Times,* March 27, 1994, p. F23; careers page on McDonald's Web site, www.mcdonalds.com, November 16, 1996; and Harriet Johnson Brackey, "Hispanic Woman Reaches Regional Manager of South Florida McDonald's," *The Miami Herald,* February 8, 2000, ptg.djnr.com.

MANAGING DISTRIBUTION CHANNELS

MANAGING CHANNEL RELATIONSHIPS: A STRATEGIC APPROACH

Companies must think strategically about relationships with intermediaries. Guidelines for channel management are outlined in Figure 12.5. Interdependence, trust, and support are prerequisites.

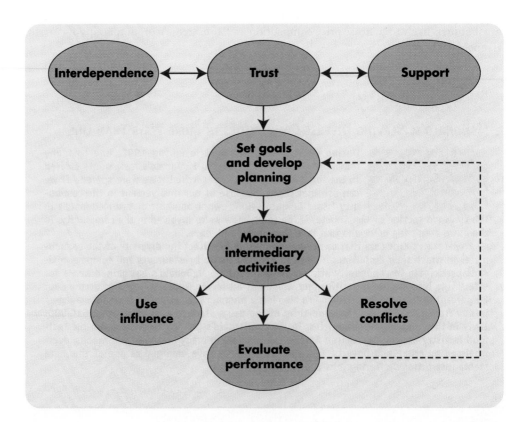

FIGURE 12.5 *A Process for Managing Channel Relationships*

Interdependence   Each channel member depends to some degree on other channel members to achieve desired goals.[25] This need is high when a large amount of a channel member's sales and profits can be attributed to the arrangement.[26] High interdependence means that each has the potential to influence the decisions of another.[27] Gaining attention and support is easier in that case because each party has a vested interest in continuing the relationship. Procter & Gamble and Wal-Mart have a highly dependent relationship, and both commit considerable effort and resources to ensuring that it works smoothly.[28] Sunbeam Corporation recently agreed to license its trademark to other corporations that manufacture complementary goods. For example, Elrene Home Fashions has received a license to manufacture BBQ Textiles, which complement Sunbeam's Grillmaster Kitchen. This licensing to manufacture complementary items requires a high degree of joint planning. Sunbeam also agreed to help these companies with advertising and retail planning.[29]

When a channel relationship is unbalanced, the firm that is less dependent has a power advantage. If the producer has the advantage, then the intermediary is likely to be very receptive to its salespeople and their plans. In the semiconductor industry, Intel has that kind of power over wholesalers such as Arrow Electronics and Hamilton-Hallmark. Sometimes the intermediary is in the driver's seat. Royal Appliance, a small manufacturer, has 27 percent of its sales in Wal-Mart stores and 16 percent in Kmart stores.[30] No doubt, Royal is very concerned about satisfying the desires of Wal-Mart and Kmart management.

When dependence is low for all parties, each lacks power in the channel relationship. All are unconcerned about the others and offer little or no support. Therefore, producers need to establish channel systems in which the dependence of associated firms is reasonably high.

Trust   Another important factor in channel relationships is trust, or confidence in the reliability and integrity of channel members.[31] High trust is the belief that words and promises can be relied upon. It makes the coordination of channel relationships much easier. The credibility of information exchanged need not be questioned. For example, Wal-Mart agreed to share point-of-sale information with VF Corporation, a leading manufacturer of jeans, because it trusted the company.[32]

Lack of trust creates serious problems. Intentions and basic honesty are likely to be questioned. Recently, Anthony Conza, a cofounder of Astor Restaurant Group, discovered he was losing the trust of many of his 600 Blimpie franchisees. He responded by improving communications. He established a franchisee advisory council, a newsletter called *No Baloney News,* and a toll-free hot line for franchisees. These changes increased trust—as well as sales growth and franchisee satisfaction.[33] Other franchise organizations use special incentives to build good relationships with franchisees; Cendant, owner of Travelodge, offers franchisees low-interest loans to improve properties in the effort to keep the franchises' quality high.[34]

Support   A company may lack power with an intermediary because of low dependence, but it can grab attention with the right kind of support. Cooperative advertising is a common means. The producer reimburses intermediaries for expenses when they submit proof of the ad along with media invoices. Usually, certain standards must be met. For example, motorcycle manufacturers do not reimburse dealers if ads mention more than one brand.[35] For eligible ads, half the expense is normally reimbursed, although limits are set on the amount per year, which are ordinarily based on the intermediary's percentage of annual sales for a product. Many manufacturers supply prepared advertising material to ensure quality.

Market development funds may be provided to intermediaries for general promotion purposes, such as brochures, mailings, and training related to a product. Even laptop computers for salespeople may qualify.[36] Again, the amount made available is usually based on the percentage of company sales the intermediary contributes.

Incentive programs offer special rewards for extraordinary commitment and effort in selling the company's products. These are often referred to as spiffs. For example, NEC of Wood Dale, Illinois, ran a 1996 spiff program for its MultiSynch XV17 computer monitor by offering wholesaler salespeople $25 for every unit sold and covering the freight charges.[37] The company DirecTV has exclusive contracts with retailers such as Best Buy and Circuit City to carry only the satellite equipment made by DirecTV's equipment partner, Thompson Consumer Electronics. DirecTV also has exclusive contracts with the NFL and NBA to distribute their games over DirecTV's service.[38]

Another form of support is to invite intermediaries to sales conferences to mingle and attend sessions devoted to new products or marketing techniques. Although some business is conducted at these events, the main purpose is to socialize and build personal relationships. As another way to foster goodwill, many companies help fund sales conferences sponsored by intermediaries. Support also may be offered through inventory management and sales training programs, hot lines, and toll-free numbers.

Goal Setting and Planning   Channel management is facilitated when members meet formally to set joint goals and develop plans for the coming year. This works best when interdependence and trust are high. During these sessions, intermediaries make a commitment to a set of goals, often including accounts and products that will get special emphasis. Specific business plans are developed regarding the activities and investments intermediaries will make to help achieve the goals. At the same time, the producer agrees to assist intermediaries through support programs and marketing efforts.

A number of companies use this approach. Honeywell's Home and Business Control division, now a part of General Electric, has a group of loyal wholesalers, many of whom are former Honeywell employees. The planning sessions are truly joint, with confidential information on new products and company strategy shared with the wholesalers. As a result, they are truly committed to the goals and business plans developed during such meetings.[39] Procter & Gamble has more than 100 sales teams that work with major wholesale and retail accounts. A key part of their mission is to reach agreement on goals and plans with these intermediaries.[40] The division of Texas Instruments that sells laptop computers and printers takes special steps. At the beginning of each year, sales personnel meet at headquarters with the top management of intermediaries to set goals and develop plans. Then other sales personnel visit individual branch managers to communicate the goals and plans and discuss how they might be fine-tuned.[41]

Monitoring Intermediary Activities   Once the business plan is in place, company sales personnel must keep abreast of the marketing and selling efforts of each intermediary. Deviations from the plan must be noted. How well the intermediary is doing in reaching the goals established must be constantly evaluated.

For example, McDonald's has company personnel visit franchisee locations and order food as a regular customer. They rate the facility on a variety of dimensions, including friendliness of the staff, quality of the food, and cleanliness. Similarly, Holiday Inn evaluators stay overnight and rate performance. Monitoring such as this gives a company leverage in channel relationships.

Conflict Resolution   Channel conflict occurs when members disagree about the course of their relationship. It often arises due to business pressures, policy changes, and the use of coercion. For example, Motorola suffered a drop in market share in cellular phones due to intense competition from European competitors, such as Finland's Nokia and Sweden's LM Ericsson. It insisted that wholesalers carry its full line before being allowed to sell StarTac, its hot new miniature. This caused a minor rebellion among some intermediaries.[42] The Video One Buying Group recently refused to follow Universal Studios Home Video's instructions and buy VHS and DVD products only from Ingram Entertainment; Video One felt that its provider of choice, Flash Electronics, could provide all of the Universal Studios titles more quickly than Ingram.[43] Selling products on the Internet has also caused channel conflicts; Rubbermaid no longer sells its products on its own Web site because retailers threatened to pull the company's products off their shelves in retaliation.[44]

Unilever Group's Elizabeth Arden division planned a September 1995 launch of Elizabeth Taylor's Black Pearls fragrance. In late summer, it began an elaborate $12 million ad campaign, featuring a blitz of 42 million scent strips and black-and-white print ads with Ms. Taylor immersed in what the company called a Tahitian lagoon. Suddenly the launch was canceled because such major department stores as Dillard's, Federated, and May refused to carry the perfume. They were retaliating against a decision by Arden's president a month earlier to cut the amount contributed to sales force salaries in cosmetic departments from 5 to 3 percent of retail sales.[45]

Some conflict is inevitable. Channel members recognize that some policies will not be changed, as in the case of Motorola, and get on with their business. Sometimes company sales personnel can help by explaining policies to intermediaries. In other cases, companies recognize they made a mistake and try to correct it. Arden's president left soon after the failed launch, the company restored the 5 percent, and Black Pearls was introduced in 1996 with some success.

U.S. antitrust laws and other regulations designed to promote competition and consumer welfare affect distribution practices. Legislation in other countries varies widely.

Resale Price Maintenance Resale price maintenance is an attempt by companies to compel channel members to charge certain prices. The practice is illegal when title to the product changes hands. Since wholesalers and retailers normally purchase the products they sell, they can charge any price they choose. If manufacturers cross the line between persuasion and coercion, then legal problems can arise. For example, a manufacturer should never threaten to take a product line away if prices are not raised.

Collusion among channel members to pressure a wholesaler or retailer to charge higher prices is against the law. Therefore, company personnel should never consult with channel members to find out whether any are discounting prices. They also should not solicit the support of intermediaries in persuading another channel member to maintain a certain price level.

Differential Pricing and Support Programs A company must give prices and support programs on proportionally equal terms to competing channel members unless two conditions are met. First, a price differential is justified if it costs less to serve one channel member versus another. Costs are usually lower in dealing with large distributors and retailers due to economies of scale. Therefore, quantity discounts are justified. Second, variations are legal if they are required to meet a competitive offer.

Companies can provide differential pricing and support programs to intermediaries who are not in competition. For example, a computer manufacturer can charge one price to a local wholesaler in San Diego and another to a local wholesaler in Seattle. Whether this makes good business sense is another matter.

Territorial and Customer Constraints A territorial constraint exists when a company assigns an intermediary a specific geographic area in which to sell its products. That is, it can sell there but nowhere else. Such constraints are legal, as they are seen as protecting the investment of all neighboring intermediaries who sell the company's products.

A class-of-customer constraint is a company limit on the customer groups to which an intermediary can sell its product. For example, a manufacturer of medical equipment may direct a wholesaler to sell to physicians and nursing homes in New York City but not to hospitals. This constraint is illegal, as the courts have found that it limits competition and harms consumer welfare. A company is allowed to suggest that an intermediary focus on certain targets: "We are looking for you to cover primarily these customer groups."

Exclusive Dealing **Exclusive dealing** occurs when a company restricts intermediaries from carrying competitive lines. Such constraints are legal, unless they are proved to be a substantial limit on competition in the marketplace. Furthermore, terminating intermediaries for failure to perform can be difficult if exclusive dealing is a requirement. The intermediary may have passed up opportunities to add other lines and may be very dependent on the channel relationship as a result.

Tying Arrangements and Full-Line Forcing A **tying arrangement** exists when a company conditions the purchase of a superior product on the purchase of a second and less desirable product. For example, a copier company may refuse to sell a high-quality machine unless the customer buys a service agreement. Such arrangements are illegal.

Full-line forcing occurs when a company requires intermediaries to carry and sell its complete line. This practice has been generally upheld in the courts, especially when it is common within an industry. It may be challenged, however, if it entails quantities to be purchased and inventory levels to be maintained. It also may be challenged as an illegal tying arrangement if it involves unrelated product lines.

Intermediary Termination In many channel systems, agreements commonly allow either party to terminate the relationship with 30 days' notice. In franchise systems, contracts are more complex. Whatever the case, companies need to document the reasons for termination. Usually, the intermediary fails to meet standards or is a poor credit risk. The termination may be challenged if based on intermediary noncompliance with illegal restraints on trade.

Ease of termination varies considerably by state. Wisconsin has a very strict law. If a company's product comprises 12 percent or more of an intermediary's sales volume, then

EXCLUSIVE DEALING
Restricting intermediaries from carrying competitive lines.

TYING ARRANGEMENT
The purchase of a superior product is conditioned on the purchase of a second product of lower quality.

FULL-LINE FORCING
Requiring intermediaries to carry and sell the company's complete line.

the company cannot terminate it. This has led many manufacturers to establish direct channels in Wisconsin, though they generally use indirect channels elsewhere.[46]

Ethics   It is illegal for companies to impose certain constraints on channel members. Other practices may not be against the law but are ethically questionable. For example, franchisers often confront the issue of how close to place outlets. Market coverage improves with a greater number, but existing franchisees may be hurt. They have committed time and money to building their business, and they do not want to be crowded out by competition from their own company.[47]

Another ethical issue arises when companies set territorial constraints and then choose to ignore them. They lack the courage to confront large intermediaries for selling outside their assigned territory. Such intermediaries often claim they will drop the product line and switch to competitors if they cannot broaden their market area.

Certain intermediaries abuse the use of market development funds. Industry analysts believe that some commonly charge about 10 to 15 percent above actual cost. Some companies go too far, however. The U.S. unit of Bayer AG was recently convicted of overcharging Medicaid for certain medications. The company was reporting inflated prices to make the drugs more attractive to doctors receiving reimbursements.[48]

Every company must take a deep look at itself. Competitive pressures aside, what is good, ethical business practice and what is not must be carefully spelled out to all employees. Companies must recognize that short-term sales increases make no sense if they weaken existing channel members. And policies must be enforced. To maintain the integrity of the entire channel system, violators must be terminated.

WHOLESALING

Wholesaling affects our lives every day, but we rarely notice. We may buy aspirin at Good Neighbor retail pharmacies, not knowing it was purchased from Bergen Brunswig Corporation, a large pharmaceutical wholesaler. We order a pepperoni pizza at a small neighborhood restaurant, not knowing most of the ingredients were acquired from SYSCO, a large wholesaler of food products, or FoodGalaxy.com, a new Web marketplace that allows independent restaurants to buy their supplies online.[49] Parents in Europe shop in retail stores for X-men action figures by Toy Biz, a U.S. company with a licensing agreement from Marvel Comics, not knowing the retailers acquired them through European toy wholesalers. Toy Biz recently received the rights to market toys based on the *Lord of the Rings* movies, set to come out in 2001 to 2003; wholesalers will distribute these toys internationally as well.[50] Most of us never see these intermediaries, but they are very important to us.

Many wholesalers are relatively small, filling a certain niche. Others are multibillion-dollar companies serving global markets. Wholesalers help thousands of companies connect with millions of customers. Whatever their size or scope, they all face competition. Their ability to make decisions about target markets, service level, pricing, business locations, merchandise assortment, credit management, use of technology, and image will influence their survival.

Wholesaling is selling goods for resale or use to retailers and other businesses. Producers have a number of options in making sales to retailers and other businesses, including company-owned sales branches, brokers, and wholesalers. The focus of this chapter is on the latter.

As mentioned earlier in the chapter, a wholesaler is an intermediary that takes title to the products it carries and makes a majority of sales to retailers or other businesses. Many wholesalers make no sales directly to consumers. For others, these sales may be a significant part of revenue. For example, Smart and Final, Inc., sells food products and related merchandise to small businesses and consumers. Since more than half of its sales come from small businesses, it is classified as a wholesaler. A pure wholesaler organization does not manufacture any goods.

THE IMPORTANCE OF WHOLESALERS

Wholesalers play an important role in the economy. The roughly 375,000 such organizations in the United States employ approximately 4 million people. Annual sales approach $2 trillion.[51] Wholesalers are prominent in a wide variety of product categories, including beverages, climate control equipment, computer hardware and software, electrical products, electronic components, fabrics, flowers and florist supplies, food, giftware, medical supplies, movies,

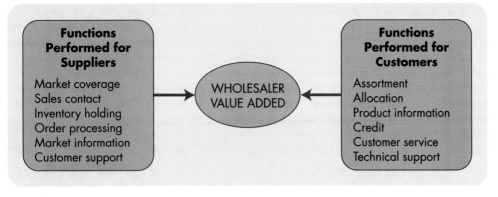

FIGURE 12.6 *Wholesalers Add Value for Suppliers and Customers by Performing Important Channel Functions*

Source: Adapted from Bert Rosenbloom, *Marketing Functions and the Wholesaler-Distributor* (Washington, DC: Distribution Research and Education Foundation, 1987), p. 26.

pharmaceuticals, telecommunications, tools, and toys. They provide value to customers and suppliers, as depicted in Figure 12.6. We will also see that they provide value for one another.

For wholesalers of consumer goods, the primary customers are retailers and service businesses, such as restaurants, hospitals, and nursing homes. In business-to-business markets, the primary customers are manufacturing organizations and service firms, such as accountants or contractors.

Wholesalers are important for product assortment and allocation. They fulfill their **assortment** function by purchasing merchandise from a variety of suppliers for resale. This makes available in one place a range of products so customers do not have to shop at many locations. They fulfill their **allocation** function by purchasing large quantities to resell in smaller amounts. This means savings for customers in both purchase price and storage costs. In essence, wholesalers make a wide variety of goods available in amounts that can be afforded and handled effectively.

Wholesalers also perform other functions, depending on customer needs. They may provide credit, education on product benefits, training in product use, and technical assistance. Hamilton-Hallmark recently opened a Technical Support Center near Phoenix staffed by electrical engineers. Customers call an 800 number if they have questions about specific applications for semiconductors.[52]

Wholesalers are needed because small or medium-sized companies in many industries cannot buy directly from manufacturers. Either direct channels are unavailable or minimum orders are too large. For example, approximately 100,000 original equipment manufacturers (OEMs) in the United States purchase semiconductors to incorporate into products such as automobiles, computers, televisions, and videocassette recorders. Roughly 96,000 of these buy from wholesalers such as Arrow Electronics, Hamilton-Hallmark, and Wyle Laboratories because manufacturers cannot afford to serve them directly.[53]

career tip Arrow Electronics says: "As our company continues to grow, we encourage qualified applicants to explore the opportunities, training programs, and career rewards available within the Arrow family." Various kinds of positions are available in five North American operating groups. For example, at Gates/Arrow Distributing, asset managers play an important role in processing daily buys, managing stock, maintaining proper inventory levels, and acting as a frontline contact for the sales department. To learn more, visit Arrow's career page at www.arrow.com/www/career_opportunities/index.html.

Some believe that wholesalers only add to the price of goods. Actually, their price is lower than what individual manufacturers would have to charge on most orders if they were made directly. Wholesalers get a discount for buying in quantity, and part of that is passed on to consumers. Furthermore, overhead is normally lower for wholesalers than for manufacturers. Therefore, wholesalers can serve small or medium-sized companies and still make a profit, whereas most manufacturers cannot.

Wholesalers often do business with one another. Sometimes this is just a matter of courtesy. A wholesaler may need a Black & Decker power drill for an important customer and can get it most quickly by calling a nearby wholesaler. In other cases, the transactions are systematic. Small wholesalers may find it easier to do business with large wholesalers than with

ASSORTMENT

A wholesaler function that entails selling a range of merchandise from a variety of sources.

ALLOCATION

A wholesaler function that entails purchasing products in large quantities and reselling them in smaller quantities.

manufacturers. As a result, in a number of industries other wholesalers are a primary target market. For example, Distributoys.com has established itself as a smaller wholesaler on the Web. The company relies on the larger wholesaler, MW Kasch, for its inventory. Smaller shops that cannot purchase in large quantities and, therefore, cannot buy from MW Kasch can go to Distributoys.com and order their inventories in smaller quantities.[54]

Master distributors are wholesaling companies given the right by manufacturers to develop certain geographical areas and recruit other distributors. These, in turn, are called subdistributors. All sales to subdistributors go through the master distributor. The system is often used by manufacturers entering a global market, especially if they lack the resources to serve it directly. Joico, Inc., a Los Angeles–based manufacturer of high-quality hair products, uses independently owned Joico-Canada, located in Vancouver, British Columbia, as its master distributor.[55]

TYPES OF WHOLESALERS

FULL-SERVICE WHOLESALER

An intermediary who performs a wide range of functions or tasks for its customers.

LIMITED-SERVICE WHOLESALER

An intermediary who performs only some of the traditional channel functions, either eliminating others or passing them on to someone else.

CONNECTED: SURFING THE NET

www.sysco.com

SYSCO is a general line wholesaler that serves approximately 260,000 operations. Visit the site of the largest marketer and distributor of food service products in North America to learn more.

Full-service wholesalers perform a wide range of tasks for their customers. **Limited-service wholesalers** provide only some of the traditional channel functions, either eliminating others entirely or passing them on to someone else to perform. Within each category, several types of wholesalers can be identified. Figure 12.7 summarizes the functions performed by different types of wholesalers.

Full-Service Wholesalers **General Line Wholesalers** carry a wide variety of products and provide a full range of services. Bosler Supply of Chicago and W. W. Grainger are good examples. They stock thousands of different industrial products, provide technical advice on product applications, and expedite shipments when necessary. Another example is SYSCO, which sells a broad array of frozen, dry, and refrigerated products to the food industry. It can provide special packaging and delivery schedules. Its cruise ship customers, for example, can receive plastic-wrapped pallets of food at any time of day or night.

Specialty Wholesalers Specialty wholesalers focus on a narrow range of products, carry them in great depth, and provide extensive services. Ryerson is the largest metals wholesaler in the world, with 50 distribution centers across the United States. It performs a variety of specialized services for customers, such as cutting metals to specification.[56] Ingram-Micro and Tech Data focus on computer hardware and software products, while providing many customer services.

Rack Jobbers Rack jobbers, who sell single product lines to retail stores on consignment, set up product displays and keep them stocked with goods. Retailers pay for the goods only after they are sold to consumers. L'eggs pantyhose are distributed this way. Rack jobbers are common in the music industry. They have had to take back new albums with offensive language. For example, Wal-Mart learned of a Sheryl Crow lyric suggesting that it sold guns to children and pulled the album from the shelves.[57]

Limited-Service Wholesalers **Cash-and-Carry Wholesalers** Cash-and-carry wholesalers are located near customers. They do not extend credit and do not use an outside sales force.

Type of Wholesaler	Personal Selling	Carry Inventory	Product Delivery	Offer Credit	Specialized Services
Full Service					
General line	yes	yes	yes	yes	yes
Specialty	yes	yes	yes	yes	yes
Rack jobbers	yes	yes	yes	yes	yes
Limited Service					
Cash and carry	yes	yes	no	no	no
Drop shippers	yes	no	no	yes	no
Truck jobbers	yes	yes	yes	no	no
Mail order	no	yes	no	sometimes	no

FIGURE 12.7 *Functions Performed by Different Wholesalers*

Rack jobbers set up product displays for L'eggs pantyhose and keep them stocked with goods.

Customers perform certain functions for themselves, such as bagging their own goods and delivery. Costs are tightly controlled in order to offer excellent prices.

Drop Shippers Drop shippers arrange for shipments directly from the manufacturer to the customer. They do not physically handle the goods but take title to them, assuming all associated risks (such as damage and theft) while in transit. They do offer credit terms. Drop shippers are prominent in the lumber, chemicals, and petroleum industries, where goods are bulky and sold in large quantity.

Truck Jobbers Truck jobbers specialize in the speedy delivery of perishables or semiperishables, such as candy, bakery goods, fresh fruits, potato chips, and tobacco products. They use their own vehicles and offer virtually all services except credit. They focus on smaller customers that full-service wholesalers tend to ignore.

Mail-Order Wholesalers Mail-order wholesalers sell through catalogs distributed to retailers and other businesses. They are most popular among small businesses in outlying areas that are not regularly contacted by salespeople. These wholesalers are prominent in the clothing, cosmetics, hardware, office supply, jewelry, sporting goods, and specialty food industries.

WHOLESALING RELATIONSHIPS

Wholesalers are successful to the extent they develop strong customer loyalty. Sometimes relationships with other wholesalers are used to serve their customers. For example, W. W. Grainger has developed alliances with a number of specialty wholesalers. The relationships feature explains Grainger's program and the special efforts of its internal sourcing group to satisfy customer needs.

Developing strong connections with suppliers is also important to more effective and efficient business operations. Southwestern Supply, an industrial products wholesaler in Las Vegas, and Milwaukee Electric Tool, a manufacturer of portable power tools, have developed an outstanding working relationship. Southwestern relies on Milwaukee to develop annual business plans, identify potential customers, develop new marketing strategies, and train its sales force. In exchange, Southwestern employees promote Milwaukee over other brands carried by the company.[58]

The decision to add new suppliers can sometimes alienate current partners. For example, when the Atlanta-based Apex Supply Co. was acquired by Home Depot, Grohe America terminated all sales relationships with Apex Supply. Grohe only sells to wholesalers; when it was bought by Home Depot, Apex no longer fit Grohe's preferred customer base.[59] In such a situation, the wholesaler must weigh the pros and cons to determine which supplier is a better match for the future.

CONNECTING THROUGH RELATIONSHIPS

W. W. GRAINGER'S ALLIANCES WITH SPECIALTY WHOLESALERS

Grainger Integrated Supply Operations (GISO) is a division of W. W. Grainger, a large industrial wholesaler. GISO's goal is to handle the acquisition, materials management, and warehouse activities for major customers through a broad range of maintenance, repair, supply, and operating services. The diverse products it provides customers include forklifts, plastic tubing, oil and grease, electric drills, road salt, and toilet tissue. It takes special requests as well. GISO's primary customers are original equipment manufacturers, such as Caterpillar and General Motors. Whenever possible, GISO fulfills customer orders from its own distribution centers, but it has relationships with a network of independent specialty wholesalers. These wholesalers focus on a narrow line of products, such as janitorial supplies or electrical products.

When GISO receives an order, it immediately checks the central computer to see whether the items are available from one of its distribution centers. If not, then GISO turns to an associated wholesaler, depending on the product and the geographical location of the customer.

Written contracts with each wholesaler specify the products it will supply. GISO pays the wholesaler, immediately upon delivery and then collects from the customers. Strong relationships have developed between GISO and its network members.

When GISO gets an order that cannot be filled by its distribution centers or aligned wholesalers, it turns to its internal sourcing group. The group routinely scours the world to satisfy requests for unusual products and services. For example, ARCO Alaska once requested bear repellent for pipeline workers. GISO's sourcing group found a small manufacturer in a remote part of Alaska. It then determined whether spray or steam applicators would be most useful and what size containers would be most economical. Once these decisions were made, GISO figured out how to get the repellent from the manufacturer to the workers as quickly as possible. Talk about going the extra mile!

W. W. Grainger is now taking advantage of Internet capabilities in its supply chain process by adding another company to Grainger called Find MRO.com. Find MRO.com leads the B-to-B arena by offering procurement solutions for maintenance repair and operating supplies that are typically difficult to find. This company began in November 1999 and offers access to more than 5 million MRO products from over 12,000 suppliers and 100,000 brands. Since 1999 it has been adding about 1,000 new products per day to its database. The purpose of Find MRO is to provide simple integration of many types of e-procurement solutions, ranging from Web portals to enterprise software vendors.

Sources: James Morgan, "Is This the Age of the Super Distributor?" *Modern Distribution Management,* April 10, 1994, pp. 5–7; James Narus and James Anderson, "Rethinking Distribution," *Harvard Business Review* (July–August 1996), p. 116; Grainger's Web site, www.grainger.com, August 15, 1996; "Find MRO.com Offers Strategic Sourcing for Indirect Materials via Commerce One.net™," *PR Newswire,* September 20, 2000; and "Smart Electrical and Graingers, Find MRO.com Join Forces to Offer Enhanced Ordering and Purchasing Capabilities for Electrical Contractors," *Business Wire,* November 13, 2000.

SUPPLY CHAIN MANAGEMENT

Incorporation of all activities concerned with planning, implementation, and control of sourcing, manufacturing, and delivery of products and services.

LOGISTICS

The movement of raw materials, components, and finished products within and between companies.

INTEGRATED LOGISTICS MANAGEMENT

The coordination of all logistical activities in a company.

SUPPLY CHAIN MANAGEMENT, LOGISTICS, AND PHYSICAL DISTRIBUTION

Supply chain management incorporates all of the activities concerned with planning, implementation, and control of sourcing, manufacturing, and delivery for products and services.[60] **Logistics** is the movement of raw materials, components, and finished products within and between companies. Physical distribution is the part of logistics that involves only finished products. **Integrated logistics management** coordinates all parts of the process. If the movement of inputs is not properly managed, then physical distribution to customers will be hindered. Coordination is equally important when goods move between plants, distribution centers, warehouses, wholesalers, and retailers. Supply chain management involves all of these elements as well as development of a network of supply and production organizations. It involves acquiring and moving products, as well as the flow of information about these activities within and across different firms. First, we will discuss supply chain management. We will then cover logistics, particularly integrated logistics management. Finally, we will address physical distribution in detail.

Supply chain management can typically lower a company's costs by 3–7 percent and increase cash flow as much as 30 percent.[61] One important aspect of supply chain management is the development of a supply network. The **supply network** consists of the organizations from which components, semi-finished products, and services are purchased. It is important to develop a network of suppliers that can provide the support required to develop excellent products. Ford has a supply network of more than two thousand companies, not including a large set of independent Ford dealers.

SUPPLY NETWORK

All of the organizations from which components, semi-finished products, and services are purchased.

Firms employ different strategies to obtain a competitive advantage in supply chain management. Many firms form strategic alliances with suppliers and distributors to optimize performance and increase customer satisfaction.[62] Raytheon uses a program to help its suppliers reduce costs and increase efficiency. This may or may not lead to a larger profit margin for Raytheon, but it invariably results in a lower cost for its end customers. This reduction in costs promotes customer loyalty.[63]

Some companies use vertical integration to control the supply chain. **Vertical integration** occurs when the buyer controls or owns the supplier or customer. This allows for great control over the supply chain, but it is expensive and leaves the firm with less flexibility. The automotive companies were vertically integrated in the past but have recently started to spin off different divisions to form new companies. In 1999 General Motors spun off Delphi, the world's largest auto supplier, and in 2000 Ford spun off Visteon, the nation's second largest auto supplier.[64] Now General Motors and Ford have no direct management responsibilities for these spin–offs and as a result are more inclined to source some components from other suppliers. At the same time, in order to achieve objectives, Delphi and Visteon must now aggressively market components to other auto manufacturers such as Volkswagen, Daimler-Chrysler, and Nissan.

VERTICAL INTEGRATION

Ownership or control of suppliers by a buying company.

Figure 12.8 shows supply chain management activities, objectives, and business performance elements. The activities are movement of products and information management. The objectives include increased efficiency and improved customer service. The resulting business performance improvements are described in the four cells.

Activities—Movement of Products and Integration of Information The movement of goods in the supply chain starts with raw materials and ends with the final consumption of the product. An important part of this process is the selection of suppliers. In the case of cereal, the chain would start with the farmer and end with the family that finally consumes the cereal. Information management includes the collection, storage, and processing of data from different departments and across firms to provide real time knowledge of the flow of goods from all sources. It also provides feedback on whether schedules are being met and the types of problems that occur as well as their remedies. This information links all parties; therefore, integration provides consumers with what they want, when they expect it, in a location that is most convenient, and at a reasonable cost.

Supply Chain Management Activities		
	Movement of Products	**Information Management**
Low Cost (Efficiency)	Improved profit	More relevant information which improves coordination and decision making
Customer Service (Effectiveness)	Rapid product delivery which improves customer satisfaction and loyalty	Better understanding of customer needs to satisfy unique customer requirements

Supply Chain Management Objectives

FIGURE 12.8 *Supply Chain Activities, Objectives, and Business Performance Improvements*

Objectives—Efficiency and Customer Service   Better efficiency occurs when unnecessary steps are avoided, delays are eliminated, and the actions of all companies are coordinated at the lowest cost while producing precisely what is intended. Customer service is all of the actions taken to meet customer expectations. This includes rapid and fair care of any problems that might occur. A firm that focuses on customer service will better meet customer needs. The initial increase in costs to the firm to meet those needs will allow the firm to capture greater rewards in the future through customer loyalty.

Business Performance Improvement   Overall there are four types of business performance improvements: decreased costs which improves profit; more relevant information which improves coordination and decision making; rapid product delivery which improves customer satisfaction and loyalty; and better understanding of customer needs to satisfy unique customer requirements.

LOGISTICS

In order to have superior supply chain management, a firm must excel at integrated logistics management.[65] The challenge of integration is to establish effective communications among companies, departments, and people whose decisions affect logistics. Even within the company, there can be problems. Salespeople may be so worried about late deliveries that they pad their forecasts. Concerned about costs, purchasing, and production departments are conservative in their projections. In many companies, the people deepest in the organization and farthest from the customer—production planners—develop the final estimates used to hire workers and build inventory.[66]

Integrated logistics management is only as strong as a company's understanding of its customers and the ability of its people to work together. Cross-functional teams in purchasing, production-warehousing, marketing, and sales often produce excellent results. By sharing information on purchasing, production schedules, marketing and sales plans, customer service standards, and customer preferences, the team can make logistical decisions that are truly integrated and beneficial to the company. Even without teams, integration can occur if communication from and about customers flows throughout the company in the form of market research reports, sales activity, forecasts, and orders. This information can be refined into specific purchasing and manufacturing plans.[67]

PHYSICAL DISTRIBUTION

Physical distribution is the movement of finished products to customers. Although the concept is simple, accomplishing this task effectively and efficiently is often complex. For example, Mattel must process and ship orders for Barbie from its four Asian factories to distribution centers, wholesalers, and retailers in 140 countries around the world.[68]

Although physical distribution obviously plays a dominant role in the operations of any wholesaling organization, it is very important to any company involved in making or selling goods. In fact, when performed well, it can provide a competitive edge.[69] For example, Domino's Pizza, with 1,160 stores in 46 countries, has achieved a leadership position in the pizza industry based on its home delivery capabilities, even while others like Pizza Hut try to emulate it.[70] Based on its strong dealer and physical distribution network, Caterpillar gets repair parts to customers the same day or the next, while it takes competitors like Samsung several days or more.

The primary objective of physical distribution is to get the right products to the right locations at the right times at the lowest total cost. An effective distribution system can contribute to customer satisfaction and, in turn, increased sales revenues. A poor performance will alienate customers, who will switch allegiance to competitors.[71]

Compaq Computer estimates it may have lost up to $1 billion in sales in the early 1990s because its laptops and desktops were not available when and where customers were ready to buy them. The company put renewed emphasis on managing its physical distribution operations with a $100 million reengineering effort. In its 350,000-square-foot Houston distribution center, sophisticated software matches customer orders to inventory on hand. Radio signals tell drivers of Aisle Rangers, the 30-foot-high trucks that run on tracks between shelves in the

Yellow Freight System promotes their excellent capabilities for physical distribution.

warehouse, which items to pick up in filling customer orders. As a result, the company's performance in making products available through approximately 31,000 wholesalers and retailers worldwide has significantly improved.[72]

While revenue generation is important, no less significant is careful control of the costs of processing orders, maintaining warehouses, carrying and handling inventory, and shipping products. Physical distribution can account for up to 40 percent of total cost and more than 25 percent of each sales dollar.[73] Achieving high customer service levels at the expense of company profitability makes no sense. Therefore, physical distribution management involves a delicate balance between effective customer service and efficient operations.

Toyota's Lexus division is an excellent example of striking the right balance. The typical car dealer has more than $200,000 in parts inventory, a heavy financial burden. At the same time, stockouts frequently occur. Understanding this, Lexus designed a system that better serves the company, its dealers, and its customers. Lexus requires dealers to have AS400 computers and satellite dishes that connect them to company headquarters in Torrance, California. Specialized inventory control software helps dealers have the right parts on hand. If an item is unavailable in inventory, then it can be ordered electronically one day and received by air freight the next. Although Lexus dealers have only $100,000 tied up in parts inventory, there are few stockouts, and customer satisfaction levels are higher.[74] The systemwide costs of computers, satellite dishes, software, and air freight are more than offset by lower inventory costs and increased sales through better customer service.

Order Management **Order management** refers to how the company receives, fills, and delivers orders to customers. The design of the physical distribution system—including order processing, warehousing, materials handling, inventory control, and transportation functions—determines how well the company manages orders, as outlined in Figure 12.9. New technologies, such as electronic data interchange and bar coding, have had a remarkable effect on system design, which in turn has improved the effectiveness and efficiency of order management. **Electronic data interchange (EDI)** is an intercompany computer-to-computer exchange of orders and other business documents in standard formats.

ORDER MANAGEMENT
The means by which a company receives, fills, and delivers orders to customers.

ELECTRONIC DATA INTERCHANGE (EDI)
Intercompany computer-to-computer exchange of orders and other business documents in standard formats.

PHYSICAL DISTRIBUTION FUNCTIONS	STEPS IN THE ORDER MANAGEMENT PROCESS
Order processing	Transmitting orders Entering orders Screening orders Prioritizing orders Invoicing orders
Warehousing	Filling orders
Materials handling	Filling orders
Inventory control	Filling orders
Transportation	Shipping orders

FIGURE 12.9 *Order Management*

Customer service standards will have a major bearing on the design of the physical distribution system. Companies that want high marks on order fill rate, order cycle time, delivery reliability, and invoice accuracy must be prepared to invest heavily in network design. Often, managers find they must lower desired standards somewhat because the costs of achieving an ideal level are prohibitive. One approach is to recognize that all customers are not equal. As a general rule, a small percentage of a company's customers, often 20 percent or less, provide over 80 percent of its revenues.[75] Customer service standards can be set higher for the firm's most important customers. Scarce resources can be saved by lowering customer service standards, at least to some extent, with less important customers.

Order Processing   The distribution of products cannot begin until the company receives an order. Order processing includes all the activities and paperwork involved in transmitting and entering, screening and prioritizing, and invoicing orders.

Orders received from customers, channel members, or company personnel are entered into the company's recordkeeping system. Traditionally, salespeople wrote the orders by hand and delivered them to the office in person or by mail, phone, or fax. New technologies have dramatically changed all that. EDI connects many companies directly with customers, who key in the order and submit it electronically. Order cycle time is significantly reduced. Furthermore, since no one has to reenter the information, errors are minimized, and invoice accuracy is improved. Labor and material costs for printing, mailing, and handling paper-based transactions are lower. An EDI system helped Texas Instruments reduce order cycle time by 57 percent, resource requirements by 70 percent, and shipping errors by 95 percent.[76] Companies such as Marshall Industries and Motorola supply their outside salespeople with laptop computers. They can access price information instantly rather than check price lists or call the office. They can enter an order, plug into phone lines, and transmit it electronically. Inside salespeople input telephone orders directly into the system. Order cycle time, invoice errors, and order processing costs are all reduced.

Orders must be screened in terms of the customer's ability to pay. Traditionally, this was done after order entry, but EDI now allows companies to screen orders immediately. For example, Vanstar's system is connected to the banks and flooring companies of its customers. (Flooring companies such as ITT grant credit lines to businesses.) If they place an order that exceeds their bank account or credit line, the order is automatically put on hold. The computer then rechecks the account or credit line twice that day to determine whether sufficient funds have been added. If so, the order is processed. If not, the order remains in limbo.[77]

The telephone-computer technology known as caller ID enables an inside salesperson to know who is calling before picking up the phone.[78] A variety of information about the caller appears on a computer screen, including payment history and credit information. If a problem is apparent, then the salesperson can notify the customer before entering the order. This avoids a good deal of wasted time on everyone's part. After screening, many companies prioritize orders based on the importance of the customer or the order cycle time requested. For example, Vanstar customers can request same-day delivery on orders at a premium price. The computer system transmits these orders to distribution ahead of next-day orders.[79]

Bills are prepared once it is known how much of the order can be filled from available inventory. Today, advanced computer systems keep track of inventory and the latest prices continuously. Invoices are automatically printed out. Order cycle time is reduced, while invoice accuracy is dramatically improved. And interestingly, invoices are becoming a hot promotion tool. They have a 100 percent readership rate, and companies are including special information and offers on them.[80]

Warehousing **Warehousing** is the storage of inventory in the physical distribution system. Many companies perform this function with a mix of distribution centers and warehouses. **Distribution centers** are where the bulk of a company's finished-goods inventory is maintained before being routed to individual sales outlets or customers. These are of two types: **Private warehouses** are owned and operated by the company, and **public warehouses** rent space to store products. Preferences for fixed versus variable costs help determine a company's mix of private and public warehousing.

With technology, many companies can provide better customer service with fewer warehouses. National Semiconductor recently closed six distribution centers around the globe and is air-freighting its microchips to customers from a new, 125,000-square-foot center in Singapore. This has cut standard delivery time 47 percent, reduced distribution costs 2.5 percent, and increased sales by 34 percent.[81] Benetton Group, Italy's integrated fashion manufacturer and retailer, ships 80 million items each year directly to 7,000 stores in 100 countries with an order cycle time of as little as seven days. Most items are sent from a single automated distribution center.[82]

Cross-docking involves sorting and reloading an incoming shipment from a supplier for delivery to customers without its being stored in any warehouse. The method is used most frequently in truck transport. EDI and specialized information systems allow for the close coordination that makes cross-docking efficient. This practice is on the increase because it reduces inventory carrying costs and order cycle time. Furthermore, the fewer times the product is handled, the lower the potential for damage. Compaq, for example, increasingly relies on cross-docking at its Houston distribution center.[83] The technique affects warehousing design: Larger parking lots are needed for transferring products from truck to truck, and buildings are smaller.

Materials Handling **Materials handling** is the moving of products in a warehouse in the process of filling orders. Traditionally, the facility manager would receive the paperwork and assign it to a worker. With a handcart or motorized forklift, the worker would go through the warehouse, picking up products and checking them off on the order forms. If some were unavailable, that would be noted on the form, and a back order would be generated. These were filled and shipped when a new supply arrived.

Bar codes, radio frequency technology, and handheld scanning devices are having a remarkable effect on materials handling. Bar code labels for identification purposes can be placed on everything from cardboard boxes to plywood sheets. Handheld scanners with display panels receive orders directly from the mainframe computer through radio waves and

WAREHOUSING
The storage of inventory in the physical distribution system.

DISTRIBUTION CENTER
A location where inventory is maintained before being routed to individual sales outlets or customers.

PRIVATE WAREHOUSE
A storage facility owned and operated by the company.

PUBLIC WAREHOUSE
A storage facility owned and operated by businesses that rent space.

CROSS-DOCKING
Sorting and loading an incoming shipment from a supplier for delivery to customers without its being stored in any warehouse.

MATERIALS HANDLING
The moving of products in and around a warehouse in the process of filling orders.

Benetton Group ships 80 million items each year directly to 7,000 stores in 100 countries with an order cycle of as little as seven days because most items are sent from a single automated distribution center.

Automated distribution centers reduce errors in filling orders and other cycle times.

guide workers to the appropriate locations. Workers then scan in the bar codes to make sure the right product and quantity are selected. If not, the scanner will beep. Errors and order cycle time are reduced. Back orders are processed much more quickly. This system is a must for any company interested in boosting quality control and customer satisfaction.[84]

INVENTORY CONTROL

Management of stock levels.

Inventory Control   **Inventory control** is the management of stock levels. For each product, company management must decide how much inventory will be carried in each distribution center and warehouse. Carrying too little inventory leads to poor order fill rates, too many back orders, and poor customer service. Carrying too much leads to higher than necessary costs. Many companies fail because they have too much capital tied up in inventory; this reduces cash flow, which means that bills cannot be paid.[85]

Inventory levels are often determined with the help of the ABC classification approach. Stockkeeping units (SKUs) are divided into three categories based on their sales volume and profitability. Inventory levels are kept relatively high for the A category, moderate for B, and relatively low for C. The trap to avoid is a large inventory of less profitable SKUs purchased by fringe or noncore customers.

Part of inventory control is to determine reorder points and order quantities. A reorder point is the inventory level at which a replenishment order is generated. The standard formula is

Reorder point = Demand or usage rate × Order cycle time + Safety stock

In other words, there should be enough inventory to supply customers during the time required to get more stock, plus a margin of safety. More formally, safety stock is the inventory kept on hand in case of forecasting error or delayed delivery of replenishment stock. For example, if the average daily demand rate is 50 units, order cycle time is 4 days, and safety stock is 20 units, then the reorder point is (50 × 4) + 20 = 220 units. Whenever inventory drops to that level, a replenishment order should be made.

ECONOMIC ORDER QUANTITY (EOQ) MODEL

A method of determining the amount of product to be ordered each time.

The **economic order quantity (EOQ) model** is a method for determining how much product to order each time. It compares ordering costs to inventory carrying costs, with the objective of minimizing total costs. The standard formula is:

$$EOQ = \frac{2 \times CO \times D}{CI \times U}$$

where CO = Cost per order

D = Annual sales volume in units

CI = Annual inventory carrying cost

U = Unit cost

The cost per order is calculated by determining purchasing costs, computer costs, and accounts payable costs associated with placing individual orders. Annual inventory carrying costs are calculated by summing expenses associated with warehouse space, insurance, taxes on inventory, obsolescence and shrinkage, materials handling (including wages and equipment), and costs of money invested. The lower the cost per order relative to inventory carrying costs, the lower the order quantity.

The EOQ method should be used only as a guideline. It works particularly well for products with consistent demand patterns throughout the year. For seasonal items or for products on which suppliers give discounts at certain order quantities, EOQ estimates need some adjustment. A just-in-time (JIT) system also skews the EOQ method. In a JIT system the necessary unit is delivered in the necessary quantity at the necessary time. The fundamental objective is to eliminate waste of all sorts, especially excess inventory. Products are delivered in just enough quantity to cover demand for a short period. Shipments are made frequently and are scheduled precisely; 100 percent delivery reliability is sought because little safety stock is carried. Total cost of ownership is stressed. Per-unit price is less important than the costs associated with extra handling, warehousing, and inventorying. JIT requires companies to meet specific deadlines, supply exact quantities, and adjust deliveries and quantities to meet changing needs, all with a minimum of paperwork. Strong relationships between the companies, including high trust, are critical to the success of such systems.

The Japanese popularized JIT delivery for materials and parts used in manufacturing, but it is now used for a variety of consumer and business-to-business products. If done well, JIT can reduce inventory carrying costs by well over half.[86] The increase in transportation costs is offset by inventory reductions. Compaq, Saturn, and Wal-Mart are among the companies that rely on JIT today.

Transportation   In a physical distribution system, transportation is the movement of goods to channel members and customer locations. That is the largest distribution expense for many manufacturers, especially if heavy, bulky products are involved, since transportation fees are charged by the pound. The cost of transporting weight-training equipment and exercise bicycles, for example, is often more than that of the equipment itself.[87] Deregulation of the transportation industry increased competition among carriers, which has led to greater efficiency and real cost savings for U.S. manufacturers, wholesalers, retailers, and consumers.

The methods for moving products are motor vehicles, railroads, airlines, water carriers, and pipelines. Figure 12.10 depicts the share of U.S. freight traffic and shipping revenues by each mode. While railroads have the highest share of traffic, trucks dominate in share of total shipping revenues in the U.S. market.

Figure 12.11 contrasts the advantages and disadvantages of the various modes. Managers choose among them based on customer service versus cost trade-offs. Different modes can be used to serve different clients. For example, orders to core customers may go via fast, reliable air service, whereas orders to noncore customers may be delivered by less expensive ground transportation.

Trucks The major advantages of trucks are door-to-door service and speed. Trucks also are dependable and widely available, making frequent shipments possible. Their major disadvantage is cost. Given these characteristics, trucks are ideally suited for high-value manufactured products. Companies can purchase and operate their own fleet of trucks or use the services of independent companies. The trade-offs have to do with level of control and fixed versus variable costs. When uncertainty is high, the use of independents is preferable. In Brazil, for example, Coca-Cola's bottler piggybacks its products on beer trucks; the Pepsi bottler owned 700 trucks until it declared insolvency.[88]

Railroads Railroads represent the most efficient mode of land transportation for bulky commodities, such as chemicals, coal, grain, iron ore, lumber, sand, and steel. Major U.S. railroads haul more than 40 percent of all freight, with coal accounting for about 64 percent of the total.[89] The major disadvantages of railroads are transit time and lack of door-to-door service,

Transportation Mode	Share of Freight Traffic (billions of ton miles)	Share of Shipping Revenues
Trucks	28%	80.2%
Railroads	38%	8.0%
Air	less than .5%	4.0%
Water carriers	15%	5.4%
Pipelines	18%	2.3%

FIGURE 12.10 *Transportation Modes: Share of U.S. Freight Traffic and Revenues*

Source: *Statistical Abstract of the United States* (Washington, DC: U.S. Department of Commerce, 1995), pp. 625, 626.

	Trucks	Railroads	Air	Water Carriers	Pipeline
Transportation cost	high	average	very high	very low	low
Door-to-door service	high	average	average	low	high
Speed of service	high	average	very high	very low	low
Dependability in meeting schedules	high	average	very high	average	high
Availability in different locations	very high	high	average	low	very low
Frequency of shipments	very high	low	average	very low	high
Need for intermodal transfer for door-to-door service	no	often	almost always	often	often
Primary advantage	door-to-door service and speed	low cost for long hauls of bulk commodities	fastest and highest quality	low cost for long hauls of bulk commodities	low cost and dependability

FIGURE 12.11   *Comparison of Different Modes of Transportation*

although rail spurs can be built to some customer locations. Unit trains run back and forth between a single loading point, such as a coal mine, and a single destination, such as a power plant, to deliver one commodity. Leading U.S. companies providing rail transportation include Burlington Northern, CSX, and Union Pacific.

Air Transport Air transport is offered by the airlines and cargo service companies. Speed and dependability in meeting schedules are very high relative to the other modes. Air is the most costly, however. Fashion merchandise, fragile and highly perishable items, emergency shipments, and expensive industrial goods account for the majority of products shipped air freight.

Water Carriers Water carriers include transoceanic ships as well as barges used on inland waterways. Their transportation cost is the lowest among the various options. However, only channel members and customers in port cities can be reached directly. Water carriers are used for bulky commodities, such as cement and petroleum. Ore barges, for example, are a common sight on the Great Lakes. The mode also is used to carry mass-produced products, such as automobiles and toys, overseas.

Pipelines Pipelines transport natural gas and petroleum by land from production fields to refineries. Up to 40 different grades of product can be shipped through the same pipeline simultaneously and separated at destination points. Pipelines are very dependable and offer door-to-door service. They are the least labor intensive of any mode, and maintenance expenses are low. They can be used only for a narrow range of products, however, and delivery speed—less than 5 miles per hour—is slow.

Intermodal transportation, the combination of two or more modes in moving freight, is gaining popularity. The objective is to exploit the major advantages of each. Piggybacking truck trailers on rail cars, for example, joins the benefits of long-haul rail movement with the door-to-door service of trucks. Express delivery often uses trucks and air to rush shipments from source to destination. Federal Express, the pioneer in overnight delivery, has developed a thriving business running transportation services for such clients as National Semiconductor, Laura Ashley, and Vanstar. Other companies offer a variety of intermodal options. For example, CNF Transportation, headquartered in Palo Alto, California, owns and operates Conway Transportation Services, which focuses on trucking services, and Emery Worldwide, which offers global air freight, ocean transport, and air charter.

The transportation modes used by companies is sometimes influenced by laws and government pressure. Coca-Cola uses three-wheeled motorbikes for deliveries in Shanghai, China, because truck use is restricted during daylight hours.[90] The Japanese government is campaigning against frequent truck deliveries because of extreme traffic congestion in major cities.[91] Many companies use bicycles to deliver products in Europe because of pollution concerns, and a few cities in the United States have recently begun delivering goods in this way for the same reason.[92]

New technologies are influencing how the transportation function is being performed. Progressive trucking companies install on-board computers in vehicles. Ryder System, which

INTERMODAL TRANSPORTATION
The combination of two or more modes in moving freight.

provides transportation services to such companies as Saturn, gives its drivers plastic keys loaded with electronic data. When these are plugged into the on-board computer, a screen informs the driver exactly where to go, which route to take, and how much time to spend getting there.[93] Manufacturers of commercial trucks, such as Kenworth, regularly make truck models with electronic tracking systems; truck drivers can enter a destination and immediately receive the best route, in the form of a map on a built-in computer screen, or verbally, from a computer-generated voice.[94]

Satellite communication systems are also having an important effect, providing a fast and high-volume channel for information movement around the globe. Wakefern Food Corp. uses a real-time global positioning system in its fleet of delivery trucks. The drivers and dispatchers can contact each other while the truck is in transit, and dispatchers always know where a truck is on the delivery route.[95] The real-time interaction provides up-to-date information to customers regarding location and delivery time. Furthermore, dispatchers can redirect trucks in response to need or traffic congestion. Federal Express, Roadway, and United Parcel Service are among the many companies that track shipments electronically to ensure that all customers remain fully informed about deliveries.

Efficient Customer Response **Efficient consumer response (ECR) programs** are designed to improve the efficiency of replenishing, delivering, and stocking inventory while promoting customer value.[96] Enhanced cooperation among channel members in order to eliminate activities that do not add value is a primary goal. A study found that ECR could yield as much as $24 billion in operating cost reductions and $6 billion in financial savings. Potential savings ranged from about 3 percent for manufacturers to 12 percent for retailers.[97]

Traditionally, retailers and wholesalers have used professional buyers to decide what and when to order from suppliers. To curry favor, suppliers frequently offered buyers price deals. Forward buying became commonplace: a large order for a product at a special price per carton and then a long delay until the next order. This led to a wide variation in order patterns for manufacturers and great uncertainty. Because of inefficiencies, stockouts occurred much too frequently, even though inventory levels for many products were high throughout the channel.

ECR requires a change in the roles played by channel members. Wholesalers and retailers give up some of their buying authority. On a daily basis, they send information on stock levels

EFFICIENT CONSUMER RESPONSE (ECR) PROGRAMS
Programs to improve the efficiency of replenishing, delivering, and stocking inventory in the distribution channel, while promoting customer value.

United States Postal Service makes it easy for Internet customers to return their goods.

and warehouse shipments to their suppliers over EDI networks. Personnel in the supplier organizations use this information to decide what and when to ship. Order quantities are determined with the objectives of providing sufficient safety stock, minimizing total logistics costs, and eliminating excess inventory in the channel. Before shipments go out, wholesalers and retailers can review and edit orders if they desire via EDI. Fewer special prices are offered by suppliers to reduce the incentive for forward buying, which is disruptive to ECR. Instead, everyday low pricing may be used.

If done effectively, ECR can reduce inventory costs and stockouts in the channel. Furthermore, wholesalers and retailers can reduce the number of professional buyers they employ, since suppliers assume more ordering responsibilities.

Procter & Gamble has been a leader in developing and implementing ECR programs with supermarket customers. In a recent five-year period, it more than doubled inventory turnover for such products as Crest, Pampers, Tide, and Prell, and order fill rates rose from 90 to 99 percent. P&G's overall sales were up 33 percent, with more than 40 percent of orders shipped automatically based on withdrawals from customer warehouses. Such moves helped the company cut its annual production and distribution costs by $1.6 billion, or about 8 percent.[98]

GLOBAL PHYSICAL DISTRIBUTION

It is difficult enough to distribute products in one's own country. When doing business abroad, the challenge is multiplied. Uncertainty increases because of greater transport distances, longer lead times, and complex customs requirements and trade restrictions. The most important factor from a physical distribution perspective, however, is a country's infrastructure, which influences how products are stored and transported.

China is the world's third largest economy, after the United States and Japan. Nearly 50 million Chinese have an annual income above $18,000 (adjusted for purchasing power). Since the early 1990s, the communist government in China has experimented with market reforms and allowing capitalist business ventures. China joined the World Trade Organization in 1999; as a part of the agreement, the Chinese government will now allow foreign firms to participate more fully in their own wholesaling, retailing, and transportation logistics processes. Foreign firms have also been successful in using businesses based in Hong Kong, recently reunited with mainland China, to distribute their products.[99] The Chinese government recently consented to help establish e-commerce and business-to-business links on the Internet by forming a partnership with the American company Buylink, as well.[100] Many practical and logistical problems will have to be improved, however, before China's potentially huge market becomes fully open to non-Chinese businesses.

The Chinese road system covers more than 600,000 miles, but only 3,600 miles are modern, paved highway. Recently, China spent $20 billion to build 50,000 kilometers of new roads in the western part of the country; about 4,500 kilometers of new expressways, 2,000 kilometers of new first-grade highways, and 8,000 kilometers of second-grade highways. China is expected to soon have 1.4 million kilometers of highways, of which 16,000 kilometers will be expressways, which will rank China third in the world.[101] By 2002, China is expected to have 70,000 kilometers of railway, but that is still not enough to integrate the country's area of 9.6 million square kilometers.[102] The State Planning Commission controls rail scheduling and gives priority to basic commodities. At certain times of the year, such as after major harvests, commercial capacity is simply unavailable. In 1998, however, the Ministry of Railways began allowing private entrepreneurs to lease railroad cars; these railroad cars have become the core of China's nascent private delivery services.[103] The number of airports is insufficient. Air freight and express services are mainly provided by passenger aircraft. Even recent expansion of air service to and from China is not enough to meet demand, according to major U.S. carriers such as Federal Express and United Airlines.[104] Domestic telecommunications are of uneven quality. Integrated information technology is improving but still is not nearly extensive enough.

Because of this infrastructure, companies find it very difficult to get their products quickly, safely, and reliably to customers in China. Customer service standards must be set with reality in mind. Proper packaging is extremely important to protect goods. Relationships must be developed with government officials to persuade them to devote resources to the infrastructure. From 2001 to 2005, foreign investment in China is expected to reach $365 billion, in part to help alleviate these continuing problems.[105] Similar problems are found in Africa, Asia, Eastern Europe, and elsewhere.[106] For example, Russia's infrastructure is aging; most of the country's transportation and telecommunications systems were built at least 20 years ago under the communist government. Today, it will take at least $100 billion to repair or rebuild Russia's crumbling infrastructure, but the government can't afford it and foreign businesses are reluctant to invest that much money in areas of the economy that don't provide immediate profits.[107]

Of course, a major challenge for many companies is moving products into other countries. **Freight forwarders** are cargo specialists, and their services are often used. Domestically, they pick up partial shipments at the customer location, consolidate all these into truckload or carload size, and arrange for delivery at destination points. Their gross margin is the difference between the rates they charge customers and what they pay carriers. Many exporters rely on freight forwarders to handle the documentation, insurance, and other aspects of delivery abroad. For example, they ensure that letters of credit are issued at the buyer's bank and properly transferred into the seller's account. Leading global freight forwarders include Nippon Express and Kintetsu World Express (Japan), Schenker (Germany), Lep International and MSAS (United Kingdom), and Burlington Air Express. The trend in air freight has been consolidation into a few large companies. For example, Deutche Post, although owned by a German national company, serves Switzerland, Sweden, and the United States, because it bought out smaller companies based in those countries.[108]

Regardless of geographic location, the ultimate goal of distribution is to make the product readily available to the consumer or end user. For the majority of consumer products, this has traditionally meant delivering goods to the retail outlets where consumers shop. Today, however, direct marketing—including sales via the Internet—is a growing force in consumer as well as business-to-business sales. In chapter 13 we will focus on retailing and direct marketing, including the distinctive strategies used by marketers in these fields.

FREIGHT FORWARDERS
Service companies specializing in the movement of cargo from one point to another, often country to country.

CONNECTED: SURFING THE NET

McDonald's
www.mcdonalds.com

THIS CHAPTER'S DIVERSITY FEATURE, "McDONALD'S: Serving Diverse Communities in More Ways Than One," discussed how the franchise thrives in inner-city locations. To expand your thinking about marketing channels and franchising, visit McDonald's Web site and answer the following questions.

1. How might McDonald's use physical distribution to bridge the separation between manufacturers and prospective customers?
2. How may channel length differ in McDonald's global markets? List several of the company's highly successful global markets.
3. As you learned in this chapter's diversity feature, McDonald's has been successful in developing a diverse mix of franchises. Read the company's franchise information. What percentage of McDonald's restaurant businesses is owned and operated by franchisees? On what premise is the corporation's franchising system based?

W. W. Grainger
www.grainger.com

THIS CHAPTER'S RELATIONSHIPS FEATURE, "ALLIANCES with Specialty Wholesalers," W. W. Grainger's discussed the company's partnerships with a number of large specialty wholesalers. To learn more about Grainger's alliances and supply operations, visit its Web site and answer the following questions.

1. W. W. Grainger's online catalog provides access to more than 189,000 items for more than 1 million customers around the world. What other services does Grainger offer? How do you think these have helped the company become a leading business-to-business distributor in the United States?
2. Read the company overview. How does Grainger meet the primary objective of physical distribution? How can an effective system impact the company? An ineffective system?
3. How does Grainger's "Green Guarantee" help to establish lasting connections with its customers?

OBJECTIVE 1: Learn why companies frequently use intermediaries to reach targeted customers.

Indirect channels involving independent intermediaries are frequently used, especially when the targeted market is small and geographically dispersed, companies face severe resource constraints, environmental uncertainty is high, the anticipated return from investments in direct channels is low, the level of value-added activities is low, and customers prefer dealing with intermediaries. Deciding whether to use direct or indirect channels in foreign markets is especially challenging, but culture, market structure, entrenched channels, and legal regulations have a significant effect on the choice.

OBJECTIVE 2: Attain insight into how channel relationships should be managed over time.

Coordinating relationships within the distribution channel is a challenge. The company must think strategically and develop a management plan. Interdependence, trust, and support will influence the success of coordination. Joint goal setting and planning, monitoring, the use of influence, conflict resolution, and performance appraisals are steps that need to be taken.

OBJECTIVE 3: Appreciate the economic importance of wholesalers.

Wholesalers are intermediaries who take title to the products they carry and make the majority of their sales to businesses. Wholesalers purchase large amounts of merchandise from a variety of suppliers and offer it for resale in smaller quantities. They often provide credit, extensive information on product benefits, training on product use, and technical assistance. They are needed because small to medium-sized companies in many industries do not buy in sufficient quantity to deal directly with manufacturers. Many large companies also buy from wholesalers because of convenience, lower personnel costs, and better customer service.

OBJECTIVE 4: Know the different types of wholesalers and the distinct roles they play.

A wide range of functions is performed for customers by full-service wholesalers, a category that includes general line wholesalers, specialty wholesalers, and rack jobbers. In contrast, limited-service wholesalers perform only some of the traditional channel functions. In this category are cash-and-carry wholesalers, drop shippers, truck jobbers, and mail-order wholesalers.

OBJECTIVE 5: Understand supply management activities and objectives, and how they improve business performance.

Supply chain management involves acquiring suppliers and moving products, as well as the flow of information about these activities within a firm and across different firms. The movement of goods in the supply chain starts with raw materials and ends with the final consumption of the product. An important part of this process is the selection of suppliers. Information management includes the collection, storage, and processing of data from different departments within and across firms to provide real time knowledge of the flow of goods from all sources. The objectives of supply chain management are low cost and customer service. Business performance improvements include: better profit; more relevant information; rapid product delivery; and better understanding of customers.

OBJECTIVE 6: Identify what physical distribution entails and why it is critical for any business organization.

Physical distribution, the movement of finished products through channels of distribution to end customers, entails order processing, warehousing, materials handling, and transportation. The primary objective is to get the right product to the right customer location at the right time at the lowest total cost. Physical distribution management involves a delicate balance between effective customer service and efficient operations. Order fill rate, order cycle time, delivery reliability, and invoice accuracy are four commonly used measures of customer service proficiency.

OBJECTIVE 7: Learn the steps in the order management process.

Order management is concerned with how the company receives, fills, and delivers orders to customers. New technologies have dramatically changed the way orders are transmitted, entered, screened, prioritized, invoiced, and filled. Many orders are now sent electronically. Handheld scanners with display panels often are used by warehouse workers in filling orders. There are automated distribution centers with mechanized picking equipment controlled by computers in conjunction with conveyor systems. Inventory control is essential to assure maximum fill rates at minimum cost. In transporting orders to customers, the major advantage of trucks and airplanes is speed, but they are relatively costly. Railroads and water carriers are the most efficient modes for the movement of bulky commodities. Gaining in popularity is intermodal transportation, the combination of two or more modes in moving freight.

Efficient consumer response programs attempt to eliminate activities that do not add value in distribution channels. Wholesalers and retailers give up some of their buying authority. They send daily information via EDI to their suppliers on stock levels and warehouse shipments. Personnel in the supplier organization then decide what and when to ship.

1. What are intermediaries? List three primary categories of intermediaries.
2. What is a reverse channel? Give an example.
3. What is a conventional channel system? Give an example.
4. What do members of an administered channel system do?
5. List three common forms of contractual channel systems. Briefly describe each.
6. What are the guidelines for managing channel relationships?
7. What is a wholesaler? Briefly explain why wholesalers are important.
8. What is a full-service wholesaler? A limited-service wholesaler? List three types for each.
9. What is integrated logistics? What is physical distribution? Name the primary objective of physical distribution.

10. What is order management? Name a technological advance that has improved its effectiveness and efficiency.
11. What is warehousing? Name two types of distribution centers.
12. What is economic order quantity? What is its formula?
13. List five modes of transportation used in a physical distribution system.
14. What is efficient consumer response?
15. Name an important factor in global physical distribution.

DISCUSSION OF CONCEPTS

1. What is a distribution channel? Why are distribution channels so important to companies and consumers?
2. How do direct channels differ from indirect channels? Under what conditions are indirect channels preferred to direct channels?
3. Why do channels vary in length or number of levels? What are multiple channels? Why are they being relied on by more and more companies today?
4. What are vertical marketing systems? Discuss the three types of VMS.
5. Describe the three distribution intensity options available to companies and give examples of each.
6. What is interdependence? Why is it such an important concept in managing channel relationships? What role do support programs play in the distribution channel?
7. Explain how conflicts can be resolved in channel relationships.
8. Compare the businesses of limited-service and full-service wholesalers. Can limited-service wholesalers be just as successful financially as full-service wholesalers?
9. What is EDI? How is it influencing the effectiveness and efficiency of order processing?
10. Explain how bar codes, radio frequency technology, and scanning devices are improving the effectiveness and efficiency of the materials handling function.
11. How are efficient consumer response programs changing the way business is conducted between manufacturers and retailers?
12. What is the major challenge to integrated logistics management? How can companies overcome this challenge?

KEY TERMS AND DEFINITIONS

Administered channel system: A vertical marketing system in which channel members devote effort to coordinating their relationships.

Allocation: A wholesaler function that entails purchasing products in large quantities and reselling them in smaller quantities.

Assortment: A wholesaler function that entails selling a range of merchandise from a variety of sources.

Broker: A firm that does not take title to the goods it handles but actively negotiates the sale of goods for its clients.

Channel levels: The number of distinct units (producers, intermediaries, and customers) in a distribution channel.

Contractual channel system: A vertical marketing system in which relationships among channel members are formalized in some fashion, often with a written contract.

Conventional channel system: A channel system in which efforts to coordinate the actions of channel members are seen as unimportant.

Corporate channel system: A vertical marketing system in which a company owns and operates organizations at other levels in the channel.

Cross-docking: Sorting and loading an incoming shipment from a supplier for delivery to customers without its being stored in any warehouse.

Direct channel: A distribution channel in which the producer uses its own employees and physical assets to distribute the product directly to the end user.

Distribution center: A location where inventory is maintained before being routed to individual sales outlets or customers.

Distribution channel: A set of interdependent organizations involved in making a product available for purchase.

Distribution intensity: The number of locations through which a company sells its product in a given market area.

Economic order quantity (EOQ) model: A method of determining the amount of product to be ordered each time.

Efficient consumer response (ECR) programs: Programs to improve the efficiency of replenishing, delivering, and stocking inventory in the distribution channel, while promoting customer value.

Electronic data interchange (EDI): Intercompany computer-to-computer exchange of orders and other business documents in standard formats.

Exclusive dealing: Restricting intermediaries from carrying competitive lines.

Exclusive distribution: Distributing a product through only one sales outlet in each trading area.

Franchise system: A type of distribution channel in which the franchiser holds the product trademark and licenses it to franchisees who contract to meet certain obligations.

Freight forwarders: Service companies specializing in the movement of cargo from one point to another, often country to country.

Full-line forcing: Requiring intermediaries to carry and sell the company's complete line.

Full-service wholesaler: An intermediary who performs a wide range of functions or tasks for its customers.

Indirect channel: A distribution channel in which the producer makes use of independent organizations to distribute the product to end users.

Integrated logistics management: The coordination of all logistical activities in a company.

Intensive distribution: Making the product available through every possible sales outlet in a trade area.

Intermediary: Independently owned organization that acts as a link to move products between the producer and the end user.

Intermodal transportation: The combination of two or more modes in moving freight.

Inventory control: Management of stock levels.

Limited-service wholesaler: An intermediary who performs only some of the traditional channel functions, either eliminating others or passing them on to someone else.

Logistics: The movement of raw materials, components, and finished products within and between companies.

Materials handling: The moving of products in and around a warehouse in the process of filling orders.

Multiple channel systems: The use of more than one channel to access markets for the same product.

Order management: The means by which a company receives, fills, and delivers orders to customers.

Physical distribution: The movement of finished products through channels of distribution to customers.

Private warehouse: A storage facility owned and operated by the company.

Public warehouse: A storage facility owned and operated by businesses that rent space.

Retailer: A firm that takes title to products for resale to ultimate consumers.

Retail cooperative: An alliance of small retailers for wholesaling purposes.

Reverse channel: A distribution channel that flows from the end user to the wholesaler and producer.

Selective distribution: The use of a limited number of sales outlets per trade area.

Supply chain management: Incorporation of all activities concerned with planning, implementation, and control of sourcing, manufacturing, and delivery of products and services.

Supply network: All the organizations from which components, semi-finished products, and services are purchased.

Tying arrangement: The purchase of a superior product is conditioned on the purchase of a second product of lower quality.

Vertical marketing system (VMS): A system in which channel members emphasize coordination of behaviors and programs.

Warehousing: The storage of inventory in the physical distribution system.

Wholesaling: Selling goods for resale or use to retailers and other businesses.

Wholesaler: A firm that takes title to products for resale to businesses, or other wholesalers or distributors, and sometimes consumers.

Wholesaler-sponsored voluntary chain: A group of retailers that have been united by a wholesaler.

REFERENCES

1. Nancy Dillon, "Coach Wears Well on Wall St.," *New York Daily News,* October 6, 2000, p. 55.
2. "Ingram Micro Inc. Net Income Declines 34% But Slightly Tops Estimates," *Wall Street Journal,* August 2, 2000, p. A6.
3. Based on consulting experiences with each company.
4. Discussion with John Thompson, Merisel vice president.
5. "Ben and Jerry's Homemade, Inc.," in Bert Rosenbloom, *Marketing Channels,* 6th ed. (Fort Worth: Dryden Press, 1995), pp. 665–670; Constance L. Hayes, "Ben & Jerry's Takeover Is Seen as Close," *New York Times,* April 12, 2000, p. C1.
6. Based on consulting experience.
7. Steve Lohr, "Computers Greening with the Times," *Chicago Tribune,* April 18, 1993, p. 3.
8. Personal conversations with Dennis Reker, head of distribution at Intel, in 1993; James Secolai, "Intel Slashes Processor Prices as AMD Readies Faster Line," *Info World,* June 5, 2000, p. 24.
9. Merrifield Consulting Group, "Infotech Applications for Distribution Channels," www.merrifield.com, August 26, 1996; Manufacturing Information Systems, www.misysinc.com/pricelist.htm, visited December 30, 2000.
10. "South Korea's Daou Data, Ingram Micro Form Alliance," *Asia Pulse,* November 24, 2000.
11. William Davidson, "Changes in Distribution Institutions," *Journal of Marketing* (January 1970): 7.
12. Rosenbloom, *Marketing Channels,* 6th ed. (Fort Worth: Dryden Press, 1995), pp. 486–487.
13. Ibid.
14. Barnaby Feder, "McKesson: No. 1 but a Doze on Wall Street," *New York Times,* March 17, 1991, p. 10; Thomas M. Burton, "Cardinal Health to Buy Bindley in Bid to Be No. 1 in Wholesale-Drug Business," *Wall Street Journal,* December 5, 2000, p. A3.
15. Louis Stern, Adel El-Ansary, and Anne Coughlan, *Marketing Channels,* 5th ed. (Upper Saddle River, NJ: Prentice Hall, 1996), p. 373.
16. Alf Nuncifora, www.bizjournals.com, visited December 30, 2000.
17. Kent Steinriedo, "Beverage Industry Top 100," *Beverage Industry,* June 2000, pp. 32–38.
18. Rosenbloom, *Marketing Channels.*
19. Gary Frazier and Walfried Lassar, "Determinants of Distribution Intensity," *Journal of Marketing* 60 (October 1996): 39–51.
20. Stern, El-Ansary, and Coughlan, *Marketing Channels.*
21. Frazier and Lassar, "Determinants of Distribution Intensity."
22. Discussions with top management in Joico, Inc., a manufacturer of hair care products, in October 1994.
23. Gretchen Morgenson, "Greener Pastures," *Forbes,* July 6, 1992, p. 48.
24. Lauren L. Rublin, "Retailers on Sale," *Barron's,* October 23, 2000, p. 23.
25. Gary Frazier and Raymond Rody, "The Use of Influence Strategies in Interfirm Relationships in Industrial Product Channels," *Journal of Marketing* 55 (January 1991): 52–69.
26. Gregory Gundlach and Ernest Cadotte, "Exchange Interdependence and Interfirm Interaction: Research in a Simulated Channel Setting," *Journal of Marketing Research* 31 (November 1994): 516–532.
27. Frazier and Rody, "Use of Influence Strategies."
28. "Wal-Mart Typifies Cooperation between Supplier, Retailer," *Commercial Appeal,* July 14, 1991, p. C1.
29. "Sunbeam Supports Its Powerful Brands in Major Licensing Initiative," *Discount Store News,* August 7, 2000, pp. 36–38.
30. Zachary Schiller and Wendy Zellner, "Clout! More and More Retail Giants Rule the Marketplace," *Business Week,* December 21, 1992, pp. 66–73.
31. Robert Morgan and Shelby Hunt, "The Commitment-Trust Theory of Relationship Marketing," *Journal of Marketing* 58 (July 1994): 20–38.
32. Liz Seymour, "Custom Tailored for Service: VF Corporation," *Hemispheres,* March 1996, pp. 25, 26, 28.
33. Laurel Touby, "Blimpie Is Trying to Be a Hero to Franchisees Again," *Business Week,* March 22, 1993, p. 70.
34. Kate Brennan, "Enticing the Elusive Franchisee," *Lodging Hospitality,* September 1, 2000, pp. 20–22.
35. Based on a consulting project for Santa Monica Honda-Kawasaki in 1996.
36. Based on a consulting project for Hewlett-Packard in 1996.
37. William Terdoslavich, "Monitors: The Squeeze Is On," *Computer Reseller News,* January 1, 1996, pp. 55, 56.
38. John M. Higgins, "Dish Dealer Drama," *Broadcasting and Cable,* February 7, 2000, p. 10.
39. Based on discussions with Steve Arnholdt, general manager of the Perfect Climate division of Honeywell, throughout 1995 and 1996.
40. "Wal-Mart Typifies Cooperation."
41. Based on a consulting assignment for Texas Instruments in 1996.
42. Leslie Helm, "Motorola Again Predicts Lower Results," *Los Angeles Times,* September 12, 1996, pp. D1, D3.
43. Seth Goldstein, "Retailers Rebel Against Uni's Distribution Plan," *Video Store,* November 5, 2000, p. 1.

44. Doug Bartholomew, "E-Commerce Bullies," *Industry Week,* September 4, 2000, pp. 48–54.

45. Teri Agins, "Arden Cancels Fall Launch of Liz Taylor's Fragrance," *Wall Street Journal,* August 30, 1995, p. B1.

46. Based on discussions with Susanne Haas, a corporate lawyer at Honeywell, in 1994.

47. Frederick Reichheld, *The Loyalty Effect* (Boston: Harvard Business School Press, 1996).

48. David S. Cloud and Laurie McGinley, "Bayer Makes Tentative Deal in Drug-Price Probe," *Wall Street Journal,* September 18, 2000, p. A30.

49. David Fondiller, "The Pizza Connection," *Forbes,* October 21, 1996, p. 202; and Missy Sullivan, "Eat This," *Forbes,* July 17, 2000, pp. 76–77.

50. Suzanne Oliver, "A Marvelous Annuity," *Forbes,* November 4, 1996, pp. 178–180; and John Lippman, "New Line Cinema Awards Toy License for 'Lord of the Rings' to Marvel Unit," *Wall Street Journal,* June 9, 2000, p. B4.

51. United States Census Bureau, 1997 projections, www.census.gov.

52. Based on consulting experience in the computer industry.

53. Ibid.

54. Molly Prior, "Wholesale Toy Distributor Launches in Time for Holidays," *DSN Retailing Today,* September 18, 2000, p. 10.

55. Based on a consulting assignment with Joico, Inc., 1995.

56. Discussion with Terrence Mulholand, vice president of western region at Ryerson, August 1996.

57. James Bates and Chuck Philips, "Wal-Mart Bans Album over Gun Sale Lyrics," *Los Angeles Times,* September 10, 1996, pp. A1, A15.

58. "Quality . . . A Critical Part of a Successful Distributor Partnership," *Today's Distributor,* June 1995, pp. 4–5.

59. Pat Lenius, "Grohe Stops Selling to Apex After Home Depot Acquisition," *Contractor,* June 2000, p. 3.

60. Donald J. Bowersox, David J. Closs, and M. Bixby Cooper, *Logistics in Supply Chain Management,* 1st ed. (McGraw-Hill: 2002).

61. Ibid.

62. Donald J. Bowersox, David J. Closs, and Theodore P. Stank, *21st Century Logistics: Making Supply Chain Integration a Reality,* Council of Logistics Management, 1999, p. 6.

63. Collin Reeves, Raytheon, from a talk given on March 12, 2001, at Michigan State University.

64. Charlotte W. Craig, "Ford Expected to Announce Spin-Off of Parts Supplier," *KRTBN Knight-Ridder Tribune Business News: Detroit Free Press,* April 14, 2000.

65. Bowersox, Closs, and Cooper, *Logistics in Supply Chain Management,* 1st ed. (McGraw-Hill, 2002).

66. Benson Shapiro, V. Kasturi Rangan, and John Sviokla, "Staple Yourself to an Order," *Harvard Business Review,* July–August 1992, pp. 113–122.

67. Donald Bowersox and David Closs, *Logistical Management* (New York: McGraw-Hill, 1996), p. 33.

68. Ron Tempest, "Barbie and the World Economy," *Wall Street Journal,* September 22, 1996, pp. A1, A20.

69. Ronald Henkoff, "Delivering the Goods," *Business Week,* November 28, 1994, pp. 64–78.

70. John Cortez, "The New Direction for Domino's," *Advertising Age,* January 4, 1993, pp. 3–5; and Jeanne Whalen, "Domino's Turnaround Master Exits," *Advertising Age,* January 24, 1994, p. 4; and Amy Zuber, "Domino's Policy Gets Government OK," *Nation's Restaurant News,* June 19, 2000, pp. 1–2.

71. Bowersox and Closs, *Logistical Management.*

72. Henkoff, "Delivering the Goods."

73. Stern, El-Ansary, and Coughlan, *Marketing Channels,* p. 119.

74. Reichheld, *Loyalty Effect,* p. 263.

75. Zachary Schiller, "Make It Simple," *Business Week,* September 9, 1996, pp. 96–104.

76. Clay Youngblood, "EDI Trial and Error," *Transportation and Distribution* 4 (1993): 46.

77. Based on consulting experience with Vanstar in 1996.

78. Gordon Graham, *Distributor Survival in the 21st Century* (Richardson, TX: Inventory Management Press, 1992), pp. 5–12.

79. Based on consulting experience with Vanstar in 1996.

80. Beth Wade, "That's No Invoice; That's a Marketing Tool," *Marketing News,* September 9, 1996, pp. 10, 11.

81. Henkoff, "Delivering the Goods."

82. "Cross-belt Sortation Maximizes Distribution Center Efficiency," *Modern Materials Handling,* June 1998, pp. 59–60.

83. Henkoff, "Delivering the Goods."

84. Merrifield Consulting Group, "Infotech Applications for Distribution Channels."

85. Graham, *Distributor Survival;* and Reichheld, *Loyalty Effect,* p. 25B.

86. Rosenbloom, *Marketing Channels.*

87. Interview with Vinny Greco, owner of Vinny's Powerhouse Gym, 1996, Watertown, MA.

88. Frank and Friedland, "How Pepsi's Charge into Brazil Fell Short."

89. American Association of Railroads, www.aar.org, 1997 statistics.

90. Joseph Kahn, "The Pioneers," *Wall Street Journal,* September 26, 1996, p. R12.

91. "Lean and Its Limits," *Economist,* September 14, 1996, p. 65.

92. Dave Block, "Bike Co-op Eliminates Pollution in Local Delivery," *In Business,* May/June 2000, p. 16.

93. Henkoff, "Delivering the Goods."

94. "Highlights from the Mid-America Trucking Show," *Fleet Equipment,* May 2000, pp. 32–33.

95. Peter Buxbaum, "Customized Technology Proves Successful," *Fleet Equipment,* August 2000, pp. 39–42.

96. Kurt Salmon Associates, *Efficient Consumer Response: Enhancing Consumer Value in the Grocery Industry* (Washington, DC: Food Marketing Institute, 1993), p. 2.

97. Stern, El-Ansary, and Coughlan, *Marketing Channels,* p. 119.

98. Schiller, "Make It Simple."

99. Tina Helsell, "China's Middlemen—New Paths to the Market," *The China Business Review,* January/February 2000, pp. 64–70.

100. "Buylink Assists Chinese Government Delegation in Seeking E-Commerce Solutions for the Textile Industry," *Businesswire,* August 10, 2000.

101. "China Boosts Highway Construction in Western Areas," *Asia Pulse,* December 28, 2000.

102. "Full Steam Ahead," *Business China,* September 11, 2000, p. 6.

103. Trish Saywell, "Express Service," *Far Eastern Economic Review,* September 3, 1998, p. 43.

104. Dennis Blank and Robert McNatt, "Gridlock to the East," *Business Week,* October 4, 1999, p. 8.

105. "State, Private Investment to Rise in China, While Foreign Investment Falls," www.chinavista.com, January 2, 2000.

106. Cyndee Miller, "Chasing Global Dream," *Marketing News,* December 2, 1996, pp. 1, 2.

107. "Cabinet Minister Offers 2001 Forecast of Calamities," *AP Worldstream,* December 25, 2000.

108. Toby G. Gooley, "Air Carriers: The Urge to Merge," *Logistics Management and Distribution Report,* July 2000, p. 74.

E-COMMERCE RAISES SUPPLY CHAIN CONCERNS

THE SUPPLY CHAIN HAS BEEN significantly altered by the advent of e-commerce. The systems that used to ship large orders to retailers are not effective for e-tailing. Companies are finding out that online selling is not as cheap as they thought it would be. Although they don't need the expensive stores, e-tailers do have to hire a large number of people to fill individual orders. This has forced companies to rethink both their supply chain strategies.

Multichannel integration has been the focus of many of the traditional bricks-and-mortar companies. The question is whether to link the supply chains of the physical stores with their dot-com divisions. Wal-Mart has outsourced its e-commerce site. The hope is that the brand recognition will spur sales and that eventually Wal-Mart.com will go public. Nordstrom has joined forces with a venture capital company to form their e-business, but unlike Wal-Mart, the intent is to keep the subsidiary in-house and maintain ownership. Some integration is necessary because over 70 percent of the brick-and-mortar companies allow its customers to return merchandise purchased online to the store. This raises implications for the integration of inventory management across the two businesses.

After the disasters of the 1999 Christmas season, when some customers did not receive their orders until January, many companies, such as Macys.com, have converted to real-time inventory management systems. This will allow customers to see exactly what is in stock, provide greater order accuracy, and lead to more efficient processing of orders.

Richard J. Sherman of EXE Technologies sums it all up when he says, "We used to deal with full truckloads and full pallets. Then in Quick Response, we were dealing with cases, less-than-truckload. In the dot-com world, we're looking at parcel management, item picks. We used to ship to 400 to 500 locations. Then in Quick Response days, we started shipping to 5,000 to 6,000 locations. In the dot-com world, you may be shipping to 80 million locations."

Sources: "Survey Reveals Need for More Channel Integration as Busy Holiday Season Approaches; Pricing and Fulfillment Seen as Largest Obstacles," *PR Newswire*, September 25, 2000, as retrieved from the World Wide Web, www.lexi-nexis.com; and Mary Aichlmayr, "Logistics Conquers a Brave New World," *Transportation and Distribution*, August 2000, pp. 29–36.

CASE 12

Texas Instruments

TEXAS INSTRUMENTS, INC. (TI), WITH headquarters in Dallas and operations in more than 30 countries, markets semiconductors, defense electronics, software, computers and peripheral products, custom engineering, electrical controls, and consumer electronics products. Recently, TI has consolidated several businesses to free up resources for the lucrative semiconductor business. In that arena, the company has transformed itself from a maker of commodity memory chips to a producer of more specialized chips that are higher in value added. For example, TI's newest chipset technology will speed up Net access and enable equipment vendors to develop their own asymmetrical digital subscriber line (ADSL) products. Although it appears that the chip industry is slowing, TI has predicted sales growth of 10 percent in 1998, double its 5 percent growth the year before. In order to reach its goal, TI had to take into account dramatic shifts in distribution in the semiconductor industry.

In the United States, most major distributors have historically carried either U.S. or Asian semiconductor products. Few distributors have carried both. The five leading U.S. chip manufacturers sold approximately 83 percent of the nearly $4 billion worth of chips sold in the United States. The five top Asian manufacturers reported selling approximately 17 percent. In

some cases, U.S. manufacturers have allowed their distributors to share shelf space with Asian manufacturers, particularly to fill out a complete line. For example, TI has been willing to share shelf space with Asian manufacturers for years. In October 1997, Motorola relaxed a decade-long prohibition against sharing space with Asian manufacturers. Thus, after decades in which OEMs had to source domestic and Asian semiconductors from two or more distributors, it is now possible to source products from both areas with a single distributor.

The ability of Japanese organizations to use distributors of U.S. products within the United States has global repercussions as well. There are obvious advantages to the Japanese chip manufacturers who have had difficulty selling to several large global OEMs with major operations in the United States. They have been inhibited because multinational customers often want a single point of contact worldwide. Now those manufacturers are able to use a single large distributor with a global presence. Dick Skipworth, managing director at Memec International Components group, Essen, Germany, a large European and PAC Rim distributor, believes that distributors everywhere now may face the problem of creating differentiation. "There is going to be an increased need for specialization as blindcards [product lines] begin to look more and more alike. I think there is going to be more specialization on the sales and marketing side of any semiconductor manufacturer that relies on distributors to actively sell their product."

The changes in distribution policies have occurred largely because of changes in OEM inventory strategies. OEMs have reduced inventories from a 10-week supply 10 years ago to a 2.2-week supply today; the brunt of the inventory reductions took place in 1996 to 1997 and the trend is continuing. Companies such as Dell, which build products to order, are demanding virtually no inventory. Consequently, there is a need for distributors that can supply customers' immediate needs while finding new ways to differentiate themselves. Arrow, for example, a large national distributor, has recently realigned itself into seven customer-driven units. Each unit is designed to provide specialized services for a unique market segment. Marshall, another large distributor, will continue to differentiate itself through technology, support, and service. Rob Rodin, chief executive of Marshall, indicates, "We are trying as always to be the low-cost producer. On the delivery front, we are trying to bring the most unique and reliable delivery systems to the marketplace, including value-added programs, programming services, JIT inventory management, 24-hour-a-day service coverage, Internet, intranets, extranets, and delivery." Arrow and Marshall both carry TI plus other major semiconductor manufacturers' products.

TI has targeted its memory chips and complex digital signal processors, high-value-added chip-based products at OEMs that incorporate semiconductors into everything from VCRs, personal computers, and toys, to navigational systems in automobiles and boats. TI sells semiconductors through two channels—direct to OEMs and indirectly to OEMs through a network of electronics distributors including Arrow and Marshall Industries. Approximately 30 percent of TI's semiconductor sales in the United States are through the distributor channel and this percentage is growing rapidly. Since distributors sell a mix of competitive products including Advanced Micro Devices, Intel, Motorola, and National Semiconductors, TI must fight to get its share. Marshall Industries, for example, emphasizes TI and Toshiba semiconductors. TI has approximately 300 field personnel who focus both on OEMs and distributors. Since the top 100 OEMs in North America use approximately 50 percent of all semiconductors, they are covered directly by TI personnel as major accounts. The next 4,000 OEMs, which use 44 percent of all semiconductors, are covered by distributors who play a vital role for TI. The remaining 6 percent in sales are made up of approximately 100,000 small OEMs, which are targeted by TI with several distributors.

Over the past several years, semiconductor manufacturers have asked distributors to develop better technical expertise, and the response has been to hire more field application engineers. Since they must deal with an array of different products from a number of manufacturers, their depth of knowledge is limited. This is even more true for ordinary sales reps, who lack the background necessary to understand the technical nuances of the complex products they are selling. Typically, distributors have about 10 sales reps for every one field application engineer, so TI devotes significant resources to helping distributor personnel when technical and sales questions arise.

Distributor personnel can contact the TI sales rep assigned to their account or geographic area, and he or she either answers the question or gets the information from others in the organization. Many distributors also inform customers about the Product Information Center at TI, accessible through an 800 number, where the staff is supposed to provide an answer within 24 hours. Marketing and product managers at TI spend considerable time on technical questions that arise in the field. Another concern is to get distributors to specify TI. An area in which distributors tend to perform poorly is getting the TI product specified during the OEM's design phase. If this does not occur, TI might not become the preferred supplier.

John Szczsponik, TI's director of North American distribution for semiconductors, has been discussing the industry changes and the specification issue with a number of people throughout the organization. Four possible options have been identified.

Option 1: Put additional pressure on distributors to enhance their technical capability. Each should hire more field application engineers and train them more effectively. TI would contribute by providing the necessary training. TI also could take the responsibility of generating sales leads for distributors through ads and bingo cards.

Option 2: Lower expectations of what distributors can accomplish. Their role should be redefined as primarily fulfilling demand. TI should be responsible for creating demand and winning designs. TI should hire at least 30 more technical and field reps and assign them accounts that appear to have greatest potential.

Option 3: Change TI's policy about sharing competitive information. Give distributor salespeople more information about product applications and hold workshops for their customers; pay distributor salespeople a bounty of $50 for every customer they can motivate to attend. Competitors like Analog Devices are making great use of tactics such as this.

Option 4: Include distributors in the design phase. They should send out direct mail to their customers not only to raise awareness of TI but also to identify application needs. With their detailed knowledge of customers, distributors can help TI focus resources on products and markets with greatest potential.

Szczsponik sees some merit in each of the options and also is trying to identify others not yet considered.

1. *Explain the basic problem(s) TI faces in its distribution channel.*
2. *How should TI address the movement toward distributors that carry both U.S. and foreign competitors' products?*
3. *Would you choose one of the four options, combine some of them, or develop a new approach? Support your recommendation.*

Sources: Discussions with Greg Delagi, Pat Moran, Briant Regan, and John Szczsponik of Texas Instruments in 1996 and 1997; Ismini Scouras, "Chain Reaction—Model Prompts OEMs to Keep Inventories Low," *Electronic Buyer News,* December 15, 1997, p. 1; Allen Myerson, "Company Reports: Chip Maker's Operating Net Is Up Sharply," *New York Times,* January 22, 1998, p. D4; Barbara Jorgensen, "New Rules Put OEMs a Step Closer to One-Stop Shopping—Industry Ponders Future as Shelf-Sharing Restrictions Ease," *Electronic Buyer News,* December 15, 1997, p. 41; and "Texas Instruments Speeds Up Net Access with New ADSL Chips," *Newsbytes News Network,* www.newsbytes.com, January 27, 1998.

RETAILING AND DIRECT MARKETING

◄ *Exterior of the Museum of Fine Arts retail store in Boston, Massachusetts*

WE ALL DREAM ABOUT A JOB that bridges the gap between our personal interests and our desire to live well. Take Cynthia Palmer, former assistant general manager of retail operations at the Museum of Fine Arts (MFA), in Boston. Her creative side loved the arts, but her practical nature led her to major in marketing. When the MFA's posting for a marketing assistant appeared at Boston University's career center, Cynthia jumped at the chance. That was back in 1983, when the MFA had a fledgling retail operation—one store and a small catalog—bringing in about $4 million. Realizing the growth potential for the market, Cynthia stayed on, steadily moving upward. And she has been a major factor in a business that now brings in $37 million a year and is one of the top museum retail operations in the world.

How can a museum succeed in the competitive world of retail? According to Palmer, "the homogenization of the market has created a demand for unique product." The MFA features some of the world's greatest French Impressionist paintings, Egyptian artifacts, and Asian treasures. Says Cynthia: "The museum's mission is to market quality products that relate to the collection, possess intrinsic beauty, educate the customer, and bring optimum revenue to the museum." MFA Enterprises consists of retailing, direct mail, and a site on the Internet that includes a corporate gift and wholesale page. Through various activities, it reaches more than 7.5 million people a year—about 2.5 percent of the U.S. population!

The MFA's retail stores have visitors estimated at more than a million annually. The flagship shop, a 5,7000-square-foot store in the museum, serves 250,000 customers a year. A smaller shop, devoted to major exhibitions, serves another 80,000 patrons a year. The MFA also has five satellites in major malls around Boston and plans to expand. In keeping with the modern retail environment, the MFA has an additional outlet near its warehouse.

The major thrust of business comes through the direct-mail catalog. The MFA sends out four editions per year, for a total of 12.5 million copies. These help the museum reach the bulk of its customers in New York and California. The target market is women (85 percent), highly educated (many have graduate degrees), in their midthirties, married, with children—people who appreciate the uniqueness of the products only a museum can offer. Catalog fulfillment is done from a 100,000-square-foot warehouse. That's also the number of mail orders the MFA receives, plus 275,000 phone orders. More than 435,000 packages are shipped each year.

The MFA began selling on the Internet in 1996. Now with significant sales, it is important to be available in multiple marketplaces. Palmer negotiated with major online services to join an electronic mall.

A major part of Cynthia's work involved creating strong ties with suppliers. She traveled to Japan and Italy to meet with long-term suppliers. Since the MFA's products are unique, and many require expert craftsmanship, "it's crucial to have good supplier relations. Good business is built upon good relationships," says Palmer. "You have to understand the capabilities and the drive behind the person on the other side of the table. Understanding what motivates them will make them excel to a greater level than they would with an ordinary customer."[1]

> *Like MFA Enterprises, modern retail organizations strive to understand and meet the needs of targeted customers. Often this requires establishing multiple channels, including direct marketing and Internet sites. Competition is too intense for retailers to ignore any viable way to connect with and serve customers.*

CONNECTED: SURFING THE NET

www.mfa.org

Check out how MFA sells on the Internet by visiting its Web site. You'll also find information on its collections, exhibitions, school, and more.

career tip Working in a museum has advantages. You can work in a field that may be of great interest to you. There is the satisfaction of bringing money to an institution devoted to making art more accessible to everyone. And from a career standpoint, nonprofits allow you to get involved with a broader spectrum of activities than is typical in for-profit organizations.

THE CONCEPTS OF RETAILING AND DIRECT MARKETING

Retailing and direct marketing touch our lives almost daily. Retailing is involved whenever you purchase a burger at McDonald's, rent a movie at Blockbuster, or buy a pair of jeans at Gap. Direct marketing is involved whenever you receive a catalog from Dell Computer, watch QVC, or place an Internet order with CDnow for Madonna's latest release. Retailers and direct marketers provide us with the goods we need to survive and prosper.

Operating a retailing organization in today's fast-paced world is challenging. Competition is intense, with different types of retailers going after many of the same customers. Retailers must make decisions about target markets, service levels, pricing, merchandise assortment, store locations, image, and the use of direct marketing, among others. They must stay abreast of new technologies that affect the efficiency and effectiveness of store operations. They must decide whether to follow increasing numbers of retailers into global markets.

More and more companies such as IBM or Wal-Mart are using direct marketing to connect with customers. And companies that specialize in this area are on the rise. Customers such as the convenience, and technologies such as the Internet are opening new avenues. Direct marketing plays an important role in selling to consumers as well as in the business-to-business market. This vibrant and exciting field has a bright future.

RETAILING

RETAILING
The activities involved in selling products and services directly to end users for personal or household use.

Retailing refers to selling products directly to consumers for personal or household use. It does not include the sale of products to other resellers or businesses, which is the domain of wholesaling. A retailer is a firm that makes the majority of its sales to consumers. Many discounters and warehouse clubs sell to small businesses as well, such as restaurants and small independent stores, but if more than half their sales are made to consumers, they are classified as retailers. CompUSA, Home Depot, Staples, and Price Club are examples of retailers that have a significant amount of sales to business customers.

As the MFA example illustrates, many retailers use direct mail and catalogs to supplement their store sales. Texas-based Neiman Marcus sends out a Christmas Book every October to its credit card customers. Over the years it has included such exotic products as camels, his-and-her airplanes, mummy cases, windmills, and submarines. In 2000, the Neiman Marcus Edition Ford Thunderbird was featured with a polished-black body finish and removable silver metallic top; all 200 of the cars sold within two hours and fifteen minutes, a record for any vehicle sold through the catalog.[2] CompUSA and Wal-Mart are among the retailers that have established Web sites on the Internet to sell select groups of products.[3]

THE IMPORTANCE OF RETAILERS

Retailers are vital to our economy. Sales in the United States through retail stores were about $3 trillion in 1999.[4] Throughout the world, retail sales exceed several trillion per year. Retailing also is one of the largest U.S. industries in terms of employment. According to the Bureau of Labor Statistics, about 22 million people work in retailing—approximately one out of every seven full-time workers.[5]

CONNECTED: SURFING THE NET

www.compusa.com

Check out the different "shops" offered by CompUSA online. You'll have access to information about the latest computer technology, as well as facts about the company and its 224 stores across the country.

Retailing is the final stage in the distribution channel for the majority of products sold to consumers, everything from chewing gum to insurance to automobiles. As retailing practices develop and become more refined, better products are provided to consumers at better prices. Retailers perform a variety of functions that increase the value of products to consumers. Similar to wholesalers, they play two critical roles in the mix of goods. They perform an allocation function by purchasing products in large quantities from suppliers (manufacturers, wholesalers, or brokers) for resale to consumers in smaller quantities. They perform an assortment function by purchasing merchandise from a variety of suppliers and offering it for sale in one location. Therefore, retailers make a broad variety of goods available to consumers in amounts they can afford and effectively handle.

Although packaged goods such as cereal, detergent, milk, and toothpaste are purchased off the shelf by consumers, retailers still provide information about such products through advertising, displays, and unit prices posted on the shelves. Other consumer products, especially durable goods and services such as insurance, require that retailers use salespeople to provide information and answer questions about product benefits.

Well-located stores increase the convenience of shopping for customers. Furthermore, many retailers facilitate transactions by investing in scanner technology and offering credit. They also may customize products, as do clothing retailers who alter suits or insurance agents who develop specialized packages. Repair services are provided by retailers such as Sears, Circuit City, and Radio Shack.

Time, place, possession, and form utilities are provided to consumers by various retailers. They help make our life more manageable and pleasurable. Without them, acquiring the basic necessities would be difficult in terms of both time and money.

Some manufacturers, such as Sherwin-Williams in the paint industry and Liz Claiborne in the apparel industry, own their outlets, at least in part. Others, such as Dell Computer, sell directly to consumers, bypassing retailers. For a majority of consumer good manufacturers, however, retailers are essential for product distribution. Most producers cannot afford to access consumer markets themselves. Their capital is tied up in operations, and it makes no sense for even large manufacturers such as Procter & Gamble to open up outlets. Retailers do this for them, investing in land, buildings, fixtures, and personnel. Furthermore, retailers typically take title to the goods they resell, incurring the inventory carrying costs and sales risks otherwise held by the manufacturer. Retailers often sell goods to consumers on credit, assuming the risks associated with accounts receivable and bad debts. Retailers also promote the products they carry. In other words, retailers make it economically feasible for manufacturers of consumer goods to operate.

RETAIL STRATEGY

The **wheel of retailing** is one way to describe how retailers emerge, evolve, and sometimes fade away. According to the theory, new retailers locate their no-frills stores in low-rent areas to keep costs down. Those that succeed start to change. They add more services, move to more expensive real estate, upgrade facilities, and raise prices. This makes them vulnerable to new low-price entrants, and the wheel goes round and round. The wheel can be broken if retailers carefully develop a strategy. They must choose a target market and create a marketing mix that satisfies it. Upgrading services, locations, and prices can be defended only if that is what the target market demands. The steps in formulating a retail strategy are shown in Figure 13.1.[6] Invariably, successful retailers have a sound retail strategy.

Target Markets and Positioning   Like any business, retailers must understand their customers to be truly successful. As a first step, they must carefully analyze the general market and decide the segment or segments on which to focus. For example, Autozone, based in Memphis, is an auto parts retailer that targets low-income consumers who repair their own cars.[7] Nordstrom's, headquartered in Seattle, is a department store chain that targets middle- to high-income households desiring superior service.[8] Wet Seal, Inc., based in Irvine, California, operates several hundred apparel stores throughout the country and targets young women ages 13 through 18.[9]

Whatever the overall targeting strategy, individual outlets may face different mixes of customers. The primary trade area is the geographic territory in which the majority of a store's customers reside. The trade area can vary in circumference from less than one mile for a convenience store to 20 miles for a specialist such as Toys "R" Us.[10] Each store manager must understand primary trade areas and react accordingly. For example, Target has a sophisticated

WHEEL OF RETAILING

A descriptive theory about how retailers emerge, evolve, and sometimes fade away.

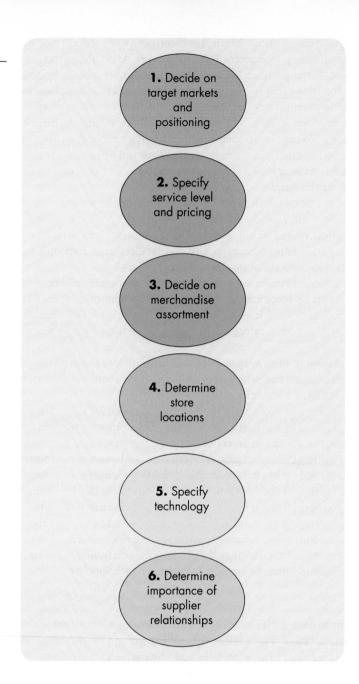

FIGURE 13.1 *Developing
a Retail Strategy*

computer system that tracks customer buying habits and tailors merchandise in each primary
trade area of over 900 stores in 44 states.[11] A Houston grocery store chain, Randall's Food
Markets, sells Hispanic specialty products to cater to the Hispanic population in the area.[12]

Retailer positioning is the mental picture consumers have of the retailer and the shopping
experiences it provides. Retailers must decide what image they want with customers—high
prestige, superior service, friendly atmosphere, low prices, or whatever. Then they must determine how to get this image established in the minds of their customers. Decisions on service
level and pricing, merchandise assortment, and store location will influence the retailer's
image.

Service Level and Pricing The target market and positioning will influence decisions on
service level and pricing. Many retailers follow a discount-oriented strategy, offering products
and service of acceptable quality at low prices. The objective is to keep service costs and
overhead down in order to make prices competitive. Lucky Stores is a supermarket chain in
southern California that offers low prices and few amenities. Wal-Mart and Kmart have a discount-oriented strategy. Crown Books offers a standard 10 percent discount in addition to
discounts up to 40 percent on *New York Times* hardback bestsellers. Competitors such as

Sears is at the forefront in connecting with diverse segments of customers.

Barnes & Noble and Borders may provide coffee shops or sell compact disks as well as offering sales and special discounts.[13]

A service-oriented strategy emphasizes quality products and value-added functions with prices to match. It is successful to the extent that this is what the target market wants. In the jewelry business, Cartier offers unique jewelry, and its well-trained sales force caters to the specific needs of each customer. Nordstrom's is well known in the Northwest for its quality of service, such as ironing shirts for customers immediately after purchase. A store's environment can also contribute to its success in competing against large competitors. The Country Market in Sandwich, Illinois, for example, offers much more than gasoline. The store's owners have created an attractive environment through their featured antiques, 10-cent Coca-Colas, wood floors, and old cereal boxes. Because of its many amenities, the gas station is much more than just a gas station and it has retained many of the same customers who look forward to running low on gas.[14]

Other retailers follow a hybrid strategy, combining quality products, value-added services, and low pricing in some manner. Autonation, Carchoice, and Carmax (a division of Circuit City) offer huge inventories of used cars marked with low, no-haggle prices. Their stores have such amenities as child care centers, coffee bars, and touch-screen computers. The well-known bookseller Borders offers more services than just selling books. The stores also feature coffee shops, sell music, have special promotions, and even coordinate products, contests, and in-store events with special events such as the Ken Burns project on jazz music. Visitors to the store in January 2001 found many jazz-related items, a limited edition Jazz Fusion Blend coffee, and could participate in workshops to learn more about the music. Borders hopes that its combination of goods and special events will distinguish it from other book and music sellers.[15]

Merchandise Assortment   Retailers must take great care in deciding what merchandise to offer. Those with the right assortment have greater sales revenues and customer satisfaction. Merchandise breadth, the variety of product lines offered, and merchandise depth, the

SCRAMBLED MERCHANDISING
A retail strategy that entails
carrying an array of product
lines that seem to be unrelated.

number of products available within each line, must be determined. Department stores have considerable breadth but only moderate depth. Retailers such as Circuit City and CompUSA have limited breadth but great depth.

A **scrambled merchandising** strategy means that the product lines carried seem to be unrelated. The goal is to facilitate one-stop shopping for customers and achieve competitive advantage. For example, in the new "Super Kmart" stores, traditional goods are combined with a well-stocked supermarket of food products. Meijer, a chain in the Midwest, has used this strategy since its inception.

Part of the assortment of many retailers is private label merchandise. JCPenney's St. John's Bay jeans and Sears, Roebuck & Company's Canyon River Blues jeans are two examples. Private labels are especially common in the apparel, food, home appliance, and drug industries. In apparel, private labels serve to build the image of the retailer rather than the manufacturer. Ann Taylor and Gap have taken this a step farther to vertical retailing. These companies design, manufacture, and market their own products in their own stores. Private label sales are growing in supermarket chains that are increasingly featuring their own products. Once supermarket retailers realized customers would buy private label products if they believed they were of good quality, the quality and marketing of these products improved. In 1999 alone, private label sales in supermarkets totaled $36 billion, 17 percent of total sales. As these labels continue to grow in acceptance and contribute to customer loyalty, it seems the trend will continue to grow.[16]

Store Location   The location decision is very important for any retailer. Among other things, it affects how convenient shopping will be for customers. The target market dictates the choice to some degree. Autozone, for example, places its stores directly in low-income neighborhoods.[17] In contrast, specialty toy stores and clothing boutiques locate in well-to-do suburbs.[18] And the location decision can be a source of competitive advantage if it preempts competitors from moving to an area with high sales and profit potential. Wal-Mart's strategy was to establish stores in small towns that could not support more than one large discount operation. It froze out competition while building a strong sales base.[19] It then spread to larger cities in the early 1990s. Dillard Department Stores concentrates primarily in secondary markets, where competition is not so fierce.[20]

Some retailers use a destination location strategy; that is, stores are put in low-rent areas off highways and some distance from other retailers.[21] Because the store is off the beaten path, consumers make it their destination when they want to shop there. In contrast, a competitor location strategy puts stores near those of major competitors. The rationale is that even more consumers will be drawn to the area. For example, Borders is likely to place its superstores as close as possible to a Barnes & Nobles outlet. They often compete for the same retail site.[22] Diamond merchants cluster along 47th Street in New York City, antique stores line the Place du Grand Sablon in Brussels, and a Planet Hollywood usually can be found near a Hard Rock Cafe.[23] In general, retailers with large stores, a large amount of merchandise, and attractive pricing can use a destination location strategy effectively. Retailers selling

Some retailers use a competitor location strategy, putting their stores near those of major competitors.

Shopping malls have immense pulling power, especially when they are as large as the Mall of America in Minneapolis.

goods that consumers want to compare on quality and price are usually wise to locate close to competitors.

Of course, many retailers choose a local or regional shopping mall rather than a freestanding location. A **shopping mall or center** is a group of retail stores in one place marketed as a unit to shoppers in a trade area. Shopping malls, especially regional ones, have immense pulling power. The diverse mix of stores offers a wide array of merchandise. Merchants can pool resources to provide entertainment, such as pianists or clowns or even a supervised indoor playground, as at the huge Mall of America in Minneapolis. This supermall has 2.5 million square feet of retail space, equivalent to four regional shopping malls, features more than 500 specialty stores and brings in over 42.5 million visitors annually, including many who charter flights from all over the world.[24] The West Edmonton Mall in Alberta, Canada, is another example of a supermall.

Technology   Retailers must keep abreast of new technologies and adopt those that promote customer satisfaction at a reasonable cost. The Big Picture, a Denver, Colorado, home theater specialty store, allows customers to develop their own customized home theater systems based on their budget and desired technology. Owner Roger Kohler says that different systems exist—from home theater in a box systems costing around $1,000 to more elaborate systems, such as the one purchased by Danny Ellrich for around $50,000. Ellrich's system includes stage and ceiling track lights, an adjacent concession room, a marquee, and top-of-the-line electronic and audio equipment that he can easily update as new technology is developed.[25]

Technology is a key tool in marketing to specific audiences. Experian, the United Kingdom's largest provider of marketing services, recently launched a new Web site at www.micromarketing-online.com as a complete resource for marketers in all industry sectors. The site is a guide to all the latest marketing tools, information on consumer profiling, and new data developments. This information can help marketers target potential customers, maintain existing customer relations, and identify potential for growth. By using technology to identify markets, micromarketing can help companies target their products in effective ways.[26]

Database marketing is the process of building, maintaining, and using computerized information to contact customers in a personalized fashion.[27] Advances in technology have enabled more and more retailers to take advantage of database marketing. A customer profile is kept on each person, which can include demographics (age, income) and past purchases as well as psychographics (activities, interests, opinions). Customized product offerings then can be developed with individualized messages and incentives. Two companies recently partnered for the specific purpose of developing targeted e-mail based on self-reported profiles. MatchLogic's global client base will be utilized by Dynamics Direct's e-mail media technology to allow the company to send personalized e-mail campaigns to customers.[28]

The technology feature describes Peapod's PC-based grocery shopping service. Several supermarket chains see it as a viable alternative channel to serve certain customers. However, many continue to be skeptical of online grocery shopping, and even Priceline.com has ended its grocery shopping features.[29]

SHOPPING MALL (SHOPPING CENTER)
A group of retail stores in one location and marketed as a unit to shoppers in a trade area.

CONNECTED: SURFING THE NET

www.micromarketing-online.com

Read the descriptions of micromarketing and learn about the technology available on Experian's site. You can even receive a free area profile.

CONNECTING THROUGH TECHNOLOGY

PEAPOD AND COMPUTER SHOPPING

 Beth Mansfield of Libertyville, Illinois, owns a sports equipment franchise and works 60-hour weeks. She also has two young daughters. Because of her hectic schedule, she used to shop at the local supermarket in the late evenings. Then a company named Peapod made her life a little easier. Beth now shops for and orders groceries from her home computer.

Peapod, Inc., headquartered in Evanston, Illinois, provides a computer shopping and delivery service to customers in eight different metropolitan areas, including Chicago, Washington, DC, and San Francisco. Peapod enables its customers to shop their local Safeway or Jewel Osco from a personal computer. Although Peapod was one of a kind at its inception in 1989, similar services such as Webvan, Shoplink, and even Priceline.com's WebHouse Club have popped up in the last few years, threatening to steal some of Peapod's thunder. In addition, Peapod has not been profitable in past years and faced the possibility of falling off the face of the online grocery market it practically invented. What really brought Peapod back to the forefront was its partnership with Dutch-owned supermarket giant Royal Ahold, which spent $73 million to gain 51 percent of the company in August 2000.

Customers can shop at any hour, sorting through the items by product category or attributes, such as cost per ounce, fat content, calories, nutritional content, and sugar. Another advantage of the online grocer is that comparison shopping is easy. Customers inform Peapod whether substitutes are acceptable if preferred items are out of stock. They also select one of six time slots for next-day delivery. Peapod forwards the order to the nearest participating store. With Ahold's merchandise storage and distribution capabilities, the speed of delivery to customers and overall efficiency of the service look to improve exponentially. "You have to guarantee 100 percent delivery excellence," states Diane Ort, consulting director for competitor HomeRuns.com. Ort felt that the problem with previous systems such as Peapod's was that they failed to configure their Web site in a way that was compatible with their business operations. That is where Peapod and Royal Ahold look to make marked improvements.

The big question that Peapod and its competitors are asking is whether a large enough demographic group exists to facilitate the time and cost-saving benefits the services offer. Large chains such as Kroger and Safeway have poked their heads into the online market and may have seen the shadow of limited success. No immediate e-commerce options are expected from either company.

So how does Peapod combat these not-so-promising outlooks? With diversification, of course. The company has branched out from offering perishable and nonperishable groceries by adding items such as *New York Times* best-sellers, magazines, baby care products, alcoholic beverages, a pet store, and a Seasonal Shop to fulfill all your holiday entertaining needs.

In June 1995, Microsoft CEO Bill Gates startled a group of top food retailers by predicting that one-third of food sales will be handled electronically by 2005. Peapod hopes he is right. At this point in time, a very small percentage of groceries are bought from home and sometimes by phone rather than computer.

Sources: "Delivery System," *Brandweek,* August 15, 1995, pp. 22, 26; Susan Chandler, "The Grocery Cart in Your PC," *Business Week,* September 11, 1995, pp. 63, 64; W. Frank Dell, "Home Delivery Gets a Reality Check," *Grocery Marketing,* February 1996, pp. 36, 37; Peapod's Web site, www.peapod.com, June 6, 1996 and December 18, 2000; "Grocery Sites Hungry for Prospects," *DSN Retailing Today,* May 8, 2000, p. 118; David Jastrow, "Reviving the Web Grocery," *Computer Reseller News,* May 8, 2000, pp. 45, 48; and Matthew Haeberle, "Ahold's Manifest Destiny," *Chain Store Age,* August 2000, pp. 52–54.

Supplier Relationships Developing strong relationships with suppliers is a strategic imperative for many retailers. Partners go out of their way to serve one another. Supplier loyalty pays off when the retailer gets the goods it needs in a quick and efficient manner. Wal-Mart has long been known as a retailer that values close partnerships with its major suppliers.[30] Whatever the strength of a relationship, however, tough bargaining issues are likely to arise between suppliers and retailers.

Cost and pricing issues are the most common areas of friction. Retailers have a targeted **markup,** the difference between merchandise cost and the retail price. For example, if Wet Seal buys blouses from California Concepts, a manufacturer in Gardena, at $12 each

MARKUP

The amount added to the cost of acquiring a product that determines its retail selling price.

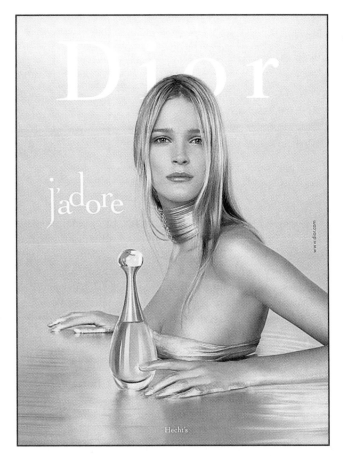

Cosmetics and perfumes generally have a high markup in the retail arena.

and prices them in stores at $20 each, the markup is $8, or 40 percent of the selling price ($8 ÷ $20 = .40). The formula is:

$$\text{Markup Percentage} = \frac{\text{Amount added to cost (markup)}}{\text{Selling price}}$$

Goods that do not sell as expected require a **markdown,** a reduction in the original retail price. Wet Seal may sell some of the blouses at $20 but then lower the price to $15 in order to sell the rest. The markdown in this case is $5, and the markdown percentage is 25 percent ($5 ÷ $20). That is the discount amount typically advertised for a sale item, and it is computed as follows:

$$\text{Markdown Percentage} = \frac{\text{Amount of markdown}}{\text{Previous selling price}}$$

The retailer typically goes back to the supplier and asks for markdown money, a credit to the retailer's account to adjust for the unanticipated price reduction.

> **MARKDOWN**
> A reduction from the original retail selling price of a product.

TYPES OF RETAILERS

There are several ways to classify retailers. Form of ownership distinguishes between small independents (often called mom-and-pop stores) and **chain stores,** which are a group of centrally owned and managed retail outlets that handle the same product lines. Level of service can be used, whether full, limited, or self. Price level can be used as well. However, the most informative classification is based on the merchandise assortment, whether retailers sell a limited line or general merchandise. Within each category, different types of retailers exist based on their service level and pricing strategy, as outlined in Figure 13.2. A number of successful companies have stores of more than one type, such as Dayton Hudson, Kmart, and Wal-Mart.

> **CHAIN STORE**
> One of a group of centrally owned and managed retail stores that handle the same product lines.

Limited-Line Retailers   Limited-line retailers focus on one product category. The four types are specialty stores, franchises, superstores, and automated vending retailers.

Limited Line	General Merchandise
Specialty stores Franchises Category killers or superstores Automatic vending retailers	Department stores Convenience stores Supermarkets Warehouse clubs Discount stores Variety stores Hypermarkets

FIGURE 13.2 *Classification of Retailers*

SPECIALTY STORE

A retailer offering merchandise in one primary product category in considerable depth.

SUPERSTORE

A retailer that focuses on a single product category but offers huge selection and low prices; also called a category killer.

AUTOMATED VENDING RETAILERS

The use of machinery operated by coins or credit cards to dispense goods.

**CONNECTED:
SURFING THE NET**

www.staples.com

With the opening of its first store on May 1, 1986, Staples, Inc., has pioneered the office products Superstore industry. The Superstore concept, for the first time, provided the same deep discounted prices to small businesses that had only been available to large corporations. Since May of 1986, Staples has expanded rapidly. To learn more, connect to the company's Web site.

DEPARTMENT STORE

A retailer with merchandise of broad variety and moderate depth and with a relatively high level of customer service.

Specialty stores offer merchandise in one primary product category in considerable depth. Examples are Wet Seal and The Limited, Florsheim and Women's Foot Locker, and Champ's Sports and Roller Skates of America. Since their strategy generally is service oriented, payroll expenses may approximate 35 percent of sales.[31] Goods are of moderate to high quality. Prices tend to be high and comparable to department stores.

Many specialty stores are run by franchisees, who sign a contractual agreement with a franchiser organization to represent and sell its products in particular retail locations. Examples include Blockbuster Video stores, the vast majority of fast-food restaurants (some outlets are company owned), and automobile dealerships.

Superstores, sometimes called category killers, focus on a single product category but offer huge selection and low prices. They tend to range in size from 50,000 to 75,000 square feet. Service levels are normally low to moderate. Examples include Barnes & Nobles, CompUSA, Home Depot, IKEA, Staples, and Sportsmart. Superstores have been particularly successful in taking business away from traditional discount stores as well as wholesalers.[32] Recently, the department store Montgomery Ward filed for bankruptcy, partially blaming its failure on the inability to counter the rise of superstores such as Wal-Mart and Circuit City.[33] Customers like the wide selection of brands that makes price and feature comparisons easy.[34]

Automated vending retailers use machinery operated by coin or credit card to dispense goods. The placement of machines is critical, and airports, hospitals, schools, and office buildings are among the most popular locations. Traditionally, vending has focused on beverages, candy, cigarettes, and food, but the industry is expanding into new areas, such as life insurance policies in airports, movie rentals in supermarkets, and lottery tickets. ARAMARK and Canteen Corporation are two leading automatic vending retailers.

In Japan, vending machines are more important in retail trade. Homes and apartments are small, with little storage space, and consumers often travel on foot or by mass transit. The convenience of location and small quantities is appealing, and a wider variety of products can be bought. Roboshop Outlets allow customers to look through displayed items, punch in the desired product's number, and then receive their purchases through a trap door. More than a dozen of these shops exist in Tokyo alone, and the Vending Machine Manufacturers Association of Japan reports that 5.5 million vending machines exist in Japan that dispense a total of $117 billion in products every year. These vending machines sell everything from alcohol to pagers and underwear.[35]

General Merchandise Retailers   General merchandise retailers carry a number of different product categories. There are seven types: department stores, convenience stores, supermarkets, warehouse clubs, discount stores, variety stores, and hypermarkets.

Department stores carry a broad array and moderate depth of merchandise, and the level of customer service is relatively high. Merchandise is grouped into well-defined departments. Both soft goods, such as apparel and linens, and hard goods, such as appliances and sporting goods, are normally sold. The intention is to provide one-stop shopping for most personal and household items. While often situated in downtown areas at a stand-alone location, department stores also are prevalent in shopping malls, where they are considered anchor tenants that draw customers.

Target markets and pricing strategies vary considerably among department stores. Some seek the upscale customer such as Bloomingdale's, Neiman Marcus, and Saks Fifth Avenue. Their decor is plush, with an ambiance and prices to match. Others such as Dillard's and May Company appeal to a somewhat broader middle-income clientele and focus on mainstream tastes.[36] Yet others, such as JCPenney and Sears, seek an even broader array of customers. Finally, department stores such as Mervyn's, Upton, and Byron's focus primarily on low-income households, featuring low prices and frequent promotions.[37] Specialty stores provide the most competition to upscale department stores, whereas at the lower end there is intense rivalry from discounters.

Convenience stores are small and have moderately low breadth and depth of merchandise. Sandwiches, soft drinks, snack foods, newspapers and magazines, milk, and beer and wine are among the most popular products carried. They are open long hours, prices are high, and their location is their primary advantage. Some are part of large corporate chains, including 7-Eleven, Circle K, and Dairy Mart. Some large oil companies have established their own operations, such as Arco's AM/PM stores and Texaco's Food Mart. Many convenience stores are mom-and-pop businesses, family owned and operated.[38]

Supermarkets are large, departmentalized, food-oriented retail establishments that sell beverages, canned goods, dairy products, frozen foods, meat, produce, and such nonfood items as health and beauty aids, kitchen utensils, magazines, pharmaceuticals, and toys. Many have in-store bakeries and delicatessens. Merchandise breadth and depth are moderately high. Since gross margins are generally low, supermarkets attempt to maximize sales volume. Typical after-tax profit is about 1.5 percent of sales.[39] In the United States, regional chains dominate, such as Hughes, Kroger, Safeway, and Winn-Dixie.

Warehouse clubs are large, no-frills stores that carry a revolving array of merchandise at low prices. They are typically 60,000 square feet or more. Consumers must become members before shopping in the clubs. Brands carried vary by day and week, depending on the deals arranged with suppliers so product selection is somewhat limited. By carrying only the most popular items in a merchandise category, clubs strive for high asset turnover (net sales divided by total assets) with gross margins as low as 8 percent. Products are often sold in bulk. Price Club/Costco and Sam's Club (part of Wal-Mart) now control 90 percent of the warehouse club industry.[40] These retailers give supermarkets stiff competition.

Discount stores offer a broad variety of merchandise, limited service, and low prices. Merchandise depth is low to moderate. Service levels are minimal. Operating costs, including payroll, are normally 20 percent or less of total sales.[41] Discounters concentrate on low- to

---

CONVENIENCE STORE

A small retailer with moderately low breadth and depth of merchandise.

SUPERMARKET

A large, departmentalized, food-oriented retail establishment that sells beverages, canned goods, dairy products, frozen foods, meat, produce, and such nonfood items as health and beauty aids, kitchen utensils, magazines, pharmaceuticals, and toys.

WAREHOUSE CLUB

A large, no-frills store that carries a revolving array of merchandise at low prices.

DISCOUNT STORE

A retailer offering a broad variety of merchandise, limited service, and low prices.

Wal-Mart is an example of a discount retailer.

OFF-PRICE RETAILER

A seller of brand-name clothing
at low prices.

CATALOG SHOWROOM

A discount retailer whose customers shop from catalogs and
can view floor samples of items
held in stock.

VARIETY STORE

A retailer offering a variety of
low-priced merchandise of low
to moderate quality.

HYPERMARKET

A giant shopping facility with
a wide selection of food and
general merchandise at low
prices.

middle-income consumers. The goal is asset turnover and sales volume per store. Wal-Mart, Kmart, and Target (a division of Dayton Hudson) are the major U.S. discount stores.

There are two specialized types of discounters. **Off-price retailers** sell brand-name clothing at low prices. Their inventory frequently changes as they take advantage of special deals from manufacturers selling excess merchandise. Examples are Loehmann's, Marshall's, Men's Warehouse, and T. J. Maxx. **Catalog showrooms** have only samples on display, and customers shop from catalogs. They often write up their own order and present it to clerks. The merchandise is then brought from the storage area. Best Products Company and Service Merchandise are examples.

Variety stores offer an array of low-priced merchandise of low to moderate quality. There is not much depth. These retailers are not as numerous as they used to be because of intense competition, mainly from larger discounters. Examples of variety stores are Everything's A Dollar and Pic'N'Save.

Hypermarkets are giant shopping facilities offering a wide selection of food and general merchandise at low prices. They have at least 100,000 square feet of space, some of them three times that. The concept was developed by a French company, Carrefour, which is very successful throughout Europe and Latin America. Hypermarkets have not thrived in the United States, partly because there is so much competition. Furthermore, consumers often complain about too much walking and limited brand selections. The costs of operating the giant facilities are high.[42] Nevertheless, hypermarkets might become more popular in the United States because they offer one-stop shopping. Existing hypermarket operations include Super Kmart Centers and Hypermarket USA.

ISSUES IN RETAILING

Retailing changes constantly and rapidly. It is important for retailers not to lose sight of such important factors as diversity, legal and ethical issues, and global retailing.

Diversity and Retailing   Because retailers deal directly with consumers, most of them realize that staffing and marketing programs must reflect the nature of the population they serve. Recognizing diversity and its implications for business practice is a must for top-performing retailers. Sears is at the forefront in connecting with diverse markets. Its stores in California serve a significant number of Hispanics, and Sears has bilingual salespeople and signage. It also advertises in Spanish in local newspapers. Sears falls only behind Procter & Gamble, AT&T, and MCI in advertising to the Hispanic market through Spanish language sources, spending $25 million in 1998 and $30 million in 1999.[43] The effort is paying off: Sales gains in its California stores with a large Latino customer base have been twice those at its other stores. Sears also is stocking smaller dress sizes in stores that serve a large Asian population.[44]

In another approach to diversity, Marriott International has a program in the inner cities called Pathways to Independence, which recently reached its 10-year anniversary. It recruits,

*Carrefour, a French company,
developed the concept of the
Hypermarket.*

screens, and trains individuals on public assistance. To qualify, applicants must have a sixth-grade reading ability, pass a drug test, and demonstrate a desire to work. Initially a program in the Atlanta Marriott Marquis hotel, the program now exists in 40 locations. The six-week program includes 60 hours of classroom instruction and 120 hours of occupational skills instruction. Over 2,700 people have graduated from the program since its inception and have assumed responsible positions in the hotel chain. Graduates of the program have among the highest retention rates in the hospitality industry. The Pathways to Independence program has been used as a model for other similar programs.[45]

Legal and Ethical Issues in Retailing   Retailers face a range of legal and ethical issues. It is important that they understand and comply with the laws applicable to them. For example, title companies perform a variety of services in consumer real estate transactions. In 1996, some California title companies were found guilty of giving kickbacks, such as cash payments, computers, and free printing of sales literature, to real estate brokers in exchange for recommending them to customers. Under federal law, no one may receive or charge any fee, kickback, or thing of value for referring business in mortgage transactions.[46]

Ethical dilemmas often arise over the goods sold by retailers. Consumer action groups often lobby them to stop carrying certain products. In an unprecedented move, Target eliminated all cigarette sales in its 714 stores in September 1996. The decision was influenced by the growing stigma attached to smoking and mounting pressure to comply with laws barring the sale of tobacco to minors.[47] Depending on community standards, many stores do not carry certain magazines, or keep them under the counter, away from children. Wal-Mart stopped carrying guns in its stores in 1994. It still sells them through catalogs and sells many shooting accessories such as gun cases, which offends many consumer advocates. The company banned Grammy winner Sheryl Crow's album in 1996 because of a lyric suggesting it sells guns to children. Record industry executives estimated this move would cost Crow a staggering 400,000 album sales.[48]

Employee relations are another area in which ethical questions arise, such as steps taken to prevent unionization or reduce employee theft. Whatever the issue, if employees are not treated with fairness and respect, then major problems can result. One recent survey found that a two-way performance review is an excellent way to retain good workers. This way both the management and the employee can comment on the employee's performance, as well as on the management's performance. Thus, the review can be just that, a "review," and not a "criticism." This plan aims to confront problems in the employee-employer relationship before they cause problems for the company.[49]

Global Retailers   A number of U.S. retailers, such as McDonald's and KFC, have had successful operations in global markets for many years. Others, such as Gap and Toys "R" Us, have only recently ventured overseas. Similar to doing business at home, the global retailer must focus on targeted customers in each market. In many cases, consumer tastes vary considerably across countries for the same product or service. McDonald's found that it had to add beer to the beverage menu in Germany and Cadbury chocolate sticks to its ice-cream cones in England.[50]

Gaining a foothold in foreign markets can be quite a challenge. It requires a strong and properly implemented retail strategy. A number of U.S. companies opened movie theaters in Japan in the mid-1990s, among them AMC Entertainment, Time Warner, and UCI (a joint

A number of U.S. retailers are building multiplexes in Japanese suburbs such as AMC theaters.

venture between Paramount and Universal Studios). They met staunch resistance from movie giants Toho and Shochiku Company, which own or control the vast majority of outlets. One of the major problems for the newcomers was obtaining a steady supply of first-rate films from Japanese film distributors. But the U.S.-owned theaters are doing well because of what they offer for the price. New theaters continue to be built in Japan and Loews Cineplex International plans to begin building its own theaters soon. They are putting up multiplexes in Japan and are locating many theaters in the suburbs. They offer advanced sound and cinematic technology, and they are open later in the evenings. Their concession stands are modern. All this is available at ticket prices as low as $10, compared to the average of $18 in theaters operated by Toho and Shochiku. Previously, movie attendance was declining in Japan due to high prices, aging theaters in downtown neighborhoods dominated by adult entertainment and bars, and competition from television and VCRs.[51] The multiplexes are beginning to yield results and admissions are increasing to the 2,000 theaters in Japan. U.S. films dominate the theaters and many worry that they are destroying smaller films.[52]

CONNECTING THROUGH RELATIONSHIPS

CDNow: Capitalizing on Internet Music Demand

Kids lining up outside their local record store, waiting for midnight and the release of their favorite band or artist's newest release. This was a common scene for decades and can still be seen even today. However, since the dawn of the Internet, companies such as CDNow have given anxious teens and even giddy adults the option of purchasing a much-anticipated album without leaving the comfort of their own home. Since its inception six years ago, CDNow has been one of the prime Internet music retailers. No longer do you have to journey to the nearest Tower Records or Sam Goody to search for CD bargains. Customers can hop onto the information superhighway and download all the information they need about an artist before making the CD purchase from their computer. By providing people easy access to their favorite music at the click of a mouse, CDNow was poised to become the next big Internet venture. However, after a few years, it began to look for an established partner in the world of CD retailing.

In March 2000, a proposed merger with Columbia House Records fell through, and CDNow saw its stock prices take a nosedive. To the rescue came German e-commerce company Bertelsmann, with a $117 million buyout proposal for CDNow. The marriage of the two high-tech media services promises to be mutually beneficial. Says CDNow CEO Jason Olim, "The market is not treating e-commerce companies very well right now, and we think we have provided the best outcome for our shareholders that was possible." Perhaps the biggest beneficiaries will be CDNow's already long list of customers. With planned "Websessions" featuring new artists, interviews, and MP3s for downloading, CDNow is looking to switch its Web site to a content focus rather than strictly a site for selling CDs and other media. Internet patrons can visit the site to get up-to-date news on their favorite musicians, hear song clips, and then purchase CDs from the same site. Also in the works is a wireless option for CDNow in conjunction with ViaFone, Inc., which could make the site accessible from PalmPilots. Users with accounts already set up through the CDNow Internet site could view and purchase CDs while on the go and also peruse the content available to traditional PC users.

For Christmas 2000, CDNow configured its shipping and warehousing operations to avoid the 1999 order delays that prompted a $100,000 fine from the Federal Trade Commission. CDNow will notify customers in advance of limited stock and plans to process orders seven times a day rather than the previous quota of two. "Close communication with our warehouse is a critical part to make sure orders are in and get out the door as soon as possible," claims vice president of customer service Amy Belew. Looking to serve customers at times when they are most demanding is one method CDNow can use to better connect with a high-tech consumer demographic.

Sources: Amy M. Mack, "New Sponsorship Model, Ad Strategy for CDNow," *Brandweek,* April 10, 2000, p. 82; Marilyn A. Gillen, "Bertelsmann Gains Web Hub with Purchase of CDNow," *Billboard,* July 29, 2000, p. 5; Matthew G. Nelson, "CDNow Takes a Leading Role in Mobile Commerce," *Informationweek,* November 6, 2000, p. 206; and Eileen Fitzpatrick, "Study Says Web Retailers Are Prepared for Holidays," *Billboard,* November 11, 2000, p. 12.

Direct marketing uses various methods to communicate with consumers, generally calling for a direct response on their part. Direct marketing is both a form of communication and a channel of distribution. Direct mail and catalogs have been used for many years. Telemarketing is another prominent method. Advertisements in print media or on television and radio that include toll-free numbers for placing orders have become very popular. The field is being revolutionized by technology—fax machines, e-mail and voice mail, electronic catalogs on diskettes and compact disks, infomercials, home television shopping channels, and the Internet.

Many organizations can benefit from direct marketing. A growing number of companies, called direct marketers, conduct business primarily or solely in this way. Excellent examples are CDNow on the Internet and Dell Computer. This kind of direct marketing is most powerful when it communicates product and pricing information, along with guidance for placing orders. The sale is completed by delivery of products via computer (such as software) or through services such as Airborne Express, DHL, and Federal Express.

According to the Direct Marketing Association, direct-marketing sales to consumers and business-to-business (B2B) markets are expected to exceed $2 trillion by the year 2005. Sales growth through direct marketing is increasing at a faster rate than consumer sales, with direct-marketing sales increasing at an annual growth rate of 8.5 percent compared to 5.5 percent for consumer sales. Similarly, business-to-business direct-marketing sales increased at 11 percent per year from 1994 to 1999 compared to a 5.6 percent growth in overall B2B sales.[53] Some industries are more affected than others. Computers, for example, are more often sold directly to the customer through the Internet rather than through retail stores. In 1999, PC sales via the Internet rose 76.4 percent compared to an 8 percent increase of sales in computer stores.[54]

VALUE TO CUSTOMERS AND MARKETING

Direct marketing offers consumers a convenient way to shop from the comfort of their home or office. The fast-paced lifestyle of many people leaves little time or energy for shopping trips. Driving costs keep increasing. Traffic congestion and parking are problems. Checkout lines are growing as many retailers reduce staff to cut costs. All these factors have increased the importance of convenience. The widespread availability of credit cards, toll-free numbers, and overnight delivery service has made direct marketing to consumers even more viable. Convenience is also important in business-to-business markets. Direct marketing allows business customers to gain information on products and place orders efficiently. It requires much less time than meeting with a variety of salespeople.

Direct marketing also can improve the quality of products offered to customers. For example, Calyx & Corolla is a mail-order florist. Its Web site claims that its flowers are generally fresher than those offered by retail outlets because its network of growers and Federal Express can get orders to customers quickly.[55] Another advantage of direct marketing is competitive prices. A company can operate out of an unadorned warehouse in an inexpensive location, keeping overhead low. Many Japanese consumers save money by ordering from U.S. catalog companies such as L.L. Bean.[56]

Direct marketing is of increasing value to many entrepreneurs as retailers cut back on inventory. For example, many music stores feature only the more mainstream artists and compilations. Music fans can, however, often find exactly what they are looking for through Internet sites such as CDNow. Wholesalers are overloaded as well. Even if they agree to add a product, there is no guarantee the product will get much support from salespeople.

Direct marketing allows small businesses to access markets without the assistance of retailers, wholesalers, or a company sales force. Consequently, the investment required for product launch is relatively low. For example, Ziff-Davis Publishing in New York City puts out a large monthly catalog, *Computer Shopper,* in which companies can advertise. A full-page ad can reach 3.34 million customers per month through the printed magazine. In addition, companies can advertise on the Web site www.zdnet.com/computershopper. *Computer Shopper* has enabled several small companies to start and successfully maintain their businesses.[57]

Large organizations also benefit from direct marketing. Some use it as their primary means of doing business. Others use it in combination with other channels. Victoria's Secret, a division of The Limited, Inc., has retail stores in major shopping malls throughout the country and also mails out several catalogs per year.

DIRECT-MARKETING DATABASES

All direct-marketing companies maintain a database with customer name, address, and purchase history. These are often supplemented with lists purchased from market research companies such as Zeller's and Dun's. Some direct marketers have taken the art of database management to a new level. The Adventa Marketplace, www.adventa.com, is a Web-based exchange for direct-marketing products and services that allows companies to rent mailing lists online. Users of the site can search for names based on hundreds of categories and then receive the list via e-mail. After a free trial period, list brokers will be charged $950 per month for the service if they join. Mailers receive the service free of charge. Adventa hopes that it is making an early move into a service that will be in need as more business is done over the Internet.[58]

DIRECT-RESPONSE MEDIA

Several media are used in direct marketing. Figure 13.3 provides estimates of sales through various direct-response media. Direct mail, including catalogs, generated the highest revenues in consumer markets, whereas telemarketing was the leader in business-to-business markets. The "other" category in Figure 13.3 includes electronic commerce over the Internet, which will grow in prominence very quickly. By 1997, direct marketers were already indicating that 40 percent of their budget would be allocated to the Internet.[59]

Direct Mail   Each year, billions of paper-based pieces are sent to prospective customers through the U.S. Postal Service. Usually, a cover letter and brochure are included but audiotapes, videotapes, and computer disks may be used. America Online mails out CDs so consumers can try the service. Orders can be placed by calling a toll-free number, filling out and mailing back an order form, or faxing the order form.

Mail contact is popular because it hits a select market at a reasonably low cost. Selective mailing lists can be developed or purchased. Direct mail also can be personalized, is flexible, and allows early testing and response measurement. Most market research projects that direct mail will continue to grow, but not as fast as it did in the 1990s. A report for the Printing Industries of America's Graphic Arts Marketing Information Services projects an annual growth of 6 percent per year from 1998 to 2008 and believes that direct mail will grow faster than other forms of marketing with the exception of the Internet.[60]

Three forms of mechanized mail are becoming popular with marketers. Fax mail is sent from one fax machine to another. Fax numbers are published in directories that can be purchased from market research companies. This method has the advantage of speed, as do the two others. E-mail is sent from one computer to another. Messages arrive almost instantly and are stored until individuals access the files. Voice mail is a verbal message sent via telephone and stored until it is retrieved. The public is less enthusiastic than direct marketers about these techniques. Many people resent paper being used to print unsolicited messages, or the time

Medium	Consumer Markets	Business-to-Business Markets
Direct mail and catalogs	$225.7	$130.4
Telemarketing	159.3	226.3
Newspapers	84.9	52.2
Magazines	30.9	29.9
Television	43.8	28.9
Radio	14.4	11.1
Other	35.6	19.4
Total	$594.4	$498.1

FIGURE 13.3   *U.S. Direct-Marketing Sales by Medium and Market (in billions of dollars)*

Source: Economic Impact: U.S. Direct Marketing Today (New York: Direct Marketing Association, 1997), p. 43.

wasted reading, listening to, and deleting messages. These forms of direct mail are best used to communicate with regular customers or people who express an interest in a product. For example, it is appropriate to send customized e-mail to people who regularly access a company's Web site or who request to be included on e-mail messages.

Catalogs **Mail-order catalogs** publish product and price information in paper form. Annually, more than 12 billion copies of more than 8,000 different paper-based catalogs are sent through the U.S. Postal Service. Some feature general merchandise, such as those by JCPenney. Others focus on a narrow range of products. Omaha Steaks sells beef, seafood, pork, lamb, chicken, pastas, and desserts in its catalog.[61] Eddie Bauer catalogs include men and women's apparel, luggage, footwear, and accessories.

Some companies, such as airlines and hotels, assemble products from various sources and hire third parties to publish paper-based catalogs. United Airlines provides SkyMall to passengers. It is a collection of upscale, unique merchandise from a number of catalogs, including Brookstone, Disney, Healthrider, Hammacher Schlemmer, and Sharper Image. Customers call an 800 number or visit www.skymall.com to order.

A major disadvantage of catalog marketing is the expense. Paper and postage prices are so high that many entrepreneurs find it impossible to issue their own, and it's very hard to get products included in brand-name catalogs. The Good Catalog Company has filled a need by partnering with producers who can't afford to publish and distribute on their own.

Electronic catalogs store product information on computer diskette or compact disk. They are becoming popular, especially in business-to-business markets. iPlanet(tm) E-Commerce Solutions, a company formed by the blending of America Online and Sun Microsystems, seeks to meet the needs of the B2B world by providing services to aid companies in becoming Internet savvy. The company collaborated with J. D. Edwards to develop "B2B in a Box," a program and electronic catalog that allows online purchasing and electronic trading.[62]

MAIL-ORDER CATALOG

A collection of product and price information that is published in paper form.

Lands' End uses mail-order catalogs to reach customers.

T̲ELEMARKETING̲

Using the telephone to contact leads (potential customers) from a list.

Telemarketing   **Telemarketing** occurs when salespeople make telephone calls to leads provided by marketing services or from other lists. The timing of calls is very important. Late morning and early afternoon are normally the best times for reaching businesses, while evenings between 7:00 and 9:00 are best for contacting households—from the marketer's standpoint. You probably have had more than a few interruptions at that time from telemarketers. When people are out, messages are often left on voice mail.

Telemarketing has a higher cost per contact than direct mail or catalogs. Furthermore, many consumers view unsolicited telephone calls as an annoyance and resent unwanted clutter on voice mail. Salespeople often are poorly trained and cannot answer questions. In fact, they may be instructed not to deviate from prearranged scripts regardless of what they are asked.

Automated telemarketing uses machines to dial numbers, play recorded messages, and take orders either via answering machines or by forwarding calls to live operators. Outbound automated calls meet with strong resistance, and the system is better used for incoming calls—that is, consumers are reached by other means and then place orders through the automated systems.

Precise list selection and development are critical for telemarketing. The sales message must be simple and strong. Salespeople must receive at least some training on how to make calls and handle customer concerns. Person-to-person telemarketing is best used in the consumer market with current customers who prefer this mode of communication. In business-to-business markets, especially when targeted at employees outside the purchasing area, telemarketing is not very successful. But some professional buyers prefer it to face-to-face dealings because less time is involved. In the business setting, it is especially important that telemarketers be carefully selected, well trained, and adequately compensated.

Advertisements in Print and Broadcast Media   Print ads in magazines and newspapers are used a great deal in direct marketing. Along with information on products and prices, toll free numbers are given. For example, Horizon Instruments of Fullerton, California, sells digital engine tachometers and other instrumentation to owners of private planes through ads in leading aviation magazines.

Direct marketers also rely on television and radio spots, usually ranging from 10 to 60 seconds. Exercise equipment from NordicTrack and Soloflex, publications such as *Sporting News* and *Sports Illustrated,* and music CDs are among the products frequently advertised on television. Oreck Corporation of New Orleans uses radio ads to sell vacuum cleaners.

I̲NFOMERCIAL̲

A programmatic advertisement of considerable length that resembles a documentary.

Infomercials are long advertisements that resemble documentaries. They range from 15 to 60 minutes and often include celebrity endorsers and testimonials from satisfied customers. Such products as smoking cessation, weight-control programs, cosmetics, and exercise equipment are promoted this way. Established companies such as Chrysler and Mattel are beginning to use the technique to communicate in depth about product benefits. Some direct marketers use it to obtain distribution in retail stores. For example, Peter Bieler's infomercials on the Thighmaster Exerciser featuring Suzanne Somers generated national publicity—including a mention in David Letterman monologues and George Bush speeches. Bieler then gained distribution through Kmart, Wal-Mart, and other big chains, selling 6 million units in less than two years.[63]

Televised Home Shopping   In the past several years, home shopping via cable television has come into prominence. The two largest marketers are Quality Value Channel (QVC) and the Home Shopping Network (HSN), with others including the Home Shopping Mall, Teleshop, and Value Club of America. Themed programs are telecast 24 hours a day, seven days a week, to more than 248 million households worldwide. Program hosts, including such celebrities as Julia Child and Hugh Downs, offer products ranging from books to computers, jewelry to lamps, clothing to power tools. Customers send orders over toll-free lines, enabling companies to adjust inventory minute by minute, not just season by season. Orders are usually shipped within 48 hours. Annual sales through this medium reached $4.28 billion in 1999. QVC and HSN also have Web sites that allow customers to shop online, track purchases, and chat with other users.[64]

Videotext links a consumer's television with a seller's computerized catalog of products by cable or telephone lines. Consumers can place orders through special keyboard devices. The use of videotext in direct marketing has not yet been successful, partly because the systems are costly to install and are available in only a few markets.

The Internet   Many companies have added e-commerce to their Web sites, allowing consumers to make purchases directly on the Web site. Consumers are already comfortable with other types of direct-response media, which helps make them receptive to the Net. Security is an issue, however. Many people are reluctant to provide credit card numbers online. Furthermore, as more and more households own computers, e-commerce is now less limited than before. And beyond our borders, the Web's heavy U.S. accent grates on many cultures. As the Web becomes more global, however, this problem also provides an opportunity for enterprising marketers who can operate across boundaries in many languages.

Companies must decide whether to set up their own Web operation or turn to a provider. The trade-off is between greater control and no fees to outside Internet resellers, on one hand, and expertise and an existing subscriber base on the other. An annual fee plus some percentage of the company's online sales, typically 2 percent, is paid to the online service.

Individuals who do not have their own Web sites, or who wish to sell their items through larger sites, can use sites such as eBay, which allows users to bid on items and then charges the seller a set amount based on the purchase price.[65]

In the consumer market, CDNow, Inc., of Fort Washington, Pennsylvania, is an Internet reseller with more than 300,000 compact disc and cassette titles, T-shirts, videos, and laser discs for sale through its site on the World Wide Web. Shoppers make purchases by credit card through a secure encryption system. CDNow owns no inventory; instead it relies on a network of wholesalers to ship orders, normally within 24 hours.[66]

The Internet is a great interactive medium. Many companies' profits are coming increasingly from Internet sales. Established mail-order catalog companies Lands' End and Spiegel are among companies whose profits are increasing because of Internet sales. Lands' End Internet sales accounted for about 10 percent of total sales in 1999 and had increased 70 percent in the first two quarters of 2000. Spiegel's Internet sales account for 6.2 percent of its total sales.[67] An Ernst & Young survey recently found that 52 percent of Americans had purchased books online, 49 percent had purchased CDs and computers, 29 percent had made reservations online, 28 percent had purchased toys and electronic equipment, and 27 percent had purchased videos online. The survey stated that online shoppers spent an average of $896 and total Internet sales for 2000 were approximately $38 billion, excluding all automobile and travel sales. Shoppers are clearly viewing the Internet as an option for making purchases in many instances.[68]

THE DIRECT-MARKETING PLAN

Direct marketers make several decisions when developing a marketing strategy. The most important relate to target markets, database management, merchandise assortment, pricing, choice of media and other channels, message design, and payment methods and delivery. The steps are depicted in Figure 13.4.

**CONNECTED:
SURFING THE NET**

www.cdnow.com

Find out more about Internet resellers by connecting to the CDNow Web site. You can place advance orders for featured items, review the weekly specials, and listen to entire albums while you shop.

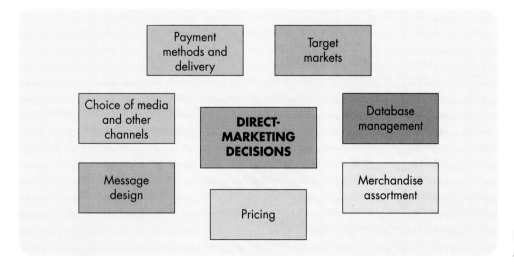

FIGURE 13.4   *Direct-Marketing Decisions*

Clinique developed a unique sun-care line to target women concerned about sun protection for every part of their body.

Target Markets   Every excellent marketing strategy begins with an understanding of the intended audience, whether baseball hobbyists, newlyweds, cooking buffs, or outdoor enthusiasts. Therefore, the first decision is which customers to target.[69] Many direct marketers are small companies content to serve a narrow group of customers in their home territory. Others expand nationally or globally once a strong business foundation is established. Dell Computer Corporation began in 1983 by serving small and medium-sized businesses in Austin, Texas, that needed upgrades on IBM-compatible computers. Dell branched out to serve large businesses and government agencies throughout the United States in the mid-1980s. Today, Dell has regional business units in the United States, England, Hong Kong, and Kawasaki, Japan.[70]

Database Management   Maintaining a strong customer database is essential. Addresses and preferences must be current. Duplicate names must be removed. Those with poor credit histories must be flagged, and inactive customers must be noted. A record must be kept of those who do not want to be contacted.

 Another critical function of a database is tracking. For example, Lids, a retailer of sports-oriented hats, has recently developed a database that will track individual stores' performances and show which are falling short of company goals. Because of the stores' limited product line, the company cannot afford to overlook missed opportunities for improvement.[71]

Merchandise Assortment   The choice of target markets goes hand in hand with decisions on merchandise assortment. Baseball enthusiasts will be attracted to fantasy baseball camps and memorabilia. Cooking buffs are interested in exotic ingredients and hard-to-get equipment. Companies need to review and adjust the assortment in light of economic trends, competition, and changes in preferences of the target market. Omaha Steaks initially sold beef but responded to the trend toward lower-fat foods by offering seafood, lamb, and chicken.[72] Dell Computer, which focused on desktop computers for years, had to add laptops and local area network (LAN) servers in the mid-1990s when it expanded to many user segments and began selling numerous handheld devices in 2000.[73]

Pricing   Direct-marketing companies often follow a low-price strategy, facilitated by their low overhead. Dell, the nation's largest producer of personal computers, ensures that customers receive quality products at low costs by eliminating unnecessary retailers. Customers can purchase custom-built computers directly through the Web site or by calling the company.[74]

In contrast, some companies emphasize merchandise quality and follow a premium price strategy. Brigandi Coin Company in New York City has a strong direct-marketing business in baseball cards, team-signed baseballs, and autographs. It has developed a reputation for selling only the finest-quality, authentic memorabilia. This is important, since fraud is a major problem in the industry. Many collectors will pay Brigandi's high prices because of their confidence in the company.

Media and Channels   Direct-marketing companies normally start with one promotion medium. QVC started with a home television shopping channel. Over time, many branch out to multiple media. Lands' End now uses the Internet as well, and QVC not only has a Web site but also sends out catalogs.

Some direct marketers continue to use traditional channels though they also operate large Internet sites. Omaha Steaks has established over 55 company-owned retail stores in 14 states in addition to its Internet-based business, including a Japanese Web site.[75]

Message Design   Whatever medium is used, message design and presentation are most important. For paper-based mail, attention must be paid to the envelope, the cover letter, and the product brochure. Envelopes of standard size and appearance are often discarded unopened, especially when mailing labels are used. An illustration or an important reason for opening the envelope often helps. The cover letter should be short and clear, using bold type to identify key product or service benefits. Brochures must be of high quality in appearance and content.[76]

Catalogs vary in quality of production depending on the company, its merchandise, and its targeted customers. For example, Victoria's Secret sells high-quality lingerie and women's apparel, targeted to an upscale market. Paper, design, and photographs are of high quality. Hello Direct sells telephone productivity tools, such as cordless headsets and speakerphones, to businesses. It emphasizes low prices, and its catalog is produced at low cost.

On the Web, the home page must be eye-catching and provide different categories of information the user can access. Sites must be easy to navigate. One rule of thumb is that content should never be more than three clicks away. Getting back to the home page must be simple. One guideline in creating content is to think of how the best salesperson would sell the company and its products. The site must provide a clear overview of the company and why its products are a good buy. Testimonials from satisfied customers are a good idea. Finally, sites must be updated regularly so that users will keep coming back to see what's new.[77]

Finally, the diversity of a company's customers must be considered when designing direct-marketing messages. A study by Skunkworks of New York said that companies can average a 20 percent increase in sales simply by advertising on Spanish-language network television instead of on English-language broadcast networks. By directly targeting Hispanic communities in ways that appeal to them, companies can increase their sales and increase customer loyalty.[78]

Payment Methods and Delivery   Direct-marketing companies serving the consumer market often offer several different payment methods—check, money order, or credit card. Installments also may be possible, especially when the product is relatively expensive, although the final cost to the consumer is greater under that option. Oreck Corporation allows a free trial period of two weeks for its vacuum cleaners.

In business-to-business markets, customers often have an account with the direct marketer, and a monthly bill is sent. Typically, if the invoice is paid within 10 days, a 2 percent credit will be applied to the next bill. Payment is normally due within 30 days.

Customers usually have several delivery options. The standard mode at Sharper Image is Federal Express second-day air; the delivery charge is based on the dollar value of the order. For an extra fee, customers can select next-day air or Saturday delivery. Eddie Bauer offers standard delivery (3 to 5 days), express (3 days), or express plus (2 days) at progressively higher charges.

ETHICS IN DIRECT MARKETING

A number of ethical problems confront the direct-marketing industry, such as the right to privacy and the confidentiality of personal information. When you order products by mail, enter a sweepstakes, apply for a credit card, or buy a magazine subscription, chances are the information is entered into a huge database that can be accessed by many companies. In September 1996, thousands of callers jammed the phone lines at the Ohio headquarters of LEXIS-NEXIS, demanding to be removed from P-Trak, a personal database offered commercially by the firm. It is targeted to law enforcement officials and lawyers trying to track down witnesses, but it can be bought by anyone willing to pay a search fee.[79] You and virtually every American adult are in P-Trak, which has current and former addresses, birth dates, and maiden names, among other information.

Another ethical issue is misrepresentation. Contests and sweepstakes are sometimes worded to make people believe they have won a prize. Only after making expensive 900-number calls do consumers discover that they have won little or nothing.

Some direct marketers bombard consumers with unwanted messages. People subscribing to one of the commercial online services often find loads of junk e-mail waiting for them, a practice called spamming in the industry.[80] In response to complaints, America Online denied access in 1996 to the biggest junk e-mailers. They filed a lawsuit, and a federal court ordered AOL to lift the blockade pending the suit's resolution.[81] A higher court finally ruled AOL had the right to protect subscribers.

In some countries, direct marketing has a very poor reputation because of past abuses. For example, many Japanese consumers view direct marketers as fly-by-night operators that cannot be trusted.[82] The industry must police itself if it is to thrive. With this in mind, the Direct Marketing Association (DMA) in Washington, DC, has established ethical guidelines, which are summarized in Figure 13.5. Companies must sign the code and agree to uphold it before becoming members of the association. The DMA has an executive committee that reviews direct-marketing materials. If any are found to be misleading, then the company is asked to change the message. The DMA also provides a service to help consumers block unwanted mail and catalogs.

You may notice that the basic principles underlying the DMA guidelines—such as honesty, clarity, fairness, and accuracy—are relevant not only to direct marketing but to marketing communications in general. In chapter 14 we will take an in-depth look at this broad and important topic. In addition to presenting an integrated conceptual framework for marketing communications, we will examine the communications process itself and the ways in which the communications mix can be orchestrated to send a powerful, unified message to the target audience.

FIGURE 13.5 *A Summary of Direct Marketing Association Guidelines for Ethical Conduct*

Source: A handout from the Direct Marketing Association, October 1996.

TERMS OF THE OFFER

HONESTY: All offers should be clear, honest, and complete so that the consumer may know the exact nature of what is being offered.

CLARITY: Simple and consistent statements of all the essential points of the offer should be clearly displayed in the promotional material. When an offer illustrates goods that are not included or that cost extra, these facts should be made clear.

PRINT SIZE: Print that by its small size, placement, or other visual characteristics is likely to substantially affect the legibility or clarity of the offer or exceptions to it should not be used.

PHOTOGRAPHS AND ARTWORK: Photographs, illustrations, artwork, and the situations they represent should be accurate portrayals and current reproductions of the products, services, or other subjects in all particulars.

SPECIAL OFFERS: When the term *free* or other similar representations are made (for example, 2-for-1, half-price, 1-cent offers), the product or service required to be purchased should not have been increased in price or decreased in quantity or quality.

PRIZES: No award should be held forth directly or by implication as having substantial monetary value if it is of nominal worth. The value of a prize given should be stated at regular retail value.

PREMIUMS: A premium, gift, or item should not be called or held out to be a "prize" if it is offered to every recipient of or participant in a promotion.

PRICE COMPARISONS: Price comparisons such as those between one's price and a former, future, or suggested price, or between one's price and the price of a competitor's comparable product should be made fairly and accurately.

CHAPTER SUMMARY

OBJECTIVE 1: Appreciate the important role retailers play in our economy and society.

Retailing is the final stage in the distribution channel for a majority of products sold to consumers. Time, place, possession, and form utilities are provided to consumers by retailers. In addition, retailers may promote the general welfare of society through efforts to recruit a diverse workforce. A number of U.S. retailers have been very successful in global markets by understanding important variations in consumer tastes across cultures.

OBJECTIVE 2: Understand strategy issues confronted by retailers when making marketing decisions.

Retailing strategy must cover a variety of issues. Each retailer must decide on the target market(s) and positioning, then adopt a distinct service level and pricing approach, and decide what type of merchandise assortment it will offer. The geographical location of stores is a very important decision. Some retailers locate stores in low-rent areas off highways and at a distance from other retailers, whereas others place stores close to competitors. Well-run shopping centers have immense pulling power and are good locations for many retailers. New technologies, such as sophisticated computer systems that allow merchandise to be tailored in individual stores, help improve retailer performance. Furthermore, effectively managing relationships with suppliers—whether manufacturers, wholesalers, or agents—is critical.

OBJECTIVE 3: Recognize the diverse array of retailers that compete with one another.

Limited-line retailers include specialty stores, superstores, and automated vending operations. General merchandise retailers include department stores, convenience stores, supermarkets, warehouse clubs, discount stores, variety stores, and hypermarkets. An understanding of each type is useful in tracking and predicting competitive trends. A number of successful retailers have stores of different types.

OBJECTIVE 4: Learn what direct marketing entails, its value, and how it differs from mass communication.

Direct marketing is a powerful selling approach, especially when media are used to communicate information on products and prices and how to place orders. Growth in sales through direct-marketing channels is outpacing growth in U.S. retail sales by about two to one. Direct marketing offers consumers and businesses a convenient way to shop. It enables many small companies to access markets they could not reach through traditional retail and wholesale organizations. It is popular in many parts of the world. In fact, the largest direct-marketing companies are based in foreign countries. International direct-marketers must adjust their strategies to the unique characteristics of each country they serve.

OBJECTIVE 5: Be familiar with the different types of direct-response media.

A large number of direct-response media are available. Paper-based mail, fax mail, e-mail, and voice mail are options. Mail-order catalogs are used by many companies, and electronic versions are gaining in popularity. Telemarketing is a major force, especially in business-to-business markets. Advertisements in print and broadcast media are important in direct-marketing activities. Infomercials can be used effectively to sell products and gain distribution through retailers. Television shopping channels have done well. The Internet is an intriguing medium still in its infancy. Each medium has its strengths and weaknesses that must be considered by companies choosing which one or which mix to use.

OBJECTIVE 6: Understand the marketing decisions made by direct-marketing companies.

Direct marketers make a number of decisions when developing a marketing strategy. They must carefully select the target market(s). Strong customer databases must be developed and maintained. In particular, direct marketers can put database marketing to great use. Decisions on target markets go hand in hand with merchandise assortment and pricing. Multiple direct-response media should be used with great attention paid to the content of messages in each medium. Each medium has unique challenges with regard to message content. Finally, payment methods and delivery options must be selected.

REVIEW YOUR UNDERSTANDING

1. What is retailing? What is a retailer? List two reasons retailers are important.
2. What are the steps in developing a retail strategy?
3. What is a markup? Markdown?
4. What are the four types of limited-line retailers? What are the seven types of general merchandise retailers?
5. List three ethical issues in retailing.
6. What is direct marketing?
7. List several ways direct marketing provides value to customers.
8. List several media used in direct marketing.
9. List the seven decisions direct marketers make when developing a marketing strategy.
10. What are two ethical problems in the direct-marketing industry? Briefly explain each.

DISCUSSION OF CONCEPTS

1. Explain the Pathways to Independence program of Marriott International, Inc. What are its main benefits?
2. Is following a hybrid strategy on service and price more difficult for a retailer than either a discount-oriented or service-oriented strategy? Explain.
3. What are the pros and cons of following a destination location strategy? Under what conditions would locating stores close to the competition be preferable?
4. Among the various types of limited-line and general merchandise retailers, which have the strongest competitive position? Why?
5. Some experts view electronic shopping over the Internet as a major threat to retailers. Do you agree or disagree?
6. What are the major reasons for the growing importance of direct marketing in the United States?
7. What are the pros and cons of using fax mail, e-mail, and voice mail? Would you recommend their use to a direct-marketing company? Why or why not?
8. What are infomercials? Can they be misused? How?
9. Explain how effective database management can improve the performance of a direct marketing company.
10. Are the efforts of the Direct Marketing Association to promote ethics among its members worthwhile? What else can be done to encourage ethical behavior in the industry?

KEY TERMS AND DEFINITIONS

Automated vending: The use of machinery operated by coins or credit cards to dispense goods.

Catalog showroom: A discount retailer whose customers shop from catalogs and can view floor samples of items held in stock.

Chain store: One of a group of centrally owned and managed retail stores that handle the same product lines.

Convenience store: A small retailer with moderately low breadth and depth of merchandise.

Department store: A retailer with merchandise of broad variety and moderate depth and with a relatively high level of customer service.

Direct marketing: The use of various communication media to interact directly with customers and generally calling for them to make a direct response.

Discount store: A retailer offering a broad variety of merchandise, limited service, and low prices.

Hypermarket: A giant shopping facility with a wide selection of food and general merchandise at low prices.

Infomercial: A programmatic advertisement of considerable length that resembles a documentary.

Mail-order catalog: A collection of product and price information that is published in paper form.

Markdown: A reduction from the original retail selling price of a product.

Markup: The amount added to the cost of acquiring a product that determines its retail selling price.

Off-price retailer: A seller of brand-name clothing at low prices.

Retailing: The activities involved in selling products and services directly to end users for personal or household use.

Scrambled merchandising: A retail strategy that entails carrying an array of product lines that seem to be unrelated.

Shopping mall (shopping center): A group of retail stores in one location and marketed as a unit to shoppers in a trade area.

Specialty store: A retailer offering merchandise in one primary product category in considerable depth.

Supermarket: A large, departmentalized, food-oriented retail establishment that sells beverages, canned goods, dairy products, frozen foods, meat, produce, and such nonfood items as health and beauty aids, kitchen utensils, magazines, pharmaceuticals, and toys.

Superstore: A retailer that focuses on a single product category but offers a huge selection and low prices; also called a category killer.

Telemarketing: Using the telephone to contact leads (potential customers) from a list.

Variety store: A retailer offering a variety of low-priced merchandise of low to moderate quality.

Warehouse club: A large, no-frills store that carries a revolving array of merchandise at low prices.

Wheel of retailing: A descriptive theory about how retailers emerge, evolve, and sometimes fade away.

REFERENCES

1. Interview with Cynthia Palmer, August 12, 1997. www.mfa.org/shop/, visited January 9, 2001.
2. www.fordvehicles.com/news/index.asp?tpt=1&aid=79&specs height=1635, site visited January 4, 2001.
3. www.walmart.com and www.compusa.com, sites visited January 4, 2001.
4. www.commerce.gov, site visited January 6, 2001.
5. www. stats.bls.gov/blshome.htm, site visited January 4, 2001.
6. Michael Levy and Barton Weitz, *Retailing Management* (Chicago: Richard D. Irwin, 1995), p. 129.
7. David Bolotsky and Matthew Fassler, *Exploring the Future of Hard Goods Specialty Retailing* (New York: Goldman, Sachs & Company, 1993), pp. 2–4; www.autozone.com, site visited January 5, 2001.
8. www.nordstrom.com, site visited January 5, 2001.
9. Conversation with Ed Thomas, president of Wet Seal, November 26, 1996; www.wetseal.com/corpinfo.asp?value=2, site visited January 5, 2001.
10. Levy and Weitz, *Retailing Management*, p. 129.
11. www.targetcorp.com/companies/target.asp#stores, site visited January 5, 2001; and Gregory Patterson, "Target Micromarketing Its Way to Success: No Two Stores are Alike," *Wall Street Journal*, May 31, 1995, pp. A1, A8.
12. Nancy Brumback, "Salsa Savvy," *Supermarket News*, March 22, 1999.
13. Zina Moukheiber, "The Price Is Right," *Forbes*, December 16, 1996, pp. 52, 53; www.crownbooks.com, www.barnesandnoble.com, www.borders.com, sites visited January 5, 2001.
14. Mike Norbut, "Gas Station as Big a Hit with History Buffs as with People Seeking Fuel, Coffee," *Associated Press Newswires*, November 7, 2000.
15. "Borders(R) Celebrates Jazz with In-Store Events, Online Contest and Interview with Ken Burns," *PR Newswire*, December 20, 2000.
16. Martin Sloane, "Making a Name for Itself," *United Features Syndicate*, July 19, 2000, p. 6.
17. Bolotsky and Fassler, *Hard Goods Specialty Retailing*, pp. 2–4.
18. Pereira, "Toys 'R' Them."
19. Levy and Weitz, *Retailing Management*, p. 258.
20. Louis Stern, Adel El-Ansary, and Anne Coughlan, *Marketing Channels*, 5th ed. (Upper Saddle River, NJ: Prentice Hall, 1996), p. 62.
21. Adam M. Brandenburger and Barry J. Nalebuff, *Co-opetition* (New York: Doubleday, 1996), p. 34.
22. Patrick Reilly, "Where Borders Group and Barnes & Noble Compete, It's a War," *Wall Street Journal*, September 3, 1996, pp. A1, A6.
23. Consulting assignment for Planet Hollywood during 1995; and Brandenburger and Nalebuff, *Co-opetition*, p. 33.
24. Paul Doocey, "Mall of America Fallout," *Stores*, May 1993, pp. 44–47; www.mallofamerica.com, site visited January 5, 2001.
25. Diane Eicher, "Now Showing a Room with a View," *Denver Post*, December 1, 2000, p. E01.
26. "Experian Launches Website for Marketers," *M2 Presswire*, November 15, 2000.
27. Don Peppers and Martha Rogers, *The One to One Future* (New York: Doubleday, 1996).
28. "Excite@Home's MatchLogic Teams with Dynamics Direct to Offer Individualized Rich Media Email," *PR Newswire*, December 5, 2000.
29. Teresa F. Lindeman, "Online Groceries More Glint Than Reality," *Pittsburgh Post-Gazette*, October 19, 2000, p. F-3.
30. "Wal-Mart Typifies Cooperation between Supplier, Retailer," *The Commercial Appeal (Memphis)*, July 14, 1991, p. C1.
31. Stern, El-Ansary, and Coughlan, *Marketing Channels*, p. 44.
32. John Cortez, "Kmart Unleashes Its Category Killer Chains," *Advertising Age*, February 1, 1993, pp. S4, S5.
33. Kevin Helliker, "Montgomery Ward to Close Its Stores," *The Asian Wall Street Journal*, January 2, 2001, p. 2.
34. Cyndee Miller, "Retailers Do What They Must to Ring Up Sales," *Marketing News*, May 22, 1995, pp. 1, 10, 11.
35. Simon Rowe, "Machine Love," *Sydney Morning Herald*, November 2, 2000, p. 26.
36. Francine Schwadel, "As Retailing's Chic and Indebted Stumble, Bland May Co. Thrives," *Wall Street Journal*, January 19, 1990, p. A1.
37. Levy and Weitz, *Retailing Management*, p. 40.
38. See, for example, Hector Saldana, "Ernie Hernandez, Owner Keeps Convenience in Jefferson Area," *San Antonio Express-News*, December 10, 2000, p. 08H.
39. William Schoell and Joseph Guiltinan, *Marketing* (Upper Saddle River, NJ: Prentice Hall, 1995), p. 408.
40. Stern, El-Ansary, and Coughlan, *Marketing Channels*, p. 43.
41. Ibid., p. 44.
42. Walter Levy, "Are Department Stores Doomed?" *Direct Marketing*, May 1991, pp. 56–60.
43. "10 Largest Advertisers to the Hispanic Market," *Marketing News*, July 3, 2000.
44. White, "Ethnic Side of Sears." *Los Angeles Times*, January 29, 1966, pp. D1, D4.
45. Dana Milbank, "Hiring Welfare People, Hotel Chain Finds, Is Tough but Rewarding," *Wall Street Journal*, October 31, 1996, pp. A1, A6; "Marriott's Welfare-to-Work Program, Pathways to Independence, Reaches 10-Year Milestone," *PR Newswire*, December 18, 2000.
46. Debora Vrana, "State Investigating Title Company Kickbacks," *Los Angeles Times*, September 11, 1996, pp. D1, D11.
47. George White and Myron Levin, "Target Stores to Stop Selling Cigarettes," *Los Angeles Times*, August 29, 1996, pp. A1, A28.
48. James Bates and Chuck Philips, "Wal-Mart Bans Album over Gun Sale Lyrics," *Los Angeles Times*, September 10, 1996, pp. A1, A15; www.walmart.com, site visited January 5, 2001.
49. Jules Steinberg, "Worker Performance Reviews Can Be a Two-Way Street," *Twice*, September 4, 2000, p. 28.
50. Tara Parker-Pope, "Custom Made," *Wall Street Journal*, September 26, 1996, pp. R22, R23.
51. Evelyn Iritani, "A Reel Challenge: U.S. Firms Make Big Push into Japan Theater Market," *Los Angeles Times*, July 28, 1996, pp. D1, D4.
52. "Big Jump in Japanese Ticket Sales," *Screen Digest*, February 1999; "Loews Cineplex International to Establish Representative Office in Japan," *Business Wire*, May 5, 2000.
53. Deborah Toth, "Direct Mail: Still Marketers' Darling," *Graphic Arts Monthly*, September 2000, pp. 79–84.
54. Doug Olenick, "Consumer-Direct PC Sales Surge in 1999," *Twice*, November 20, 2000, p. 44.
55. www.calyxandcorolla.com, site visited January 5, 2001.
56. "Japan Is Dialing 1-800 Buy America: U.S. Catalogers Offer Bargains Shoppers Can't Find at Home," *Business Week*, June 12, 1995, p. 55; and Mari Yamaguchi, "Japanese Consumers Shun Local Catalogs to Buy American," *Marketing News*, December 2, 1996, p. 12.
57. Based on consulting experience with a small direct-marketing company in the computer industry, October 1995; www.zdnet.com/computershopper.com, site visited January 5, 2001; "Computer Shopper Increases Online Shopping Emphasis with e-Link™," *PR Newswire*, January 13, 2000.
58. Patricia O'Dell, "Adventa offers an on-line marketplace for DMERS," *Direct*, July 30, 2000.
59. *Sales and Marketing Management*, April 1997, p. 14, from Cahners Business Confidence Index as reported in Robert S. Lazich, *Market Share Reporter* (New York: Gale, 1998), p. 1752.
60. Deborah Toth, "Direct Mail: Still Marketers' Darling," *Graphic Arts Monthly*, September 2000, pp. 79–84.
61. "Rare Philosophy," *Marketing Management*, Summer 1995, pp. 4–6; www.omahasteaks.com, site visited January 5, 2001.

62. Paul Mann, "The Glue That Binds the B2B World Together," *Open Manufacturing,* Summer 2000, pp. 7–9.

63. Peter Bieler, *The Business Has Legs* (New York: John Wiley & Sons, 1996).

64. Steve Sullivan, "Shopping Channels: Less of a Hard Sell," *Broadcasting and Cable,* November 27, 2000; www.qvc.com and www.hsn.com, sites visited January 5, 2001.

65. www.ebay.com, site visited January 5, 2001.

66. Karen Kaplan, "Listening Boom: Music-Oriented Sites Lead the World Wide Web Hit Parade," *Los Angeles Times,* July 12, 1995, pp. D1, D7; Kathy Rebello, "Making Money on the Net," *Business Week,* September 23, 1996, pp. 104–118.

67. Cathy Tokarski, "Online Shopping: Just What the Customers Ordered," *Crain's Chicago Business,* November 27, 2000, p. SR34.

68. Valerie Seckler, "Loyalty Is Holiday Challenge," *Women's Wear Daily,* November 27, 2000, p. 20.

69. Robert Stone, *Successful Direct Marketing Methods* (Lincolnwood, IL: NTC Business Books, 1994).

70. Das Narayandas and V. Kasturi Rangan, "Dell Computer Corporation," Case #9-596-058 (Cambridge, MA: Harvard Business School Publishing, 1996); www.dell.com, site visited January 5, 2001.

71. Kim Ann Zimmermann, "Hat's Off," *Sportstyle,* February 1999.

72. "Rare Philosophy."

73. Narayandas and Rangan, "Dell Computer Corporation"; www.dell.com, site visited January 5, 2001.

74. www.dell.com, site visited January 5, 2001.

75. www.omahasteaks.com, site visited January 5, 2001.

76. Stone, *Successful Direct Marketing Methods.*

77. Judson, *NetMarketing.*

78. Dwight Cunningham, "One Size Does Not Fit All," *Media Week,* November 15, 1999, p. 54.

79. Amy Harmon, "Public Outrage Hits Firm Selling Personal Data," *Los Angeles Times,* September 19, 1996, pp. A1, A21.

80. David Nicholson, "Spamming Spreads Over Computer Networks," *Los Angeles Times,* September 9, 1996, p. D14.

81. Jane Hodges, "AOL Takes on Bulk E-Mailers," *Advertising Age,* September 9, 1996, p. 8.

82. Alice Z. Cuneo, "Dell Joins Japan Computer Push," *Advertising Age,* September 2, 1996, p. 15.

Bricks or Clicks

WILL THE INTERNET TAKE OVER THE MALLS?

MALL OWNERS ARE NOT AFRAID of the Internet. Online sales made up less than 1 percent of total retail sales in 1999. Instead, they are jumping on the Internet bandwagon. Mills Corporation has teamed up with eBay to auction off mall shopping sprees and valuables. The goal is to get more people into the mall.

General Growth Properties and Simon Property Group, two of the largest mall owners, are both starting Internet-focused programs. Simon Property Group is testing the use of handheld scanning devices by teens to make wish lists that can then be sent to family and friends via e-mail. The program has received mixed reviews. Despite the large number of teens participating, very few retailers saw shoppers with the lists and when they did, the items were not listed with an identifying number, making it difficult to find. General Growth Properties is taking a different approach to using the Internet. It is placing kiosks with online stores in various locations throughout the mall. The online businesses are noncompeting with their physical stores. This allows the company to make a percentage of every Internet sale. In-store kiosks actually take revenue away from mall owners. The customers are buying direct from the company and not the individual store. Mall owners usually receive a percentage of a store's sales.

The dual channel strategy is working in the other direction as well. Gateway Inc., the online and catalog computer retailer, has built several physical stores across the country to tap into another subset of customers. This clicks-to-bricks shift gives the company more options and allows customers the opportunity to look, touch, and test the equipment before buying. Many customers use the Internet to research products but ultimately go to the store to purchase them. It is predicted that up to 19 percent of real-world purchases will be affected by the Internet. This supports the idea that a dual channel, bricks-and-clicks strategy is a smart one.

Sources: Christopher Heun, "The Landlords of Cyberspace," *Informationweek,* July 24, 2000, pp. RB18–RB22; Alina Matas, "Clicks and Mortar," *Broward Daily Business Review,* December 17, 1999, p. A6; and Jonathon Gaw, "Advertising and Marketing; Mall Firms Go to Net to Shop for Customers; Mills Corp. and Other Owners of Brick-and-Mortar Retail Properties Are Trying Alliances with Online Firms to Make In-Person Shopping More Attractive," *Los Angeles Times,* December 1, 1999, Business, Part C, p. 1.

CASE 13

Gateway

WOUD YOU PURCHASE YOUR FIRST computer, sight unseen, over the phone or Internet? Millions have. In 1987 Ted Waitt, founder of Gateway, Inc. (formerly Gateway 2000), recognized a neglected market that would purchase PCs through direct marketing. Aiming to "offer buyers a logical alternative to the high markups, limited choices, and inadequate support common in the PC market," Waitt and his business partner, Mike Hammond, started selling computer peripherals and software to owners of Texas Instrument PCs. Soon Gateway began assembling its own PC-compatible systems. Using the direct channel, Gateway became a *Fortune* 500 company in less than 10 years. Competing in one of the fastest-paced industries, Gateway knows how to forge relationships with customers without a strong retail presence. There were lackluster sales due to an overall decline in PC demand late in 2000, but in previous years Gateway had seen growth rates of 30 percent or more annually.

Jim Taylor, senior vice president of global marketing, says, "We ask customers to call up, spend more money on your credit card than you've ever spent before, for something you can't see and that, at the same time you order it, doesn't exist." Since Gateway only assembles computers once they have been ordered, Taylor notes, "we spend a lot of money trying to earn their trust." The investment has paid off. Gateway is now among the top personal computer retailers, and along with rival Dell, has distanced itself from mainstays such as IBM and Apple. Gateway cashed in on $3.9 billion worth of online and Gateway Country Store sales in 1999, while closest competitor Dell registered $1.3 billion. Most other competitors were stuck in the tens of millions range in sales revenue. The reason for this drastic gap is most likely due to Gateway's unique sales strategies and exemplary service. Personnel from Gateway answer every call within two minutes and strive to do even better. Gateway also has 24-hour, toll-free support seven days a week for service and questions. According to Taylor, "In the electronic world, every contact with the customer is crucial and has got to reflect your emotional and moral claims."

To maintain a high consumer response, Gateway relies heavily on such direct-response media as the Web, newspapers, television, magazines, catalogs, and others. The site enables customers to self-select according to their requirements, essentially assigning themselves to the appropriate market niche.

With an annual ad budget of more than $100 million, Gateway incorporates its South Dakota "heartland mystique" as a central part of its communications. Television is increasing in importance as a direct-response medium for the company. Traditionally relying on such print vehicles as the *Wall Street Journal* to disperse information quickly, television commercials effectively emphasize the company's values that are specifically: "Humanizing the digital revolution." Customer satisfaction is the focus of the company, and this is demonstrated in its marketing as well as its service. Gateway offers lifetime technical support on its computer systems and additional software support for at least 90 days after purchase. A recent survey in *Consumer Reports* found that Gateway was one of the highest-rated retailers in the areas of customer satisfaction and technical problem resolution among support service users. However, Gateway customers now have options other than dialing an 800 number to find out more about their computers.

Although the Gateway approach relies on dealing with consumers without the use of a retail intermediary, it is undergoing some significant changes. Gateway has established a network of 227 Country Stores to offer customers an opportunity to try different models, ask questions, and order a computer on the spot.

The stores target areas with large university populations, upper-class residents, and other characteristics of Gateway's traditional buyers. The stores, which have a "down home" appearance, are inexpensive and flexible so that displays can be changed quickly.

Gateway's success is not limited to domestic sales. In 1993, Gateway opened a direct marketing and manufacturing operation in Ireland and since then has added showrooms in France, Germany, Japan, the United Kingdom, Sweden, and Australia. It has opened a manufacturing operation in Malaysia to serve the Asia-Pacific markets. Gateway also added a call center in Cyprus to serve Greece and the United Arab Emirates (UAE). Most recently, in the summer of 2000, Gateway announced that it was teaming with Spanish-language broadcaster Univision to devise an ad campaign that will target the Hispanic marketplace. The partnership gives Gateway access to commercial airtime on the Univision network and Internet portal. In return, Univision will have its Internet portal's icon attached to Gateway computer's desktops sold in Hispanic markets in an attempt to promote Univision as the top Spanish-language Internet portal. Waitt and Hammond have often been credited with pioneering the direct-marketing growth in the PC industry. According to Waitt, Gateway's future is promising. "Our strategic focus will be on expanding our customer relationships with enhanced products and services sold via the Web, on the phone, and in our stores to home consumers and business consumers around the world."

1. *How does Gateway develop meaningful relationships with customers without a strong retail presence? What effect, if any, do you think its Country Stores will have on its direct-marketing business? Explain.*
2. *On which types of direct-response media does Gateway rely? How might its media needs differ from those of a major retailer?*
3. *This chapter discusses a number of decisions direct marketers must make when developing a marketing strategy. Discuss Gateway's decisions regarding target markets, pricing, and merchandise assortment.*

Sources: Gateway 2000 Web site, www.gw2.com, visited February 2, 1998, www.Gateway.com, visited December 18, 2000; Gerry Khermouch, "Jim Taylor," *Brandweek,* October 20, 1997, pp. 102–105; Konstantinos Karagiannis, "Buying a Computer Direct," *Popular Electronics,* January 1998, pp. 14–15; Melinda Ligos, "From the Ground Up," *Sales and Marketing Management,* January 1998, p. 13; "Gateway 2000, Inc.," *Wall Street Journal Interactive Edition, Company Briefing Book,* visited March 27, 1997; "Phone, Web Technical Support Ranked Number One," *PC Computing,* February 1998, p. 200; Tobi Elkin, "Gateway Teams with Univision for Cross-Promo," *Advertising Age,* July 31, 2000, p. 63; Kevin Ferguson, "What If It Breaks?" *Business Week,* November 13, 2000, pp. 106–108; Doug Olenick, "High-Profile PC Vendors Lose Some Sales Steam," *Twice,* November 20, 2000, p. 44; and Gary Mcwilliams, "Gateway Warns of Sales Slowdown, Expects Loss," *Wall Street Journal,* November 30, 2000, p. A3.

INTEGRATED MARKETING COMMUNICATIONS

◀ *Bill Johnson, president of the New York Stock Exchange, and Martha Stewart*

THE "*DOMINATRIX OF DOMESTICITY,*" THE NEW York Times *once called her. Some abhor her; some adore her. Like it or not, Martha Stewart's brilliant sense of publicity has people thinking about her—regularly. As with all great marketers, she saw a need, filled it with her formidable presence, and created an empire. It ranges from home improvement to interior design, gardening, cooking, entertainment, and more.*

"Stewart is one of the best self-marketers in the industry," says Steve Cohn, editor of Media Industry Newsletter. *"She's amazing—she appeals to ordinary women as well as upscale types." According to Mike McGrath, a fellow magazine editor, "In the great anonymous era, she connects with people."* The president and CEO of Time, Inc., Don Logan, *credits both the magazine Stewart created and her "tireless marketing, promotion, and publicity efforts" for her success.*

Stewart's success now includes 37 books, a daily Emmy Award–winning "how to" domestic arts television show, a daily culinary arts cable television program, a syndicated newspaper column entitled "Ask Martha," a daily radio spot, a mail-order business called Martha By Mail, a line of $110-a-gallon paints, three magazines, and marthastewart.com, which includes material from all other channels. Other strategic merchandising relationships include Martha Stewart products that are distributed through Kmart, Sears, Zellers, and P/Kaufmann. All this is more than a cash cow. Within an integrated plan that is the envy of the industry, each division is used to cross-promote the others.

"As a way to popularize the idea of information and learning, TV is second to none," says Martha. "And as people recognize the value of the TV show, they recognize the value of the magazines and the books. It's all very interrelated now." The show's promotion of the magazines is both innovative and effective. Acquiring new subscribers can be expensive—as much as $18 per name. But cross-promotion drastically lowers the cost of gaining new customers. On television, Martha points out, "We mention that all the recipes and source information are in the program guide of our monthly Martha Stewart Living magazine. At the end of the show, there's an 800 number." Material from the Martha Stewart Weddings publication is also cleverly incorporated into programs around the time of each new quarterly issue.

For her books, all of which are still in print and selling, Stewart goes beyond the traditional multicity autographing tour. For her, bookselling is a year-round event centering around her innovative monthly charity lecture. She talks to groups ranging in size from 800 to 3,000, and she gets a local bookstore involved with the promotion. Her format usually includes a lecture and lunch (proceeds going to charity), followed by a book signing. According to Stewart, around 900 books are sold at each event, but the buyers that day later purchase more copies as gifts. "These lectures have been the most effective way of keeping my books, which are up to [19] years old, totally alive."

Promoting the brand image to consumers is important, but another group is even more important. "We package our assets for advertisers," says Martha Stewart Living *publisher Shelley Lewis Waln. Martha makes personal sales calls on potential advertisers if*

THE CONCEPT OF INTEGRATED MARKETING COMMUNICATIONS

Which do you think would sell better—a poor product supported by great marketing communication or a great product supported by poor marketing communication? Actually, the product probably would not do well in either case. A good product that is poorly communicated is unlikely to be perceived appropriately by consumers. And a poor product, no matter how well it is promoted, will quickly become known for its lack of value. This is because social connections among people get the word around.

Marketers need to ensure that all elements of the marketing mix—product, price, promotion (communication), and place—are working together. This chapter deals with communication, which is broader than promotion but includes it within its scope. Recall from chapter 6 that a product's position is its image relative to competition in the minds of consumers. It would not make sense for Payless shoe stores to carry expensive brands. Nor would it make sense for Campbell's to charge less for its premium soup than its regular soup. Both would seem inconsistent in the minds of consumers. Nearly everything about a product communicates something to consumers. The gold label on Campbell's premium soups communicates quality. The very name *Payless* translates into lower-price shoes. Even where you buy a product says something. A study of doctors' offices revealed that many patients will skip the medical procedure or change physicians if they feel uneasy in the office.[2] Hackensack University Medical Center has even gone so far as to hire an interior decorator who has completely remodeled the center. By getting rid of all fluorescent lights, carpeting patient areas, and choosing floral art, she has created a more quiet and relaxing atmosphere for patients who appreciate the difference.[3]

Communication is the exchange of meaning between or among parties. It involves sharing points of view and is at the heart of forming relationships. You simply cannot connect with customers unless you communicate with them. **Promotion** is the process whereby marketers inform, educate, persuade, remind, and reinforce consumers through communication. It is designed to influence buyers and other publics. Although most marketing communications are aimed at consumers, a significant number also address shareholders, employees, channel members, suppliers, and society. In addition, we will see that effective communication is a two-way street: Receiving messages is often as important as sending them.

Integrated marketing communication (IMC) is the coordination of advertising, sales promotion, personal selling, public relations, and sponsorships to reach consumers with a powerful unified effect. These five elements should not be considered separate entities. In fact, each element of the communication plan often has a multiplier effect on the others. As we have just seen, Martha Stewart uses IMC to promote her products and brand name. Her strategic use of television, newspaper, radio, direct mail, and the Internet has resulted in an extremely successful business. Her efforts include a holiday promotion with Minute Maid, a deal with Kmart, syndication of her TV show which is aired six times a week, frequent appearances on talk shows, and being on a panel of judges to select the 2001 Miss America.[4]

The IMC concept has three parts, as depicted in Figure 14.1, which this chapter will cover in order. First, it is important to consider the objectives of IMC, which need to be related to the overall marketing strategy. Second, marketers must be familiar with the communication process in order to be effective. Third, they must understand how each type of communication in the mix accomplishes a unique task. The key is to put them all together to achieve goals; this requires planning, budgeting, implementation, and feedback. Finally, we end the chapter with a look at diversity, ethics, and technology issues as they pertain to IMC.

According to Don Schultz, coauthor of *Integrated Marketing Communications: Putting It All Together and Making It Work,* two key goals of IMC are to establish a one-to-one relationship

COMMUNICATION

The process of sending and receiving messages.

PROMOTION

The process whereby marketers inform, educate, persuade, remind, and reinforce consumers through communication.

INTEGRATED MARKETING COMMUNICATION (IMC)

The coordination of advertising, sales promotion, personal selling, public relations, and sponsorship to reach consumers with a powerful effect in the market.

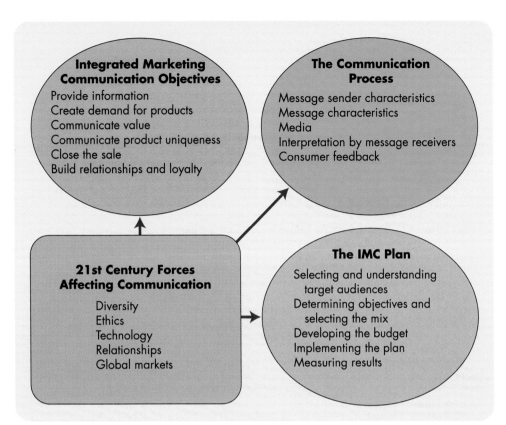

FIGURE 14.1 *The Concept of Integrated Marketing Communications (IMC)*

with consumers and to encourage two-way communication between a firm and its customers. One way companies are trying to achieve these goals is to orchestrate various elements of the promotion mix and create a brand experience directly with consumers. See the relationships feature, "Rewards of Face-to-Face Marketing."

OBJECTIVES OF INTEGRATED MARKETING COMMUNICATIONS

Integrated marketing communications has numerous objectives. The most notable are to provide information, create demand, communicate value and product uniqueness, close the sale, and build loyal customer relationships.

PROVIDE INFORMATION

Ultimately, all communication is designed to provide some form of information. It gives consumers what they need to know to make informed choices within a reasonable time frame.[5] Objectives differ depending on the target audience's familiarity with a particular product. If it is relatively unknown, then marketers need to inform and educate the target audience. Often this communication introduces consumers to the product's benefits and uses. When it is working most effectively, information helps consumers make the buying decision. It provides data on a broad range of topics, including product characteristics, uses, availability, prices, and methods of acquisition. Yet, the tremendous number and variety of sources challenge consumers to select and process the most useful information. At the same time, marketers are challenged to create communications that contribute to the consumer's search for value in the marketplace or marketspace. Consequently, communications should be designed with consumer information needs in mind.

In many cases, information is purely descriptive. Political advertisements attempt to provide information about candidates, but often they seek to provide negative information about opponents. In the 2000 election for president, Republican and Democratic advertisements often made accusatory statements about Al Gore and George W. Bush, providing biased information for very specific purposes.[6]

CONNECTED: SURFING THE NET

www.dttus.com

Learn more about one of the nation's leading professional service firms by visiting the Deloitte & Touche Web site. Find out about its specialized areas, services, solutions, and much more.

CONNECTING THROUGH RELATIONSHIPS

REWARDS OF FACE-TO-FACE MARKETING

 In fiercely contested markets, companies must find new and exciting ways to sell their products. One of these methods is face-to-face marketing, where a company actually has direct contact with the consumer. Road shows are a popular way to do this.

The Gillette Company used this strategy to introduce its Right Guard Sensitive antiperspirant brand in the United Kingdom. It is convinced that face-to-face contact is the most effective way to market a product in a highly competitive sector. When Gillette decided it was time to expand the already popular Right Guard brand to include a skin-friendly brand for women, it felt a road show was the way to go. Before this was to begin, the company ran a TV campaign to help familiarize customers with the product. This was followed by extensive in-store promotions and finally a road show initiative.

The six-week, 29-town road show included a branded four-wheel-drive vehicle that pulled a 12-foot long can of Right Guard Sensitive deodorant and a promotional team that distributed free samples to consumers. Approximately 120,000 cans of aerosol and roll-on deodorant were distributed to consumers during the road show. The locations of stops for the road show were critical in reaching the target market of 18- to 34-year-old women. The display was set up outside of stores that attract the same market that Gillette targets for this product. The display also helped to show the consumers where the new product can be purchased.

The road show is different from Gillette's traditional marketing style. Both face-to-face marketing and road shows, however, account for approximately one-fifth of all field marketing business in the United Kingdom, according to the 1999 Marketing Field Marketing League Table.

Companies are also discovering the effectiveness of face-to-face marketing in the Asian economy. Many retailers do not redeem coupons or participate in promotions, making it difficult to get consumers to try new products. Companies have learned to overcome that obstacle by going directly to the consumers with road shows or other sampling events. The advantage is that the company, not the retailer, has control over what is handed out and the discounts that are offered. Following this strategy, PepsiCo set up a marketing program in one of the poorest areas of southwestern China, offering to paint the faces of buyers of Pepsi-branded merchandise in the local soccer team's colors.

Whether a company is dealing with a competitive market or a weak retail channel, face-to-face marketing has its advantages. A great way to get consumers to become customers is to get them to try the product rather than simply seeing it on a TV ad or in a magazine. This creates a relationship between the customer and the company and the customer will be more likely to become a repeat customer.

Sources: Holly Acland, "Gillette Sensitive Takes to the Road," *Marketing; London,* April 27, 2000, pp. 27–28; and Claire Murphy, "How Face-to-Face Can Reap Rewards," *Marketing; London,* January 27, 2000, pp. 35–36.

CREATE DEMAND FOR PRODUCTS

Communication helps create demand for products in global and domestic markets. It stimulates people to desire what they do not have and inspires them to earn the money to acquire items that improve their standard of living. Communication helps assure that products will be purchased in sufficient quantities to justify their development, production, and distribution. Today, the speed of communication allows companies to obtain worldwide demand in a short period. Many products marketed globally have coordinated IMC campaigns supported by high-tech information systems. Internet working—connecting personal computers to the network—makes it possible for companies to see what demand is being created by communication in various geographic areas and adjust product availability accordingly. Cisco Systems, the largest Internet infrastructure provider, is finding that China is rapidly building Internet capabilities. Currently, the United States comprises 52 percent of Cisco's business, whereas the United Kingdom is second, and China only represents 4 percent of total business. CEO John Chambers predicts, however, that China will soon outrank the United Kingdom and account for 10 percent of business.[7] If its economy remains strong, IMC with China could provide a large market for many products.

Consider the hit television series *Survivor,* which debuted in the summer of 2000, and its follow-up series *Survivor: The Australian Outback,* which debuted after the Super Bowl on January 28, 2001. The first series cost around $10 million to make, but after doing so well, producers decided to invest $17.5 million in making the second version. Advertisers for the first series, including Reebok, Target, Budweiser, and Doritos, received great exposure because of the series' popularity all over the world. In the finale of the first series, advertisers who paid $600,000 for a commercial reached an audience of 51.7 million viewers. Demand for the second series has resulted in the increased cost of advertisements, with sponsors paying about $12 million, as opposed to the $4 million they spent for the first series. The series has been so popular and profitable that CBS approved a *Survivor III* and *Survivor IV.*[8]

COMMUNICATE VALUE

The search for value is complicated because consumers need to assess the benefits of a product relative to thousands of others. Marketers compete to provide value in keeping with consumers' willingness to pay. Consequently, much communication uses creative messages that help convey benefits. For example, Cutler-Hammer technical sales representatives learn about a broad range of sophisticated electronic products. They are taught how to communicate the benefits, functions, and features of each product to the consumer. But to communicate value they must first identify how the customer will use a product. In the case of equipment sold to contractors, they find out how it will be installed. They can then point out cost-saving product attributes due to easy installation and reliable design.

Advertisers are often careful to depict scenes of consumers clearly benefiting from products. For its Talkabout T900 personal interactive communicator, Motorola shows two young people and says that "you can exchange text messages with your friends—without wires . . . or vocal chords!" It then also suggests that its users can "Greet. Gloat. Gripe. Gossip." to convey uses and benefits at once. The ad conveys the benefits available at a reasonable cost.[9]

COMMUNICATE PRODUCT UNIQUENESS

Marketers attempt to communicate uniqueness in order to differentiate their product from others. Burger King is broiled; McDonald's is fried; Southwest Airlines is less expensive because it has no frills; Titleist is used by more professional golfers than any other ball, and so on. In each case marketers are attempting to distinguish their particular product from those of competitors. Marketers also use persuasive communication to convince consumers to switch from one brand to another. Messages compare a product's benefits, functions, and features to the competition. The goal is to illustrate their brand's unique value and build brand preference.

Dr. Martens, a shoe manufacturer, attempts to persuade consumers by using marketing communications that tell the company's history. The campaign describes how Dr. Klaus Martens, the founder, injured his foot while skiing. He then invented a rubber-soled shoe that provides comfort to people on their feet all day. The message is that Dr. Martens, having suffered foot pain himself, knows how to build a shoe superior to that of competitors.

CLOSE THE SALE

Communication also helps close the sale. Marketers want their product to be purchased. If the experience is good, chances are it will be repurchased. Thus, IMC seeks to move buyers to action the first time and then reinforce their positive experience so they will buy again and again. Today, customers are selecting when they want to receive communications, and often that is just prior to purchase. Many people use the Web to look up ads. Increasingly, newspaper, magazine, and television ads also are including Web site information so consumers can learn more or refresh their memory about what they have seen. These Web sites also are interactive, so the communication is more personal and involves the consumer. Purchasing is made easy when customers are told just where and how to buy.

BUILD RELATIONSHIPS AND LOYALTY

Once consumers have tried a particular brand, marketers remind them why they chose it in the first place and reinforce that behavior. In other words, communication helps maintain brand loyalty. Reminder communications reinforce the popularity of existing goods by reassuring loyal customers that they have made the correct choice. Because consumers tend to pay more attention to ads for products that they currently use, advertising is often meant to reinforce. For example, American Express card messages on television and in magazines remind consumers that "membership has its privileges."

THE COMMUNICATION PROCESS

The basic communication process is outlined in Figure 14.2. As you can see, messages move from the sender (marketer) to the receiver (consumer). Traditionally, communication has been seen as a one-way process. With the advent of one-to-one marketing through technologies such as the Internet, it is more useful to envision a two-way or continuous flow. Marketers need to start with a clear understanding of the target market, the objectives of the communication, and how to meet those objectives. They should also be aware that proactive customers have their own objectives and use the same process in reverse.

Let's look at the process. Effective communication can be difficult because consumers are bombarded daily by thousands of conflicting messages. Once marketers decide what to communicate, they must encode the message for the target market. It can be spoken, written, illustrated through pictures or diagrams, or conveyed by a combination of these. The encoded message then must be sent to consumers via one or more media: television, radio, newspapers, magazines, telephone, fax, personal contact, the Internet, and others.

Customers must decode, or interpret, the message that marketers send. Each customer's reaction will depend on personal background and experiences. One of the most important aspects of the communication process is feedback from the target audience. Sometimes it comes in the form of an action by the consumer. For example, if a campaign is designed to encourage product awareness, then positive feedback is an increase in the number of consumers who know about the product, and negative feedback is a flat or declining awareness. Such information is vital because it helps marketers judge whether the message accomplished its goal or needs to be adjusted.

One final element marketers must deal with when communicating to consumers is noise, that is, anything that interferes with a message being received. For example, after talking to a salesperson about a new sports car, you may want to buy it. But then a friend says, "It's a piece of junk." Your friend obviously interferes with the marketer's message. Noise can also occur if you are distracted from receiving the message or if you're not sure who sent the message. We will now look at each element of the communication process shown in Figure 14.2.

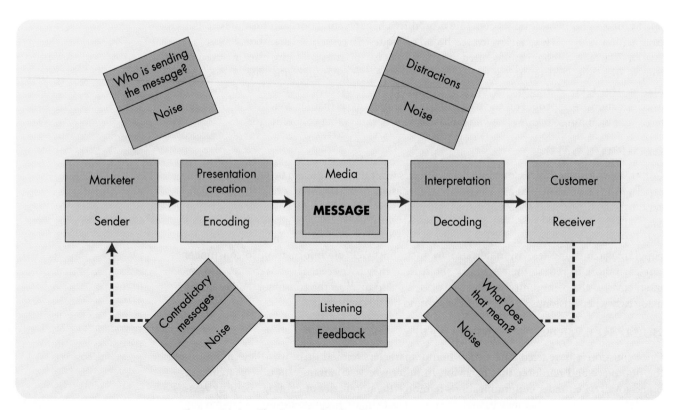

FIGURE 14.2 *The Communication Process*

Once marketers have determined that communication is in order, they initiate the process by formulating a message. As the sender, it is the marketer's responsibility to make sure the message is received by the targeted audience, is understood as intended, helps the audience become knowledgeable, and elicits an appropriate response.

Communications take valuable time from the receiver, so it is up to the sender to provide relevant information. Generally, a series of contacts is required. Once a relationship is created between the two parties, communication is much easier for two reasons: The sender learns the most useful information to supply, and the receiver is more inclined to listen. Effective communications obtain consumer responses that contribute to a company's goals. In some cases the message simply identifies the product so potential customers are more likely to include it in their set of possible choices. In other cases it may move consumers to act immediately.

The reputation of the sender—whether a person, a company, or some other organization—influences how consumers receive a message. In fact, when several sources communicate precisely the same message, it is received differently depending on the source. That's why marketers must select exactly the right person to carry their message. EAS launched a $15 million campaign that features models Cindy Crawford and Christie Brinkley to promote its nutritional bars and drinks. The advertisements, aimed at women with busy lifestyles, appeal to these women by showing Crawford and Brinkley as soccer moms who balance motherhood, work, fitness, and nutrition.[10] Reebok chose tennis star Venus Williams as its representative to launch Reebok International during the first episode of *Survivor: The Australian Outback*. Reebok International seeks to revamp its image among younger consumers.[11] One person usually does not have high credibility with all segments of the population. Different consumers respect, admire, trust, and identify with different types of people. Even within one segment, it's difficult to identify a single spokesperson to whom everyone relates. That is why the famous milk mustache appears on so many faces.

What makes a source credible with a target audience? Generally spokespersons are judged according to their expertise, trustworthiness, and attractiveness.

Expertise Consumers attribute expertise to a spokesperson for many reasons. They may believe he or she has specialized training, a great deal of experience, or a thorough knowledge. Some companies hire engineers for industrial sales positions, believing that their academic degree lends special credibility. Doctors are highly credible spokespersons in messages for pain relievers. Children's Tylenol, for example, is promoted as "the first choice of pediatricians." Robitussin notes that it is recommended by physicians, pharmacists, and "Dr. Mom." Both campaigns are based on the credibility of its sources.

Consumers also tend to rely on someone with a lifestyle similar to their own, which accounts for the surge in advertising featuring "average" people. For example, Chanel reaches consumers by using normal people who are attractive and have interesting careers in its advertisements. The company's ads show models as being people just like you, while moving toward a more casual attitude about its products.[12] Also, Luvs advertises that not only do average people use its product, but also that "smart moms know that Luvs helps stop leaks."[13]

Trustworthiness Organizations such as the Underwriter's Laboratory, American Medical Association, American Dental Association, Good Housekeeping Institute, and Consumer's Union have gained a great deal of credibility because of their trustworthiness. Not only do they have considerable technical knowledge, but also most consumers perceive them as unbiased. People tend to trust messages from "objective" sources. They also tend to discount messages from sources that stand to benefit in some way. Imagine that you are purchasing a DVD player and the salesperson constantly emphasizes the importance of an extended warranty. If you know the salesperson gets a commission on warranty sales, then you are less likely to believe what he or she is telling you. If no commission is involved, then you are more inclined to trust the person.

Attractiveness (Personal Demeanor and Appeal) It's not surprising that attractive, pleasant, likable spokespersons have influence. That's why they are selected to deliver messages. Telephone companies in particular are increasingly using famous people to endorse their products due to the heightened competition resulting from industry deregulation. Long-distance company 1-800-CALL-ATT is using David Arquette to reach the 18- to 29-year-old

**CONNECTED:
SURFING THE NET**

www.reebok.com

Visit Reebok online and check out its latest promotional activities. While you are there, look for a personal trainer in your area with Reebok University's locator.

WORLD RENOWNED SAILOR
GARY JOBSON
PUTS HIS TRUST IN
CLASSICS.

Having competed successfully in a variety of boats, Gary Jobson's choice for himself is a classic Herreshoff
28-footer whose graceful design will never go out of style. The same aesthetic is reflected in his timepiece.

Rolex Submariner Officially Certified Swiss Chronometer
For the name and location of an Official Rolex Jeweler near you, please call 1-800-36ROLEX. Rolex, ®, Oyster Perpetual and Submariner are trademarks.

ROLEX

*Rolex uses an objective
source to market their watch.
Marketers hope the consumer
would consider Gary Jobson
a trustworthy source.*

market, whereas "Advice Guy" Arsenio Hall promotes 1-800-COLLECT, and James Earl Jones continues to represent Bell Atlantic.[14]

Often celebrities gain credibility in areas outside their careers. For example, some movie stars have influenced political campaigns. When famous endorsers are also informed, their power can be substantial. For example, actor Martin Sheen has been involved in protests against the School of the Americas and increased public awareness of the issues involved through his acts of civil disobedience.[15] Athletes are obvious choices for promoting sports equipment and apparel, but the fame they have acquired on the court or playing field translates to other areas.

It's important to note that attractiveness involves all aspects of the source, whether sales personnel or any others who represent an organization. A company's general reputation also applies. Consider the damage to Exxon after 11 million gallons of oil were spilled in Alaskan waters. Since cleanup techniques are still low tech, the environmental damage probably tarnished the company's image for many consumers.[16]

PRESENTATION CREATION: ENCODING

ENCODING

Translating a message into terms
easily understood by the target
audience.

Encoding is the process of translating a message into terms easily understood by the target audience. We know from chapter 7 that information processing is a complex but very important aspect of the purchase decision. Marketers must encode messages so they are interpreted appropriately by the people for whom they are intended. For example, marketers of fine jewelry have traditionally encoded their messages to reach men—once the main purchasers of engagement rings and other gems as gifts. Today, however, women have higher disposable incomes and increasingly buy expensive presents for themselves. Also, as the baby boomer generation reaches milestone anniversaries and birthdays, jewelers expect them to celebrate with the purchase of jewelry. The Web site www.adiamondisforever.com allows visitors to create their own diamond engagement rings, encoding the message that buyers can be actively involved in creating their own dream jewelry.[17]

Many messages are screened out by consumers. Although some people seek information on their own, it is up to the sender to stimulate the consumer's interest in receiving a message.

This involves grabbing attention and keeping it while the information is processed. Messages that are boring, uninteresting, or irrelevant are tuned out. In order to facilitate consumer understanding, communications should limit the amount of information conveyed at one time. We know that consumers take in only a little and that comprehension is based on their life circumstances and experiences. Consequently, effective messages present carefully selected topics in a context relevant to the target audience.

MESSAGE CHARACTERISTICS

There are countless ways to communicate a given message. One viewpoint or several can be presented. Recommendations or conclusions may or may not be included. Key points can be made at the beginning, middle, or end. Humor or fear can be used. And messages may or may not compare a product to those of competitors.

One-Sided and Two-Sided Messages   A **one-sided message** presents only arguments favorable to the source. A **two-sided message** recognizes the arguments against a position and provides the recipient with why reasons are invalid. For example, a message for a fast-food chain might mention only the positive aspects of the ingredients and cooking methods. Or it might present both sides in response to a competitor's charge. When the source and receiver have relatively similar views, a one-sided message is more appropriate. When there is disagreement, a two-sided message often is more useful.

Recommendations or Conclusions   A message can make recommendations or offer conclusions or leave that task to the receiver. Messages with conclusions are more easily understood, but when the audience draws its own, there is a stronger likelihood of acceptance. This is particularly true for highly educated consumers. If an advertising message is repeated, then the absence of any stated conclusion is likely to make the ad more effective. Repeated exposures give the target audience an opportunity to reach its own conclusions. If the marketer wants the message to have immediate effect, then the communication probably should draw direct conclusions. Rubbermaid launched a new campaign in response to smaller competitors that were rapidly gaining market share. Since Rubbermaid wanted to influence consumers quickly, its ads were designed to focus on the numerous solutions its products provide to

ONE-SIDED MESSAGE

A message that presents only arguments favorable to the source.

TWO-SIDED MESSAGE

A message that presents arguments that are unfavorable as well as favorable to the source.

CONNECTED: SURFING THE NET

www.rubbermaid.com

Visit the Web site of the nation's number-one maker of home products. Rubbermaid sells in more than 100 countries and is noted for averaging one new product a day. Discover how it reaches consumers online— with solutions, tips, and more.

Obsessively shoe obsessed   *Madeline*
www.madelineshoes.com
At The Bon Ton & Gottschalk's

Madeline Shoes uses humor to sell their shoes.

everyday problems. The campaign was reinforced with an 89-page book, *1001 Solutions for Better Living*.[18] Rubbermaid's Web site, www.rubbermaid.com, also recommends its products to customers by providing testimonials of individuals who survived life-threatening situations with the aid of a Rubbermaid product.[19] This type of promotional effort draws direct conclusions for customers about product benefits.

Order of Presentation   The placement of the key point of a communication affects how the message is interpreted and later recalled by buyers. More is remembered about the beginning and end of a message than its middle. Therefore, effective presentations usually open and close with strong statements. Weaker arguments are most often placed in the middle.

Humor   Viewers like humorous ads because they are novel and enjoyable. But advertisers must be careful not to let humor obscure the message. There are several things to keep in mind.

- Be sure to mention the brand name within the first 10 seconds. Otherwise, the communication runs the risk of inhibiting recall of key selling points.
- Subtle humor is more effective than bizarre humor.
- Humor must be relevant to the brand or the key selling point. Without this linkage, recall and persuasion are diminished.
- It is best not to use humor that belittles or makes fun of the potential user. Jokes about the brand, the situation, or the subject matter are usually more effective.[20]

Evidence is still inconclusive as to whether a humorous approach is more effective than a serious one. Although humor tends to increase attention, it also may distract from or decrease acceptance of the message. The United Way and the National Football League have promoted the value of community service for decades but have recently begun to advertise this value through humorous commercials aired during games. One commercial features Dallas Cowboys quarterback Troy Aikman coaching a pickup football game.[21] The approach increased attention to accomplish its objective, which was to get people talking about the United Way and about the examples set by the football players.

Sometimes life insurance marketing builds public awareness by using fear appeals to persuade customers to act on the message.

Fear Appeals   Marketers sometimes use fear to gain the attention and interest of their audience. Campaigns by the American Dental Association warn that poor dental hygiene can result in tooth decay, gum disease, and loss of teeth. In some instances, advertisers play on fear for the safety of loved ones. A Michelin spot shows a baby floating in a tire and reminds parents, "You have a lot riding on them." An advertisement for seat belt use by the Michigan Association for Traffic Safety pictures a wheelchair: "It's your choice."

In many instances fear appeals are very effective. They can create higher attention and interest in the message. Consider the recent development of at-home kits testing for HIV, now marketed by companies such as Johnson & Johnson and Home Access Health Corporation. The latter runs an ad showing crossed fingers: "If this is your idea of an HIV test . . . it's time you learned about ours."[22]

Comparative Messages   In the 1970s, the Federal Trade Commission began allowing advertisers to name competitors in ads. Since then, many companies have chosen to compare their products with those of rivals. There have been sneaker wars, hamburger wars, beer wars, and cola wars. In each case, claims and counterclaims have been used in comparative messages. Do these techniques work? They certainly draw attention. Even though comparative messages allow marketers to present clear, objective arguments in favor of their product, many companies hesitate to use the technique. References to the competition may inadvertently cause the consumer to recall that product at the time of purchase. In addition, competitors may legally challenge claims of superiority or respond with comparative ads of their own.

In general, comparative messages may be more useful for companies with a lower market share, since they have little to lose by confronting the leader. For them, the potential gain in consumer awareness outweighs the likelihood that a large competitor will launch a counterattack. Royal Crown Cola used this tactic by showing Coke and Pepsi involved in a bizarre fishing contest for consumers. The intent was to remind people that there are other colas.[23]

MEDIA

The **media** are the means for transmitting messages from the sender to the receiver. There are three categories—personal, mass, and mixed—each with its advantages and disadvantages, as summarized in Figure 14.3.

Personal media involve direct contact, such as face-to-face communication or telephone conversations. These two-way exchanges allow for creative solutions to the consumer's problem. There is ample opportunity for relationships to form. Each party can assess the characteristics of the other. Although the telephone does not provide physical contact, it has dramatic cost advantages over personal encounters. Hot lines are an effective way to support customers after a sale. They not only help when problems arise with a product but also offer all kinds of advice that ultimately can maintain customer loyalty. The Microsoft Online Institute

MEDIA
The channels through which messages are communicated.

	Examples	Advantages	Disadvantages
Personal Media	Face-to-face Telephone	Two-way communication Allows for creative problem solving Flexible tailoring of messages Immediate response	Expensive Time-consuming Parties must be brought together at one time
Mass Media	Television Radio Magazines Newspapers Billboards Brochures	Messages can be developed prior to sending Low cost Many media choices Reaches most customers inexpensively	Messages tend to be one-way Preparations are expensive Harder to obtain feedback
Mixed (personal and mass combined)	Fax Internet Answering machine	Delayed or interactive Two-way communication Low cost	Receiver needs technology Lack of consumer experience

FIGURE 14.3 *Media Advantages and Disadvantages*

provides consumer assistance and product training through a combination of self-paced tutorials and live instructors.[24] The disadvantage of personal media is expense. Each representative can only have a limited number of conversations, and the costs associated with hiring, training, and motivating people can be very high.

The mass media include television, radio, magazines, billboards, and brochures. Services are readily available to help plan for and acquire space in most markets around the world. CIO Communications, Inc., for instance, offers a resource center on the Web to assist with media planning.[25] Consequently, messages can be developed prior to being communicated through a range of nonpersonal sources. Since there are many media choices, nearly all customers can be contacted at a reasonable cost. The downside of using the mass media is the lack of interactive or two-way communication. Because it is impossible to get quick feedback, a great deal is spent beforehand on research that listens to the customer. Furthermore, ad preparation can be expensive and take a long time.

The mixed media approach combines personal and mass communication and has many of the benefits of both. First, material can be developed well in advance and offered in both print (fax) and audio (via Internet) formats. Advanced technology such as the PageFast software communication tool can connect fax machines to the Web. The promotion for PageFast reads: "If your firm depends on rapid customer response, and your customer base has access to the Web, give them an alternate method of letting you know they need your attention." This use of mixed media provides effective two-way communication at a low cost.[26] Second, because mixed media can reach large numbers simultaneously, the technique is very cost-effective. A possible disadvantage is that fax and voice mail numbers are the property of the receiver, so the sender must be careful to respect privacy. A definite disadvantage is that many consumers lack the necessary technology or the experience to use it.

INTERPRETATION BY RECEIVERS: DECODING

Strong communications begin with an understanding of target audiences. People are not passive receivers of communications. In fact, they resist persuasion by refuting arguments, attacking the source, distorting messages, rationalizing, and tuning out. Many consumers regard marketing messages as "tricks" to make them purchase a particular product.

Refuting arguments is one way consumers resist persuasion. Weak messages may backfire as consumers create stronger counterarguments in their own mind. Another defense mechanism is to attack the source. Consumers may discount claims of comfort, prestige, or gas mileage because they don't trust the automobile company. All messages are automatically rejected. Attacking the source rather than the ideas being communicated is common in politics. Whenever politicians don't have a very convincing case, they are likely to strike out at the people who reject their arguments.

Intelligence and self-esteem have a lot to do with susceptibility to persuasion. Highly intelligent people are more likely to be influenced by logical, precise, and complex information. Others have to be very carefully led through an argument. Depending on the audience, marketers should let some people draw their own conclusions. It is not surprising that people with low-self esteem tend to be easily persuaded. They often rely on others in developing attitudes and making choices. Messages designed for such people should avoid complex arguments.[27]

CONSUMER FEEDBACK

Listening is an important way to learn what consumers think. Feedback is essential to a customer-focused company, and it helps the marketer adjust communications. Today, many organizations consider listening to be the first step in the communication process, even before the message is created. Through the consumer they determine needs and wants as well as how to structure communication.

THE COMMUNICATION MIX

TYPES OF COMMUNICATION ACTIVITIES

The five main types of communication activities are personal selling, sales promotion, advertising, public relations, and sponsorship. Figure 14.4 describes some characteristics of each type.

	Personal Selling	Sales Promotion	Advertising	Public Relations	Sponsorship
Focus	Person-to-person interaction	Support of sales activity	Mass communication directed at target segments	Unpaid publicity that enhances the company and its products	Cash or resources in support of an event
Objective	Develop business relationship resulting in loyal customers	Obtain immediate sale and remind after the sale	Position the product and/or increase sales	Gain a favorable impression	Be associated with influential groups
Example	Pharmaceutical salesperson	Point-of-sale displays	Billboards	Press releases	Team sponsorship
	Computer and tele-communications sales	T-shirts with company name	TV ads	Charitable projects	Sport tournaments
	Retail sales	Special sales	Magazine ads	Civic leadership	Arts events
	Consulting sales	2-for-1 offers	Direct mail	Company spokesperson gives association speech	Association events
Appeal	Personal	Move buyer to action	Mass	Mass	Market segment
Cost per customer	Very high	Low	Low to high	Very low	High to low
Amount and speed of feedback	A lot and immediately	A little and fairly fast	A little and delayed	A little and fairly fast	A lot and fast

FIGURE 14.4 *The Characteristics of Communication Activities*

Personal Selling **Personal selling** requires person-to-person communication between buyer and seller. Generally, this occurs face-to-face, although it also may involve the telephone, videoconferencing, or interactive computer linkages. Despite its relatively high cost, personal selling continues to be the most important part of business-to-business marketing and is also significant in sales of big-ticket consumer items, such as autos, computers, and housing. The objective of most personal selling is to build loyal relationships with customers that result in profitable sales volume. For example, physicians say that pharmaceutical salespersons are the most effective when they develop personal relationships and build rapport through their personal selling techniques.[28] Since personal selling provides two-way communication, it is possible to engage in a dialogue that leads to problem solving. Because this is generally the most expensive form of contact, salespeople are trained to do the best possible job of helping a customer find solutions through use of their product.

Advertising **Advertising** is paid, nonpersonal communication from an identified sponsor using mass media to persuade or influence an audience. It includes newspapers, television, radio, magazines, direct mail, billboards, the Internet, and point-of-sale displays. It is considered mass communication because the same message is sent throughout the targeted audience and the rest of the market. A major objective of advertising is to support product positioning. The same basic theme usually is sent through all advertising channels. Television ads for Charmin have been reinforced by point-of-sale displays featuring Mr. Whipple, the "don't squeeze the Charmin" grocery clerk. Depending on audience size, cost per consumer can be very low. With over 40 percent of all American households watching the Super Bowl, an estimated 130 million viewers of the Super Bowl in 2001, the cost of $2 million for a 30-second advertisement averages out to a small cost per viewer.[29] Because advertising plays a supportive role, it is sometimes difficult to determine just how well it works, in relation to other parts of the marketing mix. For example, the effects of accompanying shifts in product distribution and pricing often are felt more quickly.

PERSONAL SELLING
Face-to-face or other individual communication between a buyer and a seller.

ADVERTISING
Paid communication through nonpersonal channels.

SALES PROMOTION
Communication designed to stimulate immediate purchases, using tools such as coupons, contests, and free samples.

PUBLIC RELATIONS (PR)
Unpaid promotion designed to present the firm and its products in a positive light in the buyer's mind.

SPONSORSHIP
The exchange of money (or some other form of value) in return for a public association with an event.

CONNECTED: SURFING THE NET

www.nascar.com

How many corporate sponsors can you find on the NASCAR Web site? Not only can you check out team information, point standings, and the schedule, but also you can chat with NASCAR drivers.

Sales Promotion   **Sales promotion** is communication designed to stimulate immediate purchases using tools such as coupons, contests, and free samples. Since the approach generally is designed to stimulate immediate purchases, its effectiveness can be easily measured. Sometimes sales promotion is meant to remind customers after the sale, which contributes to relationship building. For example, a box of cookies may contain a discount coupon for the next box. Sales promotions usually last a short time. For the Summer Olympics in Atlanta, Coke's effort included a temporary theme park, in-store promotions, and a Web site, among others. To counter its rival, Pepsi made its biggest push ever with Pepsi Stuff. Consumers could use proof-of-purchase redemptions to buy brand-label merchandise unrelated to the soft drink. Although both endeavors were temporary, volume increased for both companies during the promotion.[30]

Public Relations   **Public relations** (**PR**) is the use of publicity and other nonpaid forms of communication designed to present the firm and its products positively. Because they are not paying for space, companies do not have total control over what is disseminated. The most common public relations channel is the news media. Of course, publicity can be negative. For example, news media broadcast a lot of negative information about the Ford Explorer when Firestone tires failed on the vehicle. Ford executives launched a massive public relations campaign, issuing statements to the press to counteract the negative press after the recall of over 6 million tires. Despite the PR campaign, Ford decided to launch a paid-for national mail campaign to assure owners of the vehicles' safety.[31]

Sponsorships   A major form of communication is sponsorships, which are reaching 10 to 15 percent of promotion budgets. A **sponsorship** is the exchange of money (or some other form of value) in return for a public association with an event. Reebok and Oldsmobile sponsor many Professional Golfers' Association tournaments. In fact, Oldsmobile, "The Official Car of the PGA of America," renewed its licensing agreement through 2005, a move that greatly extends the partnership that began in 1984.[32] Coca-Cola, PepsiCo, General Motors, Anheuser-Busch, United Parcel Service, and Nissan are among the largest sponsors of sports. Southwest Airlines has a four-year sponsorship of the National Hockey League, an effort that it hopes will reach males age 25 to 54 who frequently travel on business. Southwest believes that since more hockey fans have Internet access than fans of other sports, it will capitalize on the increase in sales via online reservations.[33] Virtually all sporting events are sponsored now by either corporations or dot-com companies. The 2000 college football bowl season featured games such as the GMAC Mobile Alabama Bowl, the Rose Bowl presented by AT&T, and the galleryfurniture.com Bowl, each explicitly stating its sponsor's name.[34]

Sponsorships usually are integrated with all other aspects of the communications mix. General Motors takes its key dealers and business customers to the NASCAR racing events it sponsors, features the races in its magazine ads, and cites testimonials from NASCAR drivers. This benefits both parties to the sponsorship.

FACTORS AFFECTING THE COMMUNICATION MIX

Marketers must consider several factors in selecting the communication mix. The most important are whether the audience is the business-to-business or consumer market, whether a push or pull strategy is desirable, the product's stage in the life cycle, and whether opinion leaders will play a role.

Business Versus Consumer Markets   All forms of marketing communication are important in both business-to-business and consumer marketing. Yet, the emphasis is different in each area, as seen in Figure 14.5. Personal selling is most important in marketing to businesses, whereas advertising dominates in the consumer products arena. Sales promotion is equally important in both and outweighs advertising in business markets. Public relations is relatively less important in both. One reason for these differences is costs. Mailing a catalog can cost $1 per customer; a personalized e-mail can cost $.05 per message. Pricewaterhouse Cooper predicts that Internet advertising will increase from $4.6 billion to $20.3 billion from 1999 to 2004, with the Internet accounting for 9.3 percent of all major media advertising.[35] Per exposure, television advertising can cost less than a few cents; a print ad slightly more; direct mail, a dollar or two; a telephone call, about $10; and face-to-face personal selling, more than several hundred dollars. Although public relations involves no such

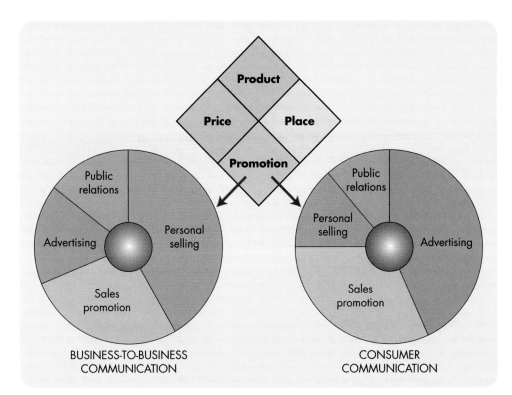

Figure 14.5 *Communication Mix for Business Versus Consumer Markets*

expenditure, it cannot compare to the other forms in terms of effectiveness and the degree of message control.

Pull Versus Push Strategies   Marketers attempt to influence the market through either a push or pull strategy, as illustrated in Figure 14.6. In many cases they use both. A **pull strategy** attempts to influence consumers directly. Communication is designed to build demand so consumers will "pull" the product through the channel of distribution. In other words, consumers ask retailers for the product, who in turn ask wholesalers, who in turn contact the manufacturer. One popular pull strategy for automakers is to offer consumers credit cards that provide rebates on new car purchases.[36]

Although pull strategies tend to be used primarily for consumer products, they also have a place in business-to-business marketing. For example, marketers of electrical control and distribution equipment often target the purchasing agent with their messages. Sales representatives call on design firms, which then specify that particular electrical equipment in the engineering design.

The **push strategy** involves communicating to distribution channel members, which in turn promote to the end user. This is particularly common in industrial or business-to-business marketing. Marketers often train distribution channel members on the sales

PULL STRATEGY

An attempt to influence consumers directly so they will "pull" the product through the distribution channel.

PUSH STRATEGY

An attempt to influence the distribution channel, which in turn will "push" the product through to the user.

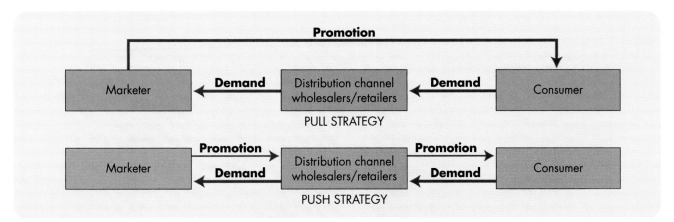

Figure 14.6 *Pull Versus Push Strategies*

techniques they believe are most suited to their products. The push technique is also used in retail marketing.

Often, a push-pull strategy is appropriate. The combination approach sells to the channel and to the end user. This can speed product adoption and strengthen market share. As we learned in chapter 12, conflicts often occur between the marketing organization and its distributors. For example, in the food industry, retailers want to carry products that yield the greatest profitability. Since these may not be brands with the strongest pull, retailers may charge marketers for shelf space. Essentially, they are being paid to push the product to the end user. Using a pull strategy to create strong demand at the consumer level makes channel members more willing to handle the product.

Product's Stage in the Life Cycle   By now it should be apparent that the communication mix is related to the product's stage in the life cycle. Consumers need to be informed and educated about new products, whereas they may need to be persuaded to purchase during growth and early maturity. Reminders and reinforcement are most appropriate in the mature and declining phases of the life cycle. Think about how companies advertise clothing styles. Most department stores or clothing stores do not advertise or promote swimwear in the winter, nor do they promote wool coats in July. Other products also have life cycles and advertisers adapt their methods to the cycles. As the Tickle Me Elmo doll began to sell out in stores at the height of its popularity, Tyco temporarily pulled its television ads. Today, the product is not marketed because its life cycle has greatly declined. In other words, communications were adjusted to match the stages of the product life cycle.

Opinion Leadership   Marketing communications reach consumers directly and indirectly. Figure 14.7 illustrates both paths. In **one-step communication,** all members of the target

ONE-STEP COMMUNICATION
Communication in which all audience members are simultaneously exposed to the same marketing message.

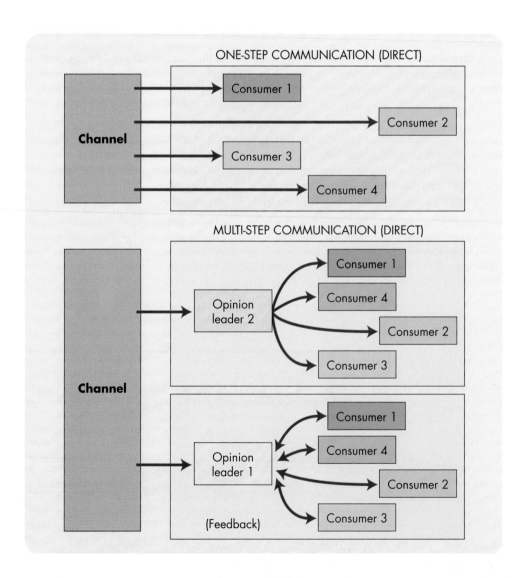

FIGURE 14.7   *Opinion Leadership*

ONE-STEP COMMUNICATION (DIRECT)

MULTI-STEP COMMUNICATION (DIRECT)

Public figures, like Oprah Winfrey, are often considered opinion leaders.

audience are simultaneously exposed to the same message. **Multiple-step communication** uses influential members of the target audience, known as **opinion leaders,** to filter a message before it reaches other group members, modifying its effect positively or negatively for the rest of the group.[37]

Because of their important role, opinion leaders have often been called gatekeepers to indicate the control they have over ideas flowing into the group. Marketers interested in maximizing communication effectiveness nearly always attempt to identify opinion leaders. Opinion leaders are open to communications from all sources. They are more inclined to be aware of information regarding a broad range of subjects. They read a lot and talk with salespeople and other people who have information about products. Opinion leaders can have a sort of multiplier effect, intensifying the strength of the message if they respond positively and pass it on to others. Consequently, the resources used to gain support from opinion leaders are probably well spent.

Public figures are often opinion leaders. Consider the sales boost for several titles after Oprah Winfrey introduced her "book of the month club" feature. She has influenced so many consumers with her highly regarded opinion that her selections have become bestsellers.[38] In January 2001, she featured the 38th book in her book club. Oprah even expanded her book club to include a "Kids' Reading List" that is coordinated with the American Library Association and allows site visitors to find suggested readings based on a child's age.[39]

MULTIPLE-STEP COMMUNICATION
Communication in which opinion leaders filter messages and modify positively or negatively their effect on the rest of the group.

OPINION LEADER
Influential member of a target audience who first screens messages sent by marketers.

CONNECTING WITH DIVERSITY

MULTINATIONALS TARGET CHINA'S "LITTLE EMPERORS" WITH ADS AND PROMOTIONS

"We used to go to dim sum on Sunday morning with the old folks," laments a Chinese mother, "but now my son is nine, he insists we go to McDonald's. Otherwise, he stays at home. What can we do?" This complaint is typical of mothers in China's cities. In urban areas, where a government policy of one child per family is strictly enforced, the one and only exerts a lot of influence on household purchasing decisions, especially if that child is a boy. These "little emperors" are also beneficiaries of the "six-pocket syndrome," with as many as six doting adults—parents and grandparents—to indulge every whim. It is easy to understand why multinational companies are aiming their promotional efforts straight for children and teenagers quickly approaching adulthood.

Danone S.A. of France, Nestlé of Switzerland, and U.S.-based H. J. Heinz Company have set up shop in China, marketing such foods as yogurt, milk, and cheese. Toy and technology companies such as Bandai, Lego, VTech Holdings, and IBM have stepped up their sales efforts. For multinationals, Chinese children are the key that will open the door

Continued

to a burgeoning market. Even companies with products that are not sold to children have redirected their promotional efforts to the younger set. General Electric sponsors China's version of Sesame Street in the hopes of instilling its corporate name in the mind of a future generation.

Many spoiled Chinese youth spend their free time in front of the television. Companies have been taking advantage of this, which is one reason why TV advertising is booming in China. And although the Chinese are less familiar with sales promotions, companies will need to provide coupons and point-of-purchase samples to spur parents to buy what they see on TV. Not much is known about the buying habits of little emperors and their parents, but advertisers have discovered several guidelines.

- Education is a key value. In China it is not uncommon for pregnant women to play English and Chinese tapes to their bellies to give their budding babies a linguistic head start. Mothers pay over $70 for a VTech English alphabet desk, even though it costs more than they earn in a week. With only one child to assure the family's future, parents of little emperors are receptive to ads that emphasize learning.
- Kids covet Western goods. Nike shoes and Western blue jeans are seen as status symbols by Chinese kids. As the first generation to grow up in a consumer society, they are tuned in to messages of Western ads and do not want to "buy Chinese." Still, as consumer culture develops, advertisers will need to differentiate their products rather than just feature the "Western" label.
- Chinese culture cannot be ignored. For thousands of years, Confucian tradition has emphasized respect for authority and family harmony. Ads in China uniformly portray happy families. Smart-aleck teens arguing with parents would not appeal to Chinese consumers. Advertisers must walk a thin line in marketing Western goods with a Chinese flavor. Coca-Cola China, Ltd., spent two years on market research before introducing a new fruit drink. Not only does Tian Yu Di (heaven and earth) feature a Chinese name, but also the attractive container has an image of China's Yellow Mountain and calligraphy by a Chinese master.

Sources: Helen Johnstone, "Little Emperors Call the Shots," *Asian Business,* September 1996, pp. 67–70; Sally D. Goll, "China's (Only) Children Get the Royal Treatment," *Wall Street Journal,* February 8, 1995, p. B1; "Wooing Little Emperors," *Business China,* July 22, 1996, pp. 1–2; and Gary Jones, "China's Little Emperors," *The Independent (London),* November 12, 2000, pp. 28, 29, 30, 32.

DEVELOPING THE IMC PLAN

Now that we have examined the factors influencing the process, let us see how an integrated marketing communication plan is built. The steps are outlined in Figure 14.8. The IMC plan should never be developed in isolation from the strategic marketing plan. It's the responsibility of strategic marketing personnel to define the role of communication in the overall marketing strategy. Usually, the IMC plan is designed to position the organization and its products in a manner consistent with that strategy.

SELECTING AND UNDERSTANDING TARGET AUDIENCES

Understanding the target audience is the most important part of communications planning. First, remember that the overall market needs to be segmented, and each segment should be treated uniquely. For every target audience, communications experts need to understand all

STEPS IN THE IMC PLAN

| **1.** Select and understand target audiences. | **2.** Determine the communication objectives and select the communication mix. | **3.** Develop the budget. | **4.** Implement. | **5.** Measure the results. |

FIGURE 14.8 *Developing the Communication Plan*

aspects of consumer behavior: where, how, and why they buy as well as how they obtain and process information. In new and developing markets, companies sometimes must operate more by trial and error as they gradually come to know buying habits. For instance, as the People's Republic of China encourages more businesses to set up shop, multinationals are learning more about the children and youth segments of this burgeoning market. See the diversity feature, "Multinationals Target China's 'Little Emperors' with Ads and Promotions."

DETERMINING OBJECTIVES AND SELECTING THE IMC MIX

Consumers move from a lack of awareness about brands to purchase and loyalty. This process of increasing involvement can be described by hierarchical models. The most straightforward of these is AIDA, which stands for attention, interest, desire, and action.[40] Figure 14.9 depicts AIDA and a more detailed version that includes awareness, knowledge, liking, preference, conviction, and purchase. For example, imagine that an in-line skater suddenly crosses your path and breaks your concentration (awareness). Next, you ask friends how they like their in-line skates, and you observe how others use the product (knowledge). Perhaps you rent a pair and have so much fun that you consider purchasing skates of your own (liking). By talking to friends and reading ads you develop a brand preference. Elaborate in-store displays and product guarantees convince you to buy a particular brand (conviction). Finally, you decide to purchase the skates with your credit card.[41]

As marketers plan their communication activities, they must keep the objective in mind. Is it to create awareness, build brand preference, or encourage purchase? The IMC mix will vary considerably depending on the objective. To create awareness and product knowledge, advertising is very effective. It gains attention and even can lead to liking and brand preference. Once desire is created, however, sales promotion may be more useful. At this point the customer is more influenced by personal selling, sales promotions, and sponsorships. Attending a sponsored event could make the product so immediately salient that the consumer decides to buy. Sales promotions involving coupons, price incentives, or in-store samples may move buyers to action by reinforcing their conviction to try the brand. The effectiveness of personal selling increases dramatically in the later stages of the buying process. This is especially true for high-priced items in consumer markets, but in some business markets personal selling may be necessary just to gain attention. Although public relations appears to be least useful—because it tapers off after the attention stage and remains low compared to the others—keep in mind the lower cost. Other than the fairly minor expense of creating the public relations message, there is no cost for delivering it.

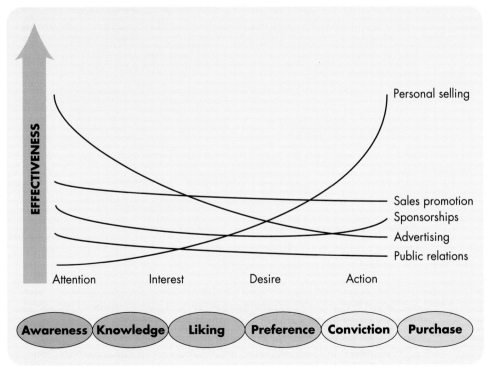

FIGURE 14.9 *Effectiveness of Main Types of Communication at Different Stages in the Consumer Buying Process*

MasterCard targets 13 million college students by using all five types of communication. It sponsors many sporting events viewed and attended by students and offers free online financial advice. Through television spots and the Internet, cards with special features, such as low finance rates and special offers on entertainment and travel, are offered to students. Often representatives visit campus to convince students to sign up for a card, for which they receive a free gift.[42]

DEVELOPING THE COMMUNICATION BUDGET

The communication budget falls within expenditures for the entire marketing mix. Consequently, establishing the specific amount for IMC requires an understanding of the overall marketing strategy, the financial resources available, and the contribution communications is expected to make. In allocating IMC money it must be remembered that some activities can be started or stopped quickly, such as advertising and sales promotion. Personal selling often must be adjusted more slowly, since time is required to hire, train, and deploy the sales force.

The IMC budget is determined in two steps. First, the total allocation is decided. Second, the amount for each type of communication is assigned.

Determining the Overall Budget   The first issue is how much it will cost to accomplish the objective. Generally, communication objectives are established once a year. Two-thirds of advertising budgets for the following year are submitted to top marketing management during September or October, and nearly 80 percent are approved by November.[43] Most IMC budgets are based on one of the following: percentage of sales, competitive budgeting, payout plan, or cost of tasks that must be performed to accomplish objectives.

Deciding precisely how much to invest in communication requires a lot of financial calculations. It is important to establish the contribution of IMC to volume objectives and determine resulting profits and cash flows. In doing these calculations, most organizations forecast sales levels based on total expenditures. The latter include all costs that can be realistically allocated to the communication campaign such as special training and compensation for the sales force. The forecasts are based on marketing research about consumer responses to communications, expected IMC spending by competitors, and product demand estimates. The percentage of sales method simply estimates the sales level and then allocates a certain percentage of sales to communications. Often the percentage is set at the industry average. Sometimes it is based on the previous year's sales. In either case, the problem is that sales are used to create the communications budget, whereas IMC should be used to create sales. Because the method is very easy to administer, however, it is used widely.

Competitive budgeting involves determining what rivals are spending and setting the budget accordingly. The deregulation of the telecommunications industry probably influenced the budgeting strategies of large companies such as AT&T and MCI. In order to maintain a strong presence in the market, such companies must be able to keep up with the IMC spending of competitors.

The payout plan method is generally used for new products that require high communication expenditures. The marketer estimates future sales and establishes the budget required to gain initial acceptance and trial of the product. Generally, IMC costs are very high relative to sales, in some cases even greater. The early expenditures are deemed reasonable because of the payback expected in later years. This is similar to investing money in product development.

The task method sets specific sales targets or other objectives and then determines what activities and amounts are required to accomplish them. This approach can be very complex and tends to be used by large organizations in highly competitive environments. Marketers must have very accurate information and considerable experience in order to develop the extensive models necessary. The task method is superior to the others because so much detailed attention is paid to how IMC contributes to accomplishing objectives.

Allocating the Budget   Communication works synergistically. In other words, as Martha Stewart suggested at the beginning of this chapter, investments in one type of communication may help other types accomplish their objectives. A salesperson benefits tremendously from awareness created by advertising and from purchase incentives due to sales promotion. The integrated aspect of marketing communication needs to be kept in mind when deciding the allocation for each activity. This process requires considerable and continuous dialogue among marketing team members. In many cases, data are fed into computer simulations that help determine the best allocations. In other cases, the team simply estimates what is required. In companies with major brands, an average of 18 executives are involved, including senior management media and advertising staff, marketing personnel, brand marketing management, and sales personnel.[44] The allocations may be determined by very specific objectives. When Nike wanted to increase traffic in retail outlets, it budgeted more for signage. When Westinghouse wanted to increase name recognition, it shifted resources from the sales force to advertising.

IMPLEMENTATION

Implementation of an IMC plan tends to be done by functional specialists with considerable experience in their field. There are ample career opportunities in these areas—such as personal selling, advertising, and public relations—because each is multifaceted and challenging. Marketers strive to obtain uniquely talented employees and suppliers to carry out communication programs. No matter how good the plan, without creative and professional implementation, all is lost.

> **career tip** The Web is an abundant source for information regarding advertising, public relations, personal selling, and other areas. Use a search engine to obtain lists of organizations worldwide. You'll have an opportunity to explore your career of interest or research a specific company. You will also discover links to networks where you can post a résumé, receive daily news briefs, or access a job information service.

The first decision is how much to do in-house and how much to outsource. For example, personal selling can be done by company personnel, manufacturer representatives (private salespersons), or distributors. Likewise, companies must decide whether to do their own advertising and sales promotion or hire outsiders. Most large and medium-sized firms outsource much of their IMC implementation. Often representatives from these advertising and promotion agencies work on-site with the client's marketing executives and personnel. Chapters 15 and 16 will explain in more detail how to implement each type of communication activity.

MEASURING IMC RESULTS

It was John Wanamaker, a famous 19th-century retailer, who first said: "I know that half of the money I spend on advertising is wasted, but I can never figure out which half." He was referring to the fact that many messages may never reach much of the target audience. Who is reached by a communication, and what does it accomplish relative to the goals established in the plan?

Why is it difficult to estimate the results of communication? The major problem is isolating the effects of one part of the IMC plan to determine its relative influence on product performance. Most marketers start by identifying criteria or measures. Performance measures are variables or factors that tell us how well the organization or product is doing. Common measures are market share, sales level, and profitability. Other factors are often used, such as number of loyal customers, amount of brand recognition, brand image, and knowledge of the product.

Once performance measures are selected, the task of assessing IMC influence can begin. Very seldom is only one part of the IMC mix adjusted at a time, and competitors' activities are virtually never stable. So determining the precise effect of communication is rarely possible. When Nike introduces a new model, how much of its success can be attributed to pricing, product distribution, customer service, or promotion? Still, by monitoring IMC expenditures and performance measures for a large number of companies and then applying statistical analysis, researchers can get a good idea of the overall effect of IMC. This information is very useful in determining whether objectives are being met and whether changes are required.

ISSUES IN COMMUNICATION

DIVERSITY

Effective communications are carefully targeted. The vast differences among consumers create opportunities for a wide variety of promotions to meet their needs. For example, 54 million Americans have some form of disability, and marketers are changing the way they communicate with these consumers. Long ignored, these Americans with disabilities represent several substantial target segments.[45] Marketers now have a new vehicle for communicating with many of these consumers—the Internet.

Until recently the Web was not very user friendly for people with limited vision or dexterity. The American Federation for the Blind (AFB) and Interliant, Inc. recently redesigned the AFB's Web site, www.afb.org, to better accommodate Internet users with disabilities. Previous assistive technologies such as screen magnifiers or screen readers did not properly read site content, but the new site allows for a much more completely accessible site. Graphics are now labeled with text that can be read by screen readers and all audio on the site is now available in text form so that it can be read by the visually impaired. The AFB's site, serves as a model for other government sites, which are required by the 1998 Rehabilitation Act to make the information they provide on their sites accessible to those with disabilities.[46]

Halftheplanet.com is a content and commerce Internet site for people with disabilities. Visitors to the site can find relevant news articles, information on technology that can make living easier, issues related to schools and child disabilities, and health and medical information. In addition, site visitors can find stories about other people with disabilities who continue to enjoy doing many things. Visitors can also become members of the site and receive e-mail updates and articles based on their interests. The site aims to assist people with disabilities in independent living.[47]

Promotions in general are becoming more inclusive by depicting people with disabilities. Insurance provider HealthExtras hired Christopher Reeve to star in its advertisements about long-term disability insurance. The former Superman has created much publicity about disabilities, particularly spinal cord injuries. The ads appeal to audiences, whether disabled or not, by using Reeve to demonstrate the possibility that tragedy can happen to anyone. Reeve has also starred in ads for Johnson & Johnson. Public tolerance of insensitivity toward people with disabilities is decreasing. When Nike ran ads that claimed its trail running shoes would prevent a jogger from running into a tree and becoming a "drooling, misshapen, non-extreme-trail-running husk of my former self," it met with swift opposition and Nike removed the advertisement with a formal apology.[48]

ETHICS

Marketers must be careful about how they communicate. The American Marketing Association Code of Ethics states that acceptable standards include "avoidance of false and misleading advertising, rejection of high-pressure manipulations, or misleading sales tactics, and avoidance of communications that use deception or manipulation." Despite these guidelines, the ethical boundaries for promotion are not always clear.

Communications targeting children have long faced public scrutiny. Under pressure from consumer groups and the federal government, R. J. Reynolds agreed to stop using the hip Joe Camel in its tobacco advertisements. In June 2000, Philip Morris Company said it would pull its tobacco ads from magazines with teenage readership of more than 15 percent, or more than 2 million teenage readers. This decision removed ads from *Sports Illustrated* and *Rolling Stone*.[49] The alcohol industry has also been accused of knowingly pushing products to minors. In September 1999, the Federal Trade Commission issued a report asking that beer, liquor, and wine companies stop the promotion of alcohol in ads that would appeal to minors, including "promotional placement" in PG and PG13 films, TV programs aimed at younger audiences, and on college campuses. At the same time, Anheuser-Busch launched its "We All Make a Difference Campaign" that salutes those who have made a difference in fighting alcohol abuse.[50]

Americans have voiced much concern about violence being marketed to children either through gun companies, violent video games, or violence on television. U.S. Surgeon General

David Satcher found that exposure to violent entertainment in childhood leads to aggressive behavior throughout life.[51] In response to attacks on the entertainment industry for marketing violence to children, ABC launched public service announcements featuring stars of the network's television series urging children to not become violent.[52]

TECHNOLOGY THAT BUILDS RELATIONSHIPS

In communications, marketers often use technology to reach consumers and establish relationships. New advances make it possible to connect with customers quickly. E-mail is rapidly becoming as common a medium for communication as the telephone. It is estimated that in 2004, marketers will send 210 billion e-mails. In addition to the Web sites already developed for promotional purposes, new graphics formats enable marketers to send advertisements directly to consumers via e-mail. Unlike traditional e-mail, the pages include the photos and advertisements just as they appear in the Web version. In addition to e-mail, consumers can receive messages via handheld organizers or cell phones.[53]

Unlike the Web, e-mail communications can be targeted more directly to a select audience, providing them with information that will be useful for making a purchase. Another use for e-mail is electronic billing. The invoice appears on the screen, and the consumer need only enter a credit card number to pay. Most sites with something to sell offer this type of service to customers, and many even allow customers to create a profile so they do not have to enter their personal information every time they make a purchase. Customers may establish loyal relationships with companies that can provide this type of convenience.[54]

Clearly, the Internet offers exciting new targeting opportunities that will increasingly affect the way marketers combine and orchestrate various communications activities to create the most effective IMC mix. In the next two chapters each of the five main activities that constitute the communications mix will be examined in more detail. Chapter 15 focuses on the mass communication activities of advertising, sales promotion, and public relations, including sponsored events. Chapter 16 is devoted to personal selling and sales force management.

E-mail has become such a common form of communication that Compaq has designed a computer small enough to put in the kitchen.

PEPSI
www.pepsi.com

THIS CHAPTER'S RELATIONSHIPS FEATURE MENTIONS a number of companies that are taking integrated marketing communications to a new level and getting consumers involved. To learn more about this type of interactive marketing, visit the Pepsi Web site and answer the following questions.

1. Once you arrive at the site, take the "Pepsi Challenge." Knowing that communication is at the heart of building relationships, explain how the "Pepsi Challenge" makes this possible.
2. Opinion leaders are an important factor in the communications mix. How does the Pepsi Web site identify and gain input from opinion leaders? Can you think of any other features the site could offer to maximize leaders' influence on others?
3. Integrated marketing communications has numerous objectives. List the objectives the Pepsi Web site accomplishes. Explain.
4. Select a press release that shows how Pepsi uses one or more of the five main types of communication. Describe the characteristics, objective, appeal, cost (low, medium, high), and amount and speed of feedback for that type or types.

IBM
www.ibm.com

THIS CHAPTER'S DIVERSITY FEATURE, "MULTINATIONALS Target China's 'Little Emperors' with Ads and Promotions," discusses the efforts of various companies to reach the millions of children in China. IBM is one of many multinationals stepping up sales efforts to plant its name in the mind of future consumers. In order to learn more, visit the IBM Web site and answer the following questions.

1. New technology often enables marketers to communicate with customers more effectively. List several products or services offered by IBM and explain how they help marketers connect with customers.
2. What does the IBM Web site offer for connecting globally? Why might message characteristics need to be adjusted for various countries?
3. The Internet is a combination of personal and mass media. What are its advantages and disadvantages? With this in mind, what features of the IBM Web site are more and less effective in communicating with customers? Explain.

CHAPTER SUMMARY

OBJECTIVE 1: **Understand the objectives of integrated marketing communication.**

Integrated marketing communication (IMC) is the coordination of all information to the market in order to provide consistent, unified messages. Since each aspect of IMC—personal selling, advertising, sales promotion, public relations, and sponsorships—tends to work synergistically, integration is very important. Marketing communication has six objectives. First, it should provide useful information that improves customer decision making and consumption. Second, it creates demand to ensure that products will be consumed in sufficient quantities to justify their development, production, and distribution. Third, it supplies knowledge about the value of products, such as their benefits, features, and functions. Fourth, it helps differentiate products by describing their uniqueness. Fifth, it helps close the sale by moving customers to action. Finally, it is critical in building the all-important relationship with customers and in securing their loyalty.

OBJECTIVE 2: **Learn how the communication process provides the intended information for the market.**

Traditionally, communication was seen as a one-way process—from seller to buyer—without a feedback loop. Today, a two-way process is more realistic. The sender needs to specify objectives, as discussed previously. The sender's characteristics are important determinants of how well messages will be received. Source credibility is determined by expertise, trustworthiness, and attractiveness (or appeal). Encoding requires translating the message into terms that will be easily understood. Since message interpretation depends on consumer life experiences, a thorough comprehension of consumer behavior is required to do an adequate job of encoding. Message characteristics also play a major role. Marketers need to decide whether a one-sided or two-sided message is better; whether to supply conclusions; the order in which information will be presented; whether to use humor or fear appeals; and whether to use comparative messages. The choice of media—mass, personal, or mixed—also influences communications. Today, mixed media such as the Internet are becoming more important. Audiences are not passive receivers; they interpret information by processing it. Their intelligence and self-esteem are important factors here.

OBJECTIVE 3: Learn about the communication mix, including personal selling, advertising, sales promotion, sponsorships, and public relations.

The communication mix has five major components. Each has particular advantages. Personal selling involves face-to-face contact or two-way technology linkages, such as the telephone or Internet. This allows dialogue and interactive problem solving. Advertising is paid, nonpersonal communication. It reaches all members of the audience with the same "mass" message. Sales promotion uses a one-way message to motivate purchase, usually in the form of short-term incentives to buy. Sponsorship is paid support of an event. It associates the sponsor with the event and its participants. Public relations is nonpaid communication (publicity) about a company and its products. These messages are sometimes broadcast by sources considered to be unbiased so they can have considerable credibility.

OBJECTIVE 4: Know the factors that influence the communications mix.

The communication mix is influenced by several factors. First, business-to-business and consumer markets use different mixes. The former are dominated by personal selling, whereas the latter are dominated by sales promotion and advertising. Second, marketers use a push or pull communication strategy. A push strategy communicates to channel members, who in turn communicate to end users. A pull strategy communicates with end users, who in turn demand products from channel members. Third, communications must be suited to the product's stage in the life cycle in order to have the greatest effectiveness. Finally, marketing communications do not always work directly on consumers. There is often a two-stage process whereby opinion leaders filter information before it reaches others in the market.

OBJECTIVE 5: Describe the steps in developing an integrated marketing communication plan.

The IMC plan is an outgrowth of the marketing plan. It has five steps. First, select and understand target markets. Second, determine communication objectives and select the IMC mix. Third, develop the IMC budget in line with the overall strategic marketing plan. Fourth, implement the plan. Fifth, measure communication results and adjust accordingly.

OBJECTIVE 6: Address diversity, ethics, and technology in communications.

Many media are not accessible to physically impaired individuals, and other avenues must be used. One is the Internet, especially through innovative software.

Marketers must be careful not to cross ethical boundaries in their communications. They should avoid false and misleading ads and sales tactics as well as high-pressure manipulation. Targeting children is a questionable practice because they may easily be misled or manipulated.

Communication technology is providing better ways to connect with consumers and create relationships. E-mail is one example. Software makes interactive communication easier and more rapid than ever before.

REVIEW YOUR UNDERSTANDING

1. What is integrated marketing communication?
2. What are the six objectives of integrated marketing communication?
3. What is the one-way communication process? How does it differ from the two-way process?
4. What are message sender characteristics and why are they important?
5. What is encoding?
6. What message characteristics should be considered? How does each influence effectiveness?
7. What are personal, mass, and mixed media? What are the characteristics of each?
8. What factors influence how messages are interpreted? Describe each.
9. What are the main categories in the communication mix?
10. What factors influence the communication mix? Describe each.
11. What are the steps in building an integrated communication plan?
12. How does diversity offer an opportunity and a challenge to communication?
13. What aspects of communication are covered by the American Marketing Association Code of Ethics?
14. Name one way that communication technology is helping to build relationships with consumers.

DISCUSSION OF CONCEPTS

1. Describe the various goals of communication. What helps determine communication objectives?
2. Why is it so important for marketers to understand the communication process? How does that process affect the development and implementation of a campaign?
3. The way in which a message is communicated to consumers is critically important to its success. Name some of the issues involved in developing a message.
4. How do consumers distort messages? Have you ever distorted a message directed at you? How can marketers combat this problem?
5. Why is the source of a message so important? What are the three characteristics of a good spokesperson? Do you think one spokesperson can communicate effectively with the entire market? Why or why not?

6. Briefly describe the five steps in developing a communication plan. How are the plan and the company's overall marketing strategy related?

7. List the pros and cons of each type of communication activity: personal selling, sales promotion, advertising, sponsorship, and public relations. What factors help determine the appropriate one to select?

KEY TERMS AND DEFINITIONS

Advertising: Paid communication through nonpersonal channels.

Communication: The process of sending and receiving messages.

Encoding: Translating a message into terms easily understood by the target audience.

Integrated marketing communication (IMC): The coordination of advertising, sales promotion, personal selling, public relations, and sponsorship to reach consumers with a powerful effect in the market.

Media: The channels through which messages are communicated.

Multiple-step communication: Communication in which opinion leaders filter messages and modify positively or negatively their effect on the rest of the group.

One-sided message: A message that presents only arguments favorable to the source.

One-step communication: Communication in which all audience members are simultaneously exposed to the same marketing message.

Opinion leader: Influential member of a target audience who first screens messages sent by marketers.

Personal selling: Face-to-face or other individual communication between a buyer and a seller.

Promotion: The process whereby marketers inform, educate, persuade, remind, and reinforce consumers through communication.

Public relations (PR): Unpaid promotion designed to present the firm and its products in a positive light in the buyer's mind.

Pull strategy: An attempt to influence consumers directly so they will "pull" the product through the distribution channel.

Push strategy: An attempt to influence the distribution channel, which in turn will "push" the product through to the user.

Sponsorship: The exchange of money (or some other form of value) in return for a public association with an event.

Sales promotion: Communication designed to stimulate immediate purchases, using tools such as coupons, contests, and free samples.

Two-sided message: A message that presents arguments that are unfavorable as well as favorable to the source.

REFERENCES

1. "Martha's Way," *Success,* January–February 1997, pp. 31–32; Keith J. Kelly, "More Martha Stewart on TV Is OK'd," *Advertising Age,* August 26, 1996, p. 4; Mark Adams, "The Franchise," *Brandweek,* March 4, 1996, pp. MR10–13; Keith J. Kelly, "Magazine of the Year," *Advertising Age,* March 11, 1996, pp. S1, S11; Martin Pedersen, "Martha Stewart Cross-Merchandising," *Publisher's Weekly,* December 12, 1994, pp. 19–20; marthastewart.com, visited December 20, 2000; Kathleen Pender, "Dueling IPOs (one year later)," *Start Tribune* (Minneapolis, MN), October 19, 2000, p. 1D; "Zeller's Collection of Martha Stewart Everyday Products Grows with Martha Stewart Everyday Kitchen," *Canada Newswire,* November 16, 2000, retrieved December 8, 2000 from the World Wide Web: web.lexis-nexis.com/universe; "Martha Stewart Living Omnimedia, Inc. Elects Arthur C. Martinez to Board of Directors," *PR Newswire,* December 7, 2000, retrieved December 8, 2000 from the World Wide Web: web.lexis-nexis.com/universe; "marthastewart.com Launches marthascards Greeting Card Service," *PR Newswire,* December 4, 2000, retrieved December 8, 2000 from the World Wide Web: web.lexis-nexis.com/universe.

2. Lisa Bannon, "Cosmetic Surgeons Need to Pay More Attention to Appearances," *Wall Street Journal Interactive Edition,* February 4, 1997, www.wsj.com.

3. Lindy Washburn, "Decor of Hackensack, NJ, Medical Center Facilitates Patient Comfort," *Knight-Ridder Tribune Business News,* January 11, 2001.

4. Judann Pollack and Alice Z. Cuneo, "Multitude of Deals Could Hurt Martha," *Advertising Age,* November 19, 1996, p. A1.

5. William Leiss, Stephen Kline, and Sut Jhally, *Social Communication in Advertising: Persons, Products, and Images of Well-Being* (Toronto: Methuen, 1986); and George Stigler, "The Economics of Information," *Journal of Political Economy.*

6. Ron Hutcheson and Chris Mondics, "Campaign Ads Get Nastier," *Pittsburgh Post-Gazette,* October 28, 2000, p. A1.

7. "Cisco CEO: China Sales Could Grow 100% a Year," *Dow Jones International News,* January 18, 2001.

8. Joe Flint, "Survivor Series Likely to Yield Windfall for CBS," *The Asian Wall Street Journal,* January 15, 2001, p. N1; " 'Survivor' Program More Than Endures in Terms of Ratings," *The Wall Street Journal Europe,* August 28, 2000, p. 23; and Mike McDaniel, "CBS Plans to Keep 'Survivor' Series on the Run," *Houston Chronicle;* January 10, 2001, p. 1.

9. www.motorola.com, site visited January 17, 2001.

10. David Goetzl, "New EAS Ads Aim to Attract Women," *Advertising Age,* January 1, 2001, p. 4.

11. Joseph Pereira, "Reebok Serves Up Tennis Star in New Ads," *Wall Street Journal,* January 18, 2001, p. B2.

12. "Chanel Finds Non-Celebrities Alluring," *Globe & Mail,* December 22, 2000, p. B12.

13. www.luvs.com, site visited January 17, 2001.

14. Mallore Dill, "Reach Out," *AdWeek Midwest,* April 24, 2000, p. 42.

15. "Martin Sheen: Prime Time Activist," *PR Newswire,* May 11, 2000; "Actor Martin Sheen Is Among 1700 Arrested at School of Americas Protest," *Star-Tribune Newspaper of the Twin Cities–Mpls.-St. Paul,* November 20, 2000, p. 11A.

16. Henry I. Miller, "Red Tape Is Blocking Oil Spill Cleanups," *Wall Street Journal Interactive Edition,* July 10, 1997.

17. Sarah Krall, "The Case for Jewelry," *Gifts & Decorative Accessories,* December 1, 2000, p. 179; www.adiamondisforever.com, site visited January 17, 2001.

18. Raju Narisetti, "Rubbermaid Opens Door to TV, Hoping to Put Houses in Order," *Wall Steet Journal Interactive Edition,* February 4, 1997.

19. www.rubbermaid.com, site visited January 17, 2001.

20. Harold L. Ross, Jr., "How to Create Effective Humorous Commercials Yielding Above Average Brand Preference Change," *Marketing News,* March 26, 1976, p. 4.

21. national.unitedway.org/nfl.cfm, site visited January 17, 2001; "Service Ads' Humor Helps Carry Message," *USA Today,* January 11, 2001, p. 2B.

22. Cyndee Miller, "HIV Kits Target Untested Market," *Marketing News,* January 20, 1997, pp. 1, 11.

23. Bob Garfield, "RC Hooks a Winner When It Goes Fishing for Some Individuality," *Advertising Age,* June 13, 1994, p. 3.

24. moli.microsoft.com/, site visited on February 10, 1997.

25. www.cio.com/marketing/commhome.html, site visited on February 10, 1997.

26. www.pagefast.com, site visited on February 10, 1997.
27. M. Zelner, "Self-Esteem, Self-Perception, and Influenceability," *Journal of Personality and Social Psychology* 25 (1973): 87–93.
28. Joel Kurth, "Suburbs Cracking Down on Door-to-Door Peddlers," *The Detroit News*, November 20, 2000; "Pharmaceutical Sales," *PR Newswire*, January 9, 2001.
29. Howard Fendrich, "Superbowl Always Produces Super Ratings," *AP Newswires*, January 18, 2001; "Superbowl: Millions Tune in, but Many Aren't There for the Watching," *Business Wire*, January 16, 2001.
30. "Heads of Top Soft Drink Brands Bring Budget Artillery, Smarts to Battlefield," *Advertising Age*, www.adage.com, site visited January 31, 1997.
31. Paul Wenske, "Reaching Out to Customers," *The Kansas City Star*, January 10, 2001, p. C1.
32. "PGA of America, Oldsmobile Renew Licensing Agreement Through 2005," *PGA News*, Issue #27, www.pga.com, site visited January 18, 2001.
33. John Evan Frook, "Southwest Hooks NHL Sponsorship," *BtoB*, September 11, 2000, p. 3.
34. Richard Sandomir, "To Track Bowl Names, A Scorecard Is Required," *The New York Times*, December 29, 2000, p. 4.
35. Tim Swanson, "A Few Words from Our Sponsors," *Variety e V Supplement*, January 2001; John Schwartz, "Marketers Turn To Simple Tool: Email," *The New York Times*, December 13, 2000, p. H1.
36. Gary Levin, "For Ford and GM Loyalty in the Cards," *Advertising Age*, March 28, 1994, pp. 5–18; Jonathan Berry et al., "Data Base Marketing: A Potent New Tool for Selling," *Business Week*, September 5, 1994, pp. 56–62.
37. Jagdish N. Sheth, "Word-of-Mouth in Low Risk Innovations," *Journal of Advertising Research* 11 (1971): 15–18.
38. Jacqueline Blais, "Oprah Nod Unnerves 'Rapture' Writer," *USA Today*, May 13, 1997, www.usatoday.com.
39. www.oprah.com, site visited January 18, 2001.
40. E. K. Strong, *The Psychology of Selling* (New York: McGraw-Hill, 1925), p. 9.
41. Robert J. Lavidge and Gary A. Steiner, "A Model for Predictive Measurements of Advertising Effectiveness," *Journal of Marketing*, October 1991, p. 61.
42. Ray Waddell, "MasterCard Music Tour Targets College Market," *Amusement Business*, April 12, 1993, p. 5; and Howard Schlossberg, "College Master Values Program Targets 13 Million 'Independents,'" *Marketing News*, March 15, 1993, p. 5; and www.mastercard.com, site visited January 19, 2001.
43. J. Thomas Russell and W. Ronald Lane, *Kleppner's Advertising Procedure* (Upper Saddle River, NJ: Prentice Hall, 1993), p. 138.
44. Fairfield Research, Inc., cited in "Beginning the End of the Seige," *Brandweek*, July 27, 1992, p. 34.
45. Associated Press, "Awareness Campaign Promotes Travel for the Disabled," *USA Today*, January 13, 1997; and www.ncd.gov, site visited January 19, 2001.
46. "AS Website for Blind," *AP Newswires*, January 17, 2001.
47. www.halftheplanet.com, site visited January 19, 2001.
48. David Goetzl, "Spokesman Reeve Stars in Effort for Disability Insurer," *Advertising Age*, February 21, 2000, p. 4; www.apacure.com, site visited January 19, 2001; and John Heinzl, "Nike Ad: Good Taste Gone in a Swoosh," *The Globe and Mail*, October 27, 2000, p. M2.
49. "Study on Teen Readership of Magazines May Step Up Pressure on Tobacco Firms," *Wall Street Journal*, October 31, 2000, p. A8.
50. Al Stamborski, "FTC Asks That Alcohol Ads Be Kept from Minors," *St. Louis Post Dispatch*, September 10, 1999, p. C10.
51. Jeff Leeds, "Surgeon General Links TV, Real Violence Entertainment," *Los Angeles Times*, January 17, 2001, p. A1; and "Youth Violence on the Decline but Surgeon General Warns of Complacency," *The Hartford Courant*, January 18, 2001, p. A10.
52. "Advertising: Hollywood Launches Messages of Peace," *Wall Street Journal*, September 14, 2000, p. B17.
53. Schwartz, "Marketers Turn to Simple Tool: Email."
54. J. William Gurley, "E-Mail Gets Rich," *Fortune*, February 17, 1997, pp. 146–148.

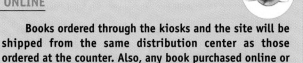

Bricks or Clicks

BORDERS GOES ONLINE

BORDERS IS ONE OF THE world's largest book retailers. Although it was comparatively slow to respond to the challenge from online sellers such as Amazon.com, it has since embraced e-commerce and has not looked back. Its site, Borders.com, is consistently ranked as one of the best for "cost (pricing), delivery, and transacting." During the summer of 2000, it decided to extend its award-winning Web site to its stores in the form of kiosks in a strategy it calls "retail convergence."

Retail convergence is "the integration of traditional and emerging retail channels and technology to provide customers with a compelling and enhanced shopping experience." Stores will soon include computers that will permit customers to search its online database via its "Title Sleuth" program. Customers will be able to search the 700,000 titles available and to order them for pickup or for home delivery. This service will be available for customers through Borders.com as well.

Books ordered through the kiosks and the site will be shipped from the same distribution center as those ordered at the counter. Also, any book purchased online or through the kiosks can be returned to a "real" storefront.

Although retail convergence is a strategy that relies on technology, "the customer is in control," according to vice president of logistics Steve McAlexander. "We allow them to make the choice of when and how they want to shop, whether it's on the Web, in the store, or any combination. The key to us is to have one brand across multiple channels."

Sources: "From Brick-and-Mortar to Click-and-Mortar," *Modern Materials Handling*, May 2000, pp. 31–33; and "Borders.com Rated #1 Online Bookseller in Forrester PowerRankings," *PR Newswire*, November 6, 2000, as retrieved from the World Wide Web: web.lexis-nexis.com.

Nike

IN 1964, PHIL KNIGHT AND his former track coach, William Bowerman, began selling shoes made by a Japanese company, Onitsuka Tiger Co., out of the back seat of Knight's car. To gain more control of their marketing efforts, Knight and Bowerman developed the Nike brand, named after the Greek goddess of victory. A Portland State University design student created the famous "swoosh" for $35. It represents a wing, to "embody the spirit of the winged goddess who inspired the most courageous and chivalrous warriors." From the onset, Knight's philosophy has been that people root for a favorite team or athlete, not a product. So Knight sold "the athletic ideals of determination, individuality, self-sacrifice, and winning." Beginning in 1973 with track star Steve Prefontaine, Nike has actively sponsored athletes with these attributes. Today, it invests hundreds of millions annually to gain sponsorship of world-class teams and players.

Nike is now the number-one shoe company in the world. It controls 45 percent of the athletic shoe market in the United States. Knight attributes success to a number of factors.

- The company is based on one brand, which has a genuine and distinct personality, and tangible, emotional connections to customers the world over.
- It is rooted in sports, the fastest-growing culture, growing so fast that it is becoming the one, true international language.
- Nike has been around for over 25 years and has grown each year because "our horizon is more than 12 months away."
- It is made up of 21,800 teammates who "stood this industry on its head."
- They include the brightest, most committed, most sought-after people in the industry.

Nike's ability to coordinate integrated marketing communication that really connects with customers is outstanding. For example, the "swoosh" is so familiar that the name no longer needs to appear along with it. The company Web site is updated constantly, announcing new products and offering more sales opportunities for the company. With features such as three-dimensional product views, a gift/product finder, Nike customization tools and the Nike TechLab, Nike is utilizing its Internet channel to the fullest.

Nike strategically coordinates its television and print ads, sponsorships, Web site, an 800 number, billboards, and other media to form an effective mix of communications. The athletes who deliver its message are a major factor. For example, Michael Jordan is generally considered to be the best basketball player in the history of the game. At a time when Nike profits were sinking, Knight selected Jordan to reestablish the company's image. Spike Lee filmed spots depicting Jordan as the basketball player whose talent (and Nike shoes) enabled him to fly. Approximately 35 ads later, Jordan was the most popular athlete in the country, according to New York–based Marketing Evaluations.

A number of other famous athletes have elicited a tremendous response from customers, including tennis players John McEnroe and André Agassi, baseball player Nolan Ryan, football's Deion Sanders, track stars Carl Lewis and Alberto Salazar, and basketball players Charles Barkley and Scottie Pippen. The young Tiger Woods has a $100 million contract with Nike. The charisma, talent, expertise, and personality of such athletes deliver Nike's message. According to its Web site, "Nike exists to be the best sports and fitness company in the world. We are here to inspire and motivate the athlete in all of us and advocate the love of sports. We live in the heart of sports and the athletes who play them."

And Nike is expanding its total market with integrated marketing communication. It is founder of P.L.A.Y. (Participate in the Lives of America's Youth), a multimillion-dollar program to promote healthy, active lifestyles among young people. There is also Niketown, a retailing effort to make a more personal connection with customers. Niketown stores feature basketball courts where customers can try out shoes, multiscreen televisions to display Nike promotions, and apparel autographed by Nike athletes.

"With the growing popularity of the WNBA, women's soccer, and such prominent female Olympians as Marion Jones, the interest in women's sports and fitness is at an all-time high. Nike has already seen the positive impact of this women's movement through such successful initiatives as 'shop-in-shop' concepts in women's sections of U.S. department stores, women's retail in Japan and women's-focused Web site sales in Hong Kong." When Nike was launched 28 years ago, a mere one in 30 school-aged girls were involved in sports. Today that number has jumped to one in five and Nike is at the forefront in sponsorships and involvement in supporting women in sports.

With a marketing budget of more than $250 million, Nike reaches consumers globally with events like Hoop Heroes. Michael Jordan, Charles Barkley, and other Nike athletes travel to help raise basketball consciousness in places such as Shanghai, Melbourne, and Seoul. In the United Kingdom, Nike has begun expansion of a Customer Service Center, while in Brazil it has formed a partnership with Confedercão Brasileira de Futbol to sponsor the national soccer team. For many major sporting events, Nike plans an array of media campaigns, product launches, and team endorsements. As Nike continues to face new competition, it will need to be the leader in not only shoes but also in integrated marketing communication.

1. *Discuss how Nike uses IMC to position the company in a manner consistent with its strategy. Give examples.*

2. *How does Nike use athletes to influence the communication process? What characteristics of message senders do you think Nike considers the most important? Why?*

3. *This chapter discussed 21st-century forces affecting communication. Based on what you have read in the case and what you know about Nike, discuss how the company addresses these forces with its marketing communications.*

Sources: Nike Web site, www.nike.com; Sarah Lorge, "Marketing a Long Shot," *Sales and Marketing Management,* June 1997, p. 20; Linda Himelstein, "The Swoosh Heard 'Round the World," *Business Week,* May 12, 1997, pp. 76–80; Randall Lane, "You Are What You Wear," *Forbes,* October 14, 1996, pp. 42–46; Steve Gelsi, "Everyone's Still Shooting at the Swoosh," *Brandweek,* February 5, 1996, pp. 30–32; www.nikebiz.com/story, visited January 7, 2001; www.hoovers.com, visited January 7, 2001; "Swoosh Through Your Holiday Gift List at Niketown.Nike.com," *PR Newswire,* December 4, 2000, retrieved December 8, 2000 from the World Wide Web: web.lexis-nexis.com/universe; "Nike to Shox the World," *PR Newswire,* November 15, 2000, retrieved December 8, 2000 from the World Wide Web: web.lexis-nexis.com/universe; and "Nike All Conditions Gear Appoints Two Nike Leaders to the ACG Business," *PR Newswire,* December 6, 2000, retrieved December 8, 2000 from the World Wide Web: web.lexis-nexis.com/universe.

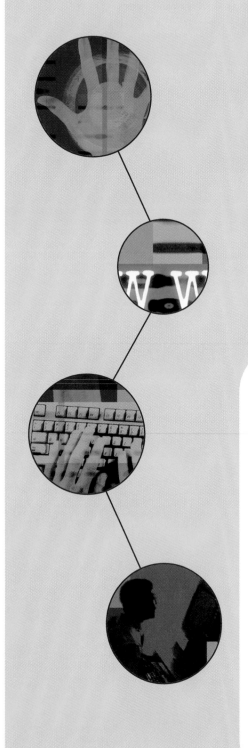

chapter 15

MASS COMMUNICATIONS: ADVERTISING, SALES PROMOTION, AND PUBLIC RELATIONS

1. Understand the concept of mass communications, including the relative use of advertising, sales promotion, and public relations.

2. Learn how technology, globalization, and ethics are playing major roles in mass communications.

3. Know the objectives, advantages, and disadvantages of advertising, as well as the sequence of steps in creating an advertising campaign.

4. Understand sales promotion objectives and what types of promotions are used to stimulate sales in business, trade, retailer, and consumer markets.

5. Understand the use of public relations in marketing.

◀ *Actor Jim Carey as the Grinch*

LIKE THE ART OF MOVIEMAKING, THE art of movie product tie-ins has matured. Studio marketers have learned they need to be more strategic as they form partnerships. Not long ago, starstruck marketers spent large amounts of money with the misguided expectation of high returns from simply putting a movie name onto their product. Now companies are becoming more selective as they choose movies with which tie-ins will be developed. Marketers are analyzing movies to determine if the themes relate to the product image they are trying to project. A recent holiday movie, How the Grinch Stole Christmas, *captured a theme that many marketers wanted to portray in their products or services. During the 2000 holiday season, the Grinch™ had movie tie-ins with Hershey Chocolate, Visa, Rite Aid, Coke, and even the U.S. Postal Service, just to name a few.*

All of these companies took the same approach to developing a movie tie-in with the Grinch by developing a monumental promotions strategy. For example, Visa U.S.A., in conjunction with Pointpathbank.com (the Internet-only bank subsidiary of Synovus Financial Corp.), ran a promotion in which game cards are randomly placed in boxes of Kellogg's cereal. These cards, worth $20, $100, $10,000, and $25,000, include the slogan "How the Grinch Stole Breakfast." The winning cards allowed the winner to withdraw cash at ATMs on Visa's Plus network. In addition, this year's Visa holiday promotion was called "Visa and the Grinch Give Back the Holidays." During November and December 2000, all purchases made on the Visa card were eligible to win.

Rite Aid has also made its first substantial movie tie-in with the Grinch. Rite Aid drugstores around the country were the exclusive vendors of the 10-inch musical Grinch doll (with and without a Santa suit) that plays the song, "You're a Mean One." Rite Aid also sold other Grinch-themed merchandise and customers were welcomed to the store by large images of the Grinch, Cindy Lou Who, and Max the Dog. Before the film was released, John K. Learish, vice president of marketing at Rite Aid stated, "This is going to be a blockbuster hit. This is bigger than life, and we're doing it to a degree that no one else has." The stores sold Hershey products that were packaged as "Grinch Stocking Stuffers," candy canes, and snowballs. Hershey also put full-page ads in Sunday newspapers to promote a deal on a Grinch candy dish and included some seasonal coupons. Why the tie-in between the Grinch and Hershey? A spokesman for Hershey, Mike Kinney, stated, "It's a fun family movie," which directly relates to the image that Hershey tries to portray.

Coca-Cola did not want to miss out on the opportunity to develop a tie-in between the Grinch and one of its products, Sprite. Coke planned a $10 million promotion using the Sprite.com site, Grinch packaging, TV ads, and $4 movie cash rebates to be used on a future ticket purchase. "Grinch represents a careful decision for Sprite since we had not tied in with films before," says Pina Sciarra, brand director of Sprite and other youth brands. "We realized that the Grinch is a good personification of what Sprite is. He helps redefine what the holidays mean to you. Even though he is the anti-Santa, he encourages teens to think for themselves."

The most unique and unexpected tie-in for the Grinch was the partnership with the U.S. Postal Service. It decorated 33,000 post offices with Whoville and Grinch decor and the cancellation stamp read "Happy Wholidays" for the 2000 Christmas season. "We are thrilled that the United States Postal Service has chosen Grinch *for their biggest-ever promotion with a motion picture release," said Beth Goss, senior vice president of national promotions for Universal Pictures. The chief marketing officer and senior vice president of the U.S. Postal Service, Allen Kane, stated, "We are delighted to be associated with the good feeling and spirit of the season the movie brings. The Whoville post office is central to the film's holiday celebration and the exchange of holiday greetings and gifts. This ties in perfectly with the image of the U.S. Postal Service as America's most trusted carrier of holiday cards and packages."[1]*

THE CONCEPT OF MASS COMMUNICATIONS: ADVERTISING, SALES PROMOTION, AND PUBLIC RELATIONS

Today, mass communication helps companies connect with customers by providing information in exciting and creative formats. It adds tremendous value by informing people about the goods and services available in today's global markets. It's so pervasive that every few seconds most of us are exposed to a message designed to influence our behavior. Consumers are bombarded by up to 3,000 marketing messages a day.[2]

In 2001 spending in the United States for mass communication will be about $628 billion, and growth is about 7 percent annually. Much of the spending is for advertising (about $262 billion) but even more is for sales promotion (about $366 billion). Public relations is a distant third. The United States accounts for about one-third of the planet's spending on mass communication. Mass communication in the rest of the world totals about $1.2 trillion, for a combined global figure of $1.8 trillion. About two-thirds is spent on consumer products, and one-third is spent by businesses marketing to other businesses.[3]

Much of the increase in mass communication is due to competitive factors, particularly the battle for brand strength. Familiar examples are Coke versus Pepsi, Kellogg versus General Mills, MCI/WorldCom versus AT&T, Barnes & Noble versus Borders, and Staples versus Office Max. Although the battle of the brands started in the United States, it has become global. Burger King and McDonald's no longer just compete at home but also in most cities around the world. And Pepsi and Coke are notorious for their vigorous rivalry in Brazil, Taiwan, and France. In fact, Coca-Cola has a worldwide ad budget of $1.3 billion—almost double Pepsi's $705 million.[4] Unilever, the Anglo-Dutch consumer goods giant, spent $3.1 billion in advertising outside of the United States in 1999.[5]

Mass communication is composed of advertising, sales promotion, and public relations, as shown in Figure 15.1. Historically, techniques have changed according to advances in

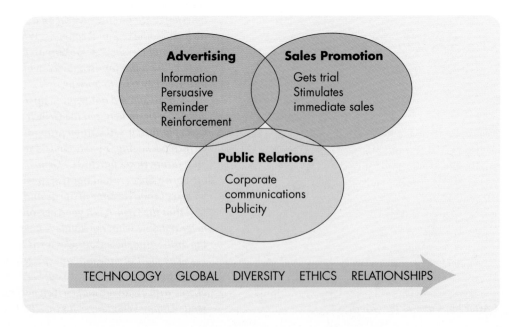

FIGURE 15.1 *The Concept of Mass Communication in Marketing*

technology. Another recent influence is the need for standardization in global markets. Because mass communication is persuasive and powerful, there are many ethical issues for marketers to consider, but it is still a key way to connect with diverse customers. This chapter first looks at technology, global aspects, and ethics. Discussion then turns to advertising and its purposes. We describe the various categories of advertising, the agencies that create and place it, and the media that carry it to the consumer. Next, sales promotion is described as a means to get trial, stimulate immediate sales, and build customer relationships. Finally, a section on public relations and publicity addresses their role in corporate communications.

MASS COMMUNICATION IN THE 21ST CENTURY

In order to understand the future of mass communication, we start with a look at the role technology has played historically and is playing in the 21st century. Second, we will see how mass communication is occurring globally. Third, we will explore several serious ethical aspects of mass communication.

TECHNOLOGICAL PERSPECTIVE

The history of mass communication mirrors a number of technological advances.[6] Before the age of printing, street criers shouted merchants' messages, and shop signs often used pictures to identify their trade to a largely illiterate public. Movable type was invented around 1440, helping to spread literacy, and 32 years later an advertisement for a prayer book was tacked to church doors. The word *advertisement* appeared in about 1665, when it was used as a header to describe announcements of commercial significance. By the mid-1700s, newspapers were popular and carried publicity and ads.

By the 1800s, mass communication through newspapers and handbills was abundant. When magazines were introduced in the mid-1800s, they provided an excellent way to communicate commercial messages. Professionals who did copywriting and advertising emerged because of this medium. By the mid-1930s, great ad agencies such as J. Walter Thompson, Rubicam, and BBDO were successful. During that era, the growth of radio provided yet another medium for promotion and quickly surpassed magazines as the leading vehicle.

Although television came along in 1939 when NBC was established, not until the 1950s did television begin to surpass radio as a promotional medium. The combination of voice and video offered greater opportunities to reach consumers with a creative message. Ronald Reagan was one of the most popular spokespersons in the early days of television. Television now dominates, but magazines, newspapers, radio, and the Internet still carry a significant proportion of promotional messages.

Whereas the traditional media revolutionized advertising and public relations, in recent years information systems based on computer technology have contributed dramatically to sales promotion growth. Computers have made it possible to track product sales globally, thus enhancing the usefulness of all forms of sales promotion. Furthermore, computers and the Internet will shape communication in even more exciting ways. Until recently the process was strictly one way. The Internet now offers a two-way exchange, which is doing for mass communication what the telephone did for interpersonal communication.

GLOBAL MASS COMMUNICATIONS

Global advertising, sales promotion, or public relations occurs when a marketing team standardizes key elements of these activities across national boundaries. Since campaigns are usually used to support global brand strategies, companies such as Coca-Cola, PepsiCo, Procter & Gamble, BMW, Nike, Toyota, and Nestlé are leaders in this arena. Today, all the large advertising agencies have offices worldwide to support clients who seek global coordination. Due to cultural differences, marketers need to assess the benefits of standardized versus localized promotion.

Because standardization provides numerous economies, the cost of developing creative promotions can be shared across many markets. For example, when Gillette introduced the Sensor razor, a worldwide campaign used the same actors and dubbed in various languages.[7] Grant Hill's fantastic slam dunks cost millions to produce, but they have the same appeal when used in Italy or Russia as in the United States to promote Sprite.

Global standardization works best when customers, not countries, are the basis for identifying segments and when the product is compatible across cultures. It is also important for the firm to have similar competitors and an equivalent competitive position in most of the markets. Finally, promotion management should be centralized so that global marketing can occur.[8] A company such as Kodak fits these criteria fairly well, although the imaging business does have regional differences. In Japan, Fuji is exceptionally strong, as is Agfa in Europe. Consequently, Kodak uses a standardized approach with adjustments for these local competitive conditions.

There are some serious drawbacks to global standardization. Cultural attitudes toward promotion differ. Although changing, Singaporeans tend to regard it negatively, whereas Russian consumers are even more positive about it than Americans.[9] In addition, local audiences have certain cultural traditions. For example, when the National Football League created an international division to market outside the United States, it had to customize its programs to appeal to different cultures. To ensure marketing success, the NFL educated foreign consumers about U.S.-style football using a region-by-region strategy. The NFL Europe Web site has results from both the American and European leagues both in English and the home country's language (e.g., the Amsterdam Admirals results given in Dutch). The NFL had also instituted one game per season called the World Bowl that pits two NFL teams in a country into which the NFL is attempting to expand. In 2000, the game was played in Tokyo, Japan, and a special NFL Japan Web site was set up to carry results in Japanese.[10]

Sales promotion and publicity often have a very local flavor. Each country has a unique promotion style, and most have legal as well as other restrictions. For example, Procter & Gamble (P&G) found it was legal to mail free samples to consumers in Poland, a practice prohibited in many countries. What surprised them was that thieves stole the samples from mailboxes before they reached intended recipients. In Germany, however, the government regulates the size of samples sent through the mail; another law prohibits advertising as a personal letter.[11] Ben & Jerry's Ice Cream ran a "Yo! I'm Your CEO" promotion in which people wrote essays about why they should be head of the company. The result was 20,000 entries from around the world. Although the new CEO was not chosen from among the entrants, considerable attention was drawn to the company's products.[12] And in England, Hoover Ltd. gave away free round-trip airplane tickets to New York or Orlando with the purchase of £250 in merchandise. The company underestimated demand and spent several million pounds more than it had budgeted. In the winter of 2000–2001, Hershey and Southwest Air announced a similar deal; consumers could get a $150 voucher for a ticket on Southwest Air by redeeming 275 wrappers of any Hershey's candy bar. Redemptions automatically enter consumers in a drawing for a free trip for two to the Super Bowl.[13]

ETHICAL ISSUES IN ADVERTISING, SALES PROMOTION, AND PUBLIC RELATIONS

The most serious ethical issue surrounding advertising, sales promotion, and public relations is deception. These communication methods are designed to be persuasive, but too much of the wrong type of persuasion can be misleading.

Deception occurs when a false belief is created or implied and interferes with the ability of consumers to make rational choices.[14] Purely descriptive information is seldom deceptive. But what about embellishment? Or what about the things left out? At what point does deception occur? Marketers must use a great amount of judgment to avoid being deceptive. An ad may show Michael Jordan soaring hundreds of feet to make a slam dunk in his Nikes, but no one is likely to believe that shoes make this possible. The exaggerated message is that Nike shoes will significantly improve the performance of the common athlete. But Nike lets you know that playing basketball well is also based on ability, training, and skill building. A more recent Nike campaign featured Marion Jones only in profile speaking into a microphone. She spoke about a variety of contemporary issues, such as the sports superstar's role as a model for children, as well as promoting Nike products.[15] And in the ads, Marion Jones and other athletes are depicted as hardworking and serious. How exciting would it be to see Nike or Reebok simply describe the materials and design for their shoes? The outlandish puffery sometimes used by Nike would not be considered deceptive by most.

Marketers must walk a fine line between producing creative, stimulating messages and being deceptive. Even company slogans can come into question when they evoke strong emotions or make comparative comments. Pantene used to urge: "Don't hate me because I'm beautiful." Hanes said: "Gentlemen prefer Hanes." Can shampoo really create jealousy, and do men really care about what brand of stockings women wear? Most consumers probably would not think these slogans seriously interfere with their ability to make informed choices. Are these catchy phrases fun and provocative or misleading?

When false information or exaggerated claims are used, deception is clear—and illegal. Microsoft found that out. Microsoft settled the Federal Trade Commission complaint without admitting or denying any of the charges. The FTC claims that Microsoft used deceptive advertising for its webtv service. It claimed that there was "virtually no place on earth you can't travel to." In reality, webtv users could not download software or display some Web pages, and they were accruing huge long-distance telephone bills.[16]

Likewise, Eggland's Best Eggs used deceptive communication: "Imagine eating delicious, real whole eggs and not raising your serum cholesterol. People did. In clinical tests of Eggland's Best Eggs they ate a dozen a week while keeping within the limits of the Surgeon General's low-fat diet. And . . . their serum cholesterol didn't go up." But the company had no evidence to substantiate its cholesterol claims, and the FTC charged that its clinical studies were false.[17] And Reynolds was recently criticized for promoting a cigarette brand, Eclipse, as being "the next best choice" to quitting claiming that the cigarette had a lower carcinogen content, when in reality Eclipse contains a higher level of three dangerous carcinogens than other cigarettes.[18] To prevent this type of problem, some countries strictly prohibit puffery, and some even ban comparative claims.

France is one of many countries that frown on deceptive advertising. A court in Paris banned the Philip Morris campaign claiming that secondhand tobacco smoke poses a smaller health risk than eating cookies or drinking milk or fluoridated water. This claim contradicts several U.S. surgeon generals, the American Medical Association, the World Health Organization, and the American Cancer Society, all of which have determined that secondhand smoke causes more than 50,000 nonsmoker deaths in the United States each year. No one has demonstrated anything like a similar risk for eating cookies or drinking milk or water. It can be concluded that Philip Morris acted unethically because it provided untrue information that some parents used to rationalize smoking around their own and other people's children.[19]

ADVERTISING

Advertising is paid, nonpersonal communication from an identified sponsor using mass media to persuade or influence an audience. The word is derived from the Latin *advertere,* "to turn toward."[20] Notice that advertising is paid for by an identified sponsor, so the audience knows the source of the message. In addition, it is a form of nonpersonal communication through mass media, such as newspapers, magazines, radio, and television. This allows advertising to be directed at relatively large audiences. But there is no opportunity for the receiver to ask questions or for the advertiser to obtain immediate feedback. Consequently, planning is extremely important in order to create a successful ad the first time.

THE MULTIPLE PURPOSES AND ROLES OF ADVERTISING

Although advertising itself is powerful, it also plays an important support role for other forms of communication. In a famous McGraw-Hill Publishing Company ad, a grumpy purchasing agent stares directly at the viewer, saying: "I don't know who you are. I don't know your company. I don't know your company's product. I don't know what your company stands for. I don't know your company's customers. I don't know your company's record. I don't know your company's reputation. Now—what was it you wanted to sell me?" The ad goes on to explain that the sales effort starts before a salesperson calls—with business publication advertising. Whether alone or in support of other promotion methods, advertising informs, persuades, reminds, or reinforces.

Informative Advertising   **Informative advertising** is designed to provide messages that consumers can store for later use. For example, an art museum may place an informative advertisement to make the community aware that a particular exhibit is on display. Often, the more information an ad provides, the better the response will be. A 6,450-word ad for Merrill Lynch brought 10,000 inquiries from interested investors. An 800-word ad for Mercedes-Benz was headlined: "You give up things when you buy the Mercedes Benz 230S. Things like rattles, rust and shabby workmanship." Sales rose from 10,000 to 40,000 cars. Many consumers want

CONNECTED: SURFING THE NET

www.mercedes.com

If you want to see some informative Mercedes-Benz communications, get connected. Visit the company's Web site, where you can find out about the latest news and events, technology and the environment, sports and leisure, the company history and future, and much more.

WHAT IF AN SUV WERE RAISED
BY A FAMILY OF SPORTS CARS?

INTRODUCING THE 200-HP MAZDA TRIBUTE LX-V6

If the company that created the legendary RX-7 and
Miata decided to build an SUV, what would you expect?
Rapid acceleration? Taut, agile handling? Pure push-
you-back-in-your-seat exhilaration?

Well, here it is. The vehicle only Mazda could have
created. The Mazda Tribute. The SUV with the soul of a
sports car. At prices that start at just $17,750 for the
Mazda Tribute DX. LX-V6 model shown $21,565.*

• 200-horsepower 3.0-liter DOHC 24-valve V6 engine.
• Electronically controlled 4-speed automatic.
• 16" alloy wheels with P235/70R16 all-season tires.
• Sport-tuned MacPherson strut front suspension
  and multilink rear suspension.
• Available Anti-lock Brake System (ABS) with Electronic
  Brakeforce Distribution (EBD).
• Available on-demand 4-wheel drive.

This ad for the 200-HP Madza Tribute is designed to be a persuasive ad.

to be provided with as much information as possible about items that interest them. A recent study found that the Internet has become the best format for informative advertising; the study showed that over half of the respondents found that Internet ads provided better information concerning products.[21]

PERSUASIVE ADVERTISING

Messages designed to change consumers' attitudes and opinions about products, often listing product attributes, pricing, and other factors that may influence consumer decisions.

Persuasive Advertising   **Persuasive advertising** is designed to change consumers' attitudes and opinions about products as well as create attitudes where none exist. These ads often list the product's attributes, pricing, and other factors that influence the buying decision. They attempt to make the product choice important so consumers will think about the subject. In this way, the message recipient is asked to form an attitude first and then buy. For example, a Land Rover ad emphasizes the ability of its Discovery and Range Rover to handle well under all conditions. The ad notes: "Weather is also a concern—no matter where you live. Whether it's snow, rain, wind, or ice, Land Rover's state-of-the-art traction technologies will help your Discovery or Range Rover stay sure-footed in all kinds of weather. Regardless of the terrain you drive or the weather you face, your Land Rover serves as a layer of comfort and stability between you and the harsh environment you're navigating."[22]

REMINDER ADVERTISING

Messages that keep the product at the forefront of the consumer's mind.

Reminder Advertising   **Reminder advertising** keeps the product at the forefront of the consumer's mind. In some cases these ads simply draw a connection between the brand and some aspect of life. In other cases they reinforce past consumer behavior to encourage the next purchase. CompuServe's reminder campaign for its online service not only aired television spots in its top 20 markets but also increased direct mail by more than 600 percent and ad inserts by 150 percent. All these told consumers that CompuServe is the solution when "life calls for deeper answers."[23] Reminder ads that stimulate the next purchase include the famous Burger King ad: "Aren't you hungry?" McDonald's tried to move consumers into its restaurants with the slogan: "You deserve a break today." The next campaign phase asked: "Have you had your break today?" "Did somebody say McDonald's?" is the most recent reminder ad used by McDonald's.[24] The reminder was intended to spur more action from the consumer.[25] Reminder ads can serve other purposes as well; Sony recently created a low-key reminder ad

A reminder ad for cheese.

campaign that would build consumer awareness of its new PlayStation II product, without creating consumer frustration over the fact that it was not widely available in stores for the Christmas shopping season. The ads included a series of billboards, that began with a giant question mark, and later morphed into the PS2 logo.[26]

Reinforcement Advertising   To encourage repeat buying behavior, **reinforcement advertising** calls attention to specific characteristics of products experienced by the user. The key here is to communicate with the consumer about product features that created the greatest amount of satisfaction. These ads also reassure customers that they made the right choice. For example, ads for Dial ask, "Aren't you glad you used Dial . . . don't you wish everyone did?"

PROS AND CONS OF ADVERTISING

Advertising has many advantages. By controlling what is said, how it is said, and where it is said, marketers can develop standardized campaigns that run for extended periods. Over time, these help build a strong brand equity position. Moreover, advertising is a very cost-effective way to reach large audiences. For example, one 30-second network TV spot in prime time reaches on average 12 million households. At current rates, that's less than 1 cent per household of coverage. No other promotional method comes close to accomplishing that kind of exposure at such low rates.

The availability of such advertising media as television, radio, newspapers, magazines, and billboards makes it easy to reach most audiences. And because advertising is used so much, it's easy for marketers to find excellent agencies that can help research markets, develop campaigns, and manage the entire process. The advantages can be summarized as follows:

- Controls the content, presentation, and placement of messages.
- Builds brand position and equity over time.
- Is cost-effective for large audiences.
- Serves many communication needs—awareness, information, reminder.
- Is easy to reach most audiences.
- Is easy to find professionals to create effective advertising.

REINFORCEMENT ADVERTISING
Messages that call attention to specific characteristics of products experienced by the user.

This informative and reinforcement ad reminds consumers about the good taste and nutrition of Campbell Soup.

Advertising does have a downside. It's difficult to direct an ad at only the target audience—many others will be exposed to it. Because many consumers distrust ads and try to avoid them, advertising campaigns may need to run for a long time to repeat the message. It is not unusual for some companies or industries to spend hundreds of millions of dollars on advertising. For consumer cleaning products and children's games and toys, more than 16 percent of sales is spent on advertising. The motion picture industry spends more than 12 percent.[27] In general, however, the retail industry spends only 2.3 percent of sales on advertising, and consumer products in general average 7.4 percent.[28] The disadvantages of advertising can be summarized as follows:

- Reaches many nonusers.
- Has high level of audience avoidance.
- Contains brief one-way messages.
- Can be costly in total.

CATEGORIES OF ADVERTISING

Advertising falls into various categories depending on its objectives, target audience, and type of message. Most marketers use one or more of the eight types described in Figure 15.2.

National or brand advertising, as the name implies, focuses on brand identity and positioning throughout the country. The aim is to develop a distinctive brand image in the mind of the consumer. Although this is often called national advertising, it is also the objective for global advertising.

Retail (local) advertising focuses attention on nearby outlets where products and services can be purchased. The emphasis is on attributes that will stimulate people to shop there, such as price, location, convenience, or customer service.

Directory advertising is a listing of businesses, their addresses, phone numbers, and sometimes brief descriptions in a publication such as the Yellow Pages. A short, differentiating message can be critical since so many competitors also advertise there. Businesses usually consider directories extremely important because most consumers use them only when they are ready to buy a product. The United States Postal Service recently began selling stamps and postal products online, in the hopes of making it easier for consumers to buy their products.

NATIONAL OR BRAND ADVERTISING

Advertising that focuses on brand identity and positioning throughout the country.

RETAIL (LOCAL) ADVERTISING

Advertising that focuses attention on nearby outlets where products and services can be purchased.

DIRECTORY ADVERTISING

A listing of businesses, their addresses, phone numbers, and sometimes brief descriptions in a publication.

Category	Description
National and Global (Brand) Advertising	Focuses on brand identity nationwide (globally). Aims to develop a distinctive brand image.
Retail (Local) Advertising	Focuses on local retail areas. Emphasizes positive attributes of retail outlets.
Directory Advertising	Company listings in a directory. Important to most businesses and retailers. Uses a short differentiating message.
Business-to-Business Advertising	Directed at professionals. Often communicates technical content. Common media include business publications and professional journals.
Institutional Advertising	Communicates corporate identity and philosophy. Describes social and ecological responsibilities of a company.
Direct-Response Advertising	Appeals directly to individual consumers. Usual delivery methods are telephone and mail.
Public Service Advertising	Supports public issues. Usually created for free and media donate space and time.
Political Advertising	Aimed at obtaining votes for issues or political candidates.

FIGURE 15.2 *Categories of Advertising*

Business-to-business advertising sends messages to a variety of organizations, ranging from health care providers to accountants, lawyers, and manufacturers. Often, technical content is communicated. In the health care field, for example, publications such as the *Journal of the American Medical Association* carry extensive advertising of pharmaceutical products of all types.

Institutional advertising is designed to communicate corporate identity and philosophy rather than messages about individual products. It describes the company's social and ecological responsibilities. For example, Toyota promotes its involvement in U.S. communities.

Direct-response advertising targets individual consumers to get immediate sales. Sales are stimulated through appeals by telephone, mail, and most recently, the Internet, and the product then is delivered to the customer's home or business. Companies such as Federal Express and UPS have helped facilitate the dramatic increase in sales through mail-order catalogs.

Public service advertising support such societal issues as the prevention of child abuse or smoking cessation. These announcements are usually created free by advertising agencies, and the space or airtime is donated by the media. Sometimes they are partially supported by charitable organizations or the government.

Political advertising is aimed at influencing voters in favor of individuals or particular ballot issues. It has come under harsh criticism for mudslinging, negative and sometimes false accusations against political candidates, and the lack of focus on substantive issues.

ADVERTISING AGENCIES

Advertising agencies are independent businesses that develop, prepare, and place advertising in the appropriate media. Most companies outsource some or all of these services. In fact, more than 90 percent of all advertising is placed through outside agencies. Even very large corporations such as General Motors outsource. The cost-effectiveness of outside agencies makes this a good choice for most companies. There are more than 10,000 ad agencies in the United States alone and probably an equal number around the world. As in any industry, there are several large agencies and many smaller ones. Big companies, such as Young & Rubicam or Saatchi and Saatchi, have offices in nearly every major country to provide the services required for global marketers.

In addition to full-service agencies, many specialize in certain advertising functions or in selected industries. For example, Creative Boutiques focuses primarily on developing ideas for advertising. In many cases, industries have certain unique needs. The health care industry is a good example. Durot, Donahoe, and Purohit of Rosemont, Illinois, is an expert in that kind of advertising, which requires knowledge of extensive regulation of health care ads by the Federal

INSTITUTIONAL ADVERTISING
Messages designed to communicate corporate identity and philosophy as opposed to product information.

DIRECT-RESPONSE ADVERTISING
Targets individual consumers to get immediate sales.

PUBLIC SERVICE ADVERTISING
Free advertising that supports societal issues.

POLITICAL ADVERTISING
Advertising to influence voters.

ADVERTISING AGENCY
A business that develops, prepares, and places advertising for sellers seeking to find customers for their products.

FIGURE 15.3 *Steps in the
Advertising Plan*

Drug Administration. Some agencies focus on certain target groups. Burmudez and Associates have expertise in the Hispanic market, and others specialize in various minorities.

THE ADVERTISING PLAN

The six major steps in developing a strong advertising plan are outlined in Figure 15.3. The process begins by setting objectives and next determining the budget. Then the theme and message are developed. The theme is the creative concept and the art and copy are used to convey the message. Next, media are selected and a schedule is set. This is followed by creation of the ads. Finally, their effectiveness is assessed.

SETTING OBJECTIVES

Each objective should be developed in such a way that its accomplishment can be measured. Remember that advertising should support the communications plan, which in turn supports the strategic marketing plan. As Figure 15.4 suggests, the goals of informing, persuading, reminding, and reinforcing should be accompanied by specific objectives, such as increase sales, establish brand position, increase awareness, support the sales force or distributors, maintain awareness, or introduce a new brand.[29]

DEVELOPING THE ADVERTISING BUDGET

As we mentioned before, advertising can be expensive in total although quite cost-effective on a per person basis. In setting the budget, the first question to answer is how much it will cost to accomplish the objective. Most advertising budgets are determined using one of the following methods: percentage of sales method, competitive budgeting method, payout plan method, or task method.

PERCENTAGE OF SALES METHOD
Allocating a percentage of estimated sales to advertising.

The **percentage of sales method** for developing the advertising budget involves simply estimating the desired sales level and then allocating a certain percentage of sales to advertising. Often this percentage is equal to the industry average. In some cases, the percentage of sales method is performed by taking a percentage of the previous year's sales and allocating it to advertising. The problem with this method is that sales are used to create the advertising budget when, in fact, advertising should be used to create sales. However, the method is used widely because it is very easy to administer.

COMPETITIVE BUDGETING METHOD
Setting the advertising expenditures relative to what competitors spend.

Competitive budgeting method involves determining what competitors are spending and setting the advertising budget accordingly. Large companies such as AT&T and MCIWorldCom use this method. In order to maintain a strong presence in the eye of the consumer, many companies try to keep up with the advertising budgets of their competitors. AT&T has an ad budget of $711.4 million, which is a large amount for many smaller competitors to attempt to match.[30]

PAYOUT METHOD
Setting the ad budget to gain initial acceptance and trial.

The **payout method** is generally used for new products that require high advertising expenditures. In this case, the marketer estimates future sales and establishes the advertising budget required to gain initial acceptance and trial of the product. Generally, these expenditures are very high relative to sales and in some cases even exceed sales. The large expenditures

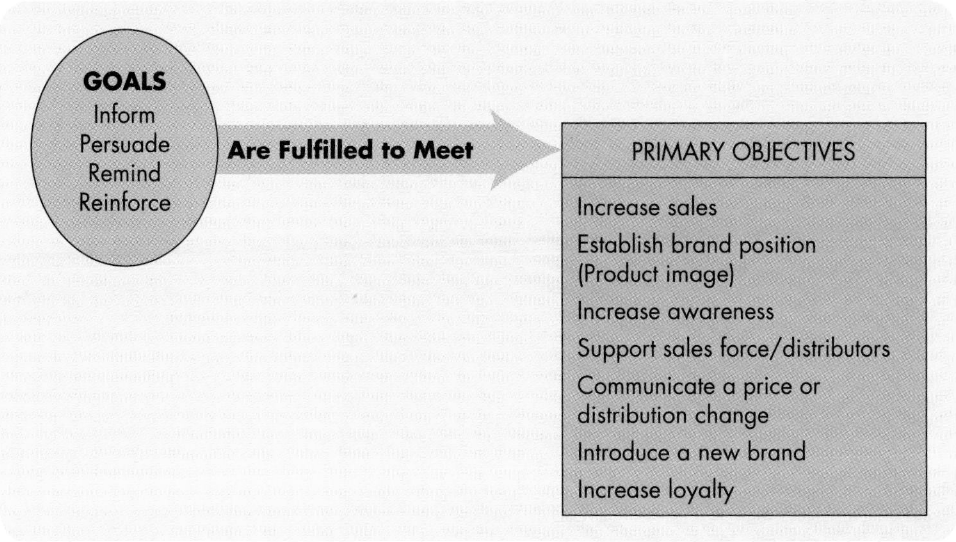

FIGURE 15.4 *Advertising Objectives*

are deemed reasonable because of the payback that occurs in later years. This is similar to investing money in product development.

The **task method** sets specific sales targets or other objectives and then determines what advertising activities and amounts are required to accomplish those objectives. This approach can be extremely complex. Advertisers who use the task method rely on very accurate information experience, and extensive models developed for the purpose. It tends to be used by large organizations in highly competitive environments. It's superior to the other methods because so much attention to detail is paid in determining how advertising contributes toward accomplishment of objectives.

TASK METHOD
Setting the advertising budget based on activities required to accomplish objectives.

DEVELOPING THE THEME AND MESSAGE

Once objectives are in place and the budget has been established, it is time to develop the theme and message—the **creative strategy** that will govern and coordinate the development of individual ads and assure that their visual images and words convey precisely and consistently what the advertiser wishes to communicate. Be careful not to confuse this overall strategy with the creative work in putting a specific ad together. The message is a fairly straightforward outgrowth of the marketer's understanding of consumer behavior, information processing, and the advertising objectives. For example, Whirlpool research found that Asian females are involved in 80 percent of household appliance purchases and that saving time is very important in their busy lifestyle. The company chose saving time as the theme. The creative strategy incorporated extremely busy Asian females and depicted their difficulty in finding time for family activities.[31] The implication is that buying a Whirlpool enables a busy woman to be with her family more often. Dunkin' Donuts recently crafted a similar ad campaign in Thailand. Noting the Thai family structure and the fact that most young Thais live with their parents, the ad campaign focused on social and familial aspects of eating out. It ran a Mother's Day promotion that included inviting patrons to sign a huge banner that was described as the "Longest Love Message to Moms," and entered patrons in a free trip sweepstakes.[32]

CREATIVE STRATEGY
The strategy that governs and coordinates the development of individual ads and assures that their visual images and words convey precisely and consistently what the advertiser wants to communicate.

An **advertising campaign** is a series of different ads with the same creative strategy. Because one ad tends to have very little effect, campaigns are required to sustain the message and accomplish the objectives. There is usually an element of continuity, such as similar characters, music, or settings. The pink Energizer bunny keeps going and going through any number of ads. Other examples are Taco Bell's talking chihuahua, the Mentos "Freshmaker" campaign, and Bounty's campaign as the "quicker picker upper."

ADVERTISING CAMPAIGN
A series of advertisements with a main theme running through them.

To be effective, the theme and message must reach the consumer and must be creative, understandable, and memorable.

Reaching the Consumer   An ad must first reach its target audience. **Exposure** is the process of putting the ad in contact with the market. Then it's up to the ad to communicate the message. A good advertisement addresses nearly every aspect of consumer behavior in a package that grabs interest and keeps it until the message is absorbed. Exposure does not

EXPOSURE
The process of putting the ad in contact with the customer.

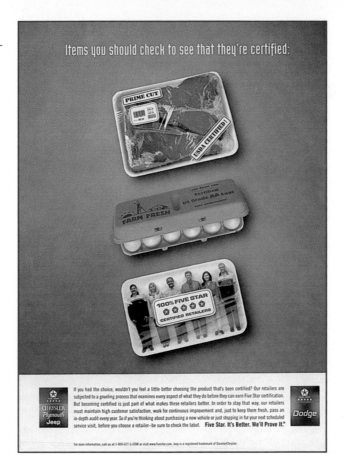

Stopping power is the key to this ad for Dodge.

ensure attention. As we learned in chapter 7, the perceptual process filters out a great deal. The ad must have what marketers call **stopping power**—the ability to gain and hold attention. Ads with stopping power are so attention getting that they interrupt whatever the person is doing. The best ads gain and hold attention because the consumer finds them interesting and relevant. They are often consistent with the buyer's lifestyle. Sometimes catchy music, humor, or an association with a celebrity works. Some phrases may gain immediate attention from certain people: *weight loss, quick cash, retire early, pay off your debts, work at home, free, new, amazing, now,* and *easy.*[33] These catch phrases have been so overused by advertisers that many people immediately tune out messages containing them.

Creativity   Originality and uniqueness are very important in advertisements. On the one hand, ads that are too unusual may not work because people have difficulty relating to them. On the other hand, creative, humorous, upbeat ads that provide some novelty tend to gain more attention than the same old thing. Recently, television ads for Energizer batteries spoofed the blockbuster movie *Twister*. A van of scientists driving around the country hoping to glimpse the famous bunny piques interest, and humor is injected when a supposed sighting turns out to be a woodchuck. Energizer's pink icon has made its alkaline battery the second best-selling battery, which shows that originality in advertising can make a difference. Coca-Cola also captured viewers with its computer-animated polar bears, considered a "heartwarmer, creative, and upbeat."[34] "Whassup?" was the catch phrase started by a series of Budweiser commercials. Bud's Web site has files you can click to hear "whassup" in several different languages.[35]

Once attention is gained, consumers are likely to become aware of the message and internalize it. **Pulling power** holds the interest of the consumer to the end of the message. Most advertisers insist that the message must relate to some aspect of the individual's life. Celebrities, for example, have reference group appeal. A Pepsi ad in the 1980s featured pop star Michael Jackson and had enormous pulling power. It was rated one of the 50 best commercials of all time by *Advertising Age.*[36]

Understandability   Although most ads don't attempt to say everything about a product, it's important that the information selected for communication be clearly understood. Otherwise, it will not be remembered. Procter & Gamble communicated the benefits of its

Slogan	Product or Brand
Where's the Beef?	Wendy's Restaurants
Reach Out and Touch Someone	AT&T
Don't Leave Home Without It	American Express
Just Do It	Nike
Generation Next	Pepsi
Enjoy the Ride	Nissan
Breakfast of Champions	Wheaties
We Bring Good Things to Life	General Electric
Did Somebody Say McDonald's?	McDonald's
I Love What You Do For Me	Toyota
Good to the Last Drop	Maxwell House
Obey Your Thirst	Sprite
Sometimes You Feel Like a Nut	Almond Joy
Fly the Friendly Skies	United Airlines

FIGURE 15.5 *Successful Advertising Slogans*

detergent Cheer through a series of ads featuring a "silent deadpan presenter" who smudges garments with terrible stains. Viewers have a clear understanding of what the product can do when the items are pulled stain free from a mixture of water, ice, and Cheer.[37] The campaign for Cascade Complete featured "skipping a step." After showing a man skip from the first date to the wedding, or a high school graduate skipping to retirement, the commercial demonstrated how consumers could "skip" rinsing dishes, put them straight into the dishwasher, and pull out sparkling clean dishes after the washing cycle.[38]

Memorability It's important that ads be memorable so that they are retained for some time. A high initial effect is useless if forgotten quickly. Consumers must remember ads until they actually purchase the product. One way to achieve this is through repetition. An ad usually must be seen at least three times before it moves into long-term memory. Jingles, slogans, and tag lines also help ensure recall. How many of the popular slogans listed in Figure 15.5 do you recognize?

CONNECTING THROUGH TECHNOLOGY

BANNER ADS OF THE NEW MILLENNIUM

 Every day 170,000 more pages are added to the World Wide Web, and every day more than 2 million visitors use search engines such as Yahoo! and Excite to locate sites ranging from "anagram insanity" to "worm world." And if the search engine companies had their way, these visitors would not just type in a keyword and vamoose. Instead, they would stay awhile to catch some music and news, play games, and glean information on topics of interest. Most important for continued profitability of these companies, these visitors would stay long enough to peruse ads from some of its 550 advertisers.

The transformation of search engines from a techie tool to a digital destination says a lot about the continuing evolution of advertising on the Web. Organizations such as Yahoo!, Lycos, and Excite sell advertising to turn a profit, and clients pay between $10 and $1,000 for every 1,000 "impressions"—Webspeak for the number of times a page is loaded by a consumer. But showing results to advertisers has been much more difficult than the companies had imagined.

Search engines were designed to get site visitors in and out as quickly as possible. For advertisers, this means that Web visitors do not linger over an ad, not the way viewers do when a commercial is right in the middle of a *Friends* episode. Companies are finding that traditional Web banners are not effective. Consumers do not pay attention to them, which means the banners do not receive the clicks companies would like. For sites such as Yahoo!, this has meant less revenue.

To improve the number of clicks a banner receives, companies such as MSN have created new types of Web banners. These banners have been developed to catch the consumer's

Continued

attention, allowing the access of more information in a convenient format. MSN says the advertisers will be given a "rich media experience, without all the costs and the heaviness of a rich-media ad."

There are currently six new types of banners that MSN has developed and started to use with clients. Each banner has been created with a unique objective. The Scrolling Graphics banner allows a consumer to scroll within the banner to see a larger product display. Another banner gives marketers the opportunity to let product descriptions and text scroll along the side of the banner. A few advertisers that have tested the new banners include American Isuzu Motors, Barnes & Noble, and Unilever's Dove brand. The interactive media manager at Unilever's Interactive Brand Center said that during the banner testing period, "click-through rates were twice what [they] normally get."

As online advertising continues to become more appealing to consumers, companies such as Yahoo! and Excite hope to see revenues once again increase. Currently, companies are spending approximately 10 percent of their advertising budgets online. But we may see this percentage increase as companies continue to find better ways of communicating effectively to consumers online.

Sources: Kim Cleland, "Searching for a Broader Role on the Web," *Advertising Age,* June 24, 1996, p. 34; Janice Maloney, "Yahoo! Still Searching for Profits on the Internet," *Fortune,* December 9, 1996, pp. 174–182; Laurie Flynn, "Market Place: A Corner Turns for Yahoo and Other Internet Search Concerns," *New York Times,* February 11, 1997, p. D8; "Online Ads Do Work, E-Marketing Survey Says," *Campaign,* October 13, 2000, retrieved December 22, 2000 from the World Wide Web: www.proquest.umi.com; Tobi Elkin, "Microsoft's MSN Fattens Banners with Rich Media," *Advertising Age,* October 30, 2000, p. 52; and Ellen Neuborne, "Beyond the Banner Ad," *Business Week,* December 11, 2000, p. 16.

SELECTING AND SCHEDULING MEDIA

MEDIA

The channels through which messages are transmitted.

Media Options   **Media** are the channels through which messages are transmitted from the sender to the receiver. Each medium has unique advantages and disadvantages, as described in Figure 15.6.

Newspapers A highly credible and flexible medium, newspapers offer wide exposure to upscale adults. Many newspapers have prestige because of their positive impact on communities. They reach 90 percent of homes in a typical location, allowing for widespread coverage. Newspapers can also facilitate coordination between local and national advertising. Some effectiveness is being lost, however, as television becomes an increasingly important news source. Another competitor is information available on the World Wide Web. Few newspaper ads are fully read, and young adults rarely read newspapers. Circulation fell 8 percent between 1990 and 1999 and the number of dailies dropped from 1,570 to 1,532 between 1992 and 1995.[39]

Television Television is also a credible source and is extremely cost efficient per person. It provides the creative flexibility to use both video and audio, allowing an unlimited range of spokespersons and themes. The disadvantages are high production costs and low recall of messages. Television is filled with advertising, which makes it difficult to gain the viewer's attention, and many consumers change the channel when commercials air. Consequently, television ads need to be rerun often to be effective. Due to increased Internet usage, television viewing may decline. A Nielsen survey reveals that television is watched less often in homes with a subscription to America Online. Although no direct link has been established, studies will continue to look for correlations.[40] As dozens of dot coms vied for business, however, the Internet came to support television for awhile, flooding the TV with advertisements for their Internet services. When these businesses crashed in the stock market, the advertising money disappeared. Now television is threatened with losing viewers to the Internet, and losing the money that came from dot coms advertising on television. And, since 1985, the number of hours spent watching TV has declined by more than one-fifth do, in part, to the Internet.[41]

Radio Very low production costs make radio an attractive medium. Furthermore, marketers can be extremely selective in targeting U.S. consumers because each market area averages 30 stations, each aimed at a specific audience. The problem has been limited research on local radio markets, but new computer systems are changing that. For example, a software program called Advance is assisting with postbuy analysis so that ad agencies can estimate the ratings for stations and specific airtimes.[42] Lacking visual content, radio spots require more

	Advantages	**Disadvantages**
Newspapers	Wide exposure for upscale adults. Flexible; timely; buyers can save for later reference. High credibility.	Few ads are fully read. Young adults don't read them. Costs are rising. Alternate media are becoming more important news sources.
Television	Creative and flexible. Cost efficient. Credible.	Message is quickly forgotten. High production cost. Difficult to get attention.
Radio	Selective targeting possible. Mobile—goes with listeners. Low production costs.	No visual content. High frequency is required to reach many people. Audience research has traditionally been difficult.
Magazines	Target narrowly defined segments. Prestigious sources. Long life—can be passed along.	Audiences declining. Long lead times to develop ads. Need to use many different magazines to reach a lot of buyers.
Outdoor Ads	Low cost per exposure. Good to supplement other media. With color, lighting, and mechanization gets attention.	Can't communicate much. Difficult to measure results.
Internet	Considerable potential. Medium for relationship marketing. Customer driven and dialogue oriented. Increasing number of users.	Little research to indicate proven effectiveness. Relies on consumers accessing the necessary technologies. Revenues still small. Difficult to target a specific audience. Difficult to measure results.

FIGURE 15.6 *Advantages and Disadvantages of Various Media*

Source: J. Thomas Russell and W. Ronald Lane, *Kleppner's Advertising Procedure*, 13th ed. © 1996. Adapted by permission of Prentice Hall, Inc., Upper Saddle River, NJ.

repetition than television ads. As methods for audience rating improve, however, it should be possible to use fewer spots and evaluate more accurately their effect on selected segments.

Magazines Magazines also target well-defined consumer segments, and professional journals reach very specific groups. Although 92 percent of adults read at least one magazine per month, overall magazine readership is declining. Most adults (about 79 percent) consider magazine ads to be positive and helpful for making purchase decisions. In fact, there is evidence that consumers pay more attention to this advertising medium than to television.[43] In the past few years, many "small" magazines have been introduced to appeal to unique tastes, which makes more finely tuned targeting possible. The disadvantages of magazines are long lead times and high production costs for ads. In efforts to target more finely, new techniques for producing special ads are being designed that will bring costs down. Ultimately, the goal is to get as close to unique customers as possible. To reach a large number of buyers, however, ads in many different magazines may be required.

Outdoor Advertising Outdoor advertisements, primarily billboards, are very inexpensive per exposure, so they provide an attractive supplement to other media. With color, lighting, and mechanization, some billboards have fantastic stopping power. Even though advertising in general has been declining, outdoor advertisements have increased steadily. This is despite the loss of tobacco ad revenue.[44] Outdoor advertisements can be so eye-catching that they distract motorists. Consider the 32-foot painting of Dennis Rodman displayed on a warehouse along the Kennedy Expressway in Chicago. It attracted so much attention in rush hour that it was removed in response to traffic officials.[45] Despite their flashiness, outdoor ads can't

The 32-foot outdoor painting of Dennis Rodman was so eye catching it caused problems with traffic.

communicate a great amount of information because people move past them so quickly. It's usually more difficult to measure the results of outdoor advertisements than other media.

The Internet The Internet provides a medium that is both customer driven and dialogue oriented. This gives companies another way to develop customer relationships. Consider that Yahoo! reaches 60 percent of Internet users and it can tailor the type of advertisements to reflect each user's preferences. It can track who is logged on and where they are coming from. Yahoo! has sold ad space to companies to customize the pages seen by their employees because 70 percent of *Fortune* 500 workers with Internet access use Yahoo! from work. This gives the Internet incredible potential.[46] A major disadvantage of Internet marketing is low click-through rates, as people are ignoring the banner ads for the most part. This has caused a slow-down in the growth rate of online advertising.[47] Viral marketing is showing a lot of promise. In this approach, advertisements are attached to the bottom of e-mail messages sent from free mail services. Procter & Gamble offered free styling spray to people who referred 10 friends to the Physique Web site. This led to over 2 million referrals and the most successful launch of a shampoo in the United States.[48]

The Internet is growing in popularity, but it relies on consumers owning or accessing the necessary equipment. As technology becomes less expensive and more user friendly, the effectiveness of this medium will improve greatly. It is difficult to target a specific audience today, but look for advances that will make it possible to attract specific segments and even specific (one-to-one) customers in the future.

career tip Go to salary.com and you can calculate your salary based on geographic location and job title. The site has information on the types of compensation packages as well as other career resources.

Media Popularity Which media do the major advertisers select? Figure 15.7 illustrates advertising expenditures for the top 100 companies. The four types of television media account for about two-thirds, followed at a great distance by magazines, newspapers, radio, and outdoor advertising.

The Media Schedule Media scheduling can be looked at as a plan within the advertising plan. This very exacting work involves a number of considerations: target audience analysis; reach, frequency, and continuity balance; media timing; and budgeting.

Target Audience As you know, the marketing plan is always directed at specific market segments. Media planning begins by addressing those segments. Marketers have developed very detailed methods for defining target markets. For example, Claritas Corporation has developed PRIZM, which uses such variables as socioeconomic status, ethnicity, family life cycle, educa-

Media	Annual Expenditure	Percent of Total
Network TV	$12.8 billion	31.4
Spot TV	$ 6.0 billion	14.7
Cable TV	$ 4.7 billion	11.5
Syndicated TV	$ 2.1 billion	5.2
Magazines	$ 6.9 billion	17.0
Sunday magazines	$ 0.3 billion	0.7
Newspapers	$ 5.0 billion	12.3
National newspapers	$ 0.9 billion	2.3
Outdoor advertising	$ 0.5 billion	1.2
Network radio	$ 0.2 billion	0.5
National spot radio	$ 0.8 billion	2.0
Yellow Pages	$ 0.1 billion	0.2
Internet	$ 0.4 billion	1.0
Total	$40.7 billion	100.0

FIGURE 15.7 *Advertising Expenditures by Media for the Top 100 Spenders*

Source: Adapted with permission from the September 30, 1996 issue of *Advertising Age.* © 1996. Crain Communications, Inc. (adage.com/dataplace/archives/dp478.html; these figures are for 1999).

tion, employment, type of housing, and location of housing to describe 40 audiences. In turn, these data are correlated with media usage patterns. The information helps determine which media are likely to influence the respective segments at various times and locations.

Media scheduling usually is done geographically and demographically. For example, Taco Bell, McDonald's, and Burger King all compete for the fast-food dollar in the United States. But Taco Bell targets males age 19 to 24, whereas the other two include families with children.[49]

Once decisions are made about target audience and geographic considerations, media planners calculate the cost of communicating with the audience through various media. Media costs are generally expressed in units of cost per thousand, abbreviated as CPM (M is the Roman numeral for 1,000). The CPM for reaching the target audience is calculated as follows:

$$\text{CPM} = \frac{\text{Advertising cost} \times 1,000}{\text{Circulation to target audience}}$$

For example, suppose we are interested in reaching women with children under two years of age. We know that *McCall's* has 600,000 readers in this category, and an advertisement there will cost $60,000. The CPM of reaching our target audience is $100 ($60,000 × 1,000 ÷ 600,000 = $100). We can then determine the cost per person by dividing CPM by 1,000. In this case it is $0.10 ($100 ÷ 1,000 = $0.10).

Reach, Frequency, and Continuity Balance Once media planners know the target audience and the cost of reaching it, they consider the reach, frequency, and continuity of the advertising campaign. **Reach** is the number of consumers in the target audience who can be contacted through a given medium. In the preceding example the reach through *McCall's* is 600,000. **Frequency** is the number of times the audience is contacted during a given period, usually over four weeks. **Continuity** is the length of time the advertising campaign will run in a given medium. It is important to select a medium with enough reach, frequency, and continuity to gain the desired effect. At the same time, agencies do not want to waste funds. **Overexposure** refers to reaching a prospect either after a purchase decision has been made or so frequently that the campaign actually wastes money.

Media Timing Products may be seasonal or purchased more frequently on certain days of the week. For example, suntan lotions are bought mainly during the summer and especially on weekends. Products such as soaps and cosmetics are purchased frequently all year round and may require constant advertising. Consider the importance of media timing for advertising weight loss products. About half of all dieters initiate programs between January and April. Weight Watchers and Jenny Craig, Inc., spent $30 million on television and print ads in January 1997 alone.[50]

To complicate matters, it's important to look at the activity of competitors. It may be necessary to counteract their campaigns or take advantage of times when they tend to promote less. Tactics include selecting media that competitors are not using or making adjustments to the scheduling, timing, and frequency of various advertisements.

REACH

The number of consumers in the target audience who can be contacted through a given medium.

FREQUENCY

The number of times the audience is reached in a given period, usually per day or per week.

CONTINUITY

The length of time the advertising campaign will run in a given medium.

OVEREXPOSURE

Continuing to reach a prospect after a buying decision has been made or to the point that the campaign becomes tedious and actually turns off some potential buyers.

CONNECTED: SURFING THE NET

www.weightwatchers.com

Has media timing brought about any changes in Weight Watchers communications recently? To find out, visit the Web site.

Media Budget Generally, the media budget is set according to the strategic marketing and communication plans. Marketers attempt to maximize the advertising effort within budget constraints, using one or a combination of media to achieve the most influence in the market. As part of the media plan, it's important to determine whether messages will be visual, verbal, or both. The amount of information to be communicated will influence the choice of media and, consequently, the budget. Recently, the costs of all forms have been escalating, so careful attention must be paid to the trade-offs among them. Fortunately, media competition helps the situation. Marketers from magazines, newspapers, television, and radio are constantly promoting their own vehicle. To accommodate clients, they are willing to provide help in media selection and scheduling.

CREATING THE ADS

This step in the ad plan involves both science and art. Creating ads can be as complicated as making a movie. The key is to know your objectives and the constraints imposed by the media, scheduling, and budget. What makes an ad outstanding and memorable? As with any creative process, it's difficult to determine precisely what people will like. To help answer that question, *Marketing*, a British journal, conducts a survey each month called "ad watch." British consumers are asked whether or not they remember a specific advertisement.

There are certainly many classics. The California raisins who "heard it through the grapevine" combined humor, visual novelty, and a great rock beat that caught the attention of millions in the 1980s. Most people still remember Mikey, who willingly ate Life cereal. And nearly everyone (if old enough) can recall the little boy sharing his Coke with Mean Joe Greene of the Pittsburgh Steelers after the game.

When diverse segments are part of the target audience, the advertisement must be created in such a way that it appeals to various tastes and preferences. Marketers also need to be aware of language differences, acceptable behaviors, ethnicity, and cultural norms. Many promotional efforts are now for a global audience, and that means communicating in as many as 3,000 different tongues and dialects.[51] To avoid costly mistakes, it is critical for marketers to research and understand the language(s) of a target market segment before they advertise to it. For example, "Pepsi Brings You Back to Life" was chosen by the company as the promotional theme in China, but the slogan translated into "Pepsi Brings Your Ancestors Back from the Grave." Coca-Cola selected Chinese characters (letters) that sound like its name but which mean "bite the wax tadpole." Imagine Chevrolet's surprise when it was reported that Nova in the Spanish market translates as "It won't go." In Italy, a campaign for Schweppes tonic water referred to the product as Schweppes toilet water, Kentucky Fried Chicken's slogan in China became "eat your fingers off" rather than "finger lickin' good."[52]

Of course, not all diversity is ethnic or linguistic. Gays and lesbians, for example, may be unresponsive to ads that employ only heterosexual couples to represent the warm, loving relationships associated with use of the product. The diversity feature discusses Subaru's advertisements targeting gays and lesbians.

ASSESSING ADVERTISING EFFECTIVENESS

The effect of advertising can be assessed at two different points: before running the ad campaign and afterward. This kind of measurement is extremely important to determine what does and doesn't work so that the campaign can be adjusted.

Individual ads and campaigns may be tested beforehand to evaluate effectiveness before committing more funds. Various tests are used on the sample audience to determine whether the ad content has been stored in the consumer's memory. Both recall and recognition are considered important by advertising researchers. One test asks the audience what it remembers about an ad after a limited run in a particular medium. Two aspects usually are measured. **Unaided recall** asks the viewer to identify any advertisements he or she can recall, such as "What commercials do you remember seeing for automobiles?" **Aided recall** refers to content that can be remembered without seeing the particular ad. An example is: "Do you recall seeing a commercial for Cadillac?" By questioning several respondents, researchers determine both the unaided and aided recall scores. These tests may be conducted immediately following exposure to the ad or up to several days thereafter.

Recognition means that you remember the ad when you see it again. This kind of remembrance is typically adequate for low-involvement products such as chewing gum or soup. To

UNAIDED RECALL

The viewer is asked to identify any advertisements he or she can remember.

AIDED RECALL

The viewer is given some specific piece of information about the ad before being asked if he or she recalls having seen it.

CONNECTING WITH DIVERSITY

BREAKING TABOOS

In 1996, Subaru of North America made a wild departure from the winding roads and dreamscapes that dominate most automobile ads. In a promotion for its all-wheel-drive Legacy station wagon, two women are pictured below a headline: "It loves camping, dogs, and long-term commitment. Too bad it's only a car." Another version features two men, and it doesn't take too much imagination to realize that the couples in these ads are not "just friends."

It seems that Subaru was targeting a segment with significant spending potential. The combined purchasing power of this segment is astounding, at approximately $340 billion for 1999, much greater than the spending potential for Hispanic consumers of the same age. The gay and lesbian market will also see significant growth at a predicted increase of 30.8 percent by 2004. On an individual basis the average annual household income for gays and lesbians is about $57,000, compared to $53,000 for an overall household average. In 1999, the reported size of self-identified gays and lesbians age 18 and older was approximately 13 million, with the potential of 15 million by 2004. Experts offer several reasons as to why this segment is growing so dramatically: ". . . a more tolerant environment in society as a whole, the expanding importance of gay and lesbian employee groups in the workplace, and the growing influence of gay and lesbian voters in the national and local elections."

Ten years ago, the number of mainstream advertisers openly targeting the gay and lesbian market was rather low. One company that did, of course, was Subaru. But at this time it was accompanied by only a few, such as Absolut vodka and American Airlines. Today, however, things have changed. Companies are increasingly willing to risk boycotts from various groups to gain favor with what many believe is a market with significant potential. The list of those targeting this segment has grown to include companies such as OfficeMax, Neiman Marcus, Hartford Insurance, Hollywood studios, Merrill Lynch & Co., Conseco Inc., American Express, and Coors Brewing Company.

Coors Brewing Company is also competing for a piece of the $340 billion market segment. The country's number-three brewer states that the gay market is a gold mine due to its brand loyalty and high disposable income levels. In the past, Coors' efforts to target the gay community included general market ads run in gay publications or ads that included the addition of a six-color rainbow flag, a symbol of the gay community. Today, its advertising to this market is much more extensive in order to set itself apart from the clutter and competition.

Witeck-Combs Communications is a company that specializes in marketing to gays and lesbians. Founder Wes Combs says "This is a very savvy and brand loyal market that is fully aware which companies are courting their business. Gays and lesbians today are highly visible within American culture, and marketers are seeking creative and cost-effective approaches to court them."

Sources: Oscar Suris, "Advertising: Mum's the Word on Subaru Ads Aimed at Homosexual Consumers," *Wall Street Journal,* March 22, 1996, p. B2, B3; "Gay and Lesbian Purchasing Power Exceeds $340 Billion," *PR Newswire,* www.prnewswire.com, July 19, 2000; Business Editors, "Harris Interactive and Witeck-Combs Collaborate to Research Gay and Lesbian Consumer Markets," April 10, 2000, www.businesswire.com; "Marketing to Gays and Lesbians Conference Held in Chicago, March 28–29, 2000," December 6, 1999, www.businesswire.com.

test recognition, audience members are shown an ad and later are asked if they remember it. In other words, the ad is a stimulus during the testing procedure. One of the most popular types of recognition test is the Starch test, which is usually conducted after an ad has been run. Respondents leaf through a magazine containing the ad and are then asked if they remember seeing it. Next, a series of questions determines whether they associated the ad with the advertiser's name or logo and whether they read at least half of the copy. Because Starch tests have been run on so many ads, marketers can compare the scores of their ad to similar types.

When persuasion is the objective of the advertisement, it is very important to go beyond simple memory tests and determine whether the ad influences attitudes or behavior. For this, marketers use persuasion tests, which essentially measure attitude change. For example, respondents may be asked to preview a particular television show with ads imbedded in it. They are then questioned about the program itself as well as brand preferences. Comparing the answers to measures taken beforehand, it's possible to determine the amount of attitude change.

SALES PROMOTION

Communications designed to stimulate immediate purchases using tools such as coupons, contests, and free samples.

SALES PROMOTION

Sales promotion is communication designed to stimulate immediate purchases using tools such as coupons, contests, and free samples.[53] It is used frequently by most companies and it accounts for about $366 billion in annual expenditures in the United States.[54] Notice that the definition focuses on immediate results and changes in the behavior of consumers or other channel members. In addition to its value as a short-term incentive, there is no doubt that sales promotion for many brands has a lot to do with long-term brand equity. This is particularly true of frequently purchased consumer items, such as Coke and Pepsi. Sales promotion plays an important role in reinforcing continuous usage and offsetting gains made by competitors. When brand switching occurs, sales promotion is a valuable way to regain consumer loyalty.

Sales promotion also stimulates trial. Many times buyers are reluctant to try a new product because it may not perform as well as their existing one. Sales promotion reduces the risk by lowering the price or creating other incentives. Most consumers are now accustomed to having a trial opportunity at little or no cost. Car dealers offer test drives, and some companies provide free samples. AOL offers 700 free minutes of online service in its trial offer.[55]

Whereas advertising and public relations increase awareness, sales promotion prompts people to action, resulting in immediate sales. By either increasing the perceived value of a product or reducing its price, sales promotion motivates customers to make an immediate purchase decision. Value is increased by providing a free gift, an unusual warranty, or some type of prize. Price may be lowered directly, with an introductory offer, or through coupons and rebates. In any case, the consumer recognizes an immediate opportunity and acts on it.

Although sales promotion generally has an immediate result, its long-term effects are less clear. It is most commonly used in conjunction with other forms of promotion, such as advertising, public relations campaigns, or personal selling. Consequently, it is usually seen as part of the total promotion package designed by the marketing communication strategists.

TYPES OF SALES PROMOTION

Figure 15.8 depicts four different types of sales promotion: business-to-business, consumer, trade, and retailer promotions.

Figure 15.9 lists typical activities in each category. Business-to-business promotions usually involve trade shows, conventions, sales contests, and specialty deals, such as volume discounts and price sales. Sales promotion in the consumer market is directed at gaining a behavioral change by way of trial or actual purchase. Manufacturers use two basic approaches to influence the consumer—the sales pull and the sales push. **Consumer promotions** are manufacturer incentives offered directly to consumers, largely bypassing the retailer. They are designed to pull the product through the retail establishment with coupons, rebates, and other means that the manufacturer can control from headquarters.

CONSUMER PROMOTION

Offer designed to pull the product through the retail establishment.

Stridex uses a sales promotion (coupon) to sell their foaming face wash.

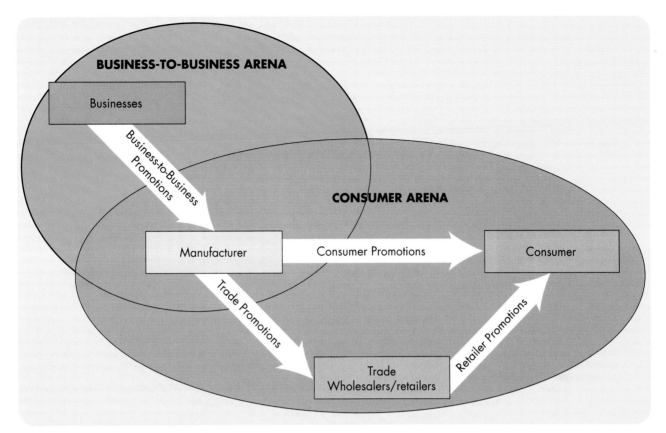

FIGURE 15.8 *Types of Sales Promotion*

Trade promotions are provided by manufacturers to distribution channel members. The objective is to give wholesalers and retailers an incentive to sell the manufacturer's brand. Essentially, these promotions make it worthwhile for the channel member to push the product to the consumer. Common incentives are advertising allowances and price reductions. For example, Ralston Purina may offer a 3 percent discount on Cat Chow to retailers. They may pass the savings on to the consumers in order to increase trade or may pocket the difference in order to increase profit.

Retailer promotions are directed at the consumer by the retail outlet. They are often confined to a local area, although large chains such as Best Buy may run many of the same promotions at all locations. This provides a sales level sufficient to obtain quantity discounts from suppliers, which enables prices to be kept low.

<u>TRADE PROMOTION</u>
An offer from a manufacturer to channel members, such as wholesalers and retailers.

<u>RETAILER PROMOTION</u>
An offer to the consumer that is sponsored by a retailer.

Business-to-Business Promotions	Manufacturer Trade Promotions	Manufacturer Consumer Promotions	Retailer Consumer Promotions
Trade shows	Discounts	Coupons	Price cuts
Conventions	• off invoice	Rebates (refunds)	Displays
Sales contests	• off list	Samples	Free goods ("trials")
Specialty items	Allowances	Price packs ("cents off")	Retailer coupons
Virtual trade shows	• advertising	Value packs ("2 for 1")	Feature advertising
	• display	Premiums (gifts)	Patronage awards
	Financing incentives	Sweepstakes (prizes and contests)	
	Contests	Point-of-purchase displays	
	Spiffs	Cross-promotion	
		Continuity programs	

FIGURE 15.9 *Major Types of Sales Promotion Activities*

Normally, the push and pull elements of the sales promotion strategy should work hand in hand. Trade promotions are usually coordinated with the firm's other sales activities. The sales force works to persuade customers (retailers or wholesalers) to purchase greater volume and push to consumers through retailer promotions. At the same time, consumer promotions are usually coordinated with ad messages about coupons and point-of-purchase displays tied into the advertising theme. This kind of one-two punch can produce dramatic results.

THE SUCCESS OF SALES PROMOTION

Sales promotion has become increasingly successful due to changing consumer lifestyles, better technology, and the changing structure of the retail industry.[56] Today's busy consumers are looking for ways to simplify purchase choices in order to save time. In addition, they want value, and they view sales promotion as a way of getting more for their money. Furthermore, one study shows that more than half of all households favor grocery brands that are supported with sales promotions.[57]

Technology helps marketers target sales promotions more precisely than ever before. Checkout scanners tell immediately which brands are purchased. Sorting machines identify which coupons and other redemption items are used, and tracking devices identify where purchases are made and by whom. It's now very easy for marketers to measure the effect of specific promotion activities on unit sales and profitability. For example, GTE developed a frequent shopper program for retailers that combine scanner data with information about consumers to reward the best customers, thereby improving relationship marketing. Companies supporting the program included RJR Nabisco, Scott Paper, and Philip Morris (for its Maxwell House and Yuban brands).[58] The Internet has also begun to track consumer spending patterns. One company, DoubleClick, has amassed 80 million profiles of consumers in order to deliver advertising tailored to the consumer's surfing patterns.[59]

Another influence on the use of promotions is the changing structure of the retail industry. As large establishments such as Wal-Mart gain market power, they can compete more effectively with manufacturers' brands. To counteract this power, manufacturers use sales promotion to create a pull through the channel to maintain their customer base. At the same time, they are engaged in competitive battles to maintain market share. A company that wants to hold share is almost compelled to use sales promotions commensurate with those of other major competitors, whether retailers or other manufacturers.

CREATING CUSTOMER RELATIONSHIPS
AND LOYALTY THROUGH SALES PROMOTION

Sales promotion is an excellent tool for organizations that want to connect with customers through relationships. The purpose of relationship marketing is to create loyal, satisfied customers. Consumers can be very fickle, however, and marketers must keep that constantly in mind. Figure 15.10 describes the four main categories of buyers and strategies for marketing to each group.[60]

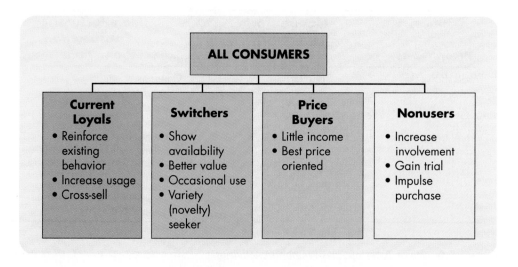

FIGURE 15.10 *Types of
Buyers*

Current Loyals   As the name implies, current loyals are presently purchasing a company's brand. They range from intensely loyal users who buy because of their relationship with the company to people who are loyal because of simple convenience or price factors. It's difficult to persuade them to switch. One strategy used to maintain these customers is to reward their loyalty with personally targeted one-to-one promotions. This encourages them to continue using the brand and reminds them about the product they have been purchasing. For example, what is more personal than a birthday? Burger King began a kid's club in January 1990, and now, as the "Big Kids" Club, more than 5 million children ages 7 to 12 receive a bimonthly newsletter and coupons on their birthday. This builds a relationship and increases the loyalty of this important segment of consumers. Sales of Burger King children's meals increased by 300 percent in the first four years of the program and the Big Kids meal has inspired competitors to target the "'tween" demographic as well.[61]

Loyal consumers also may respond to sales promotions by buying a product in larger quantities or at a time when they normally do not purchase. For example, loyal users of Chi Chi's tortilla chips are likely to buy them in bulk, and a promotion is an opportunity to stockpile the product. Users of Starkist tuna may buy several cans when the brand is on sale. Once it is available at home, it is likely to be used more often.

When a manufacturer owns two or more brands, current loyal customers are excellent candidates for **cross-selling,** promoting another of the brands or using one product to boost sales of another, often an unrelated product. Different companies also may work together to cross-sell. Procter & Gamble entered into a large cross-promotion deal with TGI Fridays' restaurant chain. The campaign highlights the effectiveness of P&G's Fit produce cleaner and how this improves the quality of food served at TGI Fridays. The campaign includes commercials that highlight both products as well as coupons. An extension of this campaign is a partnership with Tupperware. Over 200,000 Tupperware reps will demonstrate the use of Fit.[62] This campaign appeals to loyal customers of all the partners, building relationships synergistically.

Switchers   Switchers purchase a number of different brands. Loyalty has decreased in recent years, and the percentage of consumers in the switcher category has become much larger. Consequently, many manufacturers and retailers focus on this group. In many cases, switchers cut their overall expenditures by finding the best deal at the time. They may switch regularly or only when they see an opportunity to increase value or decrease price.

Switchers are not likely to wait for an out-of-stock brand. Trade promotion aimed at maximizing inventory levels and store space works well with this group. Since they are interested in price and value, they respond to even fairly complex purchase offers. For example, several units of the same product can be bundled together, the amount of product can be increased for the same price, or the price can be reduced.

Some switchers are occasional users, purchasing infrequently or according to season. This is even true of churchgoers. In England, the Churches Advertising Network launched a series of ads targeted at this group around holiday time.[63]

Other switchers are simply seeking novelty or variety and change brands to alleviate boredom or monotony. Sales promotions work particularly well on them, since they are responsive to novel purchase opportunities. If the product is noticed at the precise time the variety seeker is interested in buying, then the manufacturer benefits. 7-Up positions itself in a way that distinguishes it not only from colas but also from other uncolas. "Make 7-Up yours" is intended to reach buyers looking for a novel purchase opportunity—the use of Orlando Jones's character adding to the wackiness of the ad.[64]

Price Buyers   The price buyer's only concern is cost. Most in this category want low prices, but a few choose only the most expensive brand. People in the latter category tend to ignore nearly all sales promotion, and they consider clipping coupons a total waste of time. In contrast, buyers after low prices are likely to purchase opportunistically, when they have funds and the product is on sale. They respond very well to price promotions: cents-off, two for one, buy a second one for a penny, limited time offers, and so forth.

Nonusers   Nonusers do not currently purchase a particular brand. Sales promotions are designed to create involvement, which may stimulate purchase. Again, cross-selling works to gain trial. For example, many Barnes & Noble bookstores have Starbucks coffees in their cafes.[65] In this case, sales promotion encourages nonusers to try the product. Prego urges

CROSS-SELLING
Promotion in which the manufacturer of one brand attempts to sell another brand to the same customers, or the purchase of one product is used to stimulate the selection of another, often unrelated product.

**CONNECTED:
SURFING THE NET**

www.7up.com

See firsthand how the un-cola appeals to switchers. "Make 7-Up Yours" at the Web site. Play a game and sign up for the T-shirt promotion.

fund-raising groups to use its book of suggestions, coupons, and helpful hints for event organization, nudging nonusers to try the company's products.[66] Some companies mail samples to nonusers' homes. Rather than throw the product out, consumers are usually willing to try it. In other cases, nonusers are supplied a trial under captive circumstances. An example is the complimentary snacks offered on airlines, such as branded peanuts, pretzels, and sodas.

BUSINESS-TO-BUSINESS PROMOTIONS

The four main types of business-to-business promotion are trade shows, conventions, sales contests, and specialty items. Often volume discounts and price sales occur in conjunction with these four activities.

Trade Shows   Trade shows are designed to bring marketers and customers together at a given location for a short period. They occur around the world and are an opportunity for companies to display existing and new product lines in ways that are convenient for customers. Nearly 75 percent of all firms use trade shows as a major promotion mechanism.[67] In the United States, nearly 6,000 trade shows take place every year, attended by approximately 80 million people.

Companies set up booths that are staffed by key personnel and salespeople, and it's not unusual for retailers and distributors to select the merchandise they will carry during the coming year. Consequently, business marketers may invest a large percentage of their promotional budget in trade shows. This is a very cost-effective way to meet a great number of potential purchasers. The cost of closing a trade show sale is estimated at around $500, compared to over $1500 for a regular business-to-business sale.[68]

Today, trade show information is heavily promoted and accessed on the Internet. The Trade Show Central Web site publicizes more than 10,000 events. A directory allows companies to find shows of interest and request information as well as register.[69] Companies can quickly identify and select the event that will be the most beneficial in reaching potential customers.

Conventions   Conventions provide another opportunity for marketers and buyers to meet. They are often sponsored by professional groups, such as the American Hospital Association, the American Medical Association, or the International Association of Certified Public Accountants. It is important to note that conventions are held around the world, giving marketers the chance to assess the level of global competition and gather ideas for new strategies. Although companies attend primarily to stimulate immediate sales, they also can take the opportunity to do long-range assessments of customer and industry trends. Marketing researchers often attend conventions and trade shows because so many qualified buyers are concentrated in one place. This provides a pool of readily available respondents, and schedules often permit in-depth interviews, focus groups, and surveys. These events are considered prime opportunities for data collection.

Sales Contests   **Sales contests** for salespeople and dealers offer prizes for accomplishing specific goals. Most companies sponsor some type of sales contest from time to time and

Approximately 80 million people attend trade shows in the United States each year.

award trips, gifts, or cash, often at an annual sales convention. This type of sales promotion is designed to elicit immediate action by giving short-term rewards for short-term behavior. When incentives are tied to measurable and achievable sales objectives, they can be highly motivating.[70] Sales contests frequently are specific to product lines or market segments and are integrated into the overall selling and promotion strategy. Allied Signal designed an incentive plan targeted at its distributors, offering them a choice of gifts for increasing sales to retailers. This was an innovative way to encourage distributors to sell the product rather than just stock inventory.[71] Volkswagen rewards top sellers of the Passat with a free trip to Arizona to drive the Passat on a racetrack.[72]

Specialty Items   **Specialty items** are gifts for customers, usually sent through the mail or handed out by salespeople, with the organization's name imprinted on them. These include such items as pens, calendars, memo pads, T-shirts, sun visors, or hats. Generally there is no purchase requirement. AT&T runs a promotion on the Internet targeted at college students. The site offers links to free software, contests, and prizes as well as educational and promotional pages. The students' interactions with the site are intended to help potential customers remember AT&T.[73]

TRADE PROMOTIONS

Trade promotions are offered by the manufacturer to wholesalers or retailers. Five common types are discounts, allowances, financing incentives, sales contests, and spiffs.

Discounts   One of the most popular trade promotions is discount or price-off arrangements, which reduce either the invoice or the list price. The invoice price is what the manufacturer charges to the distributor, whereas the list price is what the end customer is charged. If distributors choose to pass the price cut on to consumers, demand may increase. If not, distributor profit margins increase. Like all trade promotions, discounts encourage distributors to handle more of the company's product and to stimulate sales to consumers.

Allowances   **Allowances** are funds given to retailers and wholesalers based on the amount of product they buy. Two typical allowances are for advertising and display purposes. For example, a retailer who purchases $5,000 worth of product may receive a $500 allowance to help pay for advertising. Display allowances work the same way, except that the funds must be used for point-of-purchase displays in the retail outlet.

Financing Incentives   **Financing incentives** help reduce the retailer's inventory carrying cost. This is commonly referred to as financing the "floor plan," which is the retailer's stock of inventory. For example, in the automobile business, dealers do not have to pay immediately for all the cars shipped to them. Instead, they pay a fee for having them in their showroom. Financing incentives come in a broad variety, but all are designed to get the manufacturer's product into the retail establishment.

Sales Contests and Spiffs   Two other types of trade promotion are sales contests and "spiffs." In this context, sales contests reward the retailer for selling a certain level of product and often extend to the salespeople within the retail establishment. Spiffs are like a commission paid to salespeople in retail outlets who sell the manufacturer's product rather than a competitor's brand. These cash incentives are not uncommon for such items as cameras, televisions, mobile homes, and cellular telephones. Many people consider spiffs unethical because they encourage the promotion of one brand over others irrespective of its value to the customer. Because consumers are not aware of the spiff, they may believe the salesperson's motives are more "pure" than is actually the case.

Trade promotions are becoming prevalent worldwide. Brand Equity sponsored Promo Power 2000, a conference dedicated entirely to promotion, in India. The focus was on promoting brands rather than on promoting sales.[74]

RETAILER PROMOTIONS

Retailer promotions are directed specifically at the end customer and originate within the retailing organization. They seek to encourage consumers to purchase a product from a given location. Consequently, retailer promotions are often in-store or specific with regard to where the promotion can be exercised. Manufacturers may help with retailer promotions. Sony's "Modern Rock Live" campaign was one of the biggest promotions ever undertaken by the

SPECIALTY ITEMS
Gifts with the organization's name that are provided to customers, usually given through the mail or by the sales force.

ALLOWANCES
Funds given to retailers and wholesalers based on the amount of product they buy.

FINANCING INCENTIVE
An offer to finance the retailer's inventory prior to its sale.

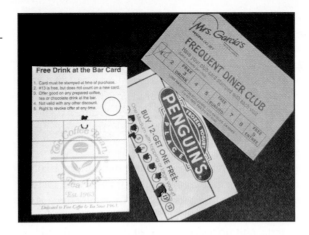

Patronage awards are very useful promotions.

company. The vice president of personal audio/video marketing called it "a real value for consumers and a great traffic and sales builder for retailers." Sony provided kits to help outlets develop local tie-ins to the national promotion campaign, which used television, radio, and print advertising as well as a consumer Web site.[75]

The most common type of retailer promotion is price cuts. Retailers are likely to use these regularly to stimulate sales of certain product lines or to reduce inventory of older products. Also common are display promotions to direct attention to particular goods. Large national retailers are likely to send teams to work with local outlets in developing similar displays across the country. These teams are likely to be dispatched on a seasonal basis. Gap takes this approach for displays. Free trials are another type of retailer promotion. Local copy shops, for example, often offer a free color copy to induce customers to try their services. Retailer coupons are used relatively frequently and are often placed in local newspapers. Also popular is feature advertising on radio or television of discounted items, such as automobiles and mobile homes. It's not unusual for the retailer to be the spokesperson in these types of ads. Finally, patronage awards are very useful promotions. Generally, a card is punched or stamped each time the consumer shops at the retail outlet. When the card is filled, it's redeemed for free merchandise. The Cappuccino Cafe in Okemos, Michigan, redeems not only its own loyalty card but also those of competitors as a way to get new trials. Patronage awards, which stimulate loyalty to a given outlet, are particularly useful in local markets for creating a bond between regular customers and the retailer.

CONSUMER PROMOTIONS

Manufacturers use consumer sales promotions to influence their market share across all retailing outlets. There are several popular forms: coupons, rebates, samples, sweepstakes, price and value packs, point-of-purchase displays, and continuity programs.

COUPON

Certificate that entitles a consumer to an incentive to buy the product, usually a price reduction or a free sample.

Coupons **Coupons** are certificates that entitle a consumer to an incentive, usually a price reduction or free sample. Trade coupons are redeemable only at a particular store or chain, whereas manufacturer coupons are redeemable at any outlet. They are particularly appealing to manufacturers because they can make a direct connection with consumers. Since manufacturers' coupons create work for retailers, they may be given incentives for handling them.

Coupons are one of the most popular forms of consumer sales promotion.[76] Some consumers purchase a large percentage of their nondurable products through coupons. Research has shown that they have higher levels of education and income, live in urban areas, and are less loyal to brands or stores.[77] Many of them decide which coupons to use before they shop.[78] A national survey by the Nielsen Co. revealed that five out of six households use grocery coupons as an important part of their shopping. Yet, although manufacturers distribute $400 billion every year, only $6.25 billion are redeemed. Often people don't like to take the time to search for and cut coupons. Brand loyalty is another factor, since coupons may not be available for the consumer's products of choice.[79]

Coupons are generally distributed as freestanding inserts (FSIs) in newspapers or magazines. They also may be sent in special mailings or as bill stuffers. Another technique is an on-shelf dispenser at the retail outlet, placed near the manufacturer's brand. Only about 2 percent of regular coupons are redeemed, 8.5 percent of checkout coupons, 9.8 percent of electronic coupons, and 13 percent of on-shelf coupons. Marketers try to identify the level of price reduction that will stimulate coupon use. If a 25-cent incentive will do as much as a 50-cent reduction, then the 25-cent incentive should be used.

Rebates   Rebates are refunds given to consumers for the purchase of particular items. Psychologically, rebates make a larger impression than price reductions. For example, let's say an automobile manufacturer offers a $1,500 rebate or a 10 percent reduction in price for a $15,000 car. Although the discount may be precisely the same, consumers are likely to see the rebate as greater. The reason is that the price discount from $15,000 to $13,500 is a perceptually smaller decrease than the $1,500 rebate. Since consumers usually have to mail a form to the manufacturer to get the rebate, they often will not bother if the amount is small. They also may lose or forget about the rebate. In those cases the company gets the sale without paying the incentive. Another advantage of rebates is that they leave higher margins for intermediaries.

Rebates tend to be particularly effective in stimulating trial of brands that are priced higher than those of competitors. Hewlett-Packard frequently runs rebate offers on its printers and other electronic devices. To get the rebate, customers have to submit a completed rebate coupon in addition to a proof-of-purchase sticker. They receive their rebate six to eight weeks after the purchase.[80]

Samples   Generally, samples are distributed via direct mail, door-to-door, or in stores. Sometimes coupons may be redeemed for free samples. This method is effective with new products or when targeted at people who lack experience with the brand. Occasionally, manufacturers attempt to renew an older product by providing samples. Co-op Promotions, which specializes in samples, packaged Off! insect repellent in 1 million Sunbeam barbecue grills for S. C. Johnson. Teledyne installed its shower massage in shower heads used by 35,000 bicyclists during a 15-city tour.[81] American Sampling, Inc., sends gift packs to 3.8 million new mothers annually, and companies such as Market Source provide samples to college freshmen.

This kind of sales promotion requires very careful attention to detail because the cost of samples is high. One study found that 51 million coupons for a free product distributed through freestanding inserts (FSIs) cost $7 per thousand, whereas 5 million samples distributed through direct mail cost $80 per thousand. But the FSIs only converted 367,200 people ($0.97 per convert), whereas the mail samples converted 800,000 ($0.50 per convert.)[82]

Sweepstakes   A sweepstakes is a contest in which participants' names are pooled, and the winner is drawn randomly. Most of you have experienced a twinge of anticipation upon receiving an envelope stating that you may have won millions of dollars. The objective of the contest is to get buyers to purchase the products included in the sweepstakes offer. Laws prevent the sponsor from requiring a purchase in order to participate. Sweepstakes promoters must provide full disclosure of the requirements for entering as well as the probabilities of winning.

A recent "Family Fantasy Sweepstakes" at Disney.com offered more than $200,000 in prizes. Participants could sign up to win Disneyland vacations among other prizes. The site encouraged consumers to enter daily, which also gave more exposure to Disney's Web site promotions.[83]

Price and Value Packs   Price and value packs are cents-off or two-for-one offers. The cents-off variety is easier to administer and receives a great deal of attention. The value pack, while more difficult to administer, gets more product in the hands of the consumer in a shorter period. Both are very flexible and relatively easy sales promotions to consumers. Value packs are different from premiums or gifts, which may not be related directly to the product. For example, in real estate sales it's not uncommon for the purchaser of a home to receive a free airline ticket to a vacation spot.

Point-of-Purchase Displays   Point-of-purchase (POP) displays exhibit products at retail locations. Since up to 70 percent of purchase decisions are made in the store, the displays can be very important. Companies spend well over $12 billion annually on POP. More than 52 percent of carbonated beverage sales, 26 percent of candy/mint sales, and 22 percent of beer/ale sales are attributed to such displays.[84] They work best when tied directly to other messages or advertising campaigns. Generally, POP displays need to have a lot of attention-getting power and must focus the consumer's interest on the sales promotion and product at hand.

Many stores are using POP to connect with customers in an interactive and exciting environment. For example, customers at Niketown can hear the sounds of bouncing tennis balls and squeaking tennis shoes. Richard Nathan, head of RTC, one of the largest POP design companies in the United States, says: "It's sensory, it's visual, but not just for amusement. The best

POP displays have a lot of attention-getting power and can increase consumer interest in a product.

POP is not just fun; it informs you and shows you how to find products in a store."[85] A point-of-purchase display for Sega of America won an award at a trade show for its innovative design and widespread retail acceptance. The display, with wing panels joined by a glass case, had visual appeal and encouraged customers to stop and look at the products.[86]

Continuity Programs   Continuity programs reward people for continued and frequent use of a particular product. A good example is the frequent flyer miles offered in the airline industry. Although these usually don't stimulate more air travel, they are an incentive for a purchaser to travel with a particular carrier. The programs also are a recognized tool for increasing customer satisfaction. Nearly every airline offers frequent flyer miles, and most hotel chains now have similar programs. Hyatt, for example, offers free room stays after a certain number of regular stays. Continuity programs tend to run longer than other types of sales promotion because their basic objective is to promote long-term usage.

PUBLIC RELATIONS AND PUBLICITY

PUBLIC RELATIONS

PUBLIC RELATIONS (PR)

The use of publicity and other nonpaid forms of communication to present the firm and its products positively.

Public relations (PR) is the use of publicity and other nonpaid forms of communication designed to present the firm and its products positively. A disadvantage is that the communication is not always controlled by the company. It can determine when to issue press releases and hold events, but it cannot control the press that independently decides whether to run the communication. Nevertheless, public relations offers several advantages not found with other types of promotion vehicles. Because gatekeepers—editors and news reporters—screen company issued communication to ensure its accuracy, the public can have some confidence that the information it receives through public relations is truthful. In addition, PR provides editorial-type messages that can break through advertising clutter. Public relations can be used to establish the social responsibility of a good corporate citizen. Because of the typical content and source of messages, it is possible to reach upscale opinion leaders, who in turn spread the message. Furthermore, there are few legal restrictions on PR activities, making it a way to address numerous issues in a more balanced light than may be possible with advertising.

Public relations is likely to focus on many publics, including employees, shareholders, community members, news media, and government. Rather than directly promote a particular product or brand, most PR messages have the appearance of objectivity. Many PR promotional campaigns center on social issues. For example, Avon supports breast cancer awareness in the United States, the prevention of violence against women in Malaysia, child nourishment in China, and AIDS prevention in Thailand. Toys "R" Us and Reebok offer gift certificates in exchange for guns. This type of public relations is known as cause marketing and costs $1 billion annually. One study found that 66 percent of consumers would switch brands if they considered the cause worthwhile. But the same study revealed that 58 percent of consumers believe cause marketing is insincere.[87] There has been a recent resurgence in cause marketing. Mutual funds that invest only in earth-friendly companies now have $12.8 billion in assets. Hewlett-Packard has begun an initiative to bring technology into rural villages.[88] Effective PR requires activities consistent with the goals and objectives of the organization.[89]

The Washington Apple Commission supported the North American Free Trade Agreement (NAFTA) because its defeat would have cost the industry $150 million a year. It developed a PR strategy with a target market of 11 members of Congress. First, it started a letter-writing campaign by sending packets to almost 4,000 apple growers and shippers. The packet contained a sample letter to editors and congressional delegates as well as a fact sheet on NAFTA. Then 51 agricultural producers in Washington State signed a letter endorsing NAFTA. Next, one apple grower went to Washington State with 150 other pro-NAFTA groups to meet with the president. This resulted in some free publicity on the television networks and the national wire services, which liked the idea of an apple grower talking to the president. The commission continued its show of public support but also focused its efforts on press conferences. Once again, two national wire services wrote stories on the industry. The PR effort resulted in a 10–1 vote in favor of NAFTA by the targeted congressional delegates. It also won an award from the National Agri-Marketing Association. Public relations supports the marketing function in several ways.

- *Corporate communication.* Messages promote a better understanding of the organization among employees, shareholders, and other relevant publics.
- *Press relations.* Newsworthy information, such as new activities and personnel promotions, are provided to the media on a timely basis.
- *Lobbying.* Communication with legislators and government officials to promote or defeat legislation is a major activity for heavily regulated industries.
- *Product publicity.* Newsworthy innovations or new attributes of products can be promoted at little cost through the media.

PUBLICITY

Publicity is what is communicated about an organization in the public news media. Publicity can be positive or negative. Negative publicity detracts from the organization's image and can have serious effects on its market position. Most PR groups attempt to generate positive publicity through news stories and public service announcements. The more common avenues are press releases, news conferences, and event sponsorship. The Internet increasingly is being used by marketers, both to spread publicity and to respond to crisis situations.

Press Releases and News Conferences   A **press release** is a statement written by company personnel and distributed to various media for publication at their discretion. It includes information about the organization or product that marketers believe will be of interest to the public. The advantage of a press release is that the marketer has control over what information is provided. Many large organizations issue press releases regularly. This type of communication is used almost invariably when negative publicity needs to be countered. Rather than leave it to the media to track down the facts, companies provide the same information to all members of the press simultaneously. Press releases must be accurate, to the point, and based on hard evidence. If not, then the media will become skeptical about any material the company issues.

PRESS RELEASE

A statement written by company personnel and distributed to various media for publication at their discretion.

News or press conferences occur when reporters are invited to a meeting at which company officials make a public statement and usually respond to questions. As with press releases, companies have some control over news conferences.

Sponsored Events or Activities   A very popular type of publicity is sponsored events or activities, especially for local promotion. Many companies sponsor rock or symphony concerts, sports teams, or youth groups. This gets their name before the public while contributing to the community. Various nontraditional activities are becoming popular publicity opportunities. To attract baby boomers, such companies as Audi, United Airlines, and Banana Republic have sponsored food and wine festivals. Ford Motor's Lincoln is associated with mountain biking, arts, and hot-air balloon events.[90] Guiness recently opened a museum in the stout's hometown of Dublin, complete with brewery tour, free samples, merchandise, and a restaurant, to overturn its stodgy image and appeal to younger customers. Coca-Cola, to relaunch the brand in Belgium after a bottling accident left hundreds ill, participated in community events by sponsoring games with Coca-Cola products as the prizes.[91]

The Internet   The Internet can be an ideal medium for publicity. In fact, it has spawned a new group of PR companies. Edelman Public Relations Worldwide is a leading creator of Web sites. Its services can be especially helpful when companies need to minimize negative publicity. For example, several bottles of Odwalla apple juice were found to contain *E. coli* bacteria. In less than three hours, Edelman created a site to provide consumers with information. It did the same for American Home Products after the death of model Chrissy Taylor, reportedly caused by inhaling Primatene Mist. The site was running within 12 hours.[92] In 2000 and 2001, Ford utilized the Internet to aid in the recall of more than 6.5 million defective tires.

Other companies use the Internet to host chat sessions, which serve as a form of positive publicity. ICMA Retirement Corporation gives consumers a chance to interact with its president and CEO, Girard Miller. Robert Barkin, the company's vice president of public relations, says: "This is an opportunity for everyone with access to the Internet, whether they work in the public sector or not, to chat with one of the nation's leading authorities on retirement issues."[93]

Marketers who skillfully blend public relations and publicity into their communications mix can underscore and intensify the positive feelings created by other mass communications activities. In chapter 16 we will turn our attention to the most personal and individualized form of marketing communication—personal selling. Although one-on-one relationship building is key to effective personal selling, mass communication provides important support. It lays the groundwork for personal sales by creating deeper receptivity toward the company and its products.

CONNECTED: SURFING THE NET

SUBARU
www.subaru.com

THIS CHAPTER'S DIVERSITY FEATURE, "BREAKING TABOOS" discussed the company's efforts to target advertisements to gays and lesbians. To expand your thinking about communication, visit Subaru's Web site and answer the following questions.

1. The Internet offers two-way interaction, making mass communication more personal. How does Subaru's site make this personal connection?
2. Whether alone or in support of other promotion vehicles, advertising informs, persuades, reminds, or reinforces. Which of these does the Subaru Web site best accomplish? Explain.
3. Each medium has unique advantages. Compare the advantages of Subaru's Web site to the other types of media discussed in the chapter. Select three that you think would be the most effective if used in combination.

MSN.COM
www.msn.com

THIS CHAPTER'S TECHNOLOGY FEATURE DISCUSSED MSN.com, a search engine on the World Wide Web. To learn more about MSN.com, visit its Web site and answer the following questions.

1. See if you can recognize MSN's new style of banner ads. Do you think this is an effective way to advertise? Why or why not?
2. How could MSN use its Web site for public relations communication? Give an example of how it could help with positive publicity and minimize negative publicity.
3. What advantages might MSN have over Yahoo!?

CHAPTER SUMMARY

OBJECTIVE 1: Understand the concept of mass communication including the relative use of advertising, sales promotion, and public relations.

Mass communication helps companies connect with customers around the world. It adds value by providing information about the goods and services available. Expenditure on mass com-munication—advertising, sales promotion, and public relations—is increasing at about 7 percent annually in the United States and at a slightly higher rate globally. Roughly the same amount is spent on sales promotion and advertising, but sales promotion is slightly ahead and is growing faster. Public relations is a distant third.

OBJECTIVE 2:   Learn how technology, globalization, and ethics are playing major roles in mass communication.

The history of mass communication coincides with the development of communications technology, particularly print, radio, and television. Today, the Internet is adding an interactive medium. Global mass communication occurs when key elements of messages are standardized across regions and nations. Standardization has cost advantages when the same customer segments are found in many countries, but it has several limitations. The primary ethical issue in mass communication is deception. Puffery may be used to make a point, but care must be taken not to be deceptive. Some countries have very strict legislation that does not allow exaggerations of any sort.

OBJECTIVE 3:   Know the objectives, advantages, and disadvantages of advertising, as well as the sequence of steps in creating an advertising campaign.

Advertising is highly controllable and works over time to build brand equity. It is cost-effective for reaching large audiences. Its primary objective may be to inform consumers, to persuade them to buy, to remind them of the product, or to reinforce buying behavior and positive feelings about the brand. Advertising media are readily available, and it's easy for marketers to find help in creating effective campaigns. But advertising reaches many people outside the target audience, encounters a high level of avoidance, and can be costly. It also can communicate only brief, one-way messages. There are several different types of advertising: national, retail (local), directory, business-to-business, institutional, direct response, public service, and political. Generally, there are five steps in developing the advertising plan: set objectives, establish the budget, create the theme and message, select and schedule media, create the ads, and assess effectiveness.

OBJECTIVE 4:   Understand sales promotion objectives and what types of promotions are used to stimulate sales in business, trade, retailer, and consumer markets.

Sales promotion is used to prompt consumers to action, resulting in immediate sales results. It is generally used with other forms of promotion, such as advertising, public relations, or personal selling. There are four types of sales promotion: business-to-business, trade, retailer, and consumer. Business-to-business promotions include trade shows, conventions, sales contests, and specialty deals. Trade promotions, which are offered by manufacturers to wholesalers or retailers, include discounts, allowances, financing incentives, sales contests, and spiffs. Retailer promotions, offered to consumers, include price cuts, displays, free trials, coupons, and patronage awards. Consumer promotions are manufacturers' offers, including coupons, rebates, free samples, sweepstakes, price and value packs, POP displays, and continuity programs.

OBJECTIVE 5:   Understand the use of public relations in marketing.

Public relations activities are used primarily to influence feelings, opinions, or beliefs about a company or its products. An attempt is made to develop messages that at least have the appearance of objectivity. PR supports the marketing function in the following ways: corporate communication, press relations, lobbying, and product publicity. Common publicity-generating activities are press releases, news conferences, and sponsorship of events or activities. Because public relations messages are placed through public channels, the messages tend to be more credible and believable. They also tend to break through the advertising clutter and are relatively low in cost. Public relations can publicize the social responsibility of a good corporate citizen.

REVIEW YOUR UNDERSTANDING

1. Why is global standardization of mass communication useful?
2. How do deception and puffery relate?
3. What is advertising? What is its overriding goal?
4. What are the objectives of advertising, which also describe types of ads?
5. What are some of the advantages and disadvantages of advertising?
6. List the eight types of advertising. What is the focus of each?
7. Name the six types of advertising media. What are the advantages and disadvantages of each?
8. What is sales promotion? How is it different from advertising?
9. Briefly describe the four different types of sales promotion. What are the most common promotional activities within each category?
10. How does sales promotion help build relationships?
11. What is public relations? How is it unique from other forms of mass communication?
12. What are the pros and cons of public relations?

DISCUSSION OF CONCEPTS

1. Describe the five steps in developing an advertising plan. On which ones would you most enjoy working? Least enjoy? Why?
2. Why is it important to develop a creative strategy before creating specific ads?
3. Which techniques are most commonly used to determine the advertising budget? Which one do you believe should be used and why?
4. What are the critical issues in selecting and scheduling the appropriate advertising media?
5. As with any creative process, it's difficult to determine precisely what people will like. When it comes to developing an advertisement, what are some of the characteristics that will tend to make the ad successful? Why?
6. In business, it's important to measure how well the organization performs certain tasks in order to make adjustments as necessary. How do marketers measure the effectiveness of advertising campaigns?
7. Marketers sometimes divide consumers into four categories of buyers. Briefly describe each type and the promotional activities that are likely to be successful with each.
8. List the most popular types of trade promotions. When is each type appropriate?
9. How do the advantages and disadvantages of public relations compare to those of other forms of promotional activities?

Advertising: Paid communication through nonpersonal channels.

Advertising agency: A business that develops, prepares, and places advertising for sellers seeking to find customers for their products.

Advertising campaign: A series of advertisements with a main theme running through them.

Aided recall: The viewer is given some specific piece of information about the ad before being asked if he or she recalls having seen it.

Allowances: Funds given to retailers and wholesalers based on the amount of product they buy.

Consumer promotion: Offer designed to pull the product through the retail establishment.

Continuity: The length of time the advertising campaign will run in a given medium.

Coupon: Certificate that entitles a consumer to an incentive to buy the product, usually a price reduction or a free sample.

Creative strategy: The strategy that governs and coordinates the development of individual ads and assures that their visual images and words convey precisely and consistently what the advertiser wants to communicate.

Cross-selling: Promotion in which the manufacturer of one brand attempts to sell another brand to the same customers, or the purchase of one product is used to stimulate the selection of another, often unrelated product.

Directory advertising: A listing of businesses, their addresses, phone numbers, and sometimes brief descriptions in a publication.

Direct response advertising: Targets individual consumers to get immediate sales.

Exposure: The process of putting the ad in contact with the consumer.

Financing incentive: An offer to finance the retailer's inventory prior to its sale.

Frequency: The number of times the audience is reached in a given period, usually per day or per week.

Informative advertising: Messages designed to provide information that consumers can store for later use.

Institutional advertising: Messages designed to communicate corporate identity and philosophy as opposed to product information.

Media: The channels through which messages are transmitted.

National or brand advertising: Advertising that focuses on brand identity and positioning throughout the country.

Overexposure: Continuing to reach a prospect after a buying decision has been made or to the point that the campaign becomes tedious and actually turns off some potential buyers.

Payout method: Setting the advertising budget to gain initial acceptance and trial.

Percentage of sales method: Allocating a percentage of anticipated sales to advertising.

Persuasive advertising: Messages designed to change consumers' attitudes and opinions about products, often listing product attributes, pricing, and other factors that may influence consumer decisions.

Political advertising: Advertising to influence voters.

Press release: A statement written by company personnel and distributed to various media for publication at their discretion.

Public relations (PR): The use of publicity and other nonpaid forms of communication to present the firm and its products positively.

Public service messages: Free advertising that supports societal issues.

Pulling power: The ability to maintain the interest of the consumer to the end of the advertising message.

Reach: The number of consumers in the target audience who can be contacted through a given medium.

Reinforcement advertising: Messages that call attention to specific characteristics of products experienced by the user.

Reminder advertising: Messages that keep the product at the forefront of the consumer's mind.

Retail (local) advertising: Advertising that focuses attention on nearby outlets where products and services can be purchased.

Retailer promotion: An offer to the consumer that is sponsored by a retailer.

Sales contest: A competition for salespeople and dealers that awards prizes for accomplishing specific goals.

Sales promotion: Communications designed to stimulate immediate purchases using tools such as coupons, contests, and free samples.

Specialty items: Gifts with the organization's name that are provided to customers, usually given through the mail or by the sales force.

Stopping power: The ability of an ad to gain and hold the consumer's attention.

Trade promotion: An offer from a manufacturer to channel members, such as wholesalers and retailers.

Unaided recall: The viewer is asked to identify any advertisements he or she can remember.

REFERENCES

1. Theresa Howard, "Products Wrapped, Tied with Film Companies Getting Savvier About Linking with Movies," *USA Today,* November 15, 2000, p. 3B; "Rite Aid 'Grinched Out' for the Holidays; Special the Grinch Toys Available Only at Rite Aid," *Business Wire,* November 17, 2000; Tom Dochat, "Rite Aid Corp. and Hershey Foods Corp. Are Hoping the Grinch Will Be a Christmas Money-Maker, Not a Thief," *The Patriot News,* November 17, 2000; W. A., Lee, "Can the Grinch Make a Market for Stored Value?" *The American Banker,* November 9, 2000, p. 11; and "Universal Pictures and Universal Studios Consumer Products Group Announce Joint Promotion with the United States Postal Service for 'Dr. Seuss,'" *PR Newswire,* July 14, 2000.

2. Regis McKenna, "Marketing Is Everything," *Harvard Business Review,* January–February 1991, pp. 65–79; Dick Morris; "Break Through the Clutter," *Chain Store Age,* December 2000, p. 260.

3. Projected based on Ian P. Murphy, "Yearly 7% Growth Seen for Communications Spending," *Marketing News,* October 7, 1996, p. 8; "Marketing Communications and Promotion Strategy," www.pcola. gulf.net/tonypitt/mk15.htm, site visited on February 20, 1997; Kip D. Cassino, "A World of Advertising," *American Demographics,* November 1997, pp. 57–60; and Robert J. Coen, "Ad Revenue Growth Hits 7% in 1997 to Surpass Forecasts," *Advertising Age,* May 18, 1998, p. 50.

4. www.adage.com/dataplace/archives/dp409.html, site visited December 23, 2000.

5. Juliana Koranteng, "Unilever takes top slot in non-U.S. spend," *Business and Industry,* November 2000, p. 36.

6. The following history is taken from William Wells, John Burnett, and Sandra Moriarty, *Advertising* (Upper Saddle River, NJ: Prentice Hall, 1992), pp. 20–29.

7. Warren J. Keegan and Mark C. Green, *Principles of Global Marketing* (Upper Saddle River, NJ: Prentice Hall, 1997), p. 355.

8. Subhash C. Jain, "Standardization of International Marketing Strategy: Some Research Hypotheses," *Journal of Marketing* 53 (January 1989): 70–79.

9. William K. Darley and Denise M. Johnson, "An Exploratory Investigation of the Dimensions of Beliefs toward Advertising in General: A Comparative Analysis of Four Developing Countries," *Journal of International Consumer Marketing* 7, no. 1 (1994): 5–21; and J. Craig Andrews, Srinivas Durvasula, and Richard G. Netemeyer, "Testing the Cross-National Applicability of U.S. and Russia Advertising Belief and Attitude Meaures," *Journal of Advertising* 23 (March 1994): 21.

10. Jeff Jensen, "New NFL Unit Goes after International Fans," *Advertising Age,* November 18, 1996, p. 10; www.nfl.com/international and www.nfleurope.com visited December 21, 2000.

11. David Wessel, "Memo to Marketers: Germany wants to Import American Junk Mail," *Wall Street Journal,* December 10, 1999, p. B1.

12. Associated Press, "Ben & Jerry's Names Odak to CEO Position," *Wall Steet Journal Interactive Edition,* January 2, 1997.

13. Mike Beirne, "Southwest Air, Hershey Link in a Sweet Deal," *Brandweek,* September 4, 2000, p. 6.

14. John R. Boatright, *Ethics and the Conduct of Business* (Upper Saddle River, NJ: Prentice Hall, 1997), p. 277.

15. Barbara Lippert, "Mouthing Off," *Adweek,* June 12, 2000, p. 40.

16. John R. Wilke and Rebecca Buckman, "Microsoft Settles Claim Alleging Deceptive Ads—U.S. Accuses WebTV of Ignoring Extra Charges," *The Wall Street Journal Europe,* October 27, 2000, p. 25.

17. Federal Trade Commission, "Eggland's Best Cholesterol Claims Called Deceptive," released March 13, 1996, www.ftc.gov, site visited February 18, 1997.

18. Gordon Fairclough, "State Disputes Reynolds Claims on New Cigarette," *Wall Street Journal,* October 4, 2000, p. B7A.

19. Federal Trade Commission, ASH (Action on Smoking and Health) Press Release, "Philip Morris Deceptive Ad Campaign Banned in France," June 1996, www.ftc.gov, site visited February 18, 1997.

20. Wells, Burnett, and Moriarty, *Advertising,* p. 10.

21. "Study Reveals the Internet is Top Advertising Medium for Information," *Business Wire,* October 2, 2000.

22. www.landrover.com visited December 21, 2000.

23. "CompuServe to Break New Branding Campaign," www.adage.com, site visited October 13, 1995.

24. Kelly Pate, "McDonalds Executives Visit Denver on Tour Promoting New Ad Campaign," *The Denver Post,* June 30, 2000, as retrieved from the World Wide Web: ptg.djnr.com.

25. Associated Press, "McDonald's New Theme Sounds Like Old Theme," *Marketing News,* March 27, 1995, p. 5.

26. Suein Hwang, "Sony Rolls out PlayStation Ads Despite Shortage," *Wall Street Journal,* October 6, 2000, p. B1.

27. "Advertising-to-Sales Ratios, 1993," *Marketing News,* August 8, 1994, p. 38.

28. Business Research Reports, 2000.

29. J. Thomas Russell and W. Ronald Lane, *Kleppner's Advertising Procedure* (Upper Saddle River, NJ: Prentice Hall, 1993), p. 24.

30. www.adage.com, site visited on December 18, 2000.

31. Richard Babyak, "Demystifying the Asian Consumer," *Appliance Manufacturer,* February 1995, pp. w25–w27.

32. Paula Lyon Andruss, "Thais Sweet on Mom, 'Love' Campaign," *Marketing News,* September 11, 2000, pp. 6–7.

33. *Marketing Update Newsletter,* exton.com, last updated January 15, 1997.

34. "Advertising Age's 50 Best Commercials," www.adage.com, site visited on February 14, 1997.

35. Kevin Merida, "Buddy-Code Lunacy," *The Washington Post,* November 19, 2000, p. W07.

36. "Advertising Age's 50 Best Commercials," www.adage.com, site visited on February 14, 1997.

37. Ibid.

38. Bob Garfield, "Let's Skip a Step: P & G Effort for Cascade Nearly Spotless," *Advertising Age,* September 28, 2000, p. 111.

39. www.ama.com, site visited December 24, 2000.

40. Chuck Ross, "Online Homes Show Lower Usage of TV," www.adage.com, site visited January 13, 1997.

41. "Business: Television Takes a Tumble," *The Economist,* January 20, 2001, pp. 59–60.

42. Chad Rubel, "Radio Tunes in to Post-Buy Analysis of Advertising," *Marketing News,* June 3, 1996, p. 7.

43. Mediamark Research, Inc., Doublebase 1988 Study: 19, cited in "Study of Media Involvement," *Audits & Surveys,* March 1988.

44. Keith L. Alexander, "Billboards Help Media Firms Weather Slowdown 'Resilient' Ad Sector Soars," *USA Today,* December 12, 2000, p. 6B.

45. Steve Kloehn and Terry Armour, "Rodman to be Yanked from Mural," *Chicage Tribune,* April 4, 1996, www.chicago.tribune.com/sports/bulls/bslnr/bsrchive/rodman9.htm.

46. Quentin Hardy, "The Killer Ad Machine," *Forbes,* December 11, 2000, p. 168.

47. "Number of Net Advertisers Quadruples—Report Finds Slowing Growth In Online Ads," *The Toronto Star,* December 5, 2000, p. BU07.

48. Erin Kelly, "This Is One Virus You Want to Spread Viral Marketing Is Cheap and Powerful, and Actually Seems to Sell Things. But Handled Wrong, it Can Be Toxic," *Fortune Magazine,* November 27, 2000, p. 297.

49. Karen Benezra and T. L. Stanley, "Slack-O Bell: Taco King Promo Tack Hits Where Gen X Lives," *Brandweek,* November 7, 1994, pp. 1, 6; Louise Kramer, "Chihuahua Gets Muzzled as Taco Bell Pushes Value," *Advertising Age,* November 29, 1999, p. 21.

50. Judann Pollack, "Weight Loss Rivals Boost Ad Budgets for New Year Rush," www.adage.com, January 6, 1997; Gail Kemp, "Radiowatch," *Marketing,* February 1, 2001, p. 8.

51. Brian Toyne and Peter G. P. Walters, *Global Market Management* (Boston: Allyn & Bacon, 1993), p. 250.

52. "International Marketing Nightmares," *Marketing Update Newsletter,* exton.com, site visited on August 15, 1996.

53. Adapted from Peter D. Bennett, *Dictionary of Marketing Terms* (Chicago: American Marketing Association, 1988), p. 179.

54. Projected based on "Marketing Communications and Promotion Strategy."

55. www.aol.com, site visited December 2000.

56. Robert D. Buzzell, John A. Quelch, and Walter J. Salmon, "The Costly Bargain of Trade Promotions," *Harvard Business Review,* March–April 1990, pp. 141–149.

57. "Consumers Remain High on Promotions," *Marketing Times,* March–April 1993, p. 11.

58. Terry Lefton, "GTE Bails Out of Scanner Based Program," *Brandweek,* March 1, 1993, pp. 1, 6.

59. "Consumers Fight Back as Online Tracking Spreads," *San Jose Mercury News,* February 12, 2000

60. Shultz, p. 31.

61. Cyndee Miller, "Marketer Hoping Kids Will Join Club, Become Lifelong Customers," *Marketing News,* January 31, 1994, pp. 1–2, www.burgerking.com and www.newstimes.com/archive99/jun1999/bzc.htm visited December 20, 2000.

62. Jack Neff, "T.G.I. Fridays, P&G Tie-In Continues with Coupons: TV Supports In-Restaurant Tie for New Produce Rinse," *Advertising Age,* August 21, 2000, p. 16.

63. "Church Reclaims Sunday with Ads," *Marketing,* December 16, 1993, p. 5.

64. Katherine Yung, "7 Up Struggles to Regain Market Share from Sprite," *The Dallas Morning News,* September 8, 1999, as retrieved from the World Wide Web: ptg.djnr.com.

65. Marijon Shearer, "New York-Based Book Retailer Opens Store in Harrisburg, PA, Area," *The Patroit News,* November 22, 2000, as retrieved from the World Wide Web: ptg.djnr.com.

66. Joan Flanagan, "Spaghetti Dinners Raising Friends and Money," *Fund Raising Management,* July 1994, pp. 29–32.

67. Business/Professional Advertising Association, 1992.

68. Projected to 2001 based on data in Pat Friedlander, "When Is It Time to Get a New Booth?" *Business Marketing,* February 1993, p. 48.

69. www.tscentral.com, site visited December 20, 2000.

70. ttisms.com/oss/contests.html, site visited on February 14, 1997.

71. "The Incentive Edge: Case Study: Establishing Goals Simple & Specific," *Sales and Marketing Management,* May 1994, p. 8.

72. Vincent Alonzo, "Showering Dealers with Incentives," *Sales and Marketing Management,* October 1999, pp. 24–26.

73. www.att.com/college, site visited December 20, 2000.

74. "Learn ABC of Promos & Add Zing to Brands," *The Economic Times,* August 9, 2000, as retrieved from the World Wide Web: ptg.djnr.com.

75. "Sony Electronics Announces National Modern Rock Live Retail Promotion," www.sel.sony.com/SEL/consumer/ss5/press_releases/mrock.htm, site visited November 16, 1997.

76. Schultz, p. 31.

77. Capil Bawa and Robert W. Shoemaker, "The Coupon-Prone Consumer," *Journal of Marketing,* October 1987, pp. 99–110.

78. "Coupon Users Need Incentive," *Promotional Sense,* June 1992, p. 1.

79. "Coupons on Demand," www.wyattweb.com/freepage/s/sjm@bright.net/home.shtml, site visited February 14, 1997.

80. www.hp.com, site visited December 2000.

81. Lefton, "Try It: You'll Like It"; Laurie Freeman, "Direct Contact Key to Building Brands," *Advertising Age,* October 25, 1993, p. S2; and "Consumer Promotional Activity Rises," *Food Institute Report,* May 31, 1993, p. 3.

82. Lefton, "Try It: You'll Like It."

83. disney.go.com/features/sweepstakes/magicsweeps00/index.html, site visited December 20, 2000.

84. Rebeca Piirto Heath, "Pop Art," *Marketing Tools,* April 1997, www.marketingtools.com.

85. Ibid.

86. "Eastar Copolyster by Eastman used in P-O-P Display for Sega of America

Products," www.eastman.com/ppbo/displays/pr/sega.shtml, site visited February 14, 1997.

87. Riccardo A. Davis, "Gun Exchange Strikes Nerve," *Advertising Age,* January 3, 1994, pp. 3, 38; Geoffrey Smith and Ron Stodghill II, "Are Good Causes Good Marketing?" *Business Week,* March 21, 1994, pp. 64–65; "Sponsors Sing a Profitable Tune in Concert with Event Promos," *Brandweek,* January 24, 1994, p. 20; and Nancy Arnott, "Marketing with a Passion," *Sales and Marketing Management,* January 1994, pp. 64–71.

88. Jane Bryant Quinn, "Cause Marketing One Way to Give to Charities," *Pittsburgh Post-Gazette,* December 18, 2000, p. E-2.

89. "Best of Show—Public Relations Sowing the Seeds of Persuasion," *Agri-Marketing,* April 1994, p. 64, www.bc.edu/bc_org/avp/csom/cccr/Publications/article_1_98.htm.

90. Elizabeth Jensen, "Marketers Lure Baby Boomers at Trendy Food-Wine Festivals," *Wall Street Journal Interactive Edition,* July 3, 1997.

91. "In the Name of Experience," *The Economist,* November 25, 2000.

92. Mark Gleason, "Edelman Sees Niche in Web Public Relations," *Advertising Age,* January 20, 1997, www.adage.com.

93. Kate Fitzsimmons, "Retirement Expert Girard Miller to Host Web Chat Session," *Wall Street Journal Interactive Edition,* July 10, 1997.

Bricks or Clicks

GAP RETAIL OUTLETS CONNECT WITH GAP.COM.

GAP HAS BEEN A RECOGNIZED name in clothing since 1969. How has Gap's image stayed fresh in the minds of consumers all these years? The answer is mass communications. Gap has continuously run advertisements and sales promotions. When Gap decided to establish a Web presence in 1997, getting the site name and address (gap.com) to the public eye was no problem. A massive advertising campaign was launched initially, and continued exposure comes in many forms.

At Gap retail outlets, the gap.com Web address is seen everywhere—display windows, computer kiosks, receipts, and printed on shopping bags. Catalogs, credit card statements, and sale postcards all prominently display the existence of the online shop. All types of media are utilized by Gap's campaign, including newspaper ads, TV commercials, billboards, and magazines. Advertisements for the store always include the Web address. Gap's advertisements tend to be institutional—the messages communicate its identity, its image, and there is less emphasis on product information. This creative strategy has helped shape all ads in a consistent manner.

Gap did have one advantage when it launched its site. It already had a recognized, respected brand. When an e-retailer has an offline brand, traffic tends to come cheaper and more is derived from each marketing dollar. But Gap has been particularly successful with gap.com, even when compared to other companies with similar brand success. The reason is its focus on simplicity.

Gap's clothing is known for its simplicity of style. The corresponding simplicity found on gap.com is simplicity of use. The chain's trademark, clean, uncluttered look has been transferred to the World Wide Web. You will find no unnecessary features on the site that may increase download time. The site's easygoing navigation and straightforward links have helped earn it a number-one ranking and numerous awards, including the 2000 Best Brick and Mortar Brand Online from IQ's Interactive Marketing Awards.

Standardization is the key to Gap's strategy. The online shopping experience parallels that of the in-store experience—there are no price discrepancies or tedious return policies. Customer service devices are easy to find on the site, which demonstrates that Gap understands the importance of building and maintaining customer relationships. In a World Wide Web of increasing complexity, gap.com has proven that it pays to keep it simple.

Sources: Ann M. Mack, "Gap.com: Best Brick and Mortar Brand Online," *Adweek,* June 5, 2000.

CASE 15

Super Bowl Advertising

AT THE END OF JANUARY every year, people all over the world gather around the television for one of the biggest events of the year: Super Bowl commercials. With some exceptions, the commercials often outweigh lopsided games for pure entertainment value and companies pay top dollar to put their best advertising efforts forth. In 2001, businesses expected to be paying $2.3 to $2.4 million for the desirable 30-second spots. Bob Scarpelli, senior vice president and chief creative officer of DDB Needham, Chicago, said: "Super Bowl day is the Super Bowl of advertising. The Super Bowl has evolved to the point where people watch the ads more than the game." CBS took full advantage of its Super Bowl coverage. The pregame show for 2001 began at noon Eastern Time, two full hours earlier than the previous year. That translated into two more hours of high-priced ad time for CBS. In addition, E-Trade headed up sponsorship of MTV's half-time show. After making a favorable impression with its ad campaign during Super Bowl XXXIV, the online brokerage firm went all out in 2001 with five pregame spots, the half-time show, and two in-game commercials.

Since many Super Bowl spots are seen just once, the punch must be exceptional. One of the statistics that sets Super Bowl Sunday so far apart from most other television programs is its holding power. The 2000 Super Bowl between the St. Louis Rams and the Tennessee Titans kept 99.4 percent of its viewing audience during commercial breaks. That means that the advertisements annually have the highest exposure of any other television event. The Super Bowl of 2000 could unofficially be dubbed "the dot-com Super Bowl," with high-tech companies wielding large amounts of advertising dollars to grab online consumers' collective attention. However, with many of the Internet start-ups sinking after taking a beating in the stock market throughout 2000, dot-com participants are way down in 2001 from the previous year's 19. Most Super Bowl ads are stand-alone spots, but a cost of $2.3 million requires more than just a typical commercial. The advertising industry sees the event as a chance to showcase talent, and risks are often taken with content and even the timing of ads. However, focusing on being the most clever or humorous commercial sometimes causes spots to lose their main objective: to convey a message to the customer.

Reviews of Super Bowl XXXIV's commercial performance showed some definite winners and losers. Ads such as Britannica.com, WebMD, and EDS may have outsmarted themselves by creating spots that had stopping power or were entertaining but failed to communicate the purpose of the business. Advertisers may be falling into the trap of chasing the unattainable ad: the "1984" Apple Macintosh computer ad. The 60-second commercial that ran during Super Bowl XVIII is thought by many to be the most innovative and effective spot of all time. It used drama, brilliant positioning, and a simple message to introduce its relatively new product as a competitor to the already established IBM. It subtly preyed on people's fears of being controlled by technology and moved them to do something while being visually appealing at the same time. Many unsuccessful ads obtain either one or the other of these factors in grand fashion but miss the other completely. With the high costs of time slots for the Super Bowl spots and high production costs for many of the more attention-grabbing commercials, one ad could send a upstart company spiraling to its doom. However, it can also be a launching pad to introduce a business or revitalize a struggling company.

Reebok ran an all-out advertising assault during high-profile television events, including the Super Bowl and *Survivor II*, to promote the strongest product line its had in years and attempt to recapture some of its former market share. Reebok budgeted for a $90 million ad campaign that doubled its previous media spending and kicked off at this year's Super Bowl. "This is really an extraordinary opportunity for us, because we are more attached to *Survivor* than any other sponsor and the Super Bowl would be a great launching pad for a new campaign," said John Wardley, vice president of global marketing at Reebok. "It won't be celebrity- or athlete-based, and [it] has to be a simple message. One of the things we've been guilty of is having complicated marketing messages and then not sticking to them." If Reebok makes a comeback and regains its position as Nike's main competitive concern, perhaps it will be looked at as the successor to Apple's "1984" campaign.

Yet, many experts believe that Super Bowl advertising may not be a smart buy. Ted Bell, vice chairman, world wide creative director of Young & Rubicam, New York, says: "It's become advertising's in-joke, all these agency guys trying to outdo each other. It's about who can have the coolest commercial. It's self-indulgence on the part of the ad industry." According to Bob Scarpelli at DDB Needham, "Many clients want to be on the Super Bowl just to be on the Super Bowl. The CEO wants his name on the Super Bowl. It's almost like bragging rights."

1. *What should a marketer consider in deciding whether to advertise at the Super Bowl? Would this differ for a smaller organization versus a larger company?*
2. *What qualities must an ad possess in order to gain attention at the Super Bowl?*
3. *Recall one of your favorite Super Bowl ads and describe what elements made it successful from your perspective.*

Sources: Ellen Newborne and Roger Crockett, "More Bang for the Super Bowl Bucks," *Business Week,* February 2, 1998, p. 70; Eleftheria Parpis, "Playing for the Ring," *AdWeek,* January 19, 1998, p. 29; Steve Hamm, "This Year's Super Bowl Hero?" *Business Week,* January 19, 1998, p. 6; Scott Andron, "Volvo Trucks Buys Super Bowl Ad," *Greensboro (North Carolina) News & Record,* November 16, 1997, p. E1; Kyle Pope, "NBC Scores Big with the Super Bowl; Game Is Among Most Watched Ever," *Wall Street Journal Interactive Edition,* January 27, 1998; Michael Kraus, "The Season Ahead; Back to Branding Basics," *Marketing News,* September 11, 2000, pp. 11–12; Terry Lefton, "Rescuing Reebok," *Brandweek,* September 18, 2000, pp. 1, 61; John Dempsey, "Top Spex Nearly Zap-Proof," *Variety,* October 16–October 22, 2000, p. 123; Richard Tedesco, "CBS Seeing $150M," *Broadcasting and Cable,* November 6, 2000, p. 34; and Michael McCarthy and Theresa Howard, "CBS Profits from Super Bowl Hype; Network Signs Sponsors for Pregame, Postgame Shows," *USA Today,* November 28, 2000, p. B3.

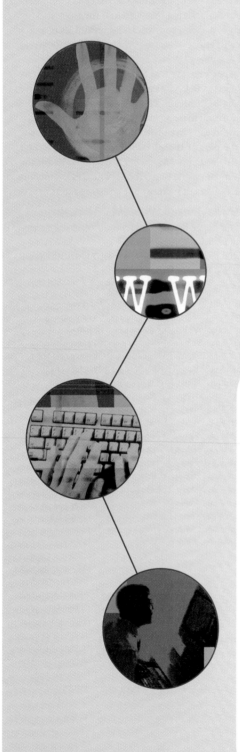

PERSONAL SELLING AND SALES FORCE MANAGEMENT

◀ *Mike Ruettgers, EMC Corp. CEO*

THE LIST OF CUSTOMERS WHO BUY *high-powered electronic data storage systems from EMC Corporation reads like a who's who of the corporate world. Traditional businesses such as Delta Air Lines, Visa International, MCI WorldCom, and Charles Schwab, as well as e-businesses such as Excite and Amazon.com, are just some of the hundreds of companies that rely on EMC products to keep their valuable data on customers, transactions, products, and Web pages safe and accessible.*

EMC, based in Hopkinton, Massachusetts, was founded in 1979 to make memory devices for minicomputers. Under the leadership of Michael Ruettgers, who became CEO in 1992, EMC refocused on large-scale storage systems for mainframe computers and added specialized software for data storage, management, and recovery. Today EMC holds an impressive 35 percent share of the data storage market, which is growing 80 percent per year. To keep up with this fast-growing demand, EMC is expanding its global workforce from 16,000 to 20,000 employees and is preparing its sales force to meet the CEO's goal of surpassing $12 billion in annual revenues.

The sales process was less complicated when EMC sold only memory enhancements. Now EMC's salespeople make multiple sales calls to forge a close working relationship with the chief information officer of each prospect firm. As the relationship develops, the sales rep learns more about the firm's data storage requirements and then recommends the appropriate combination of hardware and software components. Supporting the sales process, CEO Ruettgers spends about 20 percent of his time building relationships with customers and prospects and discussing the latest developments in storage technology.

The EMC sales force is structured according to segment, so reps become knowledgeable about the industries they service and the storage challenges their customers face. EMC's customer-focused brand of personal selling requires meticulous attention to detail and a thorough understanding of how different EMC products fit in a broad range of systems configurations. The job is so demanding, in fact, that EMC's attrition rate among sales personnel has spiked to 25 percent; by comparison, 15 percent attrition is common in the industry over all.

The company sets aggressive sales goals but provides a rich package of financial incentives for peak performance. With salary, commissions, stock options, and bonuses, EMC's top salespeople earn more than $1 million annually. In addition, Ruettgers relies on some unconventional but effective nonfinancial techniques for motivating the sales force. For example, Ruettgers recently established ambitious first-year sales goals for a new product line. However, sales lagged well below goals during the first six months of the sales campaign. So the CEO had giant cartons of unsold storage equipment delivered to each sales manager's office, along with a note explaining that the cartons would be removed when sales reached planned levels. "I wanted them to know this was not business as usual," Ruettgers remembers. Within three months, sales were back on track, and the cartons disappeared.

In recent years, EMC has been targeting a new category of prospects. Until the emergence of e-commerce, EMC's typical customer made $500 million in annual sales and employed 2,000 or more people. Now demand for data storage systems is especially strong among Internet firms, which would ordinarily be classified *as small businesses because they have fewer than 100 employees and their sales are less than $15 million. Despite these demographics, data are the lifeblood of these growing e-businesses; any disruption in the availability of information would be extremely costly. As a result, data storage and protection devices are must-haves for e-businesses—so firms in this segment turn out to be ideal prospects for EMC's sales staff.*

Competition is putting even more pressure on EMC's sales force. IBM and Compaq, two of EMC's largest rivals, recently forged an alliance to sell each other's storage systems and ensure compatibility between systems, so customers can mix and match as needed. Fighting back, EMC linked with Electronic Data Systems to jointly sell online storage systems and services for e-commerce applications. EMC also appointed dedicated teams of sales and engineering personnel to help Internet service providers, network providers, and other e-business customers set up complex online storage systems. Although these actions add another level of complexity to the sales process, they also open new opportunities for EMC's sales professionals.[1]

THE CONCEPTS OF PERSONAL SELLING AND SALES MANAGEMENT

Successful people nearly always "sell" their ideas. Broadly speaking, any time one party attempts to motivate the behavior of another party through personal contact, some form of selling takes place. When was the last time you tried to influence someone by expressing your point of view? Did you try to convince a friend to go to a movie you wanted to see or to a restaurant you wanted to visit? Whether intentional or not, you were engaged in the kind of communication that is at the heart of personal selling. It is through interpersonal contact that leaders influence the behavior of others. Although an attempt to influence people is not always labeled personal selling, it has the same characteristics. What makes personal selling a profession and not just interpersonal influence? It focuses on creating the economic exchange that is at the center of marketing. Salespeople sell customers on products.

Personal selling is one of the most prevalent and highest-paid occupations in the United States. For every person employed in advertising, there are more than 30 jobs in sales.[2] The sales and marketing sector is expanding at a great rate—by 2008, employment in marketing and sales is expected to increase by 15 percent or by 2.3 million additional workers.[3] Furthermore, personal selling pays well, and compensation is rising dramatically. In some categories, top sales executives on average earn more than $83,000 a year; the average income in 1998 was $54,600.[4] It is not unusual for salespeople to make hundreds of thousands or more than a million dollars annually. Part of Cisco Systems' success in sales is its pay plan structure in which some salespeople earn $1 million or more a year.[5]

Whether you are planning a professional sales career or simply want to sell your ideas more effectively, you'll find this chapter very helpful. We begin by describing the different types of sales personnel and selling situations. Next, a comparison of various selling approaches emphasizes the importance of relationship selling. This is followed by a section on the responsibilities of the salesperson, both to the customer and to the company. We then walk through each of the steps involved in personal selling—from planning and prospecting to closing the sale and providing follow-up service. The final personal selling section, which describes the four characteristics of strong salespeople, may help you determine if sales would be a good career choice for you.

Although a salesperson in a small start-up company may work fairly independently (recall the lone Coach salesman in chapter 12), as a company grows its management must begin to think in terms of a sales force, sales teams, and sales managers. Good sales force management is needed to coordinate and inspire the efforts of these personnel and to integrate their efforts with the overall marketing plan. In the second half of the chapter we examine the five key functions of sales management: organizing the sales force, developing diverse sales teams, preparing forecasts and budgets, implementing sales actions, and overseeing sales force activities. We conclude with information about sales force automation.

Figure 16.1 diagrams the topics in personal selling. We will examine each of these in turn.

TYPES OF SALES PERSONNEL AND SELLING SITUATIONS

The many titles for sales positions tend to describe the type of activity performed: sales executive, sales engineer, sales consultant, sales counselor, representative, account executive, account representative, territory representative, management representative, technical representative, marketing representative, agent, and sales associate. Many times the title of vice president is conferred on top-level salespeople who have important sales responsibilities but may have few if any people reporting to them.

Some common categories of salespeople are described in Figure 16.2. **Direct sales** occur when a salesperson interacts with a consumer or company in order to make a sale. **Missionary sales** are made by people who do not take orders but influence purchase by recommending or specifying a product to others. For example, textbook salespeople influence professors, who then require students to purchase a particular book for a class. Likewise, physicians prescribe drugs, golf professionals recommend a brand of clubs, and travel agents help select vacation packages.

The circumstances in which selling occurs can be categorized as executive and team selling, field selling, over-the-counter selling, inside sales, and global sales. Because each category involves a different setting, the activities of salespeople differ accordingly.

Executive and Team Selling   Although many people are employed in personal selling, the statistics don't count the numerous individuals with nonsales titles who spend much of their time on sales activities. Many executives, irrespective of their area, view personal selling as one of their primary functions. They not only communicate with the board of directors and employees in order to "sell" corporate policies but also frequently interact with major customers and suppliers.

Team selling involves people from most parts of the organization, including top executives, who work together to create relationships with the buying organization. In 2000, Boeing had 113 orders for its big airliner, the 777, a sales record at $18 billion.[6] Corporate executives were deeply committed to the effort, although most of the responsibility still remained with the sales force. In a high-technology business such as aircraft manufacturing, nearly every function gets involved in the sales process. At Boeing it is the salesperson's job to coordinate contact

DIRECT SALES

Sales that result from the salesperson's direct interaction with a consumer or company.

MISSIONARY SALES

Sales made indirectly through people who do not obtain orders but influence the buying decision of others.

TEAM SELLING

Selling that involves people from most parts of the organization, including top executives, working together to create a relationship with the buying organization.

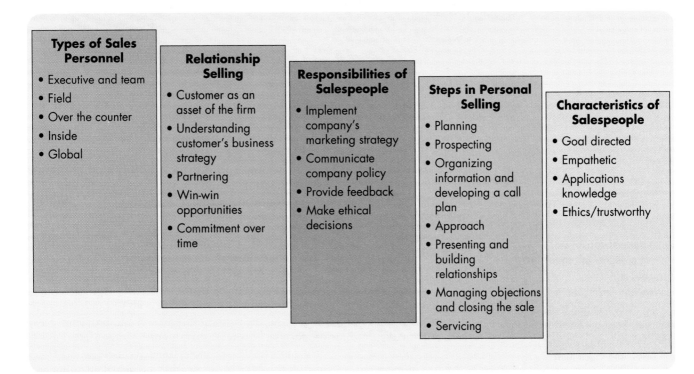

FIGURE 16.1 *The Concept of Personal Selling*

	ACTIONS	EXAMPLE
Telemarketing Representative (Direct)	Uses telephone to contact customers to receive orders.	People who respond to callers of 800 numbers (Gateway 2000).
Inside Sales Support (Missionary)	Works inside the seller's company to support the sales representatives who make face-to-face call on customer. Uses telephone and other non-face-to-face communication to help customers.	Westinghouse salesperson who sells without traveling to a customer's site.
Field Salesperson (Direct)	Meet face-to-face with customers.	Nike salesperson calling on retail sporting goods chain.
Technical Salesperson (Direct)	Meets face-to-face with customers to sell very technical products that need to be customized or explained in technical ways.	Square D salesperson (engineering background) calling on an electric utility.
Detail Person (Missionary)	Meets with people who influence the sale of a company's products but may not purchase directly.	Eli Lilly salesperson who calls on doctors to increase prescription rate for Lilly products.
Service Salesperson (Direct)	Sells intangible products, such as insurance and real estate, to a broad range of customers.	Prudential salesperson who sells a life insurance policy.
Retail Salesperson (Direct)	Associates or clerks selling items in a retail outlet.	Saturn salesperson working in showroom.

FIGURE 16.2 *Types of Sales Personnel*

CONNECTED: SURFING THE NET

www.boeing.com

Learn more about the world's leading producer of commercial airplanes and its successful team-selling effort. Go inside Boeing by connecting to its Web site. Read the latest top story, take a tour, read financial news, and much more.

between the company and the technical, financial, and planning personnel from the airline. Even if the CEO is brought in, it is not unusual for the salesperson to remain in charge of the sale using the CEO when appropriate. The salespeople perform the leadership function because they know all aspects of their customers' business. They also must be thoroughly familiar with Boeing's services. This includes cost-per-seat calculations, computerized route simulations, and many other analysis tools Boeing uses to show how it can fulfill customer needs.[7]

Field Selling   Field selling occurs at a consumer's residence or at a customer's place of business. Field representatives spend most of their time, as the name implies, away from their company and near customers. Their job is to discover prospects, make contact, and create relationships. By working with customers in their own environment, field reps have ample opportunity to understand the customer's circumstances in depth. The best performers in field selling are often skilled at learning about the customer's situation and problems. Field sales in consumer markets include products such as real estate, home building and remodeling, landscape maintenance, and even computers. For example, Hand Technologies sells personal computers in the home, where sales consultants can provide individual attention and have plenty of uninterrupted time.[8]

This Lotus ad showcases Mail Boxes Etc.'s success with their product. This is an example of missionary sales.

Field selling to businesses and distributors is also common. It is used for nearly every imaginable industrial product, for pharmaceutical sales to physicians and hospitals, and for selling consulting, accounting, and business management services to manufacturers and retailers. Merck, a leader in health care products, sends sales reps to hospitals, clinics, government agencies, drug wholesalers, and retailers, among others. In 1999, Merck salespeople sold $32.7 billion in goods and services to other businesses and organizations.[9]

career tip At Hewlett-Packard, field sales trainees are responsible for attending formal training classes and performance of appropriate projects. They develop sales through customer presentations, demos, trade shows, and territory management, as well as conduct customer and competitive research. Hewlett-Packard offers worldwide employment opportunities as well as leadership and development programs geared toward high-performing, high-potential sales professionals. If you think you might be interested in a sales career at Hewlett-Packard, connect to its Web site at www.jobs.hp.com. You will have an opportunity to learn about the company's recruiting process, events, and internships.

Field sales occur in a customer's place of business or a consumer's home.

Over-the-Counter Selling   Over-the-counter selling occurs in a retail outlet. Examples include furniture, clothing, and jewelry stores as well as auto dealerships. Customers are drawn to the salesperson by the attraction of the store itself or by advertising and sales promotion. Salespeople need to be skilled at identifying the customer's requirements quickly, often in a single encounter, and at providing the appropriate service at the point of sale. Helping consumers the first time brings them back, which provides the opportunity to gain a loyal customer. It also creates good word of mouth, which brings in friends and relatives of satisfied customers. Successful over-the-counter salespeople tend to build loyal relationships by becoming knowledgeable about the unique tastes of customers. This occurs while working with them on numerous transactions over a long period.

Inside Sales   Inside sales involve one-to-one contact with the customer via the telephone. Mail-order companies are a good example. At L.L. Bean, sales representatives know the products, how they fit, how to ship them quickly, and how to repair and care for them. L.L. Bean's Web site offers customers the opportunity to chat with salespeople online to provide them with a helpful, pleasant experience so that they will be likely to use the service again.[10] Another example is the banks of telephone sales representatives who take orders in response to advertisements and infomercials. Sometimes they perform only a clerical function, since the consumer already is sold on the product, but many of these people do an excellent job of answering questions and selling additional items. A variation is telephone marketers who solicit business by calling people at home or at work. Usually the intent is to sell products, but sometimes the purpose is to obtain a home visit for field salespeople.

Another form of inside sales is to work with established clients primarily by phone. Stock brokerage firms conduct much of their business this way. Many manufacturers and distributors have field reps and inside salespeople who work together with large customers. The reps solicit business at the customer's site, and inside sales personnel are ready at all times to provide technical support and take orders via the phone. This form of inside sales can be critical for industrial companies.[11] These inside sales people are increasingly more educated and trained about products, acting more as consultants for the customer. This service is crucial for recruiting and retaining customers. Karen Leland of the Sterling Consulting Group notes that these people become "customer advocate partners with the customer." Furthermore, notes the CEO of K.J. Electric, inside sales forces make more than five times the calls outside forces make. Inside sales forces were key to the company's growth.[12] It is also a first job for many technical salespeople, since they can learn about company policies and products while receiving plenty of help with their first customer contacts. Once experience is gained inside, these people often take a field sales position.

Global Sales   It is difficult to overstate the importance of personal selling in global markets.[13] Many of these sales involve millions or even billions of dollars. For example, YTL Corporation selected Siemens AG of Germany and General Electric of the United States, among others, as bidders on a $750 million order for power generation turbines. One reason GE lost was its failure to send a top executive to help make the sale. YTL's managing director said: "I wanted to look them in the eye to see if we can do business."[14] Even as today's communication becomes increasingly more technological, many cultures adhere to personal relationships as the foundation of business. According to John Castor, president of Teralogic, this individual attention remains crucial in Japan, where "breaking in and building is a larger exercise [. . .] You have to be willing to work for years in some cases without giving up. . . ." This includes sending top company executives abroad to meet the client.[15]

In the domestic arena, companies and their representatives often become accepted in a short period, but this may take years in a foreign environment. To overcome this resistance, many companies use domestic personnel from the host country to represent them. But this can cause problems if personal selling is not considered a prestigious occupation in that culture. Furthermore, finding and training qualified people can be challenging and expensive. Yet salespeople from the home office are less knowledgeable about the local business climate.[16]

As a compromise solution, companies often rely on nationals to provide information and make initial customer contact but send salespeople from headquarters on regular visits to establish relationships and negotiate larger contracts. Pete Macking, vice president of sales for UPS, frequently travels abroad for that purpose. Although he has considerable overseas experience, he still works with foreign nationals affiliated with UPS.[17]

Some companies find a local partner to facilitate their business abroad. Trade.com, affiliated with BlueStone Capital Partners, tried to establish its financial network worldwide, but found it impossible to do without working with financial institutions that were familiar to the local culture.[18] For tips on global etiquette, see the diversity feature, "A Few Do's and Taboos for the Round-the-World Rep."

CONNECTING WITH DIVERSITY

A Few Do's and Taboos for the Round-the-World Rep

 Many selling skills that work in the United States also work overseas, but knowing how to act in certain cultures can make the difference in closing a sale. For instance, the simple thumbs-up sign that Americans use every day may offend a customer in the Middle East. And while health nuts often sip seltzer at a U.S. business lunch, in Japan it is bad manners to refuse a stronger drink. Here are a few global p's and q's gathered from a number of international business experts:

China

- Negotiating is an art, and there's no such thing as a quick sale. According to Chin Ning Chu, author of *The Asian Mind Game,* the Chinese "map out negotiating strategies, and follow the game plan until they get a contract the way they want it."
- The more sales reps know about the culture the better. "Chinese business people will accept Americans more if they make an effort to learn about their society," says Chu.
- Printed materials presented to buyers should be in black and white, since colors can have great significance for the Chinese.

Japan

- Gift giving at a first meeting is the norm. Consultants suggest a high-quality item with a designer logo or brand name.
- The neck is considered an erogenous zone; women sales reps are advised to wear high-necked blouses or a scarf.
- The ever-accommodating Japanese will rarely say no. Instead, they will say "maybe" or "that would be very difficult"—both of which essentially mean no.

Western Europe

- Two- or three-hour meals are not uncommon. Don't be in a rush to end a meal and talk business. Follow the lead of the host.
- In France, don't schedule a breakfast meeting. The French tend not to meet before 10:00 A.M.
- Although many Europeans will discuss family matters, the Germans, the Swiss, and Scandinavians consider it rude.

Mexico

- Respect for seniors is always important. And it's customary to shake hands with everyone upon arrival and departure.
- A yes does not always mean yes. Mexican social etiquette makes it difficult to say no.
- In Mexico, as in China and Japan, business cards are used extensively. Sales reps should come armed with a large supply. Cards should be as descriptive as possible, noting any professional degrees or special titles.

Latin America

- Scheduling more than two appointments per day is unwise. Attitudes about time are casual.
- Emotions and trust are important elements in the buying process. No one purchases unless they're absolutely comfortable with the salesperson. According to David Charner of the English Resource Center in Caracas, Venezuela, which runs sales training programs: "Here we have to focus our training on searching for feelings, finding the hidden motivator that determines a buying decision."

The Middle East

- Always use the right hand to hold, offer, or receive materials. The left is used to touch toilet paper. People who write left-handed should apologize for doing so.

Continued

- In Egypt, paperwork and bureaucratic procedures make business processes slow. It may take a year or more to obtain a contract you could get in America in a week. And be careful not to tap two fingers together. It is a message that a couple is sleeping together.

Sources: Andy Cohen, "Getting to Yes, Chinese-Style," *Sales and Marketing Management,* July 1996, pp. 44–45; Andy Cohen, "Small World, Big Challenge," *Sales and Marketing Management,* June 1996, pp. 69–73; Andy Cohen, "Global Do's and Don'ts," *Sales and Marketing Management,* June 1996, p. 72; Marjorie Whigham-Desir, "Business Etiquette Overseas," *Black Enterprise,* October 1995, pp. 142–143; "Mexico: Yes Does Not Always Mean Yes," *Business America,* p. 18; and Roger E. Axtell, *Do's and Taboos Around the World* (New York: John Wiley & Sons, 1994).

RELATIONSHIP AND OTHER SELLING APPROACHES

All employees are important in building and maintaining customer relationships, but salespeople are critical because that is their primary responsibility. *One Size Fits One,* a popular book on the subject, says we are entering a world "where emphasis is less on building short-term satisfaction than on instilling long-term loyalty. And a world where relationships are the currency and the committed employees who maintain and nurture them are the primary source of competitive advantage."[19] If salespeople do not have the competencies and desire to build relationships one customer at a time, then no amount of support from all the other company employees will make up the deficit.

Today, business strategies focus on creating relationships rather than simply selling products. Companies are entering into joint activities in record numbers, and selling organizations must work closely with customers to help them accomplish their goals. Sellers must understand the consumer's lifestyle or how the customer's business works. Consequently, sales organizations are shifting from traditional ways of doing business to a new emphasis on building relationships. The three basic sales approaches are shown in Figure 16.3: traditional sales, consultative sales, and relationship selling.

TRADITIONAL SALES APPROACH
Emphasizing persuasive techniques to get consumers to buy a company's products.

The Traditional Sales Approach   The **traditional sales approach** focuses on persuading consumers to buy a company's products, thereby raising sales volume. Remember that the Industrial Revolution produced goods in record quantities. Output grew more rapidly than demand. During the first half of this century, the purpose of personal selling was to stimulate sales. Firms no longer needed to find ways to produce more in order to keep up with demand. Instead, they had to sell more in order to keep up with increased production. The salesperson's focus was on pushing the company's products, especially features and

	Traditional Sales	Consultative Sales	Relationship Selling
Focus	Understand your product	Understand customer's problems	Understand customer's business or lifestyle
Role of the customer	Prospect	Target	Asset of the business
Salesperson focus	Persuasion	Problem solving	Partnering
Salesperson role	Obtain sales volume	Advise customers	Building win-win circumstances
Objective	Profit through sales volume	Profit through problem solving	Profit through strategic relationships and customer satisfaction

FIGURE 16.3 *Major Sales Approaches*

functions, to increase the sales volume. Prospects were persuaded to buy. Techniques for persuasive selling, which taught salespeople how to negotiate, were often the dominant subject of sales training courses. Essentially, sellers and buyers tried to see who could get the best deal.

The Consultative Sales Approach   For many organizations, the traditional sales era continued well into the 1970s. As the marketing function became more important, however, the sales function also took on new responsibilities. Marketing began to focus on serving customers, and selling had to change with it. **Consultative selling** means working closely with customers to help solve their problems. Salespeople are expected to understand how their company's products can do that. Essentially, the salesperson becomes an advisor to customers rather than a negotiator seeking the best deal. In order for this type of selling to be successful, salespeople must work closely with the customer over an extended period. Customers on all levels, from individuals to businesses, are spending more time in the decision-making process, creating an "extended buying cycle."[20] Consequently, this has been dubbed long-cycle selling.[21] At Merck, salespeople are educated in medical sciences. They then act as consultants to their customers and may even suggest a competitor's product if it would better suit the customer.[22] Consultative selling stops just short of relationship selling.

Relationship Selling   **Relationship selling** attempts to forge bonds between buyers and sellers in an effort to gain loyalty and mutual satisfaction.[23] Because it promotes loyalty, it is in tune with the strategic nature of marketing. It recognizes that sellers and buyers benefit from one another's success. In today's consumer markets, people want to buy based on relationships with companies that can be counted on to enhance their lifestyle. Businesses are looking for partners who will help them compete. Relationship selling recognizes that the salesperson's role is to create value for the customer as well as the company. Typically, a great deal of work on both sides goes into building and maintaining relationships. The main aspects of relationship selling are discussed in more detail next.

Understanding the Customer's Business Strategy The focus of relationship selling is to uncover strategic needs, develop creative solutions, and arrive at mutually beneficial agreements.[24] Salespeople must recognize that companies buy products to help them run their businesses better. By understanding the customer's business, salespeople are more likely to communicate in meaningful ways with the potential buyer. A. C. Rochester, a division of General Motors that supplies engines and fuel systems to the global automotive industry, "lends" sales engineers to clients to assist with product and program development. They help create product strategies and are very familiar with confidential aspects of the client's business. In effect, they become an integral part of the customer's marketing team. Cisco Systems showed its customer-focused structure when it entered into a deal with U.S. West, a local phone company. U.S. West wanted Cisco Systems to be its infrastructure provider to be able to provide Internet access to individuals and small companies. Cisco not only provided networking hardware but also partnered with several other companies to fully serve U.S. West's needs.[25]

The Customer as an Asset Loyal customers should be viewed as an asset by the firm. Long-term contracts and repeat sales produce predictable sources of revenue. In fact, the worth of many businesses can be calculated by the size of the customer base, such as the number of subscribers of a cellular phone company. Customers are not viewed as prospects for a single sale or as targets for problem solving. Rather, they are partners in a relationship that produces long-term cash flows for the seller. In the highly competitive hotel industry, Marriott International restructured its sales program to make it possible for individuals to earn reward points at one hotel and then take their families on vacation at another. Marriott executives' belief that this would increase customer loyalty and frequency of stays proved to be true. The role of the salesperson is increasingly becoming one of service to the customer over a long time period and in many situations rather than simply selling a product.[26]

Partnering Under the traditional approach, salespeople use persuasion to obtain orders, whereas consultative selling emphasizes the ability to solve customers' problems. In contrast, relationship selling focuses on partnering. Some partnerships are contractual, established through long-term written agreements. Some are noncontractual; that is, the buyer and seller enter into an implied agreement to do business together over time. In either case, a sharing of power occurs. In traditional sales, the balance of power is typically with the salesperson; in consultative selling it is with the customer. Relationship selling involves a symmetrical

CONSULTATIVE SELLING

An approach to selling in which sales personnel work closely with customers to help solve problems.

RELATIONSHIP SELLING

Forging bonds between buyer and seller to gain loyalty and mutual satisfaction.

FIGURE 16.4 *Buyer-Seller Negotiations*

	Buyer Gains	**Buyer Loses**
Seller Gains	Win-Win	Buyer negotiates poorly
Seller Loses	Seller negotiates poorly	Lose-Lose

relationship—both parties have equal authority and responsibility. Both share information to help the other party succeed.[27]

Relationship selling replaces short-term thinking with a perspective that ensures value long after the sale is made. Consequently, just as much work is needed after the sale as before. A strong follow-through makes certain that partnerships are honored.

Building Win-Win Circumstances Historically, buying and selling have involved negotiation. **Negotiation** can be defined as discussions by two or more parties to arrange a transaction. It requires give and take. To some it means that each party tries to maximize its own benefit relative to the other through a power position obtained during the interaction. To others, negotiation is a way to build relationships. As mentioned earlier, in Japan and other cultures it is viewed as a long process that should involve every decision maker. Instead of being seen as conflict or struggle, negotiations can be regarded as information sessions that lead to win-win opportunities.[28]

Figure 16.4 describes the negotiating possibilities. When any party loses, the foundation for building a relationship diminishes greatly. And when one party gains a great deal more than the other, a relationship will not grow or will dissolve over time. A sound relationship requires that each party perceives it has gained value. In other words, lasting relationships involve win-win situations. Even in early meetings with customers, both parties need to win.

Managing Strategic Relationships Account management refers to the activities of a salesperson or sales team to build and support the relationship with a customer. Many companies have an account manager for each large customer. Hewlett-Packard's new corporate business follows this structure, which is central to the more customer-focused strategy.[29] Consulting firms, advertising agencies, and manufacturers often have account managers. Delphi assigns them to work with the Chrysler, Ford, Toyota, Volkswagen, and BMW accounts as well as with GM assembly divisions. These managers concentrate their energies on maintaining the bonds between Delphi and the client. Account managers are particularly effective when the product supplied is important to the overall strategy of the buying company. For example, Delphi's components are critical to their customers' product designs. For some auto brands, Delphi produces most of the electrical systems, brake systems, and other components. Account managers spend considerable time with customers and carefully monitor satisfaction with products and delivery.

UPS World Wide Logistics sells third-party logistical support. Some clients want only basic services, such as low-cost shipping or warehousing. Others want more. According to the company's senior vice president of business development, John Sutthoff:

> Account managers are trained to understand the business strategies of our customers and to provide solutions that contribute to the success of these strategies. Often our account managers help customers build totally new strategies that result in stronger bonds with their customers. Consequently . . . account managers need to comprehend all aspects of business strategy as well as the competitive world our clients experience.[30]

The technology feature discusses how UPS uses technology to help the sales force.

THE RESPONSIBILITIES OF A SALESPERSON

Salespeople do not simply increase sales volume. Today, most view themselves as the marketing manager of a territory. This can be a geographical area, such as a city or region, or a single large account. Essentially, a **sales territory** is all the actual and potential customers for whom the salesperson has responsibility. As marketing manager of a territory, the salesperson has several functions. The first is to implement the company's marketing strategy in that territory. The second is to communicate company policy to clients and potential customers. The third is to provide the company with feedback about the marketing

NEGOTIATION
Discussion by two or more parties to arrange a transaction.

SALES TERRITORY
All the actual and potential customers, often within a specified geographic area, for which the salesperson has responsibility.

Adobe Acrobat offers features to manage strategic relationships.

environment, including the competition and customer needs and wants. Finally, salespeople must operate ethically.

Implement the Marketing Strategy In order to translate the company's marketing strategy into action, the sales force needs to have a basic understanding of all marketing functions. In many companies, salespeople have considerable leeway in applying the entire marketing mix to their territory, including which products to emphasize, which prices and discounts to offer, and which promotional materials to distribute. In other words, although their primary responsibility is to carry out the company's strategic marketing plan, they can use considerable judgment about how that will be done. At Johnson Controls' Automotive Systems Group, an automotive parts supplier, communication between the marketing and sales teams is essential. Salespeople are able to provide the customer with information gathered by the marketing team's surveys and focus groups. Sales calls are often made by representatives from both marketing and sales divisions.[31]

Communicate Company Policy As agents of their organization, salespeople are responsible for communicating company policies to customers. A policy is a guide or set of rules the company uses in conducting business. Foot Locker's policy of total customer satisfaction means that products can be returned for a refund within 30 days.[32] Salespeople must honor this policy no matter what the circumstance. Although company policies are relatively straightforward in most consumer sales situations, they can be extremely complex in business-to-business selling. For example, pharmaceutical sales representatives usually educate doctors about the proper use of certain drugs or medical equipment, but sometimes they are present when surgeons operate in order to answer questions about products should the need arise.

Companies are likely to specify exactly what salespeople can communicate. Also common are policies on appropriate product use, warranty issues, delivery, and pricing. By communicating such policies and enforcing them, salespeople help shape customer expectations, create goodwill, and maintain positive customer relationships.

Provide Feedback Another important role of the sales force is to provide their company with information about customers, competitors, and market conditions. Salespeople are in constant contact with the market, and many companies have formal systems for collecting their information rapidly. Examples are portable personal computers with elaborate, user-friendly programs or arrangements with customers to contact their computer systems directly.

Most salespeople have an array of sophisticated communication capabilities, including voice mail, e-mail, facsimile and satellite linkages, cellular phones, and pagers. This keeps them in touch 24 hours a day, seven days a week. Customer inventory levels (stock on hand), purchase orders, price quotations, shipping data, and promotional offers can be transmitted in both directions online. In addition, salespeople usually help forecast opportunities by describing the plans of current and potential customers that may affect future sales. Many times these estimates require careful analysis of a client's strategic plan. In 1999, all UPS sales representatives received laptops loaded with programs to aid customer monitoring, sales planning, and management communication, which increased customer contact 20 to 25 percent.[33]

Salespeople also provide valuable information about competitors. By collecting and assembling this input from around the globe, Kodak can identify nearly every initiative competitors make. Let us say a salesperson in Austria identifies a rival's product introduction, new promotional campaign, or altered pricing strategy in that territory. The information can be evaluated at Kodak headquarters to determine the likelihood that markets elsewhere will be affected. In one case, Fuji strategies in one area of the world soon appeared in other areas. Because salespeople had provided an early warning, Kodak marketing executives were able to create a counterstrategy rapidly.

Make Ethical Decisions   Salespeople must exhibit excellent ethical judgment. With little supervision, they often have considerable freedom in what they do and say. Because performance evaluation frequently is tied to sales levels, there are strong pressures to put their own interests ahead of those of customers. Salespeople are likely to face ethical dilemmas regarding the company they represent and the customers they serve. It helps immensely if their company's philosophy is value creation for the customer as well as the organization. Let's look at these ethical dilemmas in greater depth.

Why does independence from supervision pose ethical issues? The company usually goes to great expense to hire, train, and support a salesperson. If he or she does not work hard, then the company may be denied sales. The amount of time spent selling is an issue of personal ethics. Most employers recognize that the job may require spending time on evenings or weekends with customers or doing paperwork. To compensate, there tends to be some flexibility regarding working hours, but an unethical salesperson may take advantage of the situation. For example, it may be relatively easy to shorten the workweek without being missed or to play golf repeatedly with clients, more with an eye to a low handicap than to building a relationship. A salesperson may add another job rather than devote full energy to the primary employer. And what about taking an MBA class during work hours without telling the company?

Other ethical issues arise with regard to performance objectives.[34] Most salespeople are evaluated at least partially on sales volume or profitability. This creates several temptations, including overstocking, overselling, or pushing brands that yield higher commissions. Overstocking occurs when customers purchase more than is required for a given period, which results in unnecessary inventory carrying charges. Imagine that you are a few thousand dollars short of your monthly sales objective. Suppose there is a distributor who relies on your estimates to restock inventory. If you put in an order for more than is needed, then you may gain a better performance evaluation, but you have behaved unethically. Overselling occurs when customers request a lower-priced product that suits their needs and budget, but the salesperson supplies a much more expensive and more profitable product. Similarly, as noted in chapter 15, some companies offer spiffs for selling their product rather than a competitor's. Another unethical practice is to promise delivery when the salesperson knows the product will be late. The customer is prevented from ordering a competitor's brand, and when the delay becomes apparent, it is too late to obtain a substitute.

What salespeople communicate can also be an ethical issue. Puffery, or sales rhetoric so obviously excessive that customers recognize it as such, may not be in good taste but rarely is considered dishonest. Misrepresentation is far more serious. Salespeople are unethical when they give incorrect information, such as claiming their product is the same as another when it is not. Selling often involves verbal communication, and there may be little documentation

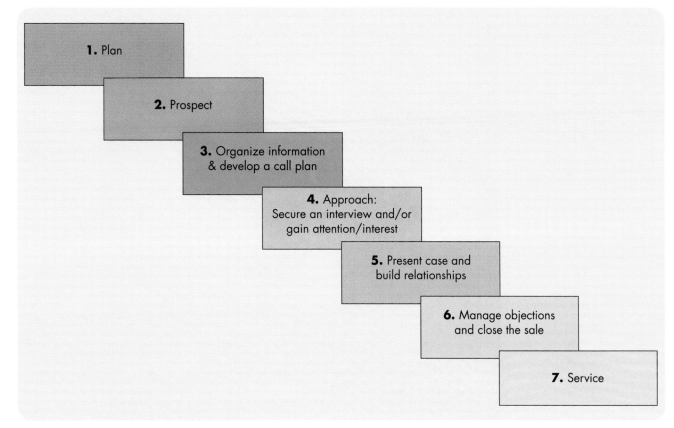

FIGURE 16.5 *Steps in Personal Selling*

other than an invoice after the sale. Whether spoken or written, intentional misrepresentation is illegal and can result in criminal or civil suits. Unintentional misrepresentation is at best a sign of incompetence in the salesperson and is grounds for canceling a contract. Ethical salespeople say, "I don't know, but I'll find out," rather than guess at the facts.

THE STEPS IN PERSONAL SELLING

Personal selling can be divided into seven stages, as outlined in Figure 16.5. Each step is explained in more detail next.

Planning　Sales planning translates the company's marketing strategy into territory plans and account plans. Territory management is extremely important. Salespeople must determine how the company's target marketing and positioning can best be applied in their territory. Because each area is different, it is important to make adjustments based on local conditions. Exceptional sales skills are of little use if calls are not made on the appropriate accounts with the right frequency and intensity. **Territory planning** determines the pool of customers, their sales potential, and the frequency with which they will be contacted about various products. The fundamental objective is to allocate sales time and use company resources to obtain the best results. Territory management is so important that many companies calculate to the minute what their salespeople do with their time. On average, salespeople spend 529 minutes per day (almost 9 hours) on the activities identified in Figure 16.6.[35]

Account planning establishes sales goals and objectives for each major customer, such as the sales volume and profitability to be obtained. Increasingly, account objectives include customer satisfaction, often measured by loyalty (repeat business). Account plans are based on an understanding of the customer's business and how the seller's products contribute to it. Elaborate account plans for major customers are common. For example, the AT&T sales team responsible for Ford Motor Company has a detailed description of its entire communication picture. This required a massive effort to develop, but the millions of dollars in revenues make it worthwhile. The plan provides all the information necessary to build and maintain the AT&T relationship with Ford.

TERRITORY PLANNING
Identifying potential customers, their sales potential, and the frequency with which they will be contacted about various products.

ACCOUNT PLANNING
Establishing sales goals and objectives for each major customer.

507

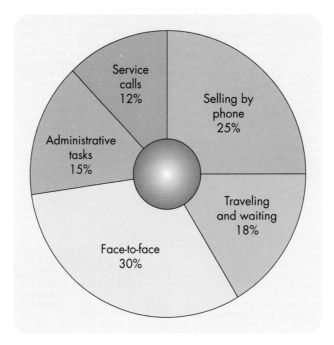

FIGURE 16.6 *Daily Activities of Salespeople*

PROSPECTING

Seeking potential customers within the company's target markets.

LEADS

All those who may have need of a company's product.

PROSPECT

A potential customer interested in the seller's product.

QUALIFYING

Examining prospects to identify those with the authority and ability to buy the product.

QUALIFIED PROSPECT

A potential buyer interested in the seller's product and with the attributes of a good customer.

Prospecting   As the name implies, **prospecting** is seeking out new customers within the company's target markets. As illustrated in Figure 16.7, it involves three steps: obtain leads, identify prospects, and qualify them. **Leads** are the names of all those who might have a need for the product, a large pool that must be narrowed down to the most likely buyers. **Prospects** are potential customers who have an interest in the product. They may currently buy from a competitor, are former customers, or have shown interest in some way. **Qualifying** is the process of determining which prospects have the authority and ability to buy the product. It also determines whether they are desirable customers. A **qualified prospect** is a potential buyer interested in the product and likely to be a reliable customer.

A number of methods are used in prospecting: cold calls (canvassing), referrals, exhibiting at trade shows, networking, telemarketing, secondary data, and coupons and ads. These are shown in Figure 16.8.

Cold calling (canvassing) is contacting the lead for the first time, either by telephone, fax, or in person. The salesperson has no idea whether the person will be interested. A few prospects are likely to be found, some of whom may be qualified. Cold calling is warranted when there is little information about the market or when the product is likely to have universal appeal. Many consumer products are sold door-to-door, and cold calling is also used in business-to-business selling. It is not very popular with customers, but it can be a useful method if not abused.[36]

A variation of cold calling is the **center of influence** method, which identifies leads by contacting opinion leaders. Recall from chapter 14 that opinion leaders are open to communications with salespeople and are considered reference group models. It is common knowledge that the pharmaceutical industry has profiled every physician in the country according to

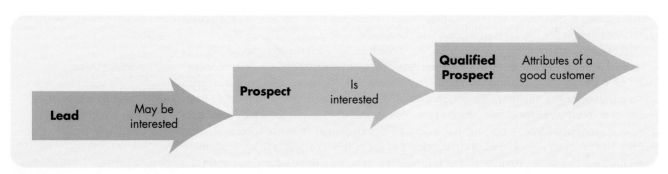

FIGURE 16.7 *Potential Customers*

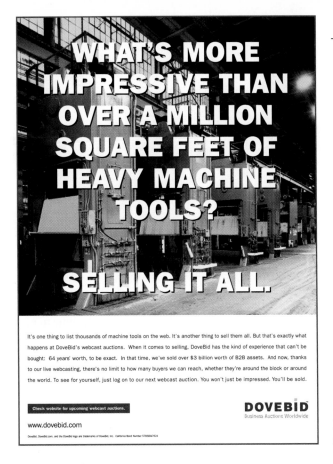

*This ad by Dovebid illustrates
their selling power.*

opinion leadership. The leaders are more open to new products and also are more likely to influence colleagues.

Referrals are names of leads provided by a qualified prospect. This method can be very effective, since qualified prospects tend to associate with those who have similar attributes. Furthermore, compared to cold calling, the referral is likely to be receptive when the salesperson mentions the name of someone they both know.

Exhibitions are an important way to obtain leads. About 85 percent of attendees significantly influence buying within their firm. This also is an inexpensive method. It costs 70 percent less to close a sale with these leads than with others.[37] In 2000, over 800,000 people attended the Detroit Auto Show.[38] In 1999, approximately 1.2 million people visited the Chicago Auto Show, one of the largest and most prestigious in the world. Participants included both domestic and foreign automakers as well as specialty manufacturers and retailers.[39] Nearly every industry sponsors a trade show. Large halls such as Madison Square Garden in New York City, the Omni in Atlanta, and McCormick Place in Chicago provide facilities for

COLD CALLING
Contacting a lead for the first time.

CENTER OF INFLUENCE
An opinion leader who can be quickly qualified as a potential customer because of his or her standing in the community.

REFERRAL
A lead provided by a qualified prospect.

Cold Calls (Canvassing)	Going door-to-door
Center of Influence	Identify opinion leaders and contact them for leads.
Referrals	Get customers or prospects to provide names of others.
Exhibitions and Demonstrations	Exhibit at trade shows or give speeches.
Networking	Contact friends, relatives, and associates to obtain leads.
Telemarketing	Phone people on lists.
Secondary Data	Obtain lists from companies such as Dun & Bradstreet.
Coupons and Ads	The prospect responds to an ad or redeems a coupon.

FIGURE 16.8 *Prospecting Methods*

*Telemarketing uses phone calls
to contact lists of leads provided by marketing services
and various directories.*

NETWORKING

Contacting friends, relatives,
and associates to obtain leads.

**CONNECTED:
SURFING THE NET**

www.amway.com

**By visiting the Amway site
you can learn more about its
extensive networking. And
for fun, play a multiple-
choice game in which you
match flags and countries.**

TELEMARKETING

Making telephone calls to leads
provided by marketing services
or from other lists.

thousands of organizations to display their products and obtain leads. Despite increasing networking through the Internet, trade shows continue to play an important role.[40]

Networking involves contacting friends, relatives, and associates to obtain leads.
Successful salespeople in most fields find this an important part of their business. Amway
Corporation has had great success obtaining sales through networking. The company uses a
system of independent agents who sell home care products directly to consumers. The agents
obtain from customers the names of additional leads to contact.[41] Amway has had incredible
success globally and has distributors in Asia, Africa, Latin America, and North America. Its
worldwide sales in fiscal year 1999 reached $5 billion.[42]

Telemarketing uses phone calls to contact lists of leads provided by marketing services
and various directories. Organizations, such as Dun & Bradstreet and Information Resources,
Inc., provide listings of nearly every private and public organization as well as the name and
title of executives, managers, and buying influencers. Many marketing services contact these
leads to determine the types of products they purchase and other information. These interviews are then turned into lists of prospects and sold to various marketing organizations.
AT&T has its own staff of telemarketers to find small business prospects for its products. Ford
hired the Phoenix Group of Farmington Hills, Michigan, to telemarket options to its leasing
customers. In an effort to maintain loyalty, calls are especially targeted to those whose lease is
about to expire.[43] Increased use and accessibility of the Internet are changing the nature of
telemarketing. Marketing services still make phone calls, but some also use real-time Internet
conversations and e-mail responses to consumer inquiries.[44]

Secondary data sources can provide thousands of lists. Chapter 5 noted categories of
secondary data, ranging from local libraries to company databases. Today, the information
highway provides access to the names of nearly all U.S. companies and most international
organizations. CD-ROM directories are another fast and effective source. Marketplace
Business and PhoneDisc PowerFinder provide millions of names and phone numbers. The
former is updated quarterly and lists 10 million U.S. businesses. The latter has search capabilities for every phone directory in the country. Both are tremendous sources for leads. They
also provide information through the Internet at www.businessmarketplace.com.[45] By using
database technologies, companies also can qualify prospects. In some cases, the selling organization manages the database, but this is a highly specialized field. Because of the very costly
technology and expertise required, most secondary data searches are outsourced.

Coupons and ads are another method for obtaining leads. Generally, coupons are
placed in newspapers or magazines or sent through the mail. People who take the time to
respond tend to be very interested and may have the attributes of a qualified prospect.
A trend in magazine advertising is response cards that consumers mail in for free information after circling a number that corresponds to a specific ad. These cards give the seller a list
of leads to pursue.

Organizing Information and Developing a Call Plan **Preapproach** refers to preparing for the initial meeting by learning about the prospect. For consumers, just their address
can yield socioeconomic information, such as the likelihood of sufficient income to purchase

PREAPPROACH

Preparation by the salesperson
for the initial meeting with
a prospect.

the product and even some general idea of tastes and preferences. Columbia TriStar Home Video has developed its own software for its sales force to use in learning about the large retail chain outlets they visit. In the case of businesses, the salesperson can obtain copies of the organization's literature and annual reports. These contain data on the firm's financial strength, organizational structure, objectives, plant locations, and sometimes even its purchasing philosophy. The salesperson's goal is to obtain enough information to develop an initial strategy for each call. An integral part of Enron Energy Services (EES) sales process is the preapproach. Salespeople research potential clients to ascertain whether they meet "hard" and "soft" criteria. Hard criteria examine the general business structure of the prospective client, whereas soft criteria consider possibilities such as already established relationships between executives.[46]

Once the preapproach phase is completed, a call plan is developed to save time and minimize travel expenses. The **routing schedule** identifies which prospects will be called on and when. There are computerized programs to help with routing, or it can be done informally.

Approach   The **approach** is the first formal contact with the customer. The objective is to secure an initial meeting and gain customer interest. It's usually a good idea to schedule an appointment; that will save time and puts the prospect in the frame of mind for a sales call. Many times, a letter of introduction before calling to schedule will help in obtaining the first appointment.

Many techniques have been developed for the initial approach. The most successful ones focus on the potential customer's business, such as a brief explanation of how or why the seller's product can help. It also is important to determine not just when the meeting will take place but how long it will last and its objective. Organizations with a strong reputation generally have an advantage in the approach stage. For example, Xerox or Kodak salespeople will have more success gaining an initial interview than will representatives of an unknown company.

Making the Case and Building Relationships   The sales **presentation** is a two-way process: The salesperson listens in order to identify customer needs and then describes how the company will fulfill them. The most important part of any good presentation is listening. In fact, it is often said that successful selling is 90 percent listening and 10 percent talking. Unfortunately, many salespeople believe their role is to tell prospects about products. Instead, by asking questions, they should put the customer first and demonstrate that they have the customer's best interest in mind. The first contact is the first opportunity to connect with a customer.

Organizations generally have to train their sales force to be good listeners. This is a trait few people possess naturally. The training identifies ways to learn about the prospect's situation. It also teaches how to communicate that the salesperson is listening and is concerned about the customer's needs and wants. **Empathy** occurs when salespeople know precisely how prospects feel. Only when prospects know that the seller understands their needs and wants are they receptive to solutions the salesperson offers.

A popular technique for interfacing with customers is SPIN selling. It stands for situation, problem, implication, and need payoff.[47] The approach resulted from research into what makes people successful at large sales. More than 35,000 sales calls were investigated. Companies such as Xerox, IBM, and Kodak supported the study and have used the system successfully for years. Considerable training is required for people to become proficient with the technique. Essentially, it employs a sequence of probing questions that enlighten the salesperson and the client at the same time.

Situation questions help discover facts about the buyer's condition. Much of this can be learned before the interview so these questions should be limited.[48] Problem questions identify dissatisfaction with the current circumstances.[49] For example, the salesperson may ask: "What makes it difficult to use this type of product?" Implication questions follow, and these are crucial. They unearth the consequences of current problems and are likely to reveal important needs. For example, in response to questions about product safety, one customer began to realize that high insurance costs, low morale, and ethical issues were consequences or hidden costs.[50] Need payoff questions then explore why it is important to solve the problem.[51] In the SPIN process, the buyer and seller establish the need for a product and the benefit of its ownership.

ROUTING SCHEDULE
A travel plan for calling on prospects that is developed to save time and minimize expenses.

APPROACH
The salesperson's first formal contact with the potential customer.

PRESENTATION
A two-way process in which the salesperson listens to the customer to identify needs and then describes how the product will fulfill them.

EMPATHY
An interpersonal connection in which the salesperson knows precisely how the prospect feels and communicates that understanding.

Follow-up occurs when a salesperson ensures after-sale satisfaction in order to obtain repeat business.

The first contact not only is an opportunity for the salesperson to make a case for a product but also may be the first step in building a relationship. Although sales sometimes are made on the first visit, most occur later. Over time, the salesperson assumes different roles as the relationship develops.

Managing Objections and Closing the Sale   One of the most important sales skills is the ability to overcome a buyer's objections. These may be raised subtly in many cultures. In the United States, for example, they often are disguised questions. A consumer may say, "I can't afford to purchase that automobile," but he or she really is asking what financing is available, or how much it costs, or what the trade-in terms are. Assertive salespeople do not let the first objection stop the dialogue; they use it to advance the discussion. Most organizations have training programs to teach salespeople how to manage objections.

Closing means getting the first order. In many cases this is simple, such as asking directly if someone wants to buy the product or whether they will use cash or credit. In other cases, it involves elaborate contracts. Good salespeople know how important it is to help the buyer toward the final decision. You have probably tried on a suit or dress and heard the salesperson say: "Shall I have that measured for alterations?" or "Shall I wrap that for you now?" In business-to-business situations, the salesperson may ask if the purchaser is ready to make a decision or would like to discuss the issue more thoroughly. A caution is in order regarding closing.[52] If a buyer is not ready to make the commitment, then asking for an order prematurely can make the salesperson appear pushy and unconcerned with the buyer's needs. A great deal of sensitivity is required for an accurate reading of the buyer's state of mind.

Service   There is a big difference between making a sale and gaining a customer. One sale equals one sale. The word *customer* implies something more than a single sale. In order to maintain relationships, salespeople spend significant time servicing accounts. They make sure products are delivered on schedule and operate to the buyer's liking. When there is a problem, the salesperson makes sure that it is resolved quickly and satisfactorily.

Follow-up occurs when a salesperson ensures after-sale satisfaction in order to obtain repeat business. Good follow-up reduces buyer's remorse. A bad feeling about spending a lot of money can be alleviated if a salesperson provides information that supports the decision. If that evidence is not forthcoming, then customers may quickly become dissatisfied. Follow-up also offers a way to identify additional sales opportunities. After the first step is taken, the second is easier. The salesperson who continues to work closely with the buying organization can uncover other needs to supply. Good service builds strong customer loyalty, which is the goal of partnership selling.

CHARACTERISTICS OF STRONG SALESPEOPLE

Hundreds, perhaps thousands, of studies have been done to determine what makes a good salesperson. Figure 16.9 describes the characteristics noted most often: goal direction, empathy, strong knowledge of applications, and ethics.[53]

CLOSING

The point at which the salesperson obtains the first order from the customer.

FOLLOW-UP

After-sales service to ensure customer satisfaction in order to obtain repeat business.

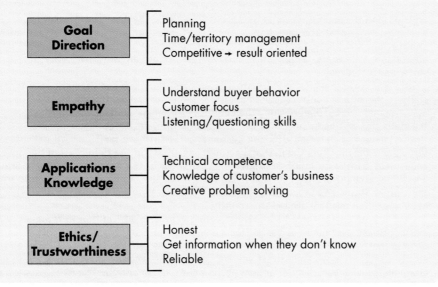

FIGURE 16.9 *Characteristics of Successful Salespeople*

First, strong sales performers tend to be goal directed. They spend adequate time on planning and then work according to the plans. They use their time effectively, which allows them to manage their territory efficiently. They are also highly competitive and obtain results in the face of stiff competition.

Second, because strong salespeople are empathetic, they are aware of the concerns and feelings of others. This means they can understand buyer behavior and have a customer focus. They see things from the customer's perspective. Most have very good listening and questioning skills that help them obtain this information.

Third, strong salespeople know how their products apply to the customer's situation. This requires technical competency as well as a good understanding of the customer's business.

That combination allows the salesperson to solve problems for the customer creatively. Since each customer has a specific set of needs, each requires special attention. A salesperson must customize or assemble a mix of products that offers the best possible answer. In essence, the strong salesperson works with the customer to tailor a solution.

Fourth, salespeople must be ethical. The nature of the job often places them in difficult situations. Since good salespeople build relationships, they must be viewed as totally trustworthy, a requisite for creating partnerships. They seek out information when they don't know the answer to a question. They provide pertinent information. They try to help customers solve problems, whether or not a sale is involved. They have a record of keeping customers informed, of facing up to mistakes, and of not promising what they can't deliver.

CONNECTING THROUGH TECHNOLOGY

UNITED PARCEL SERVICE LINKS SALES TECHNOLOGY TO PERFORMANCE

United Parcel Service (UPS) has been delivering packages for close to a century, but until about 15 years ago it didn't have a single sales rep. The world's largest shipping company had always focused on current customers, not on attracting new ones. Well, a lot has changed during the past decade. Heated competition from Federal Express, the U.S. Postal Service, and a number of small carriers has forced UPS to develop a new service menu for value-hungry businesses. Along with it has come a much more aggressive sales effort.

The company now employs about 3,000 reps and support staffers. To make sure they can keep up in the information-driven marketplace, UPS invested $5.5 million in

Continued

laptops and a communications system called LINK. By the end of 1995, everyone working on national accounts had a portable PC and training for a variety of software applications (including contact and customer management, to-do lists, contract implementation, calenders, e-mail, a report writer, faxing software, the Microsoft Office suite, and Netscape).

The shift from a paper-based system to an electronic one had dramatic results, especially in the area of contract implementation. The process used to take up to 90 days and now averages 15. Customers enjoy the benefits of the new contract that much sooner, and the transition has been smooth. LINK also allows information to flow more freely within the company and between UPS and customers. "With the e-mail . . . we get messages throughout the day from the national account executives in the field . . . and that gives us good ideas on how to build strategies for customers in the future," says David Schuler, a national account manager for UPS. "We know what the competitive situation is around the United States and around the world. So we know early what's coming next—it's like having eyes and ears all around the country."

In 1999, the sales force had an outstanding year with $27 billion in revenues, a dramatic increase over previous years. Management has also instituted a new incentive plan to help motivate the sales force. On a quarterly basis sales reps are measured on their ability to retain, grow, and attract volume and revenue. The reps are guaranteed to make more money each year if their annual performance has improved. "We froze people's pay, and then created an incentive system on top of that based on performance," says John Beystehner, senior vice president of worldwide sales for Atlanta-based UPS. Reps at UPS know what their focus is: growth.

Sources: Melanie Berger, "The Missing Link," *Sales and Marketing Management, Tools Supplement,* December 1996, pp. 18–24; and Erin Stout, Michele Marchetti, and Andy Cohen, "More Winners," *Sales and Marketing Management,* July 2000, pp. 82–83.

Relationship selling requires that salespeople be more versatile, creative, and visionary than ever before. A strong salesperson works to harness all company resources for the customer's benefit.

SALES FORCE MANAGEMENT

The sales organization connects directly with customers. Personal relationships are what it's all about. Managers develop and guide the sales organization to make sure the connections are made in the right ways with the right customers. They lead others in order to carry out the overall personal selling portion of the communications mix. **Sales force management** is the marketing function involved with planning, implementing, and adjusting sales force activities. It is a tremendously important function for companies that stress customer relationships. Nearly every dimension of how salespeople behave with customers is influenced by how they are managed. Sales management teams keep this in mind when they recruit, train, and motivate salespeople. And sales force management helps salespeople create lasting connections with customers by directing company resources to support relationship building.

Sales managers are responsible for the leadership and management of salespeople in order to accomplish the sales objectives established in the marketing plan. Sales managers make things happen through other people. They are not simply supersalespeople. They are vital in implementing the marketing strategy in companies such as General Electric, Intel, Xerox, Kodak, Eaton Corporation, and thousands of others. Many marketing executives, especially in technology-driven firms, have made their way up through the sales manager route. To do an effective job, sales managers need a full understanding of marketing strategy and planning, each aspect of the marketing mix, and personnel management in addition to the principles of selling and sales management.

Sales force managers perform many functions in support of the marketing strategy. Figure 16.10 describes the key functions: organize the sales force, develop diverse sales teams, prepare sales forecasts and budgets, implement sales actions, and oversee the sales force. These functions may be performed alone in a smaller organization or by a team of people in a larger company. The sales management team is comprised of representatives from personnel, who help with recruiting, training, and personnel records; from marketing (management)

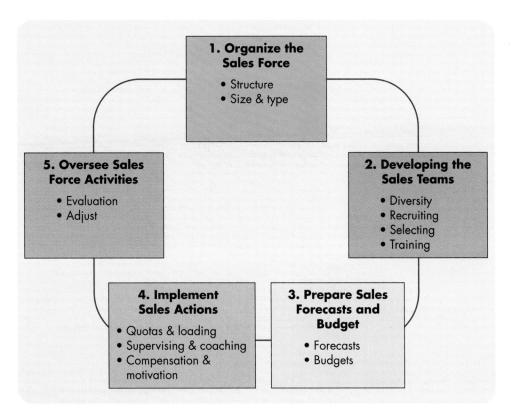

Figure 16.10 *Sales Management Functions*

information systems, who provide necessary sales data; and from customer service, who connect the sales force and their customers with manufacturing and logistics. Yet the overall responsibility for all the functions described in Figure 16.10 belongs to sales management.

Organizing the Sales Force

The characteristics of sales managers and the chain of command are important considerations in organizing the sales force. These and other concerns are of particular importance in global settings. The sales force may be structured by geography, by division or product line, or by market segment. Both the structure and the size of the sales group have a lot to do with sales coverage.

Sales Manager Types   The sales manager position can be executive, midlevel, or first line, depending on responsibilities and scope of operations. At the top are national and international sales executives, often with the title of vice president. They usually report to the top marketing executive. In most companies, only one or a few people are in this position. Their management scope covers several products across a broad territory. In large companies, executive sales managers may have several other sales managers reporting to them, and they ultimately are responsible for several thousand salespeople. Midlevel managers, called regional managers when the sales force structure is geographic, supervise several other managers, called district managers or first-line managers, in a large area, such as New England or several countries. First-line managers oversee several salespeople who handle certain products or types of accounts in a limited geographic area. First-line managers who supervise field reps and retail salespeople usually have a sales force of eight to 12; those who supervise inside sales or telemarketing personnel are likely to have more. As a first assignment, some sales managers supervise only three or four people.

Sales Force Structures   A **sales structure** is the organization of the reporting relationship between sales managers and salespeople. Sales organizations can be structured by geography, by product or division, by market segment, or by individual account. In some cases, all four are used. Figure 16.11 shows a typical geographical structure, topped by a general sales manager who reports to the vice president of marketing. Sales managers in the various geographical areas report to the general sales manager. Below them may be sales managers at the regional and district level, then territory representatives (salespersons).

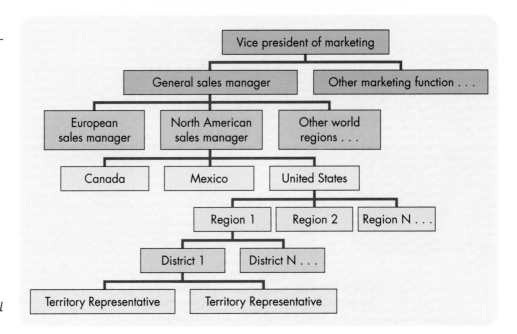

FIGURE 16.11 *A Geographical
Sales Force Structure*

Figure 16.12 illustrates the division or product line structure. Many companies are organized into divisions, and each may have a sales organization. Companies with very technical products are likely to use this sort of structure. For example, GM's Delphi division has a sales organization structured according to the components of an automobile: interior, exterior, electronics, and so forth. Each area requires a great deal of interaction among salespeople, designers, manufacturing personnel, and individual customers.

The third approach is to structure the sales force by market segment, as shown in Figure 16.13. Salespeople are focused on a given target segment, as outlined in the marketing plan. IBM has historically operated in this manner. It has one sales organization that sells to the financial community, another for universities, and yet another for manufacturing firms. The advantage is that salespeople focus on and truly understand the needs of a particular market segment. A company with a limited product line that has differing applications by segment would prefer this arrangement.

Many companies have a few customers who represent extremely large volume, called key accounts, house accounts, national accounts, or global accounts, depending on how they are managed. Major accounts may fit the 80-20 rule: About 80 percent of a company's sales volume comes from only 20 percent of its accounts. Although the percentages may differ considerably, the point is that major accounts are large, usually have unique sales needs, and are so important to volume and profitability that they require special emphasis. Major accounts are often managed by a separate sales group of a few very experienced people who report to the top sales executive. In other cases, they may be allocated to the midlevel area in which they are

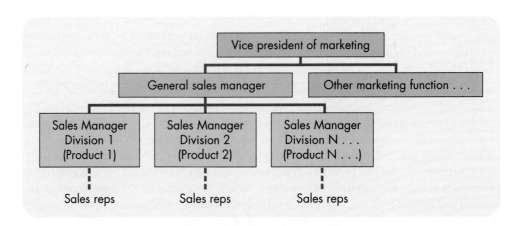

FIGURE 16.12 *A Division or
Product Line Sales Force
Structure*

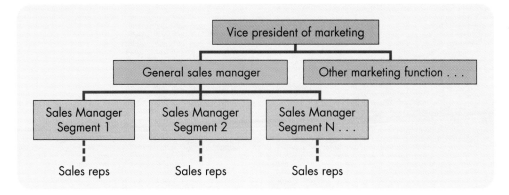

FIGURE 16.13 *A Market Segment Sales Force Structure*

located. In some companies major accounts are assigned to sales managers who split their time between these customers and their management duties.

DEVELOPING THE SALES TEAM

In order to develop the sales team, a good sales force must first be recruited, selected, and trained. Recruitment is the activity of attracting qualified prospects for the sales job. Selection involves choosing the strongest recruits for employment in the sales force. Training provides education and preparation to salespeople. In the United States it is a manager's responsibility to comply with the federal Equal Employment Opportunity Act. Hiring discrimination based on age, sex, race, national origin, religion, ethnic background, and physical handicap is strictly forbidden. Many countries have similar requirements that must be carefully followed.

Diversity in the Sales Force   Although the structure and size of the sales force are important, nothing is more critical for relationship marketing than the diversity of the sales organization. Managers must take care to develop a sales force that represents various groups. This enhances the ability of the organization to be sensitive to the needs of individual customers, thereby improving its relationship-building capacity. A diverse sales force provides a variety of insights, ideas, and perspectives, all of which make it easier to accommodate a dynamic and multicultural customer base.[54] Strong managers consider diversity in all stages of their sales force development, particularly during recruitment, selection, and training. For example, MONY Life Insurance Company in New York has a team of four "diversity recruiters" who recruit from underrepresented groups—women, African Americans, Hispanics, and Asian Americans.[55]

Although men traditionally have dominated the sales profession, many managers are finding that women have excellent relationship skills and often are more successful at selling. The mostly male readership of *Sales and Marketing Management* was asked: "Who is better at sales, women or men?" Although 70 percent ranked the sexes as equal, 17 percent said women were better, compared to 13 percent who ranked men higher. Gender-balanced sales forces were the focus of a more recent study that concluded few gender differences existed.[56] The $5.3 billion cosmetic company Avon appointed its first woman CEO in 1999, Andrea Jung, building on a tradition of a high percentage of female management.[57] Avon rewards the improved representation of women and minorities in its annual bonus plan for managers. The importance of hiring women and minorities in the workforce also is a topic at conventions and is highly publicized within and outside the company.[58]

Many companies organize committees or task forces to promote diversity in the sales force. For example, IBM set up eight task forces to evaluate diversity and determine how to make such groups as women, African Americans, gays, and lesbians feel welcome within the company and its sales force. Levi-Strauss & Co. established a committee to recruit diverse, qualified candidates for sales positions. In some cases, diversity goals are achieved by tying efforts to sales managers' compensation. This is true for Prudential Insurance.[59] In addition to organizing formal support networks for its women, African American, and gay and lesbian employees, Whirlpool Corporation sponsors community and school programs such as an Hispanic MBA Fellowship at the University of Notre Dame.[60] The most common practices

CONNECTED: SURFING THE NET

www.prudential.com

Find out more about Prudential's commitment to diversity by exploring the company's Web site. Also discover how Prudential is connecting through technology. Chairman and CEO Art Ryan says: "As we head into the next century, advances in online technology will offer us exciting, new opportunities to reach out to customers and to help them achieve financial security and peace of mind."

*Companies, such as AT&T,
have begun to recruit college
students on Spring Break.*

for insurance companies, however, include recruiting bilingual salespeople, using an affirmative action plan, and printing sales materials in languages other than English.[61] Pharmaceutical companies are also more frequently providing health information in several languages.[62]

Diversity training seeks to eliminate stereotypes and biases within the global sales force as well. It also addresses the unique tastes and preferences of the customer base as well as cultural practices that may be different. For example, Ford Motor Company uses this kind of awareness training around the globe because, according to its CEO, "it's very important for people to understand the different customer tastes around the world. People in China don't like exactly the same products as people in India."[63]

Recruiting   Effective recruitment attracts a qualified pool of candidates to fill the sales positions. The first step is to develop a job description specifying activities and qualifications. This written document spells out organizational relationships, responsibilities, and duties of the position.

The convenience of the recruiting site is important, which is why college campuses are often chosen. Many organizations use recruiting companies to find experienced candidates. Strong organizations spend a good deal of time identifying a pool of candidates. Northwestern Mutual Life Insurance has increased college hiring by 56 percent through aggressive recruiting. It offers mock interviews, career fairs, and resumé critiques on university campuses.[64] Accenture hires over 10,000 people a year and sends recruiters to over 300 universities.[65] To find out more, contact your college placement office, or visit these companies online.

Selecting   Because good sales talent is in high demand, not only the company but also the candidate does the choosing. Sales managers must demonstrate sound judgment in selecting from a broad range of talents, and they also need to sell top candidates on opportunities with their organization. FedEx sales managers see recruitment and selection of sales candidates as one of their most important functions. FedEx is considered to have one of the best global sales forces. It selects candidates who can build relationships with a dynamic customer base spread over 200 countries.[66]

Although there is no definitive list of attributes that define those likely to become successful salespeople, the attitudes, skills, and knowledge of some individuals set them apart. Important personality traits include empathy, which allows a salesperson to understand problems from another's perspective; ego drive, which ties self-image and identity to job performance; and resilience, which allows a salesperson to bounce back from defeat. Also important is the ability to communicate, think analytically, and effectively organize and manage time. Knowledge of and experience with a product, industry, competitor, or company territory are also valuable qualities. Others include self-discipline, intelligence, creativity, flexibility, self-motivation, persistence, a personable nature, and dependability.

Thingamajob.com serves as a recruiting and job search tool.

Training Even the most qualified salespeople need continuous education. New hires need the most, but seasoned veterans also can benefit from advanced training and formal practice. Many sales executives believe training is critical for developing individual and team skills. Nabisco found that it increased morale, reduced turnover, improved relationship-building skills, and developed a stronger sense of teamwork, all of which combined to increase sales dramatically.[67] Online training is combined with classroom sessions at Charles Schwab in its program LEAP (Learning for Excellence in Advice and Professionalism).[68] Training programs are usually conducted regarding company policies and procedures, product and customer applications knowledge, sales skills, and territory and account planning.

Company policies and procedures can be very elaborate, specifying the exact relationship that salespeople are expected to have with customers. Policies range from mundane matters, such as sales account and entertainment budgets, to complicated issues, such as the types of special customer requests the company will honor. In today's sales environment, procedures often are highly complex. Among other things, they may involve understanding how to enter orders, how to service accounts, and how to create and maintain reporting systems between the selling and buying organizations.

Training is necessary to understand the product's attributes and benefits. In technical sales jobs, products are often very sophisticated. In some cases training builds background information, such as a knowledge of electricity for electrical products or pharmacology for drug products. Salespeople learn not only about the technologies behind the product but also about how the product works. Teaching salespeople about new items is critical to the success of a pharmaceutical company such as Merck. There is very little time between a product's FDA approval and its introduction to customers. Approximately 90 percent of the Merck sales training program is based on classroom learning.[69]

Most organizations train new hires in basic relationship selling skills and experienced salespeople in more advanced techniques. The objective is to help the sales force do a better job of working with customers, listening, and finding ways to develop profitable relationships

**CONNECTED:
SURFING THE NET**

www.merck.com

Visit Merck's award-winning Web site to learn more about its sales training and leading pharmaceutical products.

for each party. At Saturn, all sales reps go through a five-day program at company headquarters to learn about the company's customer-focused culture. Sales skills are developed in the context of the Saturn management philosophy.[70]

Many organizations use sales certification programs to enhance the skills and credibility of their sales force. These programs are usually provided by companies or associations that specialize in sales training. In this form of training, salespeople must attend classes or in some cases take distanced learning courses offered over the Internet. Certificates are given according to the competency level attained. More than 50 percent of managers believe that a certification program would benefit their company, and 66 percent of consumers believe certified salespeople are more credible. Certification is thought to demonstrate a defined level of competency and skill. Although such training is expensive, many organizations consider it a good investment.[71]

SALES FORECASTING AND BUDGETING

Forecasting and budgeting are important steps in allocating sales resources. The forecast estimates demand based on likely responses of buyers to future market conditions, sales force, and other promotional activities and marketing actions. Sales force budgets are generally set with the sales forecast in mind. Accuracy in the forecast and budgets is important, since production is scheduled to meet demand. When forecasts are lower than actual demand, customers go unserved. When they are higher than demand, high inventory carrying costs dramatically reduce profitability. Estimation methods vary from elaborate computer programs to fairly simple questioning of potential buyers. Even small companies, which are known for their ability to adjust quickly, depend on accurate forecasts.[72]

ENVIRONMENTAL FORECAST

An estimate of the economic, political, and social factors likely to affect the level of spending for the types of products or services being forecast.

Sales Forecasting   Most companies go through three basic steps in estimating demand—an environmental forecast, an industry forecast, and a company sales forecast. The **environmental forecast** examines the economic, political, and social factors likely to affect the level of spending for a product. Factors include unemployment, consumer spending, interest rates, business investments, and inventory levels. In general, information of this type helps determine whether economic conditions for the company's products are likely to be positive or negative. Environmental forecasting can estimate not only global, international, national, and regional trends but also very localized trends. Every year *Sales and Marketing Management* prints a "Survey of Buying Power," a tool that helps marketers predict sales of products based on environmental conditions, consumer age and wealth, and distribution channels.

INDUSTRY FORECAST

An estimate of the amount and type of competitive activity likely to occur in an industry.

Sales forecasts often use the industry outlook as a key element. An **industry forecast** estimates the amount of overall demand expected based on such factors as the industry business condition, amount of spending, number of new products, and communications budgets anticipated for competitors. In other words, this forecast projects the level of sales and marketing activity for the industry as a whole as well as for competitors likely to affect the company most directly.

COMPANY SALES FORECAST

A prediction of unit or dollar sales for a given period, in total or broken down by product, segments, or other categories, and based on the marketing strategy that will be put in place.

The **company sales forecast** is based on the overall marketing strategy. It forecasts unit sales and must be in line with marketing, financial, and operations plans. If not, then adjustments must be made to the sales forecast. The marketing plan is particularly critical. For example, a product positioned as a high-priced specialty item may have a low expected sales volume. For a product positioned as a low-priced commodity, the sales volume estimate probably will be higher. In addition, in order to do a good job of developing objectives, it is important to estimate demand with other departments in mind. Sales managers communicate about forecasts with many areas of the company to reconcile any differences. Since various departments may have specific objectives, such as cost containment, brand growth, and financial targets, this interaction is necessary. Estimates may be made for the entire company, a particular product, a geographic region, a market segment, or on some other basis.

It's important to remember the more dynamic the situation, the more difficult the prediction is likely to be. Consequently, businesses in new fields may have to spend more time estimating demand than do businesses with mature product lines. Yet, even in innovative, highly competitive industries it is important to obtain reliable forecasts.

Some marketers mistakenly associate good forecasting with strong marketing. In fact, there are many examples of organizations that have forecast low sales volume and, thus, created less aggressive marketing strategies. Although they met their forecasts, they probably would have reached much higher sales levels if they had pursued an aggressive strategy. Most organizations recognize that perfect sales projections may mean the company is operating much too conservatively. Whirlpool Corporation believes a perfect forecast is possible only when a marketing group is performing below potential.

Forecasts are very important in deciding how to allocate company resources. Divisions that foresee high levels of sales are often given ample resources, such as additional salespeople, large advertising and promotion budgets, and lots of attention from product development and manufacturing. Consequently, the forecast can become a self-fulfilling prophecy. When forecasts are low, fewer resources are provided, and lower sales result.

Sales Force Budgets   One of the most important tasks of the sales manager is to create and administer the sales budget. The three most common methods for setting the budget are a percentage of overall sales, in relation to competitors in the industry, and as projected costs for the sales tasks. The first method establishes the sales budget as a percentage of the historical sales level. Although simple to use, this method has a major flaw. The estimated increase over past sales results in a larger sales budget, but the situation should be the reverse. A larger sales budget should result in a higher sales volume. Despite this problem, many sales organizations base the budget on past performance. Essentially, a sales force that produces more is rewarded more resources in the future for its past success. A variation on this is to use the sales forecast to establish the budget. This is more acceptable because it looks at the future rather than the past.

The second way to determine the sales budget is through comparison with a competitor's budget. Industry data provide the number of salespeople and sales offices as well as sales expenditures for other companies. The sales budget is then set accordingly. One advantage of this method is that it emphasizes competitive activity in the marketplace. A disadvantage is that it is not based on an understanding of the actual costs of one's own sales activities.

Task-based budgeting looks at the tasks salespeople must perform in order to accomplish objectives. Careful thought is given to each aspect of the sales process and to estimating the associated costs. The items usually considered are salaries, recruiting, training, travel, sales promotion, staff and clerical expenses, dues, and supplies.

IMPLEMENTING SALES ACTIONS

Once the sales forecast and budget have been established, sales activity can take place. Sales managers set quotas, measure performance, determine compensation, and supervise, coach, and motivate the sales organization in such a way that objectives are accomplished.

Quotas   **Quotas** are quantitative performance standards used to direct sales force activity. They also provide a way to evaluate performance. Whereas forecasts estimate results, quotas provide guidelines. They are one of the most important methods sales managers use to set and meet objectives. When quotas are exceeded, we would say that the sales force has produced beyond objectives; when quotas are not met, we would say that the sales force has fallen short of objectives. Over all, quotas are set in line with the strategic marketing plan. Most sales organizations use one of three types: sales volume, profit, or activity quotas.

Sales volume quotas establish unit or dollar objectives. Usually these are set for a market segment, product or service line, and average volume per customer. Typically, a quota for the entire sales organization is determined and then divided among the various sales regions and salespeople. During this process, salespeople and others are likely to provide feedback to sales executives regarding potential in their territory, the level of competition, and their belief about what is possible to accomplish. That information is combined with the sales forecast.

Sales profit quotas establish profitability objectives for customers, products, and market segments. Rather than volume, the focus is on the overall profit that can be made. This kind of quota is particularly important when sales actions such as price negotiations or repeat versus new customers influence profit. It is also important when different products yield different profit.

Activity quotas encourage salespeople to engage in certain tasks, such as prospecting calls, service calls, sales calls, demonstrations, and visiting new accounts. The focus is on customer contacts that will allow the company to implement its overall marketing strategy.

QUOTAS

Quantitative objectives used to direct sales force activity and evaluate performance.

SALES VOLUME QUOTAS

Unit or dollar objectives, usually set by market segment, product or service line, and average volume per customer.

SALES PROFIT QUOTAS

Profitability objectives for customers, products, and market segments.

ACTIVITY QUOTAS

Action objectives that encourage salespeople to engage in certain tasks, such as prospecting calls, service calls, sales calls, demonstrations, and visiting new accounts.

	(1) Weight	(2) Quota	(3) Performance	(4) % of Quota	(5) Contribution to Total Quota: (4) × (1)
Sales in dollars	40%	$500,000	$525,000	105%	42%
Profit margin	20%	30%	33%	110%	22%
Number of new accounts	15%	25%	20%	80%	12%
Number of accounts retained	20%	100%	120%	120%	24%
Number of new leads	5%	25%	50%	200%	10%
					TOTAL: 110%

FIGURE 16.14 *Quotas as a Measure of Performance*

Quotas are generally used to determine some portion of a salesperson's compensation. The simplest procedure is to set the same quota (such as amount of sales) for all salespeople and provide bonuses to those who exceed it. This tends to be inequitable, however, because sales potential and competition are likely to differ from one sales territory to another. Consequently, sales quotas usually vary for different parts of the organization and different salespeople. Compensation is covered in more detail in a later section.

Performance Measures Volume, profit, and activity quotas can be combined to measure performance, as shown in Figure 16.14. In this example the quota is based on sales volume, profit margin percentage, number of new accounts obtained, percentage of accounts retained, level of customer satisfaction, and number of new leads. Each factor is weighted in terms of importance. At the end of the sales period, the percentage of quota reached in each category is multiplied by the weight to determine the contribution of that category to achieving the total quota. In the example, sales are weighted at 40 percent, the quota is $500,000, and performance is $25,000 above that, leading to 105 percent of quota on that item. Multiplying by the weight, we get a 42 percent contribution to the total quota. Notice that when all these items are put together, this particular salesperson achieved 110 percent of quota (exceeded objectives by 10 percent). Performance exceeded the quota in all areas except the number of new accounts.

The performance measurement shown in Figure 16.14 can be used for several purposes. First, this person maintains loyal customers but seems to do little to increase the number of new accounts. The sales manager should discuss the situation to see whether training is needed or whether the territory has minimal potential for new customers. Second, since quotas can be used to motivate the sales force, the salesperson could be compensated for performing so well. Third, although the example provided here focuses on dollar volume, organizations often use this method to emphasize certain products or market segments consistent with their overall marketing strategy and positioning plan.

SALARY
The fixed amount of compensation paid regardless of performance.

COMMISSION
A form of sales force compensation in which the amount paid is in direct proportion to the accomplishment of specific objectives.

BONUS
A percentage of salary or a fee paid in addition to other compensation for meeting long-term or unique goals.

Compensation A well-designed compensation plan should be geared toward the needs of both the company and the sales force. It should be developed with the overall sales strategy in mind. A compensation system not only helps motivate salespeople but also is important in keeping loyal employees. For obvious reasons, turnover is harmful in relationship marketing. Furthermore, satisfied salespeople work hard to develop loyal customers. It is almost impossible to build customer loyalty with a dissatisfied sales force.

The three basic elements of sales force compensation are salaries, commissions, and bonuses. A **salary** is a fixed amount paid regardless of specific performance. Salaries are usually based on education, experience, longevity, and overall professionalism. A **commission** is an amount paid in direct proportion to the accomplishment of specific short-term sales objectives. It usually is given for meeting or exceeding a broad range of criteria, including volume and profit by product, or according to customer type and loyalty. A **bonus** is a percentage of salary or fee paid in addition to other compensation for meeting long-term or unique goals. Bonuses are often given to the entire sales team for an outstanding effort, usually quarterly or annually.[73] Compensation plans can be based on salary only, commission only, or both, and sometimes bonuses as well.

Supervision and Coaching   Supervision and coaching are face-to-face interactions between the sales manager and a salesperson. Most managers spend considerable time working with their people in the field. Good managers communicate well and help salespeople determine appropriate sales actions. They provide guidance to keep the sales force operating according to the company's philosophies, policies, and marketing plans.

A recent study defined three components central to coaching: "supervisory feedback, role modeling, and salesperson trust in manager."[74] Essentially, sales coaching occurs when the manager aids in the development of skills. Similar to a voice coach or athletic coach, the sales manager gives advice and demonstrations that enable salespeople to do a better job. Feedback should be an objective, and positive incentives should be used as progress is made. Coaching usually involves visits with customers by the manager and salesperson. The sales manager observes and gives pointers afterward on sales techniques. Good coaches also address all aspects of selling—from time management to customer sales support or even interaction with other company employees. In some cases coaching is done through role-playing. The vice president of new business partnerships at American Express says: "The sales manager's role is to add value, whether it's with the customer or whether it's helping your salespeople prepare for their next round of sales calls. It's keeping an eye out for those common problems and opportunities that are coming up . . . you're always coaching, coaching, coaching."[75]

There are many appropriate coaching styles, but good coaches usually don't simply take over. They observe, ask questions, and listen. They communicate clearly and provide positive reinforcement for the activities that salespeople carry out well. Feedback from sales managers is invaluable because it helps salespeople understand their strengths and weaknesses.

Motivation   Most top salespeople are motivated by the very nature of the job. They find selling fascinating and want to excel in a competitive environment. Still, good sales managers can add to motivation by providing a positive organizational climate as well as financial and career incentives. Since many salespeople spend little time under direct supervision, the systems for motivation must work well without the constant presence of the sales manager. A positive organizational climate exists when salespeople feel good about their opportunities and rewards. A positive climate also helps salespeople perform at the highest professional level.

Many companies use financial incentives. Money is a strong motivator, but companies are increasingly incorporating different forms of incentives. Carlson Marketing Group's (CMG) employee motivation and loyalty programs include employee rewards to each other, seminars on personal growth, and day care facilities. CMG's program "Ovation" personalizes a sales target for each salesperson, which provides incentive without creating an atmosphere of competition with coworkers. A second program, "Encore," awards top sellers with an exciting trip, such as a safari. Programs such as these have resulted in a low turnover rate of 5.2 percent.[76]

Ethical Issues in Motivation and Compensation   In striving to produce peak performers, sales managers may use several motivational approaches. If they push too hard in the wrong ways, then salespeople may be pressured to compromise ethical standards. When performance is poor, rewards may be withheld, or in extreme cases punishment may be used. Motivational techniques generally reward people for good performance. A key part of the management job, however, is to establish expectations not only in terms of sales volume but also regarding acceptable behavior. When managers focus exclusively on sales volume objectives, they are telling salespeople that the ends justify the means. This lack of attention to appropriate behavior in combination with pressure to perform can be considered unethical in itself. Let's look at three questionable practices.

- *Family pressure.* Salespeople are required to attend the annual sales meeting with their spouse (and perhaps other family members). Those performing well are rewarded publicly with free trips, gifts, or a large bonus. For the others, it is obvious to the family that they are low producers. Essentially, the company is interfering in family relationships with the intent of elevating sales.

Telcordia Technologies promotes the fact that they are an employee-owned company to attract new associates.

- *Peer pressure.* The sales manager broadcasts performance results to all salespeople or, in announcing sales contest winners, points out a few low producers. Rather than private communications between the manager and the salesperson, overt peer pressure is being used to gain behavior changes. This would be like posting student names along with grades in the student newspaper. Is that an ethical way to motivate you to learn? Could this increase the pressure on students to cheat?
- *Termination.* All salespeople are rank ordered, and the lowest performers are asked to leave even though they may be performing very profitably for the company. This keeps all salespeople pushing for fear of losing their job. Since termination is devastating for most people, to avoid it they may put undue or unscrupulous pressure on buyers.

Even quotas, though less extreme than these scenarios, can be troublesome. They are generally considered useful tools, but some sales managers believe they lead to high-pressure tactics and, thus, are harmful to relationship building. That is why Saturn moved away from quotas in favor of salary incentives. Sears auto centers got into trouble when employees were charged with performing unnecessary work in order to meet sales quotas. An embarrassed Sears eliminated the system and switched to noncommissioned rewards based on customer satisfaction.[77]

OVERSEEING SALES FORCE ACTIVITIES

Once sales operations are in effect, management needs to evaluate them and in some cases make adjustments. Evaluation and control are the final steps in the management process. Sales activities nearly always can be improved. In fact, some of the strongest sales organizations are very flexible in meeting business challenges and competitive situations. This is particularly important in industries in which changes occur rapidly. In general, most evaluation programs look at efforts and results, assess the company's influence in supporting performance, identify problems and opportunities, and take corrective action.

Salesperson performance can be evaluated behaviorally or by outcome. Behavioral performance is based on skills and the ability to meet the demands of the job. This includes such aspects as sales presentation, planning, teamwork, relationship selling, and technical knowledge. Outcome performance is measured by such customer-related factors as sales volume, market share, customer loyalty and satisfaction, and number of new accounts.[78]

In addition to evaluating individual salespeople, managers must regularly assess the entire sales force. This tells whether overall performance is strong. It may result in territory shifts, the addition of people, or other adjustments. The process gives both field reps and management an opportunity to learn whether the level of activity has produced the expected results. This often means doing productivity analysis to determine whether sales volumes have been reached, market shares have been accomplished, and the appropriate product mix has been sold to targeted segments. Usually, good evaluation requires looking behind the numbers to determine where the strongest and weakest results occurred and under what conditions.

Today, many companies use 360-degree evaluations; that is, salespeople are asked to evaluate their sales managers as well. This supports the team concept and helps break down the old barriers to joint progress. It is instrumental in helping sales managers improve. Since managerial success depends on working through others, this type of feedback is seen as absolutely critical in many companies. Tennessee Valley Authority (TVA) uses the 360-degree evaluations for employee development, both to evaluate individuals and teams. The system not only provides constructive feedback but also improves employee performance over all. In order for this method to be successful, however, the TVA stresses the need for two-way communication and absolute confidentiality and trust.[79]

SALES FORCE AUTOMATION

All sorts of high-tech tools are revolutionizing selling and sales management. **Sales force automation** is the use of technology to improve personal selling and sales management effectiveness. When Oracle Corps found demand exceeding its ability to supply, it spent millions of dollars to develop a Web-centered selling system in which customers can do the ordering themselves. Although salespeople still do the selling, they have more time to focus

SALES FORCE AUTOMATION
The use of technology to improve personal selling and sales management effectiveness.

Skyteam provides services to travelers on the go.

on the customer's needs and act as consultants. Nick Ward, CEO at MOHR Development, concludes, "People who are successful today are holding back on that sale and being careful to craft a total solution for the customer." The Oracle Web site allows salespeople to demonstrate the software immediately, and the client may also try out the product. Oracle salespeople are able to deal with a larger workload—while the number of sales representatives from 1995 to 2000 doubled from 7,000 to 14,000, Oracle's revenue tripled from $2.9 billion to $9.3 billion.[80]

According to a *Sales and Marketing Management* study, the following technologies are the most commonly used by sales personnel:[81]

- Sales automation software — 28%
- Notebook and desktop computers — 24%
- Contact management/calendaring systems — 20%
- Cellular phones — 16%
- The Internet — 15%
- Paging — 7%
- Wireless communication — 6%
- Handheld date recorders — 3%

Gateway Systems Corporation of East Lansing, Michigan, has been a pioneer in sales force automation software. According to the director of marketing, Karen Griggs:

Gateway's product, SYNERGIST Sales Portfolio (SSP), is designed to increase sales effectiveness on two levels. At the sales representative level, SSP facilitates the tracking of key account information, helps representatives monitor competitive inroads, and streamlines paperwork. At the sales management level, SSP allows managers to electronically collect critical pieces of information from the person closest to the customer—the sales representative. Furthermore, this information can be aggregated, analyzed, and provide indicators of the organization's performance within key target markets and accounts. And finally, SSP can serve as a communication vehicle from sales managers to their field sales representatives.[82]

Aether Systems Inc. offers solutions for sales force automation.

Sales force automation facilitates communication and gives salespeople fast access to necessary information. The use of notebook computers, updated software, and other technologies has improved the overall effectiveness of personal selling and sales management. Managers and salespeople alike can coordinate, plan, and interact more efficiently than ever before. This helps develop stronger relationships within the sales force and with customers. The technology feature, "United Parcel Service Links Sales Technology to Performance," further discusses the use of technology as a sales force management tool.

Personal selling, like the mass communication activities we explored in the previous chapter, is a forceful means of implementing the promotion strategy element of the marketing mix. We have now examined three of the four basic elements in the mix: product, place, and promotion. The next two chapters are devoted to the fourth element—price. Chapter 17 surveys the many factors that affect pricing, both domestically and globally. Chapter 18 focuses on price strategy—its basis in value and the ways in which it is implemented.

CONNECTED: SURFING THE NET

UPS
www.ups.com

THIS CHAPTER'S TECHNOLOGY FEATURE, "UNITED Parcel Service Links Sales Technology to Performance," discussed the company's new aggressive sales effort. To expand your thinking about UPS and personal selling, visit its Web site and answer the following questions.

1. There are many types of sales personnel. Which do you think are the most prevalent at UPS? Find information on the Web site to support your answer.
2. What interactive functions does the site offer that connect with customers through technology?
3. Which of the three major sales philosophies do you think UPS emphasizes? Explain your choice.
4. Imagine you are a salesperson at UPS. What might your responsibilities be? Give examples.

AMWAY
www.amway.com

IN THIS CHAPTER YOU LEARNED about Amway Corporation, a group of independents who sell home care products through extensive networking. To expand your thinking about this form of personal selling, visit the Amway Web site and answer the following questions.

1. Selling occurs in several circumstances. Which does Amway use? What are the advantages of this form of selling?
2. In this chapter you learned four characteristics of strong salespeople. Imagine you are an Amway distributor. How would each of these characteristics be important to your success? Give examples.
3. Connect to Amway's global village and visit Hungary. Is Amway Hungary a good business opportunity? Why or why not? What problems would a global salesperson face? What is one way companies can overcome sales resistance?

OBJECTIVE 1: Understand how selling evolved to a focus on relationships and what elements are involved in building them.

Personal selling techniques have moved through three distinct modes: the traditional persuasive approach, consultative selling, and relationship selling. The latter is strategic in nature and involves developing long-term relationships that are mutually beneficial for buyer and seller. It requires that the selling organization understand the customer's business or lifestyle and treat loyal customers as assets of the firm. Typically this leads to partnering that creates value for the customer and the selling organization. The objective of relationship selling is to create steady profit through customer loyalty and satisfaction. Interactions with customers focus on win-win situations.

OBJECTIVE 2: Know the responsibilities of salespeople and sales managers.

Most professional salespeople view themselves as the marketing manager of a territory. As such, they are responsible for implementing the company's marketing strategy within the territory. They also communicate company policy to customers and potential customers. They are important sources of feedback and have a responsibility to convey this information to their organization. Salespeople must have excellent ethical judgment since they often operate without much direct supervision, are under pressure to boost volume, and have leeway in what they say to customers.

Sales force management is the marketing function involved with planning, implementing, and adjusting sales force activities. First, sales managers work with others in their company to organize the sales force, including its structure, size, and type. Second, they develop diverse sales teams through recruiting, selecting, and training. Third, they prepare forecasts and budgets. Fourth, they implement actions by establishing quotas, assessing performance, determining compensation, and supervising, coaching, and motivating the sales force. Finally, they evaluate sales activities and make any necessary changes.

OBJECTIVE 3: Identify and understand the steps in personal selling.

The seven steps in personal selling are planning, prospecting, organizing information and developing a call plan, approaching a prospect, presenting a case and building relationships, managing objections and closing, and service. Sales planning translates the company's marketing strategy into territory and account plans. Prospecting involves seeking out new customers within the company's target markets. Next, sales personnel organize information and develop a call plan. To do this, they learn about prospects and prepare a routing schedule to identify which prospects will be called on and when. The approach is the first formal contact with the customer. The objective is to secure an initial meeting and gain customer interest. The next step is making the case and building relationships. This is done through the sales presentation. Sales personnel then manage objections and close the sale. One of the most important sales skills is the ability to overcome business objections.

Closing means getting the first order. Service follow-through is essential for developing customer loyalty.

OBJECTIVE 4: Learn the characteristics of strong salespeople.

First, strong salespeople are goal oriented. They use time well, manage their territory efficiently, and like to compete to obtain results. Second, they are empathetic; they understand buyer behavior, are customer focused, and possess excellent listening and questioning skills. Third, they have applications knowledge. They are technically competent, know their customers' business, and are good at creative problem solving. Fourth, excellent salespeople are ethical and trustworthy; they are honest, seek additional information when they don't know the answer, and make reliable partners.

OBJECTIVE 5: Understand how to develop a diverse sales organization.

Once the sales structure is determined, the sales organization is developed. Diversity is one of the most important aspects of a sales force because of its role in building relationships with multicultural customers. Strong attention must be paid to diversity when recruiting, selecting, and training salespeople. Recruitment seeks a pool of exceptional candidates and often takes place on college campuses. Selection is a choice process for the company and candidates alike, as both seek a good match. Training involves educating salespeople about company policies and procedures, product and customer application knowledge, relationship selling skills, territory and account planning, and diversity.

OBJECTIVE 6: Explore how to implement sales actions, from setting quotas and compensating salespeople to evaluating and adjusting plans.

Implementing sales actions involves several steps. Quotas establish the sales volume, profit, and activities expected from each salesperson. They are used to direct action and evaluate performance. Supervision and coaching, which involve working with salespeople to improve performance, build self-esteem and skills. Motivation is also part of the sales manager's job. It depends on a positive organizational climate in which employees feel rewarded for the effort they make. Sales force compensation is developed with the overall marketing strategy in mind. It is designed to support the development of loyal salespeople, who in turn help create loyal customers. Salaries, commissions, and bonuses are used singly or in combination. Several significant ethical issues surround motivation and compensation. Managers must be careful not to use techniques that lead to unethical actions by salespeople. The final step in sales force management is evaluation and adjustment. Organizations must be flexible in order to maintain competitive advantage. This requires an assessment of individual salespeople and each part of the sales organization. Companies are beginning to use 360-degree feedback techniques to evaluate sales managers as well as the sales force.

1. List several types of personal selling situations. Give an example of each.
2. What is relationship selling?
3. List the responsibilities of a salesperson.
4. What are the seven steps in personal selling?
5. What characterizes a strong salesperson?
6. What does closing mean?
7. Give three reasons why ethics are important to salespeople.

8. What are the five sales management functions?

9. List the types of sales forecasting. Briefly describe each.

10. What are three methods for setting a sales force budget?

11. What are quotas?

12. What is coaching?

13. What are three ethical issues surrounding sales force management?

DISCUSSION OF CONCEPTS

1. What are the key differences among the traditional, consultative, and relationship sales approaches? Which do you feel is most appropriate in a majority of circumstances? Why?

2. List the seven types of sales personnel. Under what circumstances would it make sense to have each type?

3. Why is it important for the salesperson to support the company's strategic marketing plan?

4. What is most important about each of the seven steps in personal selling? How do they form a process?

5. Describe some of the ways salespeople seek out new customers. Under what circumstances might each be appropriate?

6. Do you have the characteristics of a strong salesperson? Do you believe people are born with these, or can they be learned?

7. The job of the sales manager is to support the strategic marketing and communications plan of the organization. What are the key responsibilities of a sales manager?

8. Describe the methods a sales manager can use to set the sales budget. Which one do you feel is most effective? Why?

9. Training is now considered one of the most important factors in developing a strong sales team. What are the four major areas of training programs?

10. What is sales force automation, and how does it help sales managers and salespeople?

11. Is it acceptable to use family pressure to motivate salespeople? Why or why not?

KEY TERMS AND DEFINITIONS

Account planning: Establishing sales goals and objectives for each major customer.

Activity quotas: Action objectives that encourage salespeople to engage in certain tasks, such as prospecting calls, service calls, sales calls, demonstrations, and visiting new accounts.

Approach: The salesperson's first formal contact with the potential customer.

Bonus: A percentage of salary or a fee paid in addition to other compensation for meeting long-term or unique goals.

Center of influence: An opinion leader who can be quickly qualified as a potential customer because of his or her standing in the community.

Closing: The point at which the salesperson obtains the first order from the customer.

Cold calling: Contacting a lead for the first time.

Commission: A form of sales force compensation in which the amount paid is in direct proportion to the accomplishment of specific objectives.

Company sales forecast: A prediction of unit or dollar sales for a given period, in total or broken down by product, segments, or other categories, and based on the marketing strategy that will be put in place.

Consultative selling: An approach to selling in which sales personnel work closely with customers to help solve problems.

Direct sales: Sales that result from the salesperson's direct interaction with a consumer or company.

Empathy: An interpersonal connection in which the salesperson knows precisely how the prospect feels and communicates that understanding.

Environmental forecast: An estimate of the economic, political, and social factors likely to affect the level of spending for the types of products or services being forecast.

Follow-up: After-sales service to ensure customer satisfaction in order to obtain repeat business.

Industry forecast: An estimate of the amount and type of competitive activity that is likely to occur in an industry.

Leads: All those who may have need of a company's product.

Missionary sales: Sales made indirectly through people who do not obtain orders but influence the buying decision of others.

Negotiation: Discussion by two or more parties to arrange a transaction.

Networking: Contacting friends, relatives, and associates to obtain leads.

Preapproach: Preparation by the salesperson for the initial meeting with a prospect.

Presentation: A two-way process in which the salesperson listens to the customer to identify needs and then describes how the product will fulfill them.

Prospect: A potential customer interested in the seller's product.

Prospecting: Seeking potential customers within the company's target markets.

Qualified prospect: A potential buyer interested in the seller's product and with the attributes of a good customer.

Qualifying: Examining prospects to identify those with the authority and ability to buy the product.

Quotas: Quantitative objectives used to direct sales force activity and evaluate performance.

Referral: A lead provided by a qualified prospect.

Relationship selling: Forging bonds between buyer and seller to gain loyalty and mutual satisfaction.

Routing schedule: A travel plan for calling on prospects that is developed to save time and minimize expenses.

Salary: The fixed amount of compensation paid regardless of performance.

Sales force automation: The use of technology to improve personal selling and sales management effectiveness.

Sales force management: The marketing function involved with planning, implementing, and adjusting sales force activities.

Sales manager: The person responsible for the leadership and management of salespeople in order to accomplish the sales objectives established in the marketing plan.

Sales profit quotas: Profitability objectives for customers, products, and market segments.

Sales structure: The organization of the reporting relationship between sales managers and salespeople.

Sales territory: All the actual and potential customers, often within a specified geographic area, for which the salesperson has responsibility.

Sales volume quotas: Unit or dollar objectives, usually set by market segment, product or service line, and average volume per customer.

Team selling: Selling that involves people from most parts of the organization, including top executives, working together to create a relationship with the buying organization.

Telemarketing: Making telephone calls to leads provided by marketing services or from other lists.

Territory planning: Identifying potential customers, their sales potential, and the frequency with which they will be contacted about various products.

Traditional sales approach: Emphasizing persuasive techniques to get consumers to buy a company's products.

REFERENCES

1. Hiawatha Bray, "Hopkinton, Mass.–Based Data Storage Giant Faces Challenge from Alliance," *Knight Ridder/Tribune Business News,* July 7, 2000; John Madden, "Removable Storage: While IT Has Been Slow to Outsource Data Management, More Vendors Enter the Fray," *eWeek,* May 22, 2000, pp. 23+; Tim McLaughlin, "Rapid Expansion in Store for EMC Corp.," *Boston Herald,* March 6, 2000; Paul C. Judge, "EMC: High-Tech Star," *Business Week,* March 15, 1999, www.businessweek.com; "EMC's Ruettgers: Focus on Execution," *PC Week,* July 26, 1999, www.zdnet.com/eweek/stories/general/0,11011,2300761,00.html; Joseph F. Kovar, "Back Up to the Future—EMC Is Quietly Becoming a Top E-Business Supplier," *Computer Reseller News,* December 6, 1999, pp. 208+; EMC Web site, www.emc.com, accessed August 24, 2000.
2. Gene R. Luczniak and Patrick E. Murphy, *Ethical Marketing Decisions* (Boston: Allyn & Bacon, 1993), p. 185.
3. "Tomorrow's Jobs," *Occupational Outlook Handbook* (Washington, DC: Bureau of Labor Statistics, U.S. Department of Labor, 2000), pp. 3–4.
4. "Marketing and Sales Occupations," *Occupational Outlook Handbook* (Washington, DC: Bureau of Labor Statistics, U.S. Department of Labor, 2000), p. 271.
5. Ibid.
6. Jeff Cole, "Boeing Is Set for Record in 777 Orders—Topping $18 Billion, Results Put Pricey Plane Ahead of Rival Airbus Models," *Wall Street Journal, Eastern Edition,* November 27, 2000, p. A3.
7. Bill Kelly, "How to Sell Airplanes, Boeing-Style," *Sales and Marketing Management,* December 9, 1985, pp. 32–34; Dori Jones Yang and Andrea Rothman, "Boeing Cuts Its Altitude as the Clouds Roll In," *Business Week,* February 8, 1993, p. 25; and Shawn Tully, "Boeing: Is 'The Lazy Bee' a Bad Rap Question," *Fortune,* January 25, 1993, p. 10.
8. Chad Kaydo, "Are PCs Like Tupperware?" *Sales and Marketing Management,* June 1998, p. 20. See also its Web site at www.handteam.com.
9. Merck & Co. Annual Report, pp. 3, 31, www.merck.com/overview/99ar/pdf/99ar.pdf, site viewed December 16, 2000.
10. www.llbean.com, site visited March 5, 2001.
11. Brett A. Boyle, "The Importance of the Industrial Inside Sales Force: A Case Study," *Industrial Marketing Management* 25 (September 1996): 339–348.
12. Susan L. P. Srikonda, "No Order Number? No Problem," *Industrial Distribution,* May 2000, pp. 62–64. See also Tricia Campbell, "Getting Personal with Customers," *Sales and Marketing Management,* January 1999; p. 68.
13. Warren J. Keegan and Mark C. Green, *Principles of Global Marketing* (Upper Saddle River, NJ: Prentice Hall, 1997), p. 366.
14. Marcus W. Brauchli, "Looking East: Asia, on the Assent, Is Learning to Say No to 'Arrogant' West," *Wall Street Journal,* April 13, 1994, pp. A1, A8.
15. As cited in Marc Ferranti, "Navigating the Depths of Global Commerce," *InfoWorld,* November 27, 2000, pp. 38–40.
16. Sak Onvisit and John J. Shaw, *International Marketing* (Upper Saddle River, NJ: Prentice Hall, 1997), p. 539.
17. Interview by the author.
18. Ferranti, "Navigating the Depths of Global Commerce."
19. Gary Heil, Tom Parker, and Deborah C. Stevens, *One Size Fits One* (New York: Van Nostrand Reinhold, 1997), p. 2.
20. John R. Graham, "Successful Selling: Learning the Customer's Buying Cycle," *The American Salesman,* March 2000, pp. 3–9.
21. Gerald L. Manning and Barry L. Rease, *Selling Today* (Boston: Allyn & Bacon, 1992), pp. 17–18.
22. "Best Sales Forces, 2000," *Sales and Marketing Management,* www.salesandmarketing.com/smmnew/olexclusives/best.asp, site visited December 16, 2000.
23. See Joe Chapman and Stephanie Rauck, "Relationship Selling: A Synopsis of Recent Research," in *Developments in Marketing Science,* no. 18, ed. Roger Gomes (Coral Gables, FL: Academy of Marketing Science, 1995), p. 163.
24. Edward R. Del Gaizo, Kevin J. Corcoran, and David J. Erdman, *The Alligator Trap* (Chicago: Richard D. Irwin, 1996), p. 21.
25. "Best Sales Forces, 2000."
26. Ibid.
27. For more information, see Lisa M. Ellram, "Partnering Pitfalls and Success Factors," *International Journal of Purchasing and Materials Management* 31 (April 1995): 36–44.
28. Dean Allen Foster, "Negotiating and 'Mind-Meeting,'" *Directors and Boards,* Fall 1992, pp. 52–54. See also Sandra J. Allen, "Tactics for Success," *Communication World,* September 1999, pp. 34–37.
29. "Best Sales Forces, 2000."
30. Personal interview with John Sutthoff in Atlanta, GA, 1997.
31. "Best Sales Forces, 2000."
32. www.footlocker.com, site visited December 17, 2000.
33. "Best Sales Forces, 2000."
34. Robert J. Kapp, "Ethical Issues in Personal Selling and Sales Management," in *Ethics in Marketing,* eds. N. Craig Smith and John A. Quelch (Homewood, IL: Richard D. Irwin, 1993), pp. 539–555.
35. "Involvement of Salespeople in Different Daily Activities Varies by Industry," *Report 7023.3, Laboratory of Advertising Performance* (New York: McGraw-Hill Research, 1987).
36. Mark J. Astaria, "Cold Calling Rules and Procedures," 1995, www.seclaw.com/coldcall.htm, site visited February 21, 1997.
37. Roger S. Peterson, "Go Modular, Be Flexible to Control Exhibit Costs," *Marketing News,* December 2, 1996, p. 11.
38. Santiago Esparza, "Auto Show Sets Attendance Record," *Detroit News,* January 24, 2000 at detnews.com, visited December 16, 2000.
39. David Phillips and Mark Truby, "Trucks Rule the Roost at Chicago Auto Show," *Detroit News,* February 9, 2000, at detnews.com, visited December 16, 2000.
40. Alan Test, "Trade Show Selling," *The American Businessman,* September 2000, pp. 15–18.
41. "Richard Johnson of Amway Japan Challenging Japan's Sales Culture," *Institutional Investor,* May 1994, pp. 23–24; and "Edison Achievement Award Winners. Jay Van Andel and Richard M. De Vos," *Marketing News,* April 25, 1994, pp. E2, E8.
42. www.amway.com, site visited December 17, 2000.
43. Raymond Serafin, "Cars Look for New Lease on Loyalty," *Advertising Age,* July 11, 1994, p. 41.
44. Amanda Beeler, "Direct and Database Marketing," *Advertising Age,* October 16, 2000, p. 2.
45. "Prospecting for Business," *AT&T PowerSource Magazine,* www.att.com/hbr/check/prospect.html, site visited on February 21, 1997.
46. "Best Sales Forces, 2000."
47. Neil Rackham, *SPIN Fieldbook: Practical Tools, Methods, Exercises, and Resources* (New York: McGraw-Hill, 1996).
48. Ibid, p. 11.
49. Ibid, p. 12.
50. Role-playing with executives witnessed by the author.
51. Rackham, *SPIN Selling Fieldbook,* p. 21.
52. Jon M. Hawes, James T. Strong, and Bernard S. Winich, "Do Closing Techniques Diminish Prospect Trust?" *Industrial Marketing Management* 25 (September 1996): 349–357.
53. For additional information, see Geoffrey Brewer, "Mind Reading: What Drives Top Salespeople to Greatness," *Sales and Marketing Management,* May 1994, pp. 82–88; Bruce K. Pilling and Sevo Eroglu, "An Empirical Examination of the Impact of Salesperson Empathy and Professionalism and Merchandise Salability on Retail Buyers' Evaluations," *Journal of Personal Selling and Sales Management* 14 (Winter 1994): 45–58; Saul W. Gellerman, "The Tests of a Good Salesperson," *Harvard Business Review* 68

(May–June 1990): 64–71; George Izzo, "Compulsory Ethics Education and the Cognitive Moral Development of Salespeople: A Quasi-Experimental Assessment," *Journal of Business Ethics,* December 2000, pp. 223–241; John Farrell, "The Sweet Sound of Sales Success," *Incentive,* November 2000, p. 77; and O. C. Ferrell, Thomas N. Ingram, and Raymond W. LaForge, "Initiating Structure for Legal and Ethical Decisions in a Global Sales Organization," *Industrial Marketing Management,* November 2000, pp. 555–564.

54. Kenneth Labich, "Making Diversity Pay," *Fortune,* September 9, 1996, p. 177–180; and Louisa Wah, "Diversity at Allstate: A Competitive Weapon," *Management Review,* July/August 1999, pp. 24–30.

55. Carole Ann King, "Recruiting Women Is a Priority for MONY," *National Underwriter,* February 21, 2000, p. 23.

56. William C. Moncrief, et al., "Examining Gender Differences in Field Sales Organizations," *Journal of Business Research,* September 2000, pp. 245–257.

57. Nanette Byrnes, "Avon: The New Calling," *Business Week,* September 18, 2000, Industrial/Technology edition, p. 136.

58. "How Avon's CEO Implements Diversity," *Sales and Marketing Management,* January 1997, p. 37.

59. Lucas, "Race Matters."

60. Whirlpool Corporation at www.whirlpool.com, site visited December 18, 2000.

61. James O. Mitchel, "Winning with Diversity," *LIMRA's MarketFacts* 15 (January-February 1996): 22–26.

62. Mary Hallahan, "Bilingual Health Information Hits the Internet," *Pharmaceutical Executive,* June 2000, p. 132.

63. "Ford Motor Company: 346,990 Reasons for Success," *Special Advertising Section, Fortune,* April 15, 1996, pp. 149–192.

64. Brewer and Galea, "Best Sales Forces."

65. "Best Sales Forces, 2000."

66. Brewer and Galea, "Best Sales Forces."

67. Robert Klein, "Nabisco Sales Soar after Sales Training," *Marketing News,* January 6, 1997, p. 23.

68. "Best Sales Forces, 2000."

69. Ibid.

70. Brewer and Galea, "Best Sales Forces."

71. Earl D. Honeycutt, Jr., Ashraf M. Attia, and Angela R. O'Auria, "Sales Certification Programs," *Journal of Personal Selling and Sales Management* 16 (Summer 1996): 59–65.

72. Robin T. Peterson, "An Analysis of Contemporary Forecasting in Small Business," *Journal of Business Forecasting Methods and Systems* 15 (Summer 1996): 10–12.

73. Michele Marchetti, "Are Reps Motivated by Bonuses?" *Sales and Marketing Management,* February 1997, p. 33.

74. Gregory A. Rich, "The Constructs of Sales Coaching: Supervisory Feedback, Role Modeling, and Trust," *The Journal of Personal Selling and Sales Management,* Winter 1998, pp. 53–63.

75. "Meeting of the Minds."

76. Chad Kaydo, "A Motivation Master Class," *Sales and Marketing Management,* August 2000, pp. 88–98.

77. "What Should Sears Do? Consultants Offer Some Unsolicited Advice to Chairman Brennan," *Chain Store Age Executive,* August 1992, pp. 36–38.

78. Ken Grand and David W. Cravens, "Examining Sales Force Performance in Organizations That Use Behavior-Based Sales Management Processes," *Industrial Marketing Management* 25 (September 1996): 361–370.

79. Carey Peters, "Designing a 360(degree) Feedback System to Improve Employee Performance," *HR Focus,* September 2000, pp. 7, 10.

80. Sean Callahan, "Sales Staffs: Adapt or Die," *B to B,* April 10, 2000, pp. 1, 55ff.

81. Tom Dellecave, "Technology Update," *Sales and Marketing Management,* June 1996, p. 108.

82. Interview with Karen Griggs, March 4, 1997.

Bricks or Clicks

STAPLES, INC.

THE FIELD OF SALES FORCE management has been revolutionized by high technology. Over the past few years, a stream of innovative tools has emerged that facilitates communication and give salespeople unprecedented high-speed access to necessary information. Staples is one company that utilizes such tools. The office superstore giant recently incorporated in-store Business Solutions Centers, which bring the clicks of Staples.com to the bricks world of the store with a kiosk station.

Staples sees the Business Solutions Centers as the epitome of bricks-and-clicks retailing. By bringing the benefits of the online experience to its in-store shoppers, Staples has implemented a major transformation in its business strategy. The kiosks will be placed in up to four strategic areas of the store—furniture, the build-to-order computer kiosk, the pack-and-ship center, and the technology area. Customers that are nervous about using their credit card online can now order the products online at the kiosk and pay for their purchases at the register. This allows them access to the 45,000 items on the Web site as compared to the 7,500 items carried by a typical Staples store. One of the most important benefits of incorporating the kiosk computer stations into the store is that the salespeople are given a new tool to help increase in-store sales.

As the sales force connects directly with customers, it is crucial that they are interacting in the right way at the right time. Nearly every dimension of how salespeople behave is influenced by how they are managed. The Business Solutions Centers make it easy to plan, implement, and adjust sales force activities. Store associates can use the kiosks in many ways, which means their consultative selling skills are greatly enhanced. The associates can simply assist customers who may have problems using the system, or alternatively they can control the whole process themselves and actually perform the search for the customer. Making the customer happy is the most crucial part of sales. If customers are helped quickly and correctly the first time, they will be more likely to return in the future.

Staples seems to be ahead of the competition when it comes to integrating e-commerce with retail outlets. It is predicted that having in-store kiosks, such as the ones found in Staples Business Solutions Centers, is the wave of the future. With the click of a mouse, customers have access to information that will ultimately help them make an informed buying decision. At the same time, traditional store associates are on hand to help the customer in any way, giving the best of the clicks and bricks.

The Business Solutions Centers are also a significant way to implement the promotion strategy element of the marketing mix. When an in-store kiosk is consulted, the likelihood of a sale increases. Staples' cross-channel reach

Continued from previous page.

is increased with each new kiosk user by introducing more store customers to Staples.com. The customer base should only continue to grow.

Worldwide, Staples is currently the largest operator of office superstores. It invented the office superstore concept and will strive to stay the industry leader. As Staples founder and CEO said, "By integrating our stores with Staples.com and its extensive offering of both products and business services, [Staples is] truly becoming a one-stop destination for all the needs of small business."

Source: "Staples Merges its clicks with its bricks . . . ," *Business Wire*, August 23, 2000, www.businesswire.com; Stephanie Stoughton, "Web kiosks for consumers catch on," *The Boston Globe*, February 1, 2001, p. T4; "Staples rolls out Internet Access Points to All 954 Stores; 'Giving Customers What They Want, When They Want it,'" *Business Wire*, January 29, 2001.

CASE 16

Duracell

PEOPLE ALL OVER THE PLANET are demanding portable electronics from telephones, computers, toys, radios, and tape players to all types of handheld instruments and new forms of personal products. The variety of these devices is mind-boggling, including such items as poison gas sensors and even infusion pumps for drug treatment. While portability is booming, nothing is growing more rapidly than the need for batteries to supply power for all these gadgets. That is one reason Gillette purchased Duracell, the nation's leading supplier of batteries in the consumer market. The marriage appears to be an excellent match. Both organizations have strong sales operations targeted at retailers. And Duracell targets many other categories of accounts as well. With approximately 49 percent of the $2 billion U.S. alkaline battery market, Duracell is in a good financial position to expand and is seeking share gains. To do that, Duracell introduced Duracell Ultra in 1998, and it became the fastest growing battery in North America, stealing 13.5 percent of the market by fall 2000.

The consumer battery market, estimated at around $20 billion, is dominated by the established alkaline and zinc batteries, which sell at relatively low prices. These are the familiar AA, AAA, D, C, and rectangular nine-volt batteries. Duracell, Rayovac, Ralston Purina's Energizer, and Eveready brands are the four biggest battery companies worldwide. The U.S. manufacturers tend to be strongest in sales of the standard batteries. Panasonic and such companies as Sony, Sanyo, and Toshiba are large producers of specialized batteries for consumer products. Now Duracell has extended the line of Duracell Ultra to include a new item to better compete in the specialized battery category, Duracell Ultra with M3 technology. In September 2000 Duracell introduced the most recent generation of Ultra alkaline batteries, making the most powerful battery in the world more powerful. The improvements in performance offered by the M3 technology are very visible to the customer. These batteries offer twice the life of regular alkaline batteries in digital cameras, up to 240 more minutes of light in halogen flashlights, about 150 more pictures in flash cameras, and 180 more minutes of use in high-drain toys. The M3 technology

gets its name from the three features that create excellent performance: more power, more fuel, and more efficiency.

"Duracell's design strategy has been based on continually offering longer lasting Duracell alkaline batteries for a broad base of general purpose applications," states Ed DeGraan, president, Duracell North Atlantic Group. "But increasing power requirements from a growing and varied portable electronics device base calls for innovations beyond a single general purpose battery in order to maximize battery life and device performance."

Duracell Ultra and Duracell Ultra with M3 technology incorporate several patent-pending product features, which reduce internal resistance for improved high current flow to meet the power demands of high-tech devices. In addition, Duracell Ultra features PowerCheck, an on-battery fuel gauge tester, which has been recalibrated for use in high-tech devices.

Duracell management believes the quality of the sales organization is critical to the success of the traditional line and will be a great asset for the new-product line and product line extensions as well. Account managers work with major retailers to develop strategies uniquely suited to their competitive situation. Duracell salespeople are trained in relationship selling and play an important consultant role for major customers. Monica Botwinski, a 1994 marketing graduate from a major university, is a member of the Duracell sales team. One of her accounts was Pamida, a mass-merchandiser chain based in Omaha, Nebraska.

In order to help Pamida be successful during the Christmas season, she worked with people there to develop a strategy involving all aspects of the marketing mix. The product mix was determined by estimating potential consumer demand. The price was established on the basis of volume projections, competitor activities, and Pamida's profit objectives. The promotion strategy was developed not only around Duracell but also other products in order to increase storewide excitement and foot traffic. Finally, the location of Duracell products was carefully considered. Displays were customized to Pamida shoppers and placed in key locations to take advantage of cross-merchandising and impulse buying. The partnership approach increased Duracell dollar sales to Pamida by more than 44 percent, increased battery category sales by 20 percent, and increased battery category profitability by 38 percent. This sort of selling, which adjusts all parts of the marketing mix to the retailer's strategy and circumstance, is important to Duracell. Rather than simply sell to retail chains, which in turn have total responsibility for pushing the products, Duracell salespeople work together with the retailer's promotion personnel to develop marketing programs jointly.

1. *A key part of the Duracell sales strategy involves working jointly with retailers to create marketing strategies. What responsibilities do Duracell account managers assume when working with key retailers? How are these responsibilities carried out when introducing a new line such as Ultra?*

2. *What are the similarities and differences in selling to retail chains versus other types of accounts? For example, Duracell sales reps also sell to universities, theaters, and companies that have a broad range of battery needs.*

3. *What elements should sales managers consider in preparing the sales force for the new-product launch?*

Sources: Duracell Web site, www.duracell.com; "They Only Live Once," *Fortune,* October 27, 1997, www.fortune.com; Jennifer Kulpa, "What's Ahead in Specialty Batteries," *Drug Store News,* October 20, 1997, p. 741; RCR Radio Communications Report, September 1, 1997, p. 44; interview with Monica Botwinski, Duracell North Atlantic Group, April 1998; "Survey—Battery Industry: Consumer Demand Sparks 'Revolution': Portable Power Supply Has Come a Long Way in Recent Years," *Financial Times Surveys Edition,* April 4, 1997, p. 1; Duracell press release, *New Duracell High-Tech Alkaline Batteries Maximize Performance in High-Tech Devices,* February 18, 1998; "New Duracell Ultra With M3 Technology Is Now Available in North America," *Business Wire,* September 26, 2000; and C. William Symonds, "Can Gillette Regain Its Voltage? Duracell Acquisition Is Draining the Bottom Line," *Business Week,* October 16, 2000, p. 102.

PRICING
APPROACHES

◀ A Schwab Web site on a computer screen in the Charles Schwab online office in New York

CHARLES SCHWAB CHANGED THE STAID SECURITIES business forever in 1975, when he founded his namesake discount brokerage firm. Competing against long-established, full-commission brokerages such as Merrill Lynch, Schwab parlayed his innovative low-commission, high-volume strategy into a profitable niche business serving price-sensitive investors who don't need investment advice.

Over the years, Schwab continued to build on his discount pricing strategy by adding creative new product and service offerings. One innovation was giving customers the ability to call toll free to give brokers buy or sell orders; another was building a national chain of 300-plus Schwab offices so customers could meet with brokers in person. In yet another innovation, Schwab's brokers are on salary, not on commission as in traditional brokerages, so they can take the time to answer questions and provide information but do not recommend specific investments. Schwab also pioneered the mutual funds supermarket, an innovation that gives customers convenient access to thousands of mutual funds investments.

Then the emergence of Internet technology kicked off a new era of low-cost, brokerless trading. E*Trade and other Web-only start-ups developed software to allow customers to buy and sell securities through an automated online process. Because these brokerless trades cost much less to process than trades handled by brokers, the Web-based competitors were able to sharply undercut Schwab's discount commissions—sometimes charging less than $10 for a trade that might cost a Schwab customer $100 or more.

The Internet provided another opportunity for Schwab to continue its tradition of innovation by starting eSchwab, an online division targeting customers willing to key in their own online trades in exchange for lower commissions. Although eSchwab was positioned as a bare-bones brokerage service, customers began pushing for phone access and other features of the original Schwab service. Meanwhile, Schwab's offline customers were clamoring for eSchwab's online access and lower commissions. As Web-only rivals turned up the competitive heat by heavily promoting their deep-discount pricing, Schwab discontinued eSchwab, introduced a feature-rich new Web site, and slashed its price for online trades. Under the new price structure, customers pay a flat $29.95 commission for online trades of up to 1,000 shares, plus 3 cents per share above that level.

Now Schwab's challenge was to maintain long-term revenues and profits despite the drastic change in pricing, which cost the company about $125 million in revenues over the short run. By encouraging customers to use the Web site rather than call or visit brokers, Schwab would lower its costs. In addition, Schwab and his management team believed that the combination of low commissions, superior service, and product enhancements would build volume by attracting many new customers and reinforcing loyalty among the existing customer base. They were right: Within a year, Schwab had rocketed to the top of the online trading market and attracted millions of new customers who brought with them billions of dollars in assets, boosting Schwab's revenues as well as the bottom line.

Now almost three-quarters of the trades initiated by Schwab's 7 million customers are made online. With Schwab's increased popularity and higher trading volume, brokers and representatives are fielding more than 10 million customer calls every *month. So Schwab has installed special customer relationship management software to help employees respond to customer inquiries, track transactions, and maintain accounts. Adding to its service offerings, Schwab continues to open local offices, providing personalized service to customers in surrounding areas. It is also enhancing its Web site to offer innovations such as portfolio analysis tools, research, and customizable portfolio pages.*

True to its discount tradition, Schwab continues to stress pricing as a competitive tool. In one recent move, the company announced it will rebate automated teller machine (ATM) fees for customers who use the Schwab Access checking account and meet minimum investment or trading requirements. Elizabeth M. Stelluto, senior vice president of asset and cash management products, says the purpose is to "increase the share of wallet they hold at Schwab" by giving upscale clients another reason to bring money to Schwab.

In addition, Schwab is seeking to keep its most active online traders by cutting commissions for those who make more than 30 trades during a quarter, and cutting commissions even further for those who make more than 60 trades during a quarter. Under this pricing structure, the firm's lowest price is $14.95 per trade, half of its regular online commission rate but higher than the $4.95 some competitors charge active traders. Schwab's managers are betting that the firm's careful blend of low pricing and continuous innovation will keep customers loyal for the long term.[1]

CONNECTED: SURFING THE NET

www.schwab.com

Visit the Charles Schwab Web site and learn, research, plan, trade, invest, and connect online. Be amazed by the number of services available to you right from your own home.

THE CONCEPT OF PRICING

You can purchase a totebag for as little as $2, but you can also purchase the trendy "baguette" bag from Fendi for $1,100. A scarf can cost as little as $10, but a luxury pashmina shawl, made of cashmere, costs $300 to $400.[2] A remarkably broad range of prices is charged for items that have similar functions. Ginseng roots grown for tea in Korea and other Pacific Rim nations sell for a few dollars, but a couple of ounces found in the wild can cost nearly $50,000. New cars range from $10,000 for a Geo Metro to more than $330,000 for a Rolls-Royce Corniche.[3] Even four years of college tuition can cost from several thousand dollars to well over $100,000 at a select private school or a prestigious foreign university.

Pricing plays a critical role in the allocation of resources in free market economies. Since prices fluctuate according to competitive forces, their rise and fall directly influence the amount of goods and services consumers are willing to purchase. Pricing is also critical for the firm. The amount consumers purchase times its price determines the total revenue a company receives. Long before a sale is made, marketers forecast consumer demand at varying prices. This influences the allocation of resources used to create, promote, and distribute products. Prices have a dramatic effect in determining the overall profitability of the firm. Consequently, pricing is one of the most important and complex areas of marketing.

Seldom do we find one concept described by so many names. These "soften" the unpleasant feeling people may have when making payment. How many can you think of? Tuition is what you pay to go to school. Rent is what you pay for your apartment. An honorarium is paid for a speech. A retainer is paid to a lawyer. A fee is paid to a doctor. A premium is charged for insurance. Highways charge a toll. Dues are charged for membership. Assessments are used to calculate property taxes, the ongoing price for real estate ownership. A wage or salary is the price paid for work, and interest is the price paid for using money. Fares are charged for public transportation. Salespeople receive a commission for achieving a certain level of sales, and a bonus is the price paid for extraordinary performance. Whatever the name, price still signals that an amount is given up for the right to own or use something.

We have mentioned before that value comes from both the marketing organization and the buyer. In each case value is given up and received. **Price** is the exchange value of a good or service in the marketplace. We tend to think of price as a set amount of money that can be exchanged for a particular product. Yet, a good or service can also be exchanged for a different product through trading or bartering. Bartering simply bypasses the monetary system.

PRICE

The exchange value of a good or service in the marketplace.

Tons of killer boots starting at $27 a pair.

Payless ShoeSource

www.payless.com

Payless shoe source is known for its low priced footwear.

PRICE AS PART OF THE MARKETING MIX

We have discussed many of the decisions concerning the elements of the marketing mix. Products, logistics, and promotion create value for buyers. Price captures value from buyers for the firm. It is how the firm recovers its costs for other parts of the marketing mix. All parts of the mix interact to establish the firm's positioning. In fact, good pricing decisions require analyzing what target customers expect to pay even before products are developed, distributed, and promoted. Marketers need to understand ahead of time what customers perceive to be good value. If too much is charged, then customers perceive that they are losing value, and they will spend their money on other products or purchase the minimum amount necessary. If too little is charged, then the firm can lose money, eventually become uncompetitive, and go out of business.

This chapter's diversity feature, "Family Bargain Uses Low Prices to Court the Invisible Consumer," describes a chain whose low-price strategy is carefully blended with other mix elements—product selection, store location, targeted promotion, and service features—to create superior value.

OBJECTIVES OF PRICE SETTING

Prices are set with profit, volume, competitive, and customer objectives in mind. First, businesses need to charge enough to make a profit, which satisfies owners (shareholders) and creates the financial resources needed to grow. Even nonprofits must have excess revenues over costs in order to keep pace with inflation and expand operations. Second, prices directly influence the quantity sold. Like profit, volume maintains or increases the size of the business. In addition to pleasing owners, financial health creates opportunities for employees to progress and prosper. Third, price can prevent competitors from taking your customers. Finally, proper pricing helps build customer relationships.

As with the chicken and the egg, it is difficult to determine what comes first, but profit, volume, competitive, and customer objectives are all linked. Figure 17.1 shows that the satisfaction of all parties to the business is in some way affected by price. Most important, when relationship objectives are met, we have satisfied, loyal customers who consistently produce

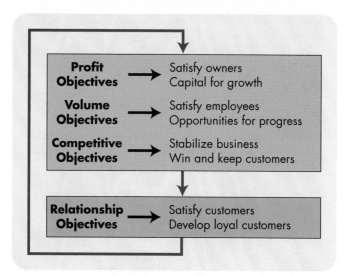

FIGURE 17.1 *Prices Serve Several Objectives*

revenues and profit. Yet it takes satisfied shareholders, contented employees, and a strong competitive position to make customers happy. Let's look at each set of objectives in turn.

PROFIT OBJECTIVES

Profit is critical for every business. Without it, investors will take their money elsewhere, and the business will cease to exist. In other words, you always need to price in order to make money. How do you do that? Simply stated, revenue minus cost equals profit. Price dramatically affects revenue. In fact, price times volume equals revenue. Later, we will see how price affects volume, which in turn affects cost. The point is that price plays a role in all the major factors that influence profit. To change profit, you simply increase or reduce price, volume, or cost. Since these three elements are so closely connected, the situation is very intriguing. Exactly how they interact is a big issue for marketers. For many businesses, a small change in price has a huge effect on profit. Let's say a business makes a 10 percent profit on sales. If nothing else changes, then a 3 percent price increase means that profits soar by 30 percent. A similar price decrease will have the opposite effect.

Price sometimes is designed to create maximum profits, but often satisfactory profits are the objective. Essentially, satisfactory means that the expectations of investors are met or exceeded. Satisfactory profits are based roughly on how much the company has historically made, plus how much similar companies make, plus the risks involved in the business. Profits are usually stated in terms of return on sales, a return on investment, or profit margin. A minimum return on investment is the amount you make when you put your money in a financial institution and earn interest. Since risks are involved in marketing a product, profits must be high enough to cover them. For example, Gateway Inc. has a profit margin of 23 percent.[4] Additionally, Gateway Inc. makes a significant profit margin of 60 percent on the maintenance packages the company offers to its customers, a major reason why the company is so successful.[5] Satisfactory profit goals are designed to reflect what shareholders, management, employees, and customers believe are fair for all parties involved.

Profit maximization is often stated as the goal of pricing, but what price will achieve this? Since price interacts with volume and cost, it is hard to say. Furthermore, there are limits to what people will pay. Theoretically, to maximize profit you would increase unit price until just before unit volume declines, and that is the point at which profit is maximized. In other words, the greatest quantity is being sold at the highest price the market will bear. Economists call this marginal analysis. But marginal analysis needs to take into account the long-term picture. Customer demand fluctuates due to economic conditions and shifts in the marketing mix. Competitive pressures also make it difficult to know exactly which price maximizes profit in dynamic markets.

VOLUME (SALES) OBJECTIVES

The price charged often affects the number of units purchased. Firms must price in such a way that production is maintained at a stable or growing level. Too high a price may result in layoffs, and too low a price may cause difficulty in meeting demand, which means lost sales and damage to the company's reputation. In either situation, employees will be unhappy. In the first case they will lose income or a job; in the second case they can't serve customers adequately. As we will see in chapter 18, too low a price can even reduce the units demanded. Because it influences the overall amount to be consumed, price must be carefully set.

COMPETITIVE OBJECTIVES

Volume translates into market share, which creates market power. Many firms have specific market share objectives and price accordingly. Of course, many factors other than price contribute to high share. Although lowering price to increase share may reduce profits in the short run, it may cause competitors to restrict activities or withdraw from markets. Prices then can be raised later in the absence of competition. But certain predatory pricing is illegal, as discussed later in this chapter. Perhaps Nintendo had a market share strategy in mind when it entered the U.S. market with its Nintendo Gamecube Game System.[6]

Aside from gaining share, pricing also can help the organization maintain its market position. Leaders try to establish the market price. Followers react to what the leaders charge. If either party wants to prevent pricing from being used to adjust demand, then it may choose one of two strategies. Status quo pricing maintains the same relative position: Every time a competitor makes a price change, rivals follow suit. Nonprice competition leaves price at a given level and adjusts other parts of the marketing mix, adding or subtracting value when appropriate. For example, advertising may be increased or decreased, extra products may be piggybacked on packages, or container size may be reduced. Of course, in the short term it is always easier to adjust price than alter other marketing mix variables.

RELATIONSHIP (CUSTOMER) OBJECTIVES

Prices can be established with customer loyalty in mind. This is at the heart of relationship marketing. The objective is to create sufficient value over time to develop repeat business. In this case, pricing signals the relationship the company desires with customers. This is called value-based pricing and is a major topic in the next chapter. Fundamentally, prices are set to

Clinique Cosmetics uses non-price competition and increases its advertising for promotional purposes.

FAMILY BARGAIN USES LOW PRICES TO COURT THE INVISIBLE CONSUMER

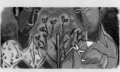 Executives at Family Bargain Center Stores want to fill a void. The population of its home state of California has changed dramatically over the last decade and most retailers are neglecting the low end of the retail spectrum. Officials at the 127-unit chain based in San Diego are targeting the low-income minority consumer groups with a strategy that stresses quality merchandise at low prices.

"We carry nationally recognized brands, essentially the same products found in major discount stores—but at prices substantially below [national chains]. We buy closeouts, overruns, and cancellations," says Family Bargain Center's president and CEO, William Mowbray. But that does not mean last season's goods. Fashion, he says, is just as important to low-income consumers as it is to more affluent shoppers. People who shop at Family Bargain know they will find a shirt for $6 that would sell in the Gap for $34, or a pair of black Vans sneakers for $10 that would sell for up to $50 in a specialty shop. Value is a powerful motivator for the market segment Family Bargain Center targets.

Unlike most discount and specialty chains that purchase goods six months in advance of the selling season, Family Bargain buys when the season opens. "Within at least 10 days from the time we order," says Mowbray, "the goods are in the stores ready to be sold." Because the chain sells only apparel, not a mix of clothing and hard goods such as most other discounters, Family Bargain's gross profit margin consistently has averaged around 35 percent, compared to the typical 28 percent.

Offering a combination of quality and current merchandise at good prices also pays off in customer loyalty. "I think one of the reasons for this is we tend to cater to our consumer more than other retailers do, building loyalty in the process," Mowbray says. The chain connects with its large Hispanic customer base by staffing stores with bilingual employees. Signs are displayed in both Spanish and English, while locally popular music, brightly colored pennants, and occasional festive outdoor promotions serve to enhance store atmosphere.

And Family Bargain does not expect customers to find its stores—it locates stores right where its target customers live. Its criteria for store sites are large Hispanic population, median household income of $25,000 (about half the national average), and a large percentage of children under age 14. Wal-Mart, Kmart, and Target should not be too surprised if a Family Bargain store appears next to them. In looking for a site, the company actually prizes locations near these discounters. "Wal-Mart in particular is a huge draw, which we typically benefit from," Mowbray says. The company's goal is to get the customer to think "I'll look for what I need in Family Bargain first, because if I find it there, I know I'll pay much less. Then I'll go to Wal-Mart."

It is quite conceivable that the Family Bargain concept may turn into a national chain. "We think our concept can extend virtually everywhere in the United States because there are low-end consumers in all parts of the country," asserts Mowbray.

Sources: Adapted from Jay L. Johnson, "The Invisible Consumer," *Discount Merchandiser,* June 1996, pp. 92–94; and PricewaterhouseCoopers EdgarScan report, 1998, retrieved December 8, 2000 from the World Wide Web: edgarscan.pwcglobal.com.

provide value for the customer in both the short term and the long run. Your most loyal customers should benefit to some degree from the extra profit generated through the relationship. This can be accomplished by lowering the price to loyal buyers or by adding value to the product they receive. Most important, you must understand your customers thoroughly in order to learn what they value.

MAJOR FACTORS INFLUENCING PRICE

Pricing according to value concepts requires a grasp of several elements, as outlined in Figure 17.2. First, economic factors explain how the demand for and supply of products relate to price. Second, legal and ethical constraints affect pricing decisions. Since price plays a major role in determining how economic resources are distributed, the government and courts have taken a particular interest in pricing. Third, the competitive environment influences price. Marketers must understand how competitors differentiate their products and the effect that substitutes have on price. Fourth, understanding how the company's cost structure is influenced by price decisions is very important. Finally, numerous global factors

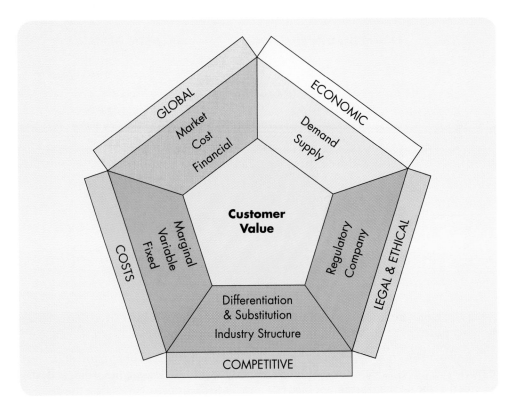

FIGURE 17.2 *Factors Influencing Price*

affect pricing in domestic and international markets. Each of these areas is addressed in the following sections.

ECONOMIC FACTORS: DEMAND AND SUPPLY

Economists have developed elaborate theories about the effect of consumer demand and product supply. Both have a significant influence on pricing.

The Demand Curve Demand is determined by the amount of product customers need, plus their willingness and ability to buy. Demand has a major influence on price. It is usually depicted by a demand curve, which is a graph showing quantity along the horizontal axis and different prices along the vertical axis. Marketers use the curve to estimate changes in total demand for a product based on differing prices. The **demand curve** describes the price elasticity of a given product. **Price elasticity** is the extent to which changes in what is charged affect the number of units sold. The formula for calculating it is

$$\text{Price elasticity of demand} = \frac{\text{Percentage change in quantity demanded}}{\text{Percentage change in price}}$$

Price elasticity is used to forecast responses to price changes and to define market segments. Knowing the price elasticity for company and competitor products is important in determining a pricing strategy.[7]

When price has a major effect on demand, the product is price elastic. When price has little effect on demand, the product is price inelastic. Figure 17.3 shows two demand curves, one for a price-elastic product (CD-ROMs) and the other for a price-inelastic product (heart surgery). CD-ROMs are useful and entertaining but are not a necessity. If their average price is high, then consumers will demand very few; if the price goes down, then demand will increase dramatically. In contrast, most consumers who need heart surgery do not care about the price, especially if government or private insurance will cover the cost. Price changes in heart surgery are not likely to influence the total demand to any large degree.

When demand is elastic, prices tend to decrease over time. As Figure 17.3 shows, when the price of CD-ROMs drops from about $250 down to $50, sales increase from 1,000 units to more than 7,000 units, reflecting elastic demand. For heart surgery, as the price drops from $2,000 to $1,000, demand stays roughly the same. There are also effects on total revenue. In the

DEMAND CURVE

A depiction of the price elasticity demand for a given product.

PRICE ELASTICITY

The extent to which changes in price affect the number of units demanded or supplied.

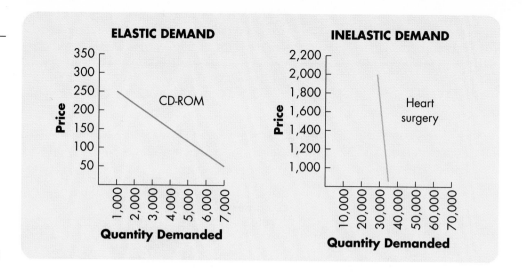

FIGURE 17.3 *Demand Curves*

elastic case it rises from $250,000 to $350,000 as increased volume more than compensates for the lower price. In the inelastic case, revenue declines from about $60 million to $35 million.

Demand Sensitivity by Market Segment In addition to the type of product, differences in market segments explain some of the variation in demand. Because the airline industry believes that the overall demand for business travel is less sensitive to price than the demand for leisure travel, pricing policies are designed specifically for each segment. Business travelers often purchase tickets at the last minute and are likely to pay full fare, whereas vacationers can plan well in advance and pay discounted rates. Fares are also lower for trips that include at least one weekend night, which seldom applies to business travelers. Their demand is inelastic because a certain amount of travel is required for the functioning of the firm. Leisure travelers not only have more elastic demand but also are more sensitive to price differences among airlines. Just before spring break, student newspapers are full of ads offering trip packages at greatly reduced prices. Yahoo Travel, for example, has cruise vacations for as low as $229 per person.[8]

CROSS-PRICE ELASTICITY OF DEMAND

The extent to which the quantity demanded of one product changes in response to changes in the price of another product.

Cross-Price Elasticity of Demand We find **cross-price elasticity of demand** when the quantity demanded of one product changes in response to price changes in another product. For example, an increase in the cost of lumber in the building industry increases the demand for substitute products made of plastic and steel. At the brand level, an increase in the price of Coke increases the demand for Pepsi. Marketers use demand curves to describe price elasticity for a product class (all brands) or for a single brand. Price elasticity may differ for the total industry (that is, for all brands) versus an individual brand. Because gasoline is a necessity, variations in the average price charged by all producers may not affect demand dramatically. But British Petroleum-Amoco may find that its demand is elastic if it charges a lot more than the industry average. In other words, cross-elasticity refers to the amount of demand for one company's product based on its difference from the average price. Therefore, the concept of elasticity applies to the total industry, whereas cross-elasticity applies to preferences for individual brands or substitutes. Several marketing factors are likely to have a significant effect on cross-elasticity. For example, customers who are brand loyal to a particular gasoline company, especially those who buy the premium grade, are less likely to buy gasoline elsewhere because of a two- or three-cent difference in price; those with little or no loyalty, and who buy the lowest grade, are more likely to shop around.[9]

career tip At British Petroleum-Amoco, pricing specialists use a combination of data to develop market-based pricing strategies and tactics for gasoline as well as metrics to measure performance for strategies and execution. They are responsible for learning about market structure, product costs, competitive retail tactics, consumer behavior patterns, and price elasticities. They are also responsible for profit, volume, and margin results as well as for achieving other strategic and tactical goals. If you are interested in this kind of job or another career at Amoco, then view the current openings at www.bpamocojobs.com.

Many marketing plans are designed to produce inelastic cross-elasticity for the brand. That means price is less important to buyers than brand attributes, so price competitors cannot lure them away. Consider Girbaud jeans, which typically retail for more than $70 per pair, whereas Levi's often sell for less than $40. Many consumers are willing to pay more for the Girbaud brand for prestige reasons or because they like its features.

To reduce the cross-price elasticity of their products, marketers may use any of the following approaches:[10]

- Position the product relative to costly substitutes. General Motors attempted this when it priced its Aurora design to be competitive with BMW, Acura, Audi, Lexus, and Infiniti in the $30,000 to $35,000 price range.[11]
- Focus attention on unique features. Boston Whaler commands a premium for its line of recreation craft due to the company's reputation for safety. The boats can't sink, which is a major reason the U.S. Coast Guard selects the brand.
- Make it costly or difficult to switch. ABB Robotics trains users of its systems in programming and maintenance. Retraining on another system is expensive and time consuming.
- Make cross-brand comparisons difficult. Prudential says "get a piece of the rock," implying that its size is an asset in financial planning.
- Use price to signal status, image, or quality. The name Mercedes is synonymous with high price. One dealer says: "If customers have to ask the price, they can't afford it."
- Put price in the context of high value. Volvo emphasizes family protection. Assuring the safety of loved ones is a benefit that customers are likely to value more highly than the money they could save by purchasing a cheaper brand.

The Supply Curve   Price, which influences profit, also has an important influence on the willingness to produce. When price is higher, producers are willing to supply more. When profit margins are low, companies are likely to produce less. The supply curves shown in Figure 17.4 depict these relationships. In the elastic curve, an increase in unit price from $30 to $280 causes a dramatic increase in CD-ROM production, from 700 units to 6,500 units. In the inelastic curve, price hikes cause only a moderate increase in supply; there are relatively few trained surgeons, and they can squeeze only so many procedures into each day's schedule.

The **supply curve** reveals the amount that producers are willing to provide at each price. Theoretically, it operates very much like a demand curve, but different factors are at work. For example, companies with high fixed investment find it extremely difficult to exit the industry, so supply is inelastic. Another example is lawyers, who are generally reluctant to switch careers because they have invested heavily in education. When the price of legal services drops dramatically because of competition, lawyers are still willing to produce the same amount, reflecting the highly inelastic supply curve. When industry entry and exit are easy, supply tends to be more elastic. As prices rise, firms are willing to produce more; as prices decline, firms produce less or switch to other products.

SUPPLY CURVE

A depiction of the price elasticity of supply for a product.

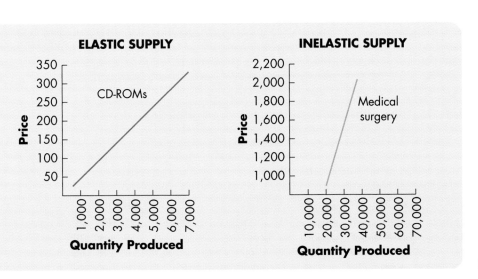

FIGURE 17.4 *Supply Curves*

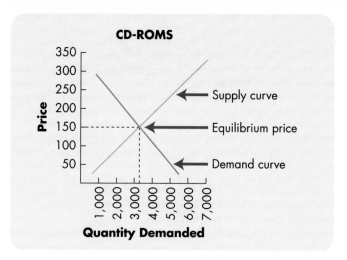

FIGURE 17.5 *Supply and Demand Equilibrium*

Equilibrium Price   In theory, price plays a role in balancing supply and demand. In Figure 17.5, the equilibrium price for CD-ROMs—the point at which the supply and demand curves cross—is $150. At prices below that point, producers are increasingly reluctant to supply CD-ROMs; at prices above it, consumers are increasingly reluctant to buy. Market forces work to help balance supply and demand so that products do not go unused and customers do not pay more than is required. Economic theory suggests that, over time, most product prices are somewhat elastic. When prices are high, supply is likely to outstrip demand. Suppliers then lower prices until supply and demand come into equilibrium. When prices are too low, less is produced. Consumers are willing to pay more for scarce products, so supply increases until it is in balance with demand. In other words, supply and demand are related because changes in price affect how both suppliers and consumers respond. For example, in 2000 the price of cranberries fell to $11 per barrel from a high of $80 in 1996. The demand for cranberries rose sharply after 1994 after a Harvard University study showed that cranberry juice soothed urinary tract infections, and cranberry growers increased their acreage by 176 percent over the next few years to match the new demand. In 1999, however, the new acreage yielded a record harvest and the supply of cranberries surpassed the demand, resulting in the low price of $11 a barrel. Many cranberry farmers are expected to go out of buisness because the price of their product does not cover the costs of growing it, much less produce a profit. With cranberry production thus scaled back, the profitability of cranberries is expected to recover by 2002.[12]

It is important to remember that supply and demand curves work perfectly only in economic theory, which assumes that most variables are held constant. In reality, the marketplace changes rapidly. Indeed, a main purpose of marketing strategy is to alter the supply and demand characteristics of an industry in the company's favor. Unfortunately, this does not always work positively for all competitors. For example, the Big Three U.S. automakers have cut their light truck production; the popularity of other light truck models from Europe and Japan has decreased the demand for those light trucks made by the Big Three.[13] In many industries the tremendous diversity in market segments and individual firms introduces more variables than can reasonably be taken into account. Furthermore, it is very difficult to forecast demand and to predict what competitors will do. For all these reasons, attempts to influence elasticities through marketing strategies may not be very effective in practice.

LEGAL AND ETHICAL INFLUENCES ON PRICING

Both federal and state laws affect pricing decisions. In fact, pricing is one of the most legally constrained areas of marketing. Most regulations are designed to allow prices to fluctuate freely so that market forces can work. Some, however, protect consumers from unfair prices—those that are higher than the value created due to the manipulation of market forces. Pricing practices that are legislatively restrained or regulated include price-fixing, price discrimination, minimum prices (unfair sales), price advertising, dumping, and unit pricing, each of which is described later. Figure 17.6 summarizes federal legislation on pricing.

Although marketers certainly must take care to avoid outlawed pricing practices, many companies are equally concerned to avoid unethical pricing that could tarnish their reputation

Act	Key Aspects
Sherman Antitrust Act 1890	Restricts predatory pricing (to drive competitors from the market) and makes it illegal to price fix.
Federal Trade Commission Act 1914	Set up the Federal Trade Commission, which is responsible for limiting unfair and anticompetitive practices in business.
Clayton Act 1914	Restricts price discrimination and purchase agreements between buyers and sellers.
Robinson-Patman Act 1936	Restricts discriminatory pricing that diminishes competition, particularly among resellers.
Wheeler-Lea Act 1938	Allows the Federal Trade Commission to investigate deceptive pricing practices and to regulate advertising of prices to help ensure that it does not deceive consumers.
Consumer Goods Pricing Act 1975	Eliminates price controls vertically and horizontally in the market so that channel members cannot set prices and so that retailers do not have to sell according to manufacturer or other channel member price schedules.

FIGURE 17.6 *Major Federal Price Legislation*

and erode consumer trust. "Pricing Ethics," the last topic in this section, describes a number of questionable practices.

Price-Fixing **Price-fixing** occurs when one party attempts to control what another party will charge in the market. There are laws against vertical and horizontal price-fixing. **Vertical price-fixing** is an attempt by a manufacturer or distributor to control the final selling price at the retail level. The Consumer Goods Pricing Act of 1975 made all interstate use of unfair trade or resale price maintenance illegal. Retailers cannot be required to use the list price (suggested retail price) set by manufacturers or resellers. Freedom for retailers to adjust prices enhances competition, thereby reducing the overall average price to consumers. The passage of this law was controversial because manufacturers and wholesalers often want to control retail prices in order to maintain consistent positioning. Several practices for controlling retail prices are legal. The manufacturer or distributor may do any of the following:

- Own the retail outlet and establish its pricing policy
- Suggest and advertise a retail price
- Preprint prices on products
- Sell on consignment (own items until they are sold)
- Screen channel members, choosing only those with a history of price maintenance in their retail outlet

PRICE-FIXING

An attempt by one party to control what another party will charge in the market.

VERTICAL PRICE-FIXING

An attempt by a manufacturer or distributor to control the final selling price at the retail level.

Preprinted-prices on products is one common legal practice for controlling retail prices.

Horizontal price-fixing is an agreement among manufacturers and other channel members to set prices at the retail level. The Sherman Act and the Federal Trade Commission Act outlaw these practices even if the prices are "reasonable." Violations of either statute can be severely punished with steep fines and prison sentences. For example, the Department of Justice is currently investigating several corporations for price-fixing through business-to-business exchanges. The largest controversy surrounds the online exchange for car suppliers, called Covisint. A joint venture among Ford, General Motors, DaimlerChrysler, and Renault/Nissan, the exchange hopes to become the preferred place for carmakers' suppliers to sell their parts to the Big Three. Some in the car industry claim that staff at one of the four car firms have implied that suppliers have no choice but to do business through this one exchange. The exchange also puts pressure on suppliers not to work with other exchanges. This set of circumstances could imply a monopoly and horizontal price-fixing.[14] The Association of Retail Travel Agents (ARTA) recently filed lawsuits in the United States and Canada for much the same reasons; ARTA believes that the "T-2" Internet site, backed by 27 global airline carriers, allows the carriers to engage in horizontal collusion and price-fixing more easily, since the individual carriers' prices are easily available to each other on the Internet.[15] Furthermore, in 2000, the world's largest and most prestigious auction houses, Sotheby's and Christie's, agreed to pay $512 million to settle claims that they cheated buyers and sellers by fixing prices as far back as 1992.[16]

Signs of price-fixing include cooperation among competitors on discounting, credit terms, or conditions of sale; any discussions about pricing at association meetings; plans to issue price lists on the same date or on given dates; plans to withhold or rotate bids on contracts; agreements to limit production in order to increase prices; and any exchange of information among competitors on pricing. The intent is to prohibit communication among competitors about pricing or any aspects of the business that may influence pricing levels.

On the international level, there are few antitrust sanctions to ensure fair competition. For example, in most countries impartial bidding processes are required, but in others the winners are secretly predetermined. In Japan this practice is called *dango* and is frequently used. In the United States and many other nations, it is known as *bid rigging*. U.S. trade officials estimate that substantial business is lost as a result of this practice. For example, U.S. builders have been prevented from competing for their share of the $500 billion Japanese construction market. The United States hired a Japanese law firm to file for $35 million in damages against 140 Japanese companies accused of rigging bids. This action resulted in a $32.6 million settlement.

Price Discrimination **Price discrimination** occurs when a manufacturer or other channel member charges different prices to retailers competing in the same marketplace. The Robinson-Patman Act of 1936 was designed to enhance competition by protecting small retailers against discounters or larger retailers that might obtain favorable treatment from suppliers. Today, this law is a major restriction on how manufacturers price. Essentially, the act permits manufacturer discounts only if the seller can demonstrate that they are available to all competing channel buyers on the same fair basis. Price fluctuations must be developed in such a way that both small and large buyers can qualify for discounts, or the discounts must be cost justified. The law specifies that it is illegal not only for sellers to engage in unfair practices but also for retailers to purchase products when they know that discrimination toward other retailers is occurring.

The Robinson-Patman Act involves a relatively complex issue. Differential pricing is allowed in many circumstances in which manufacturers are competing to gain or hold business. The law was designed to enhance competition by preventing restraint of trade. Essentially, violation occurs when manufacturers or other channel members charge differential prices that inhibit the ability of one retailer to compete with another. Acceptable price discrimination occurs when the differences are based on time, place, customer characteristics, or product distinctions. In other words, any time the marketing mix has been altered, price may reflect those changes.

Consider the annual fees associated with different credit cards. The issuer may charge affluent customers $100 a year for premium gold cards but suspend all fees for students. Discounts for senior citizens are another acceptable form of price discrimination. For instance, the Ames 55 Gold Card entitles customers age 55 and older to a 10 percent discount on merchandise bought on Tuesday.[17] These practices demonstrate how price deviates among consumer segments.

Minimum Prices   Laws against so-called minimum prices, often called unfair sales acts, have been enacted in a number of states. These prevent retailers from selling merchandise for less than the cost of the product plus a reasonable profit. More than half the states have such laws in order to protect smaller retailers from larger competitors.[18] **Predatory pricing** occurs when large firms cut prices on products in order to eliminate small local competitors. Wal-Mart was recently accused of selling certain grocery items at a loss in stores in Germany in order to unfairly undercut local business competitors.[19] At the national level, the Sherman and Clayton acts prevent this. Other laws apply to intrastate commerce.

> **PREDATORY PRICING**
> Price-cutting by large firms to eliminate small local competitors.

Loss leaders are items priced below cost to attract customers. In some states this practice is restricted. In others it is legal, particularly when it is not designed to injure specific local competitors. Most loss leaders are heavily advertised brands with strong appeal. For example, supermarkets may feature a special on brand-name laundry detergents that have wide appeal. Once in the store, customers are likely to purchase additional goods at normal or even elevated prices. McDonald's and other fast-food chains can lower prices on burgers to increase traffic because their margins on soft drinks and fries make up the difference. Even investment companies such as Charles Schwab use loss leaders. They waive fees on money funds to attract business, hoping that customers will later invest in other areas.[20]

> **LOSS LEADERS**
> Items priced below cost to attract customers.

Marketers must be careful in using loss leaders. According to Donald Hughes, a former research manager at Sears, "You have to ask yourself how much money are you willing to spend to bring people into the store, because you have the problem of cherry picking, where people come in and buy only the loss leader, which foils your strategy."[21]

Price Advertising   The Federal Trade Commission has set up permissible standards for price advertising. Essentially, these guidelines prohibit marketers from communicating price deceptively. Firms may not claim that a price is reduced unless the original price has been offered to the public regularly and recently. Price comparison with the competition cannot be made unless verification is provided. And premarked prices cannot be artificially increased as a point of comparison unless products are actually sold at that price in substantial quantities. In addition, a retailer cannot continuously advertise the same product as being on sale when that price has become standard at that outlet.

Bait-and-switch promotions are specifically outlawed by the Federal Trade Commission Act and various state statutes. **Bait and switch** occurs when the seller advertises items at extremely low prices and then informs the customer these are out of stock, offers different items, or attempts to sell the customer more expensive substitutes. In other words, when there is no intent to sell the advertised item, retailers are being dishonest.

> **BAIT AND SWITCH**
> An unethical practice in which sellers advertise items at extremely low prices and then inform the customer that the items are out of stock, offer different items, or attempt to sell the customer more expensive substitutes.

Dumping   In the international market, one of the most common regulations relates to dumping, which is a form of price discrimination. **Dumping** occurs when a product is sold in a foreign country at a price lower than in the producing country and lower than its actual cost of production. Why do companies do this? It can be a very effective way to maximize profits, since global organizations cover many of their fixed costs through product pricing in the home market; they then price according to only their variable costs in other parts of the world.

> **DUMPING**
> Selling a product in a foreign country at a price lower than in the producing country and lower than its cost of production.

Burger King lowers prices on burgers, but profits on soft drinks make up the difference.

Dumping is illegal because it puts manufacturers in the local foreign market at a disadvantage. Recently, the Department of Commerce announced that it would impose financial penalties on future imports of hot-rolled steel products coming from Japan and Brazil. Companies from these two nations had increased their steel exports to the United States by 47 percent, severely hurting the steel industry in the United States and resulting in an estimated 10,000 layoffs from 12 U.S. steel companies.[22] Many pharmaceutical companies have been accused of dumping medications in East Asia.[23] Since 1990, China has been cited in more antidumping petitions in the United States than in any other country,[24] but China recently enacted its own anitdumping laws to protect aging industries in the country that are not performing well. As a result of these new laws, China imposed punitive antidumping tariffs on newsprint imports from the United States, Canada, and South Korea.[25]

Predatory dumping is pricing designed to drive local firms out of the market. Strong market share is gained, competitors are put out of business, and then higher average prices are charged.[26] Coca-Cola, for example, dropped the price of a box of 24 bottles in Vietnam from VND 26,000 to VND 17,000. After winning a sizable share of the soft-drink market, it raised the price to VND 46,000 a box. In this way, Coca-Cola used what some claim is predatory dumping to increase sales and eventually profits.[27]

Unit Pricing   Container sizes for the same item can vary considerably. In some cases the package may have similar wording, such as "giant" or "large economy" size. This makes it difficult for consumers to compare the price of products based on the size and type of packaging. The unit pricing legislation enacted two decades ago requires that certain types of retail outlets, especially food stores, display price per unit of measure as well as total price. For example, a 4-ounce can of tuna selling for $1.00 is also priced at 25 cents per ounce. In this way consumers can clearly see whether a larger size makes a price difference. The law is designed to help cost-conscious consumers make wise decisions at the retail level. In fact, according to a survey of customers, the most important attribute in stores is unit pricing signs on the shelves.[28]

Pricing Ethics   Ethical issues in pricing abound. For price-sensitive products they revolve around the creation of demand and delivery of value based on price. For price-inelastic products, particularly because of the captive audience, gouging is an issue.

Although laws protect customers against unscrupulous pricing, we still find questionable ways of using price to increase demand. For example, an ad for dramatically reduced airfares states (in tiny print) that some restrictions may apply. When you call, you learn that so many restrictions apply that your choices are limited to a few seats and times. British Airways recently was found guilty of publishing a misleading and ambiguous advertisement. As a promotion, the airline offered free tickets to about 250,000 members of the British Airways Executive Club; the offer, however, was hedged with no less than 29 terms, conditions, and restrictions not mentioned in the promotional mailings sent to consumers.[29]

Unit price legislation requires some retail outlets to display price per unit of measure as well as item price.

Another way to increase demand is to make the product seem less expensive than it really is. Sometimes all costs are not clearly communicated. For example, you go to a car dealer and receive a price. After deciding to purchase, you notice a charge for administration expenses on the invoice. The salesperson tells you that this is standard and was stated in small print on the sheets you were shown previously.

Perhaps you have noticed that your favorite brand of paper towel or pudding seems to disappear faster than it once did. Check the package. There is a good chance that the price remained the same but the size was reduced. Rather than pass on increased costs to customers, some manufacturers reduce the amount of product contained in a package. To obscure the issue, words like "new convenience package" are printed in small type. You're getting less value but may not be aware of it, because basic package design and price stay the same.

The captive customer creates a tempting target for some marketers. Because demand is already there, the question is how much to charge. Consider the cost of automobile parts. After an accident, you find that replacing one door will cost 20 percent of what you paid for the car. Are you likely to scrap it? It is true that handling and stocking inventory has to be included in prices, but it is a known fact that many companies make a much greater percentage on replacement items than on the original product.

Another way to reduce the amount delivered is to price on an all-you-want basis and then limit the supply. For example, a golf course or tennis club has a monthly fee for unlimited usage, but there are so many customers that you must wait an exorbitant amount of time for space. Some e-tailers experienced a similar circumstance during the Christmas 1999 season, when many online stores did not have enough products, or an efficient system of delivery, to deliver items already bought and paid for by consumers. A total of 14 percent of all orders arrived late, and 6 percent did not arrive at all. Clearly, these shoppers would not have ordered the products if they had known that they would have been late for Christmas. The Federal Trade Commission fined stores such as CDNow and Macy's for failing to make good on their delivery promises. As a result, by Christmas 2000, many online retailers improved ordering and shipping practices to meet the consumer demand for their products and services.[30]

COMPETITIVE FACTORS THAT INFLUENCE PRICE

When making pricing decisions, marketers must take the competitive environment into consideration. More specifically, it's important to look at industry structure and the potential for differentiating products through pricing strategies.

Industry Structure *Industry* may be defined broadly or narrowly for marketing purposes. It refers to a group of firms offering similar products. For example, Pizza Hut executives may view their industry as only establishments that sell pizza or as all restaurants in a particular price range. As with most other tools, marketers must make sure that the industry concept they use is relevant to the situation at hand.

To understand how competition affects price, we must look at industry structure as well as the behavior of individual firms. Industry analysis examines such aspects as the number of firms, whether products are differentiated, and the freedom of firms to enter and exit. Economists have identified four basic industry structures—perfect competition, monopoly, oligopoly, and monopolistic competition. Figure 17.7 shows how each type is likely to affect pricing and other forms of competition.

Perfect Competition In an industry with **perfect competition** each firm has little if any control over prices. None is large enough relative to others to control factors of production or market demand. Usually, many small firms produce precisely the same product. Because they cannot dictate prices, their primary decisions revolve around how much to produce and how to produce it. Since firm size is small, it is generally easy to enter and exit the market. Profits tend to be generated not through price but economies of scale and cost reductions.

Monopoly At the opposite end of the spectrum from pure competition is **monopoly,** an industry structure in which one organization makes a product with no close substitutes. As the only firm in the market, the monopolist has a great deal of freedom in establishing price. Most monopolies exist because there are barriers to entry for competing firms. For example, governments in many countries establish sole providers for certain services, such as communications or public transportation. Generally, these are heavily regulated to prevent abuses, and

PERFECT COMPETITION
The industry structure in which no single firm has control over prices.

MONOPOLY
The industry structure in which one organization makes a product with no close substitutes.

Type of Structure	Number of Firms	Product Differentiated or Homogeneous	Firms Have Price-Setting Power	Free Entry	Distinguishing Characteristics	Examples
Perfect Competition	Many	Homogeneous	No	Yes	Price competition only	Wheat farmer Textile firm
Monopoly	One	A single unique product	Yes	No	Constrained by market demand	Public utility Brewery in Taiwan
Oligopoly	Few	Either	Yes	Limited	Strategic behavior	Cereal maker Primary copper producer
Monopolistic Competition	Many	Differentiated	Yes, but limited	Yes	Price and quality competition	Restaurants Music industry

FIGURE 17.7 *Industry Structure and Competition*

Source: Karl Case and Ray C. Fair, *Principles of Economics*, 3rd ed. © 1994. Adapted by permission of Prentice Hall, Inc., Upper Saddle River, NJ.

CONNECTED: SURFING THE NET

www.ticketmaster.com

See for yourself what kind of service charges apply to concerts and events. You can also check prices, order tickets, get venue and seating chart information, and much more at Ticketmaster online. See what's on sale in your area by exploring the company's weekly listing.

<u>OLIGOPOLY</u>

The industry structure in which a small number of firms compete for the same customers.

prices are set by governing boards rather than company executives. Public utilities that are established as monopolies usually must have their rates approved by a commission whose job is to protect the public interest.

From time to time private enterprises can achieve monopoly status through control of a patent or scarce raw material. Sometimes entry barriers, such as the sheer size of initial investment, may keep competitors out. Intel has been called a monopoly because of its dominance as a technology supplier. Legal experts often refer to companies such as Microsoft and Intel as essential facilities because customers have to buy their products. However, in 2000 federal court judges decided that Microsoft constituted a monopoly because the company illegally tied its Internet browser to the Windows operating system, making it difficult for consumers to buy separate operating and Internet systems. In 2001, the case is currently under appeal.[31]

Wanting lower concert prices for fans, Pearl Jam contended that Ticketmaster inflated the cost with an unwarranted charge, which added as much as 30 percent to the face value. The company argued that the service charge was used to secure venue arrangements, to guarantee performances, and sometimes for marketing purposes. It claimed that its activities may be misconstrued as anticompetitive because small-scale ticket services are unable to duplicate them. Increased competition, however, has not led to an elimination of the service charge. A number of Web sites sell concert and event tickets, such as TicketWeb.com, Ticketmaster.com, and Tickets.com, and charge a service fee; the fee has fallen, although, from the almost 30 percent Ticketmaster was charging in the early 1990s to the $2 fee charged by TicketWeb, a company that works with more than 500 clients. Ticketbroker.com, however, sometimes charges a variable fee, which is based on the demand for the tickets.[32]

Oligopoly An **oligopoly** exists when an industry has a small number of companies competing for the same customers. Firms may behave in unusual ways to gain business, such as introducing a new technology, or they may combine a number of factors that can affect their use of price as a strategic tool. They tend to be large, and old rivals engage in strategies and counterstrategies over long periods. The global auto industry is a good example. Seven major companies around the world produce nearly all motor vehicles, and each firm is large enough to commit considerable resources to differentiate itself. Each gains competitive advantage over the others from time to time. A few small firms in a local market also can be considered an oligopolistic situation.

Because oligopolies are usually well established and have strong market position, it is difficult for new firms to enter. The incumbents also get to know one another well. Through intelligence gathering, they learn about their competitors' cost structure. Their detailed market knowledge gives them insight into the amount of profitability rivals are likely to generate based on various pricing decisions. Because members of oligopolies engage in moves and countermoves, planning is essential.

Monopolistic Competition The industry structure, **monopolistic competition,** occurs when many firms compete for the same customers by differentiating their products. It falls somewhere between monopoly and pure competition but is much closer to the latter. Companies create brand loyalty to gain some of the benefits of monopoly. They control price by creating unique market offerings, such as nonfast-food restaurants in urban areas. Both price and quality are important in attracting customers and differentiating the product. Often there are numerous firms that are small or similar in size. Entry and exit are relatively easy, and the success of incumbents invites additional competitors. That's why several similar restaurants are likely to spring up when one starts doing well.

Strong marketing plans help organizations gain monopolistic advantages in highly competitive markets. They do this by creating subtle product differentiation. Rock groups are in this category. Stylistic differences enable you to differentiate among U2, Green Day, Lauryn Hill, and Brittney Spears. And each commands a price differential for concerts. Monopolistic competition also is the structure of the athletic footwear industry. Nike, Reebok, New Balance, Adidas, and a few others compete more or less on subtle differences in products.

Differentiation and Price Competition   Nonprice competition usually involves a differentiation strategy. **Differentiation** occurs when product attributes are stressed. Marketers try to demonstrate value and avoid any price reductions. In its purest form, a differentiation strategy relies on little or no mention of price. The relationships feature in this chapter, "Paying a Premium for Pet Care Nets Pampering, Too," focuses on ways in which quality pet products are differentiated beyond price considerations for many pet lovers.

Price competition adjusts prices to gain more customers or to establish a dominant position in the market. Recall that nonprice competition occurs when other marketing mix variables, such as product quality and promotion, are adjusted in response to competitors' pricing practices. Marketers need to understand the general approaches to price taken by their key competitors. This helps them anticipate overall market prices and what rivals are likely to do in response to price competition.

Marketing strategists study competitors in order to predict what they are likely to do under various conditions. Most companies respond in fairly consistent ways to price situations. Those

MONOPOLISTIC COMPETITION

The industry structure in which many firms compete for the same customers by differentiating their products and by creating unique offerings.

DIFFERENTIATION

A strategy in which product attributes that provide value are stressed.

PRICE COMPETITION

A strategy that employs price adjustments to gain more customers or to establish a dominant position in the market.

Whirlpool Corporation uses differentiation in this ad to stress product value.

that can produce at lower cost are more inclined to engage in price competition. Southwest Airlines cut costs by removing services such as in-flight meals and, therefore, is able to charge less per ticket than other airlines. Furthermore, it sells most of its tickets on the Internet; this cuts out the travel agency fees that further inflate airline ticket prices.[33] Even at lower prices Southwest Airlines can sustain a profit, whereas companies with higher costs are likely to lose money as prices drop. In countries where wage rates are low, such as Korea and Taiwan, production costs are low for many types of goods.

CONNECTING THROUGH RELATIONSHIPS

PAYING A PREMIUM FOR PET CARE NETS PAMPERING, TOO

Andrew Smithka easily drops $100 at his local pet supply store. He wants the best for his two-year-old Boston terrier, Amoosh. Andrew may spend $30 for a 40-pound bag of Nature's Choice premium dog food or $7.00 for Mr. Christal's luxury fur shampoo. While there, he may even enter Amoosh in a pet trick contest.

Americans like Smithka lavish $21 billion a year on their beloved pets for things such as food, supplies, grooming, medicine, and veterinary services. According to a 1999 survey by the American Pet Products Manufacturers' Association, 62 percent of Americans buy gifts for their pets. A *Barron's* survey showed that seven out of 10 people spend money on their pets as if they were their children. Pet care businesses are cashing in on this spending with steep prices. For instance, Colgate once sold its premium Hill's Science Diet exclusively through veterinarians. Now it is one of dozens of brands available at the vast number of pet supply and specialty stores popping up all over the country. Huge national chains such as Petco and PetsMart, as well as regional competitors, stock up to 12,000 items, and premium pet foods account for more than half their sales.

Grocery stores are losing out on this valuable product category not only because they cannot carry the huge variety but also because pet supply stores give customers added value by providing information to consumers willing to buy premium items for their pet. Customers want to know why a product is good and what it is going to do for their pet. They want knowledgeable salespeople to help them. Many specialty shops hold continuing education programs for employees to make sure they are up on topics such as premium pet food versus standard grocery store pet food.

These specialty stores also host events for owners and their pets. In this business, building customer relationships means reaching out to poodles, gerbils, iguanas, and guppies. It is not uncommon for a specialty store to conduct costume shows, pet trick contests, and portrait sessions. Sometimes the owners take center stage. One store located in Minneapolis hosted singles night on Valentine's Day, and 200 people showed up with their pets.

Aunt B's Pet Resort & Spa in DeForest, Wisconsin, is another example of the lengths pet owners will go in order to ensure the comfort and happiness of their pets. "Guests" from as far as California, Florida, and Oklahoma have come to be pampered and treated to such luxuries as massages, manicures, heated floors and furniture, and poochie Jacuzzi time. There is no doubt that pet owners who utilize such high-class kennels as these also take advantage of pet medical insurance. Veterinary Pet Insurance (VPI), the nation's number-one provider of pet insurance policies, recently announced new marketing relationships with two leading Web sites geared toward pet owners. Through various efforts, VPI and the participating sites will spread awareness about the benefits of quality pet care.

"The point is that people are taking owning a pet as a real part of their lives," says Bill Lechner, general merchandise manager of Pet Food Warehouse, now owned by Petco. "The idea of just going down to the corner and picking up a can of cat food has changed, and now there's an emotional and social aspect of pet ownership. We realize it, and we promote it, foster it, and cater to it, because if you can get the pets in the store with the owners, they are going to stay in the store a lot longer than if they simply walk in, go to the food, get it, and go out."

Sources: Jerry Minkoff, "Perking Up Pet Supplies," *Discount Merchandiser,* July 1995, pp. 30–32; Jerry Minkoff, "Pet Supply Depot: Netting a Share of the Animal-Lover Market," *Discount Merchandiser,* November 1995, pp. 46, 48; Jay Palmer, "Well, Aren't You the Cat's Meow?" *Barron's,* April 1, 1996, pp. 29–34; and Jerry Minkoff, "Pampering Pets Persistent Profits," *Discount Merchandiser,* November 1995, p. 47; www.petinsurance.com, press release, February 21, 2000, "Veterinary Pet Insurance Announces Co-Marketing Efforts with Leading Pet-Related Web Sites"; Rick Barret, "Pets Enjoy Music, Treats at DeForest, Wis. Spa," *The Wisconsin State Journal,* June 29, 2000.

Although prices should never be determined solely by cost, cost is critical information in making profitable pricing decisions. By understanding costs, marketers can judge profitability in advance. They can move resources to the highest-profit opportunities, avoid losing money, and gain better control of internal processes. By comparing costs with those of competitors, it is possible to assess production efficiency and estimate the relative profits each competitor can expect at various prices. This, in turn, helps anticipate the pricing choices available to competitors.

Types of Costs   Costs are categorized in several ways. Most simply, accountants look at fixed and variable costs. Marketers also should consider marginal and incremental costs.

Fixed and Variable Costs Most **fixed costs** do not change in the short run. These are expenditures for items such as production facilities, equipment, and salaries. Often these are called sunk costs because, once committed, nothing can be done to lower them. They do not change very much no matter how many units of a product are sold. In service industries, salaries account for a large portion of fixed (sunk) costs. For example, hospitals pay nurses irrespective of the number of patients served. For airlines, payments for aircraft and hanger space as well as salaries are fixed costs. The best you can do is use these costs more effectively. McDonald's introduced the Egg McMuffin so its facilities could produce revenues during more hours. That improved the effectiveness of the fixed costs.

Variable costs change depending on how much is produced or sold. They are usually calculated for each unit of production. These costs include raw materials, warranty costs, and the aspects of payroll (such as commissions) that rise or fall depending on the units sold. In the airline industry, for example, variable costs include the commissions paid to travel agents and food served on planes.

Total costs (*TC*) for a given period are calculated by multiplying the variable cost (*VC*) per unit times the quantity (*Q*) of units and adding the fixed costs (*FC*):

$$TC = VC \times Q + FC$$

Total revenues (*TR*) for a period are calculated by multiplying the price (*P*) per unit times the quantity (*Q*) of units sold:

$$TR = P \times Q$$

Profits (*PR*) are the difference between total revenues (*TR*) and total costs (*TC*):

$$PR = TR - TC$$

The average cost (*AC*) of each unit is the total cost (*TC*) divided by the quantity (*Q*) of units:

$$AC = TC/Q$$

The average cost of each unit doesn't provide very much useful information for pricing decisions, however, because average costs are sensitive to volume. The more units sold, the lower is the average cost.

Marginal Costs Unlike accountants, economists look at marginal costs and marginal revenues. **Marginal costs** (*MC*) are expenditures incurred in producing one additional unit of output. These costs often go down with each unit sold and stabilize at a volume of production near full capacity. Marginal cost then increases because additional fixed costs must be added, such as more production machinery. Imagine an airline with a plane that normally flies half full. It would not cost much to add one passenger—the cost of another meal and the commission paid to the travel agent who sells the ticket. Yet any price the airline can get that is greater than that marginal cost adds to profit. The price of the new ticket sold would be the **marginal revenue** (*MR*), the income from one more unit of the product sold, usually the product price. But let's say the plane is full. Would you add another aircraft to take one more passenger? Obviously not, unless that passenger is willing to pay a huge price.

Economic theory shows that profits are maximized—total revenues (*TR*) minus total costs (*TC*) are greatest—when *MR* equals *MC*. In the airline example, we can continue to lower the price until all seats are gone, or *MC* (the price of food and commissions) equals the price of a ticket. Airlines do this to a degree by offering a few discount seats. But selling a ticket for the cost of food and the agent commission (about $35) is impractical. In reality, you won't

FIXED COST
A cost that does not vary with changes in volume produced.

VARIABLE COST
A cost that changes depending on volume.

MARGINAL COSTS
The expenditures incurred in producing one additional unit of output.

MARGINAL REVENUE
The income from selling one additional unit of output.

often find many marketing executives sitting in their offices looking at graphs of marginal revenues and costs. Yet, like most good theories, this concept provides useful insights.

It was noted that fixed costs do not change with prices and sales volume. Many people assume that these are the costs of being in business. Also called overhead, these fixed costs may be higher or lower for different competitors. For example, the pharmaceutical industry has high fixed costs because of the research and development necessary to yield one profitable drug; of the 5,000 compounds tested in the laboratory, only five make it to the clinical trials, which are expensive and time-consuming to conduct. Of those five drugs, only one is approved by the FDA for patient use.[34] Fixed costs are extremely important in determining the profitability of a firm.

In practice, companies with high overhead may justify high prices if these reflect added value. Often they do not, yet decision makers push prices higher in an effort to obtain maximum revenue. The result may be even lower volume or reduced profit. If fixed costs do not add value for customers, they probably should not be a factor in pricing decisions. This is very difficult for many executives to accept because pricing to cover all costs (cost-based pricing) has been so prevalent.

INCREMENTAL COSTS

Costs that go up or down based on volume, including variable costs and certain fixed costs.

Incremental Costs Relevant costs for pricing decisions are **incremental costs,** costs that go up or down based on volume. Like variable costs, incremental costs are related to pricing because the price can affect the volume sold. Variable costs are always incremental. Only some fixed costs are incremental. For example, if a low price will increase demand to the extent that a new factory will have to be added to satisfy it, then the factory is an incremental cost and becomes a factor in the decision whether to lower the price. Once the factory is built, the cost becomes fixed or sunk. It has to be paid for no matter how much is produced. Pricing decisions that increase volume, thus, influence fixed costs, which in turn greatly influence the firm's cost structure.

Cost-Oriented Pricing Both cost-plus and rate-of-return pricing are based on the company's costs. Cost-oriented pricing adds an amount to the product cost, called a markup, which is designed to yield a profit. A percentage markup can be added directly, or additional calculations can be made to determine what percentage rate of return the seller will receive. Either approach has serious problems because each tends to ignore the customer and, to varying degrees, the competition as well.

Cost-Plus Pricing Because of its simplicity, the cost-plus approach is popular. But, as the following example shows, it doesn't necessarily assure a profit. A local furniture store pays $750 to a wholesaler for a sofa and sells it to the consumer for $1,500, a markup of 100 percent. On the surface, it appears that the store has gained $750. But it has many costs to meet, such as salaries and overhead. When these are taken into account, and depending on overall sales volume, the retailer might actually lose money on this sofa and other items. Clearly, to determine whether the sale is profitable and precisely how much is made on the sofa a portion of the retailer's costs has to be allocated to each of the products sold.

Markups are popular because they are perceived to be fair or equitable for both the buyer and the seller. Standard markups have evolved in many industries to help indicate what amount is "fair." Manufacturers or wholesalers often suggest prices to retailers, or retailers form their own conventions. For example, an auto parts dealer may mark up brake assemblies by 40 percent and consumables such as oil by 25 percent. Since all similar retailers use the same basic markup structure, all have approximately the same retail price. Notice that the calculation is based on the wholesale price, which itself is a markup on the manufacturer's price.

Government contracts and some industrial contracts often specify that the seller must use cost-plus pricing. This is full-cost pricing because the markup is based on all costs, including allocations of overhead and other fixed costs. Sellers are expected to provide an accounting upon request. The difficulty lies in determining which costs to assign to which products. Again, even full-cost pricing largely ignores the value of the product to the customer.

Rate-of-Return Pricing A variation on cost-plus pricing, rate-of-return pricing is based on the break-even point. Essentially, the method determines how many units must be sold at a particular price in order to cover fixed costs plus a profit on the investment made. The break-even point is the amount sold at a given price on which the business neither makes nor loses money. Any volume beyond that point makes money.

The break-even point is calculated by dividing the total fixed cost (*FC*) by the difference between the selling price (*P*) of one unit and the variable cost (*VC*) of one unit:

$$\text{Break-even point} = FC/(P - VC)$$

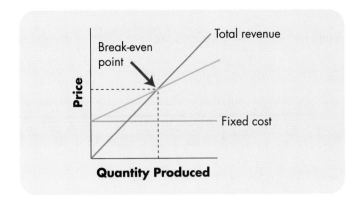

FIGURE 17.8 *Break-Even Analysis*

The difference between the price and the variable cost of a unit ($P - VC$) is called the contribution margin. It tells how much the sale of one unit contributes to covering fixed costs. Once these costs are covered, any remaining contribution is profit. Figure 17.8 shows the break-even concept graphically.

As an example of rate-of-return pricing, assume that you decide to start a small business that will offer housepainting services to homeowners during summer vacation. You calculate that you will have to invest $10,000 in fixed (sunk) costs, including advertising and promotion, insurance, equipment, truck rental, and a salary for yourself. You feel that you should earn a 20 percent return ($10,000 $\times$ 20% = $2,000) for having the idea, taking the initiative, and assuming the risk of losing your invested capital. Furthermore, you estimate that labor, paint, and other variable costs for each house will average $2,100, and with four workers your company can paint eight houses in four months. What is the average price you should charge for each house?

To answer this question, you first add your desired return to your fixed costs ($2,000 + $10,000 = $12,000) to determine the total revenue contribution required. Then you divide that sum by the number of houses (units) to find the amount that each unit must contribute ($12,000 $\div$ 8 = $1,500). Since the variable cost to paint a house is $2,100, you determine that you must charge $2,100 + $1,500 = $3,600 per house.

Notice in this example that profit is treated much like a fixed cost. This is because if you break even in a strict sense—that is, neither make nor lose money—then your project will not accomplish its profit objective.

Also notice that rate-of-return pricing ignores the customer and the competition. If homeowners consider $3,600 to be too expensive, then they may hire someone who charges less or choose to do the work themselves. If they believe the price is very low, then they may be willing to pay even more. The pricing of competitors is important. Whether competitors are willing to paint a house for $3,000 or $9,000 will influence how consumers perceive your price.

Rate-of-return pricing also tends to ignore the scale of operations you could have. For example, if eight painters rather than four were employed, the fixed costs could be spread across 16 houses rather than eight. That would lower the price, but you would have to supervise more workers while not making more profit. A major problem with the rate-of-return approach is that price will increase when demand goes down. For example, if only six houses are painted, the price for each rises by $500, to $4,100. Does this make sense? In the 1980s, U.S. auto companies lost share dramatically to foreign rivals. As demand for U.S. cars declined due to competitive pressure, Detroit increased prices to try to make up for lost unit sales, further reducing demand.

INTERNATIONAL PRICING

Pricing in global environments is affected by several factors not experienced in domestic markets. Also, because markets vary greatly among countries, international pricing is complex. Marketing executives must be knowledgeable about many issues and remain flexible in adjusting to unforeseeable circumstances. The major influencers on global pricing are market, cost, and financial factors, as outlined in Figure 17.9.

Market Factors	**Cost Factors**	**Financial Factors**
Local demand	Distance and transportation	Exchange rates
Competitive conditions	Tariffs and homologation	Inflation
Availability of substitutes	Export duties, subsidies, and controls	Government price controls
Gray marketing	Transfer pricing	

FIGURE 17.9 *Influences on Global Pricing*

GLOBAL MARKET FACTORS

Market factors such as local demand, tastes and preferences, competitor activities, and gray marketing are important. All of these elements must be considered in international pricing.

Local demand can vary dramatically due to demographic, geographic, and political conditions. For example, China is the world's most populous country and is experiencing economic growth at a staggering rate. Yet few Chinese have enough income or even the space for most of the durable goods so common in the West. Consequently, many products for the Chinese market must be designed to be priced very low.

Subtle competitive differences can influence demand, even in fairly similar economic environments. In Europe, for example, some product categories—such as electronics and pharmaceuticals—have prices that vary more than 100 percent from country to country. Although the advent of the euro has helped consumers to recognize price differences from country to country in Europe, a recent study found that the price of cars still varies on average by 19.5 percent from country to country.[35] Deodorants cost 30 percent less in Germany than the European average, and alcohol is also cheaper in Germany than elsewhere. But Nurofen tablets, a pain reliever, is 59 percent more expensive in Germany than the European average.[36]

Globally, tastes and preferences also vary dramatically. A nationalistic bias for domestic products can make them less cross-price elastic in relation to imports. For example, in France, Germany, the United Kingdom, and especially Italy, consumers prefer vehicles made in their own country even if they cost more.[37] Generally, people in countries where domestic brands are preferred have high incomes and tend to be much less price sensitive across the board.[38] That means more latitude for premium pricing. For example, companies selling consumer food products in Europe have found themselves in a difficult position recently. The economic unification of the European Union means that many global food retailers want to reduce the number of brands to streamline production processes and lower prices. The customers, however, tend to want to continue to buy specific brands and products, irrespective of price, as when British consumers protested Heinz's decision to stop manufacturing salad cream, a type of salad dressing popular among older Britons.[39] However, the advent of the euro has caused more shoppers in the United Kingdom to become price sensitive in their selections; a study done by Research International indicates that 64 percent of consumers are more price sensitive than they were two years ago.[40]

The availability of substitute products also varies widely. The most obvious case is the substitution of automation for labor. Japan—with its high education level, high labor rates, and low unemployment—is highly automated, while Chinese producers use readily available low-cost human labor whenever possible. The market for high-priced robotics is mature in Japan, where many competitors are constantly seeking an edge, but demand is weak in China.

A notable feature of many foreign economies is the gray market, which has a significant effect on pricing. Many global companies manufacture in local markets so they can sell at lower prices there, but this also may lead to gray marketing.[41] **Gray marketing** occurs when pirated products made in a foreign country are imported back to the company's home market without approval. They are then sold at reduced prices, usually by unauthorized channel members. The importation of gray market goods is prohibited in the United States by a law that forbids bringing products into the country without permission of the trademark owner. Elsewhere in the world, restrictions vary, may not exist, or may not be well enforced. Many times the foreign-made product is of a different quality but bears the company label, so consumers are confused. In other cases, prices differ because of manufacturing costs, exchange rates, or other reasons. The importation of gray market cigarettes has increased in the past two

GRAY MARKETING

Importing products made in a foreign country back to the company's home market without approval.

This FreeUK ad is from an international market but competes with price structures from around the world.

years, as some retailers try to avoid the costs of a 1998 $206 billion settlement with state governments. Gray market cigarettes sell for about 70 cents to $1 per pack less than U.S. cigarettes; these gray market cigarettes are not covered by the settlement.[42]

Gray markets can disrupt the best-laid plans of companies desiring selective or exclusive distribution. Any brand with some consumer following may find itself in this situation. For example, Continent-Wide Enterprises, a retailer of Polaroid products, was recently caught selling products priced and intended for Canada in other countries for higher profits. Continent-Wide Enterprises, which supplied Polaroid retailers overseas, was violating its franchise contract, which states it must not sell to unauthorized resellers.[43]

Companies that want to ensure selective or exclusive distribution must take steps to eliminate gray market problems. If not, then the strength and motivation of the authorized channel will be seriously impaired. The company must clearly communicate to all members of the authorized channel the importance of following policy and upholding contracts. Their activities must be monitored, especially when significant gray market activity exists. Contracts with those who violate agreements must be terminated. Companies such as Levi-Strauss and Joico, a manufacturer of hair care products, vigorously follow such steps in operating their distribution channels.[44]

GLOBAL COST FACTORS

In calculating the costs of doing business internationally, it is not just distance that matters but the expense of moving goods from one country to another. Transportation and insurance costs escalate when borders are crossed, as do tariffs and red tape. Risks also increase, so prices must cover potential adverse circumstances.

Tariffs—taxes levied against incoming goods—contribute to costs and are sometimes added to price. They affect imports in nearly every country. Vehicle prices in Turkey are elevated nearly threefold by tariffs. In the United States, importers pay an average of less than 10 percent on all items, much more for some. Producers of orange juice in Brazil pay as high a tariff as 63 percent to import orange juice into the United States; U.S. producers of orange juice claim this barrier is necessary because Brazilian companies, with their lower costs of labor and materials, could undercut U.S. producers to the point of driving them out of business.[45]

TARIFF

A tax levied against a good being imported into a country.

Bureaucratic red tape often makes it difficult and expensive to enter a market. The Japanese use it as a barrier to foreign competitors. For example, they lock out international construction companies by claiming that Japan's dirt is unique, or they require considerable testing at border entry points for all sorts of products. Recently, Vietnam rescinded hundreds of bureaucratic procedures and tariffs that prevented foreign firms from doing business in the country. Multinational companies that had tried to do business in Vietnam, such as Raytheon, Chrysler, and Sheraton Hotels, had pulled out of the country because red tape made doing business almost impossible. Vietnamese officials decided that the country needed the investments more than they needed to protect their own industries.[46] Some European pharmaceutical companies claim that FDA regulations impede their access to the U.S. market, as with the recent controversy over the morning after RU486 pill, which was finally approved after 10 years.[47]

EXPORT SUBSIDY

Funding by a government to encourage businesses to export goods.

The opposite of a tariff is an **export subsidy** paid by a government to encourage businesses to export. When you compete against these companies, essentially you're competing against their government as well. When they target a certain market, their prices can be more competitive because the subsidy covers much or all of their export costs. This may put non-subsidized exports and domestic products at a pricing disadvantage. In other cases, governments may restrict exports by adding costly duties, which raises prices in importing countries. Many countries in the world subsidize big national industries; Canada, Brazil, France, and Great Britain all subsidize their aircraft manufacturers, for example.[48]

Risk is also a factor in international business. When risk is high, prices must be raised. For example, selling in Russia is risky because of an unstable economy and the possibility of political takeovers. Anywhere in the world, a change in government can affect economic regulations and market access. Furthermore, a weak or indifferent government may permit greater corruption or lawlessness, which can mean that warehousing and distribution channels are insecure.

TRANSFER PRICE

The amount a company charges its foreign affiliate for a product.

Transfer prices are the amounts that companies charge their foreign affiliates for products. This causes some interesting price variations across countries. By altering the transfer price, both local prices and profits can be dramatically affected. In this way, companies can manipulate their price in markets globally, affecting competition and their sources of revenues. For example, Japanese auto supply companies can charge higher transfer prices for components going to assembly plants in the United States. This practice yields more profit in Japan and less profit in the United States. In turn taxes are paid in Japan, where the rate may be lower than in the United States. Ultimately, the tax savings mean that a lower price can be charged for the product in the United States.

GLOBAL FINANCIAL FACTORS

The primary financial factors influencing international prices are exchange rates, inflation, and government price controls. Exchange rates and inflation alter the value of currencies, whereas government price controls prohibit companies from moving prices upward at will. Controls are particularly troublesome when a rapid shift in exchange rates or inflation devalues the price put on a product.

EXCHANGE RATE

The worth of one currency relative to another.

Even money has a price, which is reflected in the exchange rate. The **exchange rate** is how much one currency is worth relative to another. The euro, when it was launched, was valued at 1 euro to U.S.$1.18. Since then, the euro fell to a low of 86.28 cents in November 2000. When the euro costs less, anything valued in the euro costs less. The change essentially means that anything produced in Europe costs less for Americans to buy than before the euro fell. European vacations and products, therefore, became cheaper for Americans than they had been when the euro was introduced.[49] Currency exchange rates can fluctuate considerably over time, affecting prices for imported and exported products.

INFLATION

The tendency of a currency to be worth less over time.

Inflation is the tendency of a currency to be worth less over time. When inflation occurs, product prices along the supply chain increase. These are passed on in higher prices, so consumers have to spend more money to buy the same item. Most advanced nations now have low inflation rates, often around 3 percent or even less per year. In some countries inflation is extremely high and escalates monthly or even weekly. For example, in 1990 Procter & Gamble raised prices twice a month, by 20 or 30 percent, to keep up with inflation in some Latin American countries.[50]

PRICE CONTROLS

Government restrictions on the price that can be charged for a product.

Governments often use **price controls** in an attempt to keep inflation in check. Essentially, the maximum price increase allowable is set by law. Sometimes the controls are applied to all goods, sometimes they are selective, and sometimes they apply only to imports. In any case, they can make it difficult to earn a profit, so companies may not want to sell in that market. In Russia, for example, it is not uncommon for entrepreneurs to use exclusive trade licenses to buy key raw materials, such as coal, cheaply on the local black market and sell them on the world market for a huge profit, instead of selling the products locally at a price controlled by the state.[51]

Companies use many factors when making pricing decisions locally or globally. All of these factors are likely to influence price. However, as we will see in the next chapter, the actual pricing strategy must be well grounded in an understanding of how pricing captures value from the market. This requires knowing how customers define value.

CONNECTED: SURFING THE NET

PetsMart
www.petsmart.com

This chapter's relationship feature, "Paying a Premium for Pet Care Nets Pampering, Too," discussed the segment of Americans willing to spend an amazing $20 billion a year on pets. In order to expand your thinking about pricing approaches, visit the PetsMart Web site and answer the following questions.

1. How does PetsMart use the marketing mix to persuade consumers to purchase Authority Premium Pet Nutrition? What role do you think price plays in the consumer's final decision? What should marketers do ahead of time to ensure that customers will perceive this product as a good value?
2. Prices serve several objectives. What are they? How do you think PetsMart meets or could meet relationship objectives? What aspects of the Web site help the company connect with customers?
3. Imagine you are an investor in PetsMart. Visit EdgarScan at www.edgarscan.pwcglobal.com and look up the company's financial statement. Are you satisfied with profits? Why or why not? How can price affect all major factors that influence profit?

Amoco
www.bpamoco.com

In this chapter you learned about a number of economic factors that influence price. Amoco was used to illustrate cross-price elasticity of demand. To learn more about factors influencing price as well as other pricing issues, visit the British Petroleum-Amoco Web site and answer the following questions.

1. List several products British Petroleum-Amoco sells. Do you think each product has an elastic or inelastic demand curve? Explain.
2. What determines demand elasticity? How does each relate to British Petroleum-Amoco?
3. A number of factors influence international pricing. What opportunities is British Petroleum-Amoco pursuing in China? How might demand vary there due to demographic, geographic, and political conditions?
4. Select an article from British Petroleum-Amoco's *Onstream* magazine that illustrates how the company connects with customers through relationships, technology, globalization, ethics, or diversity. Explain why this connection is beneficial to the company.

CHAPTER SUMMARY

Objective 1: Describe how pricing works with the other parts of the marketing mix.

Pricing is an important element of the marketing mix. Price decisions are made along with product, promotion, and logistics decisions. Pricing is influenced by profit, volume, competitive, and customer relationship objectives. Consequently, pricing is important for nearly all aspects of the business.

Objective 2: Learn how economic factors such as demand and supply influence prices.

The demand curve helps us understand how price influences the amount of a product customers buy. The availability of substitutes, necessity, the portion of income spent on the product, and the timing of price changes affect the price sensitivity of demand. The supply curve[51] tells how much product firms will provide at various prices. Usually, more is produced when prices are expected to rise. By analyzing the supply and demand curves, it is possible to get some idea of future prices in an industry.

OBJECTIVE 3:   Understand the legal and ethical constraints on pricing decisions.

Both legal and ethical factors affect price. Laws prohibit both vertical and horizontal price-fixing by U.S. firms. It is also illegal for manufacturers to sell to different parties at different prices, although some forms of price discrimination are acceptable. To control unfair price competition, many states regulate pricing minimums and the use of loss leaders. The Federal Trade Commission sets permissible standards for price advertising. For example, you cannot advertise a sale price unless it is really a sale and the items are available. International firms must sell at a high enough price to avoid violating antidumping laws. Finally, unit pricing regulations help consumers make comparisons. To be ethical, prices should reflect a fair exchange of value, and marketers must be careful not to misrepresent the terms of an exchange. This requires clear communication of both price and value.

OBJECTIVE 4:   Use industry structure concepts to understand how competitors in different types of industries price.

The four basic industry structures are perfect competition, monopoly, oligopoly, and monopolistic competition. In perfect competition, many firms vie to provide goods at the going price. A firm with a monopoly can set prices as high as the market will bear, although pricing by public utility monopolies is generally regulated in the public interest. In an oligopoly, a small number of competitors make pricing decisions based on their knowledge of one another's cost structures. Monopolistic competition tends to be based on product differentiation rather than price.

OBJECTIVE 5:   Use competitive factors surrounding industry structure concepts to understand how pricing works in different types of industries.

Pricing decisions must consider variable and fixed costs, marginal costs, and incremental costs. Incremental costs, which are the most important, include variable costs and, often, some fixed costs, such as the cost of building a new factory to meet increased demand. Cost-oriented methods, such as cost-plus pricing and rate-of-return pricing, have serious drawbacks because they tend to ignore the consumer and competitors.

OBJECTIVE 6:   Recognize the conditions that make international pricing complex.

Market, cost, and financial factors unique to global business must be considered in pricing. Market factors include local demand, competitive conditions, tastes and preferences, the availability of substitutes, and gray marketing. Important cost factors are transportation distance, tariffs, red tape, and export subsidies. Major financial considerations are inflation, exchange rates, and price controls. Risk is another influence on international pricing.

REVIEW YOUR UNDERSTANDING

1. List 10 names for price.
2. Which constituents of a firm can be pleased with profit objectives, volume objectives, competitive objectives, and relationship objectives?
3. What are the major factors that influence price?
4. What is elastic demand? Inelastic demand?
5. What factors influence price elasticity?
6. What is supply and demand equilibrium?
7. What are the laws that affect pricing practices? Describe the restrictions.
8. Describe dumping.
9. What are two ethical issues regarding pricing? Explain.
10. What is industry structure? What are four structures that have price implications?
11. What are fixed and variable costs?
12. What are incremental costs?
13. What is cost-plus pricing?
14. What factors influence pricing in global settings?

DISCUSSION OF CONCEPTS

1. Prices are set with several objectives in mind. What are they, and how are they important to a company?
2. A company's pricing strategy is influenced by many factors: legal and ethical issues, economic conditions, the company's costs, the global environment, and competitors. What major effect does each category have on pricing decisions?
3. Product demand is influenced by price elasticity. What does this mean, and what effect does it have on a marketer's pricing policy?
4. Federal and state laws in the United States prohibit unfair pricing. What is meant by "unfair"? Give specific examples of laws and briefly describe their objectives. Is this true of all countries?
5. How does the type of competition within an industry affect a company's ability to set prices? Briefly describe the major competitor-based pricing approaches.
6. What types of costs are relevant for pricing decisions? Which are irrelevant? Why? What are some of the main problems with cost-oriented pricing?
7. Despite its drawbacks, cost-oriented pricing is still used by many companies. Briefly describe the two types.

KEY TERMS AND DEFINITIONS

Bait and switch: An unethical practice in which sellers advertise items at extremely low prices and then inform the customer that the items are out of stock, offer different items, or attempt to sell the customer more expensive substitutes.

Cross-price elasticity of demand: The extent to which the quantity demanded of one product changes in response to changes in the price of another product.

Differentiation: A strategy stressing product attributes that provide value.

Demand curve: A depiction of the price elasticity demand for a product.

Dumping: Selling a product in a foreign country at a price lower than in the producing country and lower than its cost of production.

Exchange rate: The worth of one currency relative to another.

Export subsidy: Money paid by a government to encourage businesses to export goods.

Fixed cost: A cost that does not vary with changes in volume produced.

Gray marketing: Importing products made in a foreign country back to the company's home market without its approval.

Horizontal price-fixing: Agreement among manufacturers and channel members to set prices at the retail level.

Incremental costs: Costs that go up or down based on volume, including variable costs and certain fixed costs.

Inflation: The tendency of a currency to be worth less over time.

Loss leaders: Items priced below cost to attract customers.

Marginal costs: The expenditures incurred in producing one additional unit of output.

Marginal revenue: The income from selling one additional unit of output.

Monopolistic competition: The industry structure in which many firms compete for the same customers by differentiating their products and by creating unique offerings.

Monopoly: The industry structure in which one organization makes a product with no close substitutes.

Oligopoly: The industry structure in which a small number of firms compete for the same customers.

Perfect competition: The industry structure in which no single firm has control over prices.

Predatory dumping: Pricing below cost to drive local firms out of business.

Predatory pricing: Price-cutting by large firms to eliminate small local competitors.

Price: The exchange value of a good or service in the marketplace.

Price competition: A strategy that employs price adjustments to gain more customers or to establish a dominant position in the market.

Price controls: Government restrictions on the price that can be charged for a product.

Price discrimination: A legally restricted practice in which a manufacturer or other channel member charges different prices to different retailers in the same marketplace.

Price elasticity: The extent to which changes in price affect the number of units demanded or supplied.

Price-fixing: An attempt by one party to control what another party will charge in the market.

Supply curve: A depiction of the price elasticity of supply for a product.

Tariff: A tax levied on a good being imported into a country.

Transfer price: The amount a company charges its foreign affiliate for a product.

Variable cost: A cost that changes depending on volume.

Vertical price-fixing: An attempt by a manufacturer or distributor to control the retail selling price.

REFERENCES

1. Sebastian Rupley, "Customer Care on Wall Street," *PC Magazine*, June 27, 2000, pp. I25+; Megan Barnett, "Schwab's MVP," *Industry Standard*, May 1, 2000, p. 270; Robert Frick, "Shootout on Wall Street," *Kiplinger's Personal Finance Magazine*, March 2000, pp. 50+; "The Price Is Sliced," *Business Week*, February 14, 2000, p. 130; Katherine Fraser, "Brokers Rebating ATM Fees for High-Net-Worth Clients," *American Banker*, June 4, 1999, p. 10; "Schwab's E-Gambit," *Business Week*, January 11, 1999, p. 61.

2. Teri Agins, "All the Trimmings, Forget the Clothes," *Wall Street Journal*, November 23, 1999, p. A1.

3. www./autos/yahoo.com/newcars/details, site visited December 23, 2000.

4. David Rocks, "How PC Makers Are Reprogramming Themselves," *Business Week*, October 30, 2000, Issue 3705, p. 64.

5. Steven V. Brull, "Gateway's Big Gamble," *Business Week*, June 5, 2000, p. EB26.

6. www.nintendo.com, visited December 14, 2000 (this is its newest version, and the theory still holds).

7. James Stotter, "Applying Economics to Competitive Intelligence," *Competitive Intelligence Review*, Winter 1996, pp. 26–36.

8. www.travel.yahoo.com/tlspecials/outlet.html, site visited on December 14, 2000.

9. Keith Reid, "The Pricing Equation: Which Price Is Right," *National Petroleum News*, February 2000, Volume 92, Issue 2, pp. 16–18.

10. See Thomas T. Nagle and Reed E. Holder, *The Strategy and Tactics of Pricing* (Upper Saddle River, NJ: Prentice Hall, 1995), pp. 78–95.

11. Vanessa O'Connell and Joe White, "After Decades of Brand Bodywork, GM Parks Oldsmobile," *Wall Street Journal*, December 13, 2000, p. B1.

12. Greg Winter, "Growers Sue Ocean Spray, Seeking Possibility of Sale," *New York Times*, November 29, 2000, Section C; p. 6; Column 5.

13. Gregory L. White, "GM Will Cut North American Production as Big Three Cope with Lower Demand," *Wall Street Journal*, December 8, 2000, p. A3.

14. "A Market for Monopoly?" *The Economist*, June 17, 2000.

15. *Business Wire*, May 15, 2000.

16. *New York Times*, September 23, 2000, p. A1.

17. "Value Added Services Breed Loyal Shoppers," *Discount Store News*, May 6, 1996, pp. 56–59.

18. Richard J. Semenik and Gary J. Bamossy, *Principles of Marketing* (Cincinnati, OH: Southwestern College Publishing, 1995), p. 641.

19. "Wal-Mart Is Subject of Inquiry in Germany Over Pricing Practices," *Wall Street Journal*, June 29, 2000, p. C24.

20. Christine Dugas, "Look Beyond Yield for the Right Money Fund," *USA Today*, April 4, 1997.

21. Gene Koprowski, "The Price Is Right," *Marketing Tools*, September 1995, www.marketingtools.com.

22. Cathy Cooper with Takeshi Kamiya, "U.S. Punishes Foreign Firms Dumping Steel," *Chemical Engineering*, March 1999, Volume 106, Issue 3, p. 60.

23. Joanne McManus and Trish Saywell, "Not in Our Backyard," *Far Eastern Economic Review*, August 3, 2000, p. 56.

24. Nigel Holloway, "Sweet Smell of Excess," *Far Eastern Economic Review*, September 1996, p. 61.

25. Lester Ross and Susan Ning, "Modern Protectionism: China's Own Antidumping System," *The China Business Review*, May/June 2000, Volume 27, Issue 3, pp. 30–33.

26. Associated Press, "Japanese Company Defends Sale of Supercomputers," *USA Today*, May 12, 1997.

27. Ngo Hong Hanh, "Law to Flex Muscles with Shaddy Trading Practice," *The Vietnam Investment Review*, September 18, 2000.

28. "Consumers Are Skeptical Again," *Progressive Grocer*, April 1996, pp. 40–46.

29. "British Airways Guilty of 'Misleading' Advertising," *The London Financial Times*, July 12, 2000, p. 6.

30. Ted Kemp, "Last Chance for Grinches of '99: Deliver on Time, or Else," *Internetweek*, October 23, 2000, Issue 834, pp. 1, 90.

31. John R. Wilke, "Microsoft, Government Battle over Case, with U.S. Urging Supreme Court Review," *Wall Street Journal*, June 15, 2000, p. A3.

32. Charles Bilodeau, "Pearl Jam's War on Reality," *Consumers' Research*, June 1995, p. 24; and Chad Kaydo, "For Tickets, Get Online," *Sales and Marketing Management*, May 2000, Volume 152, Issue 5, p. 20.

33. Scott McCartney, "Computer Class: Airlines Find a Bag of High-Tech Tricks to Keep Income Aloft," *Wall Street Journal*, January 20, 2000, p. A1.

34. "Drug-Price Program Notes," *Wall Street Journal*, August 10, 2000, p. A18.

35. "Euro Narrows Differences in New-Car Sticker Prices," *Wall Street Journal*, February 8, 2000, p. A23.

36. "Finance and Economics: Price Points," *The Economist,* November 18, 2000, Volume 357, Issue 8197, p. 87.

37. Frank Verboven, "International Price Discrimination in the European Car Market," *Journal of Economics* 27 (Summer 1996): 240–268.

38. Chung Koo Kim, "The Interaction between Price and Long-Run Variables in a Multinational Brand Market," *Journal of Business Research* 37 (September 1996): 1–14.

39. Jennifer Jury, "Focus: Food and Drink—Rising to the Bait," *European Venture Capital Journal,* December 1, 1999, pp. 39–45.

40. Fiona Rule, "Consumers Wise Up," *Cabinet Maker,* September 17, 1999, Issue 5155, p. 8.

41. Paul Lansing and Joseph Gabriella, "Clarifying Gray Market Gray Areas," *American Business Law Journal,* September 1993, pp. 313–337.

42. "Cigarette Firm Wins Round in Its Gray-Marketing Case," *The Houston Chronicle,* April 16, 2000, p. 4.

43. "Polaroid Wins Major 'Grey Marketing' Battle," *Canada News Wire,* September 11, 2000.

44. Based on the author's consulting experience in these industries.

45. Anthony Depalma with Simon Romero, "Orange Juice Tariff Hinders Trade Pact for U.S. and Brazil," *New York Times,* April 24, 2000, p. A1.

46. Sheri Prasso, "Welcome Back?" *Business Week,* August 16, 2000, p. 54.

47. www.cnn.com/2000/HEALTH/women/09/28/abortion.pill, Rhonda Rowland, "Food and Drug Administration Approves 'Abortion pill'."

48. Joel Baglole and Jonathan Karp, "Canada Gets WTO Approval for Sanctions Against Brazil," *Wall Street Journal,* December 13, 2000, p. A21.

49. Dagmar Aalund, "Land Rush in Europe," *Wall Street Journal,* November 20, 2000, p. B1.

50. Alecia Swasy, "Foreign Formula: Procter & Gamble Fixes Aim on Tough Market: The Latin Americans," *Wall Street Journal,* June 15, 1990, p. A7.

51. Oleh Havrylyshyn and John Odling-Smee, "Political Economy of Stalled Reforms," *Finance and Development,* September 20, 2000, Issue 3, pp. 7–10.

Bricks or Clicks

EBAY

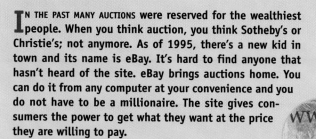

IN THE PAST MANY AUCTIONS were reserved for the wealthiest people. When you think auction, you think Sotheby's or Christie's; not anymore. As of 1995, there's a new kid in town and its name is eBay. It's hard to find anyone that hasn't heard of the site. eBay brings auctions home. You can do it from any computer at your convenience and you do not have to be a millionaire. The site gives consumers the power to get what they want at the price they are willing to pay.

eBay brings people with similar tastes and interests together. Without this service, most of these connections would never be made. For example, a golfer in Dallas is selling his old set of clubs and a golfer in Tampa is looking for a new set. If the clubs are put up for auction, these two golfers have the opportunity to connect. eBay is also a powerful tool for small business. It allows them to have a Web presence without the expense of creating their own e-tail site.

Most recently, eBay partnered with Hard Rock Café to auction music memorabilia on its Web site. Hard Rock Café will actually have its own section on the eBay site and there will be a link to the Hard Rock Café Web site, where the history of the items will be displayed. This partnership gives eBay access to the Hard Rock brand name and to the thousands of music memorabilia items collected over the years. Both companies are planning cross-promotions to increase the awareness of the partnership. In addition, special auctions of autographed merchandise will also be offered.

Several other companies have followed eBay's lead and are now offering auctions on their Web sites. Both Amazon.com and firstauction.com offer online auctions. This trend is likely to continue.

Sources: "Hard Rock Café Inks Deal with eBay to Establish Premiere Trading Community for Hard Rock Music Memorabilia and Collectibles; Agreement Marks Significant Initiative to Expand Hard Rock Brand Online," *PR Newswire,* September 14, 2000, as retrieved from the World Wide Web: www.lexis-nexis.com; and Joelle Tessler, "Online Auction Sites Create Vast Global Marketplaces," *San Jose Mercury News,* October 23, 2000, as retrieved from the World Wide Web: www.lexis-nexis.com.

CASE 17

Ty, Inc.

HOW WOULD YOU LIKE TO get $1,500 for a product that cost you only $5.99? That is exactly what happened to a Nashville couple when they sold Peanuts the Elephant, a retired Beanie Baby. Chicago entrepreneur Ty Warner has been able to match supply, pricing, and demand to achieve extraordinary growth for his lovable little creations. The palm-sized beanbag animals were developed by Warner in 1993. To date, hundreds of unique Beanie Babies have been issued, and over 100 million have been sold since 1993. Now with annual profits of over $700 million, Ty has beat out Hasbro and Mattel combined as the most profitable toy maker in America.

Chocolate the Moose, Crunch the Shark, Bernie the St. Bernard, and all the others have caught on not only with kids but also with college students, parents, and grandparents. Priced under $6, they are affordable, collectible, and tradable. Beanie Babies can be seen hanging from bookshelves, peeking out of backpacks, and sitting on school desks. How does Ty Warner cause such a sensation? He focuses on three critical elements:

a very affordable price for a quality product, the deliberate creation of scarcity, and extensive distribution that avoids large retailers.

According to *Forbes*, the empty-shelf strategy drives demand up. Warner believes careful manipulation of stock levels is important. "People are saying this Christmas will be the last, but every time we make a shipment, they want twice as many as we can possibly get to them. . . . As long as kids keep fighting over the products, and retailers are angry at us because they cannot get enough, I think those are good signs." In some parts of the country, Beanie Babies are so hard to find that a black market has developed. On several Web sites, critters such as Chilly, a white polar bear, trade for $875, and Humphry the Camel goes for $900. In Canada, Maple Bear—a white bear with a Canadian flag on its chest—is popular. Sold only north of the border, this creature is sought in the United States because of its rarity.

The distribution strategy for Beanie Babies includes no licensing deals, no big ad budgets, and no selling to large national discount chains, such as Toys "R" Us and Wal-Mart. Such megastores can sometimes get away with raising the $5.99 price as high as $35. That is why Warner has always sold and shipped directly to thousands of independent gift stores. "It's better selling 40,000 accounts than it is five accounts," he says. "It's more difficult to do, but for the longevity of the company and the profit margins, it's the better of the two." After graduating from Kalamazoo College in 1962, Warner learned to sell through a selective distribution network when he worked for Dakin Incorporated, where he sold stuffed animals to specialty shops.

In addition to carefully selecting outlets, Warner limits the number of Beanie Babies a retailer can order of each character per month. This maintains a good balance across the product line and a higher perception of value once the product is acquired. Although Beanie Babies are affordable, the restricted distribution presents a challenge in acquiring a full set, or even a particular favorite. By not selling to mass merchandisers, Warner can control demand at the retail level. Even knockoff efforts by discounters such as Wal-Mart (which sells $3.99 "Pebble Pets" made by Imperial Toy Corporation) have not had a significant effect on sales of Beanie Babies. According to Anne Nickels at Ty, Inc., the company is "very aggressive about protecting our copyright, and kids know the difference anyway, they're a lot smarter than marketers give them credit for."

After over seven years of success, Beanie Babies have shown that they have staying power. Warner's product line strategy keeps extending the life of this unique little toy. About every six months new Beanie Babies are added, while older ones are retired. The old Beanies increase in value as they become scarce and the new Beanies have investment potential. As with baseball and football cards, Warner's affordable product almost immediately has value beyond the price paid. Terry Dahlberg, a salesperson at Ellie's Hallmark store in Davie, Florida, says customers anticipate the arrival of Beanie Baby orders. "They last two hours here. All hell breaks loose when they come in." Dalberg notes that at one point there was a waiting list of 170 eager purchasers.

Keeping track of all the orders by product configuration and amount is not easy. Recently, the company selected the Design Data Systems (DDS) order entry system. Software designed by Oracle Corporation and a work group at Ty, Inc. enables up to 100,000 orders per day to be processed with outstanding customer service. The system not only allows careful tracking of demand for various Beanies but also helps with supply from the manufacturers overseas. This has provided both effectiveness and efficiency in the marketing system.

Another unique aspect of Ty, Inc. and its impressive performance is that the company does not advertise. Its Internet site, found at www.ty.com, is the company's main customer relationship tool and it includes many interactive features such as "My Tyfolio," the "Ty Talk Cyberboard," the official Beanie Baby Club home page, and "Beanie Greetings," a series of electronic cards.

A big challenge for Warner is to keep his product fresh and in demand. Certainly, the low price contributes to the toy's popularity. And there was a big boost when McDonald's gave away a scaled-down version, called Teeny Beanie Babies, in Happy Meals. For this biggest Happy Meal giveaway ever, McDonald's ordered nearly 100 million units from Ty, Inc. Despite the tremendous number, there was a sellout in many regions in the first few days of the promotion, a consumer frenzy not unlike that caused by the original Beanies. No one knows exactly how long the Beanie Baby craze may last, but for now both customers and retailers are in hot pursuit of such animals as Lips the Fish, Flitter the Butterfly, and Spinner the Spider.

1. *How has Ty Warner used demand and supply to influence the sale of Beanie Babies?*
2. *If Warner had decided to sell Beanie Babies to large retailers such as Toys "R" Us and Wal-Mart, what effect might this have had on price and demand for the toy? Is Warner's distribution strategy effective? Why or why not?*
3. *In this chapter you learned that prices serve several objectives. How has Ty, Inc. fulfilled relationship (customer) objectives?*
4. *Why do you suppose the sale of knockoffs has not adversely affected the success of Ty, Inc.?*

Sources: Gary Samuels, "Mystique Marketing," *Forbes,* October 21, 1996, pp. 276–277; Johnny Diaz, "Beanie Babies Popular in Retail and Resale," *Knight-Ridder/Tribune Business News,* April 13, 1997, p. 413B; "Boffo Business in Beanie Babies," *Maclean's,* October 6, 1997, p. 10; Randy Weston, "Beanie Babies Blitz IS," *Computerworld,* April 28, 1997, pp. 1, 2; "Beanie Mania," *People Weekly,* July 1, 1996, p. 84; Linda Kulman, "Move Over, Tickle Me Elmo," *U.S. News and World Report,* April 28, 1997, p. 14; and Cyndee Miller, "Bliss in a Niche: Toymakers Find Success by Breaking with Tradition," *Marketing News,* March 31, 1997, pp. 1, 21; Robert Dominguez, "Ty Inc. Chief Keeps Tight Hug on Beanie Babies," *Knight Ridder News Service,* retrieved on December 8, 2000 from the World Wide Web: www2.Kansas.com; and Dave Neubart, "H. Ty Warner, 58." *Chicago Sun Times,* October 29, 2000.

PRICING STRATEGY

HOW DOES A COMPANY PLAN THE pricing strategy for a new model that will replace one of its most popular and profitable products? Sony faced this challenge when preparing to launch its PlayStation2, a multimedia entertainment unit that lets users play video games, listen to music on CDs, watch films on DVDs, and—in future configurations—connect to the Internet for shopping, banking, e-mail, and other interactive functions.

Since 1994, when Sony had introduced the original PlayStation, consumers around the world had bought more than 72 million of the game consoles. The product continued in such demand that, despite widespread publicity about plans for the new multifunction model, Sony sold 18.5 million of the older units in the year before PlayStation2 was introduced. PlayStation sales contributed nearly 40 percent of the company's profits, so the product line was clearly a vital part of Sony's financial performance.

But looking ahead, industry analysts were forecasting lower revenues from higher sales of game consoles because manufacturers such as Sony tended to subsidize console prices and make up the difference through revenues from video game sales and licensing fees. In effect, the manufacturers were betting that buyers attracted by the value price of the consoles would wind up spending much more on games and accessories, which carried far higher profit margins. Building on this strategy, Sony ensured that 800 older games developed for the original PlayStation would also work on the new model, so buyers would not have to buy new versions of their favorites.

However, Sony knew that PlayStation was not the only game console in town. Nintendo, the number-two company in the video-game market, was selling its Nintendo 64 console and its handheld Gameboy, along with Mario Brothers and other game favorites. The company was going to launch its new GameCube, a more advanced game console with Internet functionality and limited DVD capabilities, months after PlayStation2's U.S. debut. Number-three Sega Enterprises, maker of the Dreamcast console and Sonic the Hedgehog games, cut its unit's price by 25 percent, from $200 to $150, to capture price-sensitive buyers just weeks before PlayStation2 became available. In addition, Microsoft had recently announced its intention to market the Xbox game console within a year.

Against this competitive backdrop, Sony planned its pricing strategy leading up to the PlayStation2 introduction in the United States, seven months after the introduction in Japan. The older unit, priced at less than $100, appealed to the lower end of the market and defended against Sega's discount pricing strategy. Sony set a price of $299 for the new unit and positioned it as a multifunction family entertainment unit, not just an improved video-game console.

The higher price did not dampen demand; in fact, Toys "R" Us and other stores that had been taking advance orders stopped when they realized how much demand they would be facing. Unfortunately, Sony experienced a components shortage and had to cut back on the number of PlayStation2 units it was shipping to retailers for the product's introductory weekend. It also pushed back the date for the model's European introduction to allow more time to boost production and restock distributors.

In another glitch, Sony had only 26 new games in production for the PlayStation2 by the launch date, much fewer than the 50 it had previously promised. Still, all 50 games would be available before the end of the holi-day selling season, with 270 more in development for release during the coming year. Despite these problems, the PlayStation2 made a major splash at its introduction, draw-ing families to stores and Internet retail sites to buy the new unit and find out more about the new games. And even before the PlayStation2 went on sale, Sony was busy planning its new, more powerful PlayStation3 model. With smart pricing and differen-tiated products, Sony has been able to maintain its worldwide leadership position in a highly competitive, fast-moving market.[1]

THE CONCEPT OF PRICE STRATEGY

This chapter could just as well be titled "Delivering Customer Value." Pricing and value are so intertwined that you cannot talk about one without the other. Customers should receive an excellent value for the price they pay, and marketers should earn a satisfactory return. The objective of marketing is not simply to sell a product but to create value for the customer and the seller. Consequently, marketers should price products fairly to reflect the value produced as well as received. Innovative marketers create value by offering, for example, a better prod-uct, faster delivery, better service, easier ordering, and more convenient locations. The greater the value perceived by customers, the more often they demand a company's products, and the higher the price they are willing to pay.

The firm is likely to incur higher costs when producing increased value. For example, it often costs more to make better products, create better distribution systems, or develop service facilities. Gillette can command higher prices because it invests in regular innovations in razor blades. In some cases, companies produce value by reducing their costs relative to those of competitors so that they can pass savings on to the customer in lower prices. That's what Procter & Gamble (P&G) did. Wal-Mart became a leading retailer by developing very focused marketing strategies that allowed dramatic cost reductions compared with rivals such as Kmart. By passing most of the savings on to customers, Wal-Mart gained considerable com-petitive advantage.

Whether a company improves its position through innovative products, distribution, communication, or cost cutting, the trick is to find a balance between what customers are will-ing to pay and the costs associated with the strategy. Essentially, the price charged is what mar-keters think their product is worth. The price paid is what the customer thinks the product is worth. If both parties have a similar price in mind, there is a strong likelihood that each party will believe it is worthwhile to trade.

It is not easy to establish precisely what price both buyers and sellers agree is fair. We need to look at how customer value is derived, recognizing that people place different values on the products they buy as well as the relationships they have with companies. Several pricing strat-egies may work. It all depends on how price is perceived, how competitors act, and how a strat-egy is designed and implemented. This chapter will deal with these issues. First, we will explore using value as the basis for pricing. We will learn how critical it is for relationship marketing. Next, we will discuss the methods used for customer, competitor, and global pricing. Finally, we will see how marketers implement the pricing strategy.

VALUE AS THE BASIS FOR PRICING

To arrive at the proper balance between the needs of the market and the needs of the firm, it is important to understand value-based pricing. **Value-based pricing** recognizes that price reflects value, not simply costs. This is contrasted with cost-based pricing in Figure 18.1. Traditionally, firms assessed the costs of doing business, added a profit, and arrived at the price. Once it was set, the marketer's job was to convince customers that the product was worth it. If the marketer was not successful, then the price was lowered. If demand turned out to be higher than anticipated, then the price was raised. An important point is that the cus-tomer was the last person to be considered in this chain of events.

Value-based pricing begins by understanding customers and the competitive market-place. The first step is to look at the value customers perceive in owning the product and to examine their options for acquiring similar products and brands. In other words, how much is

<u>VALUE-BASED PRICING</u>

A strategy that reflects value, not just cost.

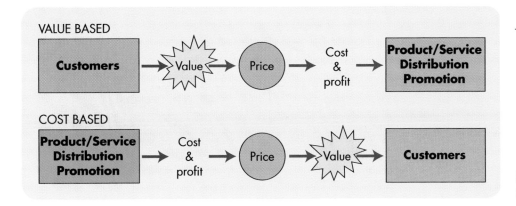

FIGURE 18.1 *Value-Based Versus Cost-Based Pricing*

the satisfaction gained from owning the product worth to them compared with what similar items or substitutes cost? Next, the marketer estimates the costs of production and necessary profit. To the extent possible, a similar analysis is usually done for each major competitor. Finally, product, distribution, and promotion decisions can be made. Notice that price is defined before developing the rest of the marketing mix. That way the marketer has a better chance of producing products at a volume competitive with rivals and of earning profits that satisfy the firm's financial objectives.

Many companies now use value-based pricing. In the summer of 2000, Ford Motor Company announced that, beginning with its 2001 models, what had been extra options would now be standard features on its cars and trucks. Although the price of a new Ford car or truck was projected to increase by 0.8 percent from 2000 to 2001, the new features meant that prices compared to those of similarly equipped vehicles would decrease by 0.3 percent. Ford anticipated that its customers would perceive more value in its products, and the company, therefore, expected an increase in sales and an increase in profits.[2] Although cost-based pricing is easier, it ignores the customer and the competition. Marketers know that it is impossible

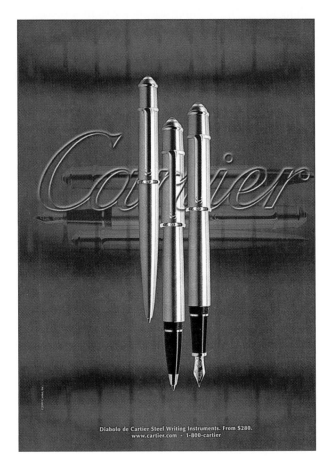

Diabolo de Cartier Steel Writing Instruments. From $280.
www.cartier.com · 1-800-cartier

Cartier's pricing strategy reflects value, not just cost.

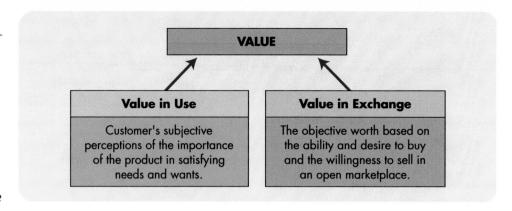

FIGURE 18.2 *Sources of Value*

to predict demand or competitors' actions simply by looking at their own costs. Consequently, cost-based pricing is becoming less popular.

Even with a good knowledge of customers, competitors, and cost, the future is always uncertain. Therefore, value-based pricing should be seen as an approach or guide for making the judgments involved in pricing decisions. It requires a lot of experience and insight, and there is always an element of chance. With this in mind, we are now ready to examine the many factors that affect value-based pricing.

SOURCES OF VALUE

What is value? Generally there are two sources: value in use and value in exchange. **Value in use** is the customer's subjective estimate of the benefits of a particular product. **Value in exchange** is the product's objective worth in the competitive marketplace. Figure 18.2 describes these two concepts. Value in use is what economists call utility. The use value of a product is based on the buyer's needs and his or her understanding of the marketplace at a given time. For example, under normal circumstances a Snickers candy bar may sell for 50 cents. But after working several hours in a location where food is unavailable, a person may be willing to pay two or three dollars for it. In this case, the use value is high because of the buyer's circumstances. The exchange value is still 50 cents, the price established by competitive forces in the market.

Although prices are often based primarily on value in exchange, companies also need to understand and manage buyer perceptions of the value of their products in use. Volvo has captured buyers at relatively high prices for years because of a reputation for durability and safety. The Volvo Saved My Life Club is not an advertising gimmick. On their own initiative, Volvo owners who had survived a wreck wrote to the company about their real-life stories. Volvo then developed a campaign of testimonial print and television ads to promote the safety and reliability of the car and enhance value-in-use perceptions of consumers.[3] Volvo continues to take vehicle safety very seriously. It has a team of accident investigators that collect data on real-life accidents and this information is used in the development of new features.[4] Volvo's Safety Concept Car has a heartbeat sensor to let you know if someone is in the car, a finger-print-activated keypad for entry, and seat belts similar to those seen in race cars.[5]

CONNECTED: SURFING THE NET

www.volvo.com

Learn more about the Volvo Saved My Life Club by visiting the company's Web site. There is also information about vehicle safety, design, and the company itself.

CUSTOMER VALUE IN PRICING

Because prices send powerful messages, it is extremely important that they reflect the customer value the company delivers. Customer value is derived from the product itself, the services surrounding it, the company–customer interaction, and the image the customer associates with the product. First, we will examine the connection between price and customer value. Second, we will find out how market leaders create customer value.

Price and Customer Value Strategies   The relationship between price and customer value is illustrated in Figure 18.3. FedEx, with its reputation for delivery 100 percent of the time by 10:00 A.M. the next day, is perceived by many consumers as having a high price and high customer value. The U.S. Postal Service (USPS) scores low on both dimensions. When FedEx introduced overnight delivery, it charged 25 times more than the USPS. Rather than undercut price, it redefined expectations of high customer value.

High price | A

• **FedEx**

• **UPS**

• **Airborne Express**

• **U.S. Postal Service**

Low price | B

Low customer value | High customer value

FIGURE 18.3 *Price and Customer Value Strategies*

Two hypothetical price strategies are indicated in Figure 18.3. Would it be practical for any company to use strategy A—high price and low perceived value? Clearly, few buyers would want to purchase from this company; they would give up more in price than they would gain in value. How about strategy B—low price and high value? Buyers would leap at the opportunity, but the company would be pricing at less than buyers are willing to pay. A strategy of this sort is called **buying market share,** that is, setting prices low for the short run in order to pull buyers away from competing brands. Japanese automobile producers used this strategy to enter the U.S. market. In the 1980s, the average Japanese import sold for nearly $2,000 below domestic makes and quickly took the lead among price-conscious consumers. By 1990, the Japanese were pricing vehicles up to $2,000 more than the Big Three but continued to sell because they had established an image of better quality.[6] During the last quarter of 2000, the U.S. car manufacturer General Motors (GM) announced its plans to introduce smaller cars at lower prices. The company targeted first-time buyers, who are more likely to purchase small cars, in an effort to increase its market share.[7]

The strategy selected depends on the company's target market and the number of buyers who desire to purchase at each value/price position. Any price strategy has the potential to produce profit or loss depending on the volumes it obtains and the marketing costs associated with it. FedEx commands the lead in volume and revenues because so many buyers are willing to pay more for its services. United Parcel Service (UPS) and Airborne Express are also successful but use different pricing strategies. In other businesses a high-value/high-price position may not appeal to many buyers. For stereo equipment, sales volumes are highest for low-price/low-value units. Nevertheless, Sony sells high-value/high-price units at a substantial profit.

Customer Value Propositions *The Discipline of Market Leaders,*[8] a best-seller, shows how product leadership, operational excellence, and customer intimacy are the three ways to deliver customer value. Because different customers buy different kinds of value, it is not necessary to be the best in all these areas. After studying 80 companies, however, the authors conclude that an organization has to be excellent in one area and good enough in the other two to deliver what buyers want. Essentially, the customer value proposition for each of the three areas is (1) customers want the best products (product leadership); (2) customers want the best price (operational excellence); and (3) customers want the best solution (customer intimacy). Figure 18.4 describes how companies gain leadership in customer value by matching their strategy with what buyers want.

Product Leadership The product leadership strategy builds customer value by differentiating the product. Nike and Intel come to mind. Both the design and functionality of their products are seen as offering high customer value, as does their overall level of customer service. Both companies invest heavily in R&D, and they stay ahead of the pack in innovation.

BUYING MARKET SHARE
A strategy in which prices are set low for the short run to pull buyers away from competing brands.

CONNECTED: SURFING THE NET

www.usps.gov

How do you rate the U.S. Postal Service on customer value? The U.S. Postal Service says, "Our goal is to evolve into a premier provider of 21st century postal communications by providing postal products and services of such quality that they will be recognized as the best value in America." Visit its Web site to learn about stamps, change of address, zip codes, postage rates, and services.

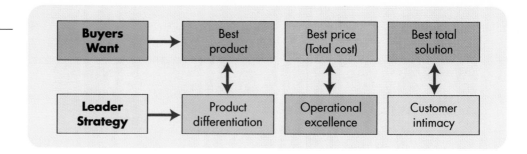

FIGURE 18.4 *Leadership in Customer Value*

Customers have grown to rely on their leadership and are willing to pay extra, knowing they will benefit from the product's supremacy. At the same time, these leaders can cut prices on old models, keeping even price competitors in check. For example, Intel dropped prices on its Pentium III by 31 percent as it prepared to introduce the Pentium 4 on the market.[9] Each company has very good operations to keep costs in line, but neither is striving for the absolute lowest cost in its field. Both also have good customer relationships, but few would describe them as pursuing customer intimacy strategies.

Operational Excellence Why can Casio sell a calculator more cheaply than Kellogg can sell a box of cornflakes?[10] For one thing, Casio's operational competencies translate into some of the lowest costs imaginable for manufacturing small objects. This means that no one can offer a lower price and sustain the same margins as Casio. Casio leads with price, its product design is adequate, and its customer service is equitable.

Stat-A-Matrix has trained employees from various companies on Six Sigma, a program to help companies achieve operational excellence. The rigorous standards of Six Sigma, or SS, a program pioneered by Motorola, begins with setting goals such as less than two late deliveries per month, one customer complaint per year, and manufacturing all parts within design tolerances. It was introduced at Libby Owens Ford, a company that supplies glass to builders and automobile manufacturers. The company's vice president Edward Kopkowski reported that after one year, Libby Owens Ford's initial investment of $1 million in the program had generated savings of $13 million.[11] This helps Libby Owens Ford establish a very competitive price while generating strong profit margins.

Customer Intimacy How does Airborne Express take business away from giants such as UPS and FedEx?[12] Certainly not through product innovation and operations. Yet, Airborne is growing faster than either rival, with revenue increases of 20 percent annually since 1985. It acquired Xerox Corporation as a client with a customer intimacy strategy. By carefully targeting a few accounts and working closely with them to identify and serve their specific needs, Airborne has eliminated services the customers do not really want, thereby saving cost. The company shares the rewards of intimacy by passing some of the savings on to customers. Both parties win.

A variation on this theme can be seen in this chapter's relationships feature, "Banks Coddle Some Customers and Make Others Pay Their Way."

CUSTOMER, COMPETITOR, AND GLOBAL PRICING

Depending on the market context, customer-oriented, competitor-oriented, or global pricing may be used. Each of these approaches involves a different set of considerations, which are discussed in more detail next.

CUSTOMER-ORIENTED PRICING

Marketers who make pricing decisions should keep in mind the effect they will have on consumer behavior. Customers can't purchase everything they want, so they have to determine what will give them the "best value"—or, at least satisfactory value—for the money. But value is relative, not absolute. That is why exact prices are not nearly as important as price differences. Assessing value is difficult because time and energy limit the amount of information we can absorb, because expectations after purchase may not be met, and because price comparisons are hard to calculate. Consumers process information about prices in the ways described in chapter 7. As you know, psychological factors affect their decisions on a variety of issues,

ChapStick products tend to fall within the acceptable price range of lip care products.

and pricing is no different. Among the most important influences on customers are reference prices, price awareness, the association between price and quality, the perception of odd-even prices, and limited offers. Also discussed at the end of this section is target pricing.

Reference Prices   Consumers try to obtain satisfactory value, not necessarily the best value. They try to determine how much satisfaction will be gained by comparing the benefits and price of one product relative to another. In most situations it is simply not worth the time to make all the calculations necessary to identify the absolute best value. Instead, buyers use reference prices and a price range. The **reference price** is what consumers expect to pay, and the **acceptable price range** is all prices around the reference point that consumers believe reflect good value.

In many airports the price of food so far exceeds consumers' reference points and acceptable range that they are dissatisfied with purchases. The Greater Pittsburgh Airport Authority requires concessionaires to use prices consistent with those in "typical" retail settings. The result is a unit volume of sales and a percentage of satisfied customers much higher there than in many other airports. An important point is that consumers respond more to price differences than to absolute prices. A reference price is often used to establish that difference. It represents the basis for judging value. For example, if a brand price is greater than a reference price, then the consumer perceives a loss in purchasing that product. If the brand price is less than the reference price, then the consumer perceives a gain.[13]

Researchers have found that consumers are likely to accept a price range for products and adjust their reference price accordingly. The brands lying outside the range will be rejected, and their prices won't be used in creating the reference price.[14] For example, you are looking for a mountain bike and expect to pay about $500 to $600. You find several bikes similar to what you want with price tags from $375 to $450. Your range shifts to about $400 to $500, and your reference price drops to around $425. You also see bikes at $200 and $800 (a midpoint of $500), but those extremes do not figure in your calculations.

The reference price gives consumers an idea about the value they can expect. They can formulate the reference price in several ways:

REFERENCE PRICE

The amount consumers expect to pay for a product.

ACCEPTABLE PRICE RANGE

All prices around the reference price that consumers believe reflect good value.

CONNECTING THROUGH RELATIONSHIPS

BANKS CODDLE SOME CUSTOMERS AND MAKE OTHERS PAY THEIR WAY

The retail banking industry has taken a sharp turn in some markets from focusing on serving its customers to focusing on its bottom line. Feeling the effects of this trend perhaps closest to home are clients of the New England banks that are being taken over by the New Jersey–based FleetBoston Financial Corp.

The general feeling of smaller account customers of these recently acquired banks is that they now need to pay for the services they may have previously enjoyed for free, while the big fish are treated like royalty. John S. Reed, the retired chairman of Citigroup, expressed his concerns by stating that financial institutions "are poorly serving their customers." The evidence? Well, in July 2000, a *Consumer Reports* study had Fleet's customer service ranked next to last for commercial banks. In some locations, customers have started to take notice of the new $2 fee for transactions made through human tellers that could have been done via phone or through electronic means. Also, the bank charges an extra dollar for every transaction made in excess of 10. What can a customer do to avoid some of these extra fees? Simply meet the $5,000 higher minimum balance.

Gerard Cassidy, a bank analyst at Tucker Anthony Capital Markets, says that banks often cater to customers with larger accounts in order to maximize profits. "Fleet is very focused on doing what airlines do with frequent fliers, those are the customers the airlines want to go out of their way to please and take care of. [This is] versus the vacation fliers who the airline is happy to have but is not paying as much attention to." Since most of a large commercial bank such as Fleet's profits come from the big-ticket clients, the attention of the tellers and staff is focused on keeping those people happy, while perhaps neglecting or charging the little guy. Because of this, banks such as Fleet look to possibly lose many customers to smaller banks that can provide the services that people are seeking. Not all banks, however, are worried about the defection or the business of the less profitable client.

HSBC's Premier global bank makes no secret of its goals and intentions. Premier targets customers with a minimum balance of $150,000 but is also trying to lure young people who are just beginning their careers with their Power Vantage account. This program carries a minimum balance of only $3,000. However, unlike Fleet, the focus of HSBC remains on servicing each client. "It's not all based on fine pricing, not all based on highly sophisticated products giving you this, that and the other. It's based on the level of service you can give," says Eric Gill, chief executive of HSBC Singapore. So the point remains that in order to effectively determine a bank's pricing policy, keeping each of its customers in mind is vitally important to success.

Sources: Siow Li Sen, "Jostling for the Lucrative Consumer Business," *Business Times (Singapore),* May 24, 2000, Banking and Finance, p. 6, retrieved November 12, 2000 from the World Wide Web: www.web.lexis-nexis.com; Geoffrey Smith, "Bigger Isn't Better for Fleet's Customers," *Business Week,* July 10, 2000, p. 64; and Don Stancavish, "Boston-Based Bank Reassures New Jersey Residents About Buyout," *The Record (New Jersey),* retrieved November 11, 2000 from the World Wide Web: web.lexis-nexis.com/universe.

- The last price paid
- The going price (amount paid most frequently)
- The believed fair price
- The average price
- The price limit (what most buyers will pay)
- The expected future price (price based on trends)[15]

Marketers also look at the differentiation value of their product's attributes to determine whether their brand is seen favorably or unfavorably. The buyer looks at the relative price and relative quality. If consumers tend to evaluate a product as better than others, then it has a positive differentiation value. This means that it may have higher demand or command a price on the upper end of the range. The opposite is true if a brand has a negative differentiation value.

Marketers often help consumers establish reference prices. How many times have you seen ads with the original price (manufacturer's suggested retail or list price) and a sale price? In this way, marketers attempt to create favorable differential price impressions. Other methods are "cents off," "everyday low prices," "new low prices," or promotions such as "2002 models at 2001 prices." Marketers must be careful, however, about price changes. If the frequency, length, and level of price promotions are not carefully managed, consumers' reference prices can be affected. As a result, consumers may lower their reference price.[16]

Price Awareness   Business-to-business customers must be very price conscious. Each item they buy contributes to their costs and, thus, to their profits and competitiveness. Many of them keep extensive records using formalized purchasing systems designed to obtain the best value for the price. Consumers tend to be less aware of actual prices. Studies of grocery shoppers have found that people are inaccurate about the exact price they paid for an item 90 percent of the time, and they err by approximately 20 percent.[17]

Price/Quality Association and Product Categorizations   When buyers have little information about a product, they often assume a relationship between its price and its quality. In other words, price is a surrogate for quality. A traveler who doesn't know the local hotels may select a medium-priced unit, expecting an average room, or the highest-priced hotel, expecting luxury accommodations. Ordinarily, the product delivered should be consistent in quality with its price relative to the competition.

Sometimes putting a very low price on a high-quality item may reduce demand by signaling low quality. Nike found that higher prices on many of its signature lines increased sales because consumers perceived that the price tag matched the company's image. Would it make sense to price Michael Jordan signature shoes the lowest? Prices that are inconsistent with perceived value can confuse buyers. Price indicates not only what we expect to give up or pay but also what we expect to gain. If these two are highly inconsistent, we distrust the seller, our own judgment, or both. The Hakeem Olajuwon brand of sneaker was priced at only $35. Hakeem's conscience would not let him endorse a more expensive product: "How can a poor working mother with three boys buy Nikes or Reeboks that cost $120? She can't. So kids steal these shoes from stores and from other kids."[18] The superstar was making a commendable effort, and buyers seemed to be perceiving the value. Spalding, marketer of the shoe, reported strong sales.[19] Early in 2000, however, Olajuwon's contract with Spalding had expired and he was seeking new shoe manufacturers with which to work.[20]

Marketers refer to the high end of a price range as the ceiling. Many companies establish ceiling prices from which reductions can be bargained.[21] In a product line with several levels of quality, there may be several ceiling prices. When consumers make few or no comparisons among brands, companies can charge prices at or near the ceiling. Companies with strong brands also can charge at the upper end. That is why Kodak is likely to price cameras at just under an $80 ceiling (or just under a $100 ceiling). It would be less profitable to charge $74.99 rather than $79.99. The $5 difference can add a lot to revenues but doesn't change the consumer's perception of value.

We know from experiments that price comparisons are made on a ratio rather than an absolute basis. If a Pontiac Firebird has a sticker price of $20,000 and is sold for $1,000 less, then that is seen as roughly a 5 percent discount. The same discount on a Firebird with a sticker price of $15,000 is seen as slightly larger, approaching 7 percent. Although consumers may not actually compute the percentages, their perception works as if rough calculations were made.[22] Pricing policy must take this into account.

Very low prices on a computer could signal low quality.

TARGET PRICING

The use of price to reach a particular market segment.

Consider the error made by a discount copying service that didn't understand how prices are perceived. Major copy centers had established copy prices of approximately 4 cents per page. The discount firm offered the same service for 3 cents a page. This attracted a lot of customers and produced a substantial amount of sales. The difference of "approximately 25 percent" was enough to entice many students. When the major centers increased price to 5 cents and then 6 cents, however, the discounter followed with two 1-cent increases. At 6 cents per page, the 1-cent differential was perceived as much smaller—only about 17 percent. The discounter's sales volume declined with each price increase, although the 1-cent absolute differential in price was maintained.

Odd-Even Price Perceptions Prices that end in odd numbers tend to be perceived differently from even-numbered prices. Consumers have learned that discounters tend to use prices ending in a 9, 7, or 5. Before sophisticated computer systems and inventory control systems were available, retailers used these endings as a code: 9 identified a markdown; 7 a second markdown, and 5 a third markdown. Early discounters adopted the odd numbers for all their products to suggest sales prices. Today, odd numbers connote lower quality and price, whereas even numbers connote higher quality and price.[23] For example, Gateway's specials advertised on its Web site all have odd prices, $799 for a desktop PC, $249 for a PDA, and $999 for a notebook computer.[24]

Limited Offers Limited offers are often used by marketers to encourage consumers to buy types or quantities of products they had not planned to purchase. The special prices are meant to persuade consumers to stock up. Consider for example, the psychology behind a limit on sales. A special promotion for sugar may read "limit 4." Why? A study has found that people are more likely to buy an item that has a limit. This is similar to children who want candy because they are told they cannot have any. Furthermore, shoppers are more likely to buy an item with a limit of four rather than two.[25]

Target Pricing Customer-oriented pricing focuses on buyers' psychological information processing and their perceptions of value in use and value in exchange. **Target pricing,** which uses price to reach a particular market segment, is a very important strategy. It is a way of matching price with the value perceived by each segment. French-made Rossignol skis are carefully marketed to various types of downhill skier. Distinct lines are priced in relation to an individual's level of interest, ability, and income. Rossignol's all-mountain, high-performance Viper X attracts aggressive, experienced skiers who are willing to pay nearly $750. The 9S Pro Race Carve 9.9, its top-of-the-line race ski, also is priced at more than $700. For beginning skiers, there is the Cut 10.4, priced at less than $400. Rossignol also markets skis such as the Cut 10.4 L that are designed especially for women.[26] As with most forms of customer-oriented pricing, target pricing requires a good understanding about what price communicates to potential buyers.

COMPETITOR-ORIENTED PRICING

Competitor-oriented pricing focuses primarily on value in exchange on the prices set by rivals. Leader-follower, going rate, discount or premium, and competitive bids are all price schemes of this type. Carried to its extreme, competitor-oriented pricing can lead to mutually destructive price wars.

Leader-Follower Pricing Duo-therm announced 10 percent higher prices for furnaces and air conditioners marketed to builders of manufactured housing. This was an invitation to others in this oligopolistic market to follow suit and increase profit for everyone. It was a large hike in an industry noted for being so price competitive that there is little or no profit. After a few days, rivals stuck to the original levels and began to win Duo-therm customers. Duo-therm then dropped prices more than 20 percent—8 percent below its original price—to show that it also could play price wars. This move won back customers and began to take some from competitors. Given the adverse effect on profitability of a prolonged price war, the major competitor then raised prices about 2 percent; Duo-therm then returned to its level before the increase. The competition followed. In the end, prices were 10 percent higher than originally. Duo-therm was the price leader, and other companies became the followers. All of them moved to a position of some profitability as average prices edged upward.

This Oldsmobile Silhouette uses target pricing to reach a market of middle-income buyers.

Competitor-oriented pricing often involves scenarios such as this. The leader-follower situation tends to occur in oligopolistic industries whose products have relatively inelastic derived demand. The leader usually has considerable strength—high market share, a loyal customer base, an efficient cost structure, moderate inventory, and a technological edge. Gas stations use price leadership to determine prices. The stations with the largest share of the market dictate the price.[27] Leaders generally can exercise power, as Duo-therm did, but often that is not necessary. The reason is that they create competitive environments, which benefit followers by providing fair profits for all. Xircom, Inc., went from a $26 million to a $131 million company in less than four years. It changed its strategy to become the price leader in the market for mobile access services.[28] Good followers can also help create a positive industry pricing climate. In banking, most small and medium-sized institutions copy the products and pricing policies of larger competitors.[29]

Price leaders must show a willingness to defend their position when price becomes an issue. Yet, across-the-board cuts may hurt larger companies more, so it's important to be selective. When America West used price against Northwest's lucrative Minneapolis–Los Angeles route, Northwest did not retaliate in that market. It could hurt America West much more by hitting its Phoenix–New York route. Northwest introduced a limited-time fare, which signaled that it was willing to back off if America West increased its Minneapolis fare.[30]

Going Rate Pricing   The **going rate** price evolves over time when no competitor has power over others so all price at a similar level. This is often the case in monopolistic competition when product differentiation is very minor and firms attempt to gain loyalty while pricing at the going rate. For example, lawyers often charge the going rate per hour, which will vary considerably from one community to another. The going rate tends to avoid price wars. Because all providers charge approximately the same, and these prices are broadly communicated, buyers' price expectations are usually met. The most recent price hikes of crude oil have had many lasting effects. The price to produce one ton of ammonia in the United States has soared to $300, but the going rate on the world market is just $200.[31]

GOING RATE

The price that evolves over time when no competitor has power over others and all price at a similar level.

Discount or Premium Pricing   Discount or premium pricing positions the company relative to competitors based solely on price. In most markets there are buyers who seek the cheapest products and those who seek the most expensive. Consider the sale of store-brand hair coloring at very low prices and L'Oréal at very high prices. L'Oréal says its hair coloring is the most expensive "because I'm worth it." The Meijer food chain establishes the lowest price possible and asks: "Why pay more?"

Competitive Bids   We tend to think of bids as related to the purchasing function, but they also are a prevalent form of competitive pricing. Sealed bids are opened at a certain time, and the low price usually is the winner. An alternative is for buyers to look at bids as they are received and perhaps give feedback to sellers indicating they are too high. This is called open bidding, and it is intended to get suppliers to lower prices.

By understanding competitors, a company can greatly enhance its ability to win contracts at the highest possible price while still being the low bidder. Competitors often scale prices up or down to meet their own volume or cost objectives. By knowing competitors' capacity and cost structure, marketers can adjust their own bids.

PRICE WAR

A cut by one company spurs similar reductions by competitors, resulting in price slashing that can lower profit margins.

Price Wars   **Price wars** occur when price cuts by one company spur similar reductions by competitors. These price-slashing battles can substantially lower profit margins. The consumer benefits, since products can be purchased below their value. The company most successful at cutting costs is usually the victor—if it can survive despite the meager profit margins. Large organizations with ample reserves have an obvious advantage.

As noted earlier, price wars have been especially common in the fast-food industry. Today, these restaurants frequently shave cents off individual items or offer larger portions at a minimal price. In 1997, McDonald's introduced its biggest discount ever, reducing the $1.90 Big Mac to 55 cents with the purchase of fries and a drink. Called "Campaign 55," for the year in which the first McDonald's franchise opened, it rotated the 55-cent price (in participating outlets) to Quarter Pounders, McRibs, the Arch Deluxe, and even the Egg McMuffin. The aggressive strategy was a response to Burger King's 99-cent Whopper and low breakfast prices, which had been gaining market share.[32] In 2000, some McDonald's restaurants offered burgers priced as low as 25 cents to compete with Burger King's Whopper promotion ("Two for $2"). Other fast-food chains such as Carl's and Hardee's avoid price wars because even though they can help companies increase market shares, they can also cut too deeply into profits.[33]

Some price wars are especially damaging. The long-distance telephone companies have cut severely into their profits to take customers away from competitors. Customers are reaping the rewards now, but that could change in the near future. The telecom climate is moving away from cutthroat competition to consolidation. This move will actually give companies the foundation to compete more effectively in the future. In 2000, AT&T, WorldCom, and Sprint have all seen substantial decreases in their stock prices. The push for new technology is forcing companies to look at the effects of the price war. Upgrading the nation's systems will require billions of dollars, and telecommunications companies must improve their performance if they want to keep up with the needs of their customer and still make a profit.[34] It can be advantageous for a company not to participate in a price war. When Heinz chose not to enter one it suffered no major losses as a result. In fact, stock price value increased.[35]

CONNECTED: SURFING THE NET

www.sprint.com

Visit the Sprint Web site to see how the company is competitively pricing its services. While there, you may also find a new phone plan for yourself.

DIVERSITY: PRICING TO ATTRACT SENIOR CITIZENS

How would you like to find a population segment that is growing more rapidly than all others combined and with a median net worth that is twice the national average? That describes U.S. senior citizens, who average a net worth of more than $73,000. Since 85 percent of them do not work, they have the time to use their significant spending power.[36] A report by the U.S. Bureau of the Census predicts that the 65 and older crowd will double in the next 25 years in Nevada, Arizona, Colorado, Georgia, Alaska, Washington, Utah, and California. It is also estimated that 19 states will have more than 1 million seniors.[37] By 2030, according to World Bank forecasts, 16 percent of the world population will be 60 or older, and most will have 25 years of retirement.[38] Even Club Med has begun focusing on price-sensitive seniors, offering discounts at 14 resorts. Working with organizations such as the American Association of Retired Persons, Club Med has been very successful in reaching this group with reduced prices.[39]

Marketing experts on the elderly caution companies that all seniors are not the same when it comes to price sensitivity. A study by Roper Starch Worldwide found that one group, called "Free Birds" (median age 69, 13 percent of the population), are very cost conscious about everyday goods so they can spend lavishly on big-ticket items for themselves.[40] There is a shift in spending that affects pricing for the age categories above and below 68 years. The older seniors "save a lot and spend a little," whereas the younger group, which has benefited from a long period of economic growth, saves some and spends some.[41]

We have already noted that the graying baby boomers do not all fit the stereotype. Americans over age 50 control 77 percent of the country's disposable income, but they make up only 27 percent of the population.[42] Seniors are the fastest-growing segment on the Internet. They spend three times more than the average online shopper. Retired.com is a Web site geared specifically to active, healthy retirees. The goal is to tap into the considerable wealth available to this generation.[43]

GLOBAL PRICING

Global pricing is complicated by many factors. One of the most important is when a government mandates that imported products cannot be paid for with cash; **countertrade** requires companies from the exporting nation to purchase products of equivalent value from the importing nation. Countertrade affects up to 30 percent of all world trade. When a nation's banking system is poor, countertrade may be the best form of pricing. It also provides government with a mechanism for stimulating exports. For example, it is estimated that 90 percent of Russian transactions for critical imports involve some form of countertrade.[44] Malaysia will likely make countertrade arrangements with Russia in an effort to increase the importation of palm oil.[45] In other words, countertrade is a simple barter, the exchange of one good for another.

Although technically the term refers to government-regulated exchanges, *countertrade* also may be initiated by trading partners. There are many arrangements similar to barter that can benefit both parties. There may be tax advantages to not using cash. Agreements to purchase like values but without exchanging money can increase demand. A countertrade deal that covers an extended period can provide a lot of flexibility in scheduling, manufacturing, and shipping. Japanese and Dutch trading companies may have hundreds of these arrangements going at one time. The Japanese *keiretsu* system relies on cross-ownership, cross-ties in banking, and discrimination against outside buyers and sellers to form huge trading organizations.[46] By locking suppliers into the organization, enormous cost savings result. The major *keiretsu* are Mitsui, Mitsubishi, Sumitomo, Fuyo, Sanwa, and Daiichi. These arrangements are slowly starting to shift in Japan as companies are starting to sell off their cross-shareholdings of other companies in the *keiretsu*.[47]

CONNECTING THROUGH TECHNOLOGY

IN LIGHT OF AOL'S MERGER WITH TIME WARNER, COMPETITORS MAY USE PRICING TO GAIN A PIECE OF THE PIE

The talk of the technology world these days is the imminent merger of media mogul Time Warner with Internet access provider AOL. Not only could the merger bring about a new era of consumer convenience and high-speed Internet access, but it also may enable AOL to branch out into various areas of communications technology. AOL gained a record 1.4 million new subscribers during the third quarter of 2000, bringing the total of AOL members to 24.6 million worldwide. Not only were new subscribers jumping on the AOL bandwagon, but current members were also taking advantage of AOL's flat monthly rate by using the Internet up to 3 minutes longer per day over the quarter. With AOL poised to roll out its new AOL Anywhere Services (such as AOLTV, AOL Mobile Services, and AOL By Phone), it would appear as if the Internet service provider is ready to become everyone's new best friend. However, some consumers and competitors are worried about the pricing strategies and possible competitive discrimination that would be made possible by the merger.

The merger between the two corporate giants has been in the negotiation stages for months due to Federal Trade Commission (FTC) and Federal Communications Commission (FCC) investigations into the possible dangers of competitive discrimination and industry domination. The government is looking to prevent a monopoly in the Internet and cable access industry that would eliminate rivals or make their ability to com-

Continued

pete much more difficult. One suggested condition that the FCC has put before AOL Time Warner, as the new company would be called, is to eliminate AOL's holdings in DirecTV. The idea is to prevent Time Warner from being able to interfere with its multichannel television competitor. Gene Kimmelman, the codirector of the Washington Office of Consumers Union, states, "High-speed Internet will be the information and entertainment highway of the future. Eliminating the competitive dangers of AOL TV dominance and the threat of discriminating practices is as important as the consequences of Microsoft."

The main fear among rival Internet service providers is that the conglomerate company may require that AOL and Time Warner advertisements or offerings appear on the desktops of competitor's Web sites. Also, Internet services or cable operators that may want to enter the fast-growing cable/Internet technology market may be shut out by the high prices demanded by Time Warner or AOL. So how do smaller rivals combat these issues? Just ask Paul Frick.

A recent article in *Inc.* magazine told the story of how Frick, who owns a public relations business, was looking for a way to save on all the company's long-distance calls. Although telecommunications services such as Startec Global, OneStar, and Qwest offer long-distance phone service, T1 Internet connection, and Web hosting needs, Frick got fed up with high prices, varying rates, and sales pitches. So Frick decided to go in a new direction—one that customers facing possibly high prices from AOL Time Warner may soon be following. He went to a Web site called TeleBright.com to find a long-distance carrier that met his needs without the hassle of wading through all the extraneous services. TeleBright promptly found a dozen long-distance companies that could beat what he was paying for his current service. Frick finally settled on a company that will save his business almost $500 a month. There are many other such Web sites waiting to bring together interested customers and businesses with services that more adequately or affordably fit their needs.

With an increasing amount of companies looking to use the Internet as a means of doing business, AOL may have to consider the efficiency of sites such as TeleBright.com before setting high prices for its business services. The government may not have to worry too much about keeping AOL Time Warner from taking over the telecommunications world—it looks like the competitors will find a way to survive on their own.

Sources: "America Online Reports Record-Breaking Results for FY2001 First Quarter in Net Income, Total Revenues, Ad/Commerce and Membership," *PR Newswire,* October 18, 2000, retrieved November 7, 2000 from the World Wide Web: web.lexis-nexis.com/universe; Sarah Fister Gale, "Lining Up Telecom Online," *Inc.,* retrieved November 9, 2000 from the World Wide Web: web.lexis-nexis.com/universe; Stephen Labaton, "FTC Review of AOL Deal in Final Stage," *New York Times,* November 6, 2000, p. C1; and B. McConnoll, "AOL/TW Gets Mega-Scrutiny," *Broadcasting & Cable,* July 31, 2000, pp. 4–8, retrieved November 7, 2000 from the World Wide Web: proquest.umi.com/.

International pricing also is complicated by the need to transfer funds. Payment is seldom direct, and generally a bank must be involved. This often requires a letter of credit that specifies the bank will pay a seller under various conditions. Because a good deal of time may pass between the settlement of an international deal and the transfer of products and funds, financing is critical. If it is poorly executed, then a lot of money can be lost.

Exchange fluctuations also influence global pricing. Companies that use value-based pricing tend to treat these fluctuations differently from those that use cost-plus pricing. As exchange rates go up and down, profit margins tend to vary. The cost-plus method simply increases or decreases price to keep the same margins, which changes what buyers pay. The value-based method tends to leave prices the same, varying instead the level of profit. Japanese companies exporting to the United States tend to maintain stable prices, reflecting their tendency to keep them in line with the market as well as profit objectives.[48] This works unless exchange rates fluctuate widely. The depreciation of the yen in relation to the dollar has meant that companies such as Nissan, Honda, and Toyota could lower U.S. prices. This has not had great effect on market share, however, because U.S. automakers have, in many cases, competitively reduced prices to maintain share. Many companies benefit in this way when the dollar is strong, but others are hurt. U.S. companies that use imported components from foreign companies have recently had to pay less, and profit has increased. Recently, some Asian currencies have been devalued. This has made U.S. products very expensive there. For example, students from Korea essentially pay much more for education in the United States now than they expected to pay a few years ago.

Once the overall pricing strategy has been chosen, it must be implemented. Since prices are easier to adjust than any other part of the marketing mix, they tend to fluctuate. Even companies with consistent pricing based on customer value make changes. Whether initiating a new strategy or adjusting an existing one, the first step in implementation is to set prices. The second step is to communicate them to the market. At both stages, ethical issues are involved.

SETTING PRICES

Fundamental Strategies for Price Setting   To set price, one of six approaches can be used: skimming, penetration, sliding down the demand curve, the price umbrella, everyday low prices, and promotional pricing. Companies can price high, low, or in between. Whatever the decision, it is sure to affect buyers and competitors. Figure 18.5 describes the fundamental strategies for price setting.

Strategy	Objective	When Typically Used
Skimming	High short-term profit without concern for the long run	No competitive products Innovation or fad Block competitor entry due to patent control, high R&D costs, high fixed costs, control of technology, government regulation, or high promotion costs Uncertain demand and/or cost Short life cycle Price-insensitive buyers
Sliding Down the Demand Curve	Gain short-term profits before competitors become entrenched without sacrificing long-term market share	Launch of high-technology innovations Slight barriers to competitive entry Medium life cycle
Price Umbrella Leadership	Encourage competitors to promote the product category to stimulate purchase of all brands and encourage competitors to follow the price leader	Several comparable competitors Growing market Stable competitors One or a few dominant competitors
Everyday Low Prices or Value Pricing	Appeal to buyers willing to shop for the "greatest" benefits for the money	Component parts in industrial markets Repurchased consumer products Mass merchandisers Established products
Promotional Pricing	Stimulate demand to introduce or reintroduce a product, neutralize a competitor, or move excess inventory	Demand fluctuates seasonally or for a certain period Marketing "wars" or head-to-head competition Mass merchandisers Fashion items
Penetration Pricing	Stimulate market growth and capture market share; become entrenched to produce long-term profits	Large markets Products of broad appeal Long product life cycle Very price-elastic demand

FIGURE 18.5 *Fundamental Strategies for Price Setting*

A strategy designed to obtain a very high price from relatively few consumers, who have the resources and desire to buy irrespective of price.

PENETRATION PRICING

A strategy that seeks the maximum number of buyers by charging low prices.

SLIDE DOWN THE DEMAND CURVE

Set a high price when a product is introduced and then lower it significantly as competitors enter the market.

PRICE UMBRELLA

The leader maintains the price at a high enough level that competitors can earn a profit at that or lower levels.

Skimming and Penetration Pricing These two approaches are discussed together because they are opposites. **Price skimming** is designed to obtain a very high price from relatively few consumers with the resources and desire to buy irrespective of price. The name is taken from the practice of dairy farmers, who once skimmed the valuable cream off the top of nonhomogenized milk and discarded the remainder or fed it to farm animals. Today, skimming is used by companies with innovations or fads. Marketers charge a very high price, thereby attracting only a small part of the total market. Because use value is high in a product's introductory period, a premium can be obtained. When more producers enter the market, prices tend to move downward as exchange value declines.

If companies perceive they can obtain a monopoly position for a short time, then they may skim to generate profits that provide investment capital for further innovations. To sustain skimming, companies must offer unusual products of the highest quality or artistic value. Many times this strategy does not produce loyal customers, since subsequent entrants eventually will offer a better value at lower price. In the past, IBM dominated personal computer sales, but as smaller companies entered the market it had to price more competitively.

In contrast to skimming, **penetration pricing** seeks the maximum number of buyers by charging a low price. This approach is used for products that are very price elastic. If costs are sensitive to volume, then these will drop dramatically as share increases relative to competitors. This is a way to keep rivals from entering the market, since many companies avoid situations in which overall prices are extremely low.

The problem with penetration pricing is that losses are likely, especially in the short term. Because profit margins tend to be very small, demand must meet expectations in order to generate enough earnings. Furthermore, when customers buy only because of price, loyalty tends to be low. They are likely to switch to competitors offering an even lower price or innovations of higher value at a higher price.

Figure 18.6 summarizes the main features of skimming and penetration pricing, which are opposite ends of a spectrum. Because neither is likely to achieve strong buyer loyalty in competitive markets, most companies use pricing approaches that fall somewhere between these extremes.

Sliding Down the Demand Curve To **slide down the demand curve** means to descend from higher to lower prices. When launching its industrial control products, Texas Instruments has been known to use this strategy. First, management establishes a high price for an innovative product to skim the market. Second, when a major competitor follows with its version, Texas Instruments drops its price—sometimes only slightly, often considerably. This aggressive strategy discourages or delays market entrants, and Texas Instruments obtains high short-term profit margins without sacrificing its long-term objective of penetrating the market.

The Price Umbrella DuPont is known for its leadership in innovations. It produces innumerable plastics, fibers, and chemicals used to create thousands of products. Because of its strength, the company is in a perfect position to use the **price umbrella;** that is, the leader prices high. Competitors can make fair profits at that level or even lower, especially if their costs are relatively low. Price leadership occurs when one or two companies price in such a way that others follow them. In DuPont's case, marketers launch innovations after careful study of the product's likely contributions to customers and society. By assessing the use value relative to substitutes and other brands, DuPont establishes a price commensurate with the high value it typically offers. Along with the product, buyers receive DuPont's uncompromising customer support, which is based on an advanced distribution system, consultative and relationship selling, and service.

	Skimming	Penetration
Intent	Capture "cream"—less price-sensitive buyers	Sell whole market at one price—no "elite" market
Focus	High profit margin sacrifice volume	High volume sacrifice profit margin
Result	Invite competitors short-term profits for reinvestment	Keep competition out achieve economies of scale

FIGURE 18.6 *Skimming Versus Penetration Pricing*

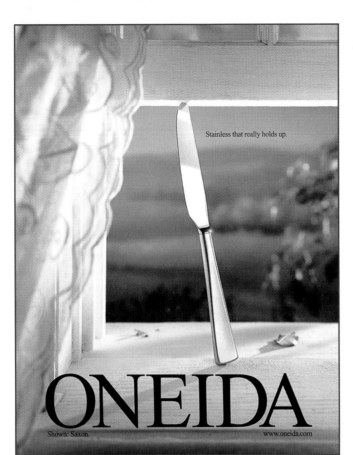

Stainless that really holds up.

ONEIDA

Shown: Saxon

www.oneida.com

Oneida establishes prices commensurate with the high value the company's product provides.

career tip "DuPont is in a time of exciting changes. We are headed into the next millennium with future-based technologies, with innovative concepts, and with businesses that are very response driven." The company actively recruits for co-op/internships and regular full-time employment. Dan Burger, DuPont's European president, says the company concentrates on two global principles. The first is "to fully engage employees by connecting them more directly to business performance. The second seeks to empower employees by providing them with the tools and working environment they need to manage their development and their careers." Go online to find out about DuPont's major recruiting events and which campuses are regularly visited: www.dupont.com/careers/index.html.

**CONNECTED:
SURFING THE NET**

www.dupont.com

DuPont says: "We're a science and technology based global company of people who make products that make a difference in everyday life." Find out more about its leadership in product innovation by visiting its Web site.

Generally, DuPont's price is high enough to encourage other healthy companies to participate in the market. At the same time, because several competitors are promoting a similar product, demand is stimulated for the product category. DuPont even licenses its products to rivals in exchange for a percentage of sales revenue. Since these competitors do not have to engage in basic R&D, DuPont's leadership in product innovation is protected.

Everyday Low Prices Wal-Mart is famous for its **everyday low prices,** which on average are consistently lower than those of competitors. Sometimes this strategy is called value pricing (not to be confused with value-based pricing). In order for it to work, retailers need to develop extremely efficient (low-cost) operations. Wal-Mart has the most advanced computerized inventory control system imaginable. Rapid turnover (products don't sit on the shelves for long) and aggressive purchasing power provide the basis for keeping prices low. Wal-Mart has most recently taken its pricing capability into groceries. It generated $75 billion in supermarket sales in 2000 and became the largest retailer of supermarket items.[49] Target and Toys "R" Us also use this strategy—and pledge to meet or beat any competitor's price on any item. In this way, they maximize volume and keep customers from shopping around. Other examples are Dollar General and Family Dollar, which target low- or fixed-income families, a market often neglected. These stores' prices are developed to match the

EVERYDAY LOW PRICES
Prices that, on average, are consistently lower than those of competitors.

needs and shopping patterns of cash-strapped target customers, who often make frequent trips for a few items.[50] The discount chain Ames likewise relies on a consistently low pricing strategy to appeal to consumers whose annual family incomes range between $25,000 and $35,000.[51]

Everyday low pricing can be highly competitive on an international scale as well. For example, Zellers, Canada's low-price leader, used the slogan "lowest price is the law." Its profit margins shrank when Wal-Mart entered the Canadian market, and the two now compete intensely with their value-pricing strategies. The Zellers slogan is "there's more than low prices," while Wal-Mart continues to implement cuts in order to offer the lowest regular prices to consumers.[52] German retailers, however, are not threatened by Wal-Mart—in fact, the company is losing money in Germany. It has been unable to increase store hours and the government has forced it to raise prices on certain staple items.[53] In an effort to keep its customers and lure customers from its rival, Zellers became the first retailer in the world to seek and gain from the International Organization for Standardization in Geneva its certification that it meets world-class standards of efficiency and quality.[54]

Promotional Pricing Companies such as Coca-Cola and PepsiCo, Burger King and McDonald's, and Toyota and Nissan are nearly always engaged in some form of **promotional pricing.** These battles serve three purposes. First, the price discount is a way to make consumers notice the product. Second, immediate purchase is encouraged because promotional pricing gives consumers the impression that the price is likely to rise in the near future. Third, consumers are kept aware of the entire product category. The "wars" between Coke and Pepsi keep buyers loyal to cola at the expense of other soft drinks. Marketers in these two companies expect continuous challenges from one another as price interacts with other parts of the marketing mix to stimulate demand and produce minor market share shifts.

One kind of promotional pricing is loss leaders, used by retailers to lure consumers into their store. As you'll remember from the previous chapter, these products are priced at or below the retailer's cost. For example, the Meijer chain often prices milk very low compared with competitors. Because this item is purchased regularly by most consumers, its price tends to be remembered. For that reason, milk and similar repeat purchases provide shoppers with a ready source of comparison among rivals. At the same time, shoppers can benefit from the price reduction on most trips. Retailers make up for loss leaders by increased volume or higher prices on other items.

There are many other forms of price promotion. Although we usually assume that price reduction is most likely to stimulate demand, sometimes any message drawing attention to the product, including a price differential, will lead to purchase. Marketing research by a major pharmaceutical company revealed some surprising news. For many years, price promotions had been used to boost sales of selected prescription drugs. Each time the product was promoted at a reduced price by sales representatives, physicians prescribed it more. The assumption was that these products were price elastic for doctors, but the research found that most of them didn't know the price of these drugs and did not much care. Then why the increase in prescriptions? The study found that the price reduction gave salespeople a reason to discuss the product with physicians; drawing their attention to the product was what increased prescriptions. Subsequent research revealed that nearly any relevant sales message led to a rise in sales because, for established and commonly used drugs, many doctors prescribe the brand that first comes to mind—often the one discussed most recently with a sales rep. The point is that price decreases often stimulate sales, but the attention drawn to a product by price promotions also may be a factor.

Product Line Pricing Strategies Consumers tend to use all products in a company's line as a way of making comparisons. Consequently, marketers use several strategies: product array, bundled, optional product, and captive product pricing.

Product Array Pricing Most companies sell several products. These may be offered within the same brand, such as different Chevy trucks, or in several lines, such as Chevy, Pontiac, and Oldsmobile. Prices need to be established across the entire product array. The difficulty arises because products are often substitutes for one another. Kodak film is sold at different prices depending on the shutter speed used to take pictures. Many speeds will work well enough for most amateur photographers, although a certain speed may be preferred for a certain shot. Many consumers select Kodak film at a premium price over rivals because of

PROMOTIONAL PRICING

A strategy in which price discounts are used to get attention and encourage immediate purchase.

its reputation for lasting quality. They then must choose among film type and speed. Pricing often plays a major role in precisely which product is bought, since all the Kodak films are likely to be displayed close together. If price differences cause confusion, then consumers may become dissatisfied. Kodak is careful to price each product so that the differences help the photographer select differing value—what is best for action photos, landscapes, or flash shots. The various price points offer value for nearly every photographer. If one average price were used for all Kodak film, then competitors would quickly take share with dramatically lower prices.

Bundled Pricing Products can be bundled or unbundled for pricing purposes. The bundled approach, which gives a single price for the entire offering, is used for standardized products, whereas unbundling is often used for customized products. For example, home builders use each method depending on the offering. Houses in a subdivision usually are priced to include carpeting, fixtures, and landscaping, whereas various items will be listed separately for custom homes. Even property and land preparation cost will be specified. The unbundling helps custom buyers assess the value to them of each item and make choices according to tastes and budgets. AT&T offers packages that bundle phone service with cable and wireless service. Several other telecom companies have followed its lead and are offering discounts to customers that buy more than one service.[55] When Cox Communications Inc., began bundling video, data, and phone services, it found that its customers were more likely to purchase bundles of two components than bundles combining all three.[56]

Optional Product Pricing Many products are sold as a base unit with optional add-ons. Cars are an obvious example. Dodge's Grand Caravan has a sticker price of about $24,000, but options may raise it as much as $6,000.[57] Add-ons for automobiles include CD players, sunroofs, and remote keys. Companies often price the base product low as a platform for selling other items. The telephone company does this. When you sign up for service, you also can buy caller ID and call waiting.

Captive Product Pricing It is pretty obvious why Gillette prices its razors low. Once you own one, you will buy blades—perhaps for years. In a sense, you're a captive customer, but since razors and blades are not very expensive, the cost to escape is minor. But how about the

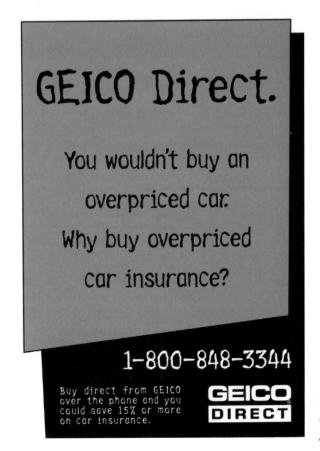

Geico Direct provides bundled pricing for its insurance packages.

cost of moving from Nintendo to Sony video games? You will need to purchase a new system (at approximately $200), and your current games no longer will be useful. New ones cost up to $70. Despite price cuts in the video game industry, you may not be able to afford switching from your Nintendo system.[58] The captive product strategy is used by many marketers. Internet-access cellular phone companies price with a variation on the captive theme. They have an installment fee, then a fixed rate plus a variable usage charge. Often the fixed rate is set very low in order to obtain the more profitable usage fees.

COMMUNICATING PRICE

The second step in price implementation is to communicate with the market. This involves more than just advertising a figure. The price may have several components that are quoted in differing ways, and various kinds of price reductions can be offered.

Price Components   Let's say that Joan Martin purchased Rossignol skis, poles, and boots at the California Ski Company outlet. The package cost $800, and the total including tax was $848. Her roommate purchased the same package at a Winter Sports Equipment store for $800, but the total including tax was $893. She was charged $30 extra for binding installation and $15 for tuning the skis. Whether the buyer or seller pays for "extras" can make a substantial difference in price.

In consumer markets, there is wide variation in what is included in the price. Foot Locker will return your money if a shoe does not meet your expectations. If the support breaks down before you think it should, then you can take the shoes back for a refund or a new pair, no questions asked. Although the Foot Locker price may be similar to that of other retailers, others may not provide the same level of customer service. Foot Locker's return policy is added value. The most common additions to price are these:

- Finance charges
- Installation fees
- Warranty charges
- 800-number assistance
- Replacement parts inventory
- Shipping and handling
- Training

It is important to communicate clearly the components that are included within a price quotation. If buyers are hit with unexpected charges for items they thought were included within the original price, dissatisfaction is likely. This is because many consumers believe this is unethical behavior on the part of the seller.

Price Quoting   Price quoting is how prices are communicated to buyers. Some companies offer price quoting services. For example, many large insurance firms use InsWeb, an online comparative shopping service. In addition, some firms offer interactive quoting and comparison systems so consumers can feel confident they are getting a fair and reliable price.[59] Sometimes prices are stated clearly and directly, but often an indirect method is used. The **list price** (or suggested retail price) set by the manufacturer usually provides the reference point by which consumers judge the fairness of the market price. The **market price** is the actual amount buyers must pay for the product. Often the list price is much higher than the market price. For example, when Sony introduces a product the list price may be over double the market price.[60] The market price is likely to result from several types of reductions, including discounts and rebates.

Price Reductions   Discounts are often given for cash payment, for purchasing large quantities, or for loyalty. Cash discounts are offered to consumers, business-to-business customers, and nearly all channel members. Many buyers look at the undiscounted price as a penalty for delayed payment. Discounts are incentives to speed cash flow from buyer to seller, and they are standard in many industries. It is common for cash discounts to be quoted in terms of a percentage reduction and a specific time for payment, most often 2/10, net 30. This says the buyer has a 2 percent discount if paid in 10 days, and full payment without a discount is due in 30 days. Many buyers pay within the first 10 days because a 2 percent discount figured over the remaining 20 days is equivalent to an interest rate of about

36 percent on an annual basis. Sellers use the discounts to speed payment and reduce losses due to bad debts. Many industries have increased their prices by nearly 2 percent to offset these cash discounts.

Quantity discounts, which are reductions for large purchases, are justified because the seller has lower costs when handling larger orders. That is, selling, order processing, billing, shipping, and inventory carrying costs are averaged over a greater volume. It is common for a supplier to use quantity discounts to entice buyers to purchase more and to achieve economies of scale for transportation and processing costs.[61] These can be offered at one time or on a cumulative basis. Eddie Bauer sells crew socks at $6 per pair, but when customers buy three pairs or more, the company only charges $4.50 per pair.[62] Another example is mutual funds, which often charge differing commissions, or "loads," depending on the amount purchased. One popular fund charges 4.25 percent for orders less than $50,000, 3.5 percent for $50,000 to $100,000, and 2.5 percent for more than $100,000. The buyer has up to one year to meet the commitment.

Patronage discounts are very similar to cumulative quantity discounts and they reward buyer loyalty. An example is a café that stamps a card for each cup of coffee bought and then gives a free cup when the card is full. Another variation is Sam's Club, a no-frills retail buying center developed by Wal-Mart, which offers discounts only to fee-paying members. Discounts should not be used, however, as the sole means for achieving customer loyalty. One study shows that in a three-year period, 60 percent of all discounted purchases were made by just 15 percent of consumers. Little market share is gained by discounts.[63] In the case of eToys, discounting has cut significantly into its revenue for 2000 and may force the company into bankruptcy.[64]

Rebates reduce prices through direct payments, usually from the manufacturer to the consumer. Chrysler popularized this tactic in the 1980s, and now it has become difficult for the company to sell some cars without this incentive. In today's competitive car market, rebates are still a popular way to move cars off the lot.[65] As we noted in chapter 15, rebates may have a greater psychological effect on customers than discounts. The buyer perceives a rebate as a large amount of money. In contrast, the discount is seen as a small percentage of the total price. Remember that price differentials make the most impression on buyers. With rebates manufacturers also are more assured that the rebates will not be partially absorbed by dealers. Sometimes, when discounts are given to dealers with the idea that they be passed along to consumers, part of the difference is kept by the dealer.

UNETHICAL PRICING PRACTICES

When marketers develop a pricing strategy, it should reflect the value perceived and received. This does not always happen. Abuses can occur through manipulation of the consumer's reference price, quoting overcharged or misleading prices, or using discriminatory pricing practices. Unethical pricing can have legal repercussions, not to mention the risk of losing valuable customers.

As mentioned earlier, the reference price serves as a guideline to consumers. What happens when marketers manipulate that price in order to change the consumer's perception of what is "fair"? Three studies have addressed this issue.[66] When a reference price is set at an implausibly high level, it can influence perceptions about a fair price as well as the highest price. Another study indicates that plausible reference prices can strongly influence customers' estimates of the highest and lowest prices for a given item, but implausible reference prices have little impact on their estimates.[67] Therefore, it is important for marketers to establish reference prices with care.

Another unethical practice is to quote unclear or misleading prices, which can have serious legal consequences. For example, a $27.5 million lawsuit was brought against several TCI cable companies for quoting prices higher than published or approved rates. Some were charging double for certain services.[68] TCI also allegedly quoted installation prices for unwired homes to consumers with homes already wired, in addition to misrepresenting the costs for reconnection.[69] More recently, in Florida and Pennsylvania, lawsuits were filed against Rite-Aid Corp. The Pennsylvania suit alleged that the company directed pharmacists to increase prices for uninsured customers, particularly when they were buying medications to treat emergency and acute conditions. Moreover, the suit claimed, Rite-Aid failed to disclose its surcharge practices. Legal action in these two states prompted investigations of the company's pricing practices by the attorney generals for the states of New York and California.[70]

Discriminatory pricing practices are often very controversial. Is it fair to charge a woman more than a man for dry-cleaning a shirt or for a haircut? This depends on a number of circumstances. Are the shirts similar, or is the service more difficult to perform for one gender versus another? Since most women have longer hair than men, perhaps it is more difficult or time-consuming to cut. Nevertheless, studies have found that women do pay more than men for products ranging from haircuts to cars.[71] In 1995, with the Gender Tax Repeal Act, California became the first state to prohibit gender discrimination in pricing for similar services.[72] Even so, a number of California businesses continue to use different prices. Three years after the passage of the act, the California Public Interest Research Group reported that many dry cleaners and hairdressers continued to charge higher prices for services to women than to men. Because of the small amounts involved in these price differences, however, very few women have chosen to take costly legal action against businesses that violate the law.[73]

CONNECTED: SURFING THE NET

AMERICA ONLINE
www.aol.com

THIS CHAPTER'S TECHNOLOGY FEATURE DISCUSSED America Online in "In Light of AOL's Merger with Time Warner, Competitors May Use Pricing to Gain a Piece of the Pie." In order to learn more about pricing changes and strategies, visit AOL's Web site and answer the following questions.

1. Read about one of AOL's new ventures, such as AOLTV or AOL By Phone. Will pricing be a major factor in the demand of these services?
2. Visit the "AOL Pricing Plans" link. Which rate do you feel is most effective? Why?
3. How might consumer factors affect AOL's pricing strategy?
4. Imagine that AOL enters a price war with a major competitor. How may it affect the company, and who may ultimately benefit?

FLEETBANK BOSTON
www.fleetbankbostonmerger.com

THIS CHAPTER'S RELATIONSHIPS FEATURE, "BANKS Coddle Some Customers and Make Others Pay Their Way," discussed the structure of many bank fees and services. To expand your thinking about pricing strategy, visit the Web site of FleetBank Boston and answer the following questions.

1. What features do you notice that help FleetBank connect with customers? Read about the company's features and how they provide service to customers. Is there an emphasis on electronic means?
2. How does the bank use limited offers to encourage customers to buy its products and services?
3. Which price-setting strategy or combination of strategies do you think would be most appropriate for FleetBank? Explain.
4. Read about FleetBank's Premier Program. Do you think this primary relationship program is suitable for all customers?

OBJECTIVE 1: Understand why an appropriate customer value proposition is a useful guide to pricing strategy.

Pricing strategies are complex and must balance the needs of both the customer and the firm. Value-based pricing, which includes the concepts of value in use and value in exchange, is increasingly popular. Since customers seek differing types of value and competitors have a broad range of choices in how to price, other strategies are viable as well. In devising a pricing strategy, it is important to identify a customer value proposition that matches the capabilities of the organization. The three types of capabilities are product leadership, operational competence, and customer intimacy.

OBJECTIVE 2: Know what factors to consider when using customer- and competitor-oriented pricing methods.

Pricing strategies may focus on customers, competitors, or global factors. Customer-oriented pricing requires an understanding of reference prices, price awareness, price/quality association, odd-even perceptions, limited offers, and target pricing. Competitor-oriented pricing considers leader-follower scenarios,

going rates, discounting, and competitive bids. Some companies engage in price wars that can seriously affect industry and company profits. On a global scale, pricing may include countertrading or barter. Funds transfer and exchange rates also affect international pricing.

OBJECTIVE 3: Learn how pricing strategy is implemented by setting prices and communicating them to the market.

Implementing a price strategy requires setting and communicating prices. One of six fundamental approaches can be used to set prices: skimming, sliding down the demand curve, price umbrella, everyday low prices, promotional pricing, and penetration pricing. Product line pricing complicates matters. Options are product array, bundled, optional product, and captive product pricing. When prices are communicated, various components may be specified or only the overall price, and various reductions may be offered. Price communication must be done carefully to avoid unethical practices, such as false impressions about price or unfair discrimination.

1. What is value-based pricing? How does it differ from cost-based pricing?
2. What is value in use? Value in exchange?
3. What three leader strategies match what buyers want?
4. What are reference prices? Give several categories.
5. What is a ceiling price, and how is it used in setting prices?
6. How are odd and even prices perceived?
7. When is going rate pricing used?
8. How is pricing used to attract senior citizens?
9. What are price skimming and penetration pricing?
10. What is umbrella pricing?
11. List three aspects of product line pricing.
12. How are prices quoted?
13. What is discriminatory pricing?

1. How are price and value related? What are the advantages of value-based pricing over the traditional cost-based approach?
2. What is the difference between value in use and value in exchange? How could a marketer use these concepts to improve profitability?
3. What is required if a company wants to use product leadership, operational competence, or customer intimacy as the basis for establishing a customer value proposition? Give examples of each.
4. How does competition affect a company's prices? Briefly describe the major competitor-based pricing approaches.
5. We know that several factors influence consumer responses to prices. What psychological factors should marketers keep in mind when using consumer-oriented pricing? Describe each.
6. How is a company's market position related to price leadership? What does this have to do with price wars?
7. Describe the six fundamental ways to set price. In what situations is each strategy typically used?
8. How does the communication of price present ethical dilemmas? Give examples of several questionable practices.

Acceptable price range: All prices around the reference price that consumers believe reflect good value.

Buying market share: A strategy in which prices are set low for the short run to pull buyers away from competing brands.

Countertrade: Government mandates that imported products cannot be paid for with cash; instead, companies from the exporting nation are required to purchase products of equivalent value from the importing nation.

Everyday low prices: Prices that, on average, are consistently lower than those of competitors.

Going rate: The price that evolves over time when no competitor has power over others and all price at a similar level.

List price: The price set by the manufacturer and used by consumers as a reference point. Also called suggested retail price.

Market price: The actual price buyers must pay for a product.

Penetration pricing: A strategy that seeks the maximum number of buyers by charging low prices.

Price skimming: A strategy to obtain a very high price from relatively few consumers, who have the resources and desire to buy irrespective of price.

Price umbrella: The leader maintains the price at a high enough level that competitors can earn a profit at that or lower levels.

Price war: A cut by one company spurs similar reductions by competitors, resulting in price slashing that can lower profit margins.

Promotional pricing: A strategy in which price discounts are used to get attention and encourage immediate purchase.

Reference price: The amount consumers expect to pay for a product.

Slide down the demand curve: Set a high price when a product is introduced and then lower it significantly as competitors enter the market.

Target pricing: The use of price to reach a particular market segment.

Value-based pricing: A strategy that reflects value, not just cost.

Value in exchange: The objective worth of a product in the competitive marketplace.

Value in use: The consumer's subjective estimate of the benefits of a particular product.

REFERENCES

1. Chris Morris, "Sony's PlayStation 2 Shortage," *CNNfn,* September 27, 2000, cnnfn.com/2000/09/27/technology/sony/; Kenneth Li, "Meet the Man Behind Sony's PlayStation," *Industry Standard,* September 1, 2000, www.cnn.com/2000/tech/computing/09/01/meet.ken.kutaragi.idg/; "Sega Announces Price Cut on Dreamcast Game System," *Los Angeles Times,* August 31, 2000, www.latimes.com/business/20000831/t000081665.html; "Sega Sees Sleepy Sales for Dreamcast," *CNet News.com,* August 17, 2000, news.cnet.com/news; "Sony to Delay European Debut of PlayStation2," *CNet News.com,* August 4, 2000, news.cnet.com/news; David Becker, "Revenue from Game Consoles Will Plunge," *CNet News.com,* July 31, 2000, news.cnet.com/news.

2. Robert L. Simison, "Ford Pricing Move Aims to Attract Buyers to Higher-End Vehicles," *Wall Street Journal,* June 23, 2000, p. B2.

3. Lindsay Chappell, "Volvo, Saturn Cultivate Their Cult Following," *Auto News,* March 28, 1994, p. 12.

4. "Volvo Traffic Accident Research Team Continues to Revolutionize Passenger Safety After 30 Years," *PR Newswire,* December 20, 2000, ptg.djnr.com.

5. "Cutting Edge: Flash—Safety-Minded Hotrod," *AsiaWeek,* December 22, 2000, ptg.djnr.com.

6. Alexander Hiam and Charles D. Schewe, *The Portable MBA* (New York: John Wiley & Sons, 1992), pp. 298–299.

7. Gregory L. White, "General Motors Plans to Rebuild Its Share of Small-Vehicle Market," *Wall Street Journal,* November 1, 2000, p. B6.

8. Michael Treacy and Fred Wiersema, *The Discipline of Market Leaders* (Reading, MA: Addison-Wesley, 1995).

9. James Niccolai, "Intel Takes the Axe to PC Chip Prices," *NetworkWorldFusion News,* www.nwfusion.com/news/10301intelcut.html, visited December 14, 2000.

10. Ken Yamada, "Intel Road Map Loaded with Chip Price Reductions," *Computer Reseller News,* August 12, 1996, p. 3.

11. Mel Mandell, "Implementing Operational Excellence," *World Trade,* December 1999, p. 84.

12. Paul C. Judge, "Digital's Struggle to Save Its Alpha Chip," *Business Week,* December 30, 1996, pp. 146–161.

13. Praveen Kopalle, Ambar G. Rao, and L. Joao Assoncao, "Asymmetric Reference Price Effects and Dynamic Pricing Policies," *Marketing Science,* 15, no. 1 (1996): 60–85.

14. Joel E. Urbany, William O. Bearden, and Dan C. Weilbaker, "The Effects of Plausible and Exaggerated Reference Prices on Consumer Perceptions and Price Search," *Journal of Consumer Research* 15 (June 1988): 95–110.

15. See Michael H. Morris and Gene Morris, *Market Oriented Pricing* (Lincolnwood, IL: NTC Business Books, 1990), pp. 5–8.

16. "Consumers' Reference Prices: Implications for Managers," *Stores* 78 (April 1996): RR4.

17. Joel E. Urbany and Peter R. Dickson, *Consumer Knowledge of Normal Prices: An Exploratory Study & Framework* (Cambridge, MA: Marketing Science Institute, 1990), pp. 7–8.

18. Brad Darrach, "A Different Kind of Superstar," *Life,* December 1995, pp. 92–93.

19. Mark Tedeschi, "Extreme Interest," *Sporting Goods Business,* February 10, 1997, p. 96.

20. Jonathan Feigen, "Rockets Notes," *Houston Chronicle Online,* January 17, 2000, www.chron.com/cs/CDA/story.hts/sports/bk/bkn/432383, visited December 14, 2000.

21. Yongmin Chen and Robert W. Rosenthal, "On the Use of Ceiling Price Commitments by Monopolies," *Rand Journal of Economics* 27 (Summer 1996): 207–220.

22. Gilbert D. Harrell, *Consumer Behavior* (New York: Harcourt Brace Jovanovich, 1986), p. 68.

23. Ibid, p. 68.

24. www.Gateway.com, site visited December 23, 2000.

25. Vince Staten, "Can You Trust a Tomato in January?" *Library Journal,* July 1993, p. 179.

26. www.goski.com/rossi/rossi1999.htm, viewed December 16, 2000.

27. "Gas Stations Sometimes Follow the Price Leader, Execs Say," *Associated Press Newswires,* July 7, 2000, as retrieved from the World Wide Web: ptg.djnr.com.

28. John T. Mulqueen, "Back on Track with Mobile Devices," *Communications Week,* September 23, 1996, pp. 73–74.

29. Robert Brooks and Darin White, "Don't Copy the Competition, Lead with New Markets," *Bank Marketing* 28 (May 1996): 13–17.

30. "Fair Game: Airlines May Be Using a Price-Data Network to Lessen Competition," *Wall Street Journal,* June 28, 1990, p. 1.

31. Masood Farivar, "Gasoline Aims Skyward as Supply Crunch Hits Pumps," *Dow Jones Energy Service,* February 15, 2000.

32. Richard Gibson, "Breakfast Takes Biggest Hit as Sales Slow across the Globe," *Wall Steet Journal Interactive Edition,* February 26, 1997.

33. "Regional Chains Get McDonald's, BK Attention," *Advertising Age,* Vol. 71, No. 40, September 25, 2000, p. s10.

34. Seth Schiesel, "New Economy: Phone Mergers That May Help Competition," *New York Times,* November 27, 2000, p. 1, column 5.

35. "Heinz Meanz Business," *Marketing,* November 21, 1996, p. 25.

36. Robert F. Fletcher, "Marketing the Experience," *Executive Speeches,* April–May 1996, p. 1–4.

37. "Census Bureau Expects Elderly Population to Double in Eight States by 2020," *Health Care Strategic Management,* 1996, p. 9.

38. Marshall Carter, "The Coming Global Pension Crisis," *Foreign Affairs* 73 (November–December 1996): S1–16.

39. Cyndee Miller, "Boomers Come of Old Age," *Marketing News,* January 15, 1996, pp. 1, 6.

40. Ibid, p. 6.

41. Faye Rice, "Come of Age," *Fortune,* June 26, 1995, pp. 110–112, 114.

42. "Seniors Ideal Customers for Drug Chains," *Chain Drug Review,* Vol. 21, No. 20, November 22, 1999, p. 41; "Aging Market Offers Opportunities, Pitfalls to Sellers," *Philadelphia Inquirer,* November 9, 1998.

43. "The Web Matures: Millenia Vision Helps Launch Retired.com; Millenia Vision Uses E-Business Talents to Create Lifestyle Web Site for Retirees," *Business Wire,* October 24, 2000, as retrieved from the World Wide Web: ptg.djnr.com.

44. Ann Ring, "Countertrade Business Opportunities in Russia," *Business America* 11 (January 1993): 15–16.

45. Fauziah Ismail, "Seeking Ways to Raise Palm Oil Exports to Russia," *Business Times (Malaysia),* October 12, 2000.

46. Genay Hesna, "Japan's Corporate Groups," *Economic Perspectives* 15 (January–February 1991): 20–30.

47. "The Unwinding of Japan Inc." *The Wall Street Journal Europe,* December 1, 2000, p. 8.

48. Onkvisit and Shaw, *International Marketing,* p. 614.

49. Lorraine Mirabella, "Wal-Mart Sees Super Future Groceries: The Retail Giant's Ambitious Expansion Plans Draw on 'Supercenters,' Which Add a Supermarket to the Regular Discount Store," *The Baltimore Sun,* October 22, 2000, p. 1C.

50. Teresa Andreoli, "Value Retailers Take the Low Income Road to New Heights," *Discount Store News,* February 19, 1996, pp. 1, 19ff.

51. Mike Duff, "Building on Core Successes Without Straining the Base," *Discount Store News,* Vol. 37, No. 6, March 23, 1998, pp. 23–24.

52. Jim Fox, "Zellers Shifts Pricing Strategy," *Discount Store News,* October 21, 1996, pp. 3, 93.

53. Carol J. Williams, "Germany Refuses to Bargain on Wal-Mart's Below-Cost Sales Retailing: U.S. Chain and Two Competitors Are Ordered to Raise Their Prices on Staple Items or Face Fines," *Los Angeles Times,* September 9, 2000, p. C-1.

54. Sean Silcoff, "They're Certifiable," *Canadian Business,* February 21, 2000, p. 14.

55. Deborah Solomon, "Tying It All Together/Companies Offer One-Stop Shopping for Local Long-Distance, Wireless Phone Service; Cable; Internet," *The San Francisco Chronicle,* March 30, 1999, p. D1.

56. Matt Stump, "Savings and Value Key to Bundling Issues," *Cable World,* Vol. 11, No. 30, July 26, 1999, p. 20.

57. Russ DeVault, "The Atlanta Journal and Constitution Test Drive Column," *The Atlanta Journal and Constitution,* October 9, 2000.

58. Prices taken from Associated Press, "Sony Slashes Price of PlayStation System," *USA Today,* March 3, 1997, web.usatoday.com.

59. Mary Brandel, "Is the World Ready for Web Quotes?" *Computerworld,* April 29, 1996, p. 12.

60. Robert A. Starrett, "First and Second Generation Recorders: Less Choice, Less Confusion," *CD-ROM Professional* 9 (September 1996): 62, 64; and www.bestbuy.com, site visited December 23, 2000.

61. W. C. Benton and Seungwook Park, "A Classification of Literature on Determining the Lot Size under Quantity Discounts," *European Journal of Operational Research,* July 19, 1996, pp. 219–238.

62. www.eddiebauer.com/eb/product/asp?product_id16957&nv=2*18*83, Web site visited December 18, 2000.

63. "Discounting Does Not Work," *Grocer,* July 27, 1996, p. 13.

64. Joelle Tessler, "Los Angeles–Based Online Toy Retailer Expects Lower Sales," *San Jose Mercury News,* December 16, 2000, as retrieved from the World Wide Web: ptg.djnr.com.

65. "Incentives Are Here to Stay," *Automotive News,* December 11, 2000, p. 42.

66. Tracy A. Suter and Scot Burton, "Believability and Consumer Perceptions of Implausible Reference Prices in Retail Advertisements," *Psychology and Marketing* 13 (January 1996): 37–54.

67. Bruce L. Alford and Brian T. Engelland, "Advertised Reference Price Effects on Consumer Price Estimates, Value Perception, and Search Intention," *Journal of Business Research,* Vol. 28, No. 2, May 2000, p. 96.

68. Price Coleman, "California Sues TCI," *Broadcasting and Cable,* May 27, 1996, p. 12.

69. Michael Katz, "TCI Accused of Customer Fraud," *Broadcasting and Cable,* May 13, 1996, pp. 50–51.

70. Harris Fleming, Jr., "Several Investigations Target Rite Aid Pricing Policies," *Drug Topics,* October 18, 1999, pp. 90–91.

71. Gerry Myers, "Why Women Pay More," *American Demographics* 18 (April 1996): 40–41.

72. "Civil Rights—Gender Discrimination," *Harvard Law Review* 109 (May 1996): 1839–1844.

73. Emily Bazar, "Women Pay More for Services, Study Finds," *The Nando Times,* October 29, 1998, www.techserver.com/newsroom/ntn/nation/102998/nation15_24075_body.html, visited December 15, 2000.

Bricks or Clicks

BEST BUY INTEGRATES BRICKS AND CLICKS WITH AN EFFECTIVE PRICE STRATEGY

E-COMPANIES HAVE COME AND GONE and researchers have gained a better understanding of what works in the virtual world and what does not. Michael Collins, a partner at the Chicago office of Bain & Co., argues "the key [to online retailing] is getting people to buy things and then getting them to come back and buy things over and over again." Price, he continues, is not the vehicle to build customer loyalty. It is only one facet of an overall marketing strategy. "Online pricing is another way to bolster your brand," says Mainspring director of eStrategy Julian Chu.

Although price is an important factor in the virtual marketplace, it is not the only factor. The elements that constitute a company's strength or weakness have changed. What many had taken to be handicaps to Best Buy's ability to compete—warehouses and "real" stores—now have become assets. The way in which the company incorporated its brick-and-mortar structure with its Internet operations was reevaluated. This led to some changes in its e-business.

When the expanded site was relaunched in June 2000, visitors to the site doubled in the normally slow summer months. The site is completely integrated with the brick-and-mortar store system, allowing the customer to pick up or return merchandise at any store. It would be impractical for BestBuy.com to compete with the brick-and-mortar stores with this level of integration.

The core objective of BestBuy.com is to be a tool to develop customer relationships and draw them to the Best Buy name. Since most consumers use the Web to gather information, but do their buying at the store, BestBuy.com maintains photos and descriptions of over 6,000 products and provides a forum for the surfer to talk with people who already use the product. Pricing is not the be-all, end-all that it was in the middle and late 1990s; it is just one facet of the overall strategy.

Sources: "The Right Pricing Strategy Can Provide Online Advantage to Clicks-and-Mortar Retailers," *Business Wire,* April 27, 2000; Eric Wieffering, "Best Buy Clicks Online; In Less Than a Year, BestBuy.com's Reputation Went From Slow-Footed and Endangered to Wise and Patient Power Player," *Star Tribune,* November 5, 2000, p. 1D; and Peter Coy, "The Power of Smart Pricing," *Business Week,* April 10, 2000, p. 160.

Harley-Davidson

IN 1903, THE FIRST HARLEY-DAVIDSON was sold—a single-cylinder, belt-driven two-wheeler. It was ridden for 100,000 miles by four owners without replacement of a single major component. The company still enjoys the reputation of producing outstanding, high-quality, high-value motorcycles. In the early days, there were 151 motorcycle manufacturers, but only Harley-Davidson and Indian came through the Great Depression, and by 1953 Harley was the sole survivor. Today, Harley controls 48 percent of the domestic market, 20 percent of the Japanese market, which traditionally prefers smaller bikes, and plans to sell over 200,000 bikes in 2001.

Much of the value of a Harley resides in its tradition—the look, sound, and heritage that have made it an all-American symbol. Customers include people such as the CEO of Southwest Airlines, the head of AT&T, and *Tonight Show* host Jay Leno. The Harley V-twin engine designed in 1909 still turns heads across America with its throaty rumble, and the bikes are easily recognized by their teardrop gas tank and oversized instruments. According to Jeffrey Bleustein, a CEO and a Harley owner, the bikes "represent something very basic—a desire for freedom, adventure, and individualism."

Harley-Davidson CEO Richard Teerlink foresees continued growth. He believes that the Harley buyer is getting older, more affluent, and much better educated. A recent study showed that the average Harley rider is now 44 years old and has a salary of over $75,000 per year. The company is no longer dependent on the Hell's Angels crowd, and it has an audience that can really afford the higher-priced products. "There's a high degree of emotion that drives our success," says Teerlink. "We symbolize the feeling of freedom and independence that people really want in this stressful world."

Harleys are expensive compared to other brands, ranging from a Sportster at about $8,995 to the 2001 custom models priced as high as $23,995. Furthermore, used bikes may cost far more than their original selling price. For example, a limited-edition model purchased new for $14,000 recently sold for more than $22,000. How is it possible to command such premium prices for a product that is slower and less fuel efficient than many of the performance bikes from Europe and Asia? Clearly, the competition has technological superiority.

Even if you were willing to pay $24,000 for a top-of-the-line Harley, until recently you would likely have to wait more than a year for delivery. However, with increased production, customers might have a chance to receive their bikes more quickly. Despite the fact that rivals such as Yamaha have started creating look-alikes, Harley enjoys brand recognition and loyalty experienced by few other products.

With supply finally catching up to demand, Harley may have some interesting marketing challenges, particularly in the area of pricing. *Forbes* asks, "Is Hog Going Soft?" Although Harley's share of its class of bikes is near 50 percent, a few years ago it exceeded 70 percent. Industry consultant Donald Brown believes the company's lead is fading fast. A few years ago, dealers could obtain premium prices for bikes they did not yet have. Now that the machines are immediately available, prices are negotiable. Dealers now have plenty of new and used bikes in stock, including some of the models traditionally hard to find. The amount of stock may mean demand has been satisfied and may present problems for future pricing. Scarcity makes buyers want Harleys more.

The price competition is also getting tougher. For example, Honda's American Classic lists for under $10,000, whereas Harley's similar Dyna Low Rider starts at about $14,595. And Yamaha has made technical improvements, such as an easy-to-maintain shaft instead of a belt drive. Does that matter to bikers who wear T-shirts that say "I'd rather push a Harley than drive a Honda"? Sales of lower-priced models, such as Harley's Sportster, which enters the market at around $8,995 have declined more than 19 percent due to inroads by Suzuki's Intruder, Kawasaki's Falcon, and Honda's American Classic, which sell between $6,500 and $11,000. According to Gil Steward, sales manager of Harleys "R" Us, "Bikes are still selling, but the price is coming down." That means reduced profit margins. Another competitor entering the market to combat Harley is Polaris's Victory Motorcycles. According to company CFO Michael Malone, ". . . we spent $3.2 million on Victory advertising and promotions in the second quarter that we had not expected to spend. We are positioning ourselves as the new American Motorcycle." Victory's strategy has been to undercut Harley's premium pricing plan while remaining above the price of most Japanese bikes.

One Harley distributor, Custom Cycle Works in Nashville, Tennessee, rents bikes to experienced riders who want the luxury of a Harley. The appeal, says Custom Cycle general manager Peggy Bowling, is that "people who ride Harleys have learned to enjoy life. I saw a T-shirt the other day that said 'If I have to explain it, you won't understand it.' That sums it up perfectly."

To compound matters for Harley retailers, most have complied with Harley-Davidson's request to upgrade their showrooms. This includes better location and decor as well as increased size to accommodate inventory in Harley accessories, clothing, and other items. So with margins shrinking at retail, dealers may be challenged to maintain their profitability. Pat Moroney, in Newburg, New York, says his store may have to increase volume: "By 2000, I may have to open an additional store to make the profit on 500 bikes that I now make on 300."

Today, Harley's overseas business is 25 percent of its annual total. Europeans like cruiser bikes but not Harley prices. In fact, some Hogs have recently been shipped back from Europe due to lack of demand. Harley may change its foreign product line in order to offer more affordable prices. But, says Teerlink, "Any softening of demand doesn't appear to be a problem because Harley will simply cut back from producing so much."

1. *Describe the Harley-Davidson pricing strategy. What does the company's positioning have to do with its pricing strategy?*
2. *How does the fact that Harley has a relatively deep line of heavy bikes influence the pricing of each product within the line?*
3. *Create the customer value proposition that would allow Harley-Davidson to continue using a premium pricing strategy.*
4. *Should Harley alter its price, given strong price pressures from rivals? If not, what strategy should it pursue in light of industry developments?*

Sources: www.harley-davidson.com; Gary Strauss, "Harley Working to Stay Leader of the Pack," *USA Today,* November 5, 1997, www.usatoday.com; "Harley Davidson Plans Marketing Tactics after Indiana Headquarters Opening," *Knight-Ridder/Tribune Business News,* November 12, 1996, pp. 11–12B; Gina Fann, "Nashville, Tenn., Cycle Shop Finds a Niche Renting Harley-Davidson Bikes," *Knight-Ridder/Tribune Business News,* April 25, 1997, p. 42B; Dyan Machan, "Is Hog Going Soft?" *Forbes,* March 10, 1997, www.forbes.com; Gary Hamel, "Killer Strategies That Make Shareholders Rich," *Fortune,* June 23, 1997, www.fortune.com; Ronald B. Lieber, "Selling the Sizzle," *Fortune,* June 23, 1997, www.fortune.com; www.harley-davidson.com, November 15, 2000; Steve Watkins, "Harley Vrooms Through Wall Street with Hog Lovers, Restless Boomers," *Investor's Business Daily,* September 1, 2000; Tony Kennedy, "Victory's Slow Start Surprises Polaris, Which Ups Incentive and Advertising," *Star Tribune (Minneapolis, MN),* August 13, 2000; and Angela Daidone, "With Baby Boomers Fueling Growth, Harley Davidson Hogs the Motorcycle Market," *The Record (New Jersey),* September 24, 2000.

photo and ad credits

Chapter 1 2 Reuters/Fred Prouser, Hulton/Archive; 7 Courtesy of United Technologies; 9 Used with permission of the Experience Network; 13 Courtesy of Martha Stewart; 20 Bob Daemmrich, The Image Works; 22 Photo by Per Nicola D'Amico; 23 Used with permission of memolink.com, and courtesy of Choice Hotels International; 24, 25 Courtesy of Centra Software; 26 Barbie® ad courtesy of Mattel, Inc.; 29 Jason Funari/Corbis Sygma.

Chapter 2 36 Randi Lynn Beach/AP/Wide World Photos; 45 Courtesy of the Daimler Chrysler Corporation, and courtesy of Snap-on Tools; 48 Courtesy of Xerox; 49 RubberMaid Home Products. A Newell RubberMaid Company; 50 Courtesy of Bloomingbags; 52 Courtesy of American Airlines; 55 Motorola, Inc.; 57 Volkswagen of America, Inc.

Chapter 3 64 Keith Hamshere/Lucasfilm Ltd./Newsmakers/Liaison Agency, Inc.; 69 Courtesy of Reebok, Inc.; 70 Dan Habib/Concord Monitor/Corbis/SABA Press Photos, Inc.; 74 Courtesy of Phoenix Wealth Management; 80 Courtesy of Sketchers, USA; 82 Darryl Bautista/The Image Works; 85 Courtesy of Philips Petroleum; 87 Robert Visser/AP/Wide World Photos.

Chapter 4 100 Richard Drew/AP/Wide World Photos; 107 Courtesy of Texaco, Inc.; 108 Courtesy of G.E. Information Services; 109 Photograph by John Huet. Used with permission of United Parcel Service; 113 Courtesy of E.I. Dupont Corp.; 116 Used with Permission of Wal-Mart; 118 Children's World Learning Center; 121 Michael Newman/PhotoEdit; 123 Laura Rauch/AP/World Wide Photos.

Chapter 5 134 Robbie McClaran/Corbis/SABA Press Photos, Inc.; 136 Courtesy of docent.com; 137 Courtesy of cPulse; 145 SuperStock, Inc.; 147 Michael Newman/PhotoEdit; 151 The Daimler Chrysler advertisements are used with permission from Daimler Chrysler; 152 Leonardi/Liaison Agency, Inc.; 155 Courtesy of Global Crossing; 156 Michael Coyne/Black Star.

Chapter 6 164 Newsmakers/Liaison Agency, Inc.; 167 Courtesy of the St. Paul Companies, Inc.; 170 Courtesy of Tropicana Products, Inc.; 173 Courtesy of the Gillette Company; 174 Courtesy of Ford Motor Company; 179 Courtesy of Pontiac; 183 Courtesy of Hi-Tec; 185 ©2000 Keebler Corporation. Used with permission; 186 Courtesy of UGG Australia; 190 Ralf-Finn Hestoft/Corbis/SABA Press Photos, Inc.

Chapter 7 198 Douglas Healey/AP/Wide World Photos; 201 Rob Goebel/AP/Wide World Photos; 205 Courtesy of Timex; 209 Courtesy of the Pilsbury Company; 212 Courtesy of Merle Norman Cosmetics; 213 Steve Rasmussen/AP/Wide World Photos; 215 Peter Menzel/Stock Boston; 219 Courtesy of Bozell Worldwide; 221 ©2000 American Baby Group. A division of Primedia Magazines, Inc.

Chapter 8 230 David Longstreath/AP/Wide World Photos; 235 Courtesy of Principle Financial Group; 236 Courtesy of Timken, Inc.; 237 Courtesy of Enron; 240 Courtesy of CNF; 242 Courtesy of Zurich-American Insurance Group; 247 Used with permission of MCI; 253 Used with Permission of 3M; 254 Courtesy of the American Arbitration Association.

Chapter 9 260 Mark Peterson/Corbis/SABA Press Photos, Inc.; 263 Courtesy of Ha-lo Industries; 264 Courtesy of Nicole Miller Eyewear; 267 Courtesy of Hershey Twizzlers, and courtesy of Avon Products, Inc.; 268 Courtesy of Mattell; 273 Courtesy of Sony; 274 Courtesy of MGM Grand; 280 Courtesy of Everready Battery Company, Inc.; 281 Courtesy of Carolina Beverage Corporation; 282 Courtesy of the Martin Agency; 285 Courtesy of Procter & Gamble Company; 286 ©2000 Callard & Bowser-Suchard Inc.

Chapter 10 294 Online USA/Liason Agency; 296 Courtesy of FedEx; 300 Courtesy of Lucent Technologies; 301 Dave Caulkin/AP/Wide World Photos; 302 ©2001 Ferrero. Photographer: Victor Schrager; 304 Courtesy of 3M; 305 © The Procter & Gamble Company. Used with permission; 310 Image ©2000; Vic Huber Photography and Martjin Oort Photography. Created by Team One Advertising.

Chapter 11 328 IBM Corporation; 330 Hernandex/Liason Agency, Inc.; 333 Courtesy of the Doner Agency; 336 Courtesy of ServerVault; 338 Courtesy of Liberty Mutual; 343 Jeff Greenberg/The Image Works; 347 Used with permission of Kinko's Venture's; 351 Courtesy of the Maui Tourist Bureau; 352 Richard Drew/AP/Wide World Photos.

Chapter 12 364 Churchill & Klehr Photography; 369 Courtesy of eSupportNow; 372 Courtesy of Maybelline; 381 Kerbs Monkmeyer Press; 385 Courtesy of Yellow Freight Systems; 387 José Goitia/AP/Wide World Photos; 388 SuperStock, Inc.; 391 Courtesy of United States Postal Service.

index

DATE DUE

OCT. 16.2002			
JAN 02.200			